China's Quest

China's Quest

THE HISTORY OF THE FOREIGN
RELATIONS OF THE PEOPLE'S
REPUBLIC OF CHINA

John W. Garver

OXFORD
UNIVERSITY PRESS

UNIVERSITY PRESS

Oxford University Press is a department of the University of
Oxford. It furthers the University's objective of excellence in research,
scholarship, and education by publishing worldwide. Oxford is a registered
trade mark of Oxford University Press in the UK and in certain other countries

Published in the United States of America by
Oxford University Press
198 Madison Avenue, New York, NY 10016, United States of America

Cataloging-in-Publication Data is on file at the Library of Congress.
ISBN 978-0-19-026105-4

9 8 7 6 5 4 3 2 1
Printed in the United States of America
on acid-free paper

To Penelope Benson Prime,
doctor and professor of economics,
mother of our two children,
and partner in a lifetime of
curiosity about and love for China

CONTENTS

LIST OF FIGURES

PREFACE

In teaching university courses on PRC foreign relations over the years, the need for a chronologically organized, synthetic overview of that topic in a single volume frequently struck me. There existed literally hundreds of first-rate studies of particular slices of PRC foreign relations: books and articles dealing with China's various bilateral relationships, the making of key Chinese decisions, various functional aspects of China's international quest, and so on. But a synthetic, historical narrative overview was lacking. A plethora of solid but narrow studies drew on materials declassified from former Soviet and East European communist archives plus rich memoir and archival materials that became available in China after 1978. Many of these materials have been made easily available by the International History of the Cold War Project (IHCWP) of the Smithsonian Institution. But a narrative mosaic combining and summarizing the insights from all these sources in a single volume was simply not available. It is such a narrative mosaic that this work undertakes to provide.

The increasing historical distance of the students in my classes from the events described made me realize how much a historical understanding of PRC foreign relations was necessary. They simply did not have any historical knowledge of the ancient (i.e., Cold War and early post–Cold War) events that had shaped the PRC: the powerful magnetic power of the communist vision of a post-capitalist society, Stalinization and de-Stalinization, the schism between Chinese and Soviet Communists, the nature of the Cold War, the global wave of liberal revolutions from 1987 to 1991, the nature of a Leninist state and its legitimization in relation to public opinion and elite conflict, and so on. In my courses I would attempt to address these gaps in historical knowledge by assigning as readings relevant journal articles and book chapters. Reading lists became longer and longer. I understood as a practical matter that the longer a reading list became, the less likely students were to engage or master it. Again I felt the need for a single-volume overview of PRC foreign relations from 1949 to the present (2015).

The profound importance of China's growing power made the absence of a comprehensive history of PRC foreign relations even more peculiar. Already in 1949, the PRC ranked as a major power—a permanent member of the Security Council and a country whose strategic weight as friend or foe was recognized by the United States and the Soviet Union. It soon showed itself willing to willing to go to war with the United States, with India, with the USSR, and with united Vietnam. Chinese armies preformed credibly in Korea, on the Indo-Tibet border, and in border battles with Soviet forces. China's power became credible. And it waxed. By the beginning of the twenty-first century, it had become clear that the PRC is a rising global power that will rival, and perhaps replace, the United States. And yet, strangely, there was no comprehensive history of PRC foreign relations.

I abstained for a number of years from tackling this task because of its sheer immensity. Finally, in the fall of 2012, my beloved wife, Penelope Prime, convinced me to go ahead. If I did not tackle the matter and give it my best effort, I would regret it in a few years when I no longer had the vigor to undertake such a task, she said. The summation of my life's study of Chinese foreign relations would remain unwritten. She convinced me to give it my best shot. The volume you have in your hands is the result.

The effort to survey in one volume sixty-six years of PRC foreign relations imposed limits in terms of scope of coverage. Thus the following work will follow China's relations with the five major Asian powers: the USSR and its successor the Russian Federation, Japan, India, Iran, and the United States. China's ties with the states of Southeast or Central Asia, or with Europe, are, with a few exceptions, not discussed. Moreover, with the exception of two "economic" chapters dealing with China's post-1978 opening and then its explosive post-1992 economic rise, the focus of the book will be on political and security aspects of PRC foreign relations. Readers should keep in mind that the focus on political and security factors is not meant to imply monocausality or to exclude economic, cultural, or other explanations. Each of Beijing's foreign policy decisions was immensely complex, and the focus on only a few political-strategic calculations is not intended to deny that many other factors were at work.

The conceptual theme providing some analytical coherence to the study is the link between PRC internal politics and its foreign relations. While foreign objectives have, of course, weighed heavily on the minds of China's leaders, domestic concerns have been paramount and have deeply impacted China's foreign ties. The way in which this domestic-international linkage worked differed over time. I discern three periods of internal-international linkage, which will be explicated in the next chapter. The broad perspective taken in this book is the relation between state formation and survival and that state's foreign relations. It seems to me that this approach situates China's experience in the context of one of the main processes of the last century of global history—the enthusiastic embrace of, and then disenchantment with, communism. It also captures a central dramatic of China's modern history. It also opens (though does not answer) the question of how a post-Leninist People's Republic of China might relate to the world.

There are, of course, other analytically useful ways of viewing any phenomenon—especially something as complex as a sixty-year slice of a big and turbulent state's foreign relations. Pursuit of national interest defined in terms of security, economic gain, status, and prestige, or merely in terms of power, is a major conceptual alternative to a focus on the domestic determinants of foreign policy. It is also apparent that national interests have frequently been important, even determinant, in many PRC foreign policy decisions. As a historical narrative of PRC foreign relations, this study will present episodes in roughly chronological fashion, sorting out the factors that seem to have been involved in making various foreign policy decisions. Although this work tries to keep a focus on the domestic-international linkage, no claim is thereby intended to monocausality. The "domestic politics as driver" approach is offered merely as a convenient and analytically insightful scaffolding on which to hang an extraordinarily colorful mosaic. I have included coverage of important episodes of PRC foreign relations even when they did not hang neatly on a domestic-international link. Yet when I could, and to the extent that it made sense, I followed the "linkage" theme. I did not want theory to overwhelm the central drama: the rise of a proud, capable, and ambitious people, the Chinese people, led by a Marxist-Leninist state, the People's Republic of China, to a position of global eminence and power.

The focus of this work is on the logic and practice of PRC foreign policy. In line with this, and in an effort to limit length, I will explain the policies of other powers only to the extent necessary to understand China's policies. This may occasionally leave readers feeling I have given the perspectives of China's counterparts short shrift. In this event, I beg the reader to keep in mind the purpose of the work—and the imperative of limiting length.

I sincerely invite fellow laborers in the academic vineyards of PRC foreign and security relations to forward to me any errors or egregious omissions they detect. These will be incorporated and will improve future editions of this work.

ACRONYMS

ADB	Asian Development Bank
ALP	Albanian Labor Party (Albania's communist party)
ASEAN	Association of South East Asian Nations
AEOI	Atomic Energy Organization of Iran
APEC	Asia Pacific Economic Cooperation (organization)
ARATS	Association for Relations Across the Taiwan Strait (Beijing)
BRICS	Brazil, Russia, India, China, and South Africa
CAC	Central Advisory Commission
CAS	Chinese Academy of Sciences
CC	Central Committee
CCP	Chinese Communist Party
CCTV	China Central Television
CDU	Christian Democratic Union (West Germany)
CMAG	Chinese Military Advisory Group (North Vietnam)
CPAFFC	Chinese People's Association for Friendship with Foreign Countries
CIA	Central Intelligence Agency
CMC	Central Military Committee
CNPC	China National Petroleum Corporation
COCOM	Coordinating Committee (NATO)
COSTIND	Commission on Science Technology and Industry for National Defense
CPB	Communist Party Burma
CPM	Communist Party of Malaya
CPSU	Communist Party of the Soviet Union
CPUSA	Communist Party United States of America
CPT	Communist Party of Thailand
CPV	Chinese People's Volunteers
CSCE	Conference on Security and Cooperation in Europe
CYL	Communist Youth League
BW	Biological Weapons
DRV	Democratic Republic of Vietnam
ENRC	Esfahan Nuclear Research Center (Iran)
EPZ	Export Processing Zone
E&R	Extension and Review (NPT)
ETIM	East Turkistan Islamic Movement

FTC	Foreign Trade Company
FDI	Foreign Direct Investment
FAW	First Auto Works
FRG	Federal Republic of Germany
FRY	Federal Republic of Yugoslavia
GATT	General Agreement on Tariffs and Trade
GDR	German Democratic Republic
G-7	Group of 7 (industrial countries)
HKSAR	Hong Kong Special Autonomous Region
HSWP	Hungarian Socialist Workers Party
IAEA	International Atomic Energy Agency
IC	integrated circuit
ICC	International Control Commission (Indochina)
ILD	International Liaison Department
IMF	International Monetary Fund
IOC	International Olympic Committee
IPR	Intellectual Property Rights
IRI	Islamic Republic of Iran
JDA	Japan Defense Agency
JIG	Joint Investigation Group (South Korea)
JMSDF	Japan Maritime Self Defense Force
JSDF	Japan Self Defense Force
JSP	Japan Socialist Party
KMT	Kuomintang (Nationalist Party of China)
KWP	Korean Worker's Party (North Korea's communist party)
LGTA	Leading Group on Taiwan Affairs
M&E	Machinery and Equipment
MFA	Ministry of Foreign Affairs
MFN	Most Favored Nation
MIIT	Ministry of Information Industry and Technology
MLP	Medium and Long Range Plan
MOFERT	Ministry of Foreign Economic Relations and Trade
MOFTEC	Ministry of Foreign Trade and Economic Cooperation
MOST	Ministry of Science and Technology
MSS	Ministry of State Security
MTCR	Missile Technology Control Regime
NATO	North Atlantic Treaty Organization
NEBDA	Northeast Border Defense Army
NEFA	North East Frontier Agency (India)
NGO	nongovernmental organization
NKCP	North Kalimantan Communist Party
NKLL	North Kalimantan Liberation League
NPA	New People's Army (Philippines)

NPC	National People's Congress
NPT	Non-Proliferation Treaty
ODA	Overseas Development Assistance (Japan)
PAP	People's Action Party (Singapore)
PAVN	People's Army of Vietnam
PBSC	Politburo Standing Committee
PKI	Parti Kommunist Indonesia (Indonesian communist party)
PNTR	Permanent Normal Trade Relations
POW	prisoner of war
PTBT	Partial (nuclear) Test Ban Treaty
PRC	People's Republic of China
PRD	Pearl River Delta
PUWP	Polish United Worker's Party (Poland communist party)
RF	Russian Federation
ROC	Republic of China
ROK	Republic of Korea
S&T	science and technology
SA-IOR	South Asia-India Ocean Region
SCO	Shanghai Cooperative Organization
SEATO	South East Asia Treaty Organization
SSTC	State Science and Technology Commission
SUP	Socialist Unity Party (East German communist party)
SEZ	Special Economic Zone
SDP	Social Democratic Party (West Germany)
SRV	Socialist Republic of Vietnam
SOE	state-owned enterprise
SEF	Straits Exchange Foundation (Taipei)
TAO	Taiwan Affairs Office
TALSG	Taiwan Affairs Leading Small Group
TPR	Taiwan Policy Review
TAR	Tibet Autonomous Region
TMD	Theater Missile Defense
TRA	Taiwan Relations Act
UAE	United Arab Emirates
UN	United Nations
UNCLOS	United Nations Convention on the Law of the Sea
UNPKO	United Nations Peacekeeping Operation
UNSC	United Nations Security Council
UNTAC	United Nations Transitional Authority Cambodia
US	United States [of America]
USSR	Union of Soviet Socialist Republic
VOA	Voice of America
VOMR	Voice of the Malayan Revolution

VOPT	Voice of People of Thailand
VWP	Vietnam Workers Party (North Vietnam communist party pre-1976)
WPC	World Peace Council
WTO	World Trade Organization

China's Quest

1 }

The Fateful Embrace of Communism and Its Consequence

State Formation and Foreign Policy

The premise of this book is that China in 1949 adopted a deeply dysfunctional political-economic model from the USSR and that this fact has deeply influenced the foreign relations of the People's Republic of China ever since. After trying for thirty years to make the Soviet economic model of comprehensive economic planning work well, China's leaders incrementally abandoned that model, starting in 1978. Over the next three-plus decades, China's leaders managed with amazing success the transition from a planned command economy to a globalized market economy—and did this while raising hundreds of millions of Chinese to midlevels of prosperity, transforming China into one of the leading economies in the world, and freeing the Chinese people from the myriad daily oppressions that were part and parcel of Mao's utopian quest. But while abandoning the economic half of the Soviet model, China retained the political half. That political half was profoundly modified as China transited from a planned to a market economy, but the core aspect remained unchanged: a Leninist state in which a centralized and disciplined party maintains perpetual control over the state while dictatorially repressing autonomous political activity. The ways in which China's Leninist party, the Chinese Communist Party (CCP), and that party's state, the People's Republic of China (PRC), relate to Chinese society shifted profoundly with the transition from a planned to a market economy. But the key mechanisms of party control over the state, tracing back to the USSR in the 1920s and 1930s, remain in place.[1] This has had profound implications for the legitimacy of the CCP party state and for PRC relations with liberal democratic powers.

It is too early to say whether China will be able to make the remaining Leninist political half of its Soviet heritage work well over the long run. The CCP itself argues, plausibly, that since 1978 it has ruled pretty well and that its

1

rule since that time demonstrates the superiority of its state system.[2] The litany of successes reprised in the previous paragraph give this claim credibility. Empirical investigations of public opinion in China suggest that a very large majority of Chinese agree with that proposition, including the middle-class professionals and private-sector entrepreneurs who considerable theory and historical experience suggests should be supporters of democratization. Chinese public opinion in the 2000s shows very little support for basic regime change.[3] There is widespread discontent and even anger at state authority in China, but remarkably little of it has translated into dissatisfaction with the party state. The CCP has indeed demonstrated remarkable willingness to adapt—and thereby survive. The Party's top-down organization was used to incrementally restructure the Chinese economy from planned to market.[4] The tribulations of other countries that have attempted to embrace liberal democracy, from Russia to Egypt to Syria, as well as China's own experience after the 1911 revolution suggest that it is very difficult to make liberal democracy work well. Fortunately, this study need not prognosticate regarding the future of China's communist-led state. I will sidestep the whole question of "will China democratize?" and focus instead on how the CCP's struggle to install and maintain its Soviet-derived Leninist state has influenced PRC foreign relations.

The focus of this book is on the foreign policy implications of the formation, transformation, and struggle for survival of the PRC, the Leninist state created and dominated by the CCP, from 1949 to 2015. During this period, there have been three stages of linkage between the internal requirements regarding the formation, transformation, and survival of the PRC on the one hand and the foreign relations of that state on the other hand. Of course, not all aspects of PRC foreign relations can be explained by domestic factors having to do with state formation and survival. States, even revolutionary states, have interests unrelated to domestic politics. In fact, external security threats may be especially severe for revolutionary states.[5] Revolutionary states that undertake to overturn existing international institutions and structures of power typically incur the hostility of established powers. If, as often happens, the revolutionary state is inspired by a universalist creed transcending national boundaries and inviting revolution in established states, foreign hostility toward the insurgent revolutionary state rises further. The early PRC fit this description to a T. Considerations of military alliances and balance of power were thus inextricably tied to the revolutionary cause. Securing the nation against foreign threat became defense of the revolution and the revolutionary state. As a survey history of PRC foreign relations, this book will deal with these externally motivated policies as they arise chronologically, without trying to fit all data into the mold of the domestic-international linkage paradigm. But focus on internal-international linkages when appropriate will provide a degree of conceptual coherence to a review of sixty-plus years of PRC foreign relations.

A number of scholars have identified formation of a new state as the core process of revolution.[6] Revolutions are made by coalitions of classes and groups, and there inevitably emerge divergent points of view within this co-alition over such matters as the political and social structure of the new rev-olutionary state, the program of the state, and its ideological underpinnings. To a significant degree, it is these divergences within the revolutionary camp over direction of the revolution which drives the foreign relations of the rev-olutionary state. Within the revolutionary leadership, radical and moderate factions emerge and struggle with one another over the direction and struc-ture of the revolution and the revolutionary state. Scholars Charles Tilly and Theda Skocpol stress mobilization of popular forces as an asset of revolution-aries in the struggle against both foreign and domestic enemies. According to Skocpol, mobilization of newly empowered citizens to participate in state-run activities is one of the key processes, and successes, of modern revolutions. Skocpol suggests that the "best task" of modern revolution is mobilizing cit-izen support across class lines for protracted and bloody wars against foreign enemies.[7] The new revolutionary state can also use the mobilization of ma-terial and human resources to defend the nation/revolution to consolidate its control over those resources. Foreign wars permit the revolutionary elite to build a strong state. Crises short of actual war might serve that purpose as well.

Scholar Richard Snyder focuses on the use of foreign conflict as a tool in struggles between rival radical and moderate groups within the revolu-tionary elite.[8] Differences inevitably emerge following the seizure of power. A key difference for modern revolutions, Snyder suggests, regards the role of the "liberal bourgeoisie," the educated middle class and capitalists who were core elements of the revolutionary coalition in its quest to seize state power. Moderates see a continuing "progressive" role for the "liberal bourgeoisie," while radicals seek to use the state to overthrow and repress it. Since the "lib-eral bourgeoisie" has ties with Western countries, confrontation with those Western countries, and especially with the United States, allows the radicals to mobilize nationalist passions and direct them against moderate leaders in the revolutionary camp.

These ideas about the potent mobilizing function of nationalist ideas and the utility of that mobilization in factional struggles within the revolutionary elite, and in consolidating control of the revolutionary state over society, work pretty well for the initial anti-US period of Mao's foreign policies. They serve pretty well too for the anti-Soviet period of Mao's foreign policy tutelage; the conflict with Moscow manufactured by Mao mobilized nationalist passions and social groups that facilitated the purge of moderate "revisionists" who were linked by Mao and his minions with Moscow. Even during the post-Mao era there have been manifestations of this domestic-international linkage.

In the early 1980s, Deng Xiaoping launched a campaign targeting Japan's history of aggression as a way of placating opposition within the Politburo to the accumulating consequences of China's opening. Several years later, conservative opponents of moderate Secretary General Hu Yaobang in the 1980s charged him with weakness in dealing with Japan to undermine his position. Still later, campaigns of hostility toward the United States were used to anathematize liberal democratic ideas espoused by the United States and intimidate people from advocating those ideas. As Skocpol points out, Leninist parties and regimes are very good at mass campaigns mobilizing popular action and passions. The adaptation of such campaigns to foreign relations has become a key survival mechanism of the PRC.

Legitimacy is another idea useful for understanding linkages between PRC foreign relations and domestic politics. Legitimacy refers to the worthiness of political authority as recognized by those subject to that authority, that is, the willingness of citizens to give loyalty and obedience to the ruling authority. Thus defined, legitimacy refers not merely to de facto acceptance of ruling power and the existing political order, but to the normative reasons given for being loyal to that ruling power.[9] During the Enlightenment, the concept of legitimacy was democratized, making it congruent with notions of popular sovereignty and shifting the focus from law or accordance with some divine or natural moral order to assent by the citizens of a polity. Max Weber further outlined three sources of legitimacy: tradition, charisma of the leader, and a rational-legal basis. During China's Mao era, the legitimacy of CCP rule came from the charisma of Chairman Mao plus an ideological but rational-legal claim that China was building socialism, moving toward the transition to communism in accord with "scientific laws of historical materialism" while re-establishing China as a great, if revolutionary, power. During the post-Mao period, legitimacy claims have been rational-legal: raising standards of living during the 1978–1989 period, and defending the nation against predatory powers during the post-1989 era.

A paradigm proposed by MIT professor Lucian Pye in 1967 provides a framework that can encompass CCP legitimacy claims of both the Mao and post-Mao periods.[10] As explicated by Pye, Chinese political culture centers around a deep-rooted belief in the grandeur and greatness of China's three-millennia-long imperial era, a period when Chinese thought of themselves as the very definition of civilization. Juxtaposed to this living recollection of China's past grandeur is China's low status in the contemporary world, a situation which Chinese attributed to the myriad injuries inflicted on China during the "Century of National Humiliation" extending from the start of the first Opium War in 1839 to the founding of the PRC in 1949. The actual main reason for foreign disesteem of China had to do, Pye argued, with China's internal arrangements, specifically absence of modern civil society and rule of law. Yet recognition of that reality would call into question the Chinese self-image of greatness. It was cognitively easier for Chinese to attribute foreigners' lack of esteem for China to anti-China hostility.

The crux of Chinese nationalism, Pye suggested, was a drive to restore China to its long-lost but well-deserved and rightful position of eminence in the world. Three legitimacy narratives corresponding to the three acts of Chinese foreign policy (described below) propose how this is to be done—and why, therefore, Chinese should be loyal to the PRC. During the Mao era, the narrative regarding the path to restored greatness centered around construction of a Soviet-socialist style political-social-economic system and "correct" leadership of the world revolutionary camp. During the 1978–1989 interregnum, the narrative focused on rapid economic development, which would deliver quick improvements in living standards followed by Chinese national power equivalent to the advanced capitalist countries by the mid-twenty-first century. During the post-1989 period, the legitimacy narrative of the second period continued but was supplemented by a struggle against putative hostile forces who were striving to return China to its pre-1949 condition of weakness, thus depriving it of its rightful place in the sun.

Creation and Maintenance of a Revolutionary State

The revolutionary upheaval of 1945–1949 shattered the institutions of the old state and formed new ruling institutions dominated by the CCP and in the form of the PRC. But China's revolutionary upheaval did not end in 1949. As long as Mao lived (he died in September 1976), the PRC remained in many ways a revolutionary state, wielding its power to transform Chinese society, and even the world, to accord with the utopian vision that had partially inspired the revolutionary upheaval. This awesome task of forging a socialist society had a deep impact on PRC foreign relations during the Mao era, moving first into confrontation with the United States and then with the Soviet Union. Eventually, as with all revolutions, the utopian élan faded and lost popular appeal. But maintaining the structures of the state created by the revolution, the PRC, remained a paramount objective. The PRC's struggle for survival in China's post-1978, post-revolutionary era was deeply shaped by the Leninist characteristics tracing to that state's gestation and birth, and by the waning of the Leninist model around the globe.

The creation of the PRC in the mid-twentieth century commingled two powerful but discrete forces: Chinese nationalism and the quest for a post-capitalist communist utopia. Chinese nationalism emerged late in the nineteenth century, when Chinese thinkers began reflecting on the deepening powerlessness of China and its growing domination by foreign states.

China's traditional social and political institutions were being thrown into disarray by deepening contact with modern industrial societies, and the resulting institutional decay interacted with foreign intrusion and domination. Eventually, the objective formulated by what became mainstream nationalist thinkers was to make China a "rich nation with a strong military" (*fu guo, qiang bing*). In line with this slogan, foreign domination of China was to be ended, and the myriad bitter humiliations of China in the decades after the First Opium War (1839–1842) were to be wiped away. China would again become a major power able to defend itself and a respected member of the international community—a status to which Chinese nationalists uniformly believed China's brilliant history and civilization entitled it.[11]

Exactly how this was to be done was the topic of considerable debate. In the early decades of the twentieth century, liberalism, republicanism, anarchism, social Darwinism, traditional and neo-Confucianism, and socialism contended with one another to explain and remedy China's fall into weakness and poverty. Virtually all of the people who founded the PRC were first drawn to politics by nationalism, by a passionate desire to "save the nation" (*jiu guo*). Only later did they discover and embrace Marxism-Leninism, the Bolshevik creed. Then, inspired by the powerful example of the Bolshevik insurrection of 1917, which led swiftly to a centralized dictatorial state, a cohort of young Chinese patriots—represented by the figures who will dominate much of this story, Mao Zedong, Zhou Enlai, and Deng Xiaoping—embraced Marxism-Leninism as the best, perhaps the only, way to "save the nation" by making it again rich and strong.[12] It was the Bolshevik model of centralized dictatorial rule, not the vision of a post-capitalist utopia, that brought these young Chinese people to political activism and to Bolshevism. Their embrace of Marxism-Leninism was initially instrumental: it offered a way to "save China." From beginning to end, the nationalist component of China's revolutionary experience was strong. When Mao proclaimed the PRC in October 1949, he declared that "the Chinese people" had stood up. Sixty-four years later, Xi Jinping, newly inaugurated as CCP paramount leader, announced that a core mission of his rule would be realization of the dream of a restored China.

After Mao and under Deng, the fact of communism's instrumentality for many Chinese nationalists facilitated the discarding of very large parts of what Mao had understood to be Marxism-Leninism. The doctrine had been adopted to make China rich and strong, but once it proved unable to do that, it was modified as necessary. But Mao was not among these people. Mao defined himself, his position in world history, in the continuum of Marx, Engels, Lenin, and Stalin. For these men, the purpose of the struggle was transition to communism, the end state of human development.

The rise and fall of the quest for post-capitalist, communist utopia was a central element of the history of the twentieth century, and PRC foreign relations must be framed by that quest if they are to be understood as Mao understood them. The vision of a post-capitalist, communist utopia was immensely attractive to many Chinese intellectuals, just as it was to intellectuals in countries around the world. In the 1950s and 1960s, PRC foreign relations and domestic politics were deeply shaped by ideological battles within the world communist movement, and within the CCP, over the "correct" line for destroying capitalism and entering a new post-capitalist era of first socialism and then, once the material and psychological conditions had been built, communism. Moreover, China's embrace and subsequent rejection of this communist vision was a key part of the global drama of enchantment and disenchantment with the communist vision. Understanding the drama of PRC foreign relations requires situating it in the context of a global embrace and then disembrace of communism.

Marxism-Leninism, the combination of philosophy and ideology worked out by Karl Marx and Vladimir Ilich Lenin, purported to lay out the scientific laws of social and historical development. These laws demonstrated to believers the inevitability of the replacement of capitalism by socialism and the subsequent replacement of socialism by communism. Capitalism, the private ownership of the means of production and market organization of economic processes, was doomed to be replaced by a superior social form, socialism, in which the means of production were owned by the state and the economy was no longer driven by blind, irrational market forces but by altruistic and wise state planners. There would be a period of "socialist construction" during which revolutionary dictatorship was "historically necessary." That period would be followed by "communism," in which economic privation, insecurity, inequality, and greedy selfish individualism, along with the state itself, would disappear. This was the communist vision: a rationally planned, highly industrialized, and technologically advanced society founded on science, but one with collective social solidarity in place of the selfish individualism of capitalism. The crux of communist philosophy was a revolutionary dictatorship which would remake every aspect of society through its exercise of dictatorial power, realizing, ultimately (and following Herbert Marcuse), the great vision of the French Revolution, a society of "liberty, equality, and fraternity," ending the long human quest for a fundamentally just society.[13] Large disparities of wealth and power would disappear along with war, imperialism, privation-driven crime, and repressive government. It was an extremely attractive, even seductive, vision.

To repeat, this utopian vision was not what drew people like Mao, Zhou, and Deng to Marxism-Leninism. Rather, it was the model of revolutionary organization that went along with Marxism-Leninism that was a large part of what made it attractive to young Chinese patriots. The type of party organization hammered out by Lenin in the two decades before the Bolshevik Revolution envisioned a relatively small cohort of completely dedicated men and women subordinating themselves absolutely to military-like discipline for the purpose of mobilizing the masses and leading them to seize and retain state power. This disciplined, centralized party was to be the revolutionary vanguard that would lead the immense task of reconstructing society. For patriotic young Chinese of the 1920s–1940s, a Leninist party offered a way to accomplishing the immense and perhaps otherwise unachievable goal of changing Chinese society. It is sometimes said that the most important Bolshevik contribution to the history of the twentieth century was the type of revolutionary organization that Lenin forged, independent of any specific end pursued via that organization. Yet while some CCP leaders were quite willing after 1949 to dilute or delay the pursuit of the communist utopia for the sake of more mundane matters like economic development, *Mao was not among them*. To the end of his days, Mao used his power to move China toward the communist utopia. Of course, another way of saying this is that a utopian vision justified Mao's absolute and ruthless dictatorship.

Exactly how socialism was to be built, and on what basis the transition from socialism to communism was to be prepared in terms of economic and political institutions, was worked out by the Communist Party of the Soviet Union (CPSU) in the Union of Soviet Socialist Republics (USSR) in the decades after 1917. By the time the CCP began setting up the PRC in 1949, the CPSU already had thirty-two years of "experience in building socialism." That experience seemed very successful to followers of the Marxist-Leninist creed. After 1949, Soviet economic and political models were imposed on China with breathtaking boldness. China's new communist leaders expected the Soviet model to quickly transform China into a rich, highly industrialized, technologically advanced, and powerful socialist state—just as they imagined had happened in the USSR. Unfortunately, the economic and political models imported by the CCP as a way of "saving China" proved to be deeply dysfunctional. To a large extent, China's subsequent history entailed modifying or discarding those dysfunctional Soviet models. This too had a deep impact on PRC foreign relations.

In the economic sphere, the Soviet socialist model centered on planning by the state. State planning replaced markets in organizing economic activity. Marx had explained how market-based production and sale of goods entailed immense waste and was full of "contradictions" and thus irrational. A planned economy would be much more rational and "scientific," Marx declared. Market-based production, Marx explained, led to underutilization of advanced machinery and technology. Markets also led to severe economic downturns, because impoverished workers were unable to purchase all the goods produced by profit-seeking capitalist enterprises. Most egregious of all, Marx taught, the selling of their labor by workers for a wage to capitalists constituted a massive transfer of wealth from the laboring to the property-owning class. The result was, inevitably, great poverty side by side with vast wealth.

A state-planned economy, on the other hand, would lead to much more rapid economic growth, driven in part by accelerated technological innovation and constant revolutionizing of the means of production, while simultaneously raising living standards and improving working conditions. Under a planned socialist economy, the wealth produced by laborers would be used to benefit the laborers, Marx explained.

Exactly how all this was to be accomplished organizationally was worked out in the Soviet Union under Stalin starting about 1928 with the initiation of the First Five Year Plan, comprehensive economic planning, and collectivization of agriculture. The high rates of growth of industrial output achieved by the USSR over the next several decades seemed to vindicate Marx's predictions and demonstrate the superiority of the socialist model. So too did the Soviet Union's pivotal role in the defeat of Nazi Germany in World War II. The industrial base built under Stalin's ruthless Five Year Plans allowed the USSR to vastly outproduce Nazi Germany in the instruments of war. The emergence of the Soviet Union after 1945 as a global rival of the capitalist United States gave further vindication of the Stalin-Soviet model. So too did Soviet prowess in nuclear bombs, intercontinental ballistic missiles, and space satellites in the 1950s.

The Soviet economic model was not without merits. Chief among these was the ability to extract wealth from every crevice of society and funnel it into projects favored by the planners. If one wanted to quickly set up a plethora of new industries and expand production of products x, y, and z by large margins in a short time, the system of state planning worked pretty well. Consumption could be restricted, even pushed down, and the resulting forced savings channeled via the central plan into investment in targeted sectors. In a classic 1956 defense of industrialization under Stalin, the CCP noted that Soviet industrial output that year was thirty times the peak pre–World War I level of 1913.[14]

Over time, however, acute problems materialized and accumulated in the planned economy. Quality of goods was often poor or not quite the type required. Efficiency in the utilization of inputs—labor, energy, material resources—was extremely low. Producers had little incentive to use inputs efficiently, but found perverse incentives to persuade the planners that they needed ever more inputs—to be supplied by the economic planners. State economic planners proved to be much inferior to entrepreneurial capitalists in accomplishing technological innovation and revolutionizing production processes on the basis of those new technologies. And standards of living for ordinary people were low. The counterpart of forced savings to achieve high rates of investment in industry was poverty for the people. The fact could be hidden from the people for a while by state control of information. But eventually, awareness of the higher standards of living in capitalist economies seeped into even closed socialist economies. During the 1980s, for example,

Chinese became aware of how fabulously wealthy even ordinary people were in advanced capitalist countries. Even war-ravaged South Korea had far higher standards of living than people in socialist China.

The PRC under Deng Xiaoping's leadership after 1978 step by step abandoned a state-planned economy and allowed a market economy to emerge and grow alongside the old state-planned sector—outgrowing the plan, one scholar called it.[15] China's economic system today may not be fully capitalist; it still favors state ownership, discriminates against private firms, allocates substantial capital on a nonmarket basis, and refuses to fully uphold private property.[16] But it most assuredly does not any longer resemble the Soviet economic model of the 1930s, imposed on China by the CCP in the 1950s. China under Deng Xiaoping's rule discarded the Soviet economic model. The same cannot be said for the PRC's political system. The political system of the PRC today is essentially the same Leninist system forged in the USSR in the 1920s and transposed to China in the early 1950s. The Chinese Communist Party that runs this out-of-date Leninist system struggles to protect its monopoly on state power ruling over an increasingly affluent and educated population that no longer believes in the myth of communism. All this has occurred in a world increasingly swept by liberal ideals, movements, and revolutions, with ideas and information carried by revolutionary technologies like the World Wide Web.

Legitimizing a Leninist Regime in a World Swept by Liberal Ideas

One dysfunctional consequence of the remaining political half of the PRC's Soviet legacy is weak legitimacy—even, after 1989, a chronic legitimacy crisis. Legitimacy in a Leninist system operates not only between the regime and the citizenry, but at the elite level as well. One of the traditional and chronic weaknesses of Leninist regimes involves the succession of paramount power from one individual to another. Peaceful and orderly transmission of supreme power is a core functional task of all political systems, but there are serious weaknesses in the way Leninist systems handle this function. In such systems—at least, ones not dominated by a supreme and charismatic dictator such as Stalin or Mao—paramount leaders depend on support by other top leaders to stay in office: the Standing Committee of five to seven men, or the Politburo of twenty-five or so, and in extremis the full Central Committee of several hundred. If an incumbent paramount leader loses the support of these few people, he may well be removed as paramount leader. Serious lapses from requirements of the narrative of legitimacy could offer a rival or political enemy a potent weapon.

The traditional set of ideas that legitimized Leninist vanguard states, including the PRC, had to do with a claim by the "proletariat vanguard" party to superior understanding of the laws of social development and a trajectory of history, through "socialist construction" to culmination in a communist society of true equality, fraternity, and justice. In the early years of the PRC, these ideas held considerable attractive power. But throughout PRC history, the standard Marxist-Leninist legitimizing narrative was supplemented by a nationalist anti-Japanese narrative. During the Mao years, the CCP stressed its putative leadership role in defeating Japan in the bitter eight-year-long war of resistance (July 1937–September 1945). In this narrative, it was the CCP, leading the heroic Chinese people, who defeated Japan. The Nationalists of Chiang Kai-shek were reduced to a marginal or even negative role. Chiang's Nationalists were supposedly fearful of Japan and/or of the roused and armed Chinese people, and prone to sympathy, and perhaps even collaboration, with Japan. The Chinese people won, defeated Japan, because they, led by the CCP, pushed aside pusillanimous KMT leadership and made revolution as well as fighting Japan.

After 1978, under Deng Xiaoping's rule, the content of the anti-Japan narrative began to change. About 1982, Deng decided that stepped-up nationalistic indoctrination of China's youth was necessary to limit the appeal of bourgeois ideas flooding into China with the opening. Nationalism, Deng realized, would constitute a more effect bulwark against "bourgeois liberal" ideas than old-style Marxism-Leninism. Gradually, during the 1980s, the CCP's ideological apparatus began to elaborate the narrative of China's century of national humiliation. The most dramatic shift was in the treatment of China's traditional heritage. During the Mao era, that heritage was rejected as "feudal" and "counterrevolutionary." After 1978, China's imperial past was rehabilitated and lauded as rich with the glory and grandeur of the Chinese people. Appropriate teaching curricula were developed and patriotic memorials and museums scattered around the country. The narrative of the anti-Japan war of resistance was also rescripted. Rather than stressing class and partisan differences and revolutionary struggle against KMT cowardice and venality, the new story line stressed the unity of all Chinese in the struggle against Japan. New historical knowledge was made available attesting to the significant role of Nationalist armies and leaders. The war became a struggle of the entire Chinese people, not a revolutionary struggle against "reactionaries" inclined toward capitulation. This new narrative also had the advantage of appealing to ethnic Chinese in Hong Kong, Taiwan, and the Southeast Asia diasporas.

After the powerful challenge to its own Leninist rule in spring 1989, followed by the collapse of Leninist parties across Eastern Europe and in the USSR, the CCP realized the diminished attractiveness of traditional Marxist ideology. It turned, instead, to intensified use of aggrieved nationalism to legitimize its power. The CCP now stressed its role as defender of China against malevolent powers seeking to injure and humiliate it. This new regime legitimization had profound implications for PRC foreign relations. Not least, the regime needed to look strong and avoid any appearance of weakness.

The great historic and philosophical alternative to both Marxism and illiberal forms of nationalism as political legitimization arises from a liberal tradition tracing to Socrates, Aristotle, Baruch Spinoza, John Locke, Jean-Jacques Rousseau, and G. W. F. Hegel. According to liberalism, individuals should be able to direct their own lives. They should be secure in their ability to reach their own conclusions about many aspects of life and to live in accord with those conclusions with due regard for the comparable rights of others. Individual freedom is the core of liberal thought. From this perspective, government becomes an act of collective self-direction by citizens participating in the process of constituting political authority via legally protected freedoms. Citizens come together and debate issues in a public space with effective legal protection, and resolve through a process of competing ideas and proposals how to constitute and wield the public power. One manifestation of this process is democracy, defined by Joseph Schumpeter as the ability of the citizenry to routinely choose and change their rulers. Democracy in the liberal tradition is the collective self-direction of free individuals.

One of the great strengths of liberal democracy is that its very processes legitimize the exercise of state power. Although liberal democracy may be very difficult to make work well, when that is accomplished, the ability of citizens to freely express their views and advocate for their interests, plus making decisions on the basis of one person one vote and majority rule, legitimizes the outcome, almost regardless of what that outcome might be. The belief that the political process is open and fair leads to acceptance by citizens. Such legitimate democratic stability is not limited to Europe, North America, and South America. Across East, Southeast and South Asia, nations have reached this modern condition. In China, however, this path to political legitimacy is precluded by the CCP's perpetual one-party rule.

The history of the past century, including China's history, indicates that liberal ideas of individual freedom have proved extremely attractive. Liberal ideas have not prevailed in any of the epic political upheavals of China, but those ideas keep reappearing, often with great power. The Chinese people may not endorse liberal ideals, but CCP leaders seem to fear that they will, perhaps suddenly and with great force, as in spring 1989. Again, the point here is not that liberal democracy will work in China—although this author believes it someday will. The point, rather, is that the old and still formal legitimization of the CCP's Leninist dictatorship, Marxism-Leninism, no longer serves well to legitimize CCP state power. Liberal ideas which might effectively relegitimize CCP rule are anathematized as leading to the slippery slope of regime change. The regime is left with aggrieved nationalism, a ruling strategy that, as this book will show, exercises a significant influence on China's foreign relations.

Three Stages of Domestic-Foreign Linkage

The link between the structures of China's Leninist state, the PRC, and that state's foreign relations differs across three periods. In each of these periods, certain patterns of cooperation with some foreign states and hostility toward other foreign states emerged. The three acts, if we can call them that because of the high drama of each period, are:

Act I: Mao Zedong era, 1949–1978. This act entailed the transfer of a large and comprehensive package of Soviet economic and political institutions to China and the launching of a totalitarian attempt to transform China via an attempt at total control into a totally new type of society—a utopian communist society—within a short period of time.

Act II: The happy interregnum, 1979–1989: This period saw the quick abandonment of Mao's totalitarian project and the creation of a wide space for individual freedom. China entered the era of what post-Stalin Eastern Europe called post-totalitarian communism. Soviet-derived economic institutions were incrementally discarded, and China began drawing on the inputs of the advanced capitalist countries via market-based transactions. The key domestic driver of China's foreign relations during this period was securing broad and deep access to inputs from the advanced capitalist countries to achieve rapid improvements on China's standard of living, thus regarnering popular support for continued CCP rule. The possibility of liberalization of the political system opened during this period because of a plurality of views within the CCP leadership combined with Deng's strategy of balancing between reformer and conservative factions. Liberal ideals exercised a strong attraction on China's youth and intellectuals, eventually confronting the regime with a stark threat to its survival in spring 1989.

Act III: The CCP Leninist state besieged, 1990–2015. In this act, the PRC became deeply integrated into the global economy and transformed that integration into rapid improvements in standards of living. Yet the world was swept by democratic movements, the collapse of world communism, and the appeal of liberal ideas carried by unprecedentedly powerful information and transportation technologies. The world was also dominated by a coalition of liberal democratic nations, with immense confidence in the wisdom and universal validity of their values and possessing historically unprecedented global power. Liberal democratic powers also showed new willingness to undertake armed intervention in ex-communist countries like Yugoslavia and Cambodia, or regional challenges like Iraq. These interventions revealed the vast military superiority of US military forces—along with the continuing backwardness of China's military. The geopolitical ballast to the PRC-US relation previously provided by joint opposition to the Soviet Union was gone, and Washington was free to press ideological concerns having to do with China's internal governance. Perhaps most dangerously, the Marxist-Leninist ideals used to legitimize CCP rule were no longer persuasive with a wide swath of the Chinese people. In this situation, the CCP effectively seized on aggrieved nationalism and itself as defender of the nation to relegitimize its rule, while waging unremitting struggle against bourgeois liberal ideas. China emerged as a nondemocratic but leading world power in a world dominated by liberal powers and swept by liberal ideas.

Act I of PRC foreign relations entailed the destruction of capitalism and the establishment of Soviet-style socialism and dictatorship. This required securing Soviet cooperation for this process and crushing opposition within China to the "transition to socialism." Confrontation with the United States created an atmosphere of crisis and fear, of imminent foreign attack, condu-cive to pushing through the monumental changes required to push China's revolution into the socialist stage. Confrontation with the United States also made Stalin and later Soviet leaders willing to help make the PRC a strong socialist power. Broad cooperation with the Soviet Union was essential to swift implantation and development in China of "advanced" socialist institu-tions. Then, once this new socialist economy and Leninist dictatorship was in place, Mao used it to impose on China a forced-march hyperindustrialization that he expected would move China rapidly toward the goal of utopian com-munism. Mao used his new Leninist state structures in a massive attempt at social engineering to guide the thinking of the entire Chinese people and transform them into a new communist person. This was China's totalitarian experiment: an attempt at total control to achieve a total transformation of society.[17] To proceed forward, that experiment had to overcome immense op-position and simple weariness.

The imposition of a Soviet-style socialist economic system on China entailed the elimination of private ownership and market-based economic activity. China's industrialists, bankers and financiers, and merchants, of course, resisted this "socialist transformation of commerce and industry." So too did the many millions of shopkeepers and innkeepers, traders and peddlers, restaurateurs, tailors, cobblers, barbers, and other skilled trades-men, who operated businesses large and small and who had often accumu-lated a modest amount of wealth. These were the sort of people who, over China's long history, had made it one of the wealthiest nations in the world, and who after 1978 would do the same again. Yet these were the groups that were "liquidated as a class" by the "transition to socialism." Of course they resisted and were bitter at the expropriation of their property by the state. As Mao explained to his comrades in the aftermath of the Hungarian anticommunist uprising of 1956, "the bourgeoisie" would resist strongly their overthrow and would need to be dealt with by the sternest repression. There were also people in the CCP leadership who believed that a longer period of "transition to socialism" was necessary, one perhaps lasting even decades.

The CCP's and Mao's efforts to impose socialism were further complicated by the fact that socialism was not what the CCP had promised when it was contesting with the Chinese Nationalist Party (Kuomintang, or KMT) for popular support from 1945 to 1949. In fact, during that period, when it still needed to court public opinion and before it had gained power and consolidated its dictatorship, the CCP had promised capitalism. Mao's April 1945 political report "On Coalition Government" to the Seventh Congress of the CCP, one of the key programmatic documents of the post–World War II CCP-KMT struggle, for instance, lauded the role of private, capitalist enterprise in China's future economic development. In it, Mao wrote:

> Some people suspect that the Chinese Communists are opposed to the development of individual initiative, the growth of private capital and the protection of private property, but they are mistaken. It is foreign oppression and feudal oppression that cruelly fetter the development of the individual initiative of the Chinese people, hamper the growth of private capital and destroy the property of the people. It is the very task of the New Democracy we advocate to remove these fetters . . . and freely develop such private capitalist economy as will benefit . . . [the people] and to protect all appropriate forms of private property. . . . It is not domestic capitalism but foreign imperialism and domestic feudalism which are superfluous in China today; indeed we have too little of capitalism . . . in China it will be necessary . . . to facilitate the development of the private capitalist sector of the economy.[18]

The program advanced by the CCP prior to the seizure of power, on the basis of which it had garnered popular support, ended once power was in its hands. After seizing power, the CCP program of "removing the fetters" on "private capitalism" quickly disappeared. Mao and many of his CCP comrades believed that both China's advance toward communism and the rise of China to a position of wealth and power required that the revolution move rapidly into its "socialist stage." The CCP dropped the 1945–1949 programs on which it had appealed to the Chinese people and instead implemented a very different and far less popular program. This too generated bitterness that had to be swept aside.

Then there were China's farmers, who with their families constituted probably well over 90 percent of China's population in 1949. The CCP's appeal to China's peasants during the 1945–1949 contest was "land to the tiller." Mao in "On Coalition Government" had said, " 'Land to the tiller' is correct for the present period of the revolution . . . 'Land to the tiller' means transferring the land from the feudal exploiters to the peasants, turning the private property of the feudal landlords into the private property of the peasants." Mao continued, "The overwhelming majority of the peasants . . . all except the rich peasants who have a feudal tail, actively demand 'land to the tiller.' "[19] In practice, the CCP's "land to the tiller" policy meant that land owned by landlords and "rich peasants" was seized and distributed among landless or poor peasants. The household property of landowners was also distributed among the village poor. The landlords themselves received rough justice by revolutionary tribunals headed by CCP activists. The result was bloody—several million landlords and their minions were killed—but probably popular, at least among poor and landless peasants.

But again, once power was in their hands, CCP policy switched. The CCP's Marxist-Leninist ideology and the workings of the Soviet socialist economic model required that China's farmers surrender to the state their recently received parcels of land along with draft animals and farm implements. All these were then merged into collective farms run by cadres appointed by and loyal to the CCP. Following collectivization in 1957–1958, China's peasants were not even employees of the state, since employees receive a wage for their labor and can switch employers if they wish. Peasants on PRC collective farms effectively became serfs who received most of their compensation in kind, in rations, and only a tiny amount in cash pay. They were fixed to the land politically and economically, requiring cadre approval to leave their collective farm or move to urban areas. Their work was supervised by cadre overlords who demanded long and hard labor to meet the quotas imposed by their superiors. Rural cadres had vast and arbitrary power over the farmers subject to them. Once the entire state system of comprehensive planning and collectivized farming was in place, wealth was sucked out of the agricultural sector to feed the hyperindustrialization drive. Urban dwellers fared somewhat better, but not much. Virtually the entire populace of China during the Mao era was poor. The wealth they produced fed voracious industrial growth, not better living standards. Several generations of Chinese were doomed to lives of state-imposed poverty for the sake of rapid growth of state-planned and mammothly inefficient industry. Close alliance with the USSR and confrontation with the United States were foreign policy correlates of this drive.

In the political arena as well, the policies pursued by the CCP before seizing power in 1949 were starkly different from the program delivered afterward. The CCP won the post–World War II contest with the KMT on the basis of a program promising "New Democracy." It was long a popular belief in the West that democracy was contrary to China's long Confucian tradition of benevolent authoritarianism and was, thus, essentially irrelevant to China's politics. Columbia University professor Andrew Nathan convincingly challenged this hoary belief by demonstrating the substantial degree to which concepts of individual civil freedom (freedom of speech, publication, correspondence, etc.) and democratic self-government (popular sovereignty, election and recall, etc.) were enshrined in China's eleven constitutions between 1908 and 1982. While those constitutions were often not implemented, or were implemented in a way distorted by dictatorial government, Nathan argued that these constitutions represented an ideal to which their drafters aspired, a goal to be achieved.[20] The fact that the CCP won power in 1949 on the basis of a promise of democracy substantiates Nathan's view.

Leninist dictatorship of the proletariat state such as the CCP imposed on China after 1949 was not what the CCP had promised during the post-1945 struggle with the KMT. In "On Coalition Government," which was the program on which the CCP challenged the KMT after 1945, Mao offered a vision of multiparty coalition government under conditions of extensive political freedom. There was to be an end to "one-party dictatorship." A broadly democratic multiparty coalition government—though one led by the Chinese Communist Party—was to be established. Secret police and concentration camps were to be abolished. All laws and decrees suppressing freedom of speech, press, assembly, association, political convictions and religious belief, and freedom of the person were to be abolished. The legal status of all "democratic" parties and groups was to be recognized. Nationalist political indoctrination in schools was to be abolished. Nor were these liberal arrangements to be a short-term expedient. In "On Coalition Government," Mao promised:

> Some people are suspicious and think that once in power the Communist Party will follow Russia's example and establish the dictatorship of the proletariat and a one-party system. Our answer is that. . . . Our system of New Democracy is different in principle from a socialist state under the dictatorship of the proletariat. . . . throughout the stage of New Democracy China cannot possibly have a . . . . one-party government and therefore should not attempt it. . . . The Russian system has been shaped by Russian history . . . The Chinese system is being shaped by the present state of Chinese history, *and for a long time to come* there will exist a special form of state . . . that is distinguished from the Russian system.[21] (Italics added)

The CCP's shift from advocacy of multiparty coalition government in 1945 to imposition of dictatorship of the proletariat in 1950 again encountered strong opposition. Many intellectuals and a large part of the population of China's internationalized coastal cities dreamed of liberal democracy, not proletarian dictatorship, for China's future. This opposition was repressed with extreme violence once the Korean War began. Opposition welled up again during the Hundred Flowers Campaign of 1957 when Mao persuaded critics of the regime to speak out. Again critics were struck down.

By 1957–1958, Mao saw that the model of socialism being imported from the Soviet Union differed significantly from the utopian vision of socialism and communism that he imagined. Mao also began to doubt the revolutionary credentials of the new Soviet leader, Nikita Khrushchev, and whether the Soviet leader was taking the USSR and the world communist movement in the "correct" direction toward communism. Mao then launched China on its own independent road to socialism and communism. A struggle against Soviet "revisionism" emerged as a corollary to Mao's struggle to move Chinese socialism away from the path being trod by Soviet socialism toward what Mao concluded was "phony communism."[22] In Mao's thinking, making revolution in China was linked to making revolution abroad. The Soviet Union's post-Stalin (de-Stalinized) socialism became the definition of what China's socialism was not, and struggling against the "negative example" of CPSU "revisionism" became central to Mao's upholding of Stalinized socialism in the PRC.

When a number of top CCP leaders broke with Mao's utopian policies after the catastrophe of the Great Leap Forward, Mao needed to crush that opposition too. Intensification of struggle against the Soviet Union was linked to Mao's efforts to speed China toward the communist utopia along with great international power. In sum, Mao needed to mobilize support in order to crush resistance to his radical restructuring of Chinese society. This imperative often and deeply influenced PRC foreign relations while Mao lived. By the early 1970s, the CCP state faced a combination of a severe threat of Soviet intervention combined with the existence of an embittered and only recently purged alternate CCP elite who doubted Mao's leadership and utopian policies, and most of whom remained alive. To protect the new, purified antirevisionist CCP elite Mao had just empowered via the Cultural Revolution, Mao engineered a rapprochement with the United States. The threat of Soviet attack in 1969–1970 was quite real, and it was exacerbated by Mao's awareness of a large cohort of CCP ex-leaders anxious to return China to more Soviet-like, development-oriented socialism.

Throughout the 1950s and 1960s, many Chinese enthusiastically anticipated the new communist era promised by Mao and the CCP, and supported policies that promised the arrival of that era. Many Chinese anticipated the swift arrival of economic prosperity and national power. It is quite possible that this revolutionary enthusiasm outweighed opposition and resentment well into the 1970s. But sustaining this revolutionary enthusiasm (including repressing the opposition) also benefited from an atmosphere of crisis and confrontation. A large portion of China's foreign relations under Mao must be understood as an effort to fan enthusiasm for China's domestic revolutionary advance, to convince China's people and skeptical leaders within the Politburo that the workers and peasants of the whole world stood beside China and its revolutionary struggle, and that internal doubters of the revolution were linked in various ways to hostile great powers who wished to abort China's bringing forth of a new order that would liberate mankind.

Act II of PRC foreign relations began after Mao's death, following a brief interregnum of neo-Maoism led by Hua Guofeng, with Deng Xiaoping's succession as paramount leader of the CCP. Deng and his reform-minded comrades understood that the regime faced an existential crisis. If it was to survive, the CCP had to fundamentally alter its method of rule. China's people circa 1978 were, with a few exceptions, tired, hungry, and poor. Both heavy industry and the defense industry had grown rapidly during 1949–1977, but very little investment had gone into improving the quality of life of the people. In the cities, housing was crowded, utility and educational services limited, and goods rationed. Even food and clothing were in short supply. In rural areas, living conditions were worse, often premodern. The promises of the 1950s for the imminent arrival of prosperity had become hollow. There was pervasive fear of being informed on, subjected to "struggle," forced to participate in labor reform, or even summary execution. The verities of Marxist-Leninist doctrine had not yet come under wide challenge; that would happen after China's opening in 1978. But the famine of the late 1950s and the widespread violence of the Cultural Revolution, along with Mao's purge of Peng Dehuai, Mao's mysterious falling out with his declared successor Lin Biao, and the Gang of Four's early 1970s vendetta against the widely loved Zhou Enlai, had led many people to question the wisdom of Mao's rule. In 1978, the PRC faced a legitimacy crisis, just as it would again in 1989. Deng Xiaoping's effort to refound CCP legitimacy focused on delivering rapid increases in standards of living, and that, in turn, drove new Chinese foreign policies.

Deng, like Mao, used the mechanisms of party control to engineer a revolution from above, but a revolution of a very different sort. In the process of reform under Deng, China would discard the Soviet economic model and the totalitarian aspect of the Stalin-Mao political model. But Deng continued the Soviet/Leninist model of a vanguard party state. He also abandoned Mao's utopian quest, vastly widening the sphere of individual freedom granted to ordinary Chinese. This abandonment of utopian totalitarianism was a profound transformation sometimes referred to as China's "second liberation." China discarded the autarkic policies of the Mao era, and began to draw broadly on the assets of global capitalism to rapidly raise the standard of living of the Chinese people. In this process, China's foreign relations were transformed and China was gradually integrated into the global economy and into global society.

The system set up by Stalin and imported by the CCP in the 1950s concentrated power in the hands of the heavy industrial ministries that were seen as the drivers of development and bore "socialist" ideological credentials.[23] Deng used the CCP's control over personnel appointments to place in positions of authority people willing to learn new ways of doing things to invigorate the economy, including the use of market mechanisms. For a number of years, these reforms did not challenge the preeminent position of the old plan-dependent heavy industrial interests. The three most notable reforms were the authorization of township and village enterprises (TVEs) in rural areas, the Shenzhen special economic zone, and a voluntary two-tier (planned and market-based) production system for industry. The crux of operation under all three approaches was that leaders at local levels could devise their own profit-making business plans, procure on markets whatever inputs they needed, sell their output on markets at market prices, and retain a hefty portion of the resulting profit. Although few at first, gradually more and more people seized the opportunities being offered. The political efficacy of this approach was that the emergence and growth of these new market-based economic elites did not immediately threaten the established plan-based heavy industrial fiefdoms. It would take well over a decade for nonplan market activity to begin to challenge the old plan firms. By then there were dynamic new elites and whole regions of the country that had a vested interest in continued opening and reform.

Again there were powerful links between China's domestic processes and foreign relations. Deng and his reformers did not have much wealth to hand out to supporters of reform. Central coffers were drained by the vast requirements of supporting inefficient heavy and defense industry. Instead of resources, Deng granted autonomy and thus opportunity for market activity. A large portion of the inputs that made market activity successful came from outside the PRC. International resources—financial, human, and technological—fueled the growth of market-based activity under Deng. Foreign capital, technology, and managerial know-how flowed in from Hong Kong, Singapore, Japan, and later South Korea and Taiwan to help make successful many of the TVEs, special economic zones, and two-tier enterprises that had dived into market activity. This was the key nexus between restructuring of the CCP's rule and PRC foreign relations during the post-1978 era.

"Opening" under Deng after 1978 meant drawing on the resources of global capitalism—markets for exports, acquisition of new technology and scientific knowledge, utilization of foreign capital—to accelerate China's development. "Reform" initially meant policy-making on the basis of pragmatic criteria of whether or not a move facilitated economic development, not whether it comported with Marxist-Leninist doctrine as under Mao. Increasingly, however, "reform" came to equal marketization. Over a decade or so, the result was an amazing economic transformation. The old Soviet-style planned economy was discarded step by step, and China developed a peculiar form of capitalism with Chinese characteristics.

This transformation was immensely popular. First tens of millions and then hundreds of millions of Chinese escaped poverty and began enjoying comfortable if still modest standards of living. At the beginning of the reform period, large quantities of consumer goods were imported to immediately motivate people and show that China was now on a different course. The dynamism and entrepreneurship of millions of Chinese given economic freedom proved far superior to guidance by economic planners in Beijing. Soon domestically produced consumer goods and food stuffs supplied by market-based firms and entrepreneurial rural families began to supply a growing torrent of goods to satisfy a vast pent-up demand. The crux of the domestic-international linkage during Act II was, in effect, a new social compact between the CCP and its subjects: if people would loyally obey the CCP, that party would allow them the autonomy and opportunities to "get rich." A large and ultimately vast array of foreign inputs flowed into the PRC to fuel Deng's revolution from above, quickly delivering economic benefits to those who were willing to participate in the dismantling of China's Soviet-style economy.

Deng's drive to reconstruct China via "opening and reform" had a profound impact on PRC foreign relations in other ways too. In order to secure broad US support for China's opening and reform, Deng used the Soviet-China-US "strategic triangle" to win US support for China's emergence as a rich and strong, yet Leninist, power. Deng transformed PRC-US relations by pouring new economic wine into the bottles of Sino-US strategic cooperation that traced to 1972. For Mao, better relations with the United States were about deterring Soviet intervention or attack and thus protecting China's uniquely antirevisionist socialism. Deng realized that, for better or worse, the United States dominated global capitalism, and that if the still-Leninist PRC was to draw deeply and broadly on inputs available in the advanced capitalist countries, it would need American goodwill. The basis of US benevolence toward socialist China's becoming a "rich and powerful" nation would be China's strategic partnership with the United States against the Soviet Union. The United States would welcome the PRC's "four modernizations" because it saw the PRC as a partner in the "triangular" conflict with the Soviet Union. Deng's diplomacy sought to create a favorable macroclimate for a multidecade drive for economic development by tilting toward the United States. Deng also sought to lessen conflicts with almost all countries, including China's traditional rivals Russia, Japan, and India. In line with this, Deng scrapped Mao's revolutionary activism. These moves allowed Deng to cut defense spending, shift resources to economic development, and expand economic cooperation with a wide range of countries.

Act II is called a "happy interregnum" for three reasons. First, the CCP abandoned its totalitarian quest, which had dominated the Mao period. No longer did the CCP attempt to engineer the transformation of the Chinese people into some sort of "new man" appropriate to the construction of a communist society according to Marxist-Leninist ideology. The CCP gradually granted the Chinese people a wide array of personal but long-prohibited freedoms: travel internationally and domestically, religious worship, romantic activity among youth, divorce, individual creativity and expression in the arts, hobbies of all sorts, the permissible scope of private and even public discussions, and not least, the freedom to form and grow private businesses. The mechanisms of CCP control over the state, and of state dictatorship over society, remained in place, and were still occasionally used. But mechanisms of state domination over society were no longer used to twist the Chinese people via thought reform into "new human beings" appropriate to an imagined utopia. Now it was enough that the people loyally obeyed the party. This sort of arrangement was named "post-totalitarian communism" by East European writers who experienced similar transformations in their countries in the 1960s. The level of personal freedom in China in the 1980s and 1990s might seem paltry compared to a liberal democracy like Taiwan, South Korea, or Japan. But compared to China's own recent past, the 1980s represented swift and substantial expansion of the sphere of personal freedom.

A second reason why Act II is "a happy interregnum" is that the door was not closed to reforming out of existence the Soviet/Leninist nature of the PRC. Indeed, that door seemed to be half open. There were high-ranking people in the CCP elite who felt that basic political reform needed to parallel economic reform—people like Hu Yaobang, appointed chairman of the CCP in 1981 and general secretary in 1982 (a post he held until 1987), and Zhao Ziyang, appointed premier in 1980 and general secretary in 1987. Deng Xiaoping did not entirely embrace the political reform ideas of Hu and Zhao. Indeed, he repeatedly warned them to avoid "western-style democracy" and "bourgeois liberalization." But Deng ruled during this decade by balancing between conservative and pro–political reform wings of the party. There were political reformers in the party leadership core, and they had a voice. The breath and speed of relaxation of party controls over society in the 1980s also gave hope, both within China and abroad, that those reforms might extend to reform of the basic structures of the party state. A significant number of Chinese intellectuals and university students openly embraced liberal democratic ideas, and were broadly tolerated—with occasional examples made to scare the rest. Still, the path to gradual, peaceful evolution of the PRC toward liberal democracy under the tutelage of a reform wing of the Chinese Communist Party seemed open. The door to that course had not yet been closed, as it would be in 1989.

A third reason why 1978–1989 was a "happy interregnum" was that it was a period of genuine and substantial cooperation between the PRC and the United States. In a number of areas, Beijing and Washington worked together effectively as genuine partners, constituting what was often called a "quasi alliance" against the Soviet Union. Most broadly, during this period each of the two countries, the United States and the PRC, looked on the power of the other as in its own interest—a situation radically different than during both the pre-1972 and the post-1989 periods. This boded well for the development of long-term peaceful and cooperative relations.

Act III of PRC foreign relations began with the crisis of global communism of 1989–1991. China's Leninist state, the PRC, found itself living in a world swept by liberal ideals carried by powerful new technologies in a world under unparalleled domination by an alliance of democratic countries. This started with the upheaval in Poland in early 1989, spread to China in April–June 1989, continued through the collapse of communist regimes in East Europe later that year, and culminated in the demise of the USSR and the CPSU in 1991. Democracy was consolidated across East Asia, and democratic uprisings erupted even in previously alien regions like Central Asia and the Middle East. The appeal of the Marxist-Leninist ideas that underpinned the CCP state continued to evaporate within China and globally, while democratic states and publics basked in confidence of the truth of their own liberal ideology. In this situation, the CCP was deeply fearful and insecure. It became imperative to inoculate China's populace against the seductive attraction of liberal ideas.

By late May 1989, what had begun as a student movement in Beijing two months earlier had developed into a large-scale movement mobilizing a large portion of Beijing's population, and then people in dozens of other major Chinese cities, challenging such traditional CCP methods of rule as intimidating free speech by "putting a [counter-revolutionary] hat" on someone, censoring journalists, and finally, using military force against Chinese citizens involved in peaceful protest. One prominent scholar judged the Chinese uprising of 1989 to be one of the most important components of the human struggle for freedom in the twentieth century.[24] Be that as it may, the powerful uprising in China in spring 1989 was a close call for the CCP regime and left its leaders deeply apprehensive about the stability of their continued rule.

CCP think tanks studied closely the overthrow of communist regimes in East Europe and the collapse of the Soviet Union. One key lesson they derived from those experiences was "don't relax control; don't let autonomous movements develop." Once autonomous movements begin, they can easily gather momentum and spread from one sector to another, with demands escalating with the growth of the movement. Soon such movements may confront the regime with the unfortunate necessity of testing the military's loyalty by calling on it to suppress popular protest. Even if successful, military suppression will erode further the legitimacy of the party. The way to avoid this is to keep tight control.

The CCP's mid-1989 turn away from political liberalization occurred as the world was increasingly swept by liberal values and institutions. As the CCP was resorting to old-style communist repression in the early 1990s, liberal democracy was being consolidated in South Korea and Taiwan. In Hong Kong, citizens marched in increasing numbers for the right to directly elect their governor and legislative council. In Japan, too, the Liberal Democratic Party, which had ruled since 1956, found itself ousted from power in 1994–1998 and again in 2009. "Color revolutions" challenging communist-derived authoritarian regimes erupted in Georgia in 2003, in the Ukraine in 2004–2005, and in Kyrgyzstan in 2005. In Iran, too, a people who had overthrown one dictatorship in 1979 only to find their revolution hijacked, Bolshevik-style, by

Islamic dictators rose in 2009 for democracy. Uprisings across the Arab world beginning in 2011—in Tunisia, Egypt, Libya, and Syria—shook a region long immune to democratic politics. The point is not that liberal democracy will work in any, let alone all, of these countries. The point, rather, is that liberal ideals are extremely attractive in today's world.

Underpinning this global contagion of liberal ideas was modern technology: jet airplanes, leading to mass tourism and foreign study; fax, photocopying machines, and digital printers; satellite communication, cell phones, and text messaging; video cameras and then digital photography; and containerization and the deepening of global economic flows. The most powerful of these new technologies was the internet and the world wide web. This revolutionary technology came of age just as the CCP was buckling down after June 1989 to counter "peaceful evolution" from "the West." It was in the late 1980s that the first commercial internet service providers appeared in the United States and Britain. The US military internet system, which had hosted and nurtured the internet since the 1960s, was decommissioned in 1990, and rapid proliferation of private, commercial internet service providers followed. By the mid-1990s, the internet revolution was well under way. Web-based blogs, chat groups, social networking, online shopping, and distribution of all sorts of hypertext documents expanded rapidly. Powerful new forms of organization and distribution of information that circumvented many forms of state control became available.

These technologies undermined the monopoly on information that had historically bolstered Leninist dictatorships. Pursuit of wealth and power, the old Chinese nationalist quest, made disengagement from this new technology impossible, but continued engagement with it carried great dangers for the legitimacy and stability of the CCP's Leninist system of rule.

Another factor feeding CCP fear in the post-1989 period was America's increasing propensity to concern itself with China's internal governance, or—even more dangerous for the CCP—the inclination of the US government to go beyond words and act on the basis of its opinions. During the Cold War, the awesome geopolitical imperative of countering the USSR had limited the US inclination to criticize China's grievous human rights shortcomings. After the end of the Cold War, that restraint was gone, freeing Americans and their elected representatives to concern themselves with China's domestic failings. The stark contrast between the nonviolent transitions from communist rule in Eastern Europe and the violent communist repression of demands for freedom in China further encouraged US concern with China's continuing repressive political arrangements—about dissidents and political prisoners, conditions in Tibet and Xinjiang and in prison camps, workers' rights, religious groups, and environmental issues.

The liberal-minded United States also occupied a position of immense, indeed unparalleled, global power. The major global rival of the United

States, the USSR, had disappeared, and for the first several years of the 1990s, there seemed to be the possibility that Russia might gravitate toward its "European home" and the Western camp. Moscow's former allies in Eastern Europe joined the US-led camp. Indeed, former Soviet satellites became some of the most enthusiastic members of the US-led NATO camp. Contrary to long-standing PRC predictions of the arrival of a multipolar era, the Western alliance system held together. Europe and Japan did not pull away from the United States. The grand America-centric alliance of Europe, North America, and democratic East Asia held firm. A new power, India, gravitated toward that camp for the first time.

Survival of the CCP regime in this newly threatening environment of Act III shaped PRC foreign relations in two main ways. First, Beijing sought to deter, constrain, and/or defeat US "interference" in China in support of dissident elements, but to do this in ways that did not undermine US willingness to continue supporting China's emergence as a rich and strong power. These conflicting objectives led to a combination of strength and toughness toward the United States on the one hand, and search for partnership with it on the other. The second key dimension has been CCP utilization of Leninist-style campaigns touting aggrieved nationalism to legitimize the CCP. Assertive nationalism uses emotionally evocative rhetoric and symbols to depict China as the victim of assaults, aggression, insults, and injury by foreign powers, especially the United States and Japan.[25] Frequently, these depictions of foreign moves and motives are grossly distorted or even downright wrong. Nonetheless, these putative foreign attacks are linked to China's "century of national shame and humiliation" in an attempt to rouse a sense of grievance and resentment against foreign enemies of China. The CCP's resort to this sort of "assertive nationalism" serves to mobilize domestic support for the regime in an era of eroding belief in Marxism.

Since China's opening, "Marxism-Leninism Mao Zedong Thought" has steadily been reduced to an intra-CCP regime credo. Party members must still master and profess belief in the ideology, and this helps provide coherence to the party, a sort of esoteric knowledge that binds its adherents together. The public legitimization of CCP rule, however, is no longer Marxism-Leninism but assertive nationalism—the propensity of hostile foreign powers to harm China and the need for a tough-minded regime like that of the CCP to defend against evil foreign transgression against China. Assertive foreign policies and nationalist rhetoric are used to appeal to injured nationalist pride, legitimizing the CCP regime that defends China so well. In line with this, the media and state-sponsored popular culture portray the world as a dark and sinister place, with the firm and steady CCP thwarting all sorts of nefarious schemes against China. CCP policies that are perceived to be inadequately resolute by the nationalist opinion fostered by the state undermine regime legitimacy.[26]

For several years after the Beijing Massacre of June 1989, the CCP clamped down on any autonomous political activity. By the 2000s, however, the CCP had adapted to a new pattern of interaction with spontaneous and independent nationalist political activity, including especially new web-based nationalism. Autonomous nationalist political activity—demonstrations, online petitions, blog activity—was now sometimes tolerated, and even occasionally rewarded with government acceptance of some of the demands advanced by that activism. Yet activists understood the limits of CCP tolerance, and the state retained the capacity to end this activity when it deemed it necessary to protect social order or important diplomatic objectives. What had developed was interaction between bottom-up nationalist activism and top-down party guidance of mass participation in political activity. In this fashion, the party diverts grievances from itself onto foreign enemies, especially Japan and the United States, while legitimizing itself as defender of China's interest and honor.[27]

ACT } I

Forging a Revolutionary State

2 }

Joining the Socialist Camp

The Decision to Join the Soviet Camp

One of the most important early foreign policy decisions of the PRC was the decision to ally with the USSR against the United States. When this decision was made in 1948–1949, the Cold War was well underway in Europe and the Middle East. The CCP decision to align with the Soviet camp placed the new-born PRC square in the middle of the intense Soviet-US conflict. In fact, the CCP decision to ally with the Soviet Union was a major factor spreading Cold War conflict to East Asia. The PRC's decision to ally with the Soviet Union had a profound impact on China's foreign relations and on the entire world situation.

According to Beijing University historian Niu Jun, the CCP decision to ally with the USSR, the socialist camp, and the world revolutionary movement against "US imperialism" arose out of the entire history of the Chinese revolutionary movement led by the CCP.[1] The Marxist-Leninist philosophy embraced by CCP leaders indicated that the Soviet model of political-economic organization was superior to the "bourgeois democratic" forms of the West. The basic question in dispute between the CCP and the KMT, according to Niu Jun, was over the type of state to be built, a western-style liberal democracy led by the KMT or a socialist people's dictatorship led by the CCP. From the CCP perspective, "bourgeois democratic" forms had been tried in China after 1911 and had failed. They were tried and failed again in the post-1945 period in China. Only "the Russian model" could pull China together and lead it forward quickly. Only the Russian-model socialist economy could quickly make China a great power. Soviet advice and assistance would be necessary in this effort.

The CCP's Marxist-Leninist ideology also indicated that capitalism led to imperialism, that the United States was now the world leader of imperialism and was oppressing virtually every country in the world, including China. Throughout the period following Japan's surrender, the United States had

supported the KMT against the CCP. When this policy of counterrevolutionary interference in China's internal affairs began to crumble, Washington,
again in the CCP view, switched to trying to split "intermediate" forces
away from the CCP-led anti-imperialist united front, to create an "opposition" within the revolutionary camp. The task of the Chinese revolution, Mao
explained, was to build socialism in China. There would be strong opposition to this from China's "liberal bourgeoisie," from wavering intermediate elements, and from outright counterrevolutionaries, all supported and
encouraged by US imperialism. Strong backing and support from the Soviet
Union would be essential to defeat US efforts to block China's advance down
its chosen revolutionary path. As Professor Chen Jian noted, Mao and the
CCP's perception of the US threat derived not primarily from US policies but
from Marxist-Leninist ideology, which taught that the United States was an
inherently aggressive and counterrevolutionary imperialist power.[2] A socialist China rapidly industrializing with Soviet assistance and supporting the
revolutionary forces of Asia could quickly emerge as the leading power in
Asia, or so CCP leaders hoped.

While CCP policy was moving toward alliance with the Soviet Union,
Washington was maneuvering toward a hoped-for opening to the emerging
CCP-led China. In late 1948, following the catastrophic KMT defeat in the
battle of Huaihai (November 6, 1948, through January 10, 1949), US policy
makers recognized that earlier US policy toward China had failed, that the
KMT was doomed, and that the CCP was likely to rule China. It was necessary, therefore, to reconsider US interests and policy. After an intense debate,
US leaders decided by the end of 1948 that the overriding US interest in the
Far East was minimizing Soviet power in that region, and that this could
best be achieved by preventing communist-ruled China from becoming an
adjunct of Soviet power. The premise underlying this policy was that conflicts
between China and the USSR—for example Soviet special privileges in China's
northeast and Xinjiang, as stipulated by documents ancillary to the August
1945 Sino-Soviet treaty—far exceeded conflicts of interests between China
and the United States. If the United States disengaged from the Chinese civil
war—that is, if it disengaged from Chiang Kai-shek, his Nationalist regime,
and the KMT bastion on Taiwan; let the dust settle from the recent conflict;
avoided making itself an enemy of new CCP-ruled China; and allowed some
time for Sino-Soviet contradictions to emerge—the opportunity for an opening to the new, communist-ruled China might materialize within a few years.
Chinese nationalist communism, "Chinese Titoism" in the parlance of that
era (and after the Yugoslav leader; see below), might be courted away from
Moscow.[3] One policy expression of this new US approach consisted of orders
to US missions in China, the embassy in Nanjing and consulates in Shenyang,
Tianjin, Shanghai, and Beiping (as Beijing was named before 1949), to remain
in place when communist forces occupied those areas, seek to avoid conflict,

open channels of communication with the new communist authorities, and strive to handle matters in a routine and businesslike manner.

These US decisions in 1948–1949 and the calculations behind them were, of course, top secret. Yet shifts in US policy were perceived and understood by CCP leaders. In January 1949, the Politburo issued a resolution warning against the "dualistic" nature of US policy. On the one hand, the United States continued to support Chiang Kai-shek. On the other hand, it was trying to bore from within the revolutionary camp. It was possible that the United States might even "recognize" new China in pursuit of this plot. It was necessary to "firmly rebuff" the US scheme, the resolution said. Two months later, a Central Committee resolution elaborated on this. The party should "take measures to thoroughly eradicate imperialist domination in China." With respect to the possibility of US imperialism recognizing new China, Mao specified that "not only should we not seek a speedy resolution now, even after our nationwide victory for a certain period we must not rush to settle the question." The question of recognition of China by the imperialist states was an element of the overall goal of "carrying the revolution through to the end," that is, consolidating CCP control and then moving the revolution into its socialist stage.[4]

The US strategy of courting nationalist Chinese communist away from Moscow posed a serious danger to CCP efforts to ally with the Soviet Union. The rebellion in 1948 of the Yugoslav League of Communists led by Josip Broz Tito against Soviet attempts to dominate Yugoslavia after World War II was a major challenge to Stalin. Yugoslavia was the one country in Eastern Europe that had independently driven out Nazi occupying forces and established a communist state without backing from Soviet armed forces. By 1948, conflicts between Tito and Stalin were sharp and public. In March, in a move similar to Khrushchev's move against China twelve years later, the Soviet Union withdrew all specialists and advisors from Yugoslavia. Economic embargo by the USSR and its East European socialist allies followed. Yugoslavia responded by reaching an accommodation with the emerging Western alliance system. Tito's rebellion against Soviet leadership raised Stalin's apprehensions that Mao might follow suit.

Stalin had long harbored doubts about Mao's and the CCP's "class character." Mao was a peasant and an intellectual, not a member of the proletariat, as Stalin fancied himself to be. Moreover, the "class basis" of the CCP revolution was the peasantry, not the urban proletariat, which Marx and Lenin had taught must be the main force of the revolution. Then there were Mao's occasional assertions of independence from Comintern direction over the years. Stalin had been tolerant of these because Mao had proven himself to be, alone among CCP leaders, a very effective military commander and ruthless ruler of men.[5] Yet Stalin suspected that Mao's inclination toward nationalist independence was evidence of a petit-bourgeois class character. Moreover, the new PRC government included democratic parties and "elements," and this, according to Wu Xiuquan, head of the PRC's Soviet desk who accompanied Zhou Enlai to Moscow in January 1950 to negotiate the terms of the new PRC-Soviet relation, roused Soviet misgivings that China might follow the pro-US and pro-Britain rather than the pro-Soviet path. "For these reasons," according to Wu, "the Soviet leadership was initially "indifferent and skeptical" toward the CCP.[6] The danger facing the CCP in 1948–1950 was that Stalin's struggle against Tito's "betrayal" might combine with the Soviet leader's doubts about Mao and the CCP, to be stirred by the new US policy of courting Chinese Titoism, and convince Stalin that it was best to keep the new CCP-led China at arm's length. This could mean only limited Soviet assistance to China's socialist transformation and construction.

These considerations led Mao to find ways of demonstrating CCP loyalty to the Soviet Union and negating Washington's efforts to open ties with China's emerging communist government. The CCP declared its support of Moscow's condemnation of Tito's ideological apostasy, and launched a campaign to educate the entire party about the need for close alignment with the Soviet Union and for Soviet leadership of the entire socialist camp. In July 1948, as part of the campaign to oppose Yugoslav-style "bourgeois nationalism" and strengthen "proletarian internationalism," the CCP recognized the leadership of the Soviet Union. A Central Committee resolution demanded that the entire party

> clearly recognize that the Soviet Union is the main force and leader of the world anti-imperialist democratic peace front, the Chinese people must form a solid fraternal alliance with the Soviet Union. Only then can the Chinese revolution achieve complete victory. Any sort of blind, anti-Soviet thinking and vestigial feelings must be eliminated and prevented.[7]

Four days after the establishment of the PRC on October 1, 1949, Liu Shaoqi declared:

> The reason we particularly emphasize and value friendly cooperation between China and the Soviet Union is that the path already traversed by the Soviet people is exactly the path we should follow. The experience of the Soviet people in national reconstruction deserves our very careful study. In the past, our Chinese people's revolution was carried on with Russia as our teacher, and that is why it could attain today's success. From now on, in our national reconstruction, we must similarly proceed with Russia as our teacher and learn from the Soviet people's experience of national reconstruction.[8]

As a popular slogan advanced by the CCP had it: "The Soviet Union of today is the China of tomorrow."

Negotiating the Alliance

On June 30, 1949, Mao declared that socialism and communism were now the goals of the Chinese revolution, to be achieved by a "people's democracy under the leadership of the working class." Externally, this required that new China "ally ourselves with the Soviet Union, with the People's Democracies and with the proletariat and the broad masses . . . in all other countries, and form an international united front" against imperialism. This meant "leaning to one side." "We are firmly convinced that in order to win victory and consolidate it we must lean to one side," Mao declared.[9] Immediately after Mao declared the CCP's determination to join the Soviet camp, Liu Shaoqi traveled to Moscow to discuss the terms of that relationship.

While Stalin did not trust Mao and the CCP, he nevertheless viewed the CCP victory in China as greatly shifting the global correlation of forces to the advantage of socialism. The creation of a communist-led and eventually socialist China would add immensely to the power of the socialist camp. As Stalin told one of his top China hands in mid-1948, "Of course we will give new China all possible help. If socialism also triumphs in China and our two countries follow the same road, the victory of socialism in the world may be considered a foregone conclusion."[10] Europe was still the center of Stalin's security concerns, and the Soviet leader believed that a general East-West war was imminent.[11] But Stalin also believed that the revolutionary upheavals underway in Asia—in China, Indochina, Korea, Indonesia, Malaya, perhaps in Japan—held the potential to divert US strength and attention away from Europe. A revolutionary offensive in Asia led by China could sap US strength in Europe. Stalin was thus willing to recognize the CCP's preeminence in Asia, even when Chinese policies occasionally clashed with Soviet interests. Another advantage for Stalin of a CCP-led revolutionary offensive in Asia was that it would drive a wedge between new China and the United States. It would be difficult for Mao to reach an accommodation with Washington while Beijing was fostering movements aimed at driving the United States out of Asia. Thirty years later, it would be exactly this logic that led Deng Xiaoping to disengage from Asian revolutionary movements.

But alliance with new China also carried dangers for Stalin. The weightiest of these was that the Soviet Union might be drawn into a war with the United States. Stalin was adamant that the East-West war he believed was inevitable would begin at a time and place of his choosing. The upheaval in China amounted to overturning understandings regarding China reached between Moscow and Washington at Yalta in 1945 (i.e. a non-communist-ruled China combined with Soviet special rights in Manchuria).[12] But the same Yalta agreement legitimized Moscow's preeminence in Eastern Europe, and the overturn of the Yalta agreement in the Far East might lead the United States to challenge the Yalta arrangements in Eastern Europe in an effort to redress the global balance in Washington's favor. Thus, Soviet interests and Stalin's attitude toward alliance with new China were equivocal.

During Liu Shaoqi's mid-1949 mission to Moscow, Stalin admitted that over the years he had made a number of mistakes in dealing with China, and had often interfered in China's internal affairs to the detriment of the CCP. "We have been a hindrance to you, and for this I am very regretful," Stalin confessed.[13] Liu diplomatically denied that Stalin had ever injured the CCP or the Chinese revolution. But Stalin's willingness to admit past mistakes deeply impressed members of the Chinese delegation.[14] Stalin also praised to Liu Shaoqi Mao's contributions in "applying" Marxism-Leninism in China—praise as a "theorist" that was very important to Mao for personal and political reasons. Stalin also stressed the world-historic importance of the CCP victory in China, and suggested that China and the CCP should play a more active role in advancing revolution in Asia. The Soviet Union would remain the leader of the global proletarian revolutionary movement, but in Asia, new China and the CCP should take the lead, Stalin said. Liu stressed the CPSU's role as undisputed leader of the world's progressive forces, but also agreed that China would try to contribute more to advance revolution in Asia.[15] This understanding would factor into CCP decisions about Korea a year later.

Mao had written Stalin frequently during the late 1940s to report on developments in China and solicit the Soviet leader's advice. This was probably part of a calculated effort to signal to the Soviet chief that Mao was willing to subordinate himself to Stalin. As the tides of war increasingly favored the CCP, Mao again solicited invitations to visit Moscow to consult with Stalin. The Soviet leader denied Mao's repeated requests to visit. Not until after the PRC was established and recognized by the USSR (on October 1 and October 3 respectively) did Stalin agreed to a visit by Mao.

Mao arrived in Moscow on December 16, accompanied by a delegation of twenty-five high-ranking officials. Li Fuchun, then head of China's Northeast (known in the West as Manchuria) and later to become one of the key PRC administrators, headed the working delegation. Virtually the entire top Soviet leadership (but not Stalin) greeted Mao at the rail station. Mao stayed in the Soviet Union until February 17, 1950, a visit of sixty-three days. This was the first time Mao had left China and the only time he met the giant leader of the world communist movement who had so deeply shaped his life.

The meeting of Stalin and Mao was a dramatic event and the subject of much and varied interpretation. Members of the Chinese delegation who later recalled the visit were struck by Stalin's efforts to show respect for Mao—housing him in Stalin's own villa outside Moscow and allocating another residence for him in the Kremlin, sending his own bodyguard to escort Mao and look after his needs, inviting Mao to stand beside him during Stalin's "birthday celebration" attended by communist leaders from around the world. Many Soviet observers, on the other hand, recalled Stalin's high-handed treatment of Mao. Perhaps the most important judgment was that by Mao himself; he believed Stalin treated him badly, keeping him waiting for over three weeks after their initial meeting and a purely formal meeting at Stalin's "birthday party," with nothing for Mao to do but, as Mao complained in his earthy fashion, "eat, sleep, and shit."[16] Stalin also declined to discuss with Mao grand problems of theory and strategy of the world revolution, discussions Mao craved. Instead, Stalin appointed a philosopher to handle such discussions, an arrangement that did not satisfy Mao. Mao craved recognition by Stalin as an equal, while Stalin kept him in the position of supplicant.

In their initial meeting, Stalin asked Mao what he hoped to accomplish from his visit. Mao replied that he hoped to accomplish something that "not only looked nice but also tasted delicious." Mao frequently used such homely circumlocutions which sometimes left even Chinese guessing as to his meaning. On this occasion Stalin and his interpreters were apparently at a loss to understand Mao's meaning. During Liu's July 1949 visit, Stalin had agreed that a new treaty would be signed replacing the August 1945 ROC-USSR Friendship Treaty, but there are many types of treaty. Mao subsequently gave an interview to the Soviet news agency TASS in which he clarified that the main object of his visit was to conclude a treaty of alliance with Stalin and the Soviet Union.[17] Uncertainty about exactly what sort of treaty Mao desired may have been one reason why Stalin suspended talks for several weeks after his initial meeting with Mao. Finally, on January 20, Mao summoned the experienced negotiator Zhou Enlai to Moscow to handle negotiation of the treaty and to sign it and other documents with foreign minister Andrei Vyshinsky. Mao was not personally involved in the negotiations, although he supervised them closely from behind the scene.

Finally, on February 14, 1950 a thirty-year treaty of friendship, alliance, and mutual assistance was signed. Article I provided that if either signatory power was attacked by "Japan or states allied with it and thus being involved in a state of war," the other signatory power "will immediately render military and other assistance with all means at its disposal."[18] "States allied with" Japan was a euphemism for the United States, which then still held sovereignty over Japan as the occupying power. (The US occupation ended and Japan recovered its sovereignty in 1952.) In the language of diplomacy, the phraseology of Article I was a strong treaty commitment. Treaties of alliance often merely provide for consultation in the event of threat. The phrase "with all means at its disposal" was introduced and insisted on by Zhou Enlai to add force and clarity to mutual obligation. The Soviet side resisted this strong formulation "for quite some time," according to Wu Xiuquan.[19] The Chinese side wanted a tight alliance. The requirement that involvement in a "state of war" was required to activate obligation under the treaty worked, on the other hand, to dilute Moscow's obligation. On the other hand, many wars were undeclared (e.g., the 1937–1941 Sino-Japan war and the then upcoming

Korean war). The requirement that a "state of war" exist to activate the treaty's mutual defense obligation worked to limit the degree of Soviet commitment under the treaty.

A secret protocol to the 1950 treaty, not revealed until 1993 after ex-Soviet archives were opened, stipulated that China would not allow third-country nationals to settle or conduct business in China's Northeast and Xinjiang. For purposes of legal equality, Moscow accepted a similar obligation regarding Russian Siberia and Central Asia, but the real purpose of this agreement was to underline that China's northeast and northwest were spheres of special Soviet security interest.[20] Separate agreements signed at the same time as the treaty of alliance provided for the broad continuation of Soviet privileges in China's Northeast—special rights tracing to the ROC-Soviet treaty of friendship of August 1945 and which Moscow and Washington had agreed at Yalta to force on China. Special privileges for Soviet shipping through Dalian were to continue for thirty years or until a peace treaty with Japan was signed. (No such treaty was ever signed between Japan and the USSR.) The new 1950 dispensation did provide, however, that Moscow was to relinquish its railway rights and its military basing right at Port Arthur (Lüshun in Chinese) "not later than the end of 1952."

After Stalin's death, Mao would condemn all these Soviet special rights as "big power national chauvinist errors" by Stalin and demand, successfully, that the post-Stalin Soviet leadership cancel most of them. Wu Xiuquan expressed in his memoir China's resentment of Stalin's niggling attitude:

> The Soviet Union should have handed [these] right[s] over to China, without any reservations. . . . but we bore in mind the overall situation and did not argue with them about such details. Stalin and the other leaders of the Soviet Communist Party seemed fairly warm toward us and they could be a potential source of help in our national construction.[21]

By swallowing Stalin's "big power chauvinist errors," Mao got what he wanted most from the Soviet Union: Soviet military protection against the United States and a commitment to large-scale and comprehensive Soviet assistance in consolidating CCP control over China and then industrializing China and modernizing the PLA. Moscow agreed to provide US$300 million of Soviet credit to finance five years' purchases of Soviet industrial machinery and equipment. The credit carried 1 percent interest and was to be repaid by shipments of Chinese raw materials, tea, gold, or US dollars over a period of ten years from 1954 to 1963. Soviet assistance would permit China's rapid socialist industrialization.

The February 1950 treaty of PRC-USSR alliance had a deep impact on US policy.

As noted earlier, from late 1948 through June 1950 Washington sought to woo Chinese communism away from Moscow. The February treaty represented the failure of that policy. As Wu Xiuquan put it: "The sign-ing of the treaty was tantamount to the complete failure of the imperialists headed by the United States to sow dissention between China and the Soviet Union."[22] The United States did not immediately shift policy, but when it did, after North Korea's June 25, 1950, attack on South Korea, the new US policy would focus on containing the Sino-Soviet bloc by building a political and military system around China's periphery.

The 1950 treaty continued the historic role of China's northeast as a plat-form for Soviet military power, a role tracing to 1896, when the Russian gov-ernment formed a secret alliance with a declining Qing government the year after China's defeat by Japan. China's obligation to "immediately render mil-itary and other assistance with all means at its disposal" under the February 1950 treaty meant that in the event of an East-West war, US positions in Japan and the Okinawa Islands would confront Soviet forces operating from bases in China's Northeast—or at least so US war planners had to assume. Throughout the 1950s, Chinese propaganda stressed the importance of the Sino-Soviet alliance to strengthening and defending the whole socialist camp, including Eastern Europe.

The 1950 treaty also profoundly altered the military significance of the island of Taiwan. If Taiwan were to be at Beijing's "disposal" following that island's conquest by the PLA, bases there would be available to Soviet air and naval forces under the provisions of the 1950 treaty. While China did not have a navy that could threaten the United States in the Pacific, the Soviet Union did. In the final days of World War II, the Soviet Union had acquired the Nazi submarine program in a fashion similar to the US acquisition of the Nazi missile program. That superior German technology was incorporated into new classes of Soviet submarines that were putting to sea by the late 1940s. In the event of a Soviet-US war, Soviet submarines in the Pacific would at-tempt to interdict US ships deploying US men and war matériel forward to bases in Japan, Okinawa, and the Philippines. Soviet submarine operations in the Pacific were greatly hampered, however, by the need for those boats to transit relatively narrow and US-monitored straits exiting the Sea of Japan before they could reach the high Pacific Ocean where their American ship-ping targets would be. Submarine operations based on Taiwan would face no dangerous straits. Soviet boats operating from Taiwan could quickly reach deep water off the continental shelf under the protection of Soviet aircraft based on Taiwan.[23] If used by the PLA, Taiwan would not be militarily signif-icant to the United States. If used by Soviet armed forces, however, it would pose a major threat to the United States in the event of a war against the Soviet Union. Beijing's close military alliance with Moscow transformed for the United States the significance of potential control of Taiwan by Beijing.

One other important element negotiated during the formation of the PRC-Soviet alliance had to do with Mongolia. Mongolia was a sovereign state allied with the Soviet Union, whose independence had been accepted by the ROC in 1945 under the terms of the Yalta settlement and as a quid pro quo for Soviet support for China's ROC government. To the end of his life (he died on Taiwan in 1975), Chiang Kai-shek believed that his 1945 accession to Soviet-American demands that he abandon China's claim to Mongolia was the major reason for his loss of popular support during the 1946–1949 contest with the CCP. This explanation was, of course, self-serving and covered up serious shortcomings in Chiang's KMT regime. On the other hand, Chiang was an ardent Chinese patriot and may have had a good sense of popular sentiment on this issue. His minister of foreign affairs, T.V. Soong (Madame Chiang's brother), resigned that office rather than affix his signature to an agreement "selling out the national territory" (*chumai guo tu*). CCP propaganda during the postwar struggle used this charge of *chumai guotu* quite effectively against Chiang.[24]

From the perspective of CCP (and KMT) leaders, Mongolians were one of China's national minorities and the large territory they inhabited was part of China. During the thirteenth through nineteenth centuries, Mongolia had frequently been part of the Chinese empire—or vice versa. But Mongolia had been directed down the socialist path circa 1921 when the Bolshevik Red Army occupied that country in the course of the Russian Civil War. Mongolian communist leaders, put in power by the Soviet Red Army at that time, saw a close relation with the Soviet Union as protection against annexation by China. Whatever other complaints Mongolia might have about Soviet policy (Stalin purged Mongolian leaders in 1937 and 1941 for criticizing his policies), at least Moscow posed no threat to Mongolian independence.[25]

Rather than approach Mongolian leaders directly with the proposal that Mongolia "return to China," CCP leaders pursued the issue with Moscow in 1949, 1950, 1954, and 1956. The CCP argument to Moscow was that Mongolia had historically been part of China, that its current independence was a great historic injustice, and that Soviet assistance in undoing that injustice would create a solid foundation for the new, fraternal relation being formed between the PRC and the USSR. Moscow declined the CCP request. Mao delivered to Anastas Mikoyan, Soviet foreign minister and Stalin's special envoy on this occasion, the first CCP request about "uniting the two parts of Mongolia" Stalin's terms were clear: if new China wanted Soviet support, it would have to recognize Mongolia's independence. Zhou and Vyshinsky exchanged notes recognizing the independence of the People's Republic of Mongolia.[26] The PRC established diplomatic relations with the People's Republic of Mongolia on October 16, 1949. Figure 2-1 shows the situation of Mongolia and Soviet special rights in China's Northeast.

After Stalin's death in 1953 and Khrushchev's denunciation of him in 1956, CCP leaders again raised the issue of Mongolia's "return to China," this time phrasing it as part of Stalin's "mistakes" that needed to be rectified. The Soviet

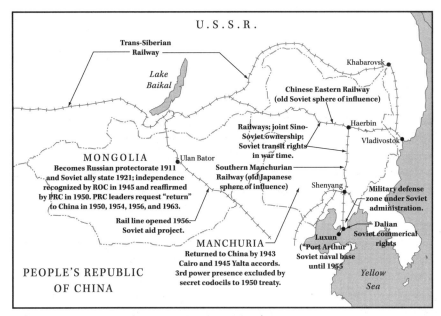

FIGURE 2-1 **Mongolia and Soviet Special Rights in China's Northeast**

Source: Chu-yuan Cheng, *Economic Relations between Peking and Moscow: 1949–1963* (New York: Praeger, 1964), pp. 28, 43.

answer was the same: no. This unspoken memory of the forced alienation of parts of "China" under intense foreign pressure is a core part of Chinese bitterness about China's "humiliation."

"Cleaning House Before Inviting Guests"

As founders of a new state, CCP leaders needed to decide when and how to establish diplomatic relations with other states. Between late 1948 and early 1950, the CCP followed several principles in this regard: distinguishing between friends and enemies, "making a fresh start," and "cleaning house before inviting guests."[27] Distinguishing between friends and enemies meant different treatment for the Soviet Union and "People's Democracies" (East European, North Korean, and North Vietnamese communist-ruled states) on the one hand, and Western countries on the other hand. For the Soviet Union and other socialist countries, new China would establish relations quickly and without negotiations. For Western countries, and especially for the United States, negotiations would be necessary to work out a new relation based on equality and noninterference in China's internal affairs. As Mao instructed a Central Committee session in March 1949, "We should not be in a hurry to solve [recognition with the United States] even for a fairly long period after country-wide victory."[28] Regarding socialist countries, Stalin promised Liu Shaoqi during their mid-1949 Moscow talks that these countries would recognize new China shortly after it was formally established. Within a week of the PRC's establishment on October 1, the Soviet Union, Bulgaria, Romania, Hungary, Czechoslovakia, and Poland had recognized and established ambassadorial relations with it. East Germany and Albania took longer (October 27 and November 23, respectively). Beijing did not establish ties with Titoist Yugoslavia, the target of Soviet and Chinese ire for "splitting the socialist camp," until January 1955. Tito offered diplomatic ties much earlier, but Mao declined the offer in order to demonstrate fealty to Stalin. The first Western country to establish ties with the PRC, at only the chargé d'affaires level, was Britain in June 1954, in spite of a British unilateral declaration of recognition in January 1950.[29]

"Making a fresh start" entailed Chinese rejection of all agreements signed by earlier Chinese governments and still valid under international law. Earlier Chinese governments, including the Qing and the ROC, had signed and ratified many treaties which were still legally valid, at least under traditional interpretations of international law. These treaties provided the legal basis for a large Western presence in China. From the CCP's perspective, this entire structure of treaties was part and parcel of China's "humiliation" and needed to be overthrown. The CCP simply did not recognize these treaties as having legal validity. New China would negotiate tabula rasa new agreements premised on equality and noninterference. This process should begin, in the CCP view, with Western powers apologizing for past "aggression" against China, accepting the complete invalidity of earlier agreements, and negotiating new treaties when China's government decided the time to do so was right. "Making a clean break" did not apply to relations with socialist countries. The August 1945 Sino-Soviet agreements formed the basis for the Sino-Soviet treaty of 1950.

The CCP's revolutionary nationalist approach clashed with the more traditional US view. Under traditional international law, new states succeeded to the obligations of their predecessors. Obligations legally agreed to by two states did not evaporate because one of those states disappeared, but passed on to successor states. The existence of US embassies, consulates, and other official offices in China, and the privileges and immunities enjoyed by those officials, were based on treaties and the customary obligations of states. US leaders were dismayed by the CCP's refusal to recognize what they felt were China's clear responsibilities under international law. They also believed that by withholding US recognition and threatening to restrict China's economic ties with the West, the United States could pressure the PRC to accept its legal responsibilities. The CCP, however, saw the entire structure of international law as it existed as part of the imperialist mechanism used to oppress and control countries like China.

The principle governing establishment of diplomatic relations was "clean house before inviting guests" (*qian dazao fangzhen, hou qing ke*). In essence this referred to pushing Western, and especially American, diplomatic presence out of China, and uprooting the vast Western cultural presence in China, before re-establishing diplomatic relations with those Western countries. In 1949, there was a huge Western-inspired and/or Western-linked cultural presence in China: businesses and companies, Christian churches, civil organizations such as YMCA and YWCAs, clubs, schools, orphanages, newspapers, political and professional associations. From the CCP's perspective, this vast matrix of civil society was unacceptable on two grounds. First, it was a social basis for imperialist influence within China. It was through these organizations that "imperialism" dominated and controlled a country, or so Marxism-Leninism taught. Second, this civil society was the core of the "bourgeois" (that is, private, voluntaristic, and self-interest-based) society that was to be destroyed as part of the construction of a socialist society. Under socialism, again as understood by Stalin's and the CCP's Marxism-Leninism, social organizations would function under the leadership of the party, thus lending their weight to achievement of the "tasks" specified by the party.

Western diplomatic missions in China had extensive contacts with this Western-influenced Chinese civil society. Allowing Western diplomatic presence to remain in China while the CCP moved to either dismantle or bring these organizations under party control would be inconvenient for two reasons. First, it would encourage resistance to China's transition to socialism by China's "bourgeois elements." Second, it would convey information about the dictatorial repression underway in China to the outside world, where the Western media would use it to "attack New China." It was better if the hard, cruel work of transition to socialism were performed without observation by Western diplomats, journalists, and missionaries.

These principles were put into practice as PLA armies swept across China. On November 2, 1948, PLA forces occupied Shenyang, capital of Liaoning province. The US consul general in that city, Angus Ward, remained at his post in that city per State Department instructions. PLA troops took up protection of the consulate grounds and initially allowed the facility to continue normal operations. For about two weeks, businesslike cooperation occurred between consular officials and the office of the new communist mayor, Zhu Qiwen. Visits were exchanged, official titles were used, and agreement was reached to issue identification cards for consulate automobiles. Then there was an abrupt hardening of CCP policy under direction of Mao and Zhou Enlai. The Center rebuked Zhu for treating US personnel as though they had some sort of special status (i.e., diplomatic status, immunities, and privileges), when in fact they were merely ordinary foreign citizens and should be treated as such. The objective, the CCP Center explained to the Party's Northeast Bureau, was to drive the US mission out of China.[30]

A short while later, the consulate was required to hand over its radio transmitter. When this was refused, the consulate was entered and the transmitter seized. Ordinary foreign citizens in China were not permitted to possess radio transmitters, Ward was told. Then consular officials were forbidden to leave the consular compound, and entry into the facility was restricted. Efforts by US diplomats elsewhere in China to contact the Shenyang consulate were thwarted. The consulate was cut off from the outside world. Then CCP media began charging (groundlessly, historians determined in retrospect) that the Shenyang consulate was a base for US espionage. In October 1949, Ward and four consular employees were arrested and charged with assaulting a Chinese employee of the consulate. Ward was put on trial and convicted. The point of all this was that US official personnel in China had no special privileges or immunities, but were mere foreign citizens subject to Chinese law and authority. Finally, on December 11, 1949, after thirteen months of detention and harassment, Ward and his consular staff were allowed to leave China.

Another "house cleaning" followed shortly after Ward's departure. On January 6, 1950, PRC authorities seized former military barracks in Beijing that had been turned into regular offices used by US diplomatic personnel. The United States held those facilities under a 1943 treaty with the ROC. In the CCP view, that treaty had no validity, and the Americans were required to vacate the facility. Shortly after the seizure of the US offices in Beijing, the United States ordered the withdrawal of all US diplomatic personnel in China. They would not return until 1973.

Two interrelated goals underlay these CCP policies: forging a close and comprehensive partnership with the Soviet Union, and preparing conditions for the movement of the revolution to its socialist stage. Stalin's deep suspicions of Mao and the CCP were discussed earlier. Allowing a US/Western diplomatic presence to remain in China would feed Stalin's paranoia, while driving them out in a revolutionary fashion would help convince Stalin that Mao and the CCP were true communists. The recommendation to seize the Shenyang consulate's radio, for example, had come from Soviet advisor Ivan Kovalev. While criticizing Shenyang mayor Zhu Qiwen for his initially cordial approach to US diplomats, Mao instructed the head of the CCP's Northeast Bureau Gao Gang to inform the Soviet Union that "So far as our foreign policy in the Northeast and the whole country is concerned, we will certainly consult with the Soviet Union in order to maintain an identical stand with it."[31] Regarding the link between eliminating the Western diplomatic presence in China and maintaining the forward momentum of the revolution, Mao informed the nation in his January 1949 New Year's address that the United States was "organizing an opposition within the revolutionary camp to strive with might and main to halt the revolution where it is or, if it must advance, to moderate it."[32] Two months later, Mao told a Central Committee session that in order to prevent the Western countries from sabotaging the revolution from within, new China must not establish diplomatic relations with the Western countries until "imperialist" privileges, power, and influences in China had been eliminated.

Uprooting the Old: Destruction of the "Imperialist" Presence in China

Uprooting the large Western presence in China and eliminating the influence of that presence on Chinese society paralleled the move toward alliance with the Soviet Union. Under the treaty system in place by 1860 that opened China to interactions with Western countries, an array of Western entities had established themselves in China. This Western presence in China probably reached its apogee in the first decade of the twentieth century and was thereafter attenuated first by China's instability and then by the long war with Japan. With a few exceptions, after the start of war with the United States and Britain in December 1941, Japan suppressed Western interests in areas under its sway, which included all of China's major coastal cities, where Western interests were concentrated. Yet China is a big country, and many Westerners, especially those associated with Christian missionary efforts, survived the Japanese wave. After Japan's surrender, many of the businesses and cultural organizations suppressed by Japan reestablished themselves in their old areas with the general welcome of China's Nationalist authorities. The Nationalist government had negotiated new treaties with the United States and Britain in 1943 which generally kept China's door open, but on the basis of equality and without such humiliating features as extraterritoriality.[33]

In 1946, there were an estimated 65,000 foreigners residing in Shanghai, down from 150,000 in 1942, but still constituting about 1 percent of a population of approximately six million in 1949.[34] That included many Russian refugees from the Bolshevik Revolution and German and Austrian Jewish refugees from Nazi rule. Chinese are rightly proud that China was one of the very few countries in the world to provide refuge to Jews fleeing the Nazi terror. Those "Shanghai Jews" were, however, driven out by the CCP along with the rest of the Westerners resident in Shanghai and China. Being mostly Caucasian and living Western lifestyles, Westerners were a highly visible minority. There were an estimated 4,000 British citizens and 2,500 Americans residing in Shanghai in the late 1940s.

Businesses and commercial interests were one major type of Western presence. Foreign investment in post–World War II China is estimated to have totaled US$1.5 billion, divided roughly equally between British and American ownership. British investment was concentrated in Shanghai and played a major role in that city's manufacturing, import-export trade, and finance. Shanghai's foreign trade represented three-quarters of all China's trade, and a large share of it was handled by long-established British merchant houses like Jardine Matheson and Butterfield & Swire. The British Hongkong and Shanghai Banking Corporation was one of the leading Western enterprises based in Shanghai, with branches in eleven Chinese cities. Shanghai's utilities—electricity, natural gas, water, streetcars, and telephone—were all run by British, US, or French firms. US investment was somewhat more geographically dispersed than British and concentrated in public utilities and distribution network of American oil giants like Standard Vacuum and Caltex. France too had significant commercial interests, worth an estimated US$200 million. French holdings were concentrated in real estate owned by the Catholic Church.

The Western religious presence was also quite large. There were an estimated 5,500 foreign Catholic missionaries and 4,000 foreign Protestant missionaries in China circa 1948. These foreign missionaries were assisted by an estimated 8,000 Chinese ordained ministers and priests. In many villages with Christian populations, the church was the largest and most prominent building. Aside from religious activities, foreign missionaries supported a number of eleemosynary activities: clinics and pharmacies in rural areas, 203 Protestant hospitals, hundreds of orphanages and foundling homes for abandoned babies, 227 middle schools, and thirteen universities. Catholic missions operated another 4,500 schools with an estimated 320,000 students, plus three universities with 4,000 students. These Western-supported Christian schools constituted in 1948 a significant portion of China's overall educational system. Ironically, a number of CCP leaders—including some who would play leading roles in shutting them down in 1949–1950—were educated in these Christian schools.

A strong media presence was another dimension of Western presence in China. Western press agencies like United Press, Associated Press, and Agence France-Presse maintained agencies there. Beijing alone had seventeen foreign correspondents circa 1948. These Western agencies were major suppliers of news about China to Western publics. Chinese-language newspapers were also major customers of the Western press agencies; Western media provided content for them. Chinese readers found interesting this Western coverage of China's affairs. There were also three English-language newspapers in Shanghai, which served to knit the foreign community together while also serving a substantial English-reading Chinese audience. The US, British, and French governments maintained cultural and information offices in many cities where their consulates were located, and offered an array of public lectures, film showings, and concerts. American jazz was popular, as were cultural performances, language lessons, and general information about the American, British, or French ways of life. Cinema was probably the Western art form with the widest appeal in China. American Hollywood movies, especially, were very popular. An investigation by CCP authorities in Shanghai in August 1949 (about four months after CCP forces occupied the city) found that 72 percent of all moviegoers in Shanghai chose US movies, in spite of a campaign by CCP media condemning US movies as instruments of US cultural imperialist aggression. American movies were so popular in Shanghai that the CCP delayed banning them for a number of months lest they generate dissent before the city was under firm control and a good supply of Soviet films were on hand as substitute.

The CCP was determined to uproot this vast Western presence, which they viewed as a form of Western aggression against China. A second CCP objective was to quick- march China into a socialist form of organization. The Western presence in China would be an obstacle to that by conveying negative information about China to foreign audiences and encouraging Westernized and/or Christian Chinese to resist communist policies. More fundamentally, there was no place in China's future socialist state for any sort of autonomous, non-state-controlled religious, business, media, educational, or even cultural activity, whether Western or Chinese. All these were to be brought under control of the CCP party state and thus directed toward fulfilling the revolutionary and socialist goals specified by the Party Center.[35]

Eradiation of the Western presence unfolded gradually. The CCP established firm control before it moved to uproot the popular but politically incorrect "imperialist presence." When PLA forces first occupied an area, they protected foreign nationals and their facilities, typically allowing normal operations to continue. The case of the US consulate in Shenyang was a marked exception. Exceptional too were foreign news services and official cultural and information offices; these were shut down as soon as PLA forces took control. Western business and religious-based activities, however, were initially left alone. Xenophobic people roused by the nationalist fervor that was sweeping China were prevented from attacking foreigners or their property. This moderation continued for a number of months, and in a few cases for a couple of years. Scholar Beverly Hooper surmised that this initial moderation was inspired by a desire to minimize disruption and opposition while the CCP had still not consolidated control and was not in a position to take over from foreigners. Then, as CCP control over an area tightened, so did the restrictions and burdens imposed on foreigners and their operations. As these burdens and restrictions grew, foreigners became increasingly aware they could no longer operate normally in China, and that attempts to do so were costly, inconvenient, and personally dangerous. The exodus of Westerners from China grew throughout the second half of 1949 and early 1950 and was well underway by the start of the Korean War in June 1950; it was not the war that triggered the exodus. The extreme hysteria and repression associated with CCP policy during that war did succeed, however, in driving out almost all Westerners. By the time the Korean War ended in

1953, only a handful of Westerners, perhaps several score, remained in China, mostly "progressive" sympathizers of the CCP who found work in the CCP's foreign-language propaganda departments.

A second characteristic of CCP eradication of the Western presence was avoidance of claims for compensation under international law by not seizing or nationalizing foreign property outright. CCP foreign policy specialists (many of whom had studied in the West) had done their homework and knew that if foreigners could be persuaded, one way or another, but via lawful means, to simply abandon their property or hand it over to a Chinese entity, China would not be liable to foreign claims to compensation for that property. Thus foreigners found themselves and their operations confronted with increasing difficulties until, finally, they simply left.

The campaign of squeezing out Western entities was paralleled by a formal pledge, stated periodically at the highest level, that the CCP and PRC would protect and not encroach on the lawful interests of foreigners in China. Hooper suggests that this declaration served as high-sounding moral camouflage to deflect criticism of the drive against Western interests. It was the proviso "lawful" that became the operative clause, as permits, taxes, wage increases, utility costs, visas, etc., stipulated by new China's legally constituted authorities that persuaded foreigners to give up and leave China. A wide array of burdens was increasingly piled on foreigners. For example, foreigners were required to obtain a residence permit from the local police office. These were for stipulated periods of time, typically three, six, or twelve months. This meant that if a permit was not renewed, as was increasingly the case, the individuals were legally required to leave China. Another permit was required to travel outside one's city of residence. Such permissions were seldom granted. This was a major difficulty for missionaries whose work required travel throughout their parishes.

Police often made "house calls" on foreign residents, searching individuals and their personal belongings and asking about activities and life histories. Chinese became the mandatory language for all interactions with officialdom, including written communications. Non-Chinese speakers were required to provide their own interpreters. The low-level government officials who handled all these transactions were often xenophobic and took easy offense, attitudes which were fanned by the anti-foreign coverage of CCP media. When foreigners gave up and were ready to leave, another exit permit was required. Before that permit was granted, the applicant was required to post a public notice in newspapers, an action that frequently resulted in claims by former employees. These claims had to be resolved, by officials who invariably ruled in favor of the Chinese claimant, before the exit permit was granted. Employees—cooks, nannies, chauffeurs, etc.—became militant, demanding large pay increases, severance pay, and compensation for past purported injuries.

Businesses, missionary schools, and hospitals found themselves subject to exorbitant taxes and fees. Workers became militant and raised costly demands. Lock-ins by militant workers would detain foreign owners or managers in their offices for long periods of time. It became virtually impossible to fire workers, even with generous severance pay. More and more economic activities were brought under government control. When taxes, wages, or fees were not paid on time, heavy fines were imposed. Appeals and explanations addressed to higher Chinese authorities were to no avail. CCP media fanned anti-foreign sentiment. When incidents involving foreigners occurred (many involving loss of tempers by foreigners), the media played them up as major examples of imperialist arrogance, and heavy fines, and sometimes jail sentences, were imposed. Foreign businessmen gradually realized that they could no longer operate profitably or even safely in China. By fall 1949, US firms were trying to get their personnel out of China as quickly and completely as they could. British firms tried to "hand on and hold out" with diplomatic support from their government, but they too soon followed US firms out China's closing door. Many firms found themselves to be "commercial hostages," with home headquarters sending money to offices in China to pay financial demands in hopes that their non-Chinese expatriate personnel might then be allowed to leave China.

In dealing with Protestant religious schools and hospitals, the CCP worked with "progressive" Chinese clergy and staff to exclude foreign personnel from any administrative or supervisory roles. Western personnel performing important functions (faculty teaching science, math, or foreign languages and medical doctors) were allowed to stay until their contracts expired. They were then replaced by Chinese personnel. "Patriotic" Chinese Protestants were then constituted as a Patriotic Chinese Protestant Church under strict state and party control. It was more difficult for the CCP to find Chinese Catholics willing to cooperate in breaking with foreign authorities, in this case the pope. But eventually this effort, too, succeeded. The last noncompliant Catholics, foreign and Chinese, were imprisoned as counterrevolutionaries or as spies during the Korean War. By 1950, the once vast Western presence in China, formed over a century, was rapidly being eliminated. By the end of the Korean War, it was gone. Deep links between China and the West would not be rebuilt for nearly forty years.

Planting the New: Transplanting the Soviet Economic Model

Within a year of the establishment of the PRC, Mao Zedong concluded that the party's earlier commitment to a ten- to fifteen-year period of capitalist development by the "national bourgeoisie" and family farming should be replaced by a drive toward socialism like that engineered by Stalin in the

Soviet Union. Mao now decided to eliminate capitalism and replace it with state-owned, state-operated, and state-planned economic activity. From the standpoint of Stalin's and Mao's Marxism-Leninism, market-based production of goods for sale, i.e., capitalism, was irrational and inhumane and must be superseded by rational, comprehensive economic planning done by the state on the basis of the interests of the working classes. In a Soviet-style comprehensively planned socialist economy, there were virtually no markets.[36] Instead, officials in state planning agencies calculated exactly how much of each particular type of good would be produced over the next several years, what factories would make exactly how much of that good, which other factories would make the necessary components for each good, and so on. All the productive resources of society, or at least the "basic" ones, were owned by the state and operated under the direction of central state planning agencies. Production quotas were assigned by the plan to each enterprise, and party committees within each enterprise ensured that enterprises complied with the plan. Effective comprehensive economic planning in a large economy was an immensely complex and difficult task. The Soviet Union had worked out practical organizational solutions to this problem starting with its First Five Year Plan in 1928. By 1951, it was beginning its Fifth Five Year Plan, giving it a quarter century of experience in "constructing socialism." It was this Soviet model of comprehensive, centralized economic planning that the CCP imposed on China in the early 1950s.

Mao's model of socialism, and the process of socialist construction which was transposed on China in the 1950s, was a copy of Soviet experience in the 1920s and 1930s. The main vehicle through which this model was conveyed to Mao and the CCP (as to communists around the world) was the *Short Course on the History of the All-Russia Communist Party (Bolshevik)*, usually known simply as the *Short Course*. This book was drafted under Stalin's close supervision in 1937 and published in the Soviet Union in 1938. Forty-two million copies would be published in sixty-seven languages between 1938 and 1953 (when Stalin died). While Stalin lived, the *Short Course* was treated by communist parties around the world as the absolute scientific truth about socialist revolution and construction and as a virtual sacred text and handbook of Marxism-Leninism. Stalin ordered the *Short Course* written for use in the ideological indoctrination of CPSU members. Mao used it for the same purpose. The book became the key vehicle for "unifying thinking" within the CCP about how socialism was to be constructed. It was translated into Chinese in 1938 and assiduously distributed around China by the CCP.[37]

Mao first encountered the *Short Course* in Yan'an in the 1930s. Once settled in Yan'an after the end of the Long March, Mao turned to study of Marxist-Leninist theory to arm himself against Soviet-trained rivals in the CCP who had a better grasp than Mao of these vital theoretical weapons.

Mao subsequently stated how deeply impressed he was by the *Short Course*'s profound Marxist-Leninist analysis. Scholar Hua-yu Li noted the irony that Mao, who frequently differed with Stalin over policy during the pre-1949 period, accepted uncritically Stalin's grossly inaccurate and distorted account of Soviet history in the 1920s and 1930s.

The *Short Course* described how Stalin had struggled against a series of "incorrect" "anti-party groups" that had (putatively) represented the bourgeoisie and other class enemies within the CPSU. By defeating these successive "incorrect and anti-party groups" within the party, Stalin had pushed the revolution forward to final victory of socialism over capitalism. According to the *Short Course*, Stalin, with profound insight, realized in the mid-1920s that the parallel existence of a state-planned sector and a private capitalist sector left open the question of "who will win, socialism or capitalism, the proletariat or the bourgeoisie?" He concluded that definitive victory for socialism and the proletariat required the complete destruction of capitalism, and moved the Soviet Union in that direction from around 1926 on. An attack on the rich peasants (known in Russia as kulaks) overcame their resistance to socialism, specifically to collective farming, and brought the agricultural sector into socialism. Three Five Year Plans fueled by extractions from agriculture then generated rapid socialist industrialization. By 1937, proclaimed the *Short Course*, the construction of socialism was basically complete, and the USSR had become a highly industrialized country with first-rate technology. Mao's 1949–1950 travels through the USSR had confirmed this conclusion for him. During those travels, Mao was shown the most modern Soviet factories and farms. Mao (unlike other top CCP leaders) had seen no capitalist country that might provide a comparison, and was very impressed by what he saw in the Soviet Union.[38]

Some of Mao's comrades on the Politburo who had themselves absorbed the *Short Course* accepted Stalin's model of socialist construction, but felt that a ten- to fifteen-year preparatory period of continued market development was necessary before China pushed ahead into the socialist stage. Ironically, Stalin himself shared this view and warned Liu Shaoqi and other CCP leaders against the abrupt expropriation of rich peasants and China's capitalist class. Stalin, after all, probably knew quite well just how far the reality of the Soviet economy differed from the rosy propaganda depicting it. During 1948–1951, Liu Shaoqi, CCP economic czar Vice Premier Chen Yun, and economic planner Bo Yibo shared Stalin's doubts about the swift destruction of capitalism in China. But the expansion of China's state sector because of Soviet assistance in industrial production in China's Northeast between 1946 and 1950 convinced Mao that the balance between the state sector and the market sector had shifted sufficiently to create the necessary industrial base for transition to socialism in China. Liu, Chen, and Bo were shocked by Mao's startling and bold conclusion, but once instructed directly by Mao, they quickly came on board with Mao's program of swift eradication of capitalism in China.[39]

Stalin's willingness to provide large-scale assistance to China's socialist industrialization was another major factor convincing Mao that a swift destruction of capitalism and the construction of socialism were possible in China. Stalin during his early 1950 Moscow talks with Mao and Zhou had pledged to assist forty-seven major industrial projects. This was the first tranche of Soviet assistance, which would grow considerably over coming years. Still, as long as Stalin was alive Mao had to move carefully to avoid antagonizing him. Stalin's death in March 1953 removed that obstacle, and in December Mao issued his "General Line for Socialist Transition." The same year, Mao launched a nationwide campaign to study the *Short Course* to "unify thinking" in the party about how to "build socialism."

The CCP viewed the Soviet model of comprehensive economic planning as the very core of socialism and transposed a nearly exact replica of that system in China. In spring 1951, the PRC began drafting its First Five Year Plan to guide the growing socialist sector. In August 1952, a large and high-level PRC delegation led by Premier Zhou Enlai, Vice Premier Chen Yun, and Li Fuchun, by then deputy director of the Central Financial and Economic Committee, traveled to Moscow.[40] The delegation included leaders from various industrial sectors: ferrous metals, energy, machine building, etc. The delegation stayed in the Soviet Union until May 1953, approximately ten months. The purpose of the delegation was to study Soviet experience with Five Year Plans. Delegation members studied components of the Soviet Fifth Five Year Plan (then underway) and related that to the First Five Year Plan underway in China. As one participant of the delegation later recalled, "By studying and discussing the draft of the Soviet Union's fifth five-year plan, we could systematically understand the formulation of the policy and content of the plan, and it helped us in enriching and improving our own five-year plan."[41]

Delegation members also received lectures by members of the Soviet economic planning commission, Gosplan. The range of lecture topics was broad: the structure and process of planning a national economy, planning budgetary resources and expenditures, pricing, labor allocation, management and cadre planning, and the planning of specific industrial sectors. The Chinese delegation members took detailed notes from the lectures which were later compiled by China's new State Planning Commission into a handbook explaining exactly how socialist economic planning worked. It was used for study by cadres involved in planning. Members of the PRC delegation also visited major industrial centers and factories to get a firsthand sense of what actual modern industrial production looked like and study the "management experience" of those factories.

Once back in China, delegation members went to work replicating the Soviet planning system. In November 1952, a Gosplan-like State Planning

Commission was established in Beijing. Specialized agencies were set up to operate various sectors of the economy. Party committees were established in factories to ensure that operations complied with plan assignments. China's neophyte economic planners also revised the First Five Year Plan in line with suggestions from Soviet planning experts. Chinese leaders were immensely excited by the setting up of a copy of Soviet economic planning to guide China's economy. In the words of one scholar, "Chinese [leaders] equated the sacred cause of socialism with the Soviet Stalinist Model, believing that it represented the material embodiment of Marxism and the truth of socialism."[42] CCP leaders uniformly expected that China's new socialist economic system would rapidly industrialize China.

Collectivized agriculture constituted the second pillar of socialism as outlined in the *Short Course*. Collectivized agriculture provided inputs for rapid industrialization via what was called "primitive socialist accumulation."[43] Mao hoped that these two foundations of a socialist economy—state-owned and -planned industry plus collectivized agriculture—would enable the PRC to accomplish industrialization. Extrapolating from Soviet experience as outlined in the *Short Course*, Mao concluded that within ten to fifteen years, but perhaps as quickly as eight years, the PRC would become a highly industrialized socialist country.[44] This paved the road for the Great Leap Forward a few years later.

The command economy Mao and the CCP imposed on China had grave defects. In effect, a deeply dysfunctional economic system was being clamped onto China. A large-scale economy is an extremely complex and dynamic thing. All the components that are used to produce a particular good must be delivered with just the right specifications at just the right time to just the right place. For each good, there may be scores, hundreds, or thousands of inputs. Goods will often be passed from one to another stage of production before arriving at a final consumer. Remote but intimately related output decisions must be coordinated over time. Requisite amounts of very specific goods must be produced and delivered so that some other good may be produced and delivered at some distant time. If everything does not fit together just right, there will be shortages of some goods, surpluses of others, and goods that don't quite meet the specifications required. Moreover, things change constantly.

In a market economy, all these decisions are handled in an extremely decentralized fashion by self-interested businessmen pursuing private and individual plans that they calculate will produce a profit for them. They buy and sell goods and services they need under terms acceptable to parties to that contract. The flow of information via a decentralized market system is far more effective than via a system of comprehensive central planning. But it would take many years for these and other fundamental drawbacks of economic planning to become apparent, and for some CCP leaders to find ways of removing "planning" from the ideological center of "socialism."

In agriculture, Stalin's model of collectivized agriculture was adopted by the CCP under Mao's leadership, in spite of warnings from Stalin to go slow, or even delay indefinitely the expropriation of rich and middle peasants via collectivization. Mao and most of his comrades were inspired by the rosy image of Soviet agriculture portrayed by the *Short Course*, and pushed ahead with the Stalinist agricultural model in spite of Stalin's warnings. Stalinist-style primitive socialist accumulation required that the state control the agricultural harvest so it could channel that wealth into industrialization.

In the Soviet Union, starting in 1928 all peasants were forced to surrender their land, farm animals, and implements, which were all merged into newly formed collective farms operating under the supervision of cadres appointed by and loyal to the party. This ensured that farms planted what higher-level planning officials specified, that work was properly done, and that crops harvested went directly from fields to warehouses controlled by other party cadres. The state asserted a monopoly on the purchase of crops, at low prices set by the planners. These arrangements gave the state control over the produce of the agricultural sector at nominal cost. Needless to say, this was not an arrangement favored by peasants, especially rich and middle peasants, who tended to be the most effective farmers, producing the greatest amount of disposable crops.

The *Short Course* described the collectivization of Soviet agriculture as a major component of the transition from capitalism to socialism, and as creating an essential basis for successful socialist industrialization. It also described the putative enthusiastic welcome for, and happy lives of Soviet peasants under, collectivized agriculture. Deeply impressed by Soviet experience as explicated in the *Short Course*, Mao came to see individual peasant farming as a backward phenomenon, and collective farming as "socialism" and as a way of "liberating" the productive forces of agriculture.

During the very early 1950s, as "land to the tiller" was being implemented across China, CCP leaders debated whether collectivization on the Soviet model should be the next step. In the CCP leadership, there were "returned students" (CCP members who had studied in the USSR) who had a better understanding of the realities of Soviet agriculture and knew that its situation was not as rosy as Soviet propaganda and the *Short Course* depicted. Most prominent among these "returned students" was Zhang Wentian (also known as Luo Fu), who had studied and taught in the Soviet Union from 1925 to 1930 (in the midst of Soviet collectivization) and had wide contacts among Soviet leaders, especially Nikolai Bukharin, who had sharply criticized Stalin's forced collectivization of agriculture. Zhang advocated the use of supply and marketing cooperatives while retaining family farming (not collectivized production and land) as the basis for socialism in China's countryside. Liu Shaoqi and Bo Yibo favored Zhang's "cooperatives" approach. Interestingly, Stalin gave subtle support to Liu. In July 1951, Mao intervened to end the debate: cooperatives were to be a transitional stage of several years, to be followed by full-scale collectivization. Liu, Zhang, and others immediately endorsed Mao's view. Collectivization of agriculture along Soviet lines became the objective.

In April 1952, the Ministry of Agriculture and the North China Bureau of the CCP sent the PRC's first major agricultural delegation to the Soviet Union. It stayed nearly six months studying the organization of collective agriculture in the Soviet Union. Upon the delegation's return to China, a full-scale propaganda campaign was launched to educate China's peasants about the bright situation of collectivized agriculture in the Soviet Union, which they, China's farmers, would soon enjoy. Members of the recently returned delegation gave talks and hosted seminars. Newspapers interviewed delegation members and wrote articles depicting the glories of Soviet collective agriculture. Soviet collective farmers were depicted as living in a virtual paradise, with big homes, private yards, and horses, sheep, and cows of their own. Soviet collective farmers had abundant food. They no longer feared natural disaster. Productivity on farms was very high. Soviet collective farming was highly mechanized. Everyone enjoyed riding on the tractor on sunny days. Soviet farmers received subsidies from the state to support raising children. Photos of happy Soviet collective farmers with their tractors accompanied articles. The point of this propaganda was that China's farmers should be joyful that they would soon follow the Soviet path of collective farming.[45]

Stalin's lukewarm attitude toward expropriation of rich and middle peasants was reflected in lack of actual movement in that direction in China while he was alive. After Stalin's death in March 1953, however, Mao began to push for quick progress toward transition to socialism, including the full collectivization of farming. By the fall of 1953, he had won acceptance from other top CCP leaders that over the next four years the CCP would push forward with progressively "higher" types of cooperatives as transitional preparatory steps for full-scale collectivization. In the meantime, propaganda educating peasants about socialism, the glories of collective farming, socialist industrialization, and China's Soviet future would continue. By the end of 1955, 63.3 percent of peasant households were members of higher-level producers' cooperatives.[46]

Mao and the CCP were imposing on China a failed agricultural model. A plausible case can be made for heavy state investment in the industrial sector, where many new industries had to be established and expanded. The same cannot be said for the collectivization of agriculture. The Soviet Union's agricultural sector was hugely unproductive. One authoritative post-Stalin Soviet study found that overall agricultural production fell from a base of 100 in 1928, the start of collectivization, to 81.5 by 1933, when collectivization was basically complete. The number of livestock fell by half. In only two years, 1937 and 1941, did collectivized agriculture exceed the precollectivization output.[47]

Stalin's and the *Short Course*'s notion of fueling industrialization by starving agriculture was among the first elements of Stalin's model to be thrown out in the Soviet Union by the post-Stalin leadership. After Stalin died, agricultural procurement prices were raised, taxes on farming cut, investment in agriculture was raised, and bureaucratic control of farming was eased.[48] In China too, collective farming was one of the first things to be thrown out after Mao died. In 1978 (perhaps a year earlier in key provinces), after twenty years of "experimentation" with Soviet-style collective farming, it was "reformed" out of existence via the "family responsibility system." Land was again parceled out to individual families, who regained wide latitude in the operation of their family plots and who profited directly from successful farming. Agricultural output began immediately to climb. Within a very few years, the chronic food shortages that had plagued China since collectivization disappeared.

In 1979, thirty years after the CCP imposed the Soviet economic model on China, Deng Xiaoping replied to a question posed by Frank Gibney of *Encyclopedia Britannica*, "Could China have been so ideologically confused initially as to have completely imitated and adopted the socialist style of the Soviet Union"? Deng replied that China's socialist road was different from the Soviet Union's "from the very start." In essence, Deng said that the CCP, unlike the CPSU, did not kill its capitalists in the process of socialist transformation, or kill oppositionists within the party. These were generally accurate judgments, although several million landlords and non-CCP dissidents were killed. Then Deng continued:

> However, some of our economic systems, especially enterprise management and organization, have been greatly influenced by the Soviet Union. For this reason it is advantageous that we inherit the advanced method of operation, management, and scientific development from advanced capitalist countries. We are still having many difficulties reforming these aspects of our economy.[49]

Soviet Economic Assistance and the Construction of Socialism

During the 1950s, the Soviet Union provided large-scale assistance to China's socialist industrialization effort.[50] Indeed, it was one of the largest transfers of capital equipment in history. China in 1949 had some industry: in the Northeast, built up by massive Japanese investment over a period of fifty years; some light industry and public utilities in China's coastal cities as part of China's integration into the global economy under the treaty system; and some defense industry in interior provinces, as part of the ROC's anti-Japan war effort. But overall, the process of China's industrialization was just beginning. Extensive Soviet assistance in the 1950s helped China greatly expand and upgrade its industrial sector. With Soviet assistance, China set up an array of industries entirely new to China: machine tools, airplanes, cars, trucks, tractors, petroleum mining and refining, precision instruments, chemicals, and many others. Via agreements signed in 1950, 1952, 1953, and 1954, the Soviet Union undertook to assist 156 major industrial projects. All Soviet assistance went to the PRC's state sector, supplying 52 percent of total capital investment during China's First Five Year Plan. Soviet assistance greatly strengthened the leading role of the centrally planned industrial sector (i.e., "socialism") in China's economy.

Soviet machinery and equipment (M&E) supplied for these projects frequently represented major technological advances for Chinese industry, resulting in major increases in productivity in those sectors. Figure 2-2 illustrates the distribution and productivity gains of the 156 Soviet aid projects. Together, these projects made up the backbone of China's industrialization efforts under the First and Second Five Year Plans (1953–1957 and 1958–1962 respectively). The Soviet role was comprehensive and included investigation of geological conditions, selection of factory sites, and assistance with actual manufacture of products.

The Soviet Union also supplied extensive human technical assistance. Between 1950 and 1960, some 11,000 Soviet specialists were sent to China. At least twenty specialists were assigned to each of the 156 key projects. Hundreds of Soviet advisors worked at big projects like new metallurgical or heavy

Industry	Number of Enterprises	Industry	% Increase Productivity Due to Soviet Assistance
iron and steel	7	iron	92.1
nonferrous metals	14	steel	82.8
electric power	24	steel products	82.8
machinery building	63	coal	22.7
coal	27	trucks	100
oil	2	electricity	45.9
chemicals	5	nitrogen fertilizer	28.5
drugs and pharmaceuticals	2	crude oil	51.4
paper	1	metallurgical equipment	50.3
textiles	1		
water conservation	1		
state farms	1		
transportation	6		
other	3		
TOTAL	156		

FIGURE 2-2 **Distribution and Productivity Contribution of 156 Key Soviet Projects**

Source: Chu–yuan Cheng, *Economic Relations Between Peking and Moscow: 1949–1963* (Praeger: New York, 1964), p. 28, 43.

machinery building complexes, or oil production in Xinjiang. Twenty-four worked on the construction of the first bridge over the Yangtze River in Wuhan, in Hubei province in central China. (The bridge opened in 1957.) One hundred and sixty Soviet specialists worked in the design bureau of the Metallurgical Ministry in Beijing. Soviet specialists helped Chinese master large and complex production processes, such as blast furnaces, hot blooming steel mills, jet airplanes, and seamless pipe. Moscow set up training programs in Soviet enterprises for Chinese personnel. By 1960, 38,000 Chinese personnel had received training in the Soviet Union, ranging from skilled workers and technicians to people receiving advanced degrees in natural sciences and engineering at Soviet universities.

A number of China's post-Mao top leaders were trained in the Soviet Union during this period. Li Peng, raised by Zhou Enlai after Li's father died in the revolutionary struggle, studied hydroelectric engineering at the Moscow Power Engineering Institute for about six years, returning to China in 1955 to work in the electrical power sector, starting in the Northeast. Jiang Zemin studied industrial management for a year at the Stalin Auto Works in the Soviet Union, returning to China circa 1955 to become a manager at China's first (and Soviet-assisted) automobile factory in Changchun, Jilin province. Hundreds of thousands of Chinese were trained in specialized programs set up in China by Soviet advisors. This deep Soviet influence would continue to be felt even in the post-Mao era. One wing of the broad reform coalition led by Deng starting in 1978 saw "planning" as the crux of "socialism" and was reluctant to reinterpret "socialism" to be compatible with markets.[51]

Soviet transfer of industrial machinery and equipment and know-how in the 1950s was an immense assist to China's industrialization effort. After the collapse of Sino-Soviet relations circa 1960, China would enter an eighteen-year-long period of relative economic isolation in which reverse engineering, copying, and dissemination across the economy of copies of Soviet equipment was the key driver of China's productivity increase and technological advance. Not until the 1980s would global inputs of advanced technology again begin to flow into China on a scale comparable to the 1950s.

Soviet models of industrial management came along with Soviet M&E. Soviet industrial organization of the 1950s was rigidly hierarchical. Enterprises were headed by a single manager with a technocratic background and wielding extensive powers over the enterprise's operation. Under the manager was a chain of command also made up of technically skilled people. The role of the party committee was limited to general oversight of the technocratic management, and most definitely did not include activities that disrupted production. Sharp wage differentials were also used to reward and motivate people.

By 1958, Mao, who was beginning to envision himself and not new CPSU leader Nikita Khrushchev as the genuine successor to Stalin in the Marxist-Leninist pantheon, would begin to find fault with the Soviet system of industrial management.[52] The Soviet model, Mao began to believe, reduced "the masses" to a passive and subordinate condition, prevented party activists ("reds") from leading and educating the masses in class struggle, and would, if allowed to continue, produce a new, extremely powerful, privileged, and relatively wealthy stratum of "expert" managers. Mao believed this process was already occurring in the Soviet Union under Khrushchev's de-Stalinized socialism, and became increasingly convinced it must not be allowed to happen in China. Consequently, Mao began to endorse experimentation with more politically correct forms of industrial organization with reds, not experts, in command and "the masses" "struggling" via "movements" to achieve economic or political objectives.

Perhaps half of all Soviet assistance in the 1950s went into military-related projects.[53] Mao and the CCP, like Stalin and the CPSU, saw development of military power as a key purpose of industrialization. The Soviet Union transferred to the PRC the production technology for almost the entire Soviet arsenal, from tanks and artillery to jet aircraft, submarines, and ballistic missiles. Nor were the technology and weapon types backward. A large portion was up to date. In some cases, production of advanced arms began in China before the Soviet Union. PLA capabilities advanced very rapidly via cooperation with the Soviet Union. Like other institutions in Chinese society, the PLA was reorganized along lines of the Soviet Army. Not until the appointment of Lin Biao to replace Peng Dehuai in 1959 would the PLA begin a systematic de-Sovietization of PLA organization and doctrine. Even then, Soviet influence in the area of doctrine, weapons, and training would remain very strong.

The Diplomacy of China's Transition to Socialism

A Soviet-style command economy, collectivized agriculture, and harsh dictatorship were not what the CCP promised when competing with the KMT for popular support after Japan's surrender. But Mao and the CCP were convinced that the Soviet path would quickly make China prosperous and strong, and place it in the vanguard of the Asian revolutionary camp. While many Chinese enthusiastically rallied to the CCP's socialist vision and program, many others did not. Mao understood that there would be strong opposition to transition to socialism ushering in a campaign of hyperindustrialization. That opposition would have to be crushed. Once power was in CCP hands, Mao began creating an international environment conducive to these immense tasks. Relations with the Western capitalist powers were ruptured and the vast Western cultural presence in China uprooted. Education of the populace, especially Westernized intellectuals, was begun regarding the nefarious crimes of the Western powers against China, as well as the benevolent and enlightened nature of Soviet influence on China. A close, thirty-year long military-political alliance with the USSR was forged, vastly strengthening the power of the socialist camp in world affairs and opening the spigot for large-scale Soviet assistance in a sweeping transfer of Soviet organizational models to China. And China chose war with the United States in Korea.

War in Korea and Indochina

Consequences of the Korean War

The war that began on June 25, 1950, with an all-out North Korean invasion of South Korea and which concluded on July 27, 1953, with an armistice (a formal ceasefire, not a peace treaty) signed by China, the United States, and North and South Korea had a deep impact on PRC foreign relations. It completed the collapse of the US strategy of driving a wedge between "Chinese Titoism" and the Soviet Union. Coming barely four months after signature of the PRC-USSR treaty of alliance, North Korea's attack signified to US leaders that Beijing and Moscow were committed to a common effort to expand the communist realm in East Asia. Washington responded by attempting to contain that expansionist push, first on the battlefields of South Korea, then in Indochina, and ultimately all around China's periphery, from Northeast Asia through the Western Pacific and Southeast Asia to South Asia. Containment became the new US strategy in Asia and was to remain in place for twenty years. The Korean War transformed the PRC into America's number one enemy in Asia, and for the next two decades the United States built up positions of military strength around China while attempting to isolate it diplomatically and economically.

The PRC responded in kind to US containment, and for two decades the PRC and the US waged an intense struggle against one another, each using virtually all means short of outright war to punish and injure the other. The Korean War marked the beginning of what historian of Sino-American relations Warren I. Cohen called the twenty-year "great aberration" in a broader pattern of generally cooperative Sino-American relations.[1] The flip side of alienation of the United States was consolidation of PRC ties with the USSR and of China's position as leader of the Asian revolutionary movement. China's decision to go to war with the United States to rescue the North Korean regime from extinction finally convinced Stalin that Mao and the

CCP were genuine communists. Soviet assistance became more generous now that there were no doubts about China's global alignment.

Another major consequence of the Korean War was the alienation of the island of Taiwan from the de facto jurisdiction of the PRC.[2] As will be discussed below, by late 1949 US leaders had decided to sacrifice Taiwan to PLA invasion and CCP rule as part of the strategy of driving a wedge between Soviet and Chinese communists. The February 1950 treaty, followed so shortly by North Korea's invasion, transformed the geopolitical significance of Taiwan, leading Washington to place Taiwan under US military protection. US re-engagement with the Nationalist regime led over several decades to the gradual transformation of the US-Taiwan relation. Sixty-five years later (in 2015), Taiwan still lies beyond the de facto sovereignty of the PRC. This traces directly to the Sino-Soviet alliance and the Korean War.

The PRC's three year war against the United States reconfirmed China's bona fides as a major power. If the Republic of China's secondary role in the defeat of Japan had left any doubt about China's right to sit at the high table of leading world powers, Mao's 1950 decision to confront the United States, and then the success of Chinese forces in fighting the US military to a standstill in Korea, removed any doubt: China was a major power, able and willing to defend its interests as it defined them.

Historiography of the Origins of the Korean War

The first question to be asked regarding the Korean War is: who started it? At the time, North Korea and its allies in Beijing and Moscow insisted that the war began with a South Korean attack on the North, which the North first rebuffed and then expanded into an all-out war to "liberate" the south, opening the way to unification of the Korean nation and peninsula under the leadership of Kim Il Sung and his Korean Workers Party (KWP). There was some market for this "the South shot first" perspective even in the United States.[3] This is still the perspective taught to Chinese citizens as part of their "patriotic education" by the CCP. The *Dictionary of Patriotic Education* published in Beijing in 1991 to "provide a complete and systematic reference book on patriotic education by the broad masses of youth . . . and workers in political thought in party organizations and enterprises," for example, says this to open the section on the Korean War: "On June 25, 1950, the United States instigated the South Korean clique of Syngman Rhee to attack the People's Democratic Republic of Korea and then sent the Seventh Fleet to China's Taiwan."[4] Another book for use in patriotic education in primary schools explains the onset of the Korean War in this way:

Foreign and domestic reactionary forces were not reconciled to their defeat [with the establishment of the PRC]. Shortly after the birth of new China, US imperialism brazenly sent troops to Korea and pushed the flames of war to the Yalu River in a wild scheme to strangle to death and uproot new China.[5]

Of course absolving Mao of responsibility for starting the Korean War neatly absolves him of responsibility for the initiation of the US protection of Taiwan that resulted from that war. While some Chinese scholars, and hopefully China's leaders, may have a more accurate understanding of the actual origins of the Korean War, mainstream political culture in the PRC still embraces the notion that the United States and/or South Korea initiated the war to injure or threaten China.

The release of ex-Soviet archives has pretty much destroyed this old "the South shot first" thesis.[6] The war that started on June 25 was a well-prepared massive invasion designed to destroy the South Korean regime and incorporate all of Korea into a single KWP-ruled state.[7] The question then becomes, what were Beijing's and Moscow's roles in the launching of Kim Il Sung's ill-fated "liberation war"? And why did Beijing decide to rescue Kim and his regime when his war plan collapsed?

The first wave of solid scholarship that attempted to answer the question of why China entered the Korean War focused on the crossing of the 38th parallel by US forces in early October 1950, and then the advance of those forces north to the Yalu River, forming the border between China and North Korea. It was the threat to China's Northeast posed by the US occupation of North Korea that impelled China to intervene, according to this interpretation.[8] China viewed North Korea as a security buffer between its main industrial bases in its Northeast and US forces ensconced in South Korea, Japan, and Okinawa. The security of the PRC simply would not permit the presence of US forces on the Yalu River within easy striking distance of China's industrial heartland. As US forces approached the 38th parallel after the successful amphibious landing at Incheon on September 15, 1950, Beijing gave warning to the United States: do not cross the 38th parallel. US leaders concluded that these warnings were a bluff. After continued US disregard for Beijing's warnings, when US forces reached the Yalu, Beijing decided to strike. On October 19, Chinese forces poured across the Yalu to push the US military to undertake the longest retreat in its history.

Much of this thesis is still sound. But more recent scholarship on the Korean War utilizing declassified Soviet documents has stressed three additional factors: 1) Stalin's and Mao's roles in approving Kim Il Sung's original decision for war, 2) the close linkages between Mao's decision to intervene late in 1950 and his efforts to consolidate CCP control over China and moving the Chinese revolution into its socialist stage, and 3) Mao's desire to establish the PRC as a strong supporter of revolutionary anti-imperialism in Asia.

China and Kim Il Sung's War Plan to "Liberate" the South

Korea moved from China's to Japan's sphere after the 1894–1895 Sino-Japan war, and was annexed by Japan in 1910. As Japan's empire was being destroyed, American, Chinese, and British leaders met at Cairo in November 1943 to outline the new postwar order in East Asia.[9] In the declaration of that conference, the three powers agreed that "in due course Korea shall become free and independent."[10] The division of the Korean peninsula into Soviet and US occupation zones came about at the Allied conference at Potsdam in August 1945 as Soviet forces were seizing control of Japanese-occupied Manchukuo. After a Soviet query at Potsdam about whether or not the United States intended to land troops in Korea, the American side proposed, and Stalin accepted without discussion, that the 38th parallel delineate Soviet and US occupation zones. Soviet forces subsequently halted at that line, even though US forces would not reach the peninsula until early September. Stalin probably hoped to secure control over North Korea, avoid conflict with the Americans, and not make himself the nemesis of Korean nationalism by blocking Korean unification.[11] The line drawn at the 38th parallel was intended as a temporary delineation of occupation zones pending the formation of an all-national government.

The Soviet armies that occupied northern Korea in 1945 brought with them a cohort of Korean communists led by the young and charismatic Kim Il Sung. As in Eastern Europe, Stalin viewed Soviet armed forces as an instrument of social revolution, and those armies put Kim and his KWP in power in North Korea and supported them as they built a Leninist socialist system. Stalin carefully avoided, however, encouragement of communist activity in the American zone south of the 38th parallel. Stalin's objective at that point was consolidation of Soviet control over North Korea.

The situation in the South was much more chaotic than in the North. In the South, civilian and military officials who had served Japanese authority vied with liberal democratic politicians, many of whom returned to Korea after Japan's surrender. There was an abundance of groups and perspectives. One of the most prominent Southern leaders was Syngman Rhee, who had a PhD, had been a prominent activist against Japanese rule in the 1910s, and headed a Korean government-in-exile in Shanghai for six years after an uprising in Korea in 1919 before going into exile in the United States for many years. Rhee returned to Korea aboard a US military aircraft in October 1945. South Korea's economy had collapsed after losing its markets in North Korea, Manchuria, and Japan. Unrest among labor and peasants was sharp in South Korea and was fanned by communist agitators. South Korea's young democracy was weak and chaotic, with many parties and individuals vying for power. Unlike in Japan, where US policy planners had given considerable wartime attention to postwar rule, in South Korea US support for the emergence of a stable democratic polity was not well thought through or particularly effective. Kim Il Sung and the KWP hoped to use this disorder in the South and seize the opportunity to "liberate" the South and unify the entire Korean nation and peninsula under communist rule. According to a top secret 1966 study by the Soviet foreign ministry intended to serve as background for Soviet negotiators, in 1948, after separate governments were formed in North and South Korea and after first Soviet and then American forces were withdrawn from their respective occupation zones, "Kim Il Sung and other Korean leaders were firmly determined to unify the country by military means." The Soviet backgrounder continues:

> Calculating that the USA would not enter a war over South Korea, Kim Il Sung persistently pressed for agreement from Stalin and Mao Zedong to reunify the country by military means. Stalin at first treated the persistent appeals of Kim Il Sung with reserve, noting that "such a large affair . . . needs much preparation," but he did not object in principle. The final agreement to support the plans of the Koreans was given by Stalin at the time of Kim Il Sung's visit to Moscow in March–April 1950. Following this, in May, Kim Il Sung visited Beijing and secured the support of Mao.[12]

Kim was confident that North Korean forces, assisted by uprisings in the South, could "liberate" the South in a week or so. The plan that Kim finally sold Stalin on in May 1950 envisioned the conquest of the South in six days. Stalin rejected Kim's proposals until early 1950. Stalin feared that an all-out attack by North Korean might trigger a war with the United States.[13] Until April 1950, Stalin vetoed Kim's plan for war. Several factors contributed to Stalin's shift and acceptance of Kim's war plan. Probably the most important were authoritative statements by top US leaders indicating that the United States would not intervene in Korea. On January 5, President Harry Truman told a press conference that the United States would not intervene in the Taiwan Straits (where the PLA was mobilizing) even if there were an attack. A more detailed exposition of US policy came onJanuary 12, 1950, when Secretary of State Dean Acheson addressed the National Press Club about the new US security strategy in the Far East following the communist victory in China. The United States had drawn a new defense perimeter in the Far East, Acheson said, running from the Aleutians to Japan, the Ryukyus, and the Philippines. Taiwan and South Korea were pointedly outside that perimeter. Regarding areas beyond the perimeter, Acheson said, "no person can guarantee these areas against military attack," and to attempt to do so was neither sensible, necessary, or practical.[14] The US sacrifice of Taiwan, combined with British January 1950 recognition of the PRC (which Stalin thought might presage a similar US move), could lead to a purely "Chinese solution" to the Taiwan question. Stalin understood that the objective of US policy was to drive a wedge between the PRC and the Soviet Union. Stalin chose a policy mirroring Truman's; Stalin now sought to drive a wedge between Washington and Beijing by involving the PRC in confrontations with the United States—in Korea as well as in the Taiwan Strait. In January 1950, the Soviet media began reporting China's preparations against Taiwan. During the negotiation of the economic aid agreement in Moscow in February 1950, Stalin agreed that half of the $300 million trade credit could be used to purchase Soviet naval equipment to outfit PLA forces for an invasion of Taiwan.[15]

Another factor contributing to Stalin's endorsement of Kim Il Sung's war plan was the conclusion of the PRC-USSR alliance in February and the understanding with Beijing, tracing to Liu Shaoqi's July 1949 talks with Stalin, that the PRC would assume prime responsibility for supporting the Asian revolution. This meant that if things did not go according to Kim's plan, it would be Chinese, not Soviet, forces who rescued Kim. Stalin made this very clear to Kim Il Sung during the latter's last pre-attack visit to Moscow from March 3 to April 25, 1950. Kim laid before Stalin a plan envisioning a six-day war to liberate all of South Korea with the assistance of an uprising by a putative 200,000 party members and peasant guerrillas in the South. The war would supposedly be over before the United States had time to intervene. Stalin accepted the plan, but told Kim that if, contrary to Kim's expectation, the United States entered the conflict, the Soviet Union would not come to Kim's rescue. That responsibility would lie with Mao and China. Stalin told Kim: "If you should get kicked in the teeth, I shall not lift a finger. You have to ask Mao for all the help."[16]

Following Stalin's suggestion, Kim Il Sung sought China's sign-off. On May 13, Kim arrived in Beijing for discussions with Mao. According to the memoir of Mao's Russian-language interpreter for that discussion, Mao asked Kim about possible US intervention in light of the fact that the United States supported the Rhee regime and that Korea was linked to Japan, where the Americans were in charge.[17] Kim was confident the Americans would not intervene. They would not have time; the operation would be over before they could deploy forces. Mao asked if Kim needed Chinese support, and offered to deploy three Chinese armies on the border with North Korea. Kim declined. North Korean forces, with the help of insurrection in the south, could solve the southern problem by themselves, Kim explained. But while asking probing questions, Mao did not directly challenge, let alone veto, Kim's plan.

After discussion with Kim, Mao cabled Stalin seeking confirmation of what Kim had told Mao about Stalin's approval of Kim's war plan. The Chinese cable reported that Kim said Stalin had indicated "that the present situation has changed from the situation in the past, and that North Korea can move toward action; however, this question should be discussed with China and personally with Comrade Mao Zedong." "Comrade Mao Zedong would like to have personal clarification of Comrade Filippov [Stalin's code name] on this question," the Chinese query to Moscow read.[18] Soviet Premier Vyshinsky replied the next day. His message read:

> In a conversation with the Korean comrades Filippov and his friends expressed the opinion that, in light of the changed international situation, they agreed with the proposal of the Koreans to move toward reunification. In this regard a qualification was made, that the question should be decided finally by the Chinese and Korean comrades together, and *in case of disagreement by the Chinese comrades, the decision on the question should be postponed until a new discussion.* . . . Filippov.[19] (Emphasis added.)

Stalin had craftily maneuvered Mao into having the final say on Kim's war plan. The Soviet leader had also made it clear that China, not the Soviet Union, would be responsible in the event that things went wrong. It was Stalin who was the undisputed leader of the socialist camp and world revolutionary movement. It would be Soviet-supplied tanks, artillery, trucks, fuel, and ammunition that would make the North Korean offense possible. It was Soviet generals, veterans of World War II offensives, who drew up the plans for the North Korean assault. And it was Soviet advisors who served with North Korean forces until shortly before the attack, when they withdrew. Yet it would be China that would fight Kim Il Sung's war for him. Mao walked into Stalin's snare.

Scholars Goncharov, Lewis, and Xue argue that Stalin had cunningly crafted a win-win situation for the Soviet Union. If the United States did not intervene and South Korea fell to the KWP, the Soviet Union would secure a stronger buffer against the Americans and a possibly rearmed Japan, plus naval bases beyond the restrictive Straits exiting the Sea of Japan. If, on the other hand and contrary to expectations, the United States intervened, China would be enmeshed in war with the United Sates. That war would draw US forces and attention away from Europe, which Stalin recognized as the center of strategic gravity in the Soviet-US contest. Once the PRC and the United States were entangled in war, it would be difficult for Washington to achieve its desired opening to "Chinese Titoism."

Mao apparently gave the green light for Kim to proceed. Goncharov, Lewis, and Xue propose several reasons why Mao did so. Kim insisted that North Korean forces could do the job alone and quickly, and would not need Chinese assistance. Stalin had several times attempted to shackle CCP revolutionary offensives, and Mao remembered those attempts bitterly. He, Mao, would not now commit the same "great power chauvinist error" as Stalin, or so Mao probably thought. Moreover, Taiwan had not yet been "liberated" by the PLA, although Stalin had agreed in early 1950 to support that invasion. If Mao said no to Kim's war plan on the obvious grounds that the United States might intervene, would not the same argument apply to Taiwan? Would not the United States be equally likely to intervene in the event of a PLA invasion of Taiwan? Mao could not warn against a war for South Korea without undermining his own case for a war for Taiwan.[20] Moreover, had either Stalin or Mao rejected Kim's plan to "liberate" the south, their credibility as a resolute supporter of world revolution, perhaps to the advantage of the other, would have been injured. From the very beginning, there was rivalry over who, Moscow or Beijing, would lead the world revolution.[21]

China's Decision to Intervene

The North Korean attack on June 25 did not go according to plan. The projected urban and peasant uprisings did not occur or were easily put down. Many South Koreans did not want to live under communist dictatorship and fought hard to prevent it. Most crucially, contrary to the signals Truman and Acheson had given in January, the United States intervened. US and South Korean resistance gradually gained in effectiveness. Still, North Korean forces pushed the defenders steadily south toward what became by August a small perimeter around the southeastern port city of Pusan.

Chinese leaders recognized as soon as the United States announced its intervention on June 27 that the balance between North and South Korean forces had altered to the North's disadvantage.[22] CCP leaders doubted the ability of North Korean forces to defeat the US reinforcements that were certain to arrive, and began considering if and how the PRC should send military forces into Korea to shift the balance back to the North's advantage. China's history had taught that Korea was an invasion corridor leading to China's Northeast. In 1592, and again in 1894, Chinese governments had sent armies to Korea to expel Japanese invaders. Now, in 1950, a North Korean defeat would leave Manchuria, China's major industrial region exposed to the threat of US imperialist attack. US defeat of North Korea would also be a major blow to the Asian revolution. The revolutionary wave in Asia might die via demoralization before it gained momentum. By September, Mao was warning his comrades that the Korean revolutionary forces would be "fundamentally destroyed" by the Americans unless China intervened. Revolutionaries elsewhere in Asia would be disheartened by an American defeat of the Korean revolutionary movement. In China itself, "reactionaries" not reconciled yet to CCP victory and socialism would be emboldened.

Kim Il Sung had not informed Chinese leaders about the configuration or the date of his invasion. Not until June 27, two days into the offensive and after Seoul was taken by Northern forces, did Kim notify Beijing of the beginning of Korea's liberation war. Kim was confident his forces could achieve complete victory, and did not request Chinese assistance. Kim may also have been leery of strengthening a pro-Chinese group that challenged his authority within the KWP. In any case, as soon as notification was received from Kim, Zhou Enlai arranged for the dispatch of a group of military intelligence officers to Pyongyang to monitor developments in Korea.

US success on June 27 in securing Security Council authorization for military intervention in Korea, and the growing flow of US reinforcements into the area (a flow apparently observed by Chinese intelligence), deepened Chinese apprehension. In early July, barely three weeks into the conflict and while US and South Korean forces were still retreating toward Pusan, Zhou Enlai convened a conference to begin preparations for intervention in Korea. A new military command, the North East Border Defense Army (NEBDA), was established and armies were redeployed from across China to that new command. By the end of July, 255,000 soldiers were in position on North Korea's borders. A large logistical effort positioned materials for NEBDA use: field hospitals, vehicles and fuel, ammunition, food, etc. Meanwhile, ferocious and repeated North Korean attacks on the Pusan perimeter failed. North Korean forces and logistic lines were subject to nearly constant US bombing, while more and more US reinforcements flowed into Japan. Still Kim Il Sung remained confident of success and did not call for Chinese help. In fact, he did not reply to a Chinese suggestion that China send a group of senior military observers to the south.

From the beginning of US intervention in Korea, Mao was acutely aware of the linkage between the war in Korea and China's domestic politics. American intervention on China's doorstep, and even more a US victory there, would encourage resistance to CCP rule by Chinese unhappy with the still-recent communist takeover. CCP control was still far from complete, and lenient CCP policies toward those who changed sides during the civil war meant that many people with an ambiguous stance toward the new CCP regime were still loose. On the other hand, if the CCP could position itself as the defender of China against American aggression, it would be able to clothe in nationalist colors its upcoming program of tightening control. If hatred could be mobilized against US imperialist aggression against China, that hatred could be used to cow the substantial number of Chinese who feared loss of their economic holdings, their American movies, or their French-language classes, or who desired liberal democratic government rather than Leninist dictatorship for China.

With North Korean forces thwarted in their repeated assaults on the Pusan perimeter, Chinese leaders accelerated preparations for Chinese entry. Mao outlined to a Politburo meeting in early August his thinking about the necessity of Chinese intervention. This was well before the US landing at Incheon, let alone the crossing of the 38th Parallel. Mao said:

> If the US imperialists won the war, they would become more arrogant and would threaten us. We should not fail to assist the Koreans. We must lend them our hand in the form of sending our military volunteers there. The timing should be further decided, but we have to prepare for this.[23]

By late August, NEBDA analysts had surmised from the buildup of US forces in Japan (in another testament to the caliber of Chinese intelligence in Japan) and the movement of ships in the Pacific that an amphibious landing by US forces was likely, outflanking the Northern forces attacking Pusan. NEBDA analysts also concluded that Incheon was the most likely location for such an enemy landing. Mao himself conveyed this warning to a North Korean representative in late August, specifically identifying Incheon as the most likely point of attack. North Korean leaders ignored the warning. Incheon was, of course, where an American invasion force landed on September 15, taking North Korean forces completely by surprise. By the end of August, CCP leaders had concluded that a major reversal of the North Korean position was likely, and that China would be required to rescue the North Korean regime. "We should prepare for the worst, and prepare quickly," Zhou instructed the NEBDA in late August.

Also in late August, the NEBDA suggested to the CCP center that linking Chinese intervention to the crossing of the 38th parallel by US forces would be politically and militarily advantageous. Politically, this would enable the CCP to cast the upcoming war as a defensive struggle to protect China's Northeast, something that would be useful with both Chinese and international audiences. Militarily, waiting for US/UN forces to cross the 38th parallel would shorten PLA logistic lines (which PLA planners knew would be exposed to US air attack). Mao and the Politburo adopted the proposal. It was essential to convince the Chinese people that the war was necessary to defend China and thus appeal to their nationalism and patriotism. In line with this tactic, in late September and early October Zhou Enlai made several statements linking possible Chinese entry to crossing of the 38th parallel by US forces. As noted earlier, US leaders regarded these warnings as a bluff; they simply did not imagine that China's leaders would feel they could gain from a war with the United States. They were also confident that US military superiority was so vast that if China did intervene, easy US victory could be achieved.

The US landing at Incheon forced a rapid northward retreat of North Korean forces. Retreat became a rout. Shortly after the Incheon landing, Stalin (not Kim Il Sung!) cabled Mao asking if China was in a position to send forces to Korea. Or, Stalin asked, would China allow Kim Il Sung to set up an exile government in China's Northeast? Kim Il Sung himself did not request foreign intervention— of Stalin, not Mao—until September 29, the day before the first South Korean forces crossed the 38th parallel. At that point, Kim cabled Stalin asking for "direct military aid" from the Soviet Union or, if that was not possible, "assistance in the creation of international volunteers in China." Stalin replied by telling Kim to address his query to Mao.[24] Kim complied.

The CCP Politburo met the next day, October 2, to consider Kim's request. Mao opened the session by saying that the question was not whether but how fast to intervene. After the session, Mao cabled Stalin that China would send forces to Korea. Mao explained why: "If Korea were completely occupied by the Americans and Korean revolutionary forces were fundamentally destroyed, the American invaders would be more rampant, and such a situation would be unfavorable to the whole East."[25] In other words, the balance between revolution and reaction across Asia would be adversely affected. At the end of another Politburo session on October 4, convened to review difficulties likely to be encountered during the upcoming Korean intervention, Mao, after listening to a long list of concerns, concluded: "All you have said is not without ground. [But] When other people are in a crisis, how can we stand aside with our arms folded?"[26] Peng Dehuai, selected by Mao to command China's forces in Korea, addressed one of the concerns raised during the Politburo session. Some comrades had expressed apprehension that war with the United States would make achievement of domestic unity difficult. In fact, Peng asserted, war would provide an opportunity to deflate the bluster of domestic reactionary forces.

On October 7, a US division crossed the 38th parallel. The next day Mao ordered 200,000 of the Chinese People's Volunteers (CPV), as the NEBDA had been renamed, to enter North Korea to assist the Korean revolutionary forces and confront the American invaders. The appellation Chinese People's Volunteers was a ploy designed to make China's entry look unofficial, making a formal state of war, and thus activation of the February 1950 treaty, somewhat less likely. The operational objective of Chinese forces when they entered Korea in October 1950 was nothing less than expulsion of US forces from the Korean peninsula. Following a decisive Politburo meeting on October 2, Mao informed Stalin of China's decision to intervene, explaining:

> [W]e shall aim at resolving the conflict, that is, *to eliminate the US troops within Korea or to drive them and other countries' aggressive forces out* [of Korea]. . . . we must prepare for the possibility that the US would declare a general war on China or it would at least bomb China's major cities and industrial base . . .[But we are] *more concerned about whether Chinese troops could wipe out the American forces within Korea's boundary* . . . As long as our troops are able to eliminate the Eighth Army [one of America's old armies, with considerable combat

effectiveness] the danger of . . . US declaration of war on China . . . would not be grave . . . In other words, since *the Korean conflict can actually be resolved on the basis of defeating the US . . . such a war would be limited in scale and would not last long.*[27] (Emphasis added.)

If the United States prevailed in Korea, Washington would become more "arrogant" and undertake increased aggression in the Taiwan Strait, Indochina, the Philippines, and elsewhere in Asia. If unchecked, US imperialism would encircle China. Then China might be compelled to fight a war on two or even several fronts. The US intervention in Korea was, Mao believed, part of a grand US strategy of encircling China. If US intervention in Korea was defeated, the United States would be more cautious, and revolutionary forces across Asia would be encouraged.[28] Allowing the United States to perennially threaten China's industrial heartland would also mean, Mao explained to the decisive Politburo session on October 2, that "We would have to wait there year after year, unsure of when the enemy will attack us."[29]

A key political objective motivating China's entry into the war was to rescue Korea's revolutionary forces from destruction. There were close ties between the CCP and the KWP. During the 1945–1947 CCP-KMT struggle for China's Northeast after Japan's surrender, North Korea had provided material assistance and sanctuary for the CCP. Then, as the CCP moved toward victory in 1949, it transferred some 50,000 to 70,000 ethnic Korean PLA soldiers to North Korean command. This very considerably increased the front-line strength of North Korean forces. The revolutionary division of labor worked out between Stalin and Liu Shaoqi in July 1949 also required that China bear the responsibility for assisting Korea's revolutionary forces. By undertaking to fight the Americans in Korea, Mao was giving substance to the CCP's pledge to take prime responsibility for supporting Asian revolution. Mao was demonstrating to Stalin that he was a resolute revolutionary not fearful of US imperialism. In effect, Mao was asserting China's bona fides as the center of the Asian international order, albeit a new revolutionary and socialist-centered order.

There was also a strong linkage between intervention in Korea and moving China's revolution "forward" into its socialist stage. The CCP's paramount objective circa 1950 was to consolidate its control over China. With war with the United States underway in Korea, ferreting out and destroying the putative agents of US imperialism within China could be cast as part of the effort to defend China from attack. On other hand, if China did not intervene in Korea, "reactionaries" within China and on Taiwan would be encouraged and emboldened. War would also facilitate establishment of state control over the economy. Integration of all China's economic resources into a single, comprehensive nationwide effort via nationalization and central planning, i.e., imposition of a Soviet-style economy, could be presented as a sensible and necessary move to defeat the American enemy. The emotional fervor, hatred, and fear that would be fostered during the war would make it clear to China's bourgeoisie that resistance would be dangerous, greatly facilitating liquidation of China's bourgeoisie as a class via transition to socialism.

Precipitating US Intervention to Shelter Taiwan

One immediate consequence of North Korea's attack on South Korea was a US decision to scrap the six-month-old policy of sacrificing Taiwan and instead use US military power to protect Taiwan from PLA invasion. North Korea's invasion, together with the conclusion of the Sino-Soviet alliance in February 1950, fundamentally altered US thinking about Taiwan's status. As noted in an earlier chapter, Soviet submarines operating from Taiwan would very substantially strengthen the threat those submarines posed to US sea lines of communications in the Western Pacific. In late 1949, US leaders had decided, after an intense and difficult debate, to abandon Taiwan to PLA takeover. This was to be done for the sake of seeking a modus vivendi with CCP-ruled China. This policy was abruptly discarded by US leaders once North Korean armies smashed across the 38th parallel with apparent Soviet and PRC support.

The US decision to abandon Taiwan was a difficult one. There was strong opposition. The US navy, which traditionally had great influence on US policy in the Pacific, and Congress, where sympathy for the KMT regime was strong, were loath to sacrifice Taiwan. There was strong sympathy for "Free China" among American communities, many of whom had long supported missionary efforts in the ROC, whose leaders, the Generalissimo and Madame Chiang, were Protestant Christians (Methodists to be precise), many Americans noted favorably. The Truman administration was also under increasing attack for being "soft on communism," and abandoning Taiwan and the KMT to the CCP would, and did, add to that criticism.

In November 1948, as KMT forces crumbled at the battle of Huaihai, the US Joint Chiefs of Staff reported to the President that a communist takeover of Taiwan would be "seriously unfavorable" to US security interests in the Far East, largely because of that island's strategic location for control of sea lines of communication.[30] These naval views contributed to a National Security Council decision of February 1949 to deny Taiwan to communist control, but only insofar as that could be achieved via "diplomatic and economic means." The State Department especially insisted that use of US military power be excluded, since that would contradict too directly the overriding strategic goal of courting "Chinese Titoism." By late 1949, however, it was clear that efforts to deny Taiwan to the PLA by purely nonmilitary means had failed, and that Taiwan would soon fall to PLA invasion unless US military forces intervened to protect it. The pros and cons of such direct military intervention were debated intensely within the Administration, but eventually it was decided not to use US military power to protect Taiwan. Stated bluntly, Taiwan was to be sacrificed for the sake of courting the PRC away from the Soviet Union. This decision was formally approved in the form of NSC memorandum 48/2 on December 30, 1949.

Opponents of this policy soon leaked news of it to the media. Once the top-level decision to sacrifice Taiwan was made late in 1949, the State Department sent a classified directive to US embassies around the world notifying them that the fall of Taiwan to communist forces was "widely anticipated," and that when it occurred, "false impressions" of the island's special military value should be countered. US missions were to explain that the disposition of Taiwan was a domestic affair of China and did not impinge on US interests. Taiwan had "no special military significance" and "is a strictly Chinese affair.... China has never been a naval power and the island is of no special strategic advantage to the Chinese communist armed forces." This ultra-sensitive directive was leaked to the *New York Times*, which published it on January 4, 1950.[31]

The day after the *Times* article appeared, Truman publicly defended the new policy. US China policy had traditionally respected the territorial unity of China and would not change now, Truman said. Referencing the Cairo Declaration of 1943, Truman noted that the United States had accepted the exercise of Chinese authority over Taiwan since Japan's surrender. The United States had no "predatory designs" on Taiwan or a desire for military bases there "at this time." Nor did the United States "have any intention of utilizing its Armed Forces to interfere in the present situation," Truman said. "The United States Government will not pursue a course which will lead to involvement in the civil conflict in China." Nor would the United States provide military aid or advice to Chinese forces on Taiwan.[32] The decision to sacrifice Taiwan was extremely controversial. There was very strong opposition founded squarely on US geostrategic interests. Still, it was a clear and authoritative decision made by the president with the support of his closest advisors and embodied in a formal NSA decision memorandum. Beijing could not have wished for a US policy more favorable to its "liberation" of Taiwan. Mao, however, bungled the opportunity.

As Washington was moving to wash its hands of Taiwan, the CCP was preparing invasion of that island, a move it considered the "last campaign to unify China."[33] On June 14, 1949, as communist armies marshaled for the push into central China, Mao ordered the commander of PLA forces moving into eastern China to plan for invasion of Taiwan in the winter of 1949–1950. Defeat of a PLA invasion of Quemoy Island in Xiamen harbor in October and an assault on the Zhoushan Islands off Zhejiang in November 1949 increased PLA awareness of the importance of air and naval capabilities in amphibious assaults, and of CCP weaknesses in these areas. Consequently, in November 1949 the CCP approved a new PLA plan for a step-by-step campaign against

Taiwan. First Jinmen and Zhoushan Islands were to be taken, then Hainan, and finally Taiwan. The invasion of Taiwan was set for mid-1951. Preparations for the Taiwan invasion continued. By early 1950, 300,000 to 380,000 troops were assembled along the central China coast training for amphibious assault operations. A CCP Central Committee meeting in early June 1950 reviewed the status of preparations for the Taiwan invasion. As a result of the review, four additional field armies were deployed opposite Taiwan for the assault, making a total of sixteen armies allocated for that mission.[34]

The critical problem confronting a PLA invasion was not troop strength but weakness of air and naval forces. In fall 1949, the CCP ordered a crash program to acquire vessels that could be used for an assault on Taiwan—build them, buy them in Hong Kong or elsewhere, refurbish captured KMT vessels, or requisition them from civilian use. As for air power, the PLA air force had only 185 aircraft of Japanese, British, and US manufacture. Far more powerful forces would be necessary to protect PLA troop transports and support forces once ashore.

Mao turned to Stalin for assistance in strengthening his air force. Securing Soviet assistance in quickly developing air and naval forces for a Taiwan invasion was high on Liu Shaoqi's Moscow agenda in mid-1949. During his Moscow talks, Liu Shaoqi requested that the Soviet Union supply the PLA with air and naval equipment for a Taiwan invasion. Stalin rejected this proposal out of hand, according to scholars Goncharov, Lewis, and Xue, because it posed too great a danger of war with the United States. It might even trigger a third world war, Stalin reportedly said.[35] Truman and Acheson's January 1950 announcement that the United States would not intervene in a PLA invasion of Taiwan led Stalin to agree to China's request for rapid creation of an air force to facilitate an assault on Taiwan. By mid-1950, Soviet training of Chinese personnel for a new PRC air force was well under way. Prospects for the successful liberation of Taiwan looked good. Then came the Korean War.

The difficult but authoritative December 1949 US decision to sacrifice Taiwan was scrapped on June 27, 1950, two days after North Korea's attack. In a statement on that day, President Truman indicated that in the new circumstances created by the Soviet- and Chinese-supported North Korean attack, "The occupation of Formosa by Communist forces would be a direct threat to the security of the Pacific area and to United States forces . . . in that area." Therefore, Truman continued, he had ordered the US Seventh Fleet to prevent any communist attack on Formosa and any attack by Chinese Nationalist forces against the mainland. The determination of the "future status" of Taiwan would have to await future developments, Truman said.[36] China had lost an opportunity to secure Taiwan without confronting the United States. It had done this in furtherance of essentially North Korean and Soviet reasons. To the extent that Mao bore responsibility for allowing Kim Il Sung to launch his war plan when and how he did, Mao must bear responsibility for US abandonment of its hands-off policy toward Taiwan.

CCP leaders did not expect US intervention and were surprised by it. The United States was in the process of demobilizing its armed forces and was too weak strategically, they had believed. The United States recognized Taiwan as part of China both in the Cairo Declaration and in post-1945 US handling ot Taiwan matters. Moreover, China was backed by the mighty Soviet Union. On June 30, 1950, three days after Truman's statement, Zhou Enlai informed the PLA navy that the invasion of Taiwan was being postponed and that forces allocated to that operation were being transferred the China–North Korea border region. Loss of a golden opportunity to secure Taiwan was the first cost to the PRC of Mao's green light to Kim Il Sung's war.

Fighting the Americans in Korea

Chinese entry into the Korean conflict took US forces by complete surprise. Chinese forces deployed forward exercised strict march discipline that prevented their discovery by US reconnaissance aircraft. They moved only at night, with camouflage netting set in place by 5:30 a.m. (before dawn) and remaining up until sundown at 7 p.m., when troops resumed their forward march. During daylight, men, equipment, vehicles, and draft animals remained immobile under camouflage nets. Unauthorized movement beyond camouflaged shelters was strictly prohibited. Individuals caught in the open when an aircraft appeared were ordered to remain completely immobile until the plane passed. Violators of march discipline were shot. Reconnaissance squads scouted ahead to find and prepare the next night's bivouac site. Such stealthy but quick movement delivered the element of surprise and gave considerable tactical success to CPV during the initial phase of combat with US and South Korean forces. Not expecting Chinese intervention, US/UN forces had allowed gaps to develop between units which CPV exploited with great skill. First CPV contact with US/UN forces came on October 25 in the Unsan area when powerful surprise assaults by CPV forces forced the United States to retreat. CPV forces then withdrew and disappeared, hiding in prepared and carefully camouflaged bivouacs in mountainous areas.[37]

A second phase of the CPV assault began on November 25 with powerful attacks at several points of the US/UN line. By mid-December, US/UN forces had been pushed south of the 38th parallel. On January 4, 1951, CPV forces retook Seoul. CPV forces often attacked at night and with overwhelmingly superior numbers. Their use of trumpets and gongs for communication and to boost morale sometimes frightened US/UN troops. By late January 1951, CPV forces had pushed US/UN forces south of Osan and Wonju, and it looked, from the perspective of both Beijing and Washington, as though the CPV might achieve their strategic objective of driving the Americans out of Korea. Figure 3-1 illustrates the tides of war in Korea.

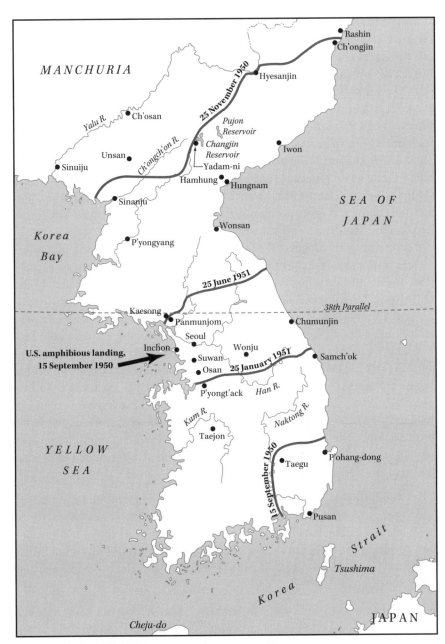

MANCHURIA

Yalu R. · Ch'osan

Ch'ongch'on R.

· Unsan

· Sinuiju

Pujon
Reservoir

Changjin
Reservoir
—Yadam-ni

25 November 1950

· Hyesanjin

· Rashin
Ch'ongjin

· Iwon

Hamhung · Hungnam

· Sinanju

Korea
Bay

· P'yongyang

· Wonsan

SEA OF
JAPAN

25 June 1951

Kaesong

Panmunjom

Seoul

38th Parallel

· Chumunjin

U.S. amphibious landing,
15 September 1950

Inchon

· Suwan
· Osan

Wonju

25 January 1951

P'yongt'ack

Han R.

· Samch'ok

Kum R.

Naktong R.

· Taejon

YELLOW
SEA

15 September 1950

· Taegu

· P'ohang-dong

· Pusan

Korea

Strait

Tsushima

Cheju-do

JAPAN

FIGURE 3-1 **Tides of War in Korea, 1950–1953**

Source: Doris M. Condit, ed., *The Test of War 1950–1953, Volume II*, Historical Office, Office of the Secretary of Defense, 1988.

By February, the battlefield balance began to shift against the CPV. The arrival of a new general for the US/UN forces, Matthew Ridgway, contributed to effective tactical responses to CPV tactics. Gaps in line that could be exploited by CPV disappeared. More artillery and machine guns were deployed to nullify CPV numerical superiority. CPV assaults with numerical superiority of even 15:1 began to fail. US forces began using defensive battles to kill large numbers of CPV, luring them into attacks on well-prepared kill zones and then quickly counterattacking to push CPV northward. US aircraft became more adept at identifying and destroying CPV bivouacs and supply depots along the long supply lines running north across the Yalu River. CPV causalities mounted. Hunger and shortage of food, clothing, ammunition, and weapons became heavy burdens on CPV forces. By June 1951, US/UN forces had retaken Seoul.

Maintaining an adequate flow of supplies to CPV forces in the face of US aerial dominance and continual bombing of Chinese logistics was a major and chronic problem for the CPV. In April 1951, deputy commander of the CPV Hong Xuezhi reported in Beijing to Zhou Enlai on the dire supply situation of Chinese forces in Korea. Food, ammunition, and medical care were all lacking.[38] Zhou responded to Hong's pleas by ordering increased production and delivery of goods, along with increased allocation of trucks and anti-aircraft guns, to Korea. Starting in September 1951, the Chinese air force began air defense operations over North Korea. Major logistical problems persisted. Zhou convened conferences in Shenyang in November 1951 and in Beijing in February 1952 to address pressing logistic problems. At the latter meeting, after listening to various government officials report all the reasons why they were unable to meet CPV requirements, CPV Commander Peng Dehuai exploded angrily:

> You have this and that problem. . . . You should go to the front and see with your own eyes what food and clothing the soldiers have. Not to speak of casualties? For what are they giving their lives? We have no aircraft. We have only a few guns. Transports are not protected. More and more soldiers are dying of starvation. Can't you overcome some of your difficulties?[39]

Beijing turned to its Soviet ally for help.[40] On October 10, 1950, after the CCP had decided to intervene but before CPV forces crossed the Yalu, Zhou Enlai flew to Stalin's Yalta villa in the Crimea to request Soviet support for the upcoming effort. Stalin agreed to supply equipment and ammunition, but only for payment. The Soviet Union would extend credits to finance Chinese purchases, Stalin said. Regarding air cover, which Zhou urgently requested, Stalin agreed to provide such support only over Chinese territory, not over Korea. Even then, Stalin said, it would take two to three months for Soviet air forces to prepare for such operations. The actual entry of CPV into North

Korea in October and the onset of heavy fighting led Stalin to modify his position and agree to provide air cover. On November 1, 1950, about a week after the CPV engaged US/UN forces, Stalin finally permitted Soviet warplanes, manned by Soviet pilots but with Soviet markings painted over, to cross the Yalu and engage US planes operating over North Korea. Still, Soviet air support was tardy and inadequate, and a source of Chinese dissatisfaction with Stalin's policies.

On March 1, 1951 Mao sent Stalin a cable emphasizing the urgent need for stronger air protection of CPV supply lines and requesting Soviet assistance in this regard. The Soviet leader agreed to deploy two air force divisions, three anti-aircraft divisions, and 6,000 trucks to Korea. Soviet assistance, along with road, railway, and bridge construction efforts by PLA engineers, improved the CPV supply situation. Throughout the war and for many years thereafter, the participation of Soviet air forces in combat with the United States over North Korea was kept top secret by both Beijing and Moscow. Although US intelligence soon determined the actual situation, it was hotly denied by Beijing and Moscow. Even after the collapse of the Sino-Soviet alliance circa 1960, Beijing and Moscow felt it best to keep secret their joint air war against the United States. Not until the post-Soviet release of Korean War documents were the inner workings of this clandestine Soviet-Chinese air war against the United States revealed.

The CPV responded to US air bombardment by building numerous camouflaged refuges for trucks in caves or gullies. A system of aircraft spotters was organized atop hills to give early warning of approaching aircraft. Once alerted, CPV trucks would quickly seek shelter. Broken-down trucks and fake bunkers were left just visible enough to attract US bombs. CPV commanders also adapted by ordering some percentage more than the amounts actually needed. Thus perhaps 20 percent more than the amount actually needed would be requisitioned, so that if 20 percent was lost en route, requirements would still be met. CPV forces adapted to heavy US air and artillery bombardment of front-line positions by digging deep tunnels and bunkers behind those positions. Main defense forces would shelter in these more protected rear positions until the US bombardment lifted, typically shortly before the US assault began, and then rush into front-line positions just before advancing US forces closed on the CPV front line. Chinese forces also waged "see-saw battles" in which they would seize US positions, withdraw when counterattacked, but then quickly counterattack themselves before the exhausted enemy had time to rest or consolidate their defenses. On other occasions, CPV forces would simulate a forced withdrawal of up to thirty kilometers, and then turn and defend strongly as US/UN forces attempted to follow through on what they supposed had been their "breakthrough."

Chinese scholar Shu Guang Zhang stresses that Mao fundamentally misunderstood the nature of modern warfare as experienced by Chinese forces in Korea.[41] Based on the CCP's own military experience up to 1950, reinforced by classic Chinese military thought that stressed tactical deception and cunning, and romantically certain of the revolutionary zeal of China's masses, Mao genuinely imagined that China's vastly undergunned forces could sweep American forces out of Korea. Mao also had an ideologically biased image of the morale and fighting capacity of US forces. This led, according to Zhang, to Chinese soldiers dying in vast numbers for objectives which were realistically beyond their capacity. According to Zhang and based on official Chinese accounts, 148,000 Chinese soldiers died in Korea, compared to 33,629 US soldiers.[42]

Ending the Korean War

Four successive waves of CPV offensives between October 1950 and March 1951 imposed very heavy causalities on Chinese forces. Peng Dehuai had proposed a fifth major offensive for April, with new Chinese divisions being sent in to replace units that had already suffered heavy casualties. Mao approved the proposal. The offensive was duly launched, only to fail with very high Chinese casualties.[43] Mao concluded that a lull in fighting via initiation of peace talks would provide a period in which CPV front lines could be reinforced, resupplied, and better linked via communications, preparing them to resume further offensive pushes.[44] Beijing had rejected a January 1951 United Nations proposal for a ceasefire because, as Zhou Enlai explained, it would only allow US/UN forces to regroup and reinforce. After the exhaustion of the CPV's fifth offensive, a ceasefire would favor China by allowing reorganization of CPV forces, Mao concluded. Talks began on July 10, 1951. They would continue for two years, until July 27, 1953.

Mao and Zhou also believed that negotiations could be exploited to political advantage. Contradictions between the United States and its European allies could be exploited. Mao and Zhou also believed that China and North Korea were better able to bear a protracted war than was the United States. The basis for this belief is not clear; probably it was due to the differing structures of power and authority in Leninist and liberal democratic systems. There would be no antiwar movements or protests in the PRC or North Korea. In any case, throughout the negotiations, Mao, Zhou, and Stalin exchanged affirmations of the belief that the United States was more afraid of protraction of the war than were China and North Korea. Of course, protraction had to be made costly for the Americans by continuing to impose battles and casualties on the United States. Fighting was integral to the Chinese process of negotiation, "talking while fighting" (*yi bian tan, yi bian da*).

Beijing's bedrock belief that the United States feared war protraction more than China did is not born out by the negotiation record. In those talks, the

Chinese side conceded far more of its demands than did the US side. On July 12, 1951, two days after the start of negotiations, Zhou Enlai laid out five conditions for peace. Beijing would achieve none of these objectives. Every one was rejected by the US/UN side, and China would, one by one, concede each point to move negotiations forward. Zhou's five conditions were:

- All foreign troops were to be withdrawn from Korea
- US military forces were to be withdrawn from the Taiwan Strait
- The Korean issue would be settled by the Korean people themselves
- The PRC would assume China's seat at the United Nations and the KMT expelled
- An international meeting would be convened to discuss signing a peace treaty with Japan[45]

Two CPV generals sat at the negotiating table for China, but negotiations were overseen by vice foreign minister and longtime head of military intelligence Li Keneng and head of the foreign ministry's International Information Bureau Qiao Guanghua. Li and Qiao guided the CPV generals from a special facility set up a kilometer or so behind the negotiating site. Zhou Enlai and, ultimately, Mao in turn guided Li and Qiao, receiving daily reports from them. Mao's instruction to his negotiating team was to wage a "political battle" and not show any hurried desire for peace. Throughout the twenty-four months of negotiations, the CPV continued limited offensive operations to keep up the American desire for a negotiated settlement by forcing them to pay a continuing price in blood.

Once talks began, it quickly became apparently that the United States would not accept consideration of any of the issues enumerated in Zhou's list of "conditions." From the US standpoint, the only issue to be settled was ending the fighting in Korea. Withdrawal of foreign (non-Korean) troops from Korea was a key Chinese objective going into the talks. The day after talks began, Mao ordered his negotiators to push hard on this: "[We] must insist that all [foreign]forces withdraw."[46] After two weeks of persistent US refusal to discuss the issue, Mao informed his negotiators that they need no longer insist on the withdrawal of foreign forces, but could leave that issue to be handled by the postarmistice conference. After several months of US refusal to pursue "political issues," Beijing again agreed to narrow the focus of the talks, assigning all "political issues" issues to a future international meeting to deliberate over them. A conference would eventually be held in Geneva in 1954, with nothing of significance regarding Korea accomplished.[47]

By July 1951, China's leaders also recognized that Chinese forces would not be able, at least as then constituted, to drive US forces out of Korea. They concluded, however, that China had already won a great victory by overcoming US technological superiority and pushing the United States out of North Korea, thereby recovering for the KWP its original territorial base north of the 38th parallel. Very early in negotiations, Mao stipulated that China's new objective was the restoration of the prewar status quo ante, that is, reestablishment of the 38th parallel as the demarcation between northern and southern zones of Korea. Mao and Zhou initially expected that the United States would accept relatively easily the restoration of the 38th parallel as the demarcation line.[48] Even though the front line of actual control was well north of the 38th parallel, Beijing believed the United States would agree to restore the status quo ante in order to end the war. The United States simply could not fight a protracted war, CCP leaders believed; it would pull back to the 38th parallel in order to secure a ceasefire. The talks could then move on to consideration of political issues underlying the war, the Chinese side agreed.[49] Again the Chinese calculations turned out to be wrong.

Washington rejected the Chinese proposition that the 38th parallel be reestablished as the demarcation line and initially insisted that a new line be drawn north of Pyongyang (the North Korean capital). Fairly quickly, the United States abandoned that demand, and insisted that the existing line of actual control between the forces of the two sides should be taken as the basis for the line. The US proposal would yield significant territorial gain north of the 38th parallel for the Republic of Korea. The land gain on the west side of the peninsula (where the North would gain some land south of the 38th parallel) was militarily useless, since those areas were peninsulas going nowhere. As Beijing became aware of the US refusal to restore the status quo ante regarding the 38th parallel, it approved a proposal by Peng Dehuai to launch a new major offensive to push US/UN forces well south of the 38th parallel. China could than agree to withdraw north of that parallel, achieving its goals. The offensive was duly launched on August 17, 1951, but achieved no success against well-prepared US/UN positions. After inflicting extremely heavy damages on CPV forces, US/UN forces counterattacked, pushing CPV forces further north. The United States claimed the new front line as the demarcation line between the two zones. Intense US bombing again had devastating effects. CCP leaders then concluded that further offensives would risk dangerous setbacks and that defensive tactics would be better. A planned further offensive was called off, and China adopted a new position at the negotiating table—a ceasefire in place. On November 27, 1951, the two sides agreed that the line of actual control would constitute the demarcation line.

Release of prisoners of war (POWs) then became the focus of the "political battle" at the negotiating table. Beijing and North Korea insisted that all POWs be handed over to their respective governments for repatriation to their countries of citizenship—"all for all," this Chinese proposal was called. US and South Korea leaders, on the other hand, insisted that POWs who did not wish to return should not be repatriated against their will. POWs should be offered a choice, and those who did not want to be repatriated should not be; there should be no involuntary repatriation. Beijing and the KWP insisted adamantly on complete repatriation without regard to individual volition. This was a matter of principle, Zhou Enlai explained to Stalin in August 1952. Therefore, China could not yield to the United States on this point. Two months later, China rejected the US/UN "final offer" on the POW issue, leading the US/UN to break off talks, to be resumed only when Beijing became willing to accept the principle of voluntary repatriation.

This, of course, was a many-layered issue. It reflected the vast difference between liberal democratic and Marxist-Leninist philosophies of the two sides. It reflected too a political struggle for moral superiority. Decisions by a significant number of Chinese and North Korean POWs not to return to their communist-ruled homes would be, and was, used by the United States and South Korea for propaganda purposes. It was also an issue touching on military discipline in future wars. If soldiers of communist armies knew—as US psychological warfare efforts would ensure they did—that they would not be returned at war's end to their communist masters, they would be more likely to surrender and to cooperate with their anticommunist captors by supplying intelligence. For seventeen months, the talks deadlocked over the POW repatriation issue.

In March 1953, after Stalin's death and with a new US president (Dwight Eisenhower) in office, Beijing proposed the resumption of talks, implicitly acceding to the US/UN position on repatriation. Beijing now accepted the principle of voluntary repatriation, but proposed that nonreturnees first be handed over to a neutral third country. This was still unacceptable to the Americans, who saw all sorts of dangers lurking in this arrangement, and the United States insisted that the issue be handled in Korea. But the shift toward a "neutral third country" option finally moved the communist side away from the "all for all" formulation. Eventually, Beijing accepted the US/UN demand; repatriation was voluntary, with "explanations" to individual POWs regarding their rights completed in Korea. Eventually 6,700 CPV POWs would choose repatriation to China, while 14,700 (or 2.2 times as many) refused repatriation.[50] Most of the Chinese nonreturnees eventually went to Taiwan.

Scholars have long believed that Stalin's death on March 5, 1953, eliminated a leader who wanted to keep the Korean conflict going as long as he could for strategic purposes. Stalin's death finally allowed Chinese leaders who longed for peace and a focus on economic development to finally bring the war to an end. Scholar Chen Jian, on the other hand, concluded that Stalin and Chinese leaders moved in tandem in late 1952–early 1953 toward ending the Korean conflict. Beijing alone was responsible for the unyielding position on the POW issue, Chen found, and there is no evidence of Soviet-Chinese disagreement on this issue that blocked settlement for seventeen months.[51] In August 1952, Stalin proposed the face-saving third-neutral-country solution that went a long way toward meeting the US/UN position. Shortly after Stalin's death, Zhou flew to Moscow to discuss matters with the Soviet Union's new leadership. The two sides agreed to end the war on the basis of "reasonable compromises with the enemy."

As noted earlier, Beijing achieved none of the negotiating objectives laid out by Zhou Enlai for the armistice talk. US forces remained in South Korea, and the United Nations remained deeply involved in the Korean question. China remained outside the UN for nearly twenty more years. US military forces remained in the Taiwan Strait. And China would not sign a peace treaty with Japan until 1978. China nonetheless deemed the war a success. There were good grounds for this judgment. Beijing had confronted the United States and fought it to a standstill on Korean battlefields. It had forced the United States to give up its demand for a demarcation line north of Pyongyang and, more substantially, to abandon its fall 1950 objective of unifying Korea under US tutelage. "Korea's revolutionary forces" were re-established in their territorial bastion. The United States was also forced to accept the PRC as an equal at the bargaining table and agree to an international conference with PRC participation to discuss a political settlement in Korea and the Far East. (This would be the 1954 Geneva Conference.)

Most substantially of all, and irrespective of the give and take at the negotiations, PRC willingness to go to war with the United States from a position of great weakness and against seemingly overwhelmingly American power profoundly altered the US perception of the PRC and its power. The United States began to take PRC power quite seriously. "Communist China" was quite ready for war with the United States, Americans concluded. The PRC was a dangerous power. This "lesson of Korea"—don't discount or underestimate China's power—would underlie two decades of US effort to "contain Communist China" and another PRC-US war, this one indirect, in Vietnam. "The lesson of Korea," underestimating communist-ruled China's readiness for war with the United States, would also be a fundamental determinant of the US strategy of "gradual, limited escalation" during the Vietnam War of the 1960s.

An interesting discrepancy exists between American and Chinese views regarding the role of US nuclear threats in ending the Korean War. US leaders of the Eisenhower Administration believed, both during the final stage of the peace negotiations and subsequently, that US threats to use nuclear weapons unless the war was swiftly concluded were instrumental in persuading Beijing to end the war. The evidence of this belief in top levels of the Eisenhower Administration is solid. Far less solid is the evidence that US nuclear threats substantially motivated China's decision to end the war. Chen Jian found no discussion of this matter in his review of Chinese documents. Other scholars have marshaled evidence of relative Chinese lack of concern with the US threat. PLA deputy chief of staff Nie Rongzhen told Indian ambassador K. M. Panikkar (India was a channel for transmission of some of the Eisenhower administration's nuclear threats) in 1953:

> The Americans can bomb us, they can destroy our industries, but they cannot defeat us on land. We have calculated all that . . . They may even drop atomic bombs on us. What then? . . . After all, China lives on the farms.[52]

The American belief in the effectiveness of atomic coercion against Beijing probably influenced subsequent resort to the same tactic by the United States during the Indochina crisis of 1953–1954 and again during both the 1954 and 1958 Taiwan Strait crises. The American use of nuclear coercion also helped convince China's leaders that China could not be without nuclear weapons of its own. In the words of a spokesperson for a Chinese scientific association, "only when we ourselves have the atomic weapon, and are fully prepared, is it possible for the frenzied warmongers to listen to our just and reasonable proposals."[53]

Germ Warfare Campaign as Negotiating Leverage

Beijing responded to US use of the POW repatriation issue to claim a position of moral superiority in the Korean War negotiations by launching a global campaign charging the United States with use of biological weapons (BW) against civilian populations of China and North Korea. Hundreds of US aircraft were reported to have dropped disease-infected insects, rodents, or other material across wide areas of northeast China and North Korea. The list of diseases allegedly spread was long: cholera, smallpox, bubonic plague, meningitis, encephalitis, hemorrhagic fever, typhoid, scarlet fever, measles, and typhus. This has long been a contentious issue, with China insisting that its charges were true, and the United States government denying it with equal vehemence. Some scholars have argued that the changes are essentially accurate.[54] Post–Cold War evidence from the Russian presidential archives, however, indicates that the Soviet government understood the charges were false, and that Soviet operatives cooperated with Chinese and North Koreans to fabricate evidence substantiating these assertions as a way of of undermining the moral position of the United States.

Initial reports of US germ warfare activities came from CPV headquarters. Mao and Zhou apparently initially credited those reports, but at some point came to understand they were bogus. They nonetheless allowed the charges to continue as part of a political strategy to undermine the US moral position in the Korean armistice talks, and indeed made them the center of a global anti-US campaign. On January 28, 1952, CPV headquarters reported that enemy aircraft had dropped material spreading smallpox virus. A more detailed report to Mao and Zhou came on February 18 from Nie Rongzhen, head of the Central Staff Department of the PLA, who reported on an investigation that was underway regarding enemy use of insects as vectors of disease.[55] Three days later, on February 21, Mao cabled Stalin to report that the Americans were using germ warfare in Korea: "In the period from 28 January to 17 February 1952 the Americans used bacteriological weapons 8 times, [dropped] from planes and through artillery shells. The Americans are equal to Japanese criminals from the 731st detachment," Mao told Stalin.[56] The reference to the "Japanese criminals" and unit 731 was to the extensive research on germ warfare conducted by Japanese units in China during World War II. Those activities had became known after 1945 and were punished as war crimes by Soviet authorities shortly after the war. US authorities, on the other hand, granted certain immunities to key Japanese participants in these activities in exchange for cooperation in understanding the scientific results achieved by these Japanese activities. The general nature of these US arrangements became known in the late 1940s, and was probably one factor inclining CCP leaders to so readily conclude that the United States was following in Japan's footsteps regarding BW. Linking putative US actions to earlier Japanese actions also greatly increased the propaganda value of these charges, both within China and globally.

To concoct evidence substantiating the BW charges, North Korean, Chinese, and Soviet officials cooperated in creating false areas of infection to be shown to two international investigation committees invited to inspect the supposedly infected areas. In the words of the deputy chief of the counter-espionage department of the Soviet Ministry of Internal Affairs and former advisor to North Korea's ministry of public health in a report to Soviet secret police head Lavrenti Beria:

> The Koreans stated that the Americans had supposedly repeatedly exposed several areas of their country to plague and cholera. To prove these facts, the North Koreans, with the assistance of our advisors, created false areas of exposure. In June–July 1952 a delegation of specialists in bacteriology from the World Peace Council arrived in North Korea. Two false areas of exposure were prepared. In connection with this, the Koreans insisted on obtaining cholera bacteria from corpses which they would get from China.[57]

A statement by another Soviet participant in the creation of these false areas of infection reported: "In the opinion of the North Korean government, this was necessary in order to compromise the Americans in this war. However, to all outward appearances, they seriously believed the information about this that they received from the Chinese."[58] Finally, on May 2, 1953, the Presidium of the Council of Ministers of the USSR sent a message to the Soviet ambassador in Beijing to be delivered to Mao Zedong. It read:

> The Soviet Government and the Central Committee of the CPSU were misled. The spread in the press of information about the use by the Americans of bacteriological weapons in Korea was based on false information. The accusations against the Americans were fictitious.[59]

Among the recommendations delivered by the Soviet ambassador and following from the above statement was the proposition: "To cease publication in the press of materials accusing the Americans of using bacteriological weapons in Korea and China." Beijing agreed with this proposal, and material about "US germ warfare" quickly disappeared from the Chinese as well as the Soviet media. According to a subsequent report by the Soviet ambassador after his May 2 delivery of this message, when he received this Soviet message Mao appeared nervous, "smoked a lot, crushed cigarettes and drank a lot of tea. Towards the end of the conversation he laughed and joked, and calmed down." Mao told the Soviet ambassador that the campaign unmasking the American use of bacteriological weapons had begun based on reports of the CPV command.[60] The comment of the North Korean KWP leader after receiving the same Soviet presentation that Mao received was instructive: "We were convinced that everything was known in Moscow. We thought that setting off this campaign would give great assistance to the cause of the struggle against American imperialism."[61]

Before Moscow pulled the plug on the anti-US germ warfare campaign, Beijing generated considerable activity promoting those accusations. On March 8, 1952, Zhou Enlai laid out the accusation: the United States had sent 448 aircraft on no less than sixty-eight occasions between February 29 and March 5 to drop germ-carrying insects. Eighteen different disease-infested insects, spiders, and ticks, as well as small rodents, had been dropped, along with germ-carrying paper and "leaflet bombs."[62] The detail of the charge lent apparent credibility to it. Following these very specific accusations, Beijing mobilized two "international commissions" to investigate American germ warfare "violations of international law" and propagate those charges to the world in a more credible fashion than statements by China's premier. One of these commissions was organized by the World Peace Council (WPC), a largely Soviet-funded and -guided peace and disarmament group founded in 1948 and based in Paris. The WPC recruited seven scientists, only one of whom was a Soviet. The head of the Chinese Academy of Sciences, Guo Morou, personally delivered to a WPC convention in Oslo the invitation to investigate "US germ warfare." Guo also persuaded his old friend, the eminent British chemist, Marxist, and Sinologist Joseph Needham, to head the investigation commission.[63]

The WPC group spent two months conducting its investigation. When members of the delegation visited the false infection areas created by the North Koreans, Soviets, and Chinese, they were discouraged from lingering too long in the area by setting off explosives in the vicinity of their lodging and by the sounding of false air raid alarms.[64] Most of the "evidence" collected by the WPC group came in the form of statements by Chinese who claimed to have witnessed insects or rodents falling from the skies and dropped by American planes. The commission took this testimony at face value and passed it on to the world in a 669-page report. Beijing bolstered the charges by securing and publicizing highly detailed "confessions" by US POWs regarding their supposed involvement in a wide array of US germ warfare activities.[65] These false "confessions" were given under extreme duress (sleep deprivation, denial of sanitary facilities, poor and unsanitary food), and were withdrawn by the POWs after their release.[66] During 1952, Chinese and Soviet media along with Moscow-linked international "peace organizations" gave extensive coverage to accusations of American germ warfare. In the four weeks between mid-March and mid-April 1952, the Soviet press devoted a full one-quarter of its coverage to germ warfare allegations. Chinese newspapers during the same period followed suit. As scholar Milton Leitenberg pointed out, April 26, 1952, was the date set for ratification of the US-Japan peace treaty, to which neither the USSR or the PRC was a party.

Chinese involvement in creation of false infection sites, help in procuring disease-infected corpses in China, and the coercing false confessions from US POWs suggests a massive disinformation campaign designed to erode the moral credentials of China's rival. Public health in war-wracked Korea and Northeast China was undoubtedly appalling, and diseases of all sorts were rampant. Convincing the Chinese people and foreign audiences that these diseases were the product of American malevolence was an effective way of undermining the United States, with its claims to stand for freedom and democracy. The apparent failure of extensive US "germ warfare" to defeat China also reinforced the CCP idea that revolutionary human spirit could overcome and defeat even the most advanced technology. If US germ warfare could not defeat China, how could US atomic bombs?

Teaching the People to Hate America

The Korean War fundamentally altered the psychology of the US-PRC relation. Traditionally, Americans had looked on China as a friendly power. Friendship quickly changed to hate. The fact that Chinese now hated the United States enough to undertake a war against it came as a shock to Americans. Most Americans, both government officials and ordinary people, saw the Korean War as masterminded by Stalin with full support by Mao. Then came the "human wave assaults" by CPV forces, demonstrating, in American eyes, stark disregard for casualties. Then the "brainwashing" of US POWs, the "germ warfare" charges, and the demand for involuntary repatriation of POWs. All these worked together to produce a deeply rooted demonic American view of "Red China."

On China's side, parallel to material preparations for military intervention in July and August, CCP leaders deliberated how to mobilize popular support for a "resist America, support Korea" campaign. The result, kicked off in July, was a full-scale, nationwide mass movement with a wide array of CCP-led mass organizations—political parties and groups, labor unions, women's and youth groups—joining an umbrella organization to educate the people of the whole country about the crimes of US imperialism against China and other countries of Asia. Central themes of this campaign were the long history of US aggression against China, the decadent and decrepit nature of US capitalism and imperialism, and the imperative need to "beat American arrogance." Many people had "illusions" about the United States, and the movement aimed to eliminate these "illusions." The anti-American movement was paralleled by another to suppress "reactionaries and reactionary activities." This movement had been launched in March, before the start of the Korean War, but did not gain momentum until the war began. By that point, all party and government offices were instructed to pursue repression of reactionaries as "one of the most important tasks." They should "lead the people to mop up ruthlessly all open and hidden reactionaries, thus establishing and consolidating the revolutionary order.[67] By May 1951, more than 2.5 million "reactionaries" had been arrested and 710,000 executed.[68] This widespread terror was justified, in part, as essential to defend new China from the US imperialism in Korea. It also encouraged people to accept the CCP's view of China and the world.

Marxist propaganda had long been critical of the United States, of course. But typically that propaganda had drawn a distinction between the US government and the people, stressing that the latter suffered oppression by the US imperialists in common with other peoples of the world. The anti-American propaganda generated by the CCP in the early 1950s depicted Americans and American society as totally corrupt, venal, bestial, brutal, and violent. American society was sunk deep in thievery, murder, lying, prostitution, rape, racial oppression, religious discrimination, starvation, poverty, and so on. One publication gives a good sense of this. The United States

> is a world of gangsters, debauchees, and murderers, a factory where criminals are made. Here morality, modesty have been thrown into the cesspool. This is a society without scruple of [sic] shame, where morality has been overwhelmed.[69]

As for the American freedom of creation and opportunity that some people touted:

> This is nothing else but a weird, empty, superficial and deformed psychological phenomenon, promoted by the American bourgeois ... [to] convert all their people into the same brainless animals as they themselves are, in order that they may be safe in their positions as keepers of the zoo.

There was absolutely nothing laudable about the United States. The essential thing was, said another publication: "After having fully understood the true facts about the US, every patriotic Chinese must hate the US, despise the US, and look with contempt upon the US." Massive amounts of propaganda of this type were produced. According to one PRC report, in the first half of 1951 New China Bookstores alone had issued over 100 million pieces of anti-US propaganda. Committees were formed at all country levels to organize anti-US speeches, rallies, parades, posters, and so on.

This sort of propaganda had two key purposes. First, to mobilize the Chinese people to support the war in Korea. Second, and probably more importantly, to re-educate many Western-educated Chinese and/or a considerable segment of China's urban middle and upper classes who looked positively on the Western ways of life symbolized by the United States. Re-educating these influential stratum of Chinese society would facilitate the elimination of Western influence in China and prepare the ground for the creation of a new socialist civilization modeled after that of the USSR.

Support for Revolution in Indochina

Indochina quickly became a second key area of PRC assistance to revolution in Asia. There was a long history of interaction between the leaders of the CCP and Vietnamese Worker's Party (VWP) leaders.[70] Vietnamese communist leader Ho Chi Minh became familiar with many of the future leaders of the CCP in France in the early 1920s. Ho then served as an operative of the Communist International for many years, and worked in that capacity with CCP leaders in Hong Kong, in south China, in the CCP Yan'an base area, and in Moscow. CCP and VWP leaders knew each other well and viewed themselves as comrades in a global anti-imperialist struggle led by the Soviet Union. Once the KMT-CCP civil war erupted in post–World War II China, the VWP assisted the CCP. When KMT forces in Guangdong moved against CCP troops in that region, CCP forces fled to a VWP base area just inside Vietnam, where they were provided with food, medicine, and supplies, along with sanctuary. In return, the CCP trained VWP forces as the latter organized as a League for Vietnamese Independence, or Viet Minh. The CCP's Hong Kong office also occasionally provided the Viet Minh with funding and organized ethnic Chinese military units which eventually amalgamated with the Viet Minh.

As soon as the People's Republic of China was founded, Ho Chi Minh sent an envoy to Beijing to request assistance in the struggle against French colonialism. France had consolidated its control over much of what later became Vietnam in the 1880s, fighting a war with Qing dynasty China in which it won hegemony over Indochina. By the 1920s, Vietnamese nationalism was taking communist forms. On the heels of Japan's surrender in August 1945, Vietnamese communists led by Ho Chi Minh seized power in Hanoi and proclaimed the independence of a new state, the Democratic Republic of Vietnam (DRV). A French attempt to reassert dominion over Vietnam soon led to fighting in which the Viet Minh did not fare very well against vastly superior French military power. CCP assistance would quickly and dramatically alter the military balance in the Viet Minh's favor.

In December 1949, Liu Shaoqi convened a Politburo meeting to consider ties with the Vietnamese revolutionary movement. Mao and Zhou Enlai were then in Moscow negotiating the February 1950 agreements with the USSR. The Politburo decided that China and Vietnam were comrades involved in a common struggle against imperialism, and that therefore the CCP should post a high-ranking liaison representative to the VWP and Viet Minh. The representative selected was General Luo Guibo, then director of the General Office of the CCP Central Military Commission. Luo would be China's main representative in Vietnam through 1957. While Mao and Zhou were still in Moscow, Ho Chi Minh flew there to discuss strategy. After talks with Ho, Mao informed Stalin that the PRC was prepared to recognize the DRV and to provide active support for the Indochinese struggle against France. Stalin approved the proposal. The PRC should recognize the DRV first, then the Soviet Union would follow suit, Stalin said, adding that the Soviet Union was also prepared to provide aid to the DRV. On January 18, 1950, the PRC became the first country to recognize the DRV. The USSR followed on January 30.

Negotiations over Chinese aid to the VWP followed, from January through April 1950. The CCP agreed to open a military training school in southern China for Viet Minh officers and cadre, and other training camps for ordinary soldiers. China also agreed to assign advisors and supply weapons to Viet Minh military units. Ho Chi Minh requested the dispatch of Chinese officers to command Viet Minh units at the regimental and battalion levels, but the CCP rejected this, agreeing to send advisors only. A Chinese Military Advisory Group (CMAG) was duly formed and began functioning at Nanning in Guangxi province in July. The CMAG was headed by General Wei Guoqing and consisted of 79 advisors with a total staff of 281 people. In terms of weapons, during 1950 China supplied the Viet Minh with rifles and pistols, machine guns and recoilless rifles, mortars, artillery, and bazookas, plus ammunition, medical supplies and communication equipment.

Before Chinese advisors deployed to Vietnam, they were instructed to avoid arrogance and attitudes of big power chauvinism. They were not to display contempt or seek to impose their views on their Vietnamese associates. Nor should they take offense if Vietnamese refused to adopt their suggestions. Mao and Luo Guibo were acutely aware of China's long history of domination of Vietnam, and strove to prevent old Chinese habits from spoiling the creation of a new era of equal cooperation.

In mid-1950, the CCP assigned another accomplished PLA general, Chen Geng, to draw up a plan for securing Viet Minh control over the mountainous terrain along Vietnam's border with China. The plan Chen Geng devised was carefully premised on the still-limited military experience and capabilities of Viet Minh forces, and would build step by step toward success in accord with the strategic principles of Mao Zedong. The offensive was successful. By October, almost the entire border region was under Viet Minh control. Transportation lines with China were no longer blocked by French forces, and Viet Minh forces were positioned to move into the more densely populated Red River delta. Chinese assistance had transformed the battlefield balance between Viet Minh and French forces. Figure 3-2 illustrates the CMAG–Viet Minh campaigns of 1950–1952.

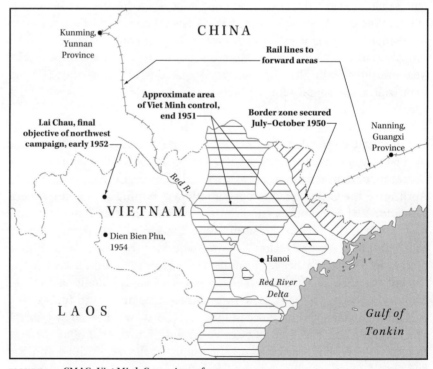

FIGURE 3-2 **CMAG–Viet Minh Campaigns of 1950–1952**

Source: Qiang Zhai, *China and the Vietnam Wars, 1950–1975*, (University of North Carolina Press: Chapel Hill, 2000), p. 27.

Early in 1952, the CMAG proposed and then drafted a plan for a major offensive to secure control over the mountainous region in northwest Vietnam. Success in this operation would secure the rear for Viet Minh forces for a subsequent thrust into the Red River delta. It would also open Laos to the "liberation struggle." It was "crucially important to help Laos achieve liberation," Liu Shaoqi told the CCP Central Military Commission in April 1952 as the CMAG proposal was under deliberation.[71] The VWP requested the deployment of PLA forces to northwestern Vietnam as part of the operation. The CCP declined that proposal, saying it was an important Chinese principle not to send Chinese forces to Vietnam. The CCP did agree, however, to deploy some units to the border to show support for the operation. The operation was launched in October 1952, and by mid-December the northwest was under Viet Minh control and liberation forces were staging for movement into Laos. Zhou Enlai briefed Stalin on the northwest offensive during August–September 1952 talks in Moscow. Stalin approved the operation, suggesting its success might help create an advantageous position for negotiations with France. In line with the spirit of the understandings of July 1949, the PRC and the USSR cooperated closely to expand the frontiers of the socialist camp in Asia.

4 }

The Bandung Era

Moscow Points a New Direction and Beijing Agrees

Stalin's death in March 1953 left a deeply divided Soviet leadership, mutually suspicious and acutely aware of the severe problems of the realm Stalin had bequeathed them. Stalin's rule had brought immense suffering and privation to the people of the USSR. Popular discontent had been repressed by police violence and sheer terror. But the post-Stalin Soviet leadership were aware that continuation of that course was likely to produce uprisings or, at best, sullen apathy. A somewhat more humane type of communist rule had to be worked out. But political relaxation also posed risks of rebellion. The problem for the new CPSU leadership was to find the appropriate level of de-Stalinization.[1] In terms of foreign policy, Stalin had managed to turn most of the USSR's neighbors into enemies. Territorial demands and confrontational policies had turned Turkey and Iran into enthusiastic participants in US collective security schemes. Stalin's wary and contemptuous attitude, plus strident condemnations by the Soviet media as tools of imperialism, had alienated potential friends like India and Indonesia. In Eastern Europe, Stalin's installation of "little Stalins" to impose harsh socialism had produced simmering discontent which was bound to produce uprisings. The uprising in East Berlin in June 1953 was a foretaste of things to come. Stalin's policies had also managed to create a military confrontation with an increasingly united and US-reinforced West, adding further danger to potential uprisings against East Europe's "little Stalins." How would the United States and Britain respond to uprisings in Eastern Europe? Even toward the PRC, Stalin's policies were unsustainable. Stalin's successors understood that Stalin's suspicious treatment of Mao, combined with Soviet insistence on special rights in China's northeast and northwest, had created a time bomb in USSR-PRC relations that needed to be defused quickly.

The day Stalin died, Mao Zedong went to the Soviet embassy in Beijing to offer condolences. For three days, Chinese national flags flew at half-mast throughout the country. A grand memorial meeting was held in Tiananmen Square.[2] Mao also wrote a eulogy for Stalin: "Let all the imperialist aggressors and warmongers tremble in the face of our great friendship."[3] Mao had good reason to stress PRC-USSR solidarity at this juncture. China and the United States were still at war in Korea, and a new American president, Dwight Eisenhower, former Supreme Commander of Allied Forces in Europe in World War II, had taken office in January 1953 and was threatening to expand the Korean conflict, possibly including the use of nuclear weapons, if the communist side did not quickly come to terms. Facing US nuclear coercion, Beijing needed at least the appearance of strong Soviet support.

Zhou Enlai, premier and foreign minister, led a Chinese delegation to Moscow for Stalin's funeral on March 9. The delegation stayed for over two weeks.[4] As mentioned in the previous chapter, Zhou and the new Soviet leaders discussed ending the Korean War, and decided to do so on the basis of "reasonable compromises with the enemy." Other major shifts occurred in Soviet foreign policy. Moscow relinquished its territorial claims against Turkey and began pursuing friendship diplomacy toward Turkey, Iran, and India.[5]

The impulse to seek a relaxation of international tensions came from Moscow, but found a ready welcome in Beijing. China was getting ready to throw its new Soviet economic model into gear, and a relaxed international environment would allow China to concentrate on making its new socialist institutions run well. Over the preceding several years, capitalist economy in the urban sector had been basically eliminated and the Soviet model of comprehensive central planning had been transplanted to China. With the new set of institutions in place, the CCP Politburo was ready to throw the switch on the new economic model, which was expected to transform China into an industrialized and technologically advanced country within a decade or so. Ending the war in Korea and averting a new war with the United States in Indochina would allow China to do this.

Relaxation of international tension via moderate policies would also facilitate escape from the diplomatic and economic isolation into which the PRC had slid during its first four years of existence. A number of factors contributed to that isolation: China's close military-political alliance with the USSR, leading Beijing to second whatever harsh rhetoric issued from Stalin's Moscow; the turn of the world communist movement in 1947 toward armed uprisings against "bourgeois democratic" (i.e., independent but noncommunist) regimes in the emerging ex-colonial nations; the ruthless uprooting of Western interests in China; and most of all, China's intervention against UN forces in Korea and the resulting embargos and sanctions. By 1953, PRC policies had nearly destroyed China's ties with countries beyond the socialist bloc. China's isolation would hinder efforts at economic growth, limit its diplomatic influence, and make it more dependent on the Soviet Union.

The United States did what it could to encourage China's isolation. China's belligerent policies in Korea and Indochina, plus its militant rhetoric, greatly facilitated Washington's efforts at isolating "Red China."

China's appeal to the emerging countries in the mid-1950s was a manifestation of Mao's thinking about an "intermediate zone" between the socialist and imperialist camps. As early as 1921, a congress of the Communist International decided to seek a broad but anti-imperialist united front in the colonies and semi-colonies, especially China, India, Persia, and Turkey. This entailed a united front with nationalist "anti-imperialist" but noncommunist movements, the most important of which was SunYat-sen's KMT in China. Then, in 1940, in debates with Stalin over whether CCP forces should focus on attacking Japanese forces (Moscow's preference) or on building base areas behind Japanese lines, Mao formulated the idea of revolutionary struggle in the intermediate zone as a way of defending the socialist countries.[6] Mao's rebuttal to Stalin was that expanding revolution in the intermediate zone between the USSR and the imperialist countries was the best way to prevent imperialist attack on the socialist citadel. In 1946, Mao announced that the countries between the socialist and imperialist camps constituted a "vast intermediate zone" which was the focus of imperialist aggression. Consolidation of imperialist control over this intermediate zone was a precondition for imperialist attack on the socialist camp.[7] China's moderate courtship of noncommunist but anti-Western governments was, in effect, an anti-imperialist united front from above.

The strategy of a broad united front mobilizing a wide array of forces but led by communists was propounded by Lenin and applied very effectively by Mao in the 1930s and 1940s. Perfected in dealings with the KMT, Japanese invaders, the United States, and various Chinese warlords and factions, Mao's united front doctrine stressed the exploitation of contradictions within the enemy camp to isolate a primary enemy, thereby defeating enemies one at a time. The widest possible array of forces were to be "united with" and the spearhead of attack directed against the primary enemy—Japan, the KMT, or the United States—as defined by the CCP for each stage of the revolution.

During the mid-1950s, Zhou Enlai was given free rein by Mao to use subtle and moderate diplomatic tactics to apply this doctrine against the United States.[8] Many of the new nations emerging out of the collapse of European and Japanese empires seemed to Zhou to offer good opportunities for application of a united front doctrine. Even within the imperialist camp, contradictions might be exploited by adroit maneuver. Britain and France, for example, might not like US policies of confrontation, and could possibly be maneuvered to oppose the United States. For such an approach to be effective, however, China and the Soviet Union would need to take more moderate, more "realistic," and less belligerent-sounding stances. Chinese and Soviet leaders agreed to implement this new approach in tandem. In September 1953,

Moscow proposed to the United States, Britain, and France the convocation of a "Five Power" conference to discuss the possibility of reducing international tensions. The "Big Five" was a formulation that included the PRC. Several days after Moscow's proposal, Beijing endorsed it. This was the beginning of a Sino-Soviet peace campaign that would lead to the Geneva conference in 1954.

The Geneva Conference on Indochina

PRC strategy at the Geneva Conference (April 20–July 20, 1954) was "fighting while talking" (*tan, tan, da, da*). Powerful military moves on Indochinese battlefields were coordinated with a diplomatic push for agreements with the Western powers to "reduce international tension." By the end of 1952, the Viet Minh campaign in northwest Tonkin had been successful.[9] Large portions of that region had been brought under Viet Minh control, opening the way for further expansion into Laos.[10] The French command responded by deciding to occupy and fortify Dienbienphu on Tonkin's westernmost border with Laos in order to block a Viet Minh linkup with communist-led forces in Laos. During the summer of 1953, just as Moscow and Beijing were planning their international peace campaign, the Chinese Military Advisory Group (CMAG) to the Viet Minh recommended that Vietnam's northwest continue to be the main theater of operation. The VWP Politburo endorsed the CMAG plan in October 1953. When French intelligence noted increased communist activity in the northwest, the French command responded by deploying large forces to Dienbienphu and strongly fortifying that position. China's top military advisor in Vietnam, General Wei Guoqing, learned of the French move and proposed that Dienbienphu be made the focus of attack; the French bastion would be surrounded and annihilated. The VWP leadership, then Mao and the CCP PBSC, approved Wei's proposal.[11] In effect, a great military victory would lay the foundation for the peace campaign at Geneva.

China provided large-scale, and probably decisive, assistance to the Viet Minh assault on Dienbienphu. Four battalions of Viet Minh anti-aircraft troops just completing training in the PRC were dispatched to the combat theater. Resupply of the Dienbienphu bastion by air, and air attacks on attacking Viet Minh forces, were crucial to the French plan, so the Viet Minh's PLA-trained anti-aircraft capabilities would play a major role in the upcoming battle. Chinese advisors also instructed Viet Minh troops in sniper tactics recently learned in Korea. PLA engineer advisors assisted the Viet Minh with construction of trenches that enabled assault forces to close on French positions before a final exposed assault. Large quantities of ammunition were forwarded by China. As the battle intensified, Mao ordered CMC vice chair Peng

Dehuai to form two new artillery divisions, using veteran Viet Minh troops advised by PLA men who had served in Korea and armed, if necessary, with cannon drawn from PLA stocks. Sufficient ammunition (Mao underlined this phrase in his directive to Peng), along with additional anti-aircraft guns and engineering equipment, was to be supplied to the new artillery divisions. Dienbienphu "should be conquered resolutely," Mao instructed Peng.

Mao also gave his thoughts about Viet Minh efforts after Dienbienphu fell. Viet Minh forces should be allowed to rest for one or one and a half months (no more than two months at most, Mao specified) before advancing on Luang Prabang on the Mekong River in the heart of northern Laos. The newly strengthened Viet Minh would also be able to assault Hanoi and Haiphong, Mao noted. He also directed that the plan to form two new artillery divisions should continue even if the conference at Geneva reached agreement. In that event, however, the training of those forces should be transferred from Chinese to Vietnamese territory as quickly as possible.[12] As the assault on Dienbienphu entered its final stage, China sent additional artillery. Mao ordered the CMAG to employ the heaviest possible bombardment. The final assault began on May 1. The last French fort surrendered on May 7, East Asia time.

A top Chinese concern during the Geneva Conference was to prevent US intervention in Indochina while maintaining North Vietnam buffer between US power and the PRC. As the French position at Dienbienphu deteriorated, US leaders considered intervening in support of the anti-communist side. In line with the strategy of containment, US leaders were loath to concede any part of Indochina to communism. US financial and logistic support for the French anti-communist effort in Indochina had begun with the Korean War, and had grown steadily. By 1954, Washington was financing most of the French effort in Indochina. Washington believed that if France would grant full independence to Vietnam, indigenous Vietnamese anti-communist forces could, with US and French support, rally and stem the communist advance. This would clearly entail a full-scale US military effort, but US leaders considered it vital to draw the line against further communist expansion. The use of atomic bombs to raise the Viet Minh siege at Dienbienphu was considered by US leaders.

In late March, with the hard battle for Dienbienphu well under way, DRV President Ho Chi Minh and Premier Pham Van Dong flew to Beijing for consultations. Chinese leaders stressed their recently acquired experience in negotiating with the Americans over Korea, and the consequent need to maintain "realistic expectations." The two sides agreed on the need to take a "realistic approach" in upcoming negotiations.[13] The day after the last French forces at Dienbienphu surrendered, the conference at Geneva began its discussion of Indochina. This portion of the conference was attended by the "big five" plus the DRV, the French-supported "State of Vietnam," the royal government of Laos, and the communist-led Laotian group the Pathet Lao, plus the royal government of Cambodia. This was the PRC's first international conference, and Chinese leaders prepared carefully. The Chinese delegation included 180 people. Zhou Enlai specified that the key objective was to break the US policy of blockade and embargo of the PRC. To this end, China should do its utmost to reach agreements, win consensus, settle disputes via consultations among the big powers, and open up new diplomatic channels, especially with Western nations.[14]

Zhou Enlai had spent the first three weeks of April in Moscow consulting with Soviet foreign minister Vyacheslav Molotov about strategy for the upcoming conference.[15] Zhou and Molotov agreed to cooperate closely at the conference and to adopt a realistic attitude to find a peaceful settlement to the Indochina problem. The United States would try to sabotage the conference to continue its policy of war and aggression in Indochina, the two agreed. Zhou and Molotov probably reached agreement that an appropriate and realistic approach would entail the establishment of two temporary regroupment zones in Vietnam, communist in the north and noncommunist in the south, to be accompanied by a French withdrawal and, after an interval, by a national plebiscite. Zhou proposed such an approach to the CCP Politburo shortly after his talks with Molotov. The Politburo, and Mao, approved Zhou's proposal for a temporary partition followed by elections.

The fall of Dienbienphu put the Viet Minh in a very strong position. Premier Pham Van Dong proposed to the conference a plan that would have given the Viet Minh sole control over all of Vietnam and perhaps Laos and Cambodia as well. The Viet Minh felt that they dominated the battlefield, that the French were defeated and demoralized, and that the Viet Minh should appropriately be rewarded with political victory. Pham refused to give ground. By mid-June, the Conference was deadlocked. Then an election in France on June 18 led to the inauguration of a new French prime minister, Pierre Mendès France, who swore upon taking office to end the war in Indochina by July 20 or resign. This deadline, and the greater French urgency to exit that it represented, gave new life to the deliberations at Geneva.

Zhou Enlai seized on the opportunity to persuade the Vietnamese to compromise. Previously, Pham had demanded that France recognize as full and legitimate governments the VWP-linked liberation movements in Laos and Cambodia and withdraw French forces completely from all of Indochina. In a meeting with Soviet and Vietnamese delegations, Zhou Enlai, with strong Soviet support, persuaded Pham that the Viet Minh should admit that it had forces in Laos and Cambodia and agree to withdraw these forces as part of the withdrawal of all foreign forces from those countries. Pham was reluctant to abandon VWP domination of Laos and Cambodia, for that was what Zhou's proposal amounted to. But confronted with Chinese and Soviet opposition,

Pham gave in and accepted the Chinese-Soviet proposal. Failure to compromise at this juncture, Zhou argued, might cause loss of the opportunity for a peaceful settlement of the Vietnam problem. The problems of Laos and Cambodia could be solved separately, Zhou argued. In Laos, where the VWP-allied Pathet Lao was relatively strong, the communist delegations would push for a regroupment zone consisting of two northern Laotian provinces contiguous to China, Sam Neua and Phong Saly. (Figure 8-1 on page 205 shows the location of these provinces.) Having secured VWP agreement, Zhou conveyed the new communist position to French and British delegations. In effect, Chinese pressure compelled the VWP to give up its plan to rule all of Indochina. Twenty-five years later, in 1979, Hanoi's pursuit of the same objective would lead Beijing to go to war with by then communist-led united Vietnam.

VWP agreement to "realistic compromise" on the Laos and Cambodian issues eliminated those problems. But the VWP still resisted the idea of partition of Vietnam into regroupment zones. In early July, Zhou met for three days on the Guangxi-Vietnam border with Ho Chi Minh, General Vo Nguyen Giap, and DRV ambassador to the PRC Huang Van Hoan.[16] Zhou's trump card was the danger of US military intervention if an agreement was not reached at Geneva. This danger was great, Zhou asserted, and would "greatly complicate" the situation. That is, the DRV and China might find themselves in a Korea-like war with the United States. Zhou persuaded Ho, and Ho in turn persuaded the VWP Politburo.

Failure to accept temporary regroupment zones in Vietnam would create a high danger of US intervention, Ho told his Politburo upon return to Vietnam. It was necessary to consider the matter at the international level. Neither the PRC nor the USSR wanted continued and possibly bigger war in Indochina. Both socialist powers wanted a period of relaxation of international tensions. The reality was that the VWP could not wage its struggles without Chinese and Soviet support, Ho said. The VWP needed to act as good communists and stay in step with the line of the world communist movement. Moreover, Ho said, it was virtually certain that the Viet Minh would win the plebiscite to be held one or two years after the French departure. The Viet Minh had led the struggle for independence from France, had organizational skills beyond any Vietnamese rival, and had Ho Chi Minh, with nationwide recognition beyond that of any other Vietnamese leader. Given this, with the French gone and the Americans held at bay, the Viet Minh were certain to win the elections, opening the way to peaceful national unification under the VWP. Ho's arguments persuaded the VWP Politburo.[17]

When Zhou initially proposed the temporary partition/regroupment zone plan to VWP leaders, he suggested the 16th parallel as the dividing line between zones. That would have pushed the VWP zone to the south, leaving in VWP hands the highway extending westward from Quang Tri on the coast into Laos. This in turn would have given the VWP a strong position for a future contest for control over southern Laos. When the Geneva Conference deliberations resumed on July 12, however, Mendès France proposed the 17th parallel rather than the 16th as the demarcation line. Zhou Enlai accepted the proposal, seconded once again by the Soviet representative. Pham was still reluctant to accept partition, even temporary, but eventually gave in to Chinese and Soviet pressure. The VWP simply could not continue its struggles without support from the two socialist great powers.

In the final agreement, signed on July 21, 1954, France granted independence to all of Vietnam. Millions of Vietnamese moved one way or the other into their desired regroupment zone. North to south movement far exceeded south to north. The VWP consolidated its control over the North and began preparing for a "transition to socialism" along Stalinist lines. In the south, anti-communists and noncommunists rallied around the regime of the last emperor of Vietnam, Bao Dai, who had abdicated in August 1945 and become a figurehead ruler maintained by the French, and sought American support to stabilize a noncommunist regime in the south. In Laos, the royal government was recognized as the sole legal authority, but VWP-affiliated Laotian forces ran Sam Neua and Phong Saly provinces. In Cambodia, the tiny Khmer communist movement was given no role, and the royal government of Norodom Sihanouk was recognized as the sole government.

Zhou had skillfully advanced China's interests at Geneva. He maintained for the PRC a territorial buffer excluding US power from PRC borders: the DRV, which emerged from the conference with wider diplomatic recognition of its territorial sovereignty. From this perspective, it did not matter greatly whether the DRV's southern boundary was on the 16th or the 17th parallel. Zhou had angered his VWP comrades by pressuring them to agree to temporary partition. But it was only later, after the promised bizonal talks and coalition government leading to a nationwide plebiscite did not occur, that the VWP began seeing Zhou's 1954 diplomacy as "betrayal" of the Vietnamese revolution.[18] In 1954, Zhou along with his VWP comrades, probably believed it when he promised Pham Van Dong that via the unification mechanisms stipulated in the Geneva agreement "all of Vietnam will be yours."[19]

Zhou, via the Geneva Conference, also opened dialogues with France, Britain, and the United States. These would grow over subsequent years, giving Beijing eyes, ears, and a voice beyond the socialist camp. The impressive caliber of Zhou Enlai's diplomatic skills was also recognized on a global stage for the first time. Both Zhou's moderate demeanor and his willingness to compromise began to send the message that he, and by extension the PRC, was reasonable and could be dealt with. This was exactly the opposite of the image of "Red China" being perpetuated by US government agencies. China's moderate tactics of the mid-1950s were approved by Mao, but just as certainly they drew on the diplomatic skill and grace of Zhou Enlai.

Search for US Disengagement from Taiwan

A key objective of China's peace offensive of 1954–1955 was securing US disengagement from Taiwan. Mao and Zhou seem to have believed at this juncture that grand strategic calculations would lead Washington to sacrifice the Taiwan pawn to influence the grand balance of the USSR, the United States, and the PRC. The US engagement with Taiwan in June 1950 had been, after all, a wartime exigency, a measure intended to prevent the war in Korea from spreading to the Taiwan Strait and to prevent US forces in Korea from being outflanked to their south. By 1954, the Korean War was over and those requirements were no longer operative. Chinese leaders were also well aware that the United States had been prepared before the Korean War to sacrifice Taiwan for the sake of influencing the PRC's international alignment vis-à-vis the United States and the Soviet Union. There were, after all, the famous January 1950 statements by Acheson and Truman, reinforced by the leaked State Department directive to overseas missions. Those profound geostrategic variables still operated. If Beijing now signaled willingness for more amicable relations with the United States, Washington would perhaps revert to its pre–June 1950 strategic calculations and disengage from Taiwan. The deliberate relaxation of international tension via moderate policies at Geneva, and later at Bandung, provided inducement for Washington to disengage from Taiwan. But that peace offensive was preceded by the powerful military offensive against Dienbienphu and would be punctuated by military demonstrations in the Taiwan Strait from September 1954 to March 1955. In the Taiwan Strait, as at Geneva and during the Korean War, Beijing followed a policy of "talking while fighting."

The negotiating aspect of Beijing's strategy focused on forty or so American citizens imprisoned in China for "economic crimes" and espionage during the campaign to uproot the Western presence in China. These hostages would be used as incentive to open a "direct channel" with the Americans. It was apparent that US leaders desired the release of these US citizens, and this desire would be used to open direct talks, creating a venue in which China could raise its demands for US disengagement from Taiwan. Once direct talks had begun, Washington was to be persuaded that there were two separate aspects of the Taiwan problem: 1) Beijing-KMT relations, which were an internal affair of China and with which the United States should not concern itself, and 2) US-PRC relations regarding Taiwan, which was clearly an international affair on which Beijing and Washington should discuss and reach agreement. Beijing proposed simultaneous talks along both dimensions, but the two tracks were separate and would remain so.[20]

Two main factors would impel Washington to disengage from Taiwan, PRC leaders calculated. US allies in Europe and in Asia did not want a US-PRC war over Taiwan, and would pressure Washington to that effect.

More importantly, the power of the PRC was a reality of which Washington would have accepted. In Korea, the PRC had denied the United States its goal of a united, US-aligned Korea and fought US forces to a standstill. In Indochina, PRC-supported Viet Minh forces had just delivered a death blow to US-backed French forces. Confronted by the reality of China's power, and with calculations of the global balance in mind, the United States would disengage from Taiwan. At least that was Beijing's plan.

Late in May 1954, at the Geneva conference, the US representative proposed, via a British intermediary, that the United States and the PRC talk about the release of US citizens being held in China. Zhou Enlai immediately convened a meeting to consider the US proposal. Here was an opportunity, Zhou said, to use the US desire for release of its citizens to open a direct channel to the Americans. Zhou proposed that China seek direct negotiations with the United States (i.e., not via the British or other intermediaries). Zhou also proposed that China link the question of the forty or so Americans held in China with the status and return to China of the 170 or so Chinese nationals being detained in the United States. These Chinese citizens had been involved in defense sector work in the United States, and once the Korean War began, Washington barred their return to China on the grounds that they would contribute to China's war effort.[21] Zhou also proposed that China's response to the United States should hint at the possibility of broader relaxation of tensions between the PRC and the United States. The CCP Politburo approved Zhou's proposal.

In June and July 1954, while the Geneva Indochina Conference was still underway, Wang Bingnan, China's ambassador to Poland, and U. Alexis Johnson, US ambassador to Czechoslovakia, met four times in Geneva. No progress was made. The United States refused to equate US prisoners in China with Chinese nationals detained in the United States and broke off the talks when Wang proposed a communiqué linking the two categories of nationals.[22] Secretary of State Dulles was aware that Beijing was using the Geneva Conference and the bilateral talks with the United States to raise its international visibility and weaken the isolation engineered by the United States over the previous several years. Dulles responded to communist successes in Korea and Indochina and to the PRC's increasing international position by building up collective security positions of strength around the periphery of the Sino-Soviet bloc. Dulles and the Eisenhower Administration generally viewed Nationalist China as an important element in "the position of strength" containing Communist China. This doomed Beijing's effort to persuade Washington to disengage from Taiwan.

Nationalist Taiwan was very much interested in participating in the US collective security structure. In March 1953, very shortly after the Eisenhower administration took office, the Republic of China (ROC—Nationalist China on Taiwan) ambassador to the United States, Wellington Koo, proposed the conclusion of a US-ROC mutual security treaty.[23] A major difficulty quickly emerged: what would be the territorial scope of such a treaty? Would it cover the Offshore Islands, scattered along the coast of continental China but still held by Nationalist forces? At the end of the Korean War, there were three main islands still in Nationalist hands: Jinmen (Quemoy) in Xiamen harbor, Mazu (Matsu) off Fuzhou harbor, and the Dachen (Tachen) group north of Wenzhou, Zhejiang province. KMT leaders, especially Chiang Kai-shek, saw retention of those islands as a symbolic and material link between Taiwan and the mainland, and were determined to defend them. US officials, however, felt that commitment of Nationalist forces to defense of the Offshores weakened the defense of Taiwan itself. Nationalist forces committed to the Offshores would be useless and cut off in the event of a communist attack on Taiwan. The islands should be defended only very lightly, US leaders thought, with Taiwan's defense perimeter drawn down the middle of the Taiwan Strait. US leaders also understood that a war with China for defense of the tiny and very far forward Offshores would be difficult to sell to the American people.

Nationalist leaders saw US unwillingness to defend the Offshores as manifestation of a desire to separate Taiwan from China, perhaps as part of a US accommodation with the communist regime. This suspicion was not entirely baseless. An independent Taiwan and comity with the communist-ruled PRC might serve US interests nicely, a fact that was occasionally deliberated in top-level US policy councils. Nationalist leaders were ardent Chinese nationalists, as strongly opposed as CCP leaders to "Taiwan independence." The dispute between the CCP and the KMT was about who should rule China, including Taiwan, not whether or not Taiwan was a part of China. US-ROC talks on a mutual security treaty continued off and on throughout 1953 and 1954. Finally, in June 1954, Chiang Kai-shek revived flagging US interest in a treaty by agreeing to seek US approval prior to undertaking major military activities (such as an attack on the mainland). US-ROC talks resumed and went into high gear.

From Beijing's perspective, a US mutual security treaty with Taiwan constituted an egregious interference in China's internal affairs. Even worse, it committed US military strength to Taiwan's defense, making virtually impossible PLA liberation of Taiwan for the foreseeable future. US Secretary of State Dulles also aspired to weave together into a comprehensive system all US mutual security agreements in East Asia—with Japan, South Korea, the Philippines, Australia and New Zealand, and SEATO. If Taiwan were included in that system, it would further institutionalize Taiwan's separation from the mainland, making seizure of the island even more difficult.

Mao decided on a military demonstration that would hopefully force the United States to reconsider its "hostile policy toward the PRC," i.e., a US alliance with Taiwan. This military demonstration would make clear that Beijing could and would adopt an even more confrontational policy if the United States continued down the path of its "anti-China policy." A military demonstration would show the United States the costs it might have to pay for hostile policies toward China. It would also exploit contradictions between Washington and Taipei. Threatening attack on the Offshores would either force the United States to keep hands off, thereby risking rupture with Chiang Kai-shek, or declare willingness to defend the Offshores, risking trying to persuade the American people that those tiny islands were worth another war with China. Either outcome could plausibly open the way to advantageous negotiations: either with the Nationalists angered by US betrayal and support for Taiwan independence, or with the Americans angered by Taipei's effort to entrap the United States in a war with the PRC.

On August 5, 1954, the Politburo agreed to Mao's proposal to launch a propaganda campaign proclaiming the need to liberate Taiwan. A month later, on September 3, only several days before the Manila treaty creating an anticommunist collective security organization in Southeast Asia was to be signed, PLA artillery began shelling Jinmen and Mazu Islands. The next day, three US aircraft carriers began converging on the area. Washington also announced the United States would concur in any defensive action taken by Nationalist forces. Shortly thereafter, Nationalist warplanes conducted intensive attacks in the Xiamen vicinity.[24] Beijing responded by escalating the conflict. On November 1, the Dachens came under very heavy bombardment. PLA air and naval activity in the vicinity of the Dachens also increased.

The PLA's bombardment of the Offshores did not deter Washington from concluding a military alliance with the Republic of China. The treaty was signed on December 2, 1954. Six days after the treaty was signed, Zhou Enlai issued a statement declaring the treaty without legal basis, null and void, and a treaty of war and aggression. Taiwan was part of China's territory, and its liberation was a matter entirely within the scope of China's sovereignty and internal affairs.[25] The shelling of Jinmen and Mazu continued until February 1955 and the seizure of the Dachen Islands. PLA forces assaulted and took, after several failed attempts, one of the islands in the Dachen group on January 18. This rendered the remaining islands in that group vulnerable, and Nationalists forces were evacuated, leaving the islands to the PLA. Then the shelling of Jinmen and Mazu ceased and Beijing shifted back to less confrontational tactics. On April 23, while attending the Bandung Conference, Zhou said: "The Chinese people are friendly with the American people and not willing to fight with them. The Chinese Government is willing to hold consultations with the US Government on relaxing the tension in the Far East, the tension in the Taiwan area in particular."[26]

Beijing followed Zhou's statement by raising the notion of a possible peaceful liberation of Taiwan. In a report to the National People's Congress, Zhou said that there were two ways China could liberate Taiwan, by war or peacefully. China would strive for a peaceful liberation, "conditions permitting." This was the first time Beijing had publicly mentioned the possibility of peaceful liberation of Taiwan.[27] It was intended to signal to Washington that US disengagement from Taiwan would not necessarily be followed by an immediate PLA attack, and to signal Taipei that Beijing was willing to negotiate the terms of Taiwan's integration into the PRC. Zhou indicated to the United States, via the British chargé in Beijing, that the basic purpose of negotiations with the United States would be to reduce or eliminate tension in the Taiwan Strait. China was willing to negotiate with the KMT regime on Taiwan, but would do that separately from talks with the United States.

In July, Washington informed Beijing, again via the British, that the United States was prepared for talks, and proposed that talks between representatives at the ambassadorial level be held in Geneva. Beijing agreed. Beijing expected that the central topic of those talks would be the relaxation and elimination of Sino-American tension in the Taiwan Strait. Significant changes in US policy toward the PRC were anticipated. Beijing also anticipated that the ambassadorial-level talks would lead fairly quickly to higher, ministerial-level talks (between Zhou and John Foster Dulles), which the MFA projected for November 1955.[28] Those ministerial-level talks would then lead to a relaxation and/or elimination of tension between the PRC and the United States in the Taiwan Strait, with the possibility of the elimination of the danger of war once the United States returned to its pre-1950 policy of handling Taiwan as an internal affair of China.

The first US-PRC meeting occurred on August 1, once again between Wang Bingnan and U. Alexis Johnson. Two days before the talks opened, Zhou Enlai in a report on foreign policy to the NPC reiterated the key themes: the people of China and the United States were friendly toward each other, China did not want a war with the United States, and China was willing to use "peaceful liberation" of Taiwan, "conditions permitting." The way to achieve these objectives, of course, was for the United States to withdraw from the Taiwan problem. On the eve of the talks, Zhou was quite optimistic about achieving improvements in ties with the United States.[29]

Beijing's hopes were disappointed. The Americans were not interested in washing their hands of Taiwan. From the perspective of the Eisenhower administration, Nationalist China had become a very important part of the strong containment structure built by the United States against expansionist Communist China.[30] The United States demanded that Beijing agree to limit itself to use of nonmilitary means toward Taiwan. Adding insult to injury, Washington proposed that this be done in the form of an agreement to that effect with the United States. These ideas were anathema to Beijing. As it turned out, the sole interest shared by the two sides was in securing the release of their respective nationals. An agreement to this effect was signed on September 10, 1955, at the fourteenth round of talks. This was the only agreement reached in the US-PRC ambassadorial talks. All told, 136 meetings would be held between 1955 and 1970. Those talks would provide an important venue for reaching mutual understandings during the Vietnam War in 1965–1967, but the breakthrough that Beijing hoped for in 1955 did not come until 1971, and then it would occur outside the venue of the ambassadorial talks.

The Bandung Conference: Reaching Out to the Third World

The world was in the midst of a profound upheaval in the late 1940s and early 1950s. The vast, globe-spanning empires of the European powers (Britain, France, and the Netherlands) that had dominated politics over the previous centuries were collapsing. In regions of Asia and Africa previously ruled from distant European capitals, new independent nations were emerging. Most of these "new emerging nations," as they were then called, were not communist. Only a few were: North Korea, North Vietnam, and China. The rest were ruled by local nationalists embracing various blends of nationalism, socialism, liberalism, and anti-imperialism, and with varying attitudes toward the institutional arrangements bequeathed by former colonial rulers. The two major powers that had long opposed European colonialism—the USSR and the United States of America—were both keenly interested in this process of decolonization, and both were attempting to direct the evolution of these "emerging countries" along lines of development comporting with their respective ideologies and national interests.

Stalin's approach to these new states had been to reject them as "bourgeois nationalist" devices cooked up by the colonialist powers to perpetuate political domination and economic exploitation. These new states were, from Stalin's perspective, a trick by the Western powers to deceive the oppressed classes. These bogus "bourgeois nationalist" regimes needed to be overthrown via revolution led by a proletariat vanguard (i.e., by a proper communist party), and directed down the path of dictatorship of the proletariat, social revolution, and socialism. Only this, Stalin believed, could truly liberate these still-enslaved emerging nations. As long as Stalin lived, this was the line of the international communist movement. This approach made the noncommunist rulers of many of the newly independent countries deeply apprehensive of ties with the USSR and the PRC. National political institutions in many of the new countries were weak, and the communist vision was often attractive to local intellectuals. In a number of new states, there were significant communist movements or uprisings—in the Philippines, India, Burma, Malaya, Indonesia, and Vietnam. Stalin's militant line combined with local communist activities to facilitate US efforts to rally the new emerging countries to a collective effort to contain communism at the boundaries of the existing Sino-Soviet camp.

The new Eisenhower administration (inaugurated in January 1953) worked to build "positions of strength" around the periphery of the Sino-Soviet camp. In September, following the expansion of Chinese influence at Geneva, the United States led the signing of a South East Asia Treaty Organization (SEATO) uniting the Philippines, Thailand, France, Britain, New Zealand, Australia, and Pakistan along with the United States in an anticommunist collective defense treaty. The new US-supported anticommunist South Vietnamese state, the Republic of Vietnam (RVN), quickly "associated" with SEATO. (Full RVN membership would have violated the Geneva agreement.) But there were a number of countries in South and Southeast Asia that were skeptical about being drawn into the intensifying Cold War between the Western and Eastern camps. A moderate and reasonable approach to these might persuade these intermediate countries to disassociate themselves from US containment schemes. It might be possible to create a "zone of peace" along China's southern borders encompassing Burma, Cambodia, Ceylon, India, Indonesia, and Nepal.[31] Cambodia, for example, had rejected "association" with SEATO, preferring to trust its security instead to China's enlightened self-interest. Further beyond China's periphery, there were other "emerging countries," in Africa for example, that might be persuaded by a moderate and reasoned approach to expand ties with the PRC, lessening its diplomatic isolation. Up to 1954, the PRC had few international contacts beyond the socialist camp.

In April 1954, the prime ministers of India, Indonesia, Burma, Pakistan, and Ceylon—all newly independent countries and (except for Pakistan) leaders in the emerging non-aligned movement—met in Ceylon and decided to convene a conference of Asian and African nations in Bandung, Indonesia, a year hence. The original Indonesian proposal was that invitations be limited to UN members, a formulation that would have excluded the PRC. Indian Prime Minister Jawaharlal Nehru urged inclusion of the PRC, and this was agreed to. Nehru imagined that drawing the PRC into the Asia-Africa movement would serve India's interests by demonstrating India's friendship for the PRC. Neither the Soviet Union nor the Western developing countries were invited—testament to the emerging non-aligned movement. The Bandung Conference is often identified as the founding event of what became the Non-Aligned Movement.

On February 10, 1955, after several weeks of deliberation, China informed the five convening countries that China accepted the invitation to attend the Bandung conference. According to Huang Hua, who served as press secretary of the Chinese delegation to the conference, Bandung was an opportunity to launch "a major counterattack" against the "US policy of hostility and isolation."[32] Mao Zedong personally presided over a Politburo meeting to work out strategy for the conference. The Politburo decided to seek a united front for international peace, unity in support of the movement for national independence in Asia and Africa, and the expansion of relations between the PRC and Asian and African countries. The Chinese delegation, led by Premier and Foreign Minister Zhou Enlai, would work to thwart efforts to inject anticommunist themes into the conference. Zhou would do this by calling for setting aside differences for the sake of unity in support of Asia-African independence movements. China, the Politburo decided, would also counter anti-PRC and anti-Soviet proposals by taking a moderate and reasonable approach, avoiding vitriol, polemics, and ideology. In line with this, Zhou attended a preconference planning session in Rangoon where he proposed, successfully, that for the sake of unity, there should be no mention of ideology and governmental system.[33]

The conference opened in April with twenty-nine nations represented. Opening speeches by Indonesia's Sukarno, Egypt's Gamal Abdel Nasser, and Cambodia's Norodom Sihanouk set a strong anticolonial tone. Some of the subsequent speakers, however, voiced "anticommunist clichés" (Huang Hua's formulation), prompting the Chinese delegation to meet to "devise countermeasures." The result was a "supplemental speech" by Zhou stressing that the purpose of the conference was unity against colonialism, and that unity could only be achieved by seeking common ground, not repelling or antagonizing one another but respecting one another. Some participants in the conference followed capitalism, Zhou said, while other participants followed socialism. But all participants should respect one another and unite against colonialism on the basis of the Five Principles of Peaceful Coexistence. The reasonable nature of Zhou's appeal, combined with his mild tone and avoidance of personal attack, was very well received by the audience. Prolonged and warm applause followed Zhou's speech, and many delegates later congratulated Zhou for an eloquent and reasonable presentation.[34]

Ceylon's prime minister, John Kotelawala, in a press conference made public positions that required Chinese counteraction. Ceylon's leader said that Taiwan should be placed under an international trusteeship pending full independence as a separate country, Soviet neocolonial rule over Eastern Europe should be condemned, and communist organizations in Asia and Africa should be disbanded. In response, Zhou met with Kotelawala and, according to Huang Hua, convinced him to "relax his position" via a combination of fact, reasonable argument, and mild attitude plus an appeal to unity.[35]

Conference organizers, and especially Nehru, favored highlighting the "Five Principles of Peaceful Coexistence" as a normative basis for state-to-state relations, putatively in contradistinction to imperialist norms of aggression, bullying, warmongering, interference, and such. Those Five Principles of Peaceful Coexistence had been agreed to by India and the PRC in an April 1954 bilateral agreement on Tibet. They were: mutual respect for territorial integrity and sovereignty, mutual nonaggression, noninterference in each other's internal affairs, equality and mutual benefit, and peaceful coexistence.

Nehru saw these as creating a moral international order different, he believed, from the power politics approach of the Western countries. Beijing saw them as a device for reassuring the newly emerged countries.[36]

A number of delegates opposed reference to the Five Principles on the grounds that "peaceful coexistence" was a concept devised by Stalin and promoted by Moscow. This criticism reportedly so angered Nehru that he left the conference hall and was persuaded to return only when told that Zhou Enlai was preparing to speak. Once again, Zhou used a moderate tone and reasonable arguments to win over his audience. The key objective, Zhou said, was unity against colonialism. Such unity could only be achieved if conference delegates put aside differences in ideology. If "peaceful coexistence" was a communist term, that term could be set aside and the text of the Preamble of the UN Charter, which called for nations to "live together in peace with one another as good neighbors," could be used instead. If reference to "five principles" was objectionable, Zhou said, other principles could be added. Zhou concluded by proposing a seven-point declaration on peaceful coexistence. Again Zhou's moderate and reasonable demeanor won the day. After Nehru strongly endorsed Zhou's speech, opposition to "peaceful coexistence" faded away. Zhou's personal demeanor—modest but self-confident, firm on principles but flexible in negotiation, treatment of others as equals open to reasonable argument and persuasion—impressed many delegates. Zhou expended considerable effort meeting and talking with delegates, both during and outside of conference sessions. As Huang Hua pointed out, China's role at the Bandung conference opened the door to increased contacts with many Asian and African countries.

Chinese breakthroughs with a number of countries followed Bandung. In August 1955, China and Egypt signed a trade agreement. Zhou and Nasser had met at Bandung. A cultural exchange agreement came the next April, and in May the two countries established diplomatic relations at the ambassadorial level. Egypt was a leader among Arab countries, and Cairo was an intellectual and political center of the Arab world. Opening ties with Egypt was, therefore, a major gain for Beijing. Syria and Yemen followed Egypt's lead in 1956. China and Nepal established diplomatic relations in August 1955. Nepal was important to Beijing both because of China's internal security concerns in Tibet, which borders Nepal to the north, and because of Indian sensitivities about Nepal's alignment vis-à-vis China and India. Two months after China and Nepal established relations, Beijing gave Nepal 60 million Indian rupees (gratis) to support that country's first five year plan.[37] This was the beginning of what would become a chronic pulling and tugging between Beijing and New Delhi for influence with Kathmandu. With Burma, too, China's relations began warming during the Geneva Conference. Zhou visited the country in June 1954, and the two sides endorsed the Five Principles of Peaceful Coexistence as the basis of bilateral relations.[38] With Cambodia,

China's relations warmed after encounters between Zhou and Sihanouk at Geneva and Bandung. Sihanouk and Zhou exchanged visits in 1956, and the two countries established diplomatic relations in 1958. With Indonesia, too, relations began to thaw. These were significant breakthroughs for Beijing.

China also achieved an important understanding with Pakistan during Bandung. Pakistan in the mid-1950s was one of the United States' most important containment partners, allied by treaty with the United States and cooperating with Turkey, Iran, and Iraq in West Asia and with SEATO in Southeast Asia. From the US perspective, these collective security structures were intended to contain communism supported by the Sino-Soviet bloc. From Pakistan's perspective, however, the key, if unstated, purpose was to strengthen Pakistan's position vis-à-vis India. At Bandung, Zhou and Pakistani Prime Minister Mohammad Ali Bogra held two private meetings during which Bogra explained the logic of Pakistan's alliances. Pakistan's alliances were not directed against the PRC, Bogra said. If the United States launched a war against China, Pakistan would not be involved in it, he assured Zhou.[39] Zhou tested the sincerity of Bogra's assurances by reporting them to the Political Committee of the Bandung conference, lauding them as creating mutual understanding and agreement among conference participants on the key question of peace and cooperation. Zhou added, "I am sure the Prime Minister of Pakistan will have no objection to these views of mine." Bogra rose to the occasion by publicly repeating his assurances to Zhou. In October of the next year, Pakistani's prime minister, by then Huseyn Suhrawardy, first visited China, a visit reciprocated by Zhou in December 1956. The joint communiqué signed at the end of Zhou's visit announced "There is no real conflict of interest between the two countries." Beijing assigned former PLA Major General Geng Biao to serve as ambassador to Pakistan from 1956 to 1960. Assigning a prominent security specialist like Geng Biao to Pakistan was evidence of Beijing's understanding of Pakistan's importance in the regional balance. It would be several years before Beijing decided that relations with India were bad enough that China should align openly and fully with Pakistan against India. But a common Chinese and Pakistani understanding of the geostrategic basis of that future entente cordiale was reached at Bandung.

Bandung and China's Relations with India

Rivalry between China and India for status among the newly emerging nations surfaced first at Bandung. Beginning with the Korean War, Nehru began courting PRC friendship by acting as China's friend and benefactor in various international fora. India opposed US-led efforts at the United Nations to condemn Chinese aggression in Korea. It voted against the United States and for the PRC on the question of Chinese representation in the UN.

It lobbied for PRC participation in the negotiations of a peace treaty with Japan and for that treaty to explicitly cede Taiwan to China. When it became clear that neither of those efforts would succeed, Nehru decided that India would not participate in the multilateral peace conference with Japan. India was a major advocate of inviting the PRC to participate, again against US urging, in what became the 1954 Geneva Conference. At Bandung, Nehru secured PRC participation and then assumed the role of introducing Zhou Enlai to other delegates, arranging a number of private gatherings calculated to bring Zhou into closer contact with other countries. The United States fumed at Nehru's efforts to help the PRC out of the isolation Washington was trying to impose on it. India's friendship diplomacy toward the PRC created major tensions in India-US relations.[40]

Several calculations underlay Nehru's effort to befriend Beijing.[41] Nehru envisioned a partnership between India and China leading Asia and the emerging nations down a path of peace and cooperation—in contrast, Nehru believed, to the path of war and hostility being charted by Washington and Moscow and their Cold War. Nehru believed that the alignments that constituted the Cold War would ultimately lead to global nuclear war. The alternate to that course, Nehru believed, was non-alignment, dialogue, and disarmament. It was India's destiny to save humanity by leading it away from the insane path toward arms races, alliances, and nuclear war being charted by Moscow and Washington. China could become a partner in this effort. As PRC rulers became more aware of the thinking of other "emerging nations" of Asia and Africa, China would draw away from close alignment with the Soviet Union and gravitate toward non-aligned cooperation with India. Nehru (and Indian nationalism generally) had deep sympathy for China's struggle against imperialism. India and China together would lead Asia and humanity away from the insanity of the Cold War.

Mao Zedong had a vision for the emerging countries that was radically different from Nehru's: not non-alignment, disarmament, and peace, but a united front against imperialism, revolutionary war, and the most powerful defense possible of the socialist camp against imperialism. Mao would not lay out this distinctly non-Nehruvian vision until 1959–1963. But when he did, it would be point by point a refutation of what Mao took to be Nehru's efforts to mislead the peoples of the intermediate zone away from the correct course of armed wars of national liberation. In 1955 at Bandung, that was still several years in the future.

A second level of logic behind Nehru's friendship policy toward the PRC had to do with persuading Beijing not to turn Tibet into a platform for Chinese military power. The centuries-long relation between Chinese emperors and Tibet's ruling monasteries did not entail the permanent stationing of large Chinese military forces in Tibet. Chinese emperors would occasionally dispatch armies to Tibet, for example to repel a Dzungar Mongol invasion in 1719 or a Nepali invasion in 1792–1793.[42] But when the mission of those Chinese armies was accomplished, they withdrew back to China proper, leaving only a small guard to protect a representative of China's emperor posted in Lhasa. As Britain consolidated its rule over India in the nineteenth century, it upheld this traditional arrangement between China and Tibet as a way of keeping Russia out of, and keeping Chinese power only weakly present in, Tibet. As the PLA marshaled to move into Tibet in 1949–1950, Indian leaders feared that Tibet would become, for the first time in history, a platform for Chinese military power. One of Nehru's closest (and more realistic) advisors, Home Minister Vallabhai Patel, argued at that juncture for a series of vigorous measures to counter the probable Chinese militarization of Tibet. Patel advocated a military buildup, road building in frontier regions, and exploration of military ties with the United States. Nehru saw Patel's course as antithetical to his vision of India's non-aligned destiny, and opted instead for a friendship offensive toward China.

Nehru hoped that Indian friendship would convince PRC leaders that there was no need to militarize Tibet, since India, a friendly power, posed no threat there, and that China should reciprocate Indian friendship by being sensitive to Indian concerns and not militarizing Tibet.[43] As part of his friendship policy toward China, on April 29, 1954, in the midst of the Geneva Conference on Indochina and the intense battle for Dienbienphu, India signed with China an eight-year agreement between India and the "Tibet region of China." The agreement used the phrase "Tibet region of China" nine times. This was the first time India recognized China's sovereignty over Tibet. India did this without demanding or receiving a quid pro quo on the border issue (or on anything else for that matter)—a source of considerable Indian criticism and lament in following decades. With the 1954 Sino-Indian agreement on Tibet, India abandoned all the special privileges in Tibet it had inherited from the British era. Nehru imagined that this statement of fine principles opened the way to India-China partnership and a new world order. The PRC would, Nehru believed, be drawn away from close alignment with the USSR and toward cooperation with India in building a new Asia and a new world. This idealistic appeal was very popular in India. Zhou Enlai visited India in June 1954 and was received by huge enthusiastic crowds shouting "Chinese and Indians are brothers." In October the same year, Nehru visited Beijing for talks with Mao and Zhou.

Cracks in the facade of India-Chinese brotherhood began to appear at Bandung. Conference participants were, as noted earlier, very impressed by Zhou Enlai's apparent humility and reasonableness, and his willingness to listen to other's arguments even when he disagreed with them. The impression left by Nehru was different. According to Carlos Romulo, the esteemed Philippine diplomat and head of the Philippine delegation at Bandung, many conference participants were "jolted by his [Nehru's] pedantry. His pronounced propensity to be dogmatic, impatient, irascible, and unyielding, especially in the face of opposition, alienated the good will of many delegates." Nehru's attitude seemed to many delegates to typify, according to Romulo, "the affectation of cultural superiority induced by a conscious identification with an ancient civilization."[44] Most delegates had gone to Bandung expecting Nehru to dominate the proceedings, according to Romulo. It was Zhou Enlai, however, who stole the show. Several years after Bandung, Nehru's preference for non-alignment in contrast to Beijing's Afro-Asian anti-imperialism would keep Nehru from sharing the stage with Zhou.

Increased Room for Maneuver, but No Breakout

Beijing's peace offensive of 1953–1957 succeeded in expanding the PRC's room for diplomatic maneuver. Beijing established ties with a number of significant newly emerging Third World countries, positioning itself as a friend of those countries. This weakened somewhat US efforts to isolate the PRC, and expanded Beijing's ties beyond the socialist camp. But Beijing's peace offensive failed to persuade Washington to distance itself from the Nationalist regime on Taiwan or to ease efforts to contain the PRC with positions of strength around its periphery. The basic reasons for this were Beijing's still-close ties with Moscow and US fears of Chinese expansionism arising out of Beijing's policies in Korea and Indochina.[45] Beijing's sole significant gain with the United States was the initiation of direct diplomatic talks via the ambassadorial talks at Geneva (later at Warsaw). This was an important mechanism which would play a valuable role during the Vietnam War, but which fell far short of Beijing's aspirations.

Within China, the relaxation of tensions during the mid-1950s paralleled the beginning of the construction of socialism. With the First Five Year Plan (1953–1957), the state-owned and -planned industrial sector grew rapidly while collectivized agriculture, the second pillar of Stalinist socialism, advanced step by step via progressively "higher" cooperatives. With the socialist camp at peace and the PRC a close ally of the Soviet Union, large-scale assistance to China's industrialization drive poured in. But even while China's construction of socialism was making great strides with generous Soviet assistance, the seeds for the breakdown of that alliance were already being sown.

The Sino-Soviet Schism

THE RACE TO COMMUNISM AND GREAT POWER STATUS

Investment Priorities and De-Stalinization

During the second half of the 1950s, there was a powerful interaction between China's drive for socialist industrialization and its ties with the Soviet Union and the United States. One driving factor was Mao's determination to substantially accelerate the pace of China's industrialization.[1] This Great Leap Forward, as Mao dubbed it, aimed to transform China into a leading industrial and military power within a few years. This was to be achieved by suppressing consumption, intensifying work effort, and pouring via comprehensive economic planning all possible resources into expansion of heavy and defense industries. Under this Great Leap, the level of state investment in industry would rise from 25 percent of total production in 1957 to 44 percent in 1959—the latter being an extremely high rate of investment typically seen in countries fighting a total war. Taking 1952 as a base year of 100, heavy industrial production rose from 311 in 1957 to 823 in 1959, a 2.7-fold leap in two years.[2] Mao's push derived from his ingestion of Stalin's economic thinking via the *Short Course*, plus a deepening rivalry with CPSU leader Nikita Khrushchev for leadership of the world communist movement. The Great Leap Forward was Mao's challenge to Khrushchev's effort to de-Stalinize socialism and achieve "peaceful coexistence" with the United States.

Mao understood that this forced march to industrialization would impose hardship on the Chinese people. But he imagined that several years of "hard struggle" would usher China into a new era of power and relative wealth. The actual results were very different. As scholar Frank Dikötter has shown, Chinese society devolved into what was probably the greatest famine in modern history, with perhaps 45 million people dying from famine. Chinese society disintegrated into a war of all against all in a desperate struggle for survival.[3] A central element of Mao's effort to herd China's people into the institutional arrangements necessary for his campaign of hyperindustrialization was military confrontation with the United States in the Taiwan Straits and ideological struggle against "revisionism."

In 1955–1956, there had been an acceleration of agricultural collectivization and reduction of wage incentives, a push known as "the Little Great Leap" and designed to raise the level of investment in industry. The result, however, had been strikes, work slowdowns, and a fall in agricultural production. Under the influence of pragmatic economic planners like Chen Yun and Bo Yibo, and backed by Premier Zhou Enlai, the CCP in late 1956 returned to policies of greater individual reward and incentive to boost output. Production rose, but so too did consumption, resulting in a slowing of investment in heavy and defense industry. Mao was dismayed by this retreat before public opposition, and seized on Khrushchev's de-Stalinization campaign and the Hungarian uprising, both of 1956, as "learning by negative example" to educate the CCP about the proper way to deal with opposition to "construction of socialism": opponents of socialist construction must be ruthlessly crushed—as Stalin had done.

Khrushchev's De-Stalinization and Mao's Reaction

Khrushchev's de-Stalinization campaign began in February 1956 with a closed-door speech to the Twentieth Congress of the CPSU.[4] As the elder brother of the world communist movement, the CPSU drew observer delegations from many communist parties to its Congress, including the Chinese. In a bombshell speech, Khrushchev told how the "cult of the person of Stalin" had produced "a whole series of exceedingly serious and grave perversions of Party principles, Party democracy, or revolutionary legality." "Accumulation of immense and limitless power in the hands of one person" had caused "great harm" and led to the "violation of the principle of collective direction of the Party." Khrushchev's "secret speech" caused great tumult in the international communist movement. This was the beginning of the CCP-CPSU ideological debate.

The CCP delegation to the Twentieth Congress, like the delegations of other communist parties, was not given advance warning of Khrushchev's criticism of Stalin. Nor was the CCP delegation, headed by Zhu De, perhaps China's most eminent military leader, given a copy of the speech afterwards. A CCP representative was permitted to read the text of the speech and was briefed on it, but the CCP's text of Khrushchev's bombshell speech came from the March 10, 1956, issue of the *New York Times*.[5] From Mao's perspective, both the process and substance of Khrushchev's speech were wrong. Not informing the CCP in advance of the speech indicated that the Soviets did not trust the CCP, in Mao's view. Issuing such a pivotal determination without prior consultation with other fraternal parties, especially the CCP, also manifested the arrogant, chauvinist way the CPSU guided the international communist movement. The substance of the speech would cause difficulties for many communist parties, yet Moscow had not taken these parties into consideration. But there was a positive aspect to Khrushchev's criticism of Stalin, Mao told a Politburo meeting convened to discuss the speech. It would allow the CCP to speak openly and frankly about Stalin's "errors" toward China—for example viewing Mao as a "Chinese Tito" before the Korean War, or demanding special privileges in China's Northeast and Xinjiang in 1950. Khrushchev's "attack" on Stalin would also puncture "superstitions" about the Soviet Union, allowing China to feel less pressure to follow Soviet advice.[6]

De-Stalinization was introduced by Khrushchev in 1956 not only as an internal policy of the Soviet Union, but also as a new line for the international communist movement. "Line" is Leninist parlance for the general analysis of the situation of the revolutionary movement and derivative strategic policy prescriptions, all as conducted by the central leadership of the proletarian vanguard party. De-Stalinization became a question of line for the international communist movement because Stalin had been, after all, the leader of the world communist movement, his ideas taken as scientific truth, and Soviet power had been used to establish Stalinist-style socialism in a half-dozen countries. Khrushchev felt that the type of socialism associated with Stalin and his repressive, dictatorial practices had seriously deformed socialism, making it less attractive than it should be. Socialism would become much more appealing, Khrushchev believed, once the Stalinist deformation was cut away and socialism returned to the putatively less repressive norms of the Lenin era. This message proved very attractive to communists around the world. By the end of the 1950s, most communist parties, especially those in both East and West Europe, followed Moscow's lead and broke with Stalinism. Those that refused to break with Stalinism rallied around the CCP. Mao's opposition to Khrushchev's de-Stalinization was thus ipso facto a critique of Khrushchev's leadership of the international communist movement. Mao soon positioned himself and the CCP as the leading opponents of Khrushchev's de-Stalinization.

The CCP Politburo decided to issue to the international communist movement a statement independently assessing the positive "contributions" and negative "errors" of Stalin—a topic that became known as the Stalin question. According to Wu Lengxi, who was the CCP's record keeper on relations with Moscow and who left a rich two-volume memoir tracing these interactions, this CCP statement on the Stalin question was the CCP's first independent declaration on major problems of the international communist movement.[7] As such, it was also the first CCP challenge to the CPSU's authority to define the line of that movement. While Khrushchev was pushing to de-Stalinize socialism, Mao believed that continued Stalinist-style dictatorship as essential for swift industrialization and transition to communism. The Politburo assigned the Marxist theoretician Chen Boda to draft the CCP statement on the "Stalin question," with instructions to stress Stalin's contributions. After extensive Politburo debate and revision, the document was released on April 5, 1956, as a *Renmin ribao* editorial entitled "On the Historical Experience of the Dictatorship of the Proletariat." The statement acknowledged many of the "errors" enumerated in Khrushchev's "secret speech," but found many factors mitigating those shortcomings:

> How could it be conceivable that a socialist state which was the first in the world to put the dictatorship of the proletariat into practice, which did not have the benefit of any precedent, should make no mistakes of one kind or another? . . . . Communists must adopt an analytical attitude to errors made in the communist movement. Some people consider that Stalin was wrong in everything; this is a grave misconception. Stalin was a great Marxist-Leninist, yet at the same time a Marxist-Leninist who committed several gross errors. We should view Stalin from an historical standpoint, make a proper and all-round analysis to see where he was right and where he was wrong, and draw useful lessons therefrom. The achievements [of the international communist movement] always exceed the defects, the things which are right always overwhelm those which are wrong . . . and the defects and mistakes are always overcome in the end.[8]

The CCP lobbied within the international communist movement on behalf of its April statement. Immediately after the statement was issued, Mao met with the leaders of six Latin American communist parties to explain the CCP analysis. Stalin's positive contributions were 70 percent, while his errors were only 30 percent, Mao told the Latin communists. Later, in October, Mao met with Soviet leader Anastas Mikoyan to discuss what Mao felt were the unequal relations that existed between fraternal parties within the international communist movement. Implicitly, Mao was asserting the CCP to be at least the coleader of the movement.

The greatest threat to Mao presented by Khrushchev's de-Stalinization was diminution of Mao's authority within the CCP elite. Khrushchev had dammed Stalin for violating Leninist norms of collective leadership, substituting his own will for the collective deliberation and wisdom of the entire Politburo, and imposing a "cult of personality" that gave him godlike status, rendering him immune from criticism. To a substantial degree, all these criticisms applied equally to Mao. During the 1942–1944 *Zheng Feng* (Party rectification) campaign, the CCP had been deliberately "Stalinized" under Mao's leadership, with Mao functioning as China's Stalin. But following and in line with Khrushchev's Twentieth Congress speech, Mao's comrades on the Politburo moved to diminish his cult of personality, for example by eliminating reference to Mao Zedong Thought from the Party constitution and strengthening the powers of the party's secretary general. Mao resented this attempt to diminish his status and power. He was beginning to think about using his immense authority as China's Stalin to eliminate, just as Stalin had, the rightist opposition among both the CCP elite and the peasantry to the drastic acceleration he envisioned for China's socialist industrialization process. Events in Eastern Europe in 1956 further divided the CCP leadership and pushed Mao's thinking leftward.

The CCP and the East European Uprisings of 1956

Within months of Khrushchev's speech denouncing Stalin, the Polish and Hungarian communist parties seized on Khrushchev's opening to begin moving toward more humane forms of socialism. China would play a significant role in both episodes, initiating a period of perhaps twenty years during which China played a role in the Eastern European socialist camp in rivalry with Moscow. Events in Poland and Hungary would also help intensify disagreements within the CCP elite over investment priorities and speed of industrialization. These East European events of 1956 also illustrate some of the problems of post-Stalinist communist rule that would plague the CCP thirty years later when, after Mao, it abandoned Stalinism and opened to the world.

In the spring of 1956, the Polish United Workers Party (PUWP—Poland's communist party) and the Hungarian Socialist Worker's Party (HSWP—Hungary's communist party) began to release political prisoners and rein in the previously ruthless political police. Many cadres purged earlier on phony charges were rehabilitated and, in some cases, reassigned to important positions. The scope of permissible speech, publication, and association was widened. An atmosphere of greater toleration and liberality developed. There was a sense that both countries were at a new point of departure, leaving behind the repressive form of socialism imposed by Soviet armies after 1945. The PUWP rehabilitated Władysław Gomułka, purged in 1954 for rightism, and elected him first secretary of the party. The HSWP rehabilitated Imre Nagy, purged in 1955 for a premature move toward de-Stalinization, And, Nagy too was made first secretary of his party during an anti-Soviet uprising of October 1956, Moscow feared that both Poland and Hungary were slipping out of control. But Khrushchev also realized that armed intervention would run counter to his push for reduced tension with the West and might even risk war with the United States.

Events in Poland reached a head somewhat before Hungary. In June 1956, protests by Polish workers erupted over shortages of food and consumer goods, declining real wages, and shipments of commodities to the USSR.

Interim First Secretary Edward Ochab favored concessions in response to the mounting discontent and pushed through the rehabilitation of Gomułka as a step in that direction. Then on October 19, as Soviet military forces mobilized on Poland's eastern borders, a majority of the PUWP Politburo, backed by Poland's army and internal security services, elected Gomułka first secretary. This was too much for Moscow, which decided to intervene. As the PUWP moved to make Gomułka its top leader, virtually the entire top CPSU leadership, including Khrushchev plus seven Soviet generals in dress uniforms, traveled to Warsaw to veto Gomułka's election. The Poles stood firm. Gomułka told the outraged Soviet delegation: "It is up to our Central Committee and to it alone to determine the membership of our Politburo . . . The composition of the leadership of a Communist Party cannot, in my opinion, be discussed with a fraternal party."[9] Gomułka told the Soviet leaders that if Soviet forces invaded, Poland would resist. But he also promised that the PUWP had no intention of discarding socialism, the dictatorship of the proletariat, or Poland's treaties with the Soviet Union.

The CCP supported the PUWP against Moscow. In September 1956, both the Polish and the Soviet parties sent delegations to the CCP's Eighth Congress. Ochab, a close supporter of Gomułka, headed the Polish delegation. Anastas Mikoyan led the Soviet delegation. On one occasion, as Mao, Ochab, and Mikoyan were discussing the situation in Poland, Mikoyan took objection to Ochab's description of events, to which Ochab replied that Poles were better judges of the Polish situation than were Soviets. "Our people will no longer tolerate taking orders from abroad," Ochab told Mikoyan. The Soviet leader thereupon became angry, leading Ochab to rise, silently shake hands with Mao, ignore Mikoyan, and leave the room. Mao too rose and silently followed Ochab out, ignoring Mikoyan.[10]

In mid-October, Moscow informed the CCP that it was considering military intervention in Poland to prevent the emergence of dangerous anti-Soviet forces there. Moscow wished to know Chinese views on this. The CCP Politburo met to consider the Soviet request for support. Mao guided discussion. Soviet military intervention in another socialist country was not appropriate, he stated. Communist parties were equal; one was not superior and the other subordinate. Soviet actions were manifestations of big power chauvinism, Mao said. Moreover, Soviet military intervention would create opportunities for imperialism. The Politburo endorsed Mao's views and decided to convey to Moscow the CCP's opposition to Soviet military intervention in Poland.[11] Mao immediately summoned Soviet ambassador Pavel Yudin to convey the Politburo decision. Mao received Yudin in pajamas. This was one of two times Mao would do this. Both times, the Soviet ambassador took it as an expression of distain by Mao. Warning the Soviet Union against military intervention in Poland, Mao said that if Moscow ignored Beijing's warning, "We will support Poland, state our opposition to you, and publicly declare our condemnation of your military intervention."[12] Confronted with firm Chinese opposition, Moscow backed down. Beijing's stance was not the only factor and probably not the most important one determining Moscow's choice, but it was one factor. While happy with Khrushchev's turnaround, Mao noted that the Soviet leader had switched positions under pressure from China.

Events in Hungary took a different direction, eventually toppling communist rule in favor of a non-communist-dominated, multiparty coalition government and a move to join the European community of states enjoying freedom and democracy. On July 18, 1956, Mátyás Rákosi, the Stalinist leader of the Hungarian Communist Party, resigned and was eventually replaced by liberal communist Imre Nagy. Nagy's new HSWP government began a dialogue with opposition groups. Inspired by events in Poland, Hungary's liberal, anticommunist movement grew rapidly. The Hungarian communist government found itself being forced to concede to liberal demands. This process was watched closely by PRC representatives in Budapest. It would be an episode recalled explicitly by CCP hardliners in May 1989 when they found themselves facing a demand for dialogue with noncommunist groups. On October 29, several days after Soviet forces had begun entering Budapest, the dismantling of the HSWP's political commissar system in the military began. This was the key mechanism through which the Hungarian communist party controlled the military. The next day, Nagy proclaimed the restoration of a multiparty political system and formation of a multiparty coalition government. The communist monopoly on state power was over. On November 1, Nagy called on the USSR to withdraw its military forces from Hungary. On the streets of Budapest, following shooting by regime security forces into a crowd of demonstrators, bands of anticommunists began to hunt down and lynch members of the regime's hated political police.

Late in October, the PRC embassy in Budapest learned that the Soviet Union was preparing to withdraw Soviet military forces from Hungary. The CCP Politburo met immediately to consider the situation. Mao again led the discussion. Moscow was once again in error, Mao said. In Poland, Moscow's error was to move to intervene. In Hungary's case, Moscow's error was to not intervene to crush the counterrevolutionary forces. It was clear that the situation in Hungary was unlike that earlier in Poland. In Poland, the communists were still in control. In Hungary, the forces of counterrevolution were moving to overthrow socialism. Proletarian internationalism required that Soviet military forces intervene in Hungary to suppress the counterrevolutionary forces and protect the achievements of socialism.[13] Mao's views were again endorsed by the Politburo, then conveyed to Moscow. Again the CCP stance influenced Moscow. In the early morning of November 4, Soviet military forces began a full-scale military assault on Budapest to oust the liberal communist Nagy government and put in power a neo-Stalinist regime led by János Kádár. Nagy was executed, in secret, seven months later. Again Khrushchev had flip-flopped, Mao noted. Mao was concluding that Khrushchev was an unprincipled opportunist who changed easily under pressure.

Shortly after the events in Hungary, the CCP invited Moscow to participate in a tripartite CPSU-CCP-PUWP meeting to discuss relations among socialist countries. Moscow agreed, and Liu Shaoqi and Deng Xiaoping flew to Moscow for the conference. On October 30, the USSR government *unilaterally* issued a declaration on relations among socialist states. The declaration proclaimed the complete equality among "the countries of the great commonwealth of socialist nations," but also that the principles of proletarian internationalism required intervention when "the forces of black reaction and counterrevolution . . . take advantage of the dissatisfaction of a part of the working people in order to undermine the foundations of the people's democratic system . . . and restore the old landowner-capitalist ways."[14] Khrushchev had essentially adopted Mao's analysis. Yet again, the Soviet leader had vacillated.

One issue left unstated by both Beijing and Moscow but clearly understood by both was the relative status of both capitals in the East European socialist camp. Was Eastern Europe to be Moscow's sphere of influence, with the CPSU calling the shots? Or was the CCP to have an equal voice in that region? Within a few years of 1956, Albania would move out of the Soviet orbit into alignment with the PRC, while Romania would balance halfway between Beijing and Moscow.[15] Several other East European regimes would play the China card to achieve a greater degree of independence from Moscow, at least until the Sino-Soviet split became too intense circa 1963 to permit that any longer. In other words, Mao and the CCP were challenging not only Soviet leadership of the international communist movement, but also Moscow's leadership of the East European socialist camp. Figure 5-1 illustrates China's position in East Europe from 1956 through 1977.

The Hungarian uprising had a major impact on CCP politics. Following the suppression of the Budapest uprising, the CCP Politburo met almost daily to discuss events. Hungarian events taught Mao that a large number of counterrevolutionaries had remained hidden under HSWP rule awaiting an opportunity to rise up. This was a lesson for China, Mao told the Politburo. It demonstrated the need for continued mass struggle against counterrevolutionaries in China and other socialist countries.[16] The central lesson of "Hungary" as defined by Mao was that the easing of repression had been wrong; it had given hidden counterrevolutionaries an opportunity to raise their heads. Expanding discussion to the "Stalin question," the Politburo agreed that Hungarian events demonstrated that Stalin's repression of counterrevolutionaries in his own time had been "basically correct," albeit expanded too far. Three CCP theoreticians—Hu Qiaomu, Tian Jiaying, and Wu Lengxi—labored for five

1956: Encourage Soviets not to intervene to oust nationalist Communist government.

1953: Support Soviet repression of worker riots.

1956: Encourage Moscow to authorize arms sale to Egypt.

1956: Urge Soviet armed intervention to oust non-Communist government, and reinstall Communist dictatorship.

1948–1953: Polemicize against Tito split with Moscow.
Jan. 1955: Establish diplomatic relations at ambassadorial level.
1956–1960: Polemicize against Tito as surrogate for Khrushchev's "revisionism".

1958: Albania aligns with CCP on destalinization and peaceful coexistence. Stands by CCP as polemic with CPSU escalates in 1960. PRC assists when Moscow cuts aid. China's closest ideological ally through Cultural Revolution. Reject Mao's pragmatic opening to the U.S. in the 1970s.

1960s: Close relationship with Stalinist nationalist regime that balances between Beijing and Moscow.

FIGURE 5-1 **China's Position in the East European Socialist Camp, 1956–1977**

days to produce a draft of another manifesto on the dictatorship of the proletariat. Two more afternoons going over the document with Mao followed, then discussion by an expanded Politburo. Mao then gave the document one final read-through, making detailed comments. Then, for two more days, expanded sessions of the Politburo deliberated the much-revised document. Mao personally guided the entire process. The amount of energy spent in working out these ideological statements indicates their profound significance in the mind of Mao, and probably other CCP leaders as well. Finally, the result was issued on December 29, 1956, under the rubric of a *Renmin ribao* editorial entitled "More on the Historical Experience of the Dictatorship of the Proletariat."[17] The CCP December Stalinist manifesto was twice as long as the one in April. It explained the Hungarian people's longing for freedom and national independence as a function of imperialist aggression:

> The activities of the imperialists in the Hungarian affair of October 1956 marked the gravest attack launched by them against the socialist

camp since the war of aggression they carried out in Korea. . . . Among the causes [of the Hungarian affair] international imperialism 'played the main and decisive part.'

The December manifesto went much further than the April document in affirming the positive, "correct" nature of Stalin's repression. By defending Lenin's line on industrialization and the collectivization of agriculture, Stalin forged socialism and "created the conditions for the victory of the Soviet Union in the war against Hitler . . . the socialist Soviet Union made tremendous progress during the period of Stalin's leadership."[18] For tactical reasons, Mao's challenge to Khrushchev's de-Stalinization as the line of the international communist movement was cast as an internal CCP affair. But "While nominally directed internally [i.e., within the CCP]," Mao told his Politburo comrades in late 1956, the CCP statements on the Stalin question were "in fact directed internationally, even though we cannot say we want to influence the international [situation]. One must understand that the Soviet Union has set up its own sausage stand and doesn't want to see China sell sausage," Mao said.[19]

Doubts of Soviet Irresolution in the Middle East

Soviet policy during the Suez crisis of 1956 was taken by Mao as further demonstration of Khrushchev's weak and irresolute response to imperialism. Simultaneously, it was a demonstration of the need for China to become a great socialist power in its own right.[20] With the Soviet Union under Khrushchev backing away from its "proletarian internationalist duty" to support the world's anti-imperialist forces, it became imperative for the PRC, still guided by genuine Marxist-Leninist principles, to step into the vacuum being created by Khrushchev's ideological apostasy. To do that, China needed to get strong quickly.

Egypt under the leadership of Gamal Abdel Nasser in the 1950s emerged as a leader of Arab nationalism and, as such, was courted by both Washington and Moscow. Nasser strongly supported Algeria's struggle for independence from France and opposed Iraq's 1955 accession to the Anglo-American backed anticommunist Baghdad Pact. Nasser was also a key figure in the emerging non-aligned movement, which, as described earlier, diluted US efforts to contain Soviet and Chinese communist influence. Several Egyptian moves in 1955–1956 tilted Egypt toward the Soviet Union: rejection of US terms for military assistance, and purchase in 1955 of Soviet-bloc arms instead; recognition of the PRC in May 1956; and nationalization of the Suez canal in July 1956. Beijing cheered all of these moves, but felt that Moscow did not go far enough in efforts to draw Egypt deeper into the world's anti-imperialist struggle.

Nasser quickly became adept at playing Beijing against Moscow. During the Bandung Conference in April 1955, Nasser had approached Zhou Enlai about Soviet reluctance to supply arms to Egypt. The Western powers were proposing an embargo on weapons sales to the Middle East as a way to tamp down tensions, and Moscow was unwilling to contradict that Western initiative. Nasser asked Zhou if China might be able to help out. China agreed to try, and raised the matter with Moscow. This led to Soviet authorization of Czechoslovak sale of weapons to Egypt.[21] Moscow's inclination to go along with Western plans for an arms embargo, and its unwillingness to directly arm Egypt for its anti-imperialist struggle, were seen by Mao as Soviet lack of resolve. From the CCP perspective, acquisition of arms was part of an Afro-Asian country's sovereign rights, essential for defense against Western imperialism. For Moscow to ignore that right in order to reduce tension with those Western imperialists was sheer, unprincipled capitulation. Under Chinese and Egyptian pressure, Moscow backed away from the arms embargo proposal, but was unwilling to itself supply arms to Egypt.

China recognized Egypt's important regional role and moved quickly to deepen ties with it following initial contacts between Zhou and Nasser at Bandung. In February 1956, the chairman of the China Islamic Association led a large Chinese delegation to Egypt. Three months later, Egypt became the first Arab country to recognize the People's Republic of China. Two days after recognition, Zhou Enlai invited Nasser to visit China, and defense minister Peng Dehuai invited Egypt's defense minister to pay a similar visit. Both invitations were accepted. In late July 1956, only a few days after China's new ambassador presented his credentials to Nasser, the Egyptian leader announced the nationalization of the Suez Canal. It took Beijing nearly three weeks to unequivocally endorse that move. This may have had to do with Zhou Enlai's Bandung-era moderation and concern for the legalities of freedom of navigation. In any case, Mao ended equivocation in his opening speech to the Eighth CCP Congress on September 15, when he declared "We firmly support the entirely lawful action of the Government of Egypt in taking back the Suez Canal company, and resolutely oppose any attempt to encroach on the sovereignty of Egypt and start armed aggression against that country."[22]

When Israel, Britain, and France invaded Egypt at the end of October to seize control of the canal, China quickly supported Egypt. A PRC government statement warned of "inestimably grave consequences" for the aggressors. Many *Renmin ribao* editorials and statements by government leaders voiced various threats and warnings to the aggressors. On October 1, Defense Minister Peng declared that the Chinese people would support Egypt in its just struggle against imperialism. During the Suez War, 250,000 Chinese reportedly registered to serve as "volunteers" in Egypt. Transport difficulties made that move purely symbolic, yet it was a potent symbol of PRC support for the Arab people's struggle against US imperialism.

Again Moscow equivocated, at least from Mao's perspective. Moscow, who unlike China did have a real ability to intervene in the Middle East, drew back from support for Egypt. Following the canal's nationalization but before the Anglo-French-Israeli attack, the Western countries proposed an international conference to deliberate on the legality of Egypt's nationalization. The Soviet Union reached an "understanding" with London to participate in such a conference. Mao saw this as unprincipled compromise with imperialism. Rather than supporting Egypt's militant struggle against imperialism, Moscow was seeking a peaceful settlement. Equally egregious, China was not invited to participate in the projected conference, and Moscow did not demand China's participation. This too represented Soviet capitulation to Western imperialism's containment of China. Again under strong Chinese and Egyptian pressure, Moscow backed away from the idea of convening an international conference.

Khrushchev did eventually threaten "to use force . . . to crush the aggressors and restore peace in the Middle East" if Anglo-French forces did not halt. During the crisis, Beijing was careful to maintain public unanimity with Moscow, and lauded Moscow's statement as a "practical threat" to Britain and France. But years later, in a long 1973 interview with an Egyptian reporter, Zhou Enlai gave the Chinese view of the Soviet warning. It was, Zhou said, an "empty shot" that was issued only once Moscow understood that Washington would intervene to force Britain and France to withdraw from Egypt. There was no risk for Moscow in making that warning, Zhou said.

In sum, Moscow had been initially unwilling to arm Egypt in the face of Western threats. Moscow had been willing to go along with imperialist diplomatic schemes to undermine Egypt. Moscow had issued "practical support" for Egypt only after US policy made clear there was no risk in giving such "support." The CCP maintained a facade of socialist unity during the crisis, but it emerged from it with deepened doubts about Khrushchev's lack of resolve in confronting imperialism. The crisis also confirmed for Mao the imperative need for China to develop as quickly as possible the practical ability to influence more decisively events in such regions as the Middle East.

Mao's Challenge to the CPSU at the 1957 Moscow Conference

By mid-1957, PRC influence was at an apex, in the estimate of Wu Lengxi who accompanied Mao to a global conference of communist parties in November of that year to celebrate the fortieth anniversary of the Bolshevik insurrection. China's successful participation in the 1954 Geneva Conference on Indochina, its 1955 participation in the Bandung Conference, its role in Eastern Europe, and its influence on Moscow's handling of relations among fraternal parties and in the debate over the "Stalin question" had enhanced Beijing's influence, in Wu's view. In June 1957, Mao had also given important support—according to Lu Lengxi's account—to Khrushchev when the Soviet leader defeated an attempt by Stalinists within the CPSU Politburo to oust him. Khrushchev felt indebted to Mao for CCP support in 1956 and 1957. China at that juncture had "extremely great influence on the world," in Wu's estimate.[23] Mao decided to use China's greater prestige to recast the way in which the international communist movement determined its "line." No longer would that line be dictated unilaterally by the CPSU. Rather, it would be determined in accord with "correct Marxist-Leninist principles" as understood by Mao. Mao worked to formulate a more equal role for all fraternal parties in setting the line for the movement, but he also insisted that those parties embrace his confrontational line, a proposition that would encounter great skepticism by the majority of parties that Mao sought to court.

Leaving China for the second and last time in his life, Mao traveled to Moscow for the conference. Sixty-four communist and workers' parties attended the conclave, making it the most extensive meeting of the world communist movement up to that time. In line with his effort to make Mao and the CCP feel comfortable within the socialist camp, Khrushchev ordered special treatment for Mao and the CCP delegation. Khrushchev sent two special aircraft to Beijing to ferry the Chinese delegation to and from Moscow. Khrushchev and most of the senior Soviet leadership were at the Moscow airport to greet Mao's arrival. Khrushchev accompanied Mao to his quarters. Alone among participating delegations, the CCP delegation was housed within the Kremlin. When conference attendees stood atop Lenin's mausoleum in Red Square to review a parade, Mao stood beside Khrushchev. "Long live Mao" and "Long live China" were popular slogans on that and other public occasions. Alone among the delegations, the CCP was not required to submit a printed draft of Mao's speech to the CPSU prior to its delivery. Alone among delegations, the CCP was allowed to meet and discuss issues with other parties' delegations. When it came time for Mao to deliver his speech, he alone among speakers delivered it sitting down. Mao took umbrage at the special treatment arranged for him by Khrushchev; it offended his communist sensibilities. "Even in this communist land, they know who is powerful and who is weak. What snobs!" Mao told his doctor.[24]

Mao's initial meetings with Khrushchev in Moscow focused on the issue of war with the United States, an issue that would dominate the conference. The socialist countries should not fear war with the Western countries, including the United States, Mao said. Not fearing war did not necessarily mean that one would have to fight a war. In fact, it would be the opposite, Mao explained to Khrushchev: fearing war would make actual war more likely. Mao referenced a speech by former Soviet marshal and defense minister Georgii Zhukov (purged by Khrushchev only weeks before), saying that if the United States launched a war, the Soviet Union should resort to a "preemptive attack" (*xin fa zhi ren*) on the United States. It might be best not to talk of this openly, Mao admitted. In public comments, it would be best to stress the defensive character of the war.[25] Mao also suggested to Khrushchev that in the event of a war with the United States, Soviet forces should withdraw eastward to the Urals in a fashion similar to the Soviet withdrawal before German armies in 1941–1943. When Khrushchev explained that that earlier withdrawal had not been voluntary but compelled by German power, Mao objected. "I don't agree," Mao said. "If you fell back to the Urals, then we Chinese could enter the war." "I looked at him closely," Khrushchev recalled, "but I couldn't tell from his face whether he was joking or not."[26] In what became the most famous portion of his prepared speech, Mao asserted that the east wind in the world now prevailed over the west wind:

> Who is stronger, the underdeveloped or advanced countries? Who is stronger, India or Britain, Indonesia or Holland, Algeria or France? To my mind all the imperialist countries are in a position which is like the position of the sun at 6 p.m., but ours is at the position of the sun at 6 a.m. Thus the tide has turned. And this means that the Western countries have been left behind, that we have outdistanced them considerably. Undoubtedly, it is not the Western wind that prevails over the Eastern wind, but the wind from the West is so weak. Undoubtedly, the Eastern wind prevails over the Western wind, for we are strong.[27]

This was Mao's call for the socialist camp to go on the offensive against imperialism across the intermediate zone. According to Wu Lengxi, Mao meant by these formulations that the strength of the socialist camp now exceeded the strength of the imperialist camp.[28] History had reached a turning point. The Red Army's destruction of German and Japanese fascism plus the "liberation" of Eastern Europe and establishment of socialist countries there, the collapse of the West European colonial empires and the victory of national liberation movements, the victory of the Chinese revolution, China's victory in the Korean War, France's defeat in Indochina, the British-French defeat by Egypt, the Soviet development of nuclear weapons and missiles like that which had just launched Sputnik (on October 14, 1957)—all indicated that the global correlation of forces now favored the socialist camp. The anti-imperialist camp was definitely stronger than the imperialist camp.

Given this, the socialist camp should adopt a militant approach toward US imperialism, maintain an intention to struggle, fight, and defeat it one piece at a time (*yi bufen yi bufen de xiaomie diren*).[29] As for US nuclear weapons, they were "paper tigers," Mao said, used to scare and intimidate people. If the United States decided to use nuclear weapons, there was nothing the socialist camp could do about it, Mao told Khrushchev, but it should not fear this possibility. If worse came to worst and US imperialism unleashed a nuclear war, perhaps half the world's population would be wiped out. But the remaining half would carry out revolutions overthrowing the imperialists who had unleashed the war. As a result, capitalism would be overthrown, and the whole world would become socialist, bringing an end to imperialism and war. Thus, fearing nuclear war was worse than not fearing it. Mao shared his thoughts about world war to the delegates this way:

> Let us imagine how many people would die if war breaks out. There are 2.7 billion people in the world, and a third would be lost. If it is a little higher it could be half. . . . I say that if the worst came to the worst and one-half dies, there will still be one-half left, but imperialism would be erased and the whole world would become socialist. After a few years there would be 2.7 billion people again.[30]

Conference delegates listened in shocked silence as Mao talked glibly about nuclear war. The Soviet and European (East and West) delegates were especially shocked. Having recently experienced the devastation of World War II, many had difficulty believing what they were hearing. Some began to doubt the mental balance of China's bold leader. While calling on the socialist camp to go on the offensive without fear of nuclear war, Mao strongly affirmed Soviet leadership of that camp

> We are so many people here, with so many parties, we must have a head . . . If the Soviet Union is not the head, then who is? Should we do it by alphabetical order? Albania? Vietnam with comrade Ho Chi Minh? Another country? China does not qualify to be the head, we do not have enough experience. We know about revolution, but not about socialist construction. Demographically we are a huge country, but economically we are small."[31]

Khrushchev initially urged that the CPSU *not* be identified as the leader, lest such identification cause apprehensions among other fraternal parties. Mao rejected this and insisted that the CPSU must be the leader. When Khrushchev proposed CPSU-CCP joint leadership, Mao declined. Only the USSR was qualified to lead the world movement; China lacked such qualifications, Mao insisted. When Khrushchev proposed that the CCP take the lead in developing ties with India, Pakistan, and Indonesia—three Asian nations with economic conditions similar to China's own, Khrushchev noted—Mao again declined: "No, it's out of the question. The leading role in Africa and Asia should belong to the Soviet Union . . . I think the CPSU should be the one and only center of the international communist movement, and the rest of us should be united around that center."[32] Eventually Khrushchev agreed. The final declaration referred to "the invincible camp of Socialist countries headed by the Soviet Union" and to "the Soviet Union, the first and mightiest Socialist power."[33] When drafting the final declaration of the conference, the CCP argued in favor of explicitly identifying US imperialism as the key enemy of the people of the world. After the Polish,

Yugoslav, and Italian parties objected, the CCP agreed to compromise.[34] The final declaration condemned "aggressive imperialist circles in the US" and used several similar circumlocutions, but eschewed the formulation "US imperialism."

Thus Mao maneuvered Khrushchev into taking responsibility for the entire revolutionary movement, which was to undertake militant confrontation with US imperialism, not fearing even nuclear war, but for which the CPSU was no longer to set policy. The line of the international revolutionary movement, of which the CPSU was the clear center, would now be set by the majority, with the CCP having a strong voice. In Khrushchev's words:

> As we listened to Mao pay recognition to [the leading role of] the Soviet Union and the CPSU, we couldn't help suspecting that his thoughts were probably very different from his words. We had the unsettling feeling that sooner or later, friction was bound to develop between our countries and our Parties. . . . there were some telltale indications of what form that friction might take. When the more than eighty delegations present turned to the possibility of thermonuclear war, Mao gave a speech [saying]. . . . We shouldn't be afraid of atomic bombs and missiles."[35]

Stripped of ambiguity, Khrushchev was beginning to wonder if Mao was not trying to maneuver the USSR into a thermonuclear war with the United States. Both of those highly urbanized countries would be utterly destroyed by such a war, while still-rural and more populous China would survive to rebuild—and seize Siberia. We will never know if such maneuvers entered Mao's mind. It is perhaps enough to say that Khrushchev suspected they did. Mao for his part was dismayed at the lukewarm reception at the Moscow conference given to his ideas about war and peace. Mao saw this as further confirmation of the apostasy from principles of Lenin and Stalin corrupting the world revolutionary movement under the misleadership of the CPSU. Mao was not yet ready to openly criticize those erroneous tendencies, because to do so would reveal "contradictions" within the anti-imperialist camp, weakening that camp in the struggle against imperialism. Besides, it was apparent that—for the time being, until China industrialized—only the Soviet Union had the capabilities to give the world revolutionary movement practical assistance in such distant regions as East Europe and the Middle East, as well as in industrializing socialist China.

One final aspect of the Moscow conference was Mao's open declaration of a race with the Soviet Union to superpower status. In May 1957, Khrushchev had declared that the Soviet Union would soon catch up with the United States in per capita agricultural production. At the Moscow conference the Soviet leader upped his claim, asserting that the Soviet Union "will . . . not only catch up with but also surpass the present [US] volume of output of important products." Mao immediately took up the challenge and announced to the conference that China would within fifteen years surpass Britain, then still seen as a major industrial power:

> Maybe I am bragging here, and maybe when we have another international meeting in future you will criticize me for being subjective, but I speak with the strength of considerable evidence ... Comrade Khrushchev tells us that the Soviet Union will overtake the United States in fifteen years. I can tell you that in fifteen years we may well catch up with and overtake Britain.[36]

The race to communism and for leadership of the world communist movement had begun. Idiosyncrasies of the psychologies of both Mao and Khrushchev contributed to the growing competition between the two leaders. Mao had long had difficulties with authority. In an essay written at the time of Mao's death, MIT professor Lucian Pye noted that at each stage of his life, Mao came into conflict with those in authority over him: his father, a school headmaster, other leaders of the CCP, Stalin, and Khrushchev.[37] In each case, Mao drew his rival into conflict and focused his psychic energy on defeating that enemy. While idealizing comradely love within revolutionary ranks, Mao seems to have been incapable of such feelings, and was prone to feel slights when he felt his voice was being ignored. Mao's personal physician, with many years of attending to Mao, also noted that Mao was subject to bouts of "irrational suspicion" of plots directed against him, and that these bouts coincided with insomnia, headaches, anxiety, depression, and bad temper.[38]

Since adolescence Mao had dreamed of being recognized as a world-historic person. He sought to achieve that by establishing himself in the Marxist-Leninist pantheon of Marx, Engels, Lenin, and Stalin.[39] Mao viewed the CCP's 1949 victory as the historical equivalent of Lenin's engineering of the Bolshevik insurrection of 1917 or Stalin's 1941–1945 defense of the Soviet state. Mao also believed that the model of revolution he had invented—protracted guerrilla war and a broad anti-imperialist united front led by a "proletarian party"—should guide the revolutionary struggle in wide swaths of the developing world. What had Khrushchev accomplished that could compare with these? There was little question in Mao's mind that he was the true, genuine successor to Lenin and Stalin. Mao soon concluded, probably at their very first meeting in October 1954 on the occasion of the PRC's Fifth National Day, that Khrushchev simply lacked the gravitas and resolution to qualify as successor to Lenin and Stalin. Khrushchev was simply not of the same caliber as Lenin, Stalin, or himself, Mao concluded, and flip-flopped constantly on issues.

Khrushchev, for his part, had survived in Stalin's murderous inner circle by playing a somewhat dim buffoon. This exterior guise hid a cunning mind, and as Khrushchev emerged as the CPSU's paramount leader he sought to escape the stereotyped image of his tutelage under Stalin. Khrushchev craved respect, while Mao doled out condescension. Khrushchev reciprocated Mao's condescension by seeing Mao as "just like Stalin," a very serious reproach for Khrushchev—arrogant and supremely ungrateful. Khrushchev had adopted a much more generous approach to China than Stalin had, and was China's benefactor in a number of ways. Yet Khrushchev saw little sign of Chinese gratitude. Mao seemed to demand ever more from the Soviet Union, while refusing reasonable moves that would benefit both the Soviet Union and China, all the while challenging the CPSU's status as leader of the socialist camp and the international communist movement, and perhaps trying to maneuver the USSR into confrontation with the United States. During their four personal encounters (in October 1954, November 1957, August 1958, and October 1959), Mao delighted in putting down Khrushchev in many ways, small and large: correcting his ideological mistakes before others; criticizing his work style, again before others; lauding CPSU leaders purged by Khrushchev; subjecting him to concerted criticism by second-rank Chinese leaders; and demonstrating his superior swimming skills while nonswimmer Khrushchev was reduced to floating with inflated water wings or sitting on the pool's edge.

The Soviet Union, the Great Leap, and the Transition to Communism

After Mao launched the Anti-Rightist Campaign in July 1957, he achieved elite unity behind the program of massive investment of resources in the expansion of heavy and defense industry known as the Great Leap Forward. Launched in January 1958 at the start of the Second Five Year Plan, the Great Leap was an all-out push to transform China within ten or fifteen years into an industrialized and technologically advanced socialist great power. The model for this great transformation was the Soviet transformation under Stalin between 1928 and 1938, when, at least according to the *Short Course*, the USSR had been transformed into an industrialized and technologically advanced and powerful country within a period of ten years. Initially framed in terms of speed of development, by 1960 Mao interpreted it in terms of movement toward or away from a utopian communist organization of society. While Khrushchev's phony communism was taking the Soviet Union away from communism, Mao's correct policies would lead China toward that desired goal.

China's ties with the Soviet Union were intertwined with the ambitious investment priorities of the Great Leap. The higher the rates of industrial growth in China, the larger the level of capital goods imports from the Soviet Union that would be required. Investment in consumer goods or foodstuffs could partially be repaid by selling the products of that investment. But investment in heavy industry typically had a longer payback time. Military industry, of course, produced no revenue at all. This meant that CCP advocates of very rapid development of heavy and defense industries needed generous Soviet support. Soviet and East European capital goods were typically not given gratis. They had to be paid for, albeit over a period of years and at a low interest rate. Since perhaps 90 percent of China's population still worked in the agricultural sector, and since China's industrialization was just beginning, most of China's capital goods imports were repaid with agricultural goods: rice, wheat, soy, seed oils, meat, eggs, pig bristles, fruits, vegetables, and nuts. The crux of trade between China and the socialist camp was Soviet and East European capital goods for Chinese foodstuffs. The larger China's demand for Soviet-bloc capital goods, the larger its exports of foodstuffs needed to be.

The Soviet-style centrally planned economy imposed on China by the CCP in 1950–1953 had the great advantage of allowing planners to concentrate resources in targeted sectors. More or less investment could be funneled to one sector or another. Following the example of Stalin's 1928–1941 crash industrialization drive, Mao believed that the largest amount of investment possible should be poured into expanding military industry and the set of heavy industries necessary to support it: mining, metal forging and working, machine building, electricity, petroleum, heavy transport, chemicals, etc. Investment in consumer goods, agriculture, housing, public sanitation, and education was held down as much as possible.

Government monopoly on the purchase of agricultural produce at government-stipulated low prices was one key mechanism of the new system of Stalinist development. The state became the sole, monopoly purchaser of a list of agricultural goods including most basic foodstuffs. Sometimes the "procurement price" paid by the state for agricultural goods was higher, sometimes lower, but it was always what the state (and not markets) said it was. Private sale of listed foods became a crime. If the state paid out higher procurement prices to the farmers, the farmers would be better off but the state would have less money to funnel into industrialization. State monopoly on agricultural produce had the great advantage, from the CCP point of view, of putting the agricultural harvest in the state's hands. One difficulty of the various cooperative systems implemented before full collectivization was that before selling their produce to state agents the peasants took the harvest home, and once at home it was liable to being underreported and eaten, hidden, or sold by the farmers on illegal markets for a price better approximating its real, market value. This "problem" would be solved by formation of the People's Communes in 1958, in which the entire production process was brought under control of CCP cadres, with the harvest going directly from fields to cadre-controlled granaries and warehouses. The agricultural harvest was taken via collectivization, with farmers living in poverty and kept in line by fear of losing their grain rations and of the political police, plus a good dose of propaganda and promise of a bright communist future.

Once in state hands, agricultural goods were used in three ways. Some small portion of it was returned by commune cadres to the farmers for subsistence rations. Another portion went to feed nonagricultural industrial and urban workers; state-supplied food rations became a major part of the income of the expanding industrial workforce. Finally, agricultural produce could be exported to pay for imports of machinery and equipment with which to industrialize China.

Marxist-Leninist doctrine linked the speed of industrialization to the transition from socialism to communism. It taught that a high level of industrialization would, under the governance of the dictatorship of the proletariat, create the material basis for transition to communism. Advocates within the CCP elite of a somewhat slower-paced approach were in favor of China's industrialization, rise as a great power, and eventual transition to communism, but favored taking a bit longer to accomplish those grand goals. Mao called this perspective "conservative, rightist opposition." The "rightist opposition" advocated greater investment in food and consumer goods, and believed that a more relaxed political atmosphere (i.e., de-Stalinization) was possible because rising living standards would generate higher levels of popular support. Defeating this "rightist opposition" was one of Mao's key domestic objectives. Struggle against Soviet "revisionism" and against US "imperialism" was an important aspect of Mao's struggle to direct the revolution in the correct direction

The program of de-Stalinization prescribed by Khrushchev was antithetical to the program of hyperindustrialization wrought by Stalin and prescribed by Mao circa 1958. De-Stalinization meant reining in the organs of repression and terror to create a more relaxed, less fearful atmosphere. De-Stalinization also involved a shift of investment from heavy and defense industries to consumer goods, agriculture, and public utilities. During a campaign of hyperindustrialization, people's lives would necessarily be harsh; they would have to work long and hard while living in extremely spartan conditions. Of course, there would be opposition and resistance that would have to be broken. People could not be motivated primarily by individual gain. Too few goods beyond bare subsistence would be available for that. Rather, people would need to be motivated by fear. Propaganda and constant exhortation would help. But those moral incentives would have to be paralleled by fear of state violence.

Mao was also beginning to see defects in the Soviet model adopted in the early 1950s. As noted earlier, by 1958 Mao had reached the conclusion that that model would not take China's revolution where Mao knew it needed to go, toward utopian communism. Mao called forth new policies designed to move China in a correct direction, toward communism: mass mobilization campaigns led by political cadres, "reds," rather than by technically competent people, "experts"; greatly intensified labor with minimal material reward; and great increases in investment in industry and capital construction. During the Great Leap Forward, these policies were implemented across the country. Mao was convinced these policies would direct China on the correct path to an industrialized, technologically advanced, socialist power in the process of transition to communism, all within a few years. Implicitly, with China and the CCP following a correct path while the USSR was increasingly in the grasp of incorrect, revisionist policies, the PRC would reach the communist stage of development before the USSR.

Mao chose policy toward the United States as the key basis on which to challenge Khrushchev's leadership of the international communist movement. Inspired by a desire to ease the heavy burden of Soviet defense spending and shift budgetary funds to raising the standards of living of the Soviet people, Khrushchev, rather like Mikhail Gorbachev thirty years later, moved to reduce tension with the United States. Khrushchev called that policy "peaceful coexistence." Khrushchev also feared that war with the United States would lead to a nuclear exchange that would destroy both the USSR and the United States. Mao saw Khrushchev's push for détente with the United States as unprincipled abandonment of the militant anti-imperialist principles followed by Lenin and Stalin.

The "Joint Fleet" Proposal and the First Mao-Khrushchev Confrontation

In October 1957, as part of Khrushchev's effort to make China feel comfortable in the Soviet camp and in the lead-up to the Moscow conference scheduled for the next month, Moscow signed with Beijing an agreement on comprehensive weapons technology transfer. One provision of that agreement dealt with nuclear weapons: Moscow was to supply full technical details for the manufacture of atomic bombs along with a prototype bomb.[40] The next month Defense Minister Peng Dehuai led a delegation to Moscow to discuss implementation of the agreement. Peng's shopping list included missiles, jet aircraft, submarines, and nuclear weapons. Again Khrushchev agreed to the Chinese requests. In this context the two sides also discussed possible increased military cooperation in the Far East.[41] Then, early in 1958, Soviet naval officers provided their PLA-navy counterparts with information about recent advances in Soviet submarine design and suggested that the PRC might consider requesting assistance in this area too.[42] In April 1958, during another visit by Peng Dehuai to Moscow, Soviet Defense Minister Rodion Malinovsky gave substance to the idea of expanded military cooperation by proposing joint USSR-PRC construction of a long-wave radio station on the south China coast to communicate with submerged Soviet submarines operating in the South Pacific. (Long radio waves penetrate water better than waves of other frequencies.) Talks on such a joint effort proceeded. It was agreed that Moscow would provide substantial and majority funding for the project. Mao insisted on full Chinese ownership of the projected facility, a demand that the Soviet side accepted.

Soviet leaders concluded from these interactions that Beijing was ready to substantially enhance the military capabilities of both countries in the Pacific Ocean via expanded cooperation.[43] China would get Soviet assistance in building modern submarines, and Soviet submarines would get improved communication via a Chinese-owned but jointly operated radio station on the south China coast. The two countries were close ideological partners; recognized a common enemy, the United States; and were bound by the 1950 military alliance. Expanded military cooperation would benefit both, Soviet leaders probably calculated.

That's where matters stood on July 21, 1958, when Soviet ambassador Pavel Yudin briefed Mao and other top CCP leaders on recent Soviet policies. After covering the situation in the Middle East and Yugoslavia, Yudin turned to the idea of a Soviet-Chinese joint submarine fleet. Yudin did not get very far into his exposition before Mao interrupted with astonishment, according to Wu Lengxi, "What! Are you proposing a 'joint company'?" "Joint company" was an allusion to the jointly owned companies set up at Soviet insistence in 1950 to exploit resources in China's northeast and Xinjiang. Mao became extremely agitated (again according to Wu Lengxi) and said that when requesting Soviet assistance in construction of submarines, he had never imagined that the Soviet Union would propose setting up a "joint company" with China. Mao then let Yudin finish his presentation, but returned to the joint fleet issue and, according to Wu, "wouldn't let it go." Yudin continued his exposition the next day, explaining that access to the high seas by Soviet submarines was dominated by Western powers, which monitored key straits. Given this, the Soviet Union very much needed ports beyond those straits, and a south Chinese port would be ideal. Mao would have none of it. Was the implication, Mao asked Yudin, that unless China accepted the joint fleet proposal, Soviet assistance in the construction of submarines would not be forthcoming? Did Moscow want to "control China?"[44]

The swiftness and highly emotional nature of Mao's response raise questions about Mao's rationality at this juncture. He apparently reached a very quick and firm judgment. Later Mao told his medical doctor that the Soviet purpose was indeed to "control China."[45] This judgment was later publicly affirmed in an authoritative CCP statement of September 1963: Moscow's "joint fleet" proposal embodied "unreasonable demands designed to bring China under Soviet military control."[46] This judgment was almost certainly wrong. The Soviet proposal was designed not to "control China," but to enhance the capabilities of the Soviet navy in the Pacific Ocean, an enhancement that Moscow believed would strengthen Chinese as well as Soviet security. A debate within Soviet military circles over the merits of submarines versus surface vessels had just been concluded in favor of submarines, as advocated by Admiral Sergey Gorshkov.[47] Large numbers of a new class of more capable submarines were to be built. But effective operation of those boats in time of war required both forward-based repair and replenishment facilities and forward-based long-wave radio stations for communication. Gorshkov had identified Hainan Island as the ideal place to meet these Soviet requirements. Yudin's proposal to Mao derived from these calculations. Khrushchev anticipated Chinese acceptance of the proposal since it would strengthen both Soviet and Chinese security, or so the Soviet leader calculated.[48]

Khrushchev's China policy had been generous in the extreme, catering to Mao's pride and bending over backward to satisfy China's various demands, all in order to make China comfortable in the socialist camp.[49] Khrushchev's whole China policy was predicated on abandoning Stalin's attempts to coerce China and instead win China to voluntary partnership. Khrushchev believed that Stalin's stingy and suspicious approach to Mao would backfire, and undertook to treat China in a generous fashion in order to make it comfortable and thus keep it in the socialist camp. Khrushchev had ended the onerous special privileges in Northeast China and Xinjiang. He had substantially increased the level of Soviet economic assistance to China. He had sought and catered to CCP opinion on Poland, Hungary, and Egypt in 1956, and again at the Moscow Conference of 1957. Khrushchev had even agreed to help the PRC build a wide array of modern weapons, including submarines, missiles, and nuclear weapons. Moreover, Soviet-Chinese negotiations over the previous eight months about expanded military cooperation formed a process leading to the "joint fleet" proposal. Any one of the PRC's astute statesmen—Premier Zhou Enlai, Foreign Minister Chen Yi, Defense Minister Peng Dehuai, or Ambassador Liu Xiao—could have explained that Moscow's proposal was not "designed to control China." But Mao's domination of China's foreign policy decision-making process was so great that once he rendered a decision, which he did very rapidly in this case, no one else, even the better-informed, was in a position to challenge that decision. China's other top leaders almost certainly understood that Mao's conclusion was faulty, but they dared not say a word. Even to this day Chinese scholars are compelled to affirm that Khrushchev sought to "control China."

On July 31, nine days after Mao's confrontation with Ambassador Yudin, Khrushchev himself arrived in Beijing to try to smooth things out. Talks extended over three days and were tense from beginning to end.[50] This direct and angry confrontation would transform the relation between Khrushchev and Mao. Khrushchev tried to explain the geographic logic behind the Soviet proposal for a jointly operated submarine fleet. Egress from Soviet ports on the Black Sea and the Baltic Sea and from Vladivostok to the high sea was restricted by passage through US-monitored straits. The port of Petropavlovsk on the Kamchatka peninsula was supplied by sea, which would render it of little use in the event of war with the US navy. Ports on the Chinese coast would greatly reduce these geographic obstacles, improving the security of both China and the Soviet Union. Mao completely rejected such logic. "You can reach the ocean from Vladivostok through the Kurile Islands. The condition is very good," Mao retorted. Mao saw such geopolitical arguments as mere pretext covering a more sinister Soviet plan to dominate China. Mao was impatient with Khrushchev's arguments and frequently interrupted him angrily. Why doesn't China simply turn over to Moscow the entire China coast?, Mao asked sarcastically. When Khrushchev said the Soviet feelings were hurt by China's suspicions that the joint fleet proposals was really an attempt "to control China," Mao, according to Wu Lengxi, "became even more angry." "Hurt your self-respect? Who hurt whose self-respect?," Mao demanded. "It's your proposal for a joint fleet that violated our self-respect." Khrushchev too had become angry by this point. He had not expected such crude treatment in China, the Soviet leader said. "What is crude?" Mao demanded. Khrushchev then withdrew the joint fleet proposal; there would be no joint fleet, he said. Deng Xiaoping, who witnessed this disintegration of the Mao-Khrushchev relation, remained quiet throughout.

Khrushchev then raised the radio station issue. Mao rejected the idea of Soviet financing. China would finance and own the facility, while the Soviet Union could cooperate with China in its operation. Fine, said Khrushchev; the Soviet Union accepted the Chinese proposal.[51] The Soviet leader then raised the possibility of the complete withdrawal of Soviet advisors from China. In the context of the tense confrontation this was clearly an implicit threat. During 1957, some of the large number of Soviet advisors in China had gotten into various sorts of trouble, and China had raised these problems with the Soviet side. Now Khrushchev escalated this to a threat of complete withdrawal. Ignoring but certainly understanding the implicit threat in Khrushchev's words, Mao replied that only a few Soviet advisors had caused trouble. China would give Moscow a list of their names. The rest should stay, Mao said.

Mao and Khrushchev also discussed the struggle against the United States. US strength was very limited, Mao insisted. The United States feared the socialist countries far more than the socialist countries feared the United States. It was necessary to intensify the struggle against the United States and in this fashion delay a war with the United States by perhaps ten, fifteen, or twenty years. International tension was disadvantageous to the United States, Mao said, because the revolutionary camp could use tension to mobilize people to oppose the United States. In his memoir, Khrushchev described this exchange beside Mao's swimming pool in Zhongnanhai. It is worth quoting at some length, because it exemplifies well the apprehensions that were to lead Moscow to draw back from alliance with the PRC:

> From what he'd said in Moscow a year earlier [at the November 1957 conference], I was already familiar with some of this ideas; but during our talks around the swimming pool . . . he went further than I'd ever heard him go before. "Let's try to imagine a future war," he began. He sounded just like Stalin, who also loved to raise hypothetical questions of that sort. 'How many divisions does the United States have? We know the population of the United States, so we can figure out how many divisions the Americans could raise if they conscripted their able-bodied men.' Then he went down the list of the other capitalist countries: England, France, and so on. 'Now,' he continued, 'how many divisions can we raise? Consider the population of China, of the Soviet Union, and the other socialist countries, and you'll see what I mean.' He smiled at me as though to say, 'See how the balance of power is in our favor?'
>
> I was too appalled and embarrassed by his line of thinking even to argue with him. To me, his words sounded like baby talk. How was it possible for a man like this to think such things? For that matter, how was it possible for him to have risen to such an important post? 'Comrade Mao,' I said, 'you're making a fundamental error in your calculations. . . . Battles are no longer won with bayonets, or bullets. . . . In the age of missiles and nuclear bombs, the number of divisions on one side or the other has practically no effect on the outcome of a battle. A hydrogen bomb can turn whole divisions into so much cooked meat. One bomb has an enormous radius of destruction.' . . . Mao's only reply was that he'd grown up as a guerrilla warrior; he was used to battles in which rifles and bayonets . . . played the key role. Later, when I informed our leadership about my conversation with Mao, everyone was perplexed; no one supported Mao's point of view. We couldn't understand how our ally, a man who we already sensed had aspirations to be the leader of the world Communist movement, could have such a childish outlook on the problem of war. Mao had given us a lot of food for thought.[52]

One crucial matter that Mao did not raise with Khrushchev during the July 31–August 3, 1958, discussions was China's plans to initiate an artillery bombardment of the Nationalist-held islands of Jinmen and Mazu (then known as Quemoy and Matsu).[53] Figure 5-2 shows the location of these two islands. While failing to inform Khrushchev about this significant point, however, Mao made clear to the Soviet leader his expectation that in the event of war with the United States, China expected to cooperate closely with the Soviet Union. Early in the discussion of the "joint fleet" during Khrushchev's visit, Ambassador Yudin, seconded by Khrushchev, said that Moscow might invite

FIGURE 5-2 The Offshore Islands

Vietnam to join the "joint fleet" in the event of war. Wartime was "another matter," Mao retorted. Mao returned to this point later in the discussion. In the event of war, Mao said, China would certainly establish a "joint company" with the Soviet Union. Mao made it clear that in the event of war with the United States, China expected the USSR and the PRC to stand together.

The 1958 Taiwan Strait Crisis and Revolutionary Mobilization

Twenty days after Khrushchev departed Beijing, Mao demonstrated what he felt was the correct way to deal with US imperialism. On August 23, PLA artillery began intense bombardment of the Nationalist islands of Jinmen and Mazu. By launching the bombardment so soon after Khrushchev's visit, Mao created the impression that the Soviet leader had agreed to the move.[54] President Eisenhower went so far as to accuse Khrushchev of instigating the move against Jinmen and Mazu. It soon became apparent to the United

States and the Chinese Nationalists that the military purpose of the bombardment was to prevent resupply of the islands, forcing their garrisons to surrender.[55] Intense artillery bombardment continued until October 6, when Defense Minister Peng Dehuai announced a ceasefire. After that, bombardment was reduced to every other day, effectively ending the danger to resupply of the island garrisons. The bombardment was preceded and paralleled by an intense propaganda campaign calling on the country to prepare to defeat a US invasion and liberate Taiwan, both of which events were proclaimed to be imminent.

In 1958, as in 1954, there were disagreements between Washington and Taipei over the wisdom of strong defense of Jinmen and Mazu. Over the preceding several years, Chiang Kai-shek had deployed to those two islands some 30 percent of Nationalist military forces, in defiance of US advice that Taiwan's defense perimeter be drawn down the middle of the Taiwan Strait. Chiang Kai-shek rejected US advice, seeing it as part of US support for "Taiwan independence" and designed to separate Taiwan from the China mainland—a perennial suspicion of Chiang's, one not entirely without some basis in US policy, and one which he shared with his hated rival in Beijing, Mao Zedong. In any case, the deployment of such a large portion of Nationalist military power to the offshore Islands meant that their fall to the PLA by blockade and non-resupply would, in fact, grievously diminish the defensibility of Taiwan itself, through both the loss of troop strength and KMT demoralization caused by anger at US betrayal. Consequently, US leaders decided to commit US power to the defense of the two tiny islands. The largest concentration of US naval power in the Pacific since 1945, and the most powerful nuclear navy yet seen, soon assembled in the vicinity of Taiwan. The United States also conspicuously deployed eight-inch howitzers capable of firing tactical nuclear warheads. The US navy drew up plans to bomb Chinese military bases as far north as Shanghai. In the event, US warships escorted convoys of Nationalist resupply ships only up to the twelve-mile territorial limit around the islands, while PLA artillery carefully abstained from targeting US warships. But while both Beijing and Washington eventually acted with restraint, the 1958 Taiwan Strait confrontation was real and carried the danger of escalation, inadvertent or possibly intentional, to the level of a PRC-US war.

As with virtually all of Mao's decision, the offshore bombardment involved a combination of international and domestic factors aimed at promoting revolution. According to Wu Lengxi, the primary objective of the 1958 bombardment was to warn the Nationalists not to make trouble along the China coast.[56] The Nationalists had been conducting small-scale intelligence and reconnaissance raids along the China coast. Mao was preparing to plunge China into the most radical phase of the Great Leap Forward and wanted to discourage the KMT from trying to utilize the inevitable discontent. A secondary objective behind Mao's launching of the crisis, according to Wu Lengxi, was to assist the Arab people's revolutionary struggle by forcing the United States to deploy forces to the western Pacific. Waves from Egypt's Nasserite revolution and the 1956 Suez War continued to shake the Middle East in 1958.[57] In July 1958, a Nasserite coup had overthrown Iraq's British-backed monarchy. The day after the Iraq coup, Lebanon requested US intervention to uphold the government. Washington agreed, and a US force of 14,000 was put ashore to defend the Lebanon government, while a fleet of seventy ships with 40,000 sailors maneuvered offshore.

Mao saw Middle East events of 1958, like the Suez crisis of 1956, as manifestations of the global struggle against US imperialism. The intensifying struggle of the Arab people against US imperialism had transformed the Middle East into a key focus of the global struggle against the United States. The tyranny of distance limited China's ability to directly assist the Arab struggle. But by opening another front of struggle in the Taiwan Strait, China would provide practical Chinese assistance.[58] Mao would tell a visiting Palestine Liberation Organization delegation in 1965: "Our artillery shelled [Jinmen] to engage the imperialists during the revolution in Iraq and the American landing in Lebanon. . . . The enemy should be engaged on all fronts."[59] Mao further elaborated the logic of the 1958 crisis to Soviet foreign minister Andrei Gromyko, who rushed secretly to Beijing on September 6–7 for consultation about the crisis in the Taiwan Strait. The United States had military bases and troops scattered all over the world, creating vulnerability, Mao explained. Causing problems for US imperialism off Taiwan while it was engaged in Lebanon was a way of "hanging" (*jiaosuo*) the United States. Increased tension would also mobilize the people of various regions to struggle against US bases while increasing the burdens born by the US people, Mao explained.[60] China's objective was to "shake up the Americans," whose people feared war with China, Mao explained to Gromyko. Mao did not make it explicit, but implicitly he was showing Khrushchev and the international communist movement how the socialist camp should deal with US imperialism.

As noted earlier, Mao had not given Khrushchev warning about the bombardment during their August meeting in Beijing. According to Wu Lengxi, the first Chinese communication with the Soviet Union regarding the bombardment came on the evening of September 5 (two weeks after the shelling began, and the day before Gromyko arrived) when Zhou Enlai briefed a counselor of the Soviet embassy on the situation. Zhou assured the Soviet representative that China's aims were limited and that it did not intend to attack Taiwan. Moreover, if the United States launched a war, China would take complete responsibility. The Soviet Union would absolutely not be involved; it would not be pulled into the water, Zhou averred.[61]

The next day, September 6, Zhou proposed resumption of US-PRC ambassadorial talks to find a peaceful solution to the problem. This move marked a shift in approach by Beijing and signaled the easing of tension. The same day as Zhou's statement, Gromyko arrived in Beijing to discuss the situation. Mao explained to Gromyko that Beijing's objective was essentially psychological. Yet Mao also reiterated Zhou's earlier assurance that in case of war with the United States, China would not expect or seek Soviet entry. Gromyko was relieved by Mao's assurances and "approved" of the Chinese approach.[62] According to Gromyko's account, Zhou indicated that China was prepared for all-out war with the United States. Gromyko paraphrased Zhou as saying, "Inflicting blows on the offshore islands, the PRC has taken into consideration the outbreak in this region of a local war between the United States and the PRC, and it is now ready to take all the hard blows, including atomic bombs and the destruction of its cities."[63] In the event of a US-PRC war, Zhou reportedly told Gromyko, the Soviet Union should remain neutral "even if the Americans used tactical nuclear weapons." Only if the United States resorted to "larger nuclear weapons" should the Soviet Union "respond with a nuclear counterstrike." Mao told Gromyko that if it came to war with the United States, China would draw US forces into China's interior. Only then should the Soviet Union strike with "all means at its disposal," a reference Gromyko understood to mean a nuclear strike.[64] According to Wu Lengxi, Mao reiterated to Gromyko that in case of war with the United States, China would bear the responsibility and not expect or seek Soviet entry. Gromyko was relieved by and approved of Mao's assurances.[65]

Gromyko also brought with him and presented to Mao a draft of a letter that Khrushchev was prepared to send to Eisenhower (which he did the next day) warning the United States that an attack on the PRC would be deemed to be an attack on the USSR. Mao found the Soviet letter to be 90 percent correct, and had Zhou revise the problematic 10 percent. Khrushchev then sent that China-revised letter to the Americans.[66] In Wu Lengxi's estimate, this and other Soviet statements were "empty cannons," fired only once Moscow understood there was little real danger that the offshore imbroglio would escalate to a PRC-US clash. Tension in the area began to dissipate further on October 6, when Defense Minister Peng Dehuai announced a ceasefire.

After reflecting on Zhou and Mao's comments to Gromyko, Soviet leaders became troubled by the reinterpretation of the terms of the 1950 treaty implicit in those comments. On September 27, the CPSU sent a letter to the CCP responding to Zhou's September 7 comments to Gromyko. What troubled Soviet leaders most was Beijing's unilateral redefinition of the 1950 alliance.[67] The 1950 treaty had stipulated, the reader will remember, that "in the event of one of the Contracting Parties being attacked by Japan or any state allied with her and thus being involved in a state of war, the other Contracting Party shall immediately render military and other assistance by all means at its disposal." Mao's and Zhou's comments to Gromyko on September 7 in effect restricted the obligation to mutual assistance to situations involving use of large-yield nuclear weapons. Zhou's suggestion that the Soviet Union would stay neutral while American armies pushed deep into China and used tactical nuclear weapons against Chinese forces was vastly different from the letter and spirit of the 1950 treaty. Moscow's September 27 letter was a plea for continued close alliance in line with the 1950 treaty. The core Soviet concern was the apparent willingness of CCP leaders to put their own views about China's interests above the solidarity of the international working class, i.e., the USSR. Soviet leaders may also have interpreted Mao's and Zhou's words as a test of Soviet commitment, requiring an unequivocal Soviet response if the alliance was to be upheld. The CPSU response to the Chinese offer said:

> We cannot allow the illusion to be created among our enemies that if an attack is launched against the PRC . . . the Soviet Union will stand on the sidelines as a passive observer. Should the adversary even presume this, a very dangerous situation would be created. It would be a great calamity for the entire Socialist camp, for the Communist working class movement, if, when atomic bombs had begun to fall on the Chinese People's Republic . . . the Soviet Union, possessing terrible weapons which could not only stop but could also devastate our common enemy, would allow itself not to come to your assistance.
>
> . . . .
>
> Thank you for your nobility, that you are ready to absorb a strike, not involving the Soviet Union. However, we believe, and are convinced that you also agree that the main thing now consists of the fact that everyone has seen—both our friends and, especially, our enemies—that we are firm and united . . . which flow from Marxism-Leninism, to defend the camp of Socialism, that the unity of all brother Communist Parties is unshakeable, that we will deliver a joint, decisive rebuff to an aggressor in the event of an attack on any Socialist state.[68]

Mao replied to the Soviet communication with a personal letter to Khrushchev, saying: "We are deeply moved by your boundless loyalty to the principles of Marxism-Leninism and internationalism. In the name of all my comrades-members of the Chinese Communist Party, I express to you my heartfelt gratitude."[69]

War Crisis and the Collectivization of Agriculture and Militarization of Labor

For Mao, international revolutionary struggle against US imperialism was linked to domestic class struggle to push the revolution forward. Mao precipitated the 1958 Straits confrontation in part to manufacture an atmosphere conducive to his program of Stalinist hyperindustrialization. Demonstrating his principled Marxist-Leninist way of dealing with US imperialism in the context of Khrushchev's deepening apostasy and striking a blow in support of the Arab people's revolutionary anti-imperialist struggle were important factors. But the concern dominating Mao's thinking was the course of China's revolution. For China to rapidly industrialize, build socialism, and prepare the transition to communism, China's peasants had to be herded into collectivized communes where their consumption could be held down and their work intensified. Resistance was certain to be strong. An atmosphere of imminent war and invasion was politically useful in overcoming all obstacles. As Mao told a leadership conference at Beidaihe in October 1958, "The bombardment of Jinmen, frankly speaking, was our turn to create international tension for a purpose." Later he told the conference, "War mobilizes the people's spiritual state. . . . Of course we do not now have war, but under this type of armed antagonism, [we] can mobilize all positive forces."[70]

Mao's program of coercive hyperindustrialization faced extremely strong resistance from the ordinary people fated to bear the heavy burdens of Mao's vast ambitions. Full collectivization of agriculture required the final obliteration of family plots and merger of all land into single collective farms. Even small family gardens were merged into collective farms. Under collectivized agriculture, the process through which labor was organized (who did what, how, and for what compensation) was organized by village-level cadres appointed on the basis of their preparedness to use brutal tactics to achieve compliance with the new arrangements. Farmers were compensated for their labor with pay determined by cadres, often in the form of rations of food or cloth and other essentials rather than in cash. Moreover, under Mao's Great Leap policies, labor was organized along military lines, with production teams and brigades working under military-like discipline. By winter 1958, three hundred million people had been enrolled in militias. Family homes were closed down and people moved to barracks segregated by sex. Husbands and wives slept separately. Wood from demolished homes provided fuel for backyard "blast furnaces" that transformed useful metal goods and tools, also taken from family homes, into crude ingots of often useless metal alloy. Meals were prepared and eaten in communal mess halls rather than in family kitchens. The quality of meals in communal mess halls was often poor and bland, while perverse incentives to eat as much as one could soon set in. Children were shuffled into collective day-care centers. One purpose of these arrangements was to free female labor from tasks like cooking, housecleaning, and tending children so they could work in the fields.

The one resource that China had in abundance, labor, was mobilized, with minimal need for the employer of that labor, the proletarian state, to pay for it. Most important of all, the agricultural harvest now went directly from fields into cadre-controlled warehouses, and was no longer subject to "theft" by those who labored to produce the crops. Levels of "procurement" demanded by state organs rose rapidly as a vicious cycle of elite hubris and lower-level toadying to superiors set in. As more and more of the agricultural produce was taken by the state, less and less was left to feed the people who grew the crops. Loss of a ration book or deprivation of a food ration because of some offense was tantamount to a death sentence. According to scholar Frank Dikötter, the very real threat of starvation via loss of one's ration card became a major mechanism of social control as agricultural production collapsed under these insane policies. Mass starvation spread. Yet the entire system worked to provide the state with large agricultural "surpluses" used to finance accelerated hyperindustrialization.

Mao could not, of course, foresee the exact parameters of popular resistance as he maneuvered China into the Great Leap Forward, but he understood quite well that farmers would resist the new arrangements. People would be reluctant to lose their homes, their family gardens, their family lands. "Land to the tiller" had been the popular slogan on which the CCP had won power after 1946. The collectivization of 1958 marked the final move by the party to take that land away. People would no longer work their own land for their own benefit; they would work collective land for the collective benefit. People would resent being separated from their spouses and their children and having their houses seized and perhaps destroyed, along with metal items. They would resent being bossed about by cadres who had the power of life and death over them. They would resent the extremely long and hard labor demanded of them, with compensation barely adequate to keep them alive. Mao understood that there would be strong resistance to "the construction of socialism." That, after all, was the lesson of Stalin's collectivization of agriculture from 1928 to 1934, of Hungary in 1956, and of the upwelling of criticism during the Hundred Flowers campaign. (The Hundred Flowers was brief period of encouragement and apparent toleration of intellectual dissent in 1957 that preceded the repression of the Great Leap.) Again, propaganda, exhortation, and terror could help control mass resistance. But it's hard to militarize a society without a military crisis. With the threat of imminent war with the United States, the justification for heavy demands on the people to finance crash industrialization and military development would be obvious. To protect the socialist motherland from attack and invasion, the people would be willing to bear even heavy sacrifices. As Mao explained to a PRC State Council meeting on September 5, 1958:

> [I]s it true that tension always harms us? Not exactly, in my opinion. How can tension benefit us instead of harming us? Because tension . . . may serve to mobilize forces and awaken inactive strata and intermediate sections. The fear of atomic war demands a second thought. Just look at the shelling of Jinmen and Mazu islands . . . Such a few shots and there was such a drastic storm and the towering smoke of gunpowder. It is because people fear war, they are afraid of disasters the United States

might randomly cause. . . . Lenin touched on this when referring to war, saying that war rallies people and intensifies man's mind. There is no war now, of course, but the tension of military confrontation can also mobilize positive elements, as well as set inactive strata to thinking.[71]

Mao's strategy achieved its purposes. The vision of US invasion and nuclear attack helped justify the misery inflicted on the Chinese people by the Great Leap Forward, perhaps the greatest famine in modern history.

6 }

Sino-Indian Conflict
and the Sino-Soviet Alliance

Eruption of the Sino-Indian Conflict

The year 1959 was a turning point in Sino-Soviet relations. Three Soviet policies touching on Moscow's commitment to China dismayed Mao. First, Moscow refused to support China in its confrontation with India. Then Moscow scrapped the 1957 nuclear weapon cooperation agreement. Finally, Khrushchev undertook a pathbreaking visit to the United States, followed by a personal effort to mediate Sino-American conflict—all this contrary to Beijing's urging of a more confrontational approach to the United States. For its part, Moscow was reevaluating the possible costs of alliance with Beijing.

By 1959, India had become an important diplomatic partner for the Soviet Union. By precipitating a conflict with India, which Khrushchev believed is what Mao did in 1959, Mao engineered a situation in which Moscow had to choose between China and India. Khrushchev refused to make such a choice. In Mao's eyes, Soviet neutrality in the Sino-Indian dispute was sheer class betrayal.

There were two aspects of the Sino-Indian conflict that flared starting in 1959: the border and Tibet. The existence of serious territorial conflict between China and India emerged in 1958 when Chinese media revealed the recent construction of a truck road from Kashgar in western Xinjiang to Lhasa, capital of the Tibet Autonomous Region (TAR). The road crossed a high, remote, desolate, and cold desert region known as Aksai Chin. China believed this region had traditionally been part of Tibet. India believed it had traditionally been part of north Indian kingdoms, abandoned by British colonial strategists who lacked loyalty to the integrity of India's national territory.[1] The road was important for the PLA, since it was the only road into Tibet open year-round when the other two routes from China proper were closed by heavy snowfall. Roads were essential for China's effective occupation of Tibet.

The subsistence economy of that poor region simply could not support large numbers of soldiers and administrative cadres. Supplies for such personnel had to be trucked in from China proper or from India via the Chumbi Valley. PLA surveying for the Aksai Chin road—which followed an old caravan route—started in October 1951. Construction on the road began in 1955, and the road was opened in October 1957. The existence of the road was unknown to India's government until 1958, when China's media carried articles about it. Revelation of China's Aksai Chin road was, in the words of the official Indian history of the 1962 war, a "rude shock to India."[2] Figure 6-1 shows the alignment of China's four supply lines into Tibet circa 1959.

Indian Prime Minister Jawaharlal Nehru had raised the territorial issue with Zhou Enlai several times during the 1950s. On those occasions, Zhou had downplayed the issue, saying that various maps objectionable to India were merely holdovers from the pre-1949 era and that the PRC had simply not yet had time to change the old maps and print new ones. On another occasion, Zhou strongly implied that China accepted a line drawn on a map along what

FIGURE 6-1 **China's Four Routes into Tibet, circa 1959**

was then understood to be the crest line of the eastern Himalayan Mountains east of Bhutan, known as the McMahon line after the British diplomat who drew it at a 1914 conference. The sudden revelation of the Aksai Chin road and the long period of previously unknown Chinese road-building activity in that region jarred India. A small map included in one of the 1958 articles showed the area south of the McMahon line—an area of about 90,000 square kilometers—as part of China. The Indian realization that from Beijing's perspective India's entire border with Tibet was undefined, with large tracts of territory claimed by China, prompted Indian efforts to actively assert control over what it felt was Indian territory. Nehru ordered Indian forces to more actively assert Indian control by patrolling and setting up outposts in territory India believed was its own.

In the midst of this escalating (but still not lethal) border conflict, an uprising against Chinese rule broke out in Lhasa, capital of Tibet, on March 10, 1959. Here a bit of background is necessary. Tibet is a vast, extremely rugged, thinly populated, and strategically located region. Since the thirteenth century, China's emperors had had a unique relation with the Buddhist monasteries that ruled Tibet. The Yuan and Qing dynasties that ruled from 1279 to 1368 and 1644 to 1911 respectively chose Tibetan "Lamaist," or more properly Vajrayana, Buddhism as their dynastic religion in order to hinder the assimilation of their native peoples by the far more numerous Chinese. In line with this, select monasteries in Tibet were invited to send priests to Beijing to instruct the imperial court and that court's non-Chinese ethnic base in religious matters and conduct religious ceremonies. Thus, for some 280 years, China's emperor and the centers of ruling monastic power in Tibet had a very close relationship—much closer, in fact, that that between the emperor and tributary rulers of kingdoms surrounding China. Imperial-Tibetan relations were both closer and more equal than China's run-of-the-mill tributary relations.

In terms of ways of life, however, Tibetans and Chinese were different in many important ways: language, diet, marriage, burial, religion, and mode of governance. With the emergence of Chinese nationalism in the early twentieth century, the Chinese reconceptualized what it meant to be Chinese, and concluded that Tibetans were part of the family of peoples that made up the new, multinational, multiethnic China. The fact that Tibet was not, and in fact had never been, under effective Chinese administration was attributed, by the Chinese nationalist narrative, to imperialist interference. This became the common Chinese nationalist narrative, but not a common Tibetan one. As CCP power swept across China in 1949, that party's leaders were determined that Tibet would be integrated into the national revolutionary process. The PLA occupied Tibet in 1951 and immediately began building a network of roads that could support a more robust military presence in the region. The Aksai Chin road was one of those roads.

Many, possibly most, Tibetans believe that they are not Chinese but Tibetan, and that their land, Tibet, has historically been and should remain distinct from China. Whatever may have been the relation between Tibetan monasteries and China's imperial court in centuries long past, many Tibetans believe the land of Tibet is the land of the Tibetan people, not part of China. These notions of Tibetan nationalism did not spring into full-blown existence in the 1950s, but emerged only gradually as Tibet was drawn into the Chinese revolutionary process. Probably few Tibetans thought in such sweeping political terms in the 1950s, and many initially welcomed the CCP as promising a materially better life. As more and more Chinese—soldiers, road construction crews, administrative cadres—poured into Tibet in the 1950s, a sense mounted among Tibetans that their land was being taken over by the Chinese. Clashes in ways of life between deeply religious Tibetans and the militant atheism of the CCP jarred. The Tibetan Autonomous Region (TAR) was exempted from the socialist reforms that began in the mid-1950s (collectivization of land, seizure of private property, suppression of religion). But ethnically Tibetan areas of Sichuan, Qinghai, Gansu, and Yunnan were not exempt and were drawn into the maelstrom of the transition to socialism. As lands and herds were collectivized and monasteries and religion repressed in those ethnically Tibetan areas outside the TAR, many Tibetans fled to the TAR, and especially its capital, Lhasa. By 1959, Lhasa's population had doubled, swollen with Tibetan refugees from communist rule. An armed insurgency among the Kham Tibetan tribes of western Sichuan added further to the sense of crisis. There was increasing Tibetan talk of armed resistance to the "Chinese invasion."

In early March a rumor began circulating in Lhasa that the PLA command in that city planned to detain the Dalai Lama, whom most Tibetans viewed as a living god, a reincarnation of a bodhisattva of compassion, and the political and spiritual head of the Tibetan government and people. As the rumor spread, crowds of Tibetans spontaneously assembled outside the Dalai Lama's palace in Lhasa to "protect" him. Demands for Tibetan independence and the withdrawal of Chinese from Tibet welled up. Crowds quickly became mobs and began attacking symbols of Chinese authority. Demonstrations spread to other towns and became a virtual national uprising of the Tibetan people. In the midst of the confusion, the Dalai Lama fled clandestinely to India. The PLA quickly went to work suppressing the rebellion in a ruthless and effective fashion. Thousands were killed, and tens of thousands of Tibetans fled to northern India.[3]

India, like China, had a long and special relation with Tibet—not political, as in China's case, but economic and religious. Trade between India and the Lhasa region was much easier than between that region and China proper. Successive waves of Indian religious ideas had shaped Tibetan Buddhism for over a millennium. Tibet's monastic system derived from India. Ordinary

Indians recognized India's long influence on Tibetan civilization. This contributed to a spontaneous eruption of sympathy for the Tibet uprising of
March 1959. Indian media and politicians strongly sympathized with the
Tibetan uprising and condemned the brutal PLA repression. Indian Prime
Minister Jawaharlal Nehru tried to moderate this criticism, but he also
accommodated it to a degree. Nehru welcomed the Dalai Lama into India,
granted him refugee status, and established camps in Indian frontier regions
for refugees from Tibet. Over the next several years, these camps would become bases of support for ongoing armed and CIA-assisted Tibetan resistance to Chinese rule in Tibet.

The CCP viewed the Tibetan uprising as an attempt by the land owning
Tibetan ruling class to uphold their system of exploitation and domination, thereby preventing the "liberation" of the Tibetan laboring class by the
Chinese Communist Party. But how was it possible that so many people in
Tibet could have been duped into opposing the CCP's enlightened path? Mao
quickly assigned responsibility for the Tibetan uprising to India and especially Nehru. Nehru was responsible for stirring up trouble in Tibet, Mao
concluded.

The Politburo met in Shanghai on March 25 to consider the situation
in Tibet. Discussion focused on the many bad things that India was doing
to encourage resistance in Tibet. But China would keep quiet for a while,
give India enough rope to hang itself, and settle accounts later, Mao ordered. Mao directed that a polemic exposing India's instigation of the
Tibet disturbance be prepared, and personally shepherded that process
over the next several weeks, intervening to make it strongly and openly
directed at Nehru.[4] When *Renmin ribao* submitted a draft of the polemic
to Mao, he rejected it. The target should not be generic "imperialists," Mao
instructed, but "Indian expansionists" who "want ardently to grab Tibet"
(*wangtu ba xizang nale guochu*). Several days later at a Politburo meeting,
Mao asked about the status of the editorial and insisted that the criticism
of Nehru should "be sharp, don't fear to irritate him, don't fear to cause
him trouble."[5] Nehru had miscalculated the situation, Mao said, believing
that China could not suppress the rebellion in Tibet and would have to beg
for India's help.

The polemic against Nehru appeared as a *Renmin ribao* editorial in May.[6]
Nehru was condemned for the "impressive welcome" he had given to the
Dalai Lama. Nehru, the polemic asserted, was barring the return of the
Dalai Lama and Tibetan refugees to China. A "tiny number of people" in
India were waging a "slander campaign against China," criticizing China's
exercise of its sovereign rights in its own territory (i.e., military repression
of the Tibetan uprising), calling for submission of the Tibet issue to the
United Nations, and calling Tibet a "country." Toward its end, the long

polemic warned the "tiny number of people trying to continue fanning the flames":

> So long as you do not end your anti-Chinese slander campaign, we will not cease hitting back. We are prepared to spend as much time on this as you want to. We are prepared, too, if you should incite other countries to raise a hue and cry against us.

The day the *Renmin ribao* polemic appeared, Zhou Enlai met with representatives of socialist countries to explain the situation and ask for solidarity. Nehru's "class nature" was counterrevolutionary, Zhou explained. Nehru opposed reform in Tibet because he wanted that region to remain backward so that it could serve as a "buffer" between India and China. This was the central aspect of the situation and of the Sino-Indian conflict, Zhou said. A section of the Indian ruling class wanted Tibetan independence so that Tibet could become an Indian protectorate.[7]

Beijing's estimates of Nehru's policy were wildly inaccurate. Nehru imagined that he was pursuing a policy of friendship toward China, including recognizing and even supporting China's control of Tibet. At the UN in 1950, Nehru declined invitations from the United States, Britain, and Central American states (who had their own reasons for opposing big-country domination of weak countries) to join in opposition to Chinese moves toward Tibet. In 1951, Nehru lobbied the Dalai Lama to return to Beijing and cut the best deal he could with the CCP, an approach that led to the seventeen-point agreement of May 1951 between Beijing and the Dalai Lama, an agreement that constituted the legal basis for China's "peaceful liberation" of Tibet. In 1954, Nehru recognized Chinese sovereignty over Tibet—without insisting on a quid pro quo on the border. Before China's new roads into Tibet opened, supplies for the growing numbers of Chinese stationed in Tibet came largely from India via the Chumbi Valley. When the CIA began operations with Tibetan rebels in 1957, Nehru may well have known about those operations, but there is no evidence he or India supported them.[8] Nehru probably saw CIA activities as a factor likely to prompt Beijing to seek Indian cooperation on Tibet. Nehru was in fact trying to persuade Beijing not to militarize the Tibet-India border region and to grant Tibet a degree of autonomy out of deference to Indian sensitivities, but to accomplish all these things on the basis of Indian acceptance of Chinese rule over Tibet. As a progressive and secular man of the left, Nehru even had a good deal of sympathy with the efforts of socialist China to reform "feudal" Tibet. Indian-Chinese solidarity was at the core of Nehru's romantic vision of the future world order, and he did not intend to have that partnership founder on Tibet. And yet Mao quickly concluded that Nehru was fanning the Tibet uprising in an effort to "grab Tibet." The vicious, direct, and open Chinese polemical attack on

Nehru brought Nehru's romantic handling of China policy under growing criticism in India. Nehru responded to that criticism by trying to show that he was tough-minded in dealing with China. Both Chinese and Indian policy were moving toward confrontation.

The uprising in Tibet and the growing movement of Tibetans to and from India caused the PLA to establish firmer control over forward areas. Simultaneously, Indian patrols were pushing into territory that New Delhi believed was Indian although previously unoccupied. The inevitable clash occurred near Longju on the eastern Himalayan border in August. One Indian soldier was killed. Another skirmish occurred in Aksai Chin in October. In these and subsequent clashes on the border, the Chinese side was invariably better prepared and acted with greater military effect than the Indian.

The day of the second clash, China's foreign ministry sought the support of Beijing's Soviet ally in the escalating conflict with India. China briefed the Soviet side on recent developments along the border and requested Soviet "understanding" of China's position. Three days later, Moscow replied. The Soviet Union "regretted" the conflict between China and India and blamed it on "those people who plot to create a tense international situation." Beijing took that as veiled attribution to China of responsibility for the clash. Moscow ignored Beijing's request for support and proclaimed itself neutral in the Sino-Indian dispute. Beijing understood Moscow's implicit message: China was to blame for the dispute. By Beijing's reckoning, this was the first time a socialist country had supported a capitalist country against a socialist one. It was also, again by Beijing's reckoning, the first open revelation of disagreements between the CCP and the CPSU.[9]

The Sino-Indian conflict put Moscow in a quandary. India was a leader among the developing countries and was favorably inclined toward the Soviet Union. Indian leftists, including Nehru, were enamored with Soviet-style economic planning and hoped to learn from the USSR in that regard. The ideal of many on the Indian left was to combine Soviet-style economic planning with British-style parliamentary democracy. Relations with the Soviet Union were thus attractive for India. After Stalin's death, India quickly emerged as a favored recipient of Soviet assistance. American aid to India could not (by US law) go to state-sector industrial projects in India. Soviet aid did. The Indian concept of non-alignment in the 1950s envisioned maintaining decent relations with both sides of the Cold War confrontation, and Moscow found this an effective counter to US efforts to "contain" Soviet influence. In 1955, there was an exchange of summit visits by Khrushchev and Nehru. Come 1959, Khrushchev was loath to choose between China and India, and unhappy with Chinese policy for putting him in that situation.

When Khrushchev arrived in Beijing at the end of September shortly after his successful tour of the United States (discussed below), he explained Soviet views in hope that Moscow could avoid a choice between its ally China and its important friend India. China should find a way to improve relations with India, an important neutral country, Khrushchev told China's leaders. Chinese leaders rejected the Soviet appeal. Chen Yi took the lead in rebutting Khrushchev's assertion. Replying "very angrily," according to Wu Lengxi, Chen said that as a socialist country and head of the socialist camp, how was it even possible that the Soviet Union was supporting a capitalist country? The atmosphere of the discussion was "extremely tense." Peng Zhen joined in, leaving an angry Khrushchev to charge the CCP with being "adventurists" and "narrow nationalists." Mao did not join in the confrontation over India, but drew it to a close by saying, "Regarding things concerning China, we hope that our Soviet comrades will listen to China's opinion, understand the situation, first of all consult China, discuss with China, and then take a position. This way will be better."[10] In other words, Mao expected its Soviet ally to follow China's lead in matters involving China's interests. This acrimonious meeting was to be the last between Mao and Khrushchev.

Soviet-American Détente and the Final Mao-Khrushchev Confrontation

In 1959, Soviet-American relations began their first thaw since the onset of the Cold War. In April, John Foster Dulles died and was replaced as Secretary of State by Christian Herter. Moscow welcomed the change as offering a more "realistic" US approach, making détente possible. Contacts between Washington and Moscow expanded rapidly. By July, Eisenhower and Khrushchev were engaged in a private correspondence. The two leaders achieved a degree of rapport and agreed on a number of issues. On August 16, reciprocal summit visits were announced. As Soviet-American ties warmed, Chinese media bitterly polemicized against unnamed people who failed to see that aggression and threat of war by US imperialism continued undiminished.

In June, Moscow had informed Beijing that it was suspending nuclear cooperation with China under the 1957 agreement. In his memoir, Khrushchev said a prototype atomic bomb was packed up and ready to send to China, when a last-minute decision was made not to send it.[11] The reason Moscow gave Beijing for the suspension was that negotiations were underway between the United States and Britain on a test ban treaty, and Soviet-Chinese nuclear cooperation might interfere with those talks.[12] Beijing asked Moscow not to sign a partial test ban treaty (PTBT) with the United States and Britain, on the grounds that such an arrangement would contradict Article III of the 1950 treaty that had provided that neither signatory "would take part in any coalition or actions or measures directed against the other." Moscow declined Beijing's request and moved ahead with the PTBT. On July 25, 1962, the PTBT was initialed by

Washington, London, and Moscow. In effect, Moscow was choosing nuclear cooperation with Washington over nuclear cooperation with the PRC.

Beijing saw Moscow's cancellation of the 1957 nuclear technology agreement with China as a Soviet "gift" to Washington opening the way to Soviet "peaceful coexistence" with the United States, although Beijing would not make this view public until several years later. When the reciprocal state visits by Khrushchev and Eisenhower were announced, *Hong qi*, the theoretical journal of the CCP, gave a detailed exposition of why "peaceful coexistence" with imperialism was impossible. A reduction of tension with imperialism might be possible, but that would only benefit imperialism itself.[13] Tension benefited the efforts of the anti-imperialist forces to mobilize the masses. On September 16, 1959, Khrushchev arrived in the United States for a two-week visit at the invitation of President Eisenhower. This was the first-ever visit by a top Soviet leader to the United States.[14] The only previous time an invitation for such a visit had been issued was in November 1946 by Truman to Stalin. The very day Khrushchev arrived in the United States, *Hong qi* attacked those who mistakenly believed that US imperialism would "lay down the butcher knife and become Buddha." The only effective way to deal with US imperialism was by repeated face-to-face struggle until it was completely defeated. As scholar Donald Zagoria pointed out, the crux of the CCP's thinly veiled criticism of Khrushchev's US policy was that it was undermining the revolutionary struggle of the people throughout the world. US aggression was still running wild, but Khrushchev was proposing that the socialist camp respond to US aggression with negotiation.

Khrushchev's visit was very well received by American people across the country. Most Americans welcomed the easing of Cold War tension, and many fondly remembered the still-recent wartime alliance against Nazi Germany. There was popular hope for a revival of Soviet-American friendship. Khrushchev basked in that warm and enthusiastic reception, and saw his visit as a major diplomatic accomplishment opening a new era in Soviet-US relations. After two weeks of travel filled with often highly emotional (and generally positive) meetings with American leaders and ordinary citizens, Khrushchev flew back to Moscow and then directly on to Beijing to attend the PRC's tenth National Day celebrations on October 1. The next day there was a long discussion between Mao and Khrushchev.[15]

The October 2, 1959, session was the mirror image of the fiery July 22, 1958, meeting between Mao and Khrushchev. In 1958, it had been Mao who provoked his counterpart. This time it was Khrushchev, inspired perhaps by his recent success in America, who was provocative and needled Mao about his shortcomings. Khrushchev raised the matter of five American citizens being held in Chinese prisons at the beginning of the talks and then returned repeatedly to it.[16] Eisenhower had brought this issue up with Khrushchev and asked him to raise it in Beijing during his upcoming visit there, Khrushchev told Mao. Mao replied to Khrushchev "with obvious displeasure and testily," according to the Russian transcript, and refused to budge on the American prisoners.

Khrushchev raised the issue of the failure of Mao to inform him in July 1958 before shelling the Offshores. Mao, backed by Zhou, insisted that the PLA General Staff Department had, in fact, informed the senior Soviet military advisor in China of those intentions a month before the bombardment began. The man had reported, Khrushchev said, but had said nothing about a plan to bombard the Offshores. Probably the notification that Mao and Zhou mentioned had been designed to be so low-key as to draw no notice that might precipitate Soviet intervention to block the planned action, but provide a basis for later insisting that notification had in fact been given. In any case, Khrushchev complained during the 1959 meeting that because a "prewar situation" had existed regarding Taiwan, and because the Soviet Union was compelled [by the 1950 treaty] to publicly declare its willingness to defend the PRC in the event of "aggravation" of the situation over Taiwan, understandings that might exist confidentially between Beijing and Moscow could be very dangerous.[17] "We would think you ought to look for ways to relax the [Taiwan] situation," Khrushchev said. The Soviet leader mentioned Lenin's establishment of an ostensibly independent Far Eastern Republic in 1920 as an example of the sort of flexibility Moscow had in mind.[18]

This suggestion was not well received by the Chinese side. Mao and Zhou both insisted that relations with Taiwan would be discussed with Chiang Kai-shek, and US relations with Taiwan would be discussed with the United States. Implicitly, Moscow didn't have a role regarding Taiwan—other than supporting Beijing when it found itself in a confrontation with the United States. "You always refuse to work out [with us] a policy on this question [of Taiwan] that we can understand," Khrushchev complained. "[W]e do not know what kind of policy you will have on this issue tomorrow." Why bombard a place and create a crisis if you didn't intend to seize that place, Khrushchev wanted to know. The Soviet leader completely failed to understand (as did almost everyone at the time) that Mao's deliberate precipitation of the Straits crisis in August 1958 was more about domestic policy than about foreign policy.

Khrushchev then turned to the clash on the Sino-Indian border in August that had left several Indians dead and precipitated a crisis. "Do you really want us to approve of your conflict with India?" Khrushchev asked Mao. "It would be stupid on our part." When the Chinese side argued that the Indian side had been the first to open fire, Khrushchev still insisted that China could and should have found a way to resolve the conflict peacefully in order to win over "fellow-traveler" Nehru to the socialist side in the world struggle. About halfway through the session, Mao became quiet and let other members of the Chinese delegation, one after the other, assault Khrushchev. Chen Yi, Lin

Biao, Peng Zhen, and Liu Shaoqi all took a shot. These angry challenges by China's second-tier leaders led Khrushchev to charge Chinese leaders with arrogance:

> KHRUSHCHEV: "Aren't you talking to us too haughtily?. . . . You do not tolerate objections, you believe you are orthodox, and this is where your haughtiness reveals itself. . . . You want to subjugate us to yourself, but nothing will come of it, we are also a party and have our own way." [Chen Yi became especially agitated, charging the Soviets with being "time-servers," i.e., opportunists.]
>
> KHRUSHCHEV: If you consider us time servers, Comrade Chen Yi, then do not offer me your hand. I will not accept it.
>
> CHEN: Neither will I. I must tell you I am not afraid of your fury.
>
> KHRUSHCHEV: You should not spit from the height of your Marshal title. You do not have enough spit. We cannot be intimidated. What a pretty situation we have. On one side, you use the formula "headed by the Soviet Union." On the other hand, you do not let me say a word. What kind of equality can we talk about?[19]

When Mao tried toward the end of the discussion to turn the discussion to Laos, where China had major and real security interests, Khrushchev replied: "Good, let us do this, but I have not [the] slightest interest in this matter, for this is a very insignificant matter, and there is much noise about it." Mao then concluded the discussion by reiterating that in August 1958 "we did not intend at all to undertake any kind of large-scale military actions there." Conveying that message to his Soviet ally two weeks before opening fire rather than a year after would perhaps have had a very different effect.

Khrushchev had planned a seven-day stay in Beijing, but left after three days.[20]

Mao sensed that a break was imminent and did not want to bear the blame for it. After this final acrimonious confrontation with Khrushchev, Mao buttonholed the Soviet chargé Sergei Antonov and told him that CCP-CPSU differences were only "one half finger" out of ten, that Khrushchev spoke very "firmly and correctly" about Taiwan in his talks with Eisenhower, and that China's bombardment of the Offshores had assisted the Soviets in Berlin and elsewhere in Europe.

Intensified Polemical Combat and the Withdrawal of Soviet Advisors

In January 1960, the CCP Politburo met to discuss relations with the United States and the Soviet Union. In spite of the serious problems associated with "food supply" (i.e., the famine sweeping the country) and in spite of the declarations by the Chinese Nationalists that their "Return to the Mainland" was not far distant, CCP leaders concluded that an American attack on China was not likely.[21] In this situation, an intensification of the polemical struggle against the revisionist mistakes of Khrushchev and the CPSU was in order. Khrushchev's errors were many and serious, and it was necessary to intensify the struggle against them. Under the guidance of Mao—who again dominated the process—the Politburo decided on a formula of "unity, struggle, unity." The purpose of intensified polemical struggle against Khrushchev's "errors" would be unity with the CPSU, but unity on the basis of principle reached by struggle.

Khrushchev was not a "systematic opportunist," Mao said, but was "easily changeable." Mao cited a number of instances in which Khrushchev had changed in response to pressure from the CCP: in 1956 over Poland and Hungary, in 1957 over the contents of the November declaration, and in 1958 over the "joint fleet." There were also a number of factors pushing Khrushchev to uphold Marxist-Leninist principles. There were still many genuine Marxist-Leninists within the CPSU. Many communist parties around the world also embraced Marxist-Leninist principles. Wars of national liberation would continue in spite of Khrushchev's efforts to stop them. Moreover, the United States would not do what Khrushchev wished. And China was a big country that Khrushchev would be reluctant to alienate. For all these reasons, Mao concluded, while there was a "relatively small" possibility that intensified polemical struggle against Khrushchev would lead to "an open split in the socialist camp." "This possibility is not very great," Mao said. This was a major miscalculation. The intensified polemic that began in April was, in fact, the straw that broke the camel's back, and it pushed Khrushchev to recall Soviet advisors from China, thereby escalating the dispute from the party-to-party to the state-to-state level.

On April 16, 1960, *Hong qi* issued a forty-page article entitled "Long Live Leninism" and commemorating the ninetieth anniversary of Lenin's birth. The article did not explicitly target the CPSU; Tito and Yugoslav "modern revisionists" were the nominal target. This too had been stipulated by Mao at the January Politburo discussion. Khrushchev understood clearly that he and the CPSU were the real targets. The core message of "Long Live Leninism" was the aggressive nature of US imperialism and how to deal with it. US imperialism was conducting all sorts of "sabotage and subversion" against the socialist countries. The way to deal with this imperialist aggression was not to talk about peace and seek to reduce tension with imperialism, but to fan revolutionary anti-imperialist wars across the intermediate zone. The "modern revisionists" aimed to "tamp down" these struggles to reduce tension with imperialism. "Peace in the mouths of Modern Revisionism is intended to whitewash the war preparations of imperialism ... designed to lower the revolutionary standards of the people of various countries and destroy their will." This approach would only encourage and embolden imperialism.

Peaceful coexistence with imperialism—preventing imperialism from attacking the socialist countries—could be achieved only by struggle.

Mao saw 1959 as a turning point for Soviet policy. Up to then, Soviet policy toward China was relatively good. In 1959, however, Khrushchev adopted a new policy, the essence of which was to stand with US imperialism against revolutionary China. For his Politburo comrades, Mao traced Khrushchev's stance to his class character: "Khrushchev represents the boss class, represents the bourgeoisie, he doesn't want revolution, does not want to continue the revolution, doesn't want communism."[22]

Khrushchev had had enough. He returned polemical fire at a Congress of the Romanian Communist Party convened in Bucharest in June 1960.[23] In a meeting with the CCP delegation to the Congress, Khrushchev bitterly attacked Mao and the CCP. If the East Wind prevailed over the West Wind, did that mean that Genghis Khan would return? the Soviet leader sneered. If the CCP esteemed Stalin so much, why didn't they take Stalin's corpse back to China to display? In his public speech to the Congress, Khrushchev clearly implied that the CCP was trying to assume leadership of the world communist movement. The head of the CCP delegation, Peng Zhen, was outraged because the applause given to his speech was noticeably less than that given for Khrushchev's, and the fact that some of the people on the dais had not paid attention while he was speaking. In Beijing, the Politburo met to consider Peng's report on the "surprise attack" underway in Bucharest. Peng was instructed to directly battle against Khrushchev's incorrect line. Peng was not to fear, but also not to push for an open split.

On July 16, 1960, Moscow notified Beijing that all 1,299 Soviet economic advisors and specialists then working in China, along with their dependents, would be withdrawn by September 1. The CCP Politburo met immediately. It decided to accelerate repayment of Soviet loans. A projected sixteen-year repayment period was to be reduced to five.[24] A "trade small group" was set up to oversee collection of commodities to accomplish this purpose. Subordinate special groups were set up in various localities. It was understood that some "hardship" would result. But Mao declared:

> The Yan'an period was hard too, but eating peppers didn't kill anybody. Our situation now is much better than then. We must tighten our belts and struggle to pay off the debt within five years.[25]

In vast areas of China, the possibility of eating peppers was then a desperate dream. By mid-1960, famine produced by Great Leap policies was sweeping China. Malnutrition, starvation, and even cannibalism were widespread. An amazing characteristic of Wu Lengxi's detailed account of CCP-CPSU relations circa 1960 is that China's leaders gave no consideration to the potential economic consequences of a split with the Soviet Union. According to Wu's detailed and authoritative account, ideological and political factors were debated at length, but the first discussion of economic costs of a split with the CPSU occurs only after Moscow's recall of Soviet economic advisors—this while China's economy was collapsing and famine sweeping the land. This oversight must have been because of the ideological fantasy world of the CCP elite. As scholar Donald Zagoria pointed out, it was extremely difficult to imagine circa 1960 that Chinese and Soviet communists, with their powerful shared beliefs, could actually come to blows.[26] One manifestation of this was the Mao-dictated CCP credo of "unity, struggle, unity." The fact that by challenging Moscow's traditional authority to define the line of the international communist movement the CCP was challenging a key instrument of Soviet global influence apparently never entered CCP minds, or if it did, it was dismissed as evidence of Khrushchev's "great power chauvinism."

China's demands on Soviet industry were heavy for the still not very developed Soviet economy to bear. The Soviet Union after 1945 was compelled to assist the development of allied socialist countries even though the Soviet economy was itself devastated by war and not yet as highly industrialized as its propaganda suggested. As Figure 6-2 indicates, China, although it was Moscow's most populous ally, received only $790 million, or about 13 percent of all Soviet aid during the period ending in 1962. China's share was considerably less than East Germany's $1,353 million or Poland's $914 million.[27] Scholar Sidney Klein suggested that resentment at this distribution of Soviet aid was one factor underlying Mao's anger toward the Soviet Union.[28]

Recipients	1945–1962	as % (rounded)	Non-Socialist	1954–1962
Socialist Countries	US$ (millions)		Developing Countries	US$ (millions)
East Germany	1,353	22		
Poland	914	15	India	811
PR China	**790**	**13**	Egypt	509
North Korea	690	11	Afghanistan	507
Outer Mongolia	658	11	Indonesia	369
Bulgaria	569	9	Cuba	300
Hungary	381	6	Iraq	183
North Vietnam	369	6	Syria	151
Albania	246	4	Ethiopia	102
Rumania	189	3		
Czechoslovakia	62	1	**PR China**	**790**
total	6,221			

FIGURE 6-2 **Distribution of Soviet Economic Assistance**

Source: U.S. Department of State, "Soviet Aid to Less-Developed Countries Through Mid-1962," Research Memorandum RSB-173, November 14, 1962. In Sidney Klein, *The Road Divides, Economic Aspects of the Sino-Soviet Dispute,* (International Studies Group: Hong Kong, 1966), p. 66, 68.

It is noteworthy that India, over which Mao presented Khrushchev an either-or choice in 1959, was a major recipient of Soviet aid. After 1954, when Moscow started giving aid to noncommunist developing countries, India's claim on Soviet aid rose rapidly. For the 1954–1962 period, India received $21 million more than the PRC, while thinly populated Afghanistan received 5/8 of the amount of credits extended to far more populous China. From Beijing's perspective, this distribution of Soviet aid reflected a lack of class perspective and was unfair to China.

From Moscow's perspective, not only were aid demands on the Soviet Union a heavy burden, but aid to China was frequently poorly used, especially during the Great Leap Forward. Many Soviet-assisted projects undertaken during the Great Leap were poorly planned. New plants often lacked requisite infrastructure or were disrupted by the demands of Great Leap mass campaigns. Expensive equipment sent from the Soviet Union often sat unused. Maintenance was often ignored to reach inflated production goals. Projects were often pushed through in mass campaign style, with the sound technical advice of Soviet advisors being ignored. Living conditions for Soviet advisors were often atrocious, and their mail, quarters, and belongings were routinely searched by Chinese agents. On several occasions, Soviet advisors were physically attacked. Nor, apparently, did Soviet aid generate a sense of Chinese gratitude toward the Soviet Union.

Nevertheless, it was not because of the misuse of Soviet aid that Moscow suspended aid to China. In a public briefing for Soviet specialists at the Soviet embassy in Beijing shortly after the announcement of the Soviet decision to withdraw advisors, Soviet ambassador Stepan Chervonenko explained that the main reasons for the Soviet decision were disagreement with China's confrontational approach toward the United States and India, the unnecessary aggravation of relations with Yugoslavia, Beijing's excessive friendship for Albania in opposition to Soviet policy, and the efforts of the Chinese Communist Party to supplant the CPSU as the leader of the socialist bloc.[29] Still, there was a positive side of the Soviet aid cutoff for the CCP. In the historical narrative the CCP formulated to explain the famine of 1959–1961, the recall of Soviet advisors was accorded the major role. The CCP was able to blame China's famine on the Soviet move, along with bad weather, rather than on its true cause, the disastrous policies of the CCP.

The Consequences of Mao's Multiple Rash Decisions

Throughout the second half of the 1950s Mao challenged Khrushchev's leadership of the international communist movement step by step. On issue after issue, Mao charged, Khrushchev had made an incorrect analysis and prescribed incorrect policies. On the Stalin question, on relations with the East

European socialist states, on relations with bourgeois nationalist states like Egypt, Iraq, and India, and most of all on relations with the United States, Khrushchev was guided, Mao increasingly concluded, by "revisionist" principles quite different from the militant approaches of Lenin and Stalin. Mao's fundamental objection to Khrushchev's approach had to do with the role of struggle and tension. Mao believed that tension and confrontation facilitated the mobilization of people, first and foremost in the intermediate zone between the West and the socialist camp, but also within the socialist states themselves and within the Western states. Mao sought global upheaval. Khrushchev, on the other hand, was more concerned with reduction of tension to keep his country out of war and ease its heavy burden of military spending.

Mao's aim through 1960 was to strengthen the revolutionary camp by convincing the CPSU that its line was "incorrect," leading that party to embrace "correct" principles advocated by the CCP. Unity, struggle via polemical combat, leading to new unity on the basis of correct principle; this was Mao's objective. Such a confession of ideological error might substantially erode the CPSU's claim to leadership of the world communist movement. To guard against this, Mao ordered that the leading position of the Soviet Union be explicitly upheld. Only the Soviet Union had the strength to provide global leadership. Indeed, the CCP became a firmer advocate of explicit Soviet leadership that Moscow itself. But while explicitly upholding Soviet leadership, Mao advocated an intra-movement decision-making process in which all fraternal parties, or at least important ruling ones, would have an equal say in setting the movement line.

On two critical issues, Mao incorrectly attributed sinister motivations to foreign leaders. First, in August 1958, when Mao determined that Moscow's "joint fleet" proposal was inspired by a "desire to control China." Second, in April 1959, when Mao determined that Nehru was trying to "seize Tibet." The swift way in which Mao arrived at these judgments suggests that they were not deeply reasoned. Had either or both of those judgments been submitted for consideration of China's more prudent leaders or their professional staffs, those judgments would almost certainly would have been discarded or greatly moderated. But Mao's preeminence within the CCP elite was such, and the fate of those who questioned his judgment grim enough, that once Mao rendered a judgment, that judgment was unassailable. Once the Chairman spoke, his words became policy.[30]

Mao also made two other major miscalculations in 1958 and 1960, both of which had dire consequences for China. First, to surprise Khrushchev with the Offshores bombardment. Second, to reckon that Moscow would not respond to intensified polemical attack with an "open break" with China. Regarding the Offshores bombardment, the fact that Mao did not inform Khrushchev of the upcoming move, let alone seek his opinion, during the

Soviet leader's early-August visit to Beijing shook Soviet confidence in Mao. Some Soviet leaders, including Khrushchev, began to suspect that Mao was trying to maneuver the USSR into confrontation with the United States. A less conspiratorial conclusion—that Mao was simply reckless—was hardly more benign. Mao's calculation that Moscow would not respond with "open split" to the April 1960 polemic was also egregiously inaccurate. Moscow responded to "Long Live Leninism" by recalling Soviet advisors.

Mao's errors and miscalculations contributed significantly to the collapse of the Sino-Soviet alliance. Although tension would escalate much further during the 1960s, and although Beijing would not formally abrogate the treaty until 1979, for all intents and purposes the alliance died when Soviet advisors withdrew in mid-1960. Had Mao intended to free himself and China from the burden of alliance with the USSR, his choices might be redeemed. But Mao's repeated references to "unity, struggle, unity" in dealing with the Soviet Union suggest that dissolving the alliance with Moscow was not Mao's objective. Mao romantically expected that the world communist movement, including the CPSU, would embrace his "correct" line and the entire revolutionary camp would struggle with greater effectiveness against US imperialism. The actual result of Mao's policies was something other than this. The schism in the communist camp created a structure of power far more favorable to the US than a relatively united Sino-Soviet camp.

Mao's rupture with Moscow also slowed the pace of China's industrial, scientific, and military development. By the end of 1962, the previously large flow of modern capital goods and military and industrial technology from the Soviet bloc to China had ended.[31] Even though Mao dressed this up in nationalist resentment, it was not at all what he had intended. For the next twenty years, China would advance slowly via an autarkic path. Not until the early 1980s would China, by then under Deng Xiaoping, find a way to again create the large-scale inflow of advanced capital goods and technology into China.

The intense if artificially generated fear of US invasion, combined with intensified struggle against moderate communism, called "revisionism," did, however, help accomplish one of Mao's key goals: moving China toward the collectivist and equalitarian order that Mao envisioned as the end goal of the Chinese revolution. China's farmers became serfs of collectivized agriculture, while the industrial workers labored long and hard for little material recompense.

Reviving Revolutionary Momentum, 1962–1965

Intensification of the Struggle against Revisionism

The economic collapse produced by the Great Leap Forward led to a brief leadership consensus that priority should be given to economic recovery. By late 1960, Mao agreed to "adjustment" of agricultural policies.[1] Communal mess halls were abolished. Private family plots and rural markets were reintroduced. Sideline occupations were again permitted. And the production team, roughly corresponding to the natural village, was made the "basic accounting unit" that determined remuneration. In terms of diplomacy, with relations with Moscow at breaking point and with India collapsing, and with the Nationalists on Taiwan contemplating the implications of the famine wracking the mainland for a Nationalist "return," Beijing sought to minimize difficulties with other neighbors. The Ministry of Foreign Affairs was authorized to reach definitive boundary settlements with Nepal in March and with Burma in April. A treaty of friendship and mutual aid was signed with Mongolia in May 1960. It was also during this period that Zhou Enlai laid before Nehru the proposal of an east-west swap of territorial claims and turning the existing line of actual control into an international boundary. Beijing also moved to reduce conflict with the CPSU. At a conference of eighty-one communist parties in Moscow in December 1960, the CCP agreed with the CPSU to "confer together on anything that might come up so as to avoid conflict."[2] President Liu Shaoqi paid a monthlong friendly visit to the Soviet Union in November–December.

The severe setbacks encountered by Mao's first attempt to forge socialist agriculture, the Great Leap Forward, combined with the apparent takeover of the CPSU by "modern revisionists" who had, Mao concluded, abandoned class struggle, led Mao to ponder the future of China's revolution. It had been clear since Defense Minister Peng Dehuai challenged Great Leap Forward policies during a CC Plenum in August 1959 that some within the CCP elite doubted the wisdom of Mao's Stalinist approach to agriculture. Once adjustment in agricultural policy began in 1961, it quickly became bolder and bolder. As this happened, Mao began to conclude that there were "hidden revisionists" within the CCP elite, people who professed loyalty to him and his correct Marxist-Leninist principles but who in fact wanted to retreat from socialism in the agricultural sector. As the *Short Course* had explained, this was what had happened in the Soviet Union in the mid-1920s during a comparable period of return to private farming and incentives. Stalin had confronted this "bourgeois line," defeated it, and pushed the socialist revolution through to the end.

Soviet experience as laid out in the *Short Course* offered Mao an example of how hidden revisionists could worm their way into a communist party, expand their influence, and ultimately take control and abandon a proletarian class perspective. Stalin had upheld proletarian principles and used the dictatorship of the proletariat to strike down "class enemies" within the party who took a "bourgeois class stance," for example by opposing agricultural collectivization.[3] Khrushchev had abandoned Stalin's intraparty class struggle, and the hidden revisionists in the CPSU had raised their heads and taken over the party. As Mao's colleagues on the CCP Politburo became more and more enthusiastic in 1961–1962 about implementation of family farming and private incentive, it began to dawn on Mao that the same thing was happening with the CCP. Just as Stalin had used the dictatorship of the proletariat to sweep aside those in the Soviet Union who had taken a bourgeois class line, Mao would sweep aside the hidden revisionists within the CCP and push China's socialist revolution "through to the end."

Khrushchev and the CPSU had criticized Great Leap policies as "unscientific" and "left-wing adventurism," although they generally kept those views to themselves until after the 1960 break. By the early 1960s, Soviet objections to the Great Leap were in the open—just as CCP advocates of family farming began to become bold in their efforts at agricultural "readjustment." This was sufficient to cause Mao see a link-up between Moscow and the CCP's "hidden revisionists." Mao also noted that some of the "hidden revisionists" in the CCP had strong Soviet connections. Defense minister and former Korean War commander Peng Dehuai had had extensive contacts and interactions with the Soviet defense establishment. Wang Jiaxiang and Wu Xiuquan (who would advance a "revisionist" program, as described below) were among the Soviet-trained cadres Moscow had tried to use to undermine Mao's leadership in the 1930s. Chen Yun, a key advocate of Soviet-style economic planning and material incentives, had spent several years in the Soviet Union.

The driving force of China's policies became Mao's effort to intensify the struggle against revisionism, international and domestic. Mao did not compartmentalize domestic from international politics. In his mind, the struggle against international revisionism was linked to the struggle against revisionism within China. Exposing and striking at the international revisionists facilitated struggle against domestic revisionists, especially those in power-ful positions within the CCP. Conversely, exposing and rooting out domes-tic revisionists undermined the ability of the international revisionists, the CPSU, to push China's off its correct nonrevisionist socialist path to communism.

Aside from China's peasantry, who Mao realized had a strong propensity to abandon collective farming, the groups in China that genuinely opposed socialism and CCP dictatorship—China's capitalists, large and small, and the intelligentsia—had been thoroughly crushed in the 1950s. By the early 1960s, those groups no longer posed much of a threat to Mao's revolution. There was, however, a truly powerful social group in China who favored abandon-ing the harsh course prescribed by Mao—the powerful people within the CCP who now doubted Mao's quest for utopia. These "hidden revisionists," as Mao called them, favored policies focused on carefully designed economic development, guided by expert managers in accord with plans worked out by experts. In many ways, their approach to development coincided with the approach of the USSR. Should the CCP's "hidden revisionists" succeed in gaining paramount power, displacing Mao one way or the other, their policies would take China down the path of Soviet-style development. Mao dubbed the economic attractiveness of this Soviet-style, revisionism "sugar-coated bullets." They posed a much greater danger to the success of the Chinese rev-olution than did the openly counterrevolutionary forces of Chiang Kai-shek and the United States. The revisionists, domestic and international, could "wave the red flag to oppose the red flag." Keeping China's revolution on the "correct" course, Mao believed by 1962, required intensifying the struggle against both the hidden revisionists within the CCP, who favored Soviet-like development policies, and the CPSU revisionists, who sympathized with the CCP's hidden revisionists and hoped someday to help them take control of China's revolutionary path.

The Wang-Wu-Liu Letter

In February 1962, a letter from the head of the CCP's International Liaison Department (ILD), Wang Jiaxiang, and signed by ILD deputy heads Wu Xiuquan and Liu Ningyi was sent to Zhou Enlai, Deng Xiaoping, and Chen Yi, then premier, secretary general, and foreign minister respectively and together having responsibility for foreign affairs.[4] Wang had trained in the USSR from 1925 to 1930 and was one of a group of Soviet-trained leaders ("the 28 Bolsheviks") foisted on the CCP by the Comintern in the early 1930s. Moscow's efforts at that earlier juncture failed; Wang had been won over by Mao and became one of Mao's main supporters in battles with Moscow-trained CCP would-be leaders. Wang then served as PRC ambassador to the Soviet Union in 1949–1951. Wu Xiuquan had studied and trained in the USSR from 1925 to 1931, becoming a probationary member of the CPSU before returning to China. When Wu signed the 1962 letter, he was an alternate member of the Politburo and first secretary of the CCP committee within the ILD. Liu Ningyi was a CC member active throughout the 1950s in international united front activities involving peace, disarmament, labor, friendship, and Afro-Asian solidarity work.[5]

The Wang-Wu-Liu letter was entirely within proper channels. It was written as China was just beginning to emerge from the Great Leap famine and while tensions with the Soviet Union, India, the United States, and the Nationalist regime on Taiwan were still high. The letter was written, too, in the context of a debate over the question of war and peace, linked to Mao's effort to re-radicalize CCP policy. The Wang-Wu-Liu letter basically argued for a relaxation of international tension and a return to Bandung-era diplomacy, allowing China to concentrate on famine relief and economic recovery. The danger of world war should not be overestimated and the possibility of peaceful coexistence with imperialism should not be underestimated, the letter argued. To facilitate peaceful coexistence, China needed to restrain aid to national liberation movements. China's ability to assist foreign movements should also be limited by its own economic abilities. China should not undertake to do what it could not afford to do, said the letter. Regarding Vietnam, China needed to be careful to avoid another Korea-style war. China should be wary of Khrushchev's efforts to drag China "into [the] trap of war," the letter said.

The Wang-Wu-Liu letter was a bold, brave move constituting, in the view of scholar and historian Zhai Qiang, the only known instance when a PRC agency under Mao offered an alternative to established policy.[6] It also made its authors the target of Mao's suspicions about hidden revisionists. Mao would not tolerate this expression of revisionist thinking. It is not entirely accurate to say that the ILD letter opposed Mao's revolutionary approach to foreign affairs. More accurately, Mao's revolutionary approach emerged, in part, out of deliberation on the Wang-Wu- Liu letter. Mao targeted the ILD letter during a Central Work Conference at Beidaihe in August 1962 as an example of revisionist trends in foreign policy. The letter advocated, Mao said, "three appeasements and one reduction" (san he, yi shao)—appeasement of Soviet revisionism, US imperialism, and Indian reaction, and reduction of aid to foreign liberation wars. This approach was completely antithetical to Marxist-Leninist principles, akin to the apostasy of the CPSU revisionists, and had to be rejected and struggled against, Mao said.

The Wang-Wu-Liu letter occurred in the context of a Soviet effort to repair Sino-Soviet relations. By 1962, Khrushchev realized that open rupture with Beijing had diminished Moscow's leverage both with the West and within the world communist movement. Many communist parties were dismayed by the disunity within the movement and thought Moscow shared some blame for it. During 1962, Khrushchev avoided further international communist conferences that would invite renewed polemical debates. His objective was to let passions burn out, opening the way to restoration of fraternal ties.[7] Khrushchev also realized that he had acted too rashly when he suspended aid in 1960. The Soviet leader saw himself as a dedicated Marxist-Leninist revolutionary, heir to Lenin and the leader of the global revolutionary struggle. The CPSU and the CCP stood on the same side of that global struggle, Khrushchev believed. It was difficult, therefore, for Khrushchev to understand why Mao and the CCP objected so strongly to Soviet policies. They must arise from Chinese misunderstandings of Soviet policy, Khrushchev concluded.

In line with this analysis, starting in August 1962 Moscow sent occasional messages to Beijing stressing the role of Soviet nuclear forces as a deterrent for the entire socialist camp, messages intended to address what Soviet leaders felt must be China's concerns about the Soviet commitment to China. During the 1962 Sino-Indian war, Moscow also stood by China against India. The culmination of Khrushchev's push for reconciliation came on February 23, 1963, with a carefully drafted letter from the CPSU to the CCP. The letter took a conciliatory tone. Differences between the two parties had been overstated, the Soviet letter said, and could be overcome by comradely discussion. Differences that existed should be understood as a function of the differing circumstances of communist parties in various countries, and not as some sort of ideological apostasy. Open polemics between the two parties should be ended.

Moscow's push for reconciliation foundered on Mao's need for a big fight against revisionism, international and within China, as part of the struggle he was waging to revive the push for socialism in China's countryside. In January 1962—the month before the Wang-Wu-Liu letter—an unprecedented conference of 7,000 cadres (virtually China's entire ruling elite) met in Beijing. President Liu Shaoqi had criticized the Great Leap Forward and called for more pragmatic, production-oriented, and humane rural policies. Other leaders supported Liu. Mao made an unprecedented self-criticism and then absented himself from the policy-making scene for several months, a ploy Mao often used to good effect, allowing his rivals to expose themselves. In the several months after the conference, agricultural policies were laid out that would have restored family farming. What was at stake, Mao believed, was whether China's agricultural sector would be socialist or capitalist—whether socialist agriculture would fuel rapid socialist industrialization, as Stalin and his *Short Course* taught was the correct way, or whether capitalism would be restored in China's countryside. Rather than restore capitalism, Mao proposed a Socialist Education Movement to teach China's peasants that collective farming was good for them. Rather than capitulate to the petit-bourgeois mentality of the peasantry, the CCP should, in Mao's view, remold their thinking and lead them forward to socialism. Mao unveiled his program at a plenary session of the Central Committee in August 1962. As Mao made clear his will, other CCP leaders fell into line behind him and his proposed ideological rejuvenation among China's farmers.[8]

The CPSU's letter of attempted reconciliation arrived while yet another CC work conference focusing on the rural Socialist Education Movement was underway in Beijing. The critical issue under discussion was the use of family farming to increase production, versus collectivized farming to move China toward socialism. Mao had already become convinced that this was a matter of "class stance" when the CPSU inadvertently injected itself into the debate with its letter. With the arrival of Moscow's letter, the focus of the conference abruptly shifted to consideration of the conflict with the CPSU. Struggle against international revisionism, the conference concluded, would be advantageous to the struggle against domestic revisionism.[9] As the work conference turned to address the Soviet letter, leading pragmatic leaders one after the other stood up to second Mao's vehement condemnation of the letter. Scholar Sergey Radchenko suggests that Liu Shaoqi and Deng Xiaoping calculated that by supporting Mao on foreign policy issues, they could secure Mao's support on domestic policy. Liu stressed the need to struggle against international revisionism. But while Liu spoke, Mao interrupted several times to link Liu's criticism of Soviet foreign policy to China's domestic situation. When Liu asserted that Moscow's "modern revisionism" concerned the revolutionary movements of all countries, Mao interjected that it also concerned the movement in China. Mao added:

> As to whether or not revisionism emerges [in China], there is a possibility that it will and there is a possibility that it will not. [B]y carrying out socialist education in the countryside, relying on the poor and lower middle peasants, and then uniting the upper middle class peasants, one can dig out the roots of revisionism.[10]

In other words, the failure to mobilize the rural poor to attack the "rich peasants" that were emerging under Liu and Deng's pragmatic policies would lead China down the same sort of "revisionist" road being followed by the Soviet Union. Conversely, exposing the errors of Soviet revisionism would create an atmosphere for exposing China's own revisionists. Deng Xiaoping followed Liu in denouncing the Soviet letter.

Suspension of open polemics as proposed by the CPSU's February 1963 letter was exactly what Mao did not want. His intensifying struggle against revisionism within China required a major fight against Soviet revisionism. Mao wanted to avoid responsibility for initiating that fight, however. Strong sentiment within the international communist movement in favor of pan-communist unity meant that whoever was assigned responsibility for a "split" would pay heavily in terms of stature within the world of global communism. Mao therefore maneuvered toward a split in the name of "unity"—but only unity on the basis of Marxist-Leninist principles as laid out by Mao. The day after the letter arrived, Mao received the Soviet ambassador Stepan Chervonenko in his, Mao's, bedroom. Once again Mao received the Soviet ambassador in pajamas. Liu Shaoqi and Zhou Enlai were also in attendance. Scholar Sergey Radchenko thought Mao's extremely casual attire was intended to demonstrate Mao's elevated status above mundane conventions like polite dress and diplomatic protocol. In any case, Mao told Chervonenko that polemical criticism was not a big deal. He himself, Mao proclaimed, was not afraid of criticism, and others should not be either:

> Indeed, because polemics [between the CCP and the CPSU] begin, will the sky fall down on earth or will grass stop growing on the Xishan Mountains? No. The sky will not fall down, grass and trees will still grow, women will bear children, and fish will swim in the water.[11]

Mao then linked the struggle against international revisionism to the struggle against revisionism within socialist countries: "In socialist countries, new bourgeois elements can appear and develop. If we do not deal with them, they could get out of hand." To demonstrate magnanimity, Mao repeatedly invited Khrushchev to visit Beijing for talks. He also said that polemics could be temporarily suspended during that visit. This invitation went nowhere, as Mao must have known it would. Khrushchev would not risk the loss of status and humiliation of appearing, once again, before Teacher Mao. The CCP did, however, accept the Soviet proposal of February 23 for bilateral talks. Eventually, July 5 was set as the starting date. Deng Xiaoping led the CCP delegation, assisted by Kang Sheng and Peng Zhen. These talks were pivotal and would mark the final rupture between the CCP and the CPSU.[12]

In the lead-up to the July 1963 talks, Moscow prepared a number of what it deemed practical proposals designed to address Chinese security concerns, albeit within the confines of continuing Sino-Soviet alliance: coordination of the air defense systems of the two countries, exchange of military intelligence, expanded economic ties, and so on. Beijing took the opposite approach. Two weeks before the scheduled start of talks, Chinese ambassador Pan Zili in Moscow handed to a top CPSU theoretician a CCP "Proposal Concerning the General Line of the Communist Movement"[13] (hereafter referred to as "Proposal"). Organized around twenty-five "questions of principle," the Proposal constituted a reply to the CPSU's conciliatory letter of February. After delivering the Proposal to the CPSU, but without waiting to hear Moscow's reply, China launched an extensive campaign to publicize it. Mao first met with foreign communist leaders visiting Beijing, gave them copies of the Proposal, and asked for their suggestions. *Renmin ribao* then published the Proposal in full. The PRC embassy in Moscow began to distribute a Russian-language translation of the document. Copies were mailed by post to Soviet organizations in Moscow and other Soviet cities. Chinese students studying in Moscow distributed copies to academic organizations. Copies were left in the hotel rooms for delegates to meetings in Moscow. These activities prompted a Soviet deputy foreign minister to call in Ambassador Pan Zili and protest. Pan rebuffed the Soviet complaint; he did not care whether the Soviet side agreed or disagreed with Chinese actions. Outraged, the Soviet representative warned the Chinese diplomat "not to forget that you are in the Soviet Union and you must respect the regulations . . . One could get the impression that the Ambassador is in charge of this country and can make whatever laws he wants."[14]

For Khrushchev, the CCP Proposal, together with the extensive effort to publicize that manifesto even before the two sides sat down to talk, was the last straw. The Soviet leader became convinced that Chinese leaders did not want reconciliation but in fact wanted a split. The conciliatory proposals prepared by Moscow were scrapped, and the CPSU began bracing for a protracted and sharp struggle with Beijing. According to CPSU Central Committee member Yuri Andropov, the CPSU should prepare for "serious and possibly long ideological struggle" with the CCP.[15]

Several days before the July meeting, CCP leaders met to determine guidelines for the Chinese delegation. It was decided that the delegation should be prepared for a split and not back down from it.[16] Once talks began, Deng Xiaoping elaborated point by point the twenty-five "points of principle" stated in the Proposal. The Soviets replied with rebuttals. In the middle of the talks, on July 15, the CPSU issued an "Open Letter to All Communists in the USSR" in response to the CCP. Like the CCP Proposal, Moscow's Open Letter was in fact directed toward communists worldwide. It addressed a number of the ideological points raised in the Proposal, as well as the illegal and provocative ways (in the Soviet view) in which the CCP had distributed that document in the Soviet Union. With Moscow's issue of the Open Letter, argument became even more acrimonious and bitter. Finally, after several weeks, Deng proposed bringing the meetings to a close, and the Soviet side agreed. The Sino-Soviet alliance was dead and now buried. When the Chinese delegation led by Deng Xiaoping returned to Beijing, they were welcomed at the Beijing airport by Mao, Liu Shaoqi, Zhou Enlai, and other top Chinese leaders. Propaganda posters of this airport reception are still widely available in antique markets in Chinese cities.

According to the CCP's Proposal, there was a global struggle underway between US imperialism and the laboring classes and exploited nations oppressed by the United States. Revolutionary struggles against the United States were sweeping the intermediate zones of Asia, Africa, and Latin America lying between the imperialist countries and the socialist countries. Peaceful coexistence of socialism with the "imperialist countries" was permissible, the CCP Proposal said, but "No one should ever demand in the name of peaceful coexistence that the oppressed people and nations should give up their revolutionary struggle." The general line of the socialist countries should be, in addition to striving for peaceful coexistence with capitalist countries, "support and assistance to revolutionary struggle of all the oppressed peoples and nations." In essence, the Proposal was a call for the Soviet Union, at the head of the socialist camp, to give bolder support for wars of national liberation in the "intermediate zone." Moscow should not pull away from such "proletarian solidarity" because of US threats, even nuclear intimidation, nor out of fear of greater tension and confrontation with United States imperialism.

Mao as Successor to Stalin as Helmsman of the Communist Movement

CCP leaders, under the stern revolutionary supervision of Mao, took the ideological debates with the CPSU very seriously. Ideology was not some sort of post hoc justification for policies worked out after calculations of national interest and power had been completed. A correct ideological analysis, as laid out by the CCP under Chairman Mao's guidance, was deemed the key to political and thus historic success in the advance of humanity toward the socialist-communist future. As recounted by the detailed memoir of Wu Lengxi, CCP record-keeper on the polemical struggle with the CPSU, China's top leaders, Mao, Liu, Deng, Zhou, and the rest, spent a great deal of time debating these polemics. Politburo or central leadership conferences debated at length, for days on end, month after month, these various polemical statements.[17] Mao participated actively in these meetings. He personally read and commented on, frequently extensively, various theoretical statements. The amount of time and energy devoted to developing these ideological polemics, at a time when China was struggling to emerge from a catastrophic famine, is amazing. Undoubtedly, it was Mao who dictated this focus on ideology. As we have seen, even the top leaders who favored more production-oriented policies felt compelled to join in the ideological chorus.

Mao saw himself as heir to Marx, Engels, Lenin, and Stalin—the titans of Marxism-Leninism. Lenin built his Bolshevik party on ideological debate. These ideological battles worked: the tight revolutionary organization built by Lenin succeeded in seizing power in 1917 and then creating history's first durable "proletarian state." Stalin saw international power politics as a manifestation of class struggle, and like Lenin, fancied himself a theorist. From the Leninist perspective, a successful revolutionary leader needed a correct theoretical analysis. Theory, ideology, was the key to historic success. With "correct" theory, all obstacles could be overcome, power seized, the revolutionary reconstruction of society undertaken, socialism created, and the transition to the final end state of human society, classless and equalitarian communism, could begin.

As successor to Marx, Engels, Lenin, and Stalin, Mao needed to establish himself as a theorist. Mao had a staff of ideologues that drafted and repeatedly redrafted the various ideological statements issued during these years. But Mao always had the final say. Even documents promulgated by other people and under other names were closely edited by Mao. But in addition to the mere creation of a body of theory, Mao needed to demonstrate the correctness of that theory in practice, through successful application. Domestically, success was measured by whether Chinese society continued to move toward the utopian vision of communism. Internationally, success was to be measured by the advance of Maoist-style wars of national liberation, with Southeast Asia the most important geographic test bed for this effort.

Mao's understanding of the international communist movement was profoundly romantic. Through his polemical struggles against the CPSU's "mistakes," Mao was in fact attacking a major mechanism of Soviet national power—Moscow's leadership of the international communist movement—but seems not to have realized this until 1961 or 1962. By 1960, there were communist parties in 100 countries.[18] In thirteen of those countries, the parties were in power. In many countries, nonruling parties were influential: Italy, France, Indonesia, Iran, and Iraq, to name a few. In others, the parties were less influential or even marginal. But even then, they typically gave Moscow the ability to inject Soviet views into the local political scene. Moscow's ability to guide the international communist movement was, in fact, a major instrument of Soviet national power, second only to the might of the Red Army. But the Soviet military was limited to lands fairly close to Soviet borders. Even utilization of Soviet armed forces (in 1956 for example) was legitimized by the international communist movement. Moscow's ability to guide the international communist movement gave Moscow a truly global voice to vindicate and support Soviet moves.

The crux of Moscow's control over the international communist movement was its ability to define that movement's line. Moscow also provided cash support, medical treatment, and other succor for foreign communist leaders who were often pariahs in their own countries.[19] Moscow also sometimes provided training, weapons, or equipment. These incentives were important. But the international communist movement was, at its core, a messianic movement inspired by a vision of a better society. For communists, at least those who looked to Moscow, the Soviet Union represented the creation-in-progress of a "new civilization," as prominent British socialists Sidney and Beatrice Webb proclaimed in the 1930s. It was this that inspired loyalty to Moscow, a willingness to accept Moscow's dictate of "line." It was this that was undermined by Beijing's polemics.

Mao recognized and deeply resented Moscow's ability to unilaterally dictate to the international communist movement, but Mao's revolutionary romanticism prevented him from understanding, at least up to 1961 or so, that his ideological challenge was actually a challenge to the global power of the Soviet state. Up to that point, Mao apparently believed that Khrushchev and the CPSU would realize their ideological "errors" and embrace Mao's "correct" ideas, permitting unity within the international communist movement to be reestablished on the basis of (Mao's) correct Marxist-Leninist principles. What was involved, Mao believed, was a party-to-party dispute over ideology, which should not and probably would not affect state-to-state relations. Mao seems to have imagined that Khrushchev would at some point say, "you are right, I am wrong," and accept the CCP's "correct" formulations of ideology. The leaders of the international communist movement would then sit down on the basis of complete equality and in deep fraternity and collectively set the line for their movement. This was a romantic perspective.

There were, of course, considerations of national power and interest underlying Mao's ideological formulations. Mao chafed at Moscow's use of aid to pressure China: the linking of submarine assistance to the radio station, the ending of nuclear weapon assistance in 1959, Khrushchev's visit to the United States, Moscow's alignment in the India-China dispute in 1959, and the abrupt cutoff of aid in 1960. Mao also resented China's subordinate status within both the Sino-Soviet alliance and the international communist movement, and the fact that the CCP was repeatedly presented with CPSU faits accomplis such as de-Stalinization, Soviet rapprochement with Yugoslavia, and pressure on Albania. But Mao viewed even these considerations of national interest through the prism of Marxist-Leninist theory. Mao saw Moscow's various objectionable moves as arising out of "mistakes" in Marxist-Leninist theory, out of an incorrect understanding of ideology. Mao concluded by 1962 or so that those ideological errors in turn arose out of the new "class character" of the CPSU. The CPSU had degenerated into a "bourgeois party," and its rule represented the "restoration of capitalism" in the USSR. Mao also chose to respond to the dispute over national interest with the Soviet Union via ideological polemics against the CPSU. Mao was an idiosyncratic combination of ideologue and revolutionary realist. He pursued realistic goals of Chinese power and greatness, but he did this in Marxist-Leninist ways and via Marxist-Leninist ideology. It *is* possible to understand the Sino-Soviet split of 1956–1963 in terms of conflicting power interests. Such an approach does not, however, put one inside the mental world of China's leaders, or at least not Mao Zedong. Mao thought in terms of the Marxist-Leninist ideology to which he had dedicated his life. And it was, Mao believed, a correct application of that ideology that would establish red, revolutionary China as the leading power in a red, revolutionary Asia.

"Khrushchevism without Khrushchev"

As conflict with the Soviet Union and within the CCP elite over agricultural policy escalated, Mao pondered the possibility that he might be removed by some sort of coup d'état. The purge of defense minister and Great Leap critic Peng Dehuai and his replacement by Mao loyalist Lin Biao in August 1959 had diminished that possibility. But the possibility still concerned Mao. At a Politburo Standing Committee meeting on military work in June 1964, Mao directed that a study of military coups be undertaken to better understand their dynamics.[20] Mao stressed the Soviet propensity for organizing coups and the imperative of learning from this. It was necessary both to step up preparations for a possible attack by the USSR and to guard against possible coup attempts by revisionists within the CCP.[21] Mao's fears were underlined in October when Khrushchev was ousted from power by a group led by Leonid Brezhnev and Alexei Kosygin. Interactions with the new Soviet leadership offered Mao further evidence that Moscow intended to oust him by coup.

Mao convened the Politburo the day after Khrushchev's ouster to discuss the new situation. It was necessary for Beijing to make a few friendly gestures toward the new Soviet leaders, Mao said, because that would be expected by "the people of China and the Soviet Union, the entire socialist world, and [Cambodian leader] Sihanouk."[22] It was thus necessary, Mao said, "to run up the flag of friendship" in Moscow. In line with this, Zhou Enlai led a delegation to Moscow in November to participate in the anniversary of the Bolshevik insurrection. In Moscow, Zhou was confronted with a Soviet proposal that Mao be ousted.

PLA Marshal General He Long was a member of the CCP delegation. He Long was a Politburo member, but also had dangerous political baggage. Following Peng Dehuai's challenge to Mao's Great Leap policies at the August 1959 Plenum, He Long was appointed to head a special commission investigating the charges against Peng. That commission found that most of the charges against Peng were baseless, and in 1965 Peng was partially rehabilitated on the basis of this determination. Of course, this meant that He Long, like Peng, was challenging the wisdom of Mao's decisions, a dangerous position to be in as Mao was maneuvering toward the purge of "hidden revisionists." He Long would be one of the first PLA leaders to be purged as the Cultural Revolution began in 1966. In any case, during one evening's festivities in Moscow, Soviet defense minister Rodion Malinovsky approached He Long and said now that the CPSU had gotten rid of Khrushchev, the CCP should get rid of Mao so that the two countries could restore friendly solidarity.[23]

He Long considered these words to be a "serious provocation" and immediately reported the matter to delegation head Zhou Enlai. Zhou, while still at the formal banquet and in a voice loud enough for others to hear, protested to Brezhnev and several other top Soviet leaders. Brezhnev expressed surprise and sent people to investigate. Brezhnev then reported to Zhou that Malinovsky had expressed his own views, not those of the Soviet leadership, and that he had been drunk. Brezhnev begged Zhou's pardon. Zhou refused to accept the apology, declaring that Malinovsky's drunkenness had permitted him to speak heartfelt words revealing the true Soviet view of China's leader, Chairman Mao. Zhou and the entire Chinese delegation then left the banquet hall and reported the incident to Beijing.[24]

In Beijing, the Politburo met immediately to discuss Malinovsky's "grave provocation." For Mao this was an extremely serious matter. Zhou Enlai had passed the test, but how might some other CCP leader, perhaps Liu Shaoqi or Deng Xiaoping, have responded to Soviet probes? The "Malinovsky incident" was, Mao declared, "brazen interference in China's internal affairs." Because of this, the CCP would not discuss other matters with the CPSU, even if they apologized for the "incident." The incident demonstrated that Khrushchev's successors would continue his anti-China line, "Khrushchevism without Khrushchev," Mao declared. Zhou in Moscow was directed to deliver a full criticism of Khrushchev's revisionist line, and to ask directly whether the CPSU was willing to abandon Khrushchev's "anti-China line" and join China in opposing US imperialism and "the reactionaries of every country." The latter formulation referred first and foremost to India's Nehru. If Moscow's new leaders expressed agreement with this position, Mao instructed, Zhou was to ask Soviet leaders to demonstrate their sincerity by actions. In reply to Zhou's diatribe, Soviet President Anastas Mikoyan said that on the question of "our differences with China," there was not the slightest difference between the new Soviet leadership and Khrushchev. All the decisions of the CPSU in this regard over the previous several years had been collective decisions. In that case, Zhou said, since the CPSU still considered itself to be the "big brother party," the CCP's polemical struggle would continue. Upon return to Beijing, Zhou reported immediately to Mao. Khrushchev's ouster had not been based on differences of line, Zhou said, but on objections to Khrushchev's personal manner and style of work. Mao proposed "Khrushchevism without Khrushchev" as a description of the new Soviet leaders, and Zhou immediately accepted.

Decision for War against the Indian Reactionaries

In 1962, Mao's intensifying struggle against Soviet and hidden revisionists within the CCP became entangled with confrontation and eventually war with India. By fall 1962, Mao had launched a nationwide Socialist Education Movement in the countryside intended to reverse the retreat from radical rural policies over the previous several years. Although the direct evidence that Mao intended a link between international confrontation and domestic radicalism in 1962 is weaker than for Korea in 1950 or the Taiwan Strait crisis in 1958, some scholars have surmised that such a link probably existed.[25] As in 1950 and 1958, an atmosphere of international crisis assisted Mao's efforts to overcome hesitation about revolutionary advance and move China down the correct road of class struggle and progress toward genuine socialism. But as in 1950 and 1958, considerations of domestic mobilization of revolutionary forces did not preclude considerations of foreign threat. In 1962, China's leaders felt they confronted sustained Indian "nibbling" of Chinese territory, which had to be dealt a strong, punitive blow.

The hard realities of military power in the high Himalayas overwhelmingly favored China in the early 1960s, and India's apparent disregard of this was part of what mystified Chinese leaders and caused them to conclude that New Delhi must be inspired by nefarious forces. PLA forces had entered Tibet in 1951 and spent the next decade building roads linking that region to China proper. By 1962, these roads kept PLA forces well supplied. Further Chinese forces entered Tibet for counterinsurgency operations as rebellion flared, and Chinese soldiers became acclimated to operations at Tibet's extremely high elevation. As part of counterinsurgency operations, PLA built roads and positions in forward areas as part of efforts to seal the border. And throughout the 1950s, the PLA underwent sweeping modernization along Soviet lines and with substantial Soviet assistance. PLA capabilities were honed in Korea. By 1962, the PLA was a well-trained and -equipped and battle-hardened force used to operations in Tibet. India, on the other hand, was led by men who believed that war was an outdated contrivance. Little attention was paid to modernization of India's military. Forward areas along the borders with China were left undeveloped, without roads, bridges, and depots to facilitate logistical movements. When Indian forces finally began advancing into forward areas in 1962, they found the going very hard. Logistical lines for Indian forces were tenuous. Nor were Indian troops acclimated to or properly equipped for high-elevation operations. When Chinese and Indian forces began encountering one another in forward areas in 1962, it was the Chinese forces who held the tactically superior positions.

In spite of its weak military position in the frontier regions, in November 1961 India adopted a new "Forward Policy" designed to establish effective Indian control over frontier territory claimed by India in the Himalayan Mountains. According to the official but long-secret Indian report on India's 1962 war with China, in fall 1961 a wide empty area existed between India's forwardmost outposts and Chinese outposts to their north. Chinese border troops were gradually pushing into this "empty area" establishing outposts, according to the Indian report. In order to demonstrate that the remaining area was not empty and thus deter Chinese advance, Indian forces were ordered to patrol as far as the crest line claimed by India as the international boundary, filling once vacant areas, in spite of the tactical superiority typically held by Chinese forces in these areas. If Indian forces encountered Chinese outposts in areas deemed to be south of the crest line, they were to build outposts encircling, cutting off, or "dominating" Chinese outposts, thus forcing them to withdraw.[26] India's Forward Policy would continue right up to the beginning of powerful Chinese offensives in October 1962. From the Indian perspective, the Forward Policy was an attempt to end ongoing Chinese encroachment on Indian territory south of the Himalayan or Kunlun crest lines (in the eastern and western sectors respectively).[27] India was doing nothing more than securing Indian territory from Chinese encroachment. India's Forward Policy was premised on the belief that Chinese forces would not resort to armed force to counter the Indian advance. China was too weak and isolated to resort to war, Indian leaders assumed. Beijing's alliance with Moscow had collapsed, and China's economy was in dire crisis.[28]

From Beijing's perspective, the legitimate border between China and India in the eastern sector ran not along the Himalayan crest line but along the foothills on the northern edge of the Brahmaputra Valley. China had nonetheless held its forces north of the Himalayan crest line in an attempt to facilitate a compromise settlement and avoid conflict with India. In October 1959, Beijing had even ordered its frontier forces not to patrol in a zone within twenty kilometers behind the line of actual control along the crest line. This act of Chinese restraint had helped create the "empty zone" into which Indian forces were now moving. India's Forward Policy entailed steady nibbling away of Chinese territory, a sort of slow-motion aggression against China conducted in spite of repeated warnings by China. Following Indian "intrusions" into the Longju region in the center of the NEFA-Tibet frontier, Beijing warned in May 1962 that unless India "desists immediately" from such intrusions, "the Chinese government will not stand idly by."[29] New Delhi ignored Chinese warnings. Indian troops continued to press forward. By the end of June 1962, the Indian foreign office reported that Forward Policy operations had brought over 2,000 square miles of territory under Indian control.[30]

From November 1961, when the Forward Policy began, until February 1962, Chinese forces were under orders to withdraw from an area when challenged by new Indian outposts. In February, Mao ordered Chinese outposts to no longer withdraw but to stand firm even when challenged by "dominating" Indian outposts. Mao dubbed this new approach "armed coexistence," saying:

> Nehru wants to move forward and we wouldn't let him. Originally, we tried to guard against this, but now it seems we cannot prevent it. If he wants to advance, we might as well adopt armed coexistence. You wave a gun, and I'll wave a gun. We'll stand face to face and each practice our courage.[31]

Rather than withdraw when challenged, Chinese forces began to build outposts counter-encircling and cutting off the new Indian positions. Mao also gave strict orders that Chinese forces were not to open fire except at his personal order. Mao did not want to stumble into an accidental war. Indian leaders were less cautious. In July 1962, Indian Army Headquarters gave discretion to post commanders to fire on Chinese troops that threatened Indian outposts.[32] In September 1962, when India's chief of General Staff gave the final orders to Indian forces to drive Chinese forces from atop the strategic Thagla Ridge that dominated the territory just east of the Bhutan, he showed immense confidence: "Experience in Ladakh [Aksai Chin] has shown that a few rounds fired at the Chinese would cause them to run away."[33]

Mao recognized early on that it would be hard to make Nehru and India change course. "A person sleeping in a comfortable bed is not easily roused by someone else's snoring," he told a CMC meeting in February 1962.[34] Beijing tried increasingly forceful methods to "wake" Nehru. In July 1962, PLA rules of engagement were altered to allow PLA forces at the frontier to open fire to defend themselves in extreme situations. Localized armed clashes proliferated. China's MFA and media carried increasingly ominous warnings. India should rein itself in at the precipice. China was prepared to wage a tit-for-tat struggle with India. If India played with fire, it would be consumed by fire. In early September, a powerful force of about 800 Chinese soldiers descended from Thagla Ridge to encircle an Indian base recently established at the bottom of that massive ridge. For twelve days, a standoff existed before the Chinese force withdrew. This was a Chinese demonstration of military preparedness—and a warning.

While trying to persuade India to abandon the Forward Policy, Beijing moved to minimize prospects for American or Soviet support for India if war became necessary. In May 1962, Zhou Enlai ordered Ambassador Wang Bingnan to return to Warsaw and reopen talks with the United States. The Nationalists on Taiwan were loudly preparing to "recover the mainland" via invasion and soliciting US support for that effort. In Laos, the United States and China were locked in confrontation, and Zhou feared that Washington might use Laos as a corridor for a Nationalist invasion of China. Wang was able to secure from the US representative at Warsaw a statement that "under present conditions" the United States would not support a Nationalist invasion.[35] Beijing also moved to reconstruct, temporarily, its security ties with the Soviet Union. The US announcement of its discovery of Soviet missiles in Cuba on October 15 initiated the Cuban missile crisis. Confronting the real possibility of war with the United States, Moscow sought Chinese support. Moscow and Beijing came together for several weeks and supported each other against the United States and India. China's assault on India came in the midst of the Cuban standoff between the Soviet Union and the United States.

On October 6, after Indian forces continued to push forward into Chinese-held territory in spite of increasingly stern Chinese warnings, Chinese leaders decided to launch a large-scale punitive war against India. According to foreign minister Chen Yi, whom Mao asked to brief the leadership meeting on that day, forty-seven Chinese personnel had been killed or wounded by Indian gunfire along the border. In all instances, Indian forces and fired first, Chen said. India was also deploying artillery to forward positions, targeting Chinese outposts. An Indian assault on Thagla Ridge seemed imminent. India had rejected Chinese efforts to begin negotiations over the border conflict and had ignored repeated Chinese warnings. After hearing Chen Yi's report, Mao declared himself for war:

> We fought a war with Japan, and with America. . . . Now the Indians want to fight a war with us. . . . We cannot give ground [because] it would be tantamount to letting them seize a big piece of land equivalent to Fujian province. . . . Since Nehru . . . insists on us fighting him, for us not to fight with him would not be friendly enough.[36]

The CMC directive resulting from the October 6 meeting ordered the PLA to prepare a large-scale attack to severely punish India, forcing it to cease its aggressive policies. Assaults should occur in both western and eastern areas, but the main blow should come in the east, where larger Indian forces made a larger target on which severe pain could be inflicted.

Forcing India to take seriously Chinese power was a central factor in Beijing's decision for war. Nehru had ignored all China's warnings out of a belief that China was bluffing. As noted earlier, the realities of the military balance in the frontier regions overwhelmingly favored China. Yet India ignored those realities and pushed forward aggressively. Nehru had concluded, Mao determined, that China "was weak and could be taken advantage of," "a dog that barks but does not bite." According to Mao: "Since Nehru says we only 'bark but don't bite,' we absolutely must fight. We have no other choice."[37] The credibility of China's warnings was at stake.

Under the PLA plan approved by the CMC, Chinese forces gave a final warning to New Delhi; Chinese forces descended from Thagla Ridge to undertake a four-day assault on an Indian outpost at the base of that ridge. Then the Chinese withdrew and there was no further Chinese action for four weeks. After no appropriate Indian response was forthcoming, and as Indian forces continued to move forward in various sectors, on November 14 a massive and well-prepared invasion force moved south, smashing into ill-prepared Indian defenses, which collapsed. Retreats by Indian forces turned into routs. Indian command and control collapsed. Key passes at Tawang, Bomdila, and Seth La were only lightly defended, allowing Chinese forces to move forward before Indian forces had time to prepare new lines of defense. By November 19, Chinese forces had taken Chako, only about fifteen miles from the edge of the Brahmaputra Valley. Panic spread across India. There were fears that Chinese forces would seize India's northeast, or perhaps march on Calcutta. Then the Chinese forces stopped. Beijing unilaterally declared a ceasefire, and Chinese forces began withdrawing over the recently won ground, back to what China said was the line of actual control prior to the beginning of India's Forward Policy. Figure 7-1 illustrates the main line of Chinese attack in 1962.

China's decision for war with India was a costly one, but it achieved the objective of making Indian leaders more soberly respectful of China's power. India abandoned its forward policy, thus stabilizing Tibet's southern frontier. The confrontations and firefights that had plagued that border since 1961 ceased, as did Indian efforts to push Chinese forces back to the line claimed by India. While Tibetan resistance fighters and probably Indian spies would continue to infiltrate across that border for many years, China did not again confront chronic fighting there. More broadly, New Delhi began paying far greater attention to Chinese warnings. 1962 was the Indian equivalent of 1950

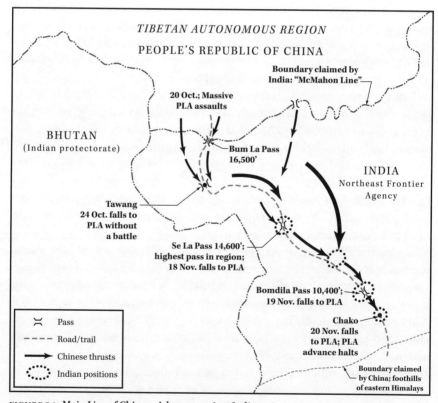

FIGURE 7-1 **Main Line of Chinese Advance against India, 1962**

Source: Allen S. Whiting, "The Sino-Soviet Split," in Roderick MacFarquhar and John King Fairbank, eds., *The Cambridge History of China, Volume 14, The People's Republic, Part I: The Emergence of Revolutionary China, 1949–1965,* (Cambridge University Press: New York, 1987), p. 522.

for the Americans. Just as the Americans learned in 1950 in Korea to take seriously Chinese power and threats, Indian leaders learned in 1962 that PRC leaders were prepared to use China's substantial military power to uphold what they deemed China's vital interests. From this perspective, both 1950 and 1962 were expensive but perhaps necessary payments for China's rise as a great power.

On the cost side of Beijing's ledger, 1962 gave rise to an enduring Indian narrative of Chinese betrayal. According to this Indian narrative, India had befriended China in the 1950s, but China had repaid Indian friendship with treacherous attack. Over the fifty years after 1962, Chinese diplomacy and propaganda would attempt to erode this Indian narrative of Chinese betrayal, but with only partial success. The memory of 1962 and the underlying sense of Chinese treachery and betrayal remains strong in India. 1962 dominates the Indian historical memory of Sino-Indian relations much as the memory of Japan's aggression in the 1930s dominates China's historical narrative of Sino-Japanese relations. Even in 2014, when Beijing was struggling to prevent India's alignment with Shinzo Abe's Japan, China's deployment of the Japanese history issue to influence Japan had little resonance in India, partly because World War II is overshadowed (in the Indian memory) by 1962. That year is the "history issue" for Indians.

The 1962 war also resulted in an Indian military development effort that turned India into a far more potent military threat to China, especially to "China's Tibet." 1962 shattered the earlier Gandhian-Nehruvian belief that war was anachronistic. India began for the first time a serious and sustained military modernization effort, so that by, say, 1971, when China feared Indian intervention in Tibet, the military balance between India and China had shifted decisively in India's favor. One component of India's post-1962 shift in defense policy was the formation of what would eventually become an eleven-battalion force (about 10,000 troops) of professionally trained and well-armed Tibetans officered by Indian Army officers and designed to conduct long-range commando and guerrilla operations deep inside Tibet.[38] This force, initially code-named Establishment 22, was maintained under conditions of deep secrecy and could work jointly with conventional Indian forces in the event of another Sino-Indian war, plus a possible call for a Tibetan national rising in an attempt to topple Chinese rule over Tibet. For several years after the 1962 war, India worked closely with the CIA in setting up Establishment 22. By 1965, the CIA had reportedly drawn up a plan for the liberation of Tibet employing Establishment 22. With Establishment 22, India had given itself a far more potent weapon that might challenge Chinese control over Tibet.

1962 also altered India's policy of non-alignment with major powers. While India continued to play a pivotal role in the non-aligned movement, it adopted a de facto policy of aligning with the superpower most willing to support it against China. From late 1962 until about 1965, that power was the United States. Then, as Sino-Soviet tensions mounted and India broke with the United States over the US intervention in Vietnam, the Soviet Union emerged as New Delhi's more reliable anti-China partner. New Delhi would maintain that alignment all the way to Mikhail Gorbachev's effort in the late 1980s to maneuver toward rapprochement with China. Gorbachev's push for rapprochement with Beijing required Moscow to dilute its security guarantee to India.[39] Then, after a period of Indian isolation in which it lacked the support of any superpower, India in the 2000s began moving into alignment with the United States.[40] The India-US strategic partnership that emerged in the 2000s cannot, of course, be reduced to 1962. Yet the lesson learned by India in that year—that China is a powerful country quite prepared to employ military force to uphold its interests and one which India must take seriously—was one significant factor in India's decision to embrace a new military, security, and strategic partnership with the United States in the first decade of the twenty-first century.

Emergence and Militarization of the Territorial Issue with the Soviet Union

Shortly after the war with India, Mao decided to escalate the conflict with Moscow from a polemic over Marxist-Leninist theory to an interstate conflict over territory. This was a momentous step. As noted earlier, one of the core political beliefs of contemporary Chinese political culture is the idea that between the start of the first Opium War in 1839 and the founding of the PRC in 1949 China experienced a Century of National Humiliation when all sorts of evils were inflicted on it by predatory Western powers and Japan. The west included tsarist Russia. One of those evils was the seizure of Chinese territory. Tsarist Russia was among the most aggressive in seizing Chinese territory.[41] In 1858, the Treaty of Aigun ceded the north bank of the Heilung or (in Russian) Amur River to Russia. In 1860, the Treaty of Beijing ceded the east bank of the Ussuri River to Russia. In 1888, tsarist Russia seized 500,000 square miles of Central Asia east of Lake Balkhash in today's Kazakhstan. In 1945, and again in 1950, Stalin had insisted that Chinese leaders, first Chiang Kai-shek and then Mao Zedong, formally recognize the independence of Mongolia. Soviet leaders were unwilling to compromise Mongolia's independence. Figure 7-2 illustrates the formation of the Sino-Russian/Soviet border.

During the period of Sino-Soviet friendship in the 1950s, commercial interaction flourished across the riverine borders of China's northeast.[42] Those borders had been fortified during the standoff between Japan's puppet state of Manchukuo and the USSR from 1931 to 1945, but during the 1950s the border was demilitarized. Customs and visa regimes were greatly simplified and

FIGURE 7-2 **Formation of the Sino-Soviet/Russian Border**

relaxed. Local governments sought expanded cooperation. Joint Soviet-PRC commissions worked out river navigation rules.

Then, in early 1963, Mao Zedong abruptly raised what seemed to be, at least to Soviet leaders, claims on the lands seized by tsarist Russia in the nineteenth century. After the Cuban missile crisis of 1962, Beijing criticized Khrushchev's "capitulation" for withdrawing Soviet missiles from Cuba: "100 percent appeasement," "a 'Munich' pure and simple," Beijing said.[43] Khrushchev responded to Beijing's charges of inadequate militancy in a speech to the Supreme Soviet. The "ultra-revolutionary loud months in Beijing," the Soviet leader noted, had not liberated Hong Kong and Macao. This failure was not some sort of "retreat from Marxism-Leninism," Khrushchev said, but simply an application of common sense—as had been his own withdrawal of missiles from Cuba to avert a possible thermonuclear war. A statement by the Communist Party of the USA (CPUSA) seconded Khrushchev's analysis of events. In March 1963, the CCP replied to the CPUSA, although it was clear to all that the real target was Khrushchev. Since the matter of the unequal treaties of the nineteenth century had been raised, the CCP statement said, China needed to put on record that none of those treaties had any validity. The PRC could not accept the validity of the "unequal treaties" of the nineteenth century. The same day, *Renmin ribao* carried an editorial saying that the nine "unequal treaties" of the nineteenth century, including the 1858, 1860, and 1888 treaties with Russia, needed to be "reexamined" and "renegotiated" and possibly "renounced" or "revised." It continued:

> You [Khrushchev] are not unaware that such questions as those of Hong Kong and Macao relate to the category of unequal treaties left over by history, treaties with the imperialists imposed on China. It may be asked: in raising questions of this kind, do you intend to raise all questions of unequal treaties and have a general settlement? Has it every entered your heads what the consequence would be? Can you seriously believe that this will do you any good?[44]

Mao personally ratcheted tension up further in a talk with a delegation of the Japan Socialist Party in July 1964, saying:

> There are too many places occupied by the Soviet Union. . . . The Soviet Union occupies an area of 22 million square kilometers while its population is only 200 million. It is time to put an end to this allotment. Japan occupies an area of 379 thousand square kilometers and its population is 100 million. About a hundred years ago the area to the east of [Lake] Baikal became Russian territory and since then Vladivostok, Khabarovsk, Kamchatka, and other areas have become Soviet territory. We have not yet presented our bill for this list.[45]

Mao's words clearly suggested that the entire territorial distribution among states in eastern Siberia needed to be revised. Many Soviet leaders, including Khrushchev, concluded that this was Mao's true aim. This was why he wanted a Soviet-American thermonuclear war. With Soviet cities and industry destroyed, the "lost territories" of eastern Siberia and Central Asia could be re-gathered by China. These fears touched on a very long failure of Russian governments to truly develop the Russian Far East, and a large and growing demographic imbalance between the Russian Far East and China's increasingly densely populated and industrialized northeastern region. It also touched on Russian memories of Adolf Hitler, who only twenty years before had also spoken in terms of ratios of populations to territory and the need for an equitable redistribution. Several months after Mao's comments to the Japanese Socialist delegation, Moscow charged that Mao's territorial demands were reminiscent of "his predecessor" (obviously Hitler) for Lebensraum. Five years later, in 1969, when some Soviet leaders favored a large-scale nuclear attack on China to reduce the Chinese population by several hundred million, these images of Mao's sweeping claims on Soviet territory were part of their cognitive map.

Mao's actual objectives in implicitly laying claim to large tracts of the USSR were probably more modest. Mao raised the territorial issue at the time and in the fashion he did as part of his competition with Moscow within the international communist movement.[46] Mao was probably trying to win the sympathy of other communist parties whose countries had also suffered from territorial aggrandizement by the Soviet Union: Japan, Poland, Germany, Finland, and Romania. This ploy also highlighted China's victimization by the Soviet Union, further winning the sympathy of communist parties and anti-imperialist nationalist movements in the Third World. It justified tighter border controls—especially in Xinjiang, where ethnic groups had links to Soviet Central Asia. Not least, by linking Russia to China's "national humiliation" and loss of territory, Mao was intensifying popular anger that could be directed against supposed Soviet-style revisionists hidden within the CCP.

As the territorial conflict emerged in 1963–1964, both Chinese and Soviet leaders began to fear infiltration and subversion, and the border regime began to change. Travel and movement of goods across the border were progressively restricted. Patrols on both sides were strengthened. Border markers and barbed wire were set up. Strips of land were again cleared for fields of observation. Watchtowers were erected. Barracks, storage depots, communication facilities, mess halls, motor pools, medical clinics, airfields, and so on were built to support the new forward presence on the border. Roads were built to supply the new border control infrastructure. This expanded infrastructure had to be protected by additional troops. And, of course, the patrols of the two sides began to encounter each other. Those encounters provided reason for additional patrols and reinforcement. Within a few years, the once-friendly border had been transformed into a militarized standoff.

Acceleration of Superpower Collusion against Revolutionary China

China's enthusiasm for revolutionary wars of national liberation in the intermediate zone and its seemingly nonchalant attitude toward nuclear war caused great concern in Washington. The administration of John Kennedy, inaugurated in January 1961, was deeply concerned with China's revolutionary activism in such places as Laos and Vietnam, and feared that Beijing might become even more assertive and bold once it acquired nuclear weapons. These concerns led the United States to intervene ever more deeply in Vietnam and—of more concern to the discussion here—to seriously consider preemptive action to abort or substantially delay China's nuclear weapons development program.[47] US leaders believed that Soviet leaders too had concerns about China's emerging nuclear capability, and understood that cooperation with the Soviet Union in this regard would be essential to successful action against China. Repeated US solicitations of Soviet cooperation in joint preemptive action to deal with China's drive for nuclear weapons were forthcoming. Fortunately for Beijing, Moscow turned out not to be interested in

American solicitations—an ironic reversal of the situation that would exist a mere six years later.

Satellite imagery of Chinese nuclear facilities became available to US leaders in August 1960. Over the next several years, US intelligence agencies put together a composite picture of China's nuclear weapons program. As soon as he took office, Kennedy was concerned about the impact of Chinese nuclear capability on that country's foreign policies, fearing that once China had nuclear bombs it would become even more supportive of wars of national liberation in such places as Laos and South Vietnam. Kennedy thus began to consider whether the split between Beijing and Moscow might make the Soviet Union willing to cooperate with the United States in stifling PRC nuclear weapons development. A number of options were considered. Veteran US diplomat Averill Harriman believed that a simple joint Soviet-American demand on Beijing, perhaps fortified with a threat of attack if China failed to comply, could induce China to back away from testing a nuclear weapon. There was also the possibility, Kennedy administration officials believed, that Moscow might agree to stand aside if the United States took unilateral military action against China's nuclear sites. There was even the possibility, some thought, that the Soviet Union might be willing to join the United States in a preemptive strike. Various methods of preemptive attack were deliberated. By September 1963, the US military had concluded that the only feasible method would entail multiple waves of strikes by US warplanes. But without at least Soviet understanding, the risks and costs of such an operation could be very high. Chairman of the Joint Chiefs of Staff Curtis LeMay warned in April 1963 that without Soviet approval, a US attack could, in fact, trigger a general East-West war. With it, however, Beijing was unlikely to retaliate in a forceful manner to a preemptive strike, LeMay maintained.

At a summit meeting in Vienna in June 1961, Kennedy broached with Khrushchev the idea of cooperation in dealing with China's nuclear program. The Soviet leader was not interested and refused to pursue the matter. In May 1963, National Security Advisor McGeorge Bundy again broached the issue with Soviet Ambassador Anatoly Dobrynin, proposing a "private and serious" discussion of China's nuclear weapons development. Again the Soviet representative demurred, diverting discussion to NATO's plan to give West Germany a limited role in the Alliance's utilization of tactical nuclear weapons, a move Moscow fiercely opposed. During the 1963 PTBT negotiations in Moscow, US Ambassador Harriman briefed Khrushchev on Kennedy's thinking about parallel Soviet and American interests regarding China and nuclear arms, and his hope either for Soviet willingness to take action with the US or at least accept unilateral US action. Khrushchev rejected the idea. A nuclear-armed China would not be a threat to the Soviet Union, Khrushchev averred. In terms of its foreign policy behavior, a nuclear-armed

China, rather than being more militant, would probably be more restrained, the Soviet leader said.

The CCP-CPSU rupture in July 1963 prompted Khrushchev to seek improved ties with the United States. The Soviet leader did not go so far as to seek US support against China, but merely sought to burnish his increasingly tarnished image among his Politburo comrades via an apparent diplomatic success.[48] Moreover, freed of the need to accommodate Chinese demands for greater Soviet militancy, Khrushchev had greater room to negotiate with the West. The key product of this new Soviet flexibility was agreement on a treaty banning atmospheric testing of nuclear weapons, and a Partial Nuclear Test Ban Treaty (PTBT) was initialed by Soviet, US, and British representatives on July 25, just five days after the end of the ill-fated CCP-CPSU Moscow conference. The idea of a PTBT had been broached in 1959, but Moscow, complying with Chinese demands that it avoid nonproliferation collaboration with the United States, had not moved forward with the idea. Then, suddenly, in July 1963, as acrimony at the Sino-Soviet Moscow meeting flared, Khrushchev surprised US and British leaders by expressing willingness to move forward with a PTBT without preconditions.

Mao saw Moscow's conclusion of a PTBT as a major advance in Soviet collusion with the US against China.[49] China then lacked the technology to conduct underground nuclear tests. (Its first underground test came only in 1969.) Banning atmospheric tests would therefore mean banning Chinese testing of nuclear weapons. Of course, the PRC would not and did not become a signatory to the treaty. But the treaty nonetheless meant that Moscow and Washington would together work to create an international climate opposing China's testing of nuclear weapons. Rather than helping socialist China become strong with a nuclear deterrent against US nuclear blackmail, Soviet "modern revisionism" colluded with US imperialism to hobble China's nuclear weapons development efforts, thereby keeping keep China vulnerable to the US nuclear threat.

Shortly before the PTBT was signed, Beijing gave Moscow a direct request that it not sign the treaty on the grounds, inter alia, that it conflicted with the provisions of the 1950 treaty. Moscow ignored Beijing's request. A Chinese statement after the treaty's signature laid out China's objections: "The Chinese government hoped that Soviet government would not infringe on China's sovereign rights and act for China in assuming an obligation to refrain from manufacturing weapons."[50] In fall 1964, following the signature of the PNBT, McGeorge Bundy tried yet again to feel out Ambassador Dobrynin regarding joint action to deal with China's incipient nuclear capacity. And once again the Soviet representative demurred. He took a nuclear China "for granted," Dobrynin said. Chinese nuclear weapons would not threaten the Soviet Union, or for that matter, the United States. China's nuclear arsenal would be too small and primitive to do that. China's nuclear weapons would have primarily a psychological impact in Asia, and were of "no importance" to the Soviet government.

There were a number of reasons why US leaders ultimately ruled out a pre-emptive strike against PRC nuclear facilities. But Moscow's attitude was a major factor. Without Soviet understanding, a US strike against China's nuclear facilities was simply too risky. Fear of another war with China was another factor. US leaders could not be confident Beijing would not respond by imposing a large-scale war on the US—perhaps in Southeast Asia. Lyndon Johnson's 1964 electoral calculations also weighed against a pre-emptive strike. Ambiguities in Chinese management of its dispute with Moscow may have played a role in the US decision. Prominent US journalists reprised for the public, including Chinese intelligence, the broad parameters of US government consideration of attack on China's nuclear sites in 1961–1963. Stewart Alsop, then one of the most prominent commentators, told readers of the *Saturday Evening Post* in fall 1963 that the "president and his inner circle . . . have agreed in principle that China must be prevented, by whatever means, from becoming a nuclear power." "Nuclear sterilization," Alsop said, would require force, which was a "technically easy problem" that could be accomplished with a "few rather small bangs."[51]

It was certainly with calculations of not antagonizing Soviet leaders too grievously that in April 1963, on the occasion of Khrushchev's seventieth birthday, Mao vetoed a highly polemical birthday greeting that a writing group had drafted. Instead, Mao mandated a much more positive reply, one promising "unity once we encounter trouble." The message ultimately read: "Once the world encounters big trouble, the two parties . . . will stand together to oppose the enemy."[52] As noted earlier, it was extremely difficult for Soviet leaders to imagine that communists could actually fight communists. By sprinkling such hints in CCP discourse with Moscow, Mao fed those Soviet illusions.

Preparing to Resist Soviet-American Collaborative Invasion

By 1964, the Sino-Soviet conflict had been transformed into a conflict between two states and was rapidly being militarized. Washington and Moscow were considering possible joint preemption of China's nuclear sites. Simultaneously, Chinese support for Hanoi's revolutionary push was increasing in tandem with increasing US support for South Vietnam's noncommunist government. Beijing and Washington were moving toward proxy war in Vietnam. Confronted with increasing tensions with both the Soviet Union and the United States, Mao resorted to two main defensive strategies: 1) building a self-reliant defense industrial base in China's interior which could sustain a protracted war to counter a Soviet and/or US attack that knocked out China's industrial capacity on the east coast, and 2) spreading anti-US wars of national liberation across Southeast Asia. The second aspect will be dealt with in the next chapter.

Regarding construction of a defense industrial base in China's interior, from August 1964 through late 1971 China undertook a huge, extremely expensive, and centrally directed effort to create a comprehensive, integrated, and self-reliant defense industrial base in China's mountainous interior. The Third Front, as this effort was called, was designed to ensure that the PLA would have industrial sources of modern weapons after China's existing industrial areas on the east coast were either occupied or destroyed by superpower air bombardment. The new military industrial base was designed to provide the PLA with tools of modern warfare—tanks, artillery, missiles, heavy trucks, airplanes, ships, atomic weapons—that could sustain a protracted war against either the United States or the Soviet Union. Or both. Mao's classic doctrine of people's war relied mainly on lightly armed small-unit guerrilla war. But that was a function of necessity, not of preference. Revolutionary armed forces should undertake, Mao believed, "mobile warfare" as soon as possible, as soon as they could procure the sophisticated arms that would allow them to wage positional battles with enemy forces. Not only heavy weapons but even rifles, machine guns, and mortars would be in short supply after China's east coast industrial areas were destroyed or occupied.[53]

By mid-1964, a draft of the Third Five Year Plan (1965–1970) had been circulating among the elite for two years. That draft provided for continued recovery from the Great Leap Forward via investment in agriculture and consumer goods. New investment was to go mostly to existing industrial areas in eastern China. Then, in May, Mao abruptly rejected that draft and called for a shift of investment to China's interior, and import not of food but of advanced industrial machinery and equipment. In August, just after the Gulf of Tonkin incident and the first US air attacks on North Vietnam, Mao proposed a massive effort to create in China's interior a "Third Front": an integrated and comprehensive defense industrial base to prepare China to resist attack from one or both superpowers. Mao's proposal was adopted without dissent or opposition. The Third Front area embraced all or part of ten provinces west of a huge mountainous escarpment running northeast to southwest across China and delineating eastern, coastal China from the interior. The land west of this escarpment is generally mountainous and above 500 meters elevation, although there are several basins, most prominently Sichuan. The many mountain valleys of this region are ideal for military defense against both land and air attack. Many of the factories built in the region during the Third Front effort were located in canyons, making air attack difficult and limiting damage. Figure 7-3 illustrates the Third Front.

During the first phase of the Third Front effort, an entire industrial structure centering on mining, metallurgy, electricity, and heavy equipment

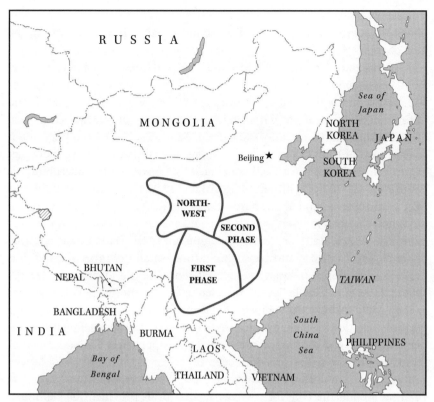

FIGURE 7-3 The Third Front, 1964–1971

manufacture (especially military equipment) was built up in Sichuan, Yunnan, and Guizhou. A mammoth new iron and steel complex was built at Panzhihua (Dukou), south of Chengdu. New West German heavy metal-working machinery was purchased for the Panzhihua complex. An aluminum and high-alloy steel industry was built, along with factories to forge those materials into planes, ships, missiles, and other weapons. Machinery in many eastern Chinese industrial centers was dismantled and shipped west, along with a portion of the eastern factory's workers and managers. Other new machinery consisted of domestic copies of older foreign equipment. The scope of the effort was enormous. All components were rushed forward simultaneously with the highest priority in 1965. Spearheaded by the PLA, hundreds of thousands of workers were mobilized for "human wave" efforts to complete projects forward. Workshops of factories were often widely separated, and situated in canyons or even caves carved into mountainsides to minimize vulnerability to air attack. Roads and rail lines had to be build connecting new facilities. Plants were typically built at considerable distance from existing populated areas, again to minimize damage from air attack. That meant that new housing and other accommodations had to be built. The

Third Front was a large-scale and systematic effort to prepare the country to wage a major war with one or both of the two superpowers.

Third Front construction during the first phase (1965–1969) facilitated China's assistance to Hanoi. Munitions from those Third Front factories could move more swiftly to North Vietnam over newly built rail lines. But scholar Barry Naughton suggests that Mao's fear was not of an American invasion of China from Indochina, but an American attack on east China's cities. Naughton points out that Mao's Third Front plan corresponded roughly to the largely successful Nationalist effort in 1937–1939 during the first years of the Sino-Japanese war to evacuate defense industrial equipment from east coast cities to China's southwest interior. It also corresponded to the Soviet effort to build a defense industrial base east of the Ural Mountains during the 1928–1941 period, an effort that contributed to the Soviet defeat of German armies during World War II. Mao was preparing China for war even as he was re-revolutionizing China via the Cultural Revolution. Yet again, international crisis paralleled domestic mobilization. By 1969, that threat was quite real.

A second stage of the Third Front began in 1969 with the confrontation with the Soviet Union. The focus of work during this period was southwestern Henan and northwestern Hubei. A new iron and steel complex was begun at Wuyang in Henan. A new heavy truck factory was set up at Shiyuan in Hubei. Workers and managers from the auto vehicle factory in Changchun in Jilin province were shifted to the new Hubei plant. New factories were set up to produce components: rubber, tires, bearings, paint. New dams were built or planned (including the huge dam at Gezhouba on the Yangtze) to supply electricity for the plants. Again, many of the workshops and factories were separated by wide distances and situated in canyons or caves. New rail lines and roads had to be built to tie facilities together. The dominant concern during this period was a possible Soviet attack.

Third Front work lost its top priority and rapidly slowed down in late 1971 with the fall of Lin Biao and the onset of PRC-US rapprochement. Regarding the latter, the improved security environment created by rapprochement with the United States and the rapid expansion of China's diplomatic relations meant that top priority on preparation for war no longer made sense. Third Front efforts had been immensely expensive. Naughton estimates that nearly 53 percent of all national investment and as much as two-thirds of the central government's investment in industry during the 1966 to 1970 period went into Third Front projects. For ordinary Chinese this meant extremely Spartan lives: cramped living spaces, poor diets, and very few consumer goods. It also meant that China's scarce capital was invested in ways that provided very low economic returns on investment. The pattern of Third Front investment was, in fact, hugely inefficient.

This crash campaign to prepare China for war was made necessary by Mao's confrontational diplomacy toward Moscow and support for revolution in Southeast Asia. The heavy demands imposed on China's people as a result contributed to the disillusion of the Chinese people from the utopian goals at the core of Mao Zedong's vast project.

China and the 1965 India-Pakistan War

China's dramatic defeat of India in 1962 established China as a viable partner of Pakistan in countering India. The Sino-Pakistan entente cordiale that resulted from this would become one of the most stable elements of PRC foreign relations. Formed in 1964 as China was on the threshold of the Cultural Revolution, the Sino-Pakistan entente was one of very few of China's diplomatic relations to survive that upheaval without disruption. During Beijing's push to propagate Marxism-Leninism and Maoist parties around the world in the 1960s, Mao advised the Pakistani Communist Party to dissolve and support the Pakistani government. Formed during a period when US imperialism was China's nemesis, China's entente with Pakistan continued unimpeded when Soviet social imperialism became Beijing's target, and continued further during the post–Cold War period when US "peaceful evolution" became Beijing's bane. The entente flourished equally under Pakistani military dictatorships and civilian parliamentary governments, as well as under more secular or more Islamicist Pakistani leaders. Forged under Mao, the Sino-Pakistan entente remained strong as Deng Xiaoping scrapped one after another of China's Mao-era policies. Even in the 2010s, as Beijing pushed for rapprochement with India, China's entente with Pakistan remained strong. The basis for this remarkable continuity is parallel Chinese and Pakistani interests in preventing Indian domination of South Asia.

Beijing did not move immediately into alignment with Pakistan after the 1962 war. Mao had hoped that after assimilating the lesson of 1962, New Delhi would be willing to return to Bandung-era-like peaceful coexistence. By 1964, it was apparent that this would not happen and that India would follow an anti-China path for some considerable time. The foundation of the partnership with Pakistan came in February 1964, when Zhou Enlai during a visit to Pakistan declared China's support for Pakistan's call for resolution of the Kashmir question on the basis of the will of the people of that region.[54]

The Kashmir issue emerged in 1947 when British India was partitioned into two separate countries, India and Pakistan. Kashmir's population was mostly Muslim, but it was ruled by a Hindu prince who opted to join India instead of Pakistan. Pakistan felt this was unjust and resorted to war to rectify the injustice. Ever since then, Pakistan has demanded that the people of Kashmir be allowed a free vote—self-determination—to decide whether they should be part of India or Pakistan. India, after briefly agreeing to a plebiscite, maintained that Kashmir's accession to the Indian union in 1947 was final and settled the matter. Since independence and partition in 1947, Kashmir has been divided between Pakistani and Indian control.

In 1964, Beijing came down squarely behind Pakistan's position on the Kashmir issue: the people of Kashmir were entitled to exercise self-determination regarding their future as a people. The same year, Pakistan's leaders devised a plan to bring Kashmir into Pakistan. Kashmiris from Pakistani Kashmir were to be given military training and arms by Pakistan's military, and infiltrated into Indian Kashmir to conduct guerrilla warfare demanding a plebiscite. Soldiers from the Pakistan army would also be infiltrated, in mufti, into Indian Kashmir to strengthen insurgent forces. Once the insurgency grew strong, a revolutionary Kashmiri government would be formed and become the center of an international campaign forcing India to consent to a plebiscite. That election would then lead Indian-controlled Kashmir to join Pakistan.[55]

China's relation to this pseudo-insurgency is unclear. Pakistan's strategy of pseudo-insurgency closely resembles Hanoi's China-supported strategy then being successfully employed in South Vietnam. Throughout 1963 and 1964, the US-supported government in Saigon tottered toward collapse before an insurgency much strengthened by infiltration of men and weapons from North Vietnam. Karachi (then Pakistan's capital) was a close US ally and member of SEATO, and thus not in a position to itself inquire of Hanoi about its strategy. Beijing, on the other hand, was well placed to inform Karachi about Hanoi's clever and apparently successful strategy. But it is also possible that Pakistani strategists independently developed this approach. Indian intelligence sources reported that Chinese personnel were involved training insurgents at camps in Pakistan, and that substantial amounts of Chinese materials were taken from insurgents: matches, flashlights, and such.[56] One critical assumption of the Pakistani plan was that India would not respond to the insurgency with a conventional attack on Pakistan. Alignment with China may have been seen as a key factor preventing this. China's ability to punish India had been demonstrated in 1962. In any event, Pakistani calculations proved wrong. India moved toward a full-scale assault on Pakistan in September. As it did, China weighed in in an effort to deter India from escalating to the level of conventional war.

In March 1965, as Karachi's pseudo-insurgency was getting under way, Pakistan leader General Ayub Khan visited Beijing to strengthen the new entente. Ayub Khan explained to Chinese leaders that Pakistan would not go along with US efforts "to make India into a counterforce to China, both economically and militarily." Khan condemned US and Soviet military aid to India, and promised that Pakistan would resist US pressure to oppose China. Khan's meeting with Mao was extremely cordial. "China and Pakistan could trust each other as neither has the intention of pulling the rug under the feet of the other," Mao told Ayub.[57] As the insurgency in Indian Kashmir flared in fall 1965 and India responded by mobilizing troops on Pakistan's borders, Beijing strengthened its deterrent support for Pakistan. On August 29, Beijing protested India's purported "flagrant disregard for Chinese sovereignty" on the Sikkim-China border at Chola Pass, where India had built "aggressive military structures on Chinese territory": "The Chinese government must warn India that if it does not immediately stop all such acts of aggression and provocation, it must bear full responsibility for the consequences that may arise there from."[58] Coming only three years after 1962, these threats were taken very seriously in India. In September, *Renmin ribao* declared China's support for the "Kashmir people's struggle for national self-determination."[59] India faced a two-front threat, in the West and in the North.

On September 6, India launched a large conventional assault on West Pakistan. Intense fighting entailed some of the largest armored battles since World War II. On September 7, Zhou Enlai termed the Indian assault on Pakistan an "act of naked aggression." Later the same day, Zhou informed the Pakistani ambassador that China was watching developments and considering its response. Zhou sought two assurances from Karachi in the event Chinese entered the war in support of Pakistan. First, Pakistan would not submit to any Kashmir solution favorable to India. Second, Pakistan would not submit to US, Soviet, or United Nations pressure for a pro-Indian Kashmir solution. In effect, Zhou was seeking a guarantee that Karachi would not abandon Beijing. Foreign Minister Chen Yi flew to Karachi to tell Pakistani foreign minister Z. A. Bhutto that China would go to any length to support Pakistan. President Ayub Khan provided the guarantees requested by Zhou Enlai.[60] On September 8, PRC President Liu Shaoqi sent a letter to Ayub promising Chinese support in the event the war continued. If India attacked East Pakistan, China would counter by opening operations in the Himalayas. The same day, Beijing radio announced that Chinese forces on the border had been put on alert and that unless India dismantled all military structures on the Sikkim-Tibet border and ceased its "frenzied provocative activities," all consequences would lie with India. A week later, at midnight on September 16, as a tank battle raged between India and Pakistan around Lahore, a deputy Chinese foreign minister summoned the Indian chargé in Beijing and informed him that unless India dismantled all military structures on the Sikkim-Tibetan border "within three days of the delivery of the present note," India would "bear full responsibility for all the grave consequences." This was an ultimatum threatening Chinese attack. Mao was apparently prepared to enter the war in support of Pakistan.[61]

China's threat of intervention produced US support for a Soviet effort to mediate the India-Pakistan conflict. Pakistan's leaders faced a choice. They could accept Chinese support and assistance, and wage a protracted war against India in alliance with China. In that event, India was likely to be backed by both Moscow and Washington. Or Pakistan could accede to US, Soviet, and United Nations pressure for a ceasefire, ending the war well short of gaining Pakistan's goals vis-à-vis Kashmir. A group within the Pakistani leadership reportedly favored a war in alliance with China in which China would seize a large chunk of India's NEFA to be exchanged for Kashmir. (It is not clear what China would get out of such a swap.) President Ayub Khan ultimately decided that protracted war beside China but with all other major powers in opposition was too risky a course, and decided on a cease-fire. Before announcing that decision, however, Khan wanted to assure that our "Chinese friends be taken into full confidence," and their reaction be given the "fullest consideration."[62] Khan himself flew to Beijing to explain his choice to Mao and Zhou. Mao gave Pakistan full freedom of action, promising to support whatever choice Pakistan made. If Pakistan chose protracted war, China was prepared to bear even the heaviest sacrifices. "Mr. President," Mao told Ayub, "if there is nuclear war, it is Beijing and not Rawalpindi [then Pakistan's provisional capital] that will be the target." Mao was apparently prepared for a second war with India. China avoided that by the decision of Pakistan's rulers.

8 }

Revolutionary China's Quest to Transform Southeast Asia

Expanding the Socialist Camp in Southeast Asia

Throughout the period of Mao's rule, the CCP encouraged and supported communist-led revolutionary movements across Southeast Asia. Starting in the early 1960s and continuing through the 1970s, the CCP gave substantial material and political support to those movements: training, radio stations, sanctuary and refuge in China, declarations of support, propaganda about revolutionary successes, and in some cases money, arms, and in one case, even Chinese volunteers. Ultimately, this support for communist-led insurgencies became one of the defining characteristics of China's ties with Southeast Asian countries during this period.

What explains this revolutionary quest? Pushing back US military encirclement and containment of China is part of the answer. In 1965, China published a major statement on international affairs that explained the proliferation of armed insurgencies in defensive terms. Entitled "Long Live the Victory of People's War," the tract argued that the proliferation of armed insurgencies across Asia, Africa, and Latin America would tie down and weaken the United States, making less likely a US attack on China or other members of the socialist camp.[1] This defensive explanation works fairly well in the cases of South Vietnam, Thailand, and the Philippines, all of which were partners of the United States in containing China. Problems emerge, however, when trying to apply the defensive "pushing back the United States" explanation to several non-aligned countries that were not part of US containment efforts: Burma, Indonesia, and Cambodia. Burma and Indonesia conspicuously disassociated themselves from US containment, yet both became major targets of CCP revolutionary activism. In Cambodia, the situation was more complex, but there too Chinese policy sought communist-led revolution, not merely containment-excluding neutrality. Moreover, Chinese support for revolutionary movements within a Southeast Asian country was likely to push that country into alignment with US containment efforts. China's diplomacy during the Bandung era had clearly recognized this and attempted to reassure countries of China's nonthreatening intentions in order to counter US efforts to contain China. Why then did Beijing discard efforts to reassure Southeast Asian governments and opt, instead, to support communist insurgencies that would push Southeast Asian countries toward Washington? Ideological commitment to spreading socialism is a large part of the explanation of China's period of revolutionary activism. Mao sought the victory of communist-led armed struggles across Southeast Asia because he believed that such victories would be a great advance for these peoples along the historical teleology laid out by Marxism-Leninism and to which Mao had dedicated his life. Mao believed that Lenin and Stalin had demonstrated their commitment to this great cause of world socialism, and he too, would establish himself as successor to those exalted demigods by making great contributions to that historic project. The CCP's December 1956 statement on the "Stalin question," for example, explained that "part of the universally applicable truth of Marxism-Leninism is that the revolutionary state firmly adheres to the principle of proletarian internationalism . . . and strives to help . . . all oppressed nations." The statement lauded the advances of socialism achieved under Stalin:

> The heroic armies of the Soviet Union liberated the East European countries and the northern part of Korea in cooperation with the popular forces of those countries. The Soviet Union has established friendly relations with the People's Democracies, and aided them in economic construction and, together with them, formed a mighty bulwark of world peace . . . the camp of socialism. The Soviet Union has also given powerful support to the independence movements of the oppressed nations . . . to the many peaceable new states in Asia and Africa established since the Second World War."[2]

If Stalin's contributions to expanding world socialism had come primarily in Eastern Europe, Mao's would come in Southeast Asia. Stalin had used Soviet armed forces as an agent of social revolution. Mao Zedong would not do that, he and his comrades decided. But that did not mean they abandoned their revolutionary duty. Revolutions in various countries would have to be made by the people of those countries. Revolution should not be exported by tanks and bayonets. But the principles of Marxism-Leninism required that China fulfill its proletarian internationalist duty by supporting revolutionary struggles. Of course, success in spreading socialism would indicate that Mao, not Khrushchev, was "correct" and thus entitled to recognition as successor to Lenin and Stalin as leader of the world communist movement. Successful revolutions in Southeast Asia would prove the correctness of Mao's Thought.

Revolutionary upheaval in Southeast Asia was also linked to revolutionary advance in China. This was perhaps the decisive factor for Mao. A powerful wave of revolutionary advance around the world, with many of those advances demonstrating the correctness of Mao Zedong's revolutionary strategies and thought, would help mobilize the Chinese people to continue the revolutionary struggle in China—to defeat revisionism and prevent the restoration of capitalism. The tyranny of distance limited China's ability to fan the flames of revolution in Africa or Latin America. Southeast Asia was nearby and had, in some cases, deep historic links with China that could be used to revolutionary advantage.

Southeast Asia as a Traditional Chinese Sphere of Influence

Southeast Asia was long a traditional area of Chinese influence. Chinese ways and techniques washed over Southeast Asia—as did those of India from a different direction. A number of Southeast Asian kingdoms found it convenient for one reason or another to enter into "tributary" relations with the Chinese emperor. For kingdoms close to China, like Vietnam or Burma, a tributary relation was often preferable to constant war with China or outright Chinese annexation. States more distant from China's borders—Thailand, Cham on the Mekong delta, or the Moslem rulers of Malacca, Java, or Sulu Island—often found other reasons to formally subordinate themselves to the emperor of China, as required by a tributary relation. A tributary relation with China typically opened the door to lucrative trade opportunities. Symbols of political legitimization—a fancy looking writ of office, an accurate calendar, and Chinese representatives at solemn ceremonies—were often useful. Chinese concubines, craftsmen, and advisors were appreciated. In certain extreme situations, a loyal tributary might call on Chinese assistance to repress a rebellion, foil or undo a coup, or repel foreign invasion, although those services were by no means automatic and depended, among other things, on how "obedient" the petitioning tributary had been in the past. Episodes of imperial expansion under the Mongol Yuan and during the first decades of the Ming Dynasty recruited more tributaries.

Commercial links between China and Southeast Asia were strong. A robust "maritime silk route" linked southeastern Chinese ports to settlements around the Strait of Malacca, and forged commercial links between these regions. Chinese tea, silk, porcelain, and lacquerware were avidly sought in Europe and supported a prosperous trade. The arrival in the seventeenth century of European ship technology and global trade networks reinforced earlier trade links. European rule over many of the lands of Southeast Asia encouraged the migration of ethnic Chinese to the new colonies for purposes of economic development. The formation of substantial communities of ethnic Chinese in almost all the lands of Southeast Asia further deepened commercial relations and the transmission of Chinese ways. By the time the People's Republic of China appeared on the scene, ethnic Chinese constituted about one-quarter of Malaysia's population, 15 percent of Brunei's, 8 percent of Thailand's, and about 3 percent of Indonesia's. In most cases, those ethnic Chinese communities controlled a hugely disproportionate share of the local economy, often serving as intermediaries between rural farmers and the urban colonial elites.

As nationalist ideologies began washing across Asia in the twentieth century, the ethnic Chinese communities of Southeast Asia had to think through where their motherland lay. Many identified with China. The revolutionary movement led by the KMT garnered much support from Southeast Asian Chinese. So too did China's long and bitter war of resistance against Japan. A sharply anti-Chinese edge to Japanese racialist thinking in that era further encouraged support for China's anti-Japan struggle. The KMT and the CCP set up organizations in Southeast Asia to court support among those communities—a competition that continues today.

Outspoken identity with China and contribution to China's various political and economic efforts exacerbated suspicions by the non-Chinese native populations of Southeast Asian countries about the loyalties of local Chinese. Were they loyal to China or to the countries where they were born (in most cases) and lived? China's revolutionary activism in Southeast Asia over a period of several decades exacerbated these local apprehensions. During the Bandung period, Beijing sought to reassure Southeast Asian governments that China had no claim on the loyalties of local ethnic Chinese. With the revolutionary thrust of the 1960s and 1970s, however, Chinese policy shifted sharply, with ethnic Chinese communities being mobilized for revolutionary struggle. After Deng Xiaoping ended the era of revolutionary activism, Chinese policy shifted again. In the 1980s, Beijing would once again look to Southeast Asia's Chinese businessmen to help jump-start China's opening to the world economy.

China's several-decade-long revolutionary thrust in Southeast Asia can be seen as an attempt to undo the "humiliation" inflicted on China during the Century of National Humiliation. Prior to the European intrusion in the nineteenth century, China had been the paramount power in this vast region. China had been toppled from that region by aggressive Western imperialism. But now China was rising, was strong once again, and was moving to restore its rightful position of regional dominance. But this effort took political forms of the twentieth century.

Beijing's Dual-Track Approach (Party and State)

Chinese support for wars of national liberation in the intermediate zone between the socialist camp and imperialism could easily spoil PRC relations with governments targeted for overthrow. The CCP attempted to manage this contradiction by insisting that government-to-government ties were separate from party-to-party ties between the CCP and foreign communist parties at the core of wars of national liberation. This was called the "dual-track approach." Under it, the MFA sought friendly, cooperative relations with the governments of various countries, even while the CCP's International Liaison Department (ILD) might be training and financing an insurgency seeking to overthrow those governments. Visits by foreign communist leaders to China for talks with CCP officials were often publicized with the party affiliation of the Chinese officials receiving them being carefully specified. Such interactions were carefully scripted as party-to-party, and not state-to-state, interactions. This did not greatly reassure governments targeted for overthrow. Memory of this twenty-year-long period of Chinese revolutionary activism, from 1960 to 1979, is an important part of the contemporary Southeast Asian perceptions of China.

Deep secrecy about China's support for foreign insurgencies was a second tactic used by Beijing to manage the contradiction between the two halves of the dual-track approach. Communist Party of Malaya chief Chin Peng outlined the scope of ILD work underway and the veil of secrecy surrounding that work when he arrived in Beijing in June 1961. Chin Peng was surprised by the extent of ILD support for various Southeast Asian communist parties: "I realised the Chinese Communists were well down the track of funding the other South East Asian fraternal parties. All had representatives in residence and large batches of people under varying training schemes."[3] The Burma, Thai, Cambodian, Laotian, and Indonesian communist parties all had "training facilities" in China, Peng discovered. Delegations of these parties were housed in a well-guarded, walled, isolated, and secret compound in central Beijing run by the CCP's International Liaison Department. To enhance secrecy, family members of the various foreign delegations lived in this walled compound, but they were not allowed to enter a separate work area. Two Politburo members, Kang Sheng and Liu Ningyi, the former being one of China's most powerful leaders, oversaw the compound and conducted discussions with the foreign partydelegations. Kang was a member of the Politburo Standing Committee with responsibility for internal security and external intelligence. He was also one of Mao's key allies in the struggle against "revisionists" within the CCP. Chin Peng assumed that Liu and Kang reported to Mao.

The CCP maintained ties with several East Asian communist parties before 1949, and those ties thickened after that pivotal year. But it was not until the early 1960s that CCP revolutionary activism went into high gear. Starting in 1962, as Mao was intensifying the struggle against domestic and international revisionism, the CCP undertook a bold and geographically wide-ranging effort to encourage and support communist-led insurgencies across Southeast Asia. This effort meshed with the CCP's rejection of the CPSU's embrace of peaceful coexistence and was, in effect, an attempt to put into practice the correct line prescribed by Mao for the international communist movement.

Wang Jiaxiang's February 1962 proposal of a return to a Bandung-era approach to foreign policy was discussed in the previous chapter. The "one reduction" component of Wang's proposal entailed reduction of support for foreign insurgencies. Wang was head of the ILD and, as such, responsible for contact with foreign revolutionary movements and communist parties. As shown in a previous chapter, Wang's proposal to reduce support for foreign wars of national liberation was decisively rejected by Mao. The CCP should increase, not decrease, support for wars of national liberation in the intermediate zone, Mao insisted. The strategy underlying this CCP revolutionary activism was outlined by Mao in talks with VWP Secretary General Le Duan in August 1964, as conveyed to and reported by Chin Peng. Revolution would soon sweep across Southeast Asia, Mao told Le Duan. Revolutionary victories would occur one after another in Vietnam, Cambodia, Thailand, and Malaysia.[4]

The CCP and Hanoi's War to "Liberate" South Vietnam

The VWP insurgency in South Vietnam constituted the central element of the CCP's Southeast Asian revolutionary offensive. In January 1959, the VWP determined that growing revolutionary activity in the South, combined with repression of the revolutionary forces by the US-supported Saigon government, required initiation of armed struggle to overthrow the Saigon regime.[5] In line with this decision, personnel and materials were infiltrated south along trails newly carved in the mountains and jungles of eastern and southern Laos and eastern Cambodia. VWP efforts met with substantial success; insurgency grew rapidly in South Vietnam. Unfortunately for Hanoi, the Kennedy administration (inaugurated in January 1961) responded by sending in ever more US military advisors to support the increasingly embattled Saigon government. Under these circumstances, Hanoi sought Chinese support. In June 1961, DRV Premier Pham Van Dong visited Beijing for talks with Chinese leaders. Mao promised support for the VWP's war to take over South Vietnam.[6]

CCP leaders urged the VWP to follow the CCP's successful path of protracted guerrilla war, avoiding large-unit battles with the enemy for a long initial period of "strategic defense."[7] Throughout Hanoi's long war with the United States, it was important to Beijing that Hanoi cleave to Mao's military strategy. Otherwise, how could Hanoi's success confirm the correctness of Mao's line? Since Vietnam's war of national liberation was the prime display of the correctness of Mao's theory, it was important to Beijing that Hanoi actually follow Mao's strategy.

The military strategy worked out by VWP General Secretary Le Duan and his chief general Nguyen Chi Thanh differed from Mao's model of protracted people's war in several ways. One was by stressing large-unit battles (battalion size and above; a battalion is roughly 1,000 men).[8] From Le Duan and Thanh's perspective, the VWP had available resources simply unavailable to Mao circa 1938 when he worked out his three-stage strategy of protracted guerrilla war. North Vietnam had an industrial base far superior to that enjoyed by the CCP in China's interior in the 1930s. Le Duan's "south first" strategy called for complete mobilization of the north's economy for war in the south.[9] Moreover, Hanoi had two powerful socialist allies, the PRC and the USSR, able and willing to supply VWP forces. The CCP in the 1930s had had to deal with a much weaker and more isolated Soviet Union which had to act cautiously in supporting anti-imperialist struggles. In the 1960s, the socialist camp was vastly stronger and more able to assist world revolutionary movements. From these differences, Le Duan and Thanh devised a strategy that mixed Maoist-style low-intensity, smaller-unit guerrilla warfare with aggressive assaults by big, well-armed units against the enemy's main forces. From the CCP perspective, this was a recipe for disaster. By massing revolutionary forces and launching fixed battles against superior enemy forces, revolutionary forces would suffer heavy losses. The CCP had experienced the consequences of such tactics in 1926–1927 when the Comintern had ordered CCP assaults on KMT-held cities. From the CCP perspective, the VWP was in danger of making the same mistake. Of course, Thanh's mixed strategy also included Maoist-style guerrilla war. When VWP leaders visited Beijing, they talked up this Maoist aspect of Vietnamese strategy.

In December 1961, PLA Marshal and General Ye Jianying visited Hanoi to discuss military strategy. The liberation wars in South Vietnam should rely on protracted guerrilla warfare and avoid battalion-size fixed battles, Ye argued. Big battles would allow the United States to target revolutionary forces with overwhelming air and artillery bombardment, producing heavy losses that could lead to demoralization.[10] DRV generals listened carefully to Ye's arguments, but Hanoi's war in the south continued along the lines of Nguyen Chi Thanh's strategy of mixing low-intensity guerrilla war and aggressive large-unit battles—at least until 1968–1969, when Hanoi gave priority to big battles. (Thanh died in July 1967.) The result of the VWP's "big battle" approach was generally what Beijing had predicted: extremely heavy casualties and demoralization. This meant that, with its guerrilla bases and forces in the south shattered, Hanoi became increasingly dependent on a "big unit, big battle" approach, and on the weaponry for such an approach that only Moscow could provide. In 1962, however, that result was still several years in the future.

In summer 1962, Ho Chi Minh and Nguyen Chi Thanh visited Beijing to seek increased Chinese help. The war in South Vietnam was going very well, the VWP leaders explained. But US intervention was also deepening. Moreover, there were indications that the United States might attack the DRV by air. In this situation, the VWP needed to further intensify the struggle, with Chinese assistance. Mao agreed. China would supply, gratis, 90,000 rifles and other equipment sufficient to arm 230 battalions.[11] During late 1962, VWP-commanded guerrilla forces in South Vietnam gave up the hodge-podge of weapons they had been using and were rearmed with Chinese AK-47 assault rifles, mortars, and machine guns.

In October 1962, another VWP delegation arrived in Beijing. This one was headed by General Vo Nguyen Giap, the mastermind of the war against the French. Giap pleaded for still greater Chinese assistance. The total mobilization of North Vietnam's economy to support the war in the south was causing increased difficulties in the north. Moreover, the United States was intervening ever more deeply. The VWP needed China's political support. Zhou Enlai promised Chinese economic, political, and military support.

It is noteworthy that the PRC's security environment was extremely poor in fall 1962 as Mao and the CCP stepped up support for Hanoi. Beijing faced a still-severe economic situation, spiraling tension with India, possible US-supported KMT invasion on China's southeast coast, and collapse of the alliance with the USSR. Yet instead of acting with greater caution in face of these difficulties, as Wang Jiaxiang's letter had recommended, the PRC, under Mao, waded deeper into support for the world revolution.

Revolutionary conditions in South Vietnam were even better by fall 1963. Deep sectarian cleavages between the Catholic-based regime of South Vietnam's President Ngo Dinh Diem and South Vietnam's Buddhist clergy flared into open confrontation. Government repression precipitated self-immolation by Buddhist monks, which in turn mobilized large and militant demonstrations. These deepening divisions culminated in the assassination of Diem in November, only weeks before the assassination of John Kennedy in Dallas, Texas. Diem's death produced a political vacuum and deeper paralysis of the South Vietnamese government. Insurgent control in the countryside expanded rapidly. The United States faced a presidential election in November 1964, and President Johnson was unlikely to want to expand intervention in Vietnam before that election. 1964 therefore seemed like a window of opportunity for Hanoi. The VWP decided to go for broke in that year in an effort to topple the weak Saigon government and bring to power a "neutralist" government in Saigon that would ask the Americans to leave before they could intervene in force. The installation of a neutralist rather than a communist government would ease the task of inviting the Americans to leave. Once the Americans were gone, and with revolutionary forces very strong, the way would be open to moving the revolution to the next stage, with the VWP assuming leadership and moving the revolution into the socialist stage. This, in any case, was VWP strategy.[12] The flow of men and materiel down the trails thus increased greatly during 1964.

The CCP again supported the VWP's war. On August 29, 1963, as the crisis in Saigon escalated, Mao Zedong issued a statement "resolutely supporting" the "just struggle" of the South Vietnamese people.[13] Several months later, the deputy chief of staff of the PLA, General Li Tianyou, spent two months in North Vietnam working out a war plan for Hanoi.[14] The plan included provisions for Chinese assistance. China would construct coastal defenses and naval bases in northeastern Vietnam near China, an effort to deter US amphibious landings or raids.

China also convened a meeting of Indochinese communist parties to work out a regional strategy. Zhou Enlai presided over the meeting in Guangdong in September 1963. Zhou was confident that the United States would be defeated in Vietnam. US manpower was overstretched. The United States was committed in too many places around the world and simply could not devote adequate manpower to Vietnam. Zhou's strategic prescription comported with Mao's model: base areas in the countryside and protracted rural guerrilla war. China would serve as the reliable rear area for fraternal Southeast Asian parties, Zhou assured the assembly.

The "Neutralization" of Laos and the Struggle for South Vietnam

One of Beijing's most important contributions to the VWP's struggle was use of the threat of Chinese intervention in a war with the United States in Laos to secure US consent to a bogus "neutralization" of Laos that secured Hanoi's vital supply lines from the north through Laos to South Vietnam. Through a strategy of "fighting while talking" with the United States, by 1962 Beijing ensured that the rugged, jungle-clad mountains of the southern Laotian panhandle would host the trails carrying men and materiel from North Vietnam to battlefields in South Vietnam.

In 1959, Hanoi set up special military units to survey and lay out trails via southeastern Laos. Securing control over those infiltration trails was absolutely vital to the VWP's war plan. Troops and material would be fed south until finally the United States was exhausted. Beijing used its military might to secure this outcome via an international conference meeting in Geneva from May 16, 1961, to July 23, 1962, that ultimately produced a de facto division of

Laos between a communist-controlled eastern zone and an anti-communist controlled western zone.[15] This arrangement left Hanoi's trails in communist hands. Figure 8-1 illustrates features pertaining to Lao's role at this juncture.

Laos was an economically primitive country, vast in size (roughly double the size of New York State), but with a population of only 2 million, most of whom lived in the Mekong River valley on the west side of the country. The Geneva conference of 1954 had designated two northern provinces, Phong Saly and Sam Neua, as regroupment zones for the communist-led Pathet Lao pending national elections that were to reunify the country.[16] Unlike in Vietnam, where such elections were never held, in Laos they were held, in May

FIGURE 8-1 **Laos and the Struggle for South Vietnam**

1958, and resulted in strong Pathet Lao representation in the new National Assembly and in a coalition government headed by a neutralist prince.

Largely because of its potential role as a transport corridor, Washington viewed the struggle for Laos as part of a broader struggle for Indochina and Southeast Asia. The United States therefore decided to use its influence to bring to power an anticommunist government which would work with the United States to sever Hanoi's trails. This was accomplished; US aid paid most of the wages of the Laotian army. US military personnel, wearing civilian clothing out of deference to the 1954 Geneva agreement, began training the Laotian military. Beijing was deeply concerned that the United States might succeed, and countered by stepping up support for the Pathet Lao. The situation in Laos reached a crisis in August 1960, when a coup by neutralist military units ousted the US-backed anticommunist leader and brought the neutralist prince back to power. That restored neutralist government in turn collapsed after only two months, and neutralist forces fled to Phong Saly and Sam Neua to join the Pathet Lao. With additional but carefully camouflaged support from both North Vietnam and China, the Pathet Lao then launched an offensive that rapidly expanded the area under communist control. By February 1961, the Pathet Lao controlled the Plain of Jars and threatened Vientiane and Luang Prabang. The next month, China established ambassadorial-level diplomatic relations with the Pathet Lao government, with the neutralist prince as a figurehead. This meant that a Chinese military presence in Laos was covered by the sovereignty of the government recognized by Beijing. China also opened a consulate in Phong Saly, headed by a PLA major general and ex-commander of the Kunming Military Region. The PLA began constructing roads linking Mengla, in Yunnan, with Phong Saly. All this signaled preparation for Chinese intervention.

As fighting in Laos flared, an international conference seeking a negotiated settlement met in Geneva from May 1961 to July 1962. China viewed the fourteen-month-long second Geneva Conference on Indochina as political warfare against US imperialism, and employed its traditional tactic of "talking while fighting." Beijing had two paramount interests at Geneva: 1) preventing Laos from being drawn into the US military system (a system that already included Thailand, South Vietnam, and the Philippines), and 2) preventing impairment of the vital trails linking North and South Vietnam. When the conference got under way, there was significant US military presence in Laos. US military advisors, economic and military aid, and air power bolstered Laotian anticommunist forces in the continually shifting alignments of Laotian politics. There were also several thousand KMT "irregular" forces in the Burma-Laos border areas that had contacts with both US and Chinese Nationalist clandestine services. All of this posed for Beijing the specter of Laos becoming a military base for the United States. Preventing this via "neutralization" of Laos and, as part of that, the elimination of a US military presence in Laos was a major Chinese objective. Keeping US forces out of Laos would also facilitate VWP and Pathet Lao control over the trails. The threat of war with China in remote and primitive Laos would eventually compel the United States to accept "neutralization" of Laos along PRC lines.

The US-PRC confrontation over Laos peaked in early 1962, when anti-communist Laotian forces launched a large offensive in Nam Tha province supported by US air power, military advisors, and troop contingents from Thailand, South Vietnam, and the Philippines, plus KMT "irregulars." The Pathet Lao, supported by 100 battalions of North Vietnamese, launched a counteroffensive. The fighting for Nam Tha was intense. US advisors saw supplies and reinforcements for the Pathet Lao crossing the border from Yunnan into Laos as part of the battle, but could not determine if the personnel were Chinese, Vietnamese, or Laotian.[17] In any case, Chinese territory served as sanctuary. As fighting flared, President Kennedy ordered US forces deployed to the Thai-Laos border, threatening intervention.[18] Beijing issued severe warnings: China could not stand idly by if the United States threatened China's security by "embarking on direct military intervention in Laos." Beijing and Hanoi stood shoulder to shoulder; both threatened that US military intervention would doom the search for "neutralization" of Laos at Geneva. Simultaneously, however, Beijing urged the Pathet Lao to suspend their offensive. The United States too drew back from overt military involvement. By mid-1962, US strategists had concluded that the coastal and more developed nature of South Vietnam made it, not Laos, the prudent location for the United States to draw the line of containment of communism in Southeast Asia. Beijing had used the threat of war to secure US acquiesce to Pathet Lao control of eastern Laos along with exclusion of a US military presence from all of Laos.

At Geneva, a number of issues touched on the integrity of Hanoi's logistical trails through Laos. Regarding withdrawal of "foreign military personnel," Beijing insisted that the only issue to be decided by the Conference was the withdrawal of US and US-aligned military forces. It was those forces, Foreign Minister Chen Yi insisted, that were interfering in Lao's internal affairs and threatening China and peace in Southeast Asia. China's representatives, along with those of the Soviet Union, the DRV, and the Pathet Lao, simply acted as though there were no North Vietnamese troops in Laos. For example, when US representatives insisted that there were, in fact, large numbers of North Vietnamese troops in eastern Laos, and that Hanoi was using Laotian territory as an avenue of transit for their guerrilla attacks on South Vietnam," China's representative Zhang Hanfu insisted that US assertions were merely a smokescreen for keeping US military forces in Laos in violation of Laos' neutrality and sovereignty.[19] When South Vietnam's representative proposed inclusion in the declaration of a prohibition on use of Laotian territory as a transport corridor between North and South Vietnam, the United

States supported the proposal. China and North Vietnam together rejected the proposal as interference with Laos' sovereignty and independence, and as a US scheme to put Laotian territory under US control. This idea too was dropped.

The issue of integration of Pathet Lao armed forces into a national Laotian army also touched on the VWP ability to control the trails. The United States argued for amalgamation of the several Laotian armies into a single national army—as had been the case with Austria in 1955—on the grounds that this was essential for a successful neutralization of Laos. Beijing and Hanoi would have none of it. The US proposal was nothing less than an attempt to wipe out Lao's "patriotic forces," Beijing said. Again the United States dropped the issue. The crux of the matter was that the VWP needed cooperation with a reliable Laotian military force to protect its trails: to garner intelligence from locals; to provide a Laotian facade when outsiders, such as Western journalists, visited; to interface with the local populace to procure labor or supplies; and to help fight whenever US covert or special forces showed up. The Pathet Lao military remained intact to serve as Hanoi's reliable partner throughout the war.

China's "fighting while talking" at the 1962 Geneva Convention made an extremely important contribution to the ultimate success of the VWP's war for South Vietnam. Together with Beijing's persuasion of Sihanouk to tolerate the trails in eastern Cambodia (a matter dealt with below), China's 1962 victory at Geneva allowed men and material to continue flowing to battlefields in South Vietnam. The United States and Saigon never succeeded in cutting that flow. Moreover, the Declaration on the Neutrality of Laos signed on July 23, 1962, gave Beijing and Hanoi a legal basis for condemnation of US efforts to disrupt the trails by air bombardment and covert special operations.

Burma

If South Vietnam was a close US ally and SEATO "associate" posing a threat to PRC security, Burma was a leading member of the non-aligned movement and a country with long cordial relations with the PRC.[20] Burma and the PRC established diplomatic relations at the ambassadorial level on June 8, 1950. Relations became warm in the early 1950s, when the two countries cooperated militarily to deal with KMT remnants in northern Burma supported by the United States and Nationalist China. Summit exchanges between Zhou Enlai and Prime Minister U Nu began in 1954 and continued through a visit by President Liu Shaoqi in 1963. In 1960, a treaty of friendship and mutual non-aggression and another treaty settling the border issue were signed.[21] Burma had no military link to the United States or the West. Non-aligned Yugoslavia was its major arms supplier. In late 1960 and early

1961, Burma's government secretly approved PLA incursions into northern Burma to degrade Nationalist forces still operating in that region.[22] In 1960, Burma and the PRC signed a boundary treaty ending a long-running territorial dispute. There were frequent high-level exchanges between Chinese and Burmese leaders. To all appearances, Sino-Burma relations were close and cordial. And yet in August 1962 the CCP began giving robust assistance to a revolutionary drive led by the Burma Communist Party (BCP).[23]

The BCP had launched armed struggle against the Rangoon government in 1948, and top leaders of the BCP had been given refuge in the PRC in the early 1950s. Neutralist Burma's non-aligned foreign policies played a significant role in the PRC's efforts to foil US containment, however, and Beijing's courtship of Rangoon limited CCP support for the BCP—until 1962. In that year, a military coup ousting a civilian government led Beijing to conclude that conditions were now ripe for revolution, and the CCP threw its support behind that revolutionary effort even though Burma's new military rulers continued the neutralist, non-aligned foreign policies of previous governments. This suggests that it was internal revolutionary transformation, not merely benign neighbors, that Beijing sought.

In August 1962, a new BCP leadership group to direct the armed struggle was set up in Beijing. The BCP was allowed to begin printing in Beijing revolutionary propaganda for distribution inside Burma. The CCP also recruited several hundred Kachin ex-insurgents to serve as a core of hardened and experienced fighters for the BCP. These men had been involved in the ethnic insurgencies of the late 1940s and early 1950s in Burma, had subsequently sought refuge in China, and had been assigned land to farm in China's Guizhou province. Circa 1962, these men were mobilized, armed, retrained, given political education by BCP cadre, and stationed in southwest Yunnan along the border with Burma. Inside Burma, small cells of ethnic Chinese communists were put in touch with the BCP for the first time, further expanding the BCP's base. Routes for motor roads along the Yunnan-Burma border were surveyed, and construction of roads pushed forward. In 1967, Chinese support increased further when PLA advisors were assigned as "volunteers" to all BCP military units. Additional manpower was provided by several thousand PRC Red Guard youth recruited and assigned to BCP units. By early 1968, preparations were complete, and a powerful BCP-PLA force pushed into northeast Burma with the objective of seizing Mandalay to serve as the capital of a liberated area. This BCP-PLA force was a conventional force with artillery, anti-aircraft guns, trucks, field communications, and medical support. Burmese armed forces were hard pressed, but eventually contained the communist advance within a 20,000 square-kilometer base area along the border with China. Fighting, often heavy, continued through the 1970s and into the 1980s. Eventually (in the late 1980s), conflicts between the BCP's ethnic Chinese leadership and the Kachins who supplied the bulk of the fighting forces undermined the revolutionary forces.

Cambodia

Sihanouk's policy of cooperation with China and North Vietnam's war effort in South Vietnam meant that the beginning of China's support for a Cambodian communist drive to seize power came later than elsewhere in Indochina. Beijing nurtured Sihanouk's "neutralism" as long as Sihanouk remained in power (he was overthrown by a coup in March 1970), but simultaneously made preparations for an eventual communist-led revolutionary uprising.

When diplomatic relations between the PRC and Cambodia were established in 1958, the new PRC embassy in Phnom Penh had a large staff under the control of Chinese intelligence rather than the Ministry of Foreign Affairs, and was responsible for contacts with Cambodian revolutionary organizations.[24] PRC agents supported creation of a Chinese Association in Cambodia to serve as a base for the Cambodian Communist Party. Some of that Association's activities were open: newspapers, schools, athletic competitions, and commerce. Other activities were semi-secret. Still others were completely secret, for example those involving use of money, manpower, and publicity to mobilize the masses to support the Cambodian revolution. All activities were under the direct leadership of the PRC embassy according to Zhou Degao, who says he was responsible for media in this arrangement. Eventually, by 1972, the leaders of the Kampuchean Communist Party (with Pol Pot as the paramount leader) concluded that China wanted to control the Cambodian revolution via the Chinese Association. Consequently, in 1972 that Association was "voluntarily self-dissolved" and its members assigned "virgin land" in areas under Khmer Rouge control. Most simply disappeared.[25]

With the onset of CCP-CPSU rivalry within the international communist movement in the late 1950s, Beijing began supporting a group of French-trained and urban-based Maoist Cambodian communists, the group that eventually became the Khmer Rouge. The mainstream of the Cambodian Communist Party was too Soviet-trained, too pro-VWP, and too moderate for Beijing's taste. This led in 1960 to the formation of a new communist group in which the returned French students played a prominent role. This group was implacably hostile to Sihanouk and called for his overthrow. In February 1962, Pol Pot became Secretary General of this new group, later renamed the Kampuchean Communist Party (KCP). In May 1963, the leadership moved to a rural border area in preparation for armed struggle. This group had China's patronage.[26] At that point, neither the CCP nor the VWP had an interest in supporting armed struggle against Cambodian leader Norodom Sihanouk. This was partially a function of the struggle underway for South Vietnam.

In the late 1950s, as the VWP began preparing logistical lines to support the armed struggle in South Vietnam, Beijing persuaded Sihanouk to turn a blind eye to the trails being laid out by North Vietnam from the southern Laotian panhandle through eastern Cambodia to South Vietnam. Persuading Sihanouk to cooperate with Hanoi's war plan may have been, along with Beijing's role in the "neutralization" of Laos, Beijing's most important political contribution to the VWP's ultimate victory. In effect, Beijing guaranteed that Vietnam would withdraw from eastern Cambodia once South Vietnam was liberated. Sihanouk was also persuaded to allow cargo destined for North Vietnamese forces in South Vietnam to enter via the port of Sihanoukville (later named Kompong Som). As long as Sihanouk was willing to cooperate with the VWP's war in this fashion, neither Hanoi nor Beijing was interested in ousting him. CCP strategy was to use Sihanouk's neutralism to safeguard the trails and defeat the United States, while supporting Pol Pot's KCP as a barrier against possible VWP domination of Cambodia in a post-Sihanouk era.

In late 1964, Pol Pot (at that time still known as Saloth Sar)—then still the leader of only one wing of the party—traveled clandestinely to Hanoi and Beijing seeking a green light for an all-out uprising against Sihanouk. Pol Pot felt that Cambodia was ripe for revolution. Hanoi was opposed, fearing it would foul up arrangements worked out with Sihanouk for sanctuary in eastern Cambodia. VWP Secretary General Le Duan stressed the importance of the Vietnamese revolution for all of Indochina, and urged that the Cambodian revolution wait until the victory of Vietnam's revolution. Pol Pot concluded from these discussions that the VWP wanted to control the Cambodian revolution, and added DRV-trained Cambodian cadres to his growing list of enemies. In Beijing, in 1964, Deng Xiaoping was Pol Pot's interlocutor. Pol Pot laid out the situation for Deng Xiaoping, including his suspicions that the VWP hoped to dominate Cambodia once Sihanouk's regime was overthrown. Deng Xiaoping seconded Pol Pot's suspicions of Hanoi, but urged him to keep those views to himself.[27] Sihanouk, according to scholar Ben Kiernan, was under the illusion that Hanoi, not Beijing, was Pol Pot's patron. This illusion was useful to Beijing because it led Sihanouk to blame Hanoi, not Beijing, for the widening scope of anti-Sihanouk activities being conducted by the KCP. Beijing was simultaneously supporting Sihanouk and laying the basis for his overthrow, but Sihanouk's belief in the VWP-KCP patron-client link blinded him to Beijing's double game, according to Kiernan.

During Pol Pot's 1964 Beijing visit, President Liu Shaoqi, Deng Xiaoping, and Politburo member and Beijing Mayor Peng Zhen flattered Pol Pot by lauding his deep understanding of Marxist-Leninist theory and the importance of the Cambodian revolution. CCP leaders promised material aid to the Kampuchean revolution, according to Zhou Degao.[28] After Pol Pot returned from Beijing, the KCP intensified preparations for armed struggle in Cambodia's countryside. In October 1966, the KCP forwarded to Beijing a plan to initiate armed struggle. The VWP intercepted this message and strongly opposed the plan out of fear it would disrupt Hanoi's vital use of eastern Cambodia for sanctuary and logistical purposes. In spite of Hanoi's efforts to abort the KCP insurgency, that rebellion was launched in April 1967. Beijing's message to the VWP was that the KCP enjoyed China's protection and should not be restricted.[29]

By mid-1967, Sihanouk was troubled enough by revolutionary agitation being conducted in Cambodia's Chinese community that he ordered an investigation of that activity. The PRC embassy, under the influence of Cultural Revolutionary pressure, issued two public letters insisting that every Chinese had the right to venerate Chairman Mao and distribute his works. Sihanouk dispatched an emissary to pursue the matter in Beijing. When Zhou Enlai requested that ethnic Chinese in Cambodia be given the right to love Chairman Mao, love the CCP, and love the PRC, the Cambodian side reacted very negatively and Zhou withdrew his request. Sihanouk then dissolved the Cambodian-Chinese friendship association and warned all media against propagating "foreign ideologies." Sihanouk went so far as to order the withdrawal of all Chinese embassy personnel, being dissuaded from this only by a personal plea by Zhou Enlai.[30] Beijing was balancing carefully between strengthening Cambodia's revolutionary forces on the one hand, and persuading Sihanouk to continue tolerating the VWP's trails on the other hand.

Sihanouk's ouster in March 1970 led the CCP and VWP to support the KCP's revolutionary push and, consequently, to a very rapid expansion of territory under KCP control. The KCP simply did not have enough cadres to administer the expanded territories. The PRC embassy chipped in by directing ethnic Chinese cadres, who had previously accepted joint control by the CCP and the KCP, to go to the new liberated areas and mobilize the "enlightened masses."[31] The CCP also reached agreement with the KCP that all "Chinese comrades" would be exclusively under the control of the KCP. Some of the Chinese comrades objected, fearing that they would not be trusted by the KCP. Such objections were overridden: "Henceforth you have no relation with China," one dissenting ex-Chinese comrade was told in Beijing.[32] When the Khmer Rouge later emptied Cambodia's cities after the collapse of the pro-US regime, those ultrarevolutionary policies fell heavy on ethnic Chinese. Zhou Degao estimates that one-third of the ethnic Chinese in Cambodia were killed in the three years and eight months of Khmer Rouge rule. Beijing's callous handling of patriotic Chinese in Cambodia was the main reason for Zhou Degao's break with Beijing. The PRC embassy in Phnom Penh saw its main mission as promoting world revolution by advancing the Kampuchean revolution, and viewed the community of ethnic Chinese in Cambodia as an expendable pawn in that game.[33]

Malaya

The Communist Party of Malaya (CPM) was formed in 1930 under Comintern guidance. The abrupt surrender of Japanese forces in August 1945 combined with delay in the arrival of British forces created a power vacuum which the CPM seized to expand their control, especially in ethnic Chinese communities of Malaya, constituting roughly one-third of the total population. With the return of British colonial authority, the CPM-led anti-Japanese wartime resistance organization was dissolved, but a secret section of that organization was held in readiness. That secret organization's first task was burial, rather than surrender, of stocks of arms and ammunition.[34] The Federation of Malaya was established under British tutelage in January 1948. (It became independent in August 1957.) Two months later, in March 1948, the CPM Central Committee endorsed the Cominform's recently promulgated view of the division of Asia into "two camps" and the corollary need for armed struggle against the imperialists. According to this new analysis, the Federation of Malaya was a puppet of imperialism in need of revolutionary overthrow. Militancy by CPM-led labor unions spiraled. Colonial authorities responded in June 1948 by proclaiming a state of emergency and arresting CPM militants. Communist survivors fled to jungle areas and began setting up base areas along the model of the increasingly successful Chinese communist model.

The CCP's drive toward victory in China's civil war led to a rapid reorientation of the CPM away from Moscow and toward China. CPM leaders were mostly ethnic Chinese. Many of them had been drawn into political struggle by China's struggles against Japan and intensely identified with China's revolutionary quest. According to long-time CPM Secretary General Chin Peng, in late 1948 CPM leaders discussed "at length" the CCP's mounting victory, and decided to push ahead "even harder with our military program."[35] By December 1948, the CPM had worked out a strategy of armed struggle "with a high expectation of success."

Close liaison with the CCP was part of the CPM's military program. The CPM set up a system of secret communications with the CCP via courier through Hong Kong, and used this system in late 1948 to request medical treatment in China for eight senior CPM cadres. Beijing agreed and proposed that after medical treatment the CPM cadres remain in Beijing and enroll in a three-year training course on communist "theory and practice, military and political."[36] By the time the Korean War began in June 1950, ten senior CPM cadres were studying in Beijing. In December 1949, PRC Vice President Liu Shaoqi gave an important speech on the revolutionary situation in the Far East in which he specifically endorsed the "liberation war" underway in Malaya. Over the next several years, according to a British intelligence report, there was "ample proof that a considerable amount of printed propaganda material of all kinds has reached the CPM from China."[37]

In September 1951, the CCP requested that the CPM post a very senior representative in Beijing. The CPM agreed, and sent Siao Chang, who reached the Chinese capital in early 1953. The CCP did not allow CPM cadres studying in China to return to Malaya while the Korean War was still underway, because it feared that discovery of links between the CCP and Asian revolutionary movements might disrupt the armistice talks underway at Panmunjom.[38] Travel and communications between CPM leaders in Malaya and CCP leaders in China was not easy. Initial efforts at radio communications failed. So too did a courier system, when a female agent compromised herself by involvement in open propaganda work. Travel overland to China required "many weeks," with considerable danger of arrest.[39] Eventually, a secure and stable system of radio communication was worked out that allowed the CPM to keep the CCP informed.[40]

Major shifts in the CPM line originated from the CPM's office in Beijing in close consultation with CCP leaders. In 1954, the two top CPM representatives in Beijing undertook an evaluation of CPM strategy and "its relationship to the overall world communist picture." This was during China's Bandung period. In consequence, the Beijing office of the CPM ordered the CPM Center in Malaya (then at Betong, just inside Malaya on the Thai border on the Kra Isthmus) to drop its earlier "emphasis on the leading role to be played by the [Malaya] Communist Party" and adopt a policy of a broad united front for national independence. According to Chin Peng, this "significant directional shift" amounted to a new strategy of seeking national independence by *"means other than armed struggle."*[41] (Emphasis added.) In his memoir, Chin Peng complained that the top CPM leaders based in Malaya "had had [no] say whatsoever in the fundamental strategic redirection. Still we found ourselves faced with the urgent requirement of devising how best to implement the Party's new approach."[42] In line with the directive from Beijing, according to Chin Peng, CPM leaders in Malaya:

> "[I]mmersed [themselves] in an extensive review of the new political position that had been imposed on us. It was very clear that neither Moscow nor Peking saw value in an armed struggle dragging on in Malaya . . . This was by far the toughest of the tough realities we had had to confront since the onset of the Emergency."[43]

Peace talks between the CPM and the Malayan government began in 1955. When those talks stalled, Beijing upped the pressure on the CPM to settle. Late in 1955, a special emissary from the CCP arrived at Betong to deliver a joint written opinion of the CPSU and the CCP. Prospects for success of the CPM's armed struggle were not good, according to the CPSU-CCP message. Topping the list of reasons for this was the absence of a common frontier with a socialist state. Later, this joint opinion was revoked due to CCP criticism.[44] By late 1958, most CPM fighters had surrendered and accepted government amnesty, while the rest had fled into southern Thailand around the town of Betong. The CPM had only 350 core fighters remaining, in deep jungle areas of Malaya, and it finally ordered them to break into small groups and infiltrate into Sumatra and Singapore.[45] In December 1959, the CPM center in Betong decided to suspend armed struggle and return to political struggle. Absence of contiguous territory controlled by a "fraternal party" was a major factor in this decision.[46] The CPM was also guilty—by its own admission—of Chinese ethnocentrism, with Chinese CPM members riding roughshod over ethnic Malays and Indians. CPM leaders in Betong reported to Beijing via radio the decision to quit armed struggle. Reports Chin Peng:

> We looked to Siao Chang [head of the CPM Beijing office] for direction. After all, he had been so long in Beijing and had established extremely good contacts with the CCP hierarchy. What was more, he was sounding out top CPC officials and interpreting their opinions on our intended return to political struggle.[47]

CPM leaders, with Siao Chang's continuing participation, drafted a demobilization plan for ending armed struggle in accord with the directive from Beijing. "Nothing could move ahead without China's consent," according to Chin Peng. Accordingly, Siao Chang began lobbying Chinese leaders. Several months passed before CCP leaders weighed in on the CPM's abandonment of armed struggle. In the meantime, Beijing accepted a CPM proposal to put in place a mechanism for CCP funding of the CPM. Two businesses were established in Bangkok, headed by Thai communists and ostensibly operating as purely commercial enterprises, to serve as conduits for funding the CPM. According to Chin Peng, the CCP allocated 4 million Thai baht (equivalent then to about US$200,000) annual subsidy for the project. The amount of cash moving from the CCP to the CPM soon exceeded the capacities of the two front companies. Movement of suitcases of cash by couriers faced multiple dangers: arrest, robbery, embezzlement, and the sheer weight of shipments. Eventually, a mechanism was established via "respectable" channels—apparently banks—which continued to function into the 1980s. Inadequate funding had been a perennial CPM problem. The flow of CCP money, US dollars actually, alleviated this previously serious problem. CCP-supplied US dollars were used to purchase arms on Southeast Asian black markets.[48] This put several degrees of distance between China and the Malaya insurgency.

Chin Peng was among those who fled to southern Thailand in late 1959. He proceeded via Bangkok and Hanoi to Beijing, arriving there in June 1961 after a long and difficult journey. He was accommodated by the CCP's International Liaison Bureau in the secret compound discussed earlier in this chapter. When he met with Secretary General Deng Xiaoping, he was astonished to hear Deng propose that the CPM resume armed struggle, relying, this time, on the experience of revolutionary forces in Vietnam. Though shocked that the CCP was now abandoning its advice, given only a year earlier, to abandon armed struggle, Chin Peng quickly recovered and asked how much support Beijing could offer if the CPM again took up arms. Without missing a beat, Deng offered a stipend of US$100,000 per year.[49] Southeast Asia was undergoing monumental changes and was ripe for armed struggle, Deng told Chin Peng. The CPM must not, Deng urged, abandon armed struggle at this point. Chin Peng felt that the reasons for the CPM's 1959 decision to end armed struggle were still sound, but he bowed to CCP wishes, and accepted Beijing's proposed reorientation of CPM strategy along with the funding. CPM leaders drew up a plan for reviving armed struggle with Chinese support.[50] It is probable that this abrupt turnaround in CCP advice to the CPM was linked, in some not-yet-understood fashion, to the "*san he, yi shao*" controversy precipitated by Wang Jiaxiang's February 1962 letter.

With improved financing, the CPM recruited 500 new fighters—mostly Muslims from the border region with southern Thailand—making a total of 800 men under arms. Four new bases were set up in jungles along the Thai-Malaysian border.[51] Further preparations were begun in August 1964 to set up a CPM-run radio station in southern China. Beijing initially turned down this request on the grounds that it might intensify US pressure against North Vietnam, or even China itself. By late 1966, however, the CCP agreed to establishment of a radio station, with China supplying the site, equipment, and technical staff, and the CPM providing broadcasting and production staff. The station, Voice of the Malayan Revolution, went into operation in November 1969. It was located in an underground bunker in a ravine inside a heavily restricted military area in a remote area of rural Hunan.[52] It took seven years to get the new insurgency up and running. On June 1, 1968, the CPM Central Command issued a declaration launching a new armed struggle. Two weeks later, CPM forces ambushed Malaysian forces, killing seventeen. The CPM's armed struggle continued throughout the 1970s.

Singapore

The majority ethnic Chinese city of Singapore offered a strategically located target for Chinese revolutionary activism. Lee Kuan Yew was the leader of an intense struggle against Singapore's communists in the late 1950s and early 1960s, first as a top leader of the People's Action Party (PAP) and then as prime minister of Singapore. Lee recounted the power and attractiveness of communism to Singapore's Chinese population in the early 1960s:

> It is impossible in ... the 1990s to imagine the psychological grip the communists had on the Chinese-speaking in the Singapore and Malaya of the 1950s and 1960s. The communists made these people believe that

what had happened in China would also come to pass in Malaya, that communism was the wave of the future and those who opposed them would be buried by history. They had then a hardcore following of some 20 to 30 percent of the electorate that we could not win over for many years, despite the economic benefits we brought them over the next decade.[53]

Singapore's communists formed the left wing of the PAP during the struggles against British authority from 1954 to 1959. The PAP was, in effect, an anti-British united front. Conflict within the PAP intensified once Singapore gained complete internal autonomy in mid-1959. In 1959–1960, as British counterinsurgency operations ground down CPM forces in Malaya, that party, as noted earlier, shifted its resources to Singapore.[54] Singapore offered an attractive field of battle, according to CPM Secretary General Chin Peng, because "The island had never become a fully fledged Emergency battlefield."[55] A group of about thirty guerrilla fighters were disguised as students and infiltrated into Singapore in cooperation with Singaporean communists. Regarding the strength of CPM assets in Singapore circa 1959, Chin Peng disclaims exact knowledge, but says "I can certainly say that most of the island's workers sympathized with the left-wing trade unions and members of the unions well appreciated [that] they [the unions] were under the control of the CPM."[56]

In mid-1961, Singaporean Communist Party leader Eu Chooi Yip, whose superior was in fact the CPM's Chin Peng, traveled to Beijing for talks with CPM leaders over the increasingly anticommunist orientation of Lee Kwan Yew and the question of Singapore's merger with the new state of Malaysia (an event that occurred in September 1963). Eu Chooi Yip and Chin Peng concluded that Lee's attempt to take Singapore into Malaysia was an attempt to draw on stronger anticommunist forces in Malaya to repress the communist forces in Singapore. Chin Peng and Eu decided to counter Lee's attempt to link up with Malaysia's anticommunist forces by stressing the anti-Chinese policies of the Malaya government—a tack that would appeal to ethnic Chinese sentiments.[57] Mounting tension within the PAP culminated in open rupture when the procommunist wing of that organization withdrew and formed a new organization, Barisan Sosialis. Lee Kuan Yew recounts:

> The skillful and tough methods of the unyielding communists . . . were unforgettable lessons in political infighting. Street fighting with them was like unarmed combat with no holds barred in a contest where winner took all. We learned not to give hostages to our adversaries or they would have destroyed us. Even after we had reduced the communist strength in the united-front organizations, their lurking presence in the underground had to be taken into our political calculations. At any time they could resort to violence or choose to rebuild their

open-front organizations, or both. Weekly intelligence reports from the Internal Security Department made us ever mindful of their presence in Singapore and their secret network that linked them to armed groups in peninsular Malaya.[58]

Labor unions and Chinese-language schools were the main organizational bases of Singapore communists into the mid-1960s. Drawing on these bases, Singapore's communists could launch effective strikes and turn out large and militant demonstrations. According to Singapore's Internal Security Department, during the late 1950s and early 1960s that organization's "Special Branch" waged "successive operations" to cripple "Communist Party of Malaya networks" in labor unions and Chinese-language schools.[59] Sweeping arrests of communists and procommunists during Operation Cold Storage in February 1962 shattered the CPM underground network in Singapore, according to Chin Peng.[60] Many communists and communist sympathizers were detained and held for long periods without trial.

There is scanty evidence regarding CCP ties to the Singapore communist movement. When Eu Chooi Yip and Chin Peng met in Beijing in mid-1961 to devise strategy, it is nearly certain that CCP ILP representatives sat in on those discussions. This, unfortunately, is surmise. Yet the absence of evidence should not, in this case, be taken as evidence of absence. Given the intensity of the struggle raging throughout the region, given the important role that Singapore played and might play in this struggle, and given what we know about CCP links with communist movements regionwide, it is probable that such links existed.

Indonesia, the PKI, and the United Front with Sukarno

Indonesia with its progressive and anti-Western President Sukarno, plus its large population and powerful communist party, offered fertile soil for Beijing's revolutionary drive. Beijing employed two major instruments toward Indonesia in 1963–1965: 1) a united front from above with Indonesian President Sukarno and leftist elements of the Indonesian military, and 2) "proletarian internationalist" ties with the Indonesian Communist Party, usually known by its initials in Dutch, PKI. Regarding the united front with Sukarno, Beijing and Djakarta shared broadly convergent interests in eliminating Western presence, especially military, from Southeast Asia. Sukarno was a proud nationalist, strongly anti-Dutch, anti-British, and anti-American, who saw Indonesia as the rightful preeminent power in Southeast Asia. Sukarno believed that the Western powers should leave the area and that the ethnically Malay peoples of Indonesia, Malaya, Borneo, and the Philippines should be united in a single Malay state, with himself as its leader, of course.

Developments in Southeast Asia moved in a different direction. Following Malaya's independence in 1957 it signed a defense agreement with Britain, and then began moving toward unity with the British protectorates of Sarawak and Sabah on the west coast of Borneo Island. Sukarno felt that all of those regions should be part of Indonesia. The new state of Malaysia was formed in September 1963 when not only Sarawak and Sabah but also Singapore joined peninsular Malaya to constitute that state. Sukarno viewed Malaysia as a British contrivance cooked up to block Indonesia's rise as the major regional power. The same month Malaysia was formed, Sukarno declared a policy of "confrontation" to "crush" that new state. Alliance with China, plus Indonesia's own military power, were the two key instruments of Sukarno's confrontation with Malaysia.[61]

Sukarno's drive to push the Western powers out of Southeast Asia fit well with Mao's plans for that region. A de facto alliance was formed in January 1963 during a visit by Sukarno to Beijing. When Malaysia was formed in September and Sukarno declared confrontation with that state, Beijing quickly supported Sukarno.[62] As the confrontation intensified in November 1964, Foreign Minister Chen Yi visited Djakarta. The press release resulting from Chen's talks declared China's full support for Indonesia's struggle to "crush" Malaysia. The entity constituted, Chen said, a direct threat to the security of the Southeast Asian countries. Moreover, the two parties, China and Indonesia, had reached a "common understanding" about the struggle against imperialism and had discussed ways to increase the level of struggle. Chen Yi also agreed to supply a much-needed US$50 million credit. In the words of scholar David Mozingo, "As a result of these accords, China became the major external force supporting Sukarno's foreign policy."[63]

By fall 1964, Indonesian commandos were conducting raids on peninsular Malaya. Indonesian military forces were also massed on the borders of Sarawak and Sabah. Chinese media gave extensive coverage to the "liberation struggle" in "North Kalimantan"—Djakarta's and Beijing's name for Sarawak and Sabah. According to CPM Secretary General Chin Peng, Beijing's objective was to precipitate a war that would radicalize the Indonesian military and society, creating fertile conditions for the PKI, either in a united front with Sukarno or otherwise. In January 1965, Indonesian Foreign Minister Subandrio, a close Sukarno ally, reciprocated Chen Yi's visit. The joint statement produced by that visit went a step further in stating China's support for Indonesia's confrontation: China solemnly declared that should the British and US imperialists dare to impose war on the Indonesian people, "the Chinese government and people would absolutely not sit idly by."[64] Following Subandrio's visit, there was a steady flow of exchange visits between the PLA and the Indonesian military. Beijing was making a concerted effort to woo the Indonesian officer class, especially its pro-Sukarno elements.

The PKI was Beijing's other policy instrument in Indonesia. In 1964–1965, the PKI was the world's largest nonruling communist party. Its position in Indonesian society had grown in the early 1960s in partnership with Sukarno's effort to create a new domestic social order. Throughout the early 1960s, as Islamic, business, and other civic organizations were steadily reduced in power, the scope of PKI influence expanded. During 1963, the PKI under the leadership of D. N. Aidit moved decisively toward the CCP's strategy of violent revolution. In the countryside, the PKI took over village committees and began to push for radical land reform. Sukarno allowed the PKI to intensify efforts to infiltrate government offices. Sukarno increasingly allied with the PKI, and used his powers as president to facilitate its expansion of influence. By early 1965, the PKI was pushing for full-blown agrarian revolution followed swiftly by the elimination of "corrupt capitalists." The Indonesian army was virtually the only organization remaining beyond PKI control. Indonesian politics was increasingly polarized between the PKI and the army.

The PKI recognized the army as the greatest obstacle to PKI rule of Indonesia. Sukarno was the PKI's major protection against the army. But what if Sukarno died or was overthrown by anticommunist generals? The PKI realized it needed an armed force under its own command if it was to push the revolution forward, perhaps even it was merely to survive. It tried several approaches. One approach was to establish a political commissar system within the army, with commissars supplied by the PKI. The army vetoed this outright. Another approach was subverting the army. In furtherance of this, the PKI established a Bureau of Special Affairs, highly secret and chaired by Aidit, to infiltrate the army. "Progressive officers" were identified, mentored by designated PKI tutors, and graded on their inclination toward cooperation with the PKI and the revolutionary cause.

The PKI's subversive efforts had some success; by mid-1965, some forty-four high-ranking officers had been won over.[65] The PKI planned to use the authority of President Sukarno to fire top conservative generals and simultaneously appoint "progressive" PKI-tutored officers to key positions controlling the armed forces. Air force head Omar Dani was deemed the most likely candidate to become the new head of the armed forces and presidential successor to Sukarno; the air force was more "progressive" than the more "reactionary" army. PKI chief Aidit was to be premier, controlling the state. PKI cadres would then be assigned to units of the army and the revolutionization of the army pushed forward. But a key weakness remained: the PKI had no armed force under its full control. The PKI decided to address this problem by forming a "workers and peasants" militia, ostensibly to defend against "imperialist" attacks from Malaysia, but in fact to safeguard Indonesia's revolutionary forces and push forward into the socialist stage.

Beijing agreed with the PKI assessment that it needed a revolutionary armed force under its command. China's role in the formation of such a force was discussed during two visits by Chen Yi to Indonesia in November and December 1964.[66] The Joint Communiqué resulting from the second of those visits provided that Indonesia and the PRC would reinforce and make more effective their cooperation. Subandrio told Indonesian ambassadors that during his talks the two sides had agreed on a division of revolutionary spheres of influence in the area. China would guide developments in the peninsular territory north of Singapore, while Indonesia would be responsible for Borneo and Singapore. Scholar Victor Fic suggests that Subandrio may have been exaggerating, yet conveying a sense of what the leaders of the two countries had in mind.[67] During a January 1965 visit to Beijing, Subandrio discussed with Zhou Enlai provision of arms for the "workers and peasants" force. Zhou agreed that China would supply 100,000 "pieces."[68] In May 1965, a high-level PRC delegation headed by Peng Zhen visited Indonesia to celebrate the PKI's anniversary. During the visit Peng openly endorsed the PKI's call for arming a "workers and peasants" force to safeguard Indonesia against imperialist invasion.[69] It is likely that Peng, Sukarno, Subandrio, and Aidit discussed modalities for delivery of arms.

By mid-1965 Sukarno understood that he could no longer balance between the PKI and the army, and that a showdown between those two was inevitable. Sukarno believed that the Indonesian revolution must move into the socialist stage, and was thus inclined toward cooperation with the PKI's plan. Sukarno was concerned, however, about his personal fate once the PKI held power. Would not the PKI get rid of him once he had served their purpose?[70] The issue was forced by Sukarno's declining health. Suffering from severe kidney disease, Sukarno had a severe attack in mid-July 1965 and then again on August 4. Sukarno's health was attended to by a team of Chinese doctors, and precise information about the attacks was passed to both Beijing and the PKI. After the August 4 attack, Sukarno's Chinese doctors reported that their patient might soon die. Since utilization of Sukarno's authority to remove "reactionary" generals and appoint "progressive" replacements was essential to the PKI's plan, action was imperative. Aidit was in Beijing at the time, and immediately discussed the issue with Chinese leaders. On August 5, the day after Sukarno's second and most serious attack, Aidit met with Mao. After being briefed by Aidit on the situation, Mao replied:

MAO: You should act quickly.

AIDIT: I am afraid the army is going to be the obstacle.

MAO: Well, do as I advise you and eliminate all the reactionary Generals and officers in one blow. The Army will be a headless dragon and follow you.

AIDIT: That would mean killing some hundreds of officers.

MAO: In Northern Shensi I killed 20,000 cadres in one stroke.[71]

A critical element of China's support for the PKI's bid for power at this juncture was a promise of safe and comfortable retirement for Sukarno in China. Sukarno was tired and worn out. Yet he feared for his life if he threw his lot unequivocally with the PKI. What would be his fate after he had played his role in the transition? A comfortable and secure in China, personally guaranteed by Mao—along the lines later granted to Cambodia's Norodom Sihanouk—was the solution.[72] This offer was reconfirmed to Aidit by Mao during their August 5 discussion. Accordingly, when Chen Yi traveled to Jakarta for Indonesia's National Day in mid-August 1965, he told Subandrio that China was prepared to provide Sukarno with a safe and secure retirement in which he would receive necessary care from Chinese medical specialists. Beijing's offer was conveyed by Aidit directly to Sukarno immediately after the PKI leader's return to Jakarta. Sukarno accepted the offer and ordered a loyal and progressive colonel to begin making preparations to act against the reactionary generals.

Mao also agreed during his August 5 discussion with Aidit to provide 30,000 weapons for the initial strike against the reactionary generals This was down from the 100,000 promised by Zhou in July—a manifestation of China's growing uncertainty about Sukarno's reliability, according to Victor Fic. Larger shipments would follow, Mao promised, once the next stage was reached and the workers' and peasants' militia was ready to be armed. Air force head Dani flew to Beijing in mid-September to expedite the shipment of Chinese arms to Indonesia via talks with Zhou Enlai and Secretary General Deng Xiaoping.[73] The first shipment of arms was carried by an Indonesian Air Force C-130 transport.[74] A second shipment arrived via a Lloyd Shipping Company ship in crates listed as "building materials" on the manifest. The cargo was given secure clearance through customs, then stored in Indonesian air force warehouses in and around Djakarta awaiting distribution to the PKI's workers' and peasants' army.[75]

China's handling of the arms transfers via Sukarno, Subandrio, and Dani—Indonesia's president, foreign minister, and air force head respectively—rather than the PKI accorded with China's dual-track approach. Technically, China's arms assistance, even though covert and carefully kept secret from Indonesia's army leadership, went to Indonesia's legal, sovereign government. Technically speaking, Beijing did not arm the PKI; it armed the Indonesian authorities. Beijing certainly knew and approved of the PKI's plan to form a red army. Indeed, Beijing's offer to supply arms, free, was intended to encourage formation of such a force. It is virtually certain that CCP and PKI leaders discussed strategy for the Indonesian revolution, and Beijing lauded and encouraged the PKI struggle. Yet there is no evidence that Beijing knew of, let alone helped plan, the calamitous PKI coup attempt that soon occurred.

The delivery of Soviet and Czechoslovak reports about Anglo-US engineering of an army coup to overthrow Sukarno prompted the PKI and its radical military officer supporters to strike preemptively. In fact, these reports were disinformation cooked up by Moscow to spoil US-Indonesian relations, but this did not become apparent until many years later.[76] At the time, Sukarno's group and the PKI credited them. Thus on October 1, 1965, PKI death squads abducted and murdered six top military commanders. Several top officers escaped, however, and organized a counterstrike against the PKI and its allies. The recently delivered Chinese arms were distributed by radical air force officers to form a hastily organized militia, but that scratch force was no match for the Indonesian army. Communists and communist sympathizers were arrested and many summarily executed. Popular anger, much of it Islamic and/or anti-Chinese in nature, began to boil over. The close identity of the PKI with Indonesia's ethnic Chinese minority produced popular anti-Chinese pogroms that raged for several months. Between 100,000 and 500,000 people, mostly suspected communists and Chinese, were massacred. By late 1965, the PKI was destroyed and its few surviving leaders, including Aidit, in exile in Beijing.

Indonesian-China relations collapsed amid popular demonstrations and army raids of PRC offices in Indonesia.[77] When Indonesian security forces raided the Chinese embassy in 1966, they found materials outlining a network of contacts between the PKI and Chinese intelligence agencies. The network was operated by Indonesians holding Chinese citizenship and eschewed all electronic communications.[78] Not until 1985 would Sino-Indonesian relations begin improving. Even then, Indonesian memory of China's deep involvement in the PKI's attempted seizure of power remained strong.

North Kalimantan

The three British protectorates of Sarawak, Sabah, and Brunei occupied the northern portion of the island of Borneo, also known as Kalimantan. The first two were integrated into the new state of Malaysia in 1963.[79] As noted previously, Indonesia's Sukarno felt that all of Borneo should be integrated into Indonesia. Prior to his ouster in September 1965, Sukarno supported the establishment of an independent North Kalimantan state as prelude to unification of that region into Indonesia. Moreover, about one-third of the population of Sarawak was ethnic Chinese, with a strong identity (in the 1950s and 1960s) with China rather than with their local host states.[80]

In 1954, the Communist Party of Malaya established an anti-British united front in Sarawak, the Sarawak Liberation League. That front, or more likely the disciplined Leninist core within it, led to the declaration in August 1964 of a North Kalimantan Liberation League (NKLL) seeking North Kalimantan independence via armed struggle. This was during the confrontation between Indonesia and Malaysia, and the NKLL was part of a Sukarno-China effort to abort Malaysia. Representatives of Indonesia's foreign ministry attended the

Year	# Reports
1962	4
1962	26
1964	20
1965	13
1966	3
1967	2
1968	6
1969	14
1970	13
1971	5
1972	2
1973	0
1974	1

FIGURE 8-2 *Renmin ribao* Reports on Armed Struggle in North Kalimantan

Source: Fujio Hara, "The North Kalimantan Communist Party and the People's Republic of China," *The Developing Economies*, vol. XLIII, issue 4 (December 2005), p. 508.

formation of military organs of the NKLL in 1964 and early 1965. Indonesia also provided military training to NKLL fighters. China and North Korea provided weapons to the NKLL by way of Indonesia.

A North Kalimantan government in exile was established in Jakarta in early 1965, but once Sukarno was overthrown in September, China quickly emerged as the main refuge for North Kalimantan insurgents. In September 1965, only about two weeks before the Indonesian coup, a North Kalimantan Communist Party (NKCP) was formed to provide leadership to the protracted armed struggle that was being planned. Shortly after the NKCP was founded, the paramount leader of that party, Wen Ming Chyuan, left for China, where he would reside for the next twenty years. Wen had abandoned his Sarawakian citizenship in 1962 and demanded and received deportation to China. Thereafter he traveled occasionally between China and Kalimantan, something that required, according to scholar Fujio Hara, "appropriate arrangements both by the Chinese and Indonesian [Sukarno] governments."[81] After the founding of the NKCP, Wen remained in Beijing, with *Renmin ribao* reporting eighteen times on his activities between June 1966 and March 1978. Figure 8-2 shows the frequency of reports by *Renmin ribao* on the North Kalimantan armed struggle in the 1960s and 1970s.

Thailand

The Communist Party of Siam (which became the Communist Party of Thailand, or CPT, in 1948) was formed in 1930 under the tutelage of Comintern agent Ho Chi Minh. Members were then mostly ethnic Chinese and Vietnamese.[82] The CCP victory in China convinced the CPT that armed struggle with a peasant base was the correct path for the CPT to follow. Debate over how that should be done in Thailand—especially over the related questions of whether a united front with capitalists was possible and whether or not Thailand was truly independent—began in the early 1950s and did not reach a conclusion until the military coups of 1957–1958. Some within the party believed a peaceful transition to socialism was possible in Thailand. CCP polemics against CPSU revisionism (the latter included the "incorrect" position that a peaceful transition to socialism was possible) helped clarify thinking within the CPT, and that Party increasingly aligned with the CCP to oppose Soviet revisionism in the debates within the world communist movement.[83] The CPT began armed struggle in 1961, but did not openly declare that path for several years. A revolutionary army was formed in 1965, and the first large-scale clash with Bangkok forces came in August of that year.[84]

Beijing supported the CPT's armed struggle. A Thai-language radio station, the Voice of the People of Thailand (VOPT), operated by CPT cadres but based in Yunnan, began operation in 1962. In March of that year, the station broadcast the CPT's embrace of a strategy of rural people's war, and in August 1965 announced the formal beginning of that struggle.[85] By 1965, the VOPT was broadcasting seven hours a day. In that year the CPT set up a united front organization modeled after the National Liberation Front of South Vietnam. The new CPT organization had an office and representatives in Beijing, who were feted frequently by CCP people's diplomacy organizations and participated in various PRC-sponsored Afro-Asian activities.[86] When CP Malaya leader Chin Peng arrived in Beijing in June 1961, he found that the CPT had a small permanent staff stationed at the International Liaison Department compound in western Beijing, and another "large group" of CPT cadres were attending a "lengthy training course."[87]

Extreme caution was a key characteristic of CCP support for the CPT. Scholars have found some evidence of weapons supply, but have also suggested that there may have been a division of labor between Beijing and Hanoi in this regard, with Hanoi supplying arms and material and Beijing supplying training, territorial sanctuary, and financial support. One close study noted that Chinese endorsements of the CPT insurgency were usually implied rather than direct. Most commonly, endorsements came in the form of republishing statements by Thai groups, reports of CPT activity, including united front activities in Beijing, or in the form of commentaries in *Renmin ribao* or *Peking Review*.[88]

By 1973, the CPT had an estimated 5,000 people under arms—a fairly significant guerrilla force.[89] Prospects looked excellent after the US abandonment of South Vietnam. Military suppression of a prodemocratic student movement in Thailand in 1976 produced a large number of student recruits for the CPT. In 1975, the year Saigon finally fell to Hanoi, the CPT asked Hanoi to supply weapons from the abundance of ex-US equipment that Hanoi had captured.[90] Things looked bright for the CPT.

Unfortunately for the CPT, escalating rivalry between Beijing and Hanoi doomed its cause.

The Philippines and Northeast India

The Communist Party of the Philippines (CPP) was formed in 1930 with Comintern support. It played a significant role in guerrilla resistance to Japanese occupation during World War II and launched an insurrection against the Manila government when the Philippines became independent in 1946. That insurgency flared briefly, but in the 1950s was worn down by a combination of land reform and counterinsurgency, both with US assistance. By the 1960s the insurgency presented little threat to the Philippine government. Nor was there evidence of Chinese support during that period. In 1969, however, a wing of the CPP undertook to revitalize the revolutionary movment with inspiration from China, Vietnam, and Cuba and enjoying Chinese material support.[91] The new party quickly formed the New People's Army (NPA) and launched an insurrection in January 1970. In 1968, apparently in preparation for the projected armed struggle, the CPP dispatched a representative to China, ostensibly to serve as a Tagalog language specialist for Radio Beijing, but actually serving as liaison to Kang Sheng and his ILD system.[92] CPP leaders had learned from PKI leader Aidit of China's generosity toward foreign revolutionary movements, and decided to apply for help. A small and highly secret CPP group flew to Macao in July 1971 and made their way to Guangdong, where they were received as revolutionary comrades and conveyed to Beijing. CPP leaders sought arms for the large numbers of new recruits who were expected to join the revolutionary movement following a planned bombing at an opposition Liberal Party rally that was to be carried out by the CPP but blamed on Ferdinand Marcos' increasingly repressive government. The provocative bombing was, in fact, carried out on August 1971. As the CPP calculated, Marcos was generally blamed for the bombing; only years later did investigation reveal CPP culpability. At the time, senior ILD cadres were deeply apprehensive that China might be implicated in the bombing. In any case, in 1971 China agreed to supply 1,200 US-designed but Chinese-manufactured (reportedly at a clandestine facility) M-14 rifles, bazookas, mortars, ammunition, communication gear, and medical kits. The ILD also provided money to purchase in Japan a 90-foot fishing trawler to deliver the munitions. The July 1972 CPP operation to land the munitions was poorly planned; the ship ran aground and was quickly reported to Philippine authorities. The designated landing zone had been inadequately reconnoitered and turned out to be populated by local fishermen. Within a few hours, most of the cargo was in the hands of the Philippine military.

A second delivery was attempted in December 1973. This time, the arms were carefully sealed in plastic at a PLA facility on Hainan Island to be dropped in shallow water off the Philippines for retrieval by CPP scuba divers. The CPP had proposed delivery by a PLAN submarine, but the ILD insisted that the CPP carry out the operation. Another ship purchased with ILD money had no more luck than the first; it ran aground well before the Philippine coast. The crew was rescued by a Hong Kong ship and delivered to that territory, where immigration officials eventually allowed them to seek asylum in China. About the same time, a CPP courier was arrested at the US-Canadian border in possession of CCP letters to CPP leaders along with $75,000. By the spring of 1976, CPP leaders in China had been assigned to agricultural work at a special compound in Hunan province and China's material support for the Philippine revolutionary movement had ended.

Regarding northeast India, following the 1962 Sino-Indian war, the CCP assisted secessionist insurgencies in northeast India. China's support for these anti-Indian insurgencies may well have had different roots than the more clearly Marxist-Leninist insurgencies of Southeast Asia. Unlike the other China-supported insurgencies in Southeast Asia, none of the northeast Indian insurgencies were Marxist-Leninist-inspired or -led. Yet this CCP support may have been part of an effort to create a new regionwide balance of power favoring revolutionary China.

Around 1967, China set up a camp near Tanzhong in southwestern Yunnan to train groups of Naga guerrillas. Naga rebels had taken up armed struggle for independence from India shortly after India's creation. Between 1967 and the mid-1970s, some eight hundred Naga fighters were trained in Yunnan, given modern arms, and reinfiltrated back to India's Nagaland via the Kachin state in north Burma.[93] Several hundred more Nagas attempted to reach Tanzhong, but were apprehended and turned back by Burmese or Kachin State military forces. In 1969, China began supplying arms to Mizo secessionist insurgents in India's Mizoram (part of Assam state until 1972). Training for small batches of Mizo insurgents at camps in Yunnan began in 1973 and continued into the mid-1970s. In May 1969, China and Pakistan set up a coordination bureau to oversee the supply of arms, training, and funding to insurgencies in northeast India. What became Bangladesh in late 1971 was then still East Pakistan, and provided easy access to India's northeastern states.

Once again, it was Deng Xiaoping who shut down this revolutionary interference. Meeting in Beijing with Indian foreign minister Atal Bihari Vajpayee in February 1979, Deng said that whatever aid China might have given to Indian rebels was now a thing of the past. When groups of Naga rebels showed up at the Yunnan border, they were refused entry by Chinese border personnel, and China refused to discuss further Naga requests for support.[94]

What Were the CCP's Objectives?

Figure 8-3 illustrates the components and geographic spread of Beijing's revolutionary quest over the entire period from 1961 to 1976. Other than in the case of Vietnam, where China circa 1978 began documenting its generous support for North Vietnam as a way of demonstrating Hanoi's subsequent ingratitude and insincerity, Beijing has released virtually no documentary material regarding exactly why China undertook the revolutionary quest of the 1960s. This episode continues to be one that the CCP finds embarrassing and best left undiscussed. In this situation, speculation is more appropriate.

A broad strategic vision or objective must have underlain an effort of this scope and duration. The CCP gave strong material and political support in the 1960s and 1970s to communist parties and movements in nine Southeast Asian countries: Vietnam, Laos, Cambodia, Thailand, Malaya and

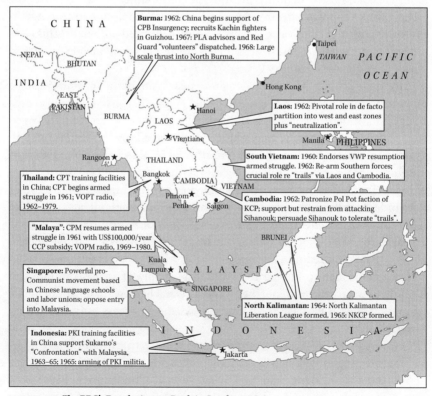

FIGURE 8-3 The PRC's Revolutionary Push in Southeast Asia

Malaysia, Singapore, Indonesia, Burma, and the Philippines, as well as the states of northeastern India. The CCP supported a coordinated offensive; indeed, it probably played the central role in coordinating that revolutionary thrust. There are occasional insights about how the pieces fit together. When Zhou Enlai and Chen Yi met with Sukarno in late 1964, they urged him to abandon commando raids on peninsular Malaya. Instead, large numbers of Indonesian communists (PKI members) should be infiltrated into Peninsular Malaya. This would help reduce the ethnically Chinese and increase the ethnically Malay complexion of the CPM insurgency. As part of this arrangement, Beijing would order the CPM to open a new front on the Malay-Thai border, appealing to the secessionist impulses of Thai Muslims. As part of these plans, China was prepared to arm 100,000 guerrilla fighters.[95] The joint communiqué issued at the end of Chen Yi's Indonesia visit called for merging Indonesia's confrontation against Malaysia with South Vietnam's struggle against the Americans, plus other anti-imperialist struggles in the region, to form a single regionwide anti-imperialist struggle.

One strategic objective of the CCP's Southeast Asian revolutionary push was to push US imperialism out of its footholds in Southeast Asia and make China's vulnerable southern flank more secure. But the way in which that was to be done was by bringing communist parties to power. Moreover, expulsion of US military presence from areas close to China was clearly not the motive with the important cases of Burma, Indonesia, or Cambodia. None of those states hosted a US presence or was aligned with the United States. Yet all three were targeted for revolutionary transformation under the tutelage of communist parties. A better approximation of Mao's grand strategic objective seems to have been the creation of a socialist camp in Southeast Asia that would look with gratitude to China for guidance, a sort of red buffer or sphere of influence for revolutionary, socialist China. China would also become the paramount power in a large region contiguous to China which had historically been within (or at least many of the states of that region were) the Sino-centric tributary system which many Chinese, perhaps including Mao, saw as the natural order of things.

Successful application of the CCP's line of protracted people's war would also demonstrate that Mao Zedong, not Nikita Khrushchev, was the "correct" theorist and thus leader of the international communist movement. The CCP's embrace of revolutionary activism circa 1960–1961 grew out of, and was an extension of, the escalating polemic between the CCP and the CPSU over the line of the international communist movement. Key "errors" of the "revisionist" line of the CPSU and Khrushchev were, in Mao's view, the notion that peaceful transition to socialism was possible, and that support by socialist countries for wars of national liberation in developing countries was too dangerous. By rejecting these propositions and by successfully applying correct Marxist-Leninist principles in Southeast Asia, Mao would garner for himself the mantle of legitimate heir, and for China glory as the red bastion of world revolution. The Marxist grail would move from Moscow to Beijing.

Establishing Mao Zedong as the fifth deity in the Marxist-Leninist pantheon (after Marx, Engels, Lenin, and Stalin) by demonstrating his unflinching adherence to revolutionary war and the "correctness" of his thought via successes in Southeast Asia was probably a strong motivation from Mao's standpoint. Success in expanding the realm of socialism was an important requirement for Marxist-Leninist sainthood, at least since Lenin. As the CCP explained in its 1956 polemic on the Stalin question, Stalin had proved his heirship to Lenin by, inter alia, expanding the socialist sphere in Eastern Europe and Korea and helping the CCP gain power in China. Because of the proximity of Southeast Asia to revolutionary China, and because of various cultural and historical factors, that region made the most sense as an arena in which China could manifest its "proletarian internationalism." East Africa was another area of Chinese revolutionary activism, but saw nothing on the scale of Southeast Asia.

Mao was, of course, concerned with the security of the PRC. He saw successful wars of national liberation as a way of driving the United States out of Southeast Asia, and believed that an American exit would strengthen PRC security. But the means they chose to achieve that was the "revolutionary transformation" of the Southeast Asian nations. Mao's objectives were, in part, realist: to make revolutionary China more secure from US pressure, threat, or attack. But another objective was to create a revolutionary China in a revolutionary world—or at least those portions of the world China could significantly influence. The fact that Indonesia and Malaya sat astride the sea lines of communication between East Asia, the Persian Gulf, and Europe would further enhance that shift.

Calculations of the correlation of forces between the revolutionary camp and the imperialist camp also factored into Mao's push for socialist revolution in Southeast Asia. If Southeast Asia joined the socialist camp, the global correlation of forces would shift even more decisively against US imperialism. Mao at the 1957 Moscow conference had enumerated the factors already accomplishing that shift. Now, if under CCP tutelage the vast area of Southeast Asia could be shifted to the revolutionary side of the global balance, that balance would further favor the revolutionary, progressive camp. China's embrace of revolutionary activism in Southeast Asia was in line with the division of labor in the world revolutionary process worked out by Stalin and Liu Shaoqi in July 1949.

Finally, the CCP's revolutionary quest also had deep roots in China's domestic politics. Mao's revolutionary activism in Southeast Asia paralleled his intensified struggle against hidden revisionists within the CCP—high-ranking leaders who favored retreat from class struggle and emphasis, instead, on improving standards of living. Mao calculated that a rising tide of revolution in Southeast Asia would encourage Chinese to "make revolution" in China by struggling against hidden revisionists who wanted to "take the capitalist road." The image of the fire of revolution spreading at China's doorstep would help inspire Chinese to overcome the setbacks of the Great Leap Forward and participate, instead, in the ideological revival of China's revolutionary élan.

Still another way to look at the thirty-year-long contest outlined in this chapter is as a struggle by two great powers, the People's Republic of China and the United States of America, to direct the development of Southeast Asia along lines compatible with their values and interests. US strategists envisioned a community of liberal, democratic, and capitalist states friendly to the United States. PRC strategists envisioned a community of Leninist proletarian dictatorships building socialism and moving toward a transition to communism.

Countering the United States in Vietnam

PROXY WAR WITH THE UNITED STATES

From Supporting Asia Revolution to Defending the PRC

Throughout the early 1960s, the revolutionary forces in South Vietnam and Laos gained ground steadily. The anti-imperialist united front founded by the VWP in December 1960, the National Liberation Front for South Vietnam (NLF), proved adept at mobilizing disparate anti-Saigon groups in South Vietnam. The NLF developed a strong organizational infrastructure across South Vietnam and effectively infiltrated the South Vietnamese government and armed forces. Cadres (still mostly southerners who had "re-grouped" north in 1954 after the Geneva agreement), along with munitions, money, and equipment, moved south from the DRV via the trails running through eastern Laos and Cambodia to South Vietnam. Hanoi carefully camouflaged its involvement in South Vietnam and Laos, including infiltration via the trails and the VWP's role in the NLF, creating and maintaining the pretense that the war in South Vietnam was a purely southern insurrection against the US-supported tyranny of the Saigon government. China's media fully cooperated with this strategic deception.

Beijing fully supported the revolutionary forces in Vietnam and Laos.[1] Politically, Beijing gave full support to the insurgency in the south. Materially, China supplied quantities of small arms and light crew-served weapons (machine guns, mortars, recoilless rifles) to the DRV, which forwarded a portion of those weapons to NLF forces in South Vietnam and the VWP-allied Pathet Lao in Laos. Between 1953 and 1971, the PRC supplied about $750 million worth of military assistance to the DRV.[2] China also assisted DRV industrialization efforts. Between 1955 and 1964, PRC aid to the DRV concentrated on transportation, communications, irrigation, and industrial sectors. After 1964, Chinese economic assistance focused on repairing damage done by US bombing and providing foodstuffs and daily necessities for the people of the

DRV. Between 1966 and 1969, China supplied an estimated $85 million per year in economic assistance to the DRV. Economic assistance was militarily important as the DRV increasingly shifted manpower and resources to the war effort in the south.

As noted in a previous chapter, in 1964 the VWP launched a major offensive push intended to topple the pro-US government in Saigon and bring to power in its place a noncommunist but neutralist government that would ask the Americans to leave South Vietnam—all this before the US presidential election scheduled for November 1964 eased political obstacles to large-scale US intervention. Several considerations underlay this crucial decision—which would, in effect, transform the DRV-aided insurgency in South Vietnam into a full-scale US-DRV war as well as a proxy war between the PRC and the United States.[3]

Early in 1964, movement of men and materiel down the trails greatly increased. Previously, people being sent south were mostly southerners who had "regrouped" north after 1954. Now that was no longer the case. Northern cadres began to go south in increased numbers. Whole units of the DRV military, the People's Army of Vietnam (PAVN), began to move south. This massive influx of men and material from the north combined with the paralysis and chaos in the south to push the Saigon government to the brink of collapse. By late 1964, there increasingly seemed to be only two realistic options for the United States in South Vietnam: to withdraw, abandoning the Saigon government to its fate, or to intervene with US combat forces to crush the insurgency or at least prevent it from consolidating control over South Vietnam. US leaders never seriously considered withdrawal, and moved steadily toward direct and large-scale US military intervention.

VWP leaders recognized the US move toward deeper intervention, but they also understood that President Lyndon Johnson would be reluctant to undertake a new war while facing the 1964 election campaign. 1964 thus became a decisive year for Hanoi.

US leaders were unwilling to concede the defeat of the nation-building and counterinsurgency efforts in South Vietnam. They were unwilling to abandon South Vietnam to communist takeover, believing that if it became communist the availability of territorial sanctuary for Thai and Cambodian communists would render those countries fatally vulnerable to communist takeover. Malaysia and other countries of Southeast Asia might then follow. The countries of Southeast Asia would fall to communism one after the other, like a line of dominos stood on end. US leaders decided, instead, to continue the de facto policy of trying to contain the expansion of the communist sphere at the 17th parallel.

The CCP's support and encouragement of revolution across Southeast Asia (reviewed in the previous chapter) was the basis for the US "domino theory." US intelligence had followed closely the polemical battle between the

CPSU and the CCP over how to defeat "US imperialism." They understood that Moscow under Khrushchev was less enthusiastic, and Beijing under Mao more enthusiastic, about supporting wars of national liberation in the intermediate zone. US intelligence also followed as closely as possible CCP aid to Southeast Asian revolutionary movements, and had at least a general idea of the scale of such assistance. Communist China, US leaders concluded, was still in the zealous ideological expansionist stage of its revolution, while the Soviets had already left that stage and begun to mellow. Until China too outgrew its revolutionary expansionist impulse, it had to be contained. To a significant degree, US leaders decided for full-scale intervention in Vietnam to contain what they perceived as Chinese communist expansionism.

US leaders during the Kennedy and Johnson administrations saw what Moscow and Beijing termed wars of national liberation as a new, more sinister type of communist expansionism. Under Stalin's global leadership, communists had relied on outright armed invasion—in Korea, for example. But that had led to war with the United States. So, US strategists concluded, the Chinese and Vietnamese communists had invented a new form of aggression: pseudo-insurgency. Rather than crash across recognized borders with uniformed troops with tanks and artillery, communist forces dressed in civilian clothing quietly infiltrated across borders, mixed with local residents, and seized upon their resentments against the local government. These were camouflaged to look like purely domestic insurrections, but were in fact manifestations of the strategic thrust of powerful states, like communist China. The insurgency in South Vietnam was a test case for this new form of communist aggression, US leaders felt. Just as the United States had learned to deal with other, earlier forms of communist aggression, it needed now to learn how to defeat this new form, externally supported wars of national liberation. This, in any case, typified the thinking of the Kennedy and Johnson administrations. Thus he PRC and the United States reciprocally matched each other in escalating commitment to Vietnam.

From both the PRC <u>and</u> the US perspectives, what was at stake was the broad path of development of many nations newly emerged from colonialism. These independent nations were seeking modernization and development. The communist powers—the USSR and the PRC, each in their own ways—were attempting to guide the development of these countries along the lines of Leninist socialism, the sort of system that existed in the USSR and the PRC. US leaders believed that the spread of Leninist socialism in Southeast Asia or elsewhere in the world did not comport with either US values or security interests, and decided to use the panoply of US power to guide these countries along liberal democratic lines. At a fundamental level, what was involved was a contest between China and the United States to shape the future political-economic evolution of Southeast Asia. Both the PRC and the United States were powerful states, governed by leaders confident of their respective universalistic creeds and believing that the future of Southeast Asia should evolve along lines comporting with their own vision of society.

US Pressure on Hanoi and China's Effort to Deter US Attack on DRV

Having decided to continue the US effort to contain communism at the 17th parallel, Washington concluded that it was crucial to compel Hanoi to suspend or at least radically reduce the infiltration of men and materiel from North to South Vietnam. This was to be achieved, US strategists concluded, by threatening to bomb the DRV's modern industrial and transportation facilities built up since 1954 with Chinese, Soviet, and East European assistance. US leaders believed that the VWP would be unwilling to risk destruction of the DRV's recently built modern sector of its economy. Once it became clear to DRV leaders that the United States was, in fact, prepared to bomb those facilities, Hanoi would move to protect them by suspending the drive to take over the south, even if only for a while. In effect, if given a choice between taking over South Vietnam and seeing the utter destruction of North Vietnam, Hanoi would stop infiltration—or so US leaders calculated. Washington's belief that infiltration was central to the deteriorating situation of the RVN was not incorrect. But the belief that US bombing, threatened or actual, of North Vietnam would persuade VWP leaders to cease such infiltration turned out to be an egregious miscalculation.

By spring 1964, US leaders were making public statements threatening US bombing of the north if infiltration continued. When this had no effect on infiltration, Washington seized the opportunity in August 1964 of an attempted attack on US destroyers by PAVN torpedo boats in the Gulf of Tonkin (the "Gulf of Tonkin incident") to bomb DRV naval facilities and ships. This bombing was intended as a warning to Hanoi that further, more devastating bombing would follow if the VWP did not suspend infiltration. Over the next four years, all the way to March 1968, the United States would gradually increase the intensity and scope of bombing of North Vietnam in search of "the breaking point" at which the VWP would call off its drive to liberate the south. That point was never reached; the VWP persisted in its quest in spite of US bombing.[4]

Beijing's policy calculus shifted with the prospect of a US attack on the DRV and the prospect of an all-out war between the United States and the DRV.[5] In its polemical argument with Khrushchev, the CCP had argued that spreading wars of national liberation in the intermediate zone would deter rather than precipitate imperialist aggression against the socialist countries. Now, in Vietnam, the United States was moving toward an attack on socialist DRV because of its pursuit of a war of national liberation. The prospect of a US attack on socialist North Vietnam required China put its strength on the line to deter such an attack, but that, in turn, opened the door to a possible US attack on China itself. Up to 1964, Beijing's key objectives in Vietnam had been to demonstrate the correctness of Mao's prescription of strategy for the international revolutionary movement—protracted people's wars of national liberation in the intermediate zone. Now Beijing's attention focused on China's own security.

The prospect of a US-DRV war raised weighty issues of China's national security. In 1954 China had won a solid buffer and ally, the DRV, standing between itself and the United States. The prospect of war between the DRV and the United States raised the prospect of the loss of that North Vietnamese buffer. The disparity in strength between the DRV and the United States was immense. If the United States directed its vast strength against North Vietnam, would the DRV be able to continue resistance? If not, would the regime surrender? Or collapse? Would the people rise up against suffering too harsh to bear? What if the United States bombed North Vietnam's population centers, as they had Japan's in 1945? What if the United States blockaded the DRV coast, shutting off its imports of fuel, food, and munitions? What if the United States bombed North Vietnam's intricate dike system, on which the country's production of paddy rice depended? What if the United States, with its South Vietnamese ally, invaded the north, as it had done in Korea in 1950, attempting to unify the country? If the DRV was defeated and/ or on the verge of collapse, would it be necessary for China to intervene, as it had in Korea, to prevent an unacceptable outcome? What if Chinese aid and support for North Vietnam led the US to bomb supply dumps and logistical lines inside China that were supporting Hanoi's war effort? Would US aircraft pursue DRV aircraft into Chinese airspace, and if so, how should the PRC respond? If the United States ignored China's warnings and crossed red lines stipulated by Beijing, what should China do? Behind the US-DRV war loomed the possibility of another war between China and the United States.

The credibility of the PRC as an ally was also newly at stake in 1964 as the United States threatened air attack on North Vietnam. The VWP was Beijing's close ally. The VWP had generally aligned with the CCP in Beijing's polemical battles with Moscow—at least until Khrushchev's ouster in October 1964 shifted Soviet policy in a more militant direction. The VWP had carefully secured CCP endorsement of initiation of armed struggle in the South in 1959. Hanoi supported Beijing on litmus test issues like the 1963 Partial Nuclear Test Ban Treaty. If Beijing did not strongly support Hanoi in the face of US pressure, China's stature as a protector of others against US imperialist threat would suffer.

China's leaders decided to use China's strength to demonstrate determination to support the DRV and implicitly threaten Chinese intervention in a US-DRV war as a way of deterring US attacks on the DRV.[6] In June 1964, the United States asked a Canadian diplomat to tell Hanoi that it was prepared to use military force if the DRV continued heavy infiltration into the south. Another US signal at the same time was heavy bombing of Pathet Lao headquarters in Laos.[7] Hanoi responded by dispatching DRV military Chief of Staff Van Tien Dung to Beijing to solicit Chinese aid and backing for ignoring US demands. Mao and Zhou promised full Chinese support. Mao told Dung that if the United States invaded the DRV, China would send troops as volunteers, as in Korea. The two parties and the two countries must cooperate in fighting the common enemy, Mao told Dong.

The next month, Zhou Enlai led a delegation to Hanoi to discuss the situation with VWP and Pathet Lao leaders. The United States was using South Vietnam as a place to test counterinsurgency war and as a base to attack socialism, Zhou said. China would support the struggles of the peoples of Southeast Asia and match US actions. If the United States sent troops, China would send troops. If the United States invaded the DRV, China would send troops to the DRV. Zhou suggested that as a political strategy the revolutionary forces uphold the Geneva agreements of 1954 and 1962. This would permit exploitation of contradictions between Washington and Paris, and would rally international public opinion against US involvement in Indochina. Publicly, Beijing warned Washington that the PRC stood behind the DRV. On July 6, Foreign Minister Chen Yi sent his DRV counterpart, Xuan Thuy, a message saying:

> US imperialism is openly clamoring for an extension of the war to the DRV and threatening to subject northern Vietnam to air and naval blockade as well as bombing . . . China and he DRV are fraternal neighbors closely related like the lips and the teeth. The Chinese people cannot be expected to look on with folded arms in the face of any aggression against the democratic Republic of Vietnam.[8]

The *Renmin ribao* commentary accompanying the publication of this note said, "The Chinese people will certainly not allow the US imperialists to play with fire right by their side."[9] The message was clear: by attacking the DRV, the United States risked a war with China.

Beijing's efforts to deter US attack on the DRV failed. In August 1964, following the Gulf of Tonkin incident, US warplanes bombed six North Vietnamese naval bases and associated fuel facilities and sank twenty DRV vessels. Coming after several months of Chinese warnings to Washington not to attack the DRV, the US attacks were a serious blow to Beijing's credibility. Beijing responded by reaffirming its determination to support Hanoi and upped the ante. A PRC statement issued just after the US bombing attacks declared that the US action "went over the brink of war." "The Chinese Government has served serious warnings on the US Government on many occasions that should it dare to launch an attack on the Democratic Republic of Vietnam, the Chinese people will absolutely not sit by with folded arms or sit idly by without lending a helping hand."[10] This choice of words echoed PRC warnings prior to China's entry into the Korean War in late 1950.

Beijing also launched vigorous military preparations following the Gulf of Tonkin incident. The PLA deployed additional interceptor aircraft to south China near the borders with the DRV. These aircraft included new model MIG-19 aircraft previously deployed in east and northeast China. China also sent MIG-15 and MIG-17 fighters to Hanoi and began training Vietnamese personnel to fly and maintain these aircraft. China established a 300-mile-wide air defense zone along China's border with the DRV. Four PLA air divisions and one anti-aircraft division were deployed to that zone. New airfields were constructed and existing ones improved. Radar stations were set up and their field of surveillance integrated and expanded to cover large portions of the DRV. This vital information guided the DRV air defense system. These preparations served the dual purpose of signaling to Washington the seriousness of China's intent and preparing to assist Hanoi's fight should the United States again ignore China's warnings and attack the north. In order to ensure the United States knew of China's military preparations, as newly deployed Chinese forces and units went into operation in the PRC's new air defense zone they broadcast in the open, easing the work of US electronic intelligence gatherers and again signaling China's resolve.[11]

Once again, Chinese efforts to deter US attack on the DRV failed. Further US strikes on the training and staging facilities of PAVN came in February 1965. In March, sustained and systematic (although not intense) bombing of the DRV began. The United States of America and the Democratic Republic of Vietnam were at war, albeit an undeclared one. The war would last ten years, until 1975, and end with the utter defeat of the United States. China's multidimensional assistance would be a major, possibly decisive, factor in Hanoi's victory.

With the beginning of sustained US bombing, the DRV sought and received PRC support. In April 1965, VWP General Secretary Le Duan and General Vo Nguyen Giap visited Beijing seeking the dispatch of PLA forces to the DRV, including volunteer pilots and engineering units. President Liu Shaoqi promised the VWP leaders that China would do its best to provide whatever was needed and that China would send the forces requested. Liu Shaoqi told Le Duan and Giap that Vietnam had complete freedom of initiative; Beijing would support whatever moves the VWP deemed necessary.[12] In June, PLA chief of staff Luo Ruiqing and PAVN chief of staff Van Tien Dung worked out a general plan for Chinese assistance. If the war remained in its current configuration, the DRV would fight by itself with the PRC providing support as needed. If the United States used air and naval forces to support a South Vietnamese attack on the DRV, China would use air and naval forces to support the DRV. If US forces attacked the DRV, China would use land forces and its strategic reserves to conduct whatever operations were necessary. In

FIGURE 9-1 PRC Military Aid to the DRV, 1964–1975

Items	1964	1965	1966	1967	1968	1969	1970	1971	1972	1973	1974	1975
Guns	80,500	220,767	141,531	146,600	219,899	139,900	101,800	143,100	189,000	233,600	164,500	141,800
Artillery pieces	1,205	4,439	3,362	3,984	7,087	3,906	2,212	7,898	9,238	9,912	6,406	4,880
Bullets (thousands)	25,240	114,010	178,120	147,000	247,920	119,170	29,010	57,190	40,000	40,000	30,000	20,060
Artillery shells (thousands)	335	1,800	1,066	1,363	2,082	1,357	397	1,899	2,210	2,210	1,390	965
Radio transmitters	426	2,779	1,568	2,464	1,854	2,210	950	2,464	4,370	4,335	5,148	2,240
Telephone sets	2,941	9,502	2,235	2,289	3,313	3,453	1,600	4,424	5,905	6,447	4,633	2,150
Tanks	16	–	–	26	18	–	–	80	220	120	80	–
Ships	–	7	14	25	–	–	–	24	71	5	6	–
Aircraft	18	2	–	70	–	–	–	4	14	36	–	20
Vehicles	25	114	96	435	454	162	–	4,011	8,758	1,210	506	–
Uniforms (thousand sets)	–	–	400	800	1,000	1,200	1,200	1,200	1,400	1,400	1,400	–

Source: Li Ke, Hao Shengzhang, *Wenhua dageming zhong de renmin jiefangjun* (The People's Liberation during the Great Cultural Revolution, Beijing: Zhonggong dangshi ziliao chubanshe, 1989), p. 416. Reproduced in Qiang Zhai, *China and the Vietnam Wars, 1950–1975*, (University of North Carolina Press: Chapel Hill, 2000), p. 136.

this latter eventuality, China was prepared to launch offensive operations to win the initiative. The two sides also worked out principles regarding air operations. PAVN warplanes would operate out of bases in south China, but would land briefly to refuel at bases in the DRV before engaging US planes in combat. Military chiefs Luo and Dung also agreed that China would send volunteer pilots to pilot DRV aircraft. China would later cancel this provision—a decision that caused Hanoi to turn increasingly to the Soviet Union for air defense capabilities.[13]

Over the next three years (between June 1965 and March 1968), China sent 320,000 PLA personnel to the DRV. The force peaked in 1967 at 170,000. About 1,100 PLA soldiers died assisting the DRV and about 4,200 were wounded. Most Chinese forces were withdrawn in 1968 for reasons having to do with shifting Chinese calculations about the relative US and Soviet threats to China, but the last Chinese forces would be withdrawn only in August 1973, following the signature of the January 1973 Vietnam peace treaty.[14] China also supplied a huge amount of military gear to the DRV, as illustrated by Figure 9-1.

PLA engineering units repaired North Vietnam's roads, bridges, and rail lines after US bombing—work critical to keeping supplies and reinforcements flowing to battlefields in the south. PLA troops assisted in the operation of North Vietnam's rail system. They organized and oversaw the movement into Vietnam of materials from China and via China from the Soviet Union and East Europe. PLA troops manned anti-aircraft guns, especially multiple heavy machine gun weapons effective against low-level attack. North Vietnam eventually developed a multilayered air defense system that became one of the best ever fielded, and Chinese gunners made an important contribution to that system. PLA gunners shot down US aircraft and took casualties in the process. All downings of US aircraft, including those by PLA gunners, were attributed to PAVN.[15] China also supplied ninety aircraft to the DRV. PLA forces helped construct and then man North Vietnam's coastal defense system to defend against US and South Vietnamese raids or landings. When the volume of foreign freight moving into the DRV exceeded its logistical capability in 1967, China supplied 500 trucks to break bottlenecks.[16]

The PRC also supported the DRV economically. PLA engineers helped bring factories back into operation after US bombing, or constructed alternate production operations in dispersed and camouflaged locations. The total mobilization of DRV manpower and industry for the war in the south, plus the destruction wrought by US bombing of industry and infrastructure, meant that the DRV could not feed its people or meet their most elemental living requirements for food, clothing, soap, kerosene, or medicine. China, along with the other socialist countries, supplied a huge amount of these daily essentials to North Vietnam. In 1978, Deng Xiaoping told Singapore leader Lee Kuan Yew that the PRC had supplied US$10 billion to the DRV, equivalent to $20 billion in current terms.[17]

The PLA also constructed a large and well-defended fortress complex at Yen Bai in northwest DRV on the main rail line and highway from China's Yunnan province to the Red River delta. Apparently intended as a territorial redoubt for PAVN in the event of a US or South Vietnamese invasion of the Red River delta, the complex ultimately included some 200 buildings and a very large runway. It was well defended by anti-aircraft guns built into caves in neighboring mountains.[18]

The air war became a hot area of US-PRC confrontation. US aircraft would occasionally enter PRC airspace, either in hot pursuit of DRV aircraft or as a result of inability to turn swiftly enough after bombing targets in the DRV. Initially, in January 1965, China's CMC ordered that PLA aircraft not attack US aircraft that intruded into Chinese airspace. Mao overruled that order, however, and directed that intruding US aircraft should be attacked.[19] The PLA would occasionally scramble fighters to intercept US planes entering China's airspace. Between September 1965 and August 1967, Beijing claimed to have shot down nine US planes in China's air space. Beijing also claimed that one PLA plane was shot down in Chinese airspace by a US warplane.[20] Most of the PLA troops killed while assisting Vietnam probably died by US bombing. In other words, in the air war over North Vietnam, PLA soldiers were killing Americans and were being killed in turn.

Defining the Limits of US Escalation

There were several key components of US strategy during 1964–1968 (i.e., the period of Lyndon Johnson's presidency). Large and heavily armed US ground forces conducted aggressive offensive operations within South Vietnam designed to find, fix, and destroy North Vietnamese and NLF main force units. This destruction of insurgent military forces was supposed to shield intensified national building and pacification efforts by the Republic of Vietnam (RVN) in South Vietnam's countryside. Beijing's main role in this regard seems to have been provision of large quantities of arms, ammunition, and military equipment to the "revolutionary forces" in South Vietnam. US strategy toward North Vietnam was to gradually and incrementally escalate the level of US bombing to the "breaking point" at which the level of death and destruction suffered by the North was too great, causing VWP leaders to pull back from their effort to topple the Saigon regime and suspend infiltration along the trails. Beijing played a critical role in persuading the United States to limit its bombing.

The ambassadorial talks in Warsaw underway since the aftermath of the 1954 Geneva Conference were the major venue for US-PRC communication

242 { China's Quest

during the 1964–1968 period. There were sixteen sessions of talks during those years, and Vietnam was on the agenda of all sessions.[21] Washington's message to Beijing during the Warsaw talks was, first of all, that the United States was determined to prevent South Vietnam from being taken over by Hanoi via armed conquest. The United States would take all measures necessary to prevent this. The United States did not, however, seek the destruction of the DRV or the communist regime ruling the north. All the United States asked, US representatives asserted, was for North Vietnam to let its southern neighbor, the Republic of Vietnam, live in peace. The United States was even willing to accept a neutral South Vietnam, if that was what the people of that country wanted. Nor did the United States seek to retain military bases in South Vietnam, or elsewhere in Southeast Asia, once the war was over. If Beijing wanted the elimination of US military bases from South Vietnam, US negotiators said, it should urge Hanoi to suspend infiltration, thus ending the war. The United States was even willing to consider extending development assistance to North Vietnam if it gave up its drive to conquer South Vietnam. On the other hand, if Hanoi persisted in its current course of aggression against its southern neighbor, US punishment of the north would continue to escalate, ultimately inflicting utter destruction on it.

Regarding China, the United States did not intend to attack, much less invade, it. The United States sought to avoid another Korea-like war with China. Nor did it intend to pose a threat to the security of China. The United States even signaled a willingness to further develop relations with the PRC. In December 1965, it proposed an exchange of journalists and doctors. And in March 1966, the US representative expressed a willingness to expand relations with "the People's Republic of China." This was the first time the US government had used the formal name of the Chinese state.[22]

Beijing rejected the premise of US policy: that the RVN was or ought to be an independent country. From Beijing's perspective, both the DRV and South Vietnam were part of the nation of Vietnam, and US presence in South Vietnam constituted illegal interference in the internal affairs of Vietnam. The United States had no right to be in South Vietnam. US involvement there was in violation of the 1954 Geneva Convention. The United States should allow the affairs of Vietnam to be determined by the Vietnamese people. It should withdraw from Vietnam immediately, completely and without condition. It should also cease all attacks on the Democratic Republic of Vietnam, again immediately and unconditionally. The defeat of the United States by the people of Vietnam was absolutely certain, China's representatives said. Moreover, China would assist the people of Vietnam in their struggle against US imperialism.

Chinese representatives ridiculed as "peace offensive frauds" various US peace proposals; for example, economic assistance to the DRV linked to an internationally supervised suspension of infiltration. The only solution to the problem, China insisted, was for the United States to accept defeat and withdraw completely from Vietnam. The tone in which these admonitions were delivered was typically strident, polemical, and acrimonious. Beijing's representatives rejected all US conciliatory gestures, such as proposed cultural exchanges and a proposed simultaneous pledge ruling out the first use of nuclear weapons. The harsh rhetoric and uncompromising positions taken by China's representatives at Warsaw reflected the content of China's media. US representatives at Warsaw found "negotiating" with the PRC equivalent to reading *Renmin ribao*.

Beijing played up the threat of Chinese intervention, even while indicating that China did not want a Korea-like war with the United States. These formulations were common in the Chinese media in 1964–1967. US imperialist aggression against Vietnam was aggression against China itself. The United States would commit a "grave historical blunder"—implicitly, as in Korea—if it underestimated the determination of the Chinese people in supporting the Vietnamese people's struggle. It could not expect the Chinese people "to stand idly by while the United States committed aggression against its fraternal neighbor, Vietnam." China and Vietnam were "like lips and teeth; they were closely linked and injury to the lips meant injury to the teeth." The United States was "playing with fire in Vietnam, and those who played with fire could expect to be consumed by fire." Washington should stop its brazen and criminal attacks on the DRV and halt at the brink of the precipice before it met catastrophe. Again, these particular choices of words echoed phrases used by China prior to its entry into the Korean War.[23]

Beijing's threat to intervene in the US-DRV war served several purposes. It helped deter a US invasion of the DRV and US attacks on facilities in China supporting Hanoi's war effort—supply dumps, roads and rail junctions, and airfields used by PAVN. It helped limit the scope and intensity of US attacks on the DRV by making the United States wary of crossing the "flash point" that would precipitate Chinese entry. China's first test of an atomic bomb in October 1964 and of a hydrogen bomb in June 1967 gave additional strength to China's warnings. The fact that China was armed with nuclear weapons weighed heavily in US calculations regarding confronting it over Vietnam during the mid-1960s.

Simultaneously with stress on the danger of Chinese entry into the war, Beijing signaled its desire to avoid a war with the United States. Interestingly, Zhou Enlai chose a mechanism other than the Warsaw ambassadorial talks to first deliver this message. In April 1965, Zhou conveyed to Pakistani president Mohammad Ayub Khan a four-point message for the United States. Pakistan was a good friend of both the PRC and the United States, and Khan was scheduled to visit Washington shortly after his visit to Beijing. Zhou's first point was that China would not take the initiative in provoking a war with the United States. Second, China meant what it said; it would stand behind the

DRV. Third, China was prepared for the eventuality of war with the United States, and Washington should not think that China would back down in the face of US provocations because of China's weakness. Fourth, if the United States provoked war with China, that war would know no boundaries.[24] This last point was an implicit threat to spread a war triggered by Vietnam into Laos, Thailand, and perhaps even Korea. When Ayub Khan later canceled his scheduled visit to Washington, Zhou repeated his four-point message to the president of Tanzania and other foreign leaders. China's representatives in Warsaw also reiterated the message.

President Johnson's fear of sparking "another Korea" exercised a significant influence on the US campaign against the DRV. Although US mastery of the sea approaches to the DRV was absolute, the United States did not—until 1972—impose a naval blockade or embargo. From 1964 until early 1972, Chinese, Soviet, East European, and some West European ships carried cargos of civilian and military goods to DRV ports, often passing within view of US warships. This forfeiting of US naval supremacy was an immense advantage to Hanoi. US forces monitored closely all maritime traffic with the DRV, and could easily have shut it off—as they did in less than one day in the spring of 1972 when finally given the order to mine DRV harbors.

Regarding the air campaign, the United States did not—again until 1972—wage all-out air war against the DRV. In 1964, Air Force Chief of Staff Curtis LeMay recommended that all available US air power be used to attack the DRV as abruptly, intensely, and completely as possible to destroy within the shortest possible time the country's ability to make war. US leaders ruled out this approach, once again until 1972, in favor of a slow and incremental expansion of the scope and intensity of bombing. This allowed Hanoi to disperse and conceal potential targets, and use frequent pauses in bombing—intended by the United States to signal the limited nature of US aims and allow VWP leaders to "cool down"—to conduct essential redeployments. It also gave Hanoi time to build up what would eventually become a world-class air defense system that posed deadly threat to US planes. The United States did not carpet bomb or fire bombed North Vietnamese population centers as it had Japanese cities in 1945. Under US war planning, DRV city centers were excluded from bombing, and a "donut" area around those centers was subject to heavily restricted bombing. This too was a boon to Hanoi. Restricted and no-bomb areas became favored locales for PAVN supply dumps, transport depots, and command centers. Some of those restrictions were incrementally lifted in line with the strategy of gradual escalation.

Further US restrictions on the war against Hanoi involved the nondeployment of US ground forces into Laos as prohibited by the 1962 "neutralization" agreement—even though the enemy's vital trails ran through the southeastern portion of that country.[25] Instead, the United States relied on indigenous Laotian anticommunist forces (especially among the Hmong mountain tribesmen) working in cooperation with nonuniformed US clandestine forces. While not entirely without effect, those indigenous forces were unable to seal off Hanoi's vital supply lines. The trails could easily have been blocked by US ground forces. Such a move would have forced PAVN to attack fixed US defensive positions, rather than having US forces trying to "find and fix" PAVN in South Vietnam, usually at places and under circumstances decided on by PAVN commanders. When the US "secret war" in Laos was discovered, as it inevitably was, it was cast as a violation of the 1962 Geneva agreement, contributing significantly to the international united front against the US effort in Vietnam. Nor did US forces invade the DRV or raid its coasts, or bomb the DRV's intricate dike system, on which its irrigated production of patty rice depended.

The highly limited way in which the United States undertook to wage its war against Hanoi was a major reason for Hanoi's ultimate victory. The self-limitation of American power allowed Hanoi to sustain a protracted war of attrition with an immensely more powerful United States, enervating the Johnson administration and a portion of the US public.[26]

The reasons why US leaders chose to wage such a highly limited war were complex. One reason, perhaps the major one, was that this approach would allow the United States to avoid triggering direct Chinese entry into the war, turning it into "another Korea"—a direct and intense war between the United States and the PRC. The lesson of Korea—ignoring China's warnings on the grounds that Beijing was bluffing—loomed large in the minds of US leaders and their advisors. They believed that the United States had inadvertently triggered war with China in Korea by advancing US forces across the 38th parallel and up to the Yalu River.[27] The strategy of gradual escalation would allow the United States and the PRC to signal and understand one another, thus avoiding "another Korea," US leaders believed. The threat of Chinese intervention thus gave Beijing leverage to influence the level of US violence directed against the North. This would allow Beijing to play a very major, perhaps decisive, role in Hanoi's defeat of the United States. But there were other reasons as well.

Another important reason for the US decision to wage such a highly limited war was the fact that the immense disparity of US and DRV power led people to believe that there was simply no way Hanoi could defeat the United States. US strength was so overwhelming that it could prevail even if used poorly. A desire to wage war in a humane and economical way (killing as few people as possible and using no more resources that necessary) was an important part of the mix. For President Johnson, a desire to keep the war small so as not to sidetrack his Great Society program of domestic reform was a high-ranking reason. But the credible threat of Chinese entry into the conflict helped persuade Washington to fight a protracted war of attrition which Hanoi could win.

China outmaneuvered the United States in the struggle for South Vietnam, only to discover that the results were not what it had hoped for, namely a friendly country allied with China, grateful for China's help, and looking to China for protection. Ironically, the outcome for the United States was also the opposite of what it had expected. Washington failed in its effort to contain communism at the 17th parallel, but found that a united communist-led Vietnam served very well to contain communist-ruled China.

Souring of the CCP-VWP Relation

Even while China was constraining US escalation against the DRV by threatening intervention, and even while China was providing large-scale assistance to Hanoi's desperate war effort, tensions were accumulating in the CCP-VWP relationship. These tensions remained below the surface until the Americans were driven out in April 1975. But they would emerge with remarkable speed after that. At that point, a powerful emotional component of the PRC-DRV relations became apparent. North Vietnamese leaders resented a long series of Chinese policies and behaviors, seeing them as "betrayal" of the sacred cause of Vietnam's struggle against the United States. CCP leaders for their part were angered by VWP ingratitude and repayment of China's generous support by adoption of policies hostile to China.

Hanoi's resentment derived from memories of Chinese and Soviet pressure during the 1954 Geneva Convention. VWP acceptance then of what was promised would be a temporary partition of Vietnam had, in fact, given the United States an opportunity to set in place a new anticommunist regime in the south that, in effect, imposed another war on the VWP—a war far more costly than the war against the French. It was true that the imposition of that bitter compromise on the VWP was the result of both Chinese and Soviet pressure, and that the CPSU was at that point the recognized leader of the international communist movement. But the CCP was the elder brother of the Asian revolutionary movement, and in that position the CCP had materially assisted the VWP struggle against the French. China was therefore in a position to deny further assistance if the VWP refused to accept China's advice in 1954. The VWP had gone along with Chinese-Soviet advice in 1954, but as the Saigon government consolidated its position in the south with American support and ignored the vague provisions of the 1954 agreement regarding unification, VWP leaders began to view the bitter compromise of 1954 as a Chinese "betrayal" of Vietnam. VWP leaders kept these views to themselves until the Americans were defeated.

The entry of large numbers of PLA troops into the DRV in June 1965 generated tensions of more mundane sorts. Mao Zedong would respond in August 1965 to VWP complaints about the behavior of PLA soldiers in Vietnam by directing them not to be "too enthusiastic" in assisting the Vietnamese struggle. "Excessive enthusiasm" seems an apt way to describe the sorts of problems that emerged. On the Vietnamese side—and perhaps subconsciously on the Chinese side too—were memories of two millennia of Chinese attempts to rule and Sinicize the Vietnamese, and of an equally long Vietnamese struggle to resist those Chinese efforts and uphold Vietnamese independence. Objectionable PLA behavior included the wearing of Mao badges and efforts to conduct anti-revisionist ideological education with Vietnamese counterparts.[28] From the VWP's perspective, the CCP's anti-revisionist ideas were completely out of place in Vietnam, a country waging a desperate, all-out struggle against the United States. Washington, not Moscow, was the target of struggle, in Hanoi's view. Chinese troops also distributed literature lauding economic construction in China. Exactly why this was objectionable is unclear. Perhaps it suggested the superior status of China. Perhaps it suggested that the DRV too should concentrate more on economic development, rather than on war to liberate the South.[29] PLA medical teams were also providing treatment to Vietnamese. VWP leaders objected to this as well. The CCP for its part objected to publication in a DRV journal of an article reprising China's invasions of Vietnam over history. Vietnamese port authorities had also refused to allow a Chinese ship refuge in a DRV port during a US bombing.

CCP General Secretary Deng Xiaoping and VWP General Secretary Le Duan discussed these issues in April 1966, about a year after PLA units entered the DRV.[30]

Deng began by recalling Mao's order directing Chinese in Vietnam not to be "too enthusiastic" about rendering assistance. Deng then mentioned the 130,000 PLA troops in the DRV, the presence of other strong Chinese forces on the DRV's northern border (ready to intervene to counter an American invasion of the DRV), and PRC-DRV planning for a joint war against the United States. Deng continued:

> Are you suspicious of us because we have so much enthusiasm? Do the Chinese want to take control over Vietnam? We would like to tell you frankly that we don't have any such intention . . . If we made a mistake thus making you suspicious, it means that Chairman Mao is really farsighted.[31]

Le Duan replied that Vietnam always appreciated China's assistance: "The more enthusiasm you have, the more beneficial it is for us. Your enthusiasm can help us to save the lives of two or three million people."[32] VWP leaders also deeply resented CCP refusal to form a united front with the Soviet Union in support of Hanoi's anti-US struggle. Following Khrushchev's ouster, the new Soviet leaders became much more supportive of Hanoi's struggle. To a considerable degree, this was a response to CCP criticism about Moscow's weak support for wars of national liberation. With the deepening of the DRV-US confrontation in 1964, Hanoi's anti-US struggle became a cause célèbre among progressive circles around the world, and the new Soviet leadership attempted to burnish its credentials as supporter of revolutionary causes by stepping up support for Hanoi. They also saw in Vietnam an opportunity to impose on the United States a war on China's flank but far from the USSR and from the strategically vital Central European front. Consequently, in February 1965 Soviet Premier Alexei Kosygin visited Beijing to propose an end to polemics between Beijing and Moscow and cooperation in support of Vietnam. Two months later, Moscow proposed convocation of a USSR-DRV-PRC summit conference to solidify support for Hanoi. Mao rejected both proposals. A year later, in March 1966, the general secretary of the Japan Communist Party, Kenji Miyamoto, launched a final effort to arrange joint CCP-CPSU support for the DRV. In talks with Liu Shaoqi and Deng Xiaoping in Beijing, Miyamoto worked out an arrangement for revolutionary solidarity in support of Hanoi. Mao intervened to squelch the deal. Liu and Deng had not been authorized to speak for China, Mao declared; the Soviet Union was the most dangerous enemy of the people of the world, and entering into united action with Moscow would only facilitate its sabotage of Vietnam's victorious revolutionary war.[33]

Mao's unstated but primary objective in rejecting "united action" with Moscow was to prepare for intensified struggle against revisionists within the CCP who, he believed, wanted to direct China's revolution along lines of "Khrushchev's phony communism." A key weapon in Mao's anti-revisionist struggle would be holding up the Soviet Union, its leaders, and its "phony communism" as negative examples from which the Chinese people were to learn. Suspension of polemics against the CPSU, affirmation that the CPSU was still communist by agreeing to cooperate with it in support of Hanoi, and reduction of tension with Moscow were exactly what Mao did not need in his effort to promote the struggle against "hidden revisionists" within the CCP. China would aid Hanoi, but on its own terms. Subsequently, Beijing agreed to transport Soviet and East European goods by rail across China to the DRV. Still later, in early 1967, Beijing agreed that DRV personnel would meet arriving cargo at the PRC's northern borders and accompany it across China to the DRV. As factional fighting escalated in China, Red Guard seizure of military cargos bound for the DRV became a serious problem.

VWP leaders were dismayed by Mao's rejection of a united front with Moscow in support of Vietnam. Hanoi's struggle against a vastly more powerful United States was a desperate one, representing, they firmly believed, the vanguard of the whole world's struggle against the common enemy, US imperialism. It was thus incumbent on all genuine revolutionaries to do whatever they could to assist Hanoi. From the perspective of Le Duan, Le Duc Tho, and other VWP leaders, Mao's narrow sectarianism, dogmatism, and left-wing extremism weakened Vietnam's struggle and helped the United

States. If a firmly united socialist camp, with PRC-USSR solidarity at its core, stood behind the DRV, the Americans would be much more cautious in their attacks. This analysis, of course, reflected DRV interests. Mao had his own views and objectives. He saw a mounting Soviet effort, internal and external, to direct the course of the Chinese revolution away from the "correct" course and toward Soviet-style "phony communism."

As long as Hanoi's war with the Americans continued, VWP leaders swallowed their bitter feelings about Mao's putting China's anti-revisionist struggle above Vietnam's anti-US struggle. Between late 1964 and mid-1975, Hanoi perfected the art of balancing between Beijing and Moscow, using the rivalry between those two powers to increase the support of each for Hanoi, and thanking and lauding both as true and reliable friends of Vietnam. Because of Hanoi's acclaim among world progressives, both Beijing and Moscow sought its affirmation. The VWP played that game well. Below the surface, however, Mao suspected the VWP's close and friendly ties with the CPSU, while Le Duan deeply resented Mao's betrayal of Vietnam.

VWP Embrace of Soviet Advice: The Growing Threat of Soviet Encirclement

In 1968, Hanoi began following Soviet advice, and rejecting Chinese advice, on key issues of war and political strategy. While the United States seemed to be drawing away from South Vietnam, the prospect was growing that the Soviet Union would replace the Americans in Vietnam. In the Chinese vernacular, Hanoi was in danger of "letting the tiger in the back door, while driving the wolf out the front door" (*qian men chu lang, hou men ru hu*).

There were two interrelated issues that defined Chinese-Soviet competition for influence in Hanoi during the 1965–1968 periods: the military strategy the VWP should use to fight the Americans, and peace negotiations with the Americans.[34] Regarding military strategy, Beijing urged Hanoi to wage a people's war with emphasis on protracted but relatively low-intensity guerrilla warfare in rural areas. This was, of course, in line with Mao's classic model of protracted war. In terms of its argument to Hanoi, Beijing warned (in lines with Mao's strategy) that big battles against main enemy forces and cities would inflict heavy casualties on the revolutionary forces and lead to demoralization. As noted earlier, VWP Secretary General Le Duan and General Nguyen Chi Thanh rejected a pure Maoist-style guerrilla war in favor of a combination of guerrilla warfare and large-unit, high-intensity, aggressive assaults by conventional PAVN forces. Chinese leaders felt this was an incorrect approach both because it was more in line with Moscow's prescriptions and because they felt it would not work. Hanoi's adherence to the Maoist prescription of people's war was especially important for Beijing.

Mao's revolutionary strategy was the very core of his ideological challenge to the CPSU. Vietnam was the test case that Beijing intended to demonstrate the correctness of Mao's strategy. Demonstrating the correctness of Mao's revolutionary line was, in turn, linked to establishing Mao Zedong as the preeminent Marxist-Leninist theorist of the communist world. While the third and final stage of a people's war envisioned offensives against enemy-occupied cities by guerrilla forces dominating surrounding rural areas, the plan developed by VWP strategists envisioned urban uprisings and seizure of cities much earlier in the revolutionary process. Rooted in the successful experience in rallying the urban populace of Hanoi in August 1945, VWP strategy envisioned a general uprising in cities precipitated by aggressive, conventional assaults by revolutionary military forces—the sort of tactics applied in the waves of assaults on South Vietnamese cities in 1968.

Moscow, for its part, urged Hanoi to consolidate forces into larger units, arm those forces with modern weapons, and wage big decisive battles, including the seizure of cities. This type of warfare required hardware that the Soviet Union was better positioned than China to supply. It was also a type of war that would require the United States to shift more big units from NATO's European front to Southeast Asia. These differences corresponded to the prescriptions of the CCP and the Brezhnev-led CPSU about the correct way to deal with US imperialism.

Up to 1964, Hanoi's war for South Vietnam largely corresponded to Mao's strategy—low-intensity guerrilla war in rural areas. It started changing in 1964, when the VWP decided to go for broke in the effort to topple the Saigon government before the United States had time to intervene. It changed even more in 1965 with Americanization and General Nguyen Chi Thanh's aggressive large-unit strategy mixed with low-intensity guerrilla tactics. It would change even more dramatically in 1968 with waves of large-unit assaults designed to seize enemy fortified cities.[35] From Mao's perspective, the VWP was gradually paying more attention to Soviet and less attention to Chinese advice.

This issue came to a head over the Tet offensive, which was launched early in 1968 but had been under discussion and planning since early 1967. The Tet offensive would eventually involve a massive conventional assault on a US base at Khe Sanh in northwest South Vietnam, combined with a general attack t on South Vietnam's cities by guerrilla forces merged into large units for open assaults. Having decided to launch the Tet Offensive, VWP leaders Pham Van Dong and Vo Nguyen Giap came to Beijing in April 1967 to inform Chinese leaders as gently as possible of Hanoi's decision to deviate from Mao's people's war strategy in 1968. After hearing out the VWP proposal, Mao warned Dong and Giap:

> We have a saying, "If you preserve the mountain green, you will never have to worry about firewood." The US is afraid of your [guerrilla]

tactics. They wish that you would order your regular forces to fight so they can destroy your main forces. But you were not deceived. Fighting a war of attrition is like having a meal: [it is best] not to have too big a bite.[36]

Mao and Zhou Enlai felt that offensives to seize cities were premature. As Zhou told Pham Van Dong and Vo Nguyen Giap during the April 1967 discussions, the war in South Vietnam was still in the second stage of strategic equilibrium. Attacks on big enemy-held and fortified cities would fail while producing heavy casualties that would demoralize revolutionary forces.[37] For Mao and Zhou, the successive big offensives launched by Hanoi in 1968, which shattered the main revolutionary forces in the south exactly as Mao had predicted, were evidence that the VWP was leaning dangerously toward acceptance of incorrect Soviet, rather than correct Chinese, advice. By the end game of the war in 1974–1975, PAVN's strategy was entirely conventional—fast-moving massed armor with mobile artillery and mechanized infantry, a very long way from Mao's model of protracted guerrilla war. Hanoi's embrace of Soviet-style warfare raised the question of how a united VWP-led Vietnam would align vis-à-vis the PRC and the USSR once America was defeated.

Regarding the issue of peace negotiations, Moscow supported and Beijing (at least up to December 1970) was deeply skeptical of Hanoi negotiating with Washington. Soviet leaders felt that it might well be possible to secure a negotiated US exit from Vietnam. Negotiations would also help prevent the Vietnam War from escalating into a great-power war, possibly involving the Soviet Union. Diplomacy was also an arena in which the USSR had vast experience and assets—in contrast to China with its isolation and seemingly irrational militancy in the middle of its Cultural Revolution. Beijing, on the other hand, adamantly opposed negotiations. Such negotiations would confuse and demoralize the revolutionary forces sapping their strength both in Vietnam and beyond, Beijing insisted. Negotiations would become a mechanism in which Moscow could bargain away Vietnam's revolutionary victory for some Soviet gains with the United States. Negotiations would become a route to Soviet betrayal of the Vietnamese revolution.[38] Unstated but clearly paramount in Chinese minds was the reality that the USSR had substantial global influence, including with the United States, while the PRC did not.

Up to 1968, VWP leaders Le Duan and Le Duc Tho, like Beijing, rejected negotiations. Most importantly, they believed that negotiations would derail the all-out war to take over the south that they advocated. They also understood that negotiations would alienate Beijing, whose support was vital. Thus, in 1967, Le Duan presided over an extensive purge of pro-peace, pro-negotiation advocates within and without the VWP. One of the intentions and results of this purge was to reassure Beijing that there would be no negotiations and, by extension, that the VWP was not about to be taken over by pro-Soviet forces. Le Duan also rejected negotiations, again up to 1968, because he believed that they would fail unless the revolutionary forces had achieved a decisive victory on the battlefield. The seizure of major cities and the toppling of the government of South Vietnamese leader Nguyen Van Thieu during the Tet offensive of 1968 were intended to be such decisive victories.

But contrary to Hanoi's expectations, the anticipated urban uprising did not occur. Neither Thieu's government nor the city of Saigon (or any other major South Vietnamese city, except Hui for a brief period) fell to communist forces during the Tet offensives. But Johnson's dramatic reorientation of American policy in the first half of 1968 indicated to Le Duan that Hanoi had achieved an advantageous position conducive to negotiations. Preliminary talks between the United States and the Democratic Republic of Vietnam began in Paris in May 1968. As noted earlier, formal talks began in October 1968.

When Hanoi announced in April 1968 that it was ready for talks with the United States, it did so without giving Beijing prior notification, let alone securing Beijing's consent. Beijing was unhappy with both the process and the substance of Hanoi's move. Ho Chi Minh was in Beijing for medical treatment when the decision was announced, and he told Chinese leaders, when asked, that he knew nothing about the decision. Hanoi compounded its mistake, in Beijing's view, in October when it agreed to the inclusion in the talks of Saigon's Nguyen van Thieu government. In November 1968, Beijing reluctantly endorsed the VWP's decision of negotiating while fighting. The VWP's double rejection of Chinese advice—on both war strategy and negotiations—in favor of Soviet advice was unacceptable to Mao and Zhou. When Le Duc Tho visited Beijing in October 1968 to brief China on negotiations with the United States, he encountered withering condemnation from Foreign Minister Chen Yi:

> At present, Washington and Saigon are publicizing the negotiations, showing the fact that you have accepted the conditions put forward by the US. Your returning home for party instructions all the more proves it to the world's people. With your acceptance of the quadripartite negotiations [i.e., including the RVN] you have handed the puppet government legal recognition, thus eliminating the National Liberation Front's status as the unique legal representative of the people of the south. . . . In our opinion, in a very short time, you have accepted the compromising and capitulationist proposals put forward by the Soviet revisionists. So between our two parties and the two governments . . . there is nothing more to talk about.[39]

Chen softened his stance at the very end of his talk by calling Vietnam and China "brothers" as well as "comrades." At the end of October, however,

Beijing used the occasion of the start of four-party negotiations to recall Chinese troops in the DRV and cut military assistance.[40] Beijing explained this move as a response to the end of US bombing: since US bombing was ended, there was no longer need for PLA anti-aircraft or engineering forces for damage repair. VWP leaders, however, understood Beijing's move as anger over Hanoi's choosing of Soviet over Chinese guidance.[41]

The withdrawal of Chinese forces from North Vietnam in 1968 meant that Chinese and American military forces were no longer fighting one another. This eliminated one potential obstacle to PRC opening of ties with the United States. That mayhave been one factor influencing Mao's thinking. The Chinese sense of betrayal by Vietnam in 1968 would be reciprocated four years later in 1972, when VWP leaders simmered in outrage over Beijing's rapprochement with Washington in the midst of intense US bombing of North Vietnam. From Beijing's perspective, the shifts in Hanoi's policy in 1968 indicated that the VWP was drifting into the CPSU's orbit. Meanwhile, a new president, Richard Nixon, had taken power in the United States in January 1969 and was giving clear signals he was interested in exploring a new relation with the PRC.

Sino-American Rapprochement and the PRC-DRV Alliance

China's opening of ties and initiation of a strategic dialogue with the United States in 1971–1972 ipso facto undercut China's deterrent support for the DRV. The fears of Chinese intervention that had haunted US leaders since 1964 were greatly eased. After rapprochement with China, the Nixon administration resorted to previously unthinkably tough military moves against the DRV. PRC-US rapprochement also undermined the VWP's effort to convince the United States people and leadership that the US cause in South Vietnam was doomed and that the United States should recognize failure and wash its hands of the Republic of Vietnam. Beijing recognized the contradiction between its US and its DRV policies, and tried to manage those contradictions by paralleling the process of rapprochement with stepped-up aid for the DRV. Hanoi accepted China's renewed assistance and thanked Beijing for it, but privately VWP leaders were furious.

Endorsement of Hanoi's negotiations with the United States was another component of Beijing's effort to manage Hanoi's anger at Beijing's opening to the United States. From 1968 through late 1970, China abstained from endorsing or criticizing Hanoi's efforts at the Paris negotiations. The Chinese media reported on those talks and Hanoi's various moves and countermoves, but in neutral tones.[42] Then, as Beijing began maneuvering toward rapprochement with the United States, it began endorsing VWP moves at the Paris talks. Mao's first overt attempt to signal Washington of his interest in improved relations with the United States came on the October 1, 1970, National Day celebrations when Mao invited American journalist Edgar Snow to stand beside him atop Tiananmen Gate.

In December 1970, Beijing shifted positions on the US-DRV peace talks in Paris. Beijing endorsed a peace plan proposed at the Paris talks by the NLF's government, the Provisional Revolutionary Government (PRG). In March the next year, a DRV-PRC joint communiqué also endorsed the PRG peace plan.[43] On July 1, 1971, the PRG issued another slightly revised Seven Point Peace Plan which the VWP intended to be the centerpiece of a global peace campaign to pressure Nixon. Hanoi's friends around the world, from the Soviet Union and its allies to the antiwar movement in the United States to the PRC, endorsed the Seven Point Plan and called for the United States to accept it. Hanoi's objective was to mobilize strong international pressure on Nixon. *Renmin ribao* endorsed the plan on July 4, 1971. This was Beijing's first endorsement of a "peaceful settlement" of the Vietnam conflict since 1965. The practical political significance of Beijing's endorsement of VWP peace proposals was overwhelmed, however, by the immense political significance of Beijing's opening to the United States.

On July 15 came the bombshell announcement by President Nixon that his national security advisor, Henry Kissinger, had been in Beijing for talks, and that Nixon himself would visit China early the next year. News of this revolution in world affairs immediately displaced the PRG's Seven Point Peace Plan in news headlines. The blossoming of a new Sino-American relation immediately became the center of global media attention. Kissinger believed that Beijing's opening to the United States would demoralize North Vietnam's populace by raising the specter of diminished Chinese support. He believed too that it would ameliorate the deep divisions in the United States that had emerged over the Vietnam War—and which had become a major component of VWP political strategy by 1971. It would also, again in Kissinger's view, undercut the VWP's belief that it could exhaust the United States. Nixon had attempted to exacerbate VWP apprehensions by hinting in his announcement that Vietnam would be a topic during his upcoming talks in Beijing.[44] Nixon's breakthrough with China also conflicted with VWP planning for a major military offensive in early 1972 prior to the US presidential election in November. Nixon's opening to China considerably strengthened his bid for re-election, undermining Hanoi's political strategy of mobilizing maximum pressure on Nixon.

Hanoi was outraged by Beijing's disregard for VWP political warfare against Nixon. The VWP's newspaper *Nhan Dan* used the metaphor of throwing a life preserver to a drowning man to characterize a policy of unprincipled reconciliation with imperialism based on "the narrow interests of one's country," which violated the "common interests of the world revolution."[45] The article did not identify the unprincipled country, but that was clear enough. A few days later *Nhan Dan* characterized Nixon's policy as:

> dividing the socialist countries, winning over one section and pitting it against another in order to oppose the national liberation movement and carry out a counter-revolutionary peace evolution in socialist countries. Nixon's policy also consists of trying to achieve a compromise between the big powers in an attempt to make smaller countries bow to their arrangements.[46]

While condemning China's policy in elliptical terms, DRV media censored until late 1971 all actual news of Kissinger's July and October 1971 visits to Beijing and Nixon's upcoming visit. Beijing did what it could to assuage VWP anger. Shortly after Kissinger's July 1971 visit, Zhou sent a message to Hanoi outlining the contents of talks with the American envoy. A PRC delegation to Hanoi followed to continue explaining China's move. When informed that Vietnam would be on the agenda of the forthcoming talks with Nixon, VWP leaders objected strongly. China had no right to negotiate for Vietnam or to discuss matters regarding Vietnam with Nixon. PRC representatives tried to persuade their VWP comrades that China still stood squarely behind the DRV.

Moscow was quick to exploit the new PRC-DRV tensions. President Podgorny arrived in Hanoi in early October 1971 to preside over agreement on new and substantial economic and military assistance programs to the DRV. A high-level Soviet military mission arrived soon after Podgorny's visit to help plan the massive offensive against South Vietnam that would begin in March 1972. That offensive would begin barely a month after Nixon's China visit and the signature of the Shanghai Communiqué with its anti-hegemony provision. Hanoi's 1972 offensive was Moscow and the DRV's response to Sino-American rapprochement.

Nixon responded to Hanoi's 1972 offensive by ordering the mining of DRV harbors, a move that effectively cut DRV sea communications for the rest of the war. Nixon also unleashed on the DRV two waves of the most intense and sustained bombing of the war. In spring and again at year's end, the United States for the first time in the entire war deployed heavy B-52 bombers against DRV military targets even in previously restricted areas, and in an intense and sustained fashion. Only the buffer zone with China was maintained. VWP leaders noted that Washington dared take these moves only after improved ties with China. Washington's fear of Chinese intervention had evaporated and with it earlier constraints on US military blows against North Vietnam.

China did what it could to help the DRV withstand the new US onslaught. The number of Soviet and East European trains carrying goods across China to the DRV was increased. Soviet and East European ships were allowed to unload goods at ports in south China for overland shipment to the DRV.

China constructed a four-inch-diameter pipeline from south China to Hanoi to deliver fuel. This was vital assistance, since Hanoi's petroleum imports by sea had been shut off. As shown in Figure 9-1, China's supply of arms and vehicles shot up in 1971 and 1972. The VWP took China's assistance and thanked Beijing for it, but Vietnamese expressions of gratitude were hollow. Privately, VWP leaders were furious at what they saw as China's "betrayal." The Americans would not have dared to take such harsh blows against the DRV as delivered in 1972 if China had not eased US fears by opening ties with the United States. As a Vietnamese White Paper published later in 1979 said, "With the Korean War, the U.S. imperialists learned the lesson that they should not wage a war on the Asian continent, especially in countries adjacent to China, less a direct military confrontation with China should take place."[47] Inviting Kissinger and Nixon to China had allowed the American imperialists to ignore those lessons. From the VWP perspective, the CCP had betrayed the world revolution and Vietnam's liberation struggle.

The Endgame at the Paris Peace Talks

As US-DRV negotiations approached their endgame in 1971–1972, Beijing followed a dual strategy. On the one hand, it refused to go along with US efforts to pressure Hanoi and deliberately disassociated itself from those efforts. It also maintained a high level of material and rhetorical support for Hanoi's war effort. On the other hand, Chinese leaders urged Hanoi to grant the United States a face-saving exit from Vietnam, leaving the incumbent Saigon government temporarily in place to be destroyed by Vietnam's revolutionary forces at some unspecified later point after the Americans had militarily withdrawn from Vietnam. This dual policy was an attempt to serve China's dual interests: building a new, cooperative relation with the United States, while not alienating DRV leaders. Ultimately, the VWP would comply with Beijing's recommendations and grant Washington a face-saving exit. But that arrangement evoked strong memories of Geneva in 1954, and left a bitter taste in the mouths of VWP leaders. With the collapse of DRV-PRC relations in 1979, Hanoi would take to calling China's role at this juncture yet another "betrayal."

US leaders hoped that their new relation with Beijing would induce China to persuade Hanoi to adopt a more moderate approach to a settlement. The crux of the US-DRV dispute at the peace talks in Paris was the relation between a military and a political settlement in Vietnam. The VWP insisted that a political settlement, including the removal of Nguyen Van Thieu's Saigon government and its replacement by an interim government, must proceed in tandem with an end to fighting. Washington insisted that military and political settlements be delinked, with an end of fighting, including the full withdrawal of US military forces from Vietnam, to be followed at some unspecified later date by a political settlement within South Vietnam and, finally, unification. From the VWP perspective, the delinked approach proposed by the United States was strongly reminiscent of the bitter medicine forced on the VWP at Geneva in 1954.

Beijing urged Hanoi to delink military and political settlements, granting the United States a face-saving exit and interval before South Vietnam fell to the revolutionary forces, as it certainly would. Mao himself told French foreign minister Maurice Schumann in July 1972 that he had advised PRG foreign minister Nguyen Thai Binh to stop demanding Thieu's removal as a precondition for a settlement with the United States.[48] Zhou Enlai later explained the logic of China's position to a group of senior CCP cadres shortly after the January 1973 peace agreement was signed:

> We told the Vietnamese comrades: we must be practical and realistic. The U.S. herself knows that to continue fighting means to stall for time with no way of knowing how long she will procrastinate. Therefore, she will make a "glorious withdrawal" through negotiations. Besides, having fought for so many years, the Vietnamese people have suffered great losses. To continue fighting will not affect the outcome for a moment. But to compel the Americans to withdraw through negotiations will leave you yourselves half to one year for rest and consolidation. You can reconsider the problem of liberating South Vietnam later. The Vietnamese comrades have accepted our suggestions.[49]

According to a VWP account, late in 1971 Mao urged Premier Pham Van Dong to postpone temporarily the liberation of the south, saying, "One can't sweep very far if the handle of the broom is too short. Taiwan is too far away for our broom to reach. Thieu in South Vietnam is also out of reach of your broom, Comrade. We must resign ourselves to this situation."[50] As a great power, Mao explained to Dong, the United States could not afford to forsake its old friends such as Nguyen van Thieu. Dong reportedly replied to Mao that Vietnam's broom had a very long handle.

Beijing matched its urging of moderation on the VWP with deliberate disassociation from US efforts to pressure the VWP. During his talks in Beijing in July and October 1971, Kissinger devoted considerable time to explaining US policy toward Indochina in hopes that Beijing could be induced to exercise some moderating influence on Hanoi.[51] Zhou rejected these overtures and replied with reiteration of China's strong support for Hanoi. When shortly before Nixon's visit to China, Kissinger sent Zhou a detailed report on Hanoi's rebuffs of US negotiating efforts at Paris, Zhou replied with an "acerbic note" accusing the United States of trying to enmesh China in the Vietnam issue.[52] During Nixon's February 1972 talks in China, Zhou declared China's sympathy and support for Hanoi and urged the United States to end the war quickly and withdraw its military forces from Vietnam. Zhou also indicated that China would not take sides in the continuing negotiations between Hanoi and the United States. Zhou also implied that China would not intervene militarily in the conflict in Indochina.[53] Kissinger had a long discussion on Vietnam with deputy foreign minister Qiao Guanhua later the same month in Vienna. Again Qiao affirmed China's moral and material support for Hanoi, while disassociating China from VWP specific negotiating positions. When the Nixon administration responded to Hanoi's spring 1972 offensive by mining and bombing the DRV, China strongly denounced US actions.

Ultimately, the DRV accepted the US proposal for separate military and political settlements. The United States withdrew its military forces with the government of Nguyen van Thieu still in place. The intention of the US administration at that point was to continue providing the RVN with robust military assistance and use US air power to enforce the provision of the peace agreement prohibiting PAVN invasion of the South.[54] These plans were later undone by congressional seizure of control over US Indochina policy. In June 1973, Congress cut off all spending for US military operations in Indochina. After that, presidential ordering of further military action in Vietnam would have been illegal. Congress also steeply cut US military assistance to the RVN. Congress's rebellion against the Nixon administration's Vietnam policy was tied to the Watergate scandal and to an underlying constitutional struggle between the executive and legislative branches over war powers. Be that as it may, when the VWP rolled the dice again in October 1974, Washington did not respond. Hanoi threw all its strength into a final assault that carried it to victory by April 1975. But all this could not be foreseen when the "peace agreement" was signed in January 1973. After fighting a ten-year-long war against the United States, the VWP was compelled to accept an agreement not too dissimilar to the 1954 Geneva settlement, leaving a hostile government in power in Saigon, and confronting it with yet another war. Again this left a strong reservoir of VWP bitterness against Beijing.

The Cultural Revolution, 1966–1969

China's Self-Isolation: Creating the Spiritual Conditions for Communism

The period from spring 1966 to late 1968 saw spreading upheaval across China. This upheaval reflected a struggle over power and policy within the top levels of the CCP. Mao had become convinced that the more development-oriented policies introduced by leaders like Liu Shaoqi after the collapse of the Great Leap Forward would, if continued, take China toward the "restoration of capitalism" he believed had already occurred in the Soviet Union. Mao also deeply resented having been pushed aside by Liu, Deng, and others. He could perhaps have used the internal security apparatus, firmly controlled by Mao loyalist Kang Sheng, to purge his rivals. Stalin had done that. Instead, Mao opted to use his immense personal authority and charisma to call forth organizations of idealistic radical youth to ferret out and hound out of office all power-holders who questioned Mao's leadership and policy directives. These "Red Guard" organizations soon gained a momentum of their own and targeted many of the privileges and abuses of power-holders empowered during the "construction of socialism" over the previous fifteen years. The Cultural Revolution became a curious phenomenon of a popular uprising against the institutions of power of a Leninist state, but an uprising led by the paramount leader of that party. Mao imagined, or at least he said, that Red Guard youth were gaining experience in "making revolution" just as he and his generation had when they were young, and this revolutionary experience would help keep China on the correct road to communism. Mao, age seventy-three in 1966, was contemplating his own mortality and sought to ensure that his spirit lived on in the course of the Chinese revolution.

The Cultural Revolution saw the most extreme efforts to force Chinese society to conform to the utopian vision of Mao. The Great Leap had been Mao's and China's first utopian thrust. But that era had concentrated on rapid increases in economic production, in Marxist terms on the economic "base." When the Great Leap ended, Mao saw China's peasants return rapidly to their traditional individualistic ways of farming. The consciousness of the Chinese people clearly remained backward, according to Mao and his supporters. During 1966 to 1969, and to some extent all the way to 1976, the emphasis was on transformation of the minds of the Chinese people, the way they thought and the cultural manifestations of their collective consciousness.[1] The transformation of the ideational "superstructure," in Marxist terms, would finally open the way to achievement of a communist utopia. It was to be achieved by intense "study," "criticism and self-criticism," and "struggle" within "small groups" in work units. Sincerity in undertaking thought reform was encouraged by a range of coercive measures that began with criticism within a small group and escalated to consignment to labor camp or summary execution as a bad element. A vast system of internal spying was mobilized to identify people whose consciousness was inadequately revolutionary. People were expected to inform on one another's ideological shortcomings. Failure to do so cast doubts on one's own ideological condition. Criticism of family members or spouses was lauded as manifestation of high class consciousness. Fear of punishment, terror, provided critical inducement for people to embrace thought reform. As often in history, terror and utopia went together.

China's foreign policies during 1966–1969 corresponded to the extremist upheaval under way domestically. During this period, the CCP positioned itself and China as the center of the world revolution, attempting to displace the USSR in that ideologically exalted role. The CCP continued the polemical struggle against the "revisionist" CPSU initiated in the early 1960s but with increased emphasis on nurturing Beijing-oriented Marxist-Leninist communist parties around the world. By the late 1960s, the world communist movement was deeply split between pro-Moscow and pro-Chinese wings—the deepest fissure since the Trotsky-Stalin split in the 1930s. China also became more vociferous in support for foreign revolutions. By the end of 1967, China had endorsed armed insurrections in twenty-nine countries.[2] China's foreign propaganda was filled with strident rhetoric and exhortation, depicting Marxism-Leninism-Mao Zedong Thought as salvation for the peoples of the world oppressed by US imperialism and Soviet revisionism. Huge amounts of inflammatory revolutionary propaganda were produced and distributed around the world. The "little red book" *Quotations of Chairman Mao* spread around the world, becoming for a while a talisman of radical youth in far-flung corners of the earth. Large color posters of Chairman Mao—also produced in large quantities by Chinese publishing companies—began to grace demonstrations from France to Mexico to the United States.

A deep strain of xenophobia in China's political culture was released during this period. Contact with foreigners, past or present, Western or socialist-camp, became grounds for suspicion of ideological shortcomings, investigation, and often "struggle" by radical youth. Gangs of radical youth were given free reign by China's internal security forces (as noted earlier, firmly under the control of Mao's ally Kang Sheng) to ransack private residences looking for foreign-language books, musical recordings, pictures, or clothing. If such were found, their possessors would typically be called to account by radical youth gangs, the incriminating items destroyed, and the culprit subjected to "struggle" in the form of verbal abuse or physical assault. On streets, young people with Western-style long hair were subject to forced haircuts. Young men wearing "Western-style" tight pants had those trousers slit open by Red Guard scissors. European classical music was banned as bourgeois and counterrevolutionary. An atmosphere of terror came to pervade China. Even Chinese scientists who had studied abroad or merely knew foreign languages or had foreign-language materials came under suspicion. Contacts with foreigners were even more strictly monitored than they had been in the 1950s. The number of foreigners allowed into China fell to probably a few thousand—resident and visiting foreign communists and progressives, some students from Africa studying agriculture or revolution, and a few carefully selected and carefully escorted "foreign guests" invited to China out of calculation that doing so would help achieve China's international objectives. Foreigners in China had already become scarce since the uprooting of the large Western presence in China in the early 1950s. By the mid-1960s, with the departure of Soviets and East European advisors, they became even scarcer.

To a very substantial degree, China's isolation of 1966–1976 was self-imposed, not imposed by hostile foreign governments. Isolation from outside influences went hand in hand with sustained propaganda, intense criticism, and struggle for ideological transformation. The objective was to create a new communist person who would, finally, make possible the realization of the Marxist utopian vision. The isolation of China kept out ideologically pernicious influences, whether Western or Soviet, and was part of a vast totalitarian effort to transform the thinking of ordinary Chinese. China's Maoist leaders, starting most importantly with Mao himself, believed that the mentality of Chinese had to be reformed (*sixiang gaizao*) to become unselfish and collective-oriented rather than selfish and individualistic. The way of thinking of Chinese had to be remade so that they would work long and hard, diligently and creatively, not for individual gain but for the sake of the revolution, Chairman Mao, and communism. Only in this fashion could the equalitarian, collectivist, altruistic, and classless society envisioned by communist theorists over the years be realized.[3] The whole of Chinese society became a Socialist Education Movement on a vast scale.

The key internal component paralleling China's external radicalism was the purge from institutions of power of all opponents of Mao and his revolutionary policies. As discussed earlier, following the economic collapse of the Great Leap Forward, many leaders of the party favored more pragmatic policies focused on economic development, policies such as had been implemented in 1953–1957 and again in 1962–1965. Mao believed that these policies would take Chinese socialism away from the utopian vision to which he was committed, and toward the corrupt, hierarchical, and unequal social system (socialist in name only, Mao believed) that existed in the USSR. The Cultural Revolution upheaval was, from one perspective, Mao's purge of those who differed from him on policy, and therefore challenged his power, within the CCP. Mao framed this purge in terms of class struggle between the bourgeoisie and the proletariat and preventing the restoration of capitalism in China. Mao and his policy preferences represented, of course, the proletariat, while his opponents and their policies stood for the bourgeoisie. As stated by a pivotal declaration "Concerning the Great Proletarian Cultural Revolution" issued in August 1966 after extensive revision by Mao:

> Although the bourgeoisie has been overthrown, it is still trying to use the old ideas, culture, customs and habits of the exploiting classes to corrupt the masses, capture their minds and endeavor to stage a come-back. The proletariat must do just the opposite: it must meet head-on every challenge of the bourgeoisie in the ideological field and use the new ideas, culture, customs, and habits of the proletariat to change the mental outlook of the whole of society. At present, our objective is to struggle against those persons in authority who are taking the capitalist road, to criticize and repudiate the reactionary bourgeois academic "authorities" and the ideology of the bourgeoisie and all other exploiting classes and to transform education, literature and art and all other parts of the superstructure that do not correspond to the socialist economic base, so as to facilitate the consolidation and development of the socialist system.[4]

When Stalin had carried out a similar purge of Soviet institutions in the 1930s, his chosen instrument was the internal security police. China's internal security forces played a critical role in the Cultural Revolution by not protecting from radical attack individuals targeted by top Maoist leaders. But the instrument of attack and removal of his opponents, real and putative, chosen by Mao was organizations of radical youth—secondary and tertiary school students, and younger workers in offices and factories. The Red Guard organizations formed by these youth attacked via criticism and then "dragged out" via "struggle" the "hidden revisionists" that had "wormed their way" into positions of power within the communist bureaucratic apparatuses that ran China. That is, they attacked CCP leaders who had had doubts (or who were suspected of having doubts) about Mao's radical policies. Mao called forth these Red Guard organizations using his immense personal authority, the cult of personality that had developed around him, backed up a by the internal security forces, and when necessary by the PLA under the control of Mao loyalist Lin Biao.

Creation of a sense of global revolutionary uprising, a sense that a tide of revolution was sweeping the world, with China the vanguard of that process, inspired and helped justify China's Red Guard uprising. Stalin in the 1930s had propagated via show trials and other means the belief that Soviet institutions were infiltrated by spies of Germany, Japan, Britain, tsarists, or Leon Trotsky. That mass psychology had paralleled the arrest and disappearance of very large numbers of people Stalin deemed of questionable loyalty. Mao's use of zealous and idealistic youth to purge his opponents required a different psychology: a sense that the world could be and was being remade in a great and beautiful manner by the brave rebellion of the noble Red Guards. Setting the world ablaze with revolution, or at least making it seem so to Chinese, inspired Chinese youth to dare to attack the powerful "hidden revisionists" seeking to take China "down the path to restoration of capitalism." To a very significant degree, the radicalism of China's foreign relations during the period 1966–1970 was an attempt to encourage and legitimize Mao's domestic policies of "continuing the revolution under the dictatorship of the proletariat"—which is how the Maoists characterized the upheaval of these years.[5]

Soviet leaders watched with dismay while the CCP's development-minded "hidden revisionists" were purged by Red Guards. From the standpoint of the CPSU, the Cultural Revolution was nothing less than a counterrevolutionary, anticommunist rebellion, an uprising against the Leninist proletarian vanguard state at the instigation of Mao and backed by the military. Moscow had been convinced since the onset of the Great Leap Forward that Mao's "unscientific" domestic policies were undermining socialism in China. Now came the Cultural Revolution, an uprising by ordinary people against long-established leaders appointed by the Chinese Communist Party organizational system. In the Soviet view, Mao's policies were clearly undermining communist rule and socialist economy in China. On the other hand, there apparently were large numbers of CCP cadres who believed Mao's policies were unwise. Might the Soviet Union be able to intervene in support of China's anti-Maoist "healthy Marxist-Leninist" forces? Fighting for their political and even their physical lives, would not China's anti-Maoist forces welcome Soviet support in the form of intervention?

The Ideological Offensive

For a period of perhaps three years during the Cultural Revolution, propagating the revolutionary ideology of Mao Zedong became China's highest foreign policy objective, outranking even national security. During the 1966–1969 period, China took a number of moves that significantly diminished its security situation. Insistence on propagating Mao Zedong Thought by Chinese representatives and students abroad, as well as by media and propaganda organs of the PRC, offended many foreign governments and publics. In pursuit of spreading Mao Zedong Thought, Beijing antagonized perhaps thirty of the fifty countries with whom the PRC had diplomatic relations in 1966. China's ties with other communist-ruled countries suffered grievously. Even China's sensitive ties with North Korea deteriorated. Among socialist countries, only Albania-China ties emerged unscathed from the upheaval of the Cultural Revolution. Even China's ties with the powerful and threatening Soviet Union were greatly and negatively affected by ideological zealotry. Ties with India became far more tense, pushing that big Asian neighbor of China into closer alignment with the USSR. Several diplomatic relations that Beijing had carefully nourished over a decade virtually collapsed: with Burma, Indonesia, and Cambodia. In terms of its judgment of foreign revolutionary movements, far greater stress was given to leadership by Marxist-Leninists, and especially groups that pledged fealty to Mao Zedong Thought, than to merely nationalist anti-imperialist groups. The importance of the global propagation of Mao Zedong Thought was laid out nicely by a *Renmin ribao* commentary of mid-1967:

> The rapid and extensive dissemination of the great, all conquering thought of Mao Zedong is the most important feature of the excellent international situation today. The world has entered a new era which has Mao Zedong's thought as its great banner. The study and application of Mao Zedong's thought has become a mass movement on a global scale, or a magnitude with far reaching influence never before witnessed in the history of the development of Marxism-Leninism.[6]

The image of a world in revolutionary upheaval led by the Thought of Mao Zedong helped inspire struggle to revolutionize China. Mao Zedong Thought was portrayed as an invincible force sweeping the world and moving it ineluctably, inevitably toward the victory of the proletariat and socialism. China's revolutionary struggle and the global revolution were linked, proclaimed Maoists. The fiercer the one struggle became, the sharper the other would become.

Assault on the Conventions of Bourgeois Diplomacy

Red Guard attacks on foreign diplomatic facilities and personnel in China were one dimension of foreign relations during the Cultural Revolution. Large crowds of demonstrators, typically involving tens of thousands, sometimes hundreds of thousands, and on several occasions millions of people, would be trucked in to assemble outside a designated foreign compound. Red Guard marshals typically directed crowd movements and sometimes led assaults breaking into the compound. These were typically not howling, frenzied mobs, although they sometimes became that, but groups of thousands of demonstrators transported in one lot after the other and cycled through demonstration sites outside one or several adjacent foreign diplomatic missions. Crowd leaders would use loudspeakers to whip up enthusiasm and anger. Bloodcurdling slogans would be shouted in unison by the throng. Posters with strident denunciations of foreign leaders and policies were plastered over the walls of the foreign compound. Effigies of other nation's leaders were burnt. Entrance and egress from the embassy became very difficult, often impossible. People or vehicles that attempted it would be cursed, spit upon, and hit. Physical violence against foreign personnel was not uncommon. Objects would be thrown at the embassy building, and occasionally the embassy compound was invaded and buildings set afire. The foreign diplomats thus besieged of course reported their situation to their governments. Many governments minimized the number of personnel and dependents thus exposed to danger by postings to China.

These Red Guard assaults were partially spontaneous expressions of the xenophobia of these mobilized youth, and partly encouraged by top Maoist leaders as a way of purifying Chinese society of the counterrevolutionary influences emanating from foreign entities to corrupt the pure, revolutionary society that the Cultural Revolution was supposedly creating. They were also ways to punish foreign governments for perceived offenses against China. Chinese importing and distributing Mao badges, little red books, or other propaganda into other countries were frequent grounds for China to take umbrage. Official foreign missions are ordinarily protected by protocols of diplomatic immunity designed to permit sovereign governments to interact with one another. These traditions of diplomatic immunity are among the oldest and most basic of the norms governing relations among of sovereign states. They were systematically violated in China for about two years, especially during 1967.

Red Guard assaults on foreign diplomatic missions in China typically took place under the watchful eye of PLA troops. These military forces were apparently under instructions not to obstruct the revolutionary actions of the Red Guards, but also to prevent the killing of foreign personnel. During 1967, Red Guards frequently beat and otherwise physically abused foreign diplomatic personnel—another egregious violation of the protocols of diplomatic immunity. But when Red Guard actions sometimes threatened foreign lives, the PLA would intervene. On occasion—such as the burning of the British mission in Beijing in August 1967—there was apparently a geographic zone designated for "revolutionary actions." Within the British compound, the Red Guard was given free reign, assaulting and humiliating the head of the British mission and other British personnel. But once British personnel escaped onto a side street outside the compound, PLA soldiers quickly took them under their protection and escorted them in a PLA truck to safety.[7]

The assaults began in January 1967 with huge, sustained, and angry demonstrations outside the Soviet embassy in northeast Beijing.[8] The minor incident that triggered the siege was a scuffle involving Chinese students returning to China from study in Eastern Europe who attempted to spread Mao Zedong Thought during a brief stopover in Moscow. The Chinese students went to Moscow's Red Square, where they unfurled radical posters at the tombs of Lenin and Stalin. When Soviet police demanded they stop their activity, which the police said was illegal, a confrontation resulted, and several Chinese students were injured. Soon after, demonstrations involving millions of Chinese assembled outside the Soviet embassy compound in Beijing.

Over a period of three weeks, millions of angry Chinese surrounded the Soviet compound. Truckloads of soldiers with bayonets fixed sometimes joined the crowds. Demonstrators were urged to frenzy by angry exportations by group leaders. Posters with vehement condemnations of Soviet leaders covered the walls of the compound. Effigies of Soviet leaders were burned. Entry and egress to the compound was virtually impossible. Inside the compound, Soviet personnel lived in fear. The street outside the Soviet compound was renamed "Anti-revisionist Street" (*fan xiu lu*) and nearby restaurants previously popular with Russians posted signs "no dogs or Russians allowed"—a reprise of a notorious sign "No dogs or Chinese allowed" believed (incorrectly) to have been posted at the entrance to the foreign park on Shanghai's waterfront in the nineteenth century. At one point, a large group of frenzied demonstrators broke into the Soviet compound and set fire to a portion of it. When Moscow ordered the withdrawal from China of spouses and children of Soviet diplomats, those people were tormented and humiliated by Red Guard crowds at the Beijing airport, forced to crawl on hands and knees under posters of Chairman Mao and between ranks of angry and abusive Red Guards. The Red Guard siege of the Soviet embassy was encouraged by an editorial in *Renmin ribao* condemning Soviet leaders as "filthy revisionist swine" whose "atrocities" against Chinese students in Moscow were akin to the actions of Hitler, the tsar, and the Ku Klux Klan.

The assault on the Soviet mission paralleled the "January storm" in which Red Guards in Beijing, Shanghai, and other key cities "seized power" from the regular CCP power-holders in offices and factories. This was a critical moment in Mao's effort to oust those perceived as disloyal to him. From Mao's perspective, the assaults on the Soviet and other foreign diplomatic missions served the critical purpose of demonstrating to the Red Guard that even those traditionally immune could now be toppled from power, that the revolutionary forces loyal to Mao Zedong, especially the PLA, would support rebellion. The world was aflame with an irresistible tide of revolution of which the Red Guard uprising was a part. That was the message.

Similar assaults followed against missions of other countries. Between January and August 1967, eleven foreign missions were besieged and often invaded by Red Guards.[9] Representatives of virtually every category of country were attacked: Yugoslavia, Bulgaria, Mongolia, and Czechoslovakia among the socialist countries; Britain, Italy, and France among the Western countries; and Indonesia, Nepal, Tunisia, Ceylon (later renamed Sri Lanka), India, Kenya, and Burma among the non-aligned countries. Parts of the Soviet, Indonesian, and British diplomatic buildings were set ablaze. PLA soldiers often stood aside, ready to intervene if foreign lives were threatened. Extreme violence just short of lethality was, however, permitted. When the car of a commercial counselor at the French embassy slightly bumped a Red Guard loudspeaker truck, for instance, the French diplomat and his wife were dragged out of the car, surrounded by a crowded tight circle of angry Red Guards, hit, yelled and cursed at, and spit upon. When it got dark, the "struggle" continued, with a spotlight being directed at the French couple. When the French ambassador protested the incident the next day at China's MFA, the Chinese brought into the room two elderly Chinese men, limping and supported by nurses, who charged that *they* had been assaulted the previous day by the French commercial counselor.[10] This blatant cynicism shocked diplomats.

China's relations with Indonesia, already tense because of events surrounding the October 1965 coup, collapsed under the impact of the Cultural Revolution. Early in 1966, *Renmin ribao* carried an article comparing Indonesia's anti-Chinese policies to those of Hitler. Shortly afterwards, Indonesian military forces surrounded the Chinese embassy in Jakarta, whereupon PRC diplomats exited the embassy to protest the military presence—and demonstrate their own brave militancy. A fight occurred between the Chinese diplomats and Indonesian soldiers. Two Chinese diplomats were subsequently declared personae non gratae and expelled from Indonesia. One of these was the chargé d'affaires at the Chinese embassy, Yao Dengshan, who would later play a prominent role in the Red Guard seizure of the foreign ministry. Yao returned to Beijing and a hero's welcome as a "red diplomatic fighter." Emerging from his airplane carrying over his head a poster of Mao garlanded with red flowers, Yao was met by Zhou Enlai and Jiang Qing, Mao's wife and key lieutenant. Yao was then taken to a meeting with Mao Zedong, and was honored by a photograph of him together with Mao and Jiang. The next day, the photo of Yao together with Mao and Jiang Qing appeared on the front page of newspapers across the country.[11] The message was clear: Yao's method of diplomatic struggle had Mao's endorsement.

Beijing added fuel to the fire in January 1967 when the PRC embassy in Djakarta received from an Indonesian group an invitation addressed to the "Republic of China" rather than the "People's Republic of China." The PRC embassy interpreted this trivial diplomatic blunder as an Indonesian plot to play the "two Chinas game" and delivered a strong protest. Demonstrations of an estimated half million people besieged the Indonesian embassy in

Beijing in April. After a week the Indonesian chargé d'affaires and atta-
ché were expelled. At the airport, they made their way to their airplane
through crowds of Red Guards who spit on, hit, and cursed them. Similar
indignities befell the Indonesian consulate in Guangzhou. Indonesia and
China severed diplomatic relations in October 1967—not to be restored
until 1990.

China's relations with Burma also deteriorated sharply. As noted earlier,
under China's "dual-track" approach, the CCP had rendered assistance to the
Communist Party of Burma since 1962. But Beijing had not publicly endorsed
the CPB's insurrection and had maintained cordial relations with Burma's
non-aligned government. Burma received Chinese aid, and there were frequent friendly interactions between Chinese and Burmese leaders throughout
the first half of the 1960s. Then, in 1967, under the influence of the Cultural
Revolution and instigation by staff of the Chinese embassy in Rangoon,
ethnic Chinese students in Rangoon began wearing Mao badges and propagating Mao Zedong Thought. Burma's government deployed soldiers to put
an end to this revolutionary agitation. Confrontations turned into clashes
and then into outright anti-Chinese riots. Over one hundred Chinese were
killed, including one Chinese aid worker. The next day, the Chinese embassy
in Rangoon was attacked by mobs. China retaliated by launching four consecutive days of demonstrations of over a million people outside the Burmese
embassy in Beijing. In Rangoon, the PRC embassy delivered a threatening
note to the Burmese government:

> Chairman Mao is the very red sun that shines most brightly in our
> hearts and Mao Zedong thought is our lifeline. We must warn you that
> we will fight to the end against anyone who dares to oppose Chairman
> Mao and Mao Zedong Thought. Anyone who dares to oppose Chairman
> Mao and Mao Zedong Thought is hitting his head against a brick wall
> and inviting his own destruction.[12]

Sino-Burma relations came close to the breaking point. Regarding India, in
June 1967 two Indian diplomats who had been following Cultural Revolution
events around Beijing were accused of spying. The Red Guard wanted to try
them before a mass assembly of 10,000 people, but the MFA ordered them
expelled instead. At the airport, the Indian diplomats were kicked and hit,
had their clothes ripped, and were dragged across the runway. The melee
ended when Red Guard leaders blew whistles, whereupon "the masses" fell
into columns and marched away. Two days later, angry Indian mobs attacked
the Chinese embassy in New Delhi.

Among the foreign and diplomatic community in Beijing, by mid-1967
there was widespread fear of attack by xenophobic and paranoid Chinese
zealots. There was also a sense of solidarity among the entire foreign diplomatic community in Beijing in the face of the seemingly irrational extremism.

An influential eight-part made-for-TV documentary film on China titled *China: The Roots of Madness* was produced in the United States in 1967.[13] The central theme was that a hundred years of national tragedy had taught the Chinese people to hate, and that this hate constituted the greatest threat to peace in the world today. To many people in the world, China had descended into national insanity—while armed with nuclear bombs and fostering armed insurrection across Southeast Asia.

The Burning of the British Mission

The most savage Red Guard violence was directed against the British mission. In May 1967, workers at a plastic-flower factory in Hong Kong went on strike. The Hong Kong Communist Party organization became involved in the strike, and the strikers adopted increasingly militant tactics. Hong Kong police thereupon arrested several militants and seventeen Chinese journalists, including several from the PRC, who had been inciting violence with inflammatory articles. The Hong Kong government also shut two procommunist newspapers and initiated lawsuits against several others. The MFA in Beijing thereupon called in the British chargé d'affaires and demanded that Britain accept the demands of the strikers, release all those arrested, punish those responsible for the "atrocities," and rescind its newspaper closures—all within forty-eight hours. Otherwise, the British government would bear full responsibility for the consequences.

Huge crowds of a million or so people over the course of several days began besieging the British mission. The Reuters correspondent in Beijing, one of only four Western journalists still stationed in Beijing, was put under house arrest. On August 22, people in the British mission noticed that the crowd outside the British mission was different: they were quiet and sat in neat rows. By chance, the chargé d'affaires, Sir Donald Hopson, a veteran of the 1944 Normandy invasion, happened to be watching and saw the crowd rise in unison and surge forward. Other observers saw a military flare signal the advance. Fire trucks were seen parked nearby, and members of the invading mob were seen carrying oil drums toward the targeted building. In other words, the invasion was planned and organized.

Inside the mission, the twenty-three British personnel quickly retreated to a prepared safe room. The Chinese mob forced their way into the building. Some proceeded to systematically search the facilities, finding and taking away the cipher encryption machine. Others set the building ablaze, at which point the British personnel exited their safe room out of fear of being burned alive. The now hysterical Chinese mob shouted "*sha, sha, sha*," "kill, kill, kill," which the Chinese-speakers in the group understood and knew was a chant of the Boxers who had massacred foreigners in 1899. Some

British personnel escaped via other exits, but the largest group, led by the chargé d'affaires Hopson, were assaulted and humiliated by the mob. Several female members of the group had their clothes torn off and were sexually molested. The British group finally made it out of the compound onto an adjacent street, at which point the PLA intervened, put the group under their protection, and arranged their safe exit from the scene. The mission building was gutted by fire, and several people, including the chargé, were seriously injured.

Several days later, Hopson was working in one of the untorched buildings in the compound when another group of Red Guards returned to call Britain to account for the recent street battle. The leader of the group demanded that Hopson bow his head and confess his "crimes." Hopson refused, whereupon the Red Guard grabbed his hair and tried to jerk his head down. The whole incident was watched by a nearby Japanese journalist, who reported it to the world.[14] Beijing expelled a number of Japanese reporters. Because of their historic familiarity with China and knowledge of Chinese, they were especially effective in reporting on the events of the Cultural Revolution.

Following the egregious violation of British diplomatic immunity in Beijing, London retaliated by imposing modest travel restrictions on Chinese diplomats in London and subjecting their movements to police surveillance. On August 29, personnel from the Chinese embassy, located on Portland Place in London, suddenly emerged from the building armed with baseball bats, axes, steel bars, and broom handles. One of them carried a camera and filmed the action. Confrontation with London police ensued, with three policeman, three Chinese, and one photographer being hospitalized as a result. The whole fight, dubbed the Battle of Portland Place by the British media, was over in about five minutes. The Chinese cameraman was captured by other photographers assiduously taking photos during the melee. Apparently, it was important to have photographic evidence of the militant spirit of China's diplomatic warriors to show to higher-ups back in Beijing.

Following the "Battle of Portland Place," the MFA called in the British chargé to protest the "barbarous atrocities" of London police who "clubs in hand, flagrantly and brutally beat up" Chinese diplomatic personnel. According to the MFA, the episode began when a London policeman wore a Mao button upside down as a deliberate insult to Chairman Mao. A Chinese diplomat had approached the policeman to protest and warn him, whereupon, according to the Chinese version, "scores of truncheon-wielding police fell upon and brutally assaulted him."[15] Chinese retaliation for the events on Portland Place came in Shanghai when the Revolutionary Committee of that city took over the British consulate. Located on the north end of the Shanghai waterfront adjacent to Suzhou Creek, the British consulate building was a quintessential symbol of Britain's role in China's "century of national humiliation." Across the street from the consulate building had once stood, at least according to popular but apocryphal legend, a sign at the entrance to the European promenade on the waterfront reading "No dogs or Chinese allowed."

Revolutionary Struggle within the Foreign Affairs System

The revolutionary extremism that seized Chinese foreign relations during the Cultural Revolution was partially a function of the political imperative that individuals in the foreign affairs system demonstrate their revolutionary bona fides. (The MFA and schools and organizations involved in foreign affairs together constituted the "foreign affairs system," or *xitong*.) Survival, let alone promotion, in the MFA now required that Chinese personnel stationed abroad prove their loyalty to Mao and his revolutionary line. This was especially the case for diplomats, who enjoyed standards of living far above those in China, who often dressed in Western-style clothes, spoke foreign languages, and had contacts with all sorts of suspicious foreigners. When they were called back home to account for their actions abroad and to criticize their own and each other's ideological shortcomings, a documented record of ardent revolutionary diplomatic struggle abroad was a good defense.

As the Cultural Revolution unfolded during the second half of 1966, the Party Committee within the MFA, headed by foreign minister Chen Yi and party secretary and vice premier Ji Pengfei, guided the Cultural Revolution within the foreign affairs system.[16] Chen and Ji tried to focus the movement on criticism of low-level cadres who had made mistakes, and on criticism of bourgeois art (a main focus of Cultural Revolution criticism at that time). At the start of the Cultural Revolution, Zhou Enlai and Chen Yi, certainly with Mao's approval, had directed that China's overseas embassies would not be involved in the Cultural Revolution. Then, in September 1966, Mao received a letter from a group of leftist foreigners who had attended an international conference in Vienna and come away dismayed at the bourgeois demeanor of China's representatives, who had arrived in expensive cars and wearing fine Western-style suits and ties. Clearly they had been corrupted by the Western, bourgeois lifestyle. Mao was struck by the letter and remarked that the staff at Chinese embassies apparently needed to be revolutionized. Mao's comments became known across the foreign affairs system and encouraged young and dissident radicals in that system who wanted to expand the range of revolutionary struggle and perhaps displace their bosses. By late 1966, radical Red Guards in organizations across China, including in the foreign affairs system, were demanding—with the encouragement of senior Maoist leaders—the targeting for struggle of top-level power holders "taking the capitalist road." Within the foreign affairs system, radical Red Guards, both in Beijing and in Chinese embassies abroad, began to criticize the bureaucratic work style and privileged, "bourgeois" life styles of top diplomats. Red Guards also began to demand the recall for examination and self-criticism of ambassadors and senior diplomatic staff posted abroad.

In January 1967, as part of a nationwide "seizure of power" by Red Guard organizations, Red Guards "seized power" in the foreign affairs system. Foreign Minister Chen Yi (still in that position) met with the newly established "revolutionary core" in the MFA and supported their "seizure of power," but insisted that conduct of foreign relations remained the exclusive domain of China's central leaders. The role of the "revolutionary core," Chen said, was to guide the Cultural Revolution in the foreign affairs system, not to conduct China's diplomacy. Chen's attempts to limit the Cultural Revolution's impact on China's diplomacy did not last long and would be the basis for Mao's ultimate loss of faith in Chen. Chen's position was weakened when he was compelled to make a self-criticism before "masses" of ten thousand for his earlier following of the Liu Shaoqi–Deng Xiaoping line in 1966 when he had attempted to limit the scope of Red Guard rebellion in the foreign affairs system. Mao had preapproved Chen's "confession," and the Maoist leader Chen Boda attended the session to ensure that it was smoothly accepted by the "revolutionary masses." Still, Chen became more vulnerable because of his moderate approach to foreign affairs. The frank-speaking Chen had this to say, for example, at a Politburo meeting in February 1967 regarding the provocative activities of Chinese students transiting Moscow that had precipitated the confrontation with the Soviet Union:

> The Chinese students took the lead in reading Chairman Mao's quotations in the Red Square. That was the beginning. Then people began to read them everywhere in the world. This means hitting in all directions and copying things [of the Cultural Revolution] in foreign countries. This gave rise to problems with the Soviet revisionists and the French imperialists. The imperialists, the revisionists and the reactionaries all fell upon us. We have landed ourselves in a passive position.[17]

Such frank criticism of radical policies led Mao to conclude that Chen was part of the "February adverse current" that had emerged to oppose the Red Guard seizure of power the previous month. This was a far more serious charge against Chen than his attempts to restrain the Red Guards in late 1966. Mao's negative judgment of Chen gave an immense boost to the Red Guards within the foreign affairs system. Zhou Enlai sought to limit radical attacks on Chen and his supporters Ji Pengfei and vice foreign minister Qiao Guanghua, but those efforts failed. Radicals then tried to attack Zhou for having supported Chen, but Mao personally intervened to veto that. Zhou Enlai was simply too important to the continued functioning of the government.

Early in 1967, Zhou ordered the recall of all China's ambassadors and up to two-thirds of embassy staff. The one exception to this recall was Huang Hua in Cairo, who was only recently been appointed ambassador and had thus not been criticized by Red Guard rebels in the Cairo embassy. In Beijing, the recalled diplomatic personnel from each country were assigned a room in a single building where they conducted criticism and self-criticism. Individuals vied in exposing one another's ideological shortcomings, bourgeois habits, and backsliding. Once they completed this course, many were dispatched to cadre schools in the countryside, where most remained for several years doing farm work.

Red Guard organizations seized power in the MFA for about two weeks in August 1967. It began with a talk on August 7 by senior Maoist leader Wang Li to leaders of the foreign affairs system's "revolutionary core" and Yao Dengshan. Wang was former deputy head of the CCP's International Liaison Department and thus a former subordinate of Kang Sheng. As noted earlier, Yao had played a militant role in Indonesia in 1967. Wang Li was a member of the central Maoist leadership group and in that capacity had played a role in dealing with a mutiny by regional military forces at Wuhan the previous month. In his talk with MFA Red Guard leaders, Wang criticized the rebels for being too lenient with conservative groups in the MFA, stated that the "seizure of power" over the MFA in January was incomplete, and urged the radicals to take control over ministry administrative and personnel matters. Wang also stated that both Mao and Zhou had said that he, Wang, should take charge of foreign affairs. A week after Wang's talk, Red Guard radicals seized control of the MFA, including its personnel department. They developed a reorganization plan which they submitted to Zhou Enlai for approval. Zhou rejected it. Meanwhile, several posters appeared around Beijing proclaiming: "Firm demand that Yao Dengshan should become foreign minister." In fact, Ji Pengfei rather than Yao had been appointed acting foreign minister. But the posters endorsing Yao were read by foreign journalists, leading to what some scholars called the "international fiction" that Yao assumed that status during the Red Guard seizure of the MFA.[18] It was, however, during the brief period of Red Guard control of the MFA that the British mission was burned and British diplomats brutalized.

By August, Mao was increasingly concerned by reports of military clashes in the provinces. In an effort to restore greater stability, Mao authorized the arrest of Wang Li, calling Wang's August 7 talk a "poisonous weed." The Maoists thus lost several of their most radical members. Zhou, with Mao's support, also moved to oust the radical Red Guards from the MFA and empower conservative Red Guards to restore regular diplomatic activity. Late in 1967, the MFA was put under a new committee composed of conservative Red Guard diplomatic personnel, but headed by Mao's grand-niece, Wang Hairong, who was one of a very few people who had direct contact with Mao. Once this new committee was in place, the purge of MFA radicals, including Yao Dengshan, began. During the upheaval of 1967, very little time and energy were devoted by the MFA to the routines of diplomacy. The number of foreign delegations and dignitaries received and the number of Chinese delegations sent abroad declined precipitously. So too did the Chinese media's coverage of foreign events. China's foreign affairs apparatus was preoccupied with the political struggles raging within that system.

By late 1967, Zhou, with Mao's support, reasserted control over China's diplomacy. In May, when Mao ordered an expansion of the Cultural Revolution in the foreign affairs system, Zhou had directed that the "power of diplomacy should not be seized and top secrets should not be captured, administration and personnel records should not be used, and the political department established by Chairman Mao should not be destroyed." By year's end, however, Zhou had determined that "a handful of class enemies and extreme left elements openly disobeyed the [May] directive" and took actions that "greatly damaged the power of diplomacy."[19] Putting affairs to rights, Zhou directed that Chinese embassies should not carry the Cultural Revolution to foreign capitals. Statements endorsing the struggles of Hong Kong communists against Britain became scarce. On China's October 1 National Day, chargés d'affaires at Chinese embassies in Nepal, Ceylon, and Cambodia held receptions, as had been usual before the Cultural Revolution. Early the next year, Beijing began to repair relations with Burma. The tone of Chinese statements about Burma moderated. A substantial contribution was made to the Burma Red Cross for typhoon disaster relief. Gradually, China's diplomacy returned to normal, though without giving the appearance of a humiliating retreat.[20]

Still, many of China's former "diplomatic fighters" languished in rural cadre schools. In May 1970 Zhou moved to restrict the scope of the purge of China's diplomatic corps by stipulating that people should be punished only for specific "crimes." Among these crimes were the "seizure of power" following Wang Li's August 7 talk and burning the British mission. Yao Dengshan would spend ten years in prison and not be rehabilitated until 1979. Chen Yi was reengaged briefly in 1969 to join other PLA marshals in evaluating the international situation, but never again held power after losing Mao's trust.[21] Chen Yi died of cancer, still in disgrace, in 1972. The "campaign to purify class ranks" in the MFA ended in October 1972, and most MFA cadre previously sent to cadre schools were recalled to diplomatic service. China needed diplomats to staff the many new embassies being opened around the world following its September 1971 admission to the United Nations.

The Mounting Threat of Soviet Intervention

In 1792, as the French Revolution approached its most radical stage, many French aristocrats targeted by the increasingly republican upheaval looked with hope to the armies of monarchical Austria and Prussia assembling in nearby Belgium. When French resistance to the foreign royalist advance faltered, fear of domestic counterrevolutionary plots swept Paris. The once formidable French army had been weakened by the emigration of many of its officers, a number of whom had joined the foreign counterrevolutionary forces marshaling in Belgium. After initial battlefield setbacks, one aristocratic officer remaining in service to revolutionary France, Marquis de Lafayette of American fame, sent an envoy to the Austrian camp offering to march on Paris and restore order if the Austrians would call off their invasion.[22] The Jacobin solution for this link-up of foreign and domestic counterrevolutionaries was the Terror, intended to ferret out and strike down hidden internal enemies of the revolution. A similar logic was at work in China during 1966–1969.

Soviet military forces deployed along China's borders grew steadily throughout the Cultural Revolution. Large units of those forces were organized and deployed for offensive operation.[23] Soviet media threatened intervention. Mao and other Chinese leaders took those threats quite seriously. This would be a major consideration inspiring China to decide to use US power to check Soviet power circa 1971. But during the period up to and including 1969, using the United States to check the Soviet Union was not part of Mao's arsenal. Instead, Mao relied on China's own inherent strength to deter the Soviet Union.

In January 1966, the Soviet Union and Mongolia signed a mutual defense pact that provided for the stationing of Soviet troops in Mongolia. Under that agreement, Soviet troops moved into Mongolia, putting them only about 500 kilometers of open terrain from Beijing. In January 1967, as Red Guards "seized power" from the established CCP apparatus in institutions across China, Wang Ming, one-time leader of pro-Soviet anti-Maoist forces in the CCP who had long since taken up residence in the Soviet Union, told officials of the CPSU Central Committee responsible for relations with socialist countries that armed intervention in support of the CCP's anti-Mao forces was imperative:

> The current situation in China is more dangerous for the socialist camp and the international communist movement than the events in Hungary in 1956 . . . We cannot let the opportunity pass by . . . we [must] provide them [the healthy forces in the CCP] not only political, but also material support via arms and possibly by sending a force composed of the proper nationalities from Central Asia and the Mongolian People's Republic.[24]

Wang proposed talks with leaders from Xinjiang and Inner Mongolia to explore possibilities for cooperation against Mao's objectively anticommunist forces. Of course, Wang did this from the safety of exile in Moscow.

PRC intelligence may not have known of Wang Ming's proposal, but similar inferences could be drawn from the abundant and vehement denunciations by Soviet media of Mao's "anticommunist," "ultra-leftist," "petti-bourgeois adventurist," and (starting in 1969, as the PLA moved in to restore order and suppress the Red Guards) "Bonapartist" forces. Parallel to these propaganda denunciations, Soviet armed forces marshaled on China's northern and western borders in configurations that suggested preparation not for border skirmishes but for deep thrusts into Chinese territory.

The mounting threat from the Soviet Union interacted with Red Guard struggle against hidden revisionists in China's structures of power. Probably very few of the CCP cadres being purged by the Red Guards sympathized with the Soviet Union or questioned the anti-revisionist campaign against the CPSU that Mao had initiated. But the policy preferences of many of the CCP leaders being purged in the Cultural Revolution were, in fact, similar to the policies of the USSR: concentration on rapid industrialization, avoidance of political campaigns that disrupted the industrialization drive, material incentives, expert and bureaucratic leadership, and so on. Many of the aspects of Mao's policies criticized by CCP "hidden revisionists" Liu Shaoqi and Deng Xiaoping were criticized equally by the Soviet Union. Moreover, the Soviet model of socialism had been extolled and inculcated in China up to about 1957. Many CCP cadres hunted by the Red Guard probably did, secretly, sympathize with Soviet-style socialism.

Some of Mao's critics, like Peng Dehuai, Wang Jiaxiang, and Chen Yun, did have considerable contact with Soviet leaders, and those contacts *may* in some cases have helped inspire opposition to Mao's policies during and after the Great Leap. There is convincing evidence that Peng's outspoken criticism of the Great Leap was motivated by concern for the suffering of China's citizens, and Peng certainly never imagined he was aligning with Moscow against Mao Zedong. Mao, on the other hand, probably believed his own charges that the Soviets were behind Peng's opposition to his Great Leap Forward policies. Moreover, in situations in which Mao's opponents, imagined and real, were struggling for their political and sometimes their natural lives, they might well welcome Soviet assistance. Lin Biao, to cite the most famous example, attempted to flee to the USSR once he fell out with Mao in 1971, even though there is no evidence of prior contact or coordination between Lin and the Soviet Union.

In Mao's mind, the congruent policy preferences of the Soviet "revisionists" and CCP "hidden revisionists" trumped the nonexistence of actual links between the two. There was little danger that "US imperialism" could infiltrate China, let alone the CCP. The social groups that supported capitalism and liberal democracy had been rooted out and liquidated in the early 1950s. There was no social base for an attempt to restore capitalism and establish liberal democracy in China. But there was a powerful social basis for a restoration of Soviet-style "capitalism"—the CCP's "hidden revisionists" who prior to Mao's Cultural Revolution had held the levers of power in the CCP's apparatus, which is to say in the PRC state.

A link-up between Mao's CCP opponents and Moscow may not have been entirely a figment of Mao's imagination. As Wang Ming's advocacy in January 1967 suggests, among the options laid before Soviet leaders circa 1967–1970 was seizure of some portion of Chinese territory, perhaps in association with bombing attacks on other targets in China. China's northeast and Xinjiang, both long-time Russian-Soviet spheres of influence, were targets commonly mentioned by Western analysts. Had Soviet leaders chosen to deal with their "Mao problem" in this way, they would almost certainly have established a satellite government run by anti-Mao Chinese communists. Another option was for Moscow to help trigger a civil war in China, and then intervene on the anti-Maoist side. Still another, perhaps more likely, scenario would have been the ousting of Mao by a group of his opponents. The ouster of CPSU General Secretary Nikita Khrushchev in October 1964 was a warning for Mao. Although the Soviet leaders that ousted Khrushchev amounted to "Khrushchev without Khrushchev," in Mao's view the earlier transition of power in the CPSU following Stalin's death had seen a radical shift in policy away from socialism and toward "revisionism." Had CCP "hidden revisionists" seized power from or after Mao, they would certainly have had the support and encouragement of the USSR. One way or the other, China's "hidden revisionists" and the Soviet "revisionists" were linked. In the words of Zhou Enlai's authoritative Chinese biographer Gao Wenqian:

> Mao succeeded in destroying the pro-Soviet [sic] faction within the Chinese Communist Party. Yet he still feared his enemies. He could envision a Soviet invasion of China ending in a vindictive comeback of all those whom he had routed.[25]

The Maoists and their policies of "seizing power" faced strong opposition from powerful veteran leaders. In February 1967, a group of Politburo members that included several top PLA leaders not closely tied to Lin Biao confronted top Maoist leaders, other than Mao of course. (The group of veteran military leaders included marshal and vice chair of the CMC Ye Jianying, marshal and head of the Science and Technology Commission and head of China's atomic weapons program Nie Rongzhen, marshal and CMC vice chair Xu Xiangqian, and marshal and foreign minister Chen Yi.) Again in July, military commanders in Wuhan in central China moved forcefully to suppress radical Red Guard organizations before troops loyal to Lin Biao moved in to disarm those anti-left regional military forces.[26] Throughout 1967, civil war conditions developed across China as moderate Red Guard organizations battled extremist Red Guard groups. Clashes were increasingly fought out with firearms. Red Guards sometimes armed themselves from trains carrying Soviet arms across China for North Vietnam. Rebels who had recently "seized power" formed armed militias to defend their hold on power. Those ousted, or threatened by being ousted, fought back in kind. PLA units increasingly took sides in these conflicts.

The crisis in relations with the USSR created a climate conducive to a purge of CCP "hidden revisionists." With Soviet armies perched on China's borders and Soviet broadcasts calling on China's "healthy Marxist-Leninist forces" to rise against Mao, it became imperative to ferret out and crush hidden revisionist elements still lurking in the CCP. The Soviet threat became a major justification for Red Guards to continue and expand the struggles against "hidden revisionists." Tarring Mao's opponents with association with the Soviet Union helped justify their removal. Thus Liu Shaoqi became "China's Khrushchev."

As Soviet forces took up positions on China's borders, Soviet propaganda began calling for Chinese to oppose Mao's rule.[27] In February 1967, *Pravda* condemned Mao and encouraged his opponents within China to "halt his erroneous course." For three consecutive days, *Pravda* and the army paper *Red Star* carried editorials saying that the Soviet Union was prepared to take any action, offensive or defensive, to help the Chinese people liberate themselves from Mao's rule. The same month, during a visit to London, Premier Kosygin said that the Soviet Union sympathized with people in the CCP struggling against "the dictatorial regime of Mao Zedong." Mandarin-language broadcasts by Soviet radio into China carried inflammatory appeals to "genuine communists" to rise up and overthrow Mao. Broadcasts in the Uighur language into Xinjiang insinuated Soviet assistance if that region's Uighurs rose in rebellion. In midyear, a series of articles in the leading Soviet papers called for opposition to Mao and implied the possibility of Soviet intervention if the situation required such action. Similar incitement and promises of support continued throughout 1967 and 1968.

The Soviet-organized Warsaw Pact military intervention in Czechoslovakia in August 1968 to oust a liberal, national communist government further exacerbated Chinese fears of Soviet intervention. The intervention in Czechoslovakia was accompanied by promulgation of a statement proclaiming the "duty" of the USSR to intervene militarily in any socialist country where the proletariat's gains of socialism were threatened by forces of counterrevolution. That was exactly what was happening in China, in the Soviet view. Moscow's new doctrine could well justify, at least in Soviet eyes, intervention in China. The Soviet position in Eastern Europe was vastly different than in China. Nonetheless, the promulgation of the Brezhnev Doctrine, as it became known, deepened Mao's apprehension of possible Soviet action. And then came a clash on the Sino-Soviet border.

The 1969 Sino-Soviet Confrontation

On March 2, 1969, a Soviet border patrol pursued a squad of Chinese soldiers across the ice covering the Ussuri River and onto Zhenbao Island (Damansky Island to the Russians) about 240 kilometers (150 miles) south of Khabarovsk.[28] The disputed islands lay on the Chinese side of the thalweg (the central line of the main navigational channel), a principle commonly recognized by international law as the basis for boundary delineation. China insisted that the border followed the thalweg, placing Zhenbao and a number of other islands in China. The Soviet Union insisted that the border followed the river's edge on the Chinese side, making all these islands Soviet territory. Figure 10-1 illustrates the situation of these islands. Since 1966, there had been an escalating but previously nonlethal confrontation over Zhenbao and other river islands. Soviet patrols had confronted Chinese patrols of these islands and insisted they stop violating Soviet territory. Chinese patrols had equally insisted that the islands were Chinese territory and that they would continue to patrol them. Confrontations escalated from swearing and shoving to beating with clubs or rifle butts, use of high-pressure water hoses and axes to cut such hoses, and threatening pointing of weapons. Finally, on two occasions in early 1969, the Soviet commander of a patrol gave warning that further Chinese patrols onto Zhenbao would be fired on by Soviet forces. Unknown to the Soviet patrol that followed the Chinese onto ice-bound Zhenbao Island on March 2, Chinese forces had prepared well-situated and camouflaged heavy weapons positions on the Chinese bank covering the anticipated path of the Chinese patrol. When firing began—the two sides dispute who fired first—the Soviet patrol was surprised to find itself enfiladed by very effective Chinese fire.

The decision to take a stand at Zhenbao in a situation tactically advantageous to China was certainly made by Mao. Mao's decision was an attempt to deter further and possibly expanded Soviet aggression against China by confronting Moscow with China's determination to stand firm and meet Soviet aggression in a tit-for-tat fashion, even if that entailed bloody military conflict with the USSR.[29] As with India in October 1962, striking first by surprise and in tactically advantageous conditions was an application of Mao's doctrine of active defense. Rather than waiting for the enemy to complete his offensive and aggressive preparations and allowing him to choose the time and place to launch his aggression, China would strike first at a time and place of its own choosing to disrupt the enemy's preparations. This bloody Chinese rebuff would cause China's rival to stop and take stock of its aggressive course. China's firm stance would make clear to the aggressor that continued aggression against China's territory would be costly, ultimately too costly to make sense.

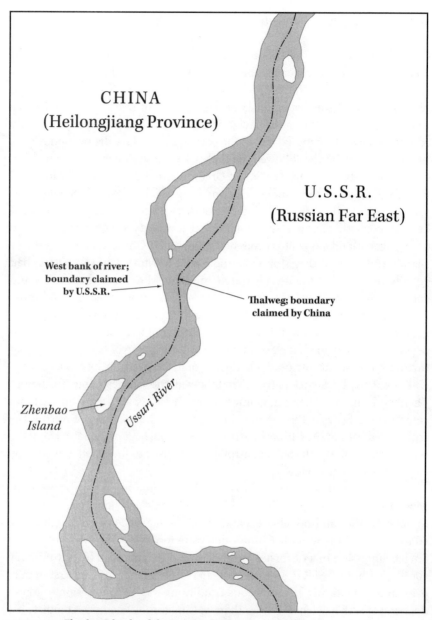

FIGURE 10-1 Zhenbao Island and the Riverine Border
Source: Down with the New Tsars! (Foreign Languages Press: Beijing, 1969).

It is likely that Mao had other deterrent objectives in mind, larger than simply persuading Moscow to stop confronting Chinese patrols on the disputed
Ussuri River islands. With the Brezhnev Doctrine and the intense factional
struggle still underway in China in mind, Mao probably also wanted to dissuade Moscow from undertaking large-scale armed intervention in support

of China's "healthy Marxist-Leninist forces." Although the PLA had been ruthlessly repressing radical Red Guards and imposing order since late 1968, the situation in China was still far from stable. Moreover, the PLA essentially took over running the country as the Red Guard upheaval was repressed. By 1969, the PLA was deeply enmeshed in administering China—and not defending China's frontiers. China's defense capabilities might look weak to Moscow, while China's Maoist forces were about to consolidate their victory in the form of a "Bonapartist" (as Moscow called it) military dictatorship. Although this is speculation, it seems likely that Mao framed the decision to use lethal force in an ambush against Soviet forces in a larger strategic context. Armed confrontation with the Soviet Union would also inoculate China's reconstructed CCP apparatus (which was being rebuilt as the Red Guard were suppressed) against reinfiltration by Soviet revisionism.

Soviet leaders responded strongly to the ambush at Zhenbao. The clash touched several Soviet sensitivities: huge numbers of Chinese pressing against the thinly populated but resource-rich Russian Far East, claimed by Beijing as "Chinese territory stolen by Czarist imperialism"; the possibility of PRC alignment with US imperialism against the Soviet Union following the model of Yugoslavia's Tito; and leadership of China by Mao Zedong, who apparently feared neither world war nor thermonuclear war. As with Mao, Soviet considerations went far beyond river islands to broader strategic calculations.

Following the first clash on March 2, Moscow prepared for a second fight at Zhenbao under conditions more advantageous to the Soviet side. Reinforcements, artillery, and tanks were rushed to the Zhenbao area. On the night of March 14–15, the Soviets unleashed a massive rocket bombardment to a depth of twenty kilometers into Chinese territory.[30] When daylight broke, Soviet forces launched a full-scale assault to secure Zhenbao, using armor and heavy artillery. The PLA responded in kind. Fighting was heavy. Following the March 15 battle, armed clashes erupted all along the Sino-Soviet border. For nearly six months, China and the Soviet Union found themselves locked in a border war. Soviet pressure was greatest in Xinjiang, where PLA logistic lines were stretched thin and where Soviet front lines were fed by the Soviet Central Asian rail and road network. On August 13, Soviet forces seized control of a disputed and sharply contested hill overlooking a strategic pass in western Xinjiang, destroying an entire Chinese regiment in the process.[31] Two weeks after the battle on the Xinjiang border, Beijing ordered all China's provinces and autonomous regions bordering the Soviet Union to enter a state of "high alertness" and "full preparation to fight a war against aggression."[32]

Soviet leaders considered a range of options. Defense Minister Andrei Grechko advocated large-scale attack against China's industrial and population centers using large thermonuclear weapons producing vast amounts of radioactive fallout that would very substantially reduce the Chinese population.[33] A war with China was inevitable, Grechko argued, and time was on

China's side, not the Soviet Union's. China was now weak, but would only grow stronger. Its international isolation would not last. A large attack now would degrade China's capabilities for a considerable time. It was irresponsible for Soviet leadership not to "solve the Chinese problem" for at least several generations while the opportunity presented itself. Soviet officials also sounded out Moscow's East European allies about possible use of nuclear weapons against China. Some of Moscow's East European consultations regarding possible use of nuclear weapons were leaked to the Western press. By mid-1969, Soviet media was making indirect threats of Soviet use of nuclear weapons against China.

A less extreme Soviet option entailed a surgical attack with conventional bombs against China's gaseous diffusion uranium enrichment plant outside Lanzhou in Gansu province.[34] Built with Soviet assistance in the 1950s as part of Moscow's aid to China's nuclear weapons program, the plant produced most if not all of the fissile material for China's atomic bombs. Involving many acres of complex machinery, the facility was highly vulnerable. Having engineered the plant, the Soviets knew exactly what points to target. Heavy conventional bombing would easily put the plant out of operation. Use of conventional rather than atomic weapons would reduce the international opprobrium resulting from an attack. The plant might eventually be rebuilt underground—possibly in caves—but that would take many years.

Preparations for attack on the Lanzhou diffusion plant proceeded in mid-1969. Advanced aircraft suitable for bombing attacks were redeployed from East Europe to China's borders;[35] they practiced bombing runs in Soviet Kazakhstan. Air bases in appropriate locations to launch and recover the strike aircraft were expanded or built in rush fashion and brought into operation. Soviet ground forces were put into position to deal with Chinese infantry attacks in retaliation for the bombing of the Lanzhou plant. Radio transmissions from these Soviet forces alerted Chinese intelligence to these preparations. Pakistan's ambassador to Moscow also reported to his government that Moscow was consulting its East European allies about a possible surgical strike against the Lanzhou facility.[36] Pakistan was, of course, China's good friend and passed on this information.

China relied on its own capabilities in 1969 to deter Soviet attack. In essence, China threatened to respond to any large Soviet attack by imposing on the Soviet Union a large-scale and costly land war that the Soviet Union would ultimately be unable to win. If the Soviet Union attacked China with nuclear weapons, China would counterattack with infantry at times and places of PLA choosing. China would use its vast geography and manpower to wage a protracted "people's war," imposing a long and costly war on Moscow. Moscow could choose to initiate a war, and perhaps when and how that was done, but it would not be able to decide when and how to end the war. As a Chinese statement of October 7 said: "China will never be intimidated by war threats, including nuclear war threats. Should a handful of war maniacs dare to raid China's strategic sites in defiance of world condemnation, that will be war, that will be aggression, and the 700 million Chinese people will rise up in resistance and use revolutionary war to eliminate the war of aggression."[37] As Lin Biao said in his report to the Ninth Party Congress in April 1969: "We will not attack unless we are attacked; if we are attacked, we will certainly counterattack."

The nature of Chinese counterattack by land was left to the imagination of Western analysts of that era. The vital Trans-Siberian rail line was vulnerable, as were a number of cities of the Russian Far East. A campaign of PLA raids in force might impose on Moscow a war of indefinite strategic defense. If Soviet forces could be lured into Chinese territory, the PLA could employ a more classic people's war. Beijing launched a mass campaign to prepare the country for war. People were mobilized to dig tunnels and construct bomb and fallout shelters. Grain and other strategic materials were stockpiled. "Dig caves deeply and store grain everywhere" became the slogan. Imports of raw rubber, a vital wartime material, from Southeast Asia rose to all-time highs.[38] Militia units were called up and training was intensified. Basic marksmanship and tactical skills were the focus of training. Defense industrial facilities were relocated to more remote and defensible locations. Caves carved into mountainsides for the purpose were a favored venue. To the extent possible, PLA units disengaged from domestic politics and concentrated on preparations for war with the Soviet Union. Two armored divisions and three anti-aircraft divisions were deployed to the region of China's nuclear research, development, and testing facilities in China's northwest.

China also used its modest nuclear arsenal to help deter Soviet attack. Though only a dozen or so in number, China's deployable atomic bombs were reportedly moved to forward positions. Means of delivery were problematic. China could not then deploy long-range missiles that might hit more distant Soviet cities. The PLA had some Chinese copies of the Soviet 1950s-style Tu-16 "Badger" bombers, but these were highly vulnerable to the Soviet Union's sophisticated air defenses. Still, one or two might get through to Soviet targets. "Exotic" modes of delivery were also discussed by Western analysts. Typically, this entailed disassembly, infiltration, and then reassembly and detonation of bombs in the vicinity of Soviet targets. As the crisis peaked in September, China tested an atomic bomb (its seventh test of a fission bomb and its first underground). A week later, it tested an immensely more powerful fusion bomb (its third such test). Beijing handled these tests very cautiously so as not to broadcast the image of reckless use of nuclear weapons. It made clear, however, that if it was attacked with nuclear weapons, it would retaliate in kind.

The 1969 crisis began to ease following a September 11 meeting of Premier Kosygin, a leader of the no-war faction in the CPSU leadership, and Zhou

Enlai. Kosygin had flown to Hanoi to attend the funeral of Vietnamese leader Ho Chi Minh, and was on his way back to Moscow when he abruptly reversed course and flew to Beijing at Zhou's invitation to discuss the escalating tension between the two countries. Zhou and Kosygin talked for three hours in the Beijing airport, reaching an oral understanding that the border dispute would be settled peacefully and without threat of any kind. Pending settlement, the status quo was to be maintained, with the armed forces of the two sides withdrawing from disputed areas. Maps exchanged in border talks in 1964 would serve as the basis for settlement—an implicit Chinese concession ruling out claims to large pieces of the Russian Far East. Zhou and Kosygin also agreed that the military forces of neither side, including nuclear forces, would attack or open fire on the other.[39] A week after the airport meeting, Zhou sent Kosygin a letter putting into print earlier verbal understandings. Zhou had expected to receive Soviet written confirmation of the agreements, but the Soviet letter of reply merely stated that orders had been issued to Soviet border forces, without mentioning the September 11 agreements.[40]

The Zhou-Kosygin meeting did not eliminate China's fears of possible attack. Those fears peaked in October and became entangled, in ways which are still not understood, with relations between Mao and Lin Biao, Mao's designated successor since the 9th Party Congress in April 1969.[41] Following the Zhou-Kosygin airport meeting, China's leadership, apparently led by Mao, greatly feared that Moscow would choose China's October 1 National Day celebration, when most people would be off work, to launch a large-scale nuclear and conventional surprise attack. At the end of September, Lin Biao became active in overseeing defense preparations, ordering the immediate dispersal of aircraft in the Beijing area, the placing of obstructions on runways, and the issue of weapons to personnel assigned to defend against Soviet parachute assault. Lin also ordered the strengthening of defenses between the Mongolian border and Beijing—an expected Soviet invasion route.

When October 1 passed without an attack, CCP leaders fixed on October 20, when a second round of talks agreed to by Zhou and Kosygin were scheduled to start, as the probable day for the anticipated Soviet attack. Zhou Enlai ordered compilation and distribution of documents regarding surprise attacks, including Pearl Harbor and the German attacks on Poland in 1939 and the USSR in 1941. Then, on October 17, PLA Chief of Staff Huang Yongsheng issued an eleven-point "First Verbal Order" from "Vice Chairman Lin" [Biao] putting the PLA and the nation on full wartime alert. Units and commanders deployed to combat positions. Weapons production, especially of anti-tank weapons, was greatly increased. Some ninety-five divisions, about 940,000 troops, 4,100 airplanes, and huge numbers of tanks and railway wagons were deployed to wartime positions. According to another Politburo session chaired by Lin Biao at Mao's request, China's central leaders evacuated

Beijing and were distributed around the country, with Mao personally deciding where each person should be sent.

Chinese sources assert that this activity was undertaken by Lin behind Mao's back and was not approved by Mao, and that these moves caused Mao to start doubting Lin's loyalty. Scholars doubt that Lin would have acted in this fashion without Mao's approval, and surmise that Mao must have endorsed this mobilization. Mao may have genuinely feared Soviet attack, or he may have generated a war crisis to mobilize the country for suppression of Red Guard disorder and consolidation of the "revolutionary committees" being put into place across the country. The episode may also reflect Mao's fear that Lin would use these sweeping moves to oust him from power. That, Mao soon concluded, was Lin's real objective.

The self-confidence of Mao Zedong during the 1969 crisis is breathtaking, bordering on recklessness. From a position of distinct material inferiority, Mao not only relied on China's lesser but vast resources to virtually dare the Soviet Union to attack China, but dared to strike first and hard at the Soviet Union (at Zhenbao Island) to drive home his deterrent message. Mao dared to "rub the [Soviet] tiger" while the PLA was still deeply enmeshed in running the country, while China had minimal and hardly credible nuclear retaliatory capability (at least by Soviet or American standards), while Soviet military capabilities were vastly superior to China's, and while China was without a friend in the world among the major powers. US policy played a role in deterring the Soviet Union, but, as discussed in the next chapter, Mao seemed not to have been in a hurry to play the American card against Moscow. After challenging Moscow's leadership of the world communist movement, declaring the USSR a capitalist country, permitting Red Guards to assault the Soviet embassy and diplomats, and ordering a bloody ambush of a Soviet border patrol, and then putting the whole country on a wartime basis, Mao faced down Soviet threats, and did this from a position of marked vulnerability and weakness. Underlying Mao's self-confidence was a belief that no nation, not even one or both of the superpowers, could defeat the Chinese people when led by a determined, revolutionary Chinese Communist Party. Conversely, China may have come very close to experiencing nuclear devastation in 1969. Had Grechko's argument prevailed in Moscow, Mao's supreme self-confidence would look a lot more like mad recklessness.

11 }

Rapprochement with the United States

End of Utopian Terror and Defense of the New Revolutionary Order

Revolutions typically reach a point when they turn away from extreme coercive measures previously deemed necessary to usher in a new equalitarian and virtuous social order. The utopian vision that earlier inspired upheaval now seems less attainable and the costs of trying unacceptably high. Revolutions also at some point turn away from direct assaults by large numbers of ordinary people on established institutions of power and privilege, and toward construction of a stable post-revolutionary order. Protecting the gains of the revolution is now deemed to require a return to stable, hierarchical bureaucratic organization. External enemies of the revolution often pose as great a threat as internal enemies.

In the French Revolution these shifts are usually traced to July 1794, the month of Thermidor under the revolutionary calendar, when Maximilien Robespierre and other leading Jacobins were arrested, then executed. The Paris Commune, center of power for the city's poor, was dissolved. Revolutionary tribunals, key instruments of the Terror, were abolished and the Committee of Public Safety, which had guided the Terror, greatly reduced in power. Mob rule, which had periodically erupted to push the revolution in radical directions, began to recede. Displays of wealth once again became common. Émigrés who had fled the Terror began to return to France. And France's leaders began worrying about how to protect the new order created by the great upheaval that had just occurred. All this happened with powerful armies of the monarchical powers of Europe still marshaled on the northern borders of the French Republic.[1]

The Thermidor of the Chinese revolution is probably best situated in fall 1968, when Mao Zedong ordered "Mao Zedong Thought Propaganda Teams" led by the PLA into schools, factories, and offices across China. Those Propaganda Teams set up new Revolutionary Committees that increasingly operated like party committees in an ordinary Leninist system. CCP

286

cadres who had passed the test of the Cultural Revolution and who pledged unequivocal loyalty to the utopian vision and policies of Mao Zedong were incorporated into the new Revolutionary Committees. Red Guard organizations were disarmed and disbanded, with a few of their leaders who were willing to accommodate the restoration of bureaucratic order being incorporated into that rebuilt order. Red Guards unwilling to abandon rebellion were dealt with very harshly by the army. Large numbers of former Red Guards were executed as vagrants and anarchists in a "purification of class ranks" campaign that stressed hierarchy and order, not rebellion against authority. The mass movements that now occurred were once again tightly controlled by party organizations, the normal arrangement in Leninist systems. After the demise of Lin Biao in September 1971, a cohort of cadres purged during 1966–1968 were restored to cadre positions under the aegis of Zhou Enlai.[2] The abrupt transformation of Lin Biao by CCP propaganda organs following his demise from close comrade-in-arms and trusted successor of Mao Zedong to long-term traitor and schemer caused many people to question for the first time the myths they had previously accepted, although this phenomenon did not become apparent until much later. By puncturing the myth of Mao's eternal correctness, the Lin Biao affair also made Mao more desirous of a grand diplomatic breakthrough with the United States that might restore his badly tarnished image. More apparent at the time, the violence, cruelty, hypocrisy, and unreason associated with the Red Guard upheaval had led many people to question the utopian ideas used to justify that violence.

While Mao faced the immense problem of consolidating the new revolutionary state the Cultural Revolution had created, the PRC faced powerful Soviet armies to its north, American military forces across the East Asian littoral, and an aggressive India (or so it seemed to Mao) to China's south. Of these several enemies, the Soviet Union posed the greatest threat to the new order just established by the Cultural Revolution upheaval. Many of the ex-cadres just purged from power sympathized with the prodevelopment policies adopted by the more pragmatic-minded CCP leaders, Mao's opponents. Unlike those purged by Stalin in the 1930s, most of those purged by Mao during the Cultural Revolution were still alive when that upheaval ebbed. Maoist charges of links between CCP pragmatists and the USSR were probably apocryphal and fabricated to malign Mao's imagined rivals. Yet the policies favored by CCP pragmatists were, in fact, similar to those being implemented in the Soviet Union. Cadres purged during the Cultural Revolution plus those who escaped the purge but who secretly doubted Mao's course constituted a social base for possible Soviet intervention in China. There was nothing comparable regarding the United States. China's "bourgeoisie" had been long since been thoroughly crushed and was far removed from the centers of power in the PRC. The prospect of a US-supported invasion to return the

KMT to power was laughable by 1969. The prospect of a Soviet intervention to return the CCP's "healthy Marxist-Leninist forces" to power was not.

The Restoration of Capitalism in the USSR

The cognitive precondition for Chinese attempts to align with the United States against the USSR was a belief that the Soviet Union was no longer a socialist country but had become a capitalist country. Mao's deep identification with Lenin and Stalin and their ideology made it cognitively impossible for him to align with "capitalist imperialist" America against "socialist" Soviet Union. It was necessary for Mao to first decide that the Soviet Union was no longer a socialist state but a capitalist and imperialist one. Once this shift in labels and their associated normative evaluations had been accomplished, whether China aligned with one or the other "imperialist capitalist" power was a matter of mere expedience. Mao's beliefs in the verities of the ideology to which he had devoted his life was no longer involved.[3] One of the core precepts of Leninism is that imperialism grows out of capitalism; imperialism is the highest stage of capitalism. The equation "capitalism = imperialism" is the very core of Leninism. Until Mao could convince himself that the USSR was not socialist, aligning with the United States against the socialist USSR was cognitively impossible. It would require that Mao discard or ignore the ideology to which he had devoted his life.

Mao achieved cognitive harmony by embracing the proposition that capitalism had been restored in the Soviet Union. Under the tutelage of Khrushchev in the 1950s, for all intents and purposes, private ownership of the means of production had been restored, Mao concluded. Drawing on the influential work of Yugoslav Marxist theorist Milovan Djilas's book *The New Class*, published in 1955, Mao concluded that the USSR had restored de facto private control over the means of production. A "red bourgeoisie" constituting the CPSU elite used its control over those means of production to provide themselves, the new red capitalist "ruling class," with luxury (at least when compared to Soviet laborers). The transformation of the Soviet Union in Mao's cognitive system from of socialist to a capitalist country made it possible to square Moscow's "class character" with Lenin's theory of imperialism, opening the way to alignment with US imperialism against Soviet "social imperialism." Since the Soviet Union was now a "red capitalist" state, it was entirely in line with Lenin's theory that its foreign policy would degenerate to the social imperialism that threatened revolutionary China. Once the normative content of the Soviet Union had been accomplished, it was a matter of tactical expediency, and not of Leninist ideology, whether China tilted toward one or the other imperialist power.

The Declining American Threat

At the end of January 1968, Hanoi launched its Tet Offensive. While the military consequences of that giant effort were much as Mao had warned (devastating and demoralizing losses and failure to take cities), the power of the assault profoundly shook the confidence of President Johnson. On March 31, two months into the offensive, Johnson announced a series of moves that together amounted to a major shift away from quest for military victory to search for a compromise negotiated settlement with Hanoi. Johnson declared a desire for a negotiated settlement. US bombing was halted, partially in March and completely in October. Cessation of bombing was Hanoi's precondition for such talks. In effect, Washington accepted Hanoi's terms, conferring very substantial military advantages on Hanoi in the process. A request from the US commander in Vietnam, William Westmoreland, for 206,000 additional troops was turned down, and then Westmoreland was relieved and replaced by Creighton Abrams, a US general who embraced a strategy of Vietnamization of combat effort paralleled by gradual withdrawal of US forces. Finally, Johnson bowed out of the 1968 presidential contest, devoting himself, he said, to the quest for a negotiated peace in Vietnam. The Nixon administration that took office in January 1969 continued these policies, although it began heavy bombing in March 1969 of North Vietnamese sanctuaries in eastern Cambodia.

From Mao's perspective, seconded by Zhou Enlai, the 1968 shifts in US policy meant that the United States was on its way out of Indochina. Washington had given up the quest to create an anticommunist, anti-China bastion in South Vietnam and was looking desperately for a face-saving exit from its positions on China's southern borders. At the same time, as noted in an earlier chapter, Hanoi was moving steadily closer to the Soviet Union in terms of military strategy. The heavy losses suffered by NLF forces during the Tet Offensive made it probable that in the future Hanoi would rely even more on regular PAVN forces outfitted by the Soviet Union.

While China's security environment was deteriorating because of Soviet moves in Czechoslovakia, in Vietnam and on China's own borders, new possibilities in the United States appeared in the form of proposals being broached by Nixon. Part of Nixon's effort to position himself for the 1968 presidential campaign was the publication in October 1967 in the journal *Foreign Affairs* of an article about US Asian policy after the Vietnam War. The American people were deeply divided over the war, and Nixon was positioning himself as the peace candidate. One section of the article dealt with China and hinted at a willingness to consider a new approach to China. It said:

> Taking the long view, we simply cannot afford to leave China forever
> outside the family of nations, there to nurture its fantasies, cherish its

hates and threaten its neighbors. There is no place on this small planet for a billion of its potentially most able people to live in angry isolation.[4]

Nixon's article was translated into Chinese and published in *Cankao ziliao* (Reference materials), a classified publication conveying foreign media coverage to China's political elite. Mao read the article and recommended it to Zhou Enlai, commenting that if Nixon was elected, US China policy might change.[5] Nixon's inaugural address on January 20, 1969, reiterated some of the same ideas as his *Foreign Affairs* article. In the speech, Nixon indicated that his administration would keep "open lines of communication" with all countries, and that the United States sought a world in which "no people, great of small, will live in angry isolation." Mao read Nixon's speech in Chinese translation and ordered that *Renmin ribao* carry the full text on its front page. The speech was accompanied by a "commentary" excoriating Nixon and his speech with the usual anti-imperialist rhetoric. Major papers across China followed the lead of *Renmin ribao*, giving the full speech by a foreign leader very rare coverage in China. Mao intended this as a signal to Nixon that he was watching Nixon's words and actions. Mao's probe was too subtle for the Americans to understand, however. The significance of *Renmin ribao*'s coverage of Nixon's speech went unnoticed in the corridors of power in Washington.[6]

In late February, shortly before the Chinese ambush and decimation of the Soviet patrol on Zhenbao Island, Mao directed Zhou to ask four of China's marshals to meet weekly to discuss and advise on "important international issues."[7] The four marshals were Chen Yi, Ye Jianying, Xu Xiangqian, and Nie Rongzhen. This group would eventually provide the strategic rationale for the opening with Washington, but it did that under the prodding of Mao and Zhou. It is possible that Mao and Zhou knew by early 1969 where they wanted to go, but needed to prepare the political conditions for that momentous shift. But it is also possible that the perceptual shift from anti-imperialism to alignment with the United States against the Soviet Union was simply too great, even for Mao and Zhou, and had to be worked out bit by bit over six months of US signaling to Beijing in the midst of the brink-of-war confrontation between Beijing and Moscow.

The first two reports of the marshals' group came after the March 2 clash at Zhenbao and as Sino-Soviet tensions were flaring along the border. The generals doubted the Soviet Union was prepared to launch a major war against China, since it had deployed far fewer than the three million soldiers that would be needed for such an effort. In terms of Soviet-American relations, the generals noted that the Middle East and its rich oil supply was the focus of superpower contention, and that it would be difficult for either superpower to tackle China before the Middle East contest had been resolved. The reports suggested no changes in China's policies toward the United States. The main policy recommendation was to accelerate preparations for war: calling up militias, strengthening defense industry, and so on.

The conclusions of the first two reports were not bold enough for Mao. In mid-May, Zhou, following Mao's directions, asked the marshals to try again. They should not be "restricted by any established framework"—such as the standard anti-imperialist and antirevisionist line just laid out at the Ninth Party Congress in April—but try to help Mao "gain command of the new tendency in the strategic development" in the world. Zhou stressed to the marshals that Mao had asked them to undertake this task because of their superior strategic vision. Zhou also appointed two senior diplomats to join the group to "assist discussion" and draft reports. These diplomats presumably would have ensured that diplomatic maneuvering would be considered as part of China's national security repertoire. Yet that does not seem to have happened. The next marshals' report came on July 11. It still did not raise the question of changes in China's foreign policies. The report declared that both the United States and the Soviet Union were "branches" of the "international bourgeoisie." Both were hostile to China, even though they were enemies of one another. Because of this, it was unlikely that the United States and the Soviet Union would launch a large-scale war against China, either jointly or separately. Still, there was no intimation of tilting toward Washington to deter Moscow.

A week after the marshals' third report, Beijing received further signals of Washington's desire for a dialogue. On July 21, the US State Department announced the relaxation of restrictions on travel by US citizens to China. On the nonpublic channel, early in 1969 the administration terminated support for Tibetan guerrillas still conducting military raids into Tibet from an isolated region in western Nepal.[8] In the Taiwan Strait, previously regular patrols by the US navy became intermittent.[9] The marshals' group reconvened late in July. This time they finally recognized the possibility of "utilizing the contradiction" between the United States and the Soviet Union, but reached the conclusion that border negotiations with the Soviet Union might strengthen China's "struggle against America." In other words, Beijing might play the Soviet card against the United States!

Before the marshals' group could draft their fourth report, the clash on the Xinjiang border on August 13 occurred. That large-scale battle between Soviet and Chinese forces finally pushed the marshals' group to conceive of using the United States to deter the Soviet Union. The report, submitted to Zhou Enlai on September 17, noted that "the card of the United States" could help China prepare for a major confrontation with the Soviet Union. In line with this, resuming the ambassadorial talks with the United States might be useful, the report suggested. Orally, Chen Yi conveyed some "unconventional thoughts" to Zhou Enlai: in addition to resuming the Warsaw ambassadorial talks, China might take the initiative in proposing talks with the United States at the ministerial level or higher so that basic and related problems could be solved. The conceptual breakthrough of aligning with the United States to deter Soviet attack had finally been made. Mao Zedong laid out for his doctor, Li Zhisui, his view of China's beleaguered situation at this juncture:

> "Think about this," [Mao] said to me one day. "We have the Soviet Union to the north and the west, India to the south, and Japan to the east. If all our enemies were to unite, attacking us from the north, south, east, and west, what do you think we should do? . . . "Think again," he said, "Beyond Japan is the United States. Didn't our ancestors counsel negotiating with faraway countries while fighting with those that are near?"[10]

When Li Zhisui asked incredulously, "How could we negotiate with the United States?" Mao replied:

> The United States and the Soviet Union are different. . . . The United States never occupied Chinese territory. America's new president, Richard Nixon, is a longtime rightist, a leader of the anti-communists there. I like to deal with rightists. They say what they really think—not like the leftists, who say one thing and mean another.

"Neither I nor Wang Dongxing [head of Mao's security unit] believed Mao," Li Zhisui recalled. "American imperialists were [being] accused of seeking hegemony by force in all of Asia. Capitalism, we were certain, was weak and dying, the victim of its own internal contradictions."

As conflict along the Sino-Soviet border spiraled upward in August–September, the United States announced a policy that amounted to pro-Chinese neutrality. Responding to intelligence from multiple sources that Moscow was seriously considering a preemptive attack on China, Nixon concluded that Soviet "smashing" of China would not be in US interests. Henry Kissinger, who was a participant and a key architect in these events as President Nixon's national security advisor, said this was a revolutionary moment in US foreign policy: a president had declared that US interests required the survival of a major communist country.[11] In line with this new thinking, on September 6, Under Secretary of State Elliot Richardson in a speech laid out the new US position:

> In the case of Communist China, long-run improvement in our relations is in our national interest. We do not seek to exploit for our own advantage the hostility between the Soviet Union and the People's Republic. Ideological differences between the two Communist giants are not our affair. We could not fail to be *deeply concerned*, however, with an escalation of this quarrel into *a massive breach of international peace and security*. Our national security would in the long run be prejudiced by associating ourselves with either side against the other. Each

is highly sensitive about American efforts to improve relations with the other. We intend, nevertheless, to pursue a long-term course of progressively developing better relations with both. We are not going to let Communist Chinese invective deter us from seeking agreements with the Soviet Union where those are in our interest. Conversely, we are not going to let Soviet apprehension prevent us from attempting to bring Communist China out of its angry alienated shell. [Emphasis added.][12]

US "deep concern" over a "massive breach of international peace" was diplomatic lingo for US opposition to a Soviet attack on China. Richardson's speech arrived in Beijing as the country was buttoning down for all-out war with the Soviet Union. From mid-1969 through the end of 1970, the Nixon Administration conveyed through various channels its desire for a high-level dialogue with China's leaders. In May 1969, for example, Secretary of State William Rogers asked Pakistani president Yahya Khan to ask Beijing about possible expanded talks on Sino-US relations. The long-standing ambassadorial talks in Warsaw offered one possible mechanism for revived Sino-US contact. Nixon and Kissinger felt strongly that that low-level venue would not succeed in achieving the breakthrough they sought. Still, lacking an apparently better channel of communication, Nixon had the State Department order the US ambassador in Warsaw, Walter Stoessel, to find an opportunity to convey to the chargé d'affaires of the PRC embassy, Lei Yang, the US desire to revive and expand talks. After several months in which no convenient opportunity presented itself, on December 3, 1969, Stoessel spied a group of PRC diplomats at a Yugoslav fashion show at Warsaw's Palace of Culture. When Stoessel approached the Chinese diplomats, they, without instructions about how to respond to an American probe and probably fearful of being criticized back in Beijing, had walked away, leaving the American representative to run to catch up and blurt out his message, in broken Polish and in a most undiplomatic fashion. The US message was nonetheless delivered and duly reported back to Zhou Enlai. Two weeks later Stoessel was invited in by Lei Yang for a chat at the Chinese embassy. This Warsaw episode later proved useful to Mao and Zhou in justifying the opening to the United States; it was the United States, not China, that was requesting a new relation, Mao and Zhou repeatedly pointed out to their skeptical comrades. Stoessel had had to run after and virtually beg Lei Yang to hear him out. Obviously this was because US weakness and decline made it convenient to alter its long-standing anti-China policies, Mao and Zhou explained.[13] Following the Stoessel-Lei meeting, Zhou reported to Mao that "the opportunity is coming; we now have a brick in our hands to knock at the door."[14] As a good-will gesture, Mao authorized the release of two US citizens detained since February 1969, when their yacht had gone off course and entered China's territorial waters near Hong Kong.

Once the Warsaw talks resumed on February 20 and March 20, 1970, they were, in Kissinger's words, "a dialogue of the deaf." At that level, both sides were still trapped in the agenda and issues that had deadlocked the previous 134 sessions, and simply unable to raise the dialogue to the strategic level that might uncover parallel interests. Nixon thus sought dispatch of a high-level envoy, such as Kissinger, to China, ideally to open the way for a visit by himself. Thus in July 1970, Nixon during a round-the-world trip asked the presidents of Pakistan and Romania, countries that were good friends with both the United States and China, to convey to Beijing the message that he, Nixon, sought a high-level exchange with China's leaders. Parallel to this diplomacy, Nixon made public statements about his desire to visit China, either while president or afterwards.

The method Mao chose to respond to Nixon's overtures—by inviting the American journalist Edgar Snow to stand beside him atop Tiananmen gate during the October 1, 1970, National Day celebrations in Beijing. Snow had traveled to the communist base area in Shaanxi province in 1936 to interview Mao. The resulting book, *Red Star over China*, gave a very positive view of China's communist movement and had a significant impact on Western and Chinese opinion about the CCP at a critical time in the party's long struggle for power.[15] Twice in the 1960s, Mao again invited Snow to China in an attempt to influence foreign opinion through him. In October 1970, Mao once again attempted to use Snow to send a message to Chinese and foreign audiences, including, most pertinently, Richard Nixon. The day after the 1970 National Day celebration, a photograph of Mao and Snow side-by-side was broadcast to the world and was intended as a display of Mao's personal regard for America. Mao also granted Snow an interview in which he made positive comments about America and the American people, and indicated that Nixon was welcome to visit China either as a president or as a private citizen.

US leaders once again missed Beijing's signal. Mao's move was too subtle for the Americans to grasp. Snow was dismissed by administration officials as a communist propagandist, and thus of little relevance to US relations with China. Snow's article conveying the contents of his interview with Mao was published, and thus became available to US leaders, only after several months' delay, by which point its relevance had already been superseded by other channels. Mao had assumed that Snow would immediately convey his comments to US officials.[16] As Kissinger stresses, after twenty years of isolation and extreme hostility that had become deeply embedded in domestic constituencies, both Chinese and US leaders struggled to establish a reliable, secure, and appropriately high-level mechanism to conduct a dialogue about setting relations in a radically new direction.

Early in December 1970, more direct high-level communication began when Zhou wrote by hand a letter to Kissinger that the Pakistani ambassador to the United States personally hand-carried from Islamabad to Washington. In the letter, Zhou acknowledged receipt of earlier messages from Nixon via intermediaries, and noted Nixon's statement to President Yahya of Pakistan that the United States would not join in a condominium with the Soviet Union against China. Zhou also agreed to the United States sending either a high-level emissary or President Nixon himself to Beijing for talks. The letter mentioned Taiwan, but in a way that Kissinger described as the mildest formulation on Taiwan that the United States had received from China in twenty years.[17] Zhou sent a second and nearly identical letter to Kissinger via the Romanian channel, but that missive arrived nearly after a month after the Pakistani one. Kissinger replied to Zhou in early January 1971 with a letter delivered via the Romanian channel, and indicating a willingness to send a high-level representative to Beijing for discussions. Then for a period of three months there was no further communication between Beijing and Washington. China's next move came in a form that came to symbolize the dramatic realignment underway: ping-pong diplomacy.

An international ping-pong tournament was taking place in Nagoya, Japan, in April 1971, and a team from China was participating—its first such participation in an international tournament—as was a team from the United States. One player on the US team, Glenn Cowan, happened one morning to miss his bus to the tournament building and was invited to board the Chinese bus to that destination by a Chinese player.[18] At the back of the bus, champion Chinese player Zhuang Zedong noted the American player, with shoulder-length hair in the style of that era, and debated in his mind for ten minutes of the fifteen-minute ride to their destination whether he should greet the American. Eventually, Zhuang remembered the photo of Mao together with Edgar Snow atop Tiananmen during the previous National Day, understood that that photo in effect authorized friendly contacts with Americans, and approached Cowan to give him a gift of a silk landscape of Huangshan Mountain. Delighted, Cowan fumbled for a gift to give in return but, on the spot, came up only with a hair comb, which he gave to Zhuang. When the bus arrived at its destination many journalists were waiting and, of course, focused on the strange sight of a long-haired young American together with Chinese athletes. One journalist asked Cowan if he would like to visit China, and Cowan replied "Of course." The next day, Japanese newspapers carried many photos of Cowan together with Zhuang and other Chinese athletes.

The foreign affairs person accompanying and responsible for the Chinese table tennis team immediately reported the episode to the MFA and Zhou Enlai. The possibility of inviting the US team to visit China for a few exhibition games after the Japan tournament thus presented itself. The MFA and Zhou Enlai, who immediately conveyed the information to Mao, recommended caution: the US team should not be invited. The decision for an invitation was Mao's alone. For two days, Mao considered the MFA and Zhou's recommendation, going back and forth in his mind. After taking some sleeping pills to get some rest, with the matter still unresolved in his mind, Mao roused himself to tell his nurse to phone the MFA and direct them to invite the American team to China. By inviting the US ping-pong team, Mao was publicly committing China to improved ties with the United States, considerably easing Nixon's concerns about possible failure and embarrassment in the radical quest for better ties with China. It also further accustomed China's public to the possibility of improved PRC-US ties. Ping-pong also happened to be a sport in which China was the world leader, allowing China to display its superiority (in at least this area) before the Americans and the world. Ping-pong also happened to be a television-friendly game that captured the mind of the American public. US views of China began to change, becoming more positive and friendly.

After the ping-pong breakthrough, the pace of high-level communication, still via the Pakistan channel, picked up. The US side proposed that Kissinger represent President Nixon in talks in Beijing to "raise the issue of principle concern to it." Mao accepted, "with great pleasure," so Zhou Enlai informed Kissinger on June 2. The driver of this push for high-level, direct dialogue was mutual desire to gain strategic advantage by recasting the Cold War international order. For China in 1969–1971 that meant primarily deterring Soviet attack. But, as Henry Kissinger pointed out, as both sides discovered the extent of their convergent views once the new strategic dialogue had begun, the new Sino-American relation would grow far beyond the narrow deterrence calculations that initially inspired it. It would become a major element of an entirely new international order involving the broad strategic alignment of the PRC and the United States—much to Moscow's disadvantage.

Kissinger's first mission to Beijing in July 1971 was clothed in secrecy to outmaneuver the many people in Washington, Moscow, and Taipei who were opposed to improved PRC-US ties. In the midst of an around-the-world trip and after stops in Guam, Saigon, and Bangkok designed to exhaust media interest, Kissinger feigned stomach problems during a stop in Islamabad and conspicuously retired to a remote chateau to recoup. Or so the press was told. In fact Kissinger was driven directly to a secure and remote military airfield to fly to Beijing. Waiting aboard the plane was a team of senior and experienced English-speaking diplomats that Zhou Enlai had dispatched to accompany Kissinger's group on their flight to a strange and unfamiliar destination, Beijing, thus helping to alleviate any tension or misgivings. The group had been selected in 1969 shortly after the four marshals' report suggesting an opening to the United States.

Zhou Enlai carefully choreographed Kissinger's visit to make it a success and to China's advantage. As with ping-pong diplomacy three months earlier, hospitality was a part of Zhou's strategy. When Kissinger's plane arrived at the Beijing airport, Marshall Ye Jianying greeted him at the bottom of the ramp.

Ye was one of China's top military leaders since the demise of Lin Biao. Ye's presence sent the message that the PLA supported China's new diplomatic track. Once the American group was ensconced in the Diaoyutai (Fisherman's Terrace) state guest house in western Beijing, Zhou Enlai paid Kissinger a visit within four hours. Zhou, a premier, was considerably higher-status than a mere presidential advisor, yet he bent diplomatic protocol to display courtesy toward the Americans. In formal talks with Kissinger, Zhou stressed his appreciation of Kissinger's "friendship" toward China, a tactic that made it psychologically harder for Kissinger to disagree with China's positions.

Mao instructed Zhou to "brag" to Kissinger about China's ability to face and defeat even an invasion by the Soviet Union, the United States, and Japan. In line with Mao's instructions, Zhou told Kissinger that in an "extreme situation," China would wage a protracted people's war to grind down the invaders and defeat them. This would be difficult, but China was confident it could do it, Zhou said on Mao's orders. Kissinger understood this as a way of eliciting the US attitude toward possible Soviet attack, and by extension US assistance in such an eventuality, without seeming to ask for US help. It was a way of asking for US assistance against the Soviet Union without appearing as a supplicant.[19] This image of China standing alone and defending itself in a self-reliant manner against all enemies became the standard line for the PRC over the next decade—while, in actuality, China was relying on US support against the Soviet Union. It became, in effect, a sort of camouflage for China's using the American barbarians to check the Soviet barbarians. On July 15, 1971, simultaneously in Beijing and Los Angeles, Kissinger's recent visit to China was announced, along with the news that President Nixon would soon visit China. That announcement was a bombshell rivaling the ping-pong diplomacy three months earlier.

The Mao-Nixon Summit

Nixon's group arrived in Beijing on February 21, 1972. The Nixon administration had positioned satellite television broadcasting equipment in Beijing, so Nixon-in-China events could be broadcast live back to the United States. Nixon, like Mao, understood the political utility of pictures as propaganda. When Nixon's airplane arrived in Beijing, at the bottom of the ramp to welcome him was Zhou Enlai.[20] The drama of the event was deliberately accentuated by Nixon descending the stairway without his entourage to the bottom to shake hands with Zhou. With careful discipline, Zhou waited until Nixon extended his hand before raising his own hand to reciprocate. Chinese audiences would notice such matters, even if Americans did not. The Nixon-Zhou handshake evoked John Foster Dulles' refusal to shake hands with Zhou at Geneva in 1954. The Nixon-Zhou handshake symbolized the abandonment of that earlier policy of hostility and the embrace of a new era of cooperation. Only after this dramatic handshake did other American personnel begin to alight. The dramatic meeting was broadcast live to US television audiences, the timing of arrival in Beijing having been arranged to fall in prime television time in the United States.

Within an hour of Nixon's settling in the Diaoyutai guesthouse, Mao summoned the US president to meet him. Kissinger, upon receiving the summons, wary of the image of the president, a barbarian envoy, being summarily called before the emperor, tried to save dignity by raising a few matters of protocol. Zhou would not have it and, showing uncharacteristic impatience, made it clear the chairman expected Nixon to arrive promptly. The Americans complied. The meeting between Mao and Nixon that followed was one of the most dramatic events of twentieth-century diplomacy. The American composer John Adams later wrote an excellent opera, *Nixon in China*, about the event, using much of the actual verbiage exchanged by the leaders.

Mao received Nixon and Kissinger in his study lined with shelves of books and manuscripts, with more of the same piled on the floor and tables. The message to the Americans was that Mao had no need for the normal trappings associated with great power. Mao, weak after a period of illness, stood to greet Nixon, took and held for some time Nixon's hand in his own hands, and smiled beamingly while photographers recorded the event. The next day, photos of Mao greeting Nixon were carried on the front pages of newspapers across China. Mao made his point: he approved of the new, friendly relation with the United States.

Mao evaded Nixon's efforts to discuss either "philosophy" (i.e., broad views of world affairs) or specific policy issues. Regarding "philosophy," when Nixon tried to turn the conversation in that direction, Mao sarcastically remarked that since Kissinger was the only doctor of philosophy present, he should be the main speaker. Regarding specific policy issues, Mao indicated that Zhou Enlai or Qiao Guanhua would discuss such matters. The symbolism of Mao's friendly reception of the American president was far more important than any verbal communication. The main point Mao made to Nixon was that China and the United States did not now threaten one another.

> At the present time, the question of aggression from the United States or aggression from China is relatively small; that is, it could be said that this is not a major issue, because the present situation is one in which a state of war does not exist between our two countries. You want to withdraw some of your troops back on your soil; ours do not go abroad.[21]

Kissinger understood Mao's reference to Chinese troops not going abroad to indicate that China would not intervene in Vietnam. China, as noted earlier, had recalled its forces from Vietnam in fall 1968. The point Mao was making was this: the PRC and the United States were not enemies, while the

Soviet Union was the enemy of both. In fifteen hours of talks, Zhou Enlai and Nixon explored the degree of convergence in world views and strategic perceptions. The two agreed at the outset that their discussions would be premised on the interests of their respective countries and not on ideologies, which, of course, differed radically. Mao and Zhou both urged the Americans to ignore the militant propaganda they saw displayed around them, and look instead at China's actions. The militant propaganda, Kissinger concluded, was for purposes of domestic control.

When it came time to draft the communiqué capping the Mao-Nixon summit, Mao proposed an innovative departure from diplomatic norms. Such communiqués usually featured platitudes about peace, cooperation, mutual trust, and so on. Kissinger had himself prepared such a draft communiqué, which he submitted to Zhou Enlai during a second visit to China in October 1971. Mao vetoed this "bullshit communiqué" and directed Zhou to propose that the two sides state their radically different views, leaving only a final concluding section to lay out their areas of agreement. Although initially surprised and skeptical, Kissinger quickly came to appreciate this unorthodox format. Blunt statement of US views would reassure audiences back home and skeptical allies in Asia that the United States had not abandoned its principles. It would also underline the importance of the final section, in which the two sides declared their areas of agreement in opposing hegemony, a code word for the Soviet Union.

Negotiating an Accommodation over Taiwan

Negotiating an accommodation of interests regarding Taiwan was the most difficult aspect of the new beginning in PRC-US relations. As discussed in an earlier chapter, PRC leaders believed that Taiwan's status as a province of China had been settled definitively by the Cairo Declaration of 1943. Beijing insisted during the 1971–1972 negotiations that the United States endorse that principle. Mao and Zhou entered the negotiations prepared to see the failure of the Nixon initiative if the United States did not adequately attest to Taiwan's status as part of China. Mao also recognized that Nixon's hopes for reelection in November 1972 put pressure on him to reach an accommodation with China. But Mao and Zhou also appreciated that Nixon was dealing personally with them and in a respectful tone as an equal.[22] Fortunately for Beijing, Nixon and Kissinger entered the negotiations with an understanding of this basic Chinese requirement for a new Sino-American relation, and had given considerable thought to how to satisfy that requirement without sacrificing US interests or destroying the political base in the United States for a new relation with Communist China. One repeated and apparently effective American argument at this juncture was that a perceived Nixon betrayal or sacrifice of the Nationalist regime on Taiwan would lead to a backlash in the United States that would destroy the new relation that Nixon and Mao were attempting to build.[23] If Mao and Zhou wanted the new relation with the United States that Nixon was risking his career to build, they would have to accommodate to some degree US interests regarding Taiwan.

Throughout the eight months of negotiations, Zhou and his diplomatic assistants deputy foreign ministers Qiao Guanhua and Huang Hua attempted to focus the talks on the issue of Taiwan. Kissinger and Nixon, on the other hand, tried to frame the issue more broadly in terms of the larger global balance of power. Beijing was intensely focused on the core issue of Taiwan, while from the US perspective, Taiwan was one of a number of issues that needed to be considered. During the first negotiating session in July 1971 between Zhou and Kissinger, Taiwan was the very first issue raised by Zhou. Kissinger had tried in his opening statement to frame the issue in terms of the withdrawal of US military forces from Taiwan. Zhou insisted that the issue be framed in a more fundamental way, in terms of the US stance on the legal status of Taiwan. Zhou told Kissinger:

> If this crucial question is not solved, then the whole question [of PRC-US relations] will be difficult to resolve. . . . In recognizing China the US must do so unreservedly. It must recognize the PRC as the sole legitimate government of China and not make any exceptions.[24]

Turning aside another attempt by Kissinger to focus on the disposition of US military forces, Zhou insisted on returning to the basic issue of principle. Relations between Beijing and Taipei were China's "internal affair," Zhou insisted, and "the United States must recognize that the PRC is the sole legal government on China and that Taiwan province is an inalienable part of Chinese territory which must be restored to the Motherland." When Zhou that evening reported to Mao this tough opening move, the Chairman directed him to take a more relaxed approach:

> There's no hurry for Taiwan, for there's no war there. A war is being fought and lives lost in Vietnam. It we want Nixon to come, we cannot think merely of ourselves.

On several other occasions during the negotiations, Mao ordered greater Chinese flexibility. During Kissinger's second visit to Beijing in October 1971, for example, when Kissinger was negotiating with Huang Hua the text of the communiqué to be issued at the conclusion of Nixon's upcoming visit, Huang insisted that the communiqué indicate that Nixon had sought the invitation. Kissinger refused Huang's proposed formulation. The issue was reported to Mao, who laughed and told Huang to revise his proposed text. This was done and agreement was swiftly reached with "both sides feeling happy," according to Huang Hua.[25] Another example of Mao's flexibility came the day before the Shanghai communiqué was to be issued, when State Department officials realized that the document contained affirmations of the continuing effectiveness of US security treaties with Japan and South Korea, but not of the treaty with Taiwan. Understanding that this would be seen as "abandonment" of Taiwan in the United States, Kissinger asked that the references to US security treaties be deleted. Qiao Guanhua adamantly refused to revisit already negotiated and agreed-upon terms. Mao, however, overruled Qiao and ordered acceptance of the US request.[26] Of course, Mao was the only person on the Chinese side who could order greater flexibility. He used that authority to guide the negotiations and his summit with Nixon to a successful conclusion.

In May 1971, after ping-pong diplomacy and in preparation for Kissinger's upcoming first and secret visit, the Politburo set up a Central Foreign Affairs Group consisting of Zhou Enlai, Ye Jianying, and Huang Hua, charged with working out guidelines for the upcoming Sino-US talks.[27] The guidelines ultimately consisted of eight points:

1. US military forces would be withdrawn from Taiwan and the Taiwan Strait within a given period of time. If no agreement could be reached on this point, it was possible that Nixon's visit could be deferred.
2. Taiwan was Chinese territory and its liberation was an internal affair of China in which no foreign interference was allowed. "Japanese militarism" should be strictly prevented from entering Taiwan.
3. China will strive to liberate Taiwan in peaceful ways. It will work carefully regarding the Taiwan issue.
4. Establishment of ambassadorial-level relations would require US recognition of the PRC as the sole legal government of China. All activities aimed at "two Chinas" or "one China, one Taiwan," should be firmly opposed.
5. If the previous three [sic] conditions could not be fully met, it would be permissible to establish liaison offices [in lieu of embassies].
6. China would not initiate discussion of the question of UN representation, but if the US side did, China would make clear the unacceptable nature of "two Chinas" or "one China, one Taiwan" arrangements.
7. Talks about trade would be entered into only after the United States accepted the principle of withdrawal of US military forces from Taiwan.
8. The Chinese government stands for the withdrawal of US forces from Indochina and all of Southeast Asia, Korea, and Japan "so that peace in the Far East will be maintained."

302 { China's Quest

As scholar Yafeng Xia pointed out, these eight points contained several implicit retreats from earlier Chinese positions. China no longer insisted that the United States sever ties with Taiwan as a precondition for discussions or even links (liaison offices) between Beijing and Washington. Comparison of the final "Taiwan text" of the Shanghai Communiqué with the Politburo's eight points indicates several further Chinese concessions. The relevant Taiwan clause of the final communiqué read:

> The US side declared: The United States acknowledges that all Chinese on either side of the Taiwan Strait maintain there is but one China and that Taiwan is a part of China. The United States government does not challenge that position. It reaffirms its interest in a peaceful settlement of the Taiwan question by the Chinese themselves. With this prospect in mind, it affirms the ultimate objective of the withdrawal of US forces and military installations from Taiwan. In the meantime, it will progressively reduce its forces and military installations on Taiwan as the tension in the area diminishes.

The United States was willing to withdraw US military forces from Taiwan and the Taiwan Strait, but contrary to the Politburo's Point One, was unwilling to set a definite date. Moreover, the clause "With this prospect in mind" referring to "the peaceful settlement of the Taiwan question by the Chinese themselves" conditioned the withdrawal of US forces on progress toward "peaceful settlement." The clause starting the next sentence, "In the meantime . . . as tension in the area diminishes," can also be read as conditioning withdrawal of US forces on reduction of tension in the area. The United States also "reaffirmed its interest in a peaceful settlement of the Taiwan question." Taken together, these several clauses imply conditionality: if the prospect for peaceful settlement evaporated, the US affirmation of withdrawal of forces might also.

The proposition that Taiwan is Chinese territory was the most difficult to negotiate. In the joint communiqué, China stated in full its claim to sovereignty over Taiwan. The problem for the US side was that unequivocal acceptance of China's claim would, under principles of international law, imply acceptance of Beijing's right to use force against Taiwan, rule out any US right to "interfere" in such an event, and imply acceptance of Beijing's authority to regulate any and all US-Taiwan ties. It would also produce a strong negative reaction among the US public. Fortunately, the two sides found formulations that satisfied China's principled demands, but also protected US interests in Taiwan. The final communiqué said the United States "acknowledges that all Chinese on either side of the Taiwan Strait maintain there is but one China and that Taiwan is a part of China. The United States Government does not challenge that position." This was an allusion to the fact that Chiang Kai-shek's Nationalist government in Taipei insisted that Taiwan and the China mainland were both part of one China, albeit the Republic of China rather than the People's Republic of China. In talks with Zhou, Nixon went further in accepting China's position, saying "There is one China and Taiwan is a part of China."[28] In the final, written agreement (the Joint Communiqué), however, the United States merely "acknowledged" and "does not challenge" the position of "all Chinese" that Taiwan is a part of China. Clearly implicit was the idea that this was not the US position. Use of the verb "acknowledge" (*renshidao* in Chinese) rather than the more potent verb "recognize" (*chengren* in Chinese)—the term used under international law to confer sovereignty upon a claimant to membership in the community of sovereign states—in both the English and Chinese texts put further distance between China's claim to Taiwan and the US position regarding that claim. Each of these manifestations of Chinese "flexibility" would have been approved by Mao.

The Shanghai communiqué did not include a Chinese pledge to rely on peaceful means to reunify Taiwan and the mainland. The contrast between the position of the two sides on this issue was glaring. The US statement stressed "peaceful solution." The Chinese statement said that "the liberation of Taiwan is China's internal affair in which no other country has the right to interfere," a formulation that contained assertion of the right to use military force. During negotiations, Zhou repeatedly underlined, in accord with Point Three of the Politburo guidelines, China's willingness "to strive" for unification by peaceful means. This was an attempt by China to address the US concern about a possible PRC attack on Taiwan, but do so in a way that did not compromise what Beijing felt was its sovereign right to use force and thus compromise China's claim to sovereignty over Taiwan. Left implicit in Zhou's statement was the proposition that nonpeaceful means might become necessary if Beijing's "striving" via peaceful means was unsuccessful.

The elements of the 1971–1972 PRC-US accommodation over Taiwan were not a victory for either side. They were, instead, a hard-bargained and delicately balanced accommodation of the interests of the two sides. As Zhou explained to Nixon toward the end of negotiations, the Chinese people had "feelings" regarding Taiwan. "But it is possible for us to persuade our people because of the prestige of the leadership of Chairman Mao."[29] As Kissinger put it, the accommodation of 1971–1972 "put the Taiwan issue in abeyance, with each side maintaining its basic principles. Despite the continuing differences over Taiwan, our rapprochement with China accelerated because we shared a common concern about the threat to the global balance of power."[30]

"Common concerns" of the PRC and the United States regarding the Soviet Union were embodied in what became known as the anti-hegemony clause of the communiqué. It read: "Neither [the PRC nor the United States] should seek hegemony in the Asia-Pacific region and each is opposed to efforts by any country or group of countries to establish such hegemony." The Soviet Union was not explicitly identified, but all savvy people understood the reference. This provision would be given considerable substance during the 1970s. According to Kissinger, one of the remarkable things about the new Sino-American relation was the extent to which the two sides agreed and were able to cooperate in area after area, once the issue of Taiwan had been set aside. The PRC-US rapprochement of 1972 was underpinned by convergent views and interests about Soviet expansionism.

In China, it was necessary to explain the new relationship with US imperialism. The day the Shanghai communiqué was released, Zhou Enlai convened a Politburo meeting to discuss the consequences that might follow from the new PRC-US dialog and decide how to explain the new relationship with the United States to the Chinese people. Eventually it was decided to explain the new relation with US imperialism to the Chinese people in terms of the exploitation of contradictions between primary and secondary enemies. Mao Zedong's united front theory from the 1930s and 1940s had explained why the CCP united with the secondary enemy, then the KMT, to defeat the primary enemy, then Japan, thus allowing the CCP to defeat enemies one at a time. Now US imperialism was cast in the role of "secondary enemy" and Soviet "social imperialism" in the role of primary enemy. Familiar categories of Mao Zedong Thought were thus used to explain "Chairman Mao's revolutionary diplomatic line" to the Chinese public and to foreign communists.

Breakthrough on China's Diplomatic Relations

During the twenty years of US-PRC confrontation from 1950 to 1971, the United States had used its vast influence to dissuade countries from establishing diplomatic relations with "Communist China" or voting to admit "Red China" to the United Nations. This effort was a major component of the US strategy of containing the PRC. Ever since the UN was formed in 1945, the Republic of China (ROC), located in Taiwan since 1949 and led by Chiang Kai-shek, had held the China seat in the UN. Keeping that so was a major objective of US containment policy. To many people, it seemed silly that a small island of then perhaps 14.8 million people held a veto as one of five permanent members of the Security Council. But keeping the ROC in the UN was a way of keeping the PRC out. Several West European countries defied Washington's wishes and opened missions or full embassies in Beijing—Britain, Denmark, and the Netherlands in 1950, France in 1964—but generally US lobbying was effective. In 1969, China had diplomatic relations with only fifty-three countries. In 1971–1972, as US-PRC rapprochement got underway, the dam broke. In those two years, thirty states recognized the PRC. With Washington itself moving to improve ties with China, American arguments against other countries following suit were no longer viable. Moreover, Nixon saw the entry of China into the United Nations and the international community as in the US interest, and decided to no longer use US influence to prevent it. In October

1971, the People's Republic of China assumed China's seat in both the United National General Assembly and the Security Council.

China was not passive in this process; it worked actively to expand its diplomatic ties.[31] Beijing sent and welcomed 290 foreign delegations from eighty countries in the one year of 1971. These delegations were honored with banquets, thereby earning the name "banquet diplomacy," and were otherwise instructed about China's desire to expand ties. China also resumed economic assistance, allocating $700 million in 1970 alone. This was a huge amount for a country as poor as China. Beijing's hospitality and largess exploited the advantageous conditions created by the shift in US policy. The need for experienced diplomatic cadres to take part in these efforts coincided with the fall of Lin Biao in September 1971. Both halves of that equation facilitated Zhou Enlai's release of many cadres from the rural cadre schools where they had been languishing since 1968 or so.

The Fallout of China's Rapprochement with the United States: Alienation of Albania

Ironically, while entering the United Nations with Albanian sponsorship, China's special, comradely relation with Albania was collapsing as a result of Beijing's rapprochement with the United States. This episode is worth exploring at some length, since from 1963 until 1971 the Sino-Albanian entente was a core part of Beijing's quest for world revolution, and the collapse of that entente was an interesting consequence of Beijing's embrace of the United States. While tensions existed in China's relations with North Vietnam and North Korea over those counties' insistence on balancing between Beijing and Moscow, no such ambiguity existed in Sino-Albanian relations. Tirana (Albania's capital) was completely in the CCP's camp as the CCP-CPSU polemic unfolded in the early 1960s. Enver Hoxha and his Albanian Labor Party (the ALP, Albania's communist party) enthusiastically supported China's Cultural Revolution as a necessary ideological purification of the proletariat vanguard along the lines of Stalin's continual purges. As China moved away from ideologically driven foreign policies toward pragmatic approaches based on China's national interest under Zhou Enlai's tutelage in 1968–1971, Albanian-Chinese relations began to deteriorate.[32]

Hoxha's objection to Zhou's pragmatic diplomacy began in fall 1968 following the Warsaw Pact invasion of Czechoslovakia. At that juncture, China began urging formation of some sort of bloc, even a military alliance if possible, between Albania, Romania, and Yugoslavia, all communist-ruled Balkan countries that hewed to lines independent of Moscow. Such an arrangement made sense to Zhou because united these Balkan countries would be better able to resist Soviet intimidation. Hoxha rejected such an arrangement because the ruling parties of Romania and Yugoslavia were revisionist and toyed with either Soviet revisionism or US imperialism, or both. Even more egregiously, Yugoslavia wanted to annex Albania into Yugoslavia, or so Hoxha believed, while oppressing ethnic Albanians in Yugoslavia's Kosovo region. Nor did China deign to discuss with Albania's leaders the idea of a Balkan tripartite alliance before publicly promulgating that proposal.

Further differences with Tirana arose over Zhou's airport summit meeting with Kosygin in September 1969. Hoxha felt that an easing of tension with Moscow would facilitate Moscow's efforts to keep the people of Eastern Europe (including potentially Albania) under Soviet control, while opening the door to expanded collaboration between Soviet and Chinese revisionists. Many revisionists were still "hidden" within the Chinese Communist Party, Hoxha feared, and would respond to the reduction of tensions with the Soviet revisionists by intensifying their schemes. Many of the "Chinese allies [of Soviet revisionism] . . . Liu Shao-chi and company" had been exposed, Hoxha wrote in his diary. But "despite the victories achieved, a great deal of work is still needed to consolidate these victories, and first of all, to ensure that the Communist Party of China is re-organized and consolidated on the Marxist-Leninist road. Has this been achieved? Regrettably, we doubt this." Many "vacillators" were still in power within the CCP but "keeping quiet," waiting for the "storm" of the Cultural Revolution to pass. "One of these may be Chou En-lai," Hoxha wrote.[33]

Albanian criticism of the Zhou-Kosygin summit stung Chinese representatives. "You are extremist," Zhou said "angrily, in an uncomradely way" to Albanian Politburo member Rita Marko when Zhou briefed him on the Zhou-Kosygin airport summit the day after it occurred and Marco rejected Zhou's justification of the airport meeting. PRC Ambassador Geng Biao in Tirana explained to Albanian leaders that China was merely using diplomacy to gain time to better prepare to resist a Soviet attack. The Soviet revisionists would attack China, but those preparations were not yet complete. The Soviet Union had marshaled troops on China's borders to attack China, but was not yet in a situation to act, Zhou explained. The Soviet leadership was also divided into "hawks" and "doves." Diplomacy would strengthen the "doves," giving China more time to arm itself. This is what Stalin had done with Hitler in 1939, Geng Biao explained.

Zhou's displeasure was manifest in a number of slights, at least as perceived by Hoxha: failure to invite Rita Marko to an exhibition, dispatch of an uncommunicative Li Xiannian (whom Hoxha took to be one of Zhou's "revisionist" supporters) to head a Chinese delegation to Albania, and so on. "The unfriendly stand of Li Hsien-nien, dictated by the group of Chou En-lai," was intended, Hoxha wrote, to let the ALP know that they were not in agreement with the activity of Chen Boda and Albanian leader Haki Toska, who had been the "warm and comradely" interlocutor of Chen Boda during an earlier visit.[34] Actually, there was a good deal of substance to the Albanian view that Chen

Boda represented a policy of ideologically based friendship with Albania, while Zhou Enlai handled Albania in a much more pragmatic fashion.

China's rapprochement with the United States pushed the Albanian-China relation to the breaking point. Following the announcement of Kissinger's first visit to Beijing in July 1971 and the revelation that Nixon would soon visit China, the ALP sent a letter to the CCP criticizing China's diplomatic direction. In his China diary, Hoxha outlined the contents of the letter. China's moves were a "major opportunist mistake," "wrong in principle, strategy and tactics." China should wage a "stern and uncompromising, blow for blow struggle . . . with American imperialism and with Soviet social-imperialism," not cavort with their leaders. Nixon was a "fascist" and a "murderer of peoples, an enemy of communism, of socialism, especially of China" and Albania. Such warm reception of US imperialist representatives as was given Kissinger would "confuse the world revolutionary movement and damp down the revolutionary impetus . . . and gravely damage the new Marxist-Leninist parties which have looked upon China and Mao Tsetung as the pillar of the revolution and defenders of Marxism-Leninism."[35] According to Hoxha, Beijing never replied to or even mentioned the ALP letter to the CCP, a treatment Hoxha termed a "silent boycott."[36] Several months after the APL letter to the CCP, the Chinese party informed Tirana that the CCP would not send a delegation to the upcoming Sixth Party Congress of the APL. Hoxha saw this as a statement of "opposition to our party on matters of principle" in response to the APL's July 1971 letter. Hoxha found China's attitude "cold" and "insulting."

Shortly before Nixon arrived in Beijing in February 1972, the Albanian newspaper *Zëri i popullit* carried an article criticizing those who failed to follow the principles of Marxism-Leninism. According to Hoxha's diary, the article was directed at the CCP's mistaken diplomacy. A "primary duty" of Marxist-Leninist parties was to assist the new Marxist-Leninist parties "which have just been formed in nearly all the countries of the world." China's recent diplomatic moves failed to do this, and were premised on "nationalist motives" camouflaged with revolutionary propaganda. "China is gradually abandoning its revolutionary line . . . and [adopting] an opportunist, liberal, revisionist line," undertaking "softening and agreement with American imperialism and the other capitalist countries."[37] After the Albanian article was published, Ambassador Geng Biao dispatched a Xinhua reporter to inquire who had authored it. From Beijing's perspective, Hoxha was waging open, polemical warfare against China's policies and principles, charging Mao and the CCP with unprincipled betrayal of the world revolution.

Beijing dispatched Qiao Guanhua to Tirana in September 1972 to attempt to persuade Albanian leaders to endorse Beijing's new relation with the United States.[38] Qiao did not mention the APL letter of July 1971, but Hoxha understood Qiao's presentation as the CCP response to that letter. Qiao explained China's new diplomatic approach as exploiting contradictions between imperialist

308 { China's Quest

and social imperialist enemies. Quotes from Lenin and Stalin were offered. Stalin's 1939 nonaggression pact with Nazi Germany was offered by Qiao as a "weighty argument." Hoxha remained unpersuaded; Qiao's arguments had "no foundation" and were "provocative," the Albanian leader said.[39] Hoxha rejected Qian's premise of a dire Soviet threat. The Soviet Union was afraid of a world war and would not attack China, the Albanian dictator believed. The next month, China informed Albania it would not be able to fulfill Tirana's request for economic aid during that country's 1975–1980 Five Year Plan.

Hoxha felt that the wrong side had won the power struggle within the CCP. Hoxha identified with the ideologically grounded Chen Boda–Jiang Qing group, and saw Zhou and his supporters as hidden rightists who should be purged by continuation of the Cultural Revolution. (Chen Boda had been purged along with Lin Biao.) Hoxha understood that Zhou Enlai favored scrapping support for the world revolution, in practice if not in rhetoric. Instead, Zhou's "opportunist, liberal" line premised China's foreign policies on China's national interests like security and development. The clash of ideas between Hoxha and China's Maoist radicals on the one hand, and Zhou Enlai and Li Xiannian on the other, reflects very nicely the movement of the PRC away from revolutionary activism.

Sino-American Rapprochement and Pakistan's Partition

While China was initiating cooperation with the United States to oppose the expansion of Soviet influence, it simultaneously suffered a serious setback to that effort in South Asia. Pakistan, a strategic partner of China since 1964 and a major factor in China's effort to constrain a hostile India, was torn apart by Soviet-backed India. The Indian-engineered secession of East Pakistan and transformation of that entity into the independent state of Bangladesh substantially diminished China's position in South Asia, putting into place one important element of the chain of Soviet "encirclement" that would come to dominate China's foreign policy for a decade.

China's strategic partnership with Pakistan developed unimpaired throughout the Cultural Revolution. Chairman Mao personally ordered that China's ties with Pakistan would be exempt from Red Guard disruption, and Zhou Enlai ensured that this directive was respected.[40] Red Guards were not allowed to organize within China's embassy in Pakistan, and Pakistan was the only Asian country not criticized by otherwise freewheeling Red Guards. Pakistan moved to improve ties with Moscow following the 1965 war, but gave Beijing assurances that these moves did not signify a weakening of Pakistan's commitment to China. Beijing in turn gave Pakistan pledges of political support on the Kashmir issue and military support in the event of an Indian attack on Pakistan.[41]

China also emerged as Pakistan's major arms supplier, supplying gratis 200 main battle tanks, 120 MiG-19 jet fighters, and arms and equipment for two infantry divisions. China also helped Pakistan build up its domestic military-industrial complex.[42] During the Cultural Revolution, China also pushed a road through the rugged Karakorum Mountains over which Chinese supplies (and perhaps forces) could reach Pakistan in the event of another war with India. Work on that road by PLA engineering troops started in 1966. Construction was difficult and dangerous, but the road was passable by truck by 1969, linking Kashgar in westernmost China to Gigot in Pakistani Kashmir. Steady improvement on the road continued over the next five decades.[43] Figure 11-1 illustrates the alignment of the Karakoram Highway

FIGURE 11-1 China, the United States, and the India-Pakistan War of 1971

and other locations relevant to the East Pakistan crisis of 1971. Indian leaders were dismayed by the formation of the China-Pakistan partnership, and that dismay contributed to India's decision to intervene in East Pakistan to separate that region from Pakistan.

The creation of Bangladesh out of East Pakistan arose out of deep ethnic cleavages between the Bengali-speaking people of East Pakistan and the Punjabis who constituted a substantial plurality in West Pakistan and dominated Pakistan's national institutions, including most importantly, the army. Those two very different peoples—Bengalis and Punjabis—had been joined together into the single nation of Pakistan in 1947 on the basis of their common Muslim religion. Islam did not prove enough to hold the nation together. A Bengali movement arose in East Pakistan in the late 1960s to push for a restructuring of relations between the two wings of the country. Gradually that movement moved from demanding greater regional autonomy to demanding independence. A turning point was reached in March 1971, when Pakistan's central government, led by General and President Yahya Khan (who had replaced Field Marshal Ayub Khan by military coup in March 1969) ordered the arrest of the leaders of the Bengali movement and the imposition of order in the turbulent east by the Pakistani army. Ruthless and frequently bloody repression spread across East Pakistan. This happened just as Beijing and Washington were maneuvering toward rapprochement.

Many national rebellions with deep historical and social roots ultimately succeed because of foreign intervention. French assistance to the American rebellion of the 1770s is one example. This was the case with Indian assistance to the Bengali rebellion. Indian intervention in East Pakistan, first in the form of covert assistance to the Bengali liberation movement and then, in December, in the form of outright invasion, was critical to the creation of Bangladesh. India acted with Soviet backing.

India had begun moving much closer to the Soviet Union in 1969 as Indira Gandhi adopted a more socialist approach to development—and as mounting Soviet-Chinese conflict prompted Moscow to look for partners to counter China. Indian-Soviet ties became closer still in 1971 as India moved toward overt intervention in East Pakistan. In August, India and the Soviet Union signed a mutual security treaty. Article IX of that treaty provided that the two countries would "immediately consult" to "remove" and "take appropriate effective measures to assure . . . the security" of the two countries, should either come under attack or threat of attack. This treaty was essentially an Indian insurance policy against Chinese intervention in the upcoming Indian intervention in East Pakistan. New Delhi calculated that the threat of Soviet intervention would deter Chinese intervention to counter India's planned action. The memory of China's threatened intervention in the 1965 India-Pakistan war was strong.

India's alignment with Moscow, and especially the conclusion of the August treaty, had a deep impact on Chinese policy. After the treaty was signed, China's media increasingly framed Indian policies as part of a Soviet effort to encircle China. India's alignment with Moscow also laid the basis for the US handling of the crisis: if China acted to support its ally Pakistan, and if the Soviet Union acted against China in accord with its obligations under the August treaty while the United States did nothing as China was "humiliated" (to use Kissinger's words) by the Soviet Union, the emerging Sino-US rapprochement could collapse and any hope of a US-PRC entente to balance the Soviet Union would be destroyed.[44] The strategic basis of the emerging PRC-US relation was common opposition to Soviet expansionism. If the United States now stood by and did nothing while Moscow and its Indian ally partitioned Pakistan, Mao and Zhou might doubt US commitment to the new anti-Soviet partnership.

Zhou Enlai saw early on that Pakistani resort to a military solution of Pakistan's deepening West-East conflict carried great dangers for that country. During a visit to China by President Yahya Khan in late 1970, Zhou urged the Pakistani leader to find a fair solution to the problems facing Pakistan. After elections in December 1970 that produced two ethnically distinct legislatures in West and East Pakistan, Zhou wrote to leaders of both wings urging them to find a satisfactory political settlement.[45] Again in April 1971, as bloodshed in the east escalated, Zhou expressed China's concern for Pakistan's future to high-level Pakistani envoys. Unless a political solution was quickly found, Zhou said, there could be grave consequences for Pakistan. The use of military force against East Pakistan's civilian population could be disastrous, Zhou warned.[46]

Zhou understood the deep roots of the Bengali rebellion and was aware that in many ways it was a classic national liberation struggle. He also apparently understood that the Bengali liberation movement might succeed, leaving China in a position of needing to court a new Bangladeshi state. And in any case, China was not in a position to prevent Indian intervention. But China could not abandon its ally Pakistan. Thus Beijing balanced between inactivity that would alienate Islamabad, and activity that would endanger China's ties with a future Bangladeshi state.[47]

In April 1971, as bloodshed in East Pakistan mounted, with Pakistani repression countered by growing Indian covert support for the Bengali resistance, China delivered a protest to India condemning India's "gross interference" in Pakistan's internal affairs. The note warned that Pakistan would have China's "firm support" if Indian expansionists dared launch aggression against Pakistan.[48] China's media and foreign propaganda polemicized against Indian and Soviet interference in East Pakistan. The same month, Pakistan's rulers sought a pledge of Chinese intervention in the event of an Indian attack. Beijing declined. After deliberating over Pakistan's request,

Beijing informed Islamabad that while Pakistan would have China's strong political and material support, China was not in a position to intervene militarily in hostilities in the subcontinent, even international hostilities.[49] China did agree, however, to provide Pakistan with substantial additional military equipment.

In November 1971, only weeks before India's outright invasion of East Pakistan, one of West Pakistan's leading civilian, populist, and pro-Chinese leaders, Zulfikar Ali Bhutto, led a high-level delegation to Beijing to plead for reversal of China's April decision against intervention. Bhutto wanted China to promise diversionary actions in the Himalayas to hold down Indian forces in the event of war. Again China declined.[50] Beijing agreed only to fire a few "empty cannons." In November, acting foreign minister Ji Pengfei (Chen Yi was dying of cancer) declared, "Our Pakistani friends may rest assured that should Pakistan be subjected to foreign aggression, the Chinese government and people will, as always, resolutely support the Pakistan government and people in their just struggle to defend their state, sovereignty and national independence.[51] Ji's statement did not mention defense of Pakistan's "territorial integrity." The themes of Ji's statement were repeated by Chinese representatives on several occasions as the crisis reached its climax. Pakistani representatives greatly exaggerated prospects for Chinese intervention. Beijing did not publicly contradict these exaggerations, probably because they were part of Pakistan's efforts to deter Indian invasion. That invasion came on December 4, following a preemptive Pakistani air strike against Indian air bases the previous day. Fighting lasted twelve days; Pakistani forces surrendered on December 16.

The most effective Chinese instrument of influence over India at this juncture was Beijing's emerging anti-hegemony partnership with the United States. Nixon and Kissinger saw parallel US and Chinese approaches toward Indian and Soviet policies as an opportunity to put into action their vision of Sino-American strategic cooperation. They also believed that if Soviet-backed India were allowed to completely eviscerate Pakistan, prospects for establish a balance constraining the Soviet Union would be greatly diminished.[52] In a meeting in New York City on December 10, in the midst of fierce fighting between Indian and Pakistani forces in East Pakistan, Kissinger met with China's newly appointed United Nations representative Huang Hua to work out a common approach to the South Asian crisis. Nixon and Kissinger had received an intelligence report indicating that Indian leader Indira Gandhi intended to turn India's military forces against West Pakistan once Pakistani forces in the east surrendered. Unless this was prevented, India would achieve, with Soviet backing, domination of South Asia.[53] Kissinger told Huang:

> The Pakistani army in the East has been destroyed. The Pakistani army in the West will run out of [gasoline] in another two or three weeks . . .

We think that the immediate objective must be to prevent an attack on the West Pakistan army by India. We are afraid that if nothing is done to stop it, East Pakistan will a Bhutan and West Pakistan will become a Nepal. And India with Soviet help would be free to turn its energies elsewhere.... It is our judgment, with great sorrow, that the Pakistan army in two weeks will disintegrate in the west as it has in the east.... We are looking for a way to protect what is left of Pakistan ... both of us must continue to bring pressure on India and the Soviet Union.... So we are prepared to listen to any practical proposals for parallel action.[54]

"When I asked for this meeting," Kissinger told Huang, "I did so to suggest Chinese military help, to be quite honest." In order to preserve West Pakistan's military strength, Kissinger continued, "We are ... prepared to attempt to assemble a maximum amount of pressure in order to deter India." While Kissinger thus pushed for Chinese military pressure on India's northern frontiers, US leaders were deciding to deploy a naval task force to the Bay of Bengal in a demonstration of force intended to deter India from striking West Pakistan. The same day Kissinger met with Huang Hua in New York, December 10, US leaders decided to move warships from the Pacific through the Malacca Strait to the Bay of Bengal as a warning to Moscow not to act militarily against China under the August treaty. Nixon and Kissinger expected China to act in support of Pakistan, and saw the naval demonstration in the Bay of Bengal as a way of encouraging the Soviets to advise New Delhi not to move against West Pakistan, or failing that, of deterring a Soviet move against China under the August treaty. Parallel military pressure from the United States and China would help prevent an Indian attack against West Pakistan that might destroy the remaining strength of that country.

Huang Hua promised to convey Kissinger's proposals to Zhou Enlai, but otherwise evaded Kissinger's call in New York for Chinese military demonstrations.[55] On December 16, however, six days after the Kissinger-Huang talks and on the very day that Pakistan's forces in the east surrendered, China issued a "strong protest" of "grave encroachments" by Indian violations of Chinese territory on the "China-Sikkim boundary."[56] By the time the Chinese protest was delivered, the Himalayan roads were already blocked by snow and thus impassable, a fact well understood by military leaders. Indian intelligence had watched carefully China's words and military movements during the East Pakistan crisis, and was confident that China would not intervene in this India-Pakistan war. But the US task force, including ten ships and headed by the aircraft carrier USS *Enterprise*, entered the Bay of Bengal on December 15. Parallel PRC and US military diplomacy during the 1971 India-Pakistan war demonstrated very clearly the possibilities for Sino-American cooperation based on common interests. Zhou Enlai later told Z. A. Bhutto that US diplomacy had saved West Pakistan.[57]

According to Kissinger, the real Chinese concern during the 1971 crisis was the precedent being set by which countries could be dismembered by Indian-Soviet collusion.[58] Beijing's specific worry was Tibet. Chinese rule in Tibet was extremely cruel during the Cultural Revolution—indeed, during the entire 1959–1978 period. Tibetan traditions were ruthlessly repressed by PLA occupation forces. Policies of "militant atheism" were imposed on a deeply religious people. The economy was ground down by collectivized agriculture, suppression of private economic activity, isolation from India, and forced agriculturalization of traditionally herding peoples. Tibetans were very poor, far worse off than people in China proper. Han Chinese cadres ruled over sullen and impoverished Tibetans. Any manifestation of protest was met with draconian punishment. Under these conditions, Tibet's indigenous population would almost certainly have welcomed Indian forces as liberators.

As noted earlier, following the 1962 war India had built up a division-size (about 10,000 men), professionally trained and armed force of ethnic Tibetans commanded by Indian Army officers. In peacetime, the Tibetan force helped patrol India's border with Tibet. But in wartime it was configured to undertake deep-penetration commando operations into Tibet, possibly in coordination with India's regular forces. In fact, during the 1960s India's Intelligence Bureau and America's Central Intelligence Agency had drafted plans for the liberation of Tibet.[59] The Dali Lama's government in exile in northern India might return to Tibet with a joyous welcome from the long-oppressed Tibetans, and build up indigenous Tibetan military forces around a core already formed from Tibetan refugees in India and armed by the Soviet Union. India's military forces had been transformed from the 1962 debacle by a decade of buildup. Those forces had just tested and vindicated in East Pakistan the strategy of intervention in support of indigenous insurrection. The Soviet Union would have been tempted to support such an Indian move in 1971–1972, since Beijing was finally moving toward the alignment with the United States that Moscow had long dreaded. Of course, if Soviet support for India in a Sino-Indian war meant, for Moscow, confrontation with the United States, that would be a very different matter. PRC alignment with the United States made Soviet-Indian intervention in Tibet far less likely.

12 }

Countering Soviet Encirclement and Trying to Preserve Mao's Legacy

Zhou's Diplomatic Skill Becomes a Liability

Zhou Enlai's handling of the rapprochement with the United States was masterful. Although Zhou ensured that each step of that process was approved in advance by Mao, Zhou carried out the very difficult and potentially risky process with considerable aplomb. Zhou was well aware of Mao's propensity to see opposition and conspiracy among his close associates, and he was careful to keep the focus of China's domestic media on Chairman Mao's role in the rapprochement process. Zhou severely rebuked Xinhua News Agency, for example, for conveying foreign media reports praising Zhou rather than Mao's role in the process of Sino-US rapprochement.[1] Abroad, opinion frequently focused on Zhou's diplomatic skill and grace, often placing him at the center of the rapprochement process. Mao assigned his two young female English interpreters, Nancy Tang and his grandniece Wang Hairong, to follow foreign coverage of Zhou and his diplomacy, and report regularly to him on it. As laudatory foreign commentary on Zhou presented by the "two Misses" accumulated, Mao began to feel that Zhou was overshadowing him. Since the demise of Lin Biao, Zhou was effectively the second-ranking person in the hierarchy—a position that always roused Mao's suspicion. Mao had already purged two of his first lieutenants, Liu Shaoqi and Lin Biao. Zhou was acutely aware of his vulnerability and did everything he could to reassure Mao of his absolute loyalty. But Zhou could not control what the foreign media said.

Mao badly needed a boost to his public standing. The falling-out between Mao and Lin Biao, followed by Lin's attempted flight to the Soviet Union and the fantastic explanation of Lin's relation with Mao released subsequent to Lin's demise, left many people in China with doubts about Mao's sagacity. If the charges against Lin were true, how was it possible that Mao had permitted a long-time traitor and schemer so close to the center of power? If the charges

315

were not true, what did that say about China's politics? The whole Lin Biao affair made Mao seem either like fool or a liar in many people's eyes. The high drama of the Sino-American rapprochement was a welcome diversion from China's unseemly domestic politics, and went some distance toward relegitimizing Mao's rule. But Zhou, it seemed to Mao, was stealing too much of the credit for China's diplomatic successes.

Mao, according to Zhou's biographer Gao Wenqian, also wanted to strengthen the position of the remaining Cultural Revolution radicals (Jiang Qing, Zhang Chunqiao, Wang Hongwen, etc.) as an ideological safeguard on Zhou and the just-rehabilitated Deng Xiaoping at the forthcoming Tenth Congress scheduled for August 1973. Mao saw Jiang Qing's radicals as the protectors of the "correct verdicts" removing revisionists during the Cultural Revolution and of the radical policies implemented during the Cultural Revolution. Mao understood that Jiang Qing's group could not run China's economy or state, and did not want to remove Zhou. Mao realized that no one except Zhou or possibly Deng could administer China's sprawling state and economy. But both Zhou and Deng had to meet Mao's test of his loyalty to the Cultural Revolution. Mao suspected that if, someday, Zhou ended up as China's top leader, perhaps merely by outliving Mao, he would focus exclusively on economic development, quickly returning China to the revisionism of the early 1960s. Greater empowerment of the radicals was thus required, and deflating Zhou's status as a diplomatic genius was part of this. Thus, Mao started a campaign criticizing Zhou's putative "rightist capitulation" to the United States.

In June 1973, Mao began to insinuate that Zhou's diplomacy had abandoned revolution to curry favor with the United States. The head of the US Liaison Office in Beijing, George H. W. Bush, delivered to Zhou a copy of the Soviet-US-British nuclear nonproliferation treaty, briefed Zhou on the contents of that treaty, and passed on a personal letter from Nixon to Zhou. Staffers in the MFA drafted a report based on these materials and passed it on to Zhou, who added some editorial commentary before passing it on to Mao. Mao crossed out all of Zhou's comments, adding that Zhou was too soft in dealing with the Americans. Mao then passed the document back to the MFA with the acid observation that "When joining hands with the bourgeoisie, one tends to forget struggle."[2]

Mao's effort to undermine Zhou's diplomacy continued the next month when the MFA drafted another report on Soviet-US nuclear nonproliferation cooperation. The two superpowers planned in this way to control the world, the MFA report concluded. Apprised of the report by Nancy Tang and Wang Hairong, Mao again condemned the MFA document for avoiding the correct view that "revolution is the basic trend in the world today." The document was revisionist, Mao concluded, as he warned others not to get on Zhou Enlai's "pirate ship"[3] Mao also had Nancy Tang and Wang Hairong spread the rumor that Zhou was frightened by Soviet nuclear threats and had committed China to military cooperation with the United States in exchange for US nuclear protection. Jiang Qing and her followers were delighted that Mao had turned against Zhou, their long-time rival for power and influence with Mao, and seized the opportunity to attack Zhou. Zhou was a "rightist capitulationist," "selling out the national autonomy," and "getting down on your hands and knees to the Americans," Jiang charged.[4] An inadvertent undermining of China's position arising out of the separation of powers in the US political system further eroded Zhou's position.

Zhou's Betrayal by the Americans in Cambodia

Policy toward Cambodia became an arena of conflict between Zhou and CCP radicals. China began supplying large-scale aid to the Khmer Rouge when Sihanouk was ousted by a coup in March 1970. Over the next five years, Beijing gave two million US dollars per year to the Khmer Rouge. Office and living accommodations in Beijing were also provided for Khmer Rouge leaders, while Sihanouk was given the old French embassy for a residence.[5] With strong Chinese support, areas under Khmer Rouge expanded rapidly. In those expanding base areas, the Khmer Rouge began implementing radical policies—collectivization of farming, communal meals, free distribution of goods, militarized labor—along with genocidal anti-Vietnamese and anti-Chinese policies. Zhou calculated that these misguided policies (similar to those of China's Great Leap Forward) would lead to economic decline and popular resistance. Later, when Khmer Rouge seized Phnom Penh and began killing off the old elites, Zhou, then in the hospital and dying of cancer, warned the Khmer leaders to avoid the mistakes of extremism committed previously by the CCP. In reply, Khmer Rouge leaders reportedly smiled condescendingly at Zhou.[6]

In mid-1973, following the January peace agreement between Hanoi, Washington, and Saigon, Beijing undertook together with the United States an effort to install in Cambodia a coalition government including most of the leaders of the US-supported Phnom Penh government but headed by Sihanouk.[7] The purpose of this arrangement was to avoid an absolute military victory and unrestricted rule by the Khmer Rouge. Zhou Enlai was the principal architect of this scheme on the Chinese side, although he would certainly not have undertaken this risky move had it not been approved by Mao. Zhou had concluded that unchecked Khmer Rouge rule of Cambodia would lead to ultraleftist and extreme anti-Vietnamese policies that would lead, in turn, to a Vietnamese takeover of Cambodia. This would indeed prove to be the case in 1978.[8] On the other hand, Sihanouk was a well-known quality to China, had proved himself to be quite amenable to China's advice over the years, and was determined to keep Vietnam from dominating his country. Putting Sihanouk back in power in Phnom Penh, strengthened by major elements of the existing Phnom Penh government plus Chinese and American support, would act as a barrier to implementation of the ultrarevolutionary policies of the Khmer Rouge and thus Vietnamese domination.

By 1973, it was clear to Zhou that Hanoi sought to bring both Cambodia and Laos under its domination once South Vietnam was conquered. With Soviet backing, this Hanoi-led "Indochinese federation" would have substantial influence in Southeast Asia. Thus, keeping Cambodia fully independent of Vietnamese domination was, Zhou concluded, a key to thwarting Hanoi's "Indochina federation" scheme, and a broad Sihanouk-led coalition government in Phnom Penh was the best way to achieve that. To this end, in May, Huang Hua, then ambassador to the United Nations, informed Henry Kissinger that China was willing to convey to Sihanouk (then residing in Beijing and nominal head of the united front that included the Khmer Rouge) an American-drafted proposal to initiate negotiations toward constituting a Sihanouk-led coalition government for Cambodia. The incentive for the Khmer Rouge to agree to this arrangement was an end to the heavy US bombing of Cambodia that had been underway for many months by mid-1973, with devastating effect on Khmer Rouge forces. The prospect of an end to that bombing was the incentive Zhou Enlai would offer to induce the Khmer Rouge to forgo total rule and accept a subordinate position in a Sihanouk-led government. By mid-1973, the United States and the PRC were working in tandem toward the common objective of keeping Cambodia free from domination by Hanoi.

The leverage of US bombing, underpinning the key role that China was to play in persuading the Khmer Rouge to compromise, evaporated when the US Congress mandated at the end of June a cutoff of all funding for US combat operations in or over all of Indochina. Two weeks after the congressional cutoff, Han Xu informed Brent Scowcroft that, for a variety of reasons, China would no longer able to communicate the US proposal to Sihanouk. When a US congressional delegation visited Beijing a month later, met with Zhou, and bragged about Congress' role in ending US bombing, Zhou became visibly angry. The US legislators could not understand why Zhou was unhappy with congressional action cutting off bombing long condemned by China, including by Zhou himself in his opening remarks to the congressional delegation.

The 1973 PRC-US effort to install a neutralist government in Phnom Penh was one of the first efforts by the two countries to work in tandem toward common objectives. It failed because of an abrupt American volte-face. After China had put its credibility with various Cambodian parties on the line by agreeing to transmit Washington's proposal to Sihanouk and the Khmer Rouge, the United States Congress jerked away the key premise of China's role in the joint effort—the prospect of an end to US bombing that would persuade the Khmer Rouge to accept a limited role in postwar Cambodia. Mao and his Politburo comrades probably understood little of the unfamiliar US system of separation of powers with its sometimes counterproductive results. It was far easier for them to see behind the US "betrayal" some grand scheme intended to undermine China's standing in Southeast Asia and deny victory to Cambodia's revolutionary forces.

Jiang Qing and her radical followers seized on Zhou's effort to "betray" Cambodia's revolutionary forces, the Khmer Rouge, by cooperating with the Americans to deny the Khmer Rouge complete victory. The way to secure the PRC, Jiang insisted in line with Mao's old tune, was by militant support for revolution in the intermediate zone, not by cutting deals with imperialism to thwart revolutionary seizure of power. In terms of China's Cambodia policy, Zhou concluded that absolute Khmer Rouge rule was inevitable, and that China had to adopt its policy to that reality. As vice foreign minister Qiao Guanghau told Kissinger in October 1973, the wise course was now to "Let the flames burning in Cambodia extinguish themselves, by themselves."[9] When Phnom Penh fell to the Khmer Rouge in April 1975, Maoist leader Zhang Chunqiao made a secret visit to Cambodia to demonstrate support for the new regime. China also agreed to give US$1 billion in assistance to the Khmer Rouge regime. This was China's largest aid pledge up to that point.[10] The Khmer Rouge victory in spite of Zhou's effort to channel them into a secondary role in a coalition government demonstrated the incorrectness of Zhou Enlai's pragmatic diplomacy—at least in the opinion of China's Maoist leaders.

The Duke of Zhou Toppled

The radicals' campaign to criticize Zhou's "right capitulationist" diplomacy gained steam with a ten-day (November 25–December 5, 1973) Politburo criticism session. Deng Xiaoping was among the participants in this session, brought back from Cultural Revolution exile in Jiangxi by Mao especially to participate in this session. This marked the beginning of Deng's rehabilitation. Mao rehabilitated Deng because he needed someone who could replace Zhou. But Mao wanted Deng to pass yet another ideological litmus test, this time by criticizing Zhou's capitulationist diplomacy. The session began with a briefing by Nancy Tang on Zhou's errors. Zhou, Tang said, was "ready to be a puppet of the Soviet invaders" and was "running an independent kingdom." Participants in the session joined in criticism of Zhou; not to have done so would have been politically risky, given that Mao had authorized the session. Zhou, following his usual practice, made a self-criticism.[11]

Deng apparently passed this test. Following the late 1973 Politburo criticism of Zhou's diplomacy, Mao designated Deng to deliver a statement by China at the April 1974 Sixth Special Session of the United Nations on raw materials and development. Mao's designation of Deng rather that Zhou to deliver this statement—the first by a top Chinese leader to the United Nations—was part of Mao's effort to degrade Zhou's position and groom Deng as a more politically reliable successor (or so Mao hoped) to manage China's state sector.[12] Mao's message to the Chinese people and the world in appointing Deng rather than Zhou to deliver this high-profile speech at the UN was this: Zhou Enlai does not speak for China. In early 1975—the last year of Zhou's life—Jiang Qing's radicals intensified their criticism of Zhou's diplomacy, making public many of the charges leveled during the closed Politburo session.

But one final effort by Zhou would later bear fruit. In January 1975, Zhou, with Deng Xiaoping's assistance, drafted a program shifting China's emphasis from political struggle to economic development. The Four Modernizations (of agriculture, industry, science and technology, and national defense) was designed to turn China into a world power. Opposition by CCP radicals and lack of interest by Mao would prevent its immediate implementation. But once Deng became paramount leader in December 1978, the Four Modernizations would be revived and driven forward with great vigor. In helping Zhou draft the Four Modernizations program, Deng convinced him that he, Deng, was committed to China's economic modernization, whatever his professed loyalty to Chairman Mao's line might be. This positioned Deng to inherit Zhou's very considerable base of support when the premier died.[13]

The conflict between Zhou and Jiang Qing over foreign policy, like Mao's effort to undercut Zhou because of his management of foreign policy, was not really about foreign policy. It was about Zhou's great prestige and influence within the CCP and PLA elite. Mao did not really disagree with Zhou's foreign policy; Zhou was, in fact, executing Mao's policies. Rather, Mao seized on diplomacy as a way of undermining Zhou because he feared Zhou would "reverse verdicts" on the Cultural Revolution if Zhou survived him with his prestige undiminished. Jiang Qing and Zhang Chunqiao attacked Zhou on his "rightist capitulationist" diplomacy, but they did so because Mao gave them a green light. Jiang's group was in no position to critique the substance of Zhou's diplomacy, because it was Mao's diplomacy. The radical attack on Zhou's diplomacy was merely a foil. The real question was who would dominate the political scene after Mao.

Nonetheless, the radical attack on Zhou's "rightist capitulationism" did influence China's diplomacy in areas other than Cambodia. Sino-US relations chilled briefly. From mid-1974 through 1976, Beijing became much more abrasive in dealings with US representatives. Acerbic rhetoric replaced earlier silky handling. The atmosphere of President Ford's December 1975 visit was chilly. Foreign Minister Qiao Guanhua felt compelled to deliver a direct critique of US foreign policy, to which Kissinger felt complied to rebut with equal directness. When a new head to the US Liaison Office was appointed in 1976, it took Hua Guofeng four months to receive him. And in mid-1976, Zhang Chunqiao gave a speech in which he offered to use bayonets to help the United States solve its Taiwan problem.[14]

Deng's Return and His Demonstrated Competence at Recovering Lost Territory

On December 22, 1973, seventeen days after the end of the Politburo criticism session of Zhou's "rightist capitulationist" diplomacy, Deng Xiaoping was appointed to the Politburo and the Central Military Commission to participate in leadership work.[15] A month later, Deng was appointed to a five-person leadership small group in military affairs, headed by Ye Jianying.[16] Deng was reportedly nominated for the group by Ye, though he was certainly approved by Mao. Deng and Ye worked closely together to conduct the recovery of lost territory in the South China Sea. In doing this, Deng was able to demonstrate to senior PLA and CCP leaders—critical constituencies if Deng was someday to succeed Zhou—that he was able to recover Chinese territory encroached on by imperialist aggression. He was a practical leader able to get things done.

The South China Sea is a shallow but much navigated body of water, with some 150 small islands plus many reefs, submerged and surface-breaking rocks, sand bars, and so on. These waters and islands have been visited for centuries by fishing and other vessels from Vietnam, the Philippines, and China. Islands in the northern group, the Paracels, and the southern group, the Spratlys, were used by various militaries (Japanese in the 1930s and 1940s, the United States in the 1950s and 1960s) for meteorological, resupply, and intelligence purposes. In the late 1960s, the region became more important when surveys indicated that the sea floor might contain large deposits of oil and gas. Additional international attention to maritime territories emerged with the onset of United Nations deliberations in 1973 that would, nearly a decade later, culminate in the Convention on the Law of the Sea.

China's government first asserted China's ownership of the islands in the South China Sea during recent times in 1939, as Japan began its fateful push into Southeast Asia. After Japan's surrender, the ROC foreign ministry again asserted China's claim, this time in the form of a dashed line drawn around the periphery of the South China Sea on a 1947 map with the apparent purpose (although it was never spelled out) of illustrating the scope of China's territorial waters. This was the origin of China's nine-dashed-line which would begin appearing routinely on PRC publications (eventually including the inside face page of Chinese passports) in the 1990s to inculcate in Chinese minds the belief that these islands and waters were Chinese.[17] While territorial nationalism would become strong in the 1990s, it was not publicly expressed in the PRC circa 1974. Yet the opportunity for China's seizure of the Paracel Islands was ripe in 1974, as described below. And seizure of the Paracels would show CCP leaders how realistic and pragmatic moves, rather than extreme ideology, could strengthen China's international position.

Hanoi, for its part, believed that most of the islands in the South China Sea belonged to Vietnam, but it kept silent about those beliefs during North Vietnam's long and desperate war with the United States—in other words, while Hanoi needed China's help. Starting in 1959, small confrontations occurred between Chinese and South Vietnamese personnel on islands in the South China Sea, leading the Chinese MFA to issue a protest against South Vietnam's violations of China's territorial sovereignty. On these occasions, Hanoi said nothing. US military forces also conducted intense operations in the South China Sea as part of the long war with North Vietnam. The fact that China believed those activities were conducted on Chinese territory deepened the "contradictions" between Washington and Hanoi. Hanoi would have gained nothing by asserting its own ownership of these territories. Thus Hanoi stayed silent—until the Americans had been defeated.

Before that happened, however, and while the US-DRV war was still underway, in 1970 the PLA navy began sending ships to the Paracels to collect meteorological and oceanic data. PLA forces then proceeded to set up small but permanent stations on islands in the eastern Amphitrite group of the Paracels. At that time, there were also a small number of South Vietnamese forces on several tiny islands in the western group of the Paracels. In 1972, the Saigon government began to contract blocks of the South China Sea floor to international oil majors for petroleum exploration.[18] In the Chinese account, in mid-January 1974 South Vietnamese forces fired on Chinese soldiers in the western Crescent group, leading PLA forces to return fire in self-defense. In response, on January 18–20, 1974, Ye Jianying and Deng Xiaoping's leadership small group ordered the occupation of the South Vietnamese–held islands. Several hundred PLA soldiers were shifted quickly from Woody Island in the eastern group to overwhelm the small South Vietnamese garrisons on islands in the western group.[19] The confrontation culminated in a thirty-seven-minute clash on January 19 in which a South Vietnamese corvette was sunk and other South Vietnamese ships retreated from the scene, leaving the contested islands under full Chinese control. An American advisor captured with the South Vietnamese was quietly repatriated to US custody in Hong Kong several weeks after Chinese forces took the islands. The PLA then moved to consolidate control over the entire Paracel group, using Woody Island as a base for a push from to the Spratlys a decade later. Figure 12-1 illustrates the Paracel and Spratly Islands.

January 1974 was an opportune time for Beijing to take the Paracels. Hanoi was still locked in confrontation with the Saigon regime. Not until October 1974 (two months after Richard Nixon's resignation as president) would the VWP decide to launch the offensive that would begin in December and end

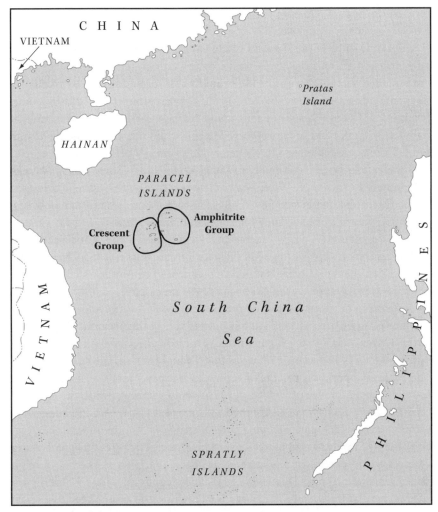

FIGURE 12-1 The Paracels Islands and the 1974 "Recovery" Operation

five months later with Hanoi's complete victory. Hanoi was already moving uncomfortably close toward Moscow, at least from Beijing's perspective. On the other hand, Beijing could be confident that the United States would not oppose China's seizure of the Paracels. Before seizing the Crescent Group, Beijing had tested the US attitude. In spring 1972, Beijing protested, privately, that US vessels had intruded into Chinese territorial waters around the Paracel Islands.[20] The United States replied to Beijing's protest by ignoring the sovereignty issue and indicating that the US navy would be instructed to stay at a distance of twelve miles from the islands. Twelve miles was the territorial limit claimed by the PRC. Washington thereby signaled acquiescence to China's claim. Beijing's rapprochement with the United States had created a much more benign American attitude toward the expansion of Chinese influence across many dimensions.

China's seizure of the Paracels made a deep impression on Hanoi. A year later, in early April 1975, three weeks before Saigon fell to northern forces but as South Vietnamese forces were rapidly disintegrating, North Vietnam's navy landed troops on six islands in the Spratly group then held by South Vietnamese forces. This move preempted Chinese seizure of these islands in a replay of January 1974. Hanoi feared that if it did not move quickly, China might. Then, a week after Saigon fell, Saigon's now VWP-controlled official newspaper published a colored map showing the Paracels and the Spratlys as Vietnamese territory. The Vietnamese view was that Southeast Asia belonged to the Southeast Asian peoples. China was not a Southeast Asian country, so China should not have such big territorial waters as it claimed.[21] China's leaders, for their part, were angered by Hanoi's insincerity: not objecting to China's claims in the South China Sea as long as they needed China's support against the Americans, but making territorial demands on China (from Beijing's view) as soon as the Americans were defeated.

The 1974 Paracels operation marked a shift away from revolution as a way of manifesting China's international influence. For the previous twenty-plus years, China's claim to greatness had primarily been its stalwart role in upholding Marxist-Leninist-Mao Zedong Thought within China and abroad. The Paracels operation marked a return to a much more traditional manifestation of the power of a state—expansion of territory under its effective control. The operation was designed and carried out by CCP leaders who wanted to end ideological struggle and campaigns—Zhou Enlai, Ye Jianying, and Deng Xiaoping—and focus instead on the practical realities of making China a world power. In a way, the Paracels operation was the first foreign policy manifestation of Zhou and Deng's Four Modernizations. Effective seizure of the Paracels made very clear why attention to China's technological and military power was important, and what the practical payoffs could be. The practical, effective conduct of the Paracels operation also highlighted for China's military and party elite Deng's strength, as opposed to the ideological rhetoric that was the forte of CCP Maoists. This did not save Deng from being purged, once again, by Mao in early 1976, but it probably strengthened Deng's appeal among China's leadership elite once Mao died and the real choice was between Deng Xiaoping, Zhang Chunqiao, and Hua Guofeng.

Mounting Fear of Soviet Encirclement

In the mid-1970s Mao became increasingly concerned with growing Soviet and declining American influence in Asia and the world. The Soviet Union seemed to be aggressively expanding its influence around the entire world, while the United States seemed to be withdrawing into isolationism, leaving power vacuums into which the Soviet Union expanded. China faced the stark possibility of becoming surrounded by the Soviet Union, or so Mao concluded. Powerful Soviet forces remained posed all along China's northern borders, from Manchuria through Mongolia to Xinjiang. New, mobile, solid-fuel and nuclear-armed intermediate range missiles, plus advanced Backfire bombers and ever more armored forces, were being deployed there by the mid-1970s. To China's south, starting in 1975, quick on the heels of Hanoi's absolute victory over Saigon, VWP-ruled Vietnam moved away from China and into alignment with the Soviet Union. Across Southeast Asia, countries began adjusting to the utter collapse of the US position in Indochina by moving toward accommodation with the powerful and very well-armed united Vietnam and its backer, the USSR. China was being placed between northern and southern jaws of a Soviet vice.

In South Asia, China's strategic partner Pakistan had been partitioned by Soviet-backed India, and India became a nuclear power in 1974 as part of what Mao saw as an Indian drive to achieve hegemony in South Asia with Soviet backing. In the Middle East, Iraq and Egypt, both major regional powers, signed friendship and cooperation treaties with the Soviet Union in 1972. Soviet naval construction programs launched after the Cuban crisis of 1962 were beginning to come on line by the late 1960s, and the Soviet naval presence in all the oceans of the world was growing rapidly. By 1968, the Soviet navy surpassed the US navy in terms of days of surface combat ships deployed in the Indian Ocean, and by 1972 it far exceeded the US navy in terms of number of port calls in the that ocean.[22] The Soviet navy had become preeminent in the Indian Ocean.

The breakup of the Portuguese empire in Africa in 1974–1975 and a Marxist military coup in Ethiopia in 1974 created opportunities that Moscow and its ally Cuba seized upon. Cuban military forces were deployed to Africa with Soviet support to bolster new Marxist allies there. By 1977, Cuba, with Soviet support, was the major extra-regional military power in Africa, with Cuban contingents supporting pro-Soviet governments in Ethiopia, Angola, and Mozambique. In Europe, NATO countries that had traditionally been bulwarks against the Soviet Union were shrinking defense budgets and military forces under the influence of détente mentality, or so it seemed to Beijing. European publics and governments were increasingly deluded, Beijing believed, into believing that concessions to the Soviet Union would render it more amicable. In fact, West European weakness would tempt the Soviet Union and make it more aggressive. All this was the Chinese view.

The seeming recession of US influence was the other half of the shift in the global correlation of forces perceived by Mao. The utter failure of the United States to support its client South Vietnamese state in 1974–1975 when Hanoi launched a large-scale conventional attack across the DMZ which overwhelmed Saigon shocked Mao. This was not how Mao had expected the United States to act. After creating the South Vietnamese state and supporting it for nineteen years (1954–1973), Mao was convinced, as he told visiting North Vietnamese leaders, that the United States would not simply abandon that state. Yet it did. The United States watched passively as North Vietnamese forces overwhelmed South Vietnam. Other US allies in Asia immediately began to question the credibility of US security guarantees. US acquiescence to Hanoi's overrunning of South Vietnam reflected congressional and public opinion in the United States. Executive power had been weakened by the Watergate episode, Nixon's impeachment and resignation, and congressional assertions of its war powers. Following the Vietnam debacle, US opinion swung sharply against US military involvement around the world, or at least in areas beyond Europe. An increasingly popular strain of thought was that the entire Cold War had been a huge mistake; there had never been a need to contain communism and/or the USSR. The entire containment project was an unnecessary, self-invented quest that had proved too costly and ultimately, in Vietnam, a failure. The United States needed to take a new course, away from being "the policeman of the world." Congress rejected President Ford's proposals for actions to counter Cuban-Soviet involvement in Africa. There was in the United States a strong desire to reap a "peace dividend." US defense budgets and size of military forces were cut.

Many of these trends contributed to the election of Jimmy Carter as president in November 1976. One of Carter's first actions as president was to order the withdrawal of US forces from Korea. (The move was soon reversed.) Carter believed that US foreign policy had long been in the grip of "an inordinate fear of communism" that had led the United States to intervene unnecessarily around the world. Many of the places that seemed to require US intervention in the 1970s, at least according to the old "inordinate fear" line of thinking, were to block Soviet advances. The United States seemed no longer willing to bear the burdens of being a world policeman, and was retreating into its traditional isolationism. A confidential report on the world situation by Foreign Minister Huang Hua in July 1977 summarized very well Beijing's concern over the direction of US policy:

> Isolationism is rising in the United States while [US] alienation of friendly nations is increasingly growing.... With American power shrinking and isolationism surging, the revisionist Soviet social-imperialists are filling the vacuum left by the United States and are taking advantage of US weakness to make expansionist and infiltrative moves. The retreat of US influence, and the policy of appeasement and conciliation fueled by Western countries, will . . . help increase the haughtiness of the revisionist Soviet social-imperialists, and confront other countries . . . with a more dangerous and horrendous enemy. It is the business of the whole

world to prevent the spread of revisionist Soviet social-imperialism's rampant aggressive forces.... We must unite with the Third World, win over the Second World, and take advantage of the splits between the two superpowers to divide them and to undermine the collusive scheme to divide the world behind the scenes. By winning the United Sates over to our side, we can concentrate all our forces to deal with the arch-enemy—revisionist Soviet social-imperialism.[23]

In response to the perceived adverse evolution of the global correlation of forces, Beijing unfolded a campaign, from roughly 1974 to about 1982, to nudge world events in a direction more favorable to China: a campaign to build a global united front against Soviet expansionism. The central idea of this campaign was that the Soviet challenge was global and had to be resisted globally. Beijing felt that the West was repeating its fatal mistake of the 1930s, when Britain and France had responded to the aggressive buildup of Germany's power with a policy of conciliation, giving in to Hitler's successive demands, and military weakness. The result had been seven years in which Hitler completed his strategic deployments and then launched a war from a very strong position. In the 1970s as in the 1930s, Beijing believed, weakness would embolden expansionism. But firm, resolute, tit-for-tat resistance by people around the world would check the Soviet Union and prevent it from launching a third world war.[24]

The conceptual framework for the global anti-Soviet front was the Three Worlds Theory announced to the world by Deng Xiaoping at the above-mentioned Special Session of the United Nations on raw materials and development in 1974. According to the Three Worlds Theory, the two superpowers, the USSR and the United States, constituted the First World. Both of these superpowers sought global hegemony and colluded and contended with each other in pursuit of that objective. The second world consisted of the industrialized countries other than the two superpowers—Western and Eastern Europe, Canada, Australia, and Japan. The Third World consisted of the developing countries of Asia, Africa, and Latin America. China was part of the Third World. Both the Second and the Third Worlds were oppressed economically and politically by the two superpowers, but the burden of oppression fell most heavily, of course, on the developing countries of the Third World. The people and countries of the world wanted liberation, and this could only come about by overthrowing the hegemonist domination of the two superpowers. The key to achieving this was to mobilize the Third World and exploit contradictions between the First and Second Worlds to win over the Second World to the anti-superpower struggle. Contradictions between the two superpowers might also be exploited, possibly aligning one of the superpowers against the other.[25] China's alignment with the United States against Soviet revisionist social imperialist expansionism would fall in this category of exploitation of contradictions between the two hegemony-seeking superpowers. In certain periods, one of the superpowers might be more aggressive than the other, and it might be possible to unite with the less aggressive superpower against the more aggressive one. This sort of exploitation of contradictions was entirely correct. Throughout the 1974–1982 period, it was apparent to China's leaders that the Soviet Union was precisely the more dangerous of the two superpowers. As Deng Xiaoping said on December 1, 1975 in a speech welcoming President Gerald Ford on his first trip to China, "the country most zealously preaching peace" was in fact the "most dangerous source of war."[26] Everyone understood these as allusions to the Soviet Union.

The Three Worlds theory placed China, along with the rest of the Third World, on a higher moral plane than the United States. It explained how China's alignment with the United States was not mere crass power politics, but served a higher moral purpose. It also provided an ideologically adequate explanation of China's return to diplomatic maneuver. While China might maneuver like the United States or the Soviet Union with diplomatic activity around the world, China would never merely seek merely its own selfish interest. China sought the emancipation of all humanity. China would never be a superpower like the United States. In practice, the theory could distinguish between the two hegemony-seeking First World superpowers.

By providing a mechanism for "mobilizing all possible forces against the primary enemy," Mao's Three Worlds Theory was similar to the anti-Japanese and then anti-KMT united fronts devised by Mao in the 1930s and 1940s. But those earlier united fronts were essentially mechanisms for mobilizing forces behind party leadership to bring about a future revolutionary restructuring of society.[27] The united front against hegemony did not function, even theoretically, as a mechanism for revolutionary mobilization. It maintained a pretense at revolution, but in fact functioned at the level of governments and states in pursuit of national security goals. Linkages with foreign revolutionary parties remained as vestiges. After 1978, under Deng Xiaoping support for foreign revolutionary struggles would be scrapped within a continuing framework of united front against Soviet expansionism.

Diplomacy was a key instrument of China's effort to counter possible Soviet encirclement. Thailand and the Philippines were early targets of China's anti-Soviet diplomatic offensive. The United States, the traditional backer of both the Philippines and Thailand, had just suffered a monumental defeat in Indochina, while Hanoi, with revolutionary and nationalist aspirations for Southeast Asia plus large, well-trained and well-armed forces, had emerged as the strongest military power in Southeast Asia. Both Bangkok and Manila were quite interested to hear what Beijing might have to say about the new situation.

Regarding Thailand, an uprising of university students in October 1974 had led to an end of decades of military domination of Thailand's governments. Thailand's new civilian government moved quickly to accommodate Hanoi after the latter's decisive military victory over Saigon. In July 1975, Thailand revoked a long-standing agreement with the United States under which US military forces had been stationed in Thailand—some 23,000 in 1975. All were to be withdrawn within one year. Bangkok began quickly expanding economic and commercial ties with the new communist governments of Indochina. Thailand was the first noncommunist country to recognize the Khmer Rouge government of Cambodia. Beijing was very concerned that Thailand might move toward the Soviet Union as part of its accommodation to the new power realities in Southeast Asia. On June 8, 1975, five weeks after Saigon's fall, a Thai parliamentary delegation visited Beijing. Thailand's prime minister soon followed. Talks with Deng Xiaoping produced an agreement to establish diplomatic relations at the ambassadorial level. Regarding the Philippines, on June 7, 1975, again about five weeks after the fall of Saigon, President and Mrs. Ferdinand Marcos visited China. The result was a similar agreement to establish diplomatic relations at the ambassadorial level. In discussions with Thailand, the Philippines, and other Southeast Asian leaders, Beijing warned against permitting the Soviet social imperialist "tiger" to enter the back door while driving the American imperialist "wolf" out the front door.

Education of foreign leaders, first and foremost those of the United States but including leaders of regional powers all around the world, was a key instrument of China's anti-Soviet effort. According to Henry Kissinger, who was the recipient of many of these Chinese lessons, "American leaders were treated by their Chinese counterparts to private seminars on Soviet intentions—often in uncharacteristically blunt language, as if the Chinese feared this topic too important to be left to their customary subtlety and indirection."[28] A good example of Beijing's pedagogic effort came in late 1975 and was directed at President Gerald Ford and Secretary of State Henry Kissinger. Beijing saw the Ford administration, and especially Kissinger, as too willing to accommodate the Soviet Union, perhaps at the expense of China.[29] During a visit by Kissinger to Beijing in October to pave the way for Ford's upcoming visit, Foreign Minister Qiao Guanhua treated his American counterpart to a thorough exposition of the dangerous illusion of detente with Soviet expansionism.[30] While Qiao excoriated the wrong way to deal with the Soviet Union, Deng Xiaoping laid out the proper way in his welcoming speech for Ford in December. Acting on the basis of the "outstanding common point" of the 1972 joint communiqué—common opposition to the hegemony of any third power—Beijing and Washington should point out the source of war, dispel illusions, make preparations, unite with all the forces that could be united with, and wage a tit-for-tat struggle. Hegemonism is weak by nature. It bullied the soft and feared the tough, Deng instructed Ford.[31]

Throughout the effort to build an anti-Soviet coalition together with the United States, Mao feared that the United States would use its new relation with China to strike a better deal with the Soviet Union. Perhaps the real US purpose, Mao feared, was to use its link with China to pressure Moscow to accommodate US interests as a quid pro quo for US support for Moscow against China. Perhaps the US intention was to encourage the Soviet Union to attack China. Both Soviet and Chinese positions would thus be greatly weakened.[32] Henry Kissinger speculated that Mao had expected China's rapprochement with the United States in 1971–1972 to torpedo US-Soviet détente. When that did not happen and Moscow-Washington ties instead continued to advance, Mao was deeply troubled. If the United States joined a Soviet-organized anti-China campaign, Beijing's position would have been dire. Ford and Kissinger attempted to assuage these Chinese fears by reiterating that further strengthening the Soviet Union was simply not an American interest.

Normalization of Relations with Japan

Starting about 1969, a central theme of Chinese commentary about Japan became the dire danger posed by the revival of Japanese militarism.[33] While highly exaggerated, this was not entirely groundless. Following Nixon's announcement of his "Guam Doctrine" in July of that year, leaders in both Japan and the United States contemplated Japan playing a greater security and defense role in East Asia.[34] Defense Secretary Melvin Laird said at one point in 1970, for example, that the United States might not oppose Japan's acquisition of nuclear weapons, while the head of Japan's Self Defense Agency, Yasuhiro Nakasone, sparked comment by saying that Japan did not "at present" desire nuclear weapons. Japan's entry into the Nuclear Nonproliferation Treaty was underway, and negotiations took six years largely because Japan insisted on acquiring its own, independent plutonium reprocessing capability.[35] With its heavy utilization of nuclear-generated electricity, Japan developed a large stockpile of unprocessed plutonium. With an independent reprocessing capability, that plutonium could be turned relatively quickly into fissile material, the essential ingredient for atomic bombs.

The July 1971 announcements that Kissinger was in Beijing and that President Nixon would soon visit China took Japanese leaders by surprise and was a deep shock. In their quest for secrecy, Nixon and Kissinger had not kept Japan apprised of steps toward rapprochement with the PRC. Prime Minister Eisaku Sato was informed of the Kissinger and Nixon visits only hours before those visits were publicly announced. This "Nixon shock" caused serious Japanese doubts about the reliability of the United States. A year later, in July 1972, Kakuei Tanaka, a somewhat unusual Japanese leader known for his bold leadership style, became Japan's prime minister. Tanaka and his foreign minister Masayoshi Ohira quickly declared their determination to normalize relations with China. US-PRC rapprochement had eliminated US opposition to Japan-China normalization, while new Japanese uncertainty regarding Washington gave Tokyo additional incentive to move in that direction.

Zhou Enlai coordinated a campaign to respond positively to the Tanaka-Ohira initiative and move it toward a successful conclusion. Zhou designated Liao Chengzhi to be China's point person in courting Japanese elite circles. Liao was born in Tokyo in 1908 as the son of Liao Zhongkai, a leading member of the KMT and close associate of Sun Yat-sen. Liao Chengzhi came under Zhou's influence in the 1920s and joined the KMT (then allied with the CCP) in 1925. Forced to flee China because of his radical political activities, Liao returned to Tokyo in 1927 and joined the CCP branch in Tokyo while studying at Waseda University in that city. For the next several decades, Liao put his linguistic skills at the service of the CCP, having picked up German, French, and English in addition to Japanese along the way. Liao spoke fluent Japanese and was well known in Japanese circles. Among Liao's effective tropes with his Japanese friends in was the proposition that history was being made, and that old friends should play an important role in the process of Sino-Japanese rapprochement.[36]

Zhou himself had visited Japan twice, in 1917 and 1919. During Beijing's 1972 courtship of Japan, Liao, Zhou, and other Chinese diplomats liaised with various Japanese political parties, especially the opposition, including but not limited to the Japan Socialist Party (JSP). Zhou found a way, however, to gracefully decline JSP solicitation of a visit to China by a large JSP delegation in the months before Tanaka's visit. Zhou thus ensured that Tanaka, representing Japan's governing party, not the JSP, would harvest the prestige for the coming breakthrough. The China-Japan Friendship Association was mobilized to lend its weight to the push for normalization. Japanese business leaders were motivated by promises of large and lucrative Chinese contracts. Zhou guided the themes stressed during the Chinese effort in Japan, playing effectively (but subtly and not harshly, as would be the case several decades later) on Japanese guilt for its aggression in the 1930s and 1940s, mingled with respect for China's ancient civilization. In the words of scholar Chae-Jin Lee, Zhou showed "keen sensitivity to . . . Japanese psychology and masterful manipulation of Japan's political and economic forces."[37]

In September 1972, seven months after Nixon's historic visit to Beijing, Prime Minister Kakuei Tanaka arrived in Beijing with an entourage of nearly fifty for a six-day visit. Tanaka was met at the Beijing airport by a large and high-ranking Chinese delegation led by Premier Zhou Enlai and Ye Jianying. Mao met with Tanaka early in the visit to signal his approval of the normalization of relations with Japan. The two sides proceeded to negotiate a nine-point communiqué that ended the "abnormal state of affairs" that existed between the two countries, established diplomatic relations at the ambassadorial level, pledged peaceful resolution and no threat of use of force in resolution of all disputes, stated that Japan "fully understands and respects" Beijing's claim to Taiwan, and copied verbatim the anti-hegemony clause of the PRC-US joint communiqué of February.

There were several points on which Zhou made concessions to Japan. In the joint communiqué, China "renounced its demand" for war indemnities from Japan.[38] This was a Chinese concession that probably did not accord with the sentiments of the Chinese people. Use of the term "demand" rather than "right" also embodied implicit Chinese acquiescence to Tokyo's argument that the Republic of China, then representing China in Tokyo's eyes, had already abandoned China's "right" to indemnities in the 1952 ROC-Japan peace treaty. In China's eyes, of course, that treaty was completely illegal. Yet Zhou Enlai agreed to the term "demand," implying at least acknowledgement of the 1952 treaty. Zhou also decided not to press the issue of the Sengaku/Diaoyutai islands. When Tanaka raised this issue, Zhou suggested that this issue not be discussed but left for some indefinite future time. In bidding farewell to Tanaka, Zhou also conveyed his best wishes to Japan's Emperor Hirohito—who had reigned throughout Japan's 1931–1945 invasion of China. Evidence from Chinese archives is not presently available, but it may be that this series of conciliatory Chinese moves toward Tokyo was part of Zhou's "rightist capitulationist diplomacy" attacked by Jiang Qing on Mao's behalf in 1973–1975.

The "history issue" (the chronicle of Japanese aggression against China) injected a sour note into the September 1972 negotiations. In the course of a welcoming banquet for the Japanese delegation, Zhou's speech touched on the history issue:

> Friendly contacts and cultural exchanges between our two countries have a history of two thousand years, and our two peoples have forged a profound friendship; all this we should treasure. However, in the half-century after 1894, owing to the Japanese militarist's aggression against China, the Chinese people were made to endure tremendous disasters and the Japanese people, too, suffered a great deal from it. The past not forgotten is a guide for the future.[39]

In his reply speech, Tanaka spoke of his "profound self-examination" of the fact that Japan had caused "*meiwaku*" to the Chinese people. The Japanese word *meiwaku* was translated as "*ma-fan*," a mild form of trouble or nuisance. The Chinese listeners in the banquet hall felt far understated the immense suffering born by Chinese as a result of Japan's invasion, and when Tanaka's reference to "*ma-fan*" reached their ears, many immediately stopped their applause and turned visibly cold. Tanaka later took great pains to explain to Zhou that *meiwaku* in Japanese means a genuine apology. It may be noted, however, that dictionaries of Japanese define *meiwaku* as "trouble, bother, nuisance, annoyance."

During his talks with Tanaka, Zhou Enlai raised but did not dwell on Japan's alliance with the United States. More pointedly, Zhou did not object to that alliance.

Japan was an important link in the anti-Soviet front Beijing was trying to assemble. During US-PRC interactions in 1971 and early 1972, Beijing had been critical of the US alliance with Japan, warning the United States that it was encouraging the revival of Japanese militarism and imperialism, which it would someday regret. The reply of US representatives was that the US alliance with Japan benefited China by limiting the development of Japanese military capabilities. By November 1973, Kissinger found that Mao and Zhou had accepted the US view. The US link with Japan was a good thing because it checked potential Japanese alignment with the Soviet Union, Mao said.[40]

Strengthening the Southern Front: Pakistan and Iran

Chinese support for Pakistan's development of nuclear weapons was apparently one component of Beijing's effort to strengthen global anti-Soviet forces.[41] Pakistan's nuclear weapons would be targeted against India, not the USSR, of course. But from the perspective of Mao and Zhou, India was a Soviet ally, while Pakistan was a quasi-ally of China. India's December 1971 partition of Pakistan had occurred with Soviet support and represented an important element of the shift in the global correlation of forces in Moscow's favor. Following Pakistan's catastrophic 1971 defeat by India, China moved quickly to assist Pakistan's rebuilding of its shattered armed forces. But India's far larger economy and population meant that Pakistan would find it difficult to match India in conventional military strength. India was also increasingly aggressive, at least from the Chinese perspective: partitioning Pakistan, annexing Sikkim in 1974–1975, testing an atomic bomb in May 1974. All these moves were, again from Beijing's perspective, aspects of an Indian drive to achieve hegemony over South Asia, turning that region into part of the Soviet-engineered encirclement of China. Indian policies had full Soviet backing. India was generally aligned with the Soviet Union in the United Nations, and most of India's weapons were purchased from the Soviet Union. Indian ports were favorite Indian Ocean ports of call for Soviet warships. A strong Pakistan was an important element countering that adverse pro-Soviet trend.

Pakistani weakness and vulnerability was also a threat to China. If Pakistan's weakness tempted another Indian attack on Pakistan, China could be confronted with the unpleasant choice of intervening to assist Pakistan, thereby risking war with both India and the Soviet Union, or not intervening and acquiescing to India's further subordination of Pakistan and, perhaps, genuine Indian hegemony over the entire subcontinent. Given the gross asymmetry between India and Pakistan in economic strength and population, it was unlikely that Pakistan could deter India via conventional military strength. A Pakistani nuclear deterrent, however, might suffice, or at least offer a stronger Pakistani deterrent. Nor would assistance to Pakistan's nuclear weapons efforts violate any international agreements signed by China. China would not sign the NPT until 1992. China's formal, declared position regarding nuclear nonproliferation in the 1970s was that it was essentially an effort by the Soviet and American hegemony-seeking superpowers to maintain their joint nuclear monopoly via collusion in order to uphold their nuclear blackmail against the Second and Third Worlds. It was, thus, a good thing if countries of the Third World, oppressed by superpower hegemony, acquired the full range of modern means of self-defense. American and Soviet hegemonists might be unhappy with efforts to undermine their joint "nuclear blackmail." But that displeasure could be offset by keeping assistance to Pakistan's nuclear program clandestine. Moreover, by officially denying nuclear cooperation with Pakistan and keeping it secret, China could plausibly deny superpower charges of Chinese proliferation.

According to a report by the US Defense Intelligence Agency, around October 1974 China dispatched twelve nuclear scientists to assist Pakistan's nuclear energy program.[42] India had tested its first atomic bomb in May. Two years later, in May 1976, Prime Minister Zulfikar Ali Bhutto led a top-level scientific-military delegation to China, including a Nobel Prize–winning Pakistani nuclear physicist who was then Bhutto's scientific advisor. Two public agreements were signed, one on military, the other on scientific cooperation. Barely a week later, a high-level Chinese scientific team arrived in Islamabad.[43] According to Indian sources, in June 1976 China and Pakistan signed a secret nuclear technology cooperation agreement. Bhutto confirmed existence of a mysterious but immensely important international agreement concluded in 1976 and related to Pakistan's nuclear capabilities. In his death cell testament (he was about to be hanged by the military group led by Mohammad Zia-ul-Haq that had ousted him from power), Bhutto referred to "the agreement of mine concluded in June 1976" which was "the single most important achievement which I believe will dominate the portrait of my public life" and which "will perhaps be my greatest achievement and contribution to the survival of our people and nation."[44] Bhutto does not say who the parties to that agreement were or what it was about other than that it related to Pakistan's nuclear program. He stresses, however, his own role in the development of Pakistan's nuclear program, from his service as head of Pakistan's Atomic Energy Commission in the 1950s to July 1977, when he was overthrown by a military coup. Bhutto believed that he was overthrown on CIA orders by military chief Zia-ul-Haq because of his efforts to push forward with Pakistan's nuclear capabilities in spite of US opposition. Bhutto insisted that Pakistan's nuclear program was "peaceful," but also said things like this: "What difference does my life make now when I can imagine eighty million of my countrymen standing under the nuclear cloud of a defenseless sky." Though written in an elliptical style probably designed to protect a Pakistani pledge of secrecy to Beijing, Bhutto clearly claims credit for laying the basis for Pakistan's production of atomic defense capability via the mysterious June 1976 international agreement.

Cooperation with China was not the only, or possibly even the most important, element of Pakistan's nuclear weapons drive in the 1970s. During that decade, Pakistani agencies began setting up a global network for clandestinely acquiring the equipment, components, and materials necessary for nuclear weapons production. Western countries—such as West Germany, the Netherlands, France, and the United States—were the key target areas for these covert acquisition efforts. China's assistance apparently supplemented these efforts. After counterproliferation efforts by US agencies in the late 1970s thwarted Pakistani efforts to extract plutonium from spent reactor fuel, Pakistan turned to uranium enrichment via gaseous diffusion. Chinese personnel reportedly helped Pakistan overcome the technical difficulties associated with gaseous diffusion, and supplied uranium hexafluoride to feed into the completed apparatus.[45] China also seems to have supplied Pakistan with the design for an atomic bomb—specifically for the type of 25-kiloton (Hiroshima-sized) atomic bomb tested by China in October 1966. CIA spies reportedly found that design, complete with Chinese script and other indications that it came from China, in the baggage of Abdul Qadir Khan when they covertly searched it during his trip abroad in the early 1980s.[46]

Chinese assistance to Pakistan's nuclear programs apparently continued throughout the 1980s. Even after China joined the NPT regime in 1992, it insisted on continuing nuclear cooperation with Pakistan, though now under IAEA inspection and confined to the nonmilitary sphere. It can be argued that China delayed entry into the NPT until it had provided Pakistan with the basics of a self-sufficient nuclear weapons capability. Even when China agreed in 1997, under great US pressure, to stop nuclear cooperation with Iran, it insisted on continuing such cooperation with Pakistan.[47] By the 1990s, the Soviet Union was no longer in the picture, but Beijing's calculations regarding maintaining a balance of power in the subcontinent favorable to China remained essentially unchanged. Those calculations trace back to 1974–1976 and were enshrined in what must have been a decision made by Mao Zedong.

The Kingdom of Iran was China's other key anti-Soviet partner in Southwest Asia. Common support for Pakistan was an important factor bringing China and Iran together in the early 1970s. China's threat to enter the 1965 India-Pakistan war had made Iran's monarch (known by the Persian title shah), Mohammed Reza Pahlavi, cognizant of China's role in the South

Asian security equation. The shah saw a strong Pakistan as a buffer between Iran and India as vital for maintaining stability on Iran's eastern borders, allowing Iran to focus on the Gulf, which the shah saw as Iran's natural sphere of influence. Pakistan then faced growing insurgencies in its southwestern province of Baluchistan and in its Pashtun-populated Northwest Frontier Agency—insurgencies supported by India and Iraq, both Soviet-aligned regional powers. In April 1973, the shah declared that Pakistan's security was vital to Iran's own security. He also ordered helicopter-borne Iranian counterinsurgency forces into Pakistan's Baluchistan to help suppress the secessionist movement there. Iran, like China, was doing what it could to keep Pakistan strong.[48]

Pakistan played a key role in bringing China and Iran together. In February 1971, Pakistan's Zulfikar Ali Bhutto passed on to Mao the information that Iran's Princess Ashraf (one of the shah's younger sisters) was interested in visiting China as an official guest of the Chinese government. The next month, while the US ping-pong team was still in Beijing, Zhou Enlai issued such an invitation. Visits by two different royal princesses followed in quick succession. Several months later, Iranian and Chinese ambassadors in Islamabad, Pakistan, negotiated the terms of a new relationship. On August 16, the two governments agreed to establish diplomatic relations at the ambassadorial level. The next month, Prime Minister Amir Abbas Hoveyda and Empress Farah visited Beijing. Talks between Abbas and Zhou clarified the wide range of convergent interests between the two sides.

Beijing cut off material and propaganda support for Marxist insurgents in Oman's southern province of Dhofar as part of its rapprochement with Tehran. Chinese support for those rebels had begun in 1969, even though the rebels were supported primarily by Soviet-backed South Yemen. (This was in line with CCP competition with the CPSU for support of the world's revolutionary forces.) Iranian forces, on the other hand, were involved in support of Oman's legitimate (royal) government in suppressing the rebellion. Iran's role in Dhofar and Pakistani Baluchistan were part of the shah's drive to establish Iran as the major power in the Gulf area. Beijing's dropping of the Dhofari rebels to eliminate friction with Iran was, in effect, a shift from competition with Moscow for global revolutionary credentials to alignment with Iran to check Moscow's use of revolution to expand the Soviet global position.

Formation of the Sino-Iranian entente in the 1970s must be seen in terms of a broader regional structure of power. Britain, the long-dominant power in the Persian Gulf and, indeed the entire Indian Ocean, announced in 1968 its determination to withdraw all its military forces from "east of Suez." That created a power vacuum to be filled. As noted earlier, the Soviet Union was vigorously trying to fill it with its navy and its alliances. The United States, for its part, moved to acquire a naval base at Diego Garcia in the middle of the Indian Ocean via agreement with Britain in December 1966.[49] But the

United States was already overstretched by commitments in Europe and the Far East, a situation that led to Nixon's "Guam Doctrine" of July 1969 declaring Washington's increased partnership with regional powers in Asia. The shah seized the opportunity to win US backing for an effort to establish Iran as the dominant military power, "the policeman," of the Gulf.

The shah was an ambitious top-down modernizer in the mold of Japan's Meiji emperor, Turkey's Mustafa Kemal Atatürk, or (later) China's Deng Xiaoping.[50] Throughout the 1960s and 1970s the shah used Iran's rapidly rising oil revenues and his royal authority to attempt to turn Iran into an industrialized, educated, urbanized, gender-equal, and, even more fatally than the last item, secular country. The shah envisioned Iran as the naturally dominant country in the Gulf region. Economic and social development were to be the foundations of this rise in national stature. So too was military development. During the 1970s, Iran's military was transformed into a large and powerful force. The diplomatic cornerstone of the shah's push for national grandeur was alliance with the United States, an alliance that went back to American efforts to secure Soviet evacuation of northern Iran in 1945 and was premised in the 1970s on Iranian fear of Soviet power on Iran's northern borders. Iran under the shah was a close and important US ally in containing the Soviet Union. Iranian partnership with the PRC was a natural extension of the shah's alliance with the United States.

From Beijing's perspective, partnership with Iran was positive for a number of reasons. Iran's alliance with the United States fit with Beijing's emerging strategy of using US power to check and counter expanding Soviet power. More importantly, Iran was a country of considerable and rapidly developing capabilities—a major regional power, whose friendship China might find useful. Iran was a close friend of Pakistan, China's close friend. Since Iran was not a First World superpower, filling the power vacuum of the Gulf with Iranian domination would help exclude superpower domination of that energy-rich region of the world. And Iran was a country with thousands of years of friendly contact and cooperation, but never conflict, with China. Unlike other major Asian powers—Japan, India, Russia—Iran had never experienced military or geopolitical conflict with China. From Beijing's perspective, Iranian preeminence in the Gulf looked benign.

Foreign Minister Ji Pengfei in June 1973 was the first high-level Chinese official to visit Iran. This was twenty-five months after the first visit by an imperial princess to Beijing, a delay that may have been partially due to the shah's insistence on maintaining balance in Iran's ties with China and the Soviet Union. His major objective in opening relations with China was to use that link as leverage to secure a degree of Soviet support for Iran's new role as policeman of the Gulf. From the shah's perspective, the Soviet Union, on Iran's northern border, was far more important than China. The shah understood that his China card should not be overplayed. Thus, while Hoveyda was in Beijing talking with Zhou Enlai, the shah himself was in Moscow discussing affairs with Soviet leaders. With Ji Pengfei's visit, China outbid Moscow by endorsing Iran's preeminence in the Gulf. Ji during his visit laid out what would become one of the fundamental and enduring principles of China's relations with Iran and the Persian Gulf. China believed, Ji stated during his visit, that the security affairs of the Persian Gulf should be handled by the countries around that Gulf, not by extra-regional powers. Iran was an "important country" in the Gulf region, Ji said, and was gravely menaced by the growing infiltration, rivalry, and expansion of "certain big powers." Ji continued:

> We have consistently held that the affairs of a given . . . region must be managed by the countries and peoples of that region. . . . Iran and some other Persian Gulf countries hold that the affairs of this region should be jointly managed by the Persian Gulf countries and brook no outside interference. This is a just position and we express our firm support for it.[51]

The "littoral principle" (as it may perhaps be called) enunciated by Ji Pengfei in 1973 represented a long-term strategic bet on Iran, and a bid for partnership with that emerging regional power.[52] While this statement implicitly gave equal standing to *all* the countries littoral to the Gulf, and could be envisioned as endorsement of some sort of cooperative collective security arrangement, the realities of power pointed in a different direction. The reality was that Iran's power far outweighed all but one power in the Gulf. Only Iraq had power adequate to rival or balance Iran. Once the realities of power are taken into consideration, in the context of 1973, Ji Pengfei's "littoral principle" represented an endorsement of the shah's push for Iran to replace Britain as the "policeman of the Gulf," a policy supported by the US as well. But the principle enunciated by Ji Pengfei in 1973 would survive the specific circumstances of 1973. As late as 1990, long after the demise of the shah's regime, during the crisis following Iraq's invasion and annexation of Kuwait, Chinese leaders would reiterate the principle during visits by Iranian leaders to Beijing.[53]

In the mid-1970s, Beijing and Tehran found a remarkable convergence of interests. Both were deeply alarmed by the vigorous advance of Soviet influence across the region: India's, Iraq's and Egypt's treaties of friendship with the Soviet Union, South Yemen's alignment with the Soviet Union and its subversion in southern Oman, and Pakistan's partition by Soviet-backed India. In 1973, Afghanistan's monarchy was overthrown and that country began to move closer to the Soviet Union, with Soviet aid and, as it turned out, subversion advancing rapidly. A 1974 coup by Marxist army officers in Ethiopia brought socialism along with Soviet advisors and Cuban military forces into that country, moving it into Moscow's camp. In 1978, Marxist circles in the

Afghani officer corps carried out a coup d'état that moved their country into Soviet-style socialism and alignment with the USSR. Throughout this period, the military capabilities of Soviet-aligned Iraq were expanding rapidly. Soviet warships were steaming around the Indian Ocean with ever-greater frequency. All this was happening while the United States, the traditional leader of the global effort to contain the Soviet Union, was distracted by Vietnam, internal political crisis, and economic "stagflation." In this increasingly dark and dangerous situation, Beijing and Tehran found a meeting of the minds. Figure 12-2 illustrates the wide convergence of Sino-Iranian interests that underpinned the formation of those two countries' entente cordiale in the 1970s.

China's partnership with the Kingdom of Iran culminated in a visit by Hua Guofeng in August 1978. This was the first-ever visit by the PRC's paramount leader to a non-communist-ruled country, a fact that Beijing intended to underline the importance it attributed to China's new, cooperative relationship with Iran. Hua's visit was also a great and dramatic diplomatic blunder that would alienate Iran's new Islamic revolutionary regime for a number of years. The policy content associated with Hua Guofeng's visit differed little from that of Ji Pengfei's 1973 visit, or of an April 1975 visit by Li Xiannian, or of

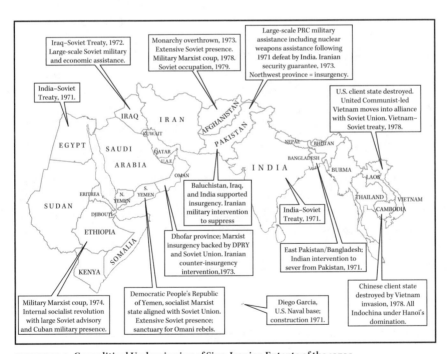

FIGURE 12-2 **Geopolitical Underpinning of Sino-Iranian Entente of the 1970s**

Source: John Garver, *China and Iran: Ancient Partners in a Post-Imperial World*, (University of Washington Press: Seattle, 2006), p. 46.

a June 1978 visit by Foreign Minister Huang Hua. The Iranian political context of Hua's visit was, however, dramatically different. By 1978, tensions generated by hyperdevelopment under the shah's ambitious programs had turned into powerful protests against his regime. By the time Hua Guofeng arrived in Tehran, large and militant crowds mobilized by radical clerics in Iran's mosques were confronting police nearly every week. The size and militancy of protests were rapidly increasing. Symbols of Western influence—cinemas, nightclubs—were targets of arson and other forms of attack. Police fired on crowds, but this only further antagonized them. The shah's regime had, in fact, entered its terminal crisis. A mere four months after Hua's visit, the shah fled Tehran for good and Islamic revolutionary leader Ayatollah Ruhollah Khomeini made a deity-like return to assume leadership of a new revolutionary Iran.

Into this revolutionary upheaval flew Hua Guofeng and his entourage. The key purpose of Hua's visit was to demonstrate China's warm and full support for the shah and his leadership of Iran. Hua praised the wise and far-sighted leadership of the shah and Iran's accomplishments under his rule. In the context of 1978, those signals conveyed to the revolution-minded people of Iran a very different message: China supported Iran's ancien régime. China's media strengthened this perception by condemning anti-shah protests for undermining order and progress, perhaps under instigation from the Soviet Union. As protests mounted in Iran, China's leaders were quick to see a nefarious Soviet hand behind them. China's diplomats and leaders were also shocked by US criticism of the shah at this juncture. Instead of giving the shah, their ally, full and unequivocal support in this crisis, American representatives undermined him with criticism, at least from Beijing's point of view. The full and robust support conveyed by Hua Guofeng was intended, in part, to stand in contradistinction to American vacillation. In this regard, China's diplomacy was successful. In his final testament, the shah wrote, "I must also pay homage to the loyalty of the Chinese leaders. When Mr. Hua Kuo-feng visited me, at a time when the Iranian crisis was reaching its peak, I had the impression that the Chinese alone were in favor of a strong Iran."[54] What caused the shah to be grateful infuriated Iranian revolutionaries. By the time the shah fled in January 1979, Chinese diplomats in Tehran were reporting posters condemning the United States, Israel, and China for their support of the shah. Hua's visit destroyed the Sino-Iranian relation. It would take Beijing five years to rebuild it.

Countering the Danger of European Appeasement

Europe, as the traditional center of Cold War tension, played an important role in Mao's effort to shift the development of the global correlation of forces in a direction favorable to China's security. Mao laid out his thinking about Europe's role in talks with Kissinger in 1973.[55] The Soviet Union would not be able to attack China until Moscow first secured control over Europe and the Middle East. Soviet forces confronting Western Europe exceeded those facing China, and redeployment of Soviet forces eastward would require prior settlement of Soviet concerns in Europe. The great danger was that Europe did not realize the dire Soviet threat it faced and would, therefore, allow the Soviets to achieve domination. Core US allies in Western Europe were wavering, Mao felt, but in the final analysis they would not abandon their vital interests by succumbing to Soviet blandishments. It was thus necessary to take a firm line with West European leaders to shake them awake. Kissinger found Mao very well informed about West European leaders and politics.

West Germany, the Federal Republic of Germany (FRG), was especially important in containing the Soviet Union because of its large population, strong economy, relatively large army, and central front-line location. Germany was also especially susceptible to Soviet blandishments because of its status as a divided country. With Moscow in firm control of East Germany, the German Democratic Republic (GDR), Moscow could loosen or tighten inter-German ties. Expansion of inter-German relations was a major FRG goal, because of both short-term issues of family reunification and long-term issues of eventual German reunification. From the FRG perspective, détente with the Soviet Union was linked to improved inter-German relations and the destiny of the German nation.[56]

West Germany was deeply divided in the 1970s over relations with the Soviet Union, the GDR, and China. Social Democratic Party (SDP) leader Willy Brandt (chancellor from 1969 to 1974) had broken with long-standing doctrine and recognized the legitimacy of the GDR, expanding relations with it in a new direction known as Ostpolitik ("East politics"). The corollary of Brandt's push for expanded inter-German relations was a push for détente with the Soviet Union. The Christian Democratic Party (CDU) and that Party's Bavarian branch, the Christian Social Union (CSU) headed by Franz Joseph Strauss, were strongly opposed to this new course, and felt that the Soviet Union had to be dealt with from a position of strength, one element of which should be close relations between the FRG and the PRC. Brandt and the SDP felt that a "Far East Policy" could not substitute for Ostpolitik, and that to try would antagonize the Soviet Union, injuring inter-German ties, and dangerously overestimate FRG capabilities. On the other hand, in the 1950s Moscow had suggested it would consent to German unification in exchange for FRG exit from NATO, and it seemed to many Germans in the 1970s that SDP Ostpolitik was moving the FRG in that direction. A West German exit from NATO would have very greatly weakened that organization.

Beijing very much agreed with the CDU's tough anti-Soviet perspective, and strove throughout the 1970s to move Germany in that direction.

Normalization of PRC-FRG relations occurred in October 1972 in the aftermath of China's entry into the United Nations and Sino-American rapprochement. As Chinese concerns with Soviet expansionism mounted in the mid-1970s, Beijing resorted to two instruments to nudge the FRG toward a more vigilant posture with the Soviet Union. The first instrument was a propaganda campaign. Large volumes of speeches, Xinhua reports, newspaper articles, and radio broadcasts pounded home the dire Soviet military threat confronting West Europe. This propaganda called for strong German and West European support for NATO, along with increased military preparations and expenditures. A favorite trope of Chinese commentary was to convey CDU views on these issues. Support for European integration and independence—but always within the context of NATO and continued presence of US military forces on the continent—was another theme of Chinese commentary.

Détente with the Soviet Union was a bête noire of Chinese propaganda at this juncture. From Beijing's perspective, détente was a gigantic Soviet deception lulling Westerners into letting down their guard while the Soviet Union built up its forces and aggressively expanded its positions around the world. It would at best result in a sort of "self-Finlandization" of West Europe, with Bonn and other European capitals doing nothing that incurred Soviet displeasure. At worst, détente could become "another Munich," with Western Europe making major concessions to Moscow's demands, allowing the Soviet Union to secure its European positions and move forces east to confront China.[57]

The Conference on Security and Cooperation in Europe (CSCE) was a special object of Chinese concern. The CSCE began with talks in Helsinki in November 1972 and culminated in the signature of the Helsinki Final Act by thirty-five states on August 1, 1975. Moscow's major objective in the CSCE process was to legitimize its control over the East European countries, while West European leaders saw it as a way of reducing tension, expanding cooperation, and securing Soviet recognition of the importance of human rights across Europe. In addition to the Helsinki Final Act, the CSCE process established an organization, although that organization was without enforcement authority. Beijing believed that the entire CSCE process was a dangerous Soviet attempt to lull the West into pacifism. Beijing's view was exemplified by an article in *Peking Review* just after the signature of the Helsinki Final Act.[58] The CSCE "will only bring a false sense of security to the West European people," the article said. Moscow was attempting to "lull the European people and split Western Europe and NATO so as to achieve domination in Europe under the smokescreen of 'détente.'" Moscow planned to use the CSCE "to disarm the West, not just militarily, but politically and psychologically as well."[59] Moscow's objective was to tranquilize West European public opinion, cut West European defense budgets, and "heighten contradictions" within NATO.

The second instrument used by Beijing to nudge Germany toward greater vigilance against the Soviet Union was invitation diplomacy.[60] Beijing sought to give weight to anti-détente views of the CSU/CDU by inviting that party's leaders to China and, of course, highlighting their anti-détente views. Even though the SDP was the FRG's ruling party during the mid-1970s, seven top CDU leaders visited Beijing compared to only three top SDP and Free Democratic Party leaders. Often CSU/CDU leaders were received shortly before SDP leaders, undercutting the perceived gravity of the second, apparently follow-on visit of the SDP leaders. CSU president Franz Joseph Strauss, an outspoken critic of Willy Brandt's foreign and defense policies, was Beijing's honored and frequent guest. During a January 1975 visit by Strauss, he was the first FRG leader to be received by Mao. This was only several months before a visit by SPD Chancellor Helmut Schmidt (who followed Brandt as head of the FRG government from 1974 to 1982) was scheduled to visit Beijing. During Strauss's visit, portrait posters of him were hung around Beijing—leading one wit to observe that he was one of only three Germans to be so honored, the other two being Marx and Engels. Chancellor Schmidt's visit had to be delayed until assurances could be secured that he, too, would be allowed to meet Mao. That is, Schmidt's treatment in Beijing would be no less than that accorded Strauss. Even then, Schmidt's reception was noticeably cool. The day after Schmidt landed in Beijing, an editorial in *Renmin ribao* welcomed him; Europe was the focus of superpower contention, the editorial informed Schmidt:

> Especially that superpower which is chanting peace psalms most loudly has become even more truculent and is baring its fangs, particularly towards Europe. It has stationed massive forces in Central Europe and is intensifying its efforts to encircle the whole of Western Europe . . . thus constituting an increasingly grave military menace to the . . . security of European countries.[61]

In his toast welcoming Schmidt, Deng Xiaoping made the same point in more poetic language:

> The trees may prefer calm but the wind will not subside . . . It is now evident that the superpower most zealously preaching detente and disarmament is . . . stepping up arms expansion and war preparations, maintaining an offensive posture far exceeding its defence needs and posing a threat to the people of Europe and the whole world . . . people must heighten their vigilance, get prepared . . . otherwise they will suffer greatly.[62]

Shortly after Schmidt's visit, Strauss paid another visit to Beijing, where he enunciated views congruent with Beijing's—and to which Chinese media gave due prominence. Beijing's attempts to manipulate German opinion and policy via invitation diplomacy became controversial in Germany. Many Germans resented what they considered to be Chinese interference in FRG internal affairs. Others saw it as an attempt to inflame Soviet-German tensions to Beijing's advantage.

The effectiveness of China's efforts to influence Germany is an interesting if ultimately unanswerable question. By the early 1980s, German opinion was in fact shifting in the direction Beijing desired—toward greater vigilance against the Soviet Union. Helmut Schmidt himself was the first European leader to propose in 1977 that NATO deploy a counter to the Soviet SS-22 intermediate-range missile deployed in East Europe, a move adopted by NATO in December 1979 and which led to actual deployment of US intermediate-range missiles in 1982–1983 against very strong opposition. To what extent did Beijing's efforts contribute to this gradual sea change in German opinion? Schmidt had long clashed with the left wing of his SDP party over defense issues. Moreover, Soviet actions, especially its December 1979 invasion of Afghanistan and its 1981 threat to invade Poland, were probably the most important factor. But it may be that an influential and respected voice coming from a source other than Washington—namely, Beijing—gave credibility to warnings about Soviet intentions. It is ironic, however, that by the time West German leaders were facing down very strong opposition to US deployments of theater nuclear forces circa 1982–1984, Beijing had shifted positions and was backing away from the concept of a global struggle against Soviet expansionist social imperialism, and toward a search for rapprochement with the Soviet Union. But this may itself be taken as testament to the effectiveness of China's policy. Confronted by increased resolution in Europe, due marginally to China's efforts, Moscow was compelled to become less hostile toward China.

China's Second Global Campaign

The PRC's 1970s push to build a global coalition to counter Soviet advances constituted Beijing's second effort to influence the evolution of the global correlation of forces. The first had been Beijing's 1960s effort to advance world revolution via Marxist-Leninist-led transitions to socialism and communism. The policy content of these two efforts differed greatly, but both were impressive deployments of national capabilities on a global basis and in accord with a broad strategic vision in an effort to create a world more in line with what China's leaders perceived as China's interests. Both efforts were based on a global analysis of China's situation and entailed a sustained, multidimensional, and substantial expenditure of national wealth and leadership attention. It seems safe to say that there was only a very small handful of states able and willing to undertake such global efforts as the PRC undertook in the 1960s and 1970s. In other words, even while young and relatively weak, the PRC tried repeatedly to shape the world to comport with its values and perceived interests. Even when weak, the PRC thought and acted like a great and global power.

With both the 1960s and 1970s pushes, there were strong links between China's domestic politics and its international policies. With the PRC's first, revolutionary, push, the key purpose was to create a rising wave of global anti-capitalist revolution that would help push China's revolution in the correct direction. With the its second, 1970s push, the key purpose was to foil the threat posed by Soviet revisionist social imperialism to the correct direction of the Chinese revolution achieved by the Cultural Revolution. Implicit in Mao's deep fear of Soviet power in the 1970s was the idea that the CPSU might, still, connive with hidden revisionists within China to reverse verdicts on the Cultural Revolution and on Mao himself, much as Khrushchev had done with Stalin, and move China once again in a revisionist direction. Outright Soviet military intervention was one possibility raised by Mao. Of greater concern, according to Gao Wenqian, was Mao's fear that focus on economic development would occur at the expense of "continuing the revolution," as Mao finally concluded would be the case if either Zhou Enlai or Deng Xiaoping succeeded him as the CCP's paramount leader. Such a development would naturally win Soviet support, and the revolutionary gains achieved via the Cultural Revolution would be washed away, China would become revisionist, and capitalism would be restored.

Another comparison between the PRC's first and second global strategic pushes is that the first, revolutionary thrust was premised on confrontation with the United States. The second, anti-Soviet-hegemony thrust was premised on cooperation with the United States. By the late 1970s, US analysts referred to China as a "quasi-ally." By that point, parallel Chinese and American policies in a wide range of geographic areas effectively countered Soviet moves. This writer would be so bold as to assert that the Sino-American anti-hegemony partnership of 1975 to 1982 was the second Sino-American alliance of the twentieth century, the first being the 1941–1945 alliance against Japan. Both partnerships were ultimately successful. When CPSU leaders decided circa 1984 to move the Soviet Union in a new direction under the leadership of the young reformist Michael Gorbachev, the fact that the USSR now faced a relatively firm and rearming coalition of China, NATO, Japan, and the United States, and could not hope to prevail over that coalition, was a major reason for that decision. All of this is to say that when China and the United States have cooperated, they have, together, been able to change the course of world history.

The Happy Interregnum, 1978–1989

13 }

Opening to the Outside World

Making the PRC a Prosperous and Powerful Socialist Country

China's foreign relations underwent a sweeping reorientation circa 1978 under the leadership of Deng Xiaoping. During the long era of Mao's rule, the CCP had sought domestic and international revolution. Under Deng, it returned to an older, pre-Mao focus that had inspired Chinese patriots since the late nineteenth century: making China rich and powerful. Deng laid out the strategic objective in March 1975 when he was drafting the "Four Modernizations" under Zhou Enlai's tutelage, while Mao was still alive:

> The whole Party must now give serious thought to our country's overall interest. What is that interest? . . . a two-stage development of our economy . . . to turn China into a powerful socialist country with modern agriculture, industry, national defense and science [i.e., the Four Modernizations] by the end of this century, that is, within the next 25 years. The entire Party and nation must strive for the attainment of this objective. This constitutes the overall national interest.[1]

One key to achieving this goal was opening to the outside world and drawing broadly and deeply on the inputs of the advanced capitalist countries: technology, science, managerial skills, machinery and equipment, capital, and export markets. As Deng explained in 1978 after Mao had died and shortly before the CCP Politburo selected Deng as paramount leader:

> For a certain period of time, learning advanced science and technology from the developed countries was criticized as 'blindly worshiping foreign things.' We have come to understand how stupid this argument is. . . . China cannot develop by closing its door, sticking to the beaten track and being self-complacent. . . . In the early 1960s, we were behind the developed countries in science and technology, but the gap was not too wide. However, over the past dozen years, the gap

has widened because the world has been developing with tremendous speed. Compared with developed countries, China's economy has fallen behind at least ten years or perhaps 20, 30, or even 50 years in some areas..... To achieve the four modernizations, we must be adept at learning from other countries and we must obtain a great deal of foreign assistance.[2]

Deng Xiaoping had a deep appreciation for the decisive role of science and technology in the process of modernization. Overseeing Soviet-Chinese technological exchanges as general secretary in the 1950s had allowed Deng to see firsthand how much Chinese science and technology advanced via cooperation with the Soviet Union during that decade.[3] Then, during his political exile in Jiangxi during the Cultural Revolution, Deng saw just how backward much of China remained. Workers had no access to even simple radios or sanitary toilets. During his 1974 trip to New York to address the UN General Assembly, with a stopover of several days in Paris added on, Deng got a glimpse of what modern cities looked like in contrast to China's or the Soviet Union's dour socialist cities. Once rehabilitated and made vice premier in January 1975, Deng chose as one of his areas of primary responsibility science and technology. Deng set up a Political Research Office staffed by a number of China's top Marxist-Leninist theoreticians to explain in acceptable theoretical terms the importance of science and technology. This office also identified various writings by Mao that could be used (and were used after Mao's death and the arrest of the Gang of Four) to stress the importance of science and technology in building socialism. A more fundamental shift can hardly be imagined. From closing off China from capitalist influences for the sake of ideological class struggle to build socialism and communism, China would open itself widely to capitalist influences for the sake of economic modernization. It is important to understand, however, that CCP leaders, especially Deng Xiaoping, did not see this as abandonment of socialism or as the restoration of capitalism—though many foreign observers mistakenly concluded that they did.[4] For China's communist leaders, it was a question of how to best build socialism in China.

CCP leaders framed the issue in Marxist-Leninist terms. Finding an ideologically satisfactory explanation of China's new course, one congruent with Marxist-Leninist ideology, was essential to achieving a broad consensus behind the new course of opening and reform. After nearly two years of intense and very genuine debate, the mainstream of CCP leaders (including the coalition that selected Deng as paramount leader in late 1978) concluded that Mao had made a fundamental error in 1956 when he concluded that antagonistic classes continued to exist even after the private ownership of the means of production had been eliminated via the socialist transformation of commerce and industry.[5] In fact, antagonistic classes no longer existed.

Under such conditions, the "fundamental contradiction" was not, as Mao had maintained, between the proletariat and the bourgeoisie, but between the underdeveloped forces of production and the material needs of the laboring classes. Rectifying Mao's error allowed the CCP to focus on the development of the productive forces.

The scrapping of class struggle, combined with a hope that Chinese in Hong Kong, Southeast Asia, and perhaps someday Taiwan could be persuaded by ethnic pride to contribute to the Four Modernizations, led to emphasis on a new variant of nationalism. There had, of course, been a strong nationalist component to the revolutionary class struggle approach of the Mao years: socialism and revolution were to make China strong and esteemed among the peoples of the earth. But that approach drew sharp lines among Chinese, with all those deemed reactionary cast into perdition. After 1978, the embrace of the Four Modernizations sought to mobilize the energies of groups previously condemned as reactionary: intellectuals, the more capable farmers, and, beyond PRC borders, the prosperous Chinese diaspora. Mobilizing these sectors required a new variant of nationalism, one that stressed not conflict between Chinese but the great unity of all Chinese people to make the "motherland" prosperous and powerful. A new narrative emerged, one stressing the glory and grandeur of imperial China—the Han, Tang, Yuan, Ming, and Qing dynasties. A new narrative of China's "five thousand years" of imperial glory—and the toppling of China from that esteemed position during the Century of National Humiliation—gradually began to be constructed.

There was a close linkage between China's foreign relations and domestic politics after 1978: China needed to find ways of acquiring inputs from the advanced countries in order to successfully and quickly accomplish the arduous task of economic modernization. But there was another powerful international-domestic linkage: CCP rule over the Chinese people was to be relegitimized via rapid improvements in the standards of living.

Scrapping Mao's Totalitarian Project

By the end of the Mao era, China's people were very poor. There had been considerable industrialization during the three decades of comprehensive economic planning, but relatively little of China's new wealth had gone into improving the lives of the Chinese people. After the state took its share, collectivized agriculture simply could not produce enough food to provide most Chinese with much above a subsistence diet. The Stalinist economy adopted by China in the early 1950s worked by sucking wealth out of every sector of the economy and channeling it via comprehensive planning to targeted industries. These industries grew rapidly, albeit with mammoth inefficiency and waste. But investment in consumer goods and public infrastructure was starved to feed expanding heavy industry. Most basic goods—grain, cooking oil, cloth—were rationed. So too were luxury goods: bicycles, watches and clocks, radios, simple box cameras, and electric fans. It typically took many years of work and a rare ration coupon to acquire one of these scarce luxuries. Electricity was available in very limited quantities. Apartments were often lit by one or a very few low-wattage light bulbs. Residential areas grew around new industrial centers, but little investment went to construct, maintain, or improve housing. Housing was bare-bones and very crowded. For most noncadre urban residents, bathing and toilets were in communal facilities. Few noncadre residences had in-home bathing, hot water, telephone, or even toilets. Transportation was by very crowded bus or train, or by bicycle. Brownouts and blackouts were common. In the countryside, conditions were even worse, often downright primitive. However, isolated from the outside world and fed a constant diet of revolutionary propaganda, most Chinese did not realize how poor they really were. As China began learning about the advanced capitalist countries after 1978, people became aware of the fabulous levels of wealth common in those countries—and of their own poverty.

Ideological belief soon began to fade. Creation of a communist society was the justification of the privation and hardship inflicted on people under the Stalinist/Maoist economy. A large portion of the Chinese people had embraced this ideal in the 1950s, but belief faded with each successive crisis: the famine of the Great Leap Forward, the violence of the Cultural Revolution, the Lin Biao affair, the disrespectful funeral given the beloved Zhou Enlai. By the late 1970s, Marxism-Leninism-Mao Zedong Thought was still used to rally popular support for the CCP, but it no longer resonated with large sections of the Chinese people. During the intense intra-CCP debate of 1977 through early 1980 about making a clean break with the Cultural Revolution and its policies, participants referred frequently to charting a new course as a matter of "life or death" and determining the "future of our party and country." The writer Zhou Yang, for example, put it this way:

> The more one looks at the progress of the debate [underway], the more one comes to see how important it is. If a political party, a state, a nation does everything according to the books, its thinking is ossified . . . then it will not move forward. Its life will stop, and the party and country will perish.[6]

Although participants in the debate did not spell out exactly how the PRC and/or the CCP regime might "perish," the implicit idea was that popular support for the regime would ebb. Unless standards of living could be raised quickly and substantially, and unless the burden of oppression laid on the Chinese people could be eased, the party would be left without popular support and would, one way or another, "die." Fear of counterrevolution haunted Mao throughout his life, and the collapse of communist party states was ultimately the common fate of nearly all such regimes around the world. Only the PRC, along with Cuba, North Korea, and Vietnam, managed to survive. The core of Deng Xiaoping's political line was to regain popular support for CCP rule by delivering rapid improvements in China's standards of living. Since the quest for the economic development that was to accomplish this relegitimation of CCP rule required major shifts in PRC foreign relations, we can say that the intertwined goals of improved living standards and regime legitimization drove those foreign policy shifts to a significant extent.

An episode during the mid-1978 debates on borrowing foreign money and importing foreign machinery exemplified the close link between inputs from the West and the CCP's efforts to forge a new social compact with the Chinese people. After agreeing that money should be borrowed to purchase and import Western industrial machinery, Deng Xiaoping proposed that fabric and clothing should be leading sectors in this process. Cloth was in short supply and available only in very limited quantities and with ration coupons, yet it was a basic necessity of life. Rapid expansion in cloth and clothing supply would, Deng suggested, quickly demonstrate to China's people the advantages of China's new course, winning popular support for the radical departures from the ideological verities of the pervious thirty years.[7] This episode exemplifies the core link between the opening to the outside world and the effort to relegitimize CCP rule of China. Drawing on the capital, technology, machinery and equipment, and managerial know-how of the advanced capitalist countries would fuel rapid economic growth, leading to improved living standards for the Chinese people and their continuing acceptance of CCP rule—while making the PRC a powerful country.

Within a very few years of Mao Zedong's death, a new cohort of CCP leaders, led and represented by Deng Xiaoping, liberated the Chinese people from highly repressive policies of the Mao era. Mao's totalitarian effort to transform the minds and habits of the Chinese people into human material appropriate to the construction of a communist society via a regimen of indoctrination, class struggle, criticism and self-criticism, small group study, and terror was abandoned. Facing strong opposition to this radical break with Marxist-Leninist ideology from more conservative members of his very broad reform coalition, Deng formulated his famous dictum: It doesn't matter if a cat is black or white, as long as it can catch mice. The "mice" were wealth and power.[8]

China's new direction slowly but ultimately vastly expanded the scope of personal freedom for individual Chinese. The scope of permissible speech gradually expanded. People less and less feared that their spoken words would land them in trouble. Published views were more tightly constrained, but there too the scope of free discussion gradually expanded. The "work unit" (*danwei*) system that had controlled people's housing, medical care, education, travel, and ration coupons, making people virtual serfs of their *danwei* during the Mao era, was dismantled step by step. People became free to change jobs without higher-level approval. Individuals (at least those with "urban" residence permits) increasingly decided where to live, where to work, and where and what their children should study. People could travel freely within China and abroad, limited in most cases (again, at least for people with urban residence permits) only by their economic capabilities. By the Twenty-first century, Chinese tourists were flooding famous sites around the world. Religious observance (if not proselytization) was increasingly tolerated. Gradually, religion came to be deemed a social stabilizing and moral leavening force. Chinese scholars were gradually freed from ideological straitjackets and allowed to again become part of their respective international epistemic communities. A vast range of private activity—in art, personal interests and hobbies, fashion, and courtship, as well as simple frivolous behavior—that had previously been suppressed as bourgeois or even counterrevolutionary was now ignored by the state.

As markets gradually expanded, so too did the ability of individual Chinese to form businesses and use their own creativity to grow those businesses, to change lines of work, to contract with others under mutually agreeable terms—the myriad small freedoms of individual choice that make up a dynamic market economy. Eventually, two or three decades into market-oriented reform, this process of marketization would overwhelm and eventually displace the old central planning system deriving from the Soviet economic model adopted in the early 1950s.[9] Discarding the Soviet model economy was not the aim of most reformers in the late 1970s–early 1980s. Indeed, a large number of prominent leaders of Deng's broad reform coalition saw the stable and methodical planning of the pre–Great Leap Forward 1950s as the golden era to which China should return.

The breathtaking scope of the emancipation of the Chinese people after 1978 is sometimes not adequately appreciated by Americans, who compare the scope of freedom in China to America's, rather than to China's own recent past. When a Chinese standard of judgment is used, the expansion of individual freedom in China under Deng Xiaoping must be recognized as one of the great expansions of human freedom in modern history. More immediately relevant to the theme of this book, the blossoming of freedom after 1978 gave many Chinese hope that the evolution of the PRC now underway would continue, eventually culminating in civic freedoms protected by rule of law. The rapid expansion of individual freedom after 1978 led to rising expectations about the trajectory of that process. History indicates that revolutions and rebellions occur not when conditions are most dire, but when things are getting better. That was the case in China in the 1980s. Within eleven years of setting out on a new course under Deng Xiaoping, China witnessed (during

April–early June 1989) a national uprising demanding that the CCP chart an even bolder course for civic freedom and democracy, and abandoning the political aspect of its Leninist legacy.

An ideological vacuum developed in China during the 1980s.[10] Marxism-Leninism-Mao Zedong Thought lost credibility with a wide swath of the Chinese people as opening brought a flood of previously forbidden knowledge about the high levels of wealth and freedom of the advanced capitalist countries. The Chinese people became aware of how poor and unfree they actually were. Liberal ideals of rule of law, freedom of speech, association, assembly, and democracy flowed into China with Western businessmen, academic exchanges, tourism, movies, and publications. On the other hand, the party's ideological apparatus continued to rely on Marxist-Leninist themes, which had less and less traction. Moreover, the narrative of national humiliation was not yet systematically used to legitimize CCP authority. Into this ideological vacuum flowed liberal ideas extolling political freedom and democracy. The CCP general secretary from 1982 to 1987, Hu Yaobang, was purged for failing to wage resolute ideological struggle against these "bourgeois liberal" ideas.

The Mechanics of Opening to the Outside World

A series of pivotal top-level CCP meetings in 1978 decided that China would open to the outside world. But how was this to be done? To a substantial degree, the opening was a policy of experimentation. Various moves, often proposed by lower-level units, were endorsed by central authorities and then implemented by localities. If the results were positive in terms of economic growth, technological acquisition, job creation, and revenue generation, the policies were often authorized on a broader scale. Yet this process of pragmatic experimentation occurred within a broader conceptual framework: learning from the positive experiences of the advanced capitalist countries to develop the PRC in the shortest time possible. Deng rejected the radical Maoist notion that adopting science and technology from advanced capitalist countries amounted to adopting capitalism. Science and technology had no "class character" according to Deng, but could be developed and used by any class. Under capitalism, they were developed and used by the bourgeoisie. In socialist China, they would be developed and used by the proletariat—to make socialist China rich and powerful. Chinese scholars later developed a narrative placing China's Maoist isolation and its post-Mao opening in a deeper historical context. China had been strong when it was open and drew deeply on the achievements of other peoples and civilizations, according to this narrative. The Han, Tang, and early Ming and Qing dynasties were identified as open and powerful periods. When China closed itself off, it became complacent and fell behind. The late Ming and Qing periods, plus the Mao era, served as examples and warnings against isolation. This framework resonated with the collective historical memory and identity of the Chinese people, providing an effective justification of the opening, with its radical break from Maoist autarky.

But exactly what should China seek to acquire from the advanced capitalist countries? The initial emphasis was on importation of modern industrial machinery, equipment, and technologies used in the West but not in China. These fit fairly neatly into the Marxist category of "forces of production," and the import of such items was an important component of the Four Modernizations plan drafted by Zhou Enlai and Deng Xiaoping in 1974–1975. But from the very beginning of his rule, Deng emphasized the need to acquire Western scientific knowledge. Deng broke with Mao regarding the class essence of China's intelligentsia. Mao had seen China's highly educated specialists, "experts," as germ seeds of a new bourgeoisie whose consciousness needed to be transformed. Deng, for his part, saw them as "workers with the mind," a respectable indeed vital, component of the working class.

What this meant in terms of PRC foreign relations was that China's scientists were allowed to engage Western scientific communities for the first time since 1949. Study of Western languages was encouraged and rewarded. Foreign publications could be acquired, paid for, and studied. Study at foreign universities was encouraged, even if and when many Chinese students and scholars opted not to return to China at the end of their studies. Cooperation with foreign scientists on joint projects, or attendance of foreign academic conferences, was encouraged and supported. Travel for such purposes was often supported financially by the state. Foreign scientific and technological literature across a wide range of areas was collected systematically. Much of it was translated into Chinese and disseminated in publications serving appropriate Chinese scientific communities.

These reforms were among the earliest following Deng's selection as paramount leader. They quickly won him a solid, supportive constituency among China's scientific and engineering elite. They also dramatically symbolized that China was headed in a new and radically different direction. Deng's broad strategic direction was clear from the beginning: to draw on the "positive" achievements of the "advanced (capitalist) countries" to make CCP-ruled, socialist China rich and strong. And relegitimize CCP rule.

Enlightening China's Elite about China's Backwardness

During the 1950s, China imported and assimilated a vast amount of Soviet and East European industrial machinery and equipment. As part of China's overall industrialization strategy, most of that relatively advanced gear was reverse-engineered, often with Soviet assistance; copied, often with simplifications; and then mass-produced in China's machine building factories and distributed across vast swaths of the economy via the central planning process. Whatever indigenous innovation occurred under comprehensive economic planning was top-down, driven by the design bureaus of various ministries and the planning organs that approved or rejected the proposals of those bureaus for incorporation into the plan. Enterprise managers, not facing competition from more efficient firms and with costs covered by planned allocations, had little incentive to innovate. Innovation was the job of higher levels in Beijing. Seeking and trying out new technologies could be dangerous for a manager whose job was to meet targets specified by higher-level planners. The incentives for managers in a planned economy were to scrupulously meet plan targets, not to take risks by trying out new innovations. Moreover, the technical experts who might have led the innovation process were politically suspect. The consequence of all this was industrialization without much subsequent innovation. Once a set of machinery or technology was put into use, it typically continued in use unchanged for decades.

This was brought home to me in the mid-1990s when I led a group of Georgia Institute of Technology students on a tour of the First Automobile Works (FAW) in Changchun, Jilin province. FAW was China's first large-scale automobile and truck factory, set up with Soviet assistance in the early 1950s. As it turned out, the factory we visited was still producing trucks based on designs supplied by the Soviet Union in the early 1950s. Those Soviet designs had, in turn, been based on General Motor's designs of the late 1930s. This meant that in the mid-1990s China's leading truck manufacturer was still producing vehicles with the power, mileage, braking, controls, and pollution standards of the late 1930s. In advanced capitalist countries, there was an immense difference between automotive technology of the late 1930s and the mid-1990s, with the latter vastly superior in all performance categories. The FAW in the 1990s was, in effect, producing obsolete vehicles in an extremely inefficient manner and foisting its inferior product on end users by government fiat and protectionism.

While the PRC during the Maoist era was isolating itself from the outside world and persecuting its engineers as bourgeois elements, the advanced capitalist countries were in the midst of a profound technological revolution. Microelectronic science, engineering, and manufacturing had matured adequately to allow integrated circuits (IC) built on silicon chips to be manufactured cheaply and reliably. IC chips were being integrated into a growing array of devices from automobiles to telecommunications to manufacturing to home appliances. Whole new industries were arising to produce IC chips and the devices that used them: computers, microwaves, laser optical devices such as printers, fax machines, video recorders, satellite television and telephones, sensing and imaging, and much more. The advanced capitalist countries were entering the "information era"—a transition of creative destruction as profound as the steam revolution of the nineteenth century or the amalgam of electricity, internal combustion engines, and radio of the early twentieth century. The military implications of this "information revolution" were also profound. By the 1980s, the United States was integrating new information technology into a revolutionary new style of war of far greater precision, speed, and lethality, radically reducing the traditional military advantage of superior numbers. The United States would not try out this new style of warfare until 1991 in Iraq. But already by the late 1970s, the implications were apparent to those who paid attention.

China in 1978 was outside of the scientific and technological revolution that was transforming the advanced capitalist countries. Most of China's leaders simply were not aware of how far behind China had fallen. Very few had had the opportunity to travel to advanced capitalist countries. What travel opportunities there were under Mao were mostly to socialist or developing countries (Burma, India, Pakistan, etc.). The few Chinese officials that traveled to capitalist countries (France or Switzerland, perhaps) were tightly constrained by both their itineraries and ideological rigidity at home. It would have been very foolish for a Chinese leader, perhaps in France in 1965, to report favorably to Beijing on the strengths of French capitalism. CCP ideology of that era declared that the working classes of advanced capitalist countries lived in privation and squalor little different than the conditions described by Karl Marx for Britain in the 1840s. In terms of level of wealth and development, how was it possible for countries with reactionary counterrevolutionary imperialist elites to be superior to progressive socialist countries led by the dictatorship of the proletariat with its "scientific" understanding of economics, society, and history? Marxist ideas of this sort were not merely one point of view at the beginning of the opening period. They were, instead, absolute scientific truth, unchallenged by other ideas and propounded nearly daily.

Profound revelation occurred when personal observation in advanced capitalist countries became possible and confronted traditional ideological verities. Again a personal antidote. In the early 1990s, my family and I lived in a neighborhood of northeast Beijing. There was one state-run store serving the neighborhood. It was a dingy single room about as big as the average American living room and was stocked with several hundred goods: pens, pencils and paper, soap and other toiletries, canned foods, thermos bottles, batteries and light bulbs, liquor, beer and soft drinks, pots and pans, etc. Such was the fare of Chinese consumers in the capital of the country. In interior regions, supply was even worse. Again, suppression of even the most basic consumer goods was a key dimension of the Stalinist strategy of hyperaccumulation. During the same era, when acquaintances from China would visit us in Atlanta during their first trip to the United States, we would take them to a typical US supermarket with its football-field-size offering of tens of thousands of brightly displayed goods. Even with a single product—toilet paper or toothpaste, perhaps—there would be scores of choices to match each individual preference. Our Chinese visitors were often shocked by this abundance.

During visits to New York in 1974 and to Paris in 1975, Deng Xiaoping had opportunities to see how far behind the advanced capitalist countries China had fallen. Deng's stay in New York City in April 1974 to propound Mao's Three Worlds theory was only for several days, but even a brief stay in that invigorating city offered a glimpse of at least the physical structure of a Western urban metropolis, so different from the low-rise, dour, low-tech cities of socialist countries. On a free day during his 1974 New York visit, Deng asked to be taken to Wall Street. It was Sunday and offices were closed, but Deng nonetheless saw the heart of US capitalism.[11] Deng returned to France in May 1975 for a six-day visit organized to give him a much closer look at advanced capitalism. Deng had lived in France for five years, from 1920 to 1925, so his return in 1975 gave him an opportunity to see the results of fifty years of capitalist development. France in that time had been completely transformed. Accompanied during his 1975 visit by a number of high-ranking cadres from China's industrial, transport, and scientific sectors, Deng and his entourage were shown a number of French factories and agricultural facilities. Deng was stuck by the high level of automation, mechanization, and efficiency of French industries. Deng also discussed trade possibilities with his French hosts and found considerable interest in this regard. Deng concluded his investigation in France acutely aware of how far behind the West China had fallen, how much it needed to race to catch up.[12] As Deng would tell a pivotal Central Work Conference in December 1978 that would lead to his appointment as the CCP's paramount leader:

> [T]he fundamental guiding principle of shifting the focus of all Party work to the four modernizations . . . has solved a host of important problems inherited from the past . . . Let us advance courageously to change the backward condition of our country and turn it into a modern and powerful socialist country.[13]

Once Deng returned to office in July 1977 after Mao's death and the arrest of Jiang Qing and her radical Maoist followers, he arranged for multiple delegations of top-level Chinese leaders to travel to advanced counties for investigation of conditions. Deng's purpose was to "emancipate the minds" of China's leaders by making them aware of how backward and poor China was and of the need to focus all party work on the Four Modernizations. In 1978, four high-level investigation groups traveled to Yugoslavia, Hong Kong, Japan, and Western Europe.[14] The delegation to Yugoslavia renormalized ties with that country and its ruling communist party and legitimized study of the socialist economies of Eastern Europe. A number of models would be debated and tried in China in the 1980s, East European models of socialism among them. The delegation to Hong Kong included leading officials from the State Planning Commission and the foreign trade ministry. It explored the possibility of expanding cross-border economic cooperation by setting up an export processing zone at Shenzhen on the Hong Kong–Guangdong border. This discussion was one origin of what would become the Shenzhen Special Economic Zone (SEZ) set up the following year.

The investigation mission to Japan in March–April 1978 stayed nearly three weeks. It included high officials from the State Planning Commission, the ministries of commerce and foreign trade, and the Bank of China. By 1978, Japan had risen from the ashes of devastating destruction in 1945 to catch up with the Western countries in terms of technological level and standard of living. Japan's government had played a key role in accomplishing this amazing recovery, though not via direct bureaucratic control over the economy as with the Soviet model. Because of Japan's distinctive state-business relation, the visiting Chinese dignitaries recognized the relevance of Japan's experience for China, and sought to understand exactly how the Japan model worked. In a report to the Politburo shortly after the mission returned to China, the delegation leader laid out the key elements. Japan had boldly used foreign technology and foreign capital. It had stressed education and scientific research. While in Japan, mission members also discussed the possibility for Japanese aid and technology transfer to China. Delegation members were stuck by how enthusiastic Japanese officials and business leaders were about the possibility of expanded Sino-Japanese economic cooperation. This was the first-ever official and high-level visit by Chinese dignitaries to Japan, and was welcomed by Japanese opinion as a harbinger of a new and friendlier era of Sino-Japanese relations.

The 1978 investigation missions to Western Europe lasted over a month (May–early June) and was led by Gu Mu, then the PRC's third highest-ranking official dealing with economic affairs (after Li Xiannian and Yu Qiuli). Gu Mu also had a long history of responsibility for technology matters. The investigation mission to Western Europe was composed of specialists from different economic sectors, and separately visited eighty different facilities in fifteen cities in France, Switzerland, West Germany, Denmark, and Belgium. This was the first state-level PRC mission to most of these countries, and host governments rolled out the red carpet. Mission members were impressed by the high level of mechanization and automation and the abundant use of computers. In Bremen, on Germany's North Sea coast, mission members saw the containerized movement of cargo for the first time. Shortly after the mission returned to China, Gu Mu reported to the Politburo on the enormous gap in technology and overall level of development between China and the West European countries. But he also reported that West European government and business leaders were friendly toward China and its development effort, and willing to lend money and transfer technologies. China should urgently investigate ways of doing this, Gu stated. Lest some leading cadres object to Gu Mu's radical conclusions, very senior supporters of Deng's opening, Ye Jianying, Li Xiannian, and Nie Rongzhen, one after the other made statements lauding Gu Mu's objectivity and clarity of presentation.

At the end of June, Gu Mu submitted a written report to the Politburo outlining how China should seek to harness the resources of advanced capitalist countries. Deng Xiaoping told the Politburo session convened to discuss Gu's proposals that China should move as quickly as possible to implement all of Gu's recommendations, including borrowing money from abroad. A two-month long forum chaired by Li Xiannian on the principles to guide the Four Modernizations followed. Gu once again reported on his West Europe mission. At the end of the forum, Li Xiannian announced the beginning of a new era of openness for China in which it would import technology, capital, machinery and equipment, and managerial know-how to rapidly achieve the Four Modernizations. Scholar Ezra Vogel noted that while China's reform leaders had embraced the principle of opening to the world by this point, there was still no discussion of the role of markets in China's new course.

The core of Deng's *political* strategy was to build voluntary constituencies supporting opening and reform by offering them particularistic arrangements that allowed them to obtain economic gain not from the central government but via activities on global and/or domestic markets. In this way, Deng did not challenge existing and still immensely powerful interests (heavy industry and the planning agencies). Rather, Deng build around these old, established interests, gradually building willing proreform constituencies engaged in opening and reform, while leaving old vested interests intact (at least until well into the reform process).[15] Nor did this arrangement require large financial support from the hard-strapped central treasury.

Deng's dispatch of "investigation missions" abroad in 1978 was a variant of this voluntary constituency creation. By sending thirteen vice premier–level officials and hundreds of first secretaries and provincial governors abroad to "investigate" in 1978, Deng was "emancipating the minds" of these officials, motivating them to grapple with the immense and still-strange difficulties of dealing with the governments and businesses of advanced capitalist countries. Calling forth a cohort of new leading officials willing to undertake this arduous task, and even the granting of lucrative autonomy to coastal areas which followed close on the heels of the 1978 investigation missions, were not the most important of constituency-building efforts by Deng in this period. Turning land over to individual farming families and authorizing private, market-based nonfarming activities, including private industrial enterprise, were probably the most important forms of constituency building in the early reform period.[16] "Reversing verdicts" on cadres unfairly purged under Mao's rule and reinterpreting the "class character" of China's intellectuals were also supremely important. But in the realm of PRC foreign relations, "emancipating the minds" of a substantial cohort of leading cadres by giving them a glimpse of China's future as a modern, technologically advanced, and industrialized country, the foreign investigation missions that began in 1978 were important. As Deng told his comrades in December 1978 as he was about to be chosen as the CCP's paramount leader: "We must acknowledge we are backward, that many of our ways of doing things are inappropriate, and that we need to change."[17]

Opening China's Door to Japan

Japan was a natural and essential partner in the Four Modernizations. By 1978, Japan's economy had become the third largest in the world (after only the United States and the USSR), and had a per capita income ranking between Britain and France. Japan was a leading export power and a world technological leader in electronic appliances, microelectronics, automation, ship building, steel, and heavy equipment. Japan was arguably the only non-Western country to have closed the economic and technological gap between the West and the non-Western countries. The importance of Japanese capital, technology, and managerial know-how to economic development in East Asia had already been demonstrated by the powerful symbiosis that developed in the 1960s and 1970s between Japan, South Korea, Taiwan, Hong Kong, and Singapore (the latter four dubbed the "Four Tigers" by the media). The same logic that welded together Japan and the Four Tigers—the combination of cheap labor and land in the Four Tigers with advanced Japanese technology to produce sophisticated, high-quality, but cheap goods for global markets—could tie together Japan and the PRC in the 1980s, if an appropriate political framework for a new Sino-Japanese economic partnership could be arranged.

No treaty existed between the PRC and Japan in 1978 to provide a framework for broad economic exchanges. The Joint Declaration of 1972, the reader will recall, had declared an end to the "abnormal situation" that had existed between the two countries up to that point and established diplomatic relations, but had only expressed a desire to terminate the state of war that still technically existed. After the 1972 breakthrough, several transportation, communications, and fisheries agreements between the two countries were signed, but a peace treaty providing, inter alia, for consular relations was still lacking. Talks on a treaty of peace and cooperation had been underway since 1972, but without much progress.

The key obstacle to such a treaty was China's insistence that it contain an anti-hegemony clause identical to the one in the 1972 Sino-Japan Joint Declaration and modeled after the anti-hegemony clause in the Sino-US

1972 Joint Communiqué. Japan resisted this, fearing that such a clause would antagonize Moscow. Japan's traditional approach to the Soviet Union and China in the late 1970s was "equidistance"—maintaining good relations with both communist powers. Inclusion of an anti-hegemony clause in a treaty with Beijing would tilt Japan toward China, possibly spoiling Soviet-Japan relations, Tokyo feared. Huang Hua, foreign minister from 1976 to 1982 and China's principal in treaty negotiations with Japan in 1978, believed that Tanaka had agreed to the anti-hegemony clause in 1972 in hopes that the specter of a Japan-Chinese alignment would pressure Moscow into returning the Northern Territories to Japan.[18] (The Northern Territories are four islands at the southern end of the Kurile Island chain seized by the Soviet Union in August 1945.) This hope had been destroyed by Moscow's refusal to return the islands. Growing Soviet military activities in the seas around Japan and increasing Soviet belligerence was making Tokyo increasingly fearful of the Soviet Union in the late 1970s, in Huang Hua's estimate. This made Tokyo reluctant to further antagonize Moscow by including an anti-hegemony clause in a treaty with China. While Mao lived, Beijing was adamantly opposed to any watering down of the anti-hegemony clause of the 1972 Joint Declaration. Speaking to a senior Japanese parliamentarian in October 1975 (while Mao was still alive, reading reports on Deng's words and actions, and watching him closely for evidence of revisionism), Deng said:

> The anti-hegemony provision in the Joint Declaration [of 1972] must be included in the treaty of peace and friendship. This is precisely the crux of . . . the treaty, and is also one of the principled positions held by China. If Japan finds it difficult to include it now, we can do it later . . . Rather than making this or that ambiguous interpretations, we would be better of postponing the talks for the time being. We can't retreat from the Joint Declaration.[19]

After Mao's death and Deng's recall to office in July 1977, Deng began working for a breakthrough in relations with Japan. In the process, and with Mao no longer looking over his shoulder, Deng would agree of inclusion of "this or that ambiguous interpretation" in the treaty in order to address Japan's concerns about antagonizing Moscow. Early in 1978, CCP leaders conducted an all-round domestic and international analysis of the situation regarding Japan. It was decided that it was time to reopen the stalled peace treaty negotiations and push for a resolution.[20] Deng began inviting to Beijing and meeting with Japanese political leaders and businessmen judged sympathetic to a treaty with China.[21] In discussions with these Japanese notables, Deng stressed the importance of Sino-Japanese cooperation for the immediate economic interests of the two countries and for the long-term peace of Asia. His message resonated with his Japanese guests. Deng also pressured Prime Minister Takeo Fukuda by identifying him to his Japanese visitors as the key obstacle to achieving a treaty. Speaking to a delegation from the opposition Japan Socialist Party, Deng expressed desire for the rapid conclusion of a treaty, said this was what the people of Japan wanted, but concluded "Now the problem is that Prime Minister Fukuda has to make a decision."[22] To a visiting former chief cabinet secretary of the Japanese government, Deng said: "The problem is that he [Fukuda] needs to make up his mind, and this takes only a single second. We are waiting in anticipation."[23]

To address Japanese fears about antagonizing Moscow, Deng also gave some critical ground on the anti-hegemony clause, permitting inclusion of an "ambiguous interpretation" that he had ruled out in October 1975 while Mao was still breathing. Beijing now informed Tokyo that, in China's view, since both countries had independent foreign policies, joint opposition to hegemonism did not mean that the two governments would take united action. When Japan conveyed this understanding to Moscow it mitigated Soviet anger. Then, shortly before the final round of talks began in Beijing between foreign ministers Huang Hua and Sunao Sonoda in August 1978, Deng Xiaoping approved Japanese-proposed phraseology that further mitigated the impact of the anti-hegemony clause. Tokyo believed that extending common opposition to hegemony in the whole world rather than restricting it to Asia-Pacific would make the clause less offensive to Moscow. Tokyo therefore proposed that the words "or in other regions" be inserted after "Asia and the Pacific" in delineating the geographic scope of their common opposition to hegemony. Those words—"or in other regions"—were not in the 1972 Joint Communiqué, but were included in the 1978 treaty. In sum, Deng had retreated from the 1972 Joint Declaration to get a deal with Japan. Huang Hua conveyed this small but significant concession to Sonoda on August 9 and portrays it as the decisive move opening the way to a treaty. According to Huang:

> Hearing my statement, Sonoda was so excited that he got to his feet and shook my hand, with tears in his eyes. He said: This visit of mine has enabled me to remove formidable difficulties. I can admit that I am gambling with . . . my political life. . . . I am deeply grateful to Huang Hua for this message that contributes greatly to the conclusion of the treaty.[24]

The Treaty of Peace and Friendship was signed by Huang Hua and Sonoda on August 12, 1978. One of the first people to pass through the now open door to Japan was Deng Xiaoping. Deng's week-long visit to Japan in October 1978 came barely two months after the signature of the Treaty of Peace and Friendship. It was the first visit by a top Chinese leader to Japan in the 2,000 years of relations between those two countries! It was also the first-ever meeting between a top Chinese leader and an emperor of Japan. In this case, the emperor was Hirohito, who had reigned during Japan's aggression against

China in the 1930s and 1940s. The formal purpose of Deng's visit was to witness ratification of the recently signed treaty. But the larger purpose was to forge a cooperative and friendly relation between the two countries, opening the way for Japanese support for China's "new long march" of the Four Modernizations. Deng's visit was a masterful display of deft diplomacy.

Deng relied on several tropes to court Japanese opinion.[25] One was his generous treatment of the history issue. During Deng's visit, many Japanese, from the emperor and prime minister to business magnates to ordinary citizens, expressed contrition and remorse for Japan's aggression. Deng accepted these expressions of apology with equanimity, forgoing innumerable opportunities to express bitterness or grievance, let alone to elaborate on Japan's crimes against China. Instead, Deng indicated that the people of both countries should not dwell on the past but look to the future. A significant element of Japan's political culture was (and remains) a feeling of remorse for Japan's aggression against China. Deng's handling of the history issue was brilliant. It was as though a high priest was offering absolution for Japan's sins. Of course, it was implicit that full remission of these sins would require atonement by assisting China on its new long march toward modernization. Many of Deng's Japanese hosts made this linkage explicit. Konosuke Matsushita, founder of the giant electronic appliance firm Panasonic and the Matsushita heavy machinery company, told Deng how deeply remorseful he was about Japan's aggression toward China. Matsushita envisioned atoning for that aggression by producing good but inexpensive televisions for China's people. Deng welcomed and encouraged such Japanese participation in China's Four Modernizations. This was an astute use of Japan's national psychology.

Another aspect of Deng's demeanor that proved effective with his Japanese audiences was his humility. Time and again, Deng referred to China's backwardness, its poverty, and its need to learn from Japan. For example, when touring Nijo Castle in Kyoto (the emperor's castle during the Tokugawa Shogunate, famous for its graceful gardens) and being told by his Japanese host that "all the culture you see here was introduced by our ancestors who learned it from China." Deng immediately replied, "Now our positions are reversed."[26] At a press conference with over 400 media people (the first such press conference ever held by a CCP leader), Deng replied to a question by saying, "We must admit our deficiencies. We are a backward country and we must learn from Japan."[27] When another reporter asked about Mao's responsibility for the horrors of the Cultural Revolution, Deng replied:

> These were not just Mao's mistakes, they were all our mistakes. Many of us made mistakes. We lacked experience and had poor judgment. . . . We are very poor. We are very backward. We have to recognize that. We have a lot to do, a long way to go, and a lot to learn.[28]

Deng's personal simplicity and apparent sincerity won Japanese sympathy. After a long discussion with Prime Minister Fukuda, Deng gave the surprised Japanese leader a bear hug (a habit Deng may have learned from Soviet leaders). During a later, more intimate meeting with Fukuda and top officials, Deng pulled out a pack of Panda cigarettes and offered them all around, saying "For years I have been looking for an opportunity to visit Japan, and finally I can realize it. I am very happy to have the chance to get to know Prime Minister Fukuda." When Fukuda later said that he knew China only from before the war and hoped someday to visit it, Deng immediately replied, "On behalf of the Chinese government, I invite you to visit at a time convenient to you."[29]

While winning Japanese opinion to support China's new modernization drive, Deng's tour of Japan "emancipated the minds" of Chinese audiences. Not many Chinese as yet had televisions, but filmed news reports and photographs documenting Deng's activities in Japan prominently displayed for Chinese the advanced levels of technology in use in Japan. They also made clear the friendly attitudes of many Japanese toward China. The point was that China could draw on the advanced aspects of modern Japan's economy to facilitate China's Four Modernizations.

Japan quickly emerged as China's second most important trade partner, ranking only behind Hong Kong. During 1978–1988, Japan accounted for roughly one-fifth of China's total trade. That was only about two-thirds of Hong Kong's level (28 percent), but double the share (about 10 percent) of China's third-ranking trade partner, the United States.[30] Japan also began giving development aid in 1979, immediately after the peace treaty was signed. Over the next twenty-five years, China was annually either the first- or second-ranking recipient of Japanese ODA. China received approximately 3.13 trillion yen in concessionary loans, 145.7 billion in grant aid (which did not need to be repaid), and 144.6 billion in technical cooperation. Japanese aid to China averaged 150 billion yen (very roughly US$1.5 billion) per year, equivalent to about 0.25 percent of China's annual GDP. Japanese assistance also supported, inter alia, the training in Japan of 37,000 Chinese specialists, the electrification of 5,000 kilometers of railway, construction of sixty large harbor berths, the Baoshan steel plant outside Shanghai, three major airports (including in Shanghai's Pudong and Beijing), five trunk highways, five power plants, three fertilizer factories, a number of pollution control projects, and a major hospital in Beijing. China was second only to Indonesia in terms of volume of Japanese development assistance.[31] Japan's assistance gave a strong boost to China's modernization drive and integration into the global economy. As Sino-Japan economic ties became closer, and as Beijing's fear of Soviet encirclement mounted, China's assessment of Japan's military alliance with the United States also shifted. Beijing began to view Japan's military strength as a positive factor countering the Soviet Union.[32]

Reform of the Trade System

A strong bias against foreign trade was built into the Soviet economic model adopted by China in the 1950s. Factory managers in a planned economy succeeded or failed professionally on the basis of whether they fulfilled the targets assigned them by annual and five year plans. If factories and their managers were to produce for export a certain quantity and type of good, that task would be assigned them by the plan. Similarly, if some particular machinery, equipment, technology, or raw material was to be imported for use in a particular factory, that too would be determined by the plan. The factory manager's job was to use the imported items or material as directed by the plan. It followed from this that exports and imports—foreign trade—were essentially plan-driven. The planners would work out their economic objectives for the next period of time. They would then calculate the materials and items necessary to achieve those objectives, along with the capabilities of various domestic firms to supply those materials and items. If required materials or items were not available domestically, the planners might opt to import them. The planners would then tabulate the sum total of all projected imports and, finally, consider what could be exported to generate the requisite amount of foreign currency to pay for the projected imports. Trade was thus essentially import-driven: goods were exported as necessary to pay for planned imports.[33]

This system had a number of disincentives to trade. Factory managers had little incentive to ensure that the goods they produced were exactly what the final customer needed, let alone redesign a product to fit the customer's need. The factory, after all, did not have to sell the goods they manufactured; their task was completed upon delivery of plan-stipulated goods. The planners were responsible for determining who would receive the products produced by a factory. And in any case, there was no direct contact between the factory and the customer. All contact was via a higher authority, most probably a trade company with a monopoly with trade in a particular range of goods. That monopoly was itself a further restraint on trade. All foreign exchange earned by trade was taken by the foreign trade ministry. This too gave little incentive for factories or even foreign trade corporations to export. Learning to operate new imported machinery could be risky and might result in non-fulfillment of plan objectives. Increases in productivity that might reward the import and utilization of new machinery in a competitive environment did not matter much in a planned economy. Costs, including losses, were covered by the state. The incentive for factory managers was to convince the planners that the items produced by the factory required as many inputs as possible. The incentives for factory managers, in other words, was to use resources inefficiently. This was yet another obstacle to trade, since success on markets required low costs, premised, in part, on efficient operations. Maoist China didn't trade much, and not only because of ideological preferences for autarky and self-reliance. Its entire Soviet-derived economic system was heavily biased against foreign trade.

China's new economic engineers understood and sought to emulate the success of Japan and the Four Tigers, which had promoted exports to generate foreign currency which was then used to import advanced machinery and equipment. Decentralization of foreign trade authority to the provinces was one of the first and most important reforms in the area of foreign trade.[34] In 1979, when reform was beginning, China had twelve foreign trade companies (FTC) under the Ministry of Foreign Trade and Economic Cooperation (MOFTEC). Each FTC had a monopoly on trade in a particular range of products. In 1979, these monopolies were abolished by granting the power to establish foreign trade companies and conduct foreign trade to provincial governments and, if the provincial governments desired, to cities under the province's administration. Authority to engage in foreign trade went to lower levels of government, not to private individuals or companies. By decentralizing foreign trade authority to provincial and city governments, Deng was, once again, creating within the state a constituency with a vested interest in opening and reform. In effect, Deng was going around China's central organs, where control-minded planners and state-owned heavy industry dominated, and empowering provinces and localities to push ahead with reform and opening as they were able. In 1986, there were about 800 foreign trade companies. By 1987, there were 5,000.[35] PRC trade began to grow rapidly, as indicated by Figure 13-1, showing trade from 1950 to 2011. Prior to opening and under a planned economy, China traded little, and there was little growth in trade. A revolutionary change began in 1979, when China's two-way trade began to

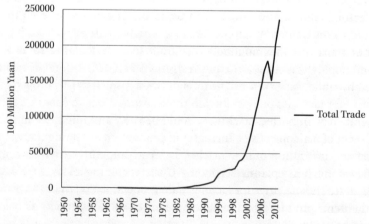

FIGURE 13-1 **PRC Foreign Trade, 1950–2011**

Source: *Xin zhongguo wushi nian tongji ziliao huibian* (Comprehensive statistical data and matierals on 50 years of new China), (China Statistics Press: Beijing, 1999), p. 60.

grow rapidly. China was on the way to restoring its historic position as one of the world's leading trading countries.

A powerful symbiosis developed between the decollectivization of China's agriculture and the growth of China's foreign trade. Once agriculture was decollectivized via the family responsibility system, China's newly liberated farmers began finding all sorts of inventive ways of enriching themselves and their country. Permitted to engage in nonagricultural lines of work, China's farmers set up small enterprises, called township and village enterprises (TVEs) because of their rural location. Many prospered and grew rapidly. Goods from the increasingly market-driven and entrepreneurial countryside began to flood into the cities, demonstrating the wealth-producing power of markets.[36] These TVEs played a leading role in China's reemergence as a trading country. Between 1980 and 1990, TVEs provided 67 percent of China's increase in exports.[37] Rural entrepreneurs, operating on a purely market basis outside the state-planned sector, were quick to recognize the opportunities presented by selling goods to rich foreign markets, and were flexible in supplying that demand. These dynamic TVEs provided local governments with tax revenue and a large portion of the locality's foreign currency, producing strong incentives for local authorities to cooperate to make firms successful. As private ownership and investment and market-based entrepreneurship became ideologically acceptable and spread ever more broadly across China's economy, the rate of growth accelerated. China had finally found the path to economic wealth.

Ten years into China's reform process, China had re-entered the global trading system. It was not yet a global trading power, but its role was growing. Trade had been decentralized to local governments hungry to expand trade, increasingly knowledgeable about how to do that, and operating in an increasingly marketized environment. China's central governmental organs had been transformed from bodies organizing and conducting foreign trade to regulatory bodies supervising trade activity by autonomous, market-based, and profit-seeking enterprises. China, following the path of earlier East Asia industrializers, had begun the path of export promotion and technology acquisition. It still had a long way to go before it became the world's leading exporter that it would eventually become. But it had begun the long march in that direction.

Foreign Investment and the Special Economic Zones

According to Marxist-Leninist theory, when capitalists from advanced capitalist countries invested in underdeveloped areas of Asia, Africa, or Latin America, the result was the transfer of wealth from these poor countries to the advanced capitalist counties. The poverty of Third World countries was a function of this private investment by the advanced capitalist countries. That was why they were poor, and the advanced capitalist countries rich. These verities of Marxism-Leninism guided China during the Maoist era. The substantial foreign investment that existed in China prior to 1949 was quickly eliminated in the process of "cleaning house" in the early 1950s. No foreign investment was permitted between 1949 and 1979.[38] While China would occasionally purchase and import foreign industrial equipment, and indeed whole factories, during the Mao era, the foreign role typically ended when the factory was "turned on" (hence "turnkey projects"). The resulting facilities were always owned by the Chinese state, never by capitalists, Chinese or foreign.

The Four Tigers followed a far different and a far more successful path. Hong Kong and Singapore welcomed foreign private capital, and this helped propel their rapid industrialization, export growth, and increase in standards of living. Taiwan and South Korea adopted state-guided industrial policy and restricted the role of foreign capital to a far larger extent than Singapore or Hong Kong in the initial states of industrialization. But in the 1960s, Taiwan and South Korea pioneered the use of designated geographic zones in which foreign direct investment (FDI) was encouraged by various preferential policies. Production in these "export processing zones" (EPZ), as they were called, was exclusively for foreign markets, thus keeping the local market protected from foreign competition as a seedbed for domestic industry. Domestic capital could be invested in the EPZ, but, again, the output was entirely for export. Technologies and processes introduced in the EPZs nonetheless tended to disseminate from the EZP into the local economy outside the zone, as ambitious local entrepreneurs first learned the secrets of commercial success inside the EPZs and then replicated them for themselves outside the zone. EPZs in Taiwan and South Korea proved very successful and served as a model for the Special Economic Zones (SEZ) set up in Guangdong province in 1979.

Guangdong had for centuries been a center of China's commercial activity with Southeast Asia. Chinese ocean-faring junks—well designed for the monsoon wind cycle of the South China Sea—would set out from Guangzhou (formerly known as Canton) and Qianzhou in Fujian province and pass through the South China Sea to the Straits to Malacca, where goods were typically handed off to Indian, Arab, or Persian merchants for the next segment of the journey west. The arrival of Europeans in the sixteenth century, with their revolutionary breakthroughs in ship design (no longer confined to monsoon seas) and more direct transoceanic trade routes to Europe and the Americas, greatly expanded this East Asian maritime economy.[39] Guangzhou was a key hub of this robust international maritime trade. Migrants followed trade routes, and Guangdong, along with Fujian, supplied a large number of migrants to Southeast Asia. There these immigrants often became commercially successful, further increasing the economic links between their new and ancestral homes. Plugged into these powerful currents of international trade, and far away from China's imperial capital in Beijing, Guangdong developed an oceanic and commercial culture distinct from the more government-centric and continental culture of North China.[40]

All this came to a stop with China's transition to socialism after 1949. China's "bourgeoisie," which had organized earlier trade, was "eliminated as a class," and foreign trade was centralized under foreign trade monopolies as described earlier. Yet, in a strange re-emergence of a practice abandoned after the First Opium War, Guangzhou was established as the sole venue for trade between China and the West. An annual Canton Trade Fair was initiated in 1957 with spring and fall sessions of about three weeks each, when foreign businesses interested in buying or selling could come, examine goods displayed in hundreds of stalls, and negotiate with representatives of state-owned trading companies operating under close party and governmental supervision. Whatever profits resulted from that trade was taken by the center. The similarity between the Canton Trade Fair of 1957 to 1979 with the Canton system of trade that functioned prior to 1842 is striking. Both characterized periods when China closed itself off from the world.

Guangdong had good reason to seize opportunities offered by the center's new approach. Guangdong had received little investment via the central planning process in the 1950s–1970s. The province was on the front line and vulnerable to attack or invasion by the United States or the Chinese Nationalists. With the Americans ensconced in Taiwan, the Philippines, and South Vietnam, and with preparation for war with the United States a constant priority during the pre-1971 era, China's planners considered it prudent not to locate new industrial facilities in the vulnerable front line. Other old industrial areas like Shanghai or Manchuria were also vulnerable to foreign threat, but they at least had the offsetting advantage of having a large, already established industrial base that yielded large returns on whatever investment the central planners chose to allocate there. Guangdong had not been a major industrial area before 1949 and lacked even this advantage. Consequently, under the planning system, when new investment came via the plan, Guangdong received very little.[41]

Guangdong did have one immense potential advantage: Hong Kong. By the late 1970s, there was a strong meshing of the comparative advantages of Hong Kong and Guangdong province. Land and labor costs in Hong Kong were rising by the late 1970s, putting sharp pressure on Hong Kong businesses exporting to highly competitive global markets. Just across the border in the PRC, labor and land were cheap. Guangdong was contiguous with Hong Kong and linked by a common variety of the Chinese language, the Guangdong dialect known as Cantonese, as different from spoken Mandarin as German is from English.

Establishment of the Shenzhen SEZ—by far the most successful of the first four SEZs set up in 1979—was the result of an initiative by leaders of Guangdong province. Early in 1979, Xi Zhongxun, then first secretary of Guangdong (and father of Xi Jinping, who would become paramount leader in 2012), proposed to Deng Xiaoping that the province be allowed to "exert its superiority" via expanded cooperation with Hong Kong.[42] Guangdong should be allowed to make its own foreign trade decisions and invite foreigners to invest, Xi suggested. In November 1977, Deng had visited Bao'an district of Guangdong, which bordered on Hong Kong, where he had been briefed by local officials on the problem of illegal flight of thousands of young people from Guangdong across the border to Hong Kong. Local officials had outlined for Deng their plans for increased use of barbed wire and patrolling to deal with this problem. This led Deng to suggest that a better method would be to find a way of creating job opportunities on the Guangdong side of the border. This in turn led to discussion of the possibility of Bao'an township becoming an assembly point for agricultural produce being supplied to Hong Kong.

Years earlier, Bao'an had built a reservoir to catch and supply fresh water to Hong Kong, and that arrangement had gone quite satisfactorily. The zone discussed in 1977–1978 went far beyond the sale of Guangdong water or food-stuffs to Hong Kong. Instead, it envisioned combining cheap Guangdong labor and land with Hong Kong's industrial manufacturing needs to produce goods for global markets. Bao'an, now a western district of Shenzhen city, was to operate along the lines of export processing zones in South Korea and Taiwan. The Gu Mu–organized State Planning Commission and MOFERT delegation to Hong Kong in 1978 (discussed earlier) further explored the idea with Hong Kong leaders. After that delegation returned to Beijing, the State Council established a Hong Kong and Macao Affairs Office to handle matters related to expanding economic cooperation with those areas.[43]

The proposal by Xi in January 1979 encapsulated these various proposals. Finally, in July the Central Committee of the party and the State Council decided to establish four special zones for export on a trial basis at Shenzhen, Macao, and Shantou, all in Guangdong province, and Xiamen in Fujian. In May 1980, they were renamed Special Economic Zones; addition of the word "economic" was an attempt to reassure conservatives who feared that the simple term "special zones" might lead people to confuse the new zones with the "special zones" under CCP control in the 1930s—and which had constituted the spearhead for transformation of the country's political-social system. Hu Yaobang, then first secretary of the Central Party School, played a key role in designing the policy framework for the SEZ. He was backed in this by Deng Xiaoping and Marshal Ye Jianying, a native of Guangdong province.

There was strong opposition to the SEZ.[44] Chen Yun, economic specialist and virtual coleader with Deng of the reform coalition in the early years after 1978, was a leading voice in opposition to the SEZ. Chen feared the SEZs would undermine China's state sector, which Chen, following Mao and Stalin, took to be the core of China's socialism. With market-based SEZ prices above planned prices in "interior provinces," enterprises would prefer to send materials to the SEZs rather than to "interior provinces" designated by the plan. In this fashion, the SEZs would undermine sound planning. SEZs would also be costly; where would the money come from? Would it not make more sense, Chen Yun said, for central planners to operate on the whole chessboard of China, allocating resources where it made the most sense, not privileging some areas over others? Smuggling and capital flight into the privileged SEZs would further bid up the cost of resources outside the Zones. The result would undermine sound economic planning, which was essential to stable growth in China.

The SEZs also violated the teachings of Marx and Lenin; China's workers would be exploited, just as Marx and Lenin said. Foreign imperialist intelligence agencies would use the zones to spy on China and undermine its socialist system. Bad things would come into China via the SEZs: corruption, organized crime, drugs, pornography, and prostitution. China had once before thrown out such imperialist decadence, while "cleaning house" in the early 1950s. Such "bourgeois filth" should not be allowed back in. The SEZs were reminiscent of the treaty ports imposed on China during its Century of National Humiliation. After wiping out those treaty ports, did China now want to reestablish them where arrogant and rich Westerners could again run wild and boss around Chinese on China's territory? Was this why the Chinese Communist Party had made the revolution? Such were the questions Chen Yun and other opponents of the SEZ asked.

These were potent arguments in the context of the late 1970s and early 1980s. Eventually, they lost out to the reformist's argument that China was poor and backward, and simply needed to earn more foreign exchange to import advanced machinery and equipment. On this basis the reformers argued: Why not try markets and cooperation with Hong Kong and foreign capitalists on an experimental basis, in an enclave literally fenced off from the rest of China and under the supervision of the PRC and the Chinese Communist Party?

Rules for the operation of the Guangdong SEZs were promulgated in August 1980.[45] Hong Kong and foreign businesses that set up factories in Shenzhen were to operate their businesses "according to their own business requirements." They could operate on a profit-seeking, market basis outside China's economic plan. They were required to hire workers via a labor service office set up by the Guangdong government, but could pay and otherwise reward those workers, and fire them, according to procedures spelled out in a contact. Basically, this meant the businesses would operate on a capitalist basis, just as they would in Hong Kong. Chinese enterprises were permitted to enter into joint ventures with foreign firms in the SEZs, and foreign firms were encouraged to purchase Chinese-origin inputs for the products they manufactured. Exports and imports for industrial production were duty-free. Goods produced in the SEZ could be sold into China with the approval of Guangdong authorities and after paying import duties. The standard tax rate was 15 percent, but lower rates were permitted for transfer of technology, projects with a longer capital turnover period, or early investment in the SEZ. Profits could be freely remitted abroad.

Once the Shenzhen SEZ was opened, Hong Kong manufacturers began shifting their labor-intensive operations there. Among the first to relocate were luggage and clothing manufacturers. An initial trickle became a steady flow and then a flood, although company headquarters and legal incorporation were typically left in Hong Kong under the protection of property- and market-friendly British law. Other Hong Kong firms secured contracts to build roads, wharf facilities, factory and apartment buildings, telecommunication systems, and other infrastructure for the Shenzhen SEZ. Hong Kong firms and been constructing such infrastructure up to world standards for decades. Now they moved into immensely larger markets in the PRC.

Relatively quickly, the integration of the Hong Kong and Guangdong economies spread beyond the Shenzhen SEZ to the entire Pearl River Delta (PRD). Other PRD cities began emulating Shenzhen. Very soon, the PRD was producing a hugely disproportionate share of China's exports. Guangdong's leadership embraced integration with Hong Kong and did what they could to encourage it. New and locally financed highways, rail lines, utility and telecommunications networks, and maritime logistical facilities increasingly tied the region together. Strong infrastructure attracted more investment. By 1997, when Hong Kong reverted to China's control, Hong Kong businesses operated over 50,000 factories across south China. Soon migrants from across China were pouring into the PRD, looking for work and higher incomes, and turning Shenzhen into the only city in Guangdong province where Mandarin, not Cantonese, was the lingua franca. This influx of labor held wages down—as did CCP control over labor unions. Guangdong quickly became the vanguard of China's new participation in the global economy and pioneered a path soon followed by cities up and down China's coast. The dynamic, globally linked economy of Hong Kong became, in effect, one of the key drivers of China's opening and reform. Shanghai, the one urban region of East China that might have challenged Hong Kong's leading role in China's opening to the world, was kept out of the reform process until 1990 because it contributed too much revenue to central government coffers. Ironically, Guangdong was able to take the lead in China's opening because it cost Beijing so little—and because of the powerful economic symbiosis it developed with Hong Kong.

Guangdong's vanguard role in China's opening is reflected in statistical data on the utilization of foreign capital (FDI and foreign loans combined),

Year	Guangdong	Jiangsu	Shanghai	Zhejiang
1978–1982	4.3%	0.4%	0.2%	N.A.
1983	11.9%	0.0%	0.5%	1.0%
1984	13.4%	0.9%	0.9%	1.0%
1985	9.3%	0.9%	1.2%	0.7%
1986	12.2%	1.6%	2.2%	0.4%
1987	10.0%	1.8%	5.8%	0.9%
1988	15.2%	1.7%	8.3%	1.2%
1989	20.9%	3.3%	10.4%	2.3%
1990	16.7%	3.6%	6.5%	1.3%
1991	13.2%	2.4%	4.4%	0.9%
1992	7.0%	2.5%	3.2%	0.6%
1993	7.8%	2.7%	2.6%	1.0%
1994	12.2%	4.8%	4.3%	1.5%
1995	11.7%	5.1%	5.1%	1.5%
1996	17.0%	6.7%	9.2%	2.9%
1997	23.3%	11.1%	10.4%	5.0%
1998	23.9%	11.0%	7.6%	3.8%

FIGURE 13-2 **Guangdong's Leading Role in Utilization of Foreign Capital. (Percentages of all FDI and foreign loans by 4 leading provinces)**

Source: *Xin zhongguo wushi nian tongji ziliao huibian* (Comprehensive statistical data on 50 years of new China), Beijing: China Statistics Press, 1999, pp. 63, 360, 385, 411, 610.

displayed in Figure 13-2. For the years 1978–1998, the first twenty years of China's opening, Guangdong's average annual share of China's total national utilization of foreign capital was 11.5 percent, more than double Shanghai's 4.1 percent, let alone Jiangsu's 3 percent or Zhejiang's 1.3 percent. (Jiangsu and Zhejiang are other coastal provinces that played leading roles in China's early opening.)

By 1984, the rapid economic development of Shenzhen had inspired cities up and down the coast to demand comparable autonomy to engage global markets. A two-week vacation by Deng Xiaoping to the southern SEZs in January 1984 helped disseminate knowledge about what was happening in Shenzhen. In May, an additional fourteen coastal cities were declared open, with fairly wide autonomy to incentivize and welcome foreign investment. The new zones thus created were named Economic and Technological Development Zones, the addition of "technology" being a response to Chen Yun's criticism that the SEZ's were attracting mainly low-tech investment. Regulations for the new open cities stated that the purpose was especially to encourage high-tech investments.[46] But these regulations were interpreted very broadly, and even low-tech assembly investments were welcomed. Gradually, the provinces forming China's east coast began engaging global markets—and forming a powerful constituency for continued opening and reform.

Re-Engaging Global Communities of Knowledge

Sending students and scholars to advanced capitalist countries for higher education and research was another core dimension of China's opening to the outside world. During the decade of 1950 to 1960, more than 38,000 Chinese had studied at Soviet universities, research institutes, or factories. Of that number, 6,561 had matriculated at Soviet institutions of higher learning.[47] After the break with Moscow, educational exchanges withered and then collapsed altogether during the Cultural Revolution. During the decade and a half between the break with Moscow and 1978, very few Chinese studied or conducted research abroad. None did so in the United States, the leading global supplier of higher education services. This changed with China's opening. Late in 1978, the first group of fifty Chinese students and scholars arrived in the United States.[48] Numbers rose rapidly, peaking at over 5,000 in 1981. As indicated by Figure 13-3, during the first five years of the new PRC-US relation, over 19,000 PRC students and scholars came to the United States for university study or advanced research.

In the early period of opening, most students and scholars were approved and financially supported by work units in China. Chinese students quickly learned to avail themselves of funding opportunities available to foreign students from US universities and foundations, however, and soon some forty ercent of financial support for these students was provided by American institutions. Two-thirds of PRC students who enrolled in US universities during this period did so in natural, physical, or life sciences; engineering; or math. Among all foreign students studying at US universities, only 8 percent choose these fields. This emphasis on hard sciences reflected the priorities of the Four Modernizations.

By the mid-1980s, a brain drain problem had emerged. A large percentage of the outstanding human talent China was sending abroad to study were

1978	50
1979	1,330
1980	4,324
1981	5,407
1982	4,480
1983	4,331
total	19,922

FIGURE 13-3 **PRC Students and Scholars in the United States, 1978–1983**

Source: David M. Lampton, *A Relationship Restored, Trends in U.S.–China Educational Exchanges, 1978–1984*, (National Academy Press: Washington, D.C., 1986), p. 32. Based on Consular report of U.S. Department of State.

not returning to China after the end of their studies. Instead, they remained in the United States to work. The US government had cooperated to address this problem in a bilateral agreement on educational exchanges by requiring that PRC students studying in the United States with official Chinese financial support (*gong fei xuesheng*) return to China for at least two years before becoming eligible to reapply for entry into the United States. As the number of "privately financed" (*zifei xuesheng*) students increased, this regulation became less effective. Moreover, some portion of Chinese students in the United States simply went "underground" after finishing their studies, living and working as illegal aliens—usually an only modestly inconvenient status. In the early decades of opening, the gap between living standards, professional opportunities, and individual freedom in the PRC and the United States was immense, offering strong incentives to remain in the United States.

As the number and percentage of nonreturning students grew, so did conservative calls for the restriction and control over educational exchange. Once again Deng took a broader view and upheld opening. Even those that did not immediately return to China would still serve as bridges assisting China's modernization. They would maintain links with Chinese colleagues in their fields, participate in China-based conferences, undertake joint projects, and sponsor other Chinese students or scholars to study in the United States. And some years down the line, perhaps after several decades, a few would return to China, bringing with them deep and mature understanding of the fields in which they had labored in America. Tightening administrative controls on overseas study and travel would create further incentives not to return, since, once having returned, it might be difficult to travel overseas once again. But, as was so often the case, Deng agreed to marginal concessions to his critics. Older, married, more established scholars (deemed more likely to return home) were preferred over younger, unmarried ones. And even older scholars were sometimes required to leave their children in China—again to increase the likelihood they would return home. But the flow was not restricted; the numbers of Chinese going overseas to study rose steadily throughout the 1980s. By the 2000s, as Chinese levels of income rose, it would become a flood. By 2013–2014, 274,439 Chinese were studying in the United States.[49] This constituted 31 percent of all foreign students in the United States and made the PRC the top consumer of US higher educational services. The second- and third-ranking consumers of US higher education were India with 12 percent and South Korea with 8 percent.[50]

From "War and Revolution" to "Peace and Development"

During the "theoretical" debates with the CPSU in the early 1960s, Mao had defined that era as one of war and revolution. The existence of imperialism made war inevitable. But war would produce revolution. It had followed from this general characterization that the PRC should prepare constantly for war and support revolutionary movements in the intermediate zone that might disrupt and divert imperialist forces, making less likely an imperialist attack on socialist China.

Redefinition of the international situation was part of the essential "theoretical work" of the early opening period. It took a while, however. The redefinition began about the time of the Twelfth CCP Congress in 1982. According to the new analysis, the forces favoring peace now so far exceeded the forces favoring war that the likelihood of a new world war, or of a large-scale attack on China, was now negligible and was likely to remain so for a fairly long time. The reinvigoration of US containment policies under the Reagan administration had shifted the balance against the Soviet Union, making new aggression by Moscow unlikely. This allowed China to concentrate on the urgent task of economic development.[51] Major reductions in the size of the armed forces allowed the shift of resources to development. And now that an imperialist attack on the PRC was no longer deemed likely, foreign wars of national liberation lost their linkage to national security. Deng Xiaoping rendered an authoritative judgment in March 1985 when he ruled that "Peace and Development are the Two Outstanding Issues of the World Today."[52]

The de-revolutionization of China's domestic politics was reflected in the de-revolutionization of its foreign relations. Since Southeast Asia had been the focus of CCP revolutionary activism during the Mao era, China's disengagement from insurgencies in that region after 1978 was the most important. Deng's economic development objectives and his concern with countering Soviet expansion in Southeast Asia were linked, but the key driver in this process circa 1978 seems to have been considerations of PRC national security.[53] Beijing's fear of expanding Soviet influence in Southeast Asia, especially in Indochina, and the consequent need to win the support of the ASEAN countries in countering Soviet advances impelled Beijing to pull away from Southeast Asian insurgencies in 1978–1981. The Soviet-backed Vietnamese invasion of Cambodia in December 1978 led to a struggle in the United Nations over which regime should represent Kampuchea (then the name for Cambodia) in the United Nations. Moscow and Hanoi favored the pro-Hanoi regime that Vietnamese forces had installed in Phnom Penh, while Beijing and Washington favored a regime led by Sihanouk and including the Khmer Rouge. Beijing desired the support of ASEAN countries for UN battles. Thailand's agreement to provide territorial sanctuary was also vital for prosecution of an armed resistance to Vietnam's occupation of Kampuchea. Winning the support of the Southeast Asian nations in this struggle caused Beijing to pull back from foreign insurgencies.

Regarding the economic development drive, the large communities of Overseas Chinese (*huaqiao*) in Southeast Asia were seen as an important source of investment and trade via Hong Kong and Shenzhen. But Southeast Asian governments would not be fully supportive of expanded economic cooperation between their ethnic Chinese citizens and the PRC if the CCP was linked to insurgencies seeking to overthrow them. CCP links with local insurgencies would make it difficult for these *huaqiao* to travel and move money and materials between Southeast Asian countries and China. A prudent desire to avoid making oneself an object of attention from local internal security agencies could easily dissuade Southeast Asian *huaqiao* from undertaking business with China. More broadly, the advanced capitalist countries from which Deng's modernizers hoped to acquire advanced technology, trade, capital, and managerial know-how would not be generous with a PRC still supporting communist insurgencies in pro-Western developing countries. Securing Southeast Asian and Western support for the Four Modernizations as well as countering Soviet/Vietnamese expansionism required that Beijing distance itself from Southeast Asian insurgencies.

Deng Xiaoping shifted China's course on the Khmer Rouge in September 1978 when Pol Pot visited Beijing to request more Chinese support. Hanoi was marshaling forces for its upcoming regime-change invasion of Cambodia (a move that came in December), and the Khmer Rouge needed assistance in countering this dire threat. Deng was not sympathetic and told Pol Pot that the KCP's difficulties were of its own making, and that if Vietnam invaded Kampuchea the Kampuchean people would have to themselves fight. China would not send soldiers. For Deng, the Khmer Rouge must have reeked of the CCP's defunct Gang of Four radicals. China continued supplying weapons to the Khmer Rouge throughout the period of Vietnamese occupation. But when Vietnam withdrew from that country in 1990, Beijing cooperated with the ASEAN countries, the United States, and the United Nations to isolate the Khmer Rouge and prevent their return to power.

Thailand was a key party to the Kampuchea issue. Prime Minister Kriangsak Chomanan visited Beijing for talks with Deng Xiaoping in March–April 1978, and Deng reciprocated that visit in November as part of a three-country Southeast Asian tour. During these talks, Deng continued to uphold the dual-track principle, but insisted that party-to-party ties should not interfere with improvement of state-to-state ties. But while upholding "principle," in July 1979 the Voice of the People of Thailand ceased operation. It was replaced by an encrypted transmission system maintaining CPT-CCP communications. But Thai-language revolutionary propaganda was no longer broadcast into Thailand from southern China.[54] When Zhao Ziyang visited Thailand in February 1981, he asserted that CCP gave only "political and moral" support (i.e., not money or arms) to Southeast Asian insurgencies, and that China would "make efforts" to ensure that party-to-party ties did not affect China's "friendship and cooperation" with ASEAN countries.

As for the Communist Party of Malaya (CPM), in December 1980 Deng Xiaoping summoned its secretary general, Chin Peng, to a meeting at the Great Hall of the People. The previous month, Singapore leader Lee Kuan Yew had visited Beijing after consulting with the leaders of Malaysia, Thailand, and Indonesia to convey Southeast Asian views about China's dual-track approach. After a few pleasantries, Deng got to the point with Chin Peng: "I have brought you here in order to talk to you about your radio station. We would like you to close it down."[55] The reader will recall that the CPM had been operating a radio station, "Voice of the Malay Revolution," from Hunan province since 1969. Now, Deng said, Lee Kuan Yew had stated that unless that radio ceased operation it would be difficult for ASEAN countries to support the Khmer Rouge claim to Cambodia's UN seat. When Chin asked "how soon," Deng, his face looking "particularly severe" according to Chin Peng, replied "the sooner the better." Deng gave the CPM until the end of June 1981 to close the radio station. That would be shortly before that year's UN General Assembly debate on Cambodia.

Deng did not leave the CPM entirely without support. Before the deadline for shutting down the VOMR, the CPM acquired, with the assistance of the CCP's International Liaison Department, a smaller, mobile radio transmitter that could broadcast from the southern Thailand base area of the CPM. Thus the day after the CPM's Hunan radio shut down, the new, smaller transmitter in southern Thailand began broadcasting. A few days later, US diplomats in Beijing protested the continuing broadcasts, according to Chin Peng. The PRC reply was that if the US side investigated the situation they would find that the broadcast did not come from China.[56] The switch of the CPM radio station from Hunan to southern Thailand did not satisfy Malaysia's leaders. When Zhao Ziyang visited Kuala Lumpur in August 1981, Prime Minister Mahathir Mohammed said that the opening of the new radio station put the whole issue "back to square one." Malaysia's foreign minister told Zhao that Malaysia was "not fully satisfied" with China's stance on the CPM insurgency. It took several years, but in response to Southeast Asian demands, China gradually dropped support for Southeast Asian revolutions. The CCP ILD still maintained contact with several of those parties, but without Chinese political and material support, the movements withered. These tiny, demanding, and troublesome parties were of little use to a Chinese government seeking expanded economic cooperation with the Southeast Asian countries and the support of those same countries in the effort to compel Hanoi to relinquish its control of Cambodia.

Burma, significantly a state not involved in the Kampuchea imbroglio, was the first state to witness CCP disengagement from foreign insurgencies. Deng Xiaoping visited Burma twice in 1978, in January and again in November, for talks with President U Ne Win. As a result of these talks, China recalled the Red Guard "volunteers" who had been serving with the Communist Party of

Burma (CPB) army since 1968, shut down the CPB radio station that had been broadcasting since 1971, and moved the entire CPB leadership from Beijing, where they had lived since the early 1960s, to a village just inside Burma on the Yunnan border. Three years later, Beijing would offer a modest pension, a house, and a plot of land in China for any veteran CPB cadre who wished to retire. The CPB insurgency continued for a few more years, but so too did Beijing's efforts to end it. In 1986, Beijing revoked the de facto monopoly on cross-border trade between Burma and Yunnan that the CPB had enjoyed since the early 1960s. This very significantly reduced the CCP subsidy to the CPB. Then, in March 1989, ethnic Wa soldiers constituting a majority of the CPB's remaining soldiers revolted against their ethnic Chinese leaders. Those leaders, now mostly elderly, fled to China.[57] By mid-1989, the CPB insurgency, the longest communist-led insurgency in history and one supported throughout by the CCP, was over. Just as China under Mao had helped sustain that insurrection, China under Deng helped shut it down.

The economic logic of improving relations with Burma was strong. If the poor provinces of Yunnan and Guizhou were to successfully open to the world, that would be most conveniently done with and through Burma (renamed Myanmar in 1989). By 1985, while China's east coast provinces were emulating Shenzhen in attracting FDI, Yunnan province was lobbying openly for the construction of an "Irrawaddy corridor" linking Yunnan with Burmese ports on the Bay of Bengal and thence the world. Kunming would eventually succeed in this lobbying effort, but only in the 1990s, after Myanmar abandoned economic isolationism and embraced the world economy.[58]

China's draw back from revolution also meant the end of China's special, ideologically based relation with Albania. In July 1978, the PRC Ministry of Foreign Affairs delivered a note to the Albanian embassy in Beijing stating that China was stopping economic and military aid to Albania and withdrawing 513 Chinese experts and engineers working on economic and military projects in Albania. Albanian students and trainers who had been working in Beijing were also being sent back to Albania. The reason for these moves was Albania's "slander" of China and its "sabotage of economic and military cooperation . . . in a planned and systematic way."[59] Albania, it will be recalled, was the CCP's close ideological supporter during Mao's anti-revisionist struggles of the 1950s–1970s. As such, it was a major recipient of Chinese economic and military assistance during those years. Albanian dictator Enver Hoxha was an ardent supporter of the Cultural Revolution and China's Maoist radicals, and had been dismayed ever since the early 1970s by the moderate, development-oriented policies of Zhou Enlai, Hua Guofeng, and Deng Xiaoping. Albania's media carried criticisms of China's domestic and foreign policies. Chinese personnel working in Albania took objection to this criticism, and this created "difficulties." By late 1977, shortly after Deng's full rehabilitation, Beijing indicated to Albania, according to Hoxha's

China diary, that until "good conditions and understanding" existed, China would not send specialists to Albania to work on "phosphorites, on PVC and other problems."[60] (PVC is polyvinyl chloride, a stock for plastics.) Albania's economic relations with China had been "greatly weakened," Hoxha wrote, because China "has taken a hostile position which is gradually extending to the field of state and economic relations." Chinese specialists, for their part, were making "rude remarks" about commentary in Albania's media, including some articles by Hoxha himself. The last article in Hoxha's China diary was a thirty-eight-page polemic of November 1977 entitled "Can the Chinese Revolution Be Called a Proletarian Revolution?" The answer was "no." The PRC had become "revisionist" and had a "bourgeois ideology." This was the same judgment that would have been rendered by Zhang Chunqiao or Jiang Qing. Deng Xiaoping apparently decided that China would not allocate scarce resources to Albanian Maoist critics of China's new Long March. China also dumped the tiny US Maoist communist party in 1979.[61]

14 }

China's Pedagogic War with Vietnam

China's "Teaching a Lesson" to Vietnam

On February 17, 1979, some 300,000 PLA troops, including thirty infantry divisions supported by 400 tanks and large concentrations of artillery, attacked border defenses and cities along the Vietnam-China border. The scope of the PLA assault initially made it difficult for PAVN commanders to determine the key lines of PLA advance and deploy reserves to defensive lines. Yet PAVN local forces, militias, and internal security units fought tenaciously against the Chinese assault, inflicting heavy losses on Chinese forces. The border towns and provincial capitals of Lao Cai on the Red River in the west and Cao Bang in the central sector were the key initial Chinese objectives. The PLA then pushed toward Cam Duong and Dong Dang to gain position for a further assault on Lang Son—the gateway to Hanoi. Seizure of Lang Son and posing a clear threat to Hanoi and the regime there was the ultimate operational objective of the PLA assault.[1] Figure 14-1 shows key locations in the 1979 war.

Fighting was intense. Many on the Vietnamese side had military training and combat experience—either against the French, the Americans, or the South Vietnamese. Far fewer on the Chinese side were combat veterans. Many had only recently received rudimentary military training, often being recently conscripted or shifted from PLA agricultural production brigades to combat units. The Chinese attack mobilized millennia-long Vietnamese passions of resistance to Chinese invasion and Vietnamese fighters were willing to sacrifice themselves to thwart the Chinese advance. The two sides frequently fought at close quarter. Cities and towns were defended house by house in fierce Vietnamese resistance.

Strategy for the eastern sector of PLA forces, as laid out by that sector's commander General Xu Shiyou, was to concentrate overwhelming superiority of troop strength and firepower on key but not heavily defended sectors of the enemy line and achieve a breakthrough, after which a second echelon

383

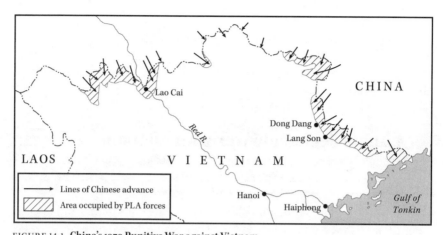

FIGURE 14-1 **China's 1979 Punitive War against Vietnam**

Source: Zygmunt Czarnotta va Zbigniew Moszumansk, p. 25, via Wikipedia Commons.

would pour through the breach in enemy lines and push deep into the enemy's rear area to encircle and annihilate enemy forces.[2] This may have been sound in theory, but proved impossible for PLA forces to achieve in practice. PLA reconnaissance of terrain was inadequate. Maps were out of date. Terrain often proved more rugged than anticipated—heavily jungled or steep mountains and few roads. This was the PLA's first attempt to apply combined arms operations in which tanks and artillery coordinated closely with infantry. Chinese infantry and tanks had not trained to cooperate together. Tanks without infantry support were vulnerable. Infantry that rode into battle on tanks were vulnerable. Tanks and infantry commanders had difficulty communicating. Vietnamese forces outflanked by the PLA withdrew into nearby mountains or forests where they knew the location of caves and tunnel complexes, and reemerged to attack the flanks and logistical lines of Chinese forces. Chinese commanders were compelled to deploy forces on search and destroy operations to hunt down Vietnamese guerrillas and bypassed units. PLA logistics services were inadequate to supply front-line forces, in spite of the fact that a substantial portion of PLA forces were devoted to that task. Communication and command problems plagued the Chinese side. Vietnamese weapons, many recently supplied by the Soviet Union and others inherited from the large US-supplied arsenals of South Vietnam, were often superior to China's. Because of these factors, Chinese forces were often unable to achieve the desired superiority of mass and firepower. In spite of these many and serious shortcomings, Chinese forces achieved their operational objectives, if not always according to the original schedule. Both sides were willing to accept heavy casualties. Attack and counterattack were nearly constant.

On February 27, ten days into the war, the battle for Lang Son began. Taking this city, thereby making clear to SRV leaders that the road to Hanoi was open, was the final PLA operational objective for the offensive phase of the war. General Xu Shiyou threw six divisions into the assault. The infantry assault was preceded by intense bombardment. Again, fighting was fierce. By March 2, PLA forces had taken the high ground on the north side of the city. This was the date originally scheduled for the end of Chinese offensive operations, but Xu Shiyou and the CMC decided to continue operations for several days to take the southern half of the city and push to the city's outskirts. After three more days of fighting, the southern half of the city was in PLA hands and Beijing announced the end of Chinese offensive operations and the beginning of withdrawal of Chinese forces from Vietnam. As Chinese forces withdrew northward, they demolished a good portion of Vietnam's transportation, communications, and governmental infrastructure. The point of the invasion was, after all, to punish Vietnam. By March 16, three weeks and six days after the beginning of the assault, Chinese forces had completed their withdrawal. Beijing proclaimed the operation over.

Chinese casualties were heavy. Vietnam at the time claimed 42,000 Chinese killed. Foreign scholars estimate 25,000 Chinese killed and another 37,000 wounded. More recent Chinese sources put PLA casualties at 6,900 dead and 15,000 wounded.[3] Keeping casualties low was not a major Chinese operational objective. Xu Shiyou and the Central Military Commission (CMC—the PLA's top, collective command) were primarily concerned with whether the PLA achieved its operational and strategic objectives—which they did—and with whether the PLA held the initiative throughout the campaign—which was also broadly the case. From the perspective of Beijing, the PLA's 1979 operations in Vietnam, while exposing many serious shortcomings in the PLA, were successful. Vietnam had learned the lesson, later voiced by a Vietnamese general, that Vietnam "must learn how to live with our big neighbor."[4] This was a lesson voiced many times over the centuries by leaders of smaller kingdoms lying to the south of giant China.[5] As this book is being written in 2015, it is a lesson mulled by Vietnam's leaders as they ponder how to respond to China's island-building activities in the South China Sea.

In the decade after the 1979 war, China maintained constant military pressure on Vietnam's northern border. Chinese military presence there, combined with frequent artillery shelling and occasional major border clashes, kept alive the threat of another Chinese 1979-style lesson, forcing Hanoi to maintain strong forces on its northern borders. Small-scale skirmishing along the border was nearly constant. Six major clashes on the border occurred: in July 1980, May 1981, April 1983, April–July 1984, June 1985, and December 1986–January 1987.[6] There were reports that the PLA cycled troops through the border fighting with Vietnam to give them combat experience.

The 1979 war is perhaps best viewed as the opening move in a decade-long campaign of attrition against the Socialist Republic of Vietnam (SRV), as Vietnam was renamed upon unification in 1976. Parallel with China's pressure on SRV northern borders, Beijing worked with the United States and Thailand to impose on Hanoi a protracted guerrilla war in Cambodia. Beijing also worked with the United States and Western countries generally to deny Vietnam economic assistance, forcing it to rely on what it could get from Moscow and Moscow's poor friends. In other words, the 1979 war was only one component of a broader, multifaceted campaign to pressure Hanoi.

Beijing's objective was to teach SRV leaders that, unlike Hanoi's earlier enemies France and the United States, China would not go away. The French and the Americans ultimately withdrew from Vietnam's vicinity when tired. China could and would not do that. A strong China living, forever, next to Vietnam was a reality that Vietnam needed to recognize and accept. Until that happened, China, together with its friends, would impose very heavy penalties on Vietnam. Things would go better for Vietnam if it learned to avoid injuring China's major interests. That was Beijing's message. Meeting with Singapore leader Lee Kuan Yew in November 1978, Deng Xiaoping estimated that it would take ten years to pull Vietnam away from the Soviet Union.[7] Deng was off by only one year. It was in 1989, following Gorbachev's reorientation of Soviet policy, that Hanoi shifted course and came to terms with China's power by withdrawing from Cambodia.

China's Decision for War

Beijing's decision for war with Vietnam evolved over six months. As early as July 1978, the Politburo discussed the Soviet Union's growing aggressiveness in the Third World and the possible utility of military measures against Vietnam as a way of disrupting Soviet strategic deployments.[8] Two months later, the PLA General Staff convened to deliberate the escalating border conflict with the SRV. The policy recommendation that emerged from this session was for a small punitive action against a Vietnamese border unit (perhaps something like the Chen Bao ambush of a Soviet patrol in 1969). Some participants, however, argued for much larger-scale actions on the grounds that such action might deter Vietnamese intervention in Cambodia.[9] By that point, Vietnamese preparations for a regime-change invasion of Cambodia were well under way, and Chinese intelligence would almost certainly have been aware of the broad parameters of those preparations.

By the time Deng Xiaoping visited Thailand and Singapore in November 1978 in a bid for understanding if not approval of China's upcoming blow against Vietnam, he had apparently already made up his mind to strike Vietnam. Deng conveyed to both Prime Minister Chomanan Kriangsak of Thailand and Prime Minister Lee Kuan Yew of Singapore his view of the gravity of a possible Vietnamese invasion of Cambodia, and his determination to counter such a move with a firm response. But Deng also assured his interlocutors that China's punishment of Vietnam would be limited in scope and duration.[10] Shortly after Deng returned from his Southeast Asian visits, the PLA General Staff Department convened another planning session. The result was a plan for much broader operations against Vietnam, including attacks on all cities and military positions along the SRV border. Strategic reserves totaling four armies and one division were shifted from Wuhan and Chengdu for the attack. The CMC met again on December 7 to consider and approve the PLA plan.[11] It then issued orders to relevant Military Regions directing them to prepare for offensive military operations into the SRV to a distance of 50 kilometers and for a duration of two weeks. Finally, on December 31, 1978, shortly after being designated China's paramount leader at a plenary meeting of the Central Committee, Deng formally proposed to the CMC a "self-defensive counterattack" against Vietnam along the lines of the PLA plan. The war would be short and swift, with Chinese forces withdrawing once the capture of Lang Son had been achieved. Chinese forces would thus avoid becoming bogged down or give the Soviet Union a chance to intervene. In addition to approving the PLA and Deng's war plan, the CMC appointed Xu Shiyou commander of the eastern Guangxi sector and Yang Dezhi commander of the western sector in Yunnan. Above them there was no unitary commander, only the CMC. This proved to be a serious shortcoming, with the two sectors fighting virtually independent wars.

A major concern was the level of PLA readiness to fight an actual war. The PLA had not fought a war since 1962 with India, seventeen years before, and had spent most of the 1965–1977 period deeply enmeshed in China's politics and civil administration. Military training had been given short shrift during the Cultural Revolution. Large-scale military operations and maneuvers had been few. Out of such concerns, Deng dispatched the director of the General Logistics Department, Zhang Zhen, to inspect the gathering Chinese forces. Zhang was shocked by what he saw, and on his return to Beijing he recommended delaying the war by a month to permit intensified training. This proposal was accepted, shifting the start of the offensive to mid-February.

Another serious concern was possible Soviet intervention. The USSR and the SRV had signed a treaty of peace and friendship in November 1978. Article Six of that treaty provided that "If either side is attacked or exposed to the threat of attack, the two signatory parties will immediately confer with each other in order to remove the threat and take appropriate and effective steps to safeguard the peace and security of both countries."[12] If Moscow did not take action to follow through on this treaty obligation, it would lose considerable credibility. Moreover, Vietnam had become Moscow's close political and military partner; failure to stand beside Hanoi could endanger that relationship, including especially Soviet access to military bases in Vietnam. Still, Chinese leaders found several reasons to conclude that forceful Soviet intervention was not likely. The brevity of the Chinese strike would end the conflict before the Soviet Union had time to act. The PLA estimated it would take Moscow at least two weeks to decide on and organize a reaction, and by that time Chinese forces would be withdrawing (at least according to the original time-table). The great distance between the USSR and the SRV would also limit the Soviet response. Moscow could send supplies and advisors by aircraft, but the route would be long and time-consuming. Sending heavy equipment and large amounts of supplies by ship would take longer than the war would last.

The only realistic form of intervention open to Moscow was to ignite a border war along China's northern or northwestern border. This was pos-sible, PRC leaders decided, and they ordered forces there to heightened levels of readiness. But fighting even a border war with China would take many weeks of preparation and the movement of units and supplies. Again, the war with Vietnam would be over by that time. If Moscow instigated some border disturbances without such preparation, they were likely to be small-scale and could be easily managed by the PLA. Moscow would also worry that China might choose to escalate a border conflict; was Vietnam worth a Soviet war with China? Chinese planners thought it unlikely Moscow would conclude that it was. Aligning the United States behind China in its upcoming punitive war—or seeming to align it—would add further to restraints on the Soviet Union. Sino-Soviet border skirmishes were one thing; a big Soviet war with China backed by the United States was something else. Securing at least the appearance of American support was one purpose of Deng's January 1979 visit to the United States.

Cambodia: China's Friend or Vietnam's Partner?

The status of Cambodia was probably the single most important cause of the 1979 war. Was Cambodia to be a fully independent state and a friend of China, or an especially close partner of Vietnam within a political structure led by the SRV? Leaders of the Communist Party of Vietnam (CPV, as the VWP was renamed in December 1976) were determined to bring Cambodia into a Vietnam-led political coalition, an "Indochina federation" as it came to be called. Beijing was equally determined to prevent that, and uphold Cambodia as an independent state able to look to China for support and protection—as Cambodian rulers had traditionally done for centuries. These conflicting objectives built on a split within the Kampuchean communist movement into China-oriented and Vietnam-oriented factions. In effect, Beijing and Hanoi each supported a faction of the Kampuchean communist movement willing to work with it.

The cleavages within the Kampuchean communist movement had deep roots. As discussed in an earlier chapter, in the late 1950s Cambodian stu-dents educated in France had imbibed Marxism and Maoism there began returning home. They entered the Kampuchean revolutionary movement and coalesced around the view that Norodom Sihanouk was a puppet of the United States who needed to be overthrown to make Cambodia truly independent. Saloth Sar, a former electrical engineering student who eventually took the nom de guerre Pol Pot, emerged as the key leader of this returned students group. They were much enamored of Mao Zedong's emphasis on class struggle and uninterrupted revolution. There was another cohort of Cambodian communists who had not been educated in France but who stayed home to work with the VWP in the struggle against the French and the Americans. Most of the work of this group had taken place in the rural areas, and these rural veteran cadres had lots of experience in hands-on grass-roots organization. They had typically worked closely with their Vietnamese comrades. The returned student group had not. The rural veteran cadres followed Hanoi in viewing Sihanouk as playing a vital role in the revolutionary struggle by condoning Hanoi's use of eastern Cambodia and the port of Kompong Som (then known as Sihanoukville) for the struggle against the Americans. From the standpoint of the VWP and their "veteran cadre" Kampuchean communist allies, the victory of the Kampuchean revolution should wait until after the victory of the Vietnamese revolution. Pol Pot's returned students group viewed this notion as nothing less than betrayal of the Kampuchea revolution. This conflict within the Kampuchean communist movement continued throughout the 1960s and 1970s. Eventually, Pol Pot's group concluded that the Vietnam-tainted "veteran cadres" were nothing less than Vietnamese agents ("Khmer bodies with Vietnamese minds") and enemies of the revolution. They were added to Pol Pot's growing list of enemies.

The overthrow of Sihanouk by a group of Cambodian generals in March 1970 led both Hanoi and Beijing to support a revolutionary offensive across Cambodia. Hanoi began allowing larger quantities of arms to reach the Khmer Rouge. The VWP and the Khmer Rouge soon fell out, however, over administration of the new territories being seized. The VWP proposed a mixed Vietnamese-Khmer military command. But Pol Pot rejected this, fearing Vietnamese infiltration of Khmer Rouge organs by Vietnamese-trained cadres. Hanoi's forces in Cambodia countered Khmer Rouge anti-Vietnamese propaganda by adopting a friendship policy toward the Cambodian population in areas under their control. The Khmer Rouge, for their part, adopted extreme radical policies in areas they ruled: collectivization of agriculture, deurbanization, suppression of markets, the banning of "extravagance," and so on. From the viewpoint of ordinary Cambodians, PAVN and "veteran cadre" rule was preferable to Khmer Rouge rule. To the Khmer Rouge, this was further evidence of Vietnamese "sabotage" and hostility to revolution.[13] Early in 1973, the Khmer Rouge launched a campaign to expel all Vietnamese and their supporters from Cambodia. Dissidents of all shades were rounded up, questioned under torture, and executed. In Khmer Rouge base areas, even more radical policies were adopted: money was abolished, and communal eating was instituted. Fighting between the Khmer Rouge and the Vietnamese in eastern Cambodia intensified. By the time the US position in Indochina collapsed in April 1975, a low-grade war between Khmer Rouge and PAVN-backed forces was underway in much of Cambodia.

The Khmer Rouge entered Phnom Penh in early April 1975, about three weeks before Saigon fell to the PAVN. The Khmer Rouge would rule Cambodia, which they renamed Democratic Kampuchea, for three years and eight months. During that period, they killed an estimated 2.4 million people, roughly one-third of Cambodia's population of 7 million.[14] The Khmer Rouge turned Cambodia into a vast prison camp in pursuit of the communist utopia. Anyone who challenged or disputed that quest in any way was executed. Under Khmer Rouge rule, the economy collapsed—in ways not too dissimilar from China's economic collapse during the Great Leap Forward. Many people died of starvation or diseases associated with malnutrition. China was the Khmer Rouge's main foreign supporter during this holocaust.

The terror-driven utopian quest of the Khmer Rouge was similar to the CCP's policies during the Great Leap and the Cultural Revolution. Such ideological affinities did not, however, determine China's efforts to keep Cambodia free from Vietnamese domination. Considerations of power and national security guided Beijing's Cambodian policies. First of all, China benefited from having more and weaker rather than fewer and stronger countries on its southern borders. If there were three states in old French Indochina, those states would each be smaller and weaker than if there were one multinational state directed by Hanoi. Three smaller and weaker states would be less likely to challenge China in various ways, and more likely to look to China for support against one another. A single strong state, on the other hand, might reject China's requests and trample on China's interests. In short, a fragmented, "balkanized" structure of power benefited China. Beijing framed this in terms of high principle.

A second reason for Beijing to object to Hanoi's attempt to dominate Cambodia was that Cambodia was a friendly state under the protection of China. In effect, Cambodia was China's protectorate, and that privileged relation was under direct challenge by Hanoi. Historically, Cambodia had looked to China for protection. In 1407, the Ming emperor Yongle sent an army of 200,000 to punish Vietnam for offenses including seizure of Champa, a kingdom bordering Cambodia on the territory of what is today southern Vietnam. A later Khmer appeal to Yongle for protection against a Champa attack yielded a Chinese envoy urging peace but no Chinese army to enforce that appeal. Nevertheless, the idea of China as regional policeman continued to inform Khmer strategic thinking.[15] Sihanouk's diplomacy of friendship with the PRC was in line with this Cambodian diplomatic tradition. As soon as Cambodia gained independence after the 1954 Geneva conference,

Sihanouk adopted a policy of friendship toward China: refusing association with SEATO, embracing non-alignment and rejecting US containment, while developing close relations with the PRC in the face of US criticism and punishment. Furthermore, as discussed in an earlier chapter, it was under Chinese prompting and with a Chinese guarantee that Sihanouk had agreed to cooperate with the VWP war effort in the 1960s.

Vietnam's leaders were convinced that they had a historical destiny to lead the peoples of Indochina in their struggle for independence, development and socialism. Their wars against the French and the Americans had led the way for the liberation of the other peoples of Indochina. Moreover, those hard struggles had been won by treating Indochina as a single battlefield, a single strategic whole, and mobilizing the strength of the whole region, under VWP leadership, to fight and defeat the imperialists. Vietnam was also more developed, and its people more disciplined, than Laos and Cambodia, so clearly, in Hanoi's view, it was Vietnam's mission to lead all the peoples of Indochina to a greater destiny, including building socialism and resisting Chinese hegemony.[16] Indochina should be a federal state—led by the VWP. Hanoi's efforts to move Indochina in this direction, toward what came to be called an Indochina federation, was seen by the Khmer Rouge as a Vietnamese attempt to take over Cambodia.

Cambodia under the Khmer Rouge was headed in the opposite direction. As soon as the Khmer Rouge entered Phnom Penh in 1975, Pol Pot issued an order expelling Cambodia's entire Vietnamese minority. Through the rest of that year over 150,000 ethnic Vietnamese were expelled and fled to South Vietnam, where they sheltered in makeshift camps or urban slums. Early in 1977, Pol Pot escalated the brutality, ordering the execution of ethnic Vietnamese remaining in Cambodia. The Khmer Rouge also turned their attention to any member of their organizations judged to have had links with or to sympathize with Vietnam. Large numbers of people were arrested and tortured until they gave "confessions" naming other people. Those people were then arrested and the process repeated. Khmer Rouge commanders, and even whole units of the Khmer Rouge army, compromised in some way by this witch hunt rebelled and, for survival, fled to South Vietnam. Any Cambodian who had had past contact with Vietnamese was likely to disappear in the Khmer Rouge killing fields. The "purification" of Cambodia from all Vietnamese influence was accompanied by escalating military conflict with Vietnam. By 1977, Khmer Rouge forces were attacking into Vietnam in an attempt to "kill the aggressors in their lair." Some Khmer Rouge dreamed of retaking the Mekong River delta south of Ho Chi Minh City, taken from Khmer rule by Vietnam only in the eighteenth century.[17]

While the Khmer Rouge were using murder to purify Cambodia of Vietnamese influence, Hanoi was moving forward with efforts to build an Indochinese federation. Laos was a more willing partner for Hanoi. In

February 1976, the general secretary of the Lao People's Revolutionary Party signed in Hanoi a communiqué declaring a "special relation" and long-term cooperation and mutual assistance between Laos and Vietnam. The next year, a twenty-five-year treaty further institutionalized Lao-Vietnam cooperation.[18]

By fall 1977, it was clear to Hanoi that Pol Pot's regime was determined to thwart development of a cooperative relation with Vietnam. Hanoi began preparing the means to oust the Khmer Rouge and install a pro-Vietnamese Khmer communist regime in Phnom Penh. In October, Hanoi began encouraging formation of an anti–Pol Pot Khmer liberation army. The small number of Khmer who had made careers in the DRV in the 1950s–1970s were inducted and given influential positions in the new organization. Former Khmer Rouge commanders and soldiers who had fled to Vietnam to escape the murderous purges underway in Cambodia were recruited. Young Khmer men were recruited from refugee camps and given military training, many at ex-US facilities in South Vietnam. The first units of the Khmer liberation army were commissioned in April 1978.[19] Many of these recruits had good reason to despise the policies of the Khmer Rouge and welcomed a chance to oust that cruel regime. Parallel with these organizational efforts, Hanoi began Khmer-language broadcasts calling for uprisings against Khmer Rouge rule. Hanoi also began intensified propaganda about the atrocities in Cambodia committed by the Khmer Rouge. Western reporters were allowed to visit the Khmer refugee camps and learn from survivors about the holocaust being wrought by Pol Pot's regime. Hanoi's calculation was that such information would generate understanding for its ouster of the Khmer Rouge.

Late in January 1978, Vietnam's senior General Vo Nguyen Giap met secretly in Laos with the commander of Soviet ground forces to consider the problem of regime change in Cambodia. The Soviet general recommended a swift armored thrust to "do a Czechoslovakia"—a reference to the 1968 Warsaw Pact intervention in Czechoslovakia to oust a liberal communist regime. Giap listened, but promised only to act in an appropriate way.[20] Prospects for an internal coup ousting Pol Pot greatly diminished in May 1978, when an attempted uprising in eastern Cambodia failed and resulted in the execution of large numbers suspected of involvement. That setback seems to have shifted Hanoi toward an externally imposed regime change. In September 1978, CPV Politburo member Le Duc Tho met with leaders of the Khmer liberation organization in Hanoi to decide on strategy. They decided on a military thrust in December to push rapidly to Phnom Penh, oust Pol Pot, and install a new communist government dedicated to more reasonable policies—including cooperation with Vietnam.[21]

That offensive thrust took place as planned in December. It looked very much like another "Czechoslovakia": armored columns with infantry in armored personnel carriers and trucks, supported by mobile artillery and aircraft. Phnom Penh was taken within a few days. "Democratic Kampuchea" was dissolved and a new state, the People's Republic of Kampuchea, was set up. Khmer Rouge forces melted into Cambodia's mountains and jungles, or across the border into Thailand.

Beijing supported the Khmer Rouge as conflict between them and Vietnam escalated. Beijing did not come down unequivocally behind Democratic Kampuchea until early 1978, but from the beginning in spring 1975, Beijing supported Khmer Rouge efforts to resist Hanoi's efforts to draw it into a "special relation." Pol Pot reported to Mao Zedong in Beijing in June 1975, some two months after taking Phnom Penh. Mao lauded Pol Pot's success in emptying the cities, something the CCP had been unable to accomplish.[22] China's leaders agreed to supply large-scale assistance to Democratic Kampuchea. A group of PLA specialists spent several months in Cambodia surveying the country's defense requirements—secretly, so as not to alarm Vietnam or Thailand. In February of the next year (1976), PLA Deputy Chief of Staff Wang Shangrong visited Phnom Penh, again secretly, to finalize a military aid package. China agreed to provide artillery, anti-aircraft weapons, patrol boats, and other equipment to transform the Khmer Rouge's guerilla force into a conventional army able to defend the state against foreign invasion.[23]

By late 1976, after Mao's death and the arrest in October of Maoist radicals, China became increasingly critical of Pol Pot's extreme policies, including harsh, coercive policies toward ethnic Chinese, who had no more place in "Democratic Kampuchea" than did ethnic Vietnamese. But Beijing did not make these criticisms public. Vietnamese Premier Pham Van Dong visited Beijing in June 1977 to see if he could use Beijing's growing unhappiness with the extremist policies of the Khmer Rouge to pry Beijing away from Phnom Penh. China was itself breaking with radical Maoist policies; perhaps they would be willing to break with similar policies being implemented by the Khmer Rouge. The result was rather different than what Dong had hoped for, and this meeting constituted a turning point in the PRC-SRV conflict. Li Xianian presented Dong with a long list of Chinese grievances: attempting to bully Cambodia, pursuing an anti-China policy regionally and globally, the growing number of bloody clashes on the PRC-Vietnam border, Hanoi's policies toward Vietnam's ethnic Chinese, and Vietnam's territorial claims in the South China Sea. Pham Van Dong gave no ground, but bitterly rebutted Li's charges. After the confrontation between Li Xiannian and Pham Van Dong, Hanoi's sense of threat from China, and consequently the felt need for Soviet support, increased considerably.[24]

In November, Le Duan tried again in Beijing to pry China away from the Khmer Rouge. He tried flattery, telling Hua Guofeng, "We are your younger brother, constantly standing on your side, and we could not do otherwise."[25] (Hua was CCP paramount leader for the two-year interregnum between Mao's death and Deng's selection.) He pointed out that Hanoi had never criticized China or sided with Moscow during the long Sino-Soviet dispute.

He also recalled that Mao and Zhou had declared assistance to Vietnam's socialist construction to be an "international obligation." Hua Guofeng responded by charging Vietnam with bullying and trying to subordinate Cambodia. The talks became acrimonious. Le Duan shocked his Chinese listeners by praising the Soviet Union by name for its assistance to Vietnam. He thereby underlined Hanoi's alternative to Chinese assistance, and the dangerous situation in which China might find itself.

Beijing tried to paper over deepening Vietnamese-Kampuchean conflicts by involving the two sides in negotiations. In January 1978, a Chinese delegation led by Zhou Enlai's widow Deng Yingchao and Vice Foreign Minister Han Nianlong visited Phnom Penh to recommend negotiations toward a settlement of disputes on the basis of the Five Principles of Peaceful Coexistence. The Khmer Rouge rejected any such moderation. The symbolism of Zhou's widow as head of the mission was not lost on Khmer Rouge leaders. They understood and hated Zhou's moderate and nonrevolutionary approach to diplomacy. The Khmer Rouge agreed with the Gang of Four in that regard. They would not accept such unprincipled and unrevolutionary compromise. Khmer Rouge media even hinted that a powerful friend (meaning China) might be bullying small, brave Kampuchea. The threat of alienating Democratic Kampuchea—China's only ally in Southeast Asia—caused Beijing to abandon its bid for negotiations and revert to full, unequivocal backing for Phnom Penh. The stage for China's punishment of Hanoi for regime change in Cambodia was set.

Vietnam's Deepening Alignment with the Soviet Union

Vietnam's deepening alignment with the USSR was a second major reason for China's decision to "teach Vietnam a lesson." As Hanoi moved toward regime change in Cambodia, it embraced military and security cooperation with the Soviet Union. Deng Xiaoping saw these processes as related: Hanoi knew China would not accept Vietnamese domination of Cambodia and sought Soviet protection to counter Chinese objections to such an effort. A hard, punitive strike against Vietnam would trump Hanoi's Soviet card, in Deng's view, and teach Hanoi that support from the faraway Soviet Union would not protect Hanoi's trampling on China's interests.[26] Vietnamese participation in what Chinese leaders deemed to be Soviet encirclement of China was unacceptable to China, and Hanoi had to be made to understand this fact of life.[27]

Moscow interpreted the DRV's dramatic 1975 victory over the United States as marking a fundamental shift in the global correlation of forces between imperialism and socialism, and moved aggressively to exploit that perceived global shift. The buildup of Soviet naval forces after the 1962 Cuban missile crisis had transformed the Soviet navy into a powerful and far-reaching force, and Moscow was anxious to acquire access to the large and modern military facilities the United States had built in South Vietnam. More broadly, Moscow aspired to replace the United States as the dominant power in Southeast Asia. Thus, shortly after the fall of Saigon in April 1975, Moscow secretly proposed to Hanoi the conclusion of a treaty of friendship and cooperation to serve as a basis for expanded military cooperation plus Soviet economic assistance to Hanoi. Hanoi sat on the Soviet proposal for nearly three years. Only in late 1978, as the SRV moved toward regime-change invasion of Cambodia, did Hanoi embrace full alliance with the USSR.[28]

It was China, or probably Mao Zedong specifically, who cut off Chinese aid to Vietnam, pushing it into close alignment with Moscow. In August 1975, four months after Hanoi's complete victory, DRV economic planner Le Thanh Nghi visited Zhou Enlai in the hospital room where he was dying from cancer. Nghi's purpose was to solicit Chinese economic assistance for Vietnam's postwar reconstruction effort. In June 1973, when Zhou had asked Le Duan to stop fighting in the south for two years, he had promised to continue aid to Vietnam at the 1973 level for five more years. When Nghi visited in 1975, however, Zhou explained that China would be unable to give assistance:

> During the war, when you were in the worst need, we took many things from our own army to give to you. We made a very great effort to help you. The sum of our aid to Vietnam still ranks first among our aid to foreign countries. You should let us have a respite and gain strength.[29]

Shortly after Nghi's visit, Le Duan arrived in Beijing to plead for a reversal of China's apparent decision to cut off aid. Deng Xiaoping used his welcoming speech to lambast superpowers seeking hegemony. Out of deference to Le Duan, Deng did not refer explicitly to the USSR, but the implication was clear enough: "The superpowers are the biggest international exploiters and oppressors of today. . . . More and more people have come to see now that to combat superpower hegemonism is a vital task facing the people of all countries."[30] In his reply, Le Duan said that Vietnam had the "warmest sentiments and heartfelt and most profound gratitude" for China's aid. But he ignored Beijing's anti-hegemony analysis entirely, and said that Vietnam's great victory would not have been possible without the "great and valuable" assistance of other fraternal socialist countries, implicitly the USSR and East European countries. He was fulsome in his praise of China's success in building socialism and for its past aid to Vietnam, but he refused to endorse China's view of the USSR as a hegemony-seeking superpower. In effect, he desired to continue Hanoi's previous arrangement of receiving aid from both the Soviet Union and China. Beijing no longer found that arrangement acceptable and, in effect, demanded that Hanoi choose between Beijing and Moscow. If it choose China, Hanoi should disassociate itself from Moscow's increasingly pernicious schemes. Le Duan left Beijing without giving the customary "thank you" banquet reciprocating the Chinese host's "welcoming" banquet—a serious breach of diplomatic protocol. Nor was a joint communiqué signed at the conclusion of the visit.

Scholar Ezra Vogel suggests that it was Jiang Qing and her radical supporters (locked then in sharp struggle with both Zhou and Deng) who insisted that Le Duan pass the "anti-hegemony" litmus test. If Deng had had control over China's foreign relations in 1975, as he had after his second rehabilitation in mid-1977, he and Le Duan might have been able to work out an accommodation, preventing Hanoi from subsequently moving into close alignment with the USSR, or so Vogel suggests.[31] By the time Deng was in charge—with Mao dead, the Gang of Four arrested, and Deng fully restored to party work, with responsibility for foreign relations—the SRV had already moved too far into alignment with the Soviet Union to be easily won back, in Vogel's view. Perhaps, but conflict between Hanoi and Beijing over other issues, and especially Cambodia, was already sharp by fall 1975. In the same month that China's leaders pleaded impecuniosity as a reason for not extending substantial aid to Vietnam, Beijing granted $1 billion in aid over a five-year period to Khmer Rouge–ruled Democratic Kampuchea. Deng Xiaoping later told Lee Kwan Yew that the reason for China's refusal to grant aid in 1975 was not lack of funds, but Vietnam's hegemonist stance.[32]

Following his failure to secure Chinese aid, Le Duan went to Moscow, arriving there late in October. Soviet leaders were quite willing to grant Vietnam large-scale aid.

Expanded military cooperation was linked to expanded economic assistance. In March and again in May 1977, Vo Nguyen Giap visited Moscow to negotiate an agreement on expanded military cooperation.[33] Hanoi joined the Soviet-led Council for Mutual Economic Assistance (COMECON), the communist response to the West's European Economic Community. Moscow accelerated delivery of industrial equipment to Vietnam and offered large, low-interest loans to cover this aid inflow. In July, a secret Soviet military delegation representing all three branches of the Soviet military arrived in Da Nang to assess Vietnam's military needs. The group visited Cam Ranh, Nha Trang, and several other places of military interest in the south. Following the Soviet visit, Moscow began supplying Vietnam with patrol boats, MIG-21 fighters, a destroyer, and two old submarines.

SRV alignment with the Soviet Union deepened still further in 1978 as Hanoi began moving toward regime change in Cambodia. Given the close relation between Beijing and the Khmer Rouge, and given China's long-standing protectorate relation with Cambodia, Hanoi knew that Vietnam's ouster of the Khmer Rouge regime risked Chinese retaliation. Alliance with the Soviet Union was Hanoi's response. The 1978 alliance consolidated Vietnam-Soviet military cooperation. By the end of 1978, there were 600 Soviet military advisors in Vietnam, and Soviet military assistance had reached $75 million per year.[34]

Ethnic Chinese in Vietnam and the South China Sea

The status of some one million ethnic Chinese in South Vietnam was yet another factor in Beijing's decision to punish Vietnam in 1979. The crudely discriminatory nature of Hanoi's policies toward Vietnam's ethnic Chinese added a near racial element to the PRC-SRV conflict, giving it a strong emotional connotation for both countries, and one that had ramifications throughout Southeast Asia, where a number of other countries shared Vietnamese prejudices against ethnic Chinese communities.

The ethnic Chinese of South Vietnam constituted a commercially successful minority. Like similar cohorts of ethnic Chinese in Indonesia, Malaysia, the Philippines, and Thailand, South Vietnam's Chinese minority played a disproportionately large role in the economic life of the country. Circa 1977, South Vietnam's Chinese businessmen, many of whom lived and conducted business in Ho Chi Minh City's "Chinatown," Cholon, controlled almost all of South Vietnam's industry and commerce, including the vital rice trade. They also held most of the liquid wealth of the country, often in gold or US dollars.[35] The US period in South Vietnam had been good for the Chinese business community, with lucrative contracts for construction, supplies, or services paid for by generous US aid or military budgets. The US-backed South Vietnamese governments had relied on these capable Chinese businessmen, but had required as a precondition for landing government contracts acceptance of Republic of Vietnam citizenship. When Saigon began this policy under Ngo Dinh Diem, the VWP-controlled NLF had protested and declared that after liberation Vietnam's ethnic Chinese would be allowed to choose their nationality, Vietnamese or Chinese.[36] Beijing took this as a pledge by the VWP to Beijing. Then in early 1976 (after South Vietnam's "liberation"), Hanoi declared that all residents of South Vietnam would be required to accept Vietnamese nationality. Beijing saw this as a breach of Hanoi's earlier promises of noncompulsory assignment of citizenship. Beijing did not make public its objections at the time, but when Li Xiannian presented his list of criticisms to Pham Van Dong in June 1977, among them was Hanoi's breaking of its promise not to force Chinese in Vietnam to accept Vietnamese citizenship.

Hanoi leaders doubted the loyalty of South Vietnam's ethnic Chinese business community. During Saigon's American period, many Cholon businessmen had maintained ties with Chiang Kai-shek's Nationalist government in Taipei. Whatever the actual reasons for that activity, from Hanoi's perspective it looked like an expression of Cholon's loyalty to "China," albeit Nationalist and not Communist China. Then when Saigon fell in April 1975, PRC flags and posters of Mao Zedong appeared in Cholon. VWP authorities ordered them removed.[37] As Hanoi began initial moves toward transition to socialism in South Vietnam in 1977, Cholon, with its abundantly stocked stores and vibrant markets, stood in stark contrast to the ill-stocked state-controlled stores that constituted the growing state sector. Hanoi saw this as a "Chinese" effort to sabotage Vietnam's economic development. Hanoi became convinced that Vietnam now faced a multifaceted Chinese pressure campaign: from the Khmer Rouge in the west, from China's PLA in the north, and the Cholon fifth column in the very heart of South Vietnam. Beijing aspired to dominate Vietnam, CPV leaders convinced themselves. Under these circumstances, what if Cholon's capitalist fifth column created economic disruptions while the Khmer Rouge, armed and financed by Beijing, attacked from the west? In February, the same session of the CPV Politburo that decided to establish an anti–Pol Pot Khmer liberation organization also considered the security implications of Cholon's control over South Vietnam's economy. The Politburo met again in mid-March 1978 to finalize an assault on Cholon's Chinese capitalists.

Early one morning in late March, Vietnamese police and militia suddenly surrounded Cholon neighborhoods. Squads of specially trained Vietnamese student volunteers then entered and searched all homes and shops. Goods were inventoried and declared state property which could not be sold. Gold and cash were confiscated on the spot. Seven tons of gold was reportedly thus nationalized.[38] The transition to socialism thus moved into high gear. Soon, young men from Cholon began to be drafted into the military, perhaps to serve in Cambodia. Many ethnically Chinese families were shipped off to "New Economic Zones" in virgin or abandoned rural areas. Life in these Zones was typically primitive and hard. Disposing of mines and unexploded ordinance was a common and highly dangerous duty. Confronting such persecution, Chinese people and families began to flee as best they could. By mid-1978, Public Security Bureaus in South Vietnamese coastal towns were building boats, filling them with ethnic Chinese, and pushing them out to sea—after demanding large payments of gold or dollars. The more fortunate among these "boat people" encountered friendly ships that took them aboard and conveyed them to refugee camps in nearby countries. Over two years, an estimated quarter million ethnic Chinese fled South Vietnam. An estimated 30,000–40,000 died at sea.[39]

It was pure serendipity that Hanoi's vicious solution to its "Chinese problem" coincided with a new Chinese appeal to Chinese communities across Southeast Asia to contribute to China's modernization drive. A January 1978 article by Liao Chengzhi in *Renmin ribao* exemplified the new appeal to Overseas Chinese. Overseas Chinese were part of the Chinese nation, and with a destiny closely linked to the motherland, Liao wrote. Overseas Chinese, including "friends of foreign [i.e., non-Chinese] nationality of Chinese descent," had an important role to play in China's development.[40]

Beijing's call for Overseas Chinese communities in Southeast Asia to contribute to China's economic modernization effort was strengthened by Beijing acting as protector of South Vietnam's ethnic Chinese. As noted earlier, a number of Southeast Asian governments shared sentiments about their ethnic Chinese communities not dissimilar from Hanoi's. There was even a regional temptation to adopt a harsh "Vietnamese-style," or perhaps an even more vicious 1965 "Indonesian-style," solution to the "Chinese question."[41] These fears were part of the political culture of Southeast Asia, for ethnic Chinese and non-Chinese alike. If Beijing responded forcefully to Hanoi's harsh anti-Chinese policies, Beijing could position itself as the protector of Southeast Asia's ethnic Chinese. Of course, if overplayed, that approach could exacerbate apprehensions of Southeast Asian governments about the loyalty of Chinese communities. Political calculations aside, Hanoi's blatantly discriminatory treatment of Vietnam's ethnic Chinese, seemingly in repayment for China's long support for Hanoi, roused deep anger among Chinese, both leaders and ordinary folk.

China's media and government strongly protested Hanoi's persecution of the ethnic Chinese. While waves of "boat people" were tempting fate in the South China Sea in 1978, Beijing dispatched two ships to evacuate any Chinese who desired to leave. Hanoi refused permission for the ships to enter Vietnamese ports, and the ships rode at anchor off those ports for several weeks. Hanoi charged Beijing with "gunboat diplomacy" and acting as though it was sovereign over Vietnam's ports. If Beijing was so concerned about overseas Chinese, Hanoi charged, it should send ships as quickly as possible to Khmer Rouge Kampuchea to rescue the Chinese being murdered there.

A final dispute underlying Beijing's decision to chastise Vietnam in 1979 was Hanoi's challenge to China's territorial claims in the South China Sea. As explained in an earlier chapter, China claimed all the islands in the South China Sea. Throughout the long DRV-US war, Hanoi did not challenge those claims. As long as Hanoi needed Beijing's help to fight the United States, it kept quiet about its opposition to Beijing's territorial claims in the South China Sea. When the PLA consolidated its control over the Paracels in 1974, the leaders in Hanoi did not publicly protest Beijing's move, but privately they saw it as the first overt act of Chinese aggression against socialist Vietnam.[42] Once the Americans were defeated, Hanoi no longer needed China's support and began protesting China's claims. A week after Saigon fell, that city's official newspaper, now under VWP control, published a colored map showing both the Paracel and Spratly Islands as Vietnamese territory. Further open claims by Vietnam to these islands followed. Hanoi's abrupt turnaround on the South China Sea angered Chinese leaders. It seemed yet another example of VWP insincerity and unprincipled hypocrisy.

Consequences of the 1979 War

The 1979 war underlined Beijing's willingness to use military power to protect what its leaders deemed China's crucial interests. Other countries understood from the 1979 demonstration the reality of the PRC's power and the preparedness of its leaders to use it when they deemed it necessary to protect China's vital interests. With 1979, Vietnam joined the list of China's neighbors who had been taught this lesson: the United States, South and North Korea, India, Taiwan, and the USSR. China's power is a reality that all its neighbors must take into account.

The 1979 war also demonstrated Chinese skill in the use of military power—not necessarily on the battlefield, but in terms of achieving political objectives. Limiting the scope of military action geographically and in duration, and lining up (or at least seeming to line up) US understanding of China's strike (discussed in the next chapter), helped to prevent Soviet intervention, in spite of the 1978 Soviet-Vietnam treaty. Beijing thus made the point to Hanoi that Vietnam could not rely on Soviet protection while it trampled on China's interests. Demonstrating the ability to march on Hanoi if that were required, and inflicting severe punishment on Vietnam as Chinese forces withdrew, and then sustaining a decade-long border war, made the point that the costs of Vietnamese defiance of China's interests would be great.

Of course, the demonstration of Chinese preparedness to use military force was not without costs. That demonstration added to regional trepidation about how China might use its even greater power in the future and the role it would then aspire to play. Beijing's "teaching Vietnam a lesson" ranks, perhaps, with China's decades-long support for communist insurgencies across Southeast Asia as historical episodes generating unease about China in Southeast Asia.

15 }

The Strategic Triangle
and the Four Modernizations

New Economic Wine in Old Strategic Bottles

The term "strategic triangle" is a useful concept referring to the pattern of cooperation and conflict between the USSR, the United States, and China during the Cold War. The basic idea is this: locked in a global protracted confrontation over power and ideology, both the Soviet and the American superpowers saw China as a significant factor, positive or negative, in that alignment. Each superpower feared China's alignment with the other superpower, and each sought China's alignment with itself. China's leaders, for their part, understood well China's role in the Soviet-US balance and sought to exploit it to China's advantage.

China's relatively substantial capabilities were the basis for its role in the strategic triangle. China played a major role in Japan's defeat in World War II by tying down about a million Japanese soldiers, helping to make feasible the Europe First strategy adopted by the Big Three Allied powers. Moreover, until the last year of the Pacific War US war planners envisioned Chinese forces, armed via a reopened Burma Road and organized and led by US military officers, providing the muscle to drive Japanese forces out of north China, opening the way for an eventual US invasion of Japan from the North China coast.[1] After Japan's defeat, as we saw in an earlier chapter, Stalin appreciated the potential for Chinese revolutionary offensives in Asia to tie down US forces in Asia, diverting US strength away from the more crucial European theater. During the 1949 interregnum, US policy sought to court "Chinese Titoism" away from close alignment with Moscow. China's willingness to go to war with the United States in Korea added to its weight in the strategic balance and paid off well in terms of the scale of Soviet assistance to China's 1950s development effort. After the Sino-Soviet split, Moscow was haunted by the possibility that China might align with the United States, while starting with Richard Nixon, US leaders sought China as a partner because of China's weight in containing the Soviet Union. Simply stated, Soviet and American leaders saw China as an important factor in the global correlation of forces.

Mao Zedong and Deng Xiaoping used China's triangular leverage in very different ways. Mao aligned with the Soviet Union and the world communist movement in a quest to build socialism, but then switched sides and aligned with the United States to deter Soviet intervention or attack. Deng maintained Mao's latter-day strategic alignment with the United States but gave it new economic content, allowing China to draw deeply on the assets of advanced capitalist countries to modernize China's economy. It is an open question whether Deng could have achieved China's alignment with the United States if Mao had not opened the way to alignment with the United States only five or so years earlier. In this regard, at least, Deng's diplomacy followed Mao's.

Deng employed triangular diplomacy for purposes radically different from Mao's: to create a favorable macroclimate for the success of China's long-term drive for economic modernization by drawing on the assets of the advanced capitalist countries. Deng reached the breathtakingly radical conclusion that the key font of assistance and inspiration for China's development should not be the USSR or the reform socialist countries of East Europe (although there was some discussion of these East European models early in the opening process). Instead, Deng concluded, China would look to the advanced capitalist countries of Western Europe, Japan, and North America for technology, scientific and managerial know-how, export markets, and capital to transform communist-ruled socialist PRC into a powerful and relatively prosperous country by the end of the twentieth century. The problem confronting Deng's radical new strategy, which he dubbed the Four Modernizations, was that the global capitalist system that made available these crucial developmental inputs was dominated, for better or worse, by the United States, which could, if it chose, substantially restrict China's access to vital developmental inputs. Why should the preeminent capitalist power, the United States, with its long history of using its vast power to oppose socialism and communism, treat benignly the rise of a strong, communist-ruled socialist China?

The other East Asian states that had successfully pioneered the developmental path China set out on under Deng—Japan, Taiwan, South Korea, Hong Kong, and Singapore—were all allies of the United States and embraced liberal ideals and institutions (at least in theory, if not yet fully in practice). The PRC, on the other hand, was and would remain communist-ruled, or so Deng was determined. The PRC had also been a vehement rival of the United States for several decades and fought wars with it in Korea and Vietnam. Even after Sino-American rapprochement in 1972, China had continued to patronize foreign revolutionary movements. How could the United States now be persuaded to look benignly on China's push for wealth and power?

Deng worked out two main policy responses to this strategic problem. First, China scrapped China's support for revolutionary anticapitalist movements, as discussed in an earlier chapter. Second, China tilted sharply toward the United States within the strategic triangle, transforming the PRC into Washington's strategic partner in countering Soviet advances. This is not to say that Deng was not deeply concerned with Soviet advances in the late 1970s. He was. By the late 1970s, Deng was concerned with Soviet advances in Afghanistan, Africa, Iran, and especially Indochina. But alignment with the United States to deal with those security concerns also served developmental purposes. Like Mao, Deng did not compartmentalize foreign and domestic issues.

Deng was more willing than Mao to enter into active and substantial cooperation with the United States. Deng seems to have been less obsessed than Mao with the possibility of US betrayal of the PRC to the USSR. Mao had been reluctant to enter into active cooperation with the United States to counter the Soviet Union. Under Mao, Beijing had been content to deliver policy seminars for visiting US dignitaries, supplemented by polemical broadsides in China's media. The one effort by Zhou Enlai to actually work together with the Americans—arranging a Sihanouk-led Cambodian coalition government in 1973—had collapsed because the Americans did not do what they said they would do, resulting in a great loss of credibility by Zhou. He was a scapegoat; the effort must have been approved by Mao, but when the scheme collapsed, Zhou bore the blame.

Underlying Mao's reluctance to actively cooperate with the United States was, in Henry Kissinger's estimate, a suspicion that the United States would ultimately strike a deal with the Soviet Union against China. Deng, on the other hand, believed that US interests in containing the Soviet Union were essentially the same as China's, and consequently was much more willing to act in unison with Washington.[2] Strategic partnership with the United States on the basis of those common interests would create a favorable macroclimate for China's effort to draw broadly and deeply on the assets of the global capitalist economy. Deng's domestic and international objectives dovetailed in the late 1970s. Partnering actively with the United States would counter Soviet expansionism while persuading the Americans that the PRC was a friendly power whose development efforts should receive generous treatment.

Strategic cooperation between the PRC and the United States against the Soviet Union from about 1978 to 1982 was so close that the Western media and analysts took to calling that partnership a quasi alliance and the PRC a quasi-member of NATO. Beijing would distance itself somewhat from the United States starting in 1982, but partnership with the United States against the Soviet Union would continue throughout the Cold War. This created a favorable macroclimate for the explosive growth of China's cooperative ties with the advanced capitalist countries led by the United States. China under

Deng did not become capitalist—at least, that was not Deng's intention—but it did wade ever deeper into the powerful currents of global capitalism, an approach vastly different than Mao's.

Normalization of Relations with the United States

Deng began pushing for normalization of ties with the United States as soon as he was fully restored to office in July 1977.[3] When Secretary of State Cyrus Vance visited Beijing in August, Deng laid out "three tasks" for the United States to achieve to make normalization possible: 1) abrogate the 1954 mutual security treaty with Taiwan, 2) withdraw all US military personnel from Taiwan, and 3) sever diplomatic relations with Taiwan. Regarding unification of Taiwan with the PRC, Deng told Vance, the Chinese people should be allowed to solve this problem by themselves.[4] In effect, Deng was asking for the United States to adopt a hands-off strategy toward cross-Strait relations. Throughout the process of PRC-US normalization, Taiwan would be the most difficult problem.

In May 1978, after President Carter resolved a policy dispute between Vance and National Security Advisor Zbigniew Brzezinski in favor of the latter's policy of aligning with Beijing against Moscow, Brzezinski arrived in Beijing with a new US approach toward normalization.[5] The United States was willing to accept the "three tasks" stipulated by Deng, Brzezinski told Deng, but hoped that when the United States said in the process of normalization that it expected a peaceful solution to the Taiwan problem, the US statement would not be refuted by China. Regarding Taiwan, Deng said: "We cannot commit ourselves to solving the Taiwan problem peacefully. With regard to this question, the two sides can express their own ideas that do not bind each other."[6] That formulation left China free to rebut US statements about peaceful resolution of the Taiwan question, an outcome contrary to Brzezinski's proposal. Still, momentum toward normalization was building.

Beijing pushed very hard for the United States to agree to a hands-off policy toward a cross-Strait military conflict. Foreign Minister Huang Hua, who had been dealing with Americans since 1936, when Zhou Enlai assigned his then-young English-speaking assistant to show the journalist Edgar Snow around the north Shaanxi base area, led the normalization negotiations on the Chinese side. The US team was led by Ambassador Leonard Woodcock, former head of the United Auto Workers union and a skilled negotiator.

The American side agreed to several small but significant changes in the verbiage used to state the US position on the status of Taiwan.[7] The English language texts of both the 1972 and 1978 PRC-US Joint Communiqués used the verb "acknowledge" to state the US position: the United States "acknowledges the Chinese position that there is but one China and Taiwan is a part of

China." The 1972 Communiqué had used the Chinese verb *renshidao* (literally "acknowledge," or see the reality of) as the predicate in the Chinese text. For the 1978 communiqué, however, American negotiators agreed to use of the Chinese verb *chengren*, which translates as "recognize." Both the English verb *recognize* and the Chinese verb *chengren* have among their several usages the conferring of the legal status of sovereignty by an established member of the community of sovereign states on an entity claiming membership in that legal community. *Chengren* is, sometimes, a precise term of diplomatic art. To "*chengren*/recognize" a state is to accept that entity's legal right to exercise sovereign control over a particular territory. Thus, the formulation (translated into English) in the Chinese-language version, "the United States *recognizes* China's view that Taiwan is a part of China," has significantly different meaning than the phrase in the US/English version, "the United States *acknowledges* China's view that Taiwan is a part of China." This is precisely why US negotiators in 1972 insisted on use of *renshidao* in the Chinese text, and why Chinese negotiators pushed so hard for use of *chengren* in the 1978 Communiqué text.[8] The change of one verb in the 1978 Chinese text led to the Chinese assertion that the United States had thereby pledged to stay out of cross-Strait relations because the United States had "recognized that Taiwan was a part of China." The English version of the 1978 communiqué, which the United States said was for it the authoritative text, continued to use the word *acknowledge*.

US agreement to the use of the verb *chengren* in the Chinese text subsequently created divergent US and Chinese views of whether the United States had "recognized that Taiwan is a part of China." The normalization documents were in two versions, English and Chinese, and each side took the version in its own language as the authoritative text. Thus, for China the United States "recognized that Taiwan was part of China," while the United States insisted it had merely "acknowledged the Chinese position that . . . Taiwan is part of China." Thus, in a January 1981 warning to Washington in the context of escalating confrontation over arms sales to Taiwan, Deng, basing his comments on the Chinese version of the normalization communiqué, asserted:

> When China and the United States established diplomatic relations in 1979, they settled the main question, the Taiwan question, and the United States *recognized* Taiwan as a part of China. Only by settling this question could the two countries establish new relations . . . Sino-US . . . relations . . . were normalized after settling the issue of *recognizing* Taiwan as part of China's territory, this remains the key issue determining whether or not Sino-US. . . . relations . . . will continue to advance.[9] [Emphasis added.]

The US request that China not contradict a statement of US "hope" (in Huang Hua's usage) or the verb "expects" (in the actual English text of the final communiqué) seemed to be resolved on November 25, when acting foreign minister Han Nianlong (standing in for Huang Hua, who was ill) informed Woodcock that if the US side made a statement expressing "hope" for a peaceful solution of the Taiwan issue, the Chinese side would not contradict it.[10] The matter was handled in two parallel unilateral statements, one by the United States and one by the PRC, issued simultaneously with the Joint Communiqué announcing establishment of diplomatic relations. This too was a modest US concession; a unilateral statement is less authoritative than a statement included in a bilateral statement. Sovereign states are bound only by their own agreements, and Beijing could argue that a unilateral US statement did not embody Chinese agreement. In the 1972 communiqué, the US statement of "its interest in a peaceful settlement of the Taiwan question by the Chinese themselves" had been in the body of the *joint* communiqué. The *unilateral* US declaration of December 1978 said:

> The United States is confident that the people of Taiwan face a peaceful and prosperous future. The United States *continues to have an interest* in the peaceful resolution of the Taiwan issue and *expects* that the Taiwan issue will be settled peacefully by the Chinese themselves.[11] (Emphasis added).

In line with Han Nianlong's statement, the PRC unilateral declaration did not directly assert China's right to use force to "solve the Taiwan question." The indirect import was clear, however. Beijing's unilateral statement in 1978 read:

> Taiwan is a part of China. The question of Taiwan ... has now been resolved between the two countries in the spirit of the Shanghai Communiqué. ... As for the way of bringing Taiwan back to the embrace of the motherland and reunifying the country, it is entirely China's internal affair.[12]

US agreement to use of the Chinese verb *chengren* in the Chinese text and to moving the US statement of its "interest in" and "expectation of" peaceful resolution from the joint communiqué to a unilateral US declaration constituted small but significant US concessions to Beijing. This established the precedent for China to subsequently press US leaders to deliver to Beijing on important occasions small Taiwan-related tokens of Washington's sincere commitment to Sino-American friendship. Beijing would subsequently push hard to continue this precedent. Nearly twenty years later, in 1996–1997, when representatives of the Jiang Zemin and William Clinton administrations were negotiating terms of a renormalization of relations, Beijing pressed for a "fourth communiqué" which would contain further "advances" regarding Taiwan. Eventually, American negotiators recognized this for what it was: salami tactics, in which individual demands are so small as to appear insignificant, but taken together can add up to something substantial. One Chinese negotiating tactic was to assert to American negotiators, who often were new to the issues and whose understanding of earlier negotiations might be weak, that earlier US negotiators had committed the United States to things that had not, in fact, been agreed to. In response, the US government commissioned an authoritative study of the PRC-US negotiating record regarding Taiwan along with typical Chinese negotiating ploys for the familiarization of neophyte US diplomats with China's methods of "diplomatic combat."[13]

Returning to the 1978 negotiations, the issue of US arms sales to Taiwan emerged as the most contentious issue and came close to deadlocking the process. Huang Hua maintained that since the United States had committed itself to a "one China policy" in the 1972 Communiqué, this required that the United States stop selling weapons to Taiwan as soon as Sino-US relations were normalized.[14] The United States found no such obligation in the 1972 Communiqué. US negotiators in 1978 agreed that the United States would not sell arms to Taiwan during 1979, the year immediately after normalization, in order to avoid highlighting the issue and embarrassing Beijing. Washington was also willing to agree that the United States would handle arms sales to Taiwan in a cautious and prudent manner and transfer only defensive weapons. But beyond that US negotiators would not go. A discussion between Brzezinski and PRC ambassador in Washington Chai Zemin, only two days before the normalization communiqué was set to be issued, left Brzezinski surprised that Chai thought the United States had agreed to end all arms sales to Taiwan.[15] This led to urgent instructions to Woodcock to seek a meeting with Deng to clarify the US stance on this crucial issue. Upon hearing Woodcock's clarification, Deng became very angry and did not calm down for ten minutes. "We cannot agree," Deng said. Deng maintained that continued US arms sales were contrary to a peaceful solution of the Taiwan question because they would dissuade Taipei from entering into negotiations with Beijing, making use of force the only way to incorporate Taiwan into the PRC. After spending almost an hour objecting to the US position, Deng said the Taiwan problem was the one problem remaining unresolved and asked, "What shall we do about it?" Ambassador Woodcock opined that with normalization and the passage of time the American people would come to accept that Taiwan was part of China. The important first task was normalization. Deng answered "*hao*" (OK), and the impasse over arms sales to Taiwan was overcome—for several years.[16]

Scholar Ezra Vogel termed Deng's decision to normalize with the United States while US arms sales to Taiwan continued "one of the most crucial decisions of his life."[17] While countering Soviet moves in Southeast Asia (where China was preparing its pedagogic war with Vietnam) was one immediate reason for this decision, another longer-range objective was gaining access to the Western capital, technology, and know-how that China needed for modernization. Deng was in a hurry. China had already lost decades and had to rush to catch up. Late in 1978, Brzezinski informed Deng that, because of the political calendar in the United States, if normalization was not achieved by the end of that year, it would need to be delayed until late 1979. What would be the situation then? Would conditions for normalization still be favorable? The PRC and the United States had been without diplomatic relations for so long already. Now the chance was at hand. Deng seized it. Deng's calculation, in Ezra Vogel's estimate, was that China lacked adequate leverage to both secure normalization and force the United States to stop arms sales to Taiwan. If he wanted normalization, continuing US arms sales to Taiwan was the price he would have to pay.[18] Two days before the issue of the PRC-US normalization communiqué, Deng gave his keynote speech to the Third Plenum of the Eleventh Central Committee announcing "the fundamental guiding principle of shifting the focus of all Party work to the Four Modernizations."[19] Deng's speech ended with the call, "Let us advance courageously to change the backward condition of our country and turn it into a modern and powerful socialist state."

Deng's American Tour: Deepening of the Triangular Partnership

Deng Xiaoping's state visit to the United States from January 29 to February 4, 1979, was the first ever by a top Chinese leader, reciprocated the 1972 and 1975 visits to China by presidents Nixon and Ford respectively, and symbolized the new era of normal Sino-US relations The visit was significant at two levels: 1) the strengthening of a PRC-US strategic triangular partnership to counter Soviet expansionism; and 2) the generation of popular American goodwill that would underpin US support for China's new long march toward modernization.

Regarding the strengthening of strategic partnership, Deng arrived in the United States seeking support, or at least understanding, for the upcoming war against Vietnam. The deterioration of PRC-Vietnamese relations during 1978 paralleled Beijing's push for normalization with the United States. As outlined in the previous chapter, Hanoi's failed efforts to engineer a coup d'état ousting the Khmer Rouge in early 1978, followed by the conclusion in November of a security treaty with the USSR and the mobilization of powerful Vietnamese military forces for a full-scale invasion of Cambodia, led the CCP to decide to "teach Vietnam a lesson" in February 1979. The Carter administration generally shared Beijing's concern about the aggressive activities of the Soviet Union and its proxies, Vietnam and Cuba, and saw deepened relations with China as one effective counter to that expansionism. In the words of National Security Advisor Brzezinski, the strategic triangle was something that he had to "think of at all times but speak of it never … publicly one had to make pious noises to the effect that US-Chinese normalization had nothing to do with US-Soviet rivalry." But in fact, "We were convinced that a genuinely cooperation relation between Washington and Beijing would . . . . be to US advantage in the global competition with the Soviet Union . . . the timing of normalization was definitely influenced by the Soviet dimension."[20]

From Beijing's perspective, deterring a Soviet military response to China's upcoming lesson to Vietnam was a key triangular objective vis-à-vis the United States in early 1979. Hanoi hoped that the threat of Soviet intervention conveyed by the November 1978 treaty would deter a Chinese military response to Vietnam's upcoming invasion and occupation of Cambodia. From Moscow's perspective, conclusion of a military alliance with Vietnam was a major step toward expansion of the Soviet military presence in Southeast Asia. This was precisely why Beijing and Washington took umbrage at the treaty. But having put Soviet credibility on the line by signing the treaty with Hanoi, failure to intervene on behalf of its client Vietnam against China would entail serious loss of credibility of the Soviet Union with its allies. This meant that, in the event of a Sino-Vietnamese war, there would be strong pressure on Moscow to act militarily in support of Vietnam. Beijing sought in January 1979 to obtain US support that would help deter Soviet intervention in China's upcoming war with Vietnam.

During private and highly confidential discussions with Carter in Washington during January 1979, Deng informed the American president of China's decision for war with Vietnam and the reasons for that decision. But Deng assured Carter that China's upcoming lesson to Vietnam would be limited in geographic scope and time. This hour-long small-group discussion had been preceded by a full day's larger group discussion during which, according to Brzezinski, "Deng minced no words, and after a vigorous denunciation of Soviet activities in the Middle East and southern Asia, he urged joint American-Chinese cooperation against the Soviets, though carefully adding that he was not proposing at this stage a formal alliance."[21] The United States and China had a common enemy and therefore should collaborate closely, Deng told the Americans. Regarding the possibility of Soviet intervention in the upcoming war, China had considered this "worst [case] possibility," Deng told Carter, and even then China would hold out and proceed to administer its lesson to Vietnam. China had considered all the alternatives and had concluded that failure to punish Vietnam would simply allow Hanoi and Moscow to run amuck in Southeast Asia. Sometimes one had to do things one would prefer not to do, Deng told Carter. He did not expect US endorsement of China's upcoming war, Deng told Carter. He desired only "moral support" from the United States.

Carter and his team took an evening to consider the matter and replied to Deng the next day. The United States could not condone open military attack by any country on another, Carter explained. Moreover, a Chinese attack on Vietnam would generate international sympathy for Vietnam, making more difficult the isolation of Vietnam over its aggression against Cambodia. A Chinese assault against Vietnam would undermine US domestic support for normalization of relations with the PRC. Deng listened carefully and noted what Carter did not say—that the United States would openly condemn China's upcoming lesson. After Carter finished his presentation, Deng expressed appreciation for Carter's comments, but reiterated his view that China found it necessary to "teach Vietnam a lesson." That "lesson" would last only ten to twenty days, Deng said. Carter told Deng he wanted China to understand that the US position was not based on fear of the Soviet Union, but on a belief that it would be better to work to internationally isolate Vietnam and the Soviet Union. Deng concluded that it was good to have a friend with whom such things could be discussed so frankly. Carter also offered Deng an intelligence briefing on the disposition of Soviet forces around China's periphery—an offer which Deng "eagerly accepted," according to Carter.[22]

Brzezinski worked out a formal US position on the war, carefully designing it to look even-handed but in fact tilting toward Beijing. The United States called for the withdrawal of Chinese troops from Vietnam and of Vietnamese troops from Cambodia. An appeal for withdrawal by both countries looked even-handed. Of course, the United States knew that China planned to withdraw its forces in ten to twenty days, while Vietnam's forces in Cambodia were digging in to stay for years. Once China's forces launched their pedagogic war, Washington sent several messages to Moscow subtly crafted to deter Soviet intervention. One message urged the Soviet Union to take no action to exacerbate the situation. The United States was prepared to act in a similar matter, the US note said. Implicit in this note, Brzezinski noted, was the message that the United States was prepared to act militarily if the Soviet Union so acted. The United States also closely monitored Soviet military moves during the war and warned the Soviet Union that any "organized Soviet military presence" in Vietnam would force the United States to reevaluate its security position in the Far East. This formulation, Brzezinski noted, carried the hint of wider US-PRC security relations.[23]

Washington used its emerging triangular leverage with Moscow in regions outside Southeast Asia. In December 1980, as Soviet forces were marshaling on Poland's borders in preparation for an invasion to oust a reformist communist government ruling that country, Brzezinski ordered the US Department of State to draw up a list of weapons to be transferred to China in the event of a Soviet invasion. "I felt fairly confident," Brzezinski reported, "that the substance of the memorandum would rapidly become more publicly known."[24] As Carter said in May 1980, "It is not bad for the Soviets to think that there is an embryonic US-Chinese military relation."[25]

China's decision to align closely with the United States in the strategic triangle soon paid off for the end goals of the Four Modernizations—national wealth and power. Washington facilitated China's smooth entry into the institutions of the global market economy. Early in 1980, China entered both the International Monetary Fund and the World Bank. Over the next thirty-two years, China would receive over $50 billion in funding for 349 infrastructure projects in China—making China one of the largest recipients of World Bank loans. In mid-1980, Washington delinked most favored nation (MFN) status for China and the Soviet Union. MFN status was essential for rapid expansion of Chinese exports to the United States. It greatly slashed import duties on Chinese goods coming into the United States, making those goods competitive. Without MFN, the market for Chinese goods in the United States would be very small. Until mid-1980, US policy had been that granting of MFN for the USSR and the PRC should proceed in tandem. Under the new policy, Chinese exports to the United States would grow steadily and rapidly over the next thirty years. The USSR, in contrast, never received MFN status from the United States. The Soviet Union posed security challenges to the United States. The PRC posed no such threats but was a partner of the United States in dealing with Soviet threats.

In terms of Chinese military power, the strategic partnership between Beijing and Washington convinced the Carter administration that more generous US support for development of Chinese military power would serve US interests. Thus, in mid-1980, Washington adopted a policy of "benign neutrality" toward weapons sales by its West European allies to the PRC.[26] Several West European states were interested in such sales, but feared legal problems under COCOM restrictions. Breaking with previous US policy, the Carter administration informed relevant countries that the United States no longer opposed these sales. A short while later, China was moved from the "Warsaw Pact countries" category under COCOM to an exclusive category of its own with much wider access to military technology. By the end of 1980, a wide array of previously forbidden military-use items were available to China: radars, electronic countermeasure equipment, radio and communications systems, and so on. This was the beginning of active US support for China military development, which would continue all the way to the Beijing Massacre of 1989. The key point here is that the basis of this new US support for China's military modernization was strategic triangular partnership.

In terms of shaping US public opinion in a direction supportive of assistance to China's new long march toward modernization, Deng's 1979 visit to the United States was a masterful display of public diplomacy comparable to his 1978 visit to Japan. Public and media attention focused on the visit. As in Japan, Deng's visit became a moment of virtual national catharsis, expressing hope for a better future. As in Japan, Deng's simplicity and directness struck a chord. At the end of a gala program at the Kennedy Center in Washington during which American children sang some songs in Chinese, Deng and President Carter together mounted the stage to congratulate the performers. When Deng hugged and kissed several of the children, the audience was deeply moved. Journalists noted that many in the audience were crying. Another moment came during a dinner at the White House with movie actress Shirley MacLaine in attendance. MacLaine had visited China during the Cultural Revolution era in the early 1970s and had been very impressed by the Maoist efforts to construct a new, model society. At the White House dinner in 1979, MacLaine recalled how, during her visit to China, she had met a university professor growing vegetables in a farm in the countryside. When asked if he felt a loss at having to do physical labor and abandon scientific research at the university, the professor had professed happiness at learning so much from the poor peasants with whom he worked. After listening to the story and pausing for a moment, Deng replied "That professor was lying." Deng's Harvard-educated English-language translator Ji Chaozhu, who witnessed this exchange, recalled: "MacLaine's jaw dropped. Carter, who had been listening, nodded gravely. I knew then that China's true liberation was finally at hand"[27] When this episode was conveyed by the media to the American public, many people reached a conclusion similar to Ji Chaozhu's.

The most famous moment of Deng's US visit came at a rodeo outside Houston, Texas. After concluding his visit and talks in Washington, DC, Deng visited Atlanta, Houston, and Seattle. Designed to give China's new leader a view of diverse aspects of American life, a cowboy rodeo was far from the ken of China's leader. Yet when one of the horse-mounted young women in the program rode up to the vice premier and offered him a ten-gallon cowboy hat, Deng readily took it and put it on. Then, accompanied by similarly hatted translator Ji Chaozhu, Deng left the stands, climbed into an old-style American stagecoach, and took a spin around the arena, waving to an audience going wild with cheers, applause, and laughter at the incongruous sight of the leader of the Chinese Communist Party, in his austere Mao tunic, decked out like an American cowboy. Deng's natural charisma, personal confidence, and willingness to be a good sport transformed an event that had the potential to make China's leader look like a fool into a brilliant public relations coup, showing a man of supreme self-confidence holding out a hand of understanding and friendship to the American people.

Throughout his American tour, Deng stressed China's backwardness, its need to work hard to catch up, and his deep interest in US technological prowess in that regard. In Atlanta, he visited a Ford automobile factory. In Houston, he visited Hughes Tool Company, manufacturing modern rigs for offshore petroleum drilling. In Seattle, he visited Boeing aircraft. In Houston, he visited the Johnson Space Center, the headquarters of the National Aeronautic and Space Administration and command center for the US space exploration program. Deng expressed deep interest in what he saw. After trying out a flight simulator modeling the landing of a spacecraft from 100,000 feet, he requested a second attempt. Even then, he was reluctant to leave the device.

Alongside such human appeal, Deng placed an appeal to the American people in plain and direct terms. In an interview with *Time* magazine, Deng said:

> If we really want to be able to place curbs on the polar bear, the only realistic thing is for us to unite. If we only depend on the strength of the US, it is not enough. If we only depend on the strength of Europe, it is not enough. We [China] are an insignificant, poor country, but if we unite, well, it will then carry weight.[28]

Active Anti-Hegemony Partnership: Cambodia and Afghanistan

Southeast Asia and Afghanistan were the two geographic foci of PRC-US strategic cooperation during the decade 1979–1989. Southeast Asia was the region that most directly engaged major Chinese security interests. Beijing responded to Hanoi's invasion and occupation of Cambodia by fostering a broad international effort to punish Hanoi. Beijing's effort began with the three-week-long war of February 1979. Throughout the remainder of the 1980s, Beijing kept up strong military pressure on Vietnam's northern borders. Chronic PLA artillery barrages and infantry incursions of greater or lesser intensity corresponded to political developments. US policy paralleled that of Beijing. Washington and Beijing also worked together to dissuade countries from supplying development assistance or loans to Vietnam, or establishing diplomatic relations with it.

Support for armed guerrilla resistance to Vietnamese forces in Cambodia was another component of Beijing's protracted campaign to punish Vietnam. Beijing worked out a deal with Thailand whereby eastern Thailand served as a territorial sanctuary for armed Khmer resistance groups, while China armed and supplied (via Thailand) the Khmer Rouge, which commanded the most potent resistance force. The strong PLA presence on Vietnam's northern borders helped dissuade Hanoi from violating Thai territory by launching military strikes into Thailand. After defeating the US-backed Saigon regime in 1975 with a powerful Soviet-armed conventional army, and inheriting in addition Saigon's huge cache of US weaponry, Vietnam was the most potent military power in Southeast Asia at that juncture. China and the United States cooperated in deterring Hanoi from using that power to move against the Khmer resistance bases along the Thai-Cambodia border.

Protraction was at the core of Beijing's strategy against Vietnam. Beijing was convinced that Hanoi would be unable to sustain the financial, political and military costs of its attempt to control Cambodia, and would ultimately be forced to come to terms with Beijing. Beijing's broad objective was to teach Hanoi that it could not afford to turn China into an enemy, and that to avoid this, Hanoi could not trample on major Chinese interests, such as violating the independence of Cambodia. In China's formulation, the 1979 war "taught Vietnam a lesson." In the words of a US diplomat, China was delivering not merely one lesson, but a whole graduate curriculum.[29] Beijing thus sought to block a "premature" political settlement. It takes time to complete a graduate curriculum.

As the political conflict with Hanoi unfolded during the 1980s, Indonesia and Malaysia—countries more apprehensive of China and of a possible Chinese advance into Southeast Asia via a Khmer Rouge return to power in Cambodia—proposed various solutions to end the conflict: a dialogue between Vietnam and ASEAN, or talks between the Vietnam-backed Phnom Penh government and the ASEAN-backed Cambodian government. Beijing worked, successfully and in tandem with the United States, to quash these moves. Beijing believed that only when Vietnam was thoroughly exhausted would it be possible to really dismantle the pro-Vietnamese political structure Hanoi had installed in Cambodia. As Deng Xiaoping told a shocked Japanese Prime Minister Masayoshi Ohira in December 1979: "It is wise for China to force the Vietnamese to stay in Kampuchea because that way they will suffer more and more and will not be able to extend their hand to Thailand, Malaysia, and Singapore."[30] Or, as Han Nianlong told journalist Nayan Chanda about the same time, nothing should be done to lighten Vietnam's burden. Only when the Soviet Union, Hanoi's backer, was exhausted would a political solution in Cambodia be possible.

China's opening gambit in its contest with Hanoi was to seek an understanding with Thailand, Vietnam's centuries-old rival for influence in Cambodia. By the seventeenth century, the Thai and the Vietnamese states were far stronger than the declining Khmer state, and both were rivals in absorbing Khmer territory. That contest had been interrupted by the arrival of the French in the nineteenth century, but had resumed, covertly, during the American war of 1964–1975. Vietnam's move to occupy Cambodia and integrate it into a Vietnamese-led Indochina bloc led Thailand to work to thwart that effort, restoring Cambodia's status as an independent and neutral buffer between Vietnam and Thailand. Bangkok's and Beijing's interests overlapped. Thus, in March 1978, as the Vietnam–Khmer Rouge conflict spiraled upward and Sino-Vietnam relations collapsed, Thai prime minister (and ex-general) Kriangsak Chomanan visited China. Deng Xiaoping reciprocated that visit in November 1978, as Vietnamese forces were marshaled for their invasion of Cambodia. During his visit, Deng stressed the need to oppose some countries' policies of domination and intervention, and the "correct conclusion" of guarding against "hegemonist expansion into the Southeast Asian region."[31] In discussion, the two sides "exchanged views on international issues of mutual concern and ways to further Sino-Thai relations." In the words of Huang Hua, both sides were "worried . . . that if

Cambodia was invaded it was likely that Thailand would be attacked." In Thailand, as in Japan in 1978 and in the United States in 1979, Deng employed his remarkable human touch. Thailand's monarch was so taken by the vice premier's simplicity and modesty that he invited Deng, along with the other male members of the Chinese entourage, to attend the induction ceremony of the crown prince's entry into a Buddhist monastery for a period of time. This was an extremely unusual invitation.[32]

Joint supply of arms to the Khmer resistance to Vietnamese occupation became one important dimension of Sino-Thai cooperation. Chinese ships would deliver PLA arms to the Thai ports of Sattahip and Khlong Yai, where they were unloaded and transported by the Thai army to Khmer resistance camps on the Thai-Cambodian border. The Thai army was allowed to keep a certain percentage of the shipments for its own use, and China paid a fee to the Thai army for transporting the weapons. The PRC also transferred technology to Thailand, allowing a Thai munitions factory to begin production of advanced anti-tank rockets, a portion of which went to the Khmer Rouge. The PRC embassy in Bangkok also purchased via Sino-Thai merchants food and medicine which went to the Khmer Rouge.[33] Again China and the United States worked in tandem. Increasingly substantial US military assistance to noncommunist Khmer resistance groups paralleled Chinese assistance to the Khmer Rouge. Generous humanitarian assistance by the US-led international community went to *all* Khmer refuge and resistance camps. US power reinforced China's in deterring Vietnamese and/or Soviet moves against Thailand for its activities in Cambodia. Had the very substantial Soviet air and naval presence established at Cam Ranh Bay in southern Vietnam by 1985, for instance, attempted to interfere with Chinese ships delivering weapons to Sattahip port, the preeminent power of the US navy in that region could easily have trumped the Soviet move.

US and PRC diplomacy generally worked in parallel in the United Nations to defeat Soviet-supported Vietnamese efforts to have its Phnom Penh client government installed as Cambodia's representative. During the late Carter administration and the period of the Reagan administration in which Al Haig was secretary of state (January 1981–July 1982), the United States sided with Beijing and against the ASEAN countries on keeping the Khmer Rouge government occupying Cambodia's seat in the UN General Assembly. Several ASEAN countries were, as noted above, troubled by the prospect of a Khmer Rouge return to power in Cambodia after a Vietnamese withdrawal, a possibility that that the US-PRC position seemed to bode. Thus, during 1981, the ASEAN counties worked out a plan under which *all* Khmer factions would be disarmed following an internationally supervised withdrawal of Vietnamese forces from Cambodia. An international peace-keeping force would simultaneously be introduced into the country and an interim government set up. Free and internationally supervised elections would then be held, and the results of those elections would determine the composition of Cambodia's future government. Implicit in this proposal was the assumption that in genuinely free elections, the Khmer Rouge would receive very few votes. Without votes or arms, the Khmer Rouge would thus be reduced to a minor role in post-withdrawal Cambodian politics. This plan would ultimately be adopted in 1990 and form the basis for successful settlement of the Cambodian question. But in 1981, both Beijing and Washington were opposed to it. The time was not yet right. Pressure on Hanoi needed to be maintained a while longer.

According to Beijing during the 1980s, the ASEAN proposal would constitute international interference in Cambodia's internal affairs. Elections were fine, Beijing said, but they should be organized by Cambodia's Khmer Rouge–led government. Cambodia's legal government, again including the Khmer Rouge, should administer Cambodia once the Vietnamese withdrew. As for disarmament, possession and utilization of military force were core elements of national sovereignty. Cambodia's legitimate government could not be denied military forces. While founded on traditional legal notions of state sovereignty, the political essence of Beijing's proposal seems to have been a Khmer Rouge return to power—albeit chastened and less extreme. In 1981, Washington opposed the ASEAN proposal in tandem with China, mainly because of a commitment to triangular partnership with Beijing. Once George Shultz became secretary of state in July 1982, however, US policy shifted to support for the ASEAN proposal. Shultz did not believe US interests, moral or geopolitical, would be served by a Khmer Rouge return to power or armed bid for power. Shultz was also less enthusiastic than Haig about the utility of triangular cooperation with the PRC. Still, PRC-US partnership over Cambodia continued until Vietnam finally became ready to withdraw in 1989. Fortunately, by that time Beijing was willing to embrace the ASEAN proposal of 1981.

Turning to Afghanistan, according to Zbigniew Brzezinski, immediately after the Soviet occupation of that country in December 1979 the Carter administration began a discussion with Pakistan about a joint response to the Soviet move that would "make the Soviets bleed for as much and as long as . . . possible."[34] President Carter signed several presidential findings that authorized covert US operations to supply munitions and other support to Afghan resistance to kill Soviet soldiers in Afghanistan—the first presidential authorization of lethal covert operations since the Vietnam War.[35] In a manner similar to Sino-American cooperation in Cambodia, the PRC and the United States jointly supported and protected a front-line state, in this case Pakistan, that was willing to allow its territory to be used as sanctuary by resistance fighters. Refugee camps were established in areas of Pakistan bordering Afghanistan, and those camps served as bases for the armed resistance struggle inside Afghanistan. The covert war in Afghanistan did not emerge full-blown all at once, but evolved through several stages. The PRC played three significant roles in the Afghan resistance war: helping to bring Pakistan and the United States together, giving a guarantee to Pakistan's security paralleling and reinforcing a US guarantee, and providing Soviet-style arms to meet huge American needs as the Afghan resistance war escalated in the mid-1980s.

On December 30, 1979, five days after the Soviet invasion, Beijing issued a statement strongly condemning the Soviet move and demanding the withdrawal of Soviet forces. From Beijing's perspective, the Soviet occupation of Afghanistan was another link in the Soviet encirclement of China. China and Afghanistan share a forty-seven-mile border abutting China's ethnically sensitive Xinjiang province. According to Huang Hua, a Soviet move against Pakistan or Iran (where the shah had just been overthrown and the pro-Soviet communist Tudeh Party was still a strong element of the revolutionary coalition) might allow Moscow to seize warm-water military ports, occupy a strategic international artery (the Strait of Hormuz), and cut connections between the Pacific countries and the oil-producing countries of the Middle East.[36] The Soviet move also put Pakistan in a vice between Soviet forces in Afghanistan and Soviet-allied India, as President Zia-ul-Haq of Pakistan explained to Huang Hua during a January 1980 visit to Pakistan.

China's initial role was in bringing Pakistan and the United States together to deal with the Soviet invasion. Pakistan-US relations were then very poor, while the risks that Pakistan would run if it undertook to provide sanctuary for Afghan resistance to Soviet occupation were very high. Washington had suspended aid to Pakistan because of Pakistan's nuclear activities and because of a military coup led by Mohammad Zia-ul-Haq in July 1977 ousting Z. A. Bhutto, a civilian and democratically elected leader who was hanged by the Pakistan military in April 1979. Then, in November 1979, a Pakistani mob stormed, sacked, and burned the US embassy in Islamabad in response to a false report by an Iranian radio station that the United States had bombed the holy Grand Mosque in Mecca. Four US and Pakistani staff personnel were killed during the embassy invasion. Pakistani leaders did not trust the United States, which, although an ally of Pakistan, had suspended military assistance in the middle of Pakistan's 1965 war with India. China, unlike the United States, had vast political capital in Islamabad. As shown in an earlier chapter, China had shown itself prepared to enter the 1965 war on Pakistan's behalf, and then had helped Pakistan rebuild its military strength (including development of nuclear weapons) after Pakistan's catastrophic 1971 partition.

Huang Hua during his January 1980 visit to Islamabad responded to Zia's complaint that the American's were "soft on the Soviets" by urging Pakistan to unite with *all countries* opposed to the Soviet Union (i.e., the United States; emphasis added).[37] Coming from Pakistan's long-time and trusted partner, this Chinese advice carried some weight. Huang and Zia discussed stepped-up Chinese economic and military aid to Pakistan. The same month that Huang

Hua was in Islamabad, US Secretary of Defense Harold Brown traveled to Beijing to discuss joint assistance to Pakistan. In those talks, Beijing agreed to supply small arms to Afghan refugees in Pakistan and to increase the supply of heavy weapons to Pakistan.[38] Although the details of these Sino-Pakistan-US discussions are still unavailable, the broad outlines are clear: the three countries were undertaking to support an Afghan armed resistance to Russian occupation, with Washington and Beijing jointly agreeing to uphold Pakistan security against Soviet incursions or even all-out invasion.

A PLA "goodwill" delegation visited Islamabad in April. After several rounds of talks, Vice Defense Minister Xiao Ke told reporters that China would "resolutely support Pakistan in its struggle to defend its sovereignty and territorial integrity."[39] President Zia visited Beijing in May to receive authoritative guarantees of Pakistan's security. In his banquet speech for Zia, Premier Hua Guofeng, speaking for China, declared: "The Chinese government and people will, as always, firmly support you in your struggle in defense of national independence and state sovereignty and will stand firmly together with you against foreign aggression and interference."[40] By late 1980, sizable quantities of Chinese air defense missiles and jet fighters began to arrive in Pakistan. In parallel with China's moves, Washington granted Pakistan large-scale economic and military aid and gave guarantees of support for Pakistan in the event of Soviet incursions or worse.

To maintain plausible deniability for China and US support for the Afghan resistance, it was necessary to supply those forces with Soviet-style weapons. Once the Afghan operation was up and running, large quantities of such weapons were required. China and the United States again cooperated. Secret CIA missions traveled to the PRC to negotiate purchase of large quantities of Soviet-style weapons: AK-47 rifles, rocket-propelled grenades, and 122- and 144-millimeter rockets. Whole PLA munitions factories were dedicated to producing the requisite Soviet-style weapons for Afghanistan. Of fifty million US dollars initially appropriated (secretly) by the US Congress for CIA purchase of arms for Afghanistan, $38 million was spent in China, which proved to be a highly reliable supplier. Within a few years, US purchases averaged US$ 100 million per year. By fall 1984, ships picked up weapons in Shanghai for shipment to Karachi, where weapons were received and allocated by the Pakistan army. The entire operation was top secret. Within the CIA, reportedly no more than ten people were briefed on the program. Even years after the Soviet withdrawal, China refused to acknowledge its involvement.[41]

China also agreed to provide training for Afghan resistance fighters. Initially, 300 Chinese military trainers operated at training camps in Pakistan. Eventually, two additional camps were established in Xinjiang outside Kashgar and Khotan.[42] Movement from Xinjiang into northeast Afghanistan via the Karakorum Highway was quite convenient. PLA forces deployed to Xinjiang to defend the camps from possible Soviet incursions.

The United States supplied military equipment to China during the 1980s to strengthen China's ability to defend against Soviet attacks in response to China's role in Afghanistan or Cambodia. The most prosaic form of Chinese support for the Afghan resistance fighters consisted of donkeys. In the rugged and underdeveloped mountainous regions in which the Afghan resistance operated, donkeys were often the most reliable form of logistic transport. As demand for these rugged beasts mounted, supply became a problem. China stepped in and conscripted donkeys from Xinjiang and China's northwest.

Throughout the 1980s, Beijing kept strong pressure on Moscow to withdraw from Afghanistan. In March 1982, following a speech by Leonid Brezhnev that hinted at a desire to improve ties with China, Deng listed Soviet withdrawal from Afghanistan as one of three tasks that had to be completed before PRC-Soviet relations could be renormalized. Eventually, Moscow acceded to this demand. The last Soviet forces left Afghanistan in April 1989, the month before Gorbachev arrived in Beijing to renormalize ties and end the long Sino-Soviet dispute.

A third arena of substantive PRC-US triangular cooperation was joint electronic monitoring of Soviet military activity in Central Asia. When Iran was ruled by the shah, Tehran permitted the CIA to maintain posts on Iran's northern borders from which US intelligence agencies monitored Soviet missile tests and electronic transmissions in the Soviet Central Asian republics. Those posts were closed down by Khomeini's revolutionary government in 1979. China under Deng Xiaoping quietly agreed to allow the United States to establish comparable posts in western Xinjiang. Two monitoring stations, operated jointly by the CIA and National Security Agency of the United States and the PLA, were built at Korla and Qitai in central Xinjiang. PLA specialists were reportedly trained at CIA facilities outside Beijing and at a special center near Palo Alto, California. Soviet activities which the Xinjiang facilities monitored included missile, space, nuclear programs, and military and commercial air flights, as well as all telecommunications in Afghanistan. The operation of these facilities was, of course, top secret at the time. These important and highly sensitive joint US-PRC operations reflected the common interests of the two countries in understanding Soviet, and perhaps later Russian, capabilities and activities. China claimed in the early 1990s that the facilities were closed, but scholar Yitzhak Shichor found evidence of their continued operation into the mid-1990s.[43]

Renegotiating the Taiwan Issue: Taiwan Relations Act and Arms Sales

Under the US legal system, legislation was necessary to allow private entities in the United States and in Taiwan to conduct relations with one another, and to authorize specific nonofficial entities of each state to represent the interests of its citizens in the other. A legal basis had to be created for "the people of the United States . . . [to] maintain cultural, commercial, and other unofficial relations with the people of Taiwan," as provided by the December 1978 US-PRC normalization communiqué. Thus, in January 1979, the Carter administration submitted a legislative proposal to Congress. Pro-Taiwan sympathies and skepticism about the PRC were strong in Congress. As a result, Congress rejected the administration proposal and crafted its own. The result was the Taiwan Relations Act (TRA), passed 345 to 55 in the House and 90 to 6 in the Senate in mid-March. The TRA was signed into law by Carter in April. Beijing demanded that Carter veto the legislation, but the lopsided votes in Congress indicate that a presidential veto would have failed.

Beijing believed the TRA seriously violated the bilaterally negotiated normalization agreement. Foreign minister Huang Hua noted (accurately) that the TRA deleted the word "unofficial" in describing the relations to be maintained between the peoples of Taiwan and the United States.[44] The TRA also stated that the US decision to open diplomatic ties with the PRC "rests on the expectation that the future of Taiwan will be determined by peaceful means." During the 1978 normalization negotiations, China had repeatedly rejected exactly this sort of explicit linkage. The TRA also said that the United States would "consider any effort to determine the future of Taiwan by other than peaceful means, including by boycotts or embargoes, a threat to the peace and security of the Western Pacific area and of grave concern to the United States." These clauses, together with the TRA stipulation that the United States would provide Taiwan with arms "necessary to enable Taiwan to maintain a sufficient self-defense capability," were taken by Beijing to be "covert" reinstitution of the US military protectorate over Taiwan that had been canceled by Washington's abrogation of the 1954 mutual security agreement. In sum, the carefully negotiated and finely balanced compromises embodied in the 1978 normalization agreement were being overturned by unilateral US action, at least in Beijing's view.

Beijing understood by this point the American system of separation of powers with its sometimes unexpected consequences, and may have taken at face value the administration's efforts to defend the original normalization agreement. Yet Beijing was determined to prevent a US retreat from the terms of the December 1978 bargain over Taiwan. The result was a forty-month diplomatic battle (from passage of the TRA in April 1979 to the signature of the "third communiqué" in August 1982) that in effect constituted a renegotiation of the Taiwan issue.

The pro-Taiwan sympathies of the Reagan administration that took office in January 1981 deeply troubled Beijing. Reagan had long and close ties with Taiwan's leaders. During his election campaign he had criticized what he viewed as Carter's betrayal of Taiwan in the US-PRC normalization process, and said that as president he would upgrade the unofficial US office in Taiwan to a liaison office such as the United States had in Beijing between 1973 and 1978. Reagan at that stage may not have understood the subtleties of the US position regarding Taiwan; in any case, he referred repeatedly to Taiwan as a separate and sovereign state. And once he won the election, it became known that two Taiwan representatives had been invited to attend his inauguration.

During the 1980 election campaign, Reagan's vice-presidential candidate George H. W. Bush, the US representative to the United Nations during the 1971 debates on PRC admission and head of the liaison office in 1973, certainly understood the ins and outs of the US stance on Taiwan, and was sent to Beijing to mollify Chinese opposition to the inaugural arrangements. Once in office, Reagan quickly became apprised of the nature of US undertakings with Beijing vis-à-vis Taiwan. Yet the issue of US arms sales to Taiwan continued to rankle Beijing. Contrary to Washington's promise during normalization negotiations, US arms sales continued during 1979. Then they increased to $276 million in 1980, compared to $208 million in 1978. Beijing decided that Washington was violating the crucial deal over US arms sales to Taiwan.[45]

Deng feared that Beijing's strategic partnership with the United States was leading Washington to conclude that the United States could force China to accept essentially unlimited arms sales to Taiwan. On January 4, 1981, after Reagan's election but before his inauguration, Deng laid before a US delegation his concerns about US belief that China's triangular dependence would compel it to acquiesce to unacceptable US moves regarding Taiwan. Deng disputed several US viewpoints that he believed mistaken and which, "if not clarified, are likely to cause regression in Sino-US relations."[46] The first US viewpoint Deng believed mistaken was that China was so poor and weak that it really didn't matter in global balance of power. People with this point of view "misjudge China's position in world politics [and] will not have a correct international strategy," Deng said. It was true that China was weak and poor, Deng said, but "China has its own advantages ... a vast territory and a large population.... Even in times of great difficulty, we dared to face reality and confronted powerful forces with our limited strength." A second mistaken US viewpoint was that, because of its drive for development, China needed US help, not vice versa. Again it was true that China was poor, but China "has a strong point: it is relatively highly capable of surviving without outside help, and "the Chinese are accustomed to being poor." A third mistaken American viewpoint was that China needed the United States to counter the Soviet Union and that therefore "if the US government adopts a hard-line policy towards the Soviet Union, China must in turn set aside such questions as ... Taiwan." "However, we simply cannot and will not do that," Deng said. Instead, "China definitely will not give way.... China will certainly make an appropriate response." Deng's fear, he told the visiting Americans, was that these mistaken views would cause the incoming Reagan administration to take actions that violated US "recognition" that Taiwan was a part of China. "We will attach great importance to the actions taken by a new administration after it assumes office." Lest the visiting Americans miss the point, Deng concluded: "What I have just said represents the official position of the Chinese government. I deem it highly important and necessary to let our American friends clearly understand the position of the Chinese government."

By fall 1981, Beijing decided that the actions of the new administration had gone too far, and attempted to secure US agreement to more restrictive guidelines limiting future US sales to Taiwan. Contrary to the TRA, which provided for open-ended US arms sales to Taiwan, Beijing demanded the United States agree to limitations on sales. In terms of quantity, Beijing pushed Washington to agree that the annual level of sales and the quality of weapons sold not exceed those of the Carter administration. Moreover, the overall quantity of US arms sales should gradually decline, eventually coming to a complete end. As Huang Hua told Secretary of State Alexander Haig in October 1981:

> The problem of arms sales to Taiwan is a remnant of the past, and it will take some time for the US to settle it. But we have been waiting in vain for three years, and the problem is still there. We are patient, but cannot wait for ever. If the US is determined . . . to remove this obstacle blocking Sino-US relations, we can give the US some more time to solve this problem. The preconditions for our flexibility are: The United States promises demonstrably that arms sales to Taiwan . . . will be reduced year by year, and finally stopped completely.[47]

The reduction of US sales should not be too gradual, Deng told Ambassador Arthur Hummel. Once final agreement had been reached, China expected that the US commitment to gradually reduce arms sales to Taiwan did not mean reduction by one dollar per year, pushing termination of sales into some distant future.[48] Beijing pushed hard to secure US agreement to a definite date for a final end to US arms sales to Taiwan.

The United States argued that by trying to secure US agreement to end arms sales to Taiwan, it was Beijing, not Washington, that was going beyond what been agreed to during the normalization negotiations. Not so, Beijing replied. During the final confrontation between Deng Xiaoping and Woodcock, when informed by Woodcock that the United States intended to resume arms sales to Taiwan after 1979, Deng had replied, "Will normalization last only one year?" This clearly implied expectation of a time limit on US sales. And in any case, it was the US side that had reopened the 1978 deal by passing the TRA.

Beijing's initial move was to assert to the newly installed Reagan admin-istration officials that the Carter administration had committed the United States to an end of arms sales to Taiwan. Upon checking the National Security Council archives, Washington found no such undertaking in the record.[49] Beijing then succeeded in persuading Haig that agreement to end arms sales to Taiwan was necessary to preserve broader triangular cooperation against the Soviet Union. Haig presented a draft memorandum to President Reagan, but Reagan rejected it and ordered another drafted without a specific cut-off date.[50] Reagan later dictated a one-page presidential statement, initialed by a new Secretary of State, George Shultz, and Secretary of Defense Caspar Weinberger, stipulating:

> The talks leading up to the signing of the [August 1982] communiqué [with Beijing] were premised on the clear understanding that any reduc-tion of such arms sales depends upon peace in the Taiwan Strait and the continuity of China's declared 'fundamental policy' of seeking a peaceful resolution of the Taiwan issue. . . . the U.S. willingness to reduce its arms sales to Taiwan is conditioned absolutely upon the continued commit-ment of China to the peaceful solution of the Taiwan–PRC differences.[51]

As the negotiations entered their final stage in August 1982, the United States asked that its commitment to solve the arms sales issue should be explicitly connected to China's policy of striving for a peaceful solution of the Taiwan question. Beijing refused.[52] Washington succeeded, however, in indirectly asserting this linkage. The final communiqué of August 17 read:

> The United States Government understands and appreciates the Chinese policy of striving for a peaceful resolution of the Taiwan ques-tion . . . The new situation which has emerged with regard to the Taiwan question also provides favorable conditions for the settlement of United States-China differences over the question of United States arms sales to Taiwan.
>
> Having in mind the foregoing statements of both sides, *the United States* Government *states that* it does not seek to carry out a long-term policy of arms sales to Taiwan . . . and that *it intends to reduce gradually its sales of arms to Taiwan, leading over a period of time to a final resolu-tion.*[53] (Emphasis added.)

Subsequently, Beijing treated the phrases italicized above in the August 1982 communiqué as the core element of the 1982 compromise. From the standpoint of China's media, domestic and international, this was virtually the only significant aspect of the 1982 communiqué, rendering US insistence on continued arms sales a clear and blatant violation—yet another—of sol-emn agreements with China. Beijing's propaganda would reiterate this sen-tence again and again, ignoring the context implied by the opening phrase of that sentence: "Having in mind the foregoing statements" about the peaceful resolution of the Taiwan question. The 1982 communiqué was the third document (after 1972 and 1978) in which the United States delivered to Beijing small but significant concessions on Taiwan. It would not be the last.

In the US view, but not in the Chinese, the 1982 communiqué established a clear if implicit linkage between US arms sales to Taiwan and the peaceful resolution of the Taiwan issue. Beijing's core objective as the talks entered their final phase was to connect the termination of US arms sales to Taiwan to the principle of mutual respect for sovereignty and territorial integrity, and mutual non-interference in internal affairs. As Huang Hua acknowledged, Beijing did not achieve this.[54] The statement in the August communiqué regarding mutual respect for sovereignty and territorial integrity concludes blandly with this sentence: "Both sides emphatically state that these principles continue to govern *all* aspects of their relations." [Emphasis added.] From Beijing's perspective, "all" included arms sales to Taiwan. From Washington's perspective, it might or might not; the matter remained vague. Washington refused to grant Beijing the right to regulate US relations with the people of Taiwan.

Both Beijing and Washington used strategic triangular leverage in their negotiating struggle. The leaders of the Reagan administration, especially Secretary of State Alexander Haig, believed that PRC reliance on US power to deter a Soviet attack and counter Soviet efforts to encircle China gave Washington leverage over the PRC. Haig understood that the basis of Sino-US rapprochement in 1972 had been Chinese fear of possible Soviet attack and noted the increased stridency of Chinese warnings against Soviet encirclement throughout the late 1970s. China needed US security support and would therefore accede to US arms sales to Taiwan, Haig maintained. He sought to persuade Beijing to accept US weapons sales to both the PRC and Taiwan.

Beijing's triangular leverage flipped the American argument: the United States needed Chinese assistance to counter Soviet advances around the world, and if Washington did not satisfy Beijing's minimal demands regarding arms sales to Taiwan, Washington might lose Chinese support in America's global contest with Moscow. In short, Washington needed Beijing more than Beijing needed Washington. The difference in triangular approach was exemplified in mid-1980, when the United States proposed that US warships visit Chinese ports in response to Soviet warships being stationed at Vietnam's ports. Ambassador Chai Zemin replied that certain aspects of US legislation regarding Taiwan made such a proposal untimely.[55] Huang Hua intensified the pressure in June 1981 by telling Haig that if the Taiwan arms sales issue could not be solved, Sino-US relations might regress, bringing "serious consequences to the strategic overall situation." Haig countered by saying that "the strategic overall situation is the big wheel, while the Taiwan question is a small wheel located inside this big wheel."[56] Huang retorted: "Arms sales to Taiwan are not . . . a small wheel, but a big wheel and a big question that influences our bilateral relations and the strategic overall situation. I hope the United States will pay serious attention to it."

The Americans tried repeatedly to insert consideration of "the international situation" in various documents regarding the arms sales issue. The Chinese side just as consistently rejected this. When Vice President George H. W. Bush arrived in China in May 1982 to discuss the increasingly tense arms sales issue, for example, he released a statement upon arrival at the airport saying that his talks would cover Argentina, Afghanistan, Poland, and Cambodia. His purpose in doing this, according to Huang Hua, was "to cover up the crisis existing in Sino-US relations and to create the false impression that China and the United States were discussing international strategy." Beijing kept all statements arising from the arms sales talks free of references to various international issues, other than pointed statements that failure to reach agreement on the arms sales issue could have adverse effects on the international situation. Beijing was in effect (i.e., not explicitly) threatening defection from its anti-Soviet/hegemony partnership with the United States to pressure Washington on the arms sales issue. In November 1980 (the same month Reagan was elected president), the Netherlands announced it intended to sell two submarines to Taiwan. After Holland moved ahead with the sale, the PRC mission in the Netherlands threatened, in March 1981, to downgrade China's mission in Holland to a chargé d'affaires. In June, Beijing followed through on its threat. Later in the year, during discussions with Haig in Washington, Huang Hua insisted that if the United States sold arms to Taiwan, Beijing would have to treat the United States the same way it had treated the Netherlands. China could not be expected to treat a great power and a small country differently, Huang insisted. "Only when the US undertook to reduce its arms sales to Taiwan on an annual basis and to stop them eventually could China treat the US and the Netherlands differently," Huang told Haig.[57]

China's position in the arms sales negotiation battle was not strong. The United States had clearly and explicitly stated during the 1978 negotiations its intention to continue selling arms to Taiwan after normalization. In the broader context, the collapse of PRC-US strategic cooperation could seriously injure the Four Modernizations, which were the core of Deng's program. These weaknesses were reflected in the outcome of the 1981–1982 arms sales negotiations. Beijing failed to directly link arms sales to territorial sovereignty. It permitted the United States to implicitly link "peaceful resolution" and arms sales in the communiqué. Moreover, this implicit linkage was translated into a presidential directive which established the US interpretation as US policy. The United States gave only a vague and temporally indefinite commitment to end arms sales. Arms sales continued. And the TRA stood, affirmed by Reagan and subsequent presidents as the law of the land and a core part of US policy toward Taiwan. Perhaps what is significant about the 1979–1982 renegotiation was how well Beijing did considering China's still very weak position.

China punished Washington for its stubbornness over arms sales by shifting to a rhetorically more middle position between the United States and the Soviet Union. Beijing hoped thereby to disabuse Washington of any notions that Beijing's triangular partnership with Washington could be used to impose harsh terms on China. Two weeks after the issue of the arms sales communiqué, Huang Hua during a visit to the UN laid out for top Reagan administration officials China's new foreign policy, adopted at the recent 12th Congress of the CCP. China followed an independent foreign policy and did not depend on any big power or group of big powers, Huang told US leaders. Huang also stated China's hope that the United States would fulfill its commitment in the August 1982 communiqué earnestly and solve this problem at an early date and thoroughly.[58] Subsequently, Chinese media stopped speaking of global united front against hegemonism, greatly toned down condemnations of Soviet "social imperialism," and began to assign greater moral equivalence to Soviet moves and American moves around the world. A new stress appeared in PRC foreign propaganda: China's independent foreign policy of seeking peaceful coexistence with all countries. Beijing also began its slow march toward re-establishing normal relations with the USSR. Close alignment with the United States circa 1978–1980 had created the appearance of dependency, which the American superpower tried to exploit over Taiwan. Beijing responded by moving toward a more balanced rhetorical position in the strategic triangle. But quiet cooperation on Cambodia and Afghanistan, and electronic monitoring of Soviet Central Asia, raised PRC-US strategic cooperation reached unprecedented levels. That cooperation helped consolidate a positive US approach toward China's Four Modernizations.

Sino-American Partnership Shapes World History

The period of PRC-US strategic partnership in the late 1970s and early 1980s constituted, in effect, the second Sino-American alliance. The first was against Japan from 1940 to 1945. Neither were formal or declared; both were informal and not based on treaties of alliance. But both were nonetheless effective. The second Sino-American alliance, or strategic partnership if one prefers, helped persuade Soviet leaders to pull back from policies of assertive use of military force by the Soviet Union and its Cuban and Vietnamese allies to expand the frontiers of socialism. Sino-Soviet strategic partnership was not the only factor, or even the most important factor, compelling Soviet leaders to undertake the fundamental shift in Soviet policy engineered by Mikhail

Gorbachev in the second half of the 1980s. The grave weaknesses of the Soviet economy were certainly the most important factor. At the international level, the reinvigoration of US containment policy during the second half of the Carter administration and during the Reagan administration, including the latter's Strategic Defense Initiative, were probably the most important international factors inducing the shift in Soviet approach. But confrontation with a very real Sino-American security partnership, which Moscow had long dreaded, was one weighty factor persuading Soviet leaders that a change of course was necessary. The quasi alliance between the People's Republic of China and the United States was one factor convincing Soviet leaders that the Brezhnev-era push to achieve a fundamental shift in the global correlation of forces to the advantage of socialism was simply beyond Soviet capabilities and was bankrupting the country.

The hemorrhaging of Soviet treasure and blood in the wars in Afghanistan and Cambodia also helped persuade Soviet leaders that a new approach was necessary to extricate the USSR from its crisis. Parallel US and Chinese security guarantees to Pakistan and Thailand underpinned the risky decisions of those two countries to provide territorial sanctuary that made possible protracted resistance wars. Parallel PRC and US diplomacy in international fora helped isolate Moscow and Hanoi over their aggressive policies. In the case of Vietnam, Beijing's tenacious insistence that an end to Soviet support for Vietnam's occupation of Cambodia was the necessary price for normalization of Sino-Soviet relations played an important role in persuading Moscow to pressure Vietnam to withdraw. In sum, the Sino-American strategic partnership of 1979–1982 (or perhaps 1972–1988) helped produce the dramatic shift in Soviet policy under Gorbachev.[59] Simply stated, the second Sino-American alliance, like the first, helped change the course of history.

The fact that there were deep rifts in the PRC-US partnership over Taiwan does not negate the reality of the strategic partnership. Many, perhaps all, alliances have internal conflicts of interest. The issue of Indian independence and decolonization, for example, divided Washington and London throughout their World War II partnership. The Sino-Soviet alliance of the 1950s was, as we have seen, wracked by conflicts over Soviet air support for China's intervention in Korea, Soviet assistance to China's nuclear weapons program, and many other factors. Eventually, those conflicts tore the PRC-USSR alliance apart, but there *was* an alliance to be torn asunder. In the case of the close Sino-American strategic partnership of 1978–1982, the two sides managed the conflict over Taiwan so as not to destabilize the larger partnership that thwarted Soviet expansionism.

Normalization with the Asian Powers

SOVIET UNION, INDIA, IRAN, AND JAPAN

Consolidation of a Favorable Macro-Climate for Development

One of the key foci of diplomatic business after the Mao era was reduction of the high levels of tension that existed in China's relations with nearly all the Asian powers: the Soviet Union, India, Iran, and, to a lesser degree of tension, Japan. The calculus of Chinese interest with each of these powers varied, but there were some common purposes underlying China's diplomatic outreach to all of them. Reducing tension and eliminating conflicts if possible would diminish chances of wars that might disrupt China's new long march toward wealth and power. Reduction of tension would also facilitate the demilitarization of China's economy, removing a heavy burden on China's economic development. This would facilitate the shift of resources to economic modernization. Improved relations would also open the door to expanded economic cooperation as part of China's opening. In short, normalization of relations and reduction of tension, where possible, were part of Deng's effort to create a favorable macro-climate for China's modernization drive.

Many of the powerful domestic objectives that had driven China's international militancy during the Mao era no longer existed. China's paramount leader no longer aspired to the status of leader of the world communist movement. Claims to legitimacy as a center of world revolution no longer needed to be validated. And confrontations with foreign powers were no longer useful for intensifying internal class struggle and "continuing the revolution under the dictatorship of the proletariat." A strong sense of modesty and humility inspired Deng's diplomacy in the early post-Mao period. Under Mao, China had attempted to seize the leadership of the world communist movement, had given vast assistance to the world's revolutionary forces, and had gone to war or the brink of war several times as part of that effort. The result, Deng concluded, was not a prosperous and strong China but a poor and weak one.

In the diplomatic sphere, "seeking truth from facts," the foundation of Deng's pragmatic policy approach, meant that China was, in fact, poor and weak, and must focus intensively on development for a very long time if it was to become prosperous and strong. In many respects, it is this sense of modest humility that distinguishes China's diplomacy during the Deng era.

Normalization of Ties with the Soviet Union

The beginning of China's quest for improved relations with the Soviet Union followed hard on the heels of the 1982 PRC-US confrontation over arms sales to Taiwan in 1982. As noted in the previous chapter, China's leaders believed that the United States was trying to use what Washington perceived as China's vulnerability within the strategic triangle to force China to bow to unacceptable US arms sales to Taiwan. Improving China's ties with Moscow would counter this by weakening Washington's ability to play the Soviet card against Beijing. Huang Hua notes that the Reagan administration's objectionable moves toward Taiwan were a main factor leading Deng to shift from rhetorical opposition to Soviet hegemonism to opposition to all hegemonism, "so as to strike a proper balance" between the two superpowers.[1] The Soviet military threat to China had diminished considerably since the 1970s. The fact that Moscow had failed to act against China during China's 1979 punitive war against Vietnam signaled the limits of Soviet power. So too did the fact that Soviet forces were bogged down in an expanding war in Afghanistan. The United States, for its part, was rapidly expanding its military forces, confronting the Soviet Union with a genuine arms race it could not hope to win. The Soviet Union clearly needed relief.

Vice Foreign Minister Qian Qichen, Soviet-educated and fluent in Russian and who was China's principal in the seven-year-long push for better relations with the Soviet Union, noted that by early 1982 Beijing had already established "a new framework" for PRC-US relations, thereby creating an opportunity to improve relations with Moscow.[2]

Modernization of China's large, Soviet-derived industrial base was one motive to expand economic cooperation with the Soviet Union. A large swath of China's industry in the early 1980s was still based on technology and machinery supplied by the USSR in the 1950s. In the intervening decades, Soviet design bureaus had upgraded much of that equipment. Incorporation of those Soviet improvements into China's industrial stock might make an important contribution toward modernization of China's industry, or so it seemed at the time. Then there was trade. For the five Chinese provinces and autonomous regions bordering the USSR or Soviet-allied Mongolia, the USSR was a natural trading partner. Most of those provinces were far from China's east coast seaports offering easy access to the global economy. For these provinces, the Soviet Union offered a path to foreign trade, perhaps allowing them to emulate, at least to some extent, the prosperous paths being pioneered by China's east coast provinces—if an amicable framework conducive to Sino-Soviet trade could be worked out.

Both Huang Hua and Qian Qichen trace the beginning of the process of Sino-Soviet rapprochement to a speech by General Secretary Leonid Brezhnev in March 1982 in Tashkent, Soviet Uzbekistan. While larded with comments highly critical of China, Brezhnev's speech recognized the PRC as a socialist country, expressed hope for improved ties with China, and noted that the Soviet Union, unlike other powers, had never denied that Taiwan was a part of the PRC. Brezhnev also proposed a revival of talks between the Soviet Union and the PRC. Deng immediately noted the Soviet leader's words and ordered the foreign ministry to prepare a reply. That reply, Deng instructed, should rebut the many anti-China attacks in Brezhnev's speech, but also hint at the awareness of possible new Soviet approaches, while stressing that China would pay attention to Soviet actions rather than words. Deng's directive resulted in a sparse three-sentence statement delivered by Qian Qichen at what was the MFA's very first international-style press conference. To reinforce Qian's message, the Chinese embassy in Moscow summoned a Soviet vice foreign minister to receive the message that the people of both countries hoped for normalization of relations, and that the time was right for such an improvement of ties.[3]

Deng convened a meeting at his home in Beijing to discuss the apparent shift in Soviet policy. Chen Yun, Li Xiannian, and several other senior leaders, plus leading cadres from the MFA, including Qian Qichen, attended. The resulting estimate was that the Soviet Union was bogged down in Afghanistan and facing a sharp global challenge from a resurgent United States now led by Ronald Reagan. Recent cooperation between the PRC and the United States was "most unfavorable" to the Soviet Union, which needed to avoid simultaneous "attacks" in East and West. Soviet harvests were poor and defense expenditures a heavy burden. Moscow's apparent search for a relaxation of tension with China was part of Moscow's response to these challenges. China should use the opportunity to improve ties with Moscow, but only on the basis of principle—specifically, Vietnam's withdrawal from Cambodia, Soviet withdrawal from Afghanistan, and reduction of the large Soviet military presence on China's northern borders. Deng termed these the "three big obstacles" to Sino-Soviet normalization. Deng also stipulated that China's policies toward the Soviet Union should be based on its national interest, not on ideology. Other participants in the meeting agreed with Deng.[4]

Brezhnev, Soviet leader since 1964, when he led a coup ousting Nikita Khrushchev, died in November 1982. His funeral offered an opportunity for Beijing to probe possibilities for improved relations. Deng decided that Huang Hua should be China's special emissary to the funeral to get a sense of the new Soviet leadership, making Huang the first Chinese ministerial-level official to visit Moscow since Zhou Enlai's 1964 attendance at the anniversary of the Bolshevik Revolution. Beijing's move was carefully planned. It began with a visit by vice chair of the NPC Standing Committee Ulanfu to the Soviet embassy in Beijing to convey condolences for Brezhnev's passing. The Soviet embassy noted Ulanfu's high rank and expressed gratitude. In Moscow, Huang Hua's delegation received red-carpet treatment. A motorcade escorted it from and back to the airport. The PRC delegation was given first rank among all foreign delegations to the funeral. China's wreath (apparently provided by the Soviet side) was the largest and placed in the most conspicuous position. All five members of Huang's delegation were allowed to stand atop the memorial stage; with other delegations, only one member was allowed this honor.[5]

Beijing responded in kind. Moscow informed Huang Hua that delegations from socialist countries would stand to the left of the Soviet delegation, while representatives from nonsocialist countries would stand to the right. On which side would the Chinese delegation like to stand, a Soviet diplomat asked? China chose to stand on the left, the socialist side, and was greeted there by leaders from other socialist countries. Huang Hua's statement commemorating Brezhnev spoke respectfully about the former Soviet leader, only generally alluding to the times of troubles in Sino-Soviet relations under him, and expressing hope for improved Sino-Soviet relations. Huang Hua also had a nearly two-hour meeting with Soviet foreign minister Andrei Gromyko. Disagreement on Vietnam in Cambodia was the main content of the discussion. But although the two sides differed, Huang found Gromyko very serious and friendly. On taking leave, Gromyko escorted Huang to the elevator and shook hands, unusual protocol for Gromyko. Huang and Gromyko agreed to open political talks at the vice foreign ministerial level.

Those talks began in October 1982. Qian Qichen was China's representative. Deng instructed Qian not to appear too enthusiastic or urgent about China and the Soviet Union getting together. Qian should "uphold principle" and insist that the Soviet Union "take a few actions," especially regarding stopping Moscow's support for Vietnam's occupation of Cambodia. Moscow should encourage Vietnam to withdraw from Cambodia, Deng instructed Qian. At the same time, however, Qian was to show friendship for the Soviet people and keep channels of communication open. Following Deng's instructions, Qian seized on the "three big obstacles" and "would not let go."[6] These talks would continue to February 1989, the very eve of the Gorbachev-Deng summit. Throughout, China's key demand, and the greatest difficulty that had to be overcome, was a Soviet commitment to bring about Vietnamese withdrawal from Cambodia. For several years, Moscow rejected Beijing's demand to discuss the Vietnam-Cambodia situation, saying that Beijing's "three obstacles" were preconditions which had no place in the talks. Beijing's demands regarding Vietnam/Cambodia "hurt the interests of third parties," and Soviet policies toward Vietnam and Cambodia in no way constituted a "threat" to China's security, Soviet representatives insisted.

Renewed economic cooperation was not held hostage to deadlock on the three obstacles. In December 1984, Soviet vice president Ivan Arkhipov, who had headed the Soviet aid mission in China in the 1950s, visited China at the invitation of CCP economic specialist Yao Yilin. During the long period of poor Sino-Soviet relations, Arkhipov had not said anything bad about China, Qian Qichen noted. Arkhipov also had many old friends in China with whom he had worked in the 1950s—Deng Xiaoping, Chen Yun, Bo Yibo, Peng Zhen— and on whom he called during his 1984 stay. Arkhipov showed great interest in China's opening and reform, and visited Shenzhen among other places in the company of Qian Qichen, who accompanied Arkhipov throughout his visit. Three agreements on economic, scientific, and technological issues were signed as a result of the visit, and a joint committee on cooperation in these areas was established. In July of the next year, Yao Yilin reciprocated Arkhipov's visit. Moscow agreed to help build seven new factories.[7]

In October 1985, following Mikhail Gorbachev's selection as the top Soviet leader the previous March, Deng upped the ante. During a visit by Romanian communist leader Nicolai Ceausescu to Beijing, Deng told his visitor that if China and the Soviet Union could reach agreement on the Soviets urging Vietnam to withdraw from Cambodia, he was willing to receive Gorbachev in Beijing. For the first time, Deng put on the table the possibility of a summit meeting with Gorbachev. Deng asked Ceausescu to convey the message to Gorbachev.[8] According to Huang Hua, only during the second half of 1986, as the USSR under Gorbachev began moving away from the Soviet Union's earlier "global offensive strategy" and "contention with the United States for world hegemony," did Moscow become willing to not only talk about removing the three obstacles, but take action to do so.[9] Gradually, according to Qian, Moscow accepted the proposition that a Vietnamese withdrawal from Cambodia was an "important factor" in Sino-Soviet relations and that both parties should do everything possible to encourage Vietnam to seek a solution to the Cambodian issue.[10] Qian again underscored Cambodia as the most important of the three obstacles.

In January 1988, Deng reiterated, via a MFA spokesman, that he was willing to meet with Gorbachev, but only on the condition that Moscow persuade Vietnam to withdraw from Cambodia. Several days earlier, Gorbachev had indicated in an interview with a Chinese magazine that he hoped for a meeting with Deng. Now Deng indicated willingness for a summit meeting, but also stated the price. "Without Soviet assistance, Vietnam could not fight a single day in Kampuchea," Deng said.[11] By September 1988, Moscow and Beijing had reached an "internal understanding" (*neibu liangjie*) regarding Vietnam and Cambodia. This seemed to open the door to a summit visit.

Even then, the diplomatic battle over Vietnam and Cambodia continued. Soviet foreign minister Eduard Shevardnadze arrived in Beijing in early December 1988 to work out details of Gorbachev's upcoming visit. Shevardnadze was the first Soviet foreign minister to visit China since Gromyko's 1958 visit in the midst of the Taiwan Strait crisis. Qian and Shevardnadze held three rounds of talks. The crux of each was Cambodia. Shevardnadze was unwilling to set a date for Vietnam's withdrawal from Cambodia. Moscow could not simply give orders to Hanoi, Shevardnadze said. Shevardnadze went home without agreement. He returned two months later, in February 1989, to try again. The Soviet foreign minister proposed May 15–18 as the date of Gorbachev's visit and suggested that it be announced in a joint statement. Shevardnadze was unwilling, however, to give a specific date for a Vietnamese withdrawal from Cambodia. Qian consulted with Deng on the issue. Deng said that while the actual date for the Gorbachev meeting could not be changed, the *announcement* of that date was a tactical matter to be decided by Qian. Qian used this flexibility to press his advantage. When Shevardnadze met Deng the next day, the Soviet envoy tried to maneuver Deng into agreeing to the May 15–18 date, but Deng sidestepped the Soviet snare and told Shevardnadze to settle the issue with Qian. Shevardnadze went to the airport to return home, but repeatedly delayed his departure while Qian lingered in the airport's waiting room. Gorbachev's summit with Deng and the full normalization of Sino-Soviet relations were in the balance. Qian says he hung tough. China had not expected such difficulties, Qian told Shevardnadze. The Soviet side had proposed issuing a joint communiqué, and the Chinese side had agreed. Now Shevardnadze refused to include in the communiqué a specific date for a Vietnamese withdrawal. Sino-Soviet relations were still not normalized, Qian said. Eventually Shevardnadze agreed to leave behind two Soviet MFA department heads to continue the talks. The next day, according to Qian's account, those representatives agreed to a joint statement giving a date for Vietnam's withdrawal from Cambodia.

The joint statement issued on February 6, 1989, regarding Cambodia provided that Beijing and Moscow "take note of the decision announced by Vietnam to withdraw all its troops from Kampuchea by the end of September 1989 at the latest." The joint statement expressed hope that this decision would be implemented and declared the willingness of the two countries "to make efforts to help attain this objective." The two sides differed over the role of the Khmer Rouge after Vietnam's withdrawal, but both sides declared in favor of "non-return to policies and practices of the recent past in Kampuchea," called for an "international control mechanism" to organize elections after Vietnam's withdrawal, and stated willingness to respect the results of that election.[12] The dates for Gorbachev's visit to Beijing were announced the same day the joint communiqué on Cambodia was issued.

Deng issued two directives in preparation for his May 1989 summit meeting with Gorbachev: "A handshake but no hugs" and "end the past, open the future." The first directive was, in part at least, an attempt to reassure Washington that the new Sino-Soviet relation would not be one of fraternal comrades as in the 1950s. The second was an attempt to draw a line under the disputes and animosity that had shaken relations over the past thirty years, and open a new era of friendly cooperation. During the meeting, Deng spoke to Gorbachev without notes, according to Qian Qichen. Deng framed Sino-Soviet relations in terms of China's century of humiliation by the great powers, and then moved on to the difficulties between Moscow and Beijing over recent decades. The core of the dispute had been, Deng judged, Moscow's attempt to put China in an unequal status. The purpose of recalling these past difficulties was not to criticize the Soviet Union, Deng told Gorbachev, but to enable the two sides to look forward rather than to the past. In spite of everything, the Chinese people had never forgotten the help the Soviet Union gave to the construction of New China in the 1950s. Regarding the ideological debates between the two parties and countries, both sides had undertaken a lot of "empty talk," Deng said. Gorbachev agreed that the Soviet Union had "definite mistakes and responsibility" for past unpleasantness. The two leaders agreed, and stated in a joint communiqué, that henceforth state-to-state relations would be based on the Five Principles of Peaceful Coexistence, which would produce normal, friendly, good-neighborly relations. Sino-Soviet relations were not directed against any third country, and would not injure the interest of any third country.[13] According to Gorbachev's account, "Deng Xiaoping was unable to refrain from commenting on the history of our relations." Gorbachev responded that one cannot rewrite or recreate history, adding: "If we started restoring boundaries on the basis of how things were in the past, which people resided on what territory, then essentially we would have to re-carve the whole world."[14]

Perhaps the most powerful linkage between the Soviet Union and the PRC at this juncture was outside the Great Hall of the People, where Deng and Gorbachev met. Students from Beijing's universities had gathered in Tiananmen to demand dialogue with the government and wider political freedoms. China's reformers were deeply inspired by the political liberalization that had occurred in the Soviet Union under Gorbachev. Taking inspiration from the oldest socialist country, with the most "experience in building socialism," China's democratic-minded youth hoped for a "Chinese Gorbachev" who might take China down the road of political liberalization and democratic socialism being followed by the Soviet Union. CCP Secretary General Zhao Ziyang "amazed" Gorbachev by the openness with which he discussed the problem of democracy and Communist Party rule during Gorbachev's May 1989 visit. According to the Soviet leader's account, Zhao posed "a seemingly rhetorical question," "Can a one-party system ensure the development of democracy?" Zhao and Gorbachev spoke about "pluralism of opinions" and about "the fact that democracy can be developed under a one-party system." From Zhao's arguments, Gorbachev noted, "It followed that the Chinese leadership was prepared to follow the path of political reform by giving the masses a chance to enjoy broad democratic rights under one-party rule." Zhao concluded, "If this did not work out, the issue of a multi-party system would inevitably arise."[15] When Zhao drew these conclusions for Gorbachev, he was only several weeks away from being purged for opposing military suppression of China's democracy movement.

The Rocky Road to Normalization with India

The high point of PRC-Indian relations during the late Mao era, such as it was, came atop Tiananmen Gate during the National Day celebration of October 1970 when Mao approached the chargé d'affaires of the Indian mission in Beijing, Brajesh Mishra, shook hands with him, and said "We cannot go on quarreling like this. We must become friends again. We will become friends again."[16] That was about as good as Sino-Indian relations got. Following China's threat to enter the 1965 India-Pakistan war, India had protested (in 1966) what it deemed a Chinese intrusion on Bhutan's northern border. Bhutan was an Indian protectorate. In 1967, China and India engaged in an intense armed clash lasting several days on the Sikkim-Tibet border—simultaneously with the mounting Sino-Soviet tension on China's northern border.[17] Beijing protested several attacks by mobs on its embassy in New Delhi.[18] In 1970, before Mao's famous comments to Mishra atop Tiananmen Gate, India had protested a particularly vicious attack in the Chinese media on Prime Minister Indira Gandhi, Mishra walked out of a speech by Zhou Enlai to protest Zhou's declaration of support for the Kashmiri people's "struggle for self-determination" (walking out in this fashion was a hardening of Indian policy from previous practice), and India noted that China was the only country with diplomatic representation in New Delhi that did not send even token representation to a celebration of the centenary of Mahatma Gandhi's birthday.[19] China watched helplessly as Indian partitioned China's strategic partner Pakistan in 1971, but then moved vigorously to assist Pakistan's rebuilding of its shattered military strength. China's help included, as we have seen, assistance with Pakistan's nuclear weapons and ballistic missile programs. India was aligned with the USSR via its August 1971 treaty and the beliefs of many Indian leaders that the Soviet Union was the natural ally of the developing countries in their struggle against the rich Western countries.

China countered Indian moves by supporting other South Asian countries against India in whatever conflicts of interest came along. India repaid the favor by hosting 100,000 or so Tibetan refugees, including a Tibetan "government in exile" in the Himalayan foothills of northwestern India. Conflicting views of Tibet generated further animosity. Indian leaders and public opinion were dismayed at the antireligious and Han Chinese chauvinist policies inflicted on the people of Tibet during the Mao era. Chinese leaders were dismayed at India's hosting of the Tibetan government in exile and allowing Tibetan refugees to conduct a wide range of what Beijing felt were anti-China political activities. Behind the scene was India's Establishment 22, the highly trained, well-armed, and Indian-commanded Tibetan force configured for commando operations in Tibet, perhaps in the event of another round of Sino-Indian war. Beijing supported, or at least maintained links with, sundry ethnic insurgencies in India's northeastern states, while in India memories of China's betrayal of Indian friendship in 1962 (or so many Indians viewed it) still rankled. The territorial issue remained unresolved, with the military forces of both sides prepared to mobilize for another round. Within the Indian military, the sting of the 1962 humiliation was still strong, as was a corresponding desire for an opportunity to redeem India's honor from that defeat.

If it came to another China-India war in the 1980s, China would not have a superpower on its side, unlike in 1962. In 1962, the Cuban missile crisis had made Moscow suddenly desirous of having China stand beside it as Moscow faced down Washington, and that had produced Soviet support for China against India for a short while. By the 1970s, Moscow was backing India against China. And while the United States might have stood behind China when it "taught (communist-ruled and Soviet-allied) Vietnam a lesson," Washington certainly would not support China against democratic India. As poor as US-Indian relations often were, with the singular exception of the December 1971 Bangladesh crisis, Washington eschewed involvement in military challenges to India.[20] If China faced a second round with India, it would do so alone, without a superpower backer. Beijing would also have to confront Indian forces in some of the most rugged and remote terrain in the world, the Himalayan-Tibetan massif, a region much closer to India's heartland than to China's.

The collapse of Indira Gandhi's quasi-dictatorial Emergency and the election of India's first-ever non–Congress Party government led by Morarji Desai in March 1977 offered Beijing an opportunity to attempt an opening to India. Deng Xiaoping was fully rehabilitated only months after Desai took over India's government. Desai came into office determined to remedy what he deemed to be a perverse pro-Soviet, anti-American and anti-Chinese tilt in Indian foreign relations under the long-ruling Indira Gandhi. Beijing moved quickly to seize the opportunity. In March 1978, Wang Bingnan, chairman and first secretary of the CCP group within the Chinese People's Association for Friendship with Foreign Countries (CPAFFC), led an "unofficial" Chinese delegation to India—the first Chinese visit in many years. In talks with Desai,

Wang expressed China's desire for improved relations and invited foreign minister Atal Bihari Vajpayee to visit China.

Unfortunately for Beijing, this initial effort at rapprochement did not go well. Vajpayee arrived in Beijing on February 12, 1979, for a weeklong visit and discussions with Premier Hua Guofeng, Vice Premier Deng Xiaoping, and Foreign Minister Huang Hua. Vajpayee's visit was the first by a high-ranking Indian official since a 1958 visit by India's vice president, and the first ministerial-level exchange since Zhou Enlai's fateful 1960 visit to India. Six days into Vajpayee's visit, on February 17, while Vajpayee was sightseeing in Hangzhou, Chinese armies attacked Vietnam. Vajpayee immediately broke off his visit and returned home. Vietnam was India's close friend. The two had drawn quite close during Hanoi's war against the United States.[21] When Beijing sought to isolate Hanoi after the latter's invasion of Cambodia, India again stood with Hanoi. India maintained robust, friendly interaction with the SRV. In the UN, India voted with Hanoi on the Cambodian issue. New Delhi did not look favorably on possible re-establishment of Chinese influence in Cambodia. From New Delhi's perspective, Southeast Asia constituted the flank of India's security zone in the South Asian–Indian Ocean region, and the growth of Chinese influence there was not desirable. From New Delhi's perspective, a Hanoi-aligned Cambodia was far preferable to a Beijing-aligned one. Between December 1978 and January 1986, there were nineteen ministerial-level or higher exchanges between India and the SRV. Prime Ministers Indira Gandhi and Rajiv Gandhi were among the visitors to Hanoi, while the SRV premier, president, and VWP secretary general were among those who visited India. India supplied the SRV with US$70 million in aid between 1978 and 1985. In short, Foreign Minister Vajpayee found himself in China while China was literally attacking India's close friend. China's 1979 attack on Vietnam also roused Indian memories of 1962. China was once again trying to bludgeon its neighbors into submission, or so it seemed to many Indians.

All this added up to great political embarrassment for Desai's coalition government. That government's Congress Party critics, including Indira Gandhi, seized on Vajpayee's embarrassment to criticize the putative naiveté of Desai's foreign policies. Some of Desai's and Vajpayee's critics even asserted that Beijing had invited Vajpayee to Beijing as a way of camouflaging the upcoming assault on Vietnam. This may or may not have been the case; we simply do not know. In any case, it seems that Vajpayee's presence in China caused Hanoi to drop its guard at that juncture,[22] and it is entirely possible that Beijing's invitation to the Indian leader was, in fact, an effort to achieve tactical surprise. Hardly less reassuring to New Delhi was the other possibility: that Vajpayee's embarrassment was merely the result of bureaucratic oversight. That would indicate how low on Beijing's foreign policy agenda India ranked. In any case, charges of Chinese duplicity reflected the depth of Indian suspicion of China. Desai's coalition fell apart in mid-1979, and Indira Gandhi and her Congress Party returned to power in January 1980. Gandhi set out to "repair the damage" to India's partnerships with the Soviet Union and Vietnam, and swung back to a much tougher approach to China. Beijing's maladroit handling of Vajpayee's visit contributed to the collapse of Deng's first attempt at rapprochement with New Delhi.

Beijing quickly tried again. With Indira Gandhi back in power, Foreign Minister Huang Hua attended a Republic Day reception at the Indian embassy in Beijing at the end of January 1980—the first time in twenty years a Chinese foreign minister had done that. Then, in June 1981, Huang Hua flew to New Delhi for talks with Foreign Minister P. V. Narasimha Rao. Huang's key proposal during the visit was that improvements of bilateral Sino-Indian relations should proceed where possible and not be linked to continuing disputes in other areas. This approach can perhaps be called "delinkage." Huang's delinkage proposal represented a response to the objections to China's military ties to Pakistan laid before Chinese leaders by Vajpayee during his January 1979 visit. More broadly, delinkage stood as a proposed alternate to India's policy, in effect since the mid-1960s, of insisting that improvements in Indian-Chinese relations were contingent on prior settlement of the territorial dispute. India's long-standing policy was that until the border issue was settled, Sino-Indian relations could not advance substantially. Huang's delinkage proposed to turn this around: advancing bilateral relations in areas where agreement could be reached would improve the situation and reduce tension, eventually creating an atmosphere in which the boundary issue might be solved.

Beijing had prepared for Huang's unveiling of the delinkage approach in New Delhi by reassuring China's other South Asian friends that improvements in Sino-Indian relations would not be at the expense of China's friendly ties with them. This was a second aspect of Beijing's delinkage approach: Sino-Indian ties should be independent of and not affected by ties between China and other South Asian countries—Nepal, Bangladesh, Sri Lanka, and, especially, Pakistan. On June 1, 1981, about three weeks before Huang Hua arrived in New Delhi, Premier Zhao Ziyang visited Pakistan for talks with President Zia-ul-Haq. After an "extensive exchange of views on international problems and relations between the two countries," the two leaders "resolved to continue efforts to further strengthen friendship and cooperation in all fields and to preserve peace and stability in South Asia."[23] At a press conference in Islamabad, Zhao explained China's desire for better relations with Pakistan as well as with India: China hoped to "solve certain problems concerning bilateral relations between China and India .... in a spirit of mutual understanding and accommodation," Zhao said.[24] From Islamabad Zhao flew to Nepal and then Bangladesh. In each capital, Zhao's message was this: China was willing to continue and advance mutually beneficial cooperation in all fields. Any improvements in Sino-Indian ties would not be at the expense of China's cooperative ties with other South Asian friends.

China also notched up its assistance to Pakistan's nuclear weapons program. According to a memorandum drafted many years later by Abdul Qadeer Khan, the mastermind of Pakistan's nuclear weapons program, in mid-1982 Pakistan began enriching weapons-grade uranium in its centrifuge plant using uranium hexafluoride supplied by China.[25] President Zia feared that India or Israel would preemptively strike Pakistan's nuclear facilities, and asked Deng Xiaoping to "loan" Pakistan enough bomb-grade uranium to fabricate several bombs to deter a preemptive strike. Deng reportedly approved the request, and fifty kilograms of highly enriched uranium (enough to fabricate two bombs) were carried by a Pakistani C-130 cargo aircraft to Pakistan. Along with the lead-lined boxes containing 1-gram ingots of highly enriched uranium came a blueprint for a simple atomic bomb of a design type already tested by China. We do not know the reasons why Deng approved the transfer; it was probably to strengthen Pakistan's deterrent capability against India and the Soviet Union and to lessen the likelihood that China might be required to fight a war to defend Pakistan. US intelligence became aware of the transaction and confronted Zhao Ziyang about it during his January 1984 visit to the White House. Zhao denied the charge: "We do not engage in nuclear proliferation ourselves, nor do we help other countries develop nuclear weapons."[26] Zhao thus fulfilled a diplomat's duty to his country. Washington knew Zhao's claim was false, but the need for continuing Pakistani and Chinese cooperation to sustain the war against the Soviets in Afghanistan led Washington not to press the issue.[27]

Another major element of Beijing's push for rapprochement with India in the 1980s was to revive and then withdraw the east-west swap proposal for settlement of the territorial dispute proposed by Zhou Enlai and rejected by Jawaharlal Nehru in 1960. The reader will recall from an earlier chapter that Zhou had unofficially proposed a package deal, with China giving up its claims in the eastern sector and accepting the McMahon Line there, while India would give up its claim to Aksai Chin in the western sector. In this fashion, the existing line of actual control would form the basis for the boundary, neither side would have to give up territory actually under its control, and each side would retain the territory most important to its national security. This proposal seemed eminently reasonable from the Chinese side, and Nehru's rejection of it in 1960 had been a major factor in the deterioration of relations leading to the 1962 war. Now, in 1980, after a hiatus of twenty years, Beijing revived the swap proposal. It would remain on the table for about five years.

In December 1980, some six months before Huang Hua's visit to New Delhi, Deng Xiaoping gave an interview to the editor of a prominent Indian defense journal outlining a compromise settlement along the same lines as

Zhou Enlai in 1960.[28] Two days after the interview, Xinhua confirmed that Deng's offer was policy. In Beijing, six months later, Huang Hua proposed the resumption of boundary talks, in hiatus since 1960.

In 1981 as in 1960, New Delhi rejected Beijing's east-west swap offer. Disputed territory in both sectors, east and west, was legally Indian territory, New Delhi insisted. The Chinese offer was like a thief entering a person's house, stealing that person's wallet and coat, and then once caught in the act, offering to return the wallet if allowed to keep the coat. It simply was not acceptable. Foreign Minister Narasimha Rao explained the Indian view to parliament in July 1980, shortly after Deng's interview with the Indian defense journal:

> The Government of India has never accepted the premise on which it [the swap proposal] is based, namely, that the Chinese side is making a concession in the eastern sector by giving up territory which they allege is illegally incorporated into India. Nevertheless, we welcome the prospect of the eastern sector being settled without any particular difficulty.[29]

From Beijing's point of view, New Delhi was pocketing China's proposed concession and asking for more. Deng Xiaoping's 1980 proposal, like Zhou Enlai's 1960 one, had been carefully unofficial—comments to journalists. There was no record of either in the official negotiating record. They could be, and were, easily withdrawn.

Boundary talks began in December 1981. They continued for thirty-plus years without substantive result. After several rounds, Beijing accepted New Delhi's proposal of a "sector by sector" approach. This meant that Chinese concessions in the eastern sector would no longer be linked to Indian concessions in some other sector. Consequently, starting with the sixth round of border talks in November 1985, Beijing began stressing the need for Indian concessions in the east. Chinese negotiators, and scholars elaborating on China's negotiating position, pointed to the Tawang sector in NEFA as the area in which Indian concessions were most clearly required by the strong documentary evidence that this region had historically been under Tibetan administration. Dropping a willingness to cede NEFA and demanding instead Indian concessions in the Tawang area represented a major hardening of China's position. Indian cession of a southward salient around Tawang would diminish India's already precarious ability to defend its northeastern states by putting Indian protectorate Bhutan between two salients of Chinese territory. Figure 16-1 illustrates the geopolitics of the Sino-Indian security situation in this region.

This toughening in China's negotiating position was soon followed by a militarized confrontation in a canyon north of Tawang and south of Thagla ridge in a region known as Sumdorong Chu. A 1980 review of Indian military

FIGURE 16-1 The Tawang Region and the Sino-Indian Military Balance

strategy by Indira Gandhi led to a decision to defend as far forward as possible in the eastern Himalayan region. This led in turn to the resumption of
Indian patrols south of the Thagla ridge in the summers of 1983, 1984, and
1985. When Indian forces arrived there in summer of 1986 as the snows in
the Himalaya melted, they found Chinese forces who had constructed semi-
permanent structures. India (then ruled by Rajiv Gandhi, Indira's son who
took over as prime minister when his mother was assassinated in October
1984), decided to respond with a large scale exercise code-named "Operation
Chequerboard" and testing the ability of Indian forces to deploy rapidly to
forward areas of the Sino-Indian border. Three full Indian divisions were
deployed forward and supported by airdrop. High-altitude heavy-lift helicopters airlifted in infantry fighting vehicles. Beijing saw the forward deployment
of heavy combat vehicles as an especially ominous sign and responded in
kind by mobilizing forces on the border. Forces on both sides took up front-
line positions and sometimes glared at one another with weapons at the ready.

Tensions rose still further in December 1986, when virtually the entire
Indian army massed swiftly in western Rajasthan on Pakistan's borders in a
military exercise codenamed "Brasstacks." Pakistan's army feared an Indian

preemptive strike against Pakistan's still embryonic nuclear arsenal (this was following the 1981 Israeli strike on Osirak in Iraq), to be followed up by a full-scale Indian invasion of Pakistan replicating New Delhi's bold thrust of 1971. In the event of a fourth round between India and Pakistan, a defensive operation in the east against China (i.e., something that would have looked a lot like Operation Chequerboard) would have made sense. We still do not know the exact rationale behind the linked Indian exercises of Chequerboard and Brasstacks. Some Indian scholars and former military leaders maintain that India's military leaders were, in fact, trying to maneuver the country into a decisive blow against Pakistan. Beijing, for its part, feared that this was India's intention.

In December 1986, in the midst of the spiraling tension associated with exercises Chequerboard and Brasstacks, the Indian government transformed NEFA into the state of Arunachal Pradesh. This added further fuel to the fire. In Beijing, an MFA spokesman declared that this move was absolutely illegal and China would never recognize the "so-called state." Two months later, when India formalized the change, Beijing expressed "indignation" at India's action, which "grossly violated China's sovereignty and territorial integrity and hurt the national feelings of the Chinese people."[30] From Beijing's perspective, New Delhi's actions were ever more reckless and brazen.

By spring 1987, as snow melted and passes reopened, the confrontation peaked. The PLA reportedly deployed 22,000 troops, along with high-altitude helicopters and jet fighters and bombers, to Tibet in response to escalating tension at Sumdorong Chu. Beijing lobbied both Washington and Moscow to rein in India. In October 1986, US Secretary of Defense Casper Weinberger carried a message from Deng Xiaoping to Indian leaders: If India did not stop "nibbling" at Indian territory, China would have to teach it a lesson. The next March, Secretary of State Shultz delivered a second, similar warning. In talks with Soviet leaders, too, Beijing made it clear that Sino-Soviet normalization would not advance if Moscow supported India against China. Gorbachev visited India in November 1986 to reassure India that recent improvements in Sino-Soviet relations would not lead to weakening of Soviet support for India. Noticeably, however, Gorbachev refused to take India's side in the confrontation at Sumdorong Chu. The Soviet leader professed ignorance of the situation on the border and called for better relations between the Soviet Union, India, and China "so no one will have to choose sides."[31] In essence, Moscow disengaged from its alliance with India to help open the door to rapprochement with Beijing.

In this context of escalating military confrontation and possible India-Pakistan-China war, in March 1987 Qiao Shi, a Politburo Standing Committee member with background in national security and intelligence, visited Burma, Nepal, and Bangladesh to discuss "international issues of mutual concern." One of Qiao's objectives was to minimize support of those countries for India in the event of a border clash. In talks with Bangladeshi President Hussain Muhammad Ershad, Qiao reportedly asked Bangladesh not to permit movement of Indian men or materiel across Bangladeshi territory in the event of a Sino-Indian clash.[32] Passage through Bangladeshi territory could well be critical for India. India's only territorial link with its northeastern states was (and remains) via an approximately twenty-five-kilometer-wide strip of territory in the vicinity of the West Bengal town of Siliguri (the Siliguri Corridor). That town itself lies only about seventy-five miles from the southern tip of China's Chumbi Valley salient with its strong PLA presence. This meant that in the event of a Sino-Indian clash, Chinese forces might easily cut the Siliguri Corridor, leaving India with no legal way to reinforce forces defending its northeastern states. Indian forces could, of course, force their way across Bangladeshi territory, but that would carry the political onus of violating the neutrality of a nonbelligerent country—a serious offense under international law. A month after Qiao Shi's visit to Dacca, President Ershad visited Beijing. Media reports indicated that he agreed to Beijing's request. As is often the case in South Asia, China was able to benefit from the deep suspicions of India among its neighbors.

Beijing's hardball tactics with India in the border negotiations and at Sumdorong Chu apparently worked. In late 1987, Prime Minister Rajiv Gandhi undertook a reevaluation of India's approach to China and the costs of a possible conflict. The young Indian leader decided that a number of shifts in India's China policy were necessary. The level of dialogue was upgraded. Gandhi sent Defense Minister K. C. Pant to Beijing in April to convey a desire to avoid conflict. India's foreign minister followed two months later. Gandhi also ordered a pullback of Indian forces from the border. Most significant of all, Gandhi decided to accept the delinkage approach suggested by Huang Hua in 1981. Sino-Indian ties would advance in areas where agreement could be reached, and would no longer be held hostage to the intractable territorial issue or Sino-Pakistan military ties. To symbolize and implement this new Indian approach, Gandhi decided to visit China for a summit meeting with Deng Xiaoping. This was the first visit by an Indian prime minister to China since a 1954 visit by Jawaharlal Nehru, Rajiv Gandhi's grandfather.

Rajiv Gandhi's December 1988 summit with Deng ranks with Nixon's 1972 and Gorbachev's 1989 visits as a reorientation of policy symbolized by a summit. Deng Xiaoping (then eighty-four years old) had a ninety-minute talk with Gandhi (then forty-four). The crux of Deng's appeal to the young Indian leader was that the two countries were both developing countries, with many common interests. It followed, Deng told Gandhi, that the two countries should work together to create a new international economic order in greater comport with the interests of the Third World developing counties and less in service of the rich Western developed countries. The two countries should also strive to create a new international political order lessening the domination of the Third World by the developed countries. Deng and Gandhi issued a joint communiqué outlining the many areas of common interest and possible cooperation and calling for the development of friendly, cooperative relations between the two countries on the basis of the Five Principles of Coexistence. The road to Sino-Indian rapprochement had been opened.

It is significant that the hardening of China's demands on the territorial issue (re Tawang) and Beijing's apparent willingness to go to war with India in 1987 precipitated the reorientation of India's China policy. This touches on an underlying Chinese perception about management of China's ties with India: India is prone to arrogantly reckless actions (the Forward Policy in 1961–1962, interference in Tibet in the 1960s, moving into Sumdorong Chu in the 1980s), and only the shock of confronting China's power will keep India sober and deter it from acting recklessly on the basis of its dangerous illusions. This may be one reason why Beijing has decided to keep the territorial issue alive by insisting on Indian concessions in the Tawang region, where Indian concessions would further aggravate India's northeastern security complex, making concessions unlikely. It may be that keeping the territorial issue open is an excellent way of keeping Indian attention focused on the reality of China's military power.[33] This, of course, is a surmise.

Establishing a Partnership with the Islamic Republic of Iran

The close anti-Soviet partnership between the Kingdom of Iran and the PRC that developed during the 1970s collapsed abruptly with the overthrow of the shah's regime in January 1979. Beijing's strong support for the shah during that monarch's final months in power deeply alienated the new rulers of Iran, constituted as the Islamic Republic of Iran (IRI) in April 1979. Aside from Hua Guofeng's ill-fated visit in August 1978 as the wave of popular revolution mounted in Iran, China's media had continued to support the forces of law and order, attributing much of the mounting instability in Iran to Soviet subversion. China's close anti-hegemony association with the United States was another source of conflict between the IRI and the PRC. From the perspective of Iran's Islamic revolutionary leaders, and especially the charismatic figure of Ayatollah Ruhollah Khomeini, who headed the coalition of revolutionary forces, the shah's regime was a US puppet government, an instrument of an infidel, demonic, and atheistic power enslaving the Muslim people of Iran. The poisonous effect of China's association with the "Great Satan" America was demonstrated by Beijing's joint effort with America to stifle Iran's Islamic revolution (i.e., Hua Guofeng's 1978 visit)—or so it seemed to Khomeini. Iran's new Islamicist rulers also knew little about China. Their worldview and experience were not wide. What they knew about China was its atheistic communist philosophy and that Muslims in China were cruelly repressed by its communist regime. In 1979, at the very beginning of Deng's rule, that image of repression by militant atheism was not necessarily inaccurate. The PRC was viewed by IRI leaders as an infidel "arrogant power" on a par with the United States, the Soviet Union, Britain, or Israel. China's relation with Iran had abruptly been transformed from close anti-hegemony partnership to cold hostility.[34]

It did not matter greatly to China's leaders whether Iran's rulers were "feudal" monarchs or Islamic revolutionaries. Beijing sought to promote Chinese interests via cooperation with whatever government ruled in Tehran. Thus, three days after the IRI was established, Premier Hua Guofeng sent a message recognizing the provisional government and congratulating its new prime minister. The PRC ambassador in Tehran also stayed at his post and managed to call on the IRI's new prime minister—who, unfortunately for Beijing, would be thrown out of office by Khomeini after several months. Beijing also drafted a letter of apology signed by Hua Guofeng and addressed to the Supreme Leader Ayatollah Khomeini. In the letter, Hua apologized for his visit of the previous year, and explained it as a function of airplane refueling ranges, diplomatic politeness, and the like, rather than as representing some deep political purpose. Khomeini merely acknowledged receipt of the letter.

Beijing's efforts to rebuild ties with Iran in the first eighteen months of the revolution were greatly hindered by the fact that China's efforts at rapprochement were targeted toward a group of IRI leaders that ultimately constituted the losing side of a struggle for power within the revolutionary camp. A realist faction believed that the IRI should use diplomatic maneuver among the powers to advance Iran's interests. The IRI prime minister, foreign minister, and later the president who solicited, received, and welcomed early Chinese diplomatic moves were members of this realist camp. But an idealist faction put Islamic values above pursuit of national interests, and believed that association with arrogant and satanic powers would lead the revolution off course. Gradually, the realists were pushed aside by the idealists, fully backed by Khomeini. One of the consequences of this for Beijing was that repeated Chinese initiatives simply did not gain traction in Tehran.

In February 1980, Beijing played its Muslim card when Chinese Hui leader Al-hajji Mohammad Ali Zhang Jie led a delegation of Chinese Muslims to the IRI—the first such delegation. Hui are Han Chinese of the Islamic faith, a religion that entered China in the Middle Ages. Zhang Jie, to use his simple Chinese name, was a longtime leader of CCP united front work among Muslims. In the 1930s, he had headed the mosque in the Yan'an capital of the CCP base area. He then led anti-Japanese united front work for the CCP among China's Muslim communities. After the establishment of the PRC, he became a key figure in PRC cultural diplomacy toward majority Muslim countries. By 1980, he had already led ten Chinese Muslim delegations to foreign countries. Zhang Jie's chief purpose in visiting Tehran was to explain to

Iran's new leaders China's new policies of religious tolerance. China's Muslims enjoyed full freedom of religion while participating in the construction of New China under the leadership of the Chinese Communist Party, Zhang explained. He also handed out invitations to IRI leaders to visit China and see for themselves the reality of religious freedom there. Zhang Jie's efforts contributed to improving the PRC image among Iran's new Islamist leaders.

It was Iran's involvement in war with Iraq which really transformed the IRI-PRC relation, however. Iraq under the leadership of Saddam Hussein launched an all-out attack on Iran starting on September 22, 1980, in an effort to seize Iran's majority-Arab and oil-rich western province of Khuzestan. (There are deep ethnic cleavages between Arabs and Persians.) The resulting eight-year war was an extremely difficult one for Iran, whose armed forces had been purged, disorganized, and demoralized by the revolution, and who were armed with American-made weapons. Iran at war needed arms, fast and in large quantities. As Iran mobilized its numerically superior and religiously zealous manpower, and as existing stockpiles of weapons were used up on the battlefield, Tehran's need for arms grew. The Soviet Union could not be a supplier; it was allied by treaty with Iraq. France too tilted toward Iraq. The United States was not a good prospect: its diplomats were still being held hostage by Iran when the war began. (Tehran's deepening estrangement from Washington was one reason why Saddam Hussein decided to grab Khuzestan.) Iran's supreme leader was also deeply hostile to the United States. China, however, was able to supply arms, fast, cheap, and relatively simple to use—exactly the type of weapons Iran needed.

China quickly proclaimed neutrality in the Iran-Iraq war. Vice Premier Ji Pengfei happened to be visiting the Yemen Arab Republic when the war broke out, and only a couple of days after the war began he announced China's neutrality. Framing the Iran-Iraq conflict in terms of Mao's Three Worlds Theory, Ji called the conflict an unfortunate and unwise one between brotherly developing countries of the Third World which could give one or both hegemony-seeking superpowers an opportunity to interfere in the affairs of the Gulf. The two warring parties should immediately cease hostilities and peacefully negotiate a settlement of the issues between them, Ji said. This stance did not please Ayatollah Khomeini. Such a stance—which more or less copied the stances of the other Permanent Members of the Security Council—failed to distinguish between the aggressor and the victim of aggression, and was the type of amoral behavior that governed the national interests calculations of the "arrogant powers" such as the United States and China. Beijing would maintain the policy of neutrality throughout the Iran-Iraq war.

The first high-level IRI delegation to the PRC came in February 1981, five months after the Iran-Iraq war began and as the vast requirements of that war were becoming apparent to Iran's leaders. The delegation was led by parliamentarian Ali Khamenei (not to be confused with Ruhollah Khomeini), a highly influential member of Khomeini's faction and ultimately (in 1989) successor to Khomeini as supreme leader. The publicly announced purpose of Khamenei's visit was to explain to China's leaders Iran's position on the war. China's efforts seem to have been somewhat successful; Khamenei later said during his visit that the fact that China had declared neutrality in the Iran-Iraq war did not mean it did not sympathize with Iran. In fact, China did sympathize with Iran, Khamenei explained, and shared with Iran similar views on a range of international issues. By 1982, US sources estimated that China and North Korea supplied 40 percent of Iran's arms imports. By 1987, that number had risen to 70 percent. Iranian infantry forces were armed increasingly with Chinese weapons in what became the largest land war since World War II. By the time the war ended in August 1988, some 262,000 Iranian soldiers had died in the war, about 2.2 percent of Iran's total population of 39 million.

Beijing rejected American pressure to stop arms sales to Iran. As the tides of war shifted in Iran's favor in 1982, and as Tehran proclaimed the objective of its revolutionary Islamic war to be liberation of Iraqi Shiites and Jerusalem from "the Zionists," Washington mobilized the international community to pressure Tehran to the negotiating table by cutting off its arms imports. Beijing refused to go along—although it did agree in 1987 to stop selling Silkworm anti-ship missiles, which Tehran was using to attack oil tankers in the Gulf. In short, Beijing stood by Tehran in the face of American pressure. The PRC thus proved to Tehran that it could be a trustworthy and reliable partner.

Beijing achieved a major breakthrough in relations with the IRI in 1983. One of the MFA's old Iran hands, He Ying, called on a new, young IRI ambassador in Beijing to confess Chinese mistakes in earlier thinking about Iranian developments. Previously, he explained, China had viewed Iranian developments from the perspective of the global struggle against Soviet hegemony and overestimated the role of Soviet subversion in Iranian affairs. China had recently undertaken a major reevaluation of events, He Ying said, and now recognized that its earlier view had been mistaken. China now had a much more positive understanding of Iran's revolutionary quest. He asked the Iranian ambassador to convey these new Chinese understandings to Tehran.[35] The Iranian ambassador, Ali Khorram (a PhD in nuclear physics from Chicago University), suggested that the new Chinese understandings were so important that He Ying himself should convey them to Iran's leaders. This he did in late January. Through meetings with Ali Khamenei, the two sides agreed on the need for a "common stand in the struggle against imperialism and colonialism." This opened the way for an exchange of foreign ministers—Ali Akbar Velayati to the PRC in September 1983 and Wu Xueqian to the IRI in October 1984. The Velayati-Wu exchanges produced several agreements on economic, cultural, and scientific and technological exchanges. A visit by President Ali Hashemi Rafsanjani in June 1985 can be taken as the symbolic renormalization of Sino-Iranian ties.

A murky but probably extremely important area of PRC-IRI cooperation was in the nuclear area, where China emerged as Iran's most important, and covert, partner starting in 1985 and continuing until 1997, when Beijing would suspend this cooperation under American pressure. Iran had had a large and active nuclear energy program under the shah. Khomeini had suspended this after the 1979 revolution, but revived it a couple of years into the war with Iraq when it became apparent that Iraq was developing nuclear weapons. Iran's nuclear partners under the shah—the United States and France—were no longer willing to cooperate. China, however, moved in, while keeping nuclear cooperation covert. Only many years later would the contours of PRC nuclear cooperation with Iran become apparent.[36] In 1984, Iran opened the Esfahan Nuclear Research Center (ENRC) to study basic reactor processes and technology, including the nuclear fuel cycle for both uranium enrichment and the chemical extraction of plutonium from depleted uranium. The next year, perhaps during Rafsanjani's visit to China in June, China and Iran signed a secret protocol for cooperation in the peaceful use of nuclear energy. Under the agreement, China supplied Iran with four small research reactors.

The Atomic Energy Organization of Iran (AEOI) also sent engineers to China for training in reactor operations. By 1987, fifteen AEOI engineers were reportedly undergoing training in China. Also in 1987, China agreed to supply ENRC with a device that uses magnetism to separate beams of uranium isotopes of varying atomic weights. This was a version of a device used by the US World War II Manhattan Project to enrich uranium. The China-supplied device could enrich up to 37 percent. In 1989, Chinese geologists began helping the AEOI prospect for uranium. Within a year, the AEOI announced that the search had been successful and that mining operations would begin at seven sites.[37] In short, during the 1980s the PRC became Tehran's major partner in the nuclear field. Locked in a desperate and bloody war with an Iraq pushing for nuclear weapons, China's support for Iran's mastery of basic nuclear processes and technology was a powerful demonstration of China's understanding of Iran's national defense concerns—and of Beijing's willingness to tell the Americans "no."

Support for Iran in United Nations action on the Iran-Iraq war was yet another dimension of China's assistance. Beijing balanced at the UN between, on the one hand, staying in step with the other Permanent Five, thus demonstrating that China was a responsible great power, and, on the other hand, differentiating itself from the United States by supporting Tehran whenever that was convenient and not too costly. In mid-1987, the Security Council began drafting a resolution demanding an immediate ceasefire to be followed by peace negotiations between Iran and Iraq. Tehran initially sought Soviet assistance in modifying some of the text of the draft, only to be told that such help was inconsistent with IRI criticism of Soviet activities in Afghanistan. IRI representatives then sought Chinese assistance, and the two countries worked together to make the draft resolution more "fair and balanced" in Tehran's view. Once Tehran and Baghdad accepted on August 8, 1987, Resolution Number 598 (endorsed by the Security Council on July 20), very difficult negotiations between Tehran and Baghdad began in Geneva. During these talks, too, Tehran turned frequently to Beijing for assistance.[38] Beijing thus made itself useful to Tehran in several ways.

Beijing also condemned US military actions in the Gulf punishing Iran for what Washington deemed illegal Iranian attacks on neutral commerce in international waters. As conflict between the US navy and the IRI navy and Revolutionary Guards escalated in mid-1987 (a conflict commonly referred to as the "tanker war"), Beijing insisted that military action by any of the Permanent Five in the Gulf required the consent of <u>all</u> the Permanent Five. After a US-flagged and -escorted Kuwaiti ship struck an Iranian mine in international waters and the United States took punitive military action against Iran, China's MFA condemned big-power interference in the Gulf and insisted that the security affairs of the Gulf should be handled by the countries of the region, i.e., the littoral principle tracing back to Ji Pengfei's 1973 visit to Tehran. Xinhua condemned US military action against Iran as big-power moves aggravating tension and creating a more explosive situation. Tehran had a few other friends who might speak up on its behalf—Libya, Syria, and North Korea. But none of these spoke with the authority or capabilities of the PRC.

As IRI leaders began to look on China as a like-minded and capable partner, Beijing had to lay down some limits on how far it was willing to go. Tehran in the mid-1980s developed a plan to expel Israel from the UN General Assembly as the first step toward destruction of the "Zionist entity." Tehran also urged Beijing to oppose the 1978 US-brokered Camp David treaty between Egypt and Israel on the grounds that it trampled on the rights of the Palestinian people. Chinese representatives listed politely to these proposals, and declined to go along. IRI media was also critical of China's warm relations with the United States. When President Ronald Reagan visited China in 1984, IRI media was strongly critical of the visit. Chinese envoys instructed Tehran regarding Chinese views of how the new PRC-IRI relation should work. Washington should not tell Tehran and Beijing what kind of relation they should have, Beijing would not tell Tehran what type of relation with the United States it should have, and Tehran should not tell Washington and Beijing what their relation should be. Each country would determine its foreign policies for itself, Beijing suggested. Gradually Iranian leaders came to understand some of the stark realities governing China's ties with the United States: China did not want to spoil its relation with the United States (or with Israel, Iraq, or any other country, for that matter) on Iran's behalf.

Within a decade, Beijing had transformed the 1979 relationship of cold isolation into one of warm partnership and mutual understanding. Beijing's long-range strategic objective was to build with Iran an all-weather partnership of mutual understanding and trust similar to the one Beijing enjoyed with Pakistan. The specific interests served by that relationship would vary, just as they had varied from containing Soviet expansion in the 1970s to minimizing American military "interference" in the Gulf in the 1980s to oil supply in the 2010s. But the relations of trust and understanding would enable the leaders of the two like-minded countries to forge cooperative programs serving the interests of both. It is interesting that an event that would transform the Sino-Iranian relation occurred the evening of June 3–4, 1989, when the PLA moved to crush China's democracy movement—the death of Ayatollah Ruhollah Khomeini. The passing of that giant figure, rather like Mao's passing, would, together with the end of the Iran-Iraq war ten months earlier, lead to profound transformations in Iran's revolutionary state. As in China after Mao, economic development became a priority in Iran. While Iran was at war, Sino-Iranian cooperation was about war and peace. As Iran turned to postwar economic development, the content of Sino-Iranian cooperation shifted to that area. But again the two powers looked on each other as like-minded cooperative partners.

Japan: Learning about History while Growing Economic Ties

Beijing's "friendship diplomacy" toward Japan, tracing back to the establishment of diplomatic relations in 1972 and the treaty of peace and friendship in 1978, continued through the last decade of the Cold War in the 1980s. As long as Beijing's concern with Soviet expansionism was strong, China tended to see Japan as part of the coalition checking the Soviet Union and consequently held a benign view of Japan's military capabilities. Priority on anti-Soviet security concerns meant that Beijing did not press too hard on the history issue. But as Sino-Soviet relations improved, the history issue became more important on Beijing's Japan agenda. Sino-Japanese friendship hobbled along through the 1990s, but in increasingly ragged shape.[39]

A shift in the narrative basis of CCP legitimacy in the early 1980s introduced a new factor into Sino-Japan relations—Chinese nationalist resentment. During the Mao era, the major CCP claim to legitimacy was that it had led the Chinese people to victory over Japan and the KMT reactionaries. This victor's narrative portrayed the Chinese people, led by the CCP, advancing from victory to victory to drive out Japan and topple the Nationalists. The desire to mobilize all possible forces, both within China and among ethnic Chinese in Hong Kong and Southeast Asia, led to the construction of a new, more broadly nationalist narrative. Dubbed the victim narrative by scholars, this narrative stressed the glories of China's millennia of imperial tradition, and the toppling of China from that exalted position by malevolent imperialists during

1978	1979	1980	1981	1982	1983	1984	1985	1986	1987
23%	23%	24%	25%	21%	23%	26%	30%	24%	20%

1988	1989	1990	1991	1992	1993	1994	1995	1996	1997
19%	17%	16%	15%	15%	20%	20%	21%	21%	19%

1998	1999	2000	2001	2002	2003	2004	2005	2006	2007
18%	18%	17%	17%	16%	16%	15%	13%	12%	11%

2008
10%

FIGURE 16-2 **Japan's Role in China's Foreign Trade, 1978–2008 (Japan as % of total two–way trade)**
Source: IMF, Direction of Trade Statistics Yearbooks. Various issues.

the Century of National Humiliation from 1839 to 1949. Japan was a key villain in both narratives, but there were important differences. In the victor's narrative, Japan had been defeated, its very villainy could be seen as opening the way to revolutionary victory, and China held the high status of shinning leader of the world revolutionary movement. In the victim's narrative, the result of Japan's villainy was still apparent in China's weakness and poverty, while rich Japan was still unrepentant for its myriad injuries against China. In 1982, the CCP launched its first anti-Japanese campaign, excoriating Tokyo for softening the language used in textbooks to discuss the 1930s.[40]

Throughout the period of Deng's reign, Beijing hoped that Japan would play an important role in China's modernization drive. Chinese leaders were critical of the tendency of Japanese firms to invest in hotels and real estate projects rather than in industrial manufacturing, and also the reluctance of Japanese firms to transfer high technology to China. Yet Japan was still an important partner in China's Four Modernizations. During the first thirty years of China's opening, Japan accounted annually for an average 21.3 percent of China's total trade. Figure 16-2 illustrates Japan's role in China's foreign trade between 1978 and 2008.

On the Japanese side, the psychological burden of guilt for Japan's aggression against China still weighed heavily on Japanese policy during the 1970s and 1980s. This helped produce greater Japanese willingness to accommodate China's demands and demonstrate Japan's friendship toward China. Japan's sense of collective guilt gradually diminished in the 1980s and 1990s due to a number of factors.[41] Among these factors was Beijing's periodic brow beating of Japan with the history issue, a process that gradually fed Japanese resentment, producing a greater Japanese willingness to say "no" to China.

Chinese foreign minister and long-time Japan hand Tang Jiaxuan explained in his memoir the logic of Beijing's Japan policy.[42] China desires friendship with various countries, including Japan, Tang explained, but the existence of "incorrect views" within those countries makes this difficult, creating obstacles. China must struggle against these incorrect ideas, correcting them and thus making friendship possible. There are two major forms of struggle, Tang explains. First, educational efforts by China's diplomats, leaders, media, scholars, and so on, explain how and why the pernicious foreign views are incorrect. Second, levying sanctions—canceling dialogues, exchanges, visits, and so on—to make clear China's unhappiness and the possible costs of that unhappiness. Tang's account of Sino-Japanese relations under his tutelage revolves around China's struggle over "history."

Beijing's understanding of this dual-track process was that through struggle against Japan's failure to recognize its past mistakes, a firmer foundation could be laid for economic and political cooperation: in Chinese, *qian shi bu wang, hou shi zhi shi* (past experiences if not forgotten may be a guide for the future). In fact, by the beginning of the post–Cold War period, Beijing's emphasis on past events would make Japan much more skeptical and guarded about cooperation with China.

In practice, Beijing's application of this unity-struggle-unity approach led not to Sino-Japanese unity but to gradually deepening estrangement of the two countries. Chinese efforts to re-educate Japan led not to amity but to growing Japanese resentment. This then combined with spontaneous eruptions of popular Chinese hatred of Japan to generate increased Japanese fear of China's growing power. Unfortunately for Beijing, its wielding of the history issue against Japan has not had the desired effect. Rather than making Japan more amenable to following Beijing's wishes, Beijing's repeated tirades about the history issue have made Japan resentful.

The history issue, as noted earlier, refers to the appraisal by Japan, China, and other Asian countries of the episode of Japanese aggression in the first half of the twentieth century. Broadly speaking, China's position has been and remains that Japan's leaders, or some of them, do not recognize the grave crimes and immense suffering their nation inflicted on the peoples of Asia in those years. Rather, they deny or beautify Japan's criminal aggression. This failure to frankly confront Japan's past—in contrast, say, to how leaders of the Federal Republic of Germany confronted Germany's responsibility for Hitler and all that he wrought—holds dangers for the future. Failure to recognize past mistakes means that those mistakes may be repeated. There is a real danger that Japan may once again pursue a course of military aggression in an effort to bring Asian countries under its sway. This, in any case, is what China's media often maintains.

The PRC's stance on the history issue must be understood at several levels. There is little doubt that individual Chinese embrace the views outlined in the last paragraph. Scholar Allen Whiting recounted the emotional responses by Chinese Japan specialists when interrogated about those beliefs during a mid-1980s research visit.[43] It may also be the case that Japanese understanding of history is inaccurate, perhaps even grossly so. But as Whiting noted, Beijing's typical response to efforts by the Japanese government to make the treatment of history more accurate, or to apologize for history, has been to stress the inadequacy of those efforts and how much remained to be done. Tokyo's efforts are never seen as adequate, the issue is never over or resolved. Japan, it seems, can never adequately atone for history.

Beijing also uses the history issue instrumentally—to achieve particular gains on other issues, such as trade, technology transfer, or aid—by pressuring Japan with "history." Domestically, stress on Japan's past aggression inculcated a sense of patriotism and national unity, *ningzhuli* in Chinese. In the context of evaporating belief in Marxism-Leninism, this was important—and became even more so after the upheaval of 1989–1991. As Minister of Defense Zhang Aiping said on the August 1985 fiftieth anniversary of Japan's World War II surrender, China's increasing standard of living could erode awareness of how bitterly earlier generations had fought to achieve the happy lives now enjoyed by Chinese. "We should not forget that once we were faced with national extinction," General Zhang said.[44] Use of Japan as object of national execration, rather than, say, the United States or Russia, had several advantages. Most obviously, neither Russia nor the United States had invaded and attempted to conquer China. Japan has. It was far easier and more effective to direct the national animus against Japan. It is also a lot safer. Japan has not been a major military power since 1945. Nor does it dominate the global order—including the Taiwan Strait—in the way the United States does.

A more important use of the history issue, at least from the standpoint of this study, has been to disqualify Japan from leadership in Asia. Japan and China have long been rivals for status in Asia. During the many centuries in which successive vast and powerful Chinese empires dominated East Asia, it was difficult for Japan to fit into that China-centric tributary system, because Japan's emperors refused to accept the ritualized subordinate status that participation in that system required. The traditional Sino-centric tributary system of East Asia was conceptually and organizationally hierarchical; the emperor of China was at the top, and other East Asian rulers were arrayed under him in subordinate order. The emperor of Japan refused to interact by these rules. He was so brazen, for example, as to style himself a "heavenly emperor" (*tianhuang* in Chinese) when all proper rulers understood, as China's Office of Rites, which functioned as the foreign ministry of China's empire ensured they did, that there was only one celestial ruler, the "son of heaven" (*tianzi*) who ruled from China's capital. Direct interaction between Chinese and Japanese rulers was thus very difficult. Official contact was usually conducted via Korean third parties who accepted vassalage to both Chinese and Japanese courts. During Japan's period of early modern national isolation (roughly 1600 to 1867), Japanese were banned from travelling abroad, while Chinese, Korean, and Dutch merchants carried on robust Sino-Japanese trade, obviating the need for contact between the Chinese and the Japanese imperial courts.[45] But starting with the Meiji Restoration, Japan challenged and ultimately destroyed the old Sino-centric Asian order. The 1894–1895 Sino-Japanese war was, in effect, a hegemonic war for pre-eminence in East Asia.[46] Then, in the 1930s, Japan attempted to build a new, hierarchical order in East Asia with itself on top and China under it. By the 1980s and 1990s, Japan was seeking to become "a normal country" with a political role more commensurate with its powerful economic role—just as China was beginning to reap accomplishments in its modernization drive. China's use of the history issue needs to be seen in the context of this centuries-old Sino-Japan rivalry for status in Asia, which began to grow intense again in the 1990s. The unstated crux of Beijing's use of the history issue was this: Japan's moral incapacity disqualified it for contesting China's rightful preeminence in Asia.

Millennia of experience suggest to many Chinese that the natural, normal, and rightful order of things, at least in East Asia, is Chinese preeminence. It is equally self-evident to Chinese that Japan simply does not have the moral bona fides to claim leadership in Asia. The history issue proves this, from the Chinese perspective. For Chinese, it is impossible that a country that committed such horrible crimes during the first half of the twentieth century, and which still refuses to fully repent and atone for those crimes, could be a leader among Asian countries. How can an unrepentant serial aggressor like Japan assume responsibility for maintaining peace in Asia? That path would too easily lead again to aggression against other Asian countries. No, in the common Chinese view, Japan must remain subordinate, either to the United States or to China. Propagating these views among the Asian countries that also experienced Japanese brutality—North and South Korea, the Philippines, Malaysia, Singapore—builds support for a lesser Japanese role in the region.

From the Japanese perspective, Japan's generous aid, its Asian Development Bank (ADB) loans and investment in China, did not seem to be building friendship. In fact, popular anti-Japan animus in China grew as Japan again and again demonstrated its friendship toward China. PRC efforts to expand friendly cooperation with Japan proceeded in tandem with periodic Chinese lessons about the history issue. Japan could never do enough to satisfy Beijing, it seemed to more and more Japanese. The history issue in Beijing's hand was not really about the past but about the future, about the role of China and Japan in Asia thirty, forty, or fifty years hence.

Leadership exchanges between China and Japan flourished in the 1980s.[47] Deng stopped in Tokyo in February 1979 on his way home from the United

States to brief Japan's leaders about the upcoming "lesson" to Vietnam. Japan disbursed loans to China every year but one between 1979 and 1988, averaging 89 billion yen per year. The ADB, in which Japan played a major role, disbursed another US$5.6 billion to China, far more than to any other country.[48] An intergovernmental conference, headed by Gu Mu on the Chinese side, met regularly. A conference of nongovernmental personages was established and met three times through 1986. There were frequent declarations of fine-sounding principles to underpin Sino-Japan relations. In June 1982, during his visit to Tokyo, Zhao Ziyang advanced three guiding principles for Sino-Japanese relations: peace and friendship, equality and mutual benefit, and long-term stability. During a November 1983 visit to Japan, Hu Yaobang spoke to Japan's parliament, saying that China would always be sincere and honest, open and aboveboard, and would act in good faith. Hu and Prime Minister Yasuhiro Nakasone agreed that future relations would be guided by the principles enunciated by Zhao Ziyang the previous year. Hu and Nakasone also agreed in 1983 to establish a 21st Century Committee for China-Japan Friendship, which met in Beijing in June 1984. The first full session met in Tokyo in September 1984 and issued yet another statement of fine-sounding principles. The same month, four groups of 3,000 Japanese youth began visiting China at the invitation of Hu Yaobang. The cornerstone for a China-Japan Youth Exchange Center in Beijing was laid in November 1986. During the 1980s, the two sides also conducted joint activities commemorating the World War II atomic bombing of Hiroshima and Nagasaki. A Japanese parliamentary delegation visited China, while the China-Japan Friendship Association held various activities.[49]

Periodic confrontations over the history issue paralleled this process of Sino-Japanese cooperation and, as it turned out, eroded mutual amity. Beijing's first "history lesson" came in 1982, when Japanese journalists discovered that the Ministry of Education had suggested that the wording used in some high school textbooks be changed to lessen the moral onus associated with Japan's actions in the 1930s and 1940s. Japan's "invasion" of China was called a "forward advance." The 1937 "Massacre" at Nanjing became the "killing of many" as a result of "fierce resistance by Chinese troops."[50] One month passed before Beijing responded. That response began with an official protest, followed by a nearly month-long media campaign excoriating in vivid terms Japan's aggression against China. The key themes of the media campaign were the danger of revival of Japanese militarism and the anger and hurt feelings of the Chinese people at the unrepentant nature of the Japanese government. China's newspapers and magazines were filled with photos of Chinese being decapitated, mutilated corpses, and the like, along with personal reminiscences from that era and cartoons lambasting the position of Japan's government and politicians. Dramatically worded headlines and

captions further roused people's ire. The Nanjing Massacre and germ warfare experiments in Manchuria were recounted. The campaign culminated
on August 15, the anniversary of Japan's surrender announcement in 1945.
A commentary in *Zhongguo qingnian bao* (China youth daily) gives a sense
of the tenor of the campaign:

> Are the officials of the Ministry of Education mentally unbal-
> anced? . . . No! Of course not, they consider themselves smart. A few
> Japanese constantly bear in mind the profit they gained from the in-
> vasion of China and the war in Southeast Asia. Their hope of realizing
> their dream of reviving militarism is indefatigable. Their attempt to
> deceive the younger generation through education is deliberate. Their
> intention to revise history and to beautify militarism under cover of
> ancestor worship is carefully thought out. Nevertheless how could his-
> torical facts written in blood be concealed by lies written in ink? Your
> 'samurai' forebears used innocent Chinese to test bacteriological war-
> fare and used them as living targets. They dismembered and chopped
> up Chinese captives who were tied to trees. You forced Chinese to dig
> holes and bury themselves alive. You adopted such savage means as the
> 'iron maiden,' pulling out fingernails, branding, belly cutting, electric
> grinding, and flesh eating to persecute Chinese compatriots.[51]

Scholar James Reilly suggests that the month-long anti-Japan propaganda
campaign of 1982 arose out of conflict between the CCP's liberal reformers
and conservatives concerned about the growing flow of Japanese investment
into China.[52] Conservatives such as Chen Yun and Bo Yipo were dismayed at
Japan's growing economic role in China, linking Japanese investment to inflation, trade deficits, growing indebtedness, and disruption of the planning
system. Conservatives also feared that Japan would exploit China's growing
dependence for political purposes, and that Japanese influence might lead
to political liberalization. Deng settled the dispute by ruling in favor of continued Japanese investment, but authorized a month-long propaganda campaign to assuage conservative fears about the political implications of Japan's
role. Reilly also suggests that calling forth Chinese animosity against Japan in
this fashion in 1982 created a space for public expression of such sentiments
that would bear fruit in the form of student demonstrations several years later.

The media campaign ended abruptly on August 15, 1982, about a month
before Prime Minister Zenko Suzuki was scheduled to visit Beijing. (August
15 is the day in 1945 the emperor announced Japan's surrender.) Beijing did
not want to spoil the atmosphere for Suzuki's visit—the first by a Japanese
prime minister since Masayoshi Ohira's December 1979 visit. During his visit,
Suzuki promised that Japan would listen fully to China's criticisms on textbook matters. "The Japanese Government will be responsible for making the
corrections [in the text books] as soon as possible, take concrete measures

sincerely and solve the question well."[53] Eight months later Japan extended a new loan of 69 billion yen. There was not a direct linkage between Chinese ire over the history issue and Japanese development assistance to China. On the other hand, Japanese assistance was clearly intended as a demonstration of Japanese friendship for China.

Three years later, the fortieth anniversary, on August 15, 1985, precipitated another flood of articles and special events portraying the horrors of Japan's history. A summer-long television program depicted the horrors of the Japanese invasion and occupation. A new museum opened in Nanjing commemorating the 1937 massacre in that city. New publications detailing the Nanjing Massacre appeared. One booklet selected the most gruesome photos from the museum collection: rows of severed heads, mutilated bodies of women and children, mass graves, and so on. Thirty-four thousand copies were printed. Other media outlets rebutted the Japanese media's focus on the atomic bombing of Hiroshima and Nagasaki. These were attempts to win sympathy for Japan and allow Japan to avoid feelings of guilt for Japan's crimes in China, China's media charged.

A visit by Prime Minister Nakasone to the Yasukuni Shrine in Tokyo on August 15, 1985, added fuel to the fire of China's anger. The Yasukuni Shinto shrine in central Tokyo was established in 1869 to commemorate and pray for all Japanese soldiers who had died in that country's wars since the Meiji Restoration.[54] Japan's government ceased financial support and involvement with Yasukuni in 1972, but the shrine continued to be controversial, partly because it contained the name plaques of fourteen Class A war criminals as determined by the post–World War II Far Eastern War Crime Trials. The museum associated with the shrine views Japan's World War II more or less as the wartime commanders of that war did: as a noble effort to liberate the colored peoples of Asia from domination by the white Western powers. Prior to 1985, other Japanese prime ministers had visited Yasukuni on August 15, but only in a nonofficial capacity. Nakasone broke with that precedent and visited in his official capacity as prime minister. China had learned of the upcoming visit before it occurred and asked Tokyo to handle it with prudence. When an official visit nonetheless transpired, the MFA declared that it had hurt the feelings of the Chinese people. The MFA did not, however, issue a formal protest, perhaps because of fear of the popular Chinese response.

The textbook issue returned in February 1986, when a tendentious textbook intended to make "young people love their country's history" came before a review commission in Tokyo. Beijing interpreted it as a violation of Suzuki's 1982 promise to correct the errors in Japanese textbooks. Instead, said the MFA, Japan's Ministry of Education had again "done something that hurts the feelings of the Chinese people."[55] The MFA then issued a "stern note" asserting that the proposed text book "grossly distorts history" and stating that "the Chinese government strongly demands that the Japanese

Government implement its 1982 commitment . . . and eliminate the negative effect caused by this issue." Nakasone acceded to Beijing's demand and directed that "certain portions of the text book should be reconsidered." Over the next months, Nakasone four times instructed and urged the Ministry of Education to revise the textbook. The final version met China's requirements on a number of issues. Beijing, however, remained unsatisfied. Xinhua elaborated on the continuing inadequacies of the text.

During 1985, popular anti-Japanese sentiment in China, fanned by Beijing's repeated campaigns against Japan on the history issue, and perhaps behind the scenes by conservative CCP leaders opposed to Deng's policy of opening, erupted into student protests.[56] In many respects, these anti-Japanese demonstrations were the genesis of the student movement that would challenge the regime so powerfully in 1989. The 1985 demonstrations showed the ability of anti-Japanese nationalism to mobilize popular sentiment in China, as well as the remarkable ease with which patriotic movements in China can transform into anti-regime movements. This factor, which would become central to China's foreign relations after the 1989–1991 upheaval, first manifested itself in 1985. As outlined by scholar James Reilly, criticism of Japan by China's government created a space for autonomous activities by freelance nationalists. CCP authorities were then faced with a choice of toleration or limitation of the activity. Toleration garnered nationalist legitimacy for the regime, but it also carried dangers of unleashing popular discontent and damaging China's foreign relations. This dynamic, first manifest in 1985–1986, would become a key dynamic in the twenty-first century.[57]

Mid-1985 opened a period of relative liberalization in Chinese society, a period that would last until January 1987 and the purge of Hu Yaobang.[58] This brief period of relative tolerance opened a space for student patriotic protest focused on the government's post-1978 policy of relying on Japan to modernize China. September 18 ("9-18"), 1985, was the anniversary of the Mukden Incident of 1931 in which elements of the Japanese army in Manchuria damaged a section of rail line to create a pretext for the seizure of that entire region by Japan. Nakasone had visited the Yasukuni Shrine only the month before, on the anniversary of Japan's 1945 surrender. On 9-18, over a thousand university students held rallies on their campuses in northwest Beijing, listened to anti-Japanese speeches, and shouted anti-Japanese slogans. The students from several universities then merged and marched the seven miles to Tiananmen Square in central Beijing. This was the same route taken by patriotic Chinese students in May 1919 when popular nationalism first emerged on China's scene. Posters in 1985 proclaimed "Down with Nakasone," "Down with the Second Occupation," and "Boycott Japanese goods." The "second occupation" referred to the growing role and highly visible presence of Japanese goods, brands, and companies in China. This was a direct challenge to one of Deng's and the CCP's core development strategies: close economic cooperation with Japan as a key driver of China's development effort.[59]

The regime mobilized to rebut the students' argument. Li Peng, then vice premier, told an assembly of student leaders that a low-keyed approach to Japan was a diplomatic necessity. Moreover, China retained the initiative in relations with Japan. China should be self-confident, Li Peng said. *Zhongguo qingnian bao* warned the students that closing China's doors to the outside world once again because of a few undesirable phenomena would be like "giving up eating for fear of choking." Gu Mu explained to student representatives that Japan's economic activity in China was not aggression but was helping China's economic development.[60]

These arguments did not suffice to end student activism. In November, students began to mobilize for further demonstrations on December 9—the day in 1935 when students had rallied to demand that Chiang Kai-shek abandon his anticommunist policies and form a united front with the communists against Japan. Clandestinely distributed publicity for the planned demonstration demonstrated how easy it was for anti-Japanese nationalism to morph into criticism of the CCP regime. Democracy was necessary to fully mobilize the Chinese people to "stand up in the world," the flyer said. "Bloodsucking princes" were "plotting their own private interests" and "taking advantage of reform" while opening the door to Japan. These were powerful echoes of the CCP's indictment of China's pre-1949 rulers—that they were partners with imperialism, enriching themselves while allowing the imperialists to run amuck in China. Once again the regime mobilized. The media's main point was that student patriotism could contribute to strengthening the nation only under the leadership of the Chinese Communist Party.[61]

Yet another round of student demonstrations spread across the campuses of Chinese universities a year later, in late 1986. These demonstrations targeted not Japan but a variety of domestic issues, with "democracy" being their common denominator.[62] The period 1985–1986 was one of intensifying conflict over the future of political reform in China. Increased contact with the outside world, relaxation of controls on speech, and increased economic dislocations associated with the monumental shift from planned to market economics led to a sense of uncertainty and questioning. Liberal intellectuals, tolerated by Hu Yaobang's lenient approach, increasingly challenged Marxist-Leninist politics and called for full democratization. One of the most prominent of these intellectuals, Fang Lizhi, a professor of astrophysics at Chinese University of Science and Technology in Hefei, Anhui province, went on a speaking tour of university campuses in late 1986. Fang was blunt in his demands. At Shanghai's Jiaotong University, for example, he said, "I am here to tell you that the socialist movement, from Marx and Lenin to Stalin and Mao, has been a failure. I think that complete Westernization [i.e., embrace of "Western-style" democracy] is the only way to modernize." Fang's ideas were well received by his university audiences, if not by the CCP authorities in charge of the schools where he was stirring up "turmoil."

CCP conservatives blamed the student demonstrations on the party's failure to wage strong and sustained struggle against "bourgeois liberalism." That failure, in turn, had been due to the influence of liberals such as Secretary General Hu Yaobang. As early as September 1986, after Hu suggested that the Four Cardinal Principles were out of date and called for reform of China's political system, Deng had identified Hu as too weak in opposition to "bourgeois liberalization." Following the wave of student demonstrations at the end of 1986, Deng agreed with the conservatives' long-standing demand that Hu be removed. The bill of particulars removing Hu in January 1987 began with the charge that for years he had failed to resist bourgeois liberalization, contributing to the demand for "total Westernization." In the debate over Hu's removal, Deng Xiaoping spoke favorably of the use of "methods of dictatorship" such as martial law, used by the Polish communists in 1981 to "bring the situation under control." Reportedly, arguments by Chen Yun had been decisive in bringing Deng to fire Hu. Hu's lax leadership, Chen told Deng, risked a split in the party and the formation of autonomous workers' unions and strikes, creating a "Chinese Gdańsk."

The Leninist State Besieged; Socialism in One Country

17 }

1989: The CCP's Near Escape and Its Aftermath

Socialism in One Country: The Last Major Leninist Regime

1989 was a turning point in PRC relations with the advanced capitalist countries.

In spring of that year, there emerged in Beijing with amazing speed a citizen's movement making a strong and increasingly nationwide demand for political reform. That movement was ultimately repressed by brute force, but only at great cost to both the domestic and international stature of the CCP. The popular and nonviolent movements that toppled the communist party states across Eastern Europe and then in Russia over the next thirty months further underlined the threat to CCP rule, as well as confirming the belief among the CCP elite that the decision to employ military repression in June 1989 had been correct. Had the CCP acted otherwise, the regime might have disintegrated, as did the Leninist states in those other countries.

Out of the events of 1989–1991 emerged a new CCP elite consensus: the "bourgeois liberal" ideas promulgated by the Western countries were dangerously seductive to China's youth and intellectuals and needed to be resisted by resolute ideological struggle. Failure to wage such struggle was one of the key mistakes committed under Hu Yaobang. A key basis for waging struggle against "bourgeois liberal" ideas was inculcation of a strong sense of Western threat and hostility to China. China's youth, especially, were to be taught that foreign powers desired to weaken and injure China for all sorts of selfish reasons; this was the real reason why these countries pressed liberal ideas on China. The "bourgeois liberal" ideals those countries peddle in various ways in China are, in fact, sugar-coated weapons designed to weaken and hurt China. In sum, the world still dominated by the advanced capitalist countries is a dark and threatening place for China, not primarily because of the threat of Western military attack or intervention, but because of the seductive power of "bourgeois liberal" ideas.[1]

Modern political systems legitimize political authority through a process of free and full debate followed by competitive and fair elections resulting in empowerment of removable political elites that derive their authority from this process. These modern processes have been embraced by most of China's neighbors: Japan, Mongolia, South Korea, Taiwan, the Philippines, Indonesia, Malaysia, Thailand, Singapore, Bangladesh, and India. But not China. There the political half of the Bolshevik legacy precluded these modern processes. This in a world in which liberal ideas are transmitted electronically at the speed of light. Ideas of all sorts, including liberal ideas, hurl across state boundaries with unprecedented speed, carried by modern communication and information technologies. Full utilization of those technologies is integral to participation in a rapidly evolving global economy and development of advanced technologies and potent military capabilities. China cannot disengage from those technologies if it hopes to achieve wealth and power. Yet engagement is potentially subversive of CCP authority. Thus a rapidly globalizing China was ruled by an anachronistic Leninist elite that saw its authority to rule profoundly threatened by the dynamics of globalization. Eventually, the CCP would develop an apparently viable nationalist and non-Marxist but antiliberal narrative. During the 1989–1991 upheaval, however, that was still years in the future.

The Global Wave of Liberal Revolutions

Nineteen eighty-nine was one of those curious years when revolution swept from country to country almost like a contagious disease. The wave began early in the year in Poland and crashed at year's end in Romania—the CCP's closest fraternal party regime in Europe. In between, a tidal-wave uprising for freedom swept across China. The CCP's violent crushing of that uprising in June played a big role in Europe's subsequent anticommunist revolution by creating the specter of a "Chinese solution" that haunted East European countries as they struggled to free themselves.

It began in Poland. Eruption of a powerful and ultimately successful anticommunist movement in Poland in late 1988 shaped the reaction of CCP leaders to the freedom movement that erupted in China in April 1989. An independent, noncommunist-led trade union, Solidarity, had emerged at Poland's Gdańsk shipyard in August 1980. Solidarity had expanded to enlist perhaps one-third of all Poland's workers by the time of imposition of military rule under the threat of Soviet invasion in March 1981. The new and intensely anticommunist US President Ronald Reagan, inaugurated in January 1981, cooperated with Polish-born Pope John Paul II (who had become pope in 1978) and with American labor unions to sustain and encourage the underground Solidarity resistance during the period of military rule. Though the full contours of this covert US-Vatican support would not become known until much later, counterintelligence organs of the Polish communist party (formally known as the Polish United Workers Party, PUWP) understood the broad contours of what was going on. Twice in 1988 Solidarity launched massive strikes and street demonstrations demanding reform.

Confronted by widespread unrest, fearing economic regression, and facing strong international criticism, the PUWP agreed in early 1989 to "Round Table" talks with Solidarity and other opposition groups. Those talks began on February 6 and continued to April 4, 1989—eleven days before Hu Yaobang's death—when an agreement was signed laying out a path for Poland's transition from Leninist dictatorship. The PUWP went into the Round Table talks confident of its continued ability to dominate Poland. The party's key strategy was to co-opt opposition leaders into the existing structures of power, thereby dividing the opposition and depriving it of key leaders. Tolerance of some opposition would, PUWP leaders calculated, assuage opposition and help legitimize continued party rule, while continued party control over traditional mechanisms of power (police, the economy, the media, etc.) would ensure that the PUWP would be able to control the process. This strategy was not much different from Zhao Ziyang's strategy of "guide and split" via "dialogue" with China's opposition in April–May 1989.

PUWP calculations soon proved wrong. Rather like the convocation of the Estates General by France's monarch in 1789, Poland's Round Table Talks quickly gained a momentum of their own. Opposition leaders refused to defect. Instead, they escalated their demands. Widespread desire for change welled up in society. Splits occurred within the PUWP. The agreement that resulted from the talks provided for a major change in the structure of power. The PUWP was compelled to abandon its monopoly on state power and accept democratic arrangements that would swiftly produce its exit from power. Labor unions and political parties independent of communist party control and in opposition to that party were legalized. New, popularly elected organs were established, and election processes reformed. Solidarity candidates routed PUWP candidates in the new, democratic elections. When elections for a new upper house of the legislature were held, Solidarity candidates won 99 percent of the seats. Poland was the first communist party–ruled country in which democratically elected representatives gained real power. Poland's pivotal elections, producing an overwhelming Solidarity victory, were held on June 4, 1989—the same day PLA forces crushed China's democracy movement. The juxtaposition of the Polish and the Chinese communist response to popular demands for liberty was graphic, and had a deep impact on Western opinion. While Polish communists were finally acceding to Polish demands for liberty, the Chinese Communist Party resorted to old-fashioned repression. The bold breakthroughs toward democracy in Poland in February and April had greatly inspired students in Beijing.

An even more powerful example of what was possible was Mikhail Gorbachev, who for several years had been introducing a liberal brand of Leninist rule in the Soviet Union. For hardliners within the CCP, the fate of the PUWP was a warning against trying the same strategy in China. Once blood flowed in Beijing streets, the specter of similar repression haunted East European capitals with the belief that the clock could be turned back to the Stalinist era as in China, if it did not move forward to freedom.

China's Democratic Uprising

In the CCP's view of things, an uprising against it cannot be democratic. Since rule by the CCP represents rule by and in the interests of the Chinese people, it is by definition "democratic." Attempts to overthrow the "people's democracy" are, again by definition, anti-democratic.[2] This Leninist sophistry met a powerful challenge in spring 1989. A powerful movement sprang into existence and assumed nationwide proportions with startling speed and demanded that the CCP abandon its traditional methods of rule, starting with its long-standing ban on independent nongovernmental organizations and control over the media. While the Chinese movement of spring 1989 did not have a single voice or set of demands, there are good grounds to credit the conclusion of the mainstream of the CCP's leaders: the movement sought nothing less than the dismantling of the CCP dictatorship.

The movement began with students memorializing the late Secretary General Hu Yaobang in Tiananmen Square on "grave sweeping day"—the traditional Confucian holiday for venerating ancestors—shortly after his death on April 15. Preparations for the officially organized funeral for Hu struck students as cursory and insincere. The student protests resonated with Beijing's populace, and soon marches of tens of thousands of people pushed to the square in protest, pushing aside police cordons in the process. The Politburo eventually responded with a harsh editorial in Renmin ribao on April 26, charging "an extremely small segment of opportunists" with "plotting to overthrow the CCP and China's political system." The editorial, pushed through while Secretary General and pro-reform leader Zhao Ziyang was visiting North Korea, was intended to scare students into ceasing protest. It backfired, angering students and creating a standing threat of punishment for the organizers of the student protests. Demonstrations swelled further; the day after the editorial, up to 100,000 people marched from Beijing's university district to Tiananmen Square. After Zhao's return from North Korea on May 1, policy shifted in a noticeably more tolerant direction. Demonstrating seemed safe, and crowds grew larger. Work units began to join in, often with banners proclaiming their units and their support for student demands. In the process, students formed independent organizations, issued demands, and called a strike of classes.

On May 17, the Politburo Standing Committee split over the question of declaring martial law to end the escalating student-led protest movement. Li Peng and vice premier Yao Yilin were in favor of martial law, Zhao Ziyang and Hu Qili were opposed. Qiao Shi, the fifth Standing Committee member, abstained. The matter was then referred to Deng, who settled the issue: martial law would be imposed in the urban districts of Beijing. The situation had gone so far, however, that when martial law was publicly declared on May 20 and convoys of troops attempted to enter the city, their advance was blocked by huge throngs of ordinary Beijing citizens. What had begun as a student movement had become a movement of the populace of Beijing. After a standoff lasting over a day, the troops withdrew. CCP leaders then mobilized troops from every Military Region and deployed them to Beijing. When those new forces entered the city on the night of June 3–4, they were authorized to use all necessary force. When crowds of Beijingers again blocked the military's advance, troops fired tear gas and rubber bullets. When that failed to disburse the crowds, around 10:30 p.m. troops began firing directly into the crowds. Enraged citizens continued to oppose them with rocks, Molotov cocktails, and angry taunts. Confrontations resulting in much bloodshed continued throughout the night and into the next morning.

Two weeks later, Beijing party secretary Li Ximing reported to the Politburo that 241 people died in the fighting on June 3–4 (known as "6-4"). The International Red Cross put the number at 2,800 killed and an equal number wounded. Another 15,000 to 20,000 people were arrested in the days after "6-4," and between 50 and 100 of these were executed (mostly for violent acts). Thousands were jailed for long terms.

As the protest movement grew in April and May, Politburo hardliners had concluded that hostile foreign forces were behind the growing challenge to party authority. On April 28, Premier Li Peng told the Politburo that the "turmoil" was "the result of long-term preparation by a tiny minority of bourgeois liberal elements hooked up with anti-China forces outside the country." "For this reason, we must fully realize the complex and protracted nature of this political struggle," Li told the PBSC.[3] "Every day," Li said, "foreigners of unclear status" came and went on Beijing college campuses to "plot strategy" with "the leaders of the illegal student organizations." At the same meeting of the PBSC, elder Bo Yibo, who served as Deng Xiaoping's representative on the Standing Committee, concurred with Li Peng's targeting of "foreign anti-China forces." Foreigners, such as the influential newsweekly *Far Eastern Economic Review*, Bo said, were "trumpeting" that China's reforms were "a dead end . . . . Because they want to encourage the students and to throw our Party and our national spirit into confusion."[4] The Ministry of State Security (MSS) supplied top CCP leaders with regular summaries of foreign media coverage of China's student movement. Unsurprisingly, most of that coverage sympathized with the students. Much of the foreign media saw the movement as a direct challenge to the party's traditional mechanisms of dictatorial rule and, explicitly or implicitly, a positive force. Andrew J. Nathan and Perry Link suggest that China's leaders paid special attention to more analytical and interpretative foreign journalistic reports, because reports from the MSS were purely descriptive in nature.

The proreform faction led by Secretary General Zhao Ziyang favored more subtle methods. This point of view was exemplified by Vice Premier Tian Jiyun at the Politburo meeting discussed above. The reason why the masses supported the student movement, Tian explained, was that the students had articulated attractive slogans that the masses identified with.[5] Zhao Ziyang did not dispute that "a tiny minority" sought an end to the CCP dictatorship or that "foreign forces" encouraged the students. Zhao believed, however, that the CCP needed to learn to rule in a new way, that the repressive ways of the past no longer worked or were acceptable to "the masses." Zhao explained at a Politburo meeting on May 1—shortly after promulgation of the pernicious *Renmin ribao* commentary of April 26, and the day after Zhao returned from his ill-timed trip to North Korea:

> Times have changed, and so have people's ideological views. Democracy is a worldwide trend, and there is an international countercurrent against communism and socialism that flies under the banner of democracy and human rights. If the Party doesn't hold up the banner of democracy in our country, someone else will, and we will lose out. I think we should grab the lead on this, not be pushed along grudgingly. We must, of course, insist on Communist Party leadership and not play around with any Western multiparty system. This basic principle can allow no compromise. . . . In sum, we must make the people feel that under the leadership of the Communist Party and the socialist system, they can truly and fully enjoy democracy and freedom. The socialist system can demonstrate its superiority only by increasing the power of its appeal to the people.[6]

The appropriate response to the student protest movement, Zhao argued to the Politburo on May 1, was to "guide and split" it. A large part of the student movement was not opposed to party leadership, Zhao believed, and via "dialogue" a substantial section could be persuaded to cooperate with the party in further reform. The crux, Zhao felt, was to convince the student "masses" that the party was willing to change and adopt new, less repressive methods or rule, and move China in the direction of democracy—albeit still socialist democracy. Zhao later, while under house arrest long after June 1989, explained his view at that time:

> My view was that the Party's ruling status need not be changed, but the way it governed had to be changed. Moreover, in order to realize "rule

of law," the existing situation of "rule by men" needed to be changed. Socialist nations should also be nations with rule of law.[7]

Independent social groups—civil society—should be allowed to exist, according to Zhao. The party should establish multiple channels for dialogue with groups. It should change China's electoral system so that "people would have a real choice." There should be "greater press freedom." The party should not be "so controlling or so severe," Zhao believed.[8] Zhao's prescription was liberal communism, the same path that the PUWP in Poland and Gorbachev's CPSU in the USSR were attempting to tread.

The problem with Zhao's reformist approach, CCP hard-liners argued, was that concessions and attempted conciliation would not satisfy but only embolden the demonstrators. "The trouble is," Li Peng explained at a key Politburo Standing Committee meeting of May 1, "there's no sign the protests are subsiding" in response to the party's heretofore relatively lenient handling of demonstrators and attempts at dialogue. Li stressed the unprecedented size and power of the movement confronting the CCP, a movement that openly advocated "bourgeois liberalism" and "absolute freedom."[9] At a crucial meeting of May 18 that decided to impose martial law, the majority view was that further concessions to the demonstrators would mean the end of CCP rule. As elder Po Bibo explained it, Western-style democracy, freedom, and human rights were the aim of the student movement:

> We have no room for any retreat. If we go one step back, they'll come one step forward; if we go back two, they'll come forward two. We're at a point of no retreat. To retreat further would be to hand China over to them.[10]

Zhao Ziyang's retort to Bo's call for repression was, "One more political mistake by the CCP might well cost us our remaining legitimacy. The Chinese people cannot take any more huge policy blunders" by the party.[11] Implicit in Zhao's warning were earlier CCP decisions for the Great Leap Forward and the Cultural Revolution. Stated simply, Zhao's position was that if the CCP continued to stand athwart the popular demand for political freedom protected by rule of law, and ultimately democracy, it would be overthrown.

By late May, the CCP faced nothing less than a nationwide—if still mainly urban—uprising for democracy. The MSS kept top leaders apprised of the rapidly burgeoning movement. On May 17, two days before the public declaration of martial law in Beijing, there were large-scale demonstrations in twenty-seven of China's then thirty-two provincial-level units.[12] Sixteen of those demonstrations involved over ten thousand people. Two days later, there were major student protests in 116 cities. Attempts by PLA forces to enter Beijing to implement martial law were once again being blocked by angry Beijing residents. Over 100,000 Beijingers were involved in such obstruction, according to the MSS. Petitions and protest telegrams were flooding into central organs, the MSS reported. There were signs, according to a MSS report on May 10, that workers were beginning to join the protests. This was an especially ominous sign for CCP leaders. "If the workers rise up, we're in big trouble," Yang Shangkun (another of Deng Xiaoping's representatives on the Standing committee) opined.[13] Deng adumbrated the party's situation this way when he decided to impose martial law: "we've never faced this kind of thing before: a small handful infiltrating into such a huge number of students and masses." Elder Li Xiannian seconded Deng's view: "If we don't put Beijing under martial law, we'll all end up under house arrest."[14] Bo Yibo concurred: "The whole imperialist Western world wants to make socialist countries leave the socialist road and become satellites in the system of international monopoly capitalism. The people with ulterior motives who are behind this student movement have support from the United States and Europe and from the Kuomintang reactionaries in Taiwan."[15] Deng Xiaoping was greatly concerned that PLA forces might become infected by the ideas of the student demonstrators and refuse to follow orders given by the CCP center.

The best demonstration of the deep challenge to the CCP in spring 1989 was the collapse of Leninist dictatorships in Eastern Europe in 1989 and then in the USSR itself over the next two years. There is no way of knowing how the CCP would have fared if Zhao Ziyang had prevailed in the critical debates of May 1989—perhaps if he had not made his ill-timed visit to North Korea, which allowed Li Peng to push through the editorial of April 26, or had not forfeited the support of Deng Xiaoping through revealing comments to Gorbachev. Zhao Ziyang's belief in 1989 was that the CCP should continue to rule China, but that it needed to learn to rule by new methods: tolerance of autonomous social groups, dialogue with various groups, more "vitality" in elections, freedom of press and artistic expression, rule by law rather than by men.[16]

As unpleasant as it may be to people of liberal democratic persuasion, it must be recognized that Li Peng, Yao Yilin, and Deng Xiaoping may have been correct; Zhao Ziyang's strategy of compromise, splitting, and guiding via dialogue might not have worked any better in China than it did in Poland or elsewhere in East Europe. Dialogue could have mobilized other groups in society and allowed them to negotiate programs that combined interests. Continuation of a permissive approach could have seen other social sectors, the urban working class or the peasants, join in the movement. New organizations could have formed alliances across social groups. Demands could have escalated further, as was already happening. The party could have split, with elements opting to secure a position in a postcommunist state. It is possible that Zhao's prescription would have led to the rapid dismantling of the CCP's Leninist state, as in Poland and the USSR.

In the event, the perspective that won out was not Zhao Ziyang's. The dominant view was that the CCP faced a powerful movement trying to undo its control over the state and hegemony over society, and that further concessions and tolerance would embolden rather than placate that movement, which was backed by a coalition of capitalist powers hostile to the very existence of CCP rule over socialist China. Internally, a protracted struggle would have to be waged against "spiritual and intellectual infiltration" by Western powers and their ideas. Externally, the PRC would need to remain vigilant and strong.

The Impact of "6-4" on China's International Status

The CCP's response to the uprising that shook China in spring 1989—a resort to military repression that left at least hundreds of civilian protestors dead, an episode widely referred to as "6-4" for "June 4" in China and as the Beijing Massacre in the West—radically redefined the PRC's relations with Western countries. In the first instance, Western public opinion was dismayed at the killing of unarmed civilian protestors in Beijing streets. The international media had flocked to Beijing to report on Gorbachev's historic summit visit to China in May. Once in that city, however, foreign journalists turned their attention to the student protest movement, and many were still on site on the night of June 3–4. Much of the violence of that night and the next day unfolded before the vigilant and shocked eyes of the international media. Brought into homes by television and firsthand newspaper reports, PLA brutality evoked deep Western sympathy for the brave Chinese freedom fighters. "Tank man," a lone civilian who blocked a column of tanks by refusing to move aside on the morning of June 4, became a powerful symbol of what Westerners perceived as China's brave resistance and the regime's brutality. Anger at the CCP leaders who ordered the use of force paralleled sympathy for China's protestors. Both impulses translated into demands on democratically elected Western governments to take action supporting China's struggle for liberty and punishing CCP rulers who seemed to stand athwart the course of history. As Figure 17-1 shows, positive US views of China fell precipitously after 6-4 to the lowest level since 1973. Fifteen years of improving American perceptions of China were wiped out in one day.

The Beijing Massacre altered Sino-US relations in another way as well. Prior to 6-4, the way had seemed open, in American eyes at least, to a gradual, step-by-step liberalization of the PRC political system via leadership by reform-minded leaders like Hu Yaobang, Zhao Ziyang, and perhaps even Deng Xiaoping himself. Modernization theory, immensely influential in the United States, had linked increased standards of living plus increased social

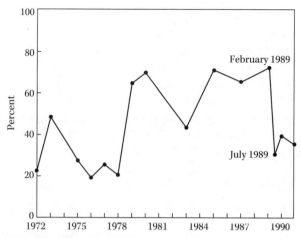

FIGURE 17-1 **Positive US perceptions of China**

Source: Harry Harding, *A Fragile Relationship: The United States and China since 1972*, (Brookings Institution: Washington, D.C., 1992), p. 372.

complexity to transition to democracy. China in the 1980s seemed to be on the right course. The experiences of the other East Asian modernizers, Taiwan and South Korea, seemed to give additional confirmation that developmental authoritarianism would lead first to liberalization and then to democracy. There was a lot of romanticism mixed in with the popular pre-6-4 American notion that China would gradually progress under enlightened CCP tutelage to liberal democracy.[17] Yet these were powerful US perceptions that were deflated by the Beijing Massacre.

The CCP's choice of military repression on 6-4, combined with the purge of top liberal leaders like Zhao Ziyang and several of his key followers, plus the anathema placed on "bourgeois liberalism," created for the United States the prospect of long-term coexistence with an authoritarian and dictatorial, but also increasingly powerful, PRC. In a way, the events of 1989 set in motion a new dynamic in PRC-US relations: an authoritarian, one-party dictatorship living in an era of global democratic revolution found itself threatened by the democratic confidence of the United States. Meanwhile, an ever more powerful anti-democratic state would appear steadily more threatening to the democratic powers. It would take two decades for Chinese power to exacerbate this fear, but once that occurred, a profound sense of American unease over the future of Chinese power would ensue. China's besieged Leninist state found deeply threatening the task of surviving in a unipolar world dominated by America with its strong sense of democratic mission and standing at the head of a broad coalition of democracies. In retrospect, the Beijing Massacre was a turning point that took China away from genuine partnership with the United States toward mutual suspicion, rivalry, and occasional confrontation.

The US Strategy of "Peaceful Evolution"

Within China, the Beijing Massacre produced a powerful need to relegitimize CCP rule among China's youth, intellectuals, and the urban populace. The result was a protracted ideological struggle waged by the CCP's propaganda apparatus against the dangerously attractive ideas of "bourgeois liberalism" that challenged the CCP dictatorship. According to this new propaganda line, the events in Beijing had been part of a US-led Western strategy to subvert and overthrow China's Communist Party in order to cast China once again into a condition of weakness such as had been its lot before 1949. This imperative of regime survival via protracted ideological struggle would lead to association of liberal ideas with Western aggression against China. To accept liberal ideas about such matters as the CCP's monopoly on state power was to support and participate in Western aggression against China. Liberal beliefs were, in fact, a sort of treason to China. This required the demonization of the West, and especially the United States, in China's media and educational systems.

The CCP's propaganda struggle against "bourgeois liberalism" and "peaceful evolution" transformed Western actions intended to express empathy with China and its people into malevolent actions intended to injure China. But deeper, more subtle psychological forces were at work too. As Lucian Pye explained in 1968, a key aspect of Chinese nationalism is a desire to be respected by the international community. In 1989, as had often been the case before, China's internal political arrangements (in this case, the violence of the June 1989 repression) denied China the respect its people craved. In a sense, responsibility for China's loss of face was due to China's own domestic shortcomings. Yet recognition of this was difficult, because it called into question the core Chinese idea that China deserved to be respected. If China's internal politics were indeed anachronistic (i.e., autocratic rule by an unelected elite), it might not deserve the respect patriotic Chinese deeply desired. Rather than recognize that China's own failure to live up to modern political norms was at the root of foreign opprobrium of China's political ways, it was much easier psychologically for Chinese to attribute criticism of China to foreign anti-China motives.[18]

On June 1, shortly before the decision to authorize use of all necessary means to achieve swift PLA control of Tiananmen Square, a report prepared by the MSS at the direction of Li Peng and sent to all members of the Politburo framed the challenge faced by the CCP in terms of a systematic offensive waged by the Western capitalist countries against all socialist countries.[19] The "Western capitalist countries headed by the United States" were seeking to overthrow China's CCP government, the report stated. "Each American administration" had aimed at "overthrowing the Communist Party and sabotaging the socialist system" in China because it was a "big socialist country," the MSS report said. The "phraseology" used by various US administrations

might vary, but the essence remained the same: "to cultivate so-called democratic forces within socialist countries and to stimulate and organize political
opposition using catchwords like 'democracy,' 'liberty,' or 'human rights.'"
"These people also try to win over and split off wavering elements within
the Party in hopes of fomenting peaceful evolution inside the Party, thereby
causing . . . changes in the nature of political power in our socialist state."[20] All
US presidents had pursued "ideological and cultural infiltration of socialist
countries," the MSS report stated. Following the failure of military encirclement and economic blockade in the 1950s and 1960s, the United States moved
"to avail itself of China's reform and opening to carry out spiritual infiltration of China through economic and cultural exchange." In other words, the
appeal of liberal ideas to many Chinese was a manifestation of US hostility
toward the CCP and its state, the PRC.

The United States used many means to carry out "spiritual infiltration,"
according to the MSS report. The United States sent professors to Chinese
universities; 162 US professors had taught at twenty-four major Chinese universities between 1979 and 1989, the report said. Even larger numbers of visiting
scholars were sent to give lectures. "The purpose of [this] is clear," according
to the report: "spiritual and ideological infiltration." Religious missionaries
were sent in the guise of teachers, doctors, or businessmen. Their goal was to
"turn Chinese students into 'new modern people with a different belief system.'" Voice of American (VOA) radio broadcasts were a "major channel" for
political and ideological infiltration into socialist countries. VOA used music,
English-language lessons, and programs introducing American life to "be-
witch the Chinese audience" and get them to accept the American viewpoint.
The US government gave money to various Chinese universities to support
"American studies institutes" for the same purpose.

The International Visitor Program through which the US government
brought to the US "young [Chinese] people who are in power or who are
soon likely to move into power" was a way of influencing China's evolution.
US leaders saw this as a "strategic" and "long-term investment." The United
States was also extending "feelers to the top Chinese leadership by every possible means," homing in on leaders affiliated with reform institutions. The
US embassy had "frequent contact with more than twenty people" at these
Chinese institutions. "The United States believes that the education, experience, and ways of thinking of these people will come to have a subtle but
strong influence on the highest Chinese leadership and decisionmaking bodies," the MSS report said. George Soros, who was active in funding proreform
activities in Hungary, was giving extensive funding to research on reform in
China. By May 1989, Soros had wired $2.5 million to China to promote insti-
tutions associated with Zhao Ziyang, the MSS report asserted.[21]

Western scholars, students and journalists were all part of "ideological and
political infiltration by U.S.-led international forces," according to the MSS

report. Western journalists were "aggressively collecting" information and "spreading it" to the "whole world." They were working overtime to depict the student struggle as heroic, thereby inflaming and encouraging the students. "US personnel and organizations" like the Committee on Scholarly Communications with the People's Republic of China, led by Princeton University professor Perry Link, were maintaining close contact with student movement leaders. Organizations in the United States were facilitating telephone and fax exchange between proreform Chinese student organizations in the United States and student movements at Chinese universities. The MSS report also raised the specter of Western military intervention to help China's antigovernment forces topple the CCP. The MSS reported that a "China Study Group" of the US Department of State had recommended in a May 1989 report that the United States prepare to provide weapons to China's floating population in order to create an antigovernment armed force.[22]

On June 2, the day after the MSS report was delivered to Politburo members, the very senior but elderly party leaders that Deng had edged out of power and replaced by younger, more reform-minded leaders in the 1980s, a group known as "the elders," met to discuss the increasingly tense situation. Deng had eased these "elders" out of active leadership as part of his leadership reforms of the first decade of reform, but brought them back to active leadership as he mobilized elite support for use of necessary force to repress the challenge to party authority. As the elders met, movement of PLA forces to Tiananmen Square to implement martial law was being blocked by demonstrations involving hundreds of thousands of Beijing citizens, and the question to be decided was whether to authorize use of "all necessary force" to achieve swift military occupation of the square. After hearing Li Peng reprise the MSS report and hearing similar reports by Beijing Party Secretary Li Ximing and Mayor Chen Xitong, the elders vented their anger. Li Xiannian—who along with Deng Xiaoping and Chen Yun was one of the three most senior elders—put the situation this way:

> The account that Comrade Li Peng just gave us shows quite clearly that Western capitalism really does want to see turmoil in China. And not only that; they'd also like to see turmoil in the Soviet Union and all the socialist countries of Eastern Europe. The United States, England, France, Japan, and some other Western counties are leaving no stone unturned in pushing peaceful evolution in the socialist counties. They've got a new saying about "fighting a smokeless world war." We had better watch out. Capitalism still wants to beat socialism in the end. None of their plots—using weapons, atomic bombs, and hydrogen bombs—ever succeeded in the past. Now they're turning to the Dulles thing. [Peaceful evolution] We can't do anything about other countries, but we have to control things in China. China can't do without

socialism.... The bottom line of this turmoil is extremely clear: Its bottom line is death to our Party and state.[23]

Deng Xiaoping seconded Li Xiannian:

> Comrade Xiannian is correct. The causes of this incident have to do with the global context. The Western world, especially the United States, has thrown its entire propaganda machine into agitation work and has given a lot of encouragement and assistance to the so-called democrats or opposition in China.... This is the root of the chaotic situation we face today. When the West stirs up turmoil in other countries, in fact it is playing power politics—hegemonism—and is only trying to control those other countries to pull into its power sphere countries that were previously beyond its control.... What they're really after is our sovereignty.... If the turmoil keeps going, it could continue until Party and state authority are worn out.[24]

The situation was clear; the CCP's rule over China was under siege by Chinese demanding freedom and democracy under the systematic instigation of the United States and other Western countries.

The Turn to Patriotic Education

Shortly after 6-4, Deng concluded that the biggest mistake he and the CCP had made since 1978 was inadequate attention to the ideological education of China's youth. The key theme that had to be taught to China's youth, Deng said, was how China had been humiliated by the foreign imperialist powers in the old days before 1949.[25] Following Deng's directive, CCP authorities soon mandated a curriculum of patriotic and national defense education to inoculate young Chinese against peaceful evolution by "Western capitalist powers led by the United States." The crux of the patriotic education curriculum was the narrative of China's victimization by predatory imperialist powers. Within a few years, this campaign gained traction and helped prepare the ground for the new nationalism that arose in China a few years later in the mid-1990s.

In March 1991, Secretary General Jiang Zemin put Deng's conclusion into a policy directive to the educational and propaganda systems outlining the content of the new patriotic education campaign. Four themes were to be stressed, according to Jiang.

1) The 100 years of bullying and humiliation of China by foreign powers
2) The bitter but widespread struggle of Chinese against foreign aggression

3) The social movement that gave rise to and then which was led by the CCP ended China's humiliation; China has stood up and cannot again be bullied; and

4) Chinese always oppose foreign aggression and never fears brutal foreign forces.

The purpose of the campaign was to reintroduce to youth born since 1949 the bitterness and shame of pre-1949 China—as interpreted by the CCP. The conclusion drawn by the campaign was that the CCP was the bearer of China's historic struggle for national independence. Without the CCP in command, China would be weak, divided, and humiliated, as it was before 1949. With the CCP in charge, China was strong and getting steadily stronger. Implicit was the idea that the world was full of strong powers hostile to China and, because of their hostility, set on undermining the CCP.

In August 1991, China's National Education Commission issued a General Outline for the new Patriotic Education curriculum for high schools.[26] A new course was to be required, of three hours per week, for a total of ninety-nine hours over two semesters. "History education reform is China's fundamental strategy to defend against the peaceful evolution plot of international hostile powers," the Outline informed school administrators. "Strengthening education on China's [pre-1949] history and national conditions is of strategic significance," the outline said.[27] By 1992, new textbooks had been published. Material from the high school patriotic education curriculum was also liberally incorporated into the national college admission exam, including the exam for people applying for science and engineering majors. This ensured that the material would be carefully studied by all youth aspiring to higher education.

Another component of the CCP's Patriotic Education campaign was establishment of "patriotic education bases" commemorating and teaching about salient events in the CCP's narrative of national humiliation and redemption. Following Jiang Zemin's March 1991 directive, the CCP Propaganda Department issued a directive calling for the exploitation of historical relics for purposes of patriotic education. Museums and memorials were to be established by local governments for this purpose. On-site education at these "bases" was to parallel classroom instruction. Indeed, on-site education was in some ways superior to classroom instruction, the Propaganda Department directive said. Thousands of memorials and museums marking various Japanese, British, Russian, or American transgressions against China were set up across China in response to these top-level calls. In 1995, the Ministry of Civil Affairs announced the selection of 100 national-level Patriotic Education Bases. These 100 sites would receive central funding, and would serve as models for local-level patriotic education bases. These model bases are listed in Figure 17-2. Two-thirds of the sites commemorate China's wars.

Category	Subject
External Conflicts (40 sites)	Anti–Japanese War, 1931–1945 (20 sites)
	Opium Wars, 1839–1842 and 1856–1860 (7 sites)
	Korean War, 1950–1953 (4 sites)
	Russian invasion, 1898 (1 site)
	China–India War, 1962 (1 site)
	War with Dutch over Taiwan, 1662 (1 site)
	Invasion by the Eight Nation Alliance, 1899–1901 (1 site)
	other general anti–imperialist museums/sites (5 sites)
Civil Wars (24 sites)	Civil wars between CCOP and KMT, 1927–1949
Myths (21 sites)	Wonders of ancient civilization and architecture (15 sites)
	Relics for prehistoric civilization (4 sites)
	Great achievements afte 1949 (2 sites)
Heroes (15 sites)	Chinese Communist Party Leaders (7 sites)
	Model Workers (4 sites)
	Patriots (4 sites)

FIGURE 17-2 **The Hundred National-Level Patriotic Education Bases**

Source: Zheng Wang, *Never Forget National Humiliation: Historical Memory in Chinese Politics and Foreign Relations,* (Columbia University Press: New York, 2012), p. 105.

Provinces established their own Patriotic Education Bases. Some provinces set up Leading Groups to promote this work. Visits to Patriotic Education Bases were organized by party branches in schools, work units, and military units. Local governments were directed to use legal holidays to carry out Patriotic Education activity such as visits to appropriate Patriotic Education Bases. The mass media also mobilized patriotic sentiments. Newspapers initiated special columns on historic patriotic themes. Increased number of television shows and movies with approved patriotic themes were produced. China's wars—the Opium War, the war against Japan, Korea—were popular themes. Attendance at these movies was organized by party branches as part of their Patriotic Education duties. Several ministries jointly published a recommended list of 100 best patriotic songs, 100 best films, and 100 best patriotic education books.

Propaganda campaigns of this sort are a forte of Leninist systems. Party branches in units organize appropriate activities that they then report to higher levels of the party. Those reports become part of the personal dossier of that party cadre. Effective accomplishment of centrally directed activities win kudos for a party member, increasing their chances of promotion to higher levels of the party apparatus.[28] An ordinary citizen would thus hear the same theme repeated from a variety of sources: in newspapers, on television, in movies, in books, from teachers in school classes, in speeches, statements, and slogans by party and government leaders, even in scholarly journals. Quite possibly, an individual would not encounter information challenging the politically correct interpretations. It thus became easy for people to conclude that the narrative they constantly heard was the way things actually had been, and were. The message of CCP propaganda became for them the truth.

Regarding the content of the campaign of "Patriotic Education," a "Dictionary of Patriotic Education" published in 1991 provided a "compete and systematic reference" for use by "educational workers of all sorts" and "propaganda workers" in party organizations and factories. It defined "peaceful evolution" thus:

> A strategic plan in which imperialist countries use methods other than war to achieve internal transformation of socialist countries. The existence of socialist countries in the world poses a severe challenge to the existence and development of capitalism. Therefore, capitalist forces will always use subversion to exterminate socialist countries and the socialist system.[29]

"Peaceful evolution" was a type of "smokeless world war" in which capitalism was trying to destroy socialism. Methods used included military pressure, ideological infiltration, seduction via economic cooperation, flying the human rights banner, and developing pro-Western forces within China. The goal was to cause socialist China to join the capitalist system.

How accurate was (and is) this vision of a long-term US strategy to undermine and ultimately overthrow China's CCP government? There is no evidence of US strategy to overthrow the CCP government or the PRC state itself. Authoritative periodic statements of US national security policy, Asian policy, and China policy consistently indicate that, since 1972, the US objective vis-à-vis the PRC has been to cooperate in areas of common interest as part of a broader effort to build a basically cooperative and friendly relationship. This finding is bolstered by the memoirs of dozens of US presidents, cabinet secretaries, national security advisors and ambassadors who also depict the US objective toward CCP-ruled China as a quest for cooperation. This conclusion is bolstered further by a half dozen studies of US China policy by reputable scholars who have delved into the histories and archives of that policy and found there essentially the same quest for cooperation with the PRC.

But that is only part of the picture. There is abundant evidence that US policies have sought and still seek to nudge China, slowly and gradually, toward liberalization and eventually democracy. When testifying before congressional committees to request funding for radio broadcasts or exchange programs with China, or justifying expanded trade with China, heads of executive agencies have frequently advanced these justifications. When leaders of liberal democratic countries decided to financially support exchanges of journalists, scholars, or aspiring young leaders, or to support "bewitching" radio broadcasts into China, dissemination of liberal democratic values was—and remains, this author submits—one of the motives for that financial support. It is also safe to say that most US leaders and officials hope that these and a myriad other interactions will, over time, lead toward China's evolution in the direction of a more liberal and democratic political system. Contrary to the MSS's assertion and later CCP propaganda, US leaders harboring such hopes did not imagine that this would make China weak or divided. More typically, they imagined it would make China more stable and stronger, as well as more attractive to the world—and eventually a better, closer, and less prickly diplomatic partner for the United States. China's political liberalization would, Americans generally imagined, increase, not diminish, China's status in the world. But they certainly did imagine that the CCP would eventually have to give up its monopoly on political power.

There is also fragmentary evidence that United States policy did, in fact, undertake covert operation to encourage China's gradual "peaceful evolution" towards liberal, democratic capitalism. According to the deputy chief of China operations in the Central Intelligence Agency in the early 1970s, that agency then operated a covert action program designed to co-opt Chinese intellectuals who were disenchanted by the excesses of the Cultural Revolution and open to ideas of democracy and market economics.[30] These operations were, apparently, conducted not inside China but in Chinese communities in Southeast Asia, North America, and Europe. But as China opened and vastly expanded the scope of freedom available to individual Chinese after 1978, it is not unlikely that similar, but probably expanded, programs would have been implemented.

US nongovernmental organizations also became quite active in China in the 1980s. Some of these were, in fact, devoted to bringing about political liberalization and democratization. One such was the organization supported by the immensely wealthy international financier George Soros. Soros was a major financier of anticommunist groups in East Europe. In the early 1980s, he supported Poland's underground Solidarity union. Soros' activities in Poland were, in fact, part of a mosaic of subversive anti-communist activities by the AFL-CIO and the Catholic Church, as well as the CIA. In 1984, Soros set up an Open Society Institute in Hungary with a budget of $3 million that, among other things, supported study at Western universities. Later, Soros supported Czechoslovakia's Charter 77, which became a germ seed of that country's reform movement. All of these efforts played a significant role in the emergence of civil society in these countries, contributing significantly to the 1989 revolutions.

Soros pursued similar activities in China. In 1987, Soros apparently took advantage of the relatively liberal atmosphere in China at the time and hired dissident writer Liang Heng to work with Chen Yizi, the head of the Research Institute for Reform of the Economic Structure under the State Council, to set up an office of Soros' Open Society Foundation in Beijing.[31] Chen Yizi was an economist, and his Research Institute served Zhao Ziyang's reform efforts. The proposed foundation was to be dedicated to promoting international exchanges and greater openness in government. The Soros–Chen Yizi link-up was approved by Zhao Ziyang's secretary Bao Tong, but rejected by a higher-level meeting where conservatives came armed with an elaborate dossier about Soros' anticommunist activities and putative CIA links. Zhao Ziyang in turn overrode this conservative move, but addressed conservative concerns by shifting the institutional sponsor for the Institute from Chen's institute to the International Cultural Exchange Center, which was part of the state security system. After 6-4, Soros' Institute and other organizations like it were shut down. Chen Yizi made his way clandestinely to Hong Kong and then to exile in the United States. Bao Tong was arrested shortly before 6-4, when Zhao Ziyang resigned his offices. Bao was among the highest-ranking officials purged after 6-4. Imprisoned till 1996, he has been held under close state supervision since then, but continues to press for political reform.

The notion that US students, professors, journalists, missionaries, and nongovernmental organizations—and even more, "Western" but non-US journalists, students, and governments—were agents of a US strategy of regime change is questionable. Such a proposition reflects deep and perhaps deliberate ignorance of how pluralistic Western societies, and relations between allied Western governments, work. Yet even here there were elements of truth in the MSS vision. Most US citizens, along with those of most other Western liberal democracies, did ardently believe that liberal democratic values and institutions were better than those of Leninist one-party dictatorship. Citizens of those democratic countries had waged centuries-long struggles to plant liberty and democracy in their own homelands, and did indeed cherish these things, at least by a large majority. In the twentieth century, citizens of democratic polities waged a seventy-year-long philosophical and political struggle against communist tyranny. Mainstream opinion in liberal democratic countries *did* believe that Marxism-Leninism would and should someday be discarded, even in China, where the Chinese people would someday step into the modern, enlightened world of freedom and democracy. Given these views, it likely that most US students, professors, missionaries, journalists, and businessmen, along with those of other Western countries, who went to China in the decade after 1978 probably did disseminate liberal democratic values and ideas in their own discrete and idiosyncratic ways.

At the broadest level, interaction with liberal democracies did, and does, undermine the CCP monopoly on political power. China's interaction with capitalist democracies is required for China's economic development, but carries strong challenges to CCP rule. Inoculating the Chinese people against "American" and "Western" ideals and arguments by attributing nefarious motives to those ideas was the first step in waging what Li Peng called a "long-term protracted political struggle" against "Western spiritual and ideological infiltration." Part of that struggle is the maintenance of the image of the United States as a power hostile to China.

The Post 6-4 Debate Over Regime Survival and Pullback from "Opening"

The bloody events of 6-4 produced deep divisions within the CCP regarding opening, reform, and the survival of China's proletarian state.[32] It seemed to many within the CCP elite that China's post-1978 opening had made possible the linkup between domestic and international counterrevolution. Marketization of the economy had produced inflation, growing unemployment, the disintegration of the social welfare net, growing economic insecurity, and the juxtaposition of new and sometimes great wealth and continuing poverty. Foreign investment and loss of control over foreign activities inside China had facilitated the spread of bourgeois ideas. The growth of market forces and withering of state control over the economy had also made available to dissidents such resources as photocopiers, fax machines and paper, public address equipment, camping tents—the latter made available for use by students on hunger strike in Tiananmen Square as a gift of people in Hong Kong. To protect China's proletarian state, influential voices within the PRC said, the CCP should reinstitute a modified command, planned economy. Market-based businesses were a sector in which "peaceful evolution" placed great hopes, and should therefore be closely watched and limited. In terms of opening, China should pull away from the global economy—not completely, perhaps, but to the degree necessary to prevent Western ideological subversion and party loss of control. Contacts between China and advanced capitalist economies needed to be more tightly controlled, more closely supervised, and used in ways that did not undermine the CCP center's ability to direct the overall economy. Westerners in China and Chinese studying in the West should be tightly vetted and carefully watched, CCP rightists said. Chinese access to Western media and Western media access to China should be tightly limited and controlled. Foreign capital should be excluded from essential sectors, and the state should maintain control over the essential sectors of the economy. Some rightists went even further. Deng Liqun, for example, maintained that the policies being implemented during the 1980s amounted to "the restoration of capitalism," which Mao had warned and struggled against. If this were the case, renewed class struggle to prevent the restoration of capitalism might be in order.

Paramount leader Deng Xiaoping believed that retreat from marketizing reform and deepening integration with the world economy was tantamount to the suicide of China's CCP state. Conservative policies would lead to economic stagnation and shortages in the supply of goods available to China's people. It was the increasing abundance of such goods due to China's post-1978 opening and reform that had allowed the CCP to survive the 1989 challenge while communist parties in Eastern Europe and the Soviet Union failed. If the CCP now retreated from opening and reform, Deng insisted, that was the road to regime collapse. From June 1989 to early 1992, conservative voices within the elite prevailed. Eventually, in 1992, Deng would wage what scholar Ezra Vogel called his "last battle," mobilizing pro-opening and reform forces to launch China boldly in that direction.

The underlying difference between Deng Xiaoping and his conservative opponents had to do with how best to ensure the survival of the CCP regime. Deng argued that delivering continued rapid increases in living standards was the only way the CCP regime could survive. Opening to the West and reform via markets were the key to rapid improvement in living standards, he believed. Socialist CCP-ruled China, therefore, had to continue to draw on the capital, technology, know-how, and export markets of the advanced capitalist countries, the West. If China once again closed itself off from the outside world, the result would be, as in Europe, collapse and extinction for the Chinese Communist Party regime.[33]

One of the sharpest and most humorous statements of the pro-opening point of view came in a defense of the Shenzhen Special Economic Zone by Vice Premier Tian Jiyun in April 1992. From the standpoint of CCP rightists, the SEZs were conduits for Western subversion and infiltration which should be closed down or at least tightly regulated. This led Tian to propose that special zones be organized along lines of China's pre-1978 policies and that traditional Marxists be invited to live in those zones. Tian suggested:

> Let us carve out a piece of land where policies favored by the leftists [i.e., conservatives] will be practiced. For example, no foreign investment will be allowed here, and all foreigners will be kept out. Inhabitants of the zone can neither go abroad or send their children overseas. There will be total state planning. Essential supplies will be rationed and citizens of the zones will have to queue up for food and other consumer products.[34]

Comments by Deng Xiaoping in the immediate aftermath of the Beijing Massacre gave credence to the hard-line view of a linkup between domestic and foreign counterrevolutionary forces. In a speech on June 9, 1989, Deng referred to the June "storm" as a product of an international macro-climate and a domestic micro-climate. A week later, he elaborated: "The entire imperialist Western world plans to make all socialist countries discard the socialist road and then bring them under the control of international monopoly capital and onto the capitalist road."[35] Rightist leaders seized on Deng's comments to push for a campaign against what they deemed the Western strategy of peaceful evolution. Ties with the United States were extremely dangerous, these rightists said. In response, China should seek to reorient its opening away from the United States and the West, toward the Third World plus the socialist countries of Eastern Europe.[36]

Deng saw the hard-line confrontational approach as a serious threat to China's opening. He countered by advancing two "basic points." First, the threat from Peaceful Evolution was a long-term one targeting future generations. It was not an immediate threat. As long as veteran revolutionaries like Deng and his fellow elders were alive, hostile foreign forces could be held in check. Second, the threat was essentially internal, not external. "The crucial factor was the ideological firmness of CCP members," Deng ruled. "If something wrong occurs in China, it will come from within the Party." As Allen Whiting noted, this formulation shifted responsibility for the 1989 uprising from the "international climate" to the "domestic climate."[37] Following this assessment, early in 1992 Deng edited out references to "peaceful evolution" in a draft of Premier Li Peng's work report to an NPC session. The same month, Deng ordered Xinhua to avoid harsh criticism of the United States:

> We should adopt a "careful and positive" policy, and report well on bilateral relations and exchanges between China and the United States. . . . As for U.S. words and deeds interfering in our internal affairs and harming our sovereignty . . . we should expose this. But we should carry out a reasonable, beneficial, restrained struggle, and not use phrases such as "Western hostile forces headed by the United States."[38]

A turning point in the struggle over "peaceful evolution" and opening apparently came in a series of Politburo meetings in February 1992, just after Deng's "southern tour" in which he highlighted the successes of south China's opening and reform, along with his own firm support for that approach. Thirty-five conservative party leaders had reportedly sent Deng a letter urging vigorous opposition to "peaceful evolution," indoctrination of communist ideology, and limitation of reform to those of a socialist (i.e., nonmarket and non–private sector) nature. Deng went all out and mobilized support to decisively reject this conservative proposal. General Secretary Jiang Zemin, who had earlier kept one foot in the conservative camp, came down squarely in support of Deng. Jiang and Yang Shangkun made self-criticisms for earlier inadequately firm support for opening. A solid majority of the Politburo lined up behind Deng. Several high-ranking Politburo members who had previously opposed Deng's approach shifted position and began openly supporting Deng and his approach.[39] China would not again close itself off. Deng had won over the civilian leadership. His next challenge would be from the PLA.

The Diplomacy of Damage Control

Differing Conceptions of Human Rights and State Sovereignty

The CCP decision in 1989 to employ military force against unarmed civilian protesters was strongly at variance with norms of state sovereignty that had evolved in the West over several centuries. Beginning with the American and French revolutions and the Enlightenment philosophies that underpinned those two upheavals, Western thinkers had embraced the notion that citizens possessed certain rights, "natural rights" they were then called, that transcended and limited state sovereignty. Gradually, the older seventeenth-century notion that the sovereignty of rulers was absolute within their specified territories was conditioned by the expectation that the ruler's sovereign powers would be exercised with due respect for the natural rights of individual citizens. These changes were linked to the transfer of the locus of sovereignty from the person of the monarch to the people of a nation, ideas associated most powerfully with the French Revolution. These ideas of conditional sovereignty were well established by the early twentieth century, but were greatly reinforced after 1945, when the peoples of the world, and especially of Europe, confronted the monstrous nature of the Nazi Holocaust, much of which took place under laws and decrees promulgated by sovereign states. The Nuremberg Tribunal institutionalized legal norms that state sovereignty did not empower violation of basic "human rights," as natural rights had come to be called.[1]

China, in contrast, was not shaken by the ideas of the Enlightenment and the American and French revolutions—at least not until the late nineteenth century, when Chinese thinkers began to conclude that China's survival required a new culture. Even then, China's trauma of humiliation at Western and Japanese hands led most Chinese to conclude that China needed a powerful, even absolutist, state that could unite and develop the country. Most Chinese patriots concluded that a strong central state was necessary to "save China."[2] The Marxist-Leninist variant of this strong-state preference went even further in subordinating individual rights to the state. Nor did Marxism-Leninism put particular stress on sovereignty. The key stress of Marxism-Leninism was on internationalism and solidarity among the oppressed laboring classes of all countries.

Developments in international legal norms associated with post–World War II decolonization strengthened PRC attempts to employ strong sovereignty norms in self-defense after 6-4. There emerged during the post-1945 period a legal philosophy that saw sovereignty as a defense of weak and poor non-Western states against the predations of the rich and powerful Western states. As scores of new states emerged during the post-1945 breakdown of the globe-spanning European empires in Asia, Africa, and Oceania, these often weak emerging nations, as they were then called, adopted norms of state sovereignty akin in many ways to the older concept of absolute sovereignty. These new and weak states did this to help protect their impoverished and often disunited nations from pressure by more powerful Western states. Previously, sovereignty norms had largely upheld the rights of major powers—concluding treaties, upholding legal rights, waging war, and such. Now norms of defensive sovereignty became a defense of weak non-Western states against powerful Western ones. The United Nations and its agencies were key mechanisms of norm creation of this new tradition of defensive sovereignty, sometimes dubbed the "revolt of the non-West."[3]

Beijing seized on and utilized this postcolonial revolution in international sovereignty norms in its defense against post-6-4 Western criticism. The philosophy and practice of defensive sovereignty was quite well developed by 1989, and the CCP grabbed this ready-made tradition to help fend off Western criticism. This trope also gave Beijing a ready-made Third World constituency and high moral ground from which to challenge Western charges of PRC human rights abuses. Before 6-4, Beijing had given occasional nods to these Third World defensive sovereignty norms as part of the anti-hegemony struggle, but it had not felt compelled to embrace them for its own defense. After June 1989, however, defensive sovereignty norms became a key arrow in the CCP's arsenal of self-defense. Well-intentioned Western sympathy for the struggle of the Chinese people for their intrinsic human rights was thus transformed into arrogant Western interference for malevolent purposes.

The Western Response to the Beijing Massacre

Widespread and strong Western criticism of the Beijing massacre erupted almost before silence fell over Beijing on June 4. That very day, President George H. W. Bush expressed "deep regret" over the Chinese government's decision to use force to suppress the peaceful protest movement. The US government had consistently urged the Chinese government to use nonviolent means to resolve the confrontation in Beijing, and regretted when this was not done. Most US allies followed suit. It would be a mistake to conclude that other Western countries were merely responding to US expectations. They were acting, rather, on the basis of the Enlightenment norms of conditional state sovereignty. Embrace of those norms was, after all, an important part of the Western struggle for individual freedom over many decades. Thus, British Prime Minister Margaret Thatcher expressed shock and indignation over the killing of unarmed civilians. French President Francois Mitterrand froze high-level contacts with China and expressed the view that a government that fired on its country's youth had no future. West German Chancellor Helmut Kohl expressed shock and outrage, saying that it was simply impermissible for states to fire on their own citizens.[4] Even Brazil departed from its long-standing practice of not commenting on the internal affairs of other countries to condemn the bloodshed in Beijing.

Sanctions gave substance to declarations of protest. On June 5, President Bush, responding to popular anger, ordered the temporary suspension of arms sales to China, the suspension of military exchanges, and the review of bilateral agreements. A short while later, the United States announced it would waive visa requirements to allow the 45,000 PRC students then studying in the United States to remain in the United States after completing their studies. The United States also announced it would oppose new loans to China by multilateral institutions such as the World Bank and the Asia Development Bank, and urged other countries to follow suit. Japan changed the status of China's exports from general to special, requiring approval on a case-by-case basis. Tokyo also suspended aid to China, freezing a large loan. Other sanctions were announced by Belgium, Portugal, Austria, Greece, the Netherlands, Denmark, Finland, Sweden, and Switzerland.[5]

Deng Xiaoping had greatly underestimated the negative international impact of the use of military force in Beijing. Shortly before 6-4, Deng had told his Politburo comrades that international negative reaction to the use of military force to re-establish control would last a mere few months and then dissipate. In fact, the moral onus of the Beijing Massacre would continue to nag China for decades.

The Beijing Massacre threatened to have disastrous consequences for the reversion of Hong Kong to Chinese sovereignty scheduled for 1997. The ongoing discussions between Britain and China over the modalities for reversion were thrown into disarray, leaving an array of crucial issues in abeyance, such as building and paying for a new airport and the inclusion in the Basic Law of the right of labor to strike and protest. Most people in Hong Kong were refugees from communist rule in China, or the descendants of such refugees, and 6-4 touched on many negative memories, raising fears that China's new hard-line leadership would dismantle Hong Kong's free economic and social system after reversion. There had been strong support in Hong Kong for China's democracy movement, and that sympathy changed into anger when it was crushed by the PLA. In the weeks after 6-4, the Hong Kong stock market lost billions of dollars in value. Real estate values fell precipitously. A huge amount of money was withdrawn from Hong Kong banks.[6] People were liquidating assets and preparing to flee. Long lines formed at foreign consulates as people applied for visas. Moreover, Beijing's key man in Hong Kong, Xu Jiatun, the director of the Xinhua News Agency in Hong Kong and head of the CCP's Hong Kong and Macao Work Committee, resigned in opposition to the resort to military force in Beijing and fled to the United States in December 1989. There was a sense in Hong Kong that China's new leaders, Jiang Zemin and Li Peng, were taking China away from opening and reform, raising grave questions about Hong Kong's return to China. Several major Hong Kong projects (a new airport and a container harbor) had been associated with Premier Zhao Ziyang, and after he was purged, there was a sense that Beijing was no longer interested in projects associated with the now-discredited Zhao. If Hong Kong's economy collapsed, with a flight of capital and talent, it would be a devastating blow to Guangdong and its vanguard role in China's opening.

The Architect of China's Post 6-4 Rehabilitation: Qian Qichen

During the turbulent decade between 1988 and 1998, Qian Qichen served as China's Minister of Foreign Affairs. During that period, Qian implemented the guidelines of China's paramount leader Deng Xiaoping, successfully guiding the PRC out of the pariah status it found itself in after 6-4. Qian was a skilled practitioner of low-profile, low-key but hard-bargaining diplomacy. Qian would carry out relatively flexible policies designed to rebuild a cooperative relation with the United States as quickly as possible. In this capacity, Qian repeatedly struck bargains, giving some ground before US pressure on Iraq, Cambodia, and North Korea. This flexibility would make Qian a target of criticism by hardliners, including many in the PLA. By 1995–1996, Qian's relatively conciliatory approach would be pushed aside in favor of confrontational policies much more in line with PLA views. After those hard-line policies carried China into military confrontation with the United States in 1996, Qian would again be called upon to normalize PRC ties with the United States.

Qian was born in Shanghai in 1928. He joined the CCP at the age of fourteen in 1942, when Shanghai along with a large part of China was under Japanese occupation. After the establishment of the PRC, when Qian was twenty-one he was assigned to work with the Communist Youth League (CYL) organization in Shanghai. In 1954, at the age of twenty-six, apparently in recognition of his administrative talents, Qian was sent to Moscow to study at its

CYL school. There, Qian was selected by the CCP organization in charge of Chinese students in Moscow to handle student affairs at the embassy. Qian became fluent in Russian and after completing his studies was assigned to the Chinese embassy in Moscow, where he served from 1955 to 1964. In 1972, after a stint at a May 7th Cadre School during the Cultural Revolution, Qian returned to China's Moscow embassy as a councilor, a position he held for another ten years. When Beijing began exploring rapprochement with Moscow in 1982, Qian was appointed "special emissary" to Moscow, and several years later headed the Chinese delegation to conduct border negotiations with the Soviet Union. When Qian took over as minister of foreign affairs and simultaneously as secretary of the CCP Committee in the MFA in 1988, he had little experience dealing with the United States or Western countries generally. His one posting beyond China or the USSR was several years as ambassador to Guinea in West Africa. Yet the negotiating skills he had learned in dealing with Russian representatives for twenty years proved transferable and served Qian, and China, well. In 1995, Qian added to his portfolio control of Hong Kong's reversion as chair of the Hong Kong Preparatory Committee. There too his efforts served China well by arranging the smooth and stable return of that rich entity to China. The diplomatic accomplishments of Qian's decade-long tutelage of China's foreign affairs are impressive.

Qian's key backer among top CCP leaders was Li Peng. Li had been head of the Chinese Student Association in the Soviet Union during his 1948–1955 study at the Moscow Power Engineering Institute. During the last year of that stay, Qian began study at the Moscow CYL school, and Li Peng got to know him then. Qian had been assigned responsibility for handling embassy matters related to Chinese students studying in the Soviet Union, and would have taken good care of the adopted son of Zhou Enlai, Li Peng.[7] Although Qian and Li were born the same year, 1928, Li's administrative superiority, and more importantly the support for him (as Zhou's adopted son) by elders Deng Xiaoping, Deng Yingchao (Zhou Enlai's wife), Chen Yun, and Peng Zhen, made him Qian's clear superior.

Once back in China, former Soviet-study students periodically got together and formed an informal network of mutual help, and this too brought Li and Qian together. Li Peng was on a fast track to the top. Entering the Central Committee in 1982, he joined the Politburo only three years later, and in 1987 joined the Politburo Standing Committee. Li became premier in April 1988 when Zhao Ziyang was promoted to replace Hu Yaobang as general secretary, and was appointed head of the Foreign Affairs Small Group after Zhao's purge in 1989, making him Qian's boss.[8] Qian repaid Li Peng's assistance over the years by refurbishing his mentor's international reputation after 6-4. In 1990, Qian arranged a flurry of international activity by Li Peng intended to obliterate any idea that Li was some sort of pariah. Qian was very different from Li Peng in terms of personality. Whereas Li tended to be awkward and frequently abrasive with foreigners, Qian had an emollient style, reminiscent, perhaps, of Zhou Enlai. Qian's equanimous personality served his harsher boss well. Within two and a half years, the chief architect of 6-4, Li Peng, would enjoy a public meeting with President Bush and visit a wide array of European capitals.

Turn to the Third World and China's Neighbors

Confronting the wave of condemnation and sanctions following 6-4, China's leaders calculated that they would find a more sympathetic reception among the socialist countries of Eastern Europe and the non-Western developing countries of the Third World. Unfortunately for Beijing, the East European communist regimes were collapsing just as Beijing began courting them. Courtship of the Third World was more successful. Many of these countries had themselves been subject to Western attitudes of moral superiority and interference in their internal affairs. Many of them also embraced norms of defensive sovereignty worked out at the UN General Assembly over the preceding decades. CCP foreign policy advisors were well aware of the new sovereignty norms elaborated by the "revolt of the non-West" over the previous decades, and calculated that arguments cast along these lines would find a warm reception in many Third World capitals. These Chinese calculations were not wrong. China also confronted the possibility that Western countries might seek to use the United Nations to condemn or punish China over human rights. Support by Third World countries would be crucial in preventing that. China had billed itself as a developing country member of the Third World both during the last decade of the Mao era (in the Three Worlds Theory) and under Deng Xiaoping. That identity had not disappeared during the late 1980s, but had been somewhat superseded by the enthusiasm of China's youth and intellectuals for China to join the ranks of the liberal, democratic countries. A deliberate turn back to the Third World would not only rally international support for China in the face of Western ostracism, but would reiterate for China's youth and intelligentsia that "Western values" were inappropriate for China.

In mid-1989 a Politburo directive declared "From now on, China will put more effort on resuming and developing relations with old friends [e.g., Pakistan and North Korea] and Third World countries."[9] A number of high-profile missions quickly reached out to these countries. In July 1989, Qian Qichen visited Botswana, Zimbabwe, Angola, Zambia, Mozambique, and Lesotho, while Deputy Foreign Minister Yang Fuchang visited Senegal, the Ivory Coast, Gambia, Sierra Leone, and Ghana. The leaders of Indonesia, Singapore, Thailand, and Malaysia visited Beijing. In March 1990, Jiang Zemin visited North Korea. In May 1990, Yang Shangkun made the first tour of Latin America by a Chinese president, visiting Mexico, Brazil, Uruguay, Argentina, and Chile. At each stop, Yang lobbied for increased trade and support for Chinese membership in GATT. The same month, Wan Li visited Pakistan. Late in 1990, Qian Qichen visited Egypt, the UAE, Sudan, Iraq, Syria, Saudi Arabia, and Jordan. In January 1991, Qian was back in Africa, visiting Ethiopia, Uganda, Kenya, and Tanzania. The leaders of seven African countries also visited China in 1990.[10] In February and March 1991, the peripatetic Qian Qichen traveled to Portugal, Spain, Poland, Bulgaria, Hungary, Greece, and Malta. This European tour made Qian the first senior PRC official to visit Western Europe since the Beijing Massacre.

Qian also engineered an end to the international ostracizing of Li Peng. As the public face of the Beijing Massacre, Li carried considerable stigma in Western countries. In November and December 1989, he was the first top-level Chinese leader to venture out of China after the Beijing massacre, traveling to Pakistan, Nepal, Bangladesh, Indonesia, Singapore, Thailand, Malaysia, the Philippines, Sri Lanka, and Laos. In April 1990, Qian arranged visits by Li to nine other South and Southeast Asian countries. Li visited India in December 1991. The capstone of Qian's effort to overcome this stigma was a nine-day tour of Italy, Switzerland, Portugal, Spain, and the United States (for a UN session) in January 1992. France declined a request to receive Li, and Portugal tried unsuccessfully to delay Li's visit. Li participated in a UN summit in January along with twelve other world leaders, and was granted a private meeting with President Bush.[11]

Qian also pushed for breakthroughs in relations with important but long-estranged countries. South Korea was an important target of these efforts. Trade and unofficial exchanges between China and South Korea began increasing in the late 1980s as the two outward-looking economies engaged under the principle of separation of politics and economics. Large delegations of Chinese athletics participated in the 1986 Asian Games in Pusan and the 1988 Summer Olympic Games in Seoul—both major steps in South Korea's recognition as a newly industrialized country. In September 1990, South Korea reciprocated China's favor by sending a 553-person team to Beijing to participate in the Asian Olympic Games. Beijing's hosting of the Asian Games was a significant element of China's effort to put behind it the onus of the Beijing Massacre, and Seoul's support in this effort was appreciated. The month after the Asian Games, Beijing and Seoul agreed to set up trade representative offices.[12]

The pace of rapprochement accelerated in 1991. In April, Vice Foreign Minister Liu Huaqiu led a delegation to Seoul for a UN meeting. This was the first ever visit by a high PRC official to South Korea. In September, Qian Qichen and Foreign Trade Minister Li Lanqing visited Seoul to attend an APEC conference. The same month, the two Korean states, the Republic of Korea and the People's Democratic Republic of Korea, simultaneously entered the UN General Assembly. This China-supported development eliminated major obstacles to China–South Korea relations. Shortly after the dual UN entry, the Chinese and South Korean foreign ministers met for the first time at an APEC ministerial session in Seoul. The two countries agreed in August 1992 to establish normal diplomatic ties.

Normalization of ties with South Korea, of course, had an economic logic. Deng's foreign policy line was premised on the expansion of economic cooperation with virtually all countries, regardless of social system or ideology, and over the next decade South Korea would emerge as one of China's most important economic partners. The changes in Sino-Korean relations in 1990–1992 also reflected the thawing wrought by Gorbachev's policies. Beijing no longer faced the risk that PRC ties with South Korea might push North Korea into alignment with Moscow. But in the context of the immediate post-6-4 period, Beijing wanted to lessen chances that South Korea, one of China's neighbors and an ally of the United States, might decide to participate in "peaceful evolution" schemes that might be cooked up by Washington.

China also moved quickly to strengthen ties with neighbors Indonesia, Singapore and India, plus regional powers like Saudi Arabia. Old grievances were quickly shelved in an effort to court new friends that might otherwise drift into alignment with Western anti-China forces. Regarding Indonesia, that powerful country had broken relations with China in 1967 over China's role in the 1965 coup. Since that time, Jakarta had demanded an explicit Chinese disavowal of support for insurgency in Southeast Asia as the sine qua non for normalization of Indonesia-China ties. In February 1989, Qian Qichen and Indonesian President Suharto had met at the funeral for Japan's Emperor Hirohito and decided to move toward normalization of ties. Talks on the "technical issues" related to normalization took place in December 1989, and the two sides apparently found a way around the history issue related to the 1965 coup. Indonesia's foreign minister visited China for further talks in July 1990, which resulted in a joint communiqué on resuming diplomatic relations. The communiqué declared the basis for relations to be the Five Principles of Peaceful Coexistence. One of those was noninterference in each other's internal affairs, and this may have been taken as a Chinese pledge not to repeat things like China's 1965 role. In any case, in August 1990 Li Peng visited Jakarta to preside over the formal renormalization of ties. Three months later, President Suharto's visit to Beijing was the capstone of the normalization process.

Two months after the Indonesia-China normalization communiqué, Singapore followed suit. With its overwhelmingly ethnic Chinese population, and confronting deep regional fears that it might become China's Trojan horse in Southeast Asia, Singapore had long held it would be the last of all the Southeast Asian countries to normalize ties with the PRC. In August 1990, Li Peng paid a formal friendship visit to Singapore. Two months later, Singapore leader Lee Kuan Yew visited Beijing to preside over formal initiation of diplomatic relations.

Chinese diplomatic reassurance of India was difficult because of the depth of the conflicts between those two countries. But even in New Delhi, Qian made gains. In March 1990, Qian visited India for talks on issues of mutual concern. The Five Principles of Peaceful Coexistence, which involved noninterference by Western powers in the internal affairs of developing countries, was a major theme of the talks. India had often been the target of Western criticism over harsh measures toward secessionist movements. Qian also stressed the desire to continue building on the agreements reached during Indian Prime Minister Rajiv Gandhi's breakthrough December 1988 visit to China. Qian signaled that Beijing hoped to settle the chronically festering territorial dispute, a gesture intended to reassure New Delhi.

The most important Chinese gesture toward India during 1989–1990 was what it did *not* do. In March 1989, India had implemented a harsh economic embargo of Nepal because of Kathmandu's initiation of military and security relations with China.[13] Chinese analysts saw India's embargo of Nepal as a manifestation of Indian hegemony and unreasonable targeting of China's friendly, cooperative ties with a South Asian neighbor, Nepal. But fearful that Chinese support for Nepal might drive India into hostility toward China at this sensitive juncture, Beijing essentially left Nepal on its own, without Chinese support. In 1988 Nepal's royal government had begun purchasing weapons from China, and then had signed a secret intelligence exchange agreement with China. Both moves went beyond Indian tolerance for China's role in strategically located Nepal, and New Delhi responded with a year-long economic embargo that had a devastating impact on Nepal's economy. In the midst of Nepal's travail, China did and said little. Chinese coverage of the India-Nepal crisis was low-key and objective. When Vice Premier Wu Xueqian stopped in New Delhi in October 1989, he meekly expressed the hope that the South Asian nations would use the Five Principles of Peaceful Coexistence to manage their relations. When Li Peng visited Kathmandu the next month, in the midst of India's economic coercion of Nepal, he merely lauded Nepal's efforts to cope with unspecified "difficulties." China did not resort to the Security Council, as it easily could have. It did not condemn Indian actions, nor use such terms as "bullying," "hegemony," or "power politics." Chinese economic aid to Nepal continued, but additional aid was minimal. In effect, Beijing stood aside as New Delhi imposed a China-exclusion policy on Nepal. Alienating India in 1989 could have been dangerous. India has a very special and sensitive relation with Tibet, and Tibet was one focus of the new Western human rights concern over China.

The culmination of Beijing's friendship offensive toward India came in December 1991, when Li Peng made the first visit by a Chinese premier to India in thirty-one years. (The previous visit in 1960 had been by Li's adoptive father, Zhou Enlai.) Li, accompanied by the inimitable Qian Qichen, secured Indian agreement that "survival" and "development" were the most important "human rights" for developing countries, and that the two countries would increase cooperation and mutual support and faced common serious challenges. Li and Qian also secured Indian reiteration that India recognized that Tibet was an autonomous region of China, and that India would not permit Tibetans in India to conduct any anti-China political activities.[14] What India received for helping Beijing escape its international opprobrium was not apparent.

In West Asia, Saudi Arabia was a major power. In July 1990, China normalized ties with it. Barely two weeks later, Iraqi forces overran Kuwait at the order of Saddam Hussein. As tension mounted over Iraq's aggression, Beijing sent several envoys to consolidate China's new ties with Riyadh. During his visit to Jakarta in August 1990 to normalize ties with Indonesia, Li Peng took note of and endorsed Saudi Arabia's decision to invite in American military forces to defend the country against a threatened Iraqi attack. "If Saudi Arabia wants to invite US armed forces to help maintain its safety out of security reasons, then we respect the decision of Saudi Arabia," Li said.[15] Li Peng also gave Saudi Arabia a pledge to stop supplying Iraq with arms, especially medium-range ballistic missiles.

With such a vigorous "neighborhood friendship policy" (*mulin youhao zhengce*), Beijing stabilized its periphery while confronting a newly hostile United States, and guarded against the possibility that China's neighbors might take part in, or turn a blind eye to, Western "peaceful evolution" activities operating from their territories.

Opening of relations with South Korea and Singapore cleared the way for those two countries to play important roles in the second state of opening and reform kicked off by Deng Xiaoping in 1992.

Japanese Assistance in "Untying the Knot" of Western Sanctions

Japan played a leading role in shelving post 6-4 sanctions. Japan's sanctions were especially severe, since Japan had emerged during the 1980s as the largest supplier of development assistance to the PRC. Following 6-4, Tokyo suspended a $6.25 billion loan that was to finance projects during China's Eighth Five Year Plan (1991–1995). During fall 1989, Tokyo used the prospect of restarting that loan as leverage to secure the lifting of martial law. Japan's leaders saw themselves as enjoying a special cultural relation with China, closer and therefore more understanding than those of Western leaders with China. Japan was well positioned, its leaders believed, to serve as a bridge between China and the West. Moreover, Japanese leaders envisioned Japan rising to play a leading role in Asia and the world, with a special partnership with China being part of that leading role. Japan had also become the largest provider of development assistance in East Asia, and envisioned China becoming a new partner with Japan. Japan's development trajectory was then still quite rapid, to the extent that many people thought of Japan as a rising number one, whose economy would soon surpass that of even the United States. Japan's growth during the 1980s had slowed from the high rates of the 1960s and 1970s, but the stagnation of the 1990s had yet to set in. Thus, while levying sanctions in the aftermath of 6-4, Japan's leaders believed they should play a leading role in bringing China back into the international community. In line with these considerations, Japan played an important role in facilitating Beijing's dissolution of post-6-4 Western sanctions.

Qian Qichen recognized Japan as "the weak link in the Western united front of sanctioning China."[16] Japan had joined in sanctioning China after 6-4 mainly in order to stay in step with other Western countries, Qian believed. Chinese diplomacy thus encouraged Japan in its desire to play an active role in restoring normal relations between China and other Western countries. In January 1990, Prime Minister Toshiki Kaifu became the first leader of a major industrial democracy to receive a Chinese leader after the Beijing Massacre when he received the head of China's State Planning Commission, Zou Jiahua. Tokyo was sensitive to US criticism, but Kaifu believed that the visit by two US presidential envoys (Brent Scowcroft and Lawrence Eagleburger) to Beijing the previous month would provide cover for an invitation to Zou.[17] In the lead up to Zou's visit, Japanese leaders told Beijing that ending martial law would help normalize the situation. Martial law was lifted in Beijing on January 11, 1990, six days before Zou arrived in Tokyo. This allowed Tokyo to take credit with its Western allies. Zou stayed in Japan for nine days to explain China's policies and call for expanded Sino-Japanese cooperation. China's government was willing to work with Japan for stable, long-term, and deeply rooted friendship between the two nations, Zou told his Japanese hosts. Japan's foreign minister told Zou that Japan's government had "without thought" imposed its own values on China, even though China had a different sort of social system. He hoped for an early restoration of normal ties, the he said.

State councilor Li Tieying went to Osaka for an *ikebana* (flower arrangement) exhibition in June, carrying an "oral letter" for Prime Minister Kaifu. China desired expanded cooperation with Japan; Sino-Japanese relations were "special," Li told Kaifu. "China's government always views the promotion of Sino-Japanese friendship as an important part of China's foreign policy," Li explained. "No matter how the world might change, no matter how much the internal conditions of the two countries might change, Sino-Japanese friendship will continue from generation to generation," Li Tieying said eloquently.[18]

China's friendship offensive toward Japan paid off in July 1990 during the G-7 summit of industrialized democracies convened in Houston, Texas.

Again, US actions provided cover for Tokyo. In late May, President Bush had extended MFN status for China and conveyed his "understanding" for Tokyo's revival of its third yen loan to China.[19] During the Houston G-7 summit, Kaifu announced Japan's decision to resume lending to China. Japan was thus the first member of the G-7 to begin dismantling sanctions imposed after 6-4. Kaifu also urged the other G-7 leaders at Houston to resume aid. Shortly after Kaifu's role at the Houston G-7 summit, a Japanese foreign ministry delegation at the vice-ministerial level arrived in Beijing to inform China that Japan was restarting its government lending to China. This was the highest-ranking Western official to visit China since 6-4. PRC Vice President Wang Zhen expressed gratitude for Kaifu's actions and emphasized the importance of Sino-Japanese friendship for world peace. In December 1990, Tokyo extended to China a new loan of 43 billion yen (about US$320 million) for seventeen major transportation and telecommunications projects.

In August 1991, Kaifu became the first top Western leader to visit Beijing since the Beijing massacre. Kaifu's visit symbolized the full normalization of Sino-Japanese relations—six years before renormalization of Sino-US relations would be achieved. During Kaifu's visit, China announced its willingness to enter the nuclear nonproliferation treaty—an act which atom-bomb-ravaged Japan greatly appreciated. An April 1992 visit by Party chief Jiang Zemin to Japan further prepared the way for an imperial visit. In October, that path-breaking visit finally transpired.

Beijing's post-6-4 friendship offensive toward Japan culminated in October 1992 with the first-ever visit by Japan's emperor to China. World War II–era Emperor Hirohito had died on January 7, 1989, and been succeeded by his son Akihito. When Japan's foreign minister visited Beijing in April 1991, Qian praised Japan's efforts on China's behalf and proposed a visit to China by Emperor Akihito. This was a bold proposal. This visit would, Qian recognized, "break the western prohibition on high-level visits with China." The Japanese side was generally positive toward the notion of an imperial visit.[20] The future of China's relations with the United States was still uncertain. A rupture with the United States was still possible, and in that event, Japan offered a viable alternative as a source of technology and capital. Thus during the imperial visit, Chinese media stressed the positive climate for investment, trade, and regional stability, along with the commonalities of the civilizations. Beijing censored popular demands for Japanese reparations to World War II victims, and did not contest Akihito's relatively vague mea culpa on the history issue: "In the long history of relationship between our two countries, there was an unfortunate period in which my country inflicted great sufferings on the people of China. I deeply deplore this."

Shortly after Akihito's visit, and after Beijing's friendship campaign toward Tokyo had served its purpose, China began to take a far more critical approach to Japan's aspirations to a regional leadership role. Tokyo's push to usher Beijing out of its post-6-4 isolation had been part of Japan's push for regional leadership. When China was isolated, it served Beijing's interest to encourage that push. Once China's need for Japanese diplomatic assistance had eased, Beijing focused more on the history issue, reflecting the clash between China's and Japan's aspirations to regional leadership.

China's European Theater

China's diplomatic almanac points out that following Japan's reviving of credits to China, the West European countries began restoring credit guarantees for exports to China, government loans, and economic cooperation with China. Japan had opened the way, but European countries soon followed Tokyo's lead.[21] In Qian Qichen's view, Sino-European diplomatic interactions combined with the rapid advance of Japanese-Chinese relations during 1989 and 1990 to convince European leaders that unless they hurried to repair ties with China, European firms would lose their share of the China market.[22] Following Tokyo's lead, in October 1990 the EU decided to cancel sanctions against China and restore normal commercial and political ties with China. EU aid, ministerial visits, and concessional lending to China resumed.

Britain led the way. London was concerned that the situation in Hong Kong might unravel and wanted Beijing's cooperation, especially regarding funding and other arrangements for a new airport and container harbor that were part of London's effort to engineer a smooth transition to Chinese rule in 1997. Britain's foreign minister in July 1990 was the first West European foreign minister to visit China after 6-4, largely because of the need to restart talks over Hong Kong's impending transition. Beijing insisted that a visit by Britain's leader to Beijing was required to pin down crucial arrangements for Hong Kong. Thus it was that Prime Minister John Major in September 1991 was the first European leader to visit Beijing after the Beijing Massacre. Major faced strong criticism from human rights groups and the political opposition over his visit to Beijing, but retorted: "I have to live in the real world. It would not be proper to sit back and strike attitudes and let the Hong Kong people pay the price."[23] On his flight to Beijing, Major assured the public of his deep concern for human rights:

> China has had a period of isolation. It needs people going in and telling them face-to-face what the rest of the world thinks. An important part of the dialogue [in Beijing] will be on human rights. I will raise the issue and I will carry it as far as I can without provoking a breakdown of communication.

Major's chief concern was arrangements for financing US$16 billion in airport and harbor projects. Major conducted those talks with Premier Li Peng.

Before the talks, Qian Qichen had arranged a formal reception for Major on Tiananmen Square, followed by a courtesy call on Li Peng by Major. Going into the talks with Major, Li Peng told the press: "Our two sides share many common points. There may be some different views, but it doesn't matter. Since we live on the same planet, we need contact."

Confronting the United States

The day after 6-4, President George H. W. Bush announced the imposition of a set of modest sanctions as an expression of US disapproval of events in Beijing.[24] At the same time, Bush attempted to telephone Deng Xiaoping to explain that the moral sentiments of the American people made unavoidable some expression of US displeasure. This was the first time an American president had attempted a direct telephone call to a Chinese leader. The Chinese side refused to put the call through.[25]

The day after Bush announced the United States' first post-6-4 sanctions, the Politburo augmented by the elders met to discuss the US move. Li Peng opined, "All the Western countries, with the United States in the lead, are issuing one or another kind of proclamation about applying sanctions against China and cutting China off from the world." Deng Xiaoping's response to Li Peng is worth quoting at length:

> Those countries like to come up with resolution after resolution about how to interfere in our internal affairs. But the interference is no big deal for us; we can ignore it if we like, or we can fight back. Those countries want to apply sanctions against us? All right, but first, let's ask them why this is any of their business. And second, if it is, then we can fight with sanctions, too. Our economic growth might suffer, but not all that much. We've done all right under international sanctions for most of the forty years of the People's Republic. So we don't have to worry too much. We can take it all calmly. This little tempest is not going to blow us over. We're not trying to offend anybody; we're just plugging away at our own work. Anybody who tries to interfere in our affairs or threaten us is going to come up empty. We Chinese have self-confidence; inferiority complexes get you nowhere. For more than a century we were forced to feel inferior, but then, under the leadership of the Communist Party, we stood up. No behemoth out there can scare us now. . . . Our people are not going to cower before foreign invasions or threats, and neither will our children or grandchildren.[26]

From the very beginning, Deng displayed the cool-headedness that would guide him, and China, through the storm. US interference was "no big deal." CCP leaders needed to remain calm, not offend anyone, and keep plugging away at economic development, reform, and opening. Deng also made clear in his June 6 talk to the Politburo meeting that an indispensable condition for China's economic development was a peaceful international environment. Implicit in this was that China should avoid confrontation with the United States if at all possible. Nor would it close its doors out of a fear of peaceful evolution:

> We won't close any doors; our biggest lesson from the past has been not to isolate ourself from the world—that only puts us out of touch and into a big sleep. If history confirms the superiority of the Chinese socialist system, that's enough for us. What happens with the social systems of other countries is none of our business.[27]

It was fortuitous that Deng had in President George H. W. Bush a leader passionately committed to a cooperative relation between China and the United States, and also an old personal friend of Deng. Bush had represented the United States in the United Nations during the September 1971 debate over Chinese representation. He had then opened and headed the US Liaison Office in Beijing in 1973–1974. This was during Deng's first rehabilitation after the Cultural Revolution. Deng and Bush had met during those years, saw in each other a potential future national leader, and mutually cultivated their friendship. Later, as Ronald Reagan's vice president from 1981 to 1988, Bush had helped smooth out the confrontation over US arms sales to Taiwan. Going even further back, Bush had served as a combat pilot with the US navy in the Pacific in World War II. These experiences had given Bush sympathy with the Chinese people and a belief that cooperation between China and the United States was in the interests of both countries and the world. During his 1979 visit to the United States—while Democrat Jimmy Carter was president and Bush was out of office—Deng nonetheless requested and was granted a private meeting with Bush in Houston, Texas. During that meeting, Deng gave Bush a frank tour d'horizon of China's foreign policies, including the then still secret plan to attack Vietnam. Later, when Bush visited Beijing as president in February 1989 prior to Gorbachev's scheduled visit and the Sino-Soviet rapprochement that that visit was expected to produce, Deng again gave Bush a frank review of Sino-Soviet relations. Over the years, Bush had also sent occasional notes to Deng in an effort to maintain their friendship. Deng did not reply to those notes, but valued Bush's effort to maintain their friendship.[28]

Yet as Deng told Bush's National Security Advisor Brent Scowcroft during the latter's December 1989 mission to Beijing, a question such as then existed between China and the United States—interference in China's internal affairs and sanctions—could not be settled on the basis of friendship between two individuals. That said, the two leaders, Deng and Bush, nonetheless worked in tandem during 1989 to normalize relations after 6-4. In doing so, Bush acted contrary to the moral sentiments of the American people, a factor that played a role in his electoral defeat by William Clinton in November 1992. Deng also came under criticism over his "conciliatory" policy toward the United States, although this criticism would crescendo only in 1995. In the face of strong domestic criticism, the two old friends, Bush and Deng, worked to rebuild a cooperative Sino-American relation.

Having failed to reach Deng by telephone on June 5, Bush sent a hand-written letter to Deng on June 21 stating Bush's firm conviction that good relations between China and the United States were a "fundamental interest of both countries," and proposing US dispatch of an emissary to Beijing to discuss ties.[29] Deng replied the very next day, indicating a willingness to receive a representative from Bush. Scowcroft was Bush's emissary; his first, secret, mission to Beijing was in July, barely six weeks after the Beijing Massacre. During their talks, Deng stressed to Scowcroft his desire for continued friendship with President Bush, but took a tough stance on US interference in China's internal affairs and sanctions. The events of June 4 were, Deng said, "an earthshaking event," in which it was "very unfortunate that the United States is too deeply involved." US foreign policy had "cornered China," Deng said. Moreover, "The aim of the counter-revolutionary rebellion was to overthrow the People's Republic of China and our socialist system. If they should succeed in obtaining that aim the world would be a different one. To be frank, this could even lead to war."[30] Deng also insisted that since it was US actions that had created the problem in relations, it was the United States that should "untie the knot." Deng reiterated that message to Richard Nixon when the latter visited Beijing a few months later:

> Please tell President Bush, let's end the past, the United States ought to take the initiative, and only the United States can take the initiative. The United States is able to take the initiative . . . China is unable to initiate. This is because the stronger is America, the weaker is China, the injured is China. If you want China to beg, it cannot be done. If it drags on a hundred years, the Chinese people can't beg [you] to end sanctions. . . . Whatever Chinese leader makes a mistake in this respect would surely fall, the Chinese people will not forgive him.[31]

Deng reached out to other influential old friends of China to convey the message that the United States needed to move first to "untie the knot." Henry Kissinger and Mike Oksenberg were among the notables invited to Beijing in 1989 to learn Beijing's view of relations.

The presence of dissident astrophysicist and professor Fang Lizhi and his wife in the US embassy in Beijing, where they had fled on the evening of June 3, was one source of Chinese grievance. CCP leaders viewed the Fang couple as major instigators and ringleaders of the recent "counterrevolutionary rebellion"—key members of the "small group with ulterior motives" that had misled the naive and inexperienced students. The invitation of Fang and his wife to a banquet at the US embassy during President Bush's visit to Beijing in February 1989 was seen by CCP conservatives as a deliberate attempt to humiliate China. In that event, the US side had rejected China's request to uninvite Fang and his wife, but their attendance was prevented by their detention (along with two American academics accompanying them) by public security the evening of the banquet. Once Fang fled to the US embassy, Chinese authorities issued an arrest warrant for him for "instigating the recent turmoil." Chinese publications began demanding that the United States turn him over to Chinese police or face deterioration of Sino-US ties. Chinese police respected the inviolability of the US diplomatic compound, but for over a year Fang was not allowed to leave for exile in the United States, as US representatives suggested. Chinese anger over "US interference in China's internal affairs" was real, but that anger was probably not the main reason for Fang's continued immobilization. Keeping Fang locked in the US embassy provided leverage with Washington.

After six months of deadlock over Fang, Deng proposed to Henry Kissinger a "package deal" that would make Fang's release more palatable by making it a quid pro quo for considerable US concessions to China. Beijing would allow Fang and his wife to leave for the United States, while the United States would then make an explicit announcement that it would lift sanctions on China. The two sides would also agree on one or two big economic projects. Finally, Jiang Zemin would make an official visit the United States.[32] Following a second visit by Scowcroft in December, Bush began lifting sanctions.[33] Beijing reciprocated by announcing the end of martial law in Beijing and releasing 573 people detained after 6-4. In May 1990, Bush announced that he would extend China's most favored nation status. The next month, over a year after they had entered the US embassy, the Fangs were allowed to leave China.

Qian Qichen took the opportunity of Scowcroft's second, December 1989, visit to engineer a public display of the US envoy honoring—perhaps *kowtowing to* is a better term—China's top leaders.[34] Scowcroft had been concerned that photographs of his toast to China's leaders during the formal banquet would become the target of criticism in the United States. He had thus insisted, and the Chinese side had agreed, that reporters would be granted a photo opportunity only before the banquet, but not during the banquet itself. This protocol was followed until Scowcroft began his toast during the banquet, at which point reporters and photographers were allowed into the hall and went to work. Rather than stop the toast and probably thereby scuttle the negotiations, Scowcroft continued with his toast, demonstrating for the whole world that US representatives respected those of China. In effect, Qian used Scowcroft's desire for successful negotiations to force him to make public a ritual he had preferred to keep private. Scowcroft refused, however, to accept the exit of Fang Lizhi as an adequate quid pro quo for lifting of US sanctions. The two matters, Scowcroft insisted, were simply not on the same level.[35] Fang and his wife were not allowed to depart China until June 1990, and then in response—according to Fang—not to American moves but to a Japanese willingness to resume loans.[36]

In the meantime, the Bush administration began to disengage from close attention to China policy. Facing an election battle in November 1992, Bush was coming under increasingly strong criticism from congressional Democrats and potential presidential rivals. Bush's efforts to quickly repair the relation with Beijing and put the Beijing Massacre behind were simply not popular with many US citizens. This was one reason why Scowcroft's first visit to Beijing in July had been kept secret. When it was revealed at the time of his second visit in December, along with the photographs of Scowcroft toasting China's leaders, a storm of criticism erupted. Bush was charged with hypocrisy or duplicity: publicly declaring suspension of high-level exchanges, then sending Scowcroft to China! The charges of weakness, appeasement, and a lack of understanding of American core values were leveled at Bush. Areas of foreign policy other than China demanded Bush's attention and were more politically profitable for him: East Europe, German unification, and the Soviet Union's mounting crisis.

Beijing's Use of Middle East Leverage against the United States

In the estimate of Qian Qichen, the 1989 upheaval in Eastern Europe, combined with focus on the upcoming 1992 elections, caused Washington to become less enthusiastic about repairing PRC-US relations.[37] Beijing offered to reciprocate Scowcroft's two 1989 missions by sending a high-ranking emissary to the United States in April 1990, but Washington declined. It was, in Qian's estimate, Iraq's invasion of Kuwait on August 2, 1990, that renewed Washington's interest in cooperation with China, offering China an "advantageous opportunity to promote the normalization of Sino-American relations." But President Bush was also happy to have a politically palatable reason to lift post 6-4 sanctions and renew the US-PRC link he valued.

Beijing saw the Iraqi invasion of Kuwait as a blunder that would give the United States an opportunity to expand its position in the Gulf, and on August 4 Vice Foreign Minister Yang Fuchang summoned the Iraqi and Kuwaiti ambassadors, one after the other, to receive China's demand for swift Iraqi withdrawal and resolution of the territorial dispute by negotiations. This put China on the moral high ground, but it also demonstrated to Middle East countries China's essential irrelevance to realistic solutions of major security problems. Once in possession of Kuwait, Iraqi forces quickly began to destroy all aspects of Kuwait's sovereignty in an effort to turn that region into an irrevocable part of Iraq. Most countries of the region quickly concluded that Saddam Hussein could not be persuaded to evacuate Kuwait by negotiations or even economic sanctions, and that military force would be necessary if Kuwaiti sovereignty was to be re-established. China was not prepared to endorse use of military force against Iraq, and this made China essentially irrelevant to the restoration of Kuwait's sovereignty. But Beijing was prepared to trade a green light in the Security Council for authorization of use of military force in exchange for US lifting of sanctions.

China voted "yes" on the first nine UN Security Council resolutions in fall 1990 condemning Iraq's action and imposing mandatory sanctions on Iraq. Voting for sanctions "was not an easy thing," Qian recounted, since the United States, France, and Britain still maintained sanctions against China for 6-4.[38] Beijing decided that a display of diplomatic involvement in the crisis would increase China's influence and status in the region over the long term, and dispatched Qian on visits to Egypt, Saudi Arabia, Jordan, and Iraq in mid-November. The explicit ostensible purpose of Qian's trip was to seek a "peaceful resolution" of Iraq's annexation of Kuwait, but the real if implicit purpose was to increase the US perception of the need for China's support in dealing with the crisis. And indeed, while Qian was in Cairo, US Secretary of State James Baker, who was also in that city, contacted Qian, asked for a meeting, and then solicited China's support for Security Council authorization of the use of force to liberate Kuwait. After Baker laid out the US view that sanctions would not work and that military force would be required to get Iraq out of Kuwait, Qian argued that sanctions should be given a longer trial, although he declined to specify how long that trial period might be. In this way, Qian made clear to the United States that there would be a price if it wanted China's cooperation in securing Security Council endorsement of the use of military force against Iraq. Baker said that if Beijing cooperated at the UN, the United States was prepared to find an opportunity to end sanctions against China.

It was clear to Qian and Baker that both sides were interested in making a deal. Discussion then focused on the price Washington would pay to secure Beijing's cooperation in the Security Council. In a letter to Qian, Baker proposed Chinese "approval" to a use-of-force resolution. Qian saw this as an attempt to raise "the price already agreed on," and insisted that China would not vote "yes" but merely abstain on the critical Security Council vote. For the US part, Baker agreed that Washington would "find an opportunity" to lift sanctions on China, including not opposing a new and large World Bank loan to China. Qian also claims that the United States agreed to support China's entry into GATT under terms regarding Taiwan that were acceptable to China, and to lift the ban on satellite sales to China. Qian points out that Baker's November 1990 visit to Beijing—the first by a US cabinet official since 6-4—represented resumption of high-level US exchanges with

China.[39] On November 29, China abstained from the Security Council vote authorizing use of force against Iraq. China's UN representative explained that Beijing's disapproval of Iraq's seizure of Kuwait suggested it could not vote against the resolution, while its opposition to the use of force to resolve disputes meant it could not vote for the resolution. Abstention was thus the logical choice.

19 }

The Crisis Deepens

COLLAPSE OF COMMUNISM IN EASTERN EUROPE
AND THE USSR

The Failed CCP Defense of Socialism in Eastern Europe

The CCP's confrontation with a powerful popular protest movement in spring 1989 and the chilling aftermath of that bloody event changed Beijing's policy toward the increasingly besieged communist party governments in Eastern Europe, especially those of East Germany, Bulgaria, Czechoslovakia, and Romania, which seemed prepared to rely on tried and proven Leninist methods of proletarian dictatorship to stay in power. By June 1989, the communist parties of Poland and Hungary were already well down the path of negotiated abandonment of their monopoly on state power. But perhaps the anticommunist tide could be halted at the borders of those countries. The CCP lent its support to this last-ditch effort to uphold proletarian state power in Eastern Europe.

The Beijing Massacre hung over the freedom movements that unfolded in Eastern Europe during the second half of 1989. The Chinese example of how an entrenched communist party apparatus could resort to old-style repression befitting Lenin or Stalin to retain their monopoly on state power became a negative example that helped convince people in Eastern Europe of the urgent need to push forward and finally topple the communist establishment. If the communist party was not stripped of control over the instruments of repression, the danger remained of a "Chinese solution," as it came to be called in East European lands during that fateful year.

Beijing adopted several key policies toward Eastern European developments in 1989. Beijing responded positively to solicitations of support from embattled communist regimes. In an attempt to replay an old game first learned in the 1950s, East European communist regimes that chose to resist Soviet pressure and growing popular demand for reform (in Berlin, Prague,

Sofia, and Bucharest) reached out to Beijing for support. Beijing responded positively to these appeals, although in a deliberately low-key manner designed to appear as normal cooperative relations between two sovereign states. In private sessions, these hard-line communists exchanged frank views about how to uphold proletarian state power in the face of counter-revolutionary challenges.

A second key CCP policy response was to accommodate swiftly to regime change. Beijing did what it could to support the embattled East European communist regimes, but when those efforts failed and regimes were toppled, Beijing moved swiftly to develop working relations with the successor governments. Refusal to come quickly to terms with the actual political outcomes of processes at work in Eastern Europe would serve little purpose other than ideological satisfaction. But delay, and still more ideological condemnation, could create opportunities for Taiwan to exploit. Unless Beijing moved swiftly to explain its One China policy to the new East European governments, Taipei might use those rulers' liberal and anticommunist views to expand ties in Europe. Delay by Beijing in recognizing the new postcommunist Eastern European regimes could also carry economic costs of lost trade and investment. The Eastern European countries were, after all, developed countries (at least by global standards), and promised to be good customers for Chinese goods. The Four Modernizations remained a top-ranked policy goal.

Nor would openly drawing ideological lines in Eastern Europe help Beijing escape the stigma of the Beijing Massacre. In furtherance of that goal, Beijing was telling the world that norms of state sovereignty precluded judgment of other state's internal developments; that each country had the right to choose its own developmental path and other states should not "interfere." Opining negatively about East European developments, or keeping the new East European governments at arm's length because of their counterrevolutionary nature, would have exposed the CCP to charges of hypocrisy, weakening its case for putting the Beijing Massacre behind. If Chinese fingerprints were found on applications of a "Chinese solution" in East Europe, the cost to China's reputation could have been heavy. Supporting embattled regimes followed by a willingness to quickly come to terms with whatever regimes emerged was a policy that seemed to serve Chinese interests well.

Because of the economic and political importance of the Federal Republic of Germany (FRG, then usually called West Germany) in Europe, Gorbachev and his reformers deemed liberal reform in the German Democratic Republic (GDR, usually called East Germany) especially important. GDR leaders were extremely reluctant to follow Gorbachev's path of perestroika (reform), convinced that the demise of their own state lay down that path. In retrospect, of course, it is apparent that these old-style communists had a realistic estimate of the situation and that Gorbachev labored under severe illusions.

By 1988, Soviet pressure on the GDR communist party, the Socialist Unity Party (SUP), to liberalize was already strong. The SUP tried to counter that pressure by reaching out to China and the CCP. PRC-GDR and CCP-SUP relations had been normalized in the early 1980s, but in 1988 East Berlin added a new dimension by reaching out to the CCP for support to counter Gorbachev's increasing pressure for political reform. In April 1988, SUP Politburo member Herman Axen visited China for political talks during which the two sides exchanged views on the reform process in socialist countries and "questions concerning the international communist movement." Qiao Shi, who had responsibility for relations with foreign fraternal parties, lauded the achievements of the GDR and the SUP in building socialism.[1] During talks with Axen, Qiao Shi and Zhao Ziyang both endorsed the principle that socialist countries have the right to independently define their own path to socialism, and that no socialist country should impose its own "experience" on another.[2] In the context of 1988–1989, that meant that the USSR should not impose its perestroika on the SUP. Securing firm CPSU agreement to the validity of multiple roads to socialism and nondictation by one fraternal party to another were high-ranking Chinese objectives during Gorbachev's May 1989 visit to China. In this, Beijing was successful. In a televised review of his just-completed meeting with Deng, Gorbachev said:

> We regard this process [of perestroika] as our national one, and do not intend in any way to foist it on anyone else. It was precisely the foisting or copying of one model . . . that in the past was the cause of many complications in the development of world socialism. We have learned that lesson well, and we build our relations with all other socialist states on the basis of complete respect for their independence and sovereign right to choose the forms and methods of their social development. . . on just such a strictly equal basis have we and our Chinese comrades agreed to develop the links between the CPSU and the CCP.[3]

From the CCP's perspective, Gorbachev's mounting pressure on East European governments to follow the path of reformed and liberal communism contradicted the principles of nondictation by one fraternal party (especially the old big-brother party, the CPSU) to other fraternal parties. Having secured firm Soviet agreement not to dictate to fraternal parties, and having just survived the upheaval in China, in June the CCP began supporting SUP efforts to resist ever stronger Soviet pressure to reform. The SUP was the first fraternal party to send a message of support to the CCP over the use of force on 6-4 to suppress opposition. That message arrived the very day the PLA occupied Tiananmen Square. A week later, the GDR legislature issued a statement justifying the CCP action in the same terms that were used by the CCP itself: the matter was China's internal affair, and the GDR opposed any foreign interference in the matter.[4]

Pressure on the GDR intensified still further in mid-1989 when thousands of its citizens began passing through Hungary and Austria in search of freedom and better lives in the FRG. Hungary had opened its borders with Austria in May, and since controls over movement within the East European socialist camp were relatively lax, GDR citizens could travel via Hungary to Austria and then to the FRG, where a promise of citizenship and government stipends awaited them. A trickle quickly became a flood. East Germans who could not make it to Hungary began to rally at the FRG embassy in Prague, also demanding transit to the West. At the same time, growing numbers of people began showing up at an old and famous Lutheran church in Leipzig (in the GDR) for a decade-long Monday evening assembly of dissidents. By October 9, a huge crowd of perhaps one hundred thousand people filled the square outside the church, ignoring warnings by internal security forces to disperse or face violence.

As the SUP crisis deepened, it reached out to the CCP for support of proletarian dictatorship. PRC and GRD national days both fell in October (on October 1 and 7, respectively) and provided an occasion for mutual support. SUP Politburo and Secretariat member Egon Krenz led the GDR delegation to China. Krenz and Qiao Shi discussed the challenges facing the GDR. China "fully understands" the current situation of the GDR, Qiao told Krenz, and "supported the GDR Party and government in upholding socialism, safeguarding state sovereignty, and fighting against all activities aimed at sabotaging socialism."[5] Hostile forces in Western countries were attempting to bring about "peaceful evolution" to capitalism in socialist countries, Qiao warned Krenz.[6]

Yao Yilin led the CCP delegation to the GDR National Day celebrations. Yao, it will be recalled, was one of two Politburo members who called for imposition of martial law in Beijing when that issue came before CCP leaders in May. During a series of meetings with GDR leaders from October 2 through 9, Yao reached a meeting of the minds on the importance of upholding socialism. He met GDR and SUP chief Eric Honecker on October 9. After the talks, Yao reported that China and the GDR shared "identical views on a series of major issues."[7] Yao was "deeply impressed" by GDR "efforts to persist in socialism." Honecker, for his part, compared the situation in the GDR to the "counterrevolutionary" activity in China before 6.4. In their joint statement, Yao and Honecker said that the lesson of both the "counterrevolutionary riot in Beijing and the current defamation campaign against the GDR" was that "socialist values should be staunchly upheld."[8]

The SUP had made preparations to use military force against demonstrators in Leipzig shortly after Yao left the country. Those preparations were complete and orders ready to go out, but at the last minute, the operation was cancelled. The party center feared that the SUP organization in Leipzig that would have responsibility for carrying out the orders would refuse to cooperate, leaving the SUP in an even worse state than had it not issued the orders.⁹ Gorbachev had also attended the GDR National Day celebration, and there was a sharp confrontation between him and Honecker over the need for reform. Gorbachev left the East German leader with the warning that "Those who are late [in reforming] will be punished by life itself."¹⁰ It was thus clear to the SUP that if they resorted to force, they would be on their own and without Soviet backup. When news spread that the demonstrators at Leipzig had not met violent repression, similar protests erupted around the country. The dam holding back popular anger burst. On October 18, Honecker resigned and was replaced by Egon Krenz, an SUP leader willing to negotiate with GDR civil society. Xinhua did not comment on Honecker's removal, but CCP Secretary General Jiang Zemin sent Krenz a message of congratulations.¹¹ Three weeks later, on November 9, the Berlin Wall opened and the final disintegration of the GDR began.

Czechoslovakia was next. Again, CCP efforts to uphold communist dictatorship came to naught. Under the impact of Gorbachev's perestroika, the first protest demonstrations occurred in Prague in 1988 and early 1989. They were easily dispersed by police. Petitions demanding sweeping political reforms and an end to censorship circulated during the summer of 1989. But it was the trauma of the GDR that sparked uprising in Czechoslovakia. During August and September, GDR citizens camped at the FRG embassy in Prague demanding transit to West Germany. After resisting for months, the Czech government finally acceded to these demands, and trainloads of German freedom-seekers began to move west. Czech citizens watched on local and foreign television the events associated with the deepening crisis of the East German regime.

A flurry of Chinese delegation diplomacy attempted to bolster Czechoslovak communist resolve. In early September, Czechoslovak Minister of Defense Milán Václavík made a visit to China. Václavík and Chinese Defense Minister Qin Jiwei discussed "matters of common concern."¹² Xinhua did not elaborate further. A delegation from the State Bank of Czechoslovakia came to China later the same month. Chinese leaders had more than economic advice. Regarding the correct relation between opening and development, Li Peng told the Czechoslovaks, "We should be on the alert against infiltration and subversion plotted by some Western countries." The Czech bankers re-endorsed the 6.4 "quelling of counterrevolutionary rebellion" and noted the "common interests of the Czechoslovak and Chinese Communist Parties in safeguarding the socialist system."¹³ PLA Deputy Chief of Staff Xu Xin arrived in Prague on October 28 after a visit to East Germany. Xu met with Czechoslovakia's president, the minister of defense, and the chief of the General Staff. Finally, Czech Foreign Minister Jaromír Johanes made a five-day visit to China on November 1–5 to discuss the state of reform in the two countries. "The two countries share identical or similar views on important international issues,"

Johanes said.[14] Qian Qichen warned him: "Some international reactionary forces are always attempting to seize opportunities to oppose or even subvert the socialist system. Socialist countries should be on guard against such attempts."[15] The two sides were clearly discussing the wisdom and modalities of using resolute measures to defend the socialist system.

Twelve days after Johanes left China, on November 17, the Czechoslovak government tried the Chinese approach when it used police force to break up an anticommunist demonstration of perhaps 15,000 in central Prague. Repression backfired. The next day, the authorities confronted an even larger and angrier crowd. Strikes and demonstrations spread. The Czechoslovak military command informed its Communist Party leadership that it was prepared to repress the opposition. But once again, as in the GDR, the Communist Party leaders decided to try compromise and conciliation with the protesters. The party elected an entirely new top leadership made up of moderate, pro-perestroika leaders. Demonstrations grew even larger. Within two weeks of the initial police firing on crowds, the Czechoslovak Federal Assembly had abolished the constitutional article providing for Communist Party leadership. Within a month, Czechoslovakia was ruled by its first noncommunist government since 1948.

Bulgaria came next. In May 1989, Todor Zhivkov, in power since 1954, dealt with growing unrest by expelling from the country one group he deemed particularly troublesome: Bulgaria's ethnic Turks. This led to strong international condemnation, which Foreign Minister Petar Mladenov had to handle. Protests over Zhivkov's harsh rule percolated through Bulgaria by mid-1989. Mladenov was a supporter of Gorbachev's perestroika, one of a handful of such supporters within the Bulgarian Communist Party. Mladenov organized a high-profile international environmental conference for October and invited a Bulgarian environmental group to participate. As in other East European countries, environmental groups were among the earliest and strongest elements of emerging civil society. When police beat up members of the Bulgarian environmental group, Mladenov resigned as foreign minister (on October 24) and issued a scathing criticism of Zhivkov's rule. Several months earlier, Mladenov and key like-minded comrades within the elite had begun plotting Zhivkov's removal, and had secured Gorbachev's tacit approval. Mladenov then made a four-day visit to Beijing for talks on the international situation with Li Peng, Jiang Zemin, Wu Xueqian, and Qian Qichen.[16] Mladenov's CCP interlocutors almost certainly urged him to stand firm against the rising forces of counterrevolution. Mladenov, however, choose not to follow that advice. Very shortly after his return from China, Zhivkov was removed from office and replaced by Mladenov, who began dismantling the party state. On December 11, Mladenov announced that the Bulgarian Communist Party was giving up its control of the state and would conduct competitive multiparty elections.

In the midst of Bulgaria's struggle, the CCP bolstered the embattled communist forces. Early in September, before the pivotal environmental conference, *Renmin ribao* carried a long interview with Zhivkov lauding Bulgaria's advances in socialist construction. In October, a large delegation from the Chinese People's Political Consultative Conference (CPPCC—the CCP's united front through which noncommunist groups and individuals participate in politics under the leadership of the CCP)—traveled to Bulgaria. The two sides exchanged views on the "active participation by social and political organizations as well as the democratic parties in running the government and assisting the Communist Party to build a socialist country." Both sides believed that "the leadership of the Communist Party and adherence to the socialist road are prerequisites for . . . development . . . and the socialist cause would suffer if those prerequisites are not met."[17]

As opposition mounted in Czechoslovakia and Bulgaria, the CCP decided to dispatch Qiao Shi and Beijing Party Secretary Li Ximing to Bucharest and Sofia to support the forces upholding proletariat state power. Li Ximing had been one of the principals who pushed through the use of all necessary means to impose martial law in Beijing. Beijing's efforts to bolster proletarian dictatorship were being overtaken by events. The day Qiao and Li left China for Bucharest, the pivotal police repression of the protest demonstration occurred in Prague and Bulgaria's Zhivkov was replaced by Mladenov. Qiao's mission was hastily planned; the visit was not announced until the day of his departure.[18] The ostensible purpose of Qiao's visit was to participate in a congress of the Romanian Communist Party (RCP). Qiao delivered a long CCP statement to that congress, lauding the great struggles and achievements of the RCP in constructing socialism. The document also pledged China's support for a "long period of common revolutionary struggle and construction."[19] Jiang Zemin sent a message to Nicolae Ceaușescu congratulating him on his re-election as RCP general secretary.

During his meeting with Qiao, Ceaușescu pleaded for the CCP to join with Romania to prevent the disintegration of socialism in the remaining East European socialist countries.[20] Qiao demurred. Beijing was not prepared to openly oppose the "counterrevolutionary movements" sweeping East Europe. Beijing offered moral and political support, plus economic and technological cooperation, as an alternative to Soviet or Western largess. CCP officials may have explained how to organize a successful armed repression of a "counterrevolutionary rebellion"; that seems likely to have been a topic of "common interests" in discussions between CCP and East European hard-line communists at this juncture. But publicly, Beijing adhered to the policy of noninterference in the internal affairs of other countries and fraternal parties.

Romania was the one East European socialist state where communist rulers in fact attempted a "Chinese solution." The result was that Romania was the only East European state which required a violent revolution to oust the communist regime, and which led to the execution of the head of the former communist state. Protests began over purely local grievances in the city of Timişoara on December 16. Initial grievances were soon irrelevant as anticommunist slogans dominated animated crowds in that city. Security personnel and, when that proved inadequate, military forces confronted the crowds. Protesters refused to scatter and fought back. Regime violence further enraged the crowds. Workers from nearby industrial centers joined the protests. Ceauşescu attempted to calm the situation by giving a televised speech before a large audience assembled by the party outside his palace in Bucharest. Ceauşescu completely misjudged the psychology of both his audience and the Romanian people. He condemned the events in Timişoara as "interference of foreign forces in Romania's internal affairs" and as "external aggression on Romania's sovereignty." Eight minutes into the speech, jeers, boos, and insults began to be heard. Some of the crowd began chanting "Ti-mi-şoa-ra." Then sounds like gunshots panicked the crowd, transforming what had become a protest demonstration into a riot. An estimated 76 percent of Romania's population had been watching Ceauşescu's televised speech and saw the situation transformed before their eyes into a riot against the regime. As in Timişoara, security and military forces were called in and used violence against the crowds. Protestors fought back, typically unarmed. An estimated 1,104 people died in the chaotic uprising. Eventually, an enraged mob broke into Ceauşescu's place, forcing the tyrant to flee. Military forces began joining the protestors or returning to their barracks under the order of their commanders. Captured in flight, Ceauşescu was given a two-hour trial and executed by firing squad on December 25.

Ceauşescu's trial and his dead body were televised, and the film was distributed around the world.[21] (The actual execution by firing squad was not taped.) In Beijing, CCP leaders assembled to watch a video of the episode shortly after it happened. After stunned silence in the darkened room, an unidentified voice opined "We'll be like this if we don't strengthen our proletarian dictatorship of reactionaries." Deng Xiaoping replied: "Yes, we'll be like this if we don't carry out reforms and bring about benefits to the people."[22] This exchange foreshadowed a sharp divide between Deng and more conservative CCP leaders over the course of post 6-4 policy.

The East European revolutions had a deep impact on CCP leaders. In the first instance, they confirmed their belief that the choice in May to refuse compromise and use "methods of dictatorship to regain control of the situation" had been correct.[23] To have followed the path of compromise and conciliation advocated by Zhao Ziyang would have led to the collapse of the CCP regime as had happened across Eastern Europe. European developments also confirmed the CCP belief that Western subversion and interference played a major role in toppling communist regimes. A visit by President George H. W. Bush to Poland and Hungary (the two leaders in the dismantling of communist rule) in July had inspired reform struggles in other East European countries. So too had a midyear G-7 summit in Paris that declared support (including debt relief) for political reform in Eastern Europe. CCP leaders compared that friendly stance of the G-7 to that Group's post-6-4 stance when it had recommended suspension of World Bank loans to China.

The CCP initial impulse was to damn Gorbachev's betrayal of the East European proletariat and the international communist movement. Conservatives insisted that open polemical struggle be waged against Gorbachev's revisionist betrayal of the international proletariat, just as Mao had struggled against Soviet revisionism in the 1950s. If Gorbachev and the Soviet Union had stood firmly behind the embattled East European proletarian states, they might well have been able to defend the "gains of the proletariat" as ably as the CCP had done in China in June, China's hardliners maintained. But without Soviet support, those states quickly succumbed. Following Ceaușescu's execution, the Politburo convened a series of meetings to discuss East European developments. Gorbachev and his policies were uniformly excoriated.[24] Chen Yun declared that "the weakness of Gorbachev's ideological line is that it is pointing in the direction of surrender and retreat. Our party cannot afford to stand idly by and watch this happen." Elder Wang Zhen seconded Chen's view and called for open criticism of Gorbachev's "revisionism." Gorbachev had deviated from the socialist path, Wang said. Jiang Zemin, just appointed in July as secretary general and designated successor to Deng as paramount leader, maintained that Gorbachev must be held fully responsible for the setbacks of the East European proletariat.[25] Gorbachev as the same type of "traitor" as Leon Trotsky and needed to be held "fully responsible" for the state of affairs in Eastern Europe, Jiang Zemin said. Fortunately for the CCP, Deng Xiaoping would veto the call for open polemical struggle against Gorbachev's "betrayal."

By early 1990, it was obvious to CCP leaders that Gorbachev was either a deliberate traitor who had infiltrated the proletariat's ranks (some believed that he was a CIA mole) or merely a blunderer whose egregious errors caused grave injury to socialist and the international proletariat cause. In February 1990, when Gorbachev announced his intention to revise the Soviet constitution to create a competitive multiparty electoral system, thus ending the CPSU's seventy-two-year-long monopoly on power, articles in PRC media denounced "bourgeois multiparty democracy." Such arrangements were sham class-based democracy run by the bourgeoisie, and far inferior to socialist democracy under the CCP. These polemics avoided, however, direct reference to the USSR or to Gorbachev and his bold constitutional reforms.[26]

The CCP's traditional dual-track approach meant that polemics against Gorbachev's betrayal of the proletariat conducted at the party-to-party level need not interfere with the establishment of normal diplomatic relations of the postcommunist successor states of East Europe at the state-to-state level.

In practice, however, such an approach would create problems—just as it once had in Southeast Asia. These difficulties might give Taiwan opportunities to expand its links with postcommunist East Europe. Even more egregious, standing vociferously against Gorbachev and his "reforms" would run counter to PRC efforts to escape the opprobrium incurred by the Beijing Massacre. And what was to be gained by polemics against Gorbachev? The costs of openly polemicizing against Gorbachev were clear. The gains from such an approach were not. Thus Deng, against apparently strong opposition, mandated a policy of "distinguishing between internal and external affairs" *(nei wai you bie)*. Within the CCP, there would be an intense educational campaign against Gorbachev's errors and ideological mistakes. This would counter the wavering that had occurred among some party members during the spring upheaval, and would unite the party for future struggle against "peaceful evolution." But externally, outside the party, and even more internationally, China would not engage in ideological struggle against Gorbachev's apostasy. Externally, China would follow a policy of noninterference in the internal affairs of other countries and avoid direct normative judgments on those affairs. The critical factor, Deng said, was the ideological strength and unity within the Chinese Communist Party. If party members understood Gorbachev's betrayal of the Four Cardinal Principles and the consequences thereof, that was sufficient. China would attend to its own affairs and let other nations attend to their affairs.

The problem with open polemical struggle against Gorbachev's "betrayal of the East European proletariat," of course, was that such a course would not serve China's, or even the CCP's, interests. It was in this context that Deng Xiaoping issued what was to become one of his most famous foreign policy dictums, his "twenty-four character directive." Translated into English, it read:

> Observe the situation calmly; stand firm in our position; deal with matters calmly; hide our capabilities and bide our time to make a comeback; maintain a low profile; never seek leadership.

The twenty-four character directive was to guide *foreign* affairs. Internally, the CCP took a far less equanimous approach. Within China, in universities, government organs, and especially within the party, an intense struggle was to be waged against the treacherous "New Thinking" of Gorbachev's liberal communism. No quarter would be given to those ideas; all their dangers would be exposed systematically and thoroughly by an ideological rectification and re-education campaign. This campaign would make sure people were clear about the "complex international background" of the contemporary challenges to proletarian power, i.e., the instigation and support of "hostile Western powers led by the United States" with the objective of destroying socialism and achieving world hegemony. Internally, the party would adopt a militant, antiliberal attitude. Externally, China would follow a nonideological and equanimous approach. China's media and officials would not express support for measures or proletarian dictatorship in other countries, nor express sorrow if and when those efforts of proletarian dictatorship failed. In terms of the slant taken by China's media, coverage was to be objective, reporting on events without siding with the healthy Marxist-Leninist forces of foreign countries, much less revealing CCP pleasure at the successes of those forces. Moreover, China would move quickly to establish normal diplomatic relations with whatever governments succeeded to power after the collapse of communist regimes. In line with this, shortly after Ceauşescu's execution, Qian Qichen sent a message to Romania's new government saying that China respected the Romanian people's choice and hoped for continued friendly relations with Romania.

Internally, the CCP moved to further inoculate the PLA against any disloyalty to the party that might be inspired by events in East Europe. On December 27, 1989, following the defection of Romania's military from party control, the PLA's General Political Department distributed a circular to commanders. Against the background of the unsettling changes in East Europe and the continuing influence of bourgeois liberalism, the circular said, it was necessary to launch a campaign to inculcate the Four Cardinal Principles throughout the PLA. Some within the military were still confused or unconvinced of the superiority or even the very future of the socialist system.[27]

The Collapse of Communism in the Soviet Union

Hot on the heels of the collapse of East European communist regimes, the most senior communist party, that of the USSR, began its slide toward extinction. 1990 and 1991 saw an increasingly desperate struggle over the future of the USSR. There were three main groups in this struggle: 1) liberal communists, led by CPSU General Secretary and USSR President Michael Gorbachev, who wanted to develop a liberal and democratic variant of communist rule—an approach not too different from those of Hu Yaobang or Zhao Ziyang; 2) conservative communists who felt Gorbachev's liberal path was an illusion that would lead ultimately to the demise of communist rule and socialism—an approach similar to that of Li Peng, Yao Yilin and other CCP hardliners; 3) noncommunist Russian nationalists, led by Boris Yeltsin, who favored Russian secession from the USSR and formation of a liberal, democratic system and a market economy.

Yeltsin, initially a protégé of Gorbachev, emerged as the leader of the noncommunist liberals during 1990. In May 1990, Yeltsin was elected chairman of the Congress of People's Deputies, a new organ of supreme state authority set up by Gorbachev in 1988 in an effort to outflank his conservative antireform

516 { China's Quest

opponents, who dominated long-established Soviet institutions of power. The new Congress of People's Deputies, unlike the old Soviets, was constituted by competitive and therefore lively elections. Yeltsin used the new Congress as a power base and as a mechanism to further amend the constitution in democratic directions. Barely two weeks after Yeltsin became its chairman, the Congress of People's Deputies issued a declaration of sovereignty. In effect, the largest and most important republic of the USSR, the Russian Republic, was seceding from the USSR. The next month, July, Yeltsin resigned from the CPSU in a dramatic speech at the 28th Congress of that party. Yeltsin took with him out of the CPSU a considerable body of Russian party members who began concentrating on consolidating control over the structures of power within the Russian Republic. Early in 1991, the institutions of the Russian Republic were reformed and a new presidency established, to be elected by direct popular vote. When the election for that office was held in June 1991, Yeltsin won 57 percent of the vote in a six-way race. The candidate supported by Gorbachev won only 16 percent of the vote. Opinion in Russia was swinging rapidly and strongly in favor of independence and thorough-going democratic reform.

By August 1991, CPSU hardliners saw the writing on the wall and attempted a coup d'état against both Yeltsin and Gorbachev. The coup attempt failed after only three days, thanks in part to the heroic actions of Yeltsin, who rushed to the Russian parliament and rallied its defense. As had happened in Romania, units of the military refused to obey Communist hardliners. The failure of the coup discredited both the hard-line communists and Gorbachev, and swung opinion further in favor of radical reform to prevent a return to old-style communist repression. Yeltsin's group proceeded to take over institutions of power in Russia ministry by ministry. In November, Yeltsin decreed a ban on all Communist Party activities in Russia, and on December 25, 1991, Gorbachev resigned all posts and the USSR ceased to function. After seventy-four years of "building socialism," the Union of Soviet Socialist Republics disappeared into the dustbin of history.

The CCP was keenly interested in Soviet developments. The collapse of communist rule, and perhaps of the communist-led state, the USSR, would erode the CCP's own legitimacy. The USSR was the oldest proletarian state, which, in the typical Marxist-Leninist formulation, had the most "experience in the construction of socialism." The CCP had numerous times exculpated itself from its failures by citing a "lack of experience in constructing socialism." Now, the party with the most "experience" was going under. China's own political system, and even still (circa 1991) to a considerable extent its economic system, was derived from the Soviet model. If that model, with its considerable "experience," had not worked in the USSR, and if it had proved itself incapable of reform, why should one think it could work or be reformed in China? There was the danger of contagion by example; if anticommunist forces could succeed even in the USSR, could not similar forces in China be inspired? Internationally, the demise of communist rule in the USSR would leave China the sole remaining major communist party state in the world. Communist-ruled socialist China would now be alone to face the entire capitalist world. Those hostile capitalist forces would be inspired by their recent victories in Eastern Europe and the Soviet Union to direct their spears against socialist China with greater vigor. And if Russia became a liberal, democratic, capitalist state, as its noncommunist reformers sought, Russia might join the West, leaving China entirely surrounded by hostile countries. On the other hand, as with Eastern Europe in 1989, open intervention in the struggle underway in the Soviet Union would be extremely dangerous.

Support for the CPSU's Marxist-Leninist Forces

Out of these contradictory interests, the CCP fell back on its dual-track approach. In terms of state-to-state relations, China continued the policy of noninterference in other countries' internal affairs that it had used during the East European revolutions of 1989. Thus, at critical junctures Beijing formally declared its noninterference and its respect for the decisions of the Russian people. In terms of party-to-party relations between the CCP and the CPSU, however, Beijing did what it could to bolster the resolve of the genuine Marxist-Leninists in the CPSU who were defending the "gains of socialism" against the forces of counterrevolution.

In April 1990, just prior to a visit to Moscow by Premier Li Peng, the CCP circulated internal documents to unify thinking on the Soviet struggle and Peng's upcoming visit. Gorbachev was a revisionist who had "completely betrayed the basic principles of Marxism-Leninism," the document said. Gorbachev "denied class struggle in the international sphere," had "changed the character of the Communist Party," and had implemented Western-style parliamentary democracy. Speaking of Gorbachev's "action program" adopted two months earlier by the CPSU, the CCP's internal guidance said:

> Facts demonstrate that Gorbachev's reforms are not some sort of perfection of the socialist system, but a basic move towards capitalism. The action program . . . can only accelerate the Soviet Union's betrayal of socialism. Not only will this not allow the Soviet Union to escape its current political, economic, and nationalities crisis, but on the contrary, will intensify all sorts of contradictions, and cause the Soviet Union and Eastern Europe to slide into a long period of instability and disorder.[28]

Deng Xiaoping wisely vetoed open polemical struggle against Gorbachev and his apostasy. But, internally, Deng was clear about the Soviet leader. In April 1990, Deng told the Politburo, "We must place our hopes in the Soviet people, place our faith in the broad masses of true Bolshevik party members."[29] Shortly before the failed coup of August 1991, the CCP reportedly distributed internal guidance saying that the CCP must "unite with the progressive elements of foreign communist parties, especially the healthy forces within the Soviet army, the KGB, and the party—and these people should be invited to visit China."[30]

The CCP used delegation diplomacy to give encouragement and support to the CPSU's Marxist-Leninist forces. Beginning in the fall of 1989, CPSU hard-liners began reaching out to the CCP in an effort to persuade Gorbachev to discontinue liberalization and put the Soviet house in order with firm methods like those used in China.[31] As illustrated by Figure 19-1, from September 1989 through the coup attempt of August 1991, conservative leaders of the CPSU hard-line faction one after the other traveled to Beijing.

The earliest of these visits was in September 1989 by Anatoly Lukyanov, a leading conservative opponent of Gorbachev's and a future leader of the August 1991 coup. During his China visit, Lukyanov praised China's model of reform, adding that the Soviet Union needed "deep insight" into it. The "specific situations" of China and the USSR differed, Lukyanov, but "one point is common: no reform is workable without the leadership of the Party."[32] Regarding the Beijing Massacre, Lukyanov expressed "understanding."[33] One of the most pointed of the CPSU delegations to China was led by Ivan Polozkov in June 1991. Polozkov was head of the CPSU organization in the Russian Republic, a position that made him the direct rival of Boris Yeltsin once the latter was elected president of the Russian Republic shortly before Polozkov's visit. Polozkov's visit to Beijing coincided with a visit by Yeltsin to Washington for talks with President Bush. The symbolism was clear: while Yeltsin looked to Washington, the heirs of Lenin looked to Beijing. Soviet Defense Minister Dmitri Yazov was in China about the same time as Polozkov. Yazov's visit was reportedly against the explicit advice of Gorbachev. Upon his return to the Soviet Union, Yazov publicized China's experience, saying it was worth thorough study.[34]

During their own visits to the Soviet Union, CCP leaders bolstered the CPSU's healthy forces. Emerging from talks with Lukyanov during his April 1990 visit to Moscow, Li Peng visited Lenin's former office, where he remarked, "full of emotion," "regrettably, now some people in the world no longer believe in Leninism." He then wrote in the guest register: "Great Lenin will forever encourage us to advance along the road of socialism."[35] A year later Li Peng told Soviet Foreign Minister Alexander Bessmertnykh in Beijing that, while "the methods of building one's own country and the kind of road to take are matters which should be decided by the people

Date	Individual	Position	Object of Visit	Role in Soviet Union
1989				
July	Song Jian	head S&T commission	S&T cooperation	
July	Tian Jiyun	vice premier	expand eco & S&T coop	
Sept.	Zhu Liang	head CCP International Liaison Dept.	strengthen party-to-party ties	
Sept.	Anatoliy Lukyanov	1st vice chair Supreme Soviet	legislative ties, reform	anti-Gorbachev
Dec.	Valentin Falin	head CPSU ILD	Inter-party ties, East Europe	Gorbachev aide
1990				
Jan.	Igor Rogachev	deputy foreign minister	Cambodia	
Mar.	K.F. Katushev	minister foreign economic relations.	trade	
Apr.	Li Peng	Premier	reform & international issues	
Apr.	Xu Xin	deputy PLA Chief of Staff	accompanies Li Peng	
Apr.	Song Wenzhong	PLA foreign affairs Dept.		
May	Boris Pugo	interior minister		member coup group
May	Liu Huaqing	vice chair CMC	mil-mil ties	
May	Hu Ping	Minister of Commerce		
Jun.	Vladimir Khuzhokov	deputy head military foreign affairs office		
Jul.	Peng Zhong	NPC vice head		
Sept.	Alex Bessmertnykh	foreign minister	Persian Gulf	
Oct.	Bessmertnykh	foreign minister	Persian Gulf	
Oct.	Zheng Tuolin	minister of eco. & trade	trade	
Dec.	Li Ruishan	NPC legal affairs vice chair	law and order	
?	Ding Guangen	Alternate Politburo member		
?	Wang Renzhi	Minister of Propaganda	ideology	
1991				
Jan.	Igor Rogachev	deputy foreign minister	Persian Gulf crisis	
Feb.	Vladimir Ivashko	dep. Secretary General CPSU	large trade credit	
Mar.	Yuriy Maslynkov	dep. Premier	economics ties	
Apr.	Alex Bessmertnykh	foreign minister		
May	Jiang Zemin	Secretary General	Party-to-party ties, reform	
May	Qin Qiwei	defense minister	accompanies Jiang Zemin	
May	Dmitriy Yazov	defense minister	arms trade	member coup group
Jun.	Li Ximing	Beijing Party Secretary	the reform process	
Jun.	Ivan Polozkov	head CPSU Russia organization		direct rival of Yeltsin
Aug.	Chi Haotian	Chief of Staff	military relations. Coup?.	conveyed alert to China?
Aug.	A.M. Belonogov	vice foreign minister	Secure endorsement of coup	

FIGURE 19-1 **Chinese Delegation Diplomacy with the Soviet Union, June 1989–December 1991**

Source: Zhongguo waijiao (China's diplomacy), Shijie zhishi chubanshe. *Foreign Broadcast Information Service, Daily Report China.*

of that country ... the Chinese side is [nevertheless] concerned about the situation in the Soviet Union, hoping that it will enjoy political stability, economic development, and national unity."[36] This was an implicit appeal for the use of whatever means necessary to repress instability and disunity. Beijing Party Secretary and Politburo member Li Ximing visited Moscow in March 1991. During the visit, Li lauded and encouraged the CPSU's healthy forces:

> The Soviet Communist Party has been leading the Soviet people in sur-
> mounting numerous difficulties in the course of their socialist revolu-
> tion and socialist construction in the past 70 years ... We sincerely hope
> that the comrades of the Soviet Communist Party will surely revolve
> the current problems ... and move the situation into a track of steady and
> healthy development.[37]

After a tour of sites associated with the Bolshevik insurrection in Leningrad, Li Ximing wrote in a visitors' register: "Members of the Chinese Communist Party will forever remember Lenin's profound remarks: forget-ting the past means betrayal."[38]

The visit by CCP Secretary General Jiang Zemin in May 1991 for a summit meeting with Secretary General Gorbachev represented a CCP endorsement of Gorbachev and, as such, a reflection of Chinese recognition of the growing weakness of the healthy hard-line forces in the Soviet Union. Jiang was not yet president of the PRC; he would not assume that post until 1993. This meant that if he were to visit the USSR and meet Gorbachev, he would have to do so in his party capacity. The CCP decision to bless Gorbachev as leader of the CPSU with Jiang's May 1991 visit reflected a judgment that Gorbachev was the lesser of two evils. The rapid growth of Yeltsin's secessionist and liberal demo-cratic forces posed the risk of victory of the anticommunist forces. Gorbachev was a liberal communist, but at least he was still a communist, one who won re-election at the 28th Congress in July 1990 (at which Yeltsin withdrew from the party) by a margin of three to one.

Jiang's May 1991 visit was the apogee of CCP delegation diplomacy. Jiang told Gorbachev, "It is our heartfelt hope and conviction that the great Soviet people, who have made a significant contribution to the cause of human prog-ress and who are imbued with a glorious revolutionary tradition, will sur-mount their existing temporary difficulties and score final victory in their social reform and construction."[39] To Soviet Vice President Gennady Yanayev, head of the future failed coup, Jiang conveyed his hope that the Soviet Union would adhere to the socialist road. Both China and the Soviet Union were facing the problem of how to preserve the socialist system, Jiang said, and should not underestimate the Western countries' efforts to take advantage of Chinese and Soviet reforms to peddle Western ideology by means of their superiority in economy and production.[40] Jiang reportedly turned down two requests by Yeltsin for a meeting.[41]

Chinese Economic Credits Counter Western Pressure

Trade credits were another form of Chinese assistance to the USSR's increasingly beleaguered communist rulers. China extended two major credits to assist the Soviet Union during its final travail. The first was associated with Li Peng's April 1990 visit and was worth approximately US$334 million, to be used for purchase of Chinese consumer goods. The second, in February 1991, was worth approximately US$700 million and was to be used to purchase Chinese foodstuffs. There was solid economic logic underlying both loans. Soviet consumers needed Chinese manufactured goods and foods. Chinese suppliers profited from meeting those needs. Leaders of both sides had agreed earlier that they should expand economic cooperation, and the loans did this. Yet the political context cannot be ignored, especially for the second credit. Coming when and how it did, the second loan was a clear signal that the Soviet Union could look to China as an alternate partner, rather than capitulate to Western pressure and let the USSR unravel.

Problems began in the Soviet Union's three Baltic republics, Latvia, Estonia, and Lithuania. Those countries had been annexed by the Soviet Union in 1940 during the period of partnership with Nazi Germany and in accord with secret codicils to the 1939 Nazi-Soviet nonaggression pact. The three Baltic states were "liberated" by the Soviet Red Army in 1944 and communist rule reimposed on them. Their indigenous nationalisms were ruthlessly suppressed. Gorbachev's liberalizing reforms, however, led to a re-emergence of that nationalism. Large demonstrations demanding greater autonomy began in late 1986. Native languages (i.e., not Russian) were instituted as state languages. Declarations of sovereignty followed: by Estonia in November 1988, Lithuania in May 1989, and Latvia in July 1989. The three Baltic republics then began negotiations with the Russian Republic over such mundane but important matters as border control and customs. The three republics increasingly demanded full independence. Negotiations deadlocked by late 1990. In January 1991, Gorbachev finally acceded to demands of CPSU hard-liners and ordered Soviet military forces to take control over Lithuania and Latvia. Twenty people were killed and hundreds wounded. Violence was especially severe in Lithuania's capital, Vilnius.

Western countries responded to the "Vilnius massacre" by suspending economic aid. The G-7 suspended US$1.5 billion in food aid and technical assistance, and canceled a meeting scheduled to discuss further assistance. The United States turned down a Soviet request for a $1.5 billion agricultural credit and postponed a Moscow summit meeting between Bush and Gorbachev. It was in this context that Beijing in February 1991 extended the US$700 million credit. It was CPSU deputy chair Vladimir Ivashko who snagged the second credit for China. Ivashko later told the Communist Party newspaper *Pravda* that the initiative for the loan came from the Chinese, not the Soviet, side. This demonstrated, Ivashko said, the "political significance" of the credit. The loan was a demonstration of China's "moral support for the renewal process" in the Soviet Union and was of "great importance."[42] *Renmin ribao* reported Ivashko's remarks without comment.

China and the Attempted August Coup

On August 19, 1991, hard-liners within the CPSU attempted a military coup to impose martial law, oust both Gorbachev and Yeltsin, and reestablish proper Soviet order. The coup organizers had long felt that Gorbachev's reform program was endangering the continued existence of the socialist system and the unity of the Soviet state. In effect, the coup was an attempt to implement a "Chinese solution" in the USSR. The Soviet coup collapsed within three days, largely because military units refused to go along.

PLA Chief of Staff Chi Haotian was in Moscow for a weeklong visit ending August 12, a week before the Soviet coup attempt began. On the evening of August 11, Soviet Defense Minister Dmitri Yazov telephoned and asked to meet with Chi. According to Hong Kong reports, at that meeting Yazov asked Chi how the CCP viewed the Soviet situation. Chi replied that China was worried about the deterioration of the Soviet economy and the possibility of a split in the nation. Yazov then said that some comrades in the army were ready to "take action." Chi reportedly replied: "We adhere to the principle of not interfering in the internal matters of the Soviet Union, but we express our understanding."[43] On August 18, the day Chi returned to Beijing, an enlarged Politburo meeting reportedly convened to hear Chi's account of the Soviet situation.

China's media responded very swiftly to news of the Soviet coup. This celerity lends credence to reports that China's media had guidance in hand when news of the coup arrived and, by extension, that China's leaders had foreknowledge of the coup that led to the dissemination of that media guidance. The day after the coup began, nearly all of China's major newspapers carried a front-page Xinhua item entitled "Gorbachev Suspended from Performing His Presidential Duties." Many also included a background account of coup leader Gennady Yanayev. Xinhua's coverage of coup activities was extensive—at least forty-two items on August 20. This also indicates that Xinhua knew in advance what slant to take. Xinhua gave extensive and factually accurate coverage to the activities of the coup leaders. It reported on their activities, including those of "Acting Soviet President Yanayev" and the "State Committee" set up by the coup. Xinhua gave lengthy descriptions of the decrees and appeals of the coup leaders, including their denunciations of Yeltsin. It conveyed statements of support for the coup by various Soviet groups and leaders. It did not, however, report on the activities or statements of Yeltsin or other opponents of the coup. Again, this strongly suggests that guidance was already in hand when the coup attempt happened.

On August 21, two days into the coup, the director of the CCP propaganda department, Wang Renzhi, convened a meeting of press officials to convey further instructions about coverage of the Soviet coup. Coverage should be inclined toward support, Wang said, but "do not be visibly pleased. Do not let others know your joy." The guiding principle should be, Wang said, "internal joy, but external worry." The current situation in the Soviet Union was favorable to China, and it was necessary to generate propaganda to stabilize the overall situation.[44]

When news of the Soviet coup arrived in Beijing on August 19, top CCP leaders had gathered at Deng Xiaoping's residence to celebrate his eighty-seventh birthday. On hearing the news of Gorbachev's overthrow, one elder, Bo Yibo, cursed the Soviet leader. Deng opined: "When Gorbachev was ousted, the Soviet Union declared to the world that Gorbachev alone cannot change the situation of a country ruled by the Communist Party for more than seventy years."[45] Later the same day, the Politburo met to discuss the Soviet situation. Defense Minister Chi Haotian reportedly advocated open declaration of support for the coup. Deng vetoed this, saying that while the Soviet coup was "a good thing," "we must not be visibly pleased but only delighted at the bottom of our hearts."[46] Publicly, China would stand by the principle that the affairs of a country are the concern of the people of that country, while also pointing out that China did not wish to see the situation in the Soviet Union deteriorate.[47] China should wait for the situation in the Soviet Union to stabilize, Deng insisted, before it openly supported the new leaders in Moscow. At a Politburo meeting the next day, Deng went a bit further: China should not enter into alignments or unite with the Soviet Union to resist the United States. This prudence served the CCP well when the coup collapsed.

The Politburo issued directives to unify thinking in the party on the Soviet hard-liners' coup. There were several points. Gorbachev's downfall was a good thing that would help the development of the international communist movement. The Soviet State Emergency Committee (the organ set up by the coup) should be recognized, because it was made up of genuine Marxists. Externally, however, party members were not to air their views or conduct private discussions on Soviet developments without authorization. Sino-Soviet relations would be strengthened because of the Soviet Union's return to the socialist camp. Party-to-party ties would not warm up immediately, because China had to consider its international image. The downfall of Gorbachev was not regarded as a good thing internationally, the directive warned CCP members, and if China rejoiced prematurely it would only isolate itself. This directive was sent out on August 20, only to be recalled when the coup collapsed two days later.[48] Immediately after the failure of the coup attempt, Qian Qichen met with the Soviet ambassador in Beijing to say, "We respect the choice the Soviet people made, and we believe . . . the good-neighborly and friendly relations between China and the Soviet Union will continue to develop on the basis of the principles set forth in the 1989 and 1991 Sino-Soviet joint communiqués."[49]

It is interesting to consider what might have been the consequences if Deng's views had not prevailed and the CCP openly polemicized against Gorbachev's "betrayal of the proletariat." The normalization of ties with Russia would probably not have been as smooth as it was. It might have been difficult for Moscow and Beijing to reach the mutual nonaggression agreement they did in December 1992 and the strategic partnership of several years later. Yeltsin might have drawn back from Beijing, rather than embrace it as he did. The cost to China's relations with the United States could have been even greater. With anticommunist "End of History" hubris rising in the United States, and with the debate over MFN–human rights linkage intensifying, if China had stood vehemently against the (largely) peaceful revolutions and with the moribund communist regimes of Eastern Europe and Russia, public opinion in the United States could have taken an even stronger negative swing. In sum, if Deng's advice about *nei wai you bie* had not prevailed, China's post-6-4 rehabilitation might have been much more difficult.

The Lessons Learned by the CCP from the Soviet Collapse

In the days after the coup collapsed, a series of emergency Politburo meetings summarized Soviet events. The failure of the coup represented a "counterrevolutionary restoration" accomplished by "peaceful evolution" engineered by hostile Western powers headed by the United States. Gorbachev had made many mistakes, but among the worst was peddling his New Thinking that denied class struggle, thereby allowing the growth of antisocialist forces. Once the coup was set in motion, its leaders did not move resolutely enough against Gorbachev, Yeltsin, and other counterrevolutionaries. Coup leaders had had blind faith in legal processes and failed to adopt effective means against Gorbachev and Yeltsin. Coup leaders failed to mobilize enough troops quickly enough. And there was Western intervention that had emboldened the anticommunist forces. The United States had even been prepared to send military forces to support the anti-coup forces, the CCP concluded.[50]

A week after the failure of the Soviet coup attempt, the editor of *Renmin ribao*, Gao Di, explained the international situation to editors and leading cadres of newspapers—the people who politically educate the Chinese pub-lic.[51] Gao Di began by informing his audience that he was conveying the views of the Central Committee. The Soviet coup failed because Gorbachev's New Thinking had abandoned the doctrine of class struggle, replacing it with the good of humankind as a whole. This switch overlooked "the fact [that] from the very day that socialism was established international imperialist and reactionary forces have constantly sought to destroy it." Most recently, those forces were using a strategy of "smokeless warfare" and "peaceful evolution." Developments in the USSR were an outcome of this ideological confusion utilized by imperialism. Gorbachev had "undertaken a wholesale repudiation of Stalin."

> The test of a true Marxist is whether or not he acknowledges the dicta-torship of the proletariat. Overthrowing the reactionary regime which Gorbachev and Yeltsin represented would have been an act of revolu-tion, a seizure of power. Revolution is merciless; if you do not overthrow him, he will overthrow you. There is no room for compromise in this, or for so-called human sympathy. Revolution is violence. Once the seizure of power had begun, they should have arrested Gorbachev and Yeltsin. You do not ask a tiger politely for its skin; either you kill him, or he will kill you.

Applying this perspective of class struggle to the international sphere, Gao continued:

> The real world is precisely this merciless. All of us hope for a peaceful international environment within which we can develop. But circum-stances to not always permit this. . . . it will take twenty years for the Soviet Union to make the transition to full market economy . . . These twenty years will be particularly important to us. We must use these twenty years to make China successful. During these twenty years the lives of the Soviet people will be very difficult, whereas the lives of the Chinese people will steadily improve. This will demonstrate that the Chinese socialist system is a good one. If we can make good use of these twenty years to manage affairs in China well, this will be beneficial to Eastern Europe and the Soviet Union, and the entire Third World. The strength of a good example will be limitless.

China should be cautious about openly expressing its views about the cur-rent nature of world affairs, but should very clear about such matters inter-nally, Gao Di told the heads of China's media. "We have our own views of what is happening in the Soviet Union, but we will not take issue with the Soviets on this. Internally we will make our own views clear. What we do internally and abroad are two different things." *Nei wai you bie.* Gao Di also explained the key reason for the CCP's low-profile approach: avoiding rivalry with the United States. The Soviet Union should have shifted economic priority to agriculture and light industry after World War II in order to raise standards of living. It did not do this, but continued to give priority to heavy industry and defense right up to the time of Gorbachev. In part this was a function of the inevitable struggle between capitalism and socialism. But it was also due to the Soviet Union's "rivalry with the United States for hegemony." This rivalry for hegemony with the United States was, according to Gao Di, a major reason for the Soviet Union's current situation. Deng's twenty-four-character directive spoke to this determination not to allow the United States to turn China into a rival and force it to assume a heavy defense burden that would hobble its development.

A book published by the Foreign Ministry just after the demise of the USSR laid out the international situation in which China now found itself.[52] China now confronted a protracted, probably decades-long, complex offensive by the Western capitalist countries, which were using economic, political, cultural, and military means to cause people—especially party members—to doubt the superiority of socialism. The most critical arena for confronting this western offensive was internal. Party organization and leadership should be strengthened, and at every level the party should grasp ideological education and struggle. Externally, the increasingly intense competition among states, some bourgeois and some proletarian, for "comprehensive national power" was a chief manifestation of the clash between socialist and capitalist systems. Western efforts at peaceful evolution took place under the threat of superior Western military power. The international situation was currently tending toward reduction of tension, but the possibility of "extreme challenges," including those of a military nature, could not be ruled out. It was absolutely essential for China to develop great "comprehensive national power" if it was to survive as a socialist state. But while maintaining great vigilance against "peaceful evolution," China could not close itself off from the world. To do that would deny China the advanced technologies and knowledge it needed to develop comprehensive national power. If opposing "peaceful evolution" meant closing China, "the more you oppose, the poorer you become, the more you oppose, the more backward you become."[53]

The collapse of the CPSU had a profound and enduring impact on the CCP worldview. Twenty-two years later, in 2013, a six-part, 100-minute video program titled *Silent Contest* and apparently intended for political education of PLA officers and CCP cadre was leaked and posted on the web.[54] The program argued in detail that the United States had defeated its greatest enemy, the Soviet Union, by nonmilitary means, including especially ideological subversion, and was now trying to do the same thing with China. Gorbachev's "New Thinking" that had erased Soviet Communist Party members' awareness of domestic and foreign class enemies and the attempted

"Westernization" that had produced Soviet weakness had all facilitated a sustained and long-term campaign of US subversion. The result was the dissolution of the Soviet Union. This had resulted in the United States shifting its spearhead toward China. The years 1978–1989 had been a "honeymoon" in US-PRC relations because of common opposition to the Soviet Union. Now the United States was using a vast array of weapons to subvert China: radio and television broadcasts, cultural and academic exchanges, the Internet, support for Tibetan or Xinjiang rebels, and even the village election program of the Carter Center in Atlanta

The trauma of postcommunist Russia generated a good deal of popular support within China for continuing CCP rule. Russia's trials under Boris Yeltsin in the 1990s were many. The economy fell to half the Soviet-era level. The social welfare net disintegrated. Organized crime boomed. Former party apparatchiks seized privatized, lucrative state assets. Russian protests were ignored by the West as East European states one after another joined NATO. Witnessing Russia's troubles, especially when juxtaposed to China's economic advance that revived circa 1992, many Chinese concluded that replacing a highly centralized communist party power system with a decentralized system of democracy led, after all, not to orderly advance but to decline and even anarchy. Lingering memories of China's own experience during the Cultural Revolution, when relaxation of central control had been paralleled by chaos, reinforced these conclusions about Russia's course. Even Chinese who had once seen Gorbachev's perestroika as an inspiration and guide for China changed their views and reluctantly concluded that the CCP under Deng, not the CPSU under Gorbachev, had followed the correct path. Continued centralized rule by the CCP was the best way to borrow heavily from the Western countries.

When Russia under Vladimir Putin in 2000 began turning away from the democratizing efforts of the previous decade, rebuilding a strong central authority, and distancing Russia from the West and from the idea of participating in a single global community, CCP leaders, and many ordinary Chinese, saw further vindication of the path the CCP had chosen. Even Russia now recognized this and was embracing a China-like course. The Soviet system could and should have been reformed under centralized Communist Party direction—as had been done in China.

Chinese drew from the Soviet collapse very different conclusions than those drawn by Americans and other Westerners. The combination of the Beijing Massacre with the collapse of communist rule in Eastern Europe and the Soviet Union had a deep impact on Western, and perhaps especially American, perceptions of China under the CCP.[55] Before those events, China had been perceived as an exemplar of wise and steady reform under far-sighted communist leaders. Afterwards, CCP-ruled China was seen as a political anachronism, and a cruel one at that.

Constraining Unipolarity in an Unbalanced International System

An "Extremely Unbalanced" International System

The end of the Cold War posed a great challenge for the PRC. Not only did the global system not move in the direction of multipolarity that China had extolled since the early 1970s as the desired future condition. Instead, the United States emerged in a position of unparalleled global preeminence. Moreover, China's relation with a newly unrestrained American hegemon had lost its vital strategic ballast; Washington no longer needed China's support to counter the Soviet Union. The basic premise of PRC-US cooperation since 1972, convergent interests in checking Soviet expansionism, was no more. Russia's new leaders were preoccupied dealing with the aftermath of state disintegration and had little time for foreign affairs. What little attention they had was mostly spent dealing with regions close to Russia. The post-Soviet Russian economy began a deeper decline than virtually anyone had expected, greatly diminishing Moscow's ability to continue to play the role of a world power. Former Soviet military forces decayed. In short, there was no longer a global power challenging the United States. Moreover, in the very early post-Soviet period, there seemed a good possibility that newly democratic Russia would become a partner of Europe and the United States, with Russia returning to what many Russians saw as "Russia's European home." A possible harbinger of closer Soviet-Western cooperation came in fall 1990, when Moscow gave a green light to Washington's military campaign to undo Iraq's attempted annexation of Kuwait.

Contrary to long-standing Chinese predictions about the imminent dawning of an era of multipolarity, Europe and Japan did not emerge as poles in a new multipolar international system, but remained comfortably within the US-led Western alliance system. The division of Europe between free self-governing democracies and communist party–ruled and mostly

Soviet-aligned dictatorships, the very cause of the Cold War, was no more. Europe was whole, united, and free—and remained allied with the United States. The Atlantic alliance between the United States and Western Europe did not split apart, as Beijing's multipolarity prognostications had predicted. Instead, the US-Europe link became stronger as the peoples of East Europe, freed at last from fifty years of Nazi and communist dictatorship, began moving toward entry into NATO and the European Union (formed by the Maastricht Treaty of February 1992) as quickly as the West European states would permit. The new East European members of NATO had a quite realistic appreciation of the security offered by European unity and the Atlantic alliance.

The fact that the defeat of communism and the USSR and the liberation of Eastern Europe had been achieved without war had a profound impact on American psychology, making it more confident of its democratic creed and more inclined to pass judgment on China's internal governance shortcomings. The monumental events of 1989–1991 were taken by a wide section of US opinion as vindication of the liberal-democratic values and institutions for which the Cold War—and for that matter, the earlier struggle against fascism, too—had been waged. A strong sense of hubris developed. The belief spread that communist rule in China too would soon disappear, or at least that the abuses of that system should no longer be minimized by the US government. Considerations of China's human rights situation that had long been subordinate in the American calculus to the awesome imperative of meeting the Soviet challenge were now greatly elevated in the calculus of US and other Western leaders. With the Soviet threat removed, Washington became much more concerned with such issues as rights for Chinese dissidents, religious groups, ethnic minorities, workers, and so on. The United States bestrode the world in a position approximating world dominance to a degree perhaps never before seen in history. Chinese analysts referred to this condition of unprecedented unipolarity as an "extremely unbalanced international system."

The great fear of China's CCP rulers was that the PRC would become the target of American power, that the United States would turn its awesome power against the world's last remaining communist party state, seeking to topple that state or injure its interests in various ways—that communist-ruled China would replace the USSR as the chief rival and opponent of US hegemony. This could destroy the favorable macro-climate for development arduously created by Chinese diplomacy over the previous decade, possibly aborting China's development drive before it advanced very far. Even more, US hostility might pose grave danger to regime survival.

Beijing's position vis-à-vis the United States deteriorated further in February 1991, when the United States decisively defeated Iraq in a 100-hour ground war to restore Kuwait's sovereignty. Shortly after that US victory, Li Peng's foreign policy advisor He Xin prepared a paper on the impact of that victory on China which was circulated among China's senior leaders. The US goal was world domination, He Xin wrote. With Iraq's defeat and the demise of the USSR, China stood as the last remaining obstacle to US realization of that goal. The United States would now turn its strength and attention against China, where Washington had "decided it must thoroughly destroy the existing order." The United States could be expected to isolate and blockade China while creating internal disorder to render it powerless via democratization.[1] The anticipated drive to overthrow the CCP and cast China into disorder came soon, under the new US president, William Clinton.

The Linkage of Human Rights and Most Favored Nation Trade Status

William Clinton assumed office in January 1993. On May 28, the new president signed an executive order indicating that if China did not demonstrate "overall significant improvement" in seven specific areas of human rights, he would not recommend to Congress the extension of China's most favored nation (MFN) trade status beyond July 3, 1994. China's continuing MFN status was thereby "linked" to its human rights status. Without MFN status, China's exports to the United States would face prohibitively high tariffs. The seven areas specified by Washington included allowing free emigration, the nonexport of goods made by prison labor, Chinese compliance with the UN Declaration on Human Rights, an end to jamming of radio and TV broadcasts into China, and the release of prisoners held for nonviolent expressions of religious or political beliefs. The logic underlying the policy of linkage was that China's dependency on exports on the US market, combined with the importance of those exports to China's continued rapid economic growth, would lead China's leaders to substantially concede to US demands. The Clinton administration expected that bilateral negotiations would begin following Clinton's executive order, with the two sides bargaining over who much "overall improvement" China would undertake to make.[2] In fact, this would not be the case. Beijing refused to negotiate over what it took to be issues of China's internal governance. CCP concerns with social stability and regime survival would dominate China's response to Washington's "linkage" effort.

From Beijing's point of view, Clinton's policy of linkage was a manifestation of the strategy of peaceful evolution designed to foster dissent and nongovernmental organizations, spread anticommunist ideas, and generally undermine Communist Party control over China. The new secretary of state, Warren Christopher, had himself declared during his Senate confirmation hearings: "Our policy will be to seek to facilitate a broad, peaceful evolution in China from communism to democracy by encouraging the forces of economic and political liberalization in that great and highly important country."[3] To underline his commitment to fostering change in China, Clinton had invited the Dalai Lama and 1989 student movement leader Chai Ling to be present when he signed his executive order. Several months later, when Clinton's National Security Advisor Anthony Lake gave a speech outlining the purposes and contours of US post–Cold War strategy, Chinese leaders were left little doubt about the nature of linkage. Core US values, Lake explained, were democracy and market economy—capitalism, in CCP terms. The highest US priority was to strengthen the bond between major market democracies and minimize the ability of nonmarket regimes to threaten them. Lake specified a number of such nonmarket regimes: Iran, Iraq, North Korea, Burma—and China, though the latter, Lake stipulated, was "opting for liberalization."[4]

No one in the Chinese hierarchy favored giving in to US human rights demands.[5] Jiang Zemin declared those demands to be a "coercive ultimatum." China's leaders decided to reject them, although they did so cautiously and while leaving room for retreat until the end of 1993, by which time it appeared clear that Clinton would be forced to abandon his own executive order. Beijing rejected US demands and, in effect, dared Clinton to follow through with his threat to revoke MFN. At a high-level meeting in September 1993, Jiang Zemin reiterated Deng Xiaoping's policy of not seeking or provoking confrontation with the United States, but added that China would neither fear nor avoid confrontation if the United States chose that path. When Jiang met Clinton for the first time in Seattle in November 1993, Jiang was tough, giving no concessions and lecturing the American president on his misunderstandings of China.[6] As a new general secretary of the CCP, Jiang could not afford to seem weak in facing down the American president.

Beijing's response to Clinton's linkage of human rights and MFN was three-pronged. First, Beijing sought to exploit contradictions in the enemy camp by mobilizing US business interests with operations in China. Scholar Mike Lampton dubs this approach the "big cake strategy."[7] Second, Beijing sought areas of cooperation with the United States on key issues of common interest, thereby underlining for US leaders the benefits of having a decent, cooperative relation with China. Cambodia, North Korea, and nonproliferation were the main areas in which this tactic was activated. Third, Beijing made very modest conciliatory moves on human rights issues to undercut assertions in the US camp that China was doing nothing in this area.

The most important of these tactics was the mobilization of the US business community. Chinese representatives visiting the United States spread the message that China's loss of MFN status would injure US business. The vice chair of the State Planning Commission, on a visit to Boeing Aircraft in Seattle in April 1993, presided over China's purchase of one large 575-model passenger jet and twenty smaller 737 jets. The 737 sale was especially important for Boeing, as demand for that model had been less than expected. Boeing estimated it would lose $5 billion in sales if China lost MFN and retaliated against the United States. In 1993, China purchased forty-seven planes from Boeing. That was 14 percent of the company's annual aircraft production for that year. The State Planning Commission delegation included representatives from China's auto as well as its aviation industry, and proceeded to visit a number of other US cities.[8] An article in the *Seattle Times* outlined the impact China's loss of MFN would have on Washington State. Weyerhaeuser would lose its second largest customer (after Japan) for wood and pulp products. Dozens of manufacturing firms would suffer. The ports of Seattle and Tacoma, which had seen Washington State's trade with China triple since 1987, would suffer greatly. "Seattle has more to lose than any other place in the United States," opined the commissioner of the Port of Seattle.[9]

When Vice Premier Zou Jiahua visited the United States in mid-1993 for the funeral of Richard Nixon, he met briefly with President Clinton and showed him a list of US goods China was prepared to purchase if PRC-US relations improved.[10] Later in 1993, President Jiang Zemin visited Seattle for the first summit of Asia Pacific Cooperation (APEC) leaders. Jiang took the opportunity to visit Boeing. In a speech to Boeing employees, Jiang spoke of the need for US businesses to work to "remove all the negative factors and artificially imposed obstacles" to PRC-US trade.[11] Jiang also dined with Boeing executives. Large numbers of US business leaders were invited to China in the second half of 1993 to be tantalized by the prospects of China's "big cake" and hear the message that enjoying that cake required joint efforts to thwart the anti-China forces in the United States.

During 1992 and the first quarter of 1993, a number of big contracts were signed with US firms: Coca Cola, AT&T, General Motors, Motorola, and ARCO. As one Chinese foreign ministry official said, "The Chinese market is a big cake. Come early and you get a big piece. I hope our two countries have good relations, but it takes two to tango."[12] In 1993, foreign investment in China reached a new peak, with 83,437 contracts with foreign companies worth $110 billion, of which 6,700 were with US companies.[13] This activity was not due entirely to an effort to entice American businesses. By 1993, following Deng Xiaoping's pivotal southern tour a year earlier, China was entering a new, expanded stage of opening and high-paced growth after the post-6.4 retrenchment, and that growth required lots of foreign cooperation. China's "big cake" was attractive to American businesses.

Beijing did not neglect to demonstrate to US business that Clinton's stance on MFN could benefit their European competitors. In November 1993, German Chancellor Helmut Kohl visited China with a delegation of forty German business leaders. Prior to the group's arrival Li Peng told the media "Chancellor Kohl is sure to fly back with a full suitcase." Sure enough, the firms in Kohl's entourage were awarded eighteen contracts worth over $2 billion. The news stories about the commercial success of Kohl's visit appeared on the same day Clinton arrived in Seattle for his meeting with Jiang Zemin. In April the next year, French Prime Minister Édouard Balladur visited Beijing, again with a large group of businessmen. Li Peng told the French guest that China planned to import $1 trillion in goods through the end of the century. "France may get some of the expanded trade," Li said.[14] The message to the Americans was clear: if they did not sell things to China, their European and Japanese competitors would. US businessmen, of course, conveyed this proposition to their representatives in government.

China's tactics were successful. A large part of the US business community mobilized to lobby against Clinton's linkage policy. That lobbying soon affected elected representatives in the US Congress and in state governments. Leading US corporate leaders undertook speaking tours as well as lobbying Clinton directly, not failing to mention their financial support during the 1992 campaign. In Washington State, for example, a statewide coalition of businesses was formed to lobby and conduct public education about the adverse economic impact of MFN revocation. In Washington, DC, agencies of the executive branch—Treasury, Commerce, Justice, the Pentagon—each of whom had issues on which they hoped for Chinese cooperation also began to find fault with the linkage approach.

By early 1994, it was clear that Clinton would not be able to follow through on his threat, even though China had not delivered "significant overall progress" on human rights. This set the stage for the public humiliation of Secretary of State Warren Christopher, one of the leading US advocates of "linkage" within the administration. Christopher's three-day visit to Beijing in March 1994 was intended to tell China's leaders precisely what they must do to achieve "significant overall progress" on human rights and thus ensure extension of MFN. An assistant secretary of state for human rights had done some advanced spadework for Christopher's visit, meeting with prominent dissident Wei Jingsheng in the process. Wei, one of the most radical advocates of democracy dating from the 1978 period, had just been released from fourteen and a half years in prison. Upon release, Wei remained an outspoken critic of CCP rule, advocate of democracy, and supporter of Clinton's "linkage" policy. Shortly after his release, Wei met with the US diplomat and expressed these views. Wei, along with fifteen other prominent dissidents, was promptly arrested. Those arrests were made on the day Christopher left Washington for China and were intended as a signal that China would not be receptive to Christopher's message.[15]

The meetings between Christopher and Li Peng were angry and confrontational, perhaps the worst meetings between Chinese and US leaders since the beginning of Sino-American rapprochement in 1971. Christopher laid out US expectations in each of the specified seven areas. Li Peng firmly replied that the United States had no standing to concern itself with China's internal affairs. Christopher described his negotiations with Li Peng this way:

> I opened ... by explaining to the premier what China needed to do if [Clinton] was to extend [MFN]. With an acerbic smile playing at the corner of his lips, Li Peng responded that China was fully prepared to lose favorable trade status, and if it did, Clinton and I could expect to be blamed [in the United States] for losing China. Li went on to make it clear that China's human rights policy was none of our business, noting that the United States had plenty of human rights problems of its own that needed attention. He made the point personal by pointing out that I had investigated the beating of Rodney King in my hometown of Los Angeles. He then said that by feeding the people, the Chinese government was dealing with the most important human rights. To ensure that I had not failed to appreciate the depth of their unhappiness, the Chinese abruptly canceled my meeting later in the day with President Jiang Zemin.[16]

"China will never accept the US concept of human rights," Li Peng told Christopher. Li also flatly told Christopher his views did not represent the entire Clinton administration. MFN would be extended in spite of Christopher's failed efforts. And as for human rights, racism in the United States should be addressed.[17]

By punishing and humiliating Christopher while rewarding and praising China's American friends, Beijing made clear the difference between enemies and friends. At a strategic level, Beijing had defeated the most aggressive US effort at "peaceful evolution" since 6-4. As scholar James Mann put it, "China had called the Administration's bluff; it had shown that America would back down from the threats it made about human rights and democracy in cases where its commercial and strategic interests were jeopardized."[18] But Beijing also doled out a modest concession. Near the end of Christopher's talks in Beijing, Foreign Minister Qian Qichen informed the American envoy that China would release two prominent organizers of the 1989 demonstrations who had been held in prison since then.

Beijing won a clear diplomatic victory over the United States in the battle over MFN linkage. On May 19, 1994, President Clinton announced that MFN was being renewed in spite of inadequate overall improvement in China's human rights situation. This diplomatic setback for the United States created a reservoir of bitterness and grievance in some quarters in Washington, and determination that the outcome would be different in the next round of confrontation with Beijing that came up. Resentment at Beijing's humiliation of Washington was added to intense dislike of the putative communist troglodytes ruling in Beijing. But while resentment was building up in the United States, the same process was underway in China too, over Beijing's application to host the 2000 Olympics.

Underlining China's Importance and Cooperativeness: Cambodia and Korea

Cambodia and Korea emerged as centers of US foreign policy attention in the early 1990s as difficult problems requiring China's cooperation. Stabilizing PRC-US ties by demonstrating to Washington America's need for China's cooperation and China's willingness to provide such cooperation given an appropriate US attitude was not the only and perhaps not even the main factor governing China's policy toward Cambodia and Korea at this juncture. Both of those countries were China's neighbors, and stability in both was important to maintaining a positive climate for China's development drive. But given the tense and precarious state of Sino-American ties, this stabilization, underlining China's substantial influence in these areas, helped remind the Americans that they occasionally needed China's cooperation—and that China was willing to cooperate with the United States on issues of convergent interests if Washington approached Beijing as a coequal great power. As Qian Qichen wrote in his memoir, the July 1989 foreign ministers' conference in Paris on Cambodia offered a good opportunity to "break the deadlock" China found itself in after 6-4. Only weeks earlier, Western nations had proclaimed their refusal to meet with high-ranking Chinese officials. Yet at the Paris conference, it was clear they would need China's cooperation and would have to meet with Foreign Minister Qian to obtain it. During the conference, Qian met with eleven foreign ministers, including those of the United States, the United Kingdom, France, Japan, and Canada. In Qian's view, China was simply too important not to be included in deliberations over Cambodia.[19]

One key to the solution of the Cambodian problem lay, in fact, in China's diplomacy with Moscow and Hanoi. As noted in an earlier chapter, throughout the 1980s China had maintained unrelenting pressure on Vietnam to abandon its quest for hegemony over Laos and Cambodia, and on Moscow to drop support for Hanoi's occupation of Cambodia, and these demands constituted the highest-ranking of the "three obstacles" in Sino-Soviet relations stipulated by Deng Xiaoping in 1982. As Gorbachev maneuvered toward normalization of Soviet-Chinese ties, he became willing to accede to this demand. In December 1988, Deng had sent Qian to Moscow with three proposals regarding Cambodia: 1) China and the Soviet Union should agree to urge Vietnam to withdraw its forces; 2) after Vietnam's withdrawal, all foreign powers would cease military aid to all Cambodian parties and would not support any party engaged in a civil war; and 3) China and Russia would support a coalition government including all four Cambodian parties and headed by Norodom Sihanouk. Deng's instructions basically brought China's policy into line with ASEAN's, and that congruence would eventually provide the basis for the Cambodian settlement. During the December 1988 Moscow talks, the Soviet Union also agreed to urge Hanoi to withdraw from Cambodia within the shortest period of time. This was formalized in the joint declaration issued at the Gorbachev-Deng summit in Beijing in May the next year.[20]

As Beijing succeeded in cutting off Soviet support for Vietnam's Cambodian occupation, China's leaders decided it was time to begin direct talks with Hanoi. Hanoi was simply no longer able to sustain its effort in Cambodia. Twice during 1988, Hanoi had expressed a desire for talks with China on Cambodia, but Beijing indicated the time was not yet right for talks. Soviet assistance to Vietnam's occupation of Cambodia was still continuing. By January 1989, Beijing judged the time propitious, and Vietnam's vice foreign minister arrived in Beijing to discuss Cambodia. In April, Hanoi finally agreed to unconditionally withdraw its forces from Cambodia. Hanoi had earlier insisted that cutoff of military aid to the three anti–Phnom Penh anti-Hanoi Cambodian factions was a precondition for Vietnam's withdrawal. Now the two sides agreed on Vietnamese withdrawal but continued to deadlock over how to guarantee peace after that. With Vietnam's withdrawal agreed on, the question of arrangements to prevent civil war among the four Cambodian parties became urgent. A Paris conference of July 1989 had deadlocked over the issue of the role of the Khmer Rouge in the transitional Cambodian authority after the withdrawal of Vietnam. Hanoi and its Cambodian ally in Phnom Penh adamantly rejected a Khmer Rouge role. Beijing, Bangkok, and the Khmer Rouge itself insisted on such a role.

In the estimate of Richard Solomon, a diplomat who was the US representative to the Cambodian negotiations, the tarnishing of China's international reputation by the bloodshed of 6-4 had significantly altered China's approach to a Cambodian settlement by strengthening Beijing's incentive to unburden itself of association with Pol Pot's Khmer Rouge.[21] When the Khmer Rouge ruled Cambodia between 1975 and 1978, that group had murdered, as noted in an earlier chapter, perhaps 2.4 million Cambodians—roughly one-third of that country's population. In the 1980s, international awareness of the murderous nature of the Khmer Rouge grew. The Hollywood film *The Killing Fields*, released in 1984, brought that awareness to a much wider audience, as did the opening of Khmer Rouge archives after 1978. China's military assistance to the Khmer Rouge continued throughout the 1980s on the grounds that they constituted the most effective armed resistance to Vietnam's occupation. During both the Reagan and Bush administrations, the United States had urged China to sever ties with the Khmer Rouge and shift its support to the two noncommunist Cambodian resistance groups, but Beijing demurred. Many people, including some in the US Congress, believed that Beijing's objective was to return the Khmer Rouge to power in Cambodia. The extremely negative impact of the Beijing Massacre on China's international reputation put continuing Chinese association with the Khmer Rouge in a very different, far more negative, light. This created a strong incentive for Beijing to sever all association with that odious group.

In fall 1989, only months after 6-4, the Bush administration began consulting with China and other permanent members of the UN Security Council (the "Perm-5") about a UN framework for a comprehensive Cambodian settlement based on the ASEAN plan of 1981. Between January and August 1990, there were six Perm-5 sessions on Cambodia. Beijing supported this process, and a Perm-5 Framework Agreement was signed in Paris in August. This Framework provided for placing the Vietnam-backed Cambodian government of Hun Sen under UN supervision and control; creating a transitional Cambodian authority headed by Norodom Sihanouk, also to be under UN supervision; the disarming of Cambodian factional armies by the UN; and the organization of free and fair elections by the UN leading to a new government. It was widely assumed that the Khmer Rouge would not fare well in free elections, as was indeed the case.

In the Cambodian negotiation process that began in fall 1989, China pushed for inclusion of the Khmer Rouge in both the transitional Cambodian authority and in the elections that were to follow. Only in this way, Beijing argued, could the Khmer Rouge be induced to give up armed struggle. According to Qian's memoir, during a meeting in New York in September 1989, US Secretary of State James Baker accepted China's demand for inclusion of the Khmer Rouge. Baker initially pushed for China to agree to exclude the Khmer Rouge, but when Qian insisted that the Khmer Rouge be given a role, Baker "reluctantly accepted."[22] Qian, however, reassured Baker "There is no possibility of the Khmer Rouge seizing power in Cambodia, and China would not support such an outcome." According to Richard Solomon, the United States accommodated these Chinese demands because the prospect of Khmer Rouge participation in the settlement process gave China the leverage necessary to persuade the Khmer Rouge to give up armed struggle. In the event, this did not happen. The Khmer Rouge refused to disarm or to participate in the electoral process. They did this, however, without China's support, and over the course of several years after the settlement the Khmer Rouge split and then disintegrated.

Arranging the structure of power among the four Cambodian factions was the most difficult part. China pushed initially for the complete dismantling of the Hun Sen government and participation of Khmer Rouge representatives in the transitional Cambodian authority. Eventually, however, Beijing agreed that the Hun Sen regime would merely be placed under the "supervision and control" of the UN. Compromise on the sensitive issue of Khmer Rouge participation was reached by allowing Khmer Rouge to participate as individuals rather than as representatives of their group. Offering a role to the Khmer Rouge met very strong opposition in the US Congress, where a China-supported Khmer Rouge return to power was deemed the greatest danger. Responding to this pressure, in mid-1990 the United States dropped its long-standing support for a UN General Assembly seat for the anti-Vietnamese Sihanouk-led coalition containing the Khmer Rouge. This important shift in US policy suggested that the United States might align with Hanoi and Hun Sen against the Khmer Rouge, a move which a number of members of Congress were in fact advocating.[23]

The prospect of a US switch of alignment to support for Hanoi and the Vietnam-supported Cambodian communists pushed Beijing to shift course and work out an accommodation with Vietnam. Beijing trumped the hinted defection of the United States to Hanoi's side by itself playing the Hanoi card. The continuing evaporation of Soviet support further induced Hanoi to compromise. Thus, in September 1990, a high-powered Vietnamese delegation headed by the Vietnam Communist Party secretary general and the premier visited Beijing for "secret talks" (*neibu huiwu*) on Cambodia with Jiang Zemin, Li Peng, and Qian Qichen. Agreement was reached on complete Vietnamese withdrawal under UN supervision. Hanoi and Beijing also agreed to send representatives to an upcoming meeting in Jakarta of the Cambodian factions, and to urge all parties to reach a settlement within the UN framework. Washington feared at this juncture that Beijing would opt for a "Red solution" between Beijing and Hanoi and drop the UN Framework Agreement. But Beijing remained true to the Agreed Framework of a year earlier.[24] In effect, Hanoi and Beijing both agreed to deliver their respective Cambodian clients for a settlement. A visit to China in November 1991 by the general secretary of the Vietnam Communist Party and the president of the Socialist Republic of Vietnam marked the normalization of Sino-Vietnam relations. Sino-Vietnam rapprochement reduced the risk that Hanoi would drift from alignment with the Soviet Union to alignment with the United States.[25]

A second Paris conference on Cambodia was held in October 1991 to formalize establishment of a United Nations Transition Authority in Cambodia (UNTAC). UNTAC was given full authority for supervising a ceasefire, repatriating refugees, disarming and demobilizing factional armies, and preparing the country for the conduct of internationally supervised free and fair elections that would produce a new government leading, in turn, to a new constitution for the nation. In March 1992, a 22,000-strong UN peacekeeping force established itself in Cambodia and began work. This was the first time the United Nations had effectively taken over administration of a whole country. UNTAC was generally effective. Elections were held in May 1993, with 90 percent of the eligible electorate voting. Sihanouk returned to preside over a coalition government that eventually gave the country peace for the first time in over twenty years.

Through its Cambodian diplomacy, Beijing freed Cambodia from Vietnamese domination, restoring an independent and China-friendly Cambodia such as had existed prior to 1970 or 1978. China had proved its effectiveness as Cambodia's protector against Vietnamese attempts to rule it. By doing this, it had secured for China a reliable and pliant ally in the heart of Southeast Asia. China's diplomacy had also helped end the civil war in Cambodia that had threatened to destabilize China's southern frontier and hinder the flow of Southeast Asian investment and trade to China. Beijing had dislodged the Soviet Union from China's southern borders. Regarding Washington, Beijing had demonstrated at a critical juncture that China had substantial influence and was quite willing to use this influence in parallel with US efforts when matters could be arranged properly via PRC-US discussions and agreement. Beijing also freed itself from association with the odious Khmer Rouge.

Regarding North Korea, that country's nuclear weapons program broke into the open in early 1993, when Pyongyang began moving toward extraction of plutonium-rich spent fuel rods from a nuclear reactor.[26] Extraction of that plutonium via chemical reprocessing would yield fissile material suitable for making atomic bombs. In March, Pyongyang declared its withdrawal from the Nuclear Non-Proliferation Treaty (NPT). Over the next eighteen months, the crisis over North Korea's nuclear program would take the United States to the brink of war with Pyongyang.

To understand China's handling of the 1993–1994 North Korean nuclear crisis, it is necessary to situate it in the broader context of China and the NPT regime. The NPT regime was a major element of the US-designed post–World War II international system, and securing the PRC's full participation in and adherence to that regime was a high-ranking US objective throughout the post-1972 period. China had begun moving toward participation in the NPT regime in 1984, when it joined the International Atomic Energy Agency (IAEA) and began putting its civilian nuclear activities under the supervision of that agency. The decisive step came on March 9, 1992 (while George H. W. Bush was still president), when China signed the NPT. China's signature of the NPT represented realization of a long-standing US policy objective and a significant step forward in PRC cooperation with the United States. In October 1993, however, a Chinese underground test of a small nuclear weapon broke an unofficial moratorium on nuclear testing and warned Washington that China could turn away from increased cooperation with the United States over nuclear nonproliferation.[27] The North Korean nuclear issue was thus a test (at least in American eyes) of Beijing's sincerity as a new and full member of the NPT. Would it work to hold Pyongyang to its NPT obligations, or would it connive at North Korea's efforts to build nuclear weapons?

As information emerged in February 1993 about Pyongyang's preparations to remove the plutonium-rich fuel rods, the IAEA Board of Governors began considering a resolution calling on North Korea to cooperate with the IAEA and meet its NPT obligations. China was a member of that board, which operates on the basis of consensus. This meant China had the power to block or facilitate the resolution. Beijing chose the latter course, agreeing to the resolution after adding modifications that lessened somewhat the stringency directed at Pyongyang.[28] For the first year of the crisis, Beijing did not play an active role. But a major shift in China's position came in March 1994 (as the confrontation over MFN linkage was peaking), when Beijing finally agreed to bring the North Korean nuclear issue before the UN Security Council. Once the issue was before the Security Council, Beijing vetted and then endorsed a US draft resolution criticizing Pyongyang. In negotiations over the text of the resolution, Beijing opposed even an implicit threat of sanctions, but agreed eventually to compromise language (suggested by New Zealand) that "further Security Council consideration will take place if necessary." The United States–sponsored resolution thus left the Security Council with unanimous, i.e. China's, support. As tension escalated during the summer of 1994, China agreed to pass a message from the United States to Pyongyang calling for negotiations about the normalization of US–North Korean relations. Chinese representatives also actively proposed solutions for defusing the mounting tension. Beijing repeatedly but quietly nudged North Korea to fulfill its NPT commitments. When the Agreed Framework was worked out in October 1994, it had China's support. China had become a "smiling dragon," in the words of one US official.[29]

Beijing's underlying strategic interest in Korea during the 1993–1994 crisis was in preventing a war that would disrupt China's development push and might lead to collapse of the North Korean regime. North Korean collapse would confront Beijing with two bad choices: allowing Korean unification, or intervening to prevent that outcome and thus risking a confrontation with South Korea and the United States. North Korean acquisition of nuclear weapons might also push Japan and/or South Korea to follow suit. But Beijing also seized on nonproliferation to remind Washington that China's cooperation was important for successful US management of international issues.

This underlined for US leaders the political costs to the United States if bilateral relations soured as a result of revocation of MFN.

Strategic Partnership with Russia: A "Far Eastern Rapallo"

Formation of a strategic partnership with the new Russian Federation was a major element of Beijing's response to the "extremely unbalanced" international system that emerged after the Cold War. The initial impulse toward that Sino-Russian partnership was the same that had inspired the Sino-Soviet rapprochement of May 1989. Both Beijing and Moscow wanted to focus on domestic issues with minimum international distractions. Each viewed economic cooperation with the other as useful. But some entirely new geostrategic calculations also entered Beijing's calculus, first and foremost preventing newly democratic Russia from moving into alignment with the West.

The overthrow of the CPSU state by Russian liberals led by Boris Yeltsin was, in fact, one of the great anticommunist revolutions of the twentieth century. The objective of many in Yeltsin's camp was to transform Russia into a European-style liberal democracy that would become part of Europe. There was a strong voice within the Russian democratic movement that insisted that Europe was Russia's natural "home," to which it should return by integrating itself with the West. If those impulses took Russia into the Western camp, the consequences for the PRC could be dire. China might find itself completely surrounded by not-very-friendly powers. Already under Gorbachev, Moscow's policy had become increasingly cooperative with Washington, for example with Moscow's support for Washington's 1991 war to restore Kuwait's sovereignty. And there was the example of the ex-communist East European countries that were moving swiftly to join the West with its prosperity, freedom, and security. Russia might switch sides and join the United States, just as China itself had done in 1972 and as Mao had long feared the United States itself would do.

On the other hand, if Russia could be persuaded to disassociate itself from the US-led camp, it might serve as a friendly rear area for China in the event that Beijing found itself in a protracted contest with the United States. These strategic calculations outweighed the dislike of CCP leaders for the Russian counterrevolutionaries who had destroyed the proletarian state of Lenin and Stalin. As often happens in history, geostrategic interest trumped ideology. It is one of the ironies of history, and also a testament to the power of national interest, that the new liberal democratic Russian state moved into alignment with the world's last remaining major Marxist-Leninist state, the PRC.[30] Although CCP leaders viewed the overthrow of the Soviet state by Boris Yeltsin's party as a monumental betrayal of world socialism, they nonetheless set aside those ideological views and worked effectively to normalize Russo-Chinese ties—and detach Russia from the emerging anti-China bloc.[31]

On December 7, 1991, as the USSR slid rapidly toward extinction, a Russian parliamentary delegation arrived in Beijing to deliver a letter from President Yeltsin to President Yang Shangkun. The letter said that Russia was the successor state to the USSR and would continue to implement that former state's treaties and undertakings. NPC head Wan Li accepted the letter and replied, "China's economic development needs a peaceful international environment. Therefore China is willing to live on good terms with all other countries."[32] On December 25, the day that Gorbachev resigned his post as president of the USSR, China recognized Russia as an independent state and the successor to the USSR. At the same time, Beijing recognized the independence of the other fourteen states that had made up the former Union of Soviet Socialist Republics. Russia for its part promised to "respect and support" Beijing's position regarding Taiwan.

Taiwan was a major obstacle in development of a new Russo-Chinese relation. As liberalization advanced in both Taiwan and the Soviet Union in the
late 1980s, people in both countries became interested in expanding ties. For
a period of several years, there was something of a Taiwan-Russia "fever" in
both countries. In May 1988, an influential Taiwan business lobbying group
visited Moscow to explore possibilities. There was strong interest from the
Soviet side. Beijing responded very harshly and demanded an explanation
from Moscow. The Soviet Union backed away from Taiwan, and during his
May 1989 Beijing visit Gorbachev re-endorsed visit Moscow's traditional
position of support for China's Taiwan claim.[33] Yet Russia-Taiwan continued
to intensify as central controls in both countries weakened. Both countries'
transition to democracy was accelerating, and there was great enthusiasm
in both for getting to know the other. During 1990, a number of Russian
groups maneuvered to monopolize the growing ties with Taiwan. One influential group was packed with former CPSU Central Committee members
and headed by foreign minister Edward Shevardnadze. Some Soviet visitors
to Taiwan spoke publicly of large-scale arms sales, representative offices, or
even full diplomatic ties.

Beijing was deeply troubled by these flourishing Soviet-Taiwan ties.
During Jiang Zemin's May 1991 visit to Moscow, Soviet leaders proposed
that Beijing agree to Moscow establishing a nonofficial representative office
in Taiwan along the lines of that maintained by the United States. Beijing
strongly objected, insisting, inter alia, that the United States was an old ally
of Taiwan while the Soviet Union was not, and that the United States was
winding down its ties to Taiwan, while the Soviet Union was expanding
them. Confronted with Beijing's opposition, Moscow dropped its proposal. In
the December 1991 renormalization joint statement, Moscow pledged again to
"respect and support" Beijing's position on Taiwan. Negotiations over Taiwan
continued into 1992. Beijing eventually agreed that nongovernmental offices
could be mutually established in Moscow and Taipei, and in September 1992
Yeltsin did this for Russia by executive order. The same order abolished an
earlier, and "official," liaison office. This agreement over Taiwan opened the
way for a December 1992 visit by Yeltsin to Beijing. The joint statement resulting from that visited stipulated Russia's "recognition" that Taiwan was "an
integral part of Chinese territory" and pledged to maintain only nongovernmental relations with Taiwan.[34] As the Russo-Chinese entente developed in
the mid-1990s, Russian enthusiasm for expanded ties with Taiwan cooled.

Yeltsin's December 1992 visit to Beijing began the process of building a
new strategic partnership. The joint communiqué signed by Jiang Zemin
and Yeltsin during that visit provided that China and Russia were "friendly
countries," that "neither party would join a "military or political alliance"
against the other, "sign any treaty or agreement with a third country preju-
dicing the sovereignty and security interests of the other party, or allow its

territory to be used by a third country to infringe on the sovereignty and security interests of the other party."[35] This was in effect a nonaggression treaty, meaning that neither country would join with the United States, or Moscow's old anti-China partners Vietnam or India, in doing anything that the other signatory deemed injurious to its security interests. The joint communiqué also contained an "antihegemony clause," stipulating the common opposition of the two signatories to "hegemonism and power politics in any form." Inclusion of an antihegemony clause in the 1992 communiqué effectively nullified the antihegemony clauses in Sino-US communiqués and the 1978 Sino-Japan agreement. The antihegemony provisions in those earlier agreements had been understood to reflect convergent interests vis-à-vis the Soviet Union. By including an antihegemony clause in the 1992 joint communiqué, Beijing universalized antihegemony, thereby draining it of its anti-Soviet essence. It pointed, in fact, toward a PRC-Russian coalition against US unipolar domination, implicitly targeting such US moves as linkage of China's MFN to human rights status, acceptance of the East European states into NATO, ballistic missile defense, and so on.

Central Asia emerged during 1993 and 1994 as an important area of Russo-Chinese cooperation. Beijing and Moscow were both astounded by the Islamic renaissance that blossomed across post-Soviet Central Asia. With the lifting of Soviet repression of Islamic activity in the former Soviet Central Asian republics, it became apparent that such activity had survived underground during seventy years of militant atheist repression. Islamic activity now burst into the open and flourished, filling a void left by the evaporation of the communist faith. Some of this new Islamic activism tended toward the extreme jihadism that had grown strong during the Afghan war of resistance. Once the Soviets were out of Afghanistan, some of the extremists, believing it was they who had defeated the Soviet Union in Afghanistan, turned their attention to post-Soviet Central Asia in an effort to replicate their Afghan victory over "infidel" regimes in Central Asia."[36] Islamic missionaries from various Islamic countries—Iran, Pakistan, Saudi Arabia, and Turkey—also became active in trying to shape the Central Asia Islamic renaissance, each trying to tie that renaissance to their own country's particular brand of Islam. In the case of Turkey (a NATO member), the old ideology of pan-Turkism played a role. Neither Beijing nor Moscow had an interest in allowing these third powers, or the United States, to muck around in their Central Asian backyard.

Beijing and Moscow soon concluded that they had a common interest in stabilizing the secular ex-CPSU-apparatchik states that ruled the post-Soviet Central Asian countries. These states had had independence suddenly thrust on them by what was in effect Russian succession from the USSR, and were vulnerable to Islamic extremism and mafia-like crime, in addition to economic retrogression and simple chaos. With Iranian, Pakistani, or Saudi

Arabian agitation mixed in, the situation could become quite complex. It soon became apparent to Beijing and Moscow that they faced common problems in Central Asia and would benefit from cooperation in dealing with them. Soon Chinese and Soviet intelligence services were exchanging information on jihadist activity in Central Asia. Thus in 1996, Russia, China, Kazakhstan, Kyrgyzstan, and Tajikistan met in Shanghai (ergo, The Shanghai Five") to develop a common approach to these problems. This was the beginning of what would ultimately become the Shanghai Cooperative Organization (SCO) in 2006. Both Beijing and Moscow also recognized a common interest in minimizing the US presence in post-Soviet Central Asia, although they choose not to say so publicly.[37]

By the mid-1990s, initial Russian enthusiasm for the West was turning to resentment. Large-scale Western economic assistance, widely anticipated at the end of the Soviet era, failed to arrive. Much US advice urging shock therapy in restructuring the economy did not work well, or even backfired, and was seen to have contributed to Russia's economic regression; many Russians wondered if this was by design. The United States and the West ignored Russian interests over German unification, over entry of East European countries into NATO, over intervention in Yugoslavia, over missile defense, and so on. Americans tended to think that they had "won the Cold War"; this seemed obvious to them. The more common Russian point of view was that there had been no winners and losers from the Cold War, and that the two sides had simply agreed to end it for their mutual benefit. These common American views infuriated Russians and explained to their satisfaction why the Americans were treating Russia like a defeated enemy, why Washington time and again violated Russia's interests. Russia was too weak to do much about US unipolar arrogance. But it could align with the other power resentful about the position of America in the world, the People's Republic of China.

There is a strong similarity between the Russo-Chinese combination that formed in the 1990s and the combination of Weimar Germany and Bolshevik Russia that formed after the Versailles settlement of 1919. Defeated Germany, reconstituted as an unstable democracy, then bore the opprobrium of war guilt, heavy reparations, and demilitarization imposed by the Versailles treaty. Bolshevik Russia was the target of intense hostility, military intervention, a cordon sanitaire, and exclusion from diplomatic circles. In the decade after Versailles, Germany and Russia, separated by a vast gulf in terms of ideology, found a convenient partnership as two powers excluded by the international dispensation set up by the victors in the recent Great War. That Russo-German partnership was formalized by a treaty signed in the northern Italian city of Rapallo in 1922. The Russo-Chinese partnership that emerged in the 1990s was a similar league of countries unhappy with the dispensation worked out by the victors in a recent epic conflict. Both Beijing and Moscow felt the United States was using its vast, historically unprecedented position of unipolarity to trample on their interests. They joined together to counter perceived US moves that injured their mutual interests.[38]

The intensification of the Sino-Russian entente was reinforced by the movement of the ex-communist East European countries toward NATO. Soviet forces began withdrawing from the former Soviet bloc countries in 1992, while Washington devised new arrangements for drawing those newly democratic countries into military partnership with NATO. The result of US planning was the proposal at an October 1993 NATO defense ministers' summit of a "Partnership for Peace" between NATO and the new East European states as a bridge to full NATO membership. Romania was the first East European country to join the Partnership for Peace, in January 1994. Ten more East European countries joined during the first three months of 1994. Russia responded to the transfer of its former East European security zone to NATO by seeking stronger Chinese support. Over the next several years, opposition to "the eastward expansion of NATO" was a significant theme of Chinese propaganda. It was curious to see China's media concerning itself with East European moves to join NATO, but China's objections made sense when seen in terms of Russo-Chinese partnership. Both Beijing and Moscow were being pressed by the United States: Moscow over East Europe, and Beijing by sanctions, MFN linkage, upgrading the US-Japan alliance, and Taiwan. The Russo-Chinese entente increasingly became a partnership in countering the US pressure.

Early in 1994, as NATO's Partnership for Peace was moving forward, Yeltsin sent a letter to Jiang Zemin proposing a "constructive partnership." Li Peng, then premier and also head of the Foreign Affairs Leadership Small Group, was very receptive to the proposal. The result was a visit by Jiang Zemin to Moscow in September. Jiang, like Li Peng, was Soviet-trained. The joint communiqué resulting from the Jiang-Yeltsin meeting provided that neither side would target their nuclear weapons against the other or be the first to use nuclear weapons against the other. These two pledges constituted a symbolic affirmation of convergent Chinese and Russian interests.

Another summit meeting of Jiang and Yeltsin occurred in April 1996 in the immediate aftermath of the US-PRC military confrontation in the Taiwan Strait. The joint communiqué resulting from this summit ratcheted up the Sino-Soviet relation to a "strategic cooperative partnership." The communiqué also pledged each signatory to support the other on territorial issues. The communiqué stated that "Taiwan is an inalienable part of the Chinese territory" and coupled this with a declaration of Chinese "support" for "measures and actions" adopted by the Russian government on the question of Chechnya. In effect, Beijing and Moscow were promising to support each other's use of military force to deal with these issues, regardless of what Washington or Europe might say. An overview of the new Russo-Chinese partnership in a January 1997 internal publication of the journal of the Peace and Development Research Center very frankly laid out the logic of that new relationship:

> As regards China, American and the other Western nations are implementing a strategy of "engagement" plus "containment," utilizing "comprehensive engagement" to promote cooperation with China and advance "Westernization." At the same time, propagating the "China threat theory" will mean setting up endless obstacles [for China] on human rights, arms sales, economics, Taiwan, Tibet, etc., [and carrying out] policies of "division" and "soft containment." China and Russia both need a stable neighborhood environment and international environment for them to achieve the strategic objectives of development, increasing comprehensive national strength, raising their international status. Both countries oppose hegemonism and power politics and advocate the establishment of a new international political order of reason and justice. America and the Western countries are implementing a policy of "containment" toward China and Russia to coerce relatively weak China and Russia, which have common interests and can strengthen their mutual position [by cooperating] and for this reason concluded a strategic cooperative partnership facing the twenty-first century.[39]

Declaration of common principles, usually in opposition to US moves and issued at Sino-Russian summit meetings, became a key modality of the Sino-Russian strategic partnership. Such declarations are listed in Figure 20-1. The statement of April 1997, issued at still another Jiang-Yeltsin summit and titled "On the Multipolarization of the World and the Establishment of a New International Order," provides a good example of these statements. It constituted a point-by-point rebuttal of US diplomatic efforts since the end of the Cold War. Point one rejected "hegemony and power politics . . . confrontation and conflict." That would be overwhelming US military power and its application, for example, in the Taiwan Strait in 1996. Point two of the declaration called for the elimination of "discriminatory policies and practices in economic relations." That would be US insistence on hard terms for entry into GATT and WTO. Point three opposed "bloc politics" and "enlarging and strengthening military blocs." That referred to the "eastward expansion of NATO" (as Chinese and Russian propaganda dubbed the process) and to the reconfiguration of the Japan-US alliance that was then underway. Point four called for strengthening the role of the UN Security Council, where both Beijing and Moscow could veto US proposed actions. "Peacekeeping operations can be undertaken only by the decision of the UN Security Council . . . and in strict compliance with the Security Council mandate and its supervision." This was an implicit criticism of UNPKO in Yugoslavia, which Beijing and Moscow felt deviated from previous principles

Date	Event	Nature of Agreement
Dec. 1992	Yeltsin to PRC	keep tranquility on borders; neither join hostile bloc
Sep. 1994	Jiang Zemin to RF	Mutual non-targeting with nuclear weapons
Apr. 1996	Yeltsin to PRC	mutual support Checnya & Taiwan + Tibet; "Strategic Partnership" proclaimed
Apr. 1997	Jiang Zemin to RF	multipolarity; non-interference internal affairs
Nov. 1998	Jiang Zemin to RF	multipolarity; non-interference; diversity of developmental paths
Dec. 1999	Yeltsin to PRC	opposition to missile defense
Jul. 2000	Putin to PRC	Opposition to missile defense; uphold ABM Treaty pro multipolarity and anti-hegemony; Taiwan part of China
Jul. 2001	Jiang Zemin to RF	oppose missile defense & weaponization of space; support UNSC role; peaceful solution in Kosovo
Dec. 2002	Putin to PRC	Mutual support on territorial integrity (Taiwan, Tibet & Chechya); oppose "double standard" on terrorism; uphold UN
May. 2003	Hu Jinao to RF	oppose power politics & unilateralism; uphold UN, oppose use of force
Oct. 2004	Putin to PRC	PRC support RF entry WTO; mutual anti-terror cooperation
Jul. 2005	Hu Jintao to RF	multipolarization of international order; oppose alliance, monopoly or dominance; call for New World Order; no rule by leading and subordinate camps; no use force
Mar. 2006	Putin to PRC	Joint Declaration; support China re Taiwan; close cooperation re Iran and North Korea
Mar. 2007	HU Jintao to RF	common stance on Iran & NK nuclear issues; strengthen leading role UNSC; Afghanistan UN reform require consensus; oppose arms race in outer space; Iran issue only = peaceful solution; UN reform via "consensus".
May. 2008	Pres. Medvedev to PRC	oppose unilateralism, power politics, & intervention; pro-mutipolarization oppose Cold War mentality and "clique politics" condemn unilateralism
Jun. 2009	Hu Jintao to RF	mutual support for sovereignty & territorial integrity (Taiwan and Caucasus) support reform World Bank to increase role of "emerging markets"
Sept. 2010	Medvedev to PRC	Comprehensively deepen strategic partnership
Jun. 2011	Hu Jintao to RF	support "package deal" re UN reform to grow representativeness attach great importance to BRICS & increase role of India
Jun. 2012	Putin to PRC	respect each other's interests; boost cooperation re security
Mar. 2013	Xi Jinping to RF	1st trip abroad since inauguration as Pres.; big powers to ditch "zero-sum mentality"; cooperate ABM development; oppose any unilateral ABM system development

FIGURE 20-1 **Sino-Russian Summit Level Joint Communiques and Declarations, 1992–2012**

of impartiality, nonuse of force, and the consent of all belligerents. The statement also proclaimed that the new Sino-Russia strategic partnership was "not directed against any third country.[40] This was diplomatic cant signaling that it was, in fact, directed against a third country.

Several years later, in July 2001, a Sino-Russian Treaty of Friendship and Cooperation came very close to being a military alliance in the event of a US-PRC clash over Taiwan. Signed by Jiang Zemin and new Russian president Vladimir Putin, Article V of the treaty provided:

> The Russian side affirms the inalterability of its principled position on the Taiwan issue as presented in the political documents signed and adopted by the heads of both states from 1992 to 2000. The Russian side recognizes that there is only one China in the world . . . and Taiwan is an integral part of China. The Russian side opposes the independence of Taiwan in any form.[41]

Article IX provided:

> If a situation emerges which, according to one of the agreeing sides, poses a danger to peace, violates peace or infringes on interests of its security and if a threat of aggression arises against one of the agreeing sides, the agreeing sides will immediately make contact with each other and hold consultations in order to eliminate the emerging threat.

This was in effect a pledge of Russian pro-Chinese neutrality in the event of a US-PRC clash over Taiwan. Russia would certainly remain neutral in such a conflict, but would, under the provisions of the 2001 treaty, continue to provide China with the material wherewithal for resistance to the United States.

"Partnerships" with Other States

The successful formation of a strategic partnership with Russia seems to have inspired a drive to form similar partnerships with other countries. Following the proclamation of the Russo-Chinese strategic partnership, between 1996 and 2005 Beijing declared "partnerships" with thirty-two countries, as outlined by Figure 20-2. These partnerships were mostly with countries that Beijing considered important, thus "strategic," and which Beijing hoped would remain committed to cooperation with China whatever vicissitudes in international affairs might arise. A key purpose of these partnerships seems to have been to insulate to some degree China's economic and political relations with these countries from any conflict that might emerge between the PRC and the United States.[42] Beijing seems to have been trying to increase the possibility that, in the event of a conflict between China and the United States, its "strategic partners" would still carry on economic and other ties with China. From

1996	Russia	Strategic Cooperative Partnership
1996	Brazil	Long-term, Stable Strategic Partnership
1997	France	Comprehensive Strategic Partnership
1997	ASEAN	Strategic Partnership for Peace and Prosperity
1997	Canada	Comprehensive Partnership for the 20th & 21st Centuries
1997	United States	Will "work toward" Comprehensive Strategic Partnership
1997	Mexico	Comprehensive Partnership Facing the 21st Century
1997	India	Partnership of Constructive Cooperation
1998	Pakistan	Partnership of Comprehensive and Cooperation for 21st Century
1998	Japan	Partnership of Friendship and Cooperation for 20th and 21st Centuries
1998	European Union	Constructive Partnership of long term and stability
1998	United Kingdom	Comprehensive Partnership
1999	Saudi Arabia	Relation of Strategic Cooperation Facing 21st Century
1999	Egypt	Relation of Strategic Cooperation Facing 21st Century
1999	South Africa	Constructive Partnership Facing 21st Century
2000	Iran	21st century oriented long-term and wide-ranging relationship of friendship and cooperation in the strategic interest of the two countries*
2000	Africa	Strategic Partnership for Sustainable Development
2003	Mexico	Comprehensive Strategic Partnership
2003	E.U.	Comprehensive Strategic Partnership
2004	South Africa	Strategic Partnership
2004	United Kingdom	Comprehensive Strategic Partnership
2004	Italy	Comprehensive Strategic Partnership
2004	Nigeria	Strategic Partnership
2004	Algeria	Strategic Partnership
2004	Germany	Global Responsible Partnership within framework of PRC–EU Strategic Partnership
2005	India	Strategic and Cooperative Partnership for Peace and Prosperity
2005	Argentina	Comprehensive Strategic Partnership
2005	Venezuela	Comprehensive Strategic Partnership
2005	Kazakhstan	Comprehensive Strategic Partnership
2005	Indonesia	Comprehensive Strategic Partnership
2005	Canada	Strategic Partnership
2005	Portugal	All Round Strategic Partnership

FIGURE 20-2 **China's Strategic Partnerships, 1996–2005**

Sources: Joseph Y. S. Cheng, Zhang Wankun, "Patterns and Dynamics of China's International Strategic Behavior," *Journal of Contemporary China*, vol. 11, no. 31 (2002), p. 237. Phillip C. Saunders, *China's Global Activism: Strategy, Drivers, and Tools*, Occasional Paper #4 National Institute for Strategic Studies, National Defense University, p.13.
*"China, Iran Joint Communique," People's Daily, June 22, 2000. http://en.people.cn/English/200006/22/eng20000622_43708.html. This obtuse phraseology is typical of the wariness with which Beijing handles relations with the Islamic Republic of Iran.

this perspective, China's partnerships can be seen as attempts to weaken US ability to use its influence to mobilize an anti-China coalition.

Partnerships were explicitly intended to counter what China dubbed "Cold War mentality," according to which pernicious distinctions were made among

550 { China's Quest

states on the basis of their social system, form of government, and values. Partnerships were intended to exclude such distinctions and recognize that each country had the right to choose its own developmental path and social-political model. Declarations of partnership were intended to delegitimize such distinctions. Differences of values and institutions were normal and unobjectionable and should be tolerated. China's partners should accept diversity and not imagine that one set of values or institutions could be used to judge other countries, draw distinctions among them, or interfere in their internal affairs. Differences in social systems and values should not affect the healthy development of state-to-state relations. Countries should respect the choices of other countries made on the basis of their national conditions and historical experience.

Partnerships were also intended as invitations to the leaders of other countries, especially important countries, to identify common interests with China and seek cooperation with China in these areas. Use of terms such as "centuries" were used to signify China's hopes for long-term, stable cooperative relations to deal with a wide range of problems, some of which were not yet known. These problems were to be dealt with on the basis of equality, mutual respect, and mutual benefit. Partnerships were also intended to assure China's neighbors that China did not constitute a threat and would not do so in even when China's national power became greater.

China's strategic partnerships would make it more difficult for Washington to line up countries against China, should the United States decide to do that. Beijing was waging a political struggle against a possible US-led new Cold War against the PRC. When doing this Beijing was careful to proclaim that its partnerships were not directed against any third country, i.e. the United States. Such disclaimers were typically a part of the declarations of Beijing's various partnerships.

UNPKOs and Multilateralism

Configuration of UN Peacekeeping Operations (UNPKO) became another venue for China's struggle against unipolarity and interference in the internal affairs of sovereign states. The nature of UNPKO changed dramatically with the end of the Cold War, and Beijing saw that shift as further strengthening the position of "the West led by the United States" in overriding strong state sovereignty norms.

For its first ten years in the UN, the PRC did not participate in UNPKO, neither voting on these issues in Security Council deliberations, nor paying the annual PKO dues assessed by the UN, nor contributing personnel for UNPKO.[43] China's position began to change in 1981, when it began to vote in favor of various PKO and pay its PKO annual assessment. China's stance changed further in 1989, when it began contributing personnel to

UNPKO and playing a much more active role in Security Council debates over the nature of those PKO. In fall 1989, China first declared its willingness to provide manpower for UNPKO, and in November it dispatched five Military Observers to the UN Truce Supervision Organization monitoring peace agreements in the Golan Heights and the Sinai.[44] Over the next decade, China would participate in nine more UNPKO. At the same time, it would abstain from or eventually distance itself from four other UNPKO, mainly because Beijing felt those operations violated the state's sovereignty. Figure 20-3 lists UNPKO supported and not supported by China. By increasing its role in PKO that it approved of, Beijing strengthened its voice in criticizing PKO to which it objected.

There seem to have been two main reasons why Beijing joined the PKO process in mid-1989: a desire to improve China's post-6-4 image in the world by demonstrating it was a reasonable power, and the need to work out a settlement of the Cambodian question once Vietnam agreed to withdraw from Cambodia. Working through a UN framework for Cambodia was especially important. Chinese diplomatic missteps there could easily alienate the Southeast Asian countries where fear of China was traditional and strong, and which Beijing hoped could be persuaded to contribute to China's development drive. Working through the UN offered a way of reassuring China's neighbors while ending the war that had raged in Indochina on China's southern borders for forty years.

Beijing also feared US manipulation of the UN to further US hegemony, and deeper engagement with the United Nations could counter US efforts to use the UN for anti-China purposes. The end of the Cold War, and the beginning of far greater cooperation among the Perm-5 that resulted, led to major shifts in UN thinking about the nature of PKO, yielding PKOs that

Supported	Dates	Abstained	Dates
Mid East Supervision Organization	1948–2013	Yugoslavia	1992–96
Iraq–Kuwait Observer Mission	1991–2003	Somalia	1992–93
Western Sahara Referendum	1991	Rwanda	1994
Mozambique	1992–1994	Haiti	1994
Advance Mission in Cambodia	1991–1992		
Transitional Authority in Cambodia	1992–93		
Observer Mission in Liberia	1993–1997		
Observer Mission in Sierra Leone	1999–?		
East Timor Transitional Administration	1999		

FIGURE 20-3 **UNPKOs Supported and Not Supported by Beijing**

Sources: Bates Gill, James Reilly, "Sovereignty, Intervention and Peacekeeping: The View from Beijing," *Survival,* vol. 42, no. 3 (Autumn 2000), p. 45. M. Taylor Fravel, "China's Attitude toward U.N. Peacekeeping Operations since 1989," *Asian Survey,* 1996, pp. 1102–21.

were of a far more aggressive, militarized, and interventionist nature. During the Cold War, the UN had drawn a sharp line between enforcement actions, which authorized the use of military force by member states against other member states, and peacekeeping operations, which required the consent of both belligerents. PKO forces were expected to be impartial between belligerents. PKO were undertaken where use of military force was unlikely to be necessary—after a ceasefire and with the consent of both belligerents. During the Cold War, the UN authorized the use of military force only once, in Korea. PKO were not understood to involve the use of military force other than for immediate self-defense.

After the Cold War and starting with the former Yugoslavia in 1992, the Security Council began to authorize a very different, nontraditional type of PKO that did not require the consent of both belligerents, that authorized the use of military force for a number of purposes other than self-defense (e.g., to protect refugees, guarantee delivery of relief aid, end mass killings and ethnic cleansing, or impose a particular government), and by doing these things effectively taking sides between warring parties. Beijing objected strongly to this trend, rejecting these PKO as violations of the sovereignty rights of states.[45] For Beijing, since 1989 upholding the principle of noninterference in the internal affairs of sovereign states had become paramount. The vitality of strong norms of state sovereignty touched on China's own security in the post–Cold War world.

China's objections to Western-driven interventionist UNPKO began with the former Yugoslavia in 1992–1993, as that ex-communist-ruled state disintegrated. China initially voted in favor of establishment of a UN Protection Force in 1992 as an "interim arrangement to create the conditions for peace and security required for the negotiation of an overall settlement of the Yugoslav crisis."[46] Subsequently, and at the instigation of Germany, France, and Britain, the Security Council expanded the mandate of the Protection Force to include establishment of safe havens for persecuted ethnic groups, no-fly zones, and armed protection of distribution of humanitarian relief. UN peacekeeping operations were also expanded from the initial Croatia to Bosnia and Herzegovina, where, unlike in Croatia, the warring parties had not concluded a ceasefire. China objected to this expansion. Use of military force to guarantee delivery of humanitarian assistance was "inappropriate," said China's Ambassador Li Daoyu. UN action had not secured the consent of the belligerents. The new role would put UNPKO in armed opposition to forces aligned with the Belgrade government. In effect, the UN was taking sides in Yugoslavia's internal conflict via armed intervention, or so Beijing believed. In 1992 and 1993, the PRC abstained eight times on Security Council resolutions expanding and strengthening the UN's role in former Yugoslavia.

In the case of Somalia, Beijing went along with the other Perm-5 members in establishing a PKO to monitor a ceasefire between warlords, and then to expand the mandate of that mission to humanitarian relief. China's attitude became more critical when the UN force (mostly American and Pakistani) began to clash with Somali militias. In Rwanda, mass killings and ethnic cleansing led the Security Council to authorize a French-led force to establish a safe zone for refuges in the southern part of the country. China abstained from supporting this effort on the grounds that it amounted to interference in a civil war. Again, in Haiti in 1994, when the Security Council authorized a PKO to restore to power a president ousted by a military coup, China abstained.

China explained its opposition to the UN's increasingly interventionist and militarized PKO in terms of opposition to use of force. Resort to military force simply was not conducive to negotiated settlement of conflicts, Beijing said. But as Taylor Fravel notes, this "tells only half the story."[47] The other half is that upholding the norm of strong state sovereignty was linked to China's own security. China's leaders feared some type of uprising in China, or possibly a conflict with Taiwan or in the South China Sea, in which the United States and other Western countries could mobilize international intervention via the United Nations. By upholding the high moral principle of strong state sovereignty in regions of the world distant from China, Beijing was eroding the ability of the US hegemonists to mobilize an international coalition and UN legitimization for some type of armed intervention against China.

It is ironic that the UNPKO that had the fullest and most important support by China—that in Cambodia—was also the most blatant example of United Nation's "nation building" and "regime change" for which Beijing would reject other UNPKO. In Cambodia the UN Transitional Authority Cambodia (UNTAC) would actually take over and administer an entire country for two years, setting up a new government and eventually a new state, dissolving and recreating a military in the process. It's hard to imagine a clearer example than UNTAC of the sort of "interference in internal affairs of a sovereign state" to which China would later repeatedly object. Yet China did not object, but fully supported UNTAC in Cambodia. Taylor Fravel's explanation is that in the Cambodian case, China's own direct national security interests trumped China's indirect security interest in upholding the global norm of strong state sovereignty.

The Serendipitous Reinforcement of the Narrative of Aggrieved Nationalism

Two of the momentous influences on China's foreign relations in the early 1990s were events that no government planned or foresaw: US congressional opposition to the city of Beijing's hosting of the 2000 International Olympics Games, and US high-sea interdiction of a Chinese merchant vessel suspected of carrying chemical-weapon precursors to Iran. Both events dovetailed nicely with the narrative of China's national humiliation propounded with added vigor by the CCP propaganda apparatus after 6-4. And these events, both in 1993, tapped sentiments of resentment of many people in China, giving real traction for the first time to CCP nationalist indoctrination efforts. For the first four years after the Beijing Massacre, CCP efforts at both intensified patriotic education and Marxist-Leninist-rooted anti–peaceful evolution propaganda produced modest results in rallying support for the regime. Sullen anger over the bloody repression of June 1989, combined with fear that the party was turning away from the popular policies of opening and reform, created a sullen atmosphere in which the diligent efforts of propaganda yielded little result. By 1994, however, the environment had changed. CCP propaganda about Western humiliation of China resonated with a much larger part of Chinese public opinion. By 1994–1995, some of China's intellectuals were spontaneously and autonomously producing a new anti-US nationalist literature. The two random events of 1993 were significant factors accomplishing this shift.

Regarding the Olympics, in 1990 Beijing Party Secretary Chen Xitong launched an application to the International Olympics Committee (IOC) for that city to host the 2000 Olympic Games. Such sponsorship would, CCP leaders calculated, help wipe out memories of the Beijing Massacre and provide the CCP will a much-needed boost in popularity. Tokyo's hosting of the 1964 Olympics and South Korea's hosting of the 1988 Olympics (the first and second times the Olympic Games were held in Asia) were recognized as major landmarks in the global rehabilitation of those countries from the ashes of war. The CCP hoped that the 2000 games would do something similarly positive for the PRC and the CCP. But Beijing city leaders were not well informed about the IOC decision process or about realistic chances for Beijing being awarded the Games so soon after the Beijing Massacre.

Once Beijing had applied with the IOC, China's government launched a three-year campaign, with rallies, billboards, and media propaganda. Beijing's lobbying campaign with the IOC was reportedly the most active and best-funded of all competitors for the 2000 games. The size of Beijing's proposed Olympics budget dwarfed competitors.[48] When an IOC inspection committee visited Beijing, large numbers of street-sweepers cleaned up the city, smog-producing factories were shut down, and throngs of cheering school children lined the streets for the IOC group. In an appeal to Third World members of the IOC, Beijing promised that it would use most of the $120 million profit estimated to result from the Games to support athletics in developing countries. Beijing also promised that, if Beijing got the 2000 Games, the names of IOC members and winners would be inscribed into the Great Wall. For ordinary Chinese, the prospect of Beijing hosting the 2000 Olympics drew considerable interest and support. By the time the IOC rendered its decision in September 1993, the Beijing Massacre was already four years in the past and China had entered a new stage of expanded opening and reform following Deng Xiaoping's successful early 1992 effort to reinvigorate those policies. When IOC head Juan Samaranch announced Sydney, Australia's selection, there was considerable disappointment among ordinary Chinese about Beijing's failure. Many blamed the outcome on the United States.[49]

In July 1993, while Beijing's Olympics campaign was in high gear, the House of Representatives of the US Congress passed a resolution calling on the IOC not to award the 2000 games to Beijing because of China's "massive violations of human rights." In the Senate, sixty senators supported a similar resolution. Chinese officials strongly denounced these resolutions as violations of the Olympics spirit of independence from politics. Beijing Deputy Mayor Zhang Baifa threatened that China would boycott the 1996 Olympics, which had already been awarded to Atlanta in the United States. This threat was later negated by other officials, but it expressed China's anger. "The American people are very good to us. It's their Congress which is stupid," Zhang Baifa told the media.[50] "Why does the U.S. go out of its way to get into other people's business?" asked one Beijing citizen interviewed by a popular US magazine.[51] Upon his return to Beijing from Monaco, where the IOC had met to make its decision, Chen Xitong briefed CCP leaders on how "hostile Western powers led by the United States" had smeared and bad-mouthed China to undermine its Olympics bid.[52] The Chinese media, guided by the CCP's propaganda department, began to stress the same theme. For the first time, CCP propaganda targeting "hostile Western powers led by the United States" began to resonate with the Chinese public.

The second incident that gave traction to the CCP's anti-US propaganda was nearly simultaneous with the Olympic imbroglio and involved a 20,000-ton Chinese containership named *Yinhe* (Galaxy). In July (while Beijing was lobbying intensely for the Olympics), the *Yinhe* loaded cargo in Dalian, Liaoning province, and set sail for Iran. Shortly after the ship's departure from Dalian, the US embassy in Beijing informed China's MFA that the *Yinhe* had loaded cargos of several chemicals used to manufacture chemical weapons, and the United States, therefore, insisted that the ship either return to port or submit to inspection. The MFA pointed out that neither the PRC nor the United States had ratified the Chemical Weapons Convention (CWC) banning trade in specified chemicals, and that no international authority had empowered the United States to conduct unilateral inspection of other country's commercial shipping. "If such behavior of a self-styled 'world cop' is to be condoned, can there still be justice, sovereign equality and normal state-to-state relations in the world?" the MFA asked the United States. Yet the Chinese government had issued "clear-cut" orders banning shipment of the indicated chemicals, it said, and would investigate whether they were included in the *Yinhe*'s cargo.[53]

Chinese authorities duly carried out an investigation, found no banned chemicals, and so informed the US embassy. Paramount leader Jiang Zemin gave a personal assurance to this effect to Ambassador Stapleton Roy, who believed that such a direct assurance from Jiang should be credited.

While all this was going on, the *Yinhe* proceeded on its journey across the Indian Ocean, closely watched by US planes and warships. International media carried photographs of the ship along with accounts of its alleged cargo. On reaching the Strait of Hormuz at the entrance to the Gulf, the ship dropped anchor and waited. It began running low on water and food, and conditions for the crew deteriorated. These hardships and US military surveillance of the *Yinhe*, along with accounts of China's protestations to the United States, were covered extensively by China's media. Eventually, an agreement was reached in which the *Yinhe* entered a Saudi Arabian port for a thorough inspection by Saudi officials under close watch by US and PRC officials. The banned chemicals were not found. China demanded a public apology, compensation for losses suffered by the Chinese shipping company, and a guarantee against future repetitions. The US State Department merely expressed "regrets" for the "inconveniences" suffered by the Chinese company, while asserting that the United States would continue vigorous enforcement of the CWC. Two weeks into the standoff, China went public about the episode, with Xinhua detailing the episode as American bullying, tarnishing China's reputation, and injuring its commerce and freedom of navigation, as well as its relations with other countries. Once again CCP propaganda resonated with public opinion. Nationalist resentment rallied around the CCP government in the face of US bullying.[54] China's media strongly condemned US policies and arrogant attitudes. "This is a show of hegemonism and power politics pure and simple," an MFA statement said.[55] As with US opposition to Beijing's Olympics bid, US handling of the *Yinhe* was deeply resented by the Chinese populace. The CCP's anti-US indoctrination began to gain traction. The crucial political logic regarding China's internal political arrangements was left unstated: what patriotic Chinese would embrace any ideas coming from a hostile power that humiliates China in these ways?

21 }

China and America in the Persian Gulf

China and the American Quest for Hegemony in the Persian Gulf

New and important energy interests entered China's diplomatic calculus in the 1990s. When China opened in 1978, it imported little crude oil and was itself a modest supplier of that product. In the late 1970s, estimates of huge deposits of offshore oil in the Bohai Gulf led to exaggerated projections that China would become a major oil exporter. These projections underlay a short-lived post-Mao but neo-Maoist approach to China's foreign orientation under Hua Guofeng's leadership before Deng's takeover in late 1978. But as China developed under Deng's policy of opening, its demand for oil rose rapidly. Most electricity was still produced by burning coal, but internal combustion–driven mobility (cars, trucks, airplanes, ships, diesel locomotives) required oil-based fuels, while petrochemical factories required petroleum feed stocks. China's domestic oil production simply could not keep pace with skyrocketing demand. Oil imports grew. In 1993, China's oil consumption surpassed domestic production. This growing dependency on imported petroleum made China vulnerable to disruption in international oil supplies. This brought the Persian Gulf into focus, since the producers of that region—Saudi Arabia, Iran, Iraq, Kuwait, the United Arab Emirates, Oman—are among the world's leading suppliers of oil.

But the Persian Gulf was also a region of war and revolution—instability that could disrupt oil supplies. It was also a region under US domination, and this reality made China's vital oil supply vulnerable to US pressure. Consequently, China tried mightily throughout the 1990s and 2000s to diversify its foreign oil supplies away from the Persian Gulf. It achieved some success in this. Angola and Sudan, the Central Asian republics, and Russia emerged as major suppliers. But after decades of attempting to diversify away from the Persian Gulf, that region's producers still supplied about the same share, some 50 percent, that they had decades earlier. The simple geological reality that a hugely disproportionate share of the world's oil was located around the Persian Gulf.

In Beijing's view, that simple reality underlay the fact (as judged by Beijing) that the Persian Gulf was a focus of rivalry between the Soviet and US superpowers. Each of the two hegemony-seeking superpowers sought to control that region's oil wealth as a stepping stone on the path to world domination. When China did not need Persian Gulf oil, it had the luxury of "sitting on the mountain top and watching the tigers fight"—in the words of an old Chinese saying—although, as discussed in an earlier chapter, Beijing decided in the 1970s that China's interests were served if Persian Gulf oil was kept out of Soviet hands. As China's need for imported oil rose in the post–Cold War period, its interests in the Persian Gulf grew. By then, however, China found that only one tiger, the United States, bestrode the Persian Gulf.[1]

The Persian Gulf became a major arena of PRC-US interaction during the post–Cold War period as frequent US sanctions, bombing, and wars touched on China's roles in the Security Council and as a partner of Iran and Iraq, the two countries targeted by US punitive measures. In these conflicts between the United States, Iran, and Iraq, Beijing encountered but rejected the option of forming with Iran an anti-US partnership along the lines of its strategic partnership with Russia. Beijing initially threatened Washington with such a bloc during the lead-up to renormalization of Sino-US relations in 1996–1997, but ultimately eschewed that option in order to avoid confrontation with the United States in the Gulf. Instead, Beijing opted to stand aside and allow the United States to run amuck in the Gulf, but simultaneously sell China's non-opposition to Washington's thrusts in the Gulf for as high a price as could be obtained from Washington.

There was a virtual consensus among Chinese analysts that the goal of US policy in the Persian Gulf was, and had always been, control over that area's rich oil supply in order to move a step closer to US global domination. Washington appealed to various themes: nonproliferation of nuclear weapons, upholding UN Security Council resolutions, antiterrorism, human rights, democracy, and the security of oil-bearing sea lanes of communication from the Gulf. But at bottom these were either nice-sounding pretexts useful for mobilizing support for US moves or second-order objectives useful as a means of achieving a deeper, more fundamental objective. The core US objective was to dominate the world by controlling the world's richest supply of crude oil in the Persian Gulf region. Controlling the oil flowing from the Gulf would give the United States the ability to coerce countries dependent on that oil: the European countries, Japan, South Korea, and, of course, China. This, Chinese analysts virtually uniformly believed, was the real, unstated but paramount, purpose of US policy in the Gulf during the post–Cold War era.

One of Beijing's elemental considerations was that in the event of a clash with the United States which became protracted, Washington might play its trump card of control of global sea lanes to enforce an embargo cutting off China's oil imports. In such an extreme situation, Beijing would face the difficulty of importing its oil needs via overland routes via rail or pipeline. But aside from transport links, China would also need, in such an extreme contingency, petroleum-rich countries willing and able to flout American demands and put large quantities of oil into China's emergency overland energy supply system. Russia (which had become a major oil producer since the end of containment), the Central Asian republics, and the Islamic Republic of Iran would be the major candidates to supply oil to China in such a dire eventuality.

China's and America's First Two Persian Gulf Wars (1987 and 1991)

The United States entered the Gulf militarily and directly only in January 1980, when President Carter proclaimed that the United States would use its military power, if necessary, to protect petroleum flows from the Persian Gulf. Prior to 1968, the United States had relied on British military dominance in that area and, after that and until 1979, on Iran under the shah. Only after the British withdrawal from "east of Suez" and the overthrow of the shah, followed quickly by the Soviet occupation of Afghanistan, did the United States undertake to use its own military power to secure control over the oil resources of the Gulf.[2] In 1980, Beijing strongly supported this, seeing it as an important and even long overdue US move to counter a Soviet expansionist offensive that had been virtually unchecked by the United States since the mid-1970s. Beijing saw the oil-rich Persian Gulf as a focal point of superpower (US and Soviet) contention, and concluded that control of those resources by US hegemony accorded with China's interests far more than would Soviet control.

China's estimate of the US role in the Gulf changed as Beijing's fear of Soviet encirclement ebbed and Sino-Soviet relations improved in the mid-1980s. As US-Iranian naval clashes escalated in 1986–1987 over Iranian challenges to oil shipping through the Gulf, Beijing reverted to its earlier position that the security affairs of the Gulf should be handled by the countries littoral to that Gulf. (The reader will recall that this principle had been endorsed by Ji Pengfei in 1973 during the period when the shah was attempting to "fill the vacuum" in the Gulf.) In 1986–1987, Beijing condemned the US resort to military force against Iranian warships, even while it rhetorically upheld the freedom of navigation of neutral shipping.[3] Beijing also advised Tehran to end the war with Iraq on the grounds that the two superpowers (obviously with the United States in the lead, although Beijing did not publicly say this) were using it as a pretext to expand their military presence in the Gulf.

The deterioration of PRC-US relations after 6-4 greatly increased the dangers to China posed by stronger US control over Gulf oil. The prospect of such strengthened US control was raised on August 2, 1990, when Iraqi military forces seized Kuwait and annexed that territory as a claimed nineteenth province of Iraq. The United States quickly condemned Iraq's action, began mobilizing UN sanctions punishing Iraq's move, and deploying military forces to the Gulf to protect Saudi Arabia, a US ally threatened by the Iraqi seizure of Kuwait. US deployments to Saudi Arabia also put in place the potential for further military action to restore Kuwaiti sovereignty should that become necessary.

Beijing condemned both Iraq's action and US military moves. Li Peng in a report to the NPC Standing Committee on August 28 (several weeks after Iraq's seizure of Kuwait) declared that China was firmly opposed both to Iraq's move and to the military involvement of the big powers. The crisis, Li said, was an indication of the imbalanced global pattern of relations following the relaxation of relations between the United States and the Soviet Union.[4] In plain language, Li was saying that the United States would not have dared to move against Iraq, a country allied with Moscow since 1972, if the USSR had been prepared, as Gorbachev was not, to stand behind Iraq. As for resolution of the dispute, Li said that it should be resolved by peaceful means among the Arab countries, utilizing the UN mediation role to the fullest—in other words, not by the United States or via the use of US military force. China, Li said, was opposed to military involvement by the big powers because such involvement would do "nothing but complicate and intensify the situation."

Chinese leaders were convinced that the United States would use the opportunity afforded by Iraq's seizure of Kuwait to advance US hegemony over the Gulf region. Iraq's invasion of Kuwait provided the United States an excellent opportunity to meddle in Middle Eastern affairs and in the domestic affairs of Middle Eastern countries, said a *Renmin ribao* article shortly after the Iraqi invasion.[5] With Soviet resolve evaporating, the United States "had nothing to fear" and was moving toward military intervention, the article said. According to a leading MFA Middle East analyst, Li Guofu, the Gulf crisis was an indication of an unbalanced global pattern following the relaxation of relations between the United States and the Soviet Union.[6]

The considerations that US leaders said (and still say) loomed large in the US decision to undo Iraq's move—not allowing violent, illegal aggression to stand, which would undermine a stable and peaceful international order—simply did not figure in Chinese analyses of US motives. There is a vast gulf between Chinese and American judgments about why the United States resorted to force in 1991.[7] The objective of US military intervention in the Iraq-Kuwait "dispute," Chinese analysts quickly concluded, was to control Persian Gulf oil in order to be able to coerce the countries dependent on that oil. "Why fight a war," an article in the MFA's magazine asked? It answered: "The reason is very simple. The Gulf oil-producing countries export 90 percent of the crude oil they produce mainly to the United States, Western Europe, and Japan."[8] The US aim was "nothing but to establish a new post-Cold-War world order," a kind of new imperialism. Another author, writing in the same issue of the MFA journal, elaborated on this conclusion: Iraq's occupation of Kuwait "presented . . . a favorable opportunity for the realization of a global strategy by the United States. The vast petroleum resources of the Gulf are of important strategic significance. Who controls the oil resources of this region controls the lifeblood of the world." The Soviet Union's decision to abandon its earlier policy of contending with the United States for control of the Middle East had given Washington an opportunity to use Iraq's move against Kuwait as an "opportunity to hit at Iraq." By controlling Persian Gulf oil and oil transport lines, the United States could "keep a tight rein on . . . rapidly rising allies like Germany and Japan."[9] Though it was left unstated, China would similarly be on the tight rein.

In Beijing's view, the 1991 Gulf war was a struggle between global and regional hegemony—US and Iraqi respectively.[10] Both countries sought to control the oil of Kuwait in order to further their hegemonistic schemes. Iraq, like the United States, was motivated by hegemonic desires, Beijing concluded. Its motives were no purer than those of the United States. The overall situation regarding the Gulf confrontation, according to a document produced by the State Council and the General Office of the Central Committee in January 1991, was a struggle between global hegemony (the United States) and regional hegemony (Iraq). The old world order had been destroyed, but a new order had not yet been established. This confrontation was over that future order. The US objective was "first to teach Saddam Hussein a lesson and then to dominate the world."[11]

Left unstated in Chinese analyses, but clearly discernable between the lines, was the proposition that the success of US schemes to control Gulf oil would render *China* more vulnerable to US pressure. China in 1991 was not yet a net oil importer, but the trend lines were clear; China's continued development would require it to import ever more oil. The United States could keep China as well as Europe and Japan "under its thumb" if it controlled the Gulf's oil. The imperative of escaping its post-6-4 isolation led China to cooperate with the United States on the Gulf Crisis. But Beijing saw US moves as deeply threatening to China's global position, although it could not say this directly.

In the conflict between what Beijing viewed as regional and global hegemonism, China's interests would not be injured by Iraqi control of Kuwaiti oil. PRC relations with both Iraq and Kuwait had been cordial. Kuwait had been generous to China, being the only Third World country to provide

China with soft loans.[12] But these were narrow interests. In broader terms, it really didn't matter to Beijing whether Kuwait's oil was controlled from Kuwait City or from Baghdad. Both were Third World developing countries with friendly relations with China. If, however, Kuwait's oil was controlled by Washington, and if Washington was able to use that control to keep Japan, Western Europe, or China itself in line, China's geostrategic interests would be injured. Yet precisely because of the centrality of the Persian Gulf in US global hegemonist strategy—as perceived by Beijing—if the PRC tried to thwart US moves, the consequences for PRC-US relations could be dire.

From Beijing's perspective, Washington was seizing on Iraq's unfortunate annexation of Kuwait to advance US control over Persian Gulf oil as a step toward achievement of a New Global Order of American global dominance. The United States, now freed of countering moves by the USSR, was focusing on the Persian Gulf and its oil in a new drive for global domination. But if the Persian Gulf was the epicenter of the current US drive for global domination, for China to oppose or thwart Washington in that region could be extremely dangerous. The more prudent course, one that characterized actual Chinese policy, was to demand and take the highest price possible that Washington was willing to pay for China's nonopposition to US moves, even while quietly laying snares for the United States when opportunities arose. Underlying Chinese policy was a conviction that US hegemonist strategy would ultimately fail. Superpower attempts to dominate the Third World would meet with the resistance of the people of the developing countries, and ultimately would be defeated. Until then, Beijing would get what it could from the United States for "allowing" the United States to run amuck in the Gulf and toward what was certain to be ultimate failure there. Until that day, China's policy of nonopposition to US moves in the Gulf would allow the energy resources China needed from that oil-rich region to continue flowing to China.

A State Council–Central Committee document of January 1991, as the US-led military assault to restore Kuwait loomed, stipulated that China would not openly criticize the United States or other coalition members during the early stage of the upcoming conflict. Chinese propaganda would maintain a neutral stance during this period. Once the battlefield situation became protracted and began to shift against the United States, China's propaganda and diplomacy would shift, and it would do what it could to contribute to the failure of the US hegemonist scheme to control Persian Gulf oil. In line with the January directive, Chinese media coverage of US moves during the 1990–1991 crises was relatively objective. Yet the assessment of US motives was overwhelmingly critical. US motives were selfish considerations of power and control. The tone, however, was not vitriolic. The war apparently never reached the second state anticipated by the State Council–CC document of January 1991.

Beijing also launched active "peace diplomacy" at this juncture to differentiate itself from the United States for Third World audiences. Beijing implicit message was that while the United States was an aggressive, war-prone country, China was a peace-loving country. Beijing was careful not to overplay its peace-diplomacy hand, however. When the Iraqi deputy prime minister arrived in China, just before the beginning of Allied ground operations, to discuss the conditions under which Iraq would withdraw from Kuwait, Li Peng urged Iraq to "take immediate and concrete measures and actions" to quit Kuwait.[13]

The Gulf war demonstrated new structural weaknesses in China's international position. The strategic triangle crucial to Chinese diplomacy from 1971 to 1989 was dead. The decline in Soviet power that underlay this transformation had been developing for years. But the alacrity of Soviet cooperation with the United States during the war spotlighted the change. No longer would Beijing be able to invite Moscow and Washington to vie for China's favor. Chinese commentary during and just after the 1991 war stressed the rivalry of Japan, Britain, France, or a revived Soviet Union with the US for domination in the Gulf. That rivalry was, however, more of a hope than a reality—far less useful to Beijing than the bitter Soviet-American rivalry of the Cold War era. The dramatic superiority of US conventional weaponry demonstrated how far behind China was militarily—thirty years, estimated one ex-PLA chief of staff. The notion that Third World countries, including China, could rely on their large populations and vast armies to defend themselves against Western power was severely undermined.

The 1991 Gulf War and China's Awareness of Its Increased Vulnerability

The quick, decisive, and low-casualty victory by US forces in early 1991 deepened the CCP's sense of insecurity and made China's leaders more acutely aware of China's own military weakness. The awesome technological superiority of US military power, plus the willingness of US leaders to use that power in so decisive a fashion, altered Chinese calculations regarding the possibility of a US decision to use military force against China. China's leaders were already convinced that the United States was pursuing a strategy of attempting to topple communist governments from Eastern Europe to China to the USSR. US leaders were showing increased concern with Tibet and encouraging dangerous political changes underway in Taiwan. The decisive military superiority the United States displayed in January–February 1991 might lead it to exploit China's military backwardness.

Before US military actions against Iraq began on January 17, many Chinese commentators believed the United States would become bogged down in a long, high-casualty, and costly war, very much like the US experience in Vietnam, and that prospects of a US defeat in such a war were high.[14] Iraq's armed forces were large (over one million men, making it the fifth largest in the world in 1990), well armed, well trained, and veteran, having only recently concluded an eight-year-long war with Iran. Iraq's army was well outfitted with Soviet, Chinese, and French weaponry. A good portion of Iraq's tanks were, in fact, Chinese exports. (China had sold arms to both sides during the 1980–1988 Iran-Iraq war.) Iraqi forces were well dug in and prepared to confront American attackers with heavy artillery, armored strikes, and line after line of trench defenses. Cities would be defended house by house. US casualties were certain to be high, Chinese analysts predicted. US forces would become bogged down in a protracted war of attrition. As causalities mounted, so too would opposition to the war in the United States. Chinese analysts fell prey to a common malady: fighting the last war. They assumed the US experience in Iraq would approximate the Vietnam War.

The conflict did not go as Chinese analysts had predicted. US forces began with thirty-eight days of intense air bombardment. Cyber attacks on Iraqi computers and information systems disabled Iraqi command, control, and communications, often in the first hours of the war. Carefully targeted attacks knocked out Iraqi telecommunications and electrical power systems. Stealth bombers conducted precision strikes of great accuracy and effectiveness while remaining invulnerable to Iraqi air defenses. Electronic warfare aircraft jammed the anti-aircraft facilities that still managed to operate. Once Iraqi air defense systems had collapsed, Iraqi ground forces were subjected to heavy, sustained, and murderous bombing by US heavy bombers. US aircraft carriers and cruise-missile ships stood a safe distance off shore, well beyond the range of Iraqi coastal defenses, and launched wave after wave of bombing and cruise missile attacks. Most aerial bombs were guided by laser or global positioning systems, and, unlike in previous wars, were highly accurate. When Saddam Hussein played his trump card of ballistic missile attacks against Israel and Saudi Arabia, US anti-missile systems proved somewhat effective against them (although not as effective as reported at the time). In space, seventy US satellites were allocated to the Iraq war, providing real-time information to US warplanes and ships, and operational commanders. An entire huge battle space, from space to far out at sea, to tactical aircraft and other "shooters," were integrated and woven together via computer networks. When US ground operations began on February 23, they lasted only 100 hours. In that period, US armored forces outflanked and enveloped Iraqi forces, slicing quickly through the best-prepared Iraqi defenses. When the fighting ended with Iraq pleading for a ceasefire, Kuwait had been liberated. US causalities were light: only 113 US personnel were killed in the war. A cohort of Chinese military officers, numbering somewhere between 20 and 300, observed the fighting from the Iraqi side.[15]

The display of US high-tech warfare had a deep and enduring impact on China's military modernization effort. The US demonstrations of military prowess in 1991 and again in 2003, as much as the Taiwan Strait confrontation of 1996, fueled the long drive for modern military power that would transform China's capabilities by the 2010s. Shortly after the ceasefire in the Gulf, the PLA's three services met to evaluate the implications of the recent conflict. The consensus was that the decisive factor in the Allied victory was the enormous superiority of their weapons. Within weeks, Beijing announced a nearly 12 percent increase in military spending, in spite of a record budget deficit that was nearly 70 percent above what had been projected.[16] Not all Chinese analysts focused on weaponry; some focused on the doctrinal shortcomings of Iraqi strategy, including especially the failure of Iraq to strike preemptively at US forces as they assembled in the Gulf region for the assault on Kuwait.[17] PLA analysts carefully studied the 1991 war.

These developments added momentum to a push for military modernization that would continue into the second decade of the twenty-first century and ultimately have a deep impact on China's foreign relations. Underlying Beijing's sweeping response to the 1991 Gulf war were apprehensions that the United States might be tempted, if China remained weak, to intervene militarily to support anti-communist forces in Tibet, or Taiwan, or maybe even in China proper. Or it might intervene in areas along China's periphery, North Korea perhaps, to establish a position from which to better pressure and subvert China. The United States was, it seemed to some of China's leaders, an aggressive interventionist country that might be tempted to take advantage of China's weaknesses, just as it had done with Iraq and Yugoslavia. The United States had to be deterred from attacking China. These, in any case, were the arguments now advanced with greater vigor by China's military leaders and heeded carefully by CCP leaders.

Many PLA leaders had long been dissatisfied with the relatively paltry military budgets of the 1980s. The Gulf War emboldened them to speak out. As part of the post-6-4 rectification campaign, the PLA's political control apparatus had insisted on the primacy of political and moral factors in war.[18] PLA professional officers, on the other hand, stressed the backwardness of PLA weaponry, strategy, and doctrine, as well as the need to spend more time on training in these areas rather than on political study. The 1991 Gulf War gave the PLA professionals both an opportunity to speak out and a powerful case study substantiating their point of view. Russia quickly emerged as the key supplier of advanced military equipment and technology for the PLA. The burgeoning arms trade between China and Russia may, in fact, have been the most important and substantial dimension of the Russo-Chinese partnership that emerged in the 1990s.

Relations between the CCP and the PLA had been altered by the events of 1989. The dependency of the CCP on PLA loyalty was now very clear. Deng

Xiaoping's prestige within the PLA had been diminished by 6-4, and PLA people were more willing to criticize him. The newly designated successor as paramount leader, Jiang Zemin, had no military background and needed to build influence with PLA officers. Heeding PLA calls for larger defense budgets and accelerated military modernization reflected all of these considerations. The military modernization that began in early 1991 was not a crash program to prepare the country for war. It was, instead, a carefully focused, incremental but sustained effort to give the PLA the ability to fight and win the type of war witnessed in 1991.[19]

China and the 2003 Regime Change War in Iraq

Beijing's policy during the United States' 2003 regime-change war in Iraq maintained the same principled opposition to US resort to military force as in 1991, while manifesting a significantly greater degree of cooperation with the United States. In 2002–2003, Beijing worked actively with the United States at certain junctures to circumvent stronger opposition from France, Russia, and Germany, and voted "yes" on the resolution that the United States (at least) saw as authorizing the use of force.

Beijing's situation in 2002 was far different than in 1990. In 1990, China's economic stakes in the Gulf were largely limited to labor service sales. By 2002, the PRC had become a major importer of Persian Gulf petroleum—about 56 percent of China's imported oil came from the Gulf region. China had also begun investing in Iraqi oil development. In 1997, the China National Petroleum Corporation (CNPC) had agreed to invest $1.26 billion in a twenty-two-year proposal in Iraq's al-Ahdab field.[20] Chinese oil majors were also negotiating with Iraq over three other development projects that, if realized, would have provided half of China's oil import needs. All these energy projects contradicted US efforts to sharply limit foreign investment in Iraq's energy sector because of Iraq's nonfulfillment of the terms of the February 1991 ceasefire agreement. Beijing's political position in 2002 was also far stronger than in 1990. Western sanctions resulting from the Beijing Massacre were long past. At the end of 2001, China had entered the WTO. Finally, the 2003 war did not erupt by surprise as had the 1990 crisis. Beijing had many months to consider its policy response to a US war to oust Saddam Hussein. These considerations seem to have led Chinese leaders to conclude that since a war seemed inevitable, China's interests would be best served by making that war as brief and as minimally disruptive as possible.[21]

During Security Council debates in October 2002 over authorization of use of force, the United States proposed a resolution giving Iraq a final warning to comply fully and completely with UN inspection efforts, and setting a firm deadline for such compliance. Failure to comply by the specified deadline would be followed by "severe consequences," according to the US draft resolution, The debate over the US proposal became very heated. France, Russia, and Germany were vehemently opposed. China, however, took a low-key approach. During a crucial Security Council meeting, for example, after the United States called for a strong resolution threatening "severe consequences" for Iraqi noncompliance, France suggested a two-stage proposal. A "final warning" if followed by Iraqi noncompliance would lead to yet another Security Council meeting to decide on a response. The Russian representative felt that no new Security Council resolution was necessary at all. During Security Council debates, China's representatives typically seconded the opinions and proposals of antiwar countries France, Russia, and Germany, but did so late in debate, and with brief statements stripped of the acrimony that often characterized the comments of French, German, and Russian representatives.

During the crucial debate on October 17, after another half dozen or so countries had spoken, China's representative weighed in. The "long absence of a solution to the Iraq question did not serve peace and stability of the region or the credibility of the [Security] Council," the Chinese representative said. Iraq should "unconditionally and without restrictions," and "at an early date," implement the resolutions of the Security Council." Under these circumstances, China "would consider" a new resolution of the question.[22] In the context of the ongoing debate, this was very close to an endorsement of the US view. At one point during the Security Council debates, a French representative asked China to take a stronger stance against the US drive for war. Beijing declined. When Resolution 1441, warning Iraq that it "will face serious consequences" if it did not promptly give UN inspectors full and effective cooperation, came to a vote on November 8, 2002, China voted "yes." Following the US overthrow of Saddam Hussein and the collapse of that regime, China worked actively, and again sometimes contrary to French and Russian moves, to quickly give the US occupation the legitimacy of UN authorization.

One way in which China's stance on the 2003 war did not differ from its position on the 1991 war was in terms of China's estimate of the hegemonic geopolitical objectives imputed to the Americans as underlying reasons for war. In 2002–2003, Chinese analysts writing in elite foreign policy journals argued that the real American motive for going to war to remove Saddam Hussein was essentially the same in 1990: to seize control of Persian Gulf oil so as to be able to coerce the consumers of that oil. Stated US concerns with nuclear weapons, chemical weapons, terrorism, democratization, and so on were all pretexts. The real US objective was world domination; Persian Gulf oil was a means to that end. Dozens of articles developed variants of this argument; only very occasionally did analysts credit professed US concern about nuclear nonproliferation or terrorism.

Shortly after the US invasion of Iraq began, several analysts from China's top think tanks outlined their estimate of US purposes in *Beijing Review*. The deputy director of the MFA research center saw two major objectives behind the US attack: to oust Saddam Hussein and to "rebuild Iraq with a democratic system" in order to diminish the Middle East's production of terrorists and "establish US oil hegemony." One of the top Middle East analysts of the MFA think tank found that the main US objective was to force Iraq into submission, and warned that Iran would be Washington's next target. The director of Tsinghua University's Institute of Strategic Studies maintained that "oil is not the only reason" the United States has attached Iraq. He continued;

> The attack is based on the desire to keep the Middle East from being dominated by an opponent and safeguard [US] oil interests in the region. I believe that the major objective of the war is to topple the totalitarian rule of Saddam and thus dominate the Middle East . . . the United States had decided to control the region first by attacking Iraq.[23]

A commentary in the PLA newspaper *Jiefangjun bao* in September 2002 saw the 2003 invasion of Iraq as part of a strategy "designed to dominate all of Eurasia." This was to be done by controlling the oil resources of the Middle East:

> Iraq's oil will have a direct impact on the . . . world economy for the next 30 years, and [will be] an important tool to decide whether the United States can control the lifeline of the world economy. The United States has always regarded oil as the lifeline of itself and the entire capitalist world. If it can prop up a pro-U.S. government in Iraq, it can ensure undisturbed oil demand [sic] for a long time.[24]

Control over Middle East oil together with control of sea transport routes for oil from the Persian Gulf and Caspian Sea littoral would allow the United States to control Eurasia from Japan through the Middle East to NATO/Europe, thus dominating "the entire world." The author did not make the point that China would thus be vulnerable to US power, but his readers would have understood that.

The contrast between the clear anti-US hegemony *perceptions* of China's foreign policy analysts regarding the 2003 war and the not-so-anti-US hegemony *policies* of the PRC in the Security Council raises the question of how to reconcile the two. One possibility is that articles in nonclassified foreign policy discussions in China's media are intended to mold the worldview of China's middle classes, instilling in that crucial readership a sense of national vigilance against malevolent foreign powers, as a way of legitimizing the CCP's continuing one-party authoritarian rule. From this perspective, the content of these journals does not reflect the thinking of China's foreign policy decision makers at the very apex of the CCP state. Rather, it is essentially a sort of Leninist "transmission belt" linking the party center with the masses. In this case, the anti-US hegemony analysis common in Chinese media does not drive Chinese foreign policy. That policy is, rather, driven by oil, expanding export and labor service markets, and mollifying the United States—all leading to low-key cooperation with the United States.

The other possibility is that the content of elite foreign policy journals does indeed reflect the thinking of the party center. In this case, Beijing's "don't bar the way" approach to US aggressiveness in the Persian Gulf may have been a way of "inviting the gentleman to enter the caldron" (*qing jun ru weng*), while demanding a price for permitting entrance.[25] In this case, China, of course, would not be the cause of American aggressiveness. But since aggression is what hegemonist superpowers like the United States do, and since American aggressiveness in the Persian Gulf is, at least, far away from China's major interests and may well help drain the American hegemonists of their appetite for aggression, having the United States rampaging around in the Gulf may serve China's interests. Of course, this type of thinking would have to be kept highly secret. Interestingly, in Chinese foreign policy accounts of US Gulf policy or US-Iraq or US-Iran relations, there is virtually nothing about how *China's* interests are affected by US policy or how *China* is in fact responding, except perhaps an affirmation of the Five Principles of Peaceful Coexistence, or the like.

Constrained Partnership with the Islamic Republic of Iran

Deterioration of PRC-US relations in the early 1990s was paralleled by intensification of cooperation between the PRC and the Islamic Republic of Iran (IRI—the formal name of the revolutionary regime established in 1979). One important reason for the latter process was an Iranian drive for economic reconstruction after the end of the long war with Iraq. That war ended in September 1988, and on the night of June 3–4, 1989—the same night the PLA carried out the Beijing Massacre—came the death of Supreme Leader Ayatollah Ruhollah Khomeini. The combination of these two events, the end of a long, impoverishing war and the death of a charismatic dictator, unleashed a powerful demand in Iran for improvement in economic conditions. Housing, energy, and infrastructure of every kind were gravely inadequate. Poverty was widespread and deep. People, including demobilized soldiers, needed jobs. As IRI leaders shifted gear to meet these dire developmental needs, China moved in to supply a large part of what Iran needed and could pay for with lucrative petroleum exports. China's post-1978 development promoted exports, and Iran offered a big market for Chinese capital goods, consumer goods, and labor and engineering services.

PRC and IRI leaders had gotten to know each other through arms sales and diplomatic maneuvering at the United Nations during the Iran-Iraq war.

During their exchanges of views on international issues of common concern, Chinese leaders discovered in the IRI an ambitious regional power deeply resentful of US domination of its region and of US efforts to spread liberal democratic values around the world. That is to say, PRC leaders discovered in the IRI a like-minded state dreaming of and willing to work toward an end to US hegemony. CCP leaders did not, of course, share, or even understand, the religious fundamentalism of IRI leaders. The notion that religious scholars should constitute the highest political authority of a state—the core notion of Ruhollah Khomeini's "rulership of the righteous jurisprudent" that inspired both the 1979 revolution and the state structure of the IRI—made no sense to the CCP, or to most ordinary Chinese for that matter. China's long tradition was, after all, one of rule by a secular, rationalistic bureaucracy. Moreover, a large portion of Chinese, certainly CCP leaders, was atheist. But Beijing was willing to set aside these divergent worldviews and build cooperation in areas of common interest and mutual agreement.

The problem for Beijing was that escalating US conflict with the IRI led Washington to object time and again to aspects of PRC-IRI cooperation, and to demand that China disengage from particular types of cooperation with the IRI. It is not possible to trace the downward trajectory of US-IRI relations here. Stated simply, those relations were bad and generally got worse. By 1995, the Clinton administration declared "dual containment" of both the IRI and Iraq under Saddam Hussein to be US policy. Often, in its effort to "contain" the IRI, Washington would ask Beijing to cooperate on this or that issue. Between the founding of the IRI in 1979 and 2014, there were at least thirteen times that Washington laid IRI-related demands before Chinese representatives, placing Beijing in the dilemma of saying no to the Americans and continuing cooperation with Iran or of acceding to American demands, thereby demonstrating to Tehran that China was really not a very reliable partner and possibly helping Washington realize its dream of hegemony over Persian Gulf oil. Figure 21-1 lists the instances of China's Persian Gulf dilemma of accepting or rejecting US demands for China's cooperation vis-à-vis the Islamic Republic of Iran.

The stakes for Beijing in managing this dilemma were potentially high. On the one hand, the favorable macro-climate for China's New Long March toward modernization depended on amicable relations with the United States. Moreover, as we have seen, Chinese leaders saw the Persian Gulf as the focus of an aggressive US drive for world hegemony in the extremely unbalanced post–Cold War international system. If China supported the IRI against the United States in the very center of Washington's drive for global hegemony, PRC-US ties could suffer considerably. The PRC might find itself in the same condition as the late USSR, with the United States viewing it as a hostile and rival power. That was ultimately one major factor bringing low the USSR which PRC leaders sought to avoid. In addition to these elemental power

Date	U.S. Policy Initiative	China's Policy Choice
1979–80	Punish Iranian seizure and detention of U.S. diplomatic personnel	condemns IRI violation of diplomatic Immunity & U.S. resort to force to free
1982–88	Push for UN-sponsored arms embargo against Iran to push it to end war with Iraq	Rejected; served as Iran's major arms supplier
1982–97	Push to end anti-ship cruise missile sales to Iran	Seemingly accepted U.S. demands but found ways to transfer to Iran
1987–88	Multilateral action to safeguard neutral oil traffic during "tanker war"	Rejected; remained disassociated from action
1990	Resort to UN-sponsored war to undo Iraqi annexation of Kuwait	Rejected and opposed, but obtained on Security Council vote
1997–2002	Use of air attack to uphold sanction and inspection regime re Iraq	Opposed
1995–2002	Maintenance of tough sanction regime against Iraq	Opposed, but let others take lead in opposition
1996–2007	Effort block large foreign investment in Iran energy sector	Rejected, but let other powers take the lead in opposing
1983–1997	End foreign assistance to Iran nuclear programs	Rejected for 13 years; agreed 1997
1989–2007	End sale of dual-use ballistic missile tech technology to Iran	Rejected, except for Category I
1989–1997	End sale of Category I related ballistic missile items	Nominally accepted; substantially accepted, 1997
2003	War for regime change in Iraq	Opposed, but let other powers take lead in countering
2004–07	Democratization and reform of middle East	Rejected and opposed
2006–2013	Push for sanctions against Iran over nuclear programs	Agreed to, but worked to weaken and delay

FIGURE 21-1 Beijing's Choices in Managing Its Persian Gulf Dilemma

calculations, there were more amorphous considerations of national reputation. To the extent that the international community (the Western countries, the Arab countries, Israel) sided with US demands on Iran, China's refusal to go along with those demands could tar China as an uncooperative and irresponsible or even "rogue" state.

On the other hand, if the United States succeeded, perhaps with indirect Chinese help, in pressuring Iran into submission, this would increase China's vulnerability to a potential US energy embargo. Most of the oil-rich countries of the Persian Gulf—Saudi Arabia, Kuwait, Oman, and the UAE—were already aligned with the United States and unlikely to stand with China against it in such an extreme situation. The IRI, alone among the Persian Gulf countries, would probably be able and willing to tell the Americans to go to hell and do what it could to assist a Chinese defeat of a US oil embargo. Perhaps even more important, Chinese capitulation to US demands regarding the IRI would undermine China's effort to gradually, over time, build with Iran an all-weather partnership based on trust and mutual understanding, a partnership like that with Pakistan but not chained to a neighboring hostile rival, as Pakistan is to India. Chinese leaders recognize Iran as a major regional power, with considerable national capacity and coherence and with no history of major conflict with, but a very long tradition of cooperation with, China. Beijing's fundamental objective vis-à-vis Iran transcends any particular type of cooperation, and seeks an enduring, cooperative partnership based on mutual understanding and trust for the coming era of China's rise. Chinese weakness in the face of US demands undermined China's attractiveness to Tehran as a long-term partner.

Another dimension of Beijing's calculations regarding management of its Persian Gulf dilemma was that a number of Arab countries, including important ones like Saudi Arabia and Egypt, were rivals of Iran, and often lobbied Beijing in the same direction as Washington. So too did Israel. This meant that saying "yes" to Tehran and "no" to the United States could negatively affect China's relations with the Arab countries. But at the end of the day, only the IRI was able and willing to challenge United States efforts to dominate the Persian Gulf. Beijing's management of its Persian Gulf dilemma tended to balance between Washington and Tehran. Beijing accommodated US demands while also finding ways of giving Tehran some level of Chinese assistance.

The period of closest and most explicitly anti-US cooperation between the PRC and the IRI came in the early 1990s as US-PRC relations were deteriorating. During this period, with MFN linkage looming, Beijing feared a genuine confrontation with the United States and saw the IRI as a partner in that unfortunate eventuality. IRI leaders, for their part, seem to have had a somewhat naive understanding of Chinese policy at this juncture, taking at face value Beijing's anti-US hegemony rhetoric. Beijing's disengagement from various types of cooperation with Tehran in the mid-1990s, as a function of US-PRC negotiations to renormalize ties, would educate Iranian leaders, giving them a much more realistic understanding of Beijing's calculus. But in the early 1990s, this Iranian learning process was just beginning.

IRI president Ali Khamenei (soon to be Khomeini's successor as Supreme Leader) visited Beijing in May 1989 shortly before Michael Gorbachev. This high-profile visit finally reciprocated Hua Guofeng's ill-fated 1978 visit to Iran, saw the formal beginning of military cooperation (in rebuilding and modernizing Iran's military forces), and vastly expanded Chinese participation in Iran's postwar economic development. When the Beijing Massacre occurred shortly after Khamenei's visit, Tehran gave China strong rhetorical support in the face of Western criticism and sanctions. Then, as US sanctions against Beijing hardened, Beijing drew still closer to Tehran.

Li Peng visited Tehran in July 1991 as part of a six-nation Middle East tour. Li was characteristically blunt in underlining the antihegemony partnership of the PRC and the IRI: "In the ever-changing international situation, the further strengthening of friendly and cooperative relations between the two countries [PRC and IRI] in all fields . . . is conducive to peace and development in the region and the world. . . . Hegemonism and power politics are the cause of world tension and turbulence, as well as a major threat to world peace and security."[26] In a talk with Iranian media, Li Peng was even blunter: "We are against the domination of the United States or of a minority over the world, and against the creation of a new order by the United States in international relations, and we are in complete agreement with the Islamic Republic of Iran on this point." Iranian leaders took Li at his word and proposed that the IRI and the PRC partner to resolve the Palestinian problem, with China doing its part by acting as a counterweight to the United States in the Middle East. Working together, "freedom fighters and justice-seeking people" would thwart the effort of "some" to stabilize their unrivaled domination in the world," Khamenei (by then Supreme Leader) told Li Peng. Third World countries, "especially those which are in sensitive areas of the globe, should have close cooperation with each other to resist the US drive for absolute domination," Khamenei told Li. In effect, Khamenei was proposing a Sino-Iranian alliance to drive the United States out of East Asia and the Gulf. Beijing politely declined the invitation. Instead, the next year the PRC normalized relations with Israel.

But while declining Tehran's invitation to openly challenge the United States in the Middle East as the USSR had once done, Beijing expanded cooperation with the IRI in other areas. Shortly after the end of the Iran-Iraq war, PRC-IRI economic cooperation began to expand. Prior to the 1979 revolution, the United States and West European countries had been Iran's major economic partners. But as the Western countries backed out of Iran under economic sanctions, political risk, and difficult business conditions, Chinese firms moved in. In 1978, the last year before the revolution, China provided less than 1 percent of Iran's imports. By 1991 that had doubled to 2 percent—compared to Germany's 8 percent. By 2003, China had captured 8 percent of Iranian demand, compared to 11 percent for Germany and 9 percent for France. Roughly half of China's exports to Iran are machinery, equipment, electrical devices, instruments, and vehicles.

China partnered with Iran in a variety of economic sectors. Chinese equipment went to a wide array of Iranian industries: glass, paper, sugar refining, fishing, canning, cigarettes, automobiles and trucks, subway locomotives and carriages, cement, railways, batteries, plastics, shipbuilding, petrochemicals, and so on. Between 1988 and 2004, China assisted more than seventy-six major Iranian industrial projects.[27] A very large swath of Iranian industry was built on the basis of Chinese machinery, equipment, and standards. It may not be too much of an overstatement to say that the IRI was coat-tailing on China's industrialization. Of course, China's support for the IRI in the

Security Council over Iran's nuclear program (discussed below) was one reason why Iranian leaders favored China as Iran's development partner.

In 1997, Beijing quietly acceded to long-standing US demands and ended
China's nuclear cooperation with Iran.[28] As discussed in an earlier chapter,
since 1985 China had been Tehran's major partner in nuclear science and
energy, and had supplied the IRI with a range of core materials, technologies, and equipment between 1985 and 1996. But in 1997, Beijing suspended
that nuclear cooperation as part of the renormalization of PRC-US ties. This
was a major Chinese concession to the United States. The American side, in a
display of deft diplomacy, said very little about this important Chinese concession. Beijing's move was motivated by a desire to avoid a confrontational
and rivalrous relation with the United States. Since the 1970s, the Americans
had argued that nuclear nonproliferation was a shared PRC and US interest
in which the two powers should cooperate, Iran and North Korea being the
two key areas in which this Sino-American cooperation was most imperative, or so said American representatives. From Beijing's perspective, with
the strategic ballast of parallel interests vis-à-vis the USSR gone, new areas
of cooperation were extremely useful to restabilize the PRC's vital relation
with the United States. Nor did there exist with Iran the hard realist calculus
of balance of power that existed with Pakistan vis-à-vis India. This strategic
logic is clear. But there may have been more. Because of its robust decade-long
cooperation with Iran in the nuclear sector (which presumably gave Chinese
intelligence a good knowledge of IRI nuclear programs and purposes), and
because of Tehran's occasional solicitations of a partnership to drive the
United States out of the Persian Gulf and East Asia, China may have concluded that the IRI was driving toward nuclear weapons and that it would be
best if China disassociated itself from that effort as soon as possible. Chinese
association with Iranian nuclear weaponization could have a seriously adverse on PRC-US relations. Earlier rather than later Chinese disassociation
from the IRI nuclear program was thus prudent.

PRC defection from nuclear cooperation with Tehran was a sharp blow to
the PRC-IRI relationship. High-level leadership exchanges withered for several years. But as with the setback in the relationship following Hua Guofeng's
disastrous 1978 visit, Beijing gradually rebuilt the partnership. Chinese support in Security Council debates over Tehran's nuclear programs now became
the major form of PRC political support for Tehran.

In the 2000s, Iran's nuclear program again came before the international
community, posing yet another set of Washington-or-Tehran choices for
Beijing. Following a series of revelations in 2001 about a large and secret
Iranian uranium enrichment facility, in 2005 the IAEA determined that
over a period of eighteen years the IRI had conducted a series of nuclear
activities that Tehran, as a NPT signatory, was obligated to report to the
IAEA, but had not. A number of these previously undisclosed nuclear

activities had involved China—prior to China's 1997 disengagement from Iran's nuclear efforts. This discovery of undisclosed Iranian nuclear activities led the United States to propose "referral" of Iran's nuclear program to the Security Council under Article VII of the UN Charter dealing with "actions with respect to threats to peace, breaches of the peace, and acts of aggression." This would open the way to sanctions or authorization of use of military force, and it was the beginning of a many-year-long process of the United States soliciting Chinese cooperation, China being compelled to respond one way or the other to those solicitations.[29]

Broadly speaking, Beijing stayed in step with the other Perm-5 powers, while finding ways to distinguish itself from the United States and assist Tehran. China initially opposed referral to the Security Council, insisting that the IAEA was the proper forum to handle the issue. Beijing also supported Iran's "right to the peaceful use of nuclear energy" under the NPT, thereby implicitly rejecting Washington's argument that Tehran had forfeited that "right" by its long history of violation of the NPT via its nonreported nuclear activities. Washington then proposed that the Perm-5 send a joint note to Tehran expressing their concern. Beijing rejected this but agreed to send a separate note. Beijing wanted to minimize the appearance that it was acting in coordination with Washington against Iran. Finally, in March 2006, Beijing agreed to "report," but not "refer," the Iran nuclear issue to the Security Council. "Refer" was objectionable because that was the word Article VII used with Security Council handling of breaches of the peace and acts of aggression.

In July 2006, the Security Council began drafting a resolution, eventually numbered 1696, demanding that Iran suspend uranium enrichment and warning Tehran of sanctions if it did not comply with Security Council demands regarding IAEA inspection of Iran's nuclear programs. Again Beijing softened the terms on Tehran's behalf. Beijing initially blocked reference to Article VII. It secured deletion of a US-proposed reference to a "threat to international peace and security" and doubled the deadline given for Tehran to respond, increasing it to thirty from fourteen days. After Tehran ignored the Security Council deadline, that body began drafting a list of Iranian individuals and entities involved in that country's nuclear programs. Over the next three years, the Security Council would pass three more resolutions imposing penalties on Iran over its nuclear programs. With each of these resolutions, Beijing ultimately voted "yes," but only after narrowing the scope of sanctions and keeping them targeted only on people and entities verifiably linked to Iran's nuclear activities, excluding sanctions targeting Iran's energy sector, the economy generally, or "normal international commerce." China thereby protected the substance of its economic partnership with Iran. Beijing insisted that normal economic interaction, including investment and involvement in Iran's energy sector, should not be targeted by UN sanctions.

Beijing also insisted that it would be bound only by sanctions agreed to by the Security Council, where China had a veto. US attempts to impose sanctions via unilateral legislation or executive decisions were denounced by Beijing as "extraterritorial," that is, attempts by a state to apply its domestic law beyond its own sovereign territory. These were manifestations of hegemony, great-power politics, and unilateral arrogance, said Beijing. China's restriction of sanctions in this fashion was of great benefit to Tehran. For several years, the United States deferred to China's (and other countries') objections to unilateral US laws and executive orders imposing sanctions on third countries for their commercial dealings with Iran that had not been proscribed by multilateral UN decisions. Only in 2010 did the United States set aside these objections and begin implementing broad and hard measures denying access to US markets to third-country firms, including China's, that conduct business with the IRI. Beijing continued to protest these US "unilateral and extraterritorial" sanctions. In spite of this, Chinese firms have often complied with US requirements to disengage from dealings with Iran. This may be because firms choose to operate in the large and rich US market in preference to the far smaller Iranian market. Be that as it may, other Chinese companies with no operations in the United States have picked up much of China's business in Iran. Coordination of Security Council activities on the Iran nuclear issue was a major aspect of the Sino-Russian strategic partnership.

Military cooperation was another dimension of PRC-IRI partnership. In 1990, China's Commission for Science Technology and Industry for National Defense (COSTIND) signed a ten-year military technology cooperation agreement with Iran. Ballistic and guided missiles as well as various types of electronic surveillance, guidance, and targeting technology were major areas of cooperation. Iran acquired from China surveillance, search, and fire control radars, along with various types of anti-ship, anti-aircraft, and surface-to-surface missiles. Among these were advanced anti-ship cruise missiles modeled after the French Exocet. These high-speed, sea-skimming anti-ship missiles could be fired from submerged submarines via torpedo tubes, from aircraft, or from surface ships, including fast attack craft, which China also supplied to Iran. This would permit targets to be attacked simultaneously from several different vectors—considerably increasing the probability of a successful strike. These were highly potent missiles, far more advanced than the Chinese-made Silkworm missiles used by Iran against tankers in the Gulf in the 1980s. One implicit target for these anti-ship cruise missiles were warships of the US Navy operating in or near the Persian Gulf. China insisted that such cooperation was part of the normal and unobjectionable range of friendly cooperation between states. The United States differed and insisted, in 1996–1997, that China abandon cooperation in the manufacture and development of advanced anti-ship cruise missiles. Beijing complied as part of the mid-1997 deal renormalizing US-PRC relations.

Beijing's handling of its Persian Gulf dilemma indicated that China ranks maintaining stable, cooperative relations with the United States above developing a strategic partnership with Iran. But Beijing has also shown determination not to sacrifice Iran and not to stand too fully with the United States against Iran. Within the parameters imposed by US minimal demands, Beijing continued to forge gradually a partnership with Iran. In the face of US pressure on Iran, the PRC assisted Iran's industrialization, scientific and technology, and military modernization efforts, while finding opportunities to befriend Tehran in Security Council debates, thereby distinguishing itself from the United States. China's foreign policy journals typically concluded that US hegemony was attempting to bludgeon the IRI into submission, but that that effort would fail. US hegemony would meet the strong resistance of the people of the region. The American people, plagued by the blunders arising out of US arrogance and ethnocentrism, would eventually grow weary of their burdens in the Gulf. Chinese analysts did not put two and two together, but if the reader will allow this author to do so, when the day arrives that the Americans decide to leave the Gulf and "go home," and the security affairs of the Persian Gulf are finally left to the countries littoral to the Gulf to deal with, China may have built a strategic partnership with the most powerful and like-minded country in that region, Iran. In effect, Beijing has placed bets on both sides of the wager, on Washington *and* on Tehran.

22 }

The Recovery of Hong Kong

Wiping Out National Humiliation

Stable recovery of control over Hong Kong on July 1, 1997, after ninety-nine years of British control was a major achievement of Chinese diplomacy. At least in the Chinese view of things. Deng Xiaoping died some four months before Hong Kong's "reversion," but he played a major role in the successful recovery of that territory. In the decade and a half before Hong Kong's reversion, Beijing demonstrated great pragmatism and flexibility by advancing and then implementing the "one country, two systems" formula that accommodated the interests of both Beijing and London and was acceptable to a majority of Hong Kong residents. In the interregnum between 6-4 and reversion, Beijing defeated what it viewed as a British scheme to plant a "time bomb" in Hong Kong that would destabilize China as part of the West's "peaceful evolution" conspiracy. These Chinese perceptions were severely distorted. British memoirs and currently available documentation indicate no British intention to use Hong Kong to destabilize China. Rather, British leaders felt a strong moral obligation to the people of Hong Kong, which Beijing dismissed as mere propaganda. British leaders also doubted that Chinese leaders understood the reason for Hong Kong's economic success, and this inspired a British effort to find ways of insulating Hong Kong from Beijing after reversion. But though Chinese perceptions of British aims may have been distorted, Beijing's policies served China's interests in Hong Kong fairly well. After reversion, Beijing's respect for Hong Kong's relative autonomy combined with deepening economic integration between Hong Kong and Guangdong province to fuel a major dynamo of China's explosive economic rise. The nexus of Hong Kong and Guangdong became a leading engine of China's export push.[1] The fact that the staunchly middle-class residents of Hong Kong were denied their aspirations of local democratic self-government was a secondary consideration, in Beijing's view. Fifteen years after Hong Kong's reversion, Beijing's denial of this aspiration became a "time bomb" of Beijing's own making.

PRC-British interactions over the reversion of Hong Kong began in the late 1970s. The story of reversion nonetheless belongs properly in the post-6-4 period of China's foreign relations, because the upheavals of 1989–1991 profoundly altered both Beijing's perception of the Western subversive threat and, consequently, Chinese handling of Hong Kong's reversion. After the Beijing Massacre, China's leaders perceived British policy toward Hong Kong as another element in the Western effort to destabilize the PRC, and dug in their heels to resist perceived British plots. The collapse in late 1993 of Sino-British cooperation over Hong Kong's reversion and subsequent nondemocratic evolution of postreversion Hong Kong must be seen in the context of China's post-6-4 struggle to ensure regime survival.

From 1842 to 1997, Hong Kong was a British colony. In the Chinese view, Britain's seizure of Hong Kong was part of China's Century of National Humiliation. One provision of the Treaty of Nanjing of 1842 that ended the First Opium War was the cession *in perpetuity* of the island of Hong Kong on the east side of the Pearl River estuary, eighty-five miles downstream from Guangzhou. Across the estuary to the west was the Portuguese enclave of Macao, granted by China's Ming Dynasty government in 1557.[2] Both enclaves, Hong Kong and Macao, gave European businessmen a base of operation beyond Chinese control but close enough to China's markets to offer convenient links. As China was forced to open ever more widely to foreign trade in the second half of the nineteenth century, Hong Kong waxed as an entrepôt for trade with south China.

A second Opium War between Qing China and Britain and France in 1856–1860 culminated in a punitive Anglo-French expedition to Beijing to punish China for various violations of diplomatic protocol. Among those punishments was the sacking of the beautiful Yuanming Yuan gardens, an imperial pleasure palace filled with exquisite architecture and gardens, in northwest Beijing. The Convention of 1860 that ended the Second Opium war ceded, again in perpetuity, the Kowloon peninsula opposite Hong Kong Island. Hong Kong Island is very mountainous—basically several steep mountains protruding from the sea—with little level ground for warehouses or other commercial facilities. Kowloon peninsula provided much more flat ground for commercial operations. The northern boundary of Kowloon peninsula is still demarcated by Boundary Street, running east-west atop Kowloon. In the Chinese historical memory—fed constantly by state patriotic indoctrination—the Opium Wars, the unequal treaties forced on China at gunpoint to end those wars, and the cession of Hong Kong Island and Kowloon peninsula are all remembered as bitter events.

A third agreement between China and Britain, in July 1898, leased to Britain for a period of ninety-nine years a swath of territory, called the New Territories, north of Kowloon peninsula to provide Hong Kong with greater defensive depth and a more secure supply of food and water. At that time, the weakness of China's Qing government had been revealed by its incompetent conduct of the 1894–1895 war with Japan.[3] Following this monumental display of Chinese weakness, various powers began scrambling to stake out an expanded position in China, a process that became known as "carving of the (Chinese) melon." Britain's demand for the New Territories was part of that "carving." The New Territories made up 90 percent of Hong Kong's total land area. The ninety-nine-year lease on the New Territories would expire on July 1, 1997. Figure 22-1 illustrates Hong Kong and its environs.

From the standpoint of the CCP, the treaties imposed on China during its Century of National Humiliation were "unequal," imposed by force and threat, and, as such, legally null and void, without any validity whatsoever. From this revolutionary perspective, Hong Kong, every part of it, was Chinese territory stolen by British imperialism, and should return to Chinese control as part of the revival of China's greatness and blotting out the shame of its national humiliation. When and how that was done was a matter for China's government to decide. In the event, after 1949 the PRC waited forty-eight

FIGURE 22-1 **Hong Kong and the Pearl River Estuary**

years to recover Hong Kong, and then did so in a pragmatic manner that did not destabilize the economic and political institutions planted by Britain in Hong Kong, at least until a belated, post-6-4 British effort to introduce democracy into Hong Kong.

In the early days of the PRC, Mao Zedong mandated a "long-range view" and "full utilization" of British rule over Hong Kong.[4] British rule over that territory was to be left intact and exploited by the PRC. Once the Korean War began, British-ruled Hong Kong became very useful to PRC efforts to circumvent US and UN embargos. Under those embargos, it became difficult for the PRC to purchase strategic materials and a wide array of industrial technology, let alone weapons and military equipment. But Hong Kong, as a British colony, was able to import many embargoed goods. Hong Kong businessmen, for reasons of Chinese patriotism and pecuniary gain, were sometimes willing to acquire needed items and find discrete ways of moving them up the Pearl River to PRC jurisdiction. The vulnerability of British Hong Kong to *Chinese* embargo, or outright military seizure, also gave Beijing leverage with London, and thus some modest degree of indirect leverage on the Anglo-American alliance. One reason why London broke ranks with the US and recognized the PRC in January 1950 was to dissuade Beijing from seizing Hong Kong.[5]

China's 1949 revolution profoundly transformed Hong Kong. Prior to 1949, Hong Kong was a center for entrepôt trade with China and a Royal Navy base, with a modest population of 1.9 million. There was very little industry. But with the CCP's post-1949 liquidation of China's bourgeoisie as a class, many Chinese capitalists moved to Hong Kong and set up shop. The British administration in Hong Kong supported private enterprise with strong legal protections for property, impartial justice, low taxes and tariffs, and a relatively incorrupt bureaucracy. Hong Kong quickly emerged as a production center for cheap, labor-intensive goods: toys, fireworks, leather items, simple electric appliances, and especially textiles, clothing, and plastic goods. Chinese shipping firms previously based in Shanghai or Ningbo moved to Hong Kong to carry much of that region's booming trade. By the 1960s, Hong Kong had become one of East Asia's leading manufacturing and logistics hubs.

Several million refugees from communist rule in China fled to Hong Kong over the years, providing a pool of cheap labor for Hong Kong's export-oriented industrialization. By 1980, the territory's population was over five million. Real estate development boomed as Hong Kong's residential and industrial areas expanded. Soon, new service industries grew strong: tourism, merchandizing, shipping, logistics and port operations, banking, finance, law, and insurance. A growing middle class of professionals developed in association with these economic changes. Wages and standards of living began to rise. Hong Kong gradually became prosperous. By the early 1970s, Hong Kong was recognized as one of East Asia's "four tigers"—along with South

Korea, Taiwan, and Singapore—which were rapidly industrializing through dynamic participation in the global economy. By 1982, when negotiations between London and Beijing over Hong Kong's reversion to China began, the average per capita annual income in Hong Kong was US$6,000, then a quite comfortable mid-level of development.

Hong Kong's growing economic prosperity offered opportunities to Beijing. Hong Kong's swelling population, combined with the mountainous nature of Hong Kong plus the greater return on level land for commercial rather than agricultural use, created a strong demand for imported food. A large portion of those foodstuffs were supplied by farms across the border in southern China. Rice, pork, chicken, fish, eggs, fruits, and vegetables, as well as electricity and potable water, came from Guangdong. By the late 1980s, half of Hong Kong's water supply came from Guangdong province.[6] All these goods were paid for in freely convertible Hong Kong dollars. Beijing was always in need of hard currency, and sales to Hong Kong supplied a substantial amount. According to a saying widely attributed to Zhou Enlai, Hong Kong was a fine machine for turning Chinese chickens and pigs into pounds sterling.

Hong Kong also served as a window on the world for the CCP. This function was especially important during the PRC's early period of relative isolation from the capitalist world. The CCP maintained an overt organization in Hong Kong, led by the Hong Kong office of Xinhua News Agency. This above-ground organization maintained liaison with leftist labor unions, patriotic capitalists, pro-PRC newspapers, and friendship associations. The CCP also maintained a covert organization in Hong Kong to conduct intelligence and other special tasks.[7] Intelligence collection was a key task of both overt and covert organizations. The staff office of China's Military Affairs Commission maintained a small team in Hong Kong to collect foreign books, newspapers, and magazines.[8] Because of Hong Kong's Chinese culture and language, it was relatively easy for CCP covert operatives to move about and avoid detection, although perhaps only seemingly so, since, according to Xu Jiatun, by the 1980s British counterintelligence in Hong Kong had a pretty good idea of CCP covert operations in the colony. Xu Jiatun was head of the Hong Kong branch of Xinhua News Agency and, as such, also the head of the CCP organization in that city from 1983 to late 1989. As late as the 1980s, the Military Intelligence Bureau of the PLA General Staff Department focused its intelligence collection operations on Hong Kong.[9]

China's post-1978 quest for foreign capital and export markets gave the PRC a different and even greater interest in maintaining the economic and political status quo of Hong Kong. Once the PRC opened to foreign investment and foreign business operations on a market basis, and once it began promoting exports, Hong Kong's dynamic and globally savvy business class contributed very substantially to the success of China's new policies. Robin McLaren, senior British representative to the Sino-British joint liaison group between 1987 and 1989 and then Britain's ambassador to Beijing from 1991 to

1994, estimated that Hong Kong supplied 60 percent of China's total direct foreign investment between 1979 and 1997.[10] After 1978, Hong Kong quickly became a preferred channel for third-country foreign investment in China. Rather than themselves investing directly in China and assuming responsibility for operations there, many third-country investors, including Overseas Chinese in Southeast Asia, invested in Hong Kong firms, allowing those firms to supervise operations in China while protecting their investment with Hong Kong's British-origin legal system.

After the opening of the Shenzhen Special Economic Zone in 1979, Hong Kong quickly emerged as one of the PRC's most important trading partners. This is illustrated by Figure 22-2. In the decade before reversion, Hong Kong accounted annually for between 26.9 and 36.3 percent of China's global merchandise trade, making it by far China's largest trade partner. Beijing's method of counting trade with Hong Kong changed in 1993, with goods transiting Hong Kong being shifted from "Hong Kong" to another country of origin.[11] Under the new statistical method, the role of Hong Kong in China's trade fell by about half. Even then, during the years 1993 through 1995, Hong Kong still ranked as the PRC's second largest trading partner, behind Japan but substantially ahead of the United States. In 1996, with 14.1 percent of China's total trade, Hong Kong fell behind the United States to third rank.

As indicated by the result of the altered statistical method in 1993, a very large percentage of PRC exports to Hong Kong were forwarded on to consumers in other areas—North America, Europe, Southeast Asia, the Middle East—perhaps after repackaging in Hong Kong and with substantial value added by Hong Kong's sophisticated marketing, insurance, advertising, shipping, and logistical services. A large portion of China's exports reach global consumers via Hong Kong intermediaries. Many of Hong Kong's exports to the PRC are high-tech components to be embedded in products assembled in the PRC for shipment to third countries, perhaps once again via Hong Kong. That city also offered a way for the PRC to conduct trade with countries

	1987	1988	1989	1990	1991	1992	1993	1994	1995	1996
Trade w/ Hong Kong as % total PRC trade	26.9%	29.4%	30.9%	35.4%	36.6%	35.1%	16.6%	17.7%	15.9%	14.1%
foreign capital actually utilized; HK as % total	N.A.	30.4%	29.0%	23.6%	24.5%	43.8%	48.5%	45.9%	42.4%	38.1%

FIGURE 22-2 **Hong Kong's Role in PRC Trade and Foreign Capital Utilization in the Decade before Reversion**

Source: Zhongguo tongji nianjian (China statistical Almanac), various years.

with which it had no diplomatic ties e.g., major trading centers South Korea, Taiwan, Israel, and South Africa in the 1970s and 1980s. This sort of politically based transit trade declined as PRC diplomatic ties widened.

Remittances by Hong Kong residents to relatives in the PRC were another way in which Hong Kong's wealth flowed to China. Since the PRC government maintained a monopoly on handling foreign currency inside China, private PRC recipients of Hong Kong or other foreign currency remittances were required to deposit them in special bank accounts at Chinese banks. Special stores stocked with foreign and luxury goods were open to holders of these foreign currency accounts. (These "friendship stores" were also open to tourists with foreign currency to spend.) These arrangements created incentives for Hong Kong residents to remit monies to relatives in the PRC, and for those PRC residents to receive remittances, while leaving the foreign currency itself in the hands of PRC banks. PRC banks operating in Hong Kong provided yet another way of shifting foreign currency from Hong Kong to the PRC. These banks accumulated foreign currency in their transactions in Hong Kong, and then remitted a substantial portion back to Beijing. In 1986, for example, it was estimated that twenty percent of all US dollar deposits in Hong Kong were held by the Bank of China. It was estimated in 1982 that invisible transfers of foreign currency by Chinese banks to the PRC amounted to US$3.2 billion.[12] Robin McLaren estimated that in the run-up to reversion, Hong Kong supplied one-third of Beijing's total foreign exchange earnings.[13] A different sort of financial incentive for China to leave Hong Kong unchanged was the heavy financial burden that would fall on Beijing if it were to assume direct responsibility for that city. Senior CCP leader Li Xiannian, who headed the Foreign Affairs Leadership Small Group in the 1980s, estimated that Beijing would have to spend US$3 billion to $5 billion per year to support Hong Kong if it assumed direct responsibility for it.[14] At the time, that amount constituted a large percentage of Beijing's budgetary expenditures.

The Imperative of "Reversion" to China

These multiple and weighty economic considerations gave Beijing a strong interest in not destabilizing the economic and political status quo of Hong Kong. At any point after 1949, Beijing could have forced the British out of Hong Kong with relative ease. Cutting off supply of food, water, electricity, and commercial intercourse would probably have been sufficient. If not, actions by CCP front groups, underground organizations, PRC banks, and Xinhua could have made Hong Kong ungovernable. Had Chinese military action been necessary, that would probably have been over in a day. Hong Kong was militarily indefensible against the PLA. And yet Beijing did not use such means. Instead, it acquiesced in British colonial rule, even while denouncing it via frequently strident propaganda.

Throughout the pre-1978 period, Chinese leaders sidestepped the issue of Hong Kong. The issue of Hong Kong's reversion was forced onto Beijing's agenda by the expiration date of the 1898 ninety-nine year lease: July 1, 1997. Many real estate leases and mortgages in Hong Kong were written for a term of fifteen years. Fifteen years from mid-1997 was mid-1982. Sino-British talks over Hong Kong's reversion had been underway without result for several years, and as the mid-1982 date came and went without any progress, uncertainty in Hong Kong began to mount. The danger of a flight of capital and human talent was quite real. Hong Kong residents kept an unusually large portion of their assets in liquid form (cash, gold, negotiable securities) because they feared it might become necessary to flee in a hurry. Hong Kong's completely open capital accounts and convertible currency made it easy to move money into or out of the city. Many Hong Kong residents had relatives in other countries, especially English-speaking Commonwealth countries—Canada, Australia, New Zealand, and Britain—with relatively open immigration policies. Many Hong Kong businessmen had wide contacts and business interests outside of Hong Kong, and could easily use those to emigrate. As 1997 approached, many Hong Kongers began to acquire foreign passports or resident permits, purchase homes abroad, and settle family members there, all in preparation for potential flight. A large portion of Hong Kong's population had already fled CCP rule once (in the 1950s through the 1970s), and many were psychologically prepared to flee again if it came to again enduring CCP rule. As July 1, 1997, drew nearer without any British-Chinese agreement or clarification of the future of Hong Kong, anxiety mounted.

CCP leaders were in a difficult situation. The completion of China's "national liberation" and extirpation of China's "national humiliation" required reversion of Hong Kong to PRC administration. Yet reversion seriously threatened the important role Hong Kong played in PRC economic development. A leader less confident than Deng Xiaoping might have acquiesced to a residual British role in Hong Kong to reassure opinion there—as London initially insisted. A leader more ideologically minded than Deng Xiaoping might have been unwilling to countenance continuation of a capitalist economic and liberal political system in Hong Kong. In the event, however, Deng Xiaoping was able to navigate the shoals with remarkable success.

Sino-British interactions over Hong Kong began in 1978 with the appointment of Percy Cradock as British ambassador to China. Cradock had served as chargé d'affaires at the British mission in Beijing during the Cultural Revolution and had considerable sympathy for the reform effort of Deng Xiaoping's leadership. Cradock helped arrange the first ever visit to Beijing by a serving British governor of Hong Kong, then Murray MacLehose, in 1979. During the visit, MacLehose proposed in talks with MFA representatives that the 1898 lease on the New Territories be extended beyond 1997. After consultation, the MFA replied that "China intends to take back Hong Kong," and asked MacLehose not to raise the matter in a scheduled meeting with Deng Xiaoping. Contrary to that advice, MacLehose broached his suggestion to Deng, who replied immediately, "At the appointed time, China will certainly take back sovereignty over Hong Kong." When MacLehose observed that that might cause anxiety among people in Hong Kong, Deng replied, "Tell the Hong Kong investors not to worry."[15] Throughout the Anglo-Chinese negotiations on Hong Kong, Deng called the shots on the Chinese side.

The issue was again engaged in September 1982 during a visit by Prime Minister Margaret Thatcher to Beijing. The fact that Thatcher had just fought and decisively won a war in April 1982 with Argentina over an illegal challenge to British ownership of the Falkland Islands complicated China's situation. The Falkland Islands had been under British control since 1690, and a treaty of territorial settlement between Britain and Argentina in 1850 implicitly ceded the islands to Britain. Thatcher responded to Argentina's seizure of the islands with a full-scale military operation to oust Argentina and restore British rule. Britain's victory in that war greatly boosted Thatcher's popularity at home. Might she use her Falkland popularity to adopt a similarly tough stance vis-à-vis Hong Kong? Beijing made it clear to Thatcher that China was fully prepared to be tough should Britain adopt a tough approach toward Hong Kong and China.

Thatcher's position during her 1982 visit was that all three conventions (of 1842, 1860, and 1898) were still legally valid, and that Hong Kong Island and Kowloon Peninsula had been ceded to Britain in perpetuity. Britain was willing to consider, however, trading sovereignty for a continuing British role in the administration of Hong Kong. From the Chinese perspective, the three conventions were unequal treaties without any legal validity whatsoever. The doctrine that treaties are legally invalid because they involved compulsion is not generally accepted under international law. That was, however, the stated position of Chinese governments, including the pre-1949 government of the Republic of China. Deng Xiaoping laid out China's position in talks with Thatcher in September 1982. Hong Kong, including the Island and Kowloon Peninsula, would revert to Chinese sovereignty:

> On the question of sovereignty, China has no room for maneuver. To be frank, the question is not open for discussion. . . . That is to say, China will recover not only the New Territories but also Hong Kong Island and Kowloon. *It must be on that understanding that China and the United Kingdom hold talks on the ways and means of settling the Hong Kong question.*[16] (Emphasis added.)

By demanding that Britain accept as a precondition for negotiations the premise that Hong Kong, all of it, was Chinese, Deng was in effect demanding that Britain give up its strongest card (swapping sovereignty of the Island and Kowloon for a continuing administrative role) before negotiations began. Beijing would try the same ploy again during the 1992–1993 negotiations, but with far less success than in 1982–1983. Deng explained this stance in 1982–1983 in terms of the force of Chinese nationalist public opinion:

> If China failed to recover Hong Kong in 1997, when the People's Republic will have been established for 48 years, no Chinese leaders or government would be able to justify themselves for that failure before the Chinese people . . . It would mean that the present Chinese government was just like the government of the late Qing Dynasty and that the present Chinese leaders were just like Li Hongzhang.[17]

Li Hongzhang was the Chinese leader who had agreed to the cession of Taiwan to Japan at the end of the 1894–1895 Sino-Japan war. Deng continued: "If we failed to recover Hong Kong in 15 years [i.e., in July 1997] the people would no longer have reason to trust us, and any Chinese government would have no alternative but to step down and . . . leave the political arena." This expression of nationalist statement was probably a combination of negotiating ploy and heartfelt belief. As noted in the first chapter of this book, Deng, like most of his comrades among the senior CCP leadership, had entered politics and embraced communism largely because of their dismay with China's traumatic and disastrous encounter with imperialism. On the other hand, with British representatives citing British and Hong Kong opinion to substantiate their positions over the modalities of reversion, it was convenient for the Chinese side to counter with its own, Chinese, public opinion.

During his 1982 talks with Thatcher, Deng called for Sino-British cooperation in managing Hong Kong's reversion: "The Chinese and British governments should work together to handle the question of Hong Kong in a satisfactory manner. We hope to have Britain's cooperation in maintaining prosperity in Hong Kong."[18] But Britain should not think that it could use China's desire for British cooperation to pressure China into accepting something less than full and complete reversion to Chinese administration. China's desire for cooperation with Britain "does not mean," Deng told Thatcher, "that continued prosperity can only be ensured under British administration." China, acting without British cooperation, was prepared to implement "principles and policies . . . acceptable not only to the people of Hong Kong but also to foreign investors," Deng told Thatcher. China was confident of its ability to successfully handle Hong Kong's reversion unilaterally, without British cooperation, if that was necessary. Deng also warned against possible British attempts to destabilize Hong Kong:

> I want to tell Madam that . . . the Chinese government . . . took all eventualities into account. We even considered the possibility of something

we would hate to see happen—that is, we considered what we should do if serious disturbances occurred in Hong Kong during the 15-year transition period. . . . If the announcement of the recovery of Hong Kong has, as Madam put it, 'a disastrous effect,' we shall face that disaster squarely and make a new policy decision. . . . I am concerned that there may be major disturbances in this [15-year] period, man-made disturbances. These could be created not just by foreigners but also by Chinese—but chiefly by Britons. It is very easy to create disturbances. This is precisely the problem our consultations will be designed to solve.[19]

But while thus making clear that there was a mailed fist inside his velvet glove, Deng indicated a willingness to cooperate with Britain in accomplishing a smooth reversion that would not destabilize Hong Kong's existing economic and political status quo. Deng proposed:

We suggest . . . that the two sides begin consultation on the question of Hong Kong through diplomatic channels. The prerequisite [for this] is the understanding that China will recover Hong Kong in 1997. On this basis we should discuss how to carry out the transition successfully in the next 15 years and what to do in Hong Kong after the end of that period."

Deng gave Thatcher a two-year deadline for the British and Chinese governments to reach agreement on Hong Kong's reversion: "in no more than one or two years—China will officially announce its decision to recover Hong Kong. We can wait another year or two, but definitely not longer." The message was that if no agreement were reached in two years, the PRC would proceed unilaterally. Within the framework of these Sino-British talks, China was prepared to be accommodating, Deng indicated. Hong Kong would remain "capitalist," and "many systems currently in use . . . will be maintained." Policies for Hong Kong "should be acceptable to the people of Hong Kong and also to foreign investors." The "main concern" was that Hong Kong remain prosperous; otherwise, Deng said, China's "drive for modernization" might be affected.[20] According to Xu Jiatun, Thatcher "who was famous for her unyielding way of handling things," was "in a dazed condition" after her "rebuff" by Deng. This caused Thatcher to stumble while going down the stairs of the Great Hall of the People after her meeting with Deng. "Although this was an accident," Xu Jiatun wrote, "it had in fact shown how seriously . . . Thatcher had been frustrated."[21]

Deng's tough approach worked. For six months, from September 1982 to March 1983, London resisted acceptance of Beijing's precondition of Chinese sovereignty over Hong Kong. Finally, in the words of McLaren, "a way was found around China's precondition," when Thatcher sent Zhao Ziyang a note saying that she was prepared to recommend to Parliament that sovereignty over the whole of Hong Kong should be transferred to China if "acceptable arrangements could be made."[22] Britain's acceptance of China's precondition opened the way to formal talks and agreement on the Joint Declaration of December 1984. In an editorial at the time of Thatcher's death in April 2013, Beijing's *Global Times* summed up Thatcher's approach in 1982: "Thatcher managed to understand that China is not Argentina and Hong Kong is not the Falklands. We can say that she made her biggest compromise as prime minster in this issue."[23] Xu Jiatun describes the Chinese reaction when he and his comrades learned of Thatcher's capitulation and acceptance of China's precondition. After Thatcher's letter was read out aloud, "laughter broke out across the meeting room, and everyone was happy about this outcome."[24] Ambassador Cradock's role in engineering this critical compromise would later become a target of criticism by both British and Hong Kong media.

Deng's "One Country, Two Systems" and Sino-British Negotiations

In 1979, in the immediate aftermath of PRC-US normalization, Deng Xiaoping began suggesting Taiwan's unification with the PRC on the basis of Taiwan maintaining political autonomy, its present capitalist economic system, and its own armed forces—a proposal that quickly became known as "one country, two systems." In December 1982, China's National People's Congress adopted a new state constitution that provided for establishment of special administrative regions along the lines of Deng's "one country, two systems" formula. Taiwan's leader Chiang Ching-kuo (Chiang Kai-shek's son) was not interested in Beijing's proposal. Instead, Chiang opted to take Taiwan down the road of democratization.[25] Unused in Taiwan, "one country, two systems" was transferred to Hong Kong. For many years, Beijing hoped that the successful application of that model in Hong Kong might, eventually, attract Taiwan.

In June 1984, after two years of consultation with leading figures in Hong Kong and deliberation among Beijing agencies, Deng Xiaoping unveiled to delegations of visiting Hong Kong businessmen the CCP's "one country, two systems" framework for governing Hong Kong after its reversion.[26] Under this framework, Hong Kong would retain its capitalist economy, free lifestyle, and noncommunist political system for fifty years after returning to China. Its legal system would remain basically unchanged. The main part of the PRC, of which Hong Kong would now become a part, would be socialist. Hong Kong, however, would remain basically unchanged for fifty years. Its status as a free port, separate customs and tariff jurisdiction, and open financial center would continue. It would continue to maintain and establish economic and cultural relations with other countries and regions. In the political sphere, Hong Kong would become a Special Administrative Region (SAR, thus "HKSAR"). Beijing would not assign officials to the HKSAR. Hong Kong would be run by Hong Kong people—the latter to be selected in a manner yet to be specified. "We are convinced that the people of Hong Kong are capable of running the affairs of Hong Kong well and want an end to foreign rule," Deng told the visiting Hong Kong magnates. The main body of Hong Kong officials should be "patriots," Deng stipulated, who respected the Chinese nation and were sincere in their support for the return of Hong Kong to the motherland. But they need not be communists or believe in socialism. They could believe in capitalism, feudalism, or even slavery, Deng suggested jocularly. "We don't demand that they be in favor of China's socialist system. We only ask them to love the motherland and Hong Kong," Deng said. Since the HKSAR would be part of the PRC, PLA forces would be stationed in Hong Kong, but only to "safeguard national security," not to interfere in Hong Kong's internal affairs. This was a shrewd appeal to Hong Kong's business and governmental elites to keep ruling Hong Kong as they had been for many decades, but now in partnership with Beijing rather than in partnership with London. While many people in Hong Kong would object to the undemocratic nature of these political arrangements, the relative stability of Hong Kong before and after reversion in July 1997 suggests that the proposal was realistic.

Sino-British negotiations began in mid-1983 and bore fruit by December 1984, when a Sino-British Joint Declaration was signed in Beijing.[27] Britain accepted Beijing's framework: Hong Kong would become a special administrative region of the PRC with a high degree of autonomy, except in areas of foreign and security affairs, where Beijing would have jurisdiction. The government of the HKSAR was to be composed of Hong Kong people, with the chief executive effectively appointed by Beijing and appointing, in turn, the chief officials of the government. Hong Kong's legislature, the Legislative Council or LegCo, was to be "constituted by elections." The meaning of this clause would be the focus of intense differences a decade later. The Joint Declaration also stipulated that "rights and freedoms" currently enjoyed by Hong Kong residents were to remain unchanged for fifty years. These "rights and freedoms" were spelled out in considerable detail in the text of the Declaration, a fact that indicated the importance of these freedoms in reassuring the people of Hong Kong. Enumerated "rights and freedoms" included: "of the person, of the press, of assembly, of association, of travel, of movement, of correspondence, of strike, of choice of occupation, of academic research and of religious belief . . . private property, ownership of enterprises, legitimate right of inheritance and foreign investment." In 1984, these guarantees delineated the great differences between life in Hong Kong and life in the rest of the PRC. By the early twenty-first century, those differences were far less—except in the area of free political activity.

The Anglo-Chinese agreement of December 1984 succeeded in reassuring people in Hong Kong. The danger of capital flight receded, and foreign investment continued to flood in. A constant pulling and tugging between Beijing and London continued over British administration of Hong Kong throughout 1985–1988, but those disagreements paled compared to the confrontation that erupted following the Beijing Massacre.

Britain's "Public Opinion Card" versus CCP United Front Work

CCP strategy for dealing with Britain was a combination of struggle and cooperation. According to Xu Jiatun, head of Xinhua's Hong Kong office and China's top official in Hong Kong, Beijing saw negotiations as a battlefield where British cooperation would be secured for the return of the territory to complete Chinese administration while maintaining Hong Kong's prosperity. Britain very much wanted to continue a direct administrative role, or failing that, to have continuing influence in Hong Kong after 1997, at least in Xu Jiatun's view of British aims. British efforts to achieve such infringements on China's sovereignty were to be defeated via struggle in diplomatic negotiations; Britain would be compelled to cooperate with China *on China's terms* and without destabilizing Hong Kong's prosperous economy. Britain repeatedly threatened that Hong Kong's economic prosperity would falter if China did not go along with London's proposals. But as in Deng's negotiations with Thatcher, China would meet British toughness with Chinese toughness. If China was prepared to walk away from negotiations, London would probably ultimately accede to China's terms for the sake of a face-saving exit from Hong Kong and future British business opportunities in China. If Britain refused to accept China's terms (which ultimately turned out to be the case), China would handle the matter unilaterally, confident that the CCP's eminently reasonable "one country, two systems" framework, combined with assiduous united front work in Hong Kong, would manage reversion without precipitating capital flight and collapse of the economy. Again, all this in Xu Jiatun's view.[28]

Subtly encased in Chinese diplomacy was the hinted threat of unilateral action, including use of military force against Britain, if things began to go wrong in Hong Kong before July 1, 1997. During their September 1982 talks, Deng had told Thatcher: "China hopes that the recovery can be accomplished in a peaceful, negotiated manner. But if negotiations fail, China will still recover Hong Kong." As Xu Jiatun pointed out, "Although . . . [Deng] had not said what means would be used, what he meant was clear," i.e., Britain would be pushed aside by unilateral Chinese moves backed as necessary by China's military power. Xu deduced several reasons why London in March 1983 abandoned its insistence on the legal validity of all three nineteenth-century conventions and agreed instead in the Joint Declaration to a smooth, negotiated return of Hong Kong to China. One reason was that a negotiated process offered Britain "retreat with honor." Implicitly, a nonnegotiated process would spoil Britain's "honor." Another reason deduced by Xu was that "China was not Argentina." Britain was not capable of using the "Falkland Island approach" with China. One component of China's preparations for reversion was preparation of PLA forces in case the failure of negotiations or riots and turmoil in Hong Kong required China to secure Hong Kong forcibly.[29] To save British face, Beijing did not publicize Deng's tough talk to Thatcher. That would be done only a decade later, when Anglo-Chinese negotiations were moving toward collapse.

In Robin McLaren's view, China's "strongest card" in the negotiations was its willingness to bear whatever economic sacrifice was necessary to assert China's sovereignty over Hong Kong. Beijing certainly hoped to keep Hong Kong economically stable and prosperous, and recognized and sought Britain's assistance in doing that. But if compelled to choose, Beijing would uphold and assert China's absolute sovereignty over the territory whatever the economic cost. The purpose of negotiations was to see how Britain could cooperate with the smooth assertion of China's control over Hong Kong.

Winning the "hearts and minds" of the people of Hong Kong in a "confrontational propaganda war" with Britain was a key CCP struggle, according to Xu Jiatun. This was one of Xu's major tasks during the 1983–1989 period of his leadership over the CCP's Hong Kong organization. This "propaganda war" paralleled and was linked to the "negotiation battle." In Xu's words, "During the negotiations, to pile more chips on the table, the British constantly tried to influence public opinion, deliberately playing their public opinion card ... The Chinese side also mobilized their media to coordinate with the negotiation struggle."[30] The British claimed that a continuing British role, or, later, a strong and democratic legislature, was necessary to maintain Hong Kong's prosperity. Without these, a capital flight would pull down Hong Kong's economy. Britain propagated these ideas among the Hong Kong populace in a number of sinister ways, according to Xu. The CCP countered British efforts via systematic united front work aimed at all strata of Hong Kong society, but especially at Hong Kong's business elite. The crux of the CCP's united front work was propagating understanding that the "one country, two systems" program was genuine and substantial, and would remain unchanged for fifty years after 1997—just as CCP leaders promised. If the people of Hong Kong could be persuaded of the sincerity of the "one country, two systems" arrangement, Britain's efforts to play the "public opinion card" would fail, and China would be able to call Britain's bluff, should that be necessary, without endangering Hong Kong's prosperity.

When Beijing opened the political battle with Britain in the early 1980s, CCP leaders grossly underestimated the magnitude of the public opinion difficulties confronting them in Hong Kong. According to Xu Jiatun, China's leaders then "assumed there was widespread support among Hong Kong compatriots for the return of Hong Kong to the motherland." After starting work in Hong Kong, however, Xu found that this was not the case: "Only after I came to Hong Kong did I realize the complicated feelings of the local countrymen. People who were truly in favor of China taking over Hong Kong did not make up a majority."[31] The prospect of China taking over Hong Kong had "badly shaken" Hong Kong. Anxiety was greatest "among the upper crust of society," who were worried that private property will be transformed or communalized by socialism and that they will lose their freedom after 1997." "Intellectuals dread brainwashing and . . . lower strata . . . are concerned that their living standards will decline." Few people in Hong Kong knew of China's "one country, two systems" proposal, and those who did worried that the arrangement would be thrown out after China took control in 1997. Critics pointed out to Xu Jiatun that the CCP had used just this sort of bait and switch maneuver when struggling for power against the KMT in 1948–1949. Xu replied that times had changed and the CCP had learned.[32]

Xu reorganized the CCP organization in Hong Kong to wage political battle with the British. The CCP had a long history of struggle with Britain in Hong Kong, Xu noted, and engaged that conflict once again in the 1980s. The staff of the Xinhua agency in Hong Kong expanded from 100 to 400. Many new staffers were tasked with investigating the backgrounds and political views of prominent Hong Kong individuals. Ostensible "roving scholars" were deployed to Hong Kong universities to collect information on people's views and activities. Party branches in PRC entities in Hong Kong (the Bank of China, China Travel Service, trading companies, a shipping company) were drawn more fully into united front work. The existing CCP underground organization, which Xu concluded was "already pretty well understood" by British counterintelligence, was reorganized. All 4,000 local Hong Kong members of the CCP (two-thirds of total CCP members in Hong Kong were from Hong Kong, the others being from "interior provinces") were examined in terms of their background and activities. Those judged not to have been compromised by British counterintelligence were reorganized into a new clandestine organization operating under "absolute secrecy" and "unified leadership."[33]

Xu Jiatun worked hard to change the united front work style of the CCP Hong Kong organization, insisting that it take a broad and tolerant approach. "Love of China" and "love of Hong Kong"—Chinese patriotism—were the key thrust of CCP united front work, Xu directed. People did not need to be "progressive" or "leftist" to be courted and won over. The objective was to "unite with centrists" and "win over rightists." CCP propagandists and activists should be tolerant and understanding of criticism of CCP history and policies, as well as of Hong Kong people's fear of CCP rule and the resulting desire for a continuing British role in Hong Kong. CCP united front work should not defend old policies, but try to convince people that the CCP had changed and was a new party that would not repeat past mistakes. Old styles of CCP operation—cursing, threatening, or attempting to suppress "incorrect" thinking—were to be set aside. CCP activists and propagandists should strive to win friends, not make enemies.

Xu himself learned a new style of politics: attending banquets large and small, giving public speeches, writing personal letters to local notables, and listening tolerantly to even the most reactionary views. Eventually Xu's New Year's card mailing list numbered three to four thousand people, with gifts going out to a smaller set of acquaintances, and potted peonies going to a still smaller set of well-known public figures. Xu's CCP organization set up delegations of Hong Kong notables, including rightists and skeptics, to visit Beijing, where Xu lobbied to have them received by top Chinese leaders who stressed the sincerity of the "one country, two systems" arrangement. Skeptics of Hong Kong's return to China were a special target of CCP united courtship. Xu lobbied effectively with Deng Xiaoping for his intervention to prevent individual and prominent CCP leaders from making offhand and unauthorized remarks about Hong Kong that sometimes contradicted the official line. Xu directed the Bank of China to increase lending to small and medium-sized Hong Kong enterprises. Left-wing labor unions held symposia and rallies supporting Hong Kong's return to China. The political message behind this conviviality was this: the "one country, two systems" arrangement fits China's interests, fits Hong Kong's interests, and comports with the interests of all Chinese patriots in ending China's Century of National Humiliation. Xu felt acutely the huge difficulty of shifting Hong Kong opinion in the CCP's favor: "I came to feel deeply that it would be easy to secure the land of Hong Kong, but very difficult to win over the people of Hong Kong."[34]

Britain tried repeatedly to play the "public opinion card" to pressure China at the negotiating table, in Xu Jiatun's view. London first proposed that a delegation representing the people of Hong Kong participate in the Anglo-Chinese negotiations on the reversion of Hong Kong, a formulation the British called a "three-legged stool." China rejected this. The talks involved the return of Hong Kong to China, and involved only the governments of the two countries. Britain's "three-legged stool" proposal was an attempt to "split" Hong Kong opinion and align a portion of that opinion against China at the negotiating table. When that ploy failed, Britain proposed that it return sovereignty to China in exchange for China granting Britain a role in administering Hong Kong beyond 1997. "Overnight Hong Kong was inundated with talk and programs representing the British stand," Xu wrote.[35] Then the British Hong Kong government remained passive—according to Xu—as the value of the Hong Kong dollar declined and long lines of panicky Hong Kongers formed outside banks to withdraw US dollars or change Hong Kong dollars into US dollars. At the negotiating table, Britain again pointed to this to argue for a continuing British role. Xu Jiatun ordered his organization to expose the British scheme via CCP-controlled media and statements by prominent PRC representatives visiting Hong Kong. London was forced to shift course and link the Hong Kong dollar to the US dollar, quickly stabilizing its value.[36] Robin McLaren, on the other hand, argues that the British Hong Kong government "intervened heavily" to support the currency, while China offered "no support" and charged that the currency crisis was "artificial, manufactured by the British to put pressure on China."[37]

The final variant of Britain's "public opinion card" was, in Xu's view, its "democracy card." This centered on transforming Hong Kong's Legislative Council (LegCo) into a center of power able to check and balance the chief executive, who was controlled, as noted earlier, by Beijing. London's "democracy card" was, in Xu Jiatun's view, a "brilliant public opinion card" which worked by intensifying Hong Kong's social divisions and unrest" over the looming China takeover. London's playing the "democracy card" "touched off a wave of democracy unparalleled in Hong Kong's history." Throughout, the British objective was to *divide* public opinion to argue for its proposals at the negotiating table. The Chinese objective was, of course, to *unite* public opinion behind it, according to Xu.

The Beijing Massacre precipitated a major challenge from PBSC conservatives to Xu Jiatun's tolerant approach to CCP united front work. Already in 1986, Xu's open-minded approach had been criticized during a Politburo retreat at Beidaihe. Lu Ping and Li Hao, director and deputy director respectively of the State Council's Office of Hong Kong and Macao Affairs, and Zhou Nan, vice foreign minister and head of China's negotiations with Britain, challenged Xu's proposition that the people of Hong Kong feared the territory's return to China. The truth, they insisted, was that the people of Hong Kong welcomed and were "impatient" for Hong Kong's return to China. Xu was betraying the country by his lenient approach toward anticommunist and other reactionary elements in Hong Kong.[38] This criticism came in the context of the push to purge Hu Yaobang for his liberal attitude toward anticommunists and other reactionaries. Xu was being tarred as one of Hu Yaobang's liberal ilk.[39] By the second half of 1989, after 6-4 and the fall of Zhao Ziyang, Xu came under increasing criticism for "right deviation."[40]

As prodemocracy demonstrations swelled in Beijing in April–May 1989, the "patriotic torrent swept most people of Hong Kong along with it and swept across every corner of Hong Kong, creating an unprecedented situation," according to Xu.[41] When the PLA crushed the Beijing demonstrations in June, "The people of Hong Kong became disappointed to an unprecedented degree" and Hong Kong was swept by democratic movement in an "unprecedented development." Xu feared the repression in Beijing would undo all that had been accomplished by six years of united front work. To make matters worse, Li Peng began ordering Xu to take a hard line toward the Hong Kong democracy demonstrations. Xu believed this was a recipe for disaster.

The dispute between Xu and Li Peng came to a head when Li directed Xu to demand that the British Hong Kong government outlaw an organization that had emerged as a very large prodemocracy united front. The movement was led by "radical democrats" who demanded complete direct election of the both the legislative and executive organs of Hong Kong. The group had succeeded in mobilizing unprecedentedly large prodemocracy demonstrations which featured denunciations of CCP policies in both the PRC and Hong Kong. Xu advised Beijing that it was unlikely that the British Hong Kong government would comply with a request to ban the group, and suggested a less confrontational wording of the Chinese note. Li Peng insisted, however, and the Chinese demand that Britain ban the organization was duly delivered. As Xu expected, it was rejected. Under British law, the organization was allowed to exist and conduct various legal activities, British representatives explained. British Hong Kong authorities encouraged the prodemocracy movement by allowing the use of the Happy Valley Race Course for rallies, yet another "unprecedented action," according to Xu.

After this and other similar encounters, Xu Jiatun requested retirement, which was eventually granted late in 1989. The next year, fearing political reprisal because of his close association with Zhao Ziyang if he remained in China, Xu fled his retirement in Shenzhen, passing through Hong Kong for political exile in the United States. A member of the CCP's Central Advisory Commission and the Central Committee, and a personal friend of Deng Xiaoping, Xu was the highest-level PRC official ever to defect to the West.[42] He would later join with other dissidents to urge the CCP to return to the policy directions of Hu Yaobang and Zhao Ziyang, and embrace freedom and democracy as China's ultimate goal.

Foiling the Putative British Scheme to Bankrupt Hong Kong

In the view of Qian Qichen, foreign minister and principal in Beijing's handling of the Hong Kong issue after June 1989, the 1984–1988 period was a "honeymoon" in Anglo-Chinese handling of Hong Kong's reversion.[43] Xu Jiatun concurred, referring to it as a "short period of cooperation" between Britain and China. Robin McLaren says that "It is hard to exaggerate the impact" of 6-4, which "made the whole relation with China far more difficult . . . Chinese authorities began to view the territory in a new and more sinister light" as a potential "base for subversion of the communist system on the mainland."[44]

Construction of a new airport on the west side of Lantao Island was one point of intense PRC-British conflict in the run-up to reversion. The need for a new airport was apparent; the old one was in a centrally located, densely populated area of high-rise apartment buildings, with the approach blocked by mountains. Mountain removal and reclamation of land from the sea on the western side of Lantao to construct a large modern airport had been considered in the early 1980s, but abandoned because of costs. The plan was revived in October 1989 as part of a British push to "restore confidence" in Hong Kong.[45]

Beijing reacted with "intense suspicion" to the revival of the airport proposal, seeing it as an attempt by London to saddle the Hong Kong government with a huge debt. Or perhaps it was a way for British companies to empty the Hong Kong treasury before Britain's departure in 1997. Eventually, an MOU on the airport was signed in August 1991 during the visit by Prime Minister John Major to Beijing. Major's visit was, according to McLaren, an "integral part of the package" and one incentive for Beijing to agree to London's airport plan. Beijing required that London guarantee a sum to be left in the Hong Kong treasury upon completion of the airport, along with tight limitations on borrowing for the airport.

The Beijing Massacre and Britain's Democratization Program

After the Beijing Massacre, London became much more concerned with creating an element of democracy (actually a rather modest element) within Hong Kong's political structure prior to reversion. London believed that the bloody repression in China in June 1989 had greatly deepened unease in Hong Kong about reversion. "The Beijing of today is the Hong Kong of tomorrow" became a popular saying in Hong Kong after 6-4. A wide section of Hong Kong's populace had watched with hope the development of China's democracy movement in April and May, and the crushing of that movement roused deep trepidation. The danger of panic and capital flight increased. John Major's election as prime minister in November 1990 contributed to the shift in British policy. Relations between Major and Thatcher's key China advisor, Percy Cradock, became strained, and Cradock soon retired. Major turned in 1992 to veteran Conservative politician Chris Patten to take over Hong Kong affairs as Britain's last governor of Hong Kong. Patten believed strongly in Britain's moral obligation to the people of Hong Kong to leave them with as much democracy and autonomy from Beijing as possible within the framework of existing Sino-British agreements. More democracy in selection of the Legislative Council (LegCo) was seen by London as a way of giving Hong Kong a hedge against harsh CCP measures after reversion, as well as of reassuring Hong Kong public opinion and thereby stabilizing Hong Kong.

According to Xu Jiatun, Beijing feared that democratization of LegCo would allow "Western and Taiwan forces" to effect a change of system in inland China and undermine inland security by turning Hong Kong into an anticommunist outpost. In fact, since "Western and Taiwan forces" had long since acted in this way, the issue was "whether they would go so far as to make things unbearable for China."[46] Britain's effort to democratize LegCo was perceived by CCP leaders as part of the Western plot to destabilize China and overthrow the CCP. Qian Qichen saw the East European upheaval of 1989 and the disintegration of the Soviet Union as the "deep international background" of Britain's newfound enthusiasm for democracy in Hong Kong. Events in Eastern Europe and Russia had led British leaders, Qian believed, to "mistakenly conclude that those events were a forecast of China's situation and [future] development."[47] British leaders believed, once again in Qian's view, that they had made too many concessions in negotiating the 1984 Joint Declaration, but that China's hard-pressed situation now gave London an opportunity to "reverse the verdict" (*fan an*) on the Joint Declaration, in effect to renegotiate that agreement. Thus Britain created a "major storm" (*da feng bo*) over Hong Kong.

Underlying Beijing's deep suspicion of London's democratization efforts was a belief that they constituted a time bomb being planted in Hong Kong to explode after reversion. Britain had never instituted democracy in Hong Kong during its 150 years of colonial rule there. Why did it become so concerned with it only as they were preparing to hand it over to China? Beijing had made clear its opposition to elections in Hong Kong in 1958 when Zhou Enlai had warned a visiting British politician that a British move to turn Hong Kong into a self-governing entity like Singapore (then being groomed for independence) would be regarded as an unfriendly act. Hong Kong's existing political arrangements (then very much those of a nondemocratic Crown Colony) should continue without change, Zhou indicated.[48] Hong Kong's LegCo had been entirely appointed by the Governor until 1985. Then, in 1985, the year after it was forced to recognize China's sovereignty in the Joint Declaration, Britain had implemented indirect elections for functional constituencies for some LegCo seats. China resisted strongly a British push in 1986–1987 to implement some directly elected LegCo seats.

London's post-6-4 push for greater democracy in Hong Kong began with a letter in December 1989 from Thatcher to Jiang Zemin, who in July 1989 had been promoted to CCP secretary general. Thatcher's letter was delivered by Percy Cradock, Britain's ambassador to Beijing from 1979 to 1984 and chief British negotiator of the Joint Declaration. Thatcher's letter and Cradock's elaboration explained that London faced increasing pressure for an expanded role for direct elections in Hong Kong, and was unable to ignore these demands. Cradock laid out the argument for more democracy in the election of LegCo as a way of stabilizing public opinion in the territory.[49] Cradock assured China's leaders that Britain had no intention of allowing Hong Kong to be a base for subversion of the authority of China's government and would do everything possible, within the limits of law, to prevent this. Cradock found Chinese leaders deeply suspicious of both British intentions and proposals for a more democratic LegCo. Cradock's presentation also conveyed to Qian Qichen the impression that China's consent to expanded direct elections in Hong Kong was a precondition for a visit by Britain's foreign secretary to Beijing.[50] Beijing was still in its immediate post-6-4 pariah status, and a visit by Britain's foreign secretary would be useful to Beijing's efforts to restore its reputation. Jiang Zemin responded to these British "pressure tactics" by indicating that the number of directly elected LegCo seats should match arrangements specified in the Basic Law (then still being drafted by the NPC).

Thatcher's letter to Jiang and Cradock's talks in Beijing led to talks between Qian Qichen and foreign secretary Douglas Hurd. In January 1990, Qian received from Hurd what Qian deemed a "detailed wish list" regarding Hong Kong. This led to the beginning of negotiations over Hong Kong that would continue for two and a half years, until their collapse in late 1992. Although the talks focused on the role of "direct elections" in constituting LegCo, in the estimate of Qian Qichen the real, underlying issue was who would guide Hong Kong's postreversion political system, London or Beijing? Eventually, Hurd and Qian agreed, via an exchange of seven letters, on the number of directly elected LegCo seats and the ratio of those seats to other "functional" LegCo seats in the elections remaining before reversion. Following this agreement, Hurd visited Beijing in July 1990. This made Hurd the first ministerial-level Western leader to visit Beijing following 6-4.[51] Beijing had leveraged London's desire for Chinese agreement to Hong Kong's legislative democratization to ease China's post-6-4 moral odium. On February 18, three months after the Hurd-Qian talks, *Renmin ribao* released the text of the Basic Law for Hong Kong, drawn up by the National People's Congress after several years of "consultation" with people in Hong Kong, especially wealthy capitalists whom the CCP saw as the true rulers of the city.[52] What Beijing would later call "the three agreements" were now in place: the Joint Declaration of 1984, the Qian-Hurd exchange of letters, and the Hong Kong Basic Law.

Up to 1992, Britain attempted to democratize Hong Kong by obtaining China's prior consent. In 1992, however, this approach was deemed by London to have yielded inadequate results, and a new approach was adopted. In July, Christopher Patten took over as Hong Kong governor. Patten would proceed with reasonable democratization measures, staying within the letter and spirit of "the three agreements" and keeping Beijing informed of British moves. But failing to obtain China's consent, Patten would move ahead with his modest democratization plans. Patten believed that Britain had the power to do this under the 1984 Joint Declaration, which had stipulated that prior to July 1, 1997, "the government of the United Kingdom will be responsible for the administration of Hong Kong with the object of maintaining and preserving its economic prosperity and social stability; and that the Government of the People's Republic of China will give its cooperation in this connection." Beijing saw this new approach as British "unilateralism."

China's view, as represented by Qian Qichen, was that Patten's approach "provoked an open dispute" with China and destroyed the possibility of Sino-British cooperation. It led ultimately to unilateral British suspension of talks (again Qian's view), and to the impossibility of "through train" arrangements for reversion.[53] In other words, and again in Qian's view, Patten and his democratization plan were instruments of Britain's new, unilateralist, and pressure-politics approach to Beijing and Hong Kong.

Chris Patten arrived in Hong Kong determined to expand the element of democracy in the election of LegCo while remaining within the parameters laid out by "the three agreements." He believed that neither the Joint Declaration, nor the Qian-Hurd letters, nor the Basic Law had specified the number and ratio of directly and indirectly elected Legislative Council (LegCo) seats or specified exactly how those seats were to be elected. That was what his reforms aimed to fill in. It was this lacuna that Patten's democratization plan proposed to fill in, in the British view.

The organization of scheduled 1995 LegCo elections became the crux of Patten's struggle with Beijing. These elections would be the last before reversion. If a "through train" was to be achieved, the terms of these legislators would have to extend beyond July 1, 1997. This was also the last chance for Britain to affect the future of Hong Kong's political set-up. Patten's reforms changed the method for electing directly elected seats from two votes to one vote per voter, a change that benefited the more popular parties—which tended not to be those closely aligned with Beijing. The most controversial of his reforms, however, focused on the method of selecting functional seats. Functional seats represented economic and social sections—business associations, professional associations, unions, etc. Prior to the reforms, votes for functional constituencies were cast by the leaders of constituent associations.[54] The number of people casting ballots was often quite small, and they were typically part of Hong Kong's economic and social elite, not average citizens. The interests of these associations were often linked to other centers of power (Hong Kong's executive organs, the CCP, powerful businesses), and the people they elected to LegCo often acted accordingly. Patten set out to make these functional constituencies more democratic. With existing functional constituencies, all the people working within that sector were now enfranchised, so that not only directors voted. Multiple votes by businessmen who directed several companies were abolished; the principle of one person, one vote was established. Nine new functional constituencies/seats were also required as part of the Qian-Hurd January 1990 agreement. For these, Patten used internationally recognized classifications of industry and commerce, enfranchising large numbers of average people working within those new sectors. Again, individual voting replaced corporate voting. In this way, election to the "functional constituencies" became significantly more democratic. Patten maintained that these reforms were within the letter of the Joint Declaration and the Qian-Hurd agreement; he believed there existed no Sino-British agreement on these matters, and that as sovereign power until July 1, 1997, Britain was acting fully within its legal rights.

Beijing responded to Patten's election reform program by demanding that London abandon its effort to "unilaterally" reform Hong Kong's prerersion political structures, that is, implementing changes without first securing Beijing's approval. The way things should work, Beijing said, was that China would lay out the parameters for postreversion Hong Kong in a Basic Law, and Britain should ensure that Hong Kong's prereversion political structures were congruent with Basic Law provisions. Such "congruence" would avoid a rupture between pre- and postreversion arrangements, thereby creating a "through train" that minimized risk of destabilizing Hong Kong. Unless Britain changed course, Beijing warned, Sino-British cooperation on the reversion of Hong Kong would be at an end. When London refused to change course, Beijing followed through on its threat, suspended cooperation, and proceeded to pressure London in various ways to accept Beijing's leadership of the reversion process. In London, Percy Cradock, then retired, joined in the criticism of Patten's approach.

Beijing waged its "negotiation battle" with Britain not on the merits of more or less democracy in Hong Kong, but on Britain's putative violation of "the three agreements," producing what Beijing called Britain's "three violations." This approach allowed Beijing to occupy the moral high ground. It was not a question of democracy, Chinese representatives said, but of British failure to comply with its agreements. This avoided casting China as an opponent to democracy in a world swept by democratic ideals.

Beijing saw Patten's reform program as an attempt to create a fait accompli which would then form a basis for discussions in which China would advance counterproposals to Patten's moves. Beijing countered by insisting that Patten abandon his reform program and "return" to the path of cooperation, i.e., of action only via agreement of the two sides, as required by the "three agreements." In the Joint Declaration, the two parties had "agreed to a proper negotiated settlement" and had set up a Joint Liaison Group to "ensure a smooth transfer." Those provisions required, or at least implied, that Britain should only act through agreement with Beijing, in China's view.

Patten believed that none of his reforms violated earlier agreements with China. According to Patten's memoir, when the matter of Chinese charges of British violations of bilateral agreements was submitted to the House of Commons and "three different teams of international lawyers were asked to say whether our electoral proposals were a breach of the [Qian-Hurd] correspondence or of the Joint Declaration and the Basic Law, they answered in the negative."[55] When Patten flew to Beijing in October 1992 to present his reform program to Beijing shortly after assuming his post in Hong Kong and announcing his political reform program, he tried to pin down exactly where and how his political reform program constituted a violation of agreements. Patten's account is interesting:

> One after another, Chinese officials—over the table or from the depths of their white-antimascassared chairs—would accuse me of having broken the Joint Declaration and the Basic Law. "How have I done so?" I would respond. "Show me where." "You know you have done so," they would reply. "You must have done so, or else we wouldn't have said it." "But where?" "It is not for us to say; you must know that you have erred." "Give me a single instance," I would argue. "Well," they would usually claim somewhat lamely, "you have at least broken the spirit of the Joint Declaration and the Basic Law." "What do you mean by the 'spirit'? Do you just mean that you disagree with me? Why not then discuss what I have done? Put forward your own proposals." "We cannot put forward our own proposals until you return to the spirit of the text. The circles spun and looped; the arguments twisted and turned . . . .[56]

When Qian met Patten during the latter's October 1992 Beijing visit, the Chinese foreign minister demanded that he publicly retract his political reform program. Failure to do so would create a "great challenge to Sino-British cooperation," Qian said. This would cause China to "quit partnership" with Britain and "start all over again." Qian viewed these harsh words as a "sincere warning" which was "not heard" by Patten and London. This failure to heed China's warning opened the way to "open confrontation."[57] As during the 1982–1983 Joint Declaration negotiations, Beijing was stipulating a precondition for negotiations—public withdrawal of Patten's election reform plan, in this case—that prejudged the outcome of talks. By withdrawing Patten's already announced reform program, London would implicitly agree to proceed with changes to Hong Kong's political set-up only after securing Beijing's consent. But in 1992–1993, unlike in 1982–1983, London refused to accept China's precondition.

Qian warned Patten that unless he abandoned his electoral reform effort, Beijing would simply ignore him and deal directly with London. Beijing followed through on this threat. Subsequently Qian handled the matter with Hurd or with the British ambassador in Beijing, Robin McLaren. Patten for his remaining years in Hong Kong was subjected to a campaign of vituperation by pro-China newspapers, by prominent figures in Hong Kong business circles, and by some British China hands, such as Cradock, who felt Patten's political reform program was simply unrealistic. Patten himself felt opinion turning against him. But Britain did not change course.

Seventeen rounds of talks between Ambassador McLaren and Zheng Junsheng (Xu Jiatun's successor as head of Xinhua in Hong Kong) began in Beijing in April and continued to late November 1993. Zhang tried to persuade McLaren that British moves in Hong Kong needed to converge with postreversion arrangements as specified by the Basic Law, and that this was required by the Joint Declaration and the Qian-Hurd correspondence. McLaren rejected the proposition that Patten's reforms violated any agreements between Beijing and London, and insisted that China should cooperate with Britain. Beijing added pressure mid-1993 by openly publishing for the first time in the text of Deng's September 1982 talk with Thatcher in which he had clearly warned the British leader that China was prepared to act unilaterally to handle any adverse situation in Hong Kong created by British-inspired disturbances there. Aside from underlining for London the possibility of unilateral Chinese recovery of Hong Kong and the possibility of humiliation of British "honor," Deng's 1982 comments made Patten's democratization program seem imprudent and unrealistic. It also reassured public opinion in Hong Kong that China was quite serious about not altering Hong Kong's economic and social systems after reversion, at least in Qian Qichen's view.[58]

By November 1993, there remained a wide and apparently unbridgeable gap between Beijing and London over issues having to do with Hong Kong elections: the size of functional constituencies, the makeup of the election committee, the voting method (one or two votes per elector) for geographic constituencies, and so on. Decision on these matters by December was essential, British representatives informed the Chinese side in November, if LegCo was to debate these proposals and translate them into law in time to guide the 1995 elections. When no further agreement was forthcoming, the talks reached an impasse and were suspended.[59] Each side blamed the other for termination of talks.

Early the next year, Patten submitted his reform proposals to LegCo for debate. As Sino-British cooperation evaporated, Beijing began unilateral preparations for reversion. In December 1996, China used the Selection Committee set up to select Hong Kong's chief executive under the Basic Law to select, as well, a "provisional legislative assembly" for the territory. Britain refused to allow that body to meet in Hong Kong, so it met in Shenzhen. Beijing declared that the portion of Hong Kong's political institutions constituted under exclusively British authority would cease to exist with the end of British authority on July 1, 1997, and that new political structures constituted according to the provisions of the Basic Law would be established.

The LegCo elected in 1995 under British authority and on the basis of Patten's election democratization effort was the first wholly elected LegCo (with both functional and geographic constituencies) in Hong Kong history, with a full one-third of its members directly elected. That body ceased to function at midnight on June 30, 1997, when it was replaced by what had been the Provisional Legislative Council. China and Britain were, however, able to agree on an intricate protocol regarding the actual conduct of the transition ceremony on June 30–July 1, 1997. That ceremony took place without major glitch, though under heavy rain, providing a transfer that was face-saving for both sides.

By confronting Britain, Beijing averted the expansion of democratic processes and institutions in Hong Kong after its reversion to China. It did this while avoiding positioning itself as an antidemocratic power. Instead, Beijing occupied the moral high ground of an agreement-abiding power insisting that Britain abide by the agreements which it had already accepted. The most crucial audience that Beijing had to convince was the people of Hong Kong. The fact that Beijing was able to abandon cooperation with Britain and unilaterally handle Hong Kong's reversion without precipitating flight of financial or human capital from Hong Kong suggests, to this author in any case, that Beijing's policies effectively served PRC and the CCP interests. Paradoxically, Beijing's relatively effective diplomacy seems to have been premised on a basic misperception of British intentions.

Chinese Misattribution of British Purposes?

How accurate were CCP views that after London's post-6-4 LegCo election proposals were part of a Western conspiracy to foment turmoil in China? The memoirs of Percy Cradock, Robin McLaren, and Chris Patten give no indication of an intention to destabilize Hong Kong or undermine the CCP government of China. Cradock and McLaren explain Britain's increased post-6-4 concern with LegCo democracy as a function of upholding Hong Kong's promised autonomy, thereby stabilizing Hong Kong.[60] Christopher Patten explains his democratic quest as a function of British public opinion and the moral obligations of Britain to the people of Hong Kong. It is possible, of course, that perfidious Albion had a secret strategy behind its bland statements and subsequent memoirs. But no documentary evidence of this exists, as far as this author is aware. I believe that the tentative conclusion must be that Chinese leaders' attributions of motives to London were inaccurate.

It is tempting to dismiss as a mere propaganda ploy the stated Chinese view of a plan or effort to destabilize Hong Kong and China, as mere attributions designed to tarnish British negotiating moves. As Xu Jiatun recognized, Chinese accusations of nefarious intent certainly were functionally useful to Beijing's struggle against London. But statements by Qian Qichen and Xu Jiatun—PRC officials responsible for handling Hong Kong—suggest that attribution of nefarious motives was not merely instrumental, but reflected genuine belief. Top Chinese leaders actually seem to have believed that directly elected LegCo seats, along with the Lantao airport scheme, were part of a British plot to destabilize China. Did Britain actually aim to destabilize Hong Kong and China? Were Chinese attributions valid? It is possible that eventual declassification of British documents will reveal otherwise, but pending that

I believe we must take Patten and McLaren at face value: Chinese leaders judged British motives incorrectly.

Steve Tsang attributed CCP misattribution of sinister motives to Britain to a combination of ideology and unfamiliarity with Hong Kong's civil service.[61] The CCP's ideology taught it that Britain had always plundered Hong Kong. No additional evidence was required to reach the conclusion that the ambitious Lantao airport plan was merely another move of this kind. CCP leaders were also extrapolating the likely Lantao construction process from how the PRC bureaucracy might handle it. CCP leaders understood well the PRC bureaucracy, and extrapolated from it to surmise that a great deal of money would disappear via corrupt officials. They did not know that Hong Kong's open tender process, its strict public oversight (including oversight by LegCo), and the independence and dedication of its civil service would prevent Hong Kong's bureaucracy from acting as the PRC's bureaucracy might.

The CCP's perception of Patten's election democratization as an instability-producing time bomb similarly arose out of its beliefs about "bourgeois democracy." Open and competitive elections and separation of powers between independent branches of government yield instability and governmental paralysis, according to the CCP's ideology. Moreover, legitimate government rests not on the consent of the governed but on superior knowledge and virtue—in this case, understanding of Marxism-Leninism and dedication to China's rise to "wealth and power." Yet while serious misperceptions marred the calculations of China's leaders, these misperceptions did not produce policy failure. The collapse of Anglo-Chinese cooperation and the absence of a "through train" did not prevent the stable transfer of Hong Kong to PRC control.

Wiping Out the Stain of National Humiliation and Opium Wars

Several years before the designated time of reversion, July 1, 1997, a huge clock was set up in Tiananmen Square showing the countdown to Hong Kong's reversion.[62] As the designated time came closer, China's media increasingly carried articles and editorials celebrating the upcoming event. Their theme was that the deep stain of China's national humiliation during the Opium Wars was being wiped away—thanks to the sagacious leadership of Deng Xiaoping, Jiang Zemin, and the CCP—and the Chinese people should celebrate this. The message resonated with the public. Two days before reversion, a crowd of over a half million gathered in Tiananmen to express their nationalist pride. Police later cleared the square. On the day before reversion, a carefully selected group of 100,000 was admitted to the square to observe patriotic festivities celebrating reversion. At zero hour, the crowd bust spontaneously into applause and mutual patriotic congratulations. Only eight years earlier, Tiananmen had evoked bitter memories. Now those were blurred by passionate nationalist joy.

Jiang Zemin led the PRC delegation to Hong Kong for the reversion ceremonies. Other leading members of the delegation were Li Peng, Qian Qichen, and Deng Yingqiao, Zhou Enlai's widow. The PRC delegation skipped the British banquet, but attended the formal midnight handover ceremony with its highly symbolic flag lowering and flag raising to the tune of the respective national anthems. Jiang Zemin gave a short speech, saying in part: "The return of Hong Kong to the motherland after going through a century of vicissitudes indicates that from now on, the Hong Kong compatriots have become true masters of this Chinese land." Hong Kong's reversion, along with that of Macao two years later, left Taiwan the only major territory remaining explicitly slated for "return to the Motherland."

Military Confrontation with the United States

Faulty Assumptions and Lessons Learned

Early in 1996, PLA lobbying for a campaign of forward-leaning military dem-onstrations designed to intimidate Taiwan's emerging democratic electorate combined with deep bitterness within the Politburo toward recent shifts in US Taiwan policy to produce the first military confrontation between the PRC and the United States since 1967, before China withdrew its forces from North Vietnam. These PLA military demonstrations were based on two assump-tions. First, that a credible threat of war with China would cause Taiwan's newly enfranchised electorate to move away from what Beijing declared to be "Taiwan independence." Second, that the United States would not inter-vene forcefully and effectively to shield Taiwan from PLA threats, and that this clarification of Taiwan's actual vulnerability would induce Taiwan's elec-torate to embrace a more prudent path of accepting Beijing's "one country, two systems" proposal. Both assumptions turned out to be wrong. PLA in-timidation angered Taiwan's voters, helping produce a landslide election for Lee Teng-hui, whom Beijing judged a "splittist." And the United States inter-vened forcefully, resulting in the third US-PRC confrontation since 6-4.

The shock of face-to-face confrontation with US military power for the first time in twenty-eight years interacted with the sobering US victory over Iraq only five years earlier to produce a "never again" resolution among China's leaders. Never again would China confront the United States from a position of military weakness. Instead, China would develop the military capabilities to match the United States in a war over Taiwan. The result was a push for carefully targeted military capabilities that could deny US forces access to the Taiwan area for the period of time necessary to bring Taiwan under PLA con-trol. Over the next two decades, that push would significantly transform the PRC-US military balance in the Western Pacific. After 1996, Chinese plan-ning for a Taiwan contingency assumed US entry, with Chinese capabilities designed to defeat that intervention.

PLA Criticism of Deng's "Weak" Taiwan Policy

In September 1992, in the midst of a campaign for re-election as president, George H. W. Bush sent an emissary to confidentially inform Deng Xiaoping that the United States would soon announce the sale of one hundred and fifty F-16 fighters to Taiwan. Bush's emissary explained that the sale was a function of the intense election campaign then underway and of Bush's desire to win the thirty-four electoral votes (second only to California's fifty-five) of Texas, where the F-16s would be produced. Bush's envoy also pointed out that Bush had a much more positive view of US relations with China than did his Democratic rival, William Clinton, who was campaigning on a promise of linking China's MFN status to human rights and getting tough on the "butchers of Beijing."[1] In line with this reasoning, Bush's representative pleaded for a restrained Chinese response to the F-16 sale. Deng Xiaoping acceded to Bush's request. Deng ruled that Bush's re-election was in China's interest, that the F-16 sale could not be undone, and that in diplomacy concessions were sometimes required; it was not possible always to attack. China's response to the F-16 sale was limited to a "strong protest" by the MFA. The F-16 was an air-superiority fighter that represented a major enhancement of air capabilities for Taiwan's air force.[2]

While explained by Bush to Deng in terms of US electoral politics, PLA leaders correctly surmised that calculations having to do with the cross-Strait military balance underlay the F-16 sale. According to James Lilley, then the assistant secretary for international security affairs in the Department of Defense, the F-16 sale originated in the Department of Defense as a response to the recent Chinese purchase from Russia of surface-to-air missiles, KILO class submarines, and advanced Su-27 air superiority fighters, and was intended to prevent the PLA from achieving clear military dominance over Taiwan.[3] PLA leaders intuited the real purpose of the F-16 sale. Deng Xiaoping's decision to credit Bush's Washington's "election tactics" explanation and his low-keyed response to the F-16 sale caused dismay in PLA circles. This was the beginning of three years of lobbying by the PLA for a tougher, military-edged policy toward Taiwan.

Enhancement of Taiwan's ability to contend for air superiority over the Taiwan Strait touched on several PLA interests. First of all, it was the PLA that would have to bear the burden of war with Taiwan if all else failed. The fact that the CCP regime was beholden to the PLA for the dirty work it did in June 1989 to keep the CCP in power emboldened PLA leaders to speak out when CCP leaders got things wrong—as with Deng's low-key response to the F-16 sale. The recent evaporation of the Soviet threat, combined with the increasing challenges from the United States and Taiwan's democratization, also prompted the PLA to focus on China's new threats. Finally, the PLA's nationalistic organizational culture led it to view itself as the defender of China's national interests.[4]

From the standpoint of all of China's leaders, not only the PLA, the F-16 sale was an unacceptable violation of the three communiqués and of China's sovereignty, and part of a US effort to encourage "Taiwan independence" separatists who wanted to permanently split Taiwan from the Chinese motherland. All of this was, in turn, part of a larger US scheme to pressure, injure and, if possible, shatter China as part of the US quest for global hegemony. The differences that emerged within the Chinese leadership at this juncture were not over the villainy of US and Taiwan moves, but over how forceful China's response to those moves should be. The MFA, supported by Deng until 1995 or so, believed that a low-keyed and nonmilitary response was appropriate. PLA leaders argued that a much stronger and military-edged rebuff was necessary—something along the lines of the military exercises that would take place in the Straits from July 1995 to March 1996.

Shortly after the 1992 announcement of the F-16 sale, the CMC convened an expanded meeting to hear and debate a report drafted by the General Staff Department. Navy and air force representatives reported on their level of preparedness for confrontation, and proposed additional measures to further heighten preparedness.[5] COSTIND, the military-industrial commission, reported on the level of preparedness for a challenge in the Strait, along with proposed research, development, and production measures to further heighten preparation. The thrust of the meeting was on preparation of a military rebuff. The atmosphere of the meeting was heated, with many speakers venting their anger at US duplicity and aggression against China. Deng Xiaoping's representative at the meeting, Yang Shangkun, tried to tamp down emotions by conveying three "instructions" from Deng: 1) except in the event of large-scale invasion of China, the focus of all work would remain on economic development; 2) military modernization should focus on quality, not quantity; and 3) China should remain calm in responding to the F-16 sale, which was motivated by Bush's re-election campaign tactics and not cooked up by the Taiwan authorities. The CCP Propaganda Department prepared an intense campaign against US hegemony and power politics. The campaign went forward, but only after propaganda chief (and Deng loyalist) Li Ruihuan deleted phrases such as "the main struggle in the world today is between hegemonism and opposition to hegemonism." Chen Yun, just below Deng in authority on the Politburo, criticized Deng's willingness to strike political deals with the Western bourgeois class.

The MFA stood its ground and argued in favor of a low-key response. If the PRC took hard moves, the MFA argued, the United States would probably respond in kind, and a cycle of mutual retaliation and escalation could result that would be disastrous for China's development. Moreover, the F-16 sale had arisen out of Bush's effort to win re-election, and his success in that effort was in China's interest. Bush was an "old friend" of China with personal connections with Deng Xiaoping and had shown a degree of understanding of China's situation after 6-4. Clinton, on the other hand, had staked his presidential campaign on hostility to China, criticizing Bush's China policy as "weak" and calling for the linkage of MFN and human rights. A tough propaganda stance regarding Washington's transgressions against China's sovereignty over Taiwan was fine, the MFA argued. But China should avoid anything that might injure PRC-US economic ties. An MFA report along these lines was approved by Deng and the Politburo Standing Committee.

Deng's personal intervention tamped down criticism for a while, but PLA criticism of the MFA and Qian Qichen continued. PLA critics could not very well attack Deng. Qian Qichen and the MFA were another matter, and they became the target of PLA criticism. At a session of the NPC in March 1994, the PLA delegation drafted a proposal of eight "suggestions" regarding the foreign policy work of the MFA. Senior Generals Li Desheng and Yang Dezhi had to visit the delegation and persuade them to drop the matter. Two months later, the PLA's Academy of Military Science (AMS) and National Defense University (NDU) convened a conference on "China's Foreign Policy and Policy toward Taiwan." The conference compiled a long list of MFA mistakes, concluded that those mistakes merited Qian's resignation as foreign minister, and embodied these views in a letter to be sent to the Central Committee. At the last minute, the heads of the AMS and NDU intervened to order the document withheld, and to explain to conference participants that the MFA was implementing policies and principles approved by the Central Committee. Deng followed up by calling on the PLA to submit at all times to party leadership. Jiang Zemin informed the Politburo, and thence the PLA, that foreign policy was decided on by the Politburo and approved by the "Central Committee" (i.e., by Deng). The MFA was not acting on its own, but had firmly implemented centrally approved policies, with Qian Qichen's efforts being lauded by Deng, Jiang informed the Politburo. Deng also dispatched close and high-level associates to key PLA generals to explain Deng's views, including the vital importance of PLA submission to party leadership on all matters.

US Upgrading of Relations with Taiwan

While pressure was building in Beijing for tougher punishment of the United States for its arms sales to Taiwan, pressure was building in Washington for greater support for democratic Taiwan. By early 1994, it was increasingly clear that Clinton's (and Congress') policy of "linkage" would fail; the costs to the United States of carrying through with MFA revocation were simply too great. Some members of Congress began looking for other ways of punishing Beijing. More importantly, Taiwan by 1994 was in the midst of a full-blown transition to democracy, a transition that generated considerable congressional sympathy for Taiwan. Congressional actions also reflected the mood of the American electorate. Taiwan, long a US friend, recently prosperous, and now a liberal democracy, had the sympathy of a wide swath of the US public. The PRC, on the other hand, seemed ruled by old-style communists.

In April 1994, Congress passed a bill containing a provision directing the State Department to review and upgrade ties with Taiwan.[6] President Clinton did not want another confrontation with China so soon after the MFN-linkage debacle. Moreover, Clinton's major focus was on healthcare reform, for which he needed congressional support. But there was overwhelming congressional support for Taiwan. A presidential veto would probably have failed, weakening the president's position on other issues. Clinton therefore signed the act. After several months, the resulting Taiwan Policy Review (TPR) marginally upgraded US ties with Taiwan. According to testimony by Assistant Secretary of State for East Asian Affairs Winston Lord to the Senate Foreign Relations committee in September 1994, the TPR was the first "systematic enhancement" of US relations with Taiwan since normalization of US-PRC relations in January 1979.[7] Through the TPR, "anomalies" in the US-Taiwan relationship were corrected and US-Taiwan ties strengthened, according to Lord. While carefully stipulating that US policy continued to be based on the Three Communiqués and that the United States would maintain merely "unofficial relations with the people of Taiwan," the TPR upgraded US ties with Taiwan in several ways. The type, level, and venue of permissible contacts between US and Taiwan officials were upgraded slightly. US officials could now, for instance, meet with Taiwan officials in their respective offices, rather than meeting in some "unofficial" venue as had previously been the case. The United States would support Taiwan's membership in international organizations open to nonstate entities and would "look for ways to have Taiwan's voice heard in organizations of states where Taiwan's membership is not possible." Taiwan was also to be allowed to use the name "Taipei" in the designation of Taiwan's office in the United States, changing that appellation of that agency from the ambiguous "Coordinating Council for North American Affairs" to "Taipei Economic and Cultural Representative Office" (TECRO). Taiwan's top leaders were also to be permitted, as they had been since 1980, to transit US territory for travel convenience and for normal periods of transits "but without undertaking any public activities." "Visits," as opposed to "transits," would not be permitted. This latter stipulation excluding "visits" would be violated within eight months.

In Beijing, the MFA issued another strong protest in response to the TPR shifts in US policy. But as with the F-16 sale in 1992, other punitive moves did not follow. On the contrary, in mid-October, only a month after the results of the TPR were announced in Washington, a US defense department delegation led by Secretary of Defense William Perry made the first visit to China by a secretary of defense since 6-4. Perry met with Jiang Zemin, Li Peng, and Liu

Huaqing, and held talks with Defense Minister Chi Haotian. In the view of some PLA leaders, China was rewarding rather than punishing Washington for upgrading US-Taiwan links via the TPR.

In August 1994, following an understanding between Deng and Chen Yun, a high-level conference of PLA, party, and state leaders was convened to respond to PLA pressure and build a consensus over policy toward the United States and Taiwan. Guided by Deng loyalists, the conference endorsed a policy of patience, forbearance, and nonuse of military force while pressing forward with new proposals for cross-Strait relations. So long as Taiwan did not split from China or experience a "foreign invasion," China would concentrate on economic development for fifteen to twenty years. By then, the standard of living on the mainland would be much higher, easing fears on Taiwan that unification might result in declining living standards—or so the conference concluded. Another fifteen to twenty years of patient waiting would also make China's eventual resort to force seem more reasonable.

Following this consensus, Jiang Zemin put his own stamp on Taiwan policy cast along the nonthreatening, more conciliatory lines favored by Deng Xiaoping. In January 1995, Jiang promulgated an eight-point proposal for development of cross-Strait relations. Drafted by the Taiwan Affairs Office of the State Council and approved by the Politburo, Jiang's eight-point proposal (*Jiang ba dian*) hewed to the "one country, two systems" rubric, but did so in moderate, nonthreatening terms, and represented a genuine attempt to appeal to the people of Taiwan. The proposal tried to assuage Taiwan concerns about unification by saying that after unification Taiwan would keep its own legislature, its own judiciary (including the power of "final adjudication"), its own armed forces, and its own government. Beijing would not station troops in Taiwan or send administrative personnel there. The proposal called for talks between the two sides, but only on the premise of "one China" and with Taiwan ceasing all words and actions aimed at "creating an independent Taiwan." Taiwan was also to stop efforts to increase its international living space. Under these conditions, Beijing was willing, Jiang's proposal said, to discuss any concerns Taiwan might have.[8] From the perspective of CCP leaders and within the context of CCP politics, "Jiang's eight-point proposal" was lenient and moderate. It would be difficult to imagine any PRC leader at that juncture issuing a more generous and lenient proposal—especially a leader who needed PLA support. Jiang took a political risk by issuing his moderate eight-point proposal. When Taipei did not respond positively to it, Jiang was out on a limb.

Taiwan's President Lee Teng-hui replied to Jiang's eight points in April. Lee, was the leader and probable presidential candidate of the Kuomintang (KMT) in the future direct popular presidential election (Taiwan's first). In his April statement, Lee endorsed the notion of unification, but ruled out "one country, two systems" as the means. The basis for unification could only be, Lee said, Beijing's acceptance of the reality of the existence of the Republic of China on Taiwan as the sovereign authority on that island. There existed on Taiwan and the mainland of China two different political entities, each of which exercised full authority over a distinct and discrete territory. Neither entity was, in fact, subordinate to the other. This was the reality that Beijing should recognize, Lee said. The governments ruling the two sides of the Taiwan Strait should establish normal relations. Meetings at "international occasions" might be an appropriate venue for beginning such normal government-to-government relations.[9]

From Beijing's perspective, Lee's formula was nothing less than a two Chinas proposal. Xinhua denounced Lee's proposal for ignoring the one country, two systems formula, which was, the news agency asserted, the common aspiration of the people on both sides of the Strait—still a rather mild rebuke. From the PLA perspective, Jiang's generous and lenient proposal had been met not with a like-minded attitude, but by a hard-line "two Chinas" response. From the PLA perspective, the weak and conciliatory approach that China had taken under MFA guidance since fall 1992 was not only permitting but actually encouraging the Taiwan splittists and their American backers. Conciliatory moves by Beijing were taken by Lee Teng-hui and his American backers as indication that yet another step toward Taiwan independence could be safely taken. Rather than moving toward peaceful unification on reasonable, even generous terms, Taiwan was moving further and further away from unification. This was being done with the support of anti-China forces in the United States, PLA leaders concluded, and was part of a plot to split Taiwan from China via institutionalization of Taiwan's separation from the PRC.

The threshold of PLA tolerance was crossed in May 1995, when the US State Department announced the issue of a visa for President Lee Teng-hui to make a "private" visit to the United States to deliver a speech at the commencement ceremony of his alma mater, Cornell University. Lee had graduated from Cornell in 1968 with a PhD in agricultural economics. This would be the first visit by a ROC president to the United States since normalization of US-PRC ties in January 1979. Lee could be expected to use, and did in fact use, his US visit to propound his views about two separate sovereign governments ruling the two sides of the Strait, i.e., "Taiwan independence" from Beijing's point of view. Allowing an incumbent president of Taiwan to visit the United States in any capacity was, from Beijing's perspective, unacceptable and a violation of the US pledge to have no official contact with Taiwan. In the context of 1995, it constituted US support for Lee Teng-hui and a turn away from peaceful unification under the "one country, two systems" framework. It must be noted that neither Lee Teng-hui nor Clinton administration officials believed that the issue of a visa for Lee or Lee's April 1995 statement on "two political entities" constituted a repudiation of peaceful cross-Strait unification or of the "one

China principle." The fact that Beijing claimed that Lee and Washington were pursuing "Taiwan independence" did not make it so.

Chinese diplomats in Washington lobbied hard and with initial success to prevent issue of a visa for Lee. In early March, the State Department announced that Lee would not receive a visa, and gave assurances to Beijing in this regard. Mounting congressional pressure, urged on by Taipei, forced Clinton to change positions. Early in May, the House of Representatives voted 396 to 1 supporting a visa for Lee. The Senate vote was 91 to 1. More broadly, Republican candidates had swept the midterm elections in November 1994, giving that party control of both houses of Congress for the first time since 1948. Confronting overwhelming congressional opposition, and in an extremely weak position, with little to gain domestically from siding with Beijing, and at a personal level not too favorably inclined toward CCP leaders, Clinton flip-flopped. Lee got his visa.

China's MFA was taken by surprise by the US issue of a visa for Lee, a fact that increased MFA vulnerability to hard-liner criticism. At an April meeting, Secretary of State Warren Christopher had attempted to signal Qian Qichen that mounting congressional pressure might undo the administration's earlier decision not to issue a visa. But Qian failed to pick up those signals. When it became apparent that the MFA had been taken by surprise, critics of that ministry got new ammunition. Qian had been duped once again by the cunning Americans, hard-line critics said. There were some analysts in the MFA and Chinese Academy of Social Science who saw US policy shifts not in terms of US efforts to "split China by encouraging Taiwan independence" but as a function of less sinister factors such as public opinion, partisan and electoral competition, and the separation of powers between executive and legislative branches. In the intensely emotional and nationalist atmosphere of internal Chinese meetings at this juncture, it was easy for advocates of a more confrontational approach to tar as unpatriotic people who tried to mitigate the evil nature of recent US policy changes toward Taiwan. The voices that had a more accurate insight into the making of US policy were often cowed by hard-liners who saw their nuanced explanation of US policy as lack of patriotism or perhaps invidious influence by the West.

The US State Department did what it could to keep Lee's June 1995 visit low-key and unofficial. Through talks with TECRO, the State Department stipulated when and how the ROC flag was to be displayed, what themes Lee's speech should and should not include, and of course, that no State Department or executive-branch officials would meet with Lee. In the event, Lee generally ignored the restrictions demanded by the State Department. Several senators and many state and local officials met with Lee. Taiwan was, after all, popular with the American public, and local governments were neither responsible for US foreign policy nor under the control of the federal government. Politicians were happy to be seen with a popular, pro-American foreign leader. Lee's speech at Cornell University proudly touted Taiwan's political and economic development, offering that experience as a guideline for the Mainland's own development. Lee used liberally the name "Republic of China," which Beijing found offensive because it connoted, in Beijing's view, de jure sovereignty. Crowds of ROC-flag-waving Taiwan and US citizens welcomed Lee in cities along his way, while the US media devoted considerable attention to his activities.

Lee's 1995 visit to Ithaca, New York, was, in effect, the kickoff of his 1996 presidential campaign.[10] Lee was running as a candidate of the KMT, a party that traditionally supported unification, but only after democratization of the mainland's political system. Lee's major opposition was the Democratic Progressive Party (DPP), which explicitly advocated Taiwan independence. Lee's successful US visit garnered support among his opposition's constituency. It was shrewd electoral politics. PLA leaders probably had little understanding of such electoral calculations; their default conclusion was that various US and Taiwan moves were manifestations of an evil anti-China scheme.

Beijing responded to the US announcement of its decision to grant Lee a visa with another MFA strong protest expressing "utmost indignation." The US move "totally contravened the fundamental principles of the three joint communiqués," the protest said. Yet on May 27, five days after the US visa announcement, the head of Beijing's Association for Relations Across the Taiwan Straits (ARATS, a nonofficial organization set up by Beijing to handle contacts with the "Taiwan authorities") arrived in Taipei for two days of talks, which resulted in the announcement of a future meeting of ARATS and Taiwan's Straits Exchange Foundation (SEF) in Beijing. (The SEF was Taipei's counterpart to ARATS.) The PLA was livid at US duplicity, at Lee Teng-hui's "splittism," and at MFA weakness. Following Lee's US visit, the PLA insisted on forceful military demonstrations to punish Lee and his US supporters. Jiang Zemin was held partially responsible for recent diplomatic weakness and failures. Jiang's political situation required him to be sensitive to PLA views. Selected as general secretary and designated successor to Deng Xiaoping only in July 1989, retaining PLA support was absolutely essential for Jiang. When Deng arranged Jiang's selection as future paramount leader shortly after 6-4, he had lobbied PLA leaders to give Jiang their full support. Deng also appointed several generals in key positions with directions to strengthen PLA support for Jiang. Following the US visa decision, the same Deng loyalists appointed in 1989 to strengthen PLA support for Jiang now conveyed to Jiang PLA views about the need for a tough response to the string of US "Taiwan independence" provocations.[11] Jiang could not afford to ignore PLA views as Deng had done in 1992. Had Jiang not heeded PLA lobbying, his continuation as paramount leader would have been in jeopardy.

Deng had immense authority both as a key member of the PRC's founding generation and as architect of China's amazingly successful about-face from the Mao era. Deng was an old military man, a political commissar with one of the PLA's key armies during the post-1945 civil war, with deep personal connections with PLA leaders. Jiang had none of this. He was a military novice. Jiang had great political need to prove his toughness to the PLA and win continued PLA support. Jiang had taken a risk and failed with the issue of his moderate-sounding eight-point proposal. Now he needed to compensate for that earlier moderation. While Deng was politically active, Jiang could borrow Deng's authority to bring the PLA into line. But by 1995, Deng was very ill and politically inactive. (Deng would die in February 1997.) Without the full support of Deng, Jiang was in no position to veto PLA demands for aggressive military exercises directed against Taiwan. Jiang thus embraced the PLA's call for a hard response, and delivered a self-criticism before an expanded meeting of the Politburo of his earlier soft approach. This was an astute move that allowed Jiang to pivot to a tougher line toward Taiwan more in accord with PLA views. Qian Qichen also made a self-criticism.[12] It was decided to stage military exercises aimed at Taiwan as proposed by the PLA. The US issue of a visa for Lee was part of a plot to encircle and split China, the Taiwan Affairs Leading Small Group (TALSG) determined, and China would respond firmly to its treacherous move.

Throughout the summer and fall of 1995, Beijing pressed Washington to give "firm commitments," ideally in the form of a "fourth communiqué," that Taiwan leaders would not again be allowed to visit the United States. Since US actions had created the problem, Beijing argued, it was up to the United States to take "concrete actions" to repair the damage. Ideally US firm guarantees would be finalized at a summit of Jiang and Clinton. Beijing indicated that if the United States accepted this Chinese proposal, there would be a rapid restoration of ties and cooperation on a whole range of issues, from nonproliferation to intellectual property rights protection, would be enhanced. Washington rejected the idea of a fourth communiqué and was only willing to offer that the United States had no plans to issue further visas to Taiwan leaders in the near future.

Taiwan's Democratic Transformation and Emergence of "Taiwan Independence"

The changes in Taiwan's long-standing policies toward unification of Taiwan and the Mainland that so deeply troubled Beijing in the early 1990s were rooted in the democratization of that island's political system. Between 1949, when the defeated remnants of the Chinese Nationalist Party (Kuomintang, or KMT) regime fled to Taiwan and the mid-1980s, Taiwan had been ruled by an authoritarian one-party dictatorship. That KMT dictatorship became less brutal over time, especially after Chiang Kai-shek died in April 1975 and power passed to his son, Chiang Ching-kuo. Scholars distinguish between an earlier stage of hard authoritarianism under Chiang Kai-shek and a latter state of soft authoritarianism under Chiang Ching-kuo. Opposition political activity gradually expanded during the latter period. By the late 1970s, the island had a vibrant island-wide opposition, commonly referred to as "outside the [KMT] party" (*dang wai*), functioning in a condition of semilegality. During the nearly forty years of KMT dictatorship over Taiwan, the proposition that the KMT-ruled Republic of China (ROC) regime represented all of China, and that Taiwan was merely a province of China—albeit a province where China's legitimate government, the ROC, happened to reside—was the philosophical underpinning of the KMT dictatorship. From this perspective, the Republic of China, not the People's Republic of China, constituted the legitimate government of China and would someday return to the mainland once the "Communist bandits" were overthrown. By the 1980s, this orthodoxy of eventual "return to the mainland" was a source of considerable humor in Taiwan, but people publicly challenged it at the risk of confronting the KMT's dreaded martial law command.

Meanwhile, throughout the nearly four decades of KMT authoritarian rule, government power promoted economic development via participation in global markets. Standards of living, levels of education, numbers of professionals, and international connectivity rose steadily. Taiwan's political culture was also deeply influenced by American and Japanese culture with their differing variants of liberal democracy. By the mid-1980s, there was widespread yearning in Taiwan for political freedom and democracy. Brave men and women periodically challenged dictatorial authority, and by the mid-1980s the "outside the party movement" was quite strong. Taiwan's leader, Chiang Ching-kuo, also recognized that US recognition of the PRC in 1979 destroyed the credibility of a KMT claim of eventual "return to the mainland," and that, consequently, the KMT would have to refound its legitimacy squarely on the consent of the people of Taiwan.[13]

Finally, in September 1986, some nine months before Chiang Ching-kuo lifted martial law, under which Taiwan had been governed since 1949, the *dangwai* movement openly declared itself to be an opposition party, the DPP, seeking power via election. The KMT government acquiesced to this move, and the process of democratization moved into high gear. Multiparty competition initiated a process of rapid and peaceful transition to democracy. Taiwan's democratic transition was continued by Chiang's successor, Lee Teng-hui, president from January 1988 to May 2000. By the time of Taiwan's presidential election of March 1996, Taiwan was a genuine and vibrant liberal democracy. It was precisely this that created difficulties for Beijing. Under a KMT dictatorship, even a "soft" one, there was the possibility of a deal between dictatorships in Taipei and Beijing. Now Beijing would have to deal with Taiwan's electorate.

Democratic self-government by the people of Taiwan required abandoning the myth that the ROC ruled over the Chinese mainland. In 1992, shortly after legalizing many cross-Strait contacts for the first time, Taipei issued "New Guidelines for National Unification" that postulated "two political entities" with "parity" within "one China," which was the ROC. The ROC still had de jure sovereignty over the mainland of China, the New Guidelines stated, but had de facto control only over Taiwan, Penghu, etc. The PRC exercised de facto control over the China mainland. These ideas were incorporated in a White Paper several days later and were again embodied in Lee Teng-hui's April 1995 response to Jiang's eight-point proposal.[14]

Democratization of Taiwan politics meant that long-taboo topics could be openly discussed. Now they were debated with enthusiasm in Taiwan. A central issue became Taiwan's group identity. Who were the people of Taiwan? Chinese? Taiwanese? Or both? And what did each of those identities signify in terms of Taiwan's relations with the ethnic Chinese people and state across the Taiwan Strait on the mainland, the PRC? And what did this signify in terms of Taiwan's own political institutions? A strong and articulate minority, represented politically by the DPP, insisted that the historical experience of the people on Taiwan was so different from that of the people on the Mainland that they had become a different people, a different nation, Taiwanese, not Chinese. As such, the people of Taiwan were entitled to the right of self-determination and to rule themselves in freedom and democracy as a sovereign, independent state accepted as a full member of the global community of sovereign states. These advocates of Taiwan independence took green as their symbolic color.[15]

A somewhat larger opinion group argued that pursuit of Taiwan independence was unrealistic and even dangerous given the established policy positions of the United States and the PRC. A quest for Taiwan independence was likely to trigger a confrontation with China, possibly even war, in which Taiwan might not have US support. Taiwan already had the substance of sovereignty, plus the support of the United States, under the existing arrangement as the Republic of China. The oldest and most fundamental meaning of sovereignty (tracing back to the formation of centralized monarchies in the fifteenth century) was that an authority was actually able to impose its will on a particular piece of territory, and by this standard there was no question that Taiwan was sovereign. The best course for Taiwan, these people urged, was to enhance the international status and recognition of the Republic of China on Taiwan. This point of view took blue as their color and was broadly represented by Lee Teng-hui's group within the KMT. From this perspective, the crucial task was to expand the international living space of the ROC. Several years later, many traditionalists who favored greater stress on eventual unification rather than enhancing Taiwan's international status would leave the KMT, creating a new meaning for "blue"—sometimes referred to as deep blue.

Intense partisan competition and constitutional reform paralleled Taiwan's identity debate. The election of Taiwan's leader by direct, popular vote (first implemented in March 1996 against the background of PLA military intimidation) meant that people aspiring to government office now had to cater to popular opinion. People on Taiwan were immensely proud of what they had achieved—first economic development and then peaceful transition to liberal democracy. Having long been forced to keep quiet and allow an authoritarian government to speak for them, the people of Taiwan now delighted in finding their own voice. Staking out positions on the identity issue and demonstrating one's effectiveness in enhancing Taiwan's international status became key ways of appealing to voters. Lee Teng-hui became an astute practitioner of this new brand of electoral politics in Taiwan. After inheriting power as Chiang Ching-kuo's designated successor, Lee refashioned himself as a popular leader capable of raising Taiwan's international status and expanding its participation in international affairs. In 1994, for example, Lee and his vice president Lian Chan made trips to Thailand, Singapore, Malaysia, and Indonesia to play golf with senior officials of those governments. This flexible "golf diplomacy" expanded Taiwan's contacts with major countries having diplomatic ties with the PRC. Lee's visit to the United States in June 1995 was the highest-profile success for Lee's "pragmatic diplomacy." One of Lee's major campaign pitches was that he had been effective in enhancing Taiwan's international status—witness the Taiwan Policy Review in the United States, golf diplomacy in Southeast Asia, and Lee's 1995 visit to the United States.

In the United States, there was strong sympathy for Taiwan and its transition to democracy. Taiwan was an old ally and friend of the United States. During the two decades of confrontation with "Communist China," Nationalist China, or Free China as it was then called, had served as an extremely important ally of the United States in containing Communist China.[16] Now that Taiwan was democratic, US values and interests were more congruent. America's friend was now a democracy, not a dictatorship. Ever since 1952, US policy had sought to nudge Taiwan slowly and incrementally in the direction of liberal democracy. Various levers of US influence in Taiwan had been used to push it slowly in that direction over several decades. Now, in the mid-1990s, that objective was finally being realized. Taiwan's democratic transition occurred about the same time that similar transitions were underway in South Korea and the Philippines, constituting a wave of liberal revolutions across the region.[17] The United States now had friendly democratic partners along the entire western Pacific littoral, from Japan through South Korea, Taiwan, and the Philippines to Australia. This created a geopolitical position of considerable strength for the United States in the western Pacific.

The view from Beijing was profoundly different. From Beijing's perspective, Taiwan was a part of the People's Republic of China. The island had been returned to China's sovereignty by the Cairo Declaration of December 1943.

The PRC was the successor state to the Republic of China and, as such and under generally accepted principles of international law, succeeded to the territory of the previous state. The whole issue of relations between Taiwan and the mainland of China, between the "Taiwan authorities" and China's legitimate government in Beijing, the PRC, was an internal affair of China. No foreign government had standing to intervene in, or even opine about, those relations. To do so constituted interference in the internal affairs of China. Part of the sovereign powers of a state over its recognized territory is the right to use military force to uphold its territorial and administrative integrity. It followed that the use or nonuse of PRC military force against Taiwan was part of China's sovereign authority, which Beijing would not bargain away. The incorporation of Taiwan into the state system of the PRC was, from the CCP perspective, the last remaining act of China's national liberation. Taiwan had been stolen from China by Japanese imperialism during China's century of weakness. But that weakness was now at an end. China was strong, and it was time for Taiwan to return to the Chinese motherland.

Continuing with the PRC view, since normalization with the United States on January 1, 1979, and out of a desire to build a cooperative relation with the United States, China had promulgated a "fundamental policy" of striving for peaceful unification of Taiwan and the "motherland." It reiterated this "fundamental policy" in the August 1982 arms sales communiqué. China had advanced the one country, two systems framework to make possible peaceful unification. The framework was applied first to Hong Kong, but was intended for use with Taiwan as well. Beijing's generous and lenient approach (as Beijing saw it) in arranging the reversion of Hong Kong was partially inspired by a calculation that such an approach would encourage Taiwan to embrace that approach. Under the framework, Taiwan would become a special autonomous region of the PRC, with foreign affairs and defense being the responsibility of Beijing, but with Taiwan enjoying a high degree of autonomy over internal affairs and international economic relations. From Beijing's perspective, the one country, two systems proposal was eminently fair and reasonable. Beijing was prepared to be very generous in accepting Taiwanese autonomy under nominal PRC sovereignty, and Taipei should enter into negotiations with Beijing to iron out these matters. The rub was that few people in Taiwan wanted to be subordinated to Beijing's authority and control.

A fundamental civilizational difference underlay discrepant mainland Chinese, Taiwanese Chinese, and American views regarding the nature of political authority. For Americans, legitimate government authority derives from the consent of the governed, that is, from the consent of those subject to that political power. This is a core American belief rooted in the very formation of the American republic. This means that the people of Taiwan should have a decisive say in whether they are ruled by the CCP government of the PRC. Anything less is literally unjust, from the American perspective. A very large percentage of people on Taiwan share the American view of the origin of legitimate government authority. Democratic self-government was, after all, the goal of a long, hard struggle under the KMT's hard and soft dictatorship.

In China's venerable political tradition, on the other hand, the legitimacy of political power never rested on the consent of the governed. In China's tradition, legitimate government derived from the superior wisdom and virtue of the rulers, and from the benevolent and orderly government that supposedly resulted from that superior virtue and understanding. Within this Confucian tradition, asking ordinary people to "consent" to the authority of the emperor and his officials was as nonsensical as asking children to consent to government by their wise and benevolent parents. The children/people simply lacked understanding. The rulers had superior understanding that vastly exceeded that of their child-like subjects.[18] Like China's great emperors of the past, the CCP believes it is ruling in the interest of all Chinese on the basis of its superior understanding and virtue. Resort to Western notions of government to "split China" is simply unacceptable.

In a way, the political psychology of Taiwan's electorate was the proximate target of the PLA military demonstrations of 1995–1996. Taiwan's democratization was moving the island's political scene into uncharted territory and seemed to be inspired by the belief that the people of Taiwan themselves could determine Taiwan's future, oblivious to the reality that that island, and all its inhabitants, were, from Beijing's point of view, under the sovereignty of Beijing. Taiwan's people needed to be instructed in this simple reality. They needed to be made aware that there were limits beyond which Beijing was prepared to go to war. A hard lesson in the realities of Taiwan's situation might also mobilize opposition to Lee Teng-hui within Taiwan. Lee Teng-hui's efforts to establish the Republic of China on Taiwan as a sovereign state, coequal to the PRC, was met with dismay by many people within the KMT, Lee's own party, who believed ardently in the old orthodoxy that Taiwan was a province of China, albeit the Republic of China.

In August 1993, a block of KMT leaders withdrew from that organization and formed a new party, called the New Party, largely out of opposition to Lee's movement away from the traditional KMT goal of reunification. Further to the left of Taiwan's political spectrum, the DPP favored a plebiscite followed by outright declaration of a Republic of Taiwan and of that entity's independence from China and the PRC. Some members of both the DPP and Lee Teng-hui's faction of the KMT believed that their policies could be implemented without war. They believed the PRC was bluffing and, if tested, would acquiesce to faits accomplis created by brave and resolute Taiwan leaders. These beliefs had to be punctured, CCP leaders concluded. Taiwan's newly empowered voters, and its newly democratically elected leaders, had to be taught that there were limits to Beijing's tolerance and quest for peaceful unification. Taiwan had to be made to understand, Beijing concluded, that China was prepared materially and psychologically for war, even for a full-scale assault on Taiwan to bring that island finally and irrevocably into the state system of the PRC, if Taipei continued to reject what Beijing believed was a reasonable and moderate one country, two systems framework. Elections of Taiwan's legislature were scheduled for December 1995, shortly before the island's first-ever direct election of a president on March 23, 1996. The 1995 Legislative Yuan (LY) election was only the second fully democratic election of Taiwan's legislature. The first had come in 1992 after constitutional reform eliminated appointed (not elected) delegates supposedly representing Mainland constituencies long since incorporated into the PRC. CCP leaders were deeply afraid that the dynamics of Taiwan's new democracy would push Taiwan toward independence. Red lines had to be made clear.

Beijing's Response to the US Visa Issuance

Washington was the second target of Beijing's coercive diplomacy. US leaders were under the false impression, China's leaders believed, that China needed US help to modernize, or that China was simply too far behind the United States in military capabilities to countenance confronting the United States. Because of these vulnerabilities, US leaders believed (continuing with Beijing's reconstruction of US views) that China would be forced to acquiesce to US interference in China's internal affairs and violation of various US-PRC agreements. General and Politburo member Liu Huaqing had expressed Beijing's intent in April 1994: China needed to send an "explicit and firm message to the United States: China will never tolerate foreign interference in its internal affairs and will never barter away its principles. China will not seek confrontation, but will not fear confrontation and will not evade any imposed confrontation."[19]

Beijing responded swiftly to the US issuance of a visa for Lee. The day after the announcement that Lee would receive a visa, a Chinese delegation in the United States headed by the PLA air force chief canceled its remaining itinerary and departed for home. A scheduled visit to the United States by Defense Minister Chi Haotian was postponed, and a scheduled visit to China by State Department nonproliferation officials was canceled. Beijing rejected an offer by Washington to send a special emissary to Beijing to explain the visa decision. Beijing also declined to approve the new US ambassador nominated by Washington, James Sasser. Stapleton Roy was scheduled to step down as US ambassador on June 17, 1995. President Clinton did not nominate a new ambassador until September 1995, and that nomination was not approved by Beijing until February 14, 1996. About a month after the visa announcement, and the day before Roy's term in Beijing expired, Beijing recalled Ambassador Li Daoyu "to report on his work." This meant that for a period of several months, for the first time since establishment of normal relations in January 1979, neither country had an ambassador posted in the other's capital. By recalling Li and delaying approval of Sasser, Beijing deliberately downgraded ties. Strident denunciations of Lee Teng-hui and of recent US shifts on Taiwan filled China's media. Shifts in US policy were depicted as efforts to encourage Taiwan independence and "split China." A long litany of US transgressions was reprised: the Taiwan Relations Act, the F-16 sale, the Taiwan Policy Review, and finally the visit of Lee Teng-hui.

But diplomatic protests and media polemics alone were deemed inadequate. This time, diplomatic protests would be given additional force by military demonstrations targeting Taiwan and gradually escalating in scope and potency. Washington did not take China's warnings seriously, Beijing felt. The United States felt it could force US-dictated terms regarding Taiwan down China's throat. It was necessary to disabuse US leaders of these illusions. Rather like the staging of a military ambush at Chen Bao Island in March 1969 in an attempt to make Moscow stop and take stock, the military demonstrations in the Strait in 1995–1996 were an attempt at active defense. Confronting Washington with China's willingness to go to war was intended to cause China's adversary, the United States in the 1990s, to "rein in at the brink of the precipice" and pull back from its unacceptable policy course regarding Taiwan. Each round of military demonstration would be followed by a hiatus and talks with the United States. This maximized opportunity for China to use the exercises to pressure Washington, and to give opportunity for China to deescalate if the United States reacted more forcefully than Beijing anticipated. Beijing did not intend to go to war with the United States, just convince Washington that it was ready to.

What eventually become eight months of on-again, off-again but gradually escalating PLA military demonstrations against Taiwan began on June 30, 1995, with routine PLA air and naval exercises simulating amphibious landings on the Fujian coast. More unusual demonstrations came in late July when the PLA conducted what Beijing called ballistic missile tests, with PLA warheads landing in a circular area twenty miles in diameter and eighty miles northeast of Taiwan. Shortly before the "tests," foreign ships and airplanes were warned to avoid the area. They complied. Over the course of a week, the PLA fired six missiles into the target zone from bases in Jiangxi and Jilin provinces at distances of up to a thousand miles. This was the first time the PLA had fired missiles into the seas adjacent to Taiwan. The missile firings effectively demonstrated PLA ability to put at risk commercial or military shipping between Taiwan and Japan. Firing exercises by coastal defense artillery and simulated air and naval strikes along China's coastal areas paralleled the missile firings. There was no military response from the United States. Beijing's campaigns of military intimidation in 1995–1996 are illustrated by Figure 23-1.

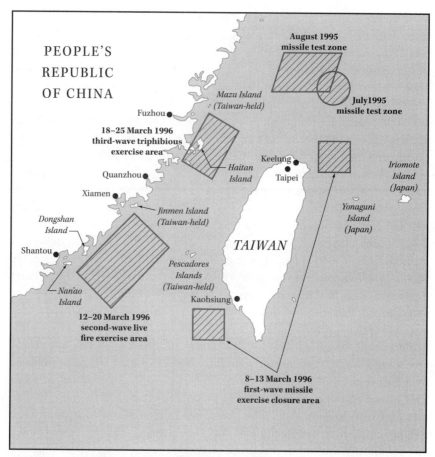

FIGURE 23-1 **PLA Military Exercises in Taiwan Straits, 1995–1996**

Source: John W. Garver, *Face Off: China, the United States, and Taiwan's Democratization* (University of Washington Press: Seattle, 1997), p. 75.

Following the July "missile tests," Beijing took stock of the US reaction. The Clinton administration responded by trying to reassure Beijing on the Taiwan issue and move beyond the Lee visa issue. The first high-level meeting of the two sides since the visa announcement and the July missile tests came in Brunei on August 1, when Qian Qichen and Warren Christopher met. During the meeting, Christopher gave Qian a letter from Clinton to Jiang Zemin. Clinton's letter restated long-standing US policy, but more directly and at the highest level.[20] As published by a pro-CCP Hong Kong newspaper, the letter said:

> The United States recognizes the PRC as the sole legitimate government of China. The United States *respects China's position* that there is only one China in the world and *that Taiwan is a part of China*. The

U.S. government will handle the Taiwan question on the basis of the one China policy. The U.S. government *is against Taiwan independence and does not support Taiwan's admission to the United Nations.*[21] (Emphasis added.)

Within the context of the subtle nuances constituting the diplomatic anatomy of the Taiwan issue, the phraseology of Clinton's letter was significant. It conceded to Beijing several new increments of political ground on the ultra-sensitive Taiwan issue. The US formulation in the 1972 Shanghai Communiqué regarding China's claim to sovereignty over Taiwan had been that the United States "does not challenge" the Chinese view. Clinton's August 1995 letter elevated "does not challenge" to "respects," implying a greater degree of acceptance than the former. Lack of support for Taiwan's entry into the UN was in line with the TPR, but had not previously been stated directly to China's leaders or embodied in a bilateral document such as a letter from one head of state to another. Two years later, during negotiations for the twin summit visits of Clinton and Jiang, Beijing would push hard for inclusion of these concessions into a fourth communiqué. Again, Washington would demure.

To Beijing, Clinton seemed pliable. After staking out a bold position on MFN linkage early in his first year in office, he backed down. Then he twice bowed before congressional pressure, once on the Taiwan Policy Review and again on the visa issue. Then, confronted with the July missile tests, Clinton offered up a set of concessions on the core issue of the legal status of Taiwan. Nor had there been any US military response to the "tests." Beijing's new policy of military coercion seemed to be working. There was little indication that a strong US reaction might maneuver China into an exposed position from which it might have to withdraw in embarrassment. China's leaders decided to move forward with a second round of slightly more provocative missile diplomacy. In mid-August 1995, Beijing announced another set of "missile tests" to take place August 15–25 in a parallelogram-shaped area ninety miles due north of Taiwan. The area of the test was considerably larger than the first "tests" in July, and continued for ten days, compared to seven for the July tests. Again, six missiles were fired. Again, foreign ships and aircraft were warned and avoided the area.

The August missile "tests" were followed by another round of negotiations with the United States, and then by a still further escalation of pressure. At his third face-to-face meeting with Clinton, on October 24 in New York City, Jiang Zemin offered increased cooperation on fighting crime, narcotics traffic, terrorism, and environmental issues, but also stressed the importance of proper handling of the Taiwan issue for smooth development of Sino-American cooperation in these areas. The Clinton administration's objective was to put the visa issue behind it and downplay conflict over Taiwan. In line with this,

Clinton reiterated the pledges made in his August letter and did not bring to Jiang's attention the US interest in peaceful resolution of the Taiwan issue. Nor had there been a US military reaction to the August "tests." This US approach satisfied Beijing. Following this Jiang-Clinton summit, Ambassador Li Daoyu returned to his posting in Washington.

Following the Jiang-Clinton meeting in New York, China's leaders met to discuss the situation. Washington had not given a pledge promising no future visits by Taiwan's leaders and also seemed to believe that the Taiwan issue was behind it. This was not satisfactory: Washington had not fully learned its lesson. Nor had Taipei shifted course. Lee Teng-hui was still pursuing his "two Chinas" and "Taiwan independence" approach in his campaign for the 1996 election. There was thus consensus within the CCP elite that further, even more threatening, measures were in order. Jiang, with PLA prompting, ordered further, more forward-leaning exercises.

In October, the PLA conducted naval exercises simulating an opposed amphibious landing on an island on the mainland coast north of the Taiwan Strait. Naval artillery and missiles bombarded coastal defenses, after which amphibious tanks and landing craft brought troops ashore while submarines and antisubmarine vessels shielded the landing force. Jiang Zemin, Liu Huaqing, and six other members of the CMC observed the simulated invasion. This underlined the importance of the exercises. China's media gave extensive coverage to the exercises, including distributing photographs to the Japanese media.

Another round of talks with the United States followed the October military demonstration. In November, a Department of Defense delegation, led by Assistant Secretary of Defense for International Security Affairs Joseph Nye, visited Beijing. This constituted the first high-level interaction of military officials since the visa announcement in May. During the talks, PLA officials pushed hard over the Taiwan issue, making clear to their US interlocutors that China was prepared for war, if necessary, and was dusting off contingency plans for Taiwan operations that had not been looked at since the 1950s. The Chinese also side probed to understand how the United States would respond to various crises in the Strait. The US side refused to be drawn into contingency scenarios, but Nye made clear at a press conference after the meetings that any use of force against Taiwan "would be a serious mistake."[22] Nye also reminded Chinese officials that both US domestic law and national security strategy indicated that instability in the Taiwan Strait could be a threat to US national security interest and hurt long-term prospects for US-PRC relations.[23]

The same month the US Defense Department delegation visited Beijing, the PLA carried out yet another, and larger, simulated amphibious invasion. This one targeted Dongshan Island, near the southern end of the Taiwan Strait. Up to 18,000 personnel from all PLA services were involved.

Air operations established air superiority over the landing zone while water obstacles were cleared by ship and helicopters. Helicopters and two hundred landing craft then ferried assault forces ashore. Those forces regrouped and expanded the beachhead, preparing the way for the landing of a second wave. Simulated enemy counterattacks on the beachhead were beaten off. These were reportedly the largest exercises the PLA had ever conducted across from Taiwan. Following these exercises, the CIA set up a special task force to monitor China's activities in the Strait on a round-the-clock basis. The US Chiefs of Staff also began contingency planning for response to various levels of Chinese escalation, up to and including use of nuclear weapons.[24]

By late 1995, PLA military demonstrations seemed to be having an impact on Taiwan politics. There was increasing crisis within Lee Teng-hui's ruling KMT, with traditionalists increasingly vocal in opposing Lee's departures from the party's traditional approach to unification. In September, seven prominent KMT leaders withdrew from the party and declared their opposition to Lee's reelection as president. They pointed to PLA exercises as evidence of the reckless and dangerous nature of his new approaches, such as talking of two equal political entities or governments. Elections for the Legislative Yuan on December 2 saw Lee's KMT lose seven seats, with its share of the total vote falling to 46 percent from the 53 percent during the previous LY election in 1993. The New Party, formed largely of ex-KMT members opposed to Lee Teng-hui's approach to cross-Strait relations, won 12 percent of LY seats in spite of that party's being only two years old. PRC media reported extensively on the deepening divisions in Taiwan's politics, damning Lee as a "100 percent traitor" and lauding his traditionalist opponents. Taiwan's leaders seemed to be coming to their senses.

In mid-December, US leaders decided that PLA maneuvers had become large and aggressive enough that a military counterdemonstration would be a prudent measure, possibly deterring further PLA demonstrations that could lead to a military clash. A navy aircraft carrier battle group built around the USS *Nimitz* was therefore ordered to transit the Taiwan Strait on its way from Japan to the Persian Gulf. This was the first such passage since the normalization of Sino-US relations in January 1979. In order to avoid public embarrassment of China's leaders, however, the *Nimitz* passage was kept very low-profile. It was not announced until six weeks later, at the end of January 1996. At that time, it was explained as a function of bad weather, necessitating use of an unusual route. PLA intelligence almost certainly monitored the ship's passage through the Strait. Beijing did not back down in the face of the *Nimitz* demonstration. Rather, it moved ahead with even more aggressive exercises. Beijing and Washington were becoming locked into a pattern of escalating military demonstrations.

Taiwan's first-ever direct and popular presidential election was scheduled for March 23, 1996. This election marked a major turning point in Taiwan's political evolution, the completion of its decade-long peaceful transition from one-party dictatorship to competitive, multiparty democracy. It was arguably the first time such a thing had happened in the several-millennia-long history of Chinese civilization—a fact of which Taiwanese were aware and proud. The ethnic Chinese on Taiwan seemed to have finally realized the century-long dream of being rich and free. These facts made the 1996 presidential election especially significant to the people of Taiwan—and to well-wishers of Taiwan's democracy around the world. Destabilizing Taiwan's democracy was probably not a CCP objective at this juncture, although that could well have been the result of PLA intimidation had it not been countered by US intervention. Beijing's objective, rather, was to influence the voting of Taiwan's electorate, to convey to them the message that a vote for Lee Teng-hui, or for his DPP rival Peng Ming-min, was a vote for confrontation and war. Prudence required voting against Lee's efforts to "split China." This was Beijing's intended message. To Washington, the message was that China was prepared for war over Taiwan.

The 1996 Exercises

PLA exercises in 1996 began on February 4, when troops from across China began arriving in an expedited fashion in Fujian province. Codenamed "Express 60," this deployment was itself a test of plans to deploy large forces to forward positions opposite Taiwan within sixty hours.[25] Exercises continued on March 8 with the launching over a six-day period of four ballistic missiles into two box-shaped target areas just beyond the ports of Keelung in the north and Kaohsiung in the south of Taiwan. These missiles were fired from deep inside Fujian province. As had been the case with the July and August 1995 missile firings, target areas were preannounced, with warnings for ships and aircraft to avoid the areas. The PLA demonstrated with these firings its ability to use complex missile firings to effectively close Taiwan's main ports.

Just before the missile bombardment off Kaohsiung ended, PLA forces began live fire exercises on Dongshan and Nan'ao Islands near the Fujian-Guangdong border at the southern end of the Taiwan Strait, just across from Kaohsiung. Once again, the exercises simulated assault from the sea on a hostile-held island. Anti-aircraft missiles were fired from shore and from frigates at sea. PLA air force B-6D heavy bombers conducted bombing runs. Anti-ship, air-to-air, and anti-submarine missiles were fired by air and sea surface forces seeking air supremacy and sea control in the landing zone. Su-27 fighters recently acquired from Russia were involved in the exercises, as were a new class of China-produced submarine and two KILO class submarines also recently acquired from Russia.

While the exercises at the southern end of the Strait were still underway, new exercises began off Haitan Island at the northern end. Once again, the exercise involved assault on a hostile shore. Again, a wide variety of warships, airplanes, and missiles sought air and sea superiority prior to the landing operation. Amphibious tanks, several new types of landing craft, and helicopters once again delivered waves of assault troops. A parachute drop was planned, but was canceled because of heavy winds. Once again, the initial assault force secured a beachhead through which a second wave was landed. As with earlier PLA exercises, the 1996 exercises were given extensive coverage by China's media. Reports to Hong Kong papers asserted that China was preparing to actually strike against Taiwan, or perhaps against Jinmen, Mazu, or the Pescadores Islands. These reports may have been part of Beijing's psychological assault on Taiwan's electorate.

PLA missile "tests" in July and August 1995 had triggered incipient panic in Taiwan. The panic touched off by the March 1996 exercises was far worse. People rushed to stores to stock up on cooking oil, rice, toilet paper, and other essentials and began withdrawing Taiwan dollars from banks and exchanging them for US dollars or gold. Demand for US dollars became so great that planeloads of dollars had to be flown in, while some banks imposed limits on the size of individual transactions. Taiwan's stock and real estate markets fell as people dumped illiquid assets. The outflow of capital from Taiwan surged, up 27 percent over the same period in 1995. Public unease lasted only about a week, however, and disappeared quickly once a US carrier deployment was announced. Had the United States not intervened swiftly and effectively, Taiwan's first-ever presidential election might have occurred in the midst of deepening panic and flight. Had the United States not intervened early and forcefully, the outcome of Beijing's military demonstrations could have been far more advantageous for Beijing than was, in fact, the case.

As the PLA prepared to begin its new exercises, US leaders decided military countermoves were prudent. On March 8, the day PLA missile firings off Kaohsiung and Keelung began, Washington announced that an aircraft carrier battle group built around the USS *Independence* would deploy to within a few hundred miles of Taiwan. The evening before that announcement, Defense Secretary William Perry told senior national security official Liu Huaqiu that missile firings so close to Taiwan "could only be considered as an act of coercion" and were reckless. About the same time, China's defense minister Chi Haotian gave a speech stressing the need to unify Taiwan and the PRC. "Without any doubt," Chi said, reunification would be achieved. "Lee Teng-hui and his gang" were "facing a grim situation" because of their attempt to "split China." Peaceful unification was the best path, Chi continued, but China would "never tolerate any attempt to split our country using all kinds of schemes." Chi quoted PLA cofounder Zhu De to the effect that "As long as Taiwan is not liberated, the Chinese people's historical humiliation is not washed away, as long as the Motherland is not reunited, our people's armed forces responsibility is not fulfilled."[26]

PLA exercises continued as planned in spite of the *Independence* deployment. China did not back down. The day after Washington announced the *Independence* movement, Beijing announced a second wave of exercises to follow the just-initiated first wave. Washington responded with further warnings. On March 10, Secretary of State Christopher appeared on the TV program *Meet the Press* to deliver clear warnings about Taiwan. Part of the US "one China policy" was Beijing's commitment to deal peacefully with the Taiwan issue, Christopher said. Implicit in these words was the warning that PLA use of force against Taiwan would call into question Washington's "one China policy." The PLA's recent exercises "smacked of intimidation and coercion," Christopher said. The situation regarding Taiwan was "of great concern" to the United States, and there would be "grave consequences" if China tried to resolve the Taiwan issue by force. "We have real interests in Taiwan and I don't want the Chinese to misunderstand about that," Christopher concluded.[27] From Beijing, Qian Qichen rebutted Christopher: "Some people ... must have forgotten the fact that Taiwan is a part of Chinese territory, not a protectorate of the United States."[28]

The day after Christopher's warning, the Pentagon announced deployment to the vicinity of Taiwan of a second aircraft carrier battle group build around the USS *Nimitz* and including seven other warships. The purpose of the deployment, the Pentagon said, was to "make sure there is no miscalculation on the part of the Chinese as to our interest in that area" and to "reassure our friends in the region that we will maintain an interest in ... peace and stability in that region."[29] The Pentagon spokesman declined to go into particulars of how the United States would respond to a Chinese attack on Taiwan other than to say that such a move would be of "grave concern" to the United States.

The US deployment of a second carrier battle group further escalated the tit-for-tat struggle underway between Beijing and Washington. Deployment of one aircraft carrier battle group could be seen as an essentially symbolic move. Dispatch of two battle groups very significantly increased the real military capabilities in the area. Each battle group included a half-dozen other warships in addition to the super-carrier itself, making a combined fleet of perhaps fifteen or so warships. This was an extremely potent display of naval power. Again, Beijing did not back down in the face of US power. The second wave of exercises began as planned on March 12. Several days later, and four days after the US announcement of the second aircraft carrier deployment, Beijing announced a third wave of exercises to begin on March 18 and ending on March 25 —two days after Taiwan's presidential elections. Tough Chinese rhetoric paralleled PLA exercises. The day before the third wave of exercises began, Li Peng warned that the US carrier deployment would be futile. "If someone threatened the use of force against China, the outcome has

already been proven by past experience. This will not bring about any beneficial result."[30] A few days later, an editorial in the CCP-controlled Hong Kong
newspaper *Dagong bao* said:

> Here it is necessary to remind certain Americans: Do not forget the
> lessons you learned from the battlefields in Korea and Vietnam. Do not
> put the interests and even lives of American people at stake. . . . Whoever
> dares to meddle in, or even invade, Taiwan, the Chinese people will
> fight them to the end until their final victory.[31]

By mid-March, the PRC and the United States were locked in an increasingly intense struggle, with both sides escalating military deployments and
threatening one another, each in its own way, with war. Neither side wanted,
expected, or was prepared for war. Both sides maneuvered very carefully to
avoid conflict, and once Taiwan's March 23 presidential elections were over,
the two sides quickly began working to repair relations. The PRC and the
United States had, however, experienced their first military confrontation in
twenty-eight years. This stark reality raised a question for the leaders of both
countries: where is the Sino-American relation going, and how will that affect
our national interests?

The confrontation of 1996 was apparently a deep shock to Beijing. Chinese
leaders went into the 1995–1996 crisis convinced that the United States would
not intervene forcefully and effectively in a cross-Strait conflict.[32] A long list
of US bugouts—Vietnam in 1974–1975, Lebanon in 1982, Haiti in 1993, and
Somalia in 1994—had convinced PLA analysts and CCP propagandists that
United States did not have the stomach any more for a major war. This belief
was reinforced by the clear desire of US leaders in the executive branch to
minimize conflict over Taiwan and cooperate in other areas. Many Chinese
leaders had convinced themselves that while the United States might protest
and take some symbolic actions in the event of a cross-Strait clash, it would
not do anything effective. The US dispatch of not one but two aircraft carrier
battle groups dispelled this belief. After the 1995–1996 confrontation, it was
clear to Chinese defense planners that the United States was likely to intervene in a cross-Strait conflict, and that the PLA was still woefully unprepared
for such an eventuality. China began developing potent new capabilities
designed to deter, delay, and downgrade US military intervention to shelter
Taiwan for long enough to allow the PLA to secure control over that island—a
PLA capability the US military came to call "anti-access area denial." This
buildup of China's anti-US military capabilities would continue into the second decade of the twenty-first century, ultimately very substantially narrowing the qualitative gap between US and PRC military capabilities.[33]

Nor was the effect of PLA exercises on Taiwan what Beijing had anticipated. In terms of the voting behavior of Taiwan's electorate, PLA intimidation backfired. In the face of blatant PLA threats, Taiwan's electorate rallied

to Lee Teng-hui, giving him a solid majority of 54 percent of the vote. The percentage of the vote won by the DPP held more or less steady at 30 percent of the vote; PLA intimidation did not cause voters to flee either Lee Teng-hui or the DPP. More broadly, Beijing's decision for military coercion of Taiwan at a crucial juncture in its evolution toward democracy reinforced Taiwanese reluctance to come under the rule of the CCP. The PLA threats of 1996 joined the Beijing Massacre as prominent reasons why Taiwanese did not favor Beijing's one country, two systems rubric.

China's military intimidation of Taiwan also scared China's neighbors, causing them to take a new interest in the peaceful resolution of the Taiwan issue and in the continued presence of the United States as a major military power in the Western Pacific. Japan especially began to make presentations to Chinese diplomats about its interest in the peaceful resolution of the Taiwan issue—much to Beijing's chagrin. In Europe, too, democratic governments and publics began to think, perhaps for the first time, about their interest in the intimidation of small but democratic Taiwan by a powerful, authoritarian, one-party dictatorship. These trends were not favorable to China's interests.[34] China's annual diplomatic almanac for 1996 concluded that China's "resolute struggle via serious negotiations" with the United States over Taiwan had "deepened the US understanding of the sensitivity and importance of the Taiwan issue."[35] This conclusion is accurate. But the political costs to China of that lesson were extremely high.

The military confrontation of 1996 enhanced the influence of the more cautious MFA in decision making. The policy debate of 1992–1995 did not boil down to a MFA-PLA dispute, with the MFA ultimately outmaneuvering the PLA. That would have been unlikely. In any case, above both the MFA and the PLA high command was the PBSC. The real question at issue was whether the PBSC would endorse the MFA's or the PLA's point of view. But as a result of the unexpected and powerful US intervention, the PLA may have become more inclined to listen to MFA warnings about the costs and risks of confrontational approaches. The PLA, after all, had as great an interest as any Chinese institution in avoiding war with the United States, and when PLA leaders realized they had miscalculated the willingness of the United States to intervene in a cross-Strait conflict, they may have become less dismissive of MFA arguments against military intimidation or coercion. At the same time, the PLA had new and persuasive arguments for accelerated military modernization efforts to close the gap between Chinese and US military capabilities.

The Sino-US confrontation of 1996 came barely eighteen months after the struggle over MFN linkage, which had in turn followed the confrontation over 6-4. The question was becoming increasingly starkly framed: was chronic confrontation the new pattern for PRC-US relations? The 1995–1996 confrontation over Taiwan shocked leaders in both Beijing and Washington, compelling them to recognize just how bad relations might become. This realization would contribute to a push in both capitals to reconstruct a more cooperative relationship.

The confrontation had a strong impact, both positive and negative, on PRC relations with the United States. On the one hand, it forced US leaders to think through the costs of confrontation with China. Even short of war, what would be the cost to the United States if China viewed the United States as a hostile power and opposed US moves around the world? Thinking through these issues helped push the United States toward a renewal of the quest for strategic partnership with China, a quest that had lapsed with the presidency of George W.H. Bush. On the negative side, the 1995–1996 confrontation alerted US leaders to the fact that China might well become a strategic competitor with the United States. There existed, in fact, deep differences in national interest and policy that could lead China to confront the United States militarily. A US desire to guard against this possibility would thereafter parallel the US quest for strategic partnership with China. Rather like the Korean War, the 1995–1996 confrontation forced the United States to recognize and respect China's great power. But the cost of that achievement was great.

China's Long Debate over Response to the US Challenge

The Vagaries of Chinese Diplomacy

There was a sharp bifurcation in China's interests vis-à-vis the United States following the upheavals of 1989–1991. On the one hand, continued success of China's monumental economic development drive—which underpinned the CCP's claim to legitimacy—required continued access to US merchandise and capital markets. China also benefited greatly from public goods supplied by the United States which might be denied by a hostile Washington: secure freedom of navigation on the high seas, a generally open global economic system, and investment opportunities in areas of special US influence such as Iraq and Kuwait. Washington also had considerable influence with allies and friends that it could use, should it so decide, to constrain China's international economic living space. Granted, US embrace of such hostile policies would cost the United States itself a lot. But governments sometimes make such choices when confronted with what they view as a dangerous rival. US hostility could conceivably abort China's development drive. Such considerations pointed toward a Chinese policy seeking continued partnership, cooperation, and friendship with the United States.

On the other hand, CCP leaders deeply feared and resented the universalistic political creed that led US voters and their elected representatives in both legislative and executive branches of the federal government to press upon China ideas of human rights, freedom, and democracy. US actors, both governmental and nongovernmental, transmitted to China such subversive ideas via radio and the internet, educational and cultural exchanges, and high-level declarations from Chinese podiums and international fora. Although intensified patriotic education combined with rising economic levels seemed remarkably successful by the twenty-first century in persuading Chinese citizens to affirm CCP leadership (at least in public opinion polls),

CCP leaders continued to fear that mass opinion might quickly shift against them as it had in spring 1989, or against authoritarian dictatorships in a score of other countries around the world in the decades after 6-4. The era of the information revolution is not comfortable for regimes based on control of information.

Some Chinese leaders went further and asserted that the United States was prepared to use military force against China (as with the US bombing of China's Yugoslav embassy, discussed below), perhaps to precipitate a popular uprising against the CCP government. Washington might be tempted to use military force in support of a popular antigovernment movement in China, perhaps in Tibet. The United States had done something along those lines in Yugoslavia and Iraq, or at least it seemed in some elite quarters in Beijing. The policy conclusion of deliberations along these lines was that China needed to remain militarily strong to deter the United States from adventurism against China. The United States also needed to be kept at arm's length to thwart its subversive efforts, and US policies needed to be "exposed" by China's media to inoculate China's citizens against attraction to notions of liberty and democracy.

These fears for regime survival were exemplified by a ninety-minute program on the vast US conspiracy to undermine and ultimately topple China's CCP government, just as "the West led by the United States" had putatively done with the USSR. The program, apparently not intended for public use but leaked and posted on the internet in fall 2013, was produced by China's National Defense University and the Institute of American Studies of the Chinese Academy of Social Sciences. Intended for use in political education of PLA officers and high-level CCP cadres, the program depicted a sweeping US strategy modeled after one putatively employed with success against the USSR and designed to weaken China, abort its rise, and thus eliminate a roadblock to Western/US global dominance.[1]

Ambivalent Chinese interests toward the United States also arose out of the dynamics of the rise and decline of great powers. With the end of the PRC-US coalition against the Soviet Union and the sudden disappearance of the USSR itself, Chinese scholars studied the ways in which new global powers emerged and become the dominant power, or declined and were superseded by rising powers. More often than not, Chinese analysts found, the rise of a new global power resulted in war between that new power and the reigning incumbent dominant power. This happened, for example, with Germany, Japan, and the USSR. Rising powers that kept on friendly terms with the incumbent paramount power were, however, sometimes able to accomplish a peaceful transition to preeminence; for example, the United States with the British Empire or, several centuries earlier, Britain with the Netherlands. War between China and the United States could be immensely costly to China's economic development effort. It was also very risky; China might lose as had Germany, Japan, and the USSR in their challenges to the United States. Starting and then losing a war with the United States could lead to the collapse of the CCP regime. Such considerations pointed toward continued cooperation, amity, and avoidance of confrontation with the United States—unless Washington imposed conflict on China.

On the other hand, China's leaders were deeply suspicious of what they perceived as US efforts to limit or thwart China's efforts to increase its global influence: encouraging Taiwan to reject Beijing's eminently reasonable (or so Beijing saw it) one country, two systems proposal; encouraging Southeast Asian countries to challenge China's just territorial rights (again, so Beijing saw it) in the South China Sea; strengthening India's military capabilities, including the nuclear; and supporting Japan's efforts to become a "normal" military power in Asia. These and many other similar policies were seen in Beijing as components of a US strategy of containing China and limiting or aborting its rise. These impulses pointed toward hard struggle with the United States.

China's post–Cold War US policies reflected these deeply discrepant interests.

A curious, almost bipolar, dynamic developed in Chinese diplomacy after the upheavals of 1989–1991. At times, Beijing spoke of friendship and partnership and invited cooperation with various powers, especially the United States, Japan, and India. At other times, Beijing spewed vitriol, backed away from cooperation, and punished foreign states, especially the United States, Japan, and India, in various creative ways. Periods of hostility alternated with charm offensives seemingly designed to repair the injury to China's foreign relations inflicted during earlier negative episodes. In part, this constant shifting was in response to foreign moves: US arms sales to Taiwan, permitting a visit by Lee Teng-hui, bombing a Chinese embassy in Belgrade, or conducting intelligence operations in China's 200-nautical-mile Exclusive Economic Zone (EEZ). But there were also factors within China that drove these policy swings. Moreover, those domestic drivers seemed to become more important as China became stronger in the twenty-first century.

One domestic driver of China's policy swings was sharply divergent views among China's foreign policy elite—divergences usefully described as between "hard-liners" and "moderates." Hard-liners tended to impute deliberate, hostile anti-China motives to foreign moves contrary to China's interests, and to prescribe harsh, frequently military-edged punitive responses to those foreign transgressions. Hard-liners tended to believe that unless China used the full scope of its growing national power, including its military, to shape its international environment, it would find itself in an environment shaped by powers hostile to China. Hardliners also tended to favor tighter internal controls to thwart what they deemed Western subversion. China's moderates did not necessarily dispute the sinister motives imputed to foreign actions (though they sometimes did), but they warned that too assertive Chinese use of its growing power could injure China in two ways: by slowing China's economic development drive, which it needed to sustain for several more decades if it was to become a true first-class world power, and by nudging China's neighbors towards a coalition to contain it, a coalition which would probably be backed by the United States. Moderate policy prescriptions tended to be in line with Deng Xiaoping's 1990 admonition that China must "keep a low profile and hide its light under a basket." The chronic debate between PRC hard-liners and moderates will be reviewed in this chapter. A second domestic driver of the bipolar nature of Chinese diplomacy has to do with growing popular nationalism and its use to legitimize the CCP regime. This aspect will be examined in subsequent chapters.

Post-Confrontation Renormalization of Ties

The 1996 military confrontation in the Taiwan Strait, the culmination of six years of mutual bitter acrimony and battles over sanctions, confronted Beijing with the real prospect that the comity with the United States that underpinned China's development drive might evaporate. Within the United States, the consensus over China policy that had developed since 1972 collapsed, giving way to a full-blown debate over whether China was a hostile power that needed to be treated as such. Many voices in this US debate asserted that the PRC was not a friendly power but a new peer competitor and strategic rival. They were critical of what they deemed to be the heretofore weak policy toward the PRC and criticized as naive the efforts of earlier presidents to treat the PRC as a cooperative partner.[2]

By 1996, the steadying hand of Deng Xiaoping that had overridden PLA demands for a tough response to Washington's F-16 sale in 1992 was no longer at work. Deng would not die until February 1997, but his health was deteriorating badly and it was clear he had fought his last political battle. Jiang Zemin was also not in a position to overrule the PLA's confrontational approach. But as soon as the military exercises that constituted the PLA's prescription ran their course in February–March 1996, Jiang put the MFA back in charge of US policy and tasked Qian Qichen with rebuilding PRC-US relations. Qian began working toward an exchange of summit visits by Presidents Jiang and Clinton.

A Politburo meeting in mid-April 1996 decided to end the confrontational approach to the United States and return primary responsibility for US affairs to the MFA.[3] Shifts in PRC media coverage of the United States soon became apparent. The emotional and antagonistic themes that had dominated since 1989 began to disappear and were replaced by more balanced and less emotional coverage. MFA dialogue with the United States soon resumed. One of the items at the top of the US agenda was securing termination of China's assistance to Iran's and Pakistan's nuclear and missile programs. Progress was rapid; Beijing expanded nonproliferation cooperation with Washington. In May, following an agreement between Qian Qichen and Warren Christopher, Xinhua announced that China would not assist any foreign nuclear facility not under IAEA safeguard and supervision. Privately, Beijing agreed to set up an effective system of export controls to give substance to this and other nonproliferation promises.

The United States considered these moves to be an important Chinese shift toward cooperation. Beijing had long responded to US complaints about Chinese proliferation by asserting that it simply lacked the ability to control China's independent economic fiefdoms. Now, under Qian and Jiang's tutelage, Beijing was agreeing to work with the Americans to figure out a way to rein in those fiefdoms. Avoiding charges of complicity with the Americans in interfering in China's domestic affairs was probably a key reason why the MFA kept this agreement confidential. Of course, Chinese concessions were not without a US quid pro quo. Washington agreed not to implement sanctions and to continue government guarantees of US business loans in China. MFA negotiators were also cooperative on US concerns about protection of intellectual property rights, at least in principle. The actual behavior of Chinese firms would turn out to be another matter. By June, MFA and US negotiators were able to reach an agreement, with the United States getting much of what it wanted. The MFA also began occasional releases of political prisoners in response to US demands, typically arranging for these people to depart for the United States. This practice satisfied some US demands and brought the release of these people to US media attention, while getting rid of some of the CCP's most troublesome dissidents.[4] By the end of 1996, the MFA had returned PRC-US relations more or less to their pre-confrontation level.

The 1997 and 1998 Summit Visits

An exchange of summit visits—Jiang to the United States in 1997 and Clinton to China in 1998—symbolized the return of PRC-US comity. Jiang's visit was the first by China's president since Li Xiannian's visit in 1985, and the first by China's paramount leader since Deng's 1979 visit. It was also the first state visit by a top-level Chinese leader to the United States since the Beijing Massacre. The summit exchanges drew a line under the post-6-4 deterioration of PRC-US relations. From the standpoint of Jiang Zemin, his 1997 US visit—which was given extensive laudatory coverage in China—symbolized his role as statesman and protector of both China's interests and its vital relation with the United States, styling himself successor to Mao and Deng in that regard. So successful was Jiang in this effort that in 2002, when he was forced to hand over to Hu Jintao the increasingly institutionalized position of paramount leader, he was able to hang on to chairmanship of the CMC for two more years largely on the grounds that that would enable him to continue to safeguard the vital PRC-US relation.

Secretary of State Christopher in a May 1996 speech had proposed "regular summit meetings" among several measures to improve Sino-American ties. During a meeting at an APEC summit in Manila, Clinton and Jiang agreed to an exchange, starting with a visit by Jiang in fall 1997. The Jiang-Clinton meeting in Manila was the second between the two men and improved the tone of the relationship. During their first meeting an APEC meeting in Seattle in November 1993, Jiang had lectured Clinton at length on US transgressions against China. Drawing on a stack of notecards, Jiang had turned aside attempts by Clinton to direct the discussion along less confrontational lines. At their Manila meeting, in contrast, the two men worked hard at overcoming differences of culture and political belief to achieve a degree of rapport, based on a mutual understanding that the personal relation between the two of them would, to some degree, set the tone for the relation between the two countries.[5]

Having scheduled a visit by Jiang to the United States, China's MFA worked hard to create a positive atmosphere for that visit by addressing US human rights concerns, creating an image of modest relaxation of China's internal political controls. In March 1997, the MFA agreed to revive talks with the International Committee of the Red Cross about periodic visitors to prisoners held for political reasons. Those talks had been in abeyance since 1995. The next month, Jiang told the visiting French defense minister that China would sign the International Covenant on Economic, Social and Cultural Rights by the end of the year. Jiang signed the Covenant in October, just before his visit to the United States. China also announced the deletion of the category of "counterrevolutionary" offences from its criminal code. Jiang agreed to meet with a delegation of US clerics for a discussion of religious freedom. Beijing released and expelled Wei Jingsheng, China's most prominent political prisoner, and revived a long-dormant dialogue on the treatment of Chinese political prisoners organized by US businessman John Kamm.[6] Chinese leaders felt that US concern with China's human rights affairs constituted interference in China's internal affairs. Yet the MFA recognized the political reality of the significance of those concerns in the United States, and took pragmatic moves to address and defuse them.

On the US side, concerns that things might go wrong with the Hong Kong reversion at the end of June delayed finalization of the Jiang visit. Clinton feared that the PLA might fire on Hong Kong demonstrations, that freedom of press might be suspended, or that police would round up dissidents, among other worries. If such things occurred, it would be embarrassing for Clinton to be locked into a firm date for meeting with Jiang. When Hong Kong's reversion went off without any such difficulties, preparations for Jiang's US visit went into high gear.[7]

Beijing pushed hard for a fourth communiqué on the Taiwan issue which would make public and enshrine in a joint document the concessions made by Clinton in his secret July 1995 letter to Jiang: the United States would not support Taiwan independence, would not support Taiwan's admission to the United Nations, and would not support creation of two Chinas—dubbed the "three nos" by China's media. Without agreement along these lines, the MFA suggested, the summit exchanges might be difficult. When the United States flatly rejected this proposal, the Chinese side expressed hope that the discussion would continue during Jiang's visit to the United States. In the event, Chinese lobbying for some statement on Taiwan along these lines continued throughout the first days of Jiang's visit and right up to two hours before Jiang was scheduled to meet Clinton at the White House.[8]

Washington, for its part, pushed for complete suspension of Chinese assistance to the nuclear and missile programs of Iran and Pakistan, even though Iran was a member of the NPT and with its known nuclear facilities under IAEA safeguards and inspections. Nor had Iran then been found by the IAEA to be in violation of its NPT obligations. (This came only after the 2002 revelation of Iran's nuclear complex at Natanz.) Yet in the negotiations over the 1997–1998 summit exchange, Beijing acceded to US demands regarding both Iran's nuclear and missile programs. We still do not know the full logic of Beijing's decision, but at a minimum, it distanced Beijing from the ever-deepening conflict between Tehran and Washington. Qian Qichen's major concern regarding this adjustment in Sino-Iran relations was confidentiality. He suggested, and the United States agreed, that the matter be dealt with in a confidential letter from him to Secretary of State Madeleine Albright.[9] The United States also agreed to handle the matter in a low-key fashion. China's media were ordered not to report on this sensitive Chinese concession. China's agreement to end nuclear cooperation with Iran opened the way to implementation of a 1985 treaty making US civilian nuclear technology available to China. It represented a major adjustment in China's policy so as to avoid confrontation with the United States in the Persian Gulf. Regarding Pakistan, however, China flatly refused US demands to suspend nuclear and missile cooperation. Pakistan was China's vital strategic ally, rather like Israel to the United States, Chinese negotiators said.

Jiang's October 1997 visit was carefully choreographed. On his way to the United States, he stopped over in Hawaii to lay a wreath at the Pearl Harbor memorial, effectively underlining the World War II Sino-US alliance against Japan. Jiang then proceeded on to Williamsburg, Virginia, where he visited a colonial-era theme park, striking another resonant chord with his American audience. While in Williamsburg, Jiang donned a colonial-era tricorn hat, replicating Deng Xiaoping's masterstroke at the Houston rodeo in 1979. Washington rolled out the red carpet for Jiang with a twenty-one-gun salute, an honor guard inspection, a reception in the White House and its Rose Garden, and a lavish state banquet. Jiang's activities during his summit visit were given fulsome media coverage in China, highlighting for Chinese audiences Jiang's, and by extension China's, equal and respected status.

This was a major political objective from Jiang's standpoint. During negotiations over the summit, Beijing had insisted on a high-level state visit, rejecting all US suggestions of a "working visit" and taking Deng Xiaoping's 1979 visit as the standard for Jiang's 1997 visit. Beijing also imported the concept of "strategic partnership" (declared in 1996 in ties with Russia) into the Joint Statement. The Joint Statement issued at the end of Jiang's White House visit on October 29, 1997, said: "The two Presidents are determined to build toward a constructive strategic partnership . . . through increasing cooperation to meet international challenges . . . to achieve this goal, they agree to approach U.S.-China relations from a long-term perspective on the basis of the principles of the three U.S.-China joint communiqués."[10] As with China's other "strategic partnerships," this declaration of principle was expected to mitigate foreign inclinations to challenge China or view its growing capabilities with suspicion.

Jiang successfully courted American public opinion during his visit by listening repeatedly to blunt American criticisms of China's human rights situation while remaining calm, not becoming angry but holding his ground on these issues and not backing down before strong and repeated US criticism. Jiang also showed an ability to use humor, often self-deprecating, to defuse criticism. Perhaps as much as any policy gains, Jiang's ability to hold his own while remaining calm and even occasionally display humor won him stature in China. It also endeared him to a section of the US public, going some distance toward rehabilitating China's image from the nadir of 6-4. The most important audience for Jang's performance in the United States was the other members of the PBSC; to them he had demonstrated he was able to manage the vital relation with the United States effectively while maintaining China's dignity.

Jiang had been carefully briefed on potentially embarrassing situations he was likely to encounter in the United States. In Williamsburg, the mayor of that city welcomed Jiang in a speech that extolled "universal principles upon which America is built—freedom, liberty, and representative democracy." Jiang replied by blandly thanking the mayor for her "heart-warming comments" and lauding Williamsburg for its role in the US struggle against British colonialism.[11] In a private tête-à-tête with Clinton, Jiang frankly disagreed with the American president on human rights, but, according to Clinton, remained calm, did not become angry, and called for increased Sino-American cooperation in spite of differences over human rights issues. In a joint press conference, the two presidents directly crossed swords on human rights and democracy, with each trying to get in the last word. Jiang stood his ground; it was natural, he said, that China and the United States should have different ideas about human rights and democracy, since they had different traditions, different levels of development, and different values. Again, he never displayed anger and remained calm and friendly. A ninety-minute session with fifty members of Congress grilled Jiang in the most direct and even baiting fashion. Jiang remained calm and refused to take the bait. At a small private dinner hosted by an eminent US strategic specialist, one American guest berated Jiang over Tibet and refused to let go of the issue. Jiang finally responded by standing up, and breaking into the American song "Home on the Range"—a move that dispelled the tension, disarmed his adversary, and delighted the other American guests, who had feared the Chinese president was about to walk out in a huff. Toward the end of his visit, in an interview on *PBS NewsHour*, moderator Jim Lehrer pressed Jiang on whether he had been disturbed by the repeated and direct US criticism of China's human rights situation. Jiang replied:

> I'm not disturbed at all. China does not feel that it has done anything wrong in the field of human rights. China has a tradition of five thousand years, and different countries have different histories and cultures.... I have already felt that I am welcomed by a majority of the American people here.[12]

Jiang's fairly good command of the English language and his willingness to employ it combined with his calm frankness and good humor to win sympathy from the American public. Jiang's visit accomplished its two major aims: to finally move the PRC-US relation out of the shadow of 6-4 and to demonstrate to the Chinese people, and more importantly to PBSC members, that Jiang was an able statesman capable of shepherding China's emergence as a great power.

In mid-1998, Clinton reciprocated Jiang's summit visit. Jiang's main objective in handling Clinton's visit was to demonstrate to China's people that China had achieved global status equal to that of the United States and that he, General Secretary and President Jiang Zemin, was largely responsible for this via the personal relation he had forged with the American president.[13] A second objective was to secure from Clinton a public statement and affirmation of the "three noes" first conveyed by Clinton to Jiang in the secret August 1, 1995, letter. Now China wanted a public, preferably written, and authoritative statement of those concessions.

Clinton's major objective in visiting China was to demonstrate that he was a strong advocate for freedom of expression, religion, assembly, and other basic human rights. Clinton saw himself as a spokesman for universal values, greatly esteemed by the American people who had twice elected him president. Clinton had been under strong criticism from people who believed that he should not bless the "butchers of Beijing" with his presence or that he was too weak in dealing with Beijing. He was also beset by a sex scandal that made it more imperative for him to take a high moral tone in China. Thus, in negotiating arrangements for Clinton's visit, his representatives pushed for broad access for Clinton to the Chinese people via China's media. Eventually, the two sides agreed to a joint press conference of Clinton and Jiang to be broadcast live on national television, a televised speech by Clinton followed by a question and answer session at Beijing University, and another televised meeting with community leaders at Fudan University in Shanghai. This was access to the Chinese people far greater than granted any previous US president. This required Jiang Zemin to persuade skeptical Politburo members, who understood that Clinton would use these occasions to make propaganda for the very bourgeois liberal ideas against which the CCP had waged resolute struggle since 6-4. In effect, allowing the American president to spread a little ideological poison was worth a successful PRC-US summit, restoring comity in the relation, and protecting the positive macro-climate for China's development drive.

Clinton, in fact, used his opportunity of speaking to the Chinese people to highlight his belief in freedom of speech, assembly, and religion. Clinton referred to 6-4 as "wrong" and "a tragic loss of life," perhaps offering to many Chinese for the first time an understanding of 6-4 different than that continually driven home by CCP propaganda. He referred to the guarantee of basic human rights, including political rights, by the UN Charter, and of the obligation of "all countries" to guarantee those rights. Clinton predicted that China's government would have to grant its people more freedom in the twenty-first century. As he had a year earlier in the United States, Jiang stood his ground during the two men's joint press conference. As one American analyst put it, ""As in 1997, the two men disagreed firmly but decorously with each other."[14]

By openly debating with Clinton in a calm but effective fashion, Jiang demonstrated to his Chinese audience his own capabilities, personal openness, and "democratic" nature. He also demonstrated China's equal status with the United States: here was China's president graciously hosting the American president, but squarely and calmly rebutting his ideas. Chinese media gave extensive coverage to Jiang's activities during Clinton's visit. Chinese television broadcast for the first time footage of Jiang swimming at Waikiki Beach in Honolulu, Hawaii, the previous year during Jiang's trip to the United States. Jiang's own swim in the Pacific Ocean was compared to Deng's occasional swims at Beidaihe on Bohai Gulf and Mao Zedong's 1966 swim in the Yangtze. The symbolic point was that Jiang was following in Mao's and Deng's footsteps by upholding China's honor and equal status while maintaining amicable relations with the Americans.

China received its quid pro quo for Clinton's broad media access when the US president publicly affirmed "the three noes" during his session at Fudan University in Shanghai. Clinton's representatives had bargained down the profile of that statement. It came in Shanghai, not Beijing; in a talk with community leaders, not with China's national leaders; and it was not in the form of a written, much less a joint statement—all the things Beijing really wanted. Yet Clinton, in response to a preplanned question by Fudan professor Wu Xinbo, publicly reaffirmed the "three noes" as US policy. China's media touted this as further evidence of the skill and success of Jiang in defending China's interests while managing ties with the Americans.

Conservatives on the Politburo Standing Committee were probably not impressed by the wisdom of allowing the American president to spread his subversive bourgeois liberal poison among the Chinese people. Li Peng had emerged since 6-4 as one of the PBSC members most opposed to concessions to the United States and most resolute in countering nefarious US moves against China. Li deeply resented the moral stigma assigned him by Western leaders and media for his role in 6-4.[15] In spite of Qian Qichen's best efforts to burnish Li's image by frequent foreign jaunts, Li still had considerable odium. From Li's perspective, this was simply unfair. Li's role in 6-4 had been secondary; the elders, including Deng Xiaoping, had been the prime movers of that event. Yet Western leaders avoided Li like the plague. While US leaders fell over themselves receiving Chinese leaders in 1996–1997, they conspicuously avoided Li. Perhaps in response, Li Peng was confrontational and acerbic in his denunciations of US transgressions. Many within the Chinese bureaucracy saw Li as a defender of China's national dignity.

America again "Attacks China": Falun Gong and the Embassy Bombing

Within a year of Clinton's mid-1998 visit, a powerful anti-US animus in Chinese policy re-emerged. In part, this was a reaction to a revival of dissident activity within China in the wake of the relaxation associated with the Jiang-Clinton exchanges. Hard-liners in the CCP saw this eruption of autonomous activity as evidence that engagement with the United States fostered oppositional activity within China. Within a year of the US president spreading his bourgeois liberal poison via China's media, the CCP confronted a powerful challenge from a group holding up the banner of religious freedom.

The most dramatic expression of the post-summit revived civil society activity was a large and very disciplined protest by the new religious group Falun Gong. This new religion combined an unusual synthesis of traditional Chinese *qi gong* (a type of slow motion and breathing exercise similar to the better-known *taiqi*) and novel beliefs. It had become popular over the preceding several years, appealing to the urban middle class, including not a few cadres. Confronting repression by local authorities for unlicensed religious activity, the group demanded official recognition. They did this by mobilizing a very large crowd of followers to rally outside CCP headquarters adjacent to Tiananmen Square in Beijing on the morning of April 25, 1999. Starting with several hundred people at dawn, by afternoon there were over 20,000 Falun Gong supporters massed outside CCP headquarters.

Aside from the large numbers and good discipline of the crowd massed at the front door of the CCP's central leadership compound, the fact that Falun Gong was able to assemble a large crowd at the very center of Chinese political power without being detected by state and party internal security organs seemed very ominous to PRC leaders. The organizational capabilities of Falun Gong impressed and frightened CCP leaders. According to an investigation by Luo Gan, secretary of the CCP's Politics and Law Commission, Falun Gong "is a highly secretive organization that includes up to 10,000 groups nationwide." Each group had ten members and a designated group leader. Groups used "modern communication equipment, such as cell phones, the internet, and long distance phones" to coordinate activities. "In sum," Luo Gang concluded, "the Falungong organization is vying with the Party not only for the masses but also for Party members. It has also infiltrated key departments. This should arouse a high degree of attention."[16] Jiang Zemin took the lead in advocating complete and firm repression of the group. At a Politburo Standing Committee meeting the day after the 25 April "convergence," Jiang said:

> Such a blatant, large-scale, and illegal convergence on Zhongnanhai for the purpose of putting on a show of force and exerting pressure on the Party and government has never taken place in the fifty years since the founding of the New China . . . Should this not have a sobering effect on us? . . . If we fail to see its political essence and do not take firm, appropriate and prompt action to resolve the issue, we will be committing a mistake of historical proportions. We must absolutely not gloss over this matter, and even less should we downplay it. . . . Comrades, we must not, under any circumstances, underestimate the appeal of Falungong, an organization with a religious patina. . . . We must not exclude the possibility of organizations beyond our borders taking a hand in this matter.[17]

Li Peng seconded Jiang Zemin in seeing the Falun Gong "convergence" as part of a vast conspiracy: "The illegal convergence on Zhongnanhai . . . is indeed not an isolated incident but has substantial political background." The "emergence of Falungong is by no means fortuitous," and the CCP must wage "grave ideological and political struggle" against it. Subsequent investigation by the MSS confirmed Jiang's and Li's suspicions regarding the foreign hand behind Falun Gong. The MSS reported that Falun Gong leader Li Hongzhi had personally been in Beijing for several days before the April 25 "convergence," Jiang told the Politburo. Moreover, "Forces abroad were involved behind the scenes in Falungong's convergence on Zhongnanhai . . . This is part of the US Central Intelligence Agency's strategy designed to split China."[18] During the same month as the Falun Gong confrontation, the United States introduced to the UN Human Rights Commission a resolution condemning human rights violations in China. The United States had abstained from such an action the previous year.[19] Here was further evidence for the PBSC that the United States was fomenting disorder in China.

Two weeks after the CIA masterminded the Falun Gong convergence on CCP headquarters, or so it apparently seemed to CCP leaders, US leaders ordered another move designed to instigate disorder in China, a bombing attack on China's embassy in Belgrade—again, so it seemed to China's leaders. From the deeply paranoid perspective of Jiang Zemin and Li Peng, the purpose of the embassy bombing, which was assumed to be intentional, was to bring Chinese into the streets so that secret underground counterrevolutionary organizations like Falun Gong could misdirect popular anger toward the regime. As Andrew Nathan concludes, "A number of the Chinese leaders seriously believed that the Americans had bombed the embassy in order to stir up a storm of nationalism that would topple the leaders from power."[20]

The international background of the CCP confrontation with Falun Gong and the bombing of the PRC Belgrade embassy was Western military intervention in the Federal Republic of Yugoslavia (FRY) to halt the ethnic cleansing underway in the Kosovo region of that state. Kosovo was an ethnically mixed Serbian and Albanian region, with many of the latter being Muslims. In 1999, the region still remained part of the rump Yugoslav state, after most of the other republics of the former Yugoslav state had already become independent. As agitation for Kosovan autonomy or independence grew in early 1999, Serbian militias linked to Slobodan Milošević, the dictator of rump Yugoslavia, began massacring ethnic Albanians in a desperate attempt to hold that region for Yugoslavia. The European nations and the United States felt strongly that ethnic cleansing, genocide in fact, could not be allowed to continue on the continent of Europe, and that effective intervention to end it was imperative. The violence associated with the breakup of Yugoslavia was the first war to stain European soil since 1945 and was deemed a major challenge to European leaders, who were loath to simply let such violence burn itself out. The tardy and often inadequate response of the Western countries to the Yugoslav civil wars earlier in the 1990s was of deep moral and political concern to European leaders, who felt that the very future of Europe as an area of peace was at stake. Western leaders concluded that military intervention was imperative to stop the massacres in Kosovo for both humanitarian and security reasons. From Beijing's perspective, this seemed like Western interference in the internal affairs of a sovereign country, an ex-communist one to boot.

The Western nations turned first to the Security Council for authorization of armed enforcement action. Chinese and Russian objections blocked that route. From Beijing's perspective, Kosovo was part of the FRY, a state recognized by the international community, and whatever was happening there, however unfortunate it might be, was an internal affair of that country. The Security Council should not become a mechanism for Western interference in the internal affairs of other countries, China's representatives at the UN said. The fact that Yugoslavia was a former socialist state and still ruled by ex-communist apparatchiks was not lost on Chinese leaders. Socialist states seemed to be especially vulnerable to Western military intervention. Rather than acquiesce to Chinese and Russian objections and let the killing in Kosovo continue, the Western countries turned to NATO and acted outside the UN framework. In mid-March 1999, NATO warplanes, mostly American, began bombing targets in the FRY in an effort to force Milošević to halt the ethnic cleansing in Kosovo. This added a further threatening element to the picture as seen from Beijing. The armed intervention in Kosovo was NATO's first-ever collective use of NATO forces under a NATO command, and it was happening in a state that was not a member of the NATO treaty. Moreover, the action was not directed toward defeating external aggression but toward rearranging the internal affairs of a non-NATO, ex-socialist state.

China's media did not inform China's people of the genocide and ethnic cleansing underway in Kosovo. Nor did it inform them of the considerations of the European nations about maintaining a regime of peace in Europe. It informed them merely that NATO warplanes were attacking the FRY without UN Security Council authorization and with devastating effect. The Western countries, led by the United States, were intervening militarily in the internal affairs of a small country yet again, and over China's principled objections, to impose Western notions of proper conduct. The instrument of this blatant aggression was NATO, which was apparently being transformed into a worldwide, aggressive military alliance, or so China's public was informed by its media.

Further apparent US insult to China came in April 1999, when Clinton turned down a set of far-reaching proposals by Premier Zhu Rongji designed to open the way to a PRC-US deal over China's entry into the WTO. Ever since the WTO was formed in 1995, Washington had insisted on market-opening measures far beyond what Beijing was prepared to accept. Premier Zhu Rongji responded in 1999 to US demands with market-opening proposals for agriculture, financial services, telecommunications, and other areas. There had been strong opposition to Zhu's proposals within China from vested industrial interests. But with backing from Jiang Zemin, Zhu was able to get his proposals approved and lay them before Clinton during an April 1999 visit to the United States. Although surprised by how far-reaching Zhu's proposal was—how far it went in addressing US demands—Clinton decided not to accept it. According to David Lampton, the main reason for this decision was Clinton's belief that he simply could not, at that juncture, secure congressional approval for granting China permanent most favored nation status—an essential quid pro quo for Zhu's concessions to US concerns. The year 2000 was also a Presidential election year, and the probable Democratic nominee, Vice President Al Gore, did not want to alienate labor union support by supporting WTO or permanent MFN status for China.[21]

China's media did not explain the nuances of Clinton's rejection of Zhu's offer—Democratic Party electoral calculations, congressional sentiment about China, or the role of Congress in the US political system. The way it was explained to them by China's media was that China's leaders had gone a very long way to meet US demands, and faced considerable internal opposition in that effort, only to have the offer rejected by the United States. It seemed to many Chinese, probably including some PBSC members, that the United States simply did not want cooperative relations with China, and that it was, after all, really hostile to China. The efforts of Jiang Zemin and Zhu Rongji to reach out to the United States and find common ground seemed naive to many Chinese who followed foreign affairs. China's leaders needed a tougher approach to dealing with American arrogance and hegemony.

Then a US warplane bombed the PRC embassy in Belgrade. On May 7, a B-2 stealth bomber operating out of an airbase in Missouri dropped laser-guided bombs on the PRC embassy in the Yugoslav capital. The bulk of them hit the intelligence section of the PRC embassy. Three Chinese personnel were killed and over twenty injured. It subsequently became clear that the maps used by the CIA to target the NATO bombing effort were out of date. The building indicated on the CIA targeting map as an office of the FRY Ministry of Defense was, in fact, now the embassy of the People's Republic of China in the FRY. The CIA officer who made this mistake was later fired. But all this would become apparent only later. At the time, all this was obscured by the fog of war. About two hours after the Belgrade embassy was bombed, an emergency Politburo session convened to discuss "countermeasures." Jiang Zemin presided, spoke first, and set the tone for deliberations:

> I was so filled with anger when I heard the news. I could not say a word, and my mind went completely blank. This crude, brutal, and evil action is a serious violation of China's sovereignty and a crime—a crime of openly trampling on international law, and one that is extremely rare in the history of foreign relations. US-led NATO must bear full responsibility for this matter. At today's meeting, we will study how to respond to this extremely abominable incident.[22]

One by one, Politburo Standing Committee members opined on the bombing. Li Peng went first. The attack was not an "isolated matter" but "a carefully crafted plot of subversion." The United States was attempting "to wantonly provoke disturbances" in China. The attack was also punishment of China for its opposition in the UN Security Council to NATO's intervention in Yugoslavia. Washington dared to do this just now because of China's eagerness to enter the WTO. "It is because the United States has this bargaining chip that it dares to brandish this big stick against our heads." Hu Jintao, already designated as Jiang's successor, spoke next. Hu stressed internal stability, urging maintaining stability and unity, restraining protest activities (against the bombing), and giving "timely guidance to the patriotic fervor of the masses," including "mobilizing organizations at all levels to do ideological work and persist in reasoning with the masses, guide their feelings, and take control over the situation." Li Lanqing (the official guiding WTO negotiations with the United States) concluded that "the current attack by the United States on our embassy in Yugoslavia is a dangerous signal! In the future, direct confrontation between China and the United States will be unavoidable." "In a word," he warned, "the United States wants to create chaos in China." Because the Falun Gong incident had just taken place, the United States "wants to sound China out and create chaos in China." Li Ruihuan warned that the United States might be attempting to "create chaos in China, to have China's young people vent their hatred on the United States on [to] the Chinese government. The Americans hope for nothing better than to provoke contradictions between the government and the broad masses of people, especially young students, and thereby shift the crisis." Zhu Rongji was the only PBSC member who acknowledged the possibility that the bombing might have been an accident. Yet even he concluded: "This is a deliberate action by the United States. Its purpose is to see China's reaction. If we submit to this humiliation without a protest, the United States will become even more unbridled in the future." Every PBSC member believed that the bombing had been a deliberate US attack on the Chinese embassy. Among the countermeasures approved by the PBSC was the organization of demonstrations against US diplomatic facilities in China, while ensuring that no one attempted to "deflect the spearhead" of the demonstrations against the government.

As soon as the news that "the United States has bombed the Chinese embassy" reached China, anger began to boil. All sorts of explanations erupted spontaneously. The Americans were punishing China for blocking Security Council authorization for the Kosovo intervention. Washington was testing China, to see how firmly it would respond to direct aggression; if China's response was weak, the Americans might move to foster Taiwan independence, or Tibetan independence, or perhaps support Chinese political dissidents. The Americans were trying to show the world that China was weak, that it could do nothing, really, in response to even such an egregious insult to China's honor. The Americans hated China and simply wanted to humiliate it. China's media fanned popular anger: the Chinese people cannot be humiliated. China will not be bullied. This was an act of new gunboat diplomacy, flagrant aggression, and a bloody atrocity. Chinese were informed by their media that the American action was a deliberate, intentional act of aggression against China. Nor did China's media inform the public about the ethnic cleansing underway in Kosovo. American bombing of Kosovo seemed like unreasonable aggression against a harmless and weak country. Now that aggression was being directed against China.

The American side moved quickly to apologize for the accidental tragedy. Ambassador James Sasser and Secretary of State Madeleine Albright quickly delivered formal apologies. President Clinton reiterated this during a stopover at an Oklahoma airport—although his seemingly casual matter of speaking on that occasion struck many Chinese as cavalier and disrespectful when videos of those comments were conveyed to them by China's media. Clinton attempted to reach Jiang by telephone to convey US apologies. The call was not accepted. A letter by Clinton met the same initial response. These multiple US efforts to apologize and make amends were not reported to the Chinese people by government officials or China's media. China's leaders apparently decided to let public anger vent for several days. As State Department official Stanley Roth would later testify before the Senate Foreign Relations Committee:

> The state-run media delayed by several crucial days publishing reports of U.S. official apologies and explanations. There was an inexplicable delay in President Jiang's willingness to accept the phone call from President Clinton . . . China failed for several days to carry out its obligations to provide for the security of US diplomatic personnel.[23]

While PRC media kept China's people ignorant of US efforts to apologize for the tragic blunder, CCP organs mobilized buses to ferry people to and from US diplomatic facilities for mass demonstrations reminiscent of the Mao era. The US embassy in Beijing and all four US consulates in China were besieged for hours or days by large, angry mobs. In scenes reminiscent of the Cultural Revolution, crowds surrounded diplomatic buildings, chanted slogans in response to leaders, and pelted buildings with rocks and paint. Considerable damage was done to the buildings. Police forces that deployed to the scene of the demonstrations seemed unconcerned with damage done to diplomatic property and did little if anything to restrain the rage of the crowds. On at least one occasion, police forces were inadequate to protect the facilities from the enraged mob. In Chengdu, Sichuan, a mob stormed and burned the US consular residence, with the US consul and family fleeing for their lives. Mobs besieged US consulates in Shanghai, Shenyang, and

Guangzhou. The US embassy in Beijing seemed for several hours to be in danger of being stormed by a mob and began to burn classified and sensitive documents.[24] Outside Xian in China's northwest, where Boeing Aircraft had a joint venture with a Chinese firm to produce airplane tail assemblies, a local official offered to provide armed escort for foreign personnel working at the facility. This led the US director to move immediately to prepare the evacuation of his expatriate personnel from China.[25] Foreign businessmen across China watched with trepidation as popular anti-US, and perhaps anti-foreign, rage gripped China for several days. Some older Chinese who remembered the xenophobia set loose by the Cultural Revolution trembled at the thought that such a force was again being unleashed.

After several days, the media conveyed news of the several US apologies, the buses no longer ferried in crowds, and the demonstrations ended. In mid-June, a US presidential special envoy arrived in Beijing to give an explanation of how the incident had occurred. Late the next month, an agreement on compensation was agreed on, with the United States providing compensation for loss of life and injury to persons and Chinese diplomatic property. A year later, the CIA analyst responsible for using out-of-date data was fired. More significantly, in November 1999 President Clinton reversed position on Zhu Rongji's WTO package deal, and accepted the Chinese offer.

The bombing of China's embassy precipitated an intense debate over policy toward the United States.[26] Though triggered by the embassy bombing, the debate touched on apprehensions about the United States that had been growing since the end of the Cold War. One opinion group in the debate pointed to a long series of US actions as proof of US hostility to China. The litany of US threats to China included (along with other items already discussed) reconfiguration of the US-Japan alliance, with China in mind; India's nuclear detonation in 1998 and improvements in US-India ties; Lee Teng-hui's "two-state" theory, announced in July 1999; and, of course, US-led NATO intervention in the internal affairs of Yugoslavia, with its ominous implications for China itself. Washington's Kosovo intervention was proof that the United States was intent on achieving global hegemony via military means. The United States and its NATO allies were bent on ignoring international sovereignty norms and the authority of the UN Security Council, and were intervening across the world to achieve domination. Taken together, these US moves indicated deep US hostility toward the PRC. A confrontation with the United States was likely or even inevitable, and China needed to prepare for it.

This conclusion touched on the balance between economic development and military modernization and preparation. Advocates of the hard-line anti-US position argued that much greater budgetary emphasis needed to be given to military preparedness. Some argued for equal emphasis on economic development and military preparedness. Others argued that the hostile international environment meant that the PRC could no longer afford to give priority to economic development, and military preparedness had to be the top priority. In terms of diplomacy, hard-liners charged that China's government had been laying too much emphasis on cultivating ties with the United States at the expense of ties with the Third World. China should also work harder to split the Europeans from Washington. The United States was in slow decline and need not be greatly feared, the hard-liners said.

Moderate voices in this debate did not dispute that the United States was doing all sorts of terrible things to the world and to China. There was a virtual consensus among participants in the debate that all major deleterious changes in China's security environment (regarding Japan, India, Taiwan, Europe, etc.) were a function of the actions and intentions of a malevolent United States. None of the participants in the debate argued that the United States genuinely sought partnership with a strong and secure China. Moderate voices differed from the hard-liners, rather, on whether a confrontation with the United States, at least in the near term, was the best course for China. Moderate voices argued that confrontation with the United States could and should be avoided. Peace and development were still the main trend in the international situation, they said. China still needed to focus on economic development for some long period of time. The regional conflicts and big-power interventions pointed to by the hard-liners did not reflect the main trend—the declining probability of war among the major powers, including a superpower attack on China. Regional wars and big-power intervention had always been going on and would probably continue for a long time yet. But the risk that China would confront a superpower attack had been greatly reduced. China was strong. All foreign sanctions imposed after 6-4 had been lifted. Hong Kong had been successfully recovered. China had forged "partnerships" with major countries around the world. The European countries were losing interest in sponsoring human rights resolutions with the United States. China had forged the Shanghai Five. Jiang Zemin had been well received in the United States, and Clinton had publicly affirmed the "three noes." In short, China was no longer weak or isolated. The United States would find little or no support for military adventures against China. China was not Serbia. China had nuclear weapons and powerful military forces. It followed that conflict with the United States was neither close at hand nor inevitable. China needed to remain vigilant against US adventurism, of course, but China's security had not deteriorated as a result of Kosovo. Other analysts pointed out that a huge gap still existed between PRC and US comprehensive national power, and that a confrontation with the United States in the near term would be a disaster for China.

The debate was drawn to a close in August 1999 at the annual leadership meeting at Beidaihe. Following that meeting, a new internal eight-character guideline was issued: "three no changes and three new changes" (*sange bu bian, sange bianhua*). Unchanged elements of the international situation were: 1) peace and development remain the main trend of the international situation, and multipolarity continues to develop; 2) economic globalization continues to expand; and 3) the major trend is toward relaxation of tension. The three new elements of the international situation were: 1) hegemonism and power politics are on the rise; 2) the trend toward military intervention is increasing; and 3) the gap between the developed and the developing countries is increasing. A premise of the new assessment was that the United States would maintain its status as the sole superpower for the next fifteen to twenty years, if not longer. The Politburo determined that the struggle with the United States would be a long-term one, and that China's guiding principle should be "struggle against, but not break with" the United States.[27]

Another Challenge to China's Security: the EP-3 Episode

The next challenge to a cooperative relation with the United States was about nineteen months in coming. At 8:15 a.m., Beijing time, on April 1, 2001, a US Navy EP-3 electronic intelligence collection aircraft collided with a PLA air force fighter jet. The PLA aircraft crashed into the sea, killing its pilot. The US aircraft, although severely damaged, managed to make an emergence landing at the nearest airfield—a PLA air force base on China's Hainan Island. As the American pilot headed toward the Hainan air base, he sent out a message of an emergency landing, but had not received verbal authorization from the Chinese side before the plane landed. The US plane thus entered Chinese territorial air space and landed on Chinese territory without Chinese permission. Once on the tarmac, the crew of the US aircraft refused to immediately open the airplane door and continued for some time to smash the sensitive electronic equipment in the plane with heavy hammers kept on board specifically for this purpose. The collision occurred 104 kilometers (65 miles) southeast of Hainan Island, well inside China's 200-nautical-mile-wide Exclusive Economic Zone (EEZ), but well outside China's twelve-nautical-mile territorial sea. The US aircraft had been collecting electronic signatures on advanced Chinese warships recently purchased from Russia, and perhaps on PLA air defense systems. The US navy could use such information for targeting the PLAN forces in the event of war. China's reading of UNCLOS, stated in a "signing statement" when it ratified that treaty in 1996, was that foreign warships and planes were required to receive Chinese permission before entering a country's EEZ. The US view of UNCLOS was that all ships and planes, including military enjoyed unrestricted right of innocent passage through the EEZ.

The EP-3 incident did not produce angry street demonstrations outside US diplomatic facilities as the embassy bombing had. It did, however, revive debate over the United States and deepen China's popular anti-American nationalism. Like earlier episodes, it also demonstrated the way in which popular anti-American nationalism generates both support for the CCP regime and pressure on that regime to act firmly to defend China's honor and interests.

The airplane collision occurred barely nine weeks after the new George W. Bush administration took office. China's leaders were apprehensive the new US leaders would shift China policy away from the cooperative approach that had once again been embraced by Washington circa 1997. During the 2000 election campaign, Bush had criticized the Clinton administration for treating the PRC as a "strategic partner" when in fact it was a "strategic competitor," or so candidate Bush said. The new Bush administration also placed greater stress on strengthening the US network of bilateral alliances in Asia— with Japan, South Korea, Australia, the Philippines, and Thailand—which Chinese leaders saw as moves designed to contain China. Many of the key leaders of the new administration were also perceived in China as "hawks," "Cold Warriors," and pro-Taiwan, further inclining them toward hostility to the PRC.[28]

The airplane collision reignited the debate over Beijing's US policies. Hard-liners on the PBSC argued that Washington's words and actions indicated that the Bush administration had already shifted policy away from cooperation toward containment. Hostile US moves included upgrading alliance partnerships in Asia, involving Japan in Theater Missile Defense, expanding arms sales to Taiwan (one of Bush's first foreign policy moves after his inauguration), and not least, Washington's arrogant and aggressive handling of the EP-3 imbroglio. It followed, CCP hard-liners said, that China should adopt a tough tit-for-tat policy.[29]

The moderate point of view, which eventually prevailed, maintained that US presidential candidates often make anti-China statements, but act differently once in the White House with full responsibility for securing US interests. These people cited Reagan and Clinton as examples of this shift toward cooperation with China once they bore the responsibilities of the presidency. Moreover, the Bush administration had not yet had time to put in place a China policy team, much less to think through and reorient US strategy toward China and Asia. If, however, China overreacted to the EP-3 collision, it could push the new Bush administration toward containment. Eventually, a consensus was reached. Positive ties with the United States were very important in maintaining a positive macro-climate for China's development drive, and China should continue to push for improvements in ties with the new administration. But it would defend its honor and its interests, and not appear weak or fearful in dealing with US provocations and insults.

It took several days for China's leaders to gather accurate information about how the collision had actually occurred. Local military authorities on Hainan apparently did not initially report the extremely close, high-speed passes that the pilot of the PLA fighter had been using to harass the EP-3. Nor did they fully inform the leadership of the flight characteristics of the large, heavily laden, propeller-driven US aircraft compared to those of the PLA inceptor. Initial local reports apparently said the US aircraft had turned sharply and suddenly toward the Chinese plane while the two were flying parallel. Special-effect animations showing this version of the collision were shown on Chinese television. The US side insisted that the EP-3 was proceeding straight and level on automatic pilot when slammed by the reckless Chinese pilot's aircraft.

Washington's handling of the collision struck Chinese, both the political elite and ordinary people, as arrogant, bullying, and crude. The US side was the first to publicly divulge the incident, at 5:30 p.m. on April 1, the day of the collision. According to Sheng Lijun, there had been a number of similar confrontations in China's EEZ (more than twenty in 2000 alone), which had been handled confidentially by the two sides.[30] The Chinese side made its first statement only five hours after the American one. From Beijing's perspective, breaking from previous practice and announcing the incident unilaterally and without consultation with Beijing was an insult and a manifestation of hostility. The US announcement made it imperative (for domestic reasons) for China's government to take a tough stance. Initial US statements were also accusatory and full of demands and implied threat. Bush's initial statement, for example, called for a "timely Chinese response" to the US request for access to the crew. The next day Bush said "it is time for our service men and women to return home," adding the threat that "the accident" had the potential to "undermine the productive relation between our two countries." Bush also insisted on the swift release of the plane "without further damage or tampering." US representatives, including members of Congress, were quick to raise threats of what might happen if US demands were not quickly complied with: weapons sales to Taiwan, opposition to Beijing's bid to host the 2008 Olympics, revocation of China's Permanent Normal Trade Relations (PNTR) status, cancellation of Bush's planned visit to Shanghai for an APEC meeting. From Beijing's perspective, this was simple bullying and power politics. It was China that had been injured and transgressed against, and yet the United States was making stern demands backed up by threats.

Beijing responded with tough policy. Beijing demanded that the United States accept full responsibility for the crash. The immediate cause of the crash, Chinese media asserted, was a sudden turn by the EP-3, resulting in its crashing into the Chinese plane. The root cause of the episode was the frequent spy activity conducted by US planes along China's coast and within its EEZ—all of which was unacceptable and must end, Beijing said. The United States should apologize to the Chinese government and people, and deliver to the Chinese government a full explanation of the incident. In spite of US demands and threats, Beijing held the twenty-four crew members for ten days, and the aircraft, which the Americans wanted to get back before PLA analysts went through it methodically, for a far longer period.

The United States hinted at use of military force. Several destroyers scheduled to return to Pearl Harbor were ordered to delay their return and linger in the region. The use of US military force to rescue the crew was not, however, an attractive option. Even if such a rescue were to be successful in securing the crewmen, the prospect of US military forces opening fire on PLA forces on Chinese soil was too serious to contemplate. Resort to other forms of US pressure—revocation of PNTR or vetoing the Beijing Olympics—could easily sour the broader relation, making cooperation in other areas very difficult or even impossible. The only realistic way Washington could secure the release of the EP-3 and its crew was through negotiations and satisfaction of Beijing's minimal demands.

The EP-3 imbroglio became a very good lesson for the new US administration: leaders with responsibility for securing US interests often found it necessary to secure China's cooperation for various purposes. Without China's cooperation, US leaders would find many matters (such as securing the release of the American crew) much more difficult. It seems likely that Chinese leaders understood that the collision was an accident (what airplane would knowingly crash into another?), but decided for reasons of tactical, and perhaps propaganda, advantage, to charge that the US pilot deliberately rammed the Chinese fighter. That echoed the Chinese charges from the 1999 embassy bombing, and would help put the Americans on the defensive.

Beijing's insistence on an American apology, and US reluctance to deliver one, quickly became the crux of the negotiations. On April 3, Ambassador Yang Jiechi, in a speech in Washington, demanded that the US government assume full responsibility for the incident and make an apology to the Chinese government and people.[31] From the US perspective, an apology was not merited, because it had been the Chinese F-8 that crashed into the EP-3, not the other way around. The US insisted that the EP-3 had been flying straight on autopilot when buzzed too closely by the PLA plane trying to harass the US craft. UNCLOS provided for overflight by military aircraft within the 200-mile EEZ, the US contended, and the unauthorized EP-3 entry into Chinese airspace and landing on Chinese territory was an emergency procedure in accord with international law and practice. Yet the situation was that unless the US apologized, the crew and the aircraft would not be released, or so it seemed to US leaders.

On April 4, Secretary of State Colin Powell sent a letter to Qian Qichen expressing his "regrets" for the death of the Chinese pilot. Qian replied that this formulation was too limited; the US side should "examine the actual situation and adopt a realistic attitude, and apologize to the Chinese people"[32] The next day President Bush for the first time expressed "regrets" for the loss of the Chinese pilot. On April 8, Powell for the first time used the world "sorry," still referring only to the collision and the loss of the Chinese pilot. Finally, on the afternoon of April 11, US Ambassador Joseph Prueher delivered a letter to Foreign Minister Tang Jiaxuan. This carefully written letter expressed "sincere regret" over the death of the Chinese pilot, and said the United States was "very sorry" that a US plane had entered China's airspace and landed without prior verbal approval. Strictly speaking, this was not a formal apology for the entire incident, but Beijing deemed the "two apologies" adequate to bring the episode to a close. The decision of China's leaders to end the confrontation even though the United States refused a genuine and unconditional "apology" attracted considerable criticism from Chinese who felt the government should be firmer in dealing with US arrogance and hegemony.

The EP-3 episode entered the popular Chinese nationalist litany of American offenses against China along with the F-16 sale, the *Yinhe*, the Beijing Olympics, Lee Teng-hui's US visit, the 1996 carrier deployment, and the Belgrade embassy bombing. Joseph Cheng and King-Lun Ngok provide a good synopsis of the popular Chinese outrage over the airplane incident:

> Chinese media widely reported the condemnation of US hegemonism by Chinese people from all walks of life, from intellectuals, university students, cadres to academics and foreign affairs specialists. At the chat rooms of various web sites in China, one could easily detect the anger toward the US from the demands to pursue the criminal responsibility of the US pilot concerned; those on the Chinese leadership to adopt a strong stand in dealing with the US, etc. The explanations offered by the US side on the air collision were typically criticized as unreasonable . . . twisting the facts . . . arrogant . . . etc. The neglect of the fate of the missing Chinese pilot by the US side was also condemned . . . as 'having lost the human conscience.'[33]

The 9-11 Attacks and Renewal of PRC-US Cooperation

The al-Qaeda attacks on the World Trade Center in New York City and the Pentagon in Washington, DC, on September 11, 2001 (hereafter "9-11"), just over five months after the EP-3 collision, was a strategic windfall for Beijing. The horrific nature of the 9-11 attacks on the American homeland focused American security concern away from China. Chinese analysts were convinced that the United States needed an enemy both to mobilize domestic support (in the form of taxes and soldiers) for US hegemonistic efforts and to keep US allies in line. China had struggled since the end of the Cold War to prevent the PRC from becoming Washington's necessary "next enemy." Now the 9-11 attacks supplied a genuine enemy for the United States. Moreover, the United States adopted an aggressive, military strategy of "war on terrorism" that took US military forces first into Afghanistan (in October 2001) to overthrow the Taliban government that had sheltered al-Qaeda, and then into Iraq (in March 2003) to oust Saddam Hussein's government, which Washington believed had colluded with terrorism. From Beijing's perspective, US energy and attention were being directed away from China. With luck, the Americans might not be able to extricate themselves from these new West Asian quagmires for many years. In fact, US forces left Iraq in December 2011, and US combat forces are scheduled to leave Afghanistan by the end of 2016. The shift in US strategic attention resulting from 9-11 eased American pressure on China for perhaps a decade.[34]

Jiang Zemin phoned President Bush before the end of the day on September 11 to convey China's condolences and condemnation of that morning's attacks. Washington's newly proclaimed "global war on terrorism" required Chinese assistance in various ways. The United States sought UN authorization for establishment of new international counterterrorism norms regarding movement of airplanes, freight containers, ships, materials, significant people, and money around the world. China, with its position on the Security Council and its prominent role in international commerce, transportation, and finance, could facilitate or obstruct those US efforts. Beijing opted to cooperate with Washington. In the Security Council, for instance, on September 12 and 28, China supported resolutions giving Washington UN authority for its response to the 9-11 attacks. At a long-scheduled APEC summit meeting in Shanghai in October, Washington wanted to set aside the originally scheduled agenda and focus instead on building a consensus on antiterrorism. China, chair of the summit, cooperated fully. President Bush reached a "consensus" with Jiang Zemin on opposing terrorism and referred to "China and other Pacific nations" as "important partners" in the antiterrorism effort.[35]

One of China's most important early forms of support for Washington's "global war on terrorism" was encouragement of Pakistan to cooperate with the United States. Having decided on military intervention to oust the al-Qaeda-harboring Taliban regime in Afghanistan, the United States needed a forward territorial operational base to support that intervention. Pakistan was geographically ideal for such a purpose; it had seaports and abutted Afghanistan. But Pakistan-US relations were very poor. In 1990, virtually as soon as the Soviets had withdrawn from Afghanistan, the United States had broken with Pakistan over its nuclear weapons programs. From the Pakistani perspective, the United States used Pakistan to support the anti-Soviet Afghan jihad, and then abandoned it as soon as it was no longer needed. Indeed, the United States began building a new cooperative relation with India in late 1998. India was, of course, Pakistan's nemesis. The Taliban in Afghanistan also had close links to Pakistan; Islamabad had supported the Taliban takeover of Afghanistan in 1994–1996 as a way of stabilizing its borders, becoming a corridor for Central Asia oil and gas to reach global markets, and gaining strategic depth against India.[36] Now, in fall 2001, Washington was demanding that Pakistan make a clear choice: abandon the Taliban and join with the United States against the Taliban, or stand with the Taliban against the United States.

In this quandary, Pakistan President Pervez Musharraf turned to China. After initial discussions with China's ambassador to Pakistan, Musharraf sought an emergency visit to China to further discuss the situation. Beijing advised against such a visit (perhaps because it would raise China's profile at this ultra-sensitive juncture).[37] Instead, in late September, as Pakistan moved toward renewed partnership with the United States, Jiang Zemin spoke with Musharraf by telephone. As reported by Xinhua, Jiang "spoke highly" of and expressed "full understanding and respect" for Pakistan's cooperation with the "international community" against terrorism.[38] In other words, Beijing endorsed Pakistan's cooperation with the United States in the "global war on terrorism." The Americans' Pakistani road to Afghanistan was open.

China's advice almost certainly played an important role in Pakistan's decision at this juncture.[39] Had China, Pakistan's main strategic backer and security partner, objected to Pakistan's re-engagement with the United States, it is doubtful that Musharraf would have said "yes" to Bush. Beijing urged Pakistan to cooperate with the United States not in order to help out the United States, but because Pakistan-US partnership comported with China's own interests at several levels. First, US re-engagement with Islamabad would strengthen Pakistan (via renewed aid, military assistance, etc.), which would help maintain Pakistan as a balancer to India—China's elemental interest in South Asia. Second, having the United States re-engage with Pakistan would make US-India ties more difficult, slowing and perhaps blocking the formation of an India-US strategic partnership. Establishing robust US-Pakistan ties would also ease Indian pressure on China over Beijing's robust ties with Pakistan. Beijing could now point to Pakistan-US cooperation when New Delhi objected to Pakistan-China cooperation. Third, helping the United States wage its global war on terrorism would divert US energies and attentions away from China while gaining US gratitude for China's assistance, perhaps extracting a few quid pro quos from the Americans for China's help.[40]

By the end of 2001, less than nine months after the airplane collision, PRC-US relations were quite cordial. Beijing's robust cooperation with Washington in the global war on terrorism delighted the Bush administration and transformed the PRC-US relation into a close partnership. A joint working group on counterterrorism was set up and met twice annually to coordinate measures in intelligence gathering, financial monitoring, and antiterrorist actions at the United Nations. Hong Kong, a vitally important transport and financial center under Chinese sovereignty, was brought into the antiterrorist fight. Beijing, of course, shared with Washington an interest in preventing al-Qaeda and like-minded groups from disrupting the global trade and financial system on which China's rise was premised. In exchange for helping Washington deal with al-Qaeda, Beijing secured US designation of the East Turkistan Islamic Movement (ETIM) as a terrorist group. This brought into play against that ethnic Uighur group all the antiterrorist measures agreed to by Beijing and Washington. Many people outside of China were sympathetic to the Uighur struggle in Xinjiang and critical of China's sometimes heavy-handed methods of dealing with people it charged as "ETIM splittists." But China rejected "double standards" for the antiterrorist struggle, and Washington acceded to Beijing's demand. By working with the United States on these common interests, Beijing recast the strategic context of the vital relation with the United States. For the first time since the end of the Cold War, the PRC and the United States were partners in struggle against a common foe, terrorism. A decade later, as the United States ended its wars in Iraq and Afghanistan and "pivoted" to Asia, tensions in PRC-US relations would again mount.

The US Financial Crisis and Beijing's Probing of US Capacity and Will

The financial crisis that began unfolding in the United States in 2007 led many in China to conclude that the extremely severe crisis had sapped US capability and will and made Washington far needier of Chinese cooperation in the economic area, and had, therefore, significantly altered the balance between Beijing and Washington. Beginning with the bursting of a housing bubble, the crisis spread to the US financial sector via rotten mortgages held by many financial institutions, hit businesses who lacked liquidity, and became a full-scale overall recession by September 2008. By October 2009, unemployment in the United States had risen to 10 percent. GDP growth collapsed, reaching a low of negative 8.9 percent in the last quarter of 2008. Overall growth for 2008 to 2012 was an anemic 1.7 percent. The United States was in deep economic crisis. US government debt spiraled up as tax revenues fell with reduced business activity and huge government expenditures for bailouts of large but deeply indebted firms, stimulus spending, and vastly expanded unemployment and welfare payments. National debt as a percent of GDP rose from 40 percent at the end of 2008 to 63 percent by the end of 2010—the highest levels of indebtedness since World War II. Mounting US government debt was partially covered by foreign purchases of US Treasury bonds. The PRC was one of the major purchasers of those US debt bonds. If China stopped buying US Treasuries, interest rates would rise greatly, further slowing investment and recovery. By late 2009, the financial crisis had spread to Europe. There a property bubble, bank bailouts, and unsustainable levels of government debt led to the potential bankruptcy of several national governments—unless averted by massive financial transfers from less prof-ligate members of the European Union, a situation that became known as Europe's sovereign debt crisis. The entire Western, capitalist world was in deep economic crisis—the worst since the 1930s.

China's economy remained strong by contrast. China's exports were hurt by the fall in consumption by developed countries, but the fall was limited by cheap renminbi and large government subsidies. China's overall economy continued to grow, unlike the economies of North America and Europe. China's annual GDP growth reached a low point of 6.2 percent growth in the second quarter of 2009, but rebounded to an average 10.2 percent in 2008, 7.5 percent in 2009, and 10.63 percent in 2010. Beijing responded to the crisis by providing massive spending for vast public works projects—high-speed rail-ways, highways, dams, and power plants—to bolster demand. Chinese banks and giant companies did not go bankrupt unless the government authorized it. Although burdened with levels of debt unsustainable in a genuine mar-ket economy, Chinese state-owned enterprises were sustained by infusions of capital from state banks. Beijing also accelerated efforts to grow China's domestic demand by acceding to demands for wage increases by workers in east coast factories, improving the social welfare net for rural residents, and accelerating the pace of urbanization. In short, while Western capitalism descended into crisis, China's economic model seemed vindicated.

Chinese analysts concluded from the deep US crisis that the relative posi-tions of the United States and the PRC had significantly changed. China was now in a much stronger position.[41] The United States needed China to con-tinue purchasing US Treasury bonds—the principal instrument for financing the US federal debt. An article by the vice president of the Shanghai Institute of International Studies, Chen Dongxiao, published in the February 2010 issue of the influential journal *Qiu Shi* (Seek truth), for example, attributed the excellent PRC-US relations that existed in 2009 during the first year of the Obama administration (discussed below) to "structural" aspects leading the two powers to adjust to one another's strategic interests. The main driver was the growth of China's international influence and power and a parallel dim-inution of US power and hegemony. The global financial crisis and the wars in Iraq and Afghanistan had thrown the United States into decline, forcing it to undertake a defensive strategic adjustment. Accordingly a "new generation leader," Obama, had emerged, looking for partners and seeking cooperation and support everywhere. In particular, the United States was compelled to rely on China to deal with its financial crisis (by purchasing US Treasury bonds). In order to secure China's support, Obama had announced a policy of "not containing China" and playing down human rights differences between China and the United States. The United States was still strong and China weak, Chen acknowledged, but recent shifts had allowed China to seize the initiative in the relationship.[42]

Sensing a shift in underlying US and PRC capabilities, along with a US administration committed to strategic reassurance of China, Beijing began pushing on issues of concern to China. In the words of one official in the Obama administration, "China senses little drops of blood in the water better than any country. They sniff out relative changes in power and pursue them."[43]

Barack Obama took office in January 2009 with a strong determination to form a cooperative partnership with China.[44] In the words of US ambassador to China Jon Huntsman, the Obama China team spent 2009 "building bridges, getting to know [China's leaders], ensuring that the new administration was able to frame our relationship going forward with China in ways meaningful to both countries."[45] Washington's "outreach" to Beijing included frequent meetings, encounters, and phone calls between Obama, President Hu Jintao, and Premier Wen Jiabao. It also included melding together two previously separate annual dialogues into a single cabinet-level Strategic and Economic Dialogue—a move welcomed by Beijing. President Hu Jintao came to Washington for the first meeting of the Strategic and Economic Dialogue in July 2009, and President Obama delivered his first major statement on China policy to a session of that Dialogue. Obama's speech was a panegyric to Sino-US cooperation, terming that relationship "as important as any bilateral relationship in the world." Obama attempted to reassure China that the United States did not seek to contain China:

> Let us be honest: We know that some are wary of the future. Some in China think that America will try to contain China's ambitions; some in America think that there is something to fear in a rising China. I take a different view. And I believe President Hu takes a different view, as well. I believe in a future where China is a strong, prosperous and successful member of the community of nations; a future when our nations are partners out of necessity, but also out of opportunity. This future is not fixed, but is a destination that can be reached if we pursue a sustained dialogue like the ones that you will commence today, and act on what we hear and what we learn.[46]

The result of the perceived shift in underlying power capabilities was a series of hard Chinese moves probing US resolve. The first came during Obama's November 2009 state visit to China. A high point of such a visit had traditionally been a public address by the American president to the Chinese people. Presidents Clinton and George W. Bush during their visits had been allowed live, nationwide television broadcasts. Obama's China team pushed for similar openness in the form of a nationally broadcast question and answer session. The US request was rejected. Obama's session was broadcast only to the Shanghai audience (the city where the event was held). Portions of it were censored. The Chinese audience was also limited to carefully screened members of the Communist Youth League (CYL) who had, moreover, been trained for the session. The questions from the CYL audience were vetted beforehand by leaders of the American Studies Center of Shanghai's Fudan University. Efforts by the US side to invite Chinese bloggers were foiled and the invitees prevented from attending.[47] Xinhua subsequently posted a transcript of the session on its website. The contrast with the broad access given Clinton in 1998 was striking.

By denying Obama media access to the Chinese people, the CCP limited the ideological poisoning of Chinese television audiences by the American president's espousal of bourgeois liberal ideas. It also avoided displaying the contrast between the open style of an American president and the more wooden style common to CCP leaders. But such considerations had existed during earlier US presidential visits and had been overridden. In 2009, the United States seemed to be in a far weaker position, so its demands were refused. Beijing also secured in the joint statement issuing from the Obama visit endorsement of a broad principle implying that each side of the US-PRC relation would abstain from actions the other deemed deeply offensive. "The two sides agreed that respecting each other's core interests is extremely important to ensure steady progress in U.S.-China relations," the statement read.[48] The US military leadership had opposed accepting this provision precisely because they understood that it invited Chinese tests of US resolve on issues such as Taiwan or the US alliance with Japan.[49]

The next demonstration of Beijing's new assertiveness came at the global climate change conference in Copenhagen, Denmark, in December 2009. Obama had announced climate change as one of his top priorities and had billed the Copenhagen meeting as a major venue for dealing with the issue. In his July 29 US-PRC Dialogue speech, Obama had identified climate change as an area of common US-PRC interest (as the two largest carbon emitters) in which he hoped for cooperation. Beijing saw the matter differently; Western demands for restrictions on carbon emissions were attempts to check China's rapid development. Consequently, China's delegation to the Copenhagen conference, led by Premier Wen Jiabao, aggressively blocked any action that might limit China's ability to emit carbon into the global atmosphere. China would play a major role at the Copenhagen conference, not in cooperation with the United States, as Obama had envisioned, but in opposition to it and by thwarting efforts by the United States and European countries to impose specific and verifiable caps on emissions of all countries.

Initial sessions at the Copenhagen meeting were conducted by second-level officials. China joined with India and Sudan to raise repeated procedural objections. An early-morning emergency meeting of top-level leaders was convened in an attempt to break the impasse. The US and French presidents, the German chancellor, and the Japanese prime minister attended. Wen Jiabao did not. China was represented by Vice Foreign Minister He Yafei.

Vice Minister He continued to raise procedural objections, backed up by developing-country representatives. China, apparently, came to the conference not to partner with the United States but to rally the Third World to defeat the attempts by the "rich countries" to hobble Third World development. In his main speech the next day, Wen Jiabiao called for voluntary targets only. In his speech following Wen, President Obama rejected the idea that developing countries' emissions promises did not need to be verifiable, adding "I don't know how you can have an international agreement where we are not sharing information and ensuring we are meeting our commitments. That doesn't make sense. It would be a hollow victory."[50]

Wen Jiabao reportedly was furious at what he saw as Obama's insinuation that China might be dishonest. Wen returned to his hotel, skipping another leaders' meeting, and sending even lower-level Chinese representatives to subsequent sessions. At a mid-afternoon US-PRC session, Obama and Secretary of State Hillary Clinton found themselves sitting across from three low-level Chinese officials. At one point in the session one of the Chinese representatives lectured Obama on what the United States needed to do, wagging his finger at Obama to stress his point. Obama took this as a deliberate slight. "It would be nice to negotiate with someone who can make political decisions," Obama said. Obama then went looking for Wen Jiabao and found him in a session with leaders of India, Brazil, and South Africa. Obama insisted on joining the session, saying he did not want them negotiating in secret. The final document issuing from the Copenhagen conference asserted that "climate change is one of the greatest challenges of our time" and stated that "deep cuts" in emissions were required. All specific numeric goals and all mandatory actions were, however, deleted.

In sum, China played a major and assertive role at the Copenhagen conference—possibly one of its most influential roles ever at a UN conference. But Beijing used its influence not in cooperation with the United States, but to block actions by the Western nations that Beijing deemed antithetical to China's interest in unrestricted and rapid industrialization. Seen from the perspective of Washington, this episode suggested China would use its growing power not as a partner of the United States to uphold a common global order, but to pursue its own narrow national interests. The next episode on the Korean peninsula would make the same point even more forcefully.

Beijing Aligns with North Korea and against the United States

In March 2010, a medium-sized South Korean warship operating in disputed waters off the west coast of Korea exploded, broke in half, and quickly sank, killing forty-six South Korean seamen. The ship, named the *Cheonan*, was recovered from the sea floor in mid-April, along with the remains of an exploded torpedo. An international Joint Investigation Group (JIG) consisting of experts from South Korea, the United States, Britain, Canada, Australia, and Sweden was assembled to conduct a forensic investigation of the sinking. After several months' intensive investigation, the JIG determined that the ship had been sunk by a torpedo fired by a North Korean submarine. The backgrounds of this incident and another in November involving North Korean bombardment of a South Korean island were complex, involving transfer of power in the North Korean regime; inter-Korean relations, including disputed maritime boundaries; and international pressure on North Korea to abandon nuclear weapons. Our concern, however, is with China's response to this North Korean attack.

North Korea had been China's ally since 1950, when Chinese intervention rescued that regime from extinction. China's post-1978 discovery of the wealth-generating potential of marketization and participation in the global economy led Beijing to urge North Korea to follow a similar path. Throughout the rule of three North Korean rulers (Kim Il-Sung, who ruled from 1948 to his death in 1994; his son Kim Jong-Il, 1994 to 2011; and Kim Jong-Il's son Kim Jong-Eun, 2011 to present), Chinese prompting went unheeded. North Korea remained isolated from the world and mired in deep poverty. After the collapse of the USSR, North Korea became highly dependent on Chinese economic support. North Korea's economy was integrated into China's economic sphere via trade and Chinese investment. Pyongyang showed little gratitude to China, and China's support earned Beijing little influence in the North Korean capital. Yet China continued to sustain the North Korean regime out of fear that its demise would lead to South Korea's annexation of the North along the lines of Germany's 1990 unification, or another Chinese military intervention in Korea to prevent that from happening. Such developments could lead to another Korean War with the United States or the inclusion of North Korea into the US-South Korean military alliance. In this context, Beijing's response to the Korea crises of 2010 signaled a strengthening of Chinese support for North Korea. Beijing signaled Washington and Seoul that retaliatory military action against North Korea risked confrontation with China.

Beijing initially responded to the *Cheonan* sinking by calling for restraint and calm by all parties.[51] It was several weeks before Beijing sent a simple message of condolence to South Korea expressing sorrow for the loss of South Korea seamen—a lapse that had a substantial impact on South Korean public opinion regarding China. Beijing also declined an invitation to send experts to join the JIG. Once the JIG had finished its work and reached a conclusion, Beijing declined an offer to send a team to Beijing to explain JIG findings. When South Korea offered to send a JIG team to New York to present its findings to the Security Council, Beijing opposed South Korea's efforts to bring the *Cheonan* incident before the Security Council, preferring to treat the matter as an inter-Korean matter that should not be "internationalized." China then demanded deferral of consideration of the issue. When Beijing's efforts to prevent United Nations action failed and the Security Council issued a statement on July 9, Beijing watered it down to hold no one responsible. Throughout, China's media suggested the JIG report was not credible but had been cooked up for ulterior purposes by Washington and Seoul. Rather than looking impartially at the forensic evidence and holding Pyongyang responsible for a reckless provocation, Beijing protected Pyongyang from responsibility, criticism, and pressure. Figure 24-1 shows the locations of the 2010 Korea events.

In late July, after the JIG had reached its conclusion, the US and South Korean navies conducted joint exercises in the Sea of Japan intended to deter North Korea from further military provocations. These exercises were initially scheduled for the Yellow Sea on the west side of the Korean peninsula, but under Chinese pressure, were shifted to the Sea of Japan, to which China is not littoral.[52] In spite of Washington's effort to assuage Chinese concerns, Beijing still strongly condemned the July exercises. *Global Times,* a nationalist newspaper under the auspices of *Renmin ribao,* said that China had worked with tolerance and patience to build strategic trust with its neighbors, but that "hard-earned trust is under threat with the US intention

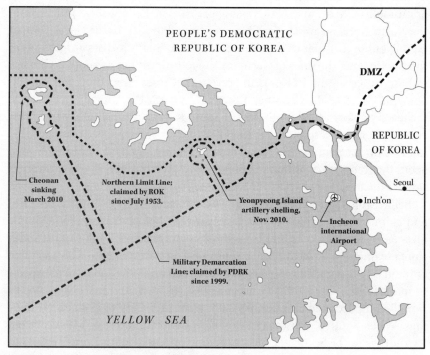

FIGURE 24-1 The 2010 Confrontations in Korea

to meddle in the region, and force countries to choose between China and the US."[53] Major General Luo Yuan, the deputy secretary general of the Chinese Association for Military Science, explained the basis for China's opposition to the July exercises in the Sea of Japan. China simply would not tolerate US military exercises near its coasts. The Yellow Sea was the gateway to China's capital and the Bohai economic circle. Historically, invaders had repeatedly used the Yellow Sea to advance on the Beijing and Tianjin areas. The strategic bottom line was to nip evil in the bud via preventive diplomacy.[54] In plain speech, Luo Yuan was saying that China needed to defend itself against a US military assault on north China's cities, or perhaps even an American expeditionary force marching to Beijing. General Luo had taken a US–South Korean military demonstration clearly directed against North Korea and transformed it into a demonstration against China. Regarding the sinking of the *Cheonan*, General Luo said that the Security Council had called on all parties to remain calm. Implicitly, the American and South Korean sea exercises were violations of the Security Council Resolution. Shortly after the US-South Korean exercises in the Sea of Japan, the PLAN conducted four days of live fire exercises in the Yellow Sea. The exercises received an unusual amount of attention from the Chinese media.[55] In effect, Beijing was countering the US–South Korean naval demonstration, intended to warn Pyongyang, with a Chinese naval demonstration warning Washington and Seoul. Beijing had aligned with Pyongyang, which had sunk the *Cheonan*, against Seoul and Washington.

By mid-2010, Washington began responding to the more assertive policies that followed Beijing's 2009 strategic recalibration. A turning point came in March 2010, when Beijing posited US noninterference in China's immediate periphery as the necessary quid pro quo for China's support for yet another US-sponsored Security Council resolution tightening sanctions on Iran. Beijing indicated it was willing to go along with another resolution on Iran's nuclear program, but insisted that, in exchange, the US promise to respect China's "core interests"—as Washington had promised to do in Obama's November 2009 joint statement with Hu Jintao. Beijing also informed US officials that China's "core interests" included the South China Sea. From Washington's perspective, unless Beijing's efforts met American pushback, East Asian countries might begin to conclude that prudence required accommodation to Beijing's demands.

US pushback began at an ASEAN Regional Forum meeting in Hanoi in July. Speaking about the South China Sea territorial disputes, Secretary of State Clinton said that while the United States did not take a side on the merits of those disputes, it had a number of interests in the region, including freedom of navigation, open access to Asia's maritime commons, and respect for international law. "We oppose the use or threat of force by any claimant," Clinton said. Rather than resorting to force or coercion, parties should pursue their claims through UNCLOS, with "legitimate claims to maritime space in the South China Sea ... derived solely from legitimate claims to land features." This was implicitly a rejection of Beijing's claim to the entire South China Sea on the basis that it is a "historic sea" belonging, by history, to China, rather than being a 200-mile EEZ drawn from terrestrial coastlines according to customary international law and UNCLOS. Finally, Clinton said that the United States was "prepared to facilitate initiatives and confidence building measures" that were consistent with the 2002 ASEAN-China declaration of conduct in the South China Sea.[56]

Washington also gave military substance to the new tougher US approach. The month after the ASEAN forum in Hanoi, the United States and Vietnam conducted their first-ever joint naval exercise in the South China Sea. The US task force was built around the aircraft carrier USS *George Washington*, which had just completed maneuvers with South Korea in the Sea of Japan.[57] After the maneuvers with Vietnam, the *George Washington* returned north for a second round of maneuvers with South Korea, but this time in the far more sensitive Yellow Sea.

Beijing objected strongly to the new US "interference" in the South China Sea disputes. Territorial conflicts should not be "internationalized" but settled by the two parties involved, Beijing asserted. China's territorial conflicts with Southeast Asian countries could not, it insisted, be dealt with on a multilateral basis with other countries ganging up against China. Nor did any extraregional power have the right to involve itself in these conflicts. Yet here was the United States doing precisely that, while encouraging the Southeast Asian countries to join together to confront China on the issue.

Then, on November 23, North Korea launched a second military strike against the south, this time with artillery bombardment of the small South Korean–held island of Yeonpyeong in the same vicinity as the *Cheonan* sinking. The bombardment went on for a day, with 170 shells and artillery rockets being fired at the island, killing four and wounding nineteen. South Korean artillery retaliated and the fighting became some of the worst since the end of the Korean War. The Yeonpyeong bombardment came five days before the start of US–South Korean naval maneuvers, this time in the Yellow Sea. That naval demonstration was a powerful demonstration of Washington's determination to uphold the right of navigation by warships in another country's EEZ, as the United States believed was permitted by customary international law. In Beijing, the MFA condemned the US-ROK maneuvers, saying "we oppose any party undertaking any military activity in our exclusive economic zone without permission." General Luo Yuan was quoted by Xinhua as saying "The United States and the ROK should not take sensitive and provocative military action at such a sensitive time and place." To do so was "pouring oil on flames."[58] As for North Korea's initiation of an artillery duel over Yeonpyeong, the MFA called for an emergency meeting of the Six Party

Talks, avoiding any condemnation of the north's responsibility for precipitating the second Korean military conflict that year.

As the dust settled from two years of pro-PDRK Chinese policies, the result was not positive for China. Beijing's policies had pushed South Korea away from China and significantly closer to the United States. In South Korea, people noted the glaring contrast between Beijing's calm response to the killing of forty-six South Koreans on the *Cheonan* and China's swift demand for a North Korean admission of guilt, assumption of responsibility, punishment of the guilty, and pledge of nonrepetition after a small clash on the PRC–North Korean border in which several Chinese were killed.[59] At the level of policy, Beijing's protection of Pyongyang challenged what had previously been conventional wisdom among South Korean foreign policy specialists—that South Korea needed to avoid being caught in the escalating US-PRC rivalry by distancing itself from Washington. That thinking did not disappear with the *Cheonan* and Yeonpyeong incidents, but South Koreans increasingly questioned whether Beijing would be an honest broker in inter-Korean relations. Many South Koreans had assumed that China's huge economic relationship with South Korea, far outweighing its economic ties to North Korea, plus the "strategic partnership" between China and South Korea agreed to in May 2008, had moved Beijing closer to Seoul, or at least toward a neutral position between the two Koreas. Beijing's protection of North Korea's provocations in 2010 demolished these beliefs. It became clear that China would do nothing to undermine its influence with Pyongyang or the existence of the North Korean state. Many in South Korea now concluded that if South and North Korea confronted one another, China would not remain neutral but would side with the north. The consequence was a renewal of South Korea's desire for a strong military alliance with the United States.[60]

As for the United States, China's policies cast doubt on China's willingness to partner with the United States on the critical issue of war and peace on the Korean peninsula. China's apparent policy was not to work with the United States to prevent or punish North Korean resort to military force, but to protect Pyongyang from pressure in response to its provocations. It was clear that China's paramount interest was protecting China's own narrow interests, not the broader stability of the Korean peninsula. It would take a while for Washington to work out a formal strategic response. When that response was laid out by Obama and Clinton in late 2011, it became known as the "pivot to Asia." In a speech to the Australian Parliament in November, Obama outlined the strategy of pivoting to Asia as the United States extricated itself from wars in Iraq and Afghanistan. "The United States has been, and always will be a Pacific nation," the American president declared.[61] In plain speech: the United States would not allow itself to be hassled out of East Asia by growing Chinese power. Secretary of State Clinton laid out the new pivot strategy in a *Foreign Policy* article the same month.[62] The first of six "lines of action" outlined by Clinton for the "pivot" had to do with strengthening bilateral security alliances in Asia. The second was deepening working relationships with emerging powers, including China. The crux of the new US approach was to clarify that the United States sought cooperation and partnership with China, but not on the basis of US acceptance of whatever Beijing defined as its core interests.

China's 2009–2011 assertiveness reverberated across East Asia. Governments watched as China confronted the United States, South Korea, and Japan (the latter discussed in the next chapter). Many countries with their own deep conflicts of interest with the PRC wondered if Beijing's newly assertive behavior foreshadowed the way Beijing would increasingly act as its power grew.

Renewed Effort to Placate the United States

Throughout the period of the US financial crisis and global economic recession, there was debate within China about whether the United States had indeed gone into terminal decline, and whether US relative capabilities had fallen sufficiently vis-à-vis China as to give Beijing a significantly more advantageous position. PRC critics of the more assertive post-2009 policies pointed to the mounting US and regional reaction to argue that China should return to Deng Xiaoping's approach of "keeping a low profile" and "keeping China's light under a basket." By using its rapidly increasing power in a more assertive fashion, Beijing was scaring China's neighbors, these moderates said, energizing the United States and creating opportunities for US efforts to contain and encircle China. This debate did not end, but by 2011 it was clear that China's more assertive policies in defense of its narrow interests were not producing the desired effect. China's assertiveness had led not to a diminishing of US influence in the Western Pacific but to a hardening of US policy, a strengthening of ties between the United States and its allies, and the threat of a US effort to build an anti-China coalition. Unless Beijing drew back and returned to a more low-profile approach, China could find itself in escalating and increasingly open rivalry with the United States for geostrategic position and influence in Asia, or so moderate Chinese analysts claimed.

Early in 2011, Beijing began an effort to restabilize ties with the United States. Although the power balance between the two countries had changed over the last few years, the mainstream of China's leaders feared that if China pushed too hard, the shift in underlying power relations could frighten the United States, pushing it toward embrace of stronger efforts to balance China. In the words of Fu Mengzi, an American specialist with the China Institute of Contemporary International Studies:

When Sino-US ties were normalized, China was just opening up its door to the world. China is now one of the world's major powers. Sino-US relations have come through many stages and come a long way. However, 2010 was a turbulent year, and we are still facing lots of challenges. Leaders of the two countries must have the courage to establish a framework for this important relationship, one that can stabilize it.[63]

Beijing's push to stabilize ties with the United States began by welcoming US Secretary of Defense Robert Gates in January 2011. Beijing's agreement to Gates' visit was a response to a request by Obama at a June 2010 G 20 Summit.[64] Hu Jintao prepared for Gates' visit by admonishing the PLA for allowing its officers to speak their own minds on sensitive issues.[65] Hu made clear to PLA leaders that China could ill afford a new round of tension with the United States. One of Gates' key messages in Beijing was that Washington would not allow the PLA to achieve supremacy in the Western Pacific. Despite economic woes and cuts in defense spending, the United States was investing in an array of new capabilities—a new generation of jamming technology, seaborne unmanned aircraft, better radar—designed to counter the PLA's rapidly improving anti-access, area-denial capabilities intended to deny the United States access to international waters near China.[66]

The PLA carried out Hu's orders to receive and talk with Gates, but it also rejected his proposal to stabilize the US-PRC military relationship by making it "consistent and not subject to shifting political winds," as Gates put it. Ending the pattern of military relations being interrupted for months or even years whenever the PLA was especially unhappy with some US move was a high US priority.[67] The PLA understood that the United States wanted military-to-military exchanges, and refused to compromise its ability to punish Washington for transgressions such as arms sales to Taiwan. As Defense Minister Liang Guanglie told a press conference during Gates' visit: "US arms sales to Taiwan seriously damage China's core interests. And we do not want to see that happen again."[68] The PLA also underlined its rapidly improving capabilities by conducting during Gates' visit the first public testing of a new stealth fighter, the J-20, a warplane that closely resembled the US F-22 Raptor stealth fighter and represented a major advance for China's power projection capabilities. The first public display of its capabilities was given wide media attention, with photos of it appearing on the website of *Global Times* shortly after the plane's public debut. When Gates raised the question of the J-20 in a meeting with Hu Jintao, it became evident that none of the civilians in the room had been informed about the test. American officials surmised that Hu Jintao, the only civilian official with authority over the PLA, had been kept uninformed about the test, and that the test was an act of PLA defiance against Hu and the civilian leadership's overly soft policy toward the United States.[69]

China's civilian leaders also used summit diplomacy to restabilize the vital US relationship. Hu Jintao's visit to Washington (reciprocating Obama's November 2009 state visit) was originally scheduled for 2010, but the policy confrontations of that year forced delay.[70] When the summit finally occurred in January 2011, one key message was directed inward, toward the Chinese people and the PLA officer corps. That message was this: China's leader was received by the United States with high esteem and respect, and the United States treats China as a coequal great power. Publication of China's three major state-owned newspapers, *Renmin ribao*, *Jiefangjun bao*, and *Jingji ribao*, was delayed up to eight hours to permit inclusion of reports on Hu's joint press conference with Obama and their joint statement. These two events were held up by China's media as tangible achievements of Hu's visit. *Renmin ribao* carried three color photographs of Hu's activities, the full text of Hu's speech on the White House South Lawn, and the Joint Statement, all under the headline "Hu Jintao Held Talks with US President Obama." Media reports stressed the fact that Hu was given the highest level of reception—and also the fact that business deals worth $45 billion were supposedly inked during Hu's visit. Anything that might imply US disrespect for China was censored by China's media. Questions by US reporters about human rights issues were blocked from Chinese websites.[71] In terms of the domestic politics of China's US policy, all paramount leaders since Deng have needed to demonstrate to the Chinese people—with the full assistance of US leaders—that a policy of cooperation and partnership with the United States is conducive to the growth of China's wealth, power, and status in the world. This is in contrast to the probable results of the confrontational approach favored by many in the PLA and by anti-US nationalist public opinion.

Xi Jinping, who succeeded Hu Jintao as President and CMC head in March 2013, took a further step toward restabilizing PRC-US ties by increasing the level of cooperation with the United States on the litmus-test North Korean nuclear issue. In May 2013, following a third nuclear weapons test by North Korea, the Bank of China announced it was closing the accounts of, and suspending transactions with, North Korea's Foreign Trade Bank. This was the first such move by a Chinese state-owned entity.[72] Given China's important role in North Korea's foreign trade, it was also a painful blow for Pyongyang. Beijing also agreed to receive a North Korean emissary and conveyed to him China's great displeasure with North Korea's continuing provocations.[73] When Xi and Obama met for their inaugural summit in June, they agreed to work more closely on North Korea. According to Obama's National Security Advisor Tom Donilon, the two agreed that the North Korean nuclear issue was "a key area of US-China enhanced cooperation, that North Korea had to denuclearize; that neither country would accept Korea as a nuclear-armed state, and that they would work together to deepen US-China cooperation and dialogue to achieve denuclearization. "I think we had quite a bit of alignment on the Korean issue," said Donilon.[74] These Chinese moves were in sharp contrast to China's alignment with Pyongyang during the 2010 incidents, and were, in part, attempts to stabilize the PRC-US relation by giving more substance to cooperation on an issue of great common concern.

Within the CCP debate over US policy, there were influential voices that advocated going further in cooperation with the Americans. The deputy editor of the weekly journal published by the Central Party School in Beijing, for instance, argued in early 2013 that China should countenance the eventual demise of the North Korean regime.[75] China's policy of support for North Korea as a buffer against the United States was an outdated policy that no longer served China's interests. Sooner or later, North Korea would have to open and reform its economy, the Chinese academic said. When that happened, the Pyongyang regime would be overthrown. Moreover, North Korea's leaders did not view China as a friend and caused China many problems. The North Korean regime might even one day use its nuclear weapons to threaten China. The author of these bold views did not explicitly call for broader partnership with the United States, but that was the clear implication. The advocate of this radical position apparently violated party discipline by openly stating such views, and was reportedly fired at the insistence of the MFA. Presumably, there are others within the CCP elite who share these views.

Some hardline PLA officers favored less rather than more cooperation with the United States. With the United States engaged in an effort to contain and encircle China via Washington's pivot to Asia, China should be strengthening, not undermining, its relations with North Korea, these voices said.[76] China should support and help defend North Korea, not join with the United States to undermine its security. North Korea sought nuclear weapons to protect itself from the United States, these analysts said. In the face of the US pivot, a strong and secure North Korea would strengthen China's position. US plans for Chinese economic pressure on the north could lead to the collapse of the northern regime, which could lead to unification of Korea as an American ally. The ring of US encirclement around China would be even tighter.[77]

For Xi Jinping, as for every CCP paramount leader, securing the loyalty of the PLA was a top priority. Satisfaction of budgetary demands and high-profile visits to military commands were key instruments of this effort. So too was giving careful consideration to PLA views about China's core interests in the face of US threats.[78] Balancing between the demands of the PLA for militancy and the myriad civilian interests who have a powerful stake in continued comity in relations with the United States has become a key dynamic of China's post–Cold War foreign policy.

China's Emergence as a Global Economic Power

China's Economic Rise

The new policy of opening and market-oriented reform adopted in 1978 transformed China over the next three decades into a leading world economic power. China transformed itself from an economically decrepit and impoverished albeit equalitarian country almost entirely outside international flows of merchandise, capital, and technology, into a leading global actor in each of those areas. In terms of overall size and rate of growth, volume of exports and role in international trade, global capital flows, and the acquisition and development of technology for industrial production, China has become a world leader, if not yet *the* world leader.

The growth and transformation of China's economy had a deep impact on China's foreign policies. As China emerged as the world's leading low-cost manufacturing center, its demand for fuels and raw materials of all sorts skyrocketed. Chinese firms increasingly went abroad, typically with government support, to secure needed raw materials wherever they might be found. Experience and economies of scale gained by Chinese firms in constructing in the 1980s and 1990s the solid infrastructure that underpinned China's development made highly competitive offers by those Chinese firms to construct similar infrastructure in other countries: harbors and cargo handling facilities, railways, highways and urban subways, high-rise buildings, telecommunications systems. China became a major supplier of engineering services for infrastructure around the world, involving its firms in sectors sometimes sensitive for other country's national security concerns. While some countries welcomed this investment, others banned Chinese investment in sensitive sectors and looked with suspicion on Chinese investment in sensitive projects in other countries.

Chinese consumer and capital goods became increasingly competitive with those of earlier Western industrializers. Chinese high-speed railway technology began to compete with that of Japan, for example. Oil-rich countries, many of which had high birth rates and therefore large young populations that needed to be employed, proved to be good customers for Chinese infrastructure and development projects. Many developing countries that had struggled for decades to industrialize (e.g., Brazil, Argentina, India, Egypt) began to fear that their domestic industrial base was being "hollowed out" by cheap Chinese imports.[1] Sometimes those countries were exporters of raw materials to China while importing Chinese manufactured goods, thereby producing a classic pattern of "dependency" that troubled many in the developing countries. China's trade boomed, especially with its neighbors. By the second decade of the twenty-first century, China was the leading trading partner with virtually all its neighbors. Countries neighboring China were increasingly drawn into its economic orbit.

Millions of young Chinese began to go abroad to seek fortune, in Africa, the Middle East, or Latin America, where modest capital might go some way. Countries around the world offered commercial opportunities to young, ambitious Chinese with a degree of commercial acumen and capital. In China, competition was often intense and profit margins low. Foreign markets sometimes offered greater opportunity. Adventuresome Chinese entrepreneurs often bore great hardship and risk, but sometimes their efforts succeeded and they prospered. Some writers have suggested that this sort of raw commercial drive was once possessed by young Americans or British in earlier eras when those nations opened commercial networks around the world.[2]

As China expanded its imports and exports, protection of the sea lines of communication (SLOC) over which that trade flowed gained importance. Greater emphasis was given to improving China's naval capability to safeguard China's SLOCs. The Indian Ocean, plagued by piracy in both its western and its eastern flanks and with a potentially hostile India square in its middle, was a primary area of Chinese concern in this regard. The presence of larger numbers of Chinese citizens and firms operating in unstable areas of the world also created new interests for China. Chinese nationals needed to be evacuated in times of crisis, and Chinese-owned property sometimes had to be protected.

The most abstract but also important way in which China's economic rise impacted its international relations was in terms of its ranking in the power hierarchy among states. The power capabilities of a state—what Chinese analysts call "comprehensive national power"—is, partially, a function of overall economic size, usually measured by gross domestic product; level of industrialization and technology; financial resources; and other economic factors. At the end of the Mao era, China ranked far below a dozen other countries in terms of comprehensive national power. That is now no longer the case. In 2010, China's GDP surpassed Japan in parity purchasing power (PPP) to become the number two economy.[3] While China is still far behind Japan and the European countries in many levels of industrial technology, it has clearly moved up in the global hierarchy of power. In terms of size and level of training of its diplomatic corps, supply of development assistance or subsidies for companies supporting government policies, the volume and quality of foreign information efforts, and not least, the quality and capabilities of its armed forces, China is already perhaps the second-ranking state in the world, second only to the United States.

The East Asian Model and the Re-emergence of Traditional Entrepreneurship

Economic historian Thomas Rawski suggested that the underlying origins of China's remarkable rise were shared with other East Asian economies such as those of Japan, Korea, Taiwan, and Hong Kong, and were rooted in a cultural tradition of families formulating strategies for commercial success on competitive and complex markets. Many of the developmental processes that transformed China's economy after 1978 were already clearly underway in the decades before 1937 (the year the Sino-Japan war began), Rawski found, and reemerged very quickly after 1978: swift dissemination of foreign-introduced technologies and techniques to Chinese firms, development of financial and transport systems to support competitive market transactions, inflow of foreign capital, and strong export growth based on intense specialization of labor. Rawski suggests that in many ways the fecund East Asian commercial tradition was suspended in China after 1949 but was restored after 1978, allowing these traditional strengths to re-emerge to propel China's economic rise, just as they propelled the economic rise of other East Asian late industrializers.[4]

As China opened, its economy grew into a specialized international division of labor between itself, the earlier East Asia industrializers (Japan and the "Four Tigers" of South Korea, Taiwan, Singapore, and Hong Kong), and the large, high-income, knowledge-intensive economies of North America and Western Europe. Driven in part by revolutionary new technologies of containerized movement of cargo and electronic information technologies that drastically reduced the transaction costs of cross-border operations, goods were increasingly produced in several countries. This combined the specialized comparative advantage of several countries into what came to be called trans-national production networks. Stated simply, the economies of North America and Europe innovated new products and held the patents, copyrights, and brands along with knowledge/science-intensive materials, technology, machinery, and components for assembly processes that took place in low-cost late industrializers, especially China. The large, high-income economies also functioned as consumers of the finished products of these global production networks. The earlier East Asian industrializers supplied high-technology, high-quality, and precision components and materials along with high-quality managerial and engineering skills—all essential to manufacturing the innovative and high-tech products innovated and designed in North America and Europe. The technology and knowledge-intensive inputs of North America and the precision parts and components produced in the earlier East Asian industrializers were then shipped to China, where they were assembled utilizing the advantage of China's cheap labor and low land costs. As the 1998 PRC White Paper on the Sino-US trade balance put it:

> Processing trade expansion is a major factor behind China's export growth in the 1990s. . . . In the 1990-96 period, the ratio of processing trade to overall Chinese exports rose from 41% to 55.8% and even amounted to 70% . . . of China's exports to the United States in 1996. The bulk of the sector has developed since the mid-1980s, when investors from developed countries including the United States and Japan as well as Singapore, the Republic of Korea, . . . Hong Kong and Taiwan . . . started to move their labor intensive industries or production procedures to China in a bid to cut production costs and enhance international competiveness.[5]

This international division of labor was, of course, not simple or static. There was intense competition between and within each pole of this division of labor. Regarding the PRC, its leaders feared that if China were locked into its current role as a low-cost manufacturing base for high-tech products invented and designed elsewhere, this would consign China to continuing dependence on the innovations and intellectual property rights of the advanced countries. It could also mean that China might become "stuck" in a mid-range of income, with its industries adding only modest value by final assembly to science and knowledge-intensive products and components invented in the high-income countries. If this occurred, China's leaders feared it might not reach its goal of becoming a leading world power.

A key mechanism of China's post-1978 economic rise was this: export growth produced foreign currency, which then, via regulated allocation by the state, financed the import of technology. Export promotion and technology acquisition: these are two key international mechanisms of China's economic rise. Technology was often a key component of foreign direct investment into China, and went, in turn, into the production of exports. A key international dynamic of China's post-1978 economic rise has thus been:

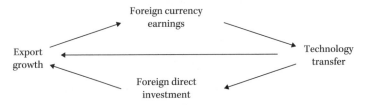

Following the example of earlier East Asian industrializing states, the PRC after 1978 adopted policies that encouraged exports. A large portion of the foreign currency generated by those exports was then taken by the state (in exchange for renminbi) and directed by an elaborate system of foreign currency allocation to import technology. Much of that new technology was then used to further strengthen China's competitive capacity to export. A powerful virtuous cycle was thereby created, all driven by the competitive zeal of Chinese entrepreneurs. There was, of course, more to China's rise than this. China's huge domestic market and the emergence of Chinese firms to supply that demand may, in fact, have been more important than export and technology import. But in terms of China's international economic relations, it is useful to focus on export growth and its link to wide-ranging technology acquisition in a virtuous cycle. This became a powerful driver of China's post-1978 rise as a leading global economic power.

The United States played an important role in the success of East Asian development, both for Japan and the Four Tigers and, later, for the PRC, by allowing exports from the East Asian economies to enter the US market on a privileged basis—as discussed earlier for Chinese textile exports during the initial stage of China's opening.

For several decades, Washington tolerated utilization of tariff and nontariff barriers that produced chronic trade imbalances that assisted the efforts of East Asian late industrializers. Washington permitted exploitation of currency rates both to encourage East Asian exports and simultaneously to limit imports. Utilization of different exchange rates for exports and imports was a key policy instrument of the East Asian model. For many years, Washington similarly acquiesced to Beijing's undervaluation of the renminbi favoring Chinese exports and limiting imports. Successive US administrations complained and threatened action unless Beijing allowed the renminbi to appreciate, but the United States never declared China a "currency manipulator," an action that would have triggered severe tariffs against Chinese goods. The United States also facilitated China's entry into the leading economic institutions—the IMT, the World Bank, and the WTO. Within the framework of these institutions, the United States helped Chinese officials gain the expertise to become effective. And in the area of higher education, the United States facilitated China's dispatch of tens and ultimately hundreds of thousands of students to US universities. There was a political quid pro quo for East Asian enjoyment of US economic beneficence: East Asian late industrializers supported the US military-political presence in East Asia.

The Economic Success of China's Opening to the Outside World

Indicators compiled by the World Bank demonstrate China's post-1978 success at economic development. Figure 25-1 illustrates the growth of China's

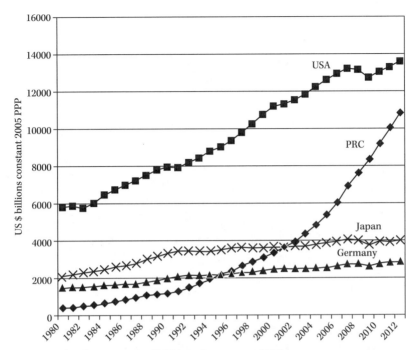

FIGURE 25-1 **China's Comparative GDP Growth, 1980–2012 (PPP)**

economy between 1980 and 2012 compared to other major economies measured in PPP. In 1980, China's GDP was roughly 9 percent of the United States',
one-third Germany's, and one-quarter of Japan's. China surpassed Germany's
PPP GDP in 1994 and Japan's in 2001. By 2012, China's economy was 79 percent the size of the US economy, 2.7 times as large as Japan's, and 3.8 times as
large as Germany's.[6] China's rate of growth remains much higher than that of
the United States, and China is expected to surpass the United States as the
world's largest economy sometime in the 2020s.

Another useful comparison is between China and other large and populous, largely agricultural, and late industrializing countries: India, Brazil,
Mexico, Indonesia, and Egypt. These countries share similar problems; modernizing such sprawling agricultural economies is an extremely difficult task.
As Figure 25-2 shows, by this measure, too, China's post-1980 performance
has been quite good. In 1980, China's economy was only 83 percent that of
India, 56 percent that of Brazil, and 73 percent that of Mexico. By 2012, it was
2.6 times that of India, 5.3 times as large as Brazil's, and seven times the size
of Mexico's economy. Indonesia and Egypt fell even further behind China. In
1980, Egypt's economy was about a quarter the size of China's. By 2012 it was
only 4.3 percent the size of China's economy.[7]

China's post-1978 development lifted hundreds of millions of Chinese out
of poverty. This may prove to be one of the most important events of the late
twentieth and early twenty-first centuries. A vast region once characterized

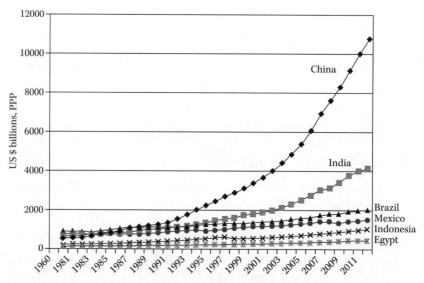

FIGURE 25-2 **China's GDP Growth Compared to Other Large Developing Countries**

by extensive and dire poverty raised itself to a quite comfortable mid-level of development. According to the World Bank, China's per capita GDP in 2012 was an "upper middle" level equivalent to US$6,188. That was up from US$3,414 in 2008—an increase of 81 percent in four years. China has replicated the developmental success of earlier East Asian modernizers, South Korea, Taiwan, and Japan. As noted earlier, it is likely that the aggregate size of China's economy will surpass that of the United States in the not too distant future. Estimates of when that will happen depend on one's assumptions. Extrapolating from recent PRC growth trends, and assuming an only somewhat more modest rate of growth, China should reach within a decade or so a standard of living comparable to that of South Korea or Japan circa 1998. Assuming a per capita GDP equivalent to South Korea's and multiplying by China's larger population produces a PRC GDP a third larger than that of the United States. Assuming a per capita GDP half the level of Japan in 1998 and accounting for China's huge population yields a GDP more than double that of the United States. Chicago University professor John Mearsheimer used these figures to issue a warning for Americans to adopt a policy of deliberately constraining the growth of Chinese power. Such an overwhelming economic position was likely to produce a drive for hegemony in Asia, Mearsheimer warned.[8] China would still be far poorer than the United States on a per capita basis. But it is principally aggregate capacity that determines a state's ability to fund foreign activities or field military forces. A Chinese economy larger than that of the United States would mean, other things being equal, that China could exceed the United States in terms of creating and deploying the normal instruments of state power.

Trade and Foreign Investment

China's re-emergence as a global trading power was one dimension of its post-1978 rise. It is useful to remember that China was historically one of the world's leading trading countries. It was really the thirty-year-long Mao era that was the exception to this historic norm. Prior to the revolution in oceanic maritime technology in the fifteenth century, the caravan trade between China and the lands to its west, often called "the Silk Road," was a key axis of the world economy.[9] The expensive luxury produce of China—silks, brocades, lacquer, and ceramic ware—were in high demand among the wealthy in Europe, Arabia, Turkey, and Persia. Large-scale factory and cottage production emerged in China to supply that demand.[10] In ancient times, the Roman demand for Chinese silk was so great that the outflow of silver to pay for those imports injured the Roman economy.[11] With the revolution in maritime technology and the rise of the oceans as highways of global commerce, craving for access to China's valued products remained strong. A dynamic maritime trading system evolved in early modern East Asia involving Dutch, Spanish, Japanese, Indian, Arab, and Chinese merchants. Revolutionary new European maritime technology combined with traditional East Asian trade patterns to produce a powerful symbiosis. Acquiring and marketing abroad the produce of China was a core element of this commercial system.[12] Indeed, it was the strong Western demand for China's products that led to the clash between China and the West in the 1840s and 1850s. By the early nineteenth century, a major trade imbalance had emerged: foreign demand for China's products was strong, but China's demand for foreign goods was weak. Resolution of this imbalance in Britain's advantage was a major cause of the first Opium War; British merchants discovered a strong Chinese demand for opium. Beyond the narrow question of trade imbalance was the prospect of access to broader trade opportunities if China were "opened" to trade. Ardent Western desire to gain access to China's markets was the major determinant of the Anglo-French onslaught to open China in the Century of National Humiliation.

China's 1978 opening led to the resumption of trends apparent in China's economy early in the twentieth century—before the liquidation of Chinese capitalism in 1949. Rawski concluded in his authoritative study of China's pre-1937 economic history:

> The sustained expansion of output per head had become a regular feature of Chinese economic life in the early decades of the [twentieth] century. This fact, with its momentous economic and social implications, represents the principal finding of my study . . . the mechanism of prewar [pre-1937] development can be specified in considerable detail. Economic growth was rooted in expansion of foreign trade. New

overseas demands for agricultural exports contributed to the acceleration of a trend toward commercial farming that predated the [1842 opening] ... The penetration of foreign goods created opportunities for introducing new products, materials, and processes into China's economy. Innovations in money and finance and in transport and communication magnified the impact of external trade on domestic economic life. Measures initially intended to smooth the path of foreign trade gradually came to affect large segments of China's economy. The impact of reduced transport costs, improved access to credit, popularization of banknotes, and expanded information flows was not limited to localities with long histories of active involvement in long-distance trade, but extended to communities that had formerly remained outside the ambit of regional and national markets.[13]

Mao and the CCP's Marxist-Leninist ideology viewed China's trade with the West as a form of exploitation and imperialist domination. During the Mao decades, China's foreign trade withered. As noted in the earlier chapter on China's opening, trade began to revive and then grew rapidly in tandem with the opening and marketization of China's economy. Perhaps the best measure of China's growing prowess as a global exporter is the value of China's exports as a percentage of global merchandise trade compared to those of other major exporters. In 1978, the PRC accounted for considerably less than 1 percent of global trade. The United States then accounted for 12.5 percent and Japan 6.7 percent of global trade. Within thirty years, China's share had risen to 8.9 percent compared to the United States' 11.6 percent and Japan's 4.6 percent. If Hong Kong's trade is added to China's (Beijing is sovereign over Hong Kong in spite of the fact that Hong Kong is a separate customs territory), China's share rises to 11.56, virtually identical with the United States. China's rise as a leading trade power has been very impressive. Figure 25-3 shows the total value of exports of China and other leading export powers.

In terms of China's export growth, there have been two inflection points since 1978, illustrated in Figure 25-3: the "second opening" launched by Deng Xiaoping in 1992, and entry into the WTO in late 2001. China has emerged within a period of twenty years as a leading exporter, second only to the United States in 2011, according to World Bank statistics. In 2004, China surpassed Japan as an exporter and in 2010 it surpassed Germany. By 2011, the United States still ranked as the world's leading exporter, according to World Bank data bank indicators, but China was closing rapidly and will almost certainly soon surpass it.

The PRC's discovery of the efficacious role of export promotion took place in a distinctive East Asian context and cannot be adequately understood outside that context. As far back as the 1870s, Japan, a small, resource-poor country, pioneered a model of state encouragement of exports as a way of paying

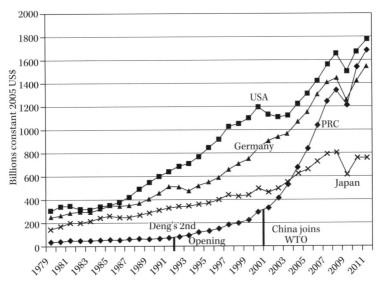

FIGURE 25-3 **Total Exports of Goods and Services**

for imports necessary for industrialization: machinery and equipment, technology and associated fees, fuels and mineral ores, components, and food for a growing urban population.[14] After 1945, post-imperial Japan redesigned this basic model on the premise of alliance with the United States.[15] Again Japan's government encouraged expansion of exports, secured control of the foreign currency gained thereby, and used it for state-guided but market-based import of items necessary for further development as determined by a technocratic and fairly autonomous state planning agency. This model again proved effective, and by the early 1960s Japan was rapidly catching up with leading European nations in terms of standard of living and levels of industrialization. Then, circa 1961, South Korea and Taiwan both began emulating Japan's path of state-guided export and import growth. Hong Kong and Singapore also participated enthusiastically in the emerging East Asian economic system, albeit with a more muted state role.

During the 1960s and 1970s, this approach, premised on state-guided but market-based development, was most definitely not the mainstream of global development efforts. Far more popular and widespread were either US-endorsed laissez-faire approaches of comparative advantage, or dependency theory, which called for developing countries to disengage or carefully limit engagement with the global economy dominated by the advanced capitalist countries. Substitution of domestic manufactures for imported goods whenever possible—import substitution—was a key component of the anti-"dependency" approach. By the late 1970s, however, people around the world, especially in China, were taking note of the impressive development of Japan and the Four Tigers.[16] Chinese leaders may not have set out to replicate the East Asian developmental state—as Japan, South Korea, and Taiwan came to be called. But that was the cumulative result of the PRC's policies and of the East Asian neighborhood in which east coast China was situated.

China's opening accelerated the process of East Asian economic integration. Huge amounts of capital from Hong Kong, Southeast Asia, Japan, Taiwan, and South Korea flowed into the PRC to produce goods for export to global markets. Circa 1978, China had abundant labor from its large and underemployed agricultural workforce. These workers were quite willing to work for wages far below those paid in Hong Kong, Taiwan, Japan, or South Korea—let alone the levels paid in North America or Europe. The PRC also had abundant land, mostly in still agricultural areas near cities and transportation links. This land could be taken by the PRC's authoritarian state for nominal compensation and made available to entrepreneurs willing to set up factories producing goods for export. Demands for costly environmental protection measures, which people and governments in Japan, South Korea, Taiwan, and Hong Kong were increasingly demanding, could also be waived by PRC governments. By thus shifting labor- and land-intensive production operations from high-cost countries to China, manufacturers could cut costs significantly. Containerized movement of freight and the electronic transmission of information also made transnational production of a single good increasingly feasible. The development of East Asian trans-national production networks, combining the specialized comparative advantage of several countries in the production of a single product, cut costs significantly. When global price competition was intense, this proved to be a very attractive option. China was on its way to becoming the global low-cost manufacturing base.

The most common understanding of the strong flow of foreign investment into China in the decades after 1978 is in terms of the competitive advantages offered to foreign firms by low land and labor costs in China. Non-PRC firms seeking profits on intensely competitive global markets invested in China as a way to cut costs. Huang Yasheng has supplemented this foreign firm "supply-driven" explanation with a Chinese firm "demand-driven" one.[17] According to Huang, because privately owned enterprises had difficulty obtaining capital from China's banks, which lent overwhelmingly to state-owned firms, private entrepreneurs turned for capital to other sources, including foreign ones. Linking up with foreign firms was a way for ambitious private Chinese entrepreneurs to procure the capital they needed to grow their enterprises.

Foreign investment into China was linked to China's emergence as an export power. Foreign direct investment (FDI) flowed into post-1978 China in huge amounts, as illustrated by Figure 25-4. Only the United States exceeded China as a destination for global FDI. If the Hong Kong Special Administrative Region is combined for this purpose into the PRC, China's

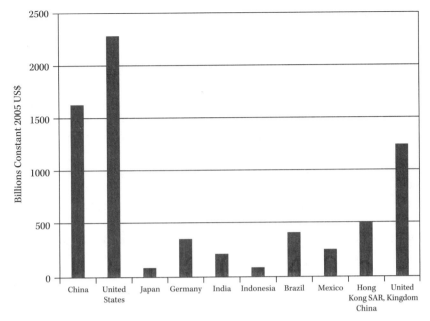

FIGURE 25-4   **FDI Cumulative Net Inflows, 2002–2012**

combined FDI almost equals that of the United States. FDI did not constitute a large percentage of China's GDP, but that relatively small percentage contributed powerfully in several main ways. FDI often transferred to China products, production techniques and technologies not previously produced or used there. Entrepreneurial Chinese businessmen learned from these foreign enterprises, frequently by working for them for a period of time and then copying or supplying the foreign enterprises. In this way, foreign-introduced modern technologies and methods spread widely across the non-foreign-invested sectors of China's economy.

Shenzhen quickly emerged as a favorite venue for FDI. The proximity of Shenzhen to Hong Kong—and to the rest of East Asia—made it fairly easy for business people to commute to factories in China. Cultural similarities among the East Asian countries, as well as linguistic and familial commonalities among the PRC, Taiwan, Hong Kong, and Singapore and the ethnic Chinese diaspora in other Southeast Asian countries, what came to be called "greater China," also encouraged investment. The strong incentives supplied by PRC governments for foreign investment (cheap land, low taxes, priority utility hook-ups, etc.) made it expedient for PRC entrepreneurs to figure out ways to channel their investment through Hong Kong. Most of these special incentives would be outlawed and phased out by China's entry into the World Trade Organization (WTO) in 2001, although actual enforcement of these laws remained problematic. Such incentives provided a powerful magnet for investment. Even after WTO accession, the stronger legal protections afforded contracts and private property under Hong Kong's British-derived law, compared to those provided under PRC law, made it attractive for PRC entrepreneurs to base their firm in Hong Kong and invest via Hong Kong. As firms, foreign and Chinese, began clustering where they could most easily obtain the human and physical resources they needed, the benefits of geographic clusters began to form. Many geographic clusters emerged to become a global manufacturing base for specific goods: overhead lighting, shoes and luggage, wicker and rattan furniture, sporting gear, disk drives, industrial fasteners, and so on. China was on its way to becoming the world's premier low-cost manufacturing base—driven in large part by a massive inflow of modern technology supplied by foreign firms seeking low costs.

The composition of China's trade changed as it industrialized and globalized after 1978. China developed a voracious demand for foreign machinery and equipment. Purchases of foreign machinery and transport equipment increased in value 107 times between 1980 and 2010, with that category of goods increasing from 26 percent to 39 percent of total imports.[18] Another major change in imports was a rapid rise in petroleum imports. Petroleum imports stood at $203 million in 1980. By 2010, they had skyrocketed to over $189 billion. As noted earlier, in 1993 China became a net importer of petroleum. China's import of mineral ores and base metals also grew rapidly to feed its metallurgical industries. Its rapidly growing demand for fuels and ores meant that China's foreign policies increasingly scoured the world for access to those vital inputs to its continued development.[19] In terms of exports, the starkest shift between 1980 and 2010 was a fall in the share constituted by agricultural goods and a rise in the share of manufactured goods. In 1980, just half of China's exports were manufactured goods. By 2010, 95 percent were. Agricultural exports fell as a percent of total exports from 17 percent to 3 percent, even though the absolute value of agricultural exports increased over fourteen times. A major task of China's diplomacy has been to open wide foreign markets for Chinese goods.[20]

China's WTO Decision

China's entry into the World Trade Organization (WTO) in November 2001 had wide-ranging implications. Established in 1995 to replace an older international organization, the General Agreement on Tariffs and Trade (GATT), which dated to 1947, the WTO represented a major step toward a more open, freer, and more market-based international trade system. While distinguishing between developing and developed countries and permitting more protectionist measures by the former, WTO lowered tariffs, restricted state intervention in markets, and banned quotas and a number of other nontariff barriers to trade. China's decision to join this system had a deep impact on its role in global trade. As shown earlier in Figure 25-3, China's exports rose rapidly after WTO entry, expanding by a yearly average of 16 percent in the decade before WTO entry compared with average growth of 19 percent in the decade after entry. Moreover, the post-entry decade included the precipitous decline in 2009 when the global recession hit. If that year is excluded, the post-entry annual export growth rate was nearly 22 percent higher than in the pre-entry decade.[21] Factors other than WTO entry were involved in this growth, but it was one important factor.

There was strong opposition within China's CCP elite to both GATT and WTO entry. According to Li Lanqing, who was the PBSC member from 1993 to 2003 in charge of overseeing the WTO negotiations, in December 1982 the Ministry of Foreign Economic Relations and Trade (MOFERT) recommended that China rejoin GATT.[22] China's top leaders endorsed the MOFERT proposal, stipulating that China would join as a "developing country" with terms to be negotiated. It took over two years for China to make a formal request for re-entry into GATT. That came only in July 1986. Negotiations then began and would continue for thirteen years.

The question of GATT and WTO entry was closely linked to the market-based reform of China's State Owned Enterprises (SOEs). The industrial ministries, already under growing competitive pressure from China's burgeoning private sector and foreign-invested joint ventures, were fearful of increased competition by foreign firms, especially large multinational firms with strong capital resources, prestige brands, and modern technology. China's industrial ministries and the enterprises they controlled had dominated the pre-1978 economy and were still immensely powerful in the 1980s. As noted in an earlier chapter, China's post-1978 opening and reform process had avoided direct challenges to these powerful vested interests. Now GATT/WTO entry presented a strong challenge to them, perhaps threatening their economic survival. Opponents of GATT/WTO entry advanced a number of arguments. Socialist ideology was one: state-owned firms were "socialist," or at least a "more advanced form of socialism" than privately owned firms, let alone foreign privately owned firms. Allowing foreign multinationals free access to China's markets would allow those firms to dominate, possibly even monopolize those markets by eliminating China's state-owned enterprises—who were still China's main suppliers of many heavy industrial goods. If that happened, opponents of WTO entry warned, foreigners would then be in a position to return China to the painful pre-1949 status of a "neo-colony," or so said opponents of GATT/WTO entry. Li Peng, who became premier in March 1988 and who had a long association with China's big industrial ministries and enterprises, was a key skeptic of WTO entry.[23]

A debate between economic nationalists and economic liberals developed in the 1990s as foreign investment by large multinational corporations (MNC) began to flood into China.[24] Between 1992 and 1996, some two hundred *Fortune* 500 MNCs began operations in China, setting up 45,000 factories, offices, and branches. As this happened, SOEs that had traditionally dominated China's markets were put under intense competitive pressures, while foreign MNCs increasingly dominated China' domestic markets. High-quality foreign brand goods proved very attractive to Chinese consumers. Nationalists and liberals had very different views of this process. Nationalists argued that foreign ownership served foreign profit-seeking rather than China's development. Foreign MNCs would never transfer advanced technology to China, nationalists said, but only second-class or even obsolete technology. Reliance on foreign technology acquired via FDI would also stifle China's domestic technological innovation. Together, these factors would consign China to a position of technological inferiority. Reliance on FDI also meant that trademarks would be foreign-owned, resulting in most of the value added going to the foreign firm rather than remaining in China. Different locales also competed with each other to shower favors on MNCs, while corrupt local officials were too frequently willing to betray China's developmental interests for personal gain, said the nationalists. The result was that the flood of FDI was locking China into a subordinate position in the emerging international division of labor. A far better course, economic nationalists argued, would be to follow the path of Japan and South Korea. Those countries had sharply limited FDI during the early stages of industrialization, relying instead on borrowing money from foreign lenders to purchase technology under state guidance, with that advanced technology being integrated into domestic industrial systems. China's SOE's would be the leaders in that process, nationalists asserted.

China's economic liberals argued that FDI was the quickest and most effective way to industrialize China. FDI was producing new factories, products and processes, jobs, exports, technology transfer, foreign currency, and government revenue. It was doing this more rapidly and effectively than China's SOEs, which simply had to become competitive and stop being dependent on government support. Allowing foreign MNCs to make a profit was the only way to encourage them to undertake operations in China. Otherwise they would go to some other country. The current domination of Chinese markets by foreign MNCs, and China's dependency on MNCs for technology development, were temporary situations. They would disappear as Chinese firms developed and became competitive. Moreover, much of the FDI coming into China was actually Chinese—from Hong Kong, Taiwan, or Chinese firms in Southeast Asia, or even PRC firms. An estimated 25 percent of investment from Hong Kong was actually from PRC entities routing capital on a "round trip" via Hong Kong to secure advantageous treatment as "foreign investment."

The modest results of efforts in the mid-1990s to vitalize SOE operations via reform of the banking system strengthened the linkage between WTO entry and SOE performance. China's top leaders recognized that the sluggish and inefficient operations of China's SOEs constituted a major drag on development and a major obstacle to China's becoming a leading global economy. In 1994–1995, a major reform of the banking and finance systems was launched to address the SOE problem. With the exception of three specifically designated policy and development banks, plus the People's Bank of China, which served as the central bank, all banks were turned into independent, profit-seeking entities responsible for profits and losses and lending money on a purely commercial basis. The intent was to compel SOEs to increase efficiency and thus generate profits to repay their bank loans. Banks were to choose lending projects with the greatest prospect for repayment. In fact, these reforms had only limited effects. SOEs continued to use their connections to local political elites to secure loans that often went unrepaid. The specter of closure of local factories and layoffs of workers frequently prompted local governments to tell banks to do whatever was necessary to keep enterprises running. As the limited results of banking reform became apparent by the late 1990s, economic liberals favoring WTO entry gained an additional powerful argument.

Both economic nationalist and liberal positions attracted support across all segments of China's society. The outcome of the protracted debate was essentially a compromise between the two positions. China would accede to WTO under terms that facilitated the flow of FDI into China. But it would also secure lengthy deadlines for market-opening measures and would marry them with indigenous innovation policies designed to address many of the concerns of economic nationalists.

From the standpoint of pro-reform leaders General Secretary and paramount leader Jiang Zemin and Vice Premier Zhu Rongji, the very competitive pressures that so threatened China's SOEs were exactly what made WTO entry a virtue. The SOEs organized under the state ministries were mammothly inefficient and inflexible, and they made chronic and huge claims on the state's resources, preventing those resources from going to other areas that would produce more growth, jobs, and wealth. Several attempts to address the SOE problem had been made in the 1980s and 1990s, but with little effect. China's reform-minded leaders realized that unless the industrial SOEs could become more efficient, dynamic, and profitable, the commanding heights of China's economy would remain a major obstacle to China emerging as a globally competitive economy. Opening China's domestic markets to foreign imports would finally force the SOEs to become more efficient—to swim or to sink.[25]

International negotiations throughout the 1990s over China's GATT or (after 1995) WTO access were complex and difficult. Initially, China was not familiar with GATT mechanisms and had much to learn. Beijing did not initially understand, for example, that re-entry into GATT would require substantial negotiations with each of that organization's major members.[26] Talks with the United States were the most difficult, according to Li Lanqing. Li describes US Trade Representative Carla Hills as a "tough talking lady" "who often wielded a stick and threatened us with sanctions at the talks."[27] During a 1991 discussion over China's protection of US intellectual property rights (IPR), for instance, Hills "not only lacked the good faith for cooperation but made an arbitrary attack on us [China], even accusing China of being an intellectual thief." Hills had not found satisfactory a promise by China to cooperate with other countries to ensure effective IPR protection. PRC representative vice premier Wu Yi, Hills' counterpart and incidentally also female, rebutted Hills' charges that China was a "thief" by recounting the alleged behavior of US forces during the 1898 eight-power intervention against the Boxers. US forces had burned, killed, and looted, behavior that was indeed that of a robber, Wu Yi stated.[28] In another negotiating session, Hills demanded monetary compensation for chemicals and pharmaceuticals produced by Chinese firms in violation of US patents. Li Lanqing dismissed the demand as "absurd," asking who could possibly know how many drugs of a particular type Chinese firms had produced. Moreover, and more interestingly, Li said that any Chinese who agreed to pay compensation to the United States "would be removed from office and punished."[29]

Li Lanqing also had to deal with Chinese resistance to WTO membership. Addressing the matter of strong opposition from "industrial departments" that feared competition and insisted that China be allowed to continue protectionist measures as a "developing country," Li told his subordinate negotiator (Long Yongtu was China's key negotiator): "Just bring these people to the negotiating table and let them speak their minds. Don't talk on their behalf. In this way, they can hear what the foreigners have to say, and the foreigners can also hear out our industrialists."[30] According to Li, this method was effective. Gradually, the "departments" adopted "a more overall perspective" less focused on protecting their narrow interests.

The strong development of market-based Chinese enterprises during the 1980s and 1990s also prepared the way for slashing tariffs, easing out quotas and bans, and otherwise opening up China's markets in preparation for WTO entry, according to Li Lanqing. China's technological level also advanced considerably. This was an especially important factor preparing the way for China's 1999 WTO proposal, again according to Li. Dynamic market-based Chinese enterprises had emerged and held the potential of moving rapidly to meet demand if China's SOE's collapsed under the competitive pressure associated with WTO accession. There was also growing recognition that insistence on national production could leave the commanding heights of China's economy burdened with poor quality and high costs. Li Lanqing cites the example of negotiations with Volkswagen circa 1978 regarding establishment of a car factory in

Shanghai. The Chinese side had insisted that maximum "domestic content" be used by the plant. Volkswagen had resisted, but finally agreed to China's demand. But the parts supplied by Chinese producers simply did not meet German standards of quality or safety. For example, the steel for the car chassis provided by China's most advanced steel rolling mill at the time was too thin to be used. The overall result was a vehicle far below the quality standards of Volkswagens produced in other countries. It gradually dawned on China's leaders that such an approach would prevent China from becoming a world leading competitor. They eventually recognized automobiles as a key leading industry, and decided that for China to succeed in that industry, it would have to be able to compete on global markets. But in tandem with the decision to subject China's auto producers to strong foreign competition, China's leaders also adopted what Li Lanqing calls China's "first industrial policy" to upgrade the "techniques" of Chinese suppliers of auto parts and components.[31]

In early 1999, Jiang Zemin decided that conditions were right for a bold push involving substantial concessions to long-standing US demands, to break the WTO deadlock with the United States. In March 1998, Zhu Rongji replaced Li Peng as premier. As significantly, Li Lanqing, with many years' experience handling trade negotiations with the United States and strongly in favor of WTO membership, was appointed executive vice premier. Relations with the United States had also improved after the difficult 1989–1996 period. In October 1997, Jiang had made a successful state visit to the United States. Vice President Al Gore had visited China in March 1998, and President Clinton was scheduled to visit in June.[32] Jiang placed great stress on stabilizing China's relation with the United States, aligning the two countries more closely in order to ensure China's stable development, and he saw WTO accession as a major way of achieving this.[33] Among other things, WTO membership would end the annual review of China's MFN status by the US Congress, a review that provided a regular venue for high-profile airing of all sorts of grievances against China.

Late in 1998 or early in 1999, Jiang Zemin endorsed a package of major concessions to be delivered to the United States by Premier Zhu Rongji.[34] In a number of these areas, China had previously steadfastly refused to compromise. China's leaders, or at least Jiang, Zhu, and Li Lanqing, expected that this package of concessions would be welcomed by the United States and would open the way to an accession agreement. Zhu was scheduled to visit Washington to deliver China's bold proposal and lobby for a final deal on WTO accession. Then, on March 24, 1999, NATO began a bombing campaign against Yugoslavia because of its ethnic cleansing of Muslims in the Kosovo region. The day after the NATO bombing campaign began, the Politburo met to deliberate whether Zhu should proceed as scheduled with his visit to Washington to deliver the package of concessions.

There was strong opposition to Zhu's proceeding as planned. Li Peng represented the views of many on the Politburo when he spoke out against a visit by Zhu:

> The Kosovo incident is bound to result in new change in the world's strategic set-up. I maintain that it is inappropriate for comrade Zhu Rongji to go to the United States at this time. [His visit] should be deferred. I have always maintained that the United States bullies the faint hearted but fears the stouthearted. Going now will reveal our hand. Others will see our bottom line, leaving us with hardly any room for maneuver.[35]

According to Zong Hairen, the center conducted a survey of the views of leading cadres in relevant "departments." Nearly two-thirds of those surveyed felt that Zhu's visit should be postponed. The decision to go ahead with the visit was made by Jiang Zemin, supported by Hu Jintao, Li Lanqing, and Zeng Qinghong, Politburo member and head of the powerful CCP Organizational Department. Jiang told the Politburo:

> Everything you comrades have said is quite to the point.... [Yet] I maintain that, proceeding from the overall situation of our national interests, the visit should proceed as planned.... We must continue to deal with the United States, and there is no need to arouse various misunderstandings on the part of the West, and especially the United States, by terminating this visit ... I believe that the Clinton administration is looking forward with eager expectancy to Comrade Rongji's visit ... On the WTO issue, we have already made substantial concessions ... In sum, there will be no change of plan for this visit to the United States ... we should continue to put our efforts into building a constructive strategic partnership between China and the United States.[36]

Clinton had sent Jiang letters early in 1999 that led him to expect a US willingness to bring the WTO issue to closure. Zhu arrived in the United States on April 6—thirteen days into the NATO bombing campaign against Serbia. Zhu found that the stance of the Clinton administration was not as positive as he had expected. A number of issues had erupted to sour the US mood on China and cause Clinton to shift with the pressure. A month before Zhu arrived in the United States, an ethnic Chinese immigrant scientist employed at the nuclear weapons research facility at Los Alamos, New Mexico, was fired from his job, and information was leaked to the media asserting that he had been involved in spying for China. In the Senate, a special committee set up the previous year was investigating alleged Chinese financial involvement in the 1996 US presidential election. In the House of Representatives, movement was underway to set up a select committee to investigate Chinese espionage activities in the United States in the area of military technologies. There was also strong opposition from US labor organizations to China's WTO accession. Labor unions, a core constituency of Clinton's Democratic Party, believed (rightly) that accession would lead to greatly expanded trade and the loss of jobs in the United States.[37] According to Zong Hairen, US trade negotiators also responded to Zhu's package of Chinese concessions by escalating US demands.[38]

Zhu's difficulties were deepened by US disclosure during his visit of the long list of concessions China was prepared to make. While Zhu was still in Washington, the office of the US Trade Representative released several quite detailed documents outlining China's proposed market opening measures. This was done without prior consultation with Zhu, much less his consent. Zhu was angered by the US move, telling his team the move was "a most arrogant and high-handed imposition, a lack of good faith. Outrageous."[39] Disappointed with the US response and angry at US unilateral disclosures, Zhu returned home without an agreement.

In China, criticism of Zhu was intense. Zong Hairen compares the impact of the US disclosure of what was, after all, China's negotiating position as "as strong as a force-six earthquake." CCP elder Song Ping (one of Li Peng's early mentors) called Zhu's proposed agreement a new "Twenty-one Demands" and warned that whoever signed that document would be "condemned through the ages as a traitor."[40] (The Twenty-one Demands were presented by Japan to China in 1915 and would have, if implemented, transformed China into a vassal state.) Li Peng reiterated his belief that "This diplomacy of mollification will not bring any good results. Make no mistake: As long as there are two different systems in the world [i.e., capitalism and socialism] there cannot be friends. One must not regard enemies as friends and blur things up."[41] Jiang Zemin distanced himself from Zhu's proposed deal. Anti-US sentiment flared further on May 8, when US warplanes engaged in the Kosovo campaign bombed China's embassy in Belgrade, producing angry Chinese mobs besieging US diplomatic missions. By mid-1999, tensions in the bilateral relation threatened to swamp WTO agreement.

Fortunately, the US side shifted during the summer and fall. The US business community recognized the significance of Beijing's proposal and began to mobilize. US pragmatic common sense began to reassert itself, and opinion gradually shifted back in favor of cooperation with China. Clinton shifted with public opinion and lobbying pressure. In fall 1999, negotiations resumed. They were intense but fruitful. In November 1999, agreement was reached; China was to become a member of the WTO. When the terrorist attacks on the United States occurred on September 11, 2001, Jiang Zemin telephoned President George W. Bush to request that China's WTO accession not be disrupted by the new US focus on counterterrorism. The United

States agreed. On December 11, 2001, the PRC entered the WTO as its 143rd member.

Foreign Investment and Technological Advance

Achieving a high level of science and technology (S&T) is essential if the PRC economy is to become a world leader. It is essential if China is to escape the middle-income trap in which it would remain an assembler of low-value-added, labor-intensive goods. It is also essential if the PLA is to become truly potent. PRC leaders, except perhaps for extreme Maoists during the Cultural Revolution, have consistently recognized this. This section will briefly survey China's S&T efforts touching on its relations with other states. Because China's technological level lagged behind both the advanced capitalist countries and the USSR in most areas, PRC technology development efforts focused on catching up with the technological levels of the leading countries. Two major international aspects of this quest were: 1) acquiring technologies available in advanced countries but not in China, indigenizing those technologies by mastering the scientific processes underlying them, and then copying or reverse-engineering them for production in China; and 2) achieving an indigenous capacity for scientific research equivalent to those of leading world scientific powers. These two thrusts continued throughout the pre and post-1978 periods, although they were pursued in very different ways in the two periods.

As part of the adoption of the Soviet model in the early 1950s, China copied the Soviet S&T system. This was a highly centralized and bureaucratically controlled system with research priorities determined by central authorities and meshed, at least in theory, to economic development objectives outlined in the Five Year Plans. A large number of research institutes were set up specializing in various areas of science and technology and funded by the state budget. Research projects and directions were decided on by the State Science and Technology Commission (SSTC), a body set up in 1958 to coordinate science and technology efforts and which continued to function until 1998, when it was replaced by a Ministry of Science and Technology (MOST). Research institutes reported upward via their organizational channels, and had little contact with the factories that might actually use the technologies they were developing. Because of lines of bureaucratic administration, research institutes also had very little interaction with other institutes working in the same field. Bureaucratic loyalties and restrictions were strong. Institute directors would often hoard resources, including personnel and facilities. Redundancy of efforts and facilities and misallocation of personnel were rife. Decisions by the SSTC regarding allocation of funds had more to do with working out a balance between politically influential organizations than with potential scientific or economic benefit. Heads of institutes were not scientists or engineers, but bureaucratic administrators. Yet they were responsible for hiring personnel, promotion, and assignment to various projects. Success or failure in innovation or discovery had little impact on an institute's budget. Employment at an institute was typically for life. There was little movement between institutes or across bureaucratic lines.[42]

The adoption of the Soviet S&T model in the 1950s, even with all its defects, contributed to China's technological advance, because it mobilized resources, including inputs from the Soviet camp, and focused them on key projects. We will never know what that model might have yielded in China had it not been devastated by the anti-intellectual policies of the Anti-Rightist Campaign, the Great Leap Forward, and the Cultural Revolution. Be that as it may, it is clear that the Soviet S&T model also imposed on China many of the same endemic weaknesses that ultimately contributed to the collapse of the Soviet Union. Outside of a few areas of military research that were privileged with the best personnel, abundant resources, and protection from political campaigns, the pace of innovation and scientific discovery was slow.[43] There were weak incentives for the successful industrial application of technologies. The system was wasteful, squandering huge amounts of money without much result. Areas of real potential were starved of resources so that unproductive institutes could continue to function. The advance of China to a world-leading S&T power required discarding the Soviet S&T model.

Increased familiarity with S&T standards of the advanced capitalist countries, and intense debate within the CCP elite and among the leaders of China's S&T sector, led to growing awareness of the weaknesses of China's pre-opening, Soviet-derived S&T system. Market-oriented reform of the S&T system began in 1985. Except for institutes involved in basic research, military areas, or public goods (environment, public health, medicine) which could not reasonably be expected to become self-financing, research institutes were to become self-supporting. Direct government funding was phased out, as was top-down designation of research direction. Institutes were to work directly with industrial enterprises on a contract basis to provide particular technological services for a fee. "Fee for service" via market contracts was to replace government budgetary allocations. Institute directors were to be younger people with science or engineering backgrounds, and were given far greater leeway in hiring, promotion, and approval of research activities. Individual remuneration and status were tied far more closely to individual scientific achievement. Institutes undertaking basic research were to compete for grants from a newly established National Science Foundation. Finally, with this redesigned, decentralized, and marketized S&T system, government funding was increased substantially.[44] Marketization and decentralization of S&T efforts were not intended as a cost-cutting measure. State funding for S&T efforts increased substantially. It is far too early to say that China's S&T efforts will succeed in catapulting it into the ranks of the world's leading technology powers, but it seems safe to conclude that the PRC has at least partially unburdened itself of the centralized bureaucratic system that helped drag down the USSR.

Foreign investment was a major mechanism for technology acquisition in post-1978 China, a mechanism that had barely functioned in China after the break with the Soviet Union in 1960. The "whole factory" approach, favored from the 1950s through the 1970s, had proved both expensive and difficult for Chinese to maintain and use at full capacity.[45] Indeed, huge imports of turnkey projects during the Great Leap Outward during the 1977–1978 interregnum nearly bankrupted the country. In 1980, the center issued guidelines for the acquisition of foreign technology. Factories should be renovated by import of select key technologies rather than by the import of whole factories. Acquisition of production technology was to be preferred over import of the finished goods; the objective was to encourage China's industrialization rather than becoming a consumer of foreign finished consumer goods. In the first decades of opening and reform, foreign investment often entailed the transfer of new products, processes, materials, machinery and equipment, and technologies to China. Overall, Chinese entities were quite willing to pay for and/or license foreign technologies.

Joint ventures (JVs) with a Chinese and a foreign party both owning equity in a business quickly became a favored form of technology transfer. Foreign investment was often synonymous with technological upgrading. In a typical JV during the first two decades of opening, the Chinese partner supplied land, labor, some resources, and components, plus official interface with the Chinese bureaucracy. The foreign party supplied product design and brands, channels to global markets, and modern technologies, both embedded within machinery, equipment, and processes and "unembedded," that is, in the minds of well-trained engineers. Chinese engineers were increasingly tempted to leave secure but low-paying jobs at state-owned enterprises for far better-paid, if riskier, positions in the private or JV sector.

As noted in the earlier discussion of the debate over WTO entry between economic nationalists and liberals, many Chinese believed that the massive inflow of foreign investment was locking China into a mid-level of S&T that would consign it to a subordinate and dependent position in the emerging international division of labor. One manifestation of this subordination was the frequent reluctance of foreign firms to transfer the most advanced technology to China. There were two main, interrelated reasons for this. First, protection of intellectual property rights was weak in China. Valuable proprietary technology transferred to China was very likely to be copied by Chinese competitors, sometimes even down to the trademarked brand name on the product. This was part of the Chinese emulation discussed above.[46] In 1984, China passed a patent law which was elaborated and strengthened in 1992, 2004, and 2009. That law provided, on paper in any case, for fairly strong protection of patents and other intellectual property rights.[47] Second, once a technology was stolen and copied, the foreign firm was likely to face a new competitor on both Chinese and international markets. That Chinese firm was often able to offer a cheaper price than the foreign competitor. The foreign firm therefore often looked on closely held technological superiority as its core competitive advantage against lower-cost Chinese imitators and competitors. Not infrequently, this made foreign firms reluctant to transfer advanced and sensitive technology to China.

One method used by Beijing to overcome this foreign reluctance to transfer advanced technology to China was to allow foreign firms access to China's domestic market in exchange for transfer of advanced technology. In their initial conception, China's Special Economic Zones were exclusively for export production. From the very beginning, some foreign-branded and SEZ-produced goods "leaked" one way or another into China's domestic markets. As coastal cities were opened to foreign investment in the mid-1980s, export mandates similar to the SEZs were applied there as well. Foreign firms soon realized there was strong demand within China for their high-quality, fashionable, and safe products, and sought ways of gaining access to these domestic markets. Agreeing to transfer of more advanced technology targeted by the MOST was one way of gaining such access: market share for technology transfer. The Chinese Academy of Science (CAS) was charged with following foreign technological and scientific developments, and identifying items and processes that should be acquired.

Targeted technologies that could not be acquired via commercial channels were sometimes sought by illegal covert means: industrial espionage.[48] The PRC, like most states, deployed clandestine operatives to foreign countries. After 1991, Chinese espionage operations soon surpassed earlier efforts by the Soviet Union. One of the distinctive features of Chinese foreign intelligence operations was that they targeted advanced industrial and military technologies rather than the political and military information typically sought formerly by Soviet intelligence. In the decades after 1978, a dozen or so Chinese spies were convicted by US courts for stealing for transfer to China various sorts of advanced technologies. As the World Wide Web developed in the 1990s, and as US businesses and governmental agencies integrated that powerful tool into their operations, Chinese intelligence agencies apparently discovered and increasingly utilized this new method of penetration. Accessing the research files of a major US corporation via the internet was, after all, far easier, faster, cheaper, safer, and probably more effective than deploying humans to undertake that task. Entities in China, which US governmental and private analysts were convinced are linked to the PRC government, successfully penetrated the cyber systems of US corporations and government defense agencies, exfiltrating vast quantities of technical and design information on the most advanced areas of science and technology. US defense contractors, including especially those working on the most advanced next-generation systems, were a major target of cyber penetration and exfiltration of data. With regard to US military capabilities, China's objective was apparently to defend against US electronic and cyber warfare capabilities, while understanding and exploiting US vulnerabilities to China's military advantage. China denied that these cyber espionage operations were authorized or conducted by government agencies, but authoritative US analysts were convinced they were.[49]

While our knowledge of this is limited, it is likely that once a new and advanced technology was acquired from abroad, research centers under CAS or MOST were responsible for studying and re-engineering and modifying it for use in China. The blueprints and technical specifications for that Chinese copy would then be passed to design bureaus of Chinese capital goods manufacturing firms, which would mass-produce the new, more technologically advanced machinery and equipment. Centrally mandated tax breaks, grants, or subsidies would then offer incentives for enterprises to acquire and utilize the new technology.

Chinese enterprises concerned with growth and profit sometimes did not have the same interest as the SSTC or MOST in acquiring more advanced technologies. New technologies could be expensive and difficult to master, and might not significantly increase productivity or efficiency for some time. Production lines and schedules with existing technologies operating quite profitably could be disrupted by a shift to new technologies. Here state agencies sometimes stepped in with monetary subventions as incentive. Party secretaries—more responsive to noneconomic directives from higher levels—also sometimes weighed in so that targeted technology would be acquired. Embodying advanced technology transfer requirements in contracts was phased out after China's WTO accession, but other means, such as grant or denial of tax breaks or subsidies, were used to achieve the same ends. The experience of General Motors (GM) of the United States offers an example.[50] When GM wanted to begin production in China of its electric car, the Volt, it was told that unless it transferred three key technologies to China—electronic controls, power storage, and motor—its products would not be eligible for a very substantial government subsidy available to other electric-car producers. That would confer a large cost advantage on GM's competitors, effectively excluding it from the China electric-car market. Foreign firms increasingly faced the choice of acceding to Beijing's technology transfer demands or being excluded from the large and rapidly expanding Chinese markets.

The Push for "Indigenous Innovation"

In 2002, a new leadership team of General Secretary and paramount leader Hu Jintao and Premier Wen Jiabao launched a push to accomplish a major upgrading of China's capacity for "indigenous innovation." Responding to many of the complaints raised by economic nationalists over the previous years, and especially after the flood of FDI into China following WTO entry, Hu and Wen elaborated a network of policies intended to transform China into a technological power house by 2020 and into a global leader in technology by 2050. In October 2005, the Politburo declared "indigenous innovation" to be a strategic equivalent equal to Deng's policy of opening and reform. Those earlier policies had been correct and would be continued and expanded, the Politburo concluded. But the older approach would now be paralleled by a systematic effort to turn the PRC into a global leader in technological innovation. The goal was to shift economic growth from reliance on import of foreign capital equipment and technology to Chinese innovation and development of those things. Reliance on foreign technology for production was to be reduced from an estimated 60 percent in 2006 to 20 percent by 2020.

In 2003, Wen Jiabao took over leadership of the Leading Group for Science and Technology with responsibility for MOST and CAS. Wen ordered the creation of twenty working groups involving CAS, MOST, the Ministry of Information Industry and Technology (MIIT), the Ministry of Education, the Ministry of Finance, and the China Development Bank, one of China's four policy banks. The working groups were charged with devising policies to accelerate domestic technological innovation. Clashing points of view regarding the scope of state control soon developed in these groups. Many scientists, including overseas ethnic Chinese recruited to the working groups, favored allocation of funds on the basis of peer review of research proposals by panels of scientists, to include foreign scientists—as was commonly done in the United States. Most funding would go to small-scale, individual-driven research projects. This arrangement, its advocates asserted, would channel resources to projects with the greatest potential for genuine innovation. State officials, on the other hand, tended to favor government selection of large-scale strategic projects which would then receive very substantial funding. Eventually, this debate began to leak into the media, and MOST stepped in to take control of and resolve the debate. The decision was in favor of the state guided "mega-project" approach. MOST together with MIIT drafted a National Medium and Long Term Plan for Development of Science and Technology, which became known at the Medium and Long-range Plan (MLP). The plan was to run through 2020. Formally promulgated in 2006, the MLP said that China's "weak innovation capacity" was to be overcome, transforming China into a leading innovation power.[51]

The core of the MLP was specification of programs and goals in eleven key sectors: energy, water, and mineral resources; the environment; agriculture; manufacturing; transportation; information and services; population and health; urbanization; public security; and national defense. Within these sectors, there were sixty-eight priority areas, with expected technology breakthroughs specified. The MLP also laid out sixteen mega projects, listed in Figure 25-5. Very generous funding was poured into these projects. Between 2000 and 2008, total spending on S&T grew by 289 percent, while spending on research and development increased by 315 percent.[52]

Ironically, perhaps, the MLP included a large web of policies intended to procure foreign inputs for China's drive for "indigenous innovation." Chinese firms were expected to "re-innovate" advanced technology imported from abroad. Such machinery was not merely to be utilized for production, but researched and mastered at a basic level. The foreign technology would then be "evolved" and changed and improved in some way, thereby "re-innovating" it. Such "re-innovated" and "evolved" technology would gain a Chinese patent and no longer need to pay intellectual property fees to foreign firms. "Indigenous technology" was defined as technology in which the ownership and intellectual property right was in Chinese hands. A mix of tax breaks, subsidies, and low-cost loans, plus exclusive or priority eligibility for procurement by government agencies, encouraged Chinese firms to comply with these objectives. China's patent rules were modified to make it more difficult for foreign firms to sue Chinese firms for IPR violations. A 2009 revision of China's patent law was intended to promote indigenous innovation

1	core electronic components, high-end chips and software
2	large scale IC manufacturing equipment and techniques
3	new generation broadband wireless mobile communication networks
4	advanced numeric-controlled machinery and basic manufacturing technology
5	oil and gas exploration: high precision seismic exploration; deep sea drilling
6	advanced nuclear reactors: 3rd generation pressurized water and gas cooled
7	water pollution control and treatment: prevention & remediation
8	genetically modified organisms: agriculture
9	Pharmaceuticals: capacity test efficacy & safety of drugs
10	control & treatment AIDS, hepatitis, etc.; independently develop vaccines
11	large aircraft: key production technologies, power and testing systems
12	earth observation system: satellites, aircraft; high definition; space data
13	Manned spaceflight and lunar probe; orbiting laboratory; moon orbital exploration
14–16	classified: presumed to be military projects

FIGURE 25-5 **16 Megaprojects Under 2006-2020 "Indigenous Innovation" MLP**

Source: James McGregor, *China's Drive for 'Indigenous Innovation,' A Web of Industrial Policies*, Global Regulataory Cooperation, US Chamber of Commerce. July 2010?, 40–42.

and reduce dependency on foreign patents. Among other things, it required that foreign holders of patents that did not "sufficiently exploit" them, they would be ordered to license the technology to Chinese firms. The China-based R&D centers of large foreign firms, previously mostly focused on modifying foreign products to suit Chinese tastes, were offered incentives to participate in major research projects targeted by the MLP.

Core infrastructure—banking, telecommunications, ports, utilities—were directed as part of the MLP to use only indigenous technology. Government agencies were to purchase indigenous technology. Catalogues were published showing long lists of goods for which government agencies should purchase only or primarily indigenous technology. Chinese firms were to work with government agencies to develop indigenous technology standards distinct from those developed by foreign firms. Japan had used this method for decades to largely exclude foreign goods from Japan's domestic markets, thereby reserving those markets for Japanese firms. Firms recognized by PRC government agencies as "innovative enterprises" were made eligible for soft loans from China's Export-Import Bank. Procedures were tightened for foreign firms to license goods for sale in Chinese markets. Foreign firms were required to reveal encryption codes and technology, a move which made theft of IPR easier. Anti-monopoly laws were increasingly applied against foreign firms that held strong positions in many Chinese markets. Sometimes these cases could be resolved by agreement on technology transfers. Foreign firms found themselves confronting all sorts of informal pressures to transfer advanced technologies.

Foreign firms and governments objected to many of these policies and pushed back against them. In some cases, policies were redrawn or implementation delayed, regarding government procurement, for example. Critics of the MLP, including Chinese critics, maintained that bureaucratic direction of research resulted in few real breakthroughs in innovation. Most of the results of massive state funding were still copies or derivatives of Western technology, critics said.[53] Other analysts doubted if China would be able to escape the mid-level *process innovation* niche China has assumed so effectively and fortuitously in the global economy.[54] Be that as it may, China's government set for the nation the objective of becoming a world leading technology innovator by the middle of the twenty-first century. It developed long-term and well-funded strategies to achieve that objective. And it drew widely on global inputs to achieve that end.

Successes of China's Technology Development Push

World Bank indicators provide a number of measures of China's relative successes in accomplishing a technological revolution together with

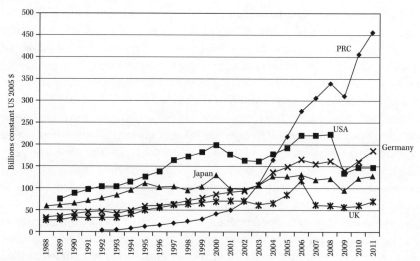

FIGURE 25-6 **High-Technology Exports (current US$)**

industrialization. China's export of high-technology goods—defined by the World Bank as goods having a high ratio of R&D expenditures relative to gross output and value added—began rising after Deng's 1992 launch of the second opening. As Figure 25-6 indicates, China's export of high-tech goods grew steadily in the decade after 1992, then began an even sharper ascent following China's WTO accession. In 2004, its high-tech exports exceeded the US level, according to World Bank indicators, and kept going. By 2011, China was by far the leading global producer of high-tech exports. In that year, China's exports of high-tech goods were 2.6 times the US level, the world's second leading high-tech exporter. Most of the PRC high-tech exports were computers, telephonic communication equipment, and other electronic goods.

Of course, most of these high-tech goods were foreign designed and branded. They were also typically produced with foreign-innovated (and therefore licensed) technology. Many of the crucial components of these "high-tech" goods (microchips and processors, special materials, etc.) that contributed most of the value added to these goods were produced outside of China (often in Taiwan or South Korea), and again under foreign patent held by a US or other Western firm. This arrangement also meant that China remained dependent on other countries, especially the United States, for innovation, and would probably continue to lag behind the United States in terms of overall technological level. It also meant that a large part of the value of these high-tech exports went to the foreign brand and patent holders. One study of one of China's high-tech exports, an Apple iPhone, found that of the $179 cost of producing an iPhone in China, only $6.50 was value added by assembly in China.[55] The other $172.50 was the cost of importing into China parts produced in other countries and sent to China

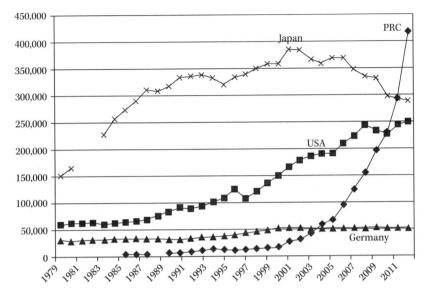

FIGURE 25-7 **Patent Applications by Residents**

for final assembly. That iPhone then sold retail in the United States for $500, meaning that China captured about 1.3 percent of the value of the iPhone. The largest share of this "Made in China" iPhone went for salaries, rents, transport, marketing, markups by wholesalers and retailers, and profits to brand-holders in the United States. A large part of the rationale of China's indigenous innovation drive is to capture for China a larger share of the value of "Made in China" goods.

The number of patent applications is another World Bank measure of technological prowess in invention of new technologies. Figure 25-7 shows that patents filed by PRC residents began rising rapidly circa 2000, about the time of WTO entry, surpassing the United States in 2009 and Japan, the previously leading country, in 2010. The quality of many of these patents is, however, questionable. Many were apparently filed in response to governmental directives and incentives for patent applications or as an attempt to undermine foreign charges of IPR infringement. Foreign firms and analysts deem many of China's new patents to be "junk" not representing any genuine innovation. Still, the steep gradient of China's upward curve indicates that at least the attention given to technological innovation has increased.

Other World Bank indicators show how far the PRC has yet to go to become a global leader in technology. In terms of research and development spending as a percentage of GDP, China spends less than half the level of Japan, and well below those of the United States and Germany. It is significant, however, that China's spending shows a steady upward slope, while the spending of the other leading countries shows greater fluctuation. Finally, in terms of number of researchers per million of population, China ranks far below the leading technological powers.

In all, China's industrialization has progressed very rapidly and successfully. But whether China will be able to realize its aspiration of becoming a world leading technology innovator remains to be seen. While recognizing that foreign investment and technology transfer helped propel China's rapid economic modernization since 1978, China's leaders are unwilling to accept the subordinate and dependent role in the international division of labor produced by those market-driven transnational flows of capital and technology. China's leaders have put in place a comprehensive set of industrial policies designed to turn it into a world leading innovator of technology by 2050. China's industrial structure will gradually be transformed—if these plans are successful—from a low-wage, labor-intensive manufacturer to a knowledge-intensive, high-value-added manufacturer. China will no longer be dependent on foreign countries, especially the United States, for technological advance, but will become self-reliant in that area, eventually becoming a major supplier of new technology to the world. These ambitious policies are underpinned by a conviction that Chinese scientists and engineers can at least equal, and perhaps exceed, the genius and creativity of scientists and engineers in Western countries. It is too early to say whether this dream will be realized. But clearly China's ambition is to become a leading world power.

26 }

Reassuring and Unnerving the Neighbors: Japan

Japan: Pressure Overwhelms Reassurance

There is a bifurcation of Chinese interests toward Japan similar to that which exists for China's relations with the United States. On the one hand, Japan is extremely important to China's economic development drive, accounting for a large portion of China's total trade and foreign investment. Japan is also a significant power that for half a century was China's rival for regional pre-eminence. This suggests that if China is to achieve preeminence in East Asia, perhaps as a stepping stone to global power, it will need to win over Japan, make it comfortable with China's growing power and ready to accept a role under China's shadow. All this suggests friendship diplomacy intended to court Japan. On the other hand, there are three structural divides separating China and Japan: competitive military modernization, overlapping maritime defense zones, and Japan's alliance with the United States. Regarding rival military development, during the 1990s both China and Japan pushed forward with military modernization, though China did so at a far more rapid pace. Some reasons for China's military modernization effort were outlined in earlier chapters. For Japan, international criticism of Japan's mere "check-book diplomacy" during the international effort in 1991 to restore Kuwait's sovereignty, plus a growing desire to be a "normal country" with political influence more commensurate with its economic power, plus the 1996 Taiwan Strait crisis and the realization that Japanese refusal to support the United States in the event of such a conflict would probably spell the effective end of Japan's alliance with the United States, all led to a steady augmentation of Japan's military capabilities.[1]

Many of the growing military capabilities of China and Japan were focused on the maritime dimension, especially submarine and antisubmarine and missile and antimissile capabilities. Each country viewed its own buildup as defensive and the other's as threatening. In a re-evaluation of maritime defense strategy in the mid-1980s, China's defense planners established a proactive strategy which laid out a new maritime defense perimeter running down the Japanese home islands, the Ryukyu Islands, Taiwan, and the Philippines, a line dubbed the first island chain and shown in Figure 26-1. This included the Sea of Japan, the East China Sea, and the South China Sea in China's new maritime defense zone.[2] In the mid-1980s, China's military capabilities were far from realizing the apparent intent of Chinese control, or domination of the waters west of the "first island chain." By the 2010s, however, with large numbers of new and modern warships, warplanes, and antiship cruise and ballistic missiles being deployed, China was much closer to supremacy in these waters. Beijing saw its expanded maritime defense zone as self-defense. Tokyo saw the PLA-N's expanding operations as putting China in a position to choke off Japan's imports and exports, and stepped up Japan's efforts to counter China and defend Japan's vital SLOCs.

FIGURE 26-1 China's First and Second Island Chain Maritime Defense

Japan's fundamental geopolitical reality is that it is a densely populated but resource-poor island nation extremely vulnerable to blockade. The increasingly militarized standoff over disputed territories in the East China Sea combined with virulent anti-Japanese sentiments that erupted periodically in China during the 2000s to cause many Japanese to wonder if Japan did not need to better defend itself against possible Chinese belligerency.

China's sentiments and interests toward Japan's alliance with the United States are also deeply conflicted. Japan's alliance with the United States brings US power into threatening proximity to China and is the keystone of a region-wide structure of US power encircling China. If China is to someday become pre-eminent in Asia, that may well require that America "go home" and leave Asians to deal with Asian security issues. From Beijing's point of view, this would ideally mean that Japan would take China as a security partner, perhaps treating China as its older brother—rather as Japan now treats the United States. On the other hand, Chinese analysts understand that over many centuries Japan's rulers were unwilling to accept a position formally subordinate to China's emperor. They realize too that rather than subordinating itself to China, Japan could well decide to arm itself to become able to defend itself independently without US support. This would mean far greater Japanese military capability—and a Japan no longer held on a leash by US desires for a cooperative relation with China.[3]

China's policy toward Japan since the upheaval of 1989–1991 has oscillated between periods of friendship diplomacy and periods of punitive pressure. Following the strategy of "unity, struggle, unity," Beijing launched periodic pressure campaigns intended to compel Japan to recognize its shortcomings and abandon policies unacceptable to Beijing. These pressure campaigns were followed by renewed campaigns of smile diplomacy designed to repair ties and avoid pushing Japan in directions adverse to China's interests. This oscillation between smile and frown diplomacy was paralleled by a steady deepening of economic relations between the two countries.

The memoir of Tang Jiaxuan, one of China's top Japan specialists and foreign minister from 1998 to 2003, offers an explanation of this oscillation between friendship and browbeating. Beijing sought friendship with its neighbors, but certain incorrect beliefs and derivative policies in neighboring countries constituted "obstacles" to friendship: visiting the Yasukuni Shrine, purchasing the Senkakus from private Japanese, detaining a Chinese trawler captain, etc. These "obstacles" had to be eliminated for friendship to flourish. There were two ways to eliminate them. First, educational work by Chinese diplomats, leaders, the media, think tanks, and so on, to explain to foreign parties the errors of their ways. Second, punitive measures: suspension of exchanges and dialogues, restricting rare-earth exports, condoning angry demonstrations by PRC citizens, military pressure on disputed territories, negative diplomatic moves, and media and cyber threats. While there was often some element of punishment and implicit Chinese military threat behind these punitive measures, their purpose was essentially psychological—to bring foreign leaders to see the error of their ways and repent, opening the way to genuine friendship, according to Tang Jiaxuan.[4]

Throughout the post–Cold War period, Beijing applied this "unity through struggle" approach to both Japan and India. It did not reassure either Japan or India about China's growing power. The result in both cases was that China's neighbors became progressively more apprehensive of China's power. Both Japan and India became more apprehensive and looked for partners who shared their concern about China. It is also interesting to note that the same "unity, struggle, unity" formula was applied by Mao to ties with India and with Moscow circa 1959–1960, did not produce positive results for China in those cases either. There may be some deep Confucian philosophical roots, or perhaps "barbarian management" origins, germinating this apparently deeply rooted diplomatic trope.

One broad consequence of Beijing's efforts to pressure and punish Japan has been growing conflict and rivalry between these two leading East Asian powers and historic rivals. In spite of periodic campaigns of friendship diplomacy, Beijing did not succeed in making Japan comfortable with China's growing power. Instead, Beijing's policies nudged Tokyo steadily closer to balancing China, both by building up its own military power and by tightening security cooperation with the United States and with other Asian nations (India, Australia, the Philippiines, Indonesia) apprehensive over China's growing power. As with China's US policies, there were moderate voices within China who urged a more consistently friendly approach to Japan. But the anti-Japanese nationalist passions fostered in China since 1978 were powerful. The link between regime legitimacy and relations with Japan was perhaps even stronger and more volatile than with Sino-US ties.

The Beijing Massacre had a strongly negative impact on Japanese public opinion toward China. Tokyo reflected popular dismay and stayed in step with Washington after 6-4 by joining international sanctions against Beijing. But, as discussed in an earlier chapter, Tokyo soon shifted gear and led the Western countries in lifting sanctions. For several years, Beijing courted Tokyo, praising its efforts on China's behalf. In the immediate aftermath of 6-4, Beijing found it useful to welcome Tokyo's desire to serve as a bridge between China and the West, and used that Japanese impulse to erode Western sanctions. This brief period of Chinese friendship diplomacy lasted until 1993. Then, less than a year after Emperor Akihito's October 1992 visit to China, Beijing's policy toward Japan began to harden. By 1993, Beijing's position was much improved. China had escaped its post-6-4 isolation by striking a bargain with Washington over the 1991 Iraq War. Deng Xiaoping's old friend, George H. W. Bush, had been replaced by a relatively "anti-China" US president, William Clinton, but China had held firm during the period of maximum danger in 1989–1991. Russian President Yeltsin's December 1992 visit to China had consolidated a friendly relation along that axis. Most important of all, China's economy was booming, entering its second period of reform following Deng's early 1992 southern tour. Japan's economy, on the other hand, was sliding into what would prove to be a very long period of stagnation. China was in an increasingly advantageous position vis-à-vis Japan.[5]

By the early 1990s, Japan was pushing to become a "normal nation" that could play a greater political and perhaps even military role in East Asia. Japan's earlier post-6-4 effort to serve as a bridge between China and the West, along with Japan's large ODA to China, had been part of Tokyo's effort to play an expanded regional role. China responded with increased emphasis on the history issue. In effect, Beijing was saying that Japan lacked the moral qualifications to play a major political, much less military, role in Asia. China's Japan hands now concluded that Japan's refusal to recognize the great crimes it had committed against the peoples of Asia during the 1894–1945 period was proof of Japan's moral incapacity. Japan's ambition was to become the hegemon of East Asia as the United States declined. But a rearmed Japan would pose a threat to China and other Asian countries. Japanese hegemony of East Asia would also deny China its rightful status in the world. Japan was also trying to lock China into a low-value, low-technology, labor-intensive niche in the emerging transnational production networks that were rapidly transforming the Asian and global economies, or so China's critics of Japan concluded. If Japan succeeded in these efforts, China's role in East Asia would be constrained. A top-level policy decision premised on such ideas resulted in a new approach toward Tokyo: China would pressure Japan to abandon its objectionable policies. PRC leaders also calculated that this new, tougher approach to Japan would win popular support from the Chinese people. Stress on the history issue was a key instrument of this new, assertive approach.[6]

One of China's early decisions regarding Japan that may have been among the most consequential was a decision not to publicize in China the large-scale Overseas Development Assistance (ODA—the formal name for Japan's economic development assistance) to China. Starting in the late 1970s and continuing through the mid-1990s, Japan provided generous development assistance to China: low-interest loans and gratis assistance. China ranked as the second top recipient of Japanese ODA. Japanese assistance supported hundreds of projects in China. Yet the Chinese government did not actively publicize Japan's assistance, and public opinion surveys in the 1990s found that most Chinese were unaware of it. Japan had initially hoped that large-scale economic assistance to China would win Chinese goodwill and help leave behind past animosities. That did not happen. In fact, anti-Japanese sentiment in China grew stronger even as Japan supplied generous ODA to China. Gradually, the Japanese began to suspect that Beijing wanted to maintain popular animosity against Japan as a way of strengthening regime legitimacy.[7]

In 1991, Japan decided to link ODA to restraint on military spending, since China's spiraling defense spending had become a major concern. The Chinese media responded by dismissing Japan's ODA as part of a Japanese bid for regional leadership. Japan gave ODA for its own selfish reasons and thus did not merit Chinese gratitude. Unstated but clearly present was the idea that Japan's ODA was a form of reparations, owed morally if not legally to China. The Chinese media began to polemicize against Japanese expression of concern about China's rapidly growing military strength. The Chinese media transformed expressions of Japanese concern about China's actions into evidence of nefarious Japanese intentions: Japan wanted to keep China weak and vulnerable while Japan itself plotted to restore militarism. Thus began a vicious cycle: Japanese expressions of concern would lead to Chinese charges of Japanese malevolent intentions, which would further increase Japanese apprehensions, leading to further accusations by the Chinese media.[8]

China's very active nuclear testing program, illustrated by Figure 26-2, became a focus of Japanese concern. Between May 1990 and July 1996, when it finally stopped nuclear tests, China exploded eleven nuclear warheads. Japan had developed a very strong aversion to nuclear weapons as a result of its suffering two atomic bombings in 1945. Many Japanese believed that as a result of their uniquely horrendous experience of having suffered atomic attack, Japan had a special mission in the world to anathematize all aspects of nuclear weapons, especially by countries next door to it. Japanese opinion was dismayed by China's nuclear tests for idealistic reasons as well as self-interest. Thus, following China's May 1995 test of a 95-kiloton bomb, Japan suspended the grant portion of ODA to China. Following another 60–80-kiloton test in August, Japan froze government grants for the remainder of 1995. The Japanese Diet also passed a resolution protesting China's continued testing.

Date	Test #	Yield	Comments
29 Jul. 1996	45	1–5 KT	
8 Jun. 1996	44	20–80 KT	detonation of two warheads
17 Aug. 1995	43	60–80 KT	Japan Diet passes resolution protesting China testing & freezes grant air for 1 month
15 May. 1995	42	95 KT	Japan suspends grant portion ODA to China
7 Oct. 1994	41	40–50 KT	
10 Jun. 1994	40	40–50 KT	
5 Oct. 1993	39	40–80 KT	
25 Sep. 1992	38	8 KT	
21 May 1992	37	650 KT	China's largest underground test (Hiroshima bomb = 13–18 KT)
16 Aug. 1990	36	189 KT	
26 May 1990	35	11.5 KT	

FIGURE 26-2 China's Nuclear Tests Since 1990

[1] Monterey Institute of International Studies database. http://www.cns.miis.edu/archives/country_China/coxrep/testlist.htm.

China showed little understanding of Japan's nuclear allergy. Its media belittled Japanese opposition to China's nuclear test program. China had made many declarations of its policy of no first use of nuclear weapons and of its peaceful intentions toward all of China's neighbors, China's media explained. Only people who were hostile to China would doubt these solemn guarantees. Japan was attempting to keep China weak so that Japan could eventually dominate East Asia—just as it had sought to do in the 1930s, or so China's media explained. Japan's media followed closely the Chinese depiction of Japan and were shocked by the negative interpretations of Japan that erupted so quickly and forcefully in 1993 only months after Japan helped China escape post 6-4 sanctions. The stated Chinese fear of revival of Japanese militarism, along with the constant exaggeration of the influence of ultranationalists in Japan's politics, struck many Japanese as incredible. China seemed obsessed by "history" even though the Japan of the 1990s was vastly different that the Japan of the 1930s. China seemed willfully unable to recognize those vast differences. It seemed to more and more Japanese that two decades of Japanese effort to build goodwill with China—lots of ODA, Japanese investment, cultural exchanges, frequent top-level exchanges—had all been for naught. China's leaders understood the importance of Japan for China's development effort, but they simply did not understand Japan's anxieties about China's own actions. Instead, Beijing decided to further intensify pressure on Tokyo.[9]

By the mid-1990s, Jiang Zemin was putting his mark on China's diplomacy. Vulnerability to criticism by Politburo rivals like Li Peng may have prompted Jiang to defend against charges of weakness before the West by adopting a tough approach toward Japan.[10] Charges of weakness in dealing with Japan had often proved to be an effective weapon in intraelite struggles. Only a decade earlier, charges that Hu Yaobang had made a misstep in inviting Japanese youth to visit China had played a role in the conservative campaign to topple Hu. Positioning himself to push forward with Deng's controversial post-1992 "second opening," Jiang needed to protect his flank from conservative criticism. A tough approach to Japan would also enhance Jiang's popularity, something that might be useful, since Jiang's only real claim to legitimacy was that he had been chosen by Deng Xiaoping. This led Jiang to put the history issue at the center of his November 1998 visit to Japan.

Japanese leaders had many times expressed remorse for Japan's history of aggression, as laid out in Figure 26-3. Before 1993, and again after 2006, these Japanese mea culpas satisfied China's leaders at least to the extent that they deemed them adequate to set aside the history issue and cooperate in other areas. Not so during the 1993–2005 period. During those years, Beijing chose to put the history issue at the core of Sino-Japan relations.

Jiang Zemin's November 1998 state visit to Japan was a disaster, deeply offending Japanese public opinion. Jiang's visit was the first by China's top leader to Japan since Deng Xiaoping's 1978 visit and was intended to commemorate the twentieth anniversary of that memorable visit. Deng, the reader will recall, had set aside the history issue during his visit and gone out of his way to convince Japanese that China was willing to close that page of history. Jiang's approach was radically different from Deng's smooth and

Sep. 1972	PM Kakuei Tanaka normalization visit to Beijing	Japan "keenly conscious ... for the serious damage caused ... to the Chinese people through war, and deeply reproaches itself."
Oct. 1992	Emperor Akihito at banquet in PRC hosted by Yang Shangkun	"In the long history of relationship between our two countries, there was an unfortunate period in which my country inflicted great sufferings on the people of China. I deeply deplore this."
Aug. 1995	PM Tomiichi Murayama (JDP) on WW II 50th anniv.	"Japan ... caused tremendous damage and suffering to the people ... particularly to those of Asian nations. ... [for these] irrefutable facts of history [I] express ... deep remorse and state my heartfelt apology." (Emphasis added)
Sep. 1997	PM Ryutaro Hashimoto press conference in Beijing	repeats Aug. 1995 formulation, addiing "I would like to repeat that this is the official position of the Government of Japan ... I have made this point very clear in a frank manner to the Chinese side. Premier Li Peng [has said] that he concurs completely in my remarks."
Nov. 1998	Jiang Zemin State Visit to Japan; joint declaration	"Keenly conscious ... for the serious distress and damage ... caused to the Chinese people through its aggression ... and expressed deep remorse for this"
Aug. 2000	Japan foreign minister Kono speech in Beijing	"Japan's perception of past history was clearly set out in the Statement by ... Murayama ... The spirit contained therein has been carried forth by successive administrations and is now the common view of the large number of Japanese people."
Oct. 2000	Premier Zhu Rongji says to media that no Japan apology exists on paper: Japan reply =	"From the perspective of the Government of Japan ... the Murayama Statement was announced in 1995 in the form of a written Statement based on a Cabinet decision.That Statement was referred to by Prime Minister Keizo Obuchi when he went to China and also by Prime Minister Mori in the meeting that took place on Friday."
Oct. 2001	PM Koizumi at WW II museum in Beijing (after visit to Yasukuni)	"deeply feel the tragedy of the past war and express heartfelt apology (dao qian) and lament (ai dao) for the Chinese who lost their lives because of aggression." (Emphasis added)
Apr. 2005	PM Koizumi at	"caused tremendous damage and suffering ... Particularly those of Asian nations. Japan

FIGURE 26-3 Japan's Apologies for Its History of Aggression

Source: Ministry of Foreign Affairs, Japan. http://www.mofa.go.jp/j_info/japan/opinion/umezu.html. The Emperor's 1992 comments in Japanese are available via the Imperial Household Agency at http://'www.kunaicho.go.jp/okobota/01/speech/speech-h04e-china.html#china.

reassuring approach. From beginning to end, Jiang bludgeoned his Japanese guests with the history issue.

In October 1998, the month before Jiang's visit to China, South Korean President Kim Dae-jung had visited Japan and secured a written apology from Prime Minister Keizo Obuchi for Japan's brutal 1905–1945 colonial rule of Korea, in exchange for a South Korean promise not to raise the issue again.[11] In the Obuchi-Kim communiqué, Japan "in a spirit of humility" expressed "deep remorse and heartfelt apology" for "tremendous damage and suffering" caused by Japan's colonial rule of Korea. The wording that was eventually used in the Jiang-Obuchi joint declaration, on the other hand, said Japan was "keenly conscious of serious distress and damages" and "expresses deep remorse for this." The key difference in the two formulations was use of the word "apology" in the Tokyo-Seoul joint declaration. In negotiations prior to Jiang's visit, Beijing demanded a written apology from Tokyo of a strength equivalent to that the Kim-Obuchi statement. Japan offered only a more equivocal expression of "remorseful repentance." No agreement had been reached when Jiang departed for Japan. In August 1995, on the fiftieth anniversary of World War II's end, an earlier Japanese prime minister Tomiichi Murayama, had issued a written statement expressing "deep remorse" and "heartfelt apology" for the sufffering caused to Asian peoples by Japan's history of colonial rule and aggression—the same phrasing used in the Kim-Obuchi declaration. Tokyo was unwilling to satisfy Beijing's demand that it "apologize" again and, perhaps, again.

Jiang could have taken what Tokyo was willing to offer on the history issue and moved on to areas of agreement and expanded cooperation. He chose not to. Instead, Jiang dwelled on the history issue throughout his visit. Upon arrival in Japan, Jiang declared in his initial statement that it was necessary to "seriously summarize the experience of the history of China-Japan relations" in order to guide the future development of ties.[12] In other words, there was a danger that Japan might again take a path of aggression. In negotiations over the apology issue, the Japanese side proposed a compromise. Obuchi would deliver an oral "apology" during his formal summit meeting with Jiang, Tokyo proposed, but the printed joint statement would mention only "remorse." After considerable wrangling, the Chinese side agreed to this arrangement. But after Obuchi delivered the agreed-upon oral apology, Jiang held forth with a twenty-five-minute lecture on the history issue. He disagreed, Jiang said disingenuously, with the "prevailing Japanese view" that there is "no more need to talk about the history issue between the two countries." As Figure 26-3 indicates, Japan's leaders had "talked about" the history issue a number of times by November 1998. The Chinese side also found Obuchi's oral statement inadequate. Obuchi had used the Japanese word *owabi* (equivalent to *dao qian* in Chinese), which the Chinese side felt was more suitable for minor, everyday offenses, such as bumping into a person. Chinese negotiators preferred that the Japanese word *shazai* (equivalent to the Chinese word *xie zui*) should be used. Each side refused to budge, delaying the issue of the joint communiqué by five hours.

With Japan's mea culpa and the joint communiqué out of the way, Jiang could have put aside the history issue. Again he chose not to. Instead, he raised the history issue at every turn, including at a formal court banquet hosted by Emperor Akihito and Empress Michiko. Japanese officials feared that Jiang might embarrass the emperor by raising the history issue during the banquet, and proposed a deal. If Jiang agreed to stop talking about "history," Japan would consider concessions on other matters. The Chinese side rejected the proposal out of hand, without inquiring what sort of concessions Japan might have in mind. When during the banquet Jiang lectured the emperor and empress on the sins of Japanese militarism, Japanese officials visibly paled.[13] The emperor is deeply revered by most Japanese, and Jiang's lèse-majesté offended many.

The contrast between Jiang's emollient behavior during his American visit in 1997 (discussed in a previous chapter) and his acerbic behavior in Japan the next year was striking. In the United States, when Jiang was subjected to repeated, blunt, even harsh and confrontational criticisms of Chinese policy. He skillfully sidestepped issues or fended them off in a low-key, friendly, and calm fashion, frequently winning over his audiences with self-deprecating humor. In Japan, in contrast, Jiang's approach was heavy-handed, seemingly designed to browbeat his Japanese audiences into submission. There is no doubt that Jiang's cold anger at Japan's unwillingness to give an unconditional apology was genuine. But with equal certainty, Jiang's demeanor in Japan was also calculated. Before 1993, and again after 2006, Beijing was satisfied with such equivocal apologies as Tokyo could be persuaded to offer. But not between those dates. Jiang probably calculated that China's position was strong and getting steadily stronger relative to Japan, and it was time for Tokyo to recognize that Japan simply did not have the moral bona fides to aspire to leadership of East Asia. That status would be held by China, and Japan should accommodate itself to that emerging reality.

China's displeasure at Japan's moral equivocation over the history issue is understandable. The Japanese self-image of World War II as a war to liberate the nonwhite races of Asia from domination by the White Powers was vastly different from the cruel reality of Japan's rule.[14] Moreover, Germany's post-1945 reflection on its aggression of the 1930s and 1940s was unquestionably more profound than Japan's. Germany's more sincere repentance has also been considerably more successful than Japan's in reassuring Germany's neighbors that its power would not again be turned to aggression. Yet it was also the case that Beijing's heavy-handed treatment of the history issue alienated many Japanese. Why did China's media and leaders refuse to recognize that the Japan of the 1990s was profoundly different from the Japan of the 1930s? Japanese asked themselves. Was it because the CCP regime fostered anti-Japanese animus to legitimize itself, or because of an inveterate hatred of Japan and Japanese? Neither answer was reassuring. Whatever the reason, Japan's twenty years of effort to win Chinese friendship had apparently failed. The history issue was not really about the past, more and more Japanese concluded, but about the future status of Japan and China in Asia. China was using the history issue to pressure Japan into accepting a position subordinate to China in the emerging East Asian order. Beijing's continual bludgeoning of Japan with the history issue also conveyed a threat. If this was the way China behaved now, how would it behave in the future when it was even stronger? Japanese asked themselves. China's nuclear weapons programs plus its large post-6-4 investment in military modernization indicated that China was determined to become a major military power. How would China deal with Japan then? Jiang's 1998 visit to Japan was a turning point for Sino-Japan relations, and not one that reassured Japan.

Following Jiang's disastrous Japan visit, China's leaders took stock and recognized the sharp deterioration of Japanese views of China. The result was another period of smile diplomacy designed to repair the damage done to Sino-Japan relations by the previous several years of Chinese harshness. US-Japanese negotiation of new guidelines for defense cooperation were under way, raising the danger of closer US-Japanese military cooperation implicitly targeted against China. NATO was expanding into Eastern Europe; Poland, Hungary, and the Czech Republic would join in 1999, the first East European states since East Germany entered via unification with West Germany in 1990. These developments raised for Beijing the specter of Japanese association with NATO. Deteriorating political ties could also adversely affect economic cooperation. Consequently, the tenor of China's media coverage of Japan shifted, becoming much more objective and less negative. Many articles now stressed the importance of friendship with Japan for China's development drive. Chinese media also began expressing appreciation of Japanese ODA.[15]

Over the next several years, China's media advanced several arguments to convince the Chinese people that cooperation with Japan was advantageous to China. Japan's power and the chances of it being used aggressively had been exaggerated, the Chinese people were now informed. It followed that China did not need to block Japan's rise as a political power, but should attempt to channel Japan's influence to create a balance of power favorable to China. It was to China's advantage for Tokyo to believe that it, Japan, could use China to offset US pressure. It would be advantageous for China if it could draw Japan away from the United States. China should therefore be sensitive to the psychology of the Japanese people and adopt a careful, reassuring approach. Finally, China needed Japan's help for economic development. Broadly speaking, China's Japan hands argued that Japan-China ties were at a turning point. Japan could become China's partner, or its opponent in cooperation with the United States. China should attempt to draw Japan into Asian regional economic integration and greater political independence of the United States.[16]

Anti-Japanese Nationalism and the End of Smile Diplomacy

Beijing's smile diplomacy lasted about two years, until a series of Japanese moves triggered an eruption of nationwide anti-Japan demonstrations. The downturn in ties started in late 2000 with the approval of new junior high school history textbooks by Japan's Ministry of Education, followed by a flurry of right-wing Japanese nationalist commentary lauding Japan's noble mission in the 1930s.[17] Against this background, Prime Minister Junichiro Koizumi, who took office in April 2001, visited the Yasukuni Shrine for the first time as prime minister in August 2001 on the anniversary of Japan's World War II surrender. Over the next five years, Koizumi would visit the shrine annually as he had promised to do during his election campaign, six times in total, with the last visit coming in August 2006. To top matters off, several big Japanese companies recalled defective products from the US market but not from China's market, implying that Chinese consumers deserved lower-quality goods than Americans.

By mid-2001, China was seized by a "Japan-bashing fever," not yet in the form of street demonstrations, but taking a myriad other forms. Virulent anti-Japanese commentary filled blogs. The Chinese media was flooded with anti-Japanese letters. China's internet and media were under state control, and toleration of this anti-Japanese activity reflected a high-level decision to permit it. Be that as it may, popular passions were real. Chinese workers at Japanese-run factories went on strike. People condemned as traitors Chinese movie stars who wore Japanese flag–themed clothing at fashion events in the United States. A man who rubbed dog excrement on one such hapless film star was widely lauded as a nationalist hero.[18] This anti-Japanese upsurge was driven in part by government propaganda, but also reflected rising popular and autonomous anti-Japanese nationalism. The CCP's anti-Japanese propaganda, like the sorcerer's apprentice, had called forth an anti-Japanese storm, which it would now struggle to control and keep from turning against itself.

Popular and autonomous anti-Japanese rage took the form of street protests in August 2004 following Japan's 3–1 victory over China in an Asian

Cup soccer match in Beijing. The Chinese audience on that occasion had set the atmosphere when it booed as the Japanese national anthem was played at the beginning of the match. Later, the Chinese audience was outraged when a referee apparently missed a hand ball by one of the Japanese players, allowing Japan to score. Japan's victory on the soccer pitch further antagonized the crowd. When the match finished, the Chinese audience turned into a mob, in spite of the presence of several thousand police dressed with riot gear and accompanied by dogs, backed up by soldiers. Thousands of Chinese jammed the streets around the stadium, in which a thousand Japanese, who had come to watch the game, were sheltered by Chinese police. The crowd chanted slogans like "Down with little Japan," "kill the dwarf pirates" (*wokou*—a strongly racist invective equivalent to "Japs" or "Chinks" in English), and singing anti-Japanese songs such as the 1930s wartime ditty "A Big Knife Chops Off the Head of the Japanese Devils." Japan's flag was burned and the windows of Japanese-brand cars smashed. After two hours, Chinese police were able to secure the exit of the Japanese sports fans, after which the mob proceeded to the Japanese embassy to continue venting their hatred of Japan.[19]

Anti-Japanese demonstrations became popular. They erupted again in April 2005 and quickly spread across China's cities, threatening to escape state control. This time the spark was Japan's push to secure a permanent seat in the UNSC, a proposal Chinese generally felt was radically inappropriate. Another visit by Koizumi to the Yasukuni Shrine further exacerbated Chinese emotions. Beijing encouraged an online petition opposing Japan's Security Council bid, and more than 22 million people quickly signed it. Chinese newspapers reported daily on the diplomatic campaign for and against Japan's Security Council bid, encouraging readers to join in. To make a strong statement, students in Beijing's university district rallied and then followed the by now traditional script of marching down Changan Avenue to Tiananmen Square and then to the Japanese embassy. Banners and posters condemned Japanese moves, called for boycotts of Japanese goods, and insulted Japan and the Japanese in often very crude terms. "Down with Japan" and "Smash Japan's dream of obtaining a Security Council seat" were poplar slogans. Windows of Japanese restaurants and Japanese-brand cars were smashed. Once the mob arrived at the Japanese embassy, that building was pelted with rocks, paint balloons, and bottles, while the mob shouted anti-Japan slogans. A heavy police presence prevented entry into the embassy compound, but did not otherwise interfere with the crowd's protests.[20]

The initial protest in Beijing ignited a flood of nationwide grass roots organizing activity, leading to anti-Japan protests a week later in twenty-one cities. Beijing sent an urgent directive to local governments ordering them to exercise vigilance and maintain public order by exercising firm control over the demonstrations. "Nationalism is a double-edged sword," one prominent campaigner for rural rights said of the upcoming anti-Japan protests. "It can help the government gain control, but it can also help people who see the government as part of the problem."[21] China's government struggled to contain the protests, shutting down anti-Japanese websites, posting lists of approved slogans, directing factory managers to ensure that their employees obeyed regulations, and directing universities to tell students to refrain from protesting or "spreading rumors."

As anti-Japanese demonstrations mounted, Tokyo asked Beijing to guarantee protection of the vast holdings of Japanese firms in China. Tokyo also asked for an apology from China for failing to prevent damage to Japan's commercial and diplomatic interests in China. Beijing flatly rejected these demands. After three weeks of demonstrations and rising tension in bilateral relations, Beijing ordered a halt to the protests after Koizumi made a public apology for Japan's aggression in Asia. The protests were getting out of hand and threatened to injure Japan-China business relations. Hu Jintao and Koizumi then met for fifty-five minutes on the sidelines of an Asia-Africa summit in Djakarta in late April. Hu asked Koizumi to "recognize history correctly," but did not demand as he had the previous November that Koizumi stop visiting Yasukuni. Hu also said that the Sino-Japan relation was "important," and that the current "difficult situation" was not one that China wanted to see.[22]

As anti-Japanese passions were peaking in 2005, Hu Jintao consolidated his hold on paramount power by securing Jiang Zemin's resignation as head of the state Military Affairs Commission in March. Hu wanted to steer relations with Japan back onto a less tumultuous path, but needed to protect himself from criticism for charting such a course. Hu adopted a twofold strategy: on the Politburo he shared power with rival factions; and he charged a new foreign minister, Li Zhaoxing, with continuing strong anti-Japanese rhetoric while quiet negotiations with Tokyo worked out terms of détente.[23]

Several years earlier, Chinese analysts writing in influential journals had warned that policies based on anti-Japanese passions were injuring China's own interests. Acting on irrational impulses such as hatred would prevent China from being guided by sound strategic calculation and would end up injuring China, the influential commentator Ma Licheng argued. Rather than treating Japan in a harsh and ungenerous fashion, as anti-Japanese activists urged, China should have the generosity of a great, powerful, and victorious nation. It should not be harsh toward Japan. The emotional hatred of Japan sweeping across urban China could end up injuring China by isolating it from the outside world, Ma warned. The xenophobic "Spirit of the Boxers" which had sought to seal China off from corrupting foreign influences could be detected in the current "Japan-bashing fever," Ma argued.

Another analyst, professor Shi Yinhong of People's University in Beijing, argued that China's overriding strategic interest was to draw Japan away from the United States and balance it against the United States. The scope of American global dominance was historically unprecedented, Shi warned, and Washington would use its power to try to stifle China's rise. If China could use Japan to balance the United States, that would be greatly to China's advantage, Shi argued. Unfortunately, China's emotional Japan bashing had the opposite effect, driving Japan into Washington's arms. Shi's policy recommendations were bold. China should accept for now such apologies over "history" as Japan was willing to offer, essentially putting that issue on hold. China should publicly thank Japan for its large ODA, stop stressing exaggerated and alarmist predictions of the restoration of Japanese militarism, welcome Japan as a "great power," and stop giving Japan the notion that China was trying to hold it down or keep it in an inferior status relative to China. Shi went so far as to recommend that Beijing support Japan's UNSC permanent membership. This would be a small price to pay, Shi argued, for a "diplomatic revolution" that would change Japan's position and role in the US-Japan-PRC triangle.[24]

Hu Jintao inducted former ambassador to the United States Li Zhaoxing as foreign minister in March 2003, and assigned him responsibility for continuing to voice nationalist resentment over various "history issues" while also reigning in anti-Japan demonstrations. Substantive negotiations with Japan took place through low-profile channels. In fall 2004, Hu appointed Vice Foreign Minister Wang Yi, a fluent Japanese speaker, as ambassador to Japan. In the MFA, Dai Bingguo, with rich experience in foreign affairs and one of Hu's closest foreign policy advisors, became vice foreign minister. Together Wang and Dai steered Sino-Japan relations in a more amiable direction.[25] The resignation of Koizumi in September 2006 and his replacement by Shinzo Abe provided Beijing with an opportunity to shift policies back toward friendship. In 2007 and 2008, tensions eased, creating conditions for a visit by Hu Jintao to Japan in May 2008. Shifts in Japanese policy also played a role. Abe's first visit as prime minister was to Beijing. He also visited the Meiji Shrine in Tokyo to commemorate war dead rather than the Yasukuni Shrine.

Hu's 2008 visit was the first by China's top leader since Jiang Zemin's ill-fated visit a decade earlier. It was carefully choreographed to send a different message than had Jiang's abrasive visit. A new prime minister, Yasuo Fukuda, was in office (Abe had resigned in September 2007 after only a year in office) and was recognized by Beijing as belonging to the "Asian school" rather that the "Western school" of Japanese diplomacy, and this facilitated Beijing's effort to rebuild Sino-Japanese ties. In a speech at Waseda University in Tokyo, Hu noted the "unfortunate history" that "caused not only great misfortunes among China's people, but also great suffering for the Japanese people," thereby taking an even-handed approach that recognized that "history" had been cruel to Japanese too. In a television broadcast to the Japanese people, Hu lavished praise on Japan's post–World War II development. Regarding history, Hu said that the reason to remember history was not to nurse hatred but to better "look forward to the future." In contrast to earlier warnings about the danger of revived Japanese militarism, Hu lauded Japan's adherence to the "path of a peaceful country over the past six decades and more." The Joint Communiqué signed by Hu and Fukuda stated that China "values Japan's status and role in the United Nations and is willing to see Japan play a bigger and more constructive role in international affairs." Hu and Fukuda agreed to increase the exchange of high-level visits in the security sector to "promote mutual understanding and trust." This would lead later in 2008 to the scheduling of a friendship visit by a Japanese warship to a Chinese harbor—the first such visit since 1945. The Joint Communiqué also pledged to make the East China Sea "a sea of peace, cooperation and friendship."[26] This provision would lead to an agreement later in the year for Japanese investment in a joint development zone in a rich natural gas field on the Chinese side of the mid-line in the East China Sea claimed by Japan as the boundary. In sum, Hu's 2008 visit was an impressive attempt to reassure Japan of China's friendship. Unfortunately, before the projected friendship visit by the Japanese warship and joint development project in the East China Sea could occur, another eruption of anti-Japanese nationalism made both of those gestures of reassurance appear as traitorous weakness to much Chinese anti-Japanese patriotic opinion. Starting in December 2008, tension flared over the Senkaku Islands, and by 2013–2014 it would carry the two countries into a tense and increasingly militarized confrontation in the East China Sea.

Intensification of the Territorial Conflict

China and Japan dispute ownership of a cluster of five small islands situated 170 kilometers northeast of Taiwan, about the same distance northwest of Japan's Ishigaki Island at the southern end of the Ryukyu archipelago, and 330 kilometers from the coast of continental China. China contends that the islands—known as Diaoyu in Chinese and Senkaku in Japanese—are Chinese territory stolen by Japan in the 1890s and definitively transferred back to China by the Cairo Declaration of 1943. Tokyo contends that the islands were administered by no state until incorporated into Japan as part of the Ryukyu archipelago in the 1870s—that is, well before the 1894 Sino-Japan war. The Cairo Declaration has nothing to do with the Senkakus, Japan insists. The United States administered the islands until 1972, when it handed the Ryukyu Islands, including the Senkakus, over to Japan. There had been flare-ups of tension over the disputed Senkaku/Diaoyu Islands in 1970–1972, 1978, 1990 and 1996–1997, but the growth of maritime capabilities of both China and Japan along with the growing energy needs of both those countries in the twenty-first century increased the sharpness of the confrontation over these tiny islands and their surrounding sea floor. Conflicting territorial claims in the East China Sea emerged as a serious irritant in Sino-Japan relations in 2004 as both countries moved to develop the natural gas reserves under that sea's floor.[27]

China claims that the boundary in the East China Sea runs along the outermost edge of the continental shelf, making the largest portion of that sea and its resources China's. Japan, on the other hand, insists that the boundary follows a line equidistant between the coast of mainland China and a western baseline of the Ryukyu archipelago, dividing the sea equally between China and Japan. A rich natural gas field, Chunxiao in Chinese, more or less straddles the median line claimed by Japan. The Chunxiao field is estimated to contain a huge amount of natural gas. Both China and Japan have a great and growing demand for energy, especially for natural gas, which is environmentally cleaner than either oil or coal. With energy prices rising rapidly in the 2000s, both countries sought to expand supply. Both China and Japan were also trying to diversify away from the unstable Persian Gulf, which supplied a large share of both countries' imported oil. Both countries were also concerned with "energy security" in which they control their own energy supply. These factors meant that the Chunxiao field was ardently desired by both Tokyo and Beijing. This situation would have been difficult to handle through dispassionate diplomatic negotiations in any case. Once nationalist passion entered the equation, it became far more difficult. Figure 26-4 illustrates these respective claims in the East China Sea.

In August 2003, China signed contracts with several international oil companies, including British and US firms, to explore resources in Chunxiao. Although the area designated for development was west of the midline claimed by Japan as the boundary, it was close enough to that line that since the deposits straddle the Japanese claim line, extraction from wells sunk on the Chinese side held the potential of siphoning gas from the Japanese-claimed area, or at least so Tokyo believed.[28] Japan responded to China's moves by commissioning a Norwegian ship to undertake seismic surveys of the Chunxiao area. Chinese coast guard vessels treated the Japan-commissioned Norwegian ship as a spy, radioed warnings to it, and shadowed it. At one point, a Chinese coast guard ship nearly collided with the vessel. Meanwhile, China finished work on a gas production platform just a mile west of Japan's claim line, with a pipeline extending westward across 300 miles of sea floor to deliver pumped gas to Shanghai. Japan's trade minister inspected the Chinese production platform from a Japan coast guard airplane, then demanded that China either cease work on the project or share its seismic and drilling data with Japan. (Such data would presumably show whether gas in the Japan-claimed area was being pumped by the Chinese rig.) China rejected these demands and reiterated earlier calls for a joint venture to develop resources in the area. Tokyo rejected that proposal and began moving toward a Japanese-only

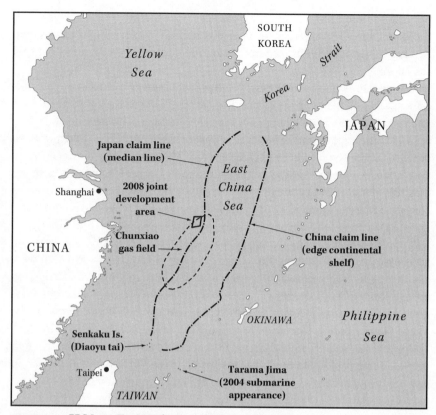

FIGURE 26-4 **PRC-Japan Territorial Dispute in the East China Sea**

Source: "Zhong ri zai donghai xunqiu huli gongying (China and Japan search for mutual interest and dual win in the East Sea), *Renmin Ribao*, June 19, 2006, p. 7. James Brook, "Drawing the Line," *New York Times*, March 29, 2005, p. C1.

exploitation of the Chunxiao field. Tokyo tripled its East China Sea research budget and ordered construction of Japan's own seismic survey ship.[29]

Tension over the Chunxiao field increased further in April 2008, when Tokyo countered China's move to develop it by authorizing Japanese companies to begin drilling in the Japan-claimed portion (that is, east of the mid-line claimed by Tokyo but on the continental shelf claimed by China). China's MFA termed Tokyo's move a "serious provocation," protested, and reserved "the right to take further action."[30] When Japan's foreign minister visited China to discuss the matter, Beijing authorized demonstrations at Japan's consulate in Shanghai. Over ten thousand people gathered at the consulate, pelting it with bricks, paint balloons, and bottles and chanting anti-Japan slogans.[31] Several months later, Beijing openly applied military pressure when a squadron of five PLA-N warships maneuvered near the Chunxiao field—reportedly the first time Chinese warships had done that. This display of gunboat diplomacy came shortly before China's Chunxiao production platform was to begin pumping gas, shortly after Tokyo had granted a Japanese company rights to test drill in Chunxiao, and two days before a general election in Japan.[32]

Parallel to the East China Sea territorial dispute, a low-profile but strategically significant contest over PLA-N access to the seas beyond China's first island chain was underway.[33] The first observed passage of a PLA-N vessel through a Japanese strait in recent years came in 2000, when a Chinese icebreaker and intelligence gathering ship transited the Tsugami Strait between Hokkaido and Honshu to reach the high Pacific. Five more transits (confirmed and unconfirmed) occurred through late 2008. PLA-N vessels were believed to be scouting the seas east of Japan where combat might someday occur. Another component of the escalating naval rivalry had to do with whether PLA-N submarines could transit various Japanese-controlled straits submerged. UNCLOS permitted submerged passage in "international straits" but not other straits. Japan recognizes only five "international straits" among its many intra-archipelagic straits. China counts many more and insists on upholding rights of submerged passage by PLA-N submarines. Japan tries to force Chinese subs to access the high Pacific only by recognized—and presumably well-monitored—international straits. What were involved in these cat and mouse interactions were the capabilities of PLA-N submarines and JMSDF anti-submarine forces to conduct operations on Japan's SLOCs between the first and second island chains. From Japan's perspective, the PLA was tightening its hold on Japan's vital SLOCs.

A typical incident occurred in November 2004, when JMSDF ships forced a PLA submarine in Japan's territorial waters near Tarama Jima (shown earlier in Figure 26-4) in the southern Ryukyus to surface and display its flag. The Chinese sub then exited the area escorted by JMSDF helicopters and destroyers. Japan formally protested the incursion. After several days, China's MFA informed Japan that the intrusion was the result of a "technical error," and apologized for the accidental intrusion. That apology was not reported by China's media, thus sheltering the MFA from criticism for the decision to apologize.[34] Japanese defense officials were skeptical of Beijing's assertion that the intrusion was accidental, noting that that had always been the excuse when Soviet aircraft and warships violated Japanese territory during the Cold War. Japanese officials suspected that Chinese submarines were familiarizing themselves with Japanese waters in preparation for possible combat operations. When Hu Jintao and Koizumi met on the sidelines of an APEC conference in Chile in November 2004, Hu called on Koizumi to stop visiting the Yasukuni Shrine. Koizumi responded by asking Hu to take preventive measures to ensure that Chinese warships did not again "mistakenly" enter Japan's territorial waters.[35]

Tension in the East China Sea eased as Hu Jintao's foreign policy team of Dai Bingguo and Wang Yi maneuvered toward improved relations with Japan, culminating in Hu's May 2008 visit to Japan. But after that brief respite, tension flared again. In December, two Chinese government vessels entered into the twelve-nautical-mile territorial zone around the Senkakus. According to Japan's Ministry of Foreign Affairs, it was the first time this had happened.[36] The Chinese government vessels remained in the area for some nine hours in spite of calls by the Japan Coast Guard to leave the area. A "strong protest" made to China via diplomatic channels. Tokyo saw this as an attempt to change the territorial status quo through force and coercion. The frequency of entry by "Chinese government and other" vessels into waters around the Senkakus, according to Japan's MFA, is shown by Figure 26-5.

A spike in Chinese intrusions (numbering twenty-four) occurred in September 2010, when a Chinese fishing trawler rammed a Japanese coast guard vessel. Following the Japanese detention of that boat's captain in September 2010, fourteen intrusions into the Senkakus' twenty-nautical-mile contiguous zone occurred in October, followed by eight in November. Prior to September 2010, Chinese boats had left the area when warned to do so by Japanese coast guard vessels.[37] On this occasion, however, instead of departing, one Chinese vessel rammed a Japanese coast guard ship, as clearly shown by video documentation released by Japan.[38] The Japanese thereupon detained the captain and crew of the Chinese boat, taking them to Ishigaki in the southern Ryukyus. The captain was charged with obstructing officers in their line of duty, while the crew was released six days after the incident.[39] The ramming was an escalation of China's practice, although it is still unclear whether it was the result of a high-level policy decision. *Global Times* reported one Chinese vessel replying this way to a Japanese order to leave: "We are a Chinese fisheries administration boat. The Diaoyu Islands are China's indigenous territory, and we are carrying out our official duties in Chinese territorial waters. We ask you to leave immediately."[40]

China's pressure succeeded. Seventeen days after Tokyo's detention of the trawler captain, Japan's prosecutors announced that he would be released. In view of Beijing's strong reaction, Tokyo understood that unless he was released, it faced a major downturn in China-Japan relations. Rather than face those consequences, Tokyo backed down. Beijing's tough handling of Japan had been vindicated. The same day the captain arrived back in China to media acclaim as a national hero, Beijing demanded a Japanese apology for the incident and monetary compensation. The demand was met in Japan with anger and disbelief, and promptly rejected. Dropping usual diplomatic opacity, the Japanese foreign ministry statement said "The demand of the Chinese side for apology and compensation is completely groundless and utterly unacceptable to Japan."[41]

Beijing saw Japan's attempt to try a Chinese fishing boat captain before Japanese court (the first time Japan had done this) as an attempt to raise the

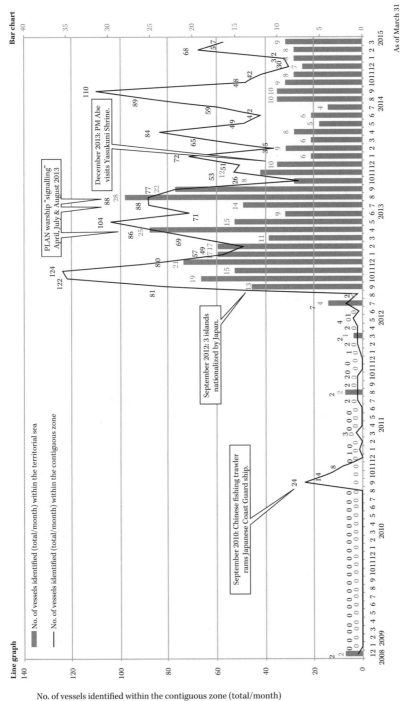

No. of vessels identified within the territorial sea (total/month)

No. of vessels identified within the contiguous zone (total/month)

Line graph
▬ No. of vessels identified (total/month) within the territorial sea
— No. of vessels identified (total/month) within the contiguous zone

Bar chart

As of March 31

December 2013: PM Abe visits Yasukuni Shrine.

PLAN warship "signalling" April, July & August 2013

September 2012: 3 islands nationalized by Japan.

September 2010: Chinese fishing trawler rams Japanese Coast Guard ship.

FIGURE 26-5   Chinese Vessels Entering Senkaku Territorial Sea and Contiguous Zone

Source: "Trends in Chinese Government and Other Vessels in the Waters Surrounding the Senkaku Islands and Japan's Response" (Ministry of Foreign Affairs: Tokyo, February 18, 2015), (http://www.mofa.go.jp/region/page23e_000021.html).

legal status quo of Japan's hold over the disputed islands. Beijing's response was swift and hard. The Japanese ambassador in Beijing was summoned to the MFA six times to receive Chinese protests. One of those summonses was in the early morning, a move Tokyo took as a deliberate slap in the face. Beijing broke off high-level talks underway with Japan on expanding aviation routes, coal technologies, and joint development of the Chunxiao field. Beijing also ordered all central and provincial government offices to suspend interactions with their Japanese counterparts. After the captain had been detained for several days, Chinese authorities detained and launched an investigation of four employees of a Japanese construction company for allegedly entering and filming in a military zone.[42] Chinese travel agencies began to cancel tour groups to Japan. Premier Wen Jiabao refused to meet with Prime Minister Naoto Kan on the sidelines of a UN summit in New York City. Instead, Wen threatened additional actions if Japan did not quickly release the trawler's captain. Beijing also began restricting the export of Chinese rare earths, a move that seriously threatened major Japanese industries dependent on these exports. Japanese opinion at the time saw this as part of China's effort to punish Japan, although China subsequently argued that the export restrictions were unrelated to Sino-Japan conflict but were routine industrial policy.[43] "The de facto ban on rare earths export that China has imposed could have a very big impact on Japan's economy," said Japan's economic and fiscal policy minister Banri Kaieda shortly after industry executives began reporting that customs officials had begun blocking rare-earth exports.[44] The politics behind the shift in China's rare-earth policies are not clear. In Tokyo, in any case, the export restriction was widely seen as part of Beijing's campaign to force Japan to release the captain and, beyond that, to cease contesting Beijing's effort to gradually change the terms of administration of the disputed territories by establishing a permanent and significant physical presence in the seas just off the islands. The contrast between China's reassuring words during Hu Jintao's May 2008 visit and the forceful actions during the September 2010 confrontation jarred Japan.

Chinese maritime pressure in the Senkakus reached unprecedented intensity beginning in September 2012 after Japan's government purchased three privately owned Senkaku Islands as a way of preempting a proposal by the nationalist governor of Tokyo to purchase and then commercially develop those islands. Beijing ignored the rationale for Tokyo's move and declared it a unilateral Japanese attempt to change the legal status quo of the islands. Chinese maritime pressure on Japan's administration of the islands intensified. Chinese intrusion into the contiguous zone occurred almost daily and intrusions into the territorial sea almost five times per month. Frequent Chinese intrusions then became standard. Beijing had established a new status quo. As intrusions by Chinese ships into the disputed islands' twelve-nautical-mile territorial sea spiked in 2013, on three occasions PLAN warships maneuvered near the islands, actions that a careful study by the US navy determined were "signaling" to Japan.[45]

Beijing's tough handling of Senkaku disputes with Japan was popular with China's nationalist public opinion. During the September 2010 confrontation over the detention of the Chinese fishing boat captain, the purchase of Japanese-brand goods by Chinese consumers fell off considerably. Japanese companies worried that the fall in sales would be permanent. Chinese tourism to Japan also declined precipitously. Demonstrations called for boycott of Japanese goods while condemning "Japanese bastards" and "Japanese militarism." But while Beijing's pressure campaign proved popular in China, in Japan it reinforced growing apprehension about China's increasing power. The fact that China's high-pressure tactics against Japan were successful did not reassure Japan—or other Asian countries for that matter. Was this the way China would deal with territorial and other disputes as its power grew? China's neighbors asked. Again, some wise heads in China worried that strident anti-Japanese sentiments might injure China. Wu Jianmin, former ambassador to several European nations and to the United Nations and ex-president of China's Foreign Affairs University, pleaded in an interview for a "rational" type of patriotism. Strained Sino-Japanese relations would injure China's development effort, Wu warned.[46] These moderate sentiments, while they may have been common among China's top leaders, did not reflect either mainstream public opinion or Chinese policy.

Large, angry anti-Japanese street demonstrations erupted again in August 2012, when Japanese authorities detained and then deported a group of Chinese activists who had landed on one of the Senkaku Islands. Protests took place in a dozen east China cities. Chinese media reported the crowd size at several hundred, but photos posted on websites showed vastly larger crowds. When a group of Japanese activists swam ashore on one of the disputed islands (also to be detained and sent home by the Japanese coast guard), Chinese protests grew larger, more numerous, and angrier. Vicious banners declared things like "Japan must be extinguished" and "Noda [then Japan's prime minister] must die." Japanese-brand cars and Japanese stores, restaurants, and even factories were attacked. Demonstrations continued for a week, spread to over eighty cities, and reached a peak on September 18, the anniversary of the "Mukden Incident" in 1931. Streets full of angry demonstrators scared some. An editor of *Global Times*, usually an outlet for strongly nationalist views, urged restraint on the crowd: "Chinese people, please don't be overly angered by this. We should have more confidence and view Japan from a global perspective." On the other hand, Major General Luo Yuan suggested the PLA declare the islands to be a bombing target range and plant naval mines around them. Western journalists in Beijing speculated that the

CCP decision to allow the demonstrations to continue for a full week was related in some still not understood way to the transfer of power from Hu Jintao to Xi Jinping.[47]

Large anti-Japanese demonstrations—the largest since 2005—erupted across China following Tokyo's September 2012 nationalization of the three islands. Vicious placards like "Japan must be wiped out" and "Kill Japanese robbers" were popular with protestors. Police struggled to restrain the angry mobs. "Wisdom is needed in the expression of patriotism," Xinhua urged."[48] When the CCP center decided to bring the demonstrations to a close, it accompanied directives to that effect with hard-edged diplomacy toward Japan: more Chinese ships were dispatched to the disputed islands.[49] Roused nationalist opinion would not countenance weakness. Throughout 2013, the intensity and forcefulness of Chinese military activity over and around the Senkaku gradually but steadily increased. PLA reconnaissance aircraft flew over the disputed islands, causing Japan's SDF to scramble fighters from Okinawa. A PLA-N frigate locked its fire control radar onto a JMSDF destroyer. PLA aircraft challenged Japanese warplanes with recklessly close high-speed passes.[50]

Beijing's strategy toward Japan seems to be to slowly and incrementally use China's growing military power to challenge Japan's claims to the East China Sea.[51] From 2010 through 2015, Beijing had, in fact, established a nearly constant Chinese presence in these disputed areas, altering the status quo from a few years ago, when they were under nearly unchallenged Japanese control. Beijing's calculus seems to have been that by slowly escalating its military and paramilitary presence in these contested areas, chances of provoking a strong Japanese counteraction is reduced. Tension and conflict may gradually increase but will remain manageable at levels below outright military conflict. This tough approach to Japan's transgressions will validate Beijing's and Xi Jinping's nationalist credentials both to potential Politburo rivals and to China's public.

Meanwhile, China's continued enhancement of its overall military power vis-à-vis the United States and Japan creates increasing doubt in those countries about whether they could prevail in a military conflict with China over these islands and waters, and whether or not the United States would deem them worth a war with a strong China, especially the tiny Senkaku Islands.[52] Crisis over the Senkakus might exacerbate tensions within the US-Japan alliance, with one side or the other eventually deciding to back away from the alliance for the sake of improved relations with China. Were this to happen, China's position would be greatly strengthened, at least according to Beijing's calculations. Parallel to increased military pressure, Beijing engages Japan's leaders and society, promising far better bilateral relations if Japan accedes to China's demands in the East China Sea. Beijing's objective seems to be to win control over the East China Sea without fighting.

Japan's Search for Security in the Face of Mounting Chinese Pressure

The maritime confrontations that flared in 2010 were a lost opportunity for Beijing. In a major rupture in Japan's tradition of domination by the Liberal Democratic Party, an opposition party, the Democratic Party of Japan (DJP), led by Yukio Hatoyama, took over Japan's government starting in September 2009. (He remained in office until June 2010.) The DJP and Hatoyama had campaigned and won election on a program of a less America-centric and more Asia-centric orientation for Japan. The US-Japan relation was not an equal one and could ensnare Japan in conflicts with China over conflicts not related to Japan's own interests, Hatoyama said. Japan needed a greater degree of independence from the United States and better ties with China. Hatoyama promised to revise a 2006 deal with the United States over an air base on Okinawa, and once in office he ended the refueling mission of JMSDF in the Indian Ocean in support of US operations in Afghanistan. By early 2010, Hatoyama's government was reportedly negotiating with Beijing over a visit by him to Nanjing (site of the infamous 1937 massacre) to deliver a statement on the history issue.

Hatoyama's brief leadership and courtship of China was doomed by several factors. One factor was a change of mind regarding the Okinawa air base issue, a shift directly linked to North Korea's sinking of the *Cheonan* in March 2010. The *Cheonan* sinking convinced Hatoyama that retention of the US base was prudent. Hatoyama's gestures of friendship toward Beijing also did not produce the positive Chinese response that Hatoyama had hoped for. An effort by Hatoyama's foreign minister in May 2010 to initiate better ties with China, for example, foundered in a confrontation with Foreign Minister Yang Jiechi. The Japanese official had been so bold as to suggest that China should consider joining the global nuclear disarmament process by reducing rather than continually expanding its stockpile of nuclear weapons. Rather than using the opportunity to explore development of an "East Asian community" with China and Japan at its core—one of Hatoyama's themes—Yang delivered a "pretty severe" rebuttal of Japan's right to challenge China on this topic, since it was under the US "nuclear umbrella."[53] Yang also undertook a "robust exchange" when his Japanese counterpart raised the issue of PLA activities in the East China Sea. In short, Beijing did not exploit the potential offered by Hatoyama's desire to rebalance the Japan-US relation.

Hatoyama's DJP successor Naoto Kan (in office from June 2010 to September 2011) was less determined than Hatoyama to move toward greater equidistance in the China-Japan-US triangle. Moreover, Kan's tenure saw China's tacit defense of North Korea's bombardment of Yeonpyeong Island and the "trawler captain incident," episodes that helped convince Kan, along with mainstream Japanese opinion, that prudence required continued close military alliance with the United States. There is, of course, no way of knowing if stronger Chinese friendship policies could have driven a wedge between Tokyo and Washington. It is pretty clear, however, that while aware of this possibility and of its desirability for China's geostrategic position, the broader thrust of China's Japan policy was to intimidate Japan into submission—a course popular with nationalist opinion in China.

Throughout the post–Cold War period, Japan became steadily more apprehensive of China's growing power combined with the anti-Japanese passions that flared again and again in China.[54] In January 1994, against the background of the "Japan-bashing fever" sweeping across China plus China's vigorous nuclear weapons testing program, the annual defense White Paper of Japan's Self Defense Agency (JSDA—Japan's de facto ministry of defense) for the first time expressed concern about the development of China's military power. By 2013, the White Paper referred directly and explicitly to the threat posed by Chinese action:

> China has rapidly expanded and intensified its activities in the waters and airspace surrounding Japan as exemplified by its intrusions into Japan's territorial waters and airspace. . . . China has attempted to change the status quo by force based on its own assertion which is incompatible with the existing order of international law. . . . China has been broadly and rapidly modernizing its military forces, and has been expanding and intensifying its activities in its surrounding waters and airspace. These moves . . . are a matter of concern for the region and the international community, including Japan.[55]

Japan's 2013 defense White Paper aggregated the PLAN's gradually intensifying activity in waters near Japan to depict a pattern of creeping Chinese maritime encirclement. This is shown in Figure 26-6. The White Paper identified five objectives inspiring these expanding PLAN activities. First, to intercept hostile naval operations in waters as far as possible from China's coast and territorial waters. Second, to prevent Taiwan independence, including preventing or defeating intervention by a foreign power in a cross-Strait conflict. Third, to undermine the effective control of other countries over territories claimed by China. Fourth, to protect and expand China's energy exploitation efforts. Finally, to defend China's sea lines of communication, including those delivering Gulf energy resources to China. Several of these Chinese objectives touched on Japan's interests. The 2013 White Paper continued: "Given these objectives and recent trends in China's maritime activities, it is believed that China plans to further expand the sphere of its maritime activities, and expand its operations . . . in waters surrounding Japan, including the East China Sea and the Pacific Ocean as well as the South China Sea."[56]

Japan's leaders are acutely aware of their island country's vulnerability to hostile blockade. The blockade imposed by the US navy in 1944–1945 was a

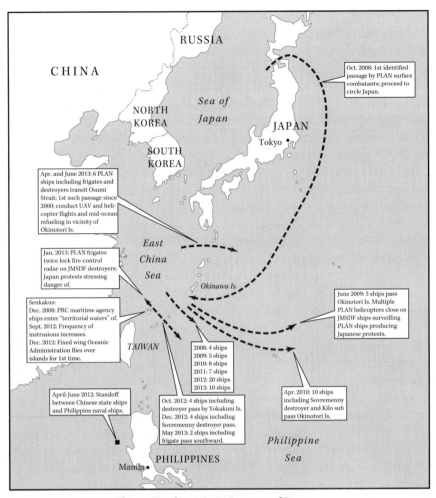

FIGURE 26-6 **Mounting Chinese Naval Activity in Seas around Japan**

Source: Defense of Japan 2013 (Minstry of Defense: Tokyo), (www.mod.go.jp/e/publ/w_paper/pdf/2013).

major factor bringing about the collapse of the Japanese Empire. During the Cold War, Japan once again faced danger from Soviet submarines that might attempt to sever Japan's sea communications with the rest of the world. In response, the JMSDF became a substantial and effective partner of the US navy in countering the Soviet submarine threat by keeping those boats bottled up in the Seas of Okhotsk and Japan.[57] Many of the antisubmarine and antimine capabilities developed by Japan to counter Soviet submarines during the Cold War are broadly applicable to dealing with the threat of encirclement and possible blockade by the PLA-N.

Japan responded to China's growing assertiveness in the East China Sea (and to the evaporation of the threat of a Russian invasion of Hokkaido) by reorienting its national security strategy. In December 2010, Japan adopted new Defense Guidelines to replace ones dating to 2004. While the new guidelines had been developed over many months, the flaring confrontation over the Senkakus, plus China's growing maritime activism, made clear their relevance to China. The new guidelines shifted the focus of Japan's defense effort from Hokkaido in the north to the islands and waters lying between Kyushu and the Senkakus. Ground forces designed to cope with a Russian invasion from the north were cut, while maritime and air surveillance capabilities in the Ryukyus were strengthened. Under the new guidelines, the JSDF was to build permanent stations, including missile defense bases, on several of the Ryukyu Islands beyond the main island of Okinawa, which already had a strong US defense presence. Vietnam War–era F-4 fighters in the Ryukyus were to be replaced with newer F-15s. Six new Aegis-equipped ballistic missile defense destroyers were to be added to the JMSDF. The JMSDF was to develop a specialized amphibious assault force comparable to the US marines, including small, highly flexible forces that could be quickly deployed by aircraft or by amphibious landing to contested islands. Japan's submarine fleet was to grow from sixteen to twenty-two, and additional small helicopter carriers dedicated to antisubmarine operations were to be added. Integration of US and Japanese forces was to be boosted by sharing command centers and intelligence. Japan's MSDF would assume increased responsibility for antisubmarine operations, freeing the US navy for other operations. The guidelines also called for "deepening and developing" Japan's military alliance with the United States and enhancing security cooperation with South Korea, Australia, ASEAN countries, and India. From the perspective of Japan's security, priority was to be placed on "improving capabilities to respond to attacks on offshore islands." By early 2011, JMSDF aircraft were conducting regular air patrols of the Chunxiao field and the Senkakus.[58] Japan was preparing for possible military conflict with China in the East China Sea.

This shift in Japanese policy was not due entirely to China's policies. Political forces within Japan that favored a more nationalist course and a stronger military seized on China's words and actions to move Japan in the direction they desired. But mainstream Japanese also shifted to become, step by step, more apprehensive of how China would use its steadily growing strength. These apprehensions were reflected in the evolution of Japanese defense and security policy. In sum, Beijing's combination of friendship diplomacy and pressure did not succeed in reassuring Japan, in making it feel comfortable with and not threatened by China's growing power. In fact, Beijing's words and actions pushed Japan in the opposite direction, toward greater military preparedness plus alignment with other countries similarly apprehensive about China's future course.

China's media did not recognize that Japan's reorientation of military strategy was a response to China's actions. Instead, it blamed the shift on evil

Japanese intentions and US "divide and rule" machinations. According to an article in *China Daily*, Tokyo's new policy "baldly plays up the so-called 'China threat' . . . [and] calls China's normal military development 'a matter of concern for the region and the international community'." This made "crystal clear" Japan's intention to "contain China" in cooperation with the United States, South Korea, Australia, and "other countries." The new guidelines and the anti-China views underpinning them seriously damaged and undermined the consensus (stated during Hu Jintao's 2008 visit) that "China and Japan are not each other's threat." The shift in Japan's policy indicated that the JSDF "will become more aggressive."[59]

Japan responded to China's mounting military pressure by drawing closer to other Asian countries with similar apprehensions about China's growing power: Australia, the Philippines, Vietnam, Myanmar, and India. The most important of these countries, and the only one with capabilities adequate to shape the regional environment, was India. By 2015, the formation of a strategic entente between Japan and India in response to Beijing's use of China's growing power had become the potential core of an Asian coalition fearful of China's possible future course. It is thus to India that this study now turns. There, too, China's policies did not reassure its neighbor.

Reassuring and Unnerving the Neighbors: India

The Piddling Success of the Quest for Friendship with India

India is the other great Asian power that, like Japan, has a history of difficult relations with China. China's leaders have undertaken periodic efforts
to improve Sino-Indian ties and reassure India that China's growing power
and influence in South Asia and the Indian Ocean Region (SA-IOR) does not,
and will not, constitute a threat to India. But these Chinese efforts have had
limited success. As with China's policies toward Japan, with India one also
finds an oscillating pattern of friendship diplomacy interspersed with periods of Chinese anger and pressure. One key result of this pattern has been
deepening Indian apprehension over China's rise and expanding discussions
of those apprehensions with other like-minded countries. First among these
has been the United States, but concerns over the recession of US power in
the twenty-first century alongside the sustained growth of Chinese power
brought India and Japan together in an incipient coalition to balance China.
Yet steadily deepening Sino-Indian economic interdependency parallels this
slowly deepening security dilemma.

The collapse of the USSR and the emergence of US unipolar dominance
circa 1991 was a deep shock to India. The Soviet Union had been India's major
backer against China since the mid-1960s, while the United States had been
aligned with China, India's nemesis, since 1971. The US deployment of the
Enterprise task force to the Bay of Bengal during the India-Pakistan war still
rankled Indian opinion. A strong strain of anti-US resentment characterized
India's political and intellectual elite. Broadly speaking, India's long-ruling
Congress Party had undertaken to emulate Soviet economic planning, combining it with parliamentary democracy as in British Fabian socialism, and
this had generated sympathy for the Soviet Union. By 1991, India's socialist
model slid toward national bankruptcy as Indian workers in the Persian Gulf
fled the upcoming war in that region, cutting off the vital flow of remittances
to India. Events compelled India to rethink its position in the world.

China reached out to New Delhi. The upheavals of 1989–1991 reinforced Beijing's desire for friendly ties with India. With its long border with Tibet, large community of Tibetan refugees, and close ties with the Dalai Lama's Tibetan government in exile, India could cause considerable trouble for China if it chose. Chinese leaders considered the developing countries of the Third World to be China's natural constituency, more concerned with stability and development than with Western notions of human rights and often resentful of Western interference in their internal affairs. India fit this to a T. New Delhi had often been stung by Western criticism of its handling of internal security matters in Kashmir, Punjab, or elsewhere in its sprawling territory. India was also influential among non-aligned countries. Mobilizing India's voice to speak against Western interference in internal affairs of the Third World and in favor of strong sovereignty norms would strengthen China's defenses against Western "intervention" in China's internal affairs.

Beijing's appeal to India in the aftermath of the Beijing Massacre was this: both India and China were poor developing countries seeking to pull themselves out of poverty in a world economic order set up by, dominated by, and working primarily to the advantage of the rich Western counties. The whole global economic order discriminated against the developing countries. Developing countries, especially big and important ones like India and China, should unite in struggle to create a new international economic order more in accord with the interests of the developing countries. India and China both had great traditions of civilization, but had been subjected to over a century of national humiliation by aggressive and arrogant Western powers. Those Western powers, now led by the United States, were so brazen as to tell non-Western developing countries how to govern themselves. The Western countries constantly interfered in the internal affairs of the non-Western developing countries. India and China should return to the spirit of "China and India are brothers" of the halcyon days of India-Chinese friendship of 1954–1956, and struggle together against the unfair international order set up by the West. As part of Beijing's turn to the Third World to counter Western criticism, Li Peng visited India in December 1991. During his visit, Li dwelled on the need for Sino-Indian cooperation in building a "new international political and economic order" favoring the developing countries. Six full paragraphs in the joint communiqué resulting from Li's visit fleshed out that joint effort. Point three gives the flavor of these principles:

> Efforts should be made to address the growing gap between the North and the South, and achieve the settlement of global economic, social, demographic and environmental problems in a manner which would benefit all members of the world community.... The developed countries are urged to address the question of the mounting debt burdens

of the developing countries, worsening terms of trade, inadequacy of financial flows and obstacles to technology transfers.[1]

Beijing's Third World narrative had considerable appeal in India in the 1990s. This worldview corresponded roughly to the views of Jawaharlal Nehru, India's visionary leader from 1947 to 1964. It was also the view of Nehru's daughter, Indira Gandhi, who dominated India's political scene from 1966 to her assassination in 1984. This Third Worldist narrative had also underpinned India's strategic partnership with the USSR during the 1970s and 1980s, transforming the Soviet Union into the "natural partner" of the Third World in its struggle against the rich capitalist countries of the West— or so many Nehruvians maintained. Beijing's post–Cold War appeal to these traditional Nehruvian/Third Worldist themes was, thus, not unreasonable.

Unfortunately for Beijing, there was a contrary tradition in India's political culture, a tradition which may accurately be called realist.[2] From this perspective, founding Indian foreign policy on romantic notions of Third World solidarity led Indian leaders to ignore India's hard interests, including security interests. Wooly-headed Third Worldism had in fact blinded India to moves by China that diminished India's security, Indian realists argued—for example, in 1954, when Nehru recognized China's sovereignty over Tibet, thereby granting China's major objective and legitimizing China's military occupation of Tibet, all in hopes of Sino-Indian solidarity and all without a Chinese quid pro quo such as acceptance of the McMahon line as the boundary. Third Worldism was, in fact, realist critics said, an illusion shrewdly manipulated by Beijing to strengthen China's position and undermine India's security. According to Indian realists, India needed to abandon illusions of Third World solidarity and predicate India's policies squarely on the pragmatic pursuit of India's national interests.[3] Realism was a nearly constant critique of India's dominant Third Worldist approach throughout India's post-1947 history. But through the end of the Cold War, idealistic Third Worldism continued to dominate Indian politics and diplomacy. Only in the mid-1990s did the realist critique begin to gain real traction in India. One of the most radical proposals of Indian realists was that India strengthen its position vis-à-vis China by reaching a strategic understanding with the United States.

China's entente cordiale with Pakistan was a major concern of Indians pretty much across the political spectrum. As noted earlier, China's entente with Pakistan was one of the most stable elements of China's foreign relations, remaining constant across regime changes in both China and Pakistan, reorientation of China's relations with the United States and the USSR, and in good times and bad in China-India relations. Yet as part of its post-6-4 outreach to New Delhi, Beijing made a significant shift in policy on the litmus-test Kashmir issue. In 1947, Nehru had agreed to refer the Kashmir issue to the United Nations (against the advice of his realist-minded Interior Minister

Sardar Vallabhi Patel). The UN then decided that the disposition of the disputed Kashmir territory should be determined by a plebiscite. Nehru had agreed to that as well. Ever since, Pakistan had demanded a Kashmir plebiscite held under UN auspices. India, on the other hand, maintained, inter alia, that Pakistan had agreed at the end of the December 1971 war that the future of Kashmir would be determined via bilateral negotiations between India and Pakistan, thus rendering obsolete the notion of a UN plebiscite. Alignment on Kashmir became a litmus issue for all countries in the India-Pakistan relation, including China.

In 1964, at the inception of the Sino-Pakistan entente cordiale, China came down squarely on Pakistan's side of this issue: the people of Kashmir were entitled to exercise self-determination regarding their future as a people. Once China entered the United Nations, it began framing self-determination in terms of UN resolutions. Then, in the lead-up to Li Peng's 1991 visit, India had weighed in, leveraged Beijing's desire for better ties, and demanded Chinese neutrality on the Kashmir issue. Out of a strong desire for a breakthrough in relations with India, Beijing agreed, and for a period of several months, references to the United Nations disappeared from China's statements on Kashmir. Pakistan countered Indian lobbying, and references to UN resolutions reappeared in Chinese statements, before finally disappearing for good except for rare occasions when Beijing wished to give New Delhi a shock, as after India's May 1998 "China threat" justification of its nuclear tests.

Li Peng delivered what became the authoritative Chinese statement on Kashmir during his 1991 visit: "As for disputes between India and Pakistan, we hope the two countries will settle them properly through negotiation . . . and will not resort to force."[4] Several years later, just prior to a 1996 visit by Jiang Zemin to India (the first ever visit by China's paramount leader to India) and Pakistan, and in the midst of a Pakistani effort to "internationalize the Kashmir issue," China's ambassador to India stated "We do not stand for the internationalization of the Kashmir question," thereby quietly but publicly rejecting Pakistan's appeal for support on its "internationalization" push. Regarding "disputes" between Indian and Pakistan, they should be resolved via "consultation and negotiation," Jiang said during his visit. Beijing had become neutral on the Kashmir question as part of its effort to open the door to better Sino-Indian relations.

But China's assistance to Pakistan's military development continued unimpaired by China's push for improved relations with India. This was one of several shoals upon which China's friendship diplomacy toward India foundered. Beijing insisted that Sino-Pakistan and Sino-Indian relations were not linked, but were independent of each other. China sought to develop multidimensional friendly cooperative relations with *all* it's neighbors, Beijing said, and none of China's cooperative relations with any neighbor were directed against or threatened any other neighbor.

If someone suggested otherwise, they were either misinformed or sought to spoil China-Indian friendship, Beijing insisted. During most of the 1990s, Indian leaders publicly complied with Beijing's demand for political correctness. Indian realists, who dominated Indian policy starting in 1998, insisted, however, on focusing on such impolite realities as China's strong support for Pakistan's military development.

Between 1993 and 1997, Pakistan purchased a whopping fifty one percent of all PRC arms exports. This included hundreds of main battle tanks, jet fighter aircraft, antiaircraft and antiship missiles both aircraft- and ship-fired, and surface-to-surface ballistic missiles, as well as shorter-range artillery missiles. China supplied fast attack craft to shoot antiship missiles, considerably enhancing Pakistan's naval capabilities. China supplied machinery, equipment, and technical assistance for Pakistan to indigenize defense productions. China also undertook with Pakistan joint research and development of new and more advanced tanks, missiles, and jet aircraft. As the United States disengaged from Pakistan circa 1990 over Pakistan's uranium enrichment program, China remained Pakistan's major nuclear partner, rejecting US demands during the 1996–1997 negotiations that China suspend cooperation with Pakistan.[5] Pakistan was China's vital strategic partner, Beijing told Washington during those pivotal negotiations. China agreed to suspend nuclear cooperation with Iran, but not with Pakistan. Stripped of diplomatic ambiguity, what Beijing meant was that a strong Pakistan was essential to China's effort to constrain India. US disengagement from Pakistan also removed a major obstacle to formation of a new US-India relation, further raising the danger confronting Beijing—and giving additional importance to Pakistan as a balance against India.

Coupled with China's assistance to Pakistan's military development was a standing threat of Pakistani entry into a China-India conflict, or Chinese entry into an India-Pakistan conflict arising out of the still unresolved territorial dispute. Beijing would be loath to enter a war between India and Pakistan, and would certainly do what it could to avoid it. The costs to China of another war with India would be heavy, perhaps resulting in several more generations of Indian animosity toward China. But if India were posed to overwhelm Pakistan, possibly resulting in the further partition of Pakistan and consequent elimination of the standing threat of a two-front war that India now faces, China's leaders might choose to intervene. A war with India might be deemed necessary to maintain Pakistan's independence of India and strength adequate to continue balancing it. A war with India with all its consequent and heavy costs might be the lesser of two evils. Maintaining a regional balance of power favorable to China was exactly why China was prepared to enter the 1965 India-Pakistan war and why it attacked Vietnam in 1979. It is also, as already argued, the basis for the exceptional stability of China's entente with Pakistan.

A nuclearized Pakistan might have been the best way of avoiding confronting China with the unfortunate choice between a war with India and loss of Pakistan as a balance to India. No one outside the CCP elite, including this author, knows the rationale for Mao's decision circa 1975, reaffirmed by Deng in 1982, to assist Pakistan's nuclear weapons program, both discussed in earlier chapters.[6] This author's informed guess is that China's leaders calculated that a nuclear-armed Pakistan was the least risky way of keeping Pakistan free from Indian domination, thus maintaining a balance of power in South Asia and reducing the likelihood that Beijing would face the undesirable choice between war with India or Indian subordination of Pakistan. Sustaining a non-nuclear Pakistan would require that China be prepared to assume the heavy burden of another war with India. A nuclear-armed Pakistan was a less costly way of maintaining the Pakistani balancer than was another war with India. These calculations seem to have worked thus far. But if, at some point, things went awry and Pakistan was on the verge of utter defeat by India, China might well decide to act. There is also the contingency of Pakistani entrance into another India-China war, perhaps over Arunachal Pradesh. If China became heavily engaged in conflict with India, Beijing might call on Pakistan to open a second front, and Pakistan's army might welcome the opportunity to seize "Indian-occupied Kashmir," finally making Pakistan whole. Victorious China and Pakistan might then negotiate peace terms with a defeated India. It is elemental calculations of this sort that, in part, underlay India's 1998 decision to acquire and deploy nuclear weapons.

There existed a deep security dilemma between China and India across the South Asia-Indian Ocean Region.[7] India was deeply apprehensive of China's expanding military presence, security roles, and involvement in dual-use (civilian and military) infrastructure projects in the SA-IOR. Countries other than India across that region frequently looked on China as a balancer against regional hegemon India and welcomed ties with China for that reason among others. China's rapid economic growth meant that it was able to subsidize large Chinese infrastructural projects in SA-IOR countries—harbors, highways, and telecommunications systems—projects which often had the effect of integrating the economies of those countries into China's economic sphere. The result has been that China steadily expanded what it styled "friendly, multidimensional cooperation, based on mutual agreement and mutual interest" with countries across the SA-IOR: Bangladesh, Nepal, Myanmar, Sri Lanka, Afghanistan, the Seychelles, and Iran—and, of course, Pakistan. China's relations with these countries were close and growing rapidly, including in many cases in the military and security fields.

Beijing's view was that China could and would expand multifaceted cooperative relations with *all* the countries of the SA-IOR as it and the governments of those countries might deem appropriate. Military and security ties and cooperation—military-to-military exchanges, security dialogues, arms sales and training, intelligence cooperation, financing and construction of dual-use infrastructural projects—were part of the normal panoply of relations between sovereign states, Beijing insisted. Military and security ties between China and various SA-IOR countries were purely defensive and did not threaten India or any other country. India should understand this and take China's assurances at face value. To do otherwise was evidence of hostility toward China, or of influence by a hostile great power, the United States, which cooked up and peddled ideas of a "China threat" in order to divide and rule. To question such normal cooperation between China and its SA-IOR neighbors, after professing a desire for friendship with China, was a manifestation of Indian insincerity, Beijing insisted.[8]

India, for its part, watched with trepidation the seemingly inexorable growth of Chinese influence in the SA-IOR. It sought to counter China's advances by opening Indian markets and higher education to SA-IOR countries, stepping up infrastructure development in and supply of economic assistance to neighboring countries. Many Indian analysts spoke of China's "creeping encirclement." Historically, India's profound advantage over China in the SA-IOR was the tyranny of distance: India was at the center of the SA-IOR, while China was far away and separated by very difficult terrain. That traditional Indian geopolitical advantage was now being dissolved by modern transportation and communications technologies. As high-speed rail lines and modern highways linked Kunming in Yunnan to Kyaukpyu on Myanmar's Bay of Bengal coast or Kashgar in western Xinjiang to Gwadar on Pakistan's Baluchi coast, distance becomes less relevant. As had happened many times in history, the geopolitical significance of advanced transportation technology was transforming the significance of terrain. China was becoming a SA-IOR country, much to India's unease.[9]

The territorial conflict between China and India also remained unresolved. The Sino-Indian border remained undefined and undemarcated. China claimed ownership of some 90,000 square kilometers constituting the Indian state of Arunachal Pradesh. The two sides did not agree where the line of actual control lay. Except for the middle sector, which was the least important, as of 2014 the two sides had not exchanged maps showing where each believed the LOC actually was. What India deemed to be Chinese incursions into the Indian side of the LAC typically occurred scores of times a year, sometimes more. The frequency and depth of penetration of these incursions seemed, in the Indian view, to be proportional to levels of Chinese displeasure with India. Across the Himalayan frontier in Tibet, India saw steadily improving PLA capabilities. The opening in 2006 of a high-speed rail line from Xining in Qinghai to Lhasa in Tibet caused Indian military planners to reduce from ninety to twenty days the estimated time it would take China to mobilize two divisions on India's northeastern borders. New Delhi responded by strengthening its defenses. In the early 2010s, India deployed its most capable multirole combat aircraft, the Russian-made Sukhoi-30MKI Flanker, to the northeast to defend Arunachal Pradesh. Old airbases in India's northeast were reopened and refurbished to host those aircraft. (These locations are shown on Figure 16-1 on page 441.) India also established two new mountain divisions to serve as a mountain strike force to India's northeast.[10]

Nuclear Weapons and the PRC-India-US Triangle

China's nightmare regarding India since the 1989–1991 upheaval has been that India would join with the United States, as it had once joined with the USSR, to encircle China. This fear did not spring immediately into existence, however, but was acquired by Beijing over a period of several years in mid-1990s, as New Delhi and Washington adapted to the new post–Cold War era. The 1990s constituted for Beijing, for New Delhi, and for Washington a crucial learning period. Within a decade of the Soviet Union's demise, however, all three capitals were aware of convergent Indian and US concerns regarding the growth of China's power, and were pondering the implications of an emerging India-US alignment.

As Beijing scored modest improvements in its ties with India in the mid-1990s, it also expanded cooperation with the United States on South Asian nuclear proliferation issues. This cooperation would eventually explode in Beijing's face, producing consequences very different than those anticipated by Beijing or by Washington. Simply stated, Sino-US cooperation on South Asian nonproliferation issues would ultimately confront New Delhi with the specter of a China-US condominium, leading both New Delhi and Washington to rethink their interests and policies, leading in turn to emergence of an India-US alignment based, in part, on common apprehensions about China's rise.

Sino-US nuclear nonproliferation cooperation in South Asia occurred in three venues in the mid-1990s: the 1995 NPT Extension and Review (E&R) conference and the 1996 Comprehensive Test Ban Treaty (CTBT) negotiations, and in the Security Council in the aftermath of India's nuclear tests in 1998.[11] Regarding the E&R Conference, the term of the NPT that took effect in 1970 was for twenty-five years, meaning it expired in 1995 unless extended. It was also time for a "review" conference of the NPT, held every five years. A major US objective going into the NPT E&R Conference was to secure entry into the NPT regime of India and Pakistan, both of which were threshold nuclear weapons powers with "screwdriver bombs" that could be assembled in short periods of time. But neither country had deployed nuclear weapons, and neither was a signatory of the NPT. As a non-NPT signatory power, India did not attend or participate in the E&R conference, but followed it very closely, since India was a major object of conference deliberations.

Regarding Sino-US interactions, at the very beginning of Sino-US normalization in the early 1980s US leaders had identified nuclear nonproliferation as a common interest on which a more cooperative US-PRC relation could be built. During the 1980s that aspiration seemed to come to fruition as Beijing step by step entered the IAEA (the part of the NPT structure that actually implements the treaty), and finally signed the NPT in 1992. US leaders also understood that China played an important role in South Asian nuclear politics, both via its cooperation with Pakistan's nuclear programs and as a threat inspiring India to acquire nuclear weapons. It thus seemed logical that the United States should partner with China to help persuade Pakistan and India to enter the NPT system as non-nuclear weapons states, that is, as states not legitimately possessing nuclear weapons under the imprimatur of the NPT.

Prior to the opening of the NPT E&R Conference, Washington persuaded Beijing to issue a statement giving to non-nuclear weapons members of the NPT assurances against nuclear threat or attack. This Beijing did in April 1995.[12] In the Security Council, too, Washington and Beijing worked together to reassure non-nuclear-weapons states, notably India and Pakistan, in order to put pressure on them to accede to the NPT. Thus Security Council Resolution 984 of April 1995, supported by Washington and Beijing, recognizes "the legitimate interest of non-nuclear-weapon States Parties to the Treaty on the Non-Proliferation of Nuclear Weapons to receive assurances that the Security Council, and above all its nuclear-weapon State permanent members, will act immediately in accordance with the relevant provisions of the Charter of the United Nations, in the event that such States are the victim of an act of, or object of a threat of, aggression in which nuclear weapons are used."[13]

From an Indian perspective these were extremely dangerous moves. If India did not join the NPT as a non-nuclear weapons state—which it certainly would not, since long-standing Indian policy was to keep open its nuclear option—the use or threatened use of nuclear force against it was, at least partially and implicitly, legitimized by Resolution 984. India's representative at the UN objected strongly, saying: "One would hope that by offering a draft resolution of this kind, the nuclear weapons States are not telling the non-members of the NPT that they, the nuclear weapons States, are free to use nuclear weapons against them [non-NPT signatories], because this would have implications which are too frightening to contemplate."[14] In other words, Resolution 984 might legitimize nuclear coercion by NPT-signatory China against non-signatory India—at least so Indian leaders feared. The intense pressure India faced at the NPT E&R Conference led India's government to decide to conduct a nuclear test as a definitive rejection of the multiple pressures being applied to India to renounce its nuclear weapon option. Foreign governments learned of the plan, however, and heavy international pressure forced its cancellation.[15]

In mid-1996, Beijing moved to expand nonproliferation with the United States as part of the effort to normalize Sino-US ties after the confrontations of 1989–1996. Beijing dropped its previous demand that China be allowed to continue nuclear testing for "peaceful purposes." Instead, Beijing now informed Washington that it would suspend nuclear testing by September 1996, when the CTBT was scheduled to take effect. Achieving a CTBT was a high priority of the Clinton administration, which was happy that Beijing had shifted to support it. Beijing became an active participant of the CTBT Conference, working closely with the United States. China became an advocate of strong "entry into force" provisions designed to pressure countries like India to join the emerging CTBT. India tried to block progress by refusing to assent to the draft CTBT in the UN Disarmament Conference where the negotiations were being held and whose rules required unanimity. Washington and Beijing then outmaneuvered New Delhi by referring the draft treaty to the General Assembly, which operates by majority vote. There the CTBT was approved by a vote of 158 to 3. Only India, Bhutan, and Libya voted against it.

India was dismayed and outraged by US and Chinese circumvention of its objections. It was even more dismayed by the reality of PRC-US cooperation against it. India had just lost its Soviet backer and was isolated, while China and the United States seemed to be moving closer and cooperating to arrange the security affairs of South Asia. India, without backing from any major power, faced a China-US condominium trying to force India into a nonnuclear status, abandoning even the option of a nuclear deterrent against China, and accepting a nonnuclear status parity with Pakistan. As India's representative to the UN said, "a very small group of countries" had tried to "enforce obligations on India without its consent." The Indian representative explained India's security situation vis-à-vis nuclear China and Pakistan:

> Our security environment has obliged us to maintain the nuclear option.... Countries around us continue their weapons program either openly or in a clandestine manner. In such an environment, we cannot permit our options to be constrained or checked in any manner as long as nuclear weapons states remain unwilling to accept the obligation to eliminate their nuclear arsenals.[16]

Two years later, in May 1998, a different Indian government, headed by self-defined realists led by Prime Minister Atal Bihari Vajpayee, ordered underground tests of three nuclear weapons. Two days later, two more bombs were tested, including one hydrogen bomb. On the day of the second set of tests, Vajpayee—the Indian defense minister who had been caught in Hangzhou nineteen years earlier when China attacked Vietnam—sent a letter to US President Clinton and other world leaders. Vajpayee's letter did not explicitly name China, but the implication was so clear that it was considered a major lapse of diplomatic protocol, which typically requires obfuscation of unpleasant facts. India had on one border "an overt nuclear state" "which [had] committed armed aggression upon India in 1962," Vajpayee's letter said. Although Indian relations with "that country" had improved in the past decade, "an atmosphere of distrust persists mainly due to the unresolved border problem." Referring to China's assistance to Pakistan's nuclear weapons program, Vajpayee's letter continued: "To add to the distrust that country has materially helped another neighbour of ours to become a covert nuclear weapons state." Vajpayee's letter then solicited US understanding and proposed closer India-US ties: "We value our friendship and cooperation with your country and with you personally. We hope that you will show understanding of our concerns for India's security."[17]

Beijing took umbrage not at India's decision to acquire nuclear weapons, but at the "anti-China" justification New Delhi gave for that decision.[18] If New Delhi had alluded to a vague US threat, Beijing would probably have been quite content with New Delhi's move. A stable nuclear deterrent balance between India and Pakistan would serve quite well China's interest in maintaining Pakistan as a balance to India, while reducing the chances that China would have to go to war with India to uphold Pakistan as a balancer. Chinese leaders must have calculated in the mid-1970s, when China began covert assistance to Pakistan's nuclear weapons program in order to maintain Pakistan as a balance to India, that New Delhi would at some point follow Pakistan's lead in developing weapons (something India had not done after an initial 1974 test). Beijing viewed a bilaterally nuclear-armed South Asia as less of a threat to China than possible Indian domination of Pakistan, which could result if Pakistan was without nuclear arms to prevent India from overwhelming it. It was Vajpayee's appeal to the United States that Beijing deemed threatening. Vajpayee was appealing for US understanding of India's need to defend itself against threats from China. At bottom, what Beijing found objectionable was an India-US understanding regarding China's threat to Indian security.

Following India's China-threat justification of India's decision to acquire nuclear weapons, Beijing launched a pressure campaign that lasted about eighteen months and punished New Delhi in various ways.[19] Beijing lobbied the United States to sanction India only, and not Pakistan, on grounds that India had tested first. Beijing lobbied Moscow and France for stronger sanctions against India. It supported strong Security Council resolutions condemning India's tests. It rejected an Indian proposal for a no-first-use agreement on the grounds that India must first abandon its nuclear weapons program and unconditionally sign the NPT and the CTBT. It suspended a Joint [Sino-Indian] Working Group on the territorial issue. China's ambassador to the UN, Qin Huasun, referred to UN resolutions on Kashmir for the first time in many years, hinting that China might shift back to a pro-Pakistan stance on that critical issue. China's media again began using the invective "hegemonist" to refer to India. That term had disappeared from Chinese commentary in the 1980s; now it briefly reappeared. China also conspicu-ously increased its military cooperation with Pakistan, supplying missile guidance systems, motors, and specialty steel. Finally, after Indian leaders adequately ate Vajpayee's words by declaring publicly that China was not a threat to India, the normal condition of Sino-Indian "friendship" returned. Of course, Beijing's pressure campaign made New Delhi even more appre-hensive of Beijing's ire.

US policy inertia for the several months after India's May 1998 tests led to continued US nonproliferation cooperation with China against India. Shortly after India's initial round of tests, Clinton used the recently installed hotline to Beijing (this was the first time it was used) to call Jiang Zemin, urging him to use his influence to dissuade Pakistan from following India's lead in testing nuclear weapons. Jiang agreed to write a letter to Pakistan, and Beijing later told Washington that the letter had been sent. Secretary of State Madeleine Albright and Foreign Minister Qian Qichen worked together to hammer out benchmarks for India's roll-back from nuclear weapons. Beijing and Washington worked together to draft and pass Security Council Resolution 1172 demanding that both India and Pakistan immediately suspend their nu-clear weapons program, refrain from weaponization, and cease production of fissile material and missiles capable of delivering nuclear bombs.

The high point of PRC-US cooperation against India came with the prom-ulgation of a Sino-US Presidential Joint Statement on South Asia during Clinton's state visit to China in June 1998. In it, the two countries pledged to "continue to work closely together to prevent an accelerating nuclear and missile arms race in South Asia." The two countries were committed to "as-sist where possible, peaceful resolution of difficult and long standing differ-ences" between India and Pakistan, "including the issue of Kashmir." India had long opposed Pakistani efforts to internationalize the Kashmir issue and insisted instead on settling that issue bilaterally with Pakistan. Now China and the United States were together proposing to "internationalize" the issue. The Presidential Joint Statement also "recognized" the respective "responsi-bilities" of the two countries in South Asia and pledged to "contribute actively to the maintenance of peace, stability, and security in the region."[20] From the Indian perspective, the United States was inviting China to assume a security role in South Asia!

It is difficult to overstate Indian dismay at the US-PRC Joint Presidential Statement on South Asia. The United States was responding to India's request for US understanding about China's threat by declaring China a major actor in South Asian security affairs! While trying to lock India to a nonnuclear status together with Pakistan, Washington was presuming to dictate to India in cooperation with Beijing! One good thing about the Joint Presidential Statement was that the Indian anger it triggered forced Americans to think through, really for the first time, US geostrategic interests regarding India in the era of China's rise. The conclusion reached via this American recalculation was that a strong, self-confident, and globally engaged India would help prevent China from achieving hegemony over greater East Asia, and was therefore (among other reasons; no claim of monocausality is intended here) in the US interest. Rather than viewing India in a regional context and linked to Pakistan, as the United States had done previously, US leaders (or at least the dominant group in both the Clinton and George W. Bush administrations) began viewing Indian in a global context and as a potential balancer in an era when China was emerging as an ambitious Asian and global power. On the basis of this recalibration, the United States shifted first toward neutrality in India-China affairs, and then toward broad support for India's emergence as a major power to keep a powerful China from achieving hegemony in Asia.[21]

In effect, a new post–Cold War US-India-China triangle was in the process of formation. As a new India-US alignment formed in the early 2000s, as soon as the Vajpayee government had retracted its "China threat" justification of India's nuclearization and embraced once again the politically correct but hollow professions of China's non-threat, Beijing revived its friendship offensive toward New Delhi. Now that formation of a genuine India-US strategic partnership was underway, keeping India from aligning too closely with the United States was important to China. Frequent visits to India by top Chinese leaders were one component of Beijing's friendship diplomacy. Li Peng visited in 2001 as head of the NPC, Premier Zhu Rongji visited in 2002, Premier Wen Jiabao in 2005, and finally Hu Jintao in 2006. Military-to-military ties were expanded in an effort to assuage apprehensions about China's intentions among India's military establishment, traditionally one of the most anti-China constituencies in India. A Sino-Indian security dialogue was launched in March 2000 (the same month President Clinton made a pathbreaking visit to India). Second and third rounds of that dialogue occurred in 2001 and 2002. A PLA-N squadron visited India in 2001. (This was the second such visit; the first had been in 1993.) In 2003, Indian and Chinese navies conducted their first-ever joint exercise. A second set of joint naval exercises was held in 2005. The PLA deputy chief of staff, chief of staff, and defense minister visited India. In 2005, China agreed to a "strategic dialogue" with India—a forum Beijing had long resisted on the grounds that India was not a nuclear weapons state under the NPT.

Beijing also made several concessions on territorial issues as part of its courtship of India. In 2005, the two sides agreed to a set of Guiding Principles and Parameters for settlement of the territorial issue. Article 7 provided that a settlement "shall safeguard due interests of . . . settled populations in the border areas." Since Arunachal Pradesh had a population of one million, while Tawang district had a population of some 39,000, this implied that those areas would remain with India. This proviso also hinted at a Chinese return to the old notion of transforming the existing Line of Actual Control into the international boundary. Another Chinese concession involved recognition of Indian sovereignty over Sikkim. That entity, situated on the west side of the strategic Chumbi Pass—the best pass between the subcontinent and the Tibetan plateau—had been annexed by India in 1974 after a long process of constitutional reform and democratization.[22] From Beijing's perspective, Sikkim was a sovereign, independent state that had historically engaged in friendly relations with "China's Tibet" tracing back to the eighth century. Beijing deemed the PRC to be the legal successor state to the traditional "local government of Tibet." Indian annexation of Sikkim was thus, from the Chinese point of view, a blatant act of aggression and hegemony. Through 2002, the diplomatic almanac published annually by China's MFA carried under the heading "Sikkim" the one sentence declaration: "The government of China does not recognize India's illegal annexation of Sikkim."[23] Starting in 2003, that statement disappeared from the MFA almanac. The joint declaration issued during Wen Jiabao's April 2005 visit to India referred to "Sikkim state of the Republic of India." China's ambassador to India told the media that the matter of sovereignty over Sikkim "has been completely settled."[24]

The Failure of Beijing's Friendship Offensive and Return to a Punitive Approach

Beijing hoped that its reassurance of India via friendship diplomacy would dissuade New Delhi from joining an anti-China combination with the United States—just as Russia had promised to do with the December 1992 joint communiqué and again with the 2001 treaty of friendship. Nonalignment with powers hostile to China was the sine qua non of China's friendship with its neighbors, in Beijing's view. Unfortunately for Beijing's anti-encirclement friendship diplomacy, India ignored China's professions of friendship and moved into deeper and deeper military partnership with the United States. India also began forging military and security links with Japan, hinting at a US-Japan-India "anti-China" linkup.

A new, more cooperative India-US relation began to form during the last two years of the Clinton presidency (1999–2000). It was given a great boost by the George W. Bush administration, which took office in January 2001. Over the eight years of the George W. Bush presidency, India-US cooperation, especially in the military and security areas, expanded rapidly. Exchanges of high- and working-level military personnel reached unprecedented intensity. A wide array of defense and security dialogues was set in motion. India was one of only a few countries to enthusiastically welcome the Bush administration's ambitious plans for ballistic missile defense (BMD); joint development efforts were followed by deployment, with US assistance, of an integrated Indian

BMD system in 2011. Joint research and development efforts in space and a range of other high-tech areas began. The two militaries began joint training exercises in a range of areas: high altitude operations, air defense, command post, and naval maneuvers. The two navies began coordinating their patrolling activities in the Indian Ocean, including the Strait of Malacca. India began to purchase US arms. The two sides coordinated efforts in Afghanistan, though quietly so as to minimize Pakistani unease. In June 2005, India and the United States signed a New Framework for Defense Relations laying out a ten-year program of expanded cooperation. Washington also offered India an exception to NPT requirements that would allow the United States to begin civilian nuclear cooperation with India. Talk on such an exception began in 2005 and culminated in a March 2006 agreement on India-US civilian nuclear cooperation.

The India-US security partnership was a truly revolutionary development in the international system. As noted earlier, the USSR had been India's major security backer during the Cold War, while China had been the US partner since 1971. In the 2000s, international alignments shifted on the fulcrum of common US and Indian concern about China's growing power. India was delighted to find the United States a new and powerful backer of Indian security. Beijing, however, watched with dismay as the United States and India forged an entirely new military and strategic partnership. Washington and New Delhi were careful, of course, to deny that the new relationship was aimed in any way against China. But China's representatives knew that it was.[25] In April 2002, when US Chairman of the Joint Chief of Staff visited India to expand military relations, a commentary in *Renmin ribao* charged that the purpose of the visit was to send "a clear message to China ... The United States is expanding its sphere of influence in Asia [into] China's back yard." Yet it was hard to predict, the paper said, whether India would "become a strategic ally of the United States or a strategic ally of China." The US goal, however, was clear: "establishing a bastion for containing China; checking and containing the Islamic fundamentalists in Central Asia; and promoting democratic politics in South Asia."[26] Another *Renmin ribao* article said regarding the New Framework for Defense Relations that it was "partly intended to diminish China's influence in this region and to safeguard and expand US strategic interest in Asia." It continued:

> Although both sides say the agreement has nothing to do with China ... The China factor is only too obvious.... [the US and India] felt keenly uneasy about China's development, though neither of them mentioned it. US neo-cons have long been insisting that the long-term threat is from China, while India apparently senses that China is a neighbor stronger than itself in both economic and military strength.[27]

From Beijing's perspective, India was responding to China's friendship diplomacy of 2000–2005 by aligning with the United States against China. China's quest for friendship with India was being repaid by Indian anti-China alignment with the United States. The key political purpose of China's friendly approach was to reassure India, thereby dissuading it from aligning with the United States. But India responded to China's friendship not in kind, but by partnering with Washington to encircle and contain China. A firmer approach to India was merited. China's friendship effort was being taken by Indian leaders as Chinese weakness. India had to be shown that friendship with China needed to be a two-way street. If New Delhi wanted China's friendship, it would have to abstain from actions hostile to China. New Delhi had to be made to understand that there would be heavy costs for rejecting China's friendship. It is important to note that at this juncture Beijing would not play the one card that might have made a major difference to India: settlement of the territorial dispute. That approach was probably impossible because of nationalist sentiment within China, both within the Politburo and among ordinary citizens.

Starting in 2006, Chinese policy toward India hardened. Beijing withdrew the suggestion in Article 7 of the Guidelines and Parameters of the previous year that China might be prepared to give up its claim to all of Arunachal Pradesh. Speaking shortly before Hu Jintao's November 2006 visit to India, PRC Ambassador to India Sun Yuxi told the international press: "In our position, the whole of what you call the state of Arunachal Pradesh is Chinese territory and Tawang is only one place in it and we are claiming all of that—that's our position."[28] The point was reiterated by foreign minister Yang Jiechi in talks with his Indian counterpart six months later: the "mere presence" of settled population did not affect China's territorial claims. Beijing also told Indian leaders that China had been moving toward a settlement of the territorial question until New Delhi decided to align with the United States against China. Whether or not Beijing was actually prepared to settle the territorial dispute, it was in China's interest that Indian leaders believe that it was. Meanwhile, on the border, Chinese incursions into the Tawang and Ladakh sectors increased, according to the Indian government.

Beijing also opposed lending in the Asian Development Bank during 2009 for projects in Arunachal Pradesh. It worked in the Nuclear Suppliers Group (a forty-five-member group that regulates trade in nuclear materials) during a 2008 meeting in Vienna against a ruling that would open the way to implementation of the India-US nuclear technology agreement. China's representative lobbied against a special exemption for India and insisted on a similar exemption for Pakistan. When deliberations became protracted, the Chinese delegation prepared to leave the conference and return home. Eventually, only a direct appeal from President Bush to Hu Jintao secured China's return to the conference and nonblocking of the exemption for India.

The most unnerving aspect of Beijing's pressure campaign was an eruption of commentary on Chinese websites, including some linked to the PLA, about a possible war between China and India. One article posted on the website of the International Institute for Strategic Studies in Beijing, a PLA-linked think tank, for example, warning that India could respond to China's planned damning of the upper Brahmaputra River with a military strike that could lead to a war larger than that of 1962. In this war, India would have "much support," while China would face a two-front war, since the United States was likely to make a move regarding Taiwan in order to "contain China."[29] Many inventive scenarios of PRC-Indian war were posted online during the 2005–2009 period. This effort was probably a type of psychological operation intended to make India think about how heavy the costs to India might be if New Delhi continued to display such an unfriendly approach to China. Cyber threats of war dovetailed with increased forward-leaning patrolling on the border.

India-Japan Relations: Inception of a Countervailing Coalition

Beijing's mix of reassurance and pressure toward Japan and India was not sufficient to keep those two Asian powers from pulling together and hewing more closely to the United States out of common concern over how China had used and would use its growing power. Step by step, a loose coalition of Japan and India formed to balance China's growing strength. Washington quietly encouraged this emerging Asian coalition as well as the efforts of Tokyo and New Delhi to expand dialogue with other like-minded countries: Australia, Vietnam, the Philippines, and Indonesia. Rather than becoming comfortable with China's rapidly growing power, Japan and India drew closer to one another, and to the United States, out of common concern about China's growing power and assertive behavior.

According to Richard Samuels, by the mid-1990s Japan began incrementally to embrace the practice of de facto collective security. Apprehension over China's growing strength was central to this course.[30] China's actions helped create a deep congruence of Indian and Japanese views regarding China's rise. Both Tokyo and New Delhi aspired to play a greater role in Asia and saw China as attempting to prevent that: by blocking permanent Security Council membership for both, by emphasizing the history issue with Japan and by arming Pakistan in the case of India, by taking hard lines on territorial disputes. The history issue that weighed so heavily in Sino-Japan relations did not exist in Indo-Japan ties. In fact, the anti-European colonial aspect of World War II in Asia produced a feeling of kinship between India and Japan. Both worried that China's growing naval strength and activity astride vital sea lines of communication with the Persian Gulf and the Suez Canal, and eastward with Guam, Hawaii, and North America. Both Tokyo and New Delhi worried that China might opt to use military force to resolve territorial disputes, and in such a situation, the timely exchange of intelligence on Chinese ship movements between the Indian and Pacific Oceans would considerably strengthen the efforts of both Tokyo and New Delhi to keep track of those movements. More broadly, Tokyo and New Delhi each saw the other as sharing an interest in preventing emergence of a China-centric Asia, and in maintaining a pluralistic multipolar system in Asia. Both Tokyo and New Delhi worried that Beijing's efforts to expand cooperative ties with various Asian countries could, if not balanced, lead to a China-centered Asia. Tokyo and New Delhi each looked favorably on the military capabilities of the other, seeing them as enhancing its own security. In economic terms, Indo-Japanese ties expanded, with both Tokyo and New Delhi gradually discovering that cooperation averted certain shortcomings encountered with economic cooperation with China. As Japan cut economic assistance to China, aid to India rose.[31] Factors other than China's growing power influenced some of these developments. But Beijing's periodic campaigns to pressure and intimidate Japan and India contributed significantly to the glacial movement of the two countries toward a loose coalition intended to prevent eventual Chinese domination of Asia.

Defense cooperation between India and Japan began in August 2000, when Prime Minister Yoshiro Mori visited India to sign with Prime Minister Vajpayee an agreement declaring a "Global Partnership between Japan and India in the Twenty-first Century." This was in the aftermath of New Delhi's China-threat justification of India's nuclearization, and was part of Vajpayee's effort to strengthen India's global position. Indian warships began visiting Japan in 2000 as gestures of goodwill, and the first exchange of defense ministers came in July the next year.[32] In 2006, "strategic" was added to the official description of the Indo-Japanese relationship, reflecting growing interest in military and security cooperation. Between 2006 and 2014, a dozen or so statements and declarations of strategic partnership were issued during nearly annual exchange visits by Japanese and Indian prime ministers. In August 2007, Japan and India agreed on a Roadmap for New Dimensions to the Strategic and Global Partnership. The Roadmap declared that the partnership was founded on "universal values of democracy, open society, human rights, rule of law and market economy"—formulations that sharply distinguished those two countries from China. The Roadmap also proclaimed "common interests in promoting peace, stability and prosperity in Asia and the world." Moreover: "A strong . . . India is in the interest of Japan and a strong . . . Japan is in the interest of India." "Japan and India share a convergence of interests," the Roadmap declared.[33]

A year after the "Roadmap," the two countries signed an agreement on security cooperation—only Japan's third such agreement, after ones with the

United States and Australia. The Joint Declaration on the security agreement proclaimed that India and Japan were: "partners with a mutual stake in each other's progress and prosperity . . . . that a strong and prosperous India is in the interests of Japan and that a strong and prosperous Japan is in the interests of India." Because of this, the Declaration said, the two countries had "decided to create a comprehensive framework for the enhancement of security cooperation between the two countries."[34] All sorts of cooperation "mechanisms" were set up under these agreements: annual strategic dialogues at the foreign minister level, regular consultations between the national security advisors of the two governments, annual sub-minister meetings of Foreign and Defense Ministry officials, a maritime security dialogue, and so on.[35] In July 2010, regular combined dialogues between the defense and foreign ministers ("two plus two") of the two sides began.

None of these Indo-Japanese Declarations or "cooperation mechanisms" mentioned China, let alone identified China as a matter of common concern. That country could, however, be discerned between the lines. The Joint Statement Vision for Japan-India Strategic and Global Partnership in the Next Decade signed by Prime Ministers Manmohan Singh and Naoto Kan in October 2010, for instance, referred to "a changing and dynamic Asia" that led both countries to value bilateral cooperation in "sustaining peace and prosperity." China's rise would clearly be a major factor of change and dynamism in Asia. The Vision welcomed the launch of a India-Japan "dialogue on Africa at the official level" to achieve "wider policy consultation and cooperation on foreign policy and security issues." Implicit was the fact that China's assertive push for African resources posed challenges to both India and Japan, which themselves sought those resources. The Vision called for increased cooperation between the Indian navy and the JMSDF in the Gulf of Aden. Unstated but implicit was the fact that the PLA-N had only two years before begun sustained operations in the Gulf of Aden—astride both Japan and India's sea lines of communication with the Persian Gulf. The Vision called for inclusion of the United States in the East Asia Summit—something China opposed.[36]

Practical military cooperation between India and Japan began in 2001, when, following the 9-11 attacks and the US-led intervention in Afghanistan, Japan's navy entered the Indian Ocean for the first time since World War II, as a small squadron of JMSDF vessels took up station to provide refueling support for Allied anti-Taliban operations. Japanese warships began quietly refueling and resupplying at Indian ports. Following the US-led 2003 regime-change war in Iraq, Japan's military role in the Indian Ocean rose another notch when Tokyo sent a contingent of military engineers to assist with the reconstruction effort in Iraq. Japan's deployments in 2001 and 2003 marked major departures for Japan's military role in SA-IOR and for the Japan-India military relationship.

Late in 2008, China initiated a major increase in its naval presence and capabilities in the Indian Ocean when it decided to send PLA-N warships to participate in international antipiracy efforts that had been underway for several years in the Gulf of Aden. Economic considerations partially motivated this move. Insurance costs were rising for unescorted Chinese vessels and delivery schedules were being disrupted putting Chinese businesses at a competitive disadvantage.[37] Whether or not China's leaders considered the strategic impact of this decision, those impacts were substantial. PLA-N warships established a permanent and robust presence in the Indian Ocean. PLA-N warships had visited Indian Ocean ports a dozen or so times since the first visit in 1985, but those visits had been transitory. Beginning in 2009, the PLA-N presence was enduring, with one PLA-N task force replacing another after serving on station for four months. PLA-N warships began frequent calls at ports all around the Indian Ocean littoral, as illustrated by Figure 27-1. PLA-N commanders thus gained useful knowledge of where they could get various supplies, replacement personnel, maintenance, or repairs. PLA-N warships also began investigating such factors as currents, temperature and salinity gradients, and sea floor terrain, knowledge essential for effective operations, especially submarine and antisubmarine operations.

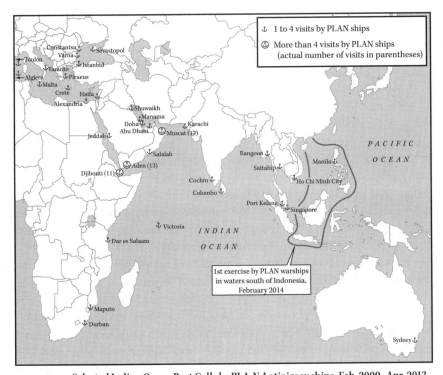

FIGURE 27-1 **Selected Indian Ocean Port Calls by PLA-N Antipiracy ships, Feb. 2009–Apr. 2013**

Source: Andrew S. Erickson, Austin M. Strange, *No Substitute for Experience: Chinese Antipiracy Operations in the Gulf of Aden,* (China Maritime Studies Institute monograph no. 10, U.S. Naval War College, November 2013); Trefor Moss, "Beijing's Power Play Exposes Anxieties," *Wall Street Journal,* February 20, 2014, A10.

Early in 2014, the PLA-N pushed still further into new maritime territory when three ships that were part of the antipiracy patrols transited the Sunda and Lombok straights for the first time, as shown in Figure 27-1. From India's perspective, it faced a much denser Chinese military presence virtually all around its perimeter.

In fall 2013, President Xi Jinping unveiled a plan for large-scale construction of ports and associated free trade zones at ports in Pakistan, Sri Lanka, Bangladesh, and Myanmar. Dubbed a "maritime Silk Road," the plan called for funding by China's government, to be followed by Chinese investment and expanded trade.[38]

China's escalating naval presence in the Indian Ocean caused unease in India. The traditional advantages the Indian navy held arising from the tyranny of distance confronting the PLA-N in that ocean was steadily being eroded. As a former Indian foreign secretary wrote:

> The port facilities China is obtaining or building [around the Indian Ocean littoral] ... raise concerns about China encircling us physically and politically, changing our bilateral equation further to our disadvantage. . . China will, inevitably, follow up with its commercial footholds in the Indian Ocean with naval ones. The purpose of China's naval expansion is precisely to create strategic space for itself in [the] Western Pacific and then move into the Indian Ocean gradually, in preparation for which China is learning to operate far from its shores for quite some time now, in the Gulf of Aden, for instance.[39]

India responded to China's growing Indian Ocean activity by stepping up maritime cooperation with the United States and with Japan. The United States was India's most important security partner, but it was the India-Japan link that pointed most clearly toward the deepening alignment of China's neighbors to countervail its growing strength. India-Japan naval cooperation began in 2000 and expanded slowly over the next decade.[40] In 2012, the Indian and Japanese navies conducted their first-ever bilateral exercise off Japan's east coast. The next year, the two countries began a maritime affairs dialogue. Significantly, the Indian delegation to the dialogue included representatives from the Ministry of Earth Sciences, a body with responsibilities for satellite remote sensing, a core technology for finding and tracking ships at sea (or undersea). In 2013, the second Japan-India joint naval exercise took place in the Bay of Bengal. The next year, India agreed to Japan's participation in the Indo-US Malabar naval exercises. India had first consented to Japanese participation in the Malabar exercises in 2007 and again in 2009, but Beijing's protests had caused New Delhi to pull back from such forward-leaning cooperation. India's 2014 acceptance of Japan's participation in the annual Indo-US exercise was a move to offset the escalating PLA-N presence in the Indian Ocean. The big picture was this: confronting growing

Chinese naval power, Japan and India recognized convergent interests and pulled together to deal with their common challenge. Washington quietly supported this process.

Beijing lobbied New Delhi not to align with Japan. Shortly before visits by Japan's defense minister and Prime Minister Abe in January 2014, China's ambassador to India authored an op-ed that appeared in a leading Indian English-language newspaper. Ambassador Wei Wei's article called on India to stand with China, not Japan, in shaping Asia's future. The ambassador offered two key arguments: the history issue and the rapidly deepening and mutually beneficial Sino-Indian economic relations. Regarding "history," Japan was again trying to develop into a "military power," even though visits to Yasukuni Shrine showed Japan was unrepentant. China and India had stood together against Japan in the 1930s, and should again stand shoulder to shoulder to block Japan's nefarious efforts.[41] In Beijing, an MFA spokesman said China hoped that Japan-Indian defense cooperation would "be conducive to peace, stability and security of the whole region."[42] To give substance to these warnings, Chinese forces on the border stepped up patrol activity.[43] A prominent member of India's National Security Advisory Board saw that one purpose of China's increased border "intrusions" was to "caution India against drawing closer to the U.S., Japan or Vietnam as China could exert military pressure on India at a place and time of its choosing anywhere along the countries' long border."[44]

During a May 2015 visit to Beijing, Indian Prime Minister Narendra Modi, who had taken office a year earlier, pressed China to show greater consideration for India's security concerns and, thus, sincere friendship for India. Speaking to reporters after talks with Xi Jinping, Modi said, "I stressed the need for China to reconsider its approach on some of the issues that hold us back from realizing the full potential of our partnership."[45] "We covered all issues, including those that trouble smooth development of our relations," Modi said.[46] Behind closed doors, Modi urged Xi to work toward fixing the Line of Actual Control along the border as a step toward an early and final settlement of the territorial dispute. Modi's key leverage in persuading Beijing to pay greater heed to India's security concerns, is Beijing's awareness that, without such reassurance, India may well drift further into alignment with Japan and the United States.

There are major obstacles in both Japan and India to genuine alignment against China. In India there remains a deep strain of nonalignment and strategic autonomy in the political culture. This, combined with the reality that Indian alignment with US-allied Japan would be tantamount to Indian alignment with the United States, constitutes a powerful Indian argument for keeping Japan at arm's length, at least in strategic if not in economic terms. Many Indians fear getting dragged into US conflicts with China. There is also fear that angering Beijing could lead to a genuine confrontation with China.

India, unlike Japan, is not protected by alliance with the United States, and in a situation of looming "encirclement" Beijing might well target India as the weakest, most vulnerable link. New Delhi's strategy thus seems to be to use the threat of Indian alignment with the United States and Japan to induce Beijing to adopt more conciliatory policies toward India, especially on the territorial dispute. This is a tack that requires a tilt toward Washington and Tokyo adequate to rouse Chinese apprehensions, but not so pronounced as to produce Chinese hostility and punitive measures. Overplaying the US-Japan card could induce the Chinese hostility toward India it was intended to avoid. Yet Indian fears of China's growing presence in SA-IOR are real and strong and could lead, if not handled properly by Beijing, to emergence of a counter-vailing India-Japan coalition.

In Japan, there remains a strong aversion to Japanese military power and the practice of power politics. Memory of the catastrophic consequences of those things in the 1930s remains strong. So too does guilt for Japan's actions in that era, guilt that comingles with esteem for China's civilizational achieve-ments. There is also recognition of the deep economic ties between Japan and China, and of the potential heavy costs if political conflict disrupts those ties. It thus remains unclear how far and how fast even a determined Japanese leader like Shinzo Abe will be able to go in forging a security partnership with India. What is clear, however, is that China's growing power and the assertive application of that power are not reassuring Japan and India, but are nudging those countries together out of common apprehensions.

China's Quandary

Beijing will have to move deftly to avoid pushing its two apprehensive neigh-bors into a coalition to contain it. A major thrust of Chinese diplomacy will have to be reassurance of Japan and India. The track record of China's efforts in this regard indicates that China's leaders and diplomats are cognizant of this fact. Overall, however, Chinese efforts to reassure Tokyo and New Delhi have not been highly successful.

Nationalist passions and elite competition in China make difficult a shift by Beijing to policies better designed to reassure China's neighbors. Any CCP administration that pulled back from the current strategy of assert-ively establishing an ongoing and de facto Chinese presence in the disputed East China Sea would be charged with weakness and lack of patriotic zeal by a rival in the Politburo, by the PLA, by bloggers, by impassioned mobs in the streets of China's cities, or by some combination of these. How could rising China allow itself to be pinned in by "little Japan"? ardent Chinese nationalists would say. Similarly, a Chinese leader who advocated abandon-ing China's claim to the southern slope of the eastern Himalayas and drawing the boundary along the detested McMahon Line would face similar charges. In addition, a conciliatory Chinese leader—perhaps along the lines of Zhou Enlai or Deng Xiaoping—who was willing to "abandon" that territory would be charged with endangering the Sino-Pakistan entente, thereby founding the security of "China's Tibet" not on a solid balance of power favoring China but on Indian pledges of friendship that could easily shift.

China's leaders certainly recognize as well as foreign analysts the tectonic shifts underway in response to China's growing power. The outcomes of these shifts could well be the most decisive factor in determining the course of human events in the twenty-first century. The good outcome would be that China finds another statesman of the caliber of Zhou Enlai or Deng Xiaoping who can succeed in reassuring its neighbors. The bad outcome would be an ambitious politician who rides the wave of nationalism to lead an effort to break out of the anti-China encirclement that Chinese nationalists imagine malevolent American hegemonists have engineered around China.

28 }

China's Quest for Modernity and the Tides of World History

First a Scary Story: Will China Be Another "Germany"?

Once upon a time there was a great, rich and powerful people who had raised themselves to a high position by hard work and tenacity. They were ruled, however, by a small group of men who claimed for themselves the power to govern, and who crushed all who challenged that claim. Many among the talented and hard-working people resented the arrogance of their self-appointed rulers, and dreamed of the day when the people would be able to chose their rulers and change them when they saw fit, as many of the neighboring peoples already did. The challenge to the rulers was great, for few among the people any longer believed the myths used by the rulers to justify their rule. For a while the rulers of the land were modest, concentrated on improving the lives of the people, and avoided giving offense to their neighbors. But the rulers remained fearful that the people might rise against them. Then one day a clever man among the rulers discovered a way to rally the people around the rulers—expand the glory and might of the kingdom so that it might warm the hearts of the people. And the people rallied to the cause of glory, for they were proud of all they had accomplished and had long believed that their treatment among the nations had been unfair. But it came to pass that the many nations who lived around the mighty kingdom grew fearful and united together to defeat their proud neighbor. The name of the people was Germany. The clever ruler who sought their glory was Kaiser Wilhelm II (reign 1888–1918). His failed quest for glory became known as World War I.

History, of course, never repeats itself, and there are great differences between Germany in the early twentieth century and China in the early twenty-first century. Yet there are also multiple striking similarities between the two, and framing a discussion of the domestic determinants of contemporary China's foreign policies by comparison with Wilhelmine Germany

(1871–1918) is a useful heuristic exercise.[1] Among the similarities between Wilhelmine Germany and post-Mao China, the one most directly relevant to this study is the resort to both aggressive and aggrieved nationalism to mobilize domestic support for the regime. But it is useful to review the other similarities first.

At the top of the list of other similarities is the fact that the politically dominant elites in both countries are noncapitalist or even anticapitalist, yet both elites preside over extremely rapid processes of capitalist economic development. In Wilhelmine Germany, a landed aristocracy called Junkers dominated the highest levels of state power. In China, the CCP dominates the state. Both elites were noncapitalist in terms of historic origins, social composition, and ideology. Regarding The Junkers, they emerged as holders of agricultural manors enfeoffed to them for hereditary military service tracing back to the Germanic conquest of Slavic lands east of the Elbe River under Charlemagne in the ninth century.[2] As towns based on maritime trade—the germ seeds of modern capitalism—emerged around the Baltic in the late medieval period, the Junker estates became suppliers of grain for those towns. A centuries-long struggle between the Junker aristocracy and the trade towns ensued. In this region of Europe, the landed aristocracy won, unlike German towns further west on the Baltic, where leagues of trade towns were able to defy sovereign monarchs and their noble supporters for several more centuries.[3] The Crusading Order of Teutonic Knights gave rise in 1525 to a centralizing state centered on the Hohenzollern dynasty, and the Junkers transferred their loyalty to that dynasty, becoming the major social base of the emerging Prussian state. Since estates went to the eldest son via primogeniture, many younger sons, all well-educated and with a sense of noble ancestry, went into military or government service, where they came to dominate the Prussian state. When Germany was unified under Prussian hegemony in 1871, the new state structure was carefully designed to ensure continuing Prussian dominance within Germany and Junker dominance within Prussia. The capitalist industrial and financial elite of united Germany was given a role in the new Germany, leading to the famous duopoly of "iron and rye." But within that partnership, the Hohenzollern dynasty and the Junkers dominated. Germany's capitalists played second fiddle. Regarding the CCP, its historic origin was, of course, the global Marxist-Leninist communist movement of the twentieth century. The CCP arose and waxed as part of a worldwide movement to destroy capitalism and replace it with a postcapitalist, socialist society. The CCP still prides itself on its destruction of capitalism and China's capitalist class in the 1950s. Twentieth-century communism ranks with much of Europe's feudal aristocratic class as a historic enemy of capitalism.

In terms of social composition (family origins and career paths), the top leaders of both Wilhelmine Germany and post-Deng China were/are noncapitalist. The Junkers were a legally privileged aristocracy based on agriculture and heredity, with strict rules of marriage and imperial ennoble-ment governing admission into that closed elite. Commoners and capitalists could and sometimes did manage ennoblement into the Junkers, but those cases were rare. The typical path of advance for CCP members has been via promotion by the CCP's nomenklatura to ever higher levels of power and responsibility in China's state and party administrative systems. Virtually none of the top CCP leaders are from capitalist families—although that may change in years ahead. There are great differences between the Junker and the CCP elites in terms of openness of recruitment and the role of profes-sional meritocracy. The point here, however, is that in terms of social com-position, neither Junkers nor CCP leaders were linked to capitalist economic success, although with both it can be argued that political success required fostering and assisting capitalist industrialization. In China, the relation between the CCP and successful capitalists was modified in 2000 when Jiang Zemin persuaded the CCP to open to party membership successful private sector entrepreneurs. To date, however, this had had little impact on the top levels of power.

The formal legitimizing ideology of both the Junkers and the CCP is anti-capitalist. The Junker claim to legitimacy was based on the antiquity of enfeoffment, long loyalty and service to the liege lord and later the sover-eign, military prowess, family heraldry, and simple tradition. Junkers typi-cally disdained commercial activity as beneath their status. As for the CCP, its formal ideology remains Marxism-Leninism–Mao Zedong Thought, with its belief in the evil nature of capitalism, the superiority of socialism over capitalism, and so on. This creed serves today largely as a device for strength-ening intraparty unity and for solemn high rituals legitimizing the CCP's permanent domination of the state. Yet is remains the formal ideology of the CCP, embodied, for example, in the Four Cardinal Principles.

The Junkers of Wilhelmine Germany and the post-Deng CCP are similar too in that they are essentially extrastate elites that maintain permanent con-trol over the state. The mechanisms through which they do this differ. The devices used by the CCP were enumerated in note 1 in chapter 1. Regarding Germany, the Junkers ensured their dominance via the Hohenzollern dy-nasty, control over the top levels of the state bureaucracy, and the domination of the officer corps of the German army. Prussia also had a privileged pos-ition within the Wilhelmine state via certain constitutional arrangements. Repression was a key ruling strategy relied on by both the Wilhelmine and the CCP states. In both, opponents of the established order were subject to harassment or imprisonment. Police powers were great and informants were pervasive. There was the ever-present threat of martial law. In Wilhelmine Germany and perhaps in the PRC today, over all loomed the threat of a "coup d'état from above" in which the rulers would suspend constitutional forms and rule by direct dictatorship.

In both the Wilhelmine and CCP states, elections were not designed to allow the people to remove one elite and install another to govern them—Joseph Schumpeter's famous definition of democracy. Rather, elections were intended and designed merely to improve the quality of administration by self-selected rulers. The Wilhelmine state had a national legislative body constituted by election based on universal male suffrage and exercising certain powers of legislation. But the government was responsible not to the legislature but to the monarch, whose court was packed with high aristocrats. Historian Richard Evans calls the Wilhelmine set-up "a pseudo-constitutional semi-absolutist" system.⁴ In the PRC, the electoral process is still modeled after that of the USSR. The nomination process is controlled by the CCP and filters out oppositional elements. Legislative bodies produced by elections are guided by embedded party organs and serve, at most, as sounding boards for proposed legislation. Usually People's Congresses function as rubber stamps for decisions made by party organs. The purpose of elections is to strengthen and improve CCP rule, not to provide a mechanism for the Chinese people to genuinely choose and change their rulers.

Another similarity between the Wilhelmine and current CCP elite is fear of rebellion. Germany's working class was then large, growing rapidly, discontented, and enamored with ideas of democracy, socialism, and revolution. The examples of 1789, 1848, and the Paris uprising of 1871 loomed large, as did the myth of a general strike that would topple capitalism. The Wilhelmine regime lived in constant fear of a workers' rebellion, and this was a key reason for its highly repressive nature. China's situation is paradoxical. On the one hand, as noted in chapter 1, attitudinal surveys among the Chinese populace—including middle-class professionals and private-sector entrepreneurs who modernization theory indicates should be supporters of democratization—show remarkably little support for basic regime change. Chinese public opinion, across virtually all social groups, supports continuing authoritarian CCP rule. Most Chinese have apparently been convinced that liberal democracy would not work for China. There *is* great discontent in China. In 2012, there were reportedly around 150,000 protests over all sorts of complaints: state seizure of property, police brutality, environmental degradation, wage and pension disputes, official corruption, etc. But the anger underlying these demonstrations does not seem to translate into a desire for regime change. Nonetheless, CCP leaders seem transfixed by the danger of a popular uprising against them. The trauma of the 1989–1991 upheavals, the intense CCP concern for internal stability, and careful cultivation of the PLA as ultimate guardian of the CCP state strongly suggest that CCP leaders, like those of Wilhelmine Germany, fear uprising. There seems to be a sense among CCP leaders that public opinion might shift rapidly, and that events might quickly mobilize diverse sectors of society, and demands escalate, confronting them with another 6-4-like challenge. The entire internal security apparatus of the post-6-4 CCP state seems designed to prevent that from happening. The abrupt emergence and rapid growth of anti-regime movements in Eastern Europe, Soviet Russia, the "color revolutions" of the former Soviet area and the Arab Spring undoubtedly play a role in fostering regime fears, as may Confucian concepts of loss of the Mandate of Heaven and China's own history of not infrequent rebellion. In any case, in today's China, as in Wilhelmine Germany, the constant threat of direct dictatorial rule, imposed as necessary by internal security forces and ultimately the army, stands ready to repress opposition to the ruling elite's control over the state.

There are similarities too in terms of the military's role as protector of the authoritarian state. The army of Prussia-Germany was a "state within a state," virtually immune from governmental direction and loyal only to the kaiser. The German army was deeply conservative and stood not only as a bulwark against liberal reform but as an advocate of the development and utilization of military power in foreign affairs.[5] The PLA, for its part, houses a political work system tightly controlled by the CCP center and designed to ensure that "the Party controls the gun."[6] The primary loyalty of the PLA high command is to the party center, with state institutions typically formalizing and legitimizing decisions already reached by the CCP Politburo or the Central Military Commission. And as we have seen, since the upheavals of 1989–1991 the PLA has been both the ultimate guardian of CCP rule and a major source of demands for a more confrontational and forceful foreign policy backed up by displays of military force. On at least one occasion (1995–1996), the PLA succeeded in translating its policy preferences into national policy. This is not to say that PLA leaders favor war. Their assessment of the actual military balance between the PLA and, say, Japan and the United States is probably quite sober and realistic, leading to a desire to avoid actual conflict. But there are many ways to use military force below the threshold of outright belligerency.

Still another eerie similarity between Wilhelmine Germany and the PRC is a strong sense of historically rooted national victimization. China's narrative of "the Century of National Humiliation" has been dealt with elsewhere in this book. Regarding Germany, Wilhelm II's *"Weltpolitik"* fed upon and encouraged a belief in Germany's victimization, a strong sense that Germany had not been treated fairly by the great powers. The small German states had been the main battleground for the religious wars of the seventeenth century known as the Thirty Years War (1618–1648). Powerful armies of the major European states—Spain, Sweden, Austria, France, and Britain—marched back and forth across Germany. Foraging by armies, looting, disease, famine, rape, and war depopulated whole regions, reducing the population of the German states by perhaps as much as half. French diplomacy fueled resistance by the feuding German states with the objective of using German resistance to grind down the strength of France's major European rivals. In consequence of the resulting devastation and disunity, while other European powers—Spain, Portugal, France, Russia, Britain, and the Netherlands—built national states and then seized vast, far-flung overseas empires, Germany did not. French policy sought to keep the German lands disunited. Not until 1871 did Germany achieve national unification, several centuries after the other leading European states. The other powers had not been fair to Germany, German patriots ardently believed. Germany had been conspired against and denied her proper place in the sun. People from Germany's middle class flocked to patriotic societies that gave voice to these sentiments of grievance and entitlement. This mobilization of popular patriotic passion encouraged bold diplomatic moves that won patriotic applause: seizure of a sphere of influence in China, a naval demonstration in support of the ethnically Dutch Boer settlers in South Africa, confrontation with France over influence in Morocco, dispatch of a force to chastise the Boxers in China. Mobilization of popular patriotic fashion also made it difficult for Germany's leaders to back down once they found themselves in the confrontations that often resulted from bold diplomatic moves against ever more fearful neighboring governments. Compromise and conciliation were easily depicted as betrayal of the nation.

The Problem of Great Power and the Need for Caution

From an international perspective, the "problem" of Wilhelmine Germany was that its strength was so great that, when not used with great restraint, it frightened its neighbors, causing them to join together against it. This seems to be a core problem of the contemporary PRC as well. Regarding Germany, the unification under Prussian tutelage of German states in 1871 created a new state, Germany, which with a population of 41 million became the most populous European country west of Russia. United Germany also had high levels of literacy and education (measured by number of universities and books published), as well as strong commercial and scientific development. In the brief forty-seven-year existence of the Wilhelmine regime, scientists from Wilhelmine Germany received more Nobel prizes than Britain, France, and the United States combined. Germany was a leading world center in many areas of scientific and medical research, as well as industrial engineering and manufacturing. German industrialization proceeded very rapidly after 1871. By 1913, Germany was the leading industrial power of Europe (although barely so), with 15.7 percent of world manufacturing, compared to Britain's 14 percent, France's 6.4 percent, and Russia's 6.4 percent.[7] Germany's army was also far more potent than those of the other European powers.

Under Wilhelm I and his cautious chancellor Otto von Bismarck, German foreign policy was successful in reassuring Germany's neighbors Russia,

Austria-Hungary, and Britain that Germany's growing power would not threaten them. Bismarck sought to isolate France, whom he viewed as the inveterate enemy of a unified Germany, from potential partners in containing Germany. Restraint and reassurance were key characteristic of Bismarck's diplomacy.[8] Bismarck eschewed colonial conquest precisely because he feared it would turn Britain against Germany and push it toward alignment with France. Most significant of all, Bismarck reassured Russia that German power would not be directed against it. He did this by signing a treaty with Russia that, in effect, meant that Germany's other ally, Austria-Hungary, had only a *conditional* guarantee by Germany against Russia, Austria-Hungary's rival in the Balkans.

There are strong similarities between Bismarck's and Deng Xiaoping's low-profile and restrained diplomacy. Deng quickly scrapped the revolutionary activism that had alienated China's Southeast Asian neighbors, pushed for rapprochement with all China's major neighbors (Japan, India, Islamic Iran, the Soviet Union), and exploited the strategic triangle to reassure the United States.

After a period of self-restraint under Wilhelm I and Bismarck, new German leaders shifted course and pursued an assertive policy of *Weltmacht* or "world power." In 1890, Wilhelm II fired Bismarck and took personal control of Germany's diplomacy. He then charted a new course for Germany in world affairs, *Weltpolitik* or world policy—an effort to establish Germany as a world power fully equal to other first-rate powers in the world. This meant inter alia construction of a powerful high-seas fleet of modern battleships that could threaten Britain's Royal Navy and thus its ability to maintain communication with its far-flung global empire. German strategists imagined that this threat would deter British from a war in support of France. In fact, it produced the opposite result and pushed Britain toward entente with France. *Weltmacht* meant too the pursuit of colonies and other foreign holdings in Asia and Africa. *Weltpolitik* brought Germany into frequent conflicts with Britain and France over their respective holdings in Asia and Africa—just as Bismarck had feared. Even more fatally, Wilhelm II abandoned the treaty with Russia for the sake of an unequivocal alliance with Vienna. Conflicting treaty obligations with Petersburg and Vienna seemed illogical and confusing to Germany's new leader. Standing alone and now confronting German power behind Austria in the Balkans, Russia soon moved into alliance with France. Then Britain joined them, largely out of fear of the threat Germany's new high seas battleships posed to Britain's global empire. This created the "Triple Entente" of France, Russia, and Britain. Germany had precipitated its own encirclement by its assertive policies combined with great industrial and military power. Fearing Germany's ever-growing power and assertive policies, the Triple Entente joined together to counter Germany. Germans at the time, however, viewed the anti-German coalition not as a response to

Germany's moves, but as the result of deep anti-German animus inspired by a determination to return Germany to the status of weak victimhood that had been its fate before 1871. This "encirclement" had to be smashed by bold policy moves, Germany's leaders and nationalist public opinion concluded. The stage was set for Germany's effort to break out of Franco-Russian-British "encirclement" and World War I.

Several historians who have studied Germany's fatal embrace of *Weltmacht* have concluded that it was driven largely by domestic factors. By the mid-1890s, the deep divisions of German society could no longer be papered over by the compromise arrangements of the 1870s. Germany's Junker elite and Hohenzollern dynasty faced mounting demands for reform requiring them to give up control of the state. Rather than accede to these demands, Germany's rulers decided to divert public attention outward, toward Germany's growing global majesty, generating popular appreciation for the strong state that was delivering that glory. In the words of Imanuel Geiss, "Weltpolitik came into existence as a red herring of the ruling class to distract the middle and working classes from social and political problems at home at the risk of war, of losing war, monarchy and all. . . . A breathtaking foreign policy was intended to unite the nation and, through mobilization of the masses, would increase her power."[9] As one of the architects of *Weltmacht*, German Chancellor Johannes von Miquel, put it in 1901 (shortly before Germany's move to break out of encirclement by the Triple Entente), the way to win popular support for the monarchy was to "revive the national ideal" by "a victorious war." Just as the victorious wars of German unification in 1866–1870 had revived the dynasty from a steady decline, "A victorious war would solve many problems" within Germany, Miquel said.[10]

Bismarck's moderate course did not prove popular with nationalist German opinion in the decades before 1914. A question haunting governments around the world today is whether a diplomacy of moderation, restraint, and reassurance will prove more acceptable to Chinese ardent and mobilized nationalist opinion in the 2020s than it did to Germany's nationalists in the 1900s. Will China someday embrace a *Weltmacht* diplomacy to replace the cautious Bismarck-like diplomacy of Deng Xiaoping? Perhaps such a shift has already begun with the strategic adjustment of 2009 followed by the rise of Xi Jinping. China's blunt and frequently intimidating diplomacy toward Japan and India is not reassuring (here used in its Bismarckian sense). Assertive policies toward Japan and India are undoubtedly popular with China's nationalists. But they also seem to be precipitating the same sort of countervailing coalition that Germany faced by the 1910s. And like those of Germany, China's nationalists blame the formation of that countervailing coalition not on China's own actions but on malevolent foreign powers; behind the growing Japanese-Indian coalition is the nefarious instigation of the United States.

The Fabrication of Chinese Patriotism: The CCP as the Sorcerer's Apprentice?

In 1797, Johann Wolfgang von Goethe wrote a poem titled "The Sorcerer's Apprentice." In it, a semiskilled apprentice magician, tired of daily chores, takes advantage of his master's temporary absence to magically empower a broom to carry water and mop the floor. Once empowered, the broom soon escapes the apprentice's control, threatening him with disaster. Finally, the master sorcerer returns to break the spell and save the day. The story stands as a warning to those who unleash forces, especially in politics, that they cannot control. In 1797, the revolutionary spell of nationalism was sweeping Europe, toppling regimes and mobilizing whole populations for revolution and war. Might the CCP have called forth a militant Chinese nationalism that it will be unable to control?

The emergence of nationalism both as the major legitimization of CCP authority and as an autonomous social force voicing foreign policy demands on the CCP is a major characteristics of China's post-1989 period. Nationalism has been defined as any behavior designed to restore, maintain, or advance the public image of a nation. *Chinese* nationalism is defined as determination to wipe out the dishonor of the Century of National Humiliation and restore China to its rightful position of high international esteem. The instrumental goals for achieving this are national prosperity and power.[11]

Patriotism in the form of a burning desire to drive all foreign imperialists out of China was a primary driving force of the whole Chinese communist movement. But during the post-1949 Mao era, the CCP advanced what has been called a "victor's narrative," with the Chinese people, under the correct leadership of Mao Zedong and the CCP, advancing from victory to victory: defeating Japan, driving out the KMT puppets of imperialism, overthrowing the landlords and comprador capitalists linked to imperialism, building socialism, rectifying ideological errors within the international communist movement, winning the esteem of the revolutionary peoples of the whole world, preparing to lead the world to the transition to communism, and so on. Within the framework of Mao's victor narrative, the Chinese revolution had made China strong. China, led by the CCP, had defeated the Japanese and their KMT lackeys. China, under Mao and the CCP, was showing the oppressed people of the world how to defeat imperialism, establish socialism, and move toward the transition to communism. China, under the correct leadership of Mao, was the leader of the whole world's revolutionary forces. The laboring classes of the whole world loved and esteemed Chairman Mao, in the Maoist narrative of that era. These were heady ideas.

After 1978, this victor's narrative faded with growing awareness of how poor and backward China actually was—a reality stressed by Deng Xiaoping and driven home by growing contact with the advanced capitalist countries and the rapidly modernizing countries of East Asia. Themes of revolution—the CCP defeating the KMT, China's proletarian victory over feudal landlords and the bourgeoisie, class struggle against hidden revisionists within the party—faded. New nationalist themes of the century of national humiliation and the struggle of all Chinese against that humiliation emerged. The new nationalist narrative had the advantage of including and appealing to ethnically proud Chinese in Taiwan, Hong Kong, and Southeast Asia. Marxism-Leninism–Mao Zedong Thought remained the formal ideology for performing formal political rituals or for justifying the repression of dissent.

In terms of societal processes during the 1978–1989 period, perhaps the most significant development was the embrace of liberal democratic ideas by a large portion of China's intelligentsia and youth. Within the top party leadership there was also a set of leaders, represented by Hu Yaobang and Zhao Ziyang, who felt the party needed to learn a new, less repressive way of ruling, pointing toward greater political relaxation. Following 6-4, CCP leaders concluded that the major political mistake purged General Secretary Hu Yaobang had made was failure to inculcate the danger of foreign threat posing the danger of returning China to its pre-1949 condition of weakness. They set out to rectify that mistake by a systematic "patriotic education" campaign.

After 6-4, the CCP mobilized its entire apparatus to indoctrinate via patriotic education the carefully crafted historical narrative of "national humiliation." But there also existed by the mid-1990s a genuine and vibrant nationalism which was independent of the regime, and though generally supportive of the regime, at times became critical of it. It is this autonomous and occasionally antiregime aspect of China's new nationalism that sometimes placed foreign policy demands and pressures on the government and was potentially dangerous for the CCP. Anti-Japanese nationalist sentiments genuinely felt among the populace, especially Internet nationalists prone to criticism of regime policies, also created a potent weapon for use in struggles between members of the CCP elite.[12] Charges that a leader is irresolute in confronting injury to China's interests and honor, especially insults by hated Japan, are potent precisely because anti-Japanese passions are so genuine and widespread. Thus encouragement of petitions, letter-writing campaigns, or demonstrations may be a tool in intraelite struggle.

The CCP's Patriotic Education Campaign and repression of liberal ideas and individuals cannot fully account for the rise of nationalist, anti-Western, and anti-US nationalism in the 1990s. More important than governmental moves may have been broad intellectual deliberations underway within China during the 1990s.[13] The difficulties encountered by Russia after embracing liberal institutions made a deep impact on Chinese intellectuals. The Russian economy shrank by perhaps half in the years after 1991—in contrast to China's economy, which boomed under the guidance of its authoritarian state. The phenomenal post-1992 pace of China's economic growth contrasted sharply with Russia's economic regression. Criminal syndicates became powerful in post-communist Russia. The dearth of Western aid to newly democratic Russia was also noted, as were frequent Western efforts to further diminish Russia's international influence. The West was still hostile to Russia, Chinese observers concluded, in spite of Russia's embrace of liberal democracy. Moscow's loss of sovereignty over the former Soviet republics also raised the specter for Chinese intellectuals of Tibetan, Xinjiang, or Taiwanese independence if China followed the Russian path of adopting liberal democratic institutions.

The experience of the East Asian "tigers" which had gone through long periods of developmental authoritarianism also pointed toward the need for continued authoritarian government in China. The real danger, many Chinese intellectuals concluded, was that China's state was too weak, especially in terms of revenues and control over the economy. To continue rapid development, the state needed to be strengthened, not weakened by liberal reform. Politically speaking, this could be done only through the utilization of nationalism. Traditional Marxist-Leninist themes were simply no longer effective in legitimizing state authority. Only nationalism would suffice to strengthen the state in post–Cold War China.

Repeated clashes with the United States over both interests and ideology also pushed Chinese intellectuals toward nationalistic conclusions. Many of these conflicts seemed to be over ideological issues—Beijing's bid to host the Olympics Games, MFN–human rights linkage, Tibet and treatment of dissidents, upgrading ties with newly democratic Taiwan, and sanctions in response to 6-4. Between 1972 and 1988, there had been few disputes with the United States over issues of China's internal governance. After 1989, they proliferated. Why had the United States become so much more concerned with human rights conditions after the end of the Soviet Union, even though human rights conditions in China were steadily improving? Chinese wondered. Even intellectuals who did not draw sweeping conclusions about US ulterior motives became tired of continually hearing Western, and especially American, lectures about how China should reform its backward institutions to comport with international values. Did not China's very remarkable development record mean there were at least some laudable elements to China's system? And why was it that no Chinese economists had won a Nobel Prize for economics for their contribution to China's breathtaking developmental achievements? There seemed to be a pervasive Western bias against China.

Greater familiarity with US society not infrequently contributed to stronger Chinese nationalism. The number of Chinese scholars who visited US universities greatly increased during the 1990s. Their experiences were often difficult. Language and financial burdens confronted them. The highly competitive and individualistic nature of US society sometimes combined with the aloofness of American professors to cause unease. Chinese scholars who came to US universities had often achieved some degree of renown in their field in China and expected to be received with an appropriate level of esteem by their American institutional hosts—as would have been the case with a Chinese university receiving an American "foreign guest." When this did not happen, as was often the case, Chinese scholars felt slighted. As these experiences and associated feelings of resentment permeated back to China, they inclined people to believe the worst about the United States. Returnees from the United States often spoke with special authority because of their first-hand experience. Of course the many Chinese scholars who did not return to China were generally the ones who were more successful in adapting to American ways.

By the mid-1990s, Chinese intellectuals were authoring popular books with anti-US and anti-Western themes. This development was a function of the commercialization of the publishing business in the 1990s. These books were often sensationalistic, emotional, one-sided, and not academically sound. But they sold very well. Publishing companies printed large quantities both to make a profit and to please CCP higher-ups who might be watching. The state approved dissemination of these popular books—of which there were hundreds—because they chimed with the patriotic education campaign. Books challenging the official narrative, perhaps by arguing that the United States actually and deliberately supported China's emergence as a rich and strong power, simply were not published. Xinhua wrote favorable reviews of many of these nationalist anti-US tracts, further encouraging people to read them. By the mid-1990s, a culture of anti-US nationalism permeated China. Challenges to the official narrative of assertive nationalism were not tolerated.

According to an authoritative summary of Chinese views of US intentions in 2011, sinister interpretations of US intentions were pervasive.[14] According to that report, it was "strongly" believed in China that the US objective was to contain or abort China's rise in order to maintain US global dominance and hegemony. The United States viewed China as a dangerous competitor and was striving in many ways to prevent China from becoming rich and strong, a first-class world power. In the common Chinese view, US politicians were true believers in the law of the jungle, that might makes right. The US objective was to overthrow China's CCP government so that China would again become faction-ridden and divided, and thereby unable to continue the rapid development that might enable it to challenge the United States. US demands regarding human rights were really mere instruments used by the United States to undermine China, create disorder, and malign China's image before the world. This Chinese cynicism regarding US motives was so widespread, the report said, that no one would openly affirm that the Americans truly believed what they said about human rights.[15] The American strategy of subverting rivals or potential rivals and bringing countries under US domination had a proven track record of success, in Chinese eyes: in Eastern Europe, in the Soviet Union, in the "color revolutions" of post-Soviet Central Asia and during the Arab Spring in 2011. The function of many US-linked NGOs operating in China was to spy on China in order to better carry out the strategy of peaceful evolution.

The sinister state-promulgated view of US China policy was not without some basis in reality.[16] Ever since 1972, US China policy has sought coopera-tion with the PRC in areas of common interest. One reason for this search for cooperation (aside from the specific interests furthered) was to build a stable, long-term, amicable Sino-US relation. This traditional US approach continued into the twenty-first century, when China was clearly emerging as a leading global power. But at the same time that the United States sought cooperation, it also sought to nudge China incrementally and peacefully toward political liberalization and ultimately basic political change. Deputy Secretary of State Robert Zoellick, for example, in a major 2005 call for broadly expanded cooperation between the United States and the PRC under the rubric of China as a "responsible stakeholder" in the international system, made clear the US view:

> China needs a peaceful political transition to make its government re-sponsible and accountable to its people. . . . China needs to reform its ju-diciary. It should open government processes to the involvement of civil society and stop harassing journalists who point out problems. China should also expand religious freedom and make real the guarantees of rights that exist on paper—but not in practice.[17]

"We do not urge the cause of freedom to weaken China," Zoellick said, but because these were core US values. Moreover, political transformation within China would lay a more solid foundation for amicable Sino-American rela-tions. Said Zoellick: "Relationships built only on a coincidence of interests have shallow roots. Relationships built on shared interests *and* shared values are deep and lasting. We can cooperate with the emerging China of today, even as we work for the democratic China of tomorrow." Several years later, during the Obama administration, Deputy Secretary of State James Steinberg advanced the notion of "strategic reassurance" in an attempt to persuade Beijing that the United States welcomed China as "a prosperous and successful power." Again, Steinberg, while calling for broader and deeper US-PRC coop-eration, also called for basic political change in China. Some people said that US interests in China's internal governance issues were "designed to weaken China" and were inconsistent with PRC-US partnership. "I couldn't disagree more," Steinberg said. He continued:

> We stand up for human rights because, as President Obama has said, it is who we are as a people. But we also believe that a China that respects

the rule of law and universal norms provides reassurance to others that it will bring the same approach to its international behavior, as well as providing greater stability and growth for its own people.[18]

As suggested by Steinberg's acknowledgement of "some people" who believed US concern for China's internal governance was designed to "weaken China," a major difference in US and Chinese views had to do with the *intentions* inspiring US concerns for China's internal governance. In the American view, individual freedom and democratic self-government were intrinsically good things which, if implemented gradually and prudently, would strengthen China's status in the world and, not least, lay a basis for closer, more stable cooperation between China and the United States. This optimistic view of liberal institutions arose, of course, out of the US experience and worldview. China's experience and worldview were very different.

Several factors converged to shape China's view of the "real," sinister US purposes that most Chinese believe are behind US advocacy of political change in China.[19] Many Chinese had a strong perception of China as an intrinsically peaceful, defense-oriented, and ethically minded country. The United States and the West generally, on the other hand, were widely perceived in China as militaristic, aggressive, and selfish. Since China cannot, by cultural self-perception, give offense, conflicts with the United States must arise out of US aggressiveness. These perceptions may have roots in China's centuries of management of barbarian powers in which China was the paragon of virtue and barbarian rulers were, or at least should be, humble students of China's superior ways, in the Chinese view of things. The lingering influence of Marxist thinking also leads to the conclusion that the United States seeks to dominate and exploit China along with the rest of the world. The influence of US hard realist theorizing about international relations also feeds sinister views of US intentions. Imbibed by Chinese analysts, many with backgrounds in the PLA or security organs, via books or study at US universities, this hard realist perspective postulated that states would seek to control their security environment to the full extent that their capabilities permit. It was thus to be expected that the United States would oppose China's rise, and seek to weaken and undermine it—although Washington would seek to camouflage those aims with a sugarcoating of high-sounding rhetoric. China's own failed experiment with liberal democracy in the early twentieth century—as interpreted by the CCP—was yet another taproot of China's sinister perception of US efforts to liberalize China. As laid out in Beijing's White Paper on Political Democracy:

> In [the] movement to save China from destruction, some of the elite turned their eyes to the West for a road that would save the country .... But the bourgeois republic, including the parliamentarian and multi-party system that were ... established after the Revolution of 1911

in imitation of the mode of Western democracy, did not fulfill the fervent desire of the Chinese people for independence and democracy. The new republic soon collapsed under the onslaught of domestic and foreign reactionary forces.... The Chinese people had still not shaken off oppression, slavery, and exploitation.... [T]he Chinese people finally came to realize that mechanically copying the Western bourgeois political system and applying it to China would lead them nowhere. To accomplish the historical task of saving China and triumphing over imperialism and feudalism, the Chinese people needed ... a totally new political system.[20]

This interpretation justified the CCP's continued insistence on a Leninist state. But there was also little doubt that CCP leaders believed these strictures. There was even less doubt that these strictures were taught to China's citizens in classrooms and via China's media. In consequence, US advocacy of basic civil and political rights for China's citizens is transformed into an instrument of hegemonist aggression against China. Since Leninism "saved" China, the US insistence that China abandon Leninism must mean that the United States wants to again enslave and dominate China.

Aggrieved Nationalism and Chinese Foreign Policy

The use of aggrieved nationalism to legitimize the authority of the CCP and individual leaders generated pressure for the CCP to be seen as a tough and resolute defender of China's honor and interests. As one scholar put it, "Because the CCP has built its legitimacy on a reputation as the righter of past wrongs, it cannot afford to allow the country to be humiliated again."[21] Having fostered a culture of insecurity and resentment over the many transgressions inflicted on China over the past 150 years, the CCP cannot afford to be seen as weak in response to contemporary "humiliations." Not all of China's policy disputes with the United States became entangled in the national humiliation complex. During the 1990s, for example, while confrontations with Washington flared over MFN linkage, Taiwan, and the Belgrade embassy bombing, Beijing reached agreement with Washington on a number of issues without mobilizing popular passions, even though negotiations were sometimes long and contentious: accession to the NPT in 1993, compliance with the MTCR in 1992, signature of the CTBT in 1996, and accession to the WTO in 1999. In none of these latter policy conflicts did Beijing mobilize Chinese nationalist anger or try to escalate tensions. It was events which occurred abruptly and forced themselves onto Chinese public attention through the use or threatened use of military force—"hot conflicts"—that led Beijing to escalate the conflict and mobilize popular anger against Washington.[22]

In hot confrontations that touched on historic memories of "humiliation" and appeared to the public as contemporary humiliation, Beijing actually *escalated* tension and confrontation with the United States. With the Taiwan Strait confrontation in 1995–1996, for example, it was Beijing that escalated the conflict from the political-diplomatic level to the military level with its July–August missile "tests," and then ratcheted up the level of military tension by steadily expanding the scope of its military exercises. With the 1999 Belgrade embassy bombing, Beijing unleashed demonstrations that brought US diplomatic buildings under siege and posed real physical danger to US personnel, while Jiang Zemin twice refused hotline calls from Clinton intended to defuse the situation. In the meantime, China's media withheld from the Chinese public information about repeated US apologies, apparently in order to give time for hatred of the United States to vent. In the case of the 2001 airplane collision, Beijing escalated the conflict by immediately demanding an apology before the crash was investigated, and by detaining the US crew. In all three "hot confrontations" (Taiwan in 1995–1996, Belgrade in 1999, EP-3 in 2001), Beijing ordered the media to frame US actions as part of a broad pattern of US hostility and insult of China. Explanations of US moves as stupid US accidents (as with the embassy bombing) or as manifestations of the US system of separation of powers (as with the Lee Teng-hui visa decision) were dismissed out of hand and the matter seen, instead, as part of a long and vast US strategy of aggression against China.

Analysts differ about the extent to which autonomous (non-state-directed) popular nationalism influences CCP foreign policy decisions. One scholar argued that web-based popular nationalism constitutes a sort of echo chamber that significantly influenced foreign policy decisions.[23] The twenty-four-hour cable news cycle, combined with the availability of that coverage via Internet and Hong Kong broadcasts, meant that news of international events reached China's public quickly and unfiltered by government censors. The ability of the state to restrict or ban access to information had been greatly reduced. This meant that when a hot crisis occurred, party leaders were aware that news of the event would almost immediately spread through the Chinese public. News presented by foreign news sources would probably be sensationalistic and focus on violence, since that attracts readers in China as in other countries. Once the news of some insult of China hit the streets, there would be a strong impulse for the leaders to make known their own position, stressing their anger over the newest insult of China. There would be a strong tendency for the government, and for individual leaders vulnerable to challenge by rivals, to try to put themselves at the head of nationalist public opinion, lest they become the target of that public opinion for being slow and weak in defense of China's honor. To position itself before mobilized nationalist opinion as a resolute defender of China's interests and honor, the government would probably define the offensive episode as part of a deliberate long-term strategy. The government would probably demand a change in the policies of the foreign transgressing state, along with an apology for the transgression. Communication with the offending party may well be refused, since even to speak with the foreign transgressor can be seen as a sign of weakness. There were two faces of China's power. One face was calm and reasonable, and sought to reassure other countries, both the United States and China's neighbors, that China was and would remain peaceful and nonbelligerent. China showed its other face, an aggressive and threatening face, in response to hot crises, when China's government was acting under the mobilized attention of its nationalist public. In these cases, the government could not afford to be seen as weak. The incentive was to be stern and tough defenders of China against ruthless foreign aggression.

It may be that nationalist bloggers critical of Beijing's foreign policies functioned as a sort of pressure group. Nationalist bloggers who felt that Beijing's, or perhaps the MFA's, policies were not tough enough were, of course, a relatively small number of people (perhaps a few tens of thousands). Yet when their views were aggregated, systematized, and put in a top-secret report under the imprimatur of the MSS, Politburo members paid considerable attention to them. China's leaders would make foreign policy moves with an awareness of how moves would be received by a handful of cyber nationalists. Those cyber nationalists soon come to understand this, and this sense of importance and actual influence might inspire them to take even more extreme positions.

Other scholars stress that party leaders, while using web nationalism to legitimize party rule and mobilize support, remained in full charge of foreign policy and continued to act on the basis of interests associated with China's long-term development.[24] A sort of state-tolerated civil society evolved around this popular and spontaneous, bottom-up nationalism. Spontaneous web-based nationalist activism, including demands for tougher state policies, erupted in response to various issues reported by the international and Chinese media. Web-based nationalists formed organizations and undertook a range of independent activities: circulating petitions; organizing boycotts, demonstrations and protests; and lobbying state legislative bodies and party-directed mass organizations to adopt more assertive policies on nationalist issues. The state legitimized and in effect authorized this activity by its own criticism of foreign actions. The state then tolerated popular nationalist agitation, or even encouraged it, as long as it stayed within bounds of not endangering social order or party authority. Freelance nationalist groups watched state policy closely for clues of official toleration, perhaps even conditional support, and responded quickly when they saw such signs. Cyber nationalist efforts to mobilize opinion were often assisted by China's commercial press, which understood that sensationalist, nationalist content sold papers. The state set parameters for permissible nationalist agitation, but editors learned to navigate between "the party line" and "the bottom line," selling papers by peddling fire-breathing nationalist resentment against foreign transgressors. The commercial press was considerably more nationalist than the party press, which is less dependent on market appeal. The CCP state used this popular nationalist activism to legitimize its authority and to gain leverage in negotiating with foreign governments. But CCP leaders clearly understood that the costs of belligerent and confrontational policies might be heavy, and calmly and reasonably settled disputes with foreign states—although they sometimes insisted on doing this behind closed doors and while concealing from China's popular nationalists their reasonable, nonconfrontational approach.

The PRC state attempted to bring nationalist cyber discussion under its control in a number of ways. One was insulation of China's Internet from the World Wide Web. Chinese web users were routed through Chinese servers, where access to politically objectionable content on the World Wide Web was blocked. Sophisticated Chinese web users, armed with special software, could circumvent these obstacles, but for the great majority of Chinese web users this "great firewall of China" was effective in blocking access to material that might challenge the orthodox narrative. The Ministry of State Security also employed a large number of people (reportedly over one million) to censor online commentary—probably routing it for further analysis and investigation. The MFA also set up a website of its own to host a discussion of China's foreign affairs. Critical questions and comments were invited and responded to by MFA specialists. Finally, special reports on the substance of online criticism of China's foreign policies were routinely prepared by the MSS for perusal by the Politburo.

Beijing's handling of conflict with other states sometimes touched on the political survival of the incumbent paramount leader. Susan Shirk outlined several ways in which perceived weakness in dealing with foreign "humiliation" might lead to leadership change. Rivals within the Politburo might use the opportunity to oust the incumbent paramount leader. The PLA might withdraw its support for the incumbent paramount leader—a development which would almost certainly lead to the removal of that leader—or hesitate to carry out an order by the paramount leader to use violent force to suppress nationalist demonstrations and movements. Developments along these lines could compel the CCP to enter a path of dialogue with the opposition, a path that would probably lead to a power-sharing arrangement, effectively ending the CCP's monopoly control over state power.

The likely trigger of any of these forms of regime change would be nationalist street demonstrations followed by quick emergence of nationalist movements. Nationalist street demonstrations are potentially very dangerous to the party. The center's handling of the Belgrade embassy bombing, the Falun Gong convergence, the EP-3 episode, and the fishing-boat captain incident all demonstrate the deep elite apprehension that foreign transgressions might be transformed into challenges to the party-state. Once people are in the streets venting hatred against Japanese or US transgressions, it is very easy for the target of anger to shift from those countries to China's internal shortcomings, with CCP leaders held responsible. State-condoned nationalist demonstrations are virtually the only form of organized public political activity tolerated in China, and people quickly seize such opportunities to raise other grievances. Any hint of weakness by the CCP in confronting the foreign "humiliation" du jour could prompt a shift from foreign to internal demands. Shirk imagines Chinese students once again swarming from Beijing's university district to Tiananmen Square carrying posters saying "Down with the America-loving CCP toadies."[25]

Protests over nationalist issues are also dangerous because those causes cut across social groups and regions. Protests against land seizures or environmental hot spots are intrinsically parochial, although there are sometimes copycat actions in other cities. Nationalist issues appeal instantaneously to people in different cities, regions, and groups. Protests over nationalist causes are also more dangerous for China's central authorities because nationalist causes are able to tap into deep emotions of group identity and individual meaning in ways that mere "economic" issues cannot. Nationalist appeals can rouse in people intense anger and a deep sense of identification that makes them willing to kill and even sacrifice their own lives to avenge the insults against "their" nation. Lost wages or pensions, official corruption, or environmental pollution is less likely to rouse such passion. The mob psychology associated with large street protests also enhances their volatility. Passions are contagious, and people feel empowered by numbers and protected by seeming anonymity. Seemingly lost in a crowd, people may do things that would be unthinkable under normal circumstances, perhaps introduce anti-regime slogans into a protest or confront the police.

A final linkage between China's aggrieved nationalism and foreign policy is the interaction between PLA views and CCP elite politics. While there is no evidence of PLA foreign policy lobbying since the 1995–1996 Taiwan Strait situation, there is abundant evidence of expression of hard-line PLA views on how to deal with the United States and Japan. In just one year, 2010, for example, on seven occasions PLA officers either called for or themselves dealt out tougher treatment of the United States: calling for China to sell off US Treasury bonds in retaliation for US arms sales to Taiwan, calling the United States "hegemonist" at the Security and Economic Dialogue, verbally challenging US Secretary of Defense Robert Gates at a Singapore conference, protesting Secretary of State Clinton's assertion that the United States had a national interest in freedom of navigation in the South China Sea, warning the United States and South Korea that joint military exercises threatened China, calling for PLA-N warships to be deployed to the Senkaku/Diaoyu

Islands, and reprimanding a former Japanese foreign minister at a conference in Singapore.[26] The CCP center is extremely lenient in its handling of this sort of expression of PLA views. In 2005, for instance, General Zhu Chenghu told a foreign reporter that in the event the United States intervened in a cross-Strait conflict and attacked China with conventional weapons, China should respond by being willing to sacrifice "every city east of Xian."[27] Implicitly but clearly, Zhu was suggesting a Chinese nuclear strike on the United States, moreover a first strike. The MFA explained Zhu's comments as "his personal views," and several weeks later it stated that China's policy continued to be "no first use" of nuclear weapons. Regarding General Zhu, five months later he received one demerit, which meant no promotion for one year.

Two main factors incline the Politburo to be attentive to and solicitous of PLA views on foreign policy issues. The first factor is the method of selecting China's—that is the CCP's—paramount leader. There is a group of several hundred people, civilian and military leaders at the apex of the organizations that run Chinese society, who have an effective vote in what individual will become paramount leader.[28] Top leaders of the PLA are among this "selectorate." Ambitious CCP leaders who aspire to the position of highest power, and to consolidate that power, need to pay close attention to PLA views. A second major reason for the Politburo to heed PLA views on foreign policy is that at some point it might again become necessary for CCP leaders to call on the PLA to repress a challenge to the regime. A paramilitary People's Armed Police, initially set up in 1982, has been vastly strengthened for use as an internal stability force since 1989. Still, the multiple lessons of the years 1989–1991 indicate that the military is the ultimate guarantee of the Communist Party's dictatorship of the proletariat. Only with complete military loyalty to the party is the survival of the regime ensured. Thus, the Politburo must pay close heed to PLA views.

China's Embrace of Marxism-Leninism and Its Quest for Modernity

A central aspect of the past century was a struggle between the philosophy of individual freedom—liberalism—and its philosophical rivals. Fascism, which saw individual identification with a racial or national community as the vital aspect of human meaning, was one powerful challenge to liberal democracy, defeated only with great effort. Today, in the 2010s, Islamism with its insistence on the sovereignty of God, not of mere humans, is the most powerful rival of liberalism. But the most powerful and long-lived challenge to liberalism came from Marxism-Leninism, or simply communism. For Chinese patriots, communism had the potent advantage of imposing unity and order on their chaotic land and quick-marching it toward wealth and power.

The communist vision was immensely attractive in many lands and for many years. In China, many high-minded, energetic, and intelligent people embraced it as the solution to their country's woes and imported into China Leninist-Stalinist economic and political models in the belief that this would "save China." Imposition of those institutions had to overcome strong resistance from many sectors of the Chinese people and occasionally (as with the rapid transition to the socialist stage) from within the CCP elite. Mobilization of nationalist sentiments via international confrontation, war, and preparation for war, facilitated crushing that resistance. Domestic opponents were linked to foreign enemies. Since those dangerous enemies had to be defeated, immense sacrifices had to be borne by the Chinese people: lives of privation and hardship to fuel the maw of Stalinist hyperaccumulation that was supposed to propel China to great-power status and communism. Linking the myriad hardships imposed on the Chinese people to foreign threats and malevolence helped persuade people to endure those heavy burdens. Mao saw war and international tension as essential tools in the destruction of structures of power in China's presocialist society, crushing the forces of counterrevolution and overwhelming all opposition, within and outside the CCP, to the repeated coercive campaigns necessary to twist China into the communist utopian mold. Fear and hatred of foreign enemies helped create domestic conditions allowing the revolution's "advance." Thus the Korean War paralleled the liquidation of the bourgeoisie and transition to socialism. The Taiwan Straits crisis paralleled the collectivization of agriculture, and the war with India paralleled the leftist push toward the Cultural Revolution. Polemical struggle against the CPSU paralleled the internal struggle to "prevent the restoration of capitalism" in China. Creation of a vision of global revolutionary wave inspired by and looking to China's revolution also helped generate internal revolutionary impetus. The result of this was the isolation of China from the world and deep poverty and bitterness among the Chinese people.

After thirty years of attempting to force Chinese society and individual Chinese human beings to conform to Mao's utopian vision of communism, the Chinese people turned away from the Lenin-Stalin *economic* model. Under the leadership of Deng Xiaoping—a man who for all his grave shortcomings must, I believe, be recognized as one of the giant liberators of humankind in the twentieth century—China took a new path. Step by step, Deng and his reform-minded comrades rolled back state control, creating and expanding a sphere of individual freedom, albeit not one yet protected by rule of law or encompassing autonomous political activity. Rapid improvement in the standards of living of the Chinese people—driven largely by market-based entrepreneurial activity—became the new basis for legitimacy of the CCP regime under Deng. Achieving this required drawing broadly and deeply on the capital, technology, export markets, and scientific and managerial knowledge of the advanced capitalist countries. The inputs of the advanced capitalist countries were to be harnessed to modernize socialist China. Persuading the capitalist countries to agree to this arrangement required abandoning the push for world revolution to overthrow capitalism around the world. Step by step, China deradicalized its foreign relations, and one by one normalized ties with its neighbors. Postrevolutionary China gradually entered the global institutions set up and dominated by the Western countries. Perhaps most important of all, as China's economy "outgrew the plan," the Chinese people witnessed with their own eyes the wealth-generating power of the market-based private initiative and entrepreneurship of capitalism. As the amazing transformation wrought by markets was comprehended, belief in the superiority of socialism over capitalism faded.

But the revolutionary dictatorship, the Leninist state—the *political* half of the Lenin-Stalin model imported circa 1950—remained in place. That party-state no longer used its powers to twist and torture Chinese into "new, communist people." It was satisfied if the people merely obeyed and submitted. But it was not a liberal state. This in a world increasingly swept by demands for freedom, individual and collective. Expanding contact with capitalist countries, and comparison of the freedom of peoples in those countries with conditions in China, made liberal ideals more attractive and communist and Leninist ideas steadily less so. Secretary General Hu Yaobang also failed to wage intense and sustained ideological struggle against liberal ideas infiltrating the party.

The global upheavals of 1989–1991 ushered in a world that was profoundly threatening to the CCP. The third act of PRC foreign relations, from 1989 to today (2015), has been a period in which powerful tides of liberal revolution have swept the world. The CCP's state is one of only four surviving communist-party states.[29] The global tide of liberal revolution has been powerful: South Korea, Taiwan, Indonesia, Thailand, and Myanmar in East Asia; Eastern Europe; Russia; the "color revolutions" of Ukraine, Georgia, Kyrgyzstan, and Azerbaijan; Nepal and Bangladesh in South Asia; Tunisia, Libya, and Egypt in the Arab world; the struggles for democracy of the people of Iran and in Hong Kong; even Afghanistan and Iraq, courtesy of US intervention and regime change. China's 1989 uprising was part of this global wave. This is not to say the inculcation of liberal institutions in any or all of these countries has been easy or even successful. Many, perhaps all, of these new democracies will fail. Many countries, Germany for example, make democratic institutions work well only after several failed attempts.[30] The point, rather, is that liberal ideas carried by modern technologies are extremely attractive to people around the world. Twenty-four-hour cable news, beautifully crafted and emotionally gripping Hollywood movies with special effects and magnetic appeal, the Internet and World Wide Web, satellite telecommunications, jet travel and mass tourism, containerization and accelerated globalization, the powerful global leading role of US higher education—these and scores of other technologies spread ideas rapidly from one country to another almost like a highly contagious disease. Sometimes the ideas carried by these technologies are illiberal. Jihadist Islamism today and fascism and Marxism-Leninism in the past, for example. But it is liberal movements and revolutions that are shaking and remaking the world. Regimes topple, or nearly so, right and left. Civil war becomes a real danger, and civil wars sometimes invite foreign intervention.

The CCP Politburo sees the United States as the source of the ideological onslaught confronting it. While somewhat distorted, this perception is not entirely unjustified. The immensely powerful and dynamic American republic *does* propagate and radiate liberal democratic ideas in scores of powerful ways. There is also little question that stable liberal democratic countries *are* convinced of the superiority of their ways and that some of those democracies (France, Britain, and the United States) sometimes feel compelled to rebuke the PRC for its failure to live up to modern, global, liberal standards. And among the liberal democratic countries, the United States feels a special mission, its historic or even God-imposed duty , to vindicate liberal values to the whole world. However one feels about this excentric American sense of mission, one must recognize its powerful influence on the US role in the world. The United States *is*, or so it seems to this author, a liberal missionary country, although it must constantly balance those ideological impulses with the realities of power.

Since 1989, a diaspora of Chinese intellectuals and activists dedicated to basic reform of the CCP regime has developed in Europe and North America. This diaspora is tiny in number and has very limited contact with people in China. Yet in earlier eras, tiny groups of foreign-based political activists exercised significant influence on China's political evolution. In the run-up to the 1911 revolution, for example, small groups of revolutionary activists in the United States, Europe, and Japan with only tenuous links to communities in China played an important role in toppling the Qing dynasty.[31] In the 1930s, anti-Japanese patriotism among Overseas Chinese in Southeast Asia boosted communist growth in China. Today, more and more Chinese trained in the West return to China, inculcated (perhaps) with a democratic ethos that conflicts with the communist creed. These people occupy more and more positions of influence, and may even enter the party. But their ideological loyalty to the party, or at least its formal Marxist-Leninist creed, is questionable. As for China's entrepreneurs, professionals, middle class, and youth, while it is true that they do not now call for basic political change, that may be contingent on continuing rapid growth or other contingent factors. Attitudes can shift rapidly, as they did in China between 1989 and 1993.

The CCP is in a profound quandary. It cannot disengage from the global economic and technological processes that generate development but also carry liberal ideas. To withdraw would be to once again shut China off from the world, as happened to disastrous effect during the late Ming and Qing dynasties and the Mao era. China's leaders recognize that its isolation during those periods was a great blunder, constituting a major reason why China fell behind the West. China's leaders understand that self-isolation is the road to national decline, not national revival. And yet global engagement opens China to the contagion of liberal ideas.

The CCP's key defense against this ideological infection has been indoctrination that anathematizes liberal ideals as "Western," foreign to China's tradition, and putatively peddled by "the West," especially the United States, as part of an aggressive campaign to humiliate and belittle China. In this fashion, responsibility for foreign disesteem for China's political setup is translated from China's own illiberal domestic arrangements onto foreign powers. The anger of Chinese people is directed outward. To recognize China's own illiberal political institutions as the root of many of its international status problems is cognitively difficult, because it calls into question the core belief in the superiority of China's tradition.

Combining all these factors yields a specter that seems to haunt the regime and perhaps especially the paramount leader: some "hot transgression" against China's honor or interests by Japan or the United States occurs, to which the government response is seen as inadequately firm, leading to redirection of mobilized and perhaps widespread nationalist outrage away from the foreign transgressor toward China's "weak" government. The demonstrations spread from city to city and region to region. Demands on the government shift from the original foreign issues to domestic demands. Once millions of angry and agitated people are in the streets, former indifference toward democracy evaporates. Some people in the crowd, protected perhaps by a sense of anonymity, raise political demands. Others echo those demands. Demands then escalate and displace the original parochial grievances in importance. Revolutions are almost by definition periods when values and perspectives change with great rapidity. In such a situation, would employment of police force be successful? Or would it backfire? In either case, what will PLA leaders say and do? Would the PLA remain loyal to the regime? This creates strong incentives not to trigger such a potentially disastrous chain of events by being perceived as weak in dealing with foreign powers, especially Japan and the United States.

Awareness of the possibly catastrophic consequences of defeat in war is a major restraint on CCP foreign policy moves. While the authoritarian CCP regime must pose as a forceful defender of China's honor and interests, overly assertive moves that involved China in a military conflict that it might lose could be a disaster for the CCP, possibly precipitating the sort of snowballing nationalist protests described in the previous paragraph. There are many cases of lost wars delegitimizing a regime: France in 1791, China in 1895, Russia in 1905 and again in 1917, Germany in 1918, France in 1940, and Argentina in 1982. Defeat in war, inability to defend the nation, is immediately understandable evidence of terminal ineptitude. Were China to get involved in a military clash with, say, Japan over the Senkaku/Diaoyu Islands and lose to a technologically very potent Japanese Maritime Self Defense Force, the result could be large and highly emotional protests across China against the apparent inability of the CCP to defend China's interests. In such a situation, escalation might be preferable to conceding defeat. This would only further increase the stakes for the CCP. That regime might conclude it had a choice between a full-scale war with the United States and Japan that it might lose, and confronting a powerful domestic nationalist movement determined to oust it from office for being too weak. In such circumstances, a lost war with the United States might appear the lesser of two evils. CCP leaders might calculate their regime could survive an all-out but losing war with Japan and the United States, but could not survive the internal challenge that would result from backing away from such a war out of fear.

Defeat of China in war with Japan and the United States could lead to even worse outcomes for the twenty-first century. Very probably, an even more enraged nationalistic China would prepare for the next round, determined not to lose again. An extreme form of Chinese nationalism could develop that sees the CCP regime as an obstacle to China's rise and realization of its true historic destiny of greatness. A Chinese attempt at political liberalization that produced not stability but instability could also push China in a more radical nationalist direction. Here again we return to the sad German paradigm, not of the Wilhelmine but of a later period.

At the end of the nineteenth and in the early twentieth century there arose in Germany a form of radical nationalism that argued that the aristocratic and capitalist duumvirate that had dominated Germany since 1871 prevented Germany from mobilizing the full strength of the German people, thereby keeping it from achieving its rightful place of eminence in the world. Bourgeois political parties squabbled with one another and thwarted strong leadership. Aristocrats kept out of office nonaristocratic Germans of greater capability and merit. A dynastic monarchy feared the people and could not rouse and harness their full emotional passion. Big capitalists and financiers kept many German workers in poor health and privation. Divisions over class, religion, and region that pitted Germans against one another, rather than uniting them to reach their common destiny of greatness, needed to be overcome. The preachers of division—the socialists, communists, political parties—needed to be banished. What was needed was not liberal democracy, but strong, firm leadership. What was needed was a new culture, a new national revolution that would create a true national community and mobilize the energies of the entire German people, and lead them to their destiny of greatness. This was the cultural soil upon which German fascism, National

Socialism, fed.[32] Germans embraced the radical antiestablishment nationalism of National Socialism only after the old order proved itself unable to secure victory in World War I or to rid Germany of the "national humiliation" of the Versailles Treaty. If the CCP gets China involved in a war with Japan over the Senkaku/Diaoyu Islands, or perhaps in a stark and ultimately humiliating confrontation with the United States, and loses that conflict, the prospects for embrace of radical anti-CCP establishment nationalism would become much greater. The result might be a populist, antidemocratic, and radical Chinese nationalism determined to mobilize the full strength of the great Chinese people to win the next round against China's enemies. It might look a lot like fascism.

One of contemporary China's leading advocates of China's modernization via democratization, Li Shenzhi (1923–2003), warned against such a possibility. Li was purged as a "rightist" in 1957 for advocating democracy but rehabilitated in the late 1970s, and served as advisor on foreign affairs to Deng Xiaoping during the latter's visit to the United States. The year before his death, Li wrote:

> Recent years . . . . have seen the appearance of some extreme nationalists, who think the United States is too dominant in the world and too overbearing and aggressive toward China. . . . they have revisited Lenin and Mao Zedong's theory that imperialism embodies wars, and they want China to say no to the United States. They question Deng Xiaoping's two main goals of "peace and development" and criticize the Chinese government's foreign policies as being too weak. This tendency requires our attention. China is a big country . . . with the largest population and longest history in the world. A national mentality of self-importance has been deeply rooted in people's minds as a result of over five decades of propaganda. Following the Reform and Open Door Policy the economy has improved and with it has come a blind arrogance and pride. This extreme nationalism has a market in China, especially among young students with a lack of common sense. If we allow it to evolve freely, it may put the future of the nation at risk. This should be brought to everyone's attention.[33]

But perhaps China will not democratize. Perhaps it will be an exception to an otherwise global demand for democracy. Perhaps China will go its own way based on its unique millennia-long political traditions. Americans have had a strong tendency to see in China what they want to see, and this American scholar is perhaps not immune to this malady.[34] A strong and quite plausible argument can be made that China's current CCP regime is highly meritocratic, selecting and advancing people to positions of power on the basis of demonstrated performance.[35] This cohort of CCP-selected cadres has, since 1978, achieved an impressive record of accomplishments addressing quite effectively the pressing needs of the Chinese people—greatly increased wealth, expanded opportunities, stability combined with expanding personal freedoms, rapid scientific and technological advance, national power. True, the CCP's Leninist authoritarian state is neither liberal nor democratic, but neither were China's traditional political arrangements. Benevolent authoritarianism characterized China's long Confucian tradition, and today's CCP regime approximates those traditional arrangements, at least according to this line of argument. Moreover, as noted at the outset of this book, multiple surveys of public opinion in China indicate very high levels of public acceptance of CCP rule and the CCP-led state—levels of satisfaction far higher than found in leading liberal democratic states, in fact. Grievances among ordinary Chinese are many, but those are typically not directed against the fundamental structures of the regime. If this line of argument is correct, the world may witness a long period of coexistence between an extremely powerful authoritarian China and a coalition of democracies each of which may be individually less powerful that the Chinese superpower.

One approach to peaceful coexistence in such a situation might be for the United States and other democratic powers to deliberately set aside their own normative expectations and deal with China on its own terms. Leninist PRC would thus be treated as an exception to the otherwise universal expectations and normative affirmation of liberal democratic values. After all, dealing with antidemocratic regimes in the Middle East or Africa is, in reality, quite different than dealing with an antidemocratic power that is the world's strongest state built on a two-millennia heritage of relatively successful authoritarian government. It thus might make sense for democratic powers to suspend efforts to nudge China toward liberalization and democratization.

Such an approach would encounter a number of difficulties. Would it not encourage and facilitate a Chinese effort to establish new global norms based on benevolent authoritarianism? With "the West" stepping back from China's great power, why should China retreat? Would not the result, then, be a protracted and probably worldwide ideological struggle, a new Cold War? But that might be the best we can realistically hope for. Acceptance of Chinese exceptionalism would also require a significant change in the US sense of a God-given mission to uphold liberty and democracy. Other proud democratic powers similarly convinced of the principles of human liberty—France, Britain, Germany—would also need to greatly qualify their embrace of universal norms of human rights, at the very time in history when those values are under challenge by an authoritarian Chinese superpower. This is difficult to imagine.

This American author believes, perhaps as an act of faith, that the Chinese people will eventually secure for themselves and their posterity the blessings of individual liberty and collective self-government protected by law. These are the common inheritance of all humanity, and the Chinese people are simply too intelligent and creative not to claim them as their own. But "eventually" may be a while. Anti-liberal thought has already won several rounds of struggle for the soul of China, as it has in other lands. There may be further detours, even, God forbid, disastrous ones, before China becomes a modern nation in which its citizens enjoy political rights protected by law from the state and in which its citizens can choose and change their rulers. But when that happens, China will become a true world leader.

NOTES

Chapter 1. The Fateful Embrace of Communism and Its Consequence

1. Mechanisms of party control are these: embedding of party organizations within state organs and supervision of government work by these party organizations; party control over elections and the judicial system to ensure that these strengthen rather than undermine party leadership; party control over cadre assignments via a personnel system that gives the party control over the assignment, promotion, and removal of decision-making positions within the state (called the nomenklatura after the Soviet name for this system) party control over the mass media and schools combined with a party propaganda and ideology system; dictatorial repression of recalcitrant opposition; and party control over the military via a political work system. Regarding party-state relations in the contemporary PRC, see David Shambaugh, *China's Communist Party: Atrophy and Adaptation*, Berkeley: University of California Press, 2008. Richard McGregor, *The Party: The Secret World of China's Communist Rulers*, New York: Harper Collins, 2010. Kenneth Lieberthal, *Governing China; From Revolution Through Reform*, New York: W. W. Norton, 1995.

2. An extremely articulate presentation of this view by a PRC entrepreneur was posted online in June 2013. Eric X. Li, "A Tale of Two Political Systems." http://www.ted.com/talks/eric_x_li_a_tale_of_two_political_systems?language=en.

3. A number of empirical studies reach this or similar conclusions. Teresa Wright, *Accepting Authoritarianism: State-Society Relations in China's Reform Era*, Stanford: Stanford University Press, 2010. Jie Chen, *Popular Political Support in Urban China*, Stanford: Stanford University Press, 2004. Kellie S. Tsai, *Capitalism without Democracy: The Private Sector in Contemporary China*, Ithaca, NY: Cornell University Press, 2007. Bruce J. Dickson, *Red Capitalists in China: The Party, Private Enterprise and Prospects for Political Change*, Cambridge: Cambridge University Press, 2003.

4. Susan Shirk, *The Political Logic of Economic Reform in China*, Berkeley: University of California Press, 1993.

5. John David Armstrong, *Revolution and World Order: The Revolutionary State in International Society*, Oxford: Clarendon Press, 1993.

6. Charles Tilly, *From Mobilization to Revolution*, Reading: Addison-Wesley, 1978. Barrington Moore, *Social Origins of Dictatorship and Democracy*, Boston: Beacon, 1967. Theda Skocpol, *States and Social Revolutions*, Cambridge: Cambridge University Press, 1979.

7. Theda Skocpol, "Social Revolution and Mass Military Mobilization," *World Politics*, vol. 40 (1988), pp. 147–68.

8. Robert S. Snyder, "The U.S. and Third World Revolutionary States: Understanding the Breakdown of Relations," *International Studies Quarterly*, no. 43 (1999), pp. 265–90.

9. Kenneth Bayner, *The Oxford Companion to Politics and the World*, 2nd ed., London: Oxford University Press, 2001, pp. 495–6.

10. Lucian Pye, *The Spirit of Chinese Politics: A Psycho-cultural Study of the Authority Crisis in Political Development*, Cambridge: MIT Press, 1967.

11. Regarding the formation of the PRC, see Jonathan D. Spence, *The Search for Modern China*, New York: W. W. Norton, 1990. Michael Gasster, *China's Struggle to Modernize*, New York: Knopf, 1972.

12. Regarding Mao's political evolution from nationalism to communism, see Maurice Meisner, *Mao Zedong, a Political and Intellectual Portrait*, Cambridge: Polity, 2007, pp. 11–41. Jonathan Spence, *Mao Zedong, a Life*, New York: Penguin, 2006, pp. 18–51. Regarding Zhou Enlai, see Gao Wenqian, *Zhou Enlai: The Last Perfect Revolutionary*, New York: Public Affairs, 2007, pp. 21–37. Kuo-Kang Shao, *Zhou Enlai and the Foundations of Chinese Foreign Policy*, New York: St. Martin's Press, 1996, pp. 3–72. Regarding Deng, see Ezra F. Vogel, *Deng Xiaoping and the Transformation of China*, Cambridge: Belknap Press, 2011, 15–25.

13. Herbert Marcuse argued that the failure of the French Revolution to live up to its professed ideals of "liberty, equality, and fraternity" was the organizing question Marx sought to answer. Marx's solution to this problem, according to Marcuse, was the proletariat. Achievement of these ideals could only be realized via the abolition of the private ownership of the means of production, and accoomplishment of which was the historical destiny of the proletariat. Herbert Marcuse, *Soviet Marxism: A Critical Analysis*, New York: Columbia University Press, 1958.

14. "More on the Historical Experience of the Dictatorship of the Proletariat," in *The Historical Experience of the Dictatorship of the Proletariat*, Beijing: Foreign Languages Press, 1959, p. 27.

15. Barry Naughton, *Growing Out of the Plan; Chinese Economic Reform, 1978–1993*, Cambridge: Cambridge University Press, 1996.

16. Huang Yasheng, *Capitalism with Chinese Characteristics: Entrepreneurship and the State*, Cambridge: Cambridge University Press, 2008.

17. The classic analysis of totalitarianism is Carl J. Friedrich and Zbigniew K. Brezinski, *Totalitarian Dictatorship and Autocracy*, New York: Praeger, 1966.

18. Mao Zedong, "On Coalition Government," April 24, 1945, in *Selected Works of Mao Tse-tung*, Vol. 3, Beijing: Foreign Languages Press, 1967, pp. 205–68, 231, 233.

19. Mao, "On Coalition Government," p. 247.

20. Andrew J. Nathan, *Chinese Democracy*, Berkeley: University of California Press, 1985.

21. Mao, "On Coalition Government," pp. 234–35.

22. "Phony Communism" was the title of the ninth and final CCP polemic against the CPSU in 1964. See "On Khrushchov's Phony Communism and Its Historical Lessons for the World," July 14, 1964, in *The Polemic on the General Line of the International Communist Movement*, Beijing: Foreign Language Press, 1964, pp. 415–94.

23. Shirk, *Political Logic*.

24. Andrew J. Nathan and Perry Link, *The Tiananmen Papers*, New York: Public Affairs, 2001, p. xi. The introduction is authored by Nathan alone.

25. Allen S. Whiting, "Assertive Nationalism in Chinese Foreign Policy," *Asian Survey*, vol. 23, no. 8 (August 1983), pp. 913–33.

26. Susan Shirk, *Fragile Superpower*, New York: Oxford University Press, 2007.

27. James Reilly, *Strong Society, Smart State: The Rise of Public Opinion in China's Japan Policy*, New York: Columbia University Press, 2013.

Chapter 2. Joining the Socialist Camp

1. Niu Jun, *From Yan'an to the World, the Origins and Development of Chinese Communist Foreign Policy,* translated and edited by Steven I. Levine, Northwalk, CT: EastBridge, 2005, pp. 316–43.

2. Chen Jian, *Mao's China and the Cold War,* Chapel Hill: University of North Carolina Press, 2001, p. 50.

3. Regarding the US "wedge strategy," see John Lewis Gaddis, "The American 'Wedge' Strategy, 1949–1955," in *Sino-American Relations, 1945–1955: A Joint Reassessment of a Critical Decade,* edited by Harry Harding and Yuan Ming, Wilmington, DE: SR Books, 1989, pp. 157–83. This US "wedge strategy" can be seen as an expression of the approach that had dominated US China policy since the 1890s, that of using and supporting China as a check on other powers deemed more offensive to US interests—Russia, Japan, etc. See Warren I. Cohen, *America's Response to China,* 5th ed., New York: Columbia University Press, 2010.

4. Niu Jun, *From Yan'an,* pp. 332–33.

5. This is a central theme of Alexander V. Pantsov and Steven I. Levine, *Mao: The Real Story,* New York: Simon and Schuster, 2012.

6. Wu Xiuquan, *Eight Years in the Ministry of Foreign Affairs (January 1950–October 1958)—Memoirs of a Diplomat,* Beijing: New World Press, 1985, p. 10.

7. Quoted in Niu Jun, *From Yan'an,* p. 323.

8. *Renmin ribao,* October 8, 1949. Quoted in Chu-yuan Cheng, *Economic Relations between Peking and Moscow: 1949–1963,* New York: Praeger, 1964, p. 91.

9. Mao Zedong, "On the People's Democratic Dictatorship," *Selected Writings of Mao Tse-tung,* Vol. 4, Beijing: Foreign Languages Press, 1961, p. 415.

10. Hua-yu Li, *Mao and the Economic Stalinization of China, 1948–1953,* Lanham, MD: Rowman and Littlefield, 2006, p. 24.

11. Regarding the negotiation of the 1950 treaty, see Sergei Goncharov, John W. Lewis, and Xue Litai, *Uncertain Partners: Stalin, Mao, and the Korean War,* Palo Alto, CA: Stanford University Press, 1994, pp. 81–109. Chen Jian, *China's Road to the Korean War; the Making of the Sino-American Confrontation,* New York: Columbia University Press, 1994, p. 64–91.

12. The Far Eastern component of the Soviet-US agreement at Yalta in February 1945 had provided for Soviet entry into the war against Japan following Germany's surrender. In exchange for this Soviet assistance, the US agreed to help pressure Chiang Kai-shek and his ROC to grant the USSR certain special rights in China's Northeast. Stalin also pledged, as part of this arrangement, to support Chiang Kai-shek's ROC to the detriment of the CCP. Yalta was in many regards China's, and the CCP's, first experience of a Soviet-American condominium.

13. Wu Xiuquan, *Eight Years,* pp. 9–10.

14. Hua-yu Li, *Stalinization,* p. 28.

15. Chen Jian, *China's Road,* pp. 74–5.

16. Hua-yu Li, *Stalinization,* p. 30. Gancharov, Lewis, Xue, *Uncertain Partners,* pp. 82–97.

17. Wu Xiuquan, *Eight Years,* p. 10.

18. A source containing the texts of both the 1945 and the 1950 Sino-Soviet agreements is Aitchen K. Wu, *China and the Soviet Union,* London: Methuen, 1950.

19. Wu Xiuquan, *Eight Years*, p. 13.

20. Goncharov et al., *Uncertain Partners*, p. 122.

21. Wu Xiuquan, *Eight Years*, pp. 17–8.

22. Wu Xiuquan, *Eight Years*, p. 16.

23. Taiwan lies on the eastern edge of the continental shelf, allowing submarines based in Taiwan to quickly enter deep water. Regarding the reorientation of US strategy as a result of the 1950 treaty, see John W. Garver, *The Sino-American Alliance, Nationalist China and U.S. Cold War Strategy in Asia*, Amok: ME Sharpe, 1997, pp. 21–31.

24. Emily Yaung, "The Impact of the Yalta Agreement on China's Domestic Politics, 1945–1946," PhD diss., Kent State University, 1979.

25. This section is based on Sergey Radchenko, "New Documents on Mongolia and the Cold War," *CWIHP Bulletin*, issue 16 (Fall 2007/Winter 2008), pp. 341–66. This contains the text of nine documents.

26. *China's Foreign Relations: A Chronology of Events (1949–1988)*, Beijing: Foreign Languages Press, 1989, p. 453.

27. This section is based on Chen Jian, *China's Road*, pp. 33–63. Also Chen Xiaolu, "China's Policy toward the United States, 1949–1955," in Harding and Ming, *Sino-American Relations, 1945–1955*, pp. 184–97.

28. Quoted in Chen, *China's Road*, p. 40.

29. A convenient handbook of recognition data is *China's Foreign Relations: A Chronology of Events*.

30. Chen, *China's Road*, pp. 33–8.

31. Quoted in Chen, *China's Road*, p. 37.

32. Quoted in Chen Xiaolu, "China's Policy," p. 185.

33. This section is based on Beverly Hooper, *China Stands Up: Ending the Western Presence, 1948–1950*, Sydney: Allen and Unwin, 1986. Extraterritoriality was a legal arrangement that placed citizens of certain nationalities in China and certain designated areas of Chinese cities beyond the jurisdiction of Chinese governmental authority.

34. The estimate of foreigner population is from my Georgia Tech Shanghai history colleague Professor Hanchao Lu. In 1919, there were over 350,000 officially registered foreigners living in all of China.

35. There are scholars of the "lost chance" school who argue that CCP uprooting of the Western presence was a response to the hostile policies of Western governments. Had Western governments adopted policies friendlier to the PRC, for example by immediately recognizing it, the CCP might have tolerated portions of the Western presence longer than it actually did. Hooper debates these scholarly views passim, concluding in favor of the deep historical forces outlined above. Among the evidence for her conclusion reached by Hooper is the British case. British business decided early on, with support from London, to do their utmost to cooperate with China's new government. This included a declaration of recognition of the PRC by London on January 6, 1950, a diplomatic act that London anticipated would lead swiftly to the establishment of ambassadorial relations (as was usually the case). Beijing was not interested in London's bid, and British interests in China fared little better than their American counterparts.

36. Stalin, like the CCP and even Mao during certain periods, reluctantly allowed peasants to market "sideline" produce grown on small private plots. Regarding the Soviet experience, see Alec Nove, *An Economic History of the U.S.S.R.*, New York: Pelican, 1972,

pp. 184–85. "Black markets" of course emerged, but participation in those markets became, under both Stalin and Mao, a criminal offense.

37. Xiaojia Hou, "'Get Organized': The Impact of two Soviet Models in the CCP's Rural Strategy, 1949–1953," in *China Learns From the Soviet Union, 1949–Present*, edited by Thomas P. Bernstein and Hua-yu Li, Lanham, MD: Lexington Books, 2011, pp. 167–96.

38. Quoted in Xiaojia Hou, "'Get Organized,'" pp. 175–76.

39. This is a central thesis of Hua-yu Li's book *Stalinization*.

40. Kong Hanbing, "The Transplantation and Entrenchment of the Soviet Economic Model in China," in Bernstein and Li, *China Learns*, pp. 153–66.

41. Quoted in Kong Hanbing, "Transplantation," p. 158.

42. Kong, "Transplantation," p. 162.

43. Primitive socialist accumulation was a concept proposed by Bolshevik economist Yevgeny Preobrazhensky in the mid-1920s according to which wealth produced by private agriculture and industry would be siphoned off, with violence, to grow the socialist sector. The concept became associated with Trotsky and was thus renounced by Soviet authority. In fact, Stalin's policies conformed well to Preobrazhensky's concept. See, Alexander Erlich, *The Soviet Industrialization Debate, 1921–1928*, Cambridge, MA: Harvard University Press, 1960.

44. Hua-yu Li, *Stalinization*, pp. 108–09, 116.

45. Xiaojie Hou, "Get Organized," pp. 182–85.

46. Johathan D. Spence, *In Search of Modern China*, New York: W. W. Norton, 1990, p. 550.

47. Roy A. Medvedev, *Let History Judge: The Origins and Consequences of Stalinism*, New York: Alfred Knopf, 1971, pp. 90–1.

48. Nove, *An Economic History of the U.S.S.R.*, p. 299.

49. Deng Xiaoping, "We Can Develop a Market Economy Under Socialism," November 26, 1979, in *Selected Works of Deng Xiaoping*, Vol. 2, Beijing: Foreign Languages Press, 1995, p. 238.

50. This section draws on Chu-yuan Cheng, *Economic Relations between Peking and Moscow: 1949–63*, New York: Praeger, 1964.

51. This is a key theme of Richard Baum, *Burying Mao; Chinese Politics in the Age of Deng Xiaoping*, Princeton: Princeton University Press, 1994.

52. For an exposition of the Soviet model of industrial organization and Mao's critique of it, see Franz Schurmann, *Ideology and Organization in Communist China*, Berkeley: University of California Press, 1968, pp. 239–62.

53. This section draws on Sergei Goncharov, "Sino-Soviet Military Cooperation," in Odd Arne Westad, *Brothers in Arms; the Rise and Fall of the Sino-Soviet Alliance, 1945–1962*, Washington, DC: Washington Wilson Center Press, 1998, pp. 141–69.

Chapter 3. War in Korea and Indochina

1. Warren I. Cohen, *America's Response to China*, 5th ed., New York: Columbia University Press, 2010. It was an aberration because the broader pattern of Sino-American relations, according to Cohen, was a pattern of cooperation from the 1890s to the 1980s, with the United States looking on a strong China as a balance to other East Asian powers, Japan and Russia, while Chinese governments from Qing to Republican looked on the United States as the least threatening of the imperialist powers.

2. There are two aspects to state sovereignty under international law: actual ability to control a piece of territory and the people who live there (de facto sovereignty) and recognition as a member of the community of sovereign states by existing members of that community (de jure sovereignty). Broadly speaking, the PRC has deprived Taiwan of de jure sovereignty since about 1971, but it has never exercised de facto sovereignty over Taiwan.

3. One of the most influential left-wing commentators of the 1950s and 1960s, I. F. Stone, wrote a book marshalling the evidence behind this thesis, *Hidden History of the Korean War*, New York: Monthly Review Press, 1951. One of the most detailed studies of the origins of the war followed Stone in concluding that the North did *not* launch a well-prepared and large-scale attack on the morning of June 25; instead, South Korea and the United States probably provoked a Northern counterattack and the fighting then spread to other sectors of the DMZ. See Bruce Cumings, *The Origins of the Korean War*, Vol. 2, *The Roaring of the Cataract, 1947–1950*, Princeton: Princeton University Press, 1990, pp. 568–621. Neither of these "revisionist" studies were able to make use of post-Soviet documents on interactions between Kim, Stalin, and Mao.

4. *Aiguo zhuyi jiaoyu cidian* (Dictionary of patriotic education), Dalian: Dalian chubanshe, 1991, p. 472.

5. *Zu guo wan sui* (Long live the motherland), primary school textbook, Beijing: China Youth Publishing Company, 1993, pp. 74–5.

6. When South Korean president Kim Young Sam visited Moscow in June 1994, shortly after the normalization of Russian–South Korean relations, he asked Russian president Boris Yeltsin to declassify documents dealing with the Korean War. Yeltsin agreed, and 200 documents totaling 600 pages were delivered. These have progressively been made available. These documents reveal Kim Il Sung's prolonged efforts to secure Stalin's and Mao's approval and material support for an offensive. The Cold War International History Project (*CWIHP*) *Bulletin* published by the Woodrow Wilson International Center for Scholars has been the major English-language venue for their publication.

7. The Korean Communist Party renamed itself the Korean Worker's Party in 1946 in an attempt to give itself a seemingly broader appeal.

8. Allen S. Whiting, *China Crosses the Yalu: The Decision to Enter the Korean War*, Stanford: Stanford University Press, 1960.

9. This was the only Allied summit conference in which Chiang Kai-shek participated. Stalin refused to meet with Chiang out of fear it might provoke Japan to attack Siberia, confronting the USSR with a two-front war. This was the conference at which Taiwan was stripped from Japan's sovereignty and returned to China.

10. Liu Xiaoyuan argued that more effective US-ROC cooperation during 1944–1945 could have avoided the tragedy of Korean division: *Partnership for Disorder; China, the United States and their Policies for Postwar Disposition of the Japanese Empire, 1941–1945*, New York: Cambridge University Press, 1996.

11. Katherine Weathersby, "Soviet Aims in Korea and the Origins of the Korean War, 1945–1950: New Evidence From Russian Archives," CWIHP Working Paper No. 8, November 1993.

12. "On the Korean War," Top Secret, for Brezhnev, Kosygin, et al., August 9, 1966. In CWIHP *Bulletin*, Issue 3 (Fall 1993), pp. 15–6.

13. Sergei Goncharov, John W. Lewis, and Xue Litai, *Uncertain Partners*, Stanford: Stanford University Press, 1993. Chen Jian, *China's Road to the Korean War*, New York: Columbia University Press, 1994, pp. 134–35.

14. *US Department of State Bulletin*, January 23, 1950, pp. 111–2.

15. Goncharov, *Uncertain Partners*, p. 100.

16. Goncharov, *Uncertain Partners*, pp. 142–45.

17. Chen Jian, *China's Road*, p. 112. According to Chen Jian, writing in 1994, no Chinese study has touched on the Kim-Mao meeting of May 13–16, 1950.

18. Soviet ambassador Nikolai Roshchin to Stalin, May 13, 1950, in CWIHP *Bulletin*, No. 4 (Fall 1994), p. 61.

19. "Filippov" (Stalin) to Mao Zedong, May 14, 1950, in "Documentation," *CWIHP Bulletin*, Issue 4, Fall 1994, p. 61.

20. Goncharov et al., *Uncertain Partners*, p. 146.

21. Katherine Weathersby makes this important point.

22. Four key works based on declassified Soviet documents generally agree on these events and were relied on for this section: Chen Jian, *China's Road*. Weathersby, "Soviet Aims in Korea." Goncharov et al, *Uncertain Partners*. Shu Guang Zhang, *Mao's Military Romanticism; China and the Korean War, 1950–1953*, Lawrence: University of Kansas Press, 1995.

23. Chen Jian, *China's Road*, p. 143.

24. Chen Jian, *China's Road*, p. 171.

25. Chen Jian, *China's Road*, p. 175.

26. Chen Jian, *China's Road*, p. 182. Shu Guan Zhang argues that genuine and strong opposition to entry was expressed at this meeting. *Military Romanticism*, pp. 80–81.

27. Zhang, *Military Romanticism*, p. 78.

28. Zhang, *Military Romanticism*, p. 81.

29. Zhang, *Military Romanticism*, p. 85.

30. This section follows John Garver, *The Sino-American Alliance; Nationalist China and U.S. Cold War Strategy in Asia*, Armonk, NY: M. E. Sharpe, 1997, pp. 15–21.

31. "Fall of Formosa Expected, Says U.S.," *New York Times*, January 4, 1950.

32. Harry Truman Presidential Library, www.trumanlibrary.org.

33. This section follows He Di, "The Last Campaign to Unify China: The CCP's Unmaterialized Plan to Liberate Taiwan, 1949–50," *Chinese Historians*, Issue 5 (Spring 1990), pp. 1–16.

34. He De, "The Last Campaign," p. 11.

35. Goncharov et al. and Chen Jian disagree about whether Stalin agreed in mid-1949 to equip a Taiwan invasion force. Goncharov et al. say Stalin refused such aid and only changed his mind after the January 1950 clarification of US policy by Truman and Acheson. Chen Jian says that Stalin agreed to arm an invasion force during his July 1949 talks with Liu Shaoqi, and that such equipment was arriving by September–October 1949. *Uncertain Partners*, pp. 98–101. *China's Road*, p. 98. Given what we know of Stalin's caution in confronting the United States in Korea, I believe Goncharov's account is more probable.

36. Document 173, Statement by President on the Situation in Korea, June 27, 1950. Truman Library, www.trumanlibrary.org.

37. Allen Whiting interpreted this initial and brief contact as a final Chinese warning. Chinese sources attribute the break to logistical difficulties.

38. This section follows Barbara Barnouin and Changgeng Yu, *Zhou Enlai; A Political Life*, Hong Kong: Chinese University Press, 2006, pp. 148–9.

39. Barnouin and Yu, *Zhou Enlai*, pp. 148–9.

40. Shen Zhihua, "China and the Dispatch of the Soviet Air Force: The Formation of the Chinese-Soviet Korean Alliance in the Early Stage of the Korean War," *Journal of Strategic Studies*, vol. 33, no. 2 (April 2010), pp. 211–30.

41. This is Zhang's central thesis in *Mao's Military Romanticism*.

42. Another authoritative source drawing on official Chinese data puts the figure at 152,000: Xu Yan, "The Chinese Forces and their Casualties in the Korean War: Facts and Statistics," *Chinese Historians*, vol. 6, no. 2 (Fall 1993), pp. 45–58.

43. Chen Jian, *Mao's China and the Cold War*, Chapel Hill: University of North Carolina Press, pp. 87–114.

44. This section follows Yafeng Xia, *Negotiating with the Enemy; U.S.–China Talks during the Cold War, 1949–1972*, Bloomington: Indiana University Press, 2006.

45. Xia, *Negotiating*, pp. 44–5.

46. Xia, *Negotiating*, pp. 57–8.

47. Deliberations on Indochina, however, were critically significant.

48. Xia, *Negotiating*, pp. 51, 53.

49. Xia, *Negotiating*, pp. 51, 53.

50. Xia, *Negotiating*, p. 73.

51. Chen Jian, *Mao's China*, pp. 112–7. Kathryn Weathersby, using essentially the same sources as Chen, concluded that Stalin's death eliminated a key factor keeping the war going for geostrategic purposes. See "Stalin, Mao, and the End of the Korean War," in *Brothers in Arms; The Rise and Fall of the Sino-Soviet Alliance, 1945–1963*, Washington: Woodrow Wilson Center Press, 1998, pp. 90–116.

52. Quoted in Rosemary J. Foot, "Nuclear Coercion and the Ending of the Korean Conflict," *International Security*, vol. 13, no. 3 (Winter 1988–1989), pp. 93–106, 105. For an exposition of US views on the efficacy of nuclear coercion, see Roger Dingman, "Atomic Diplomacy during the Korean War," in the same issue of *International Security*, pp. 50–91. Dingman argues that US nuclear threats had no noticeable impact on China's decision to end the war; Foot argues that they played a role in that decision.

53. William R. Harris, "Chinese Nuclear Doctrine: The Decade Prior to Weapons Development, 1945–1955," *China Quarterly*, No. 21 (January–March 1965), pp. 87–95.

54. Proponents of the theory that the United States used BW in Korea include Stephan L. Endicott, "Germ Warfare and 'Plausible Denial,' the Korean War, 1952–1953," *Modern China*, vol. 5, no. 1 (January 1975), pp. 79–104. Jon Halliday and Bruce Cumings, in their influential 1988 book *Korea: the Unknown War*, New York: Pantheon Books, 1988 (p. 185), maintain that the issue of US conduct of biological warfare in Korea "is open." A careful and persuasive rebuttal of this hypothesis drawing, inter alia, on evidence from the Russian presidential archives is Milton Leitenberg, "New Russian Evidence on the Korean War Biological Warfare Allegations: Background and Analysis," CWIHP *Bulletin*, issue 11 (Winter 1998), pp. 185–99. Numbered documents below are from this collection.

55. Quoted in Shu Guang Zhang, *Mao's Military Romanticism*, p. 182.

56. Document No. 1, *Bulletin*, op. cit., p. 180.

57. Document No. 2, *Bulletin*, op. cit., p. 180. The conduct of these investigations was apparently linked to the succession struggle among Stalin's heirs. Weathersby and Leitenberg conclude that while this may cast doubts on the putative motives attributed to Soviet participants in these activities, the outline of events presented in the documents stands.

58. Document No. 3, *Bulletin*, p. 181.

59. Document No. 8, *Bulletin*, p. 183.

60. Document No. 9, *Bulletin*, p. 183.

61. Document No. 11, *Bulletin*, p. 184.

62. Quoted in Leitenberg, "New Russian Evidence," p. 186.

63. Guo's solicitation of Needham, and Needham's deeply flawed role in the subsequent "investigation," are narrated in Simon Winchester, *The Man Who Loved China*, New York: Harper Collins, 2008, pp. 199–216.

64. Document No. 2, *Bulletin*, pp. 180–2.

65. *The Hate Campaign in Communist China*, Hong Kong: US Consulate. No date (1953?). This is a 210-page compilation of materials from the PRC media. A number of these "confessions" are included in *The Hate Campaign in Communist China*, cited above.

66. "National Affairs: Germ Warfare: Forged Evidence," *Time*, March 9, 1953. www.time.com/time/priintout/0,8816,819144,00.html.

67. Chen Jian, *China's Road*, p. 141.

68. Chen Jian, *China's Road*, p. 194.

69. *The Hate Campaign in Communist China*, p. 213.

70. This section follows Qiang Zhai, *China and the Vietnam Wars, 1950–1975*, Chapel Hill: University of North Carolina Press, 2000, pp. 10–42. The name of the Vietnamese communist movement was considerably more variable than that of the Chinese. From 1931 to 1945, it was known as the Indochina Communist Party. From February 1951 to 1976, it was known as the Vietnamese Workers Party (VWP). In 1976, the name was changed to Vietnam Communist Party. For simplicity, I will refer to the pre-1976 party as the VWP.

71. Zhai, *China and Vietnam Wars*, p. 37.

Chapter 4. The Bandung Era

1. Adam B. Ulam, *Expansion and Coexistence; A History of Soviet Foreign Policy, 1917–1967*, New York: Praeger, 1968, pp. 539–71. This discussion follows Ulam.

2. *China's Foreign Relations, a Chronology of Events (1949–1988)*, Beijing: Foreign Languages Press, 1989, pp. 454–5.

3. Ulam, *Expansion*, p. 544.

4. *China's Foreign Relations*, p. 455.

5. Ulam, *Expansion*, p. 546.

6. John Garver, *Chinese-Soviet Relations, 1937–1945, the Diplomacy of Chinese Nationalism*, London: Oxford University Press, 1988, pp. 137–40.

7. Mao Zedong, "Talk with the American Correspondent Anna Louise Strong, August 1946, *Selected Works of Mao Tse-tung*, Vol. 4, Beijing: Foreign Languages Press, 1961, pp. 97–101.

8. Kuo-Kang Shao, *Zhou Enlai and the Foundations of Chinese Foreign Policy*, New York: St Martins Press, 1996, pp. 210–37. Nineo Nakajima, "Foreign Relations: From the Korean War to the Bandung Line," *The Cambridge History of China*, Vol. 14, *The People's Republic of China, Part I: The Emergence of Revolutionary China, 1949–1965*, edited by Roderick MacFarquhar and John King Fairbank, New York: Cambridge University Press, 1987, pp. 259–89. The strategy of a united front has deep roots tracing

back to Lenin's thinking about how communists could mobilize and guide the strength of more numerous noncommunists.

9. French rule over Vietnam consisted of three zones: Tonkin in northern Vietnam, Annam in the central, narrow coastal region, and Cochin China encompassing the Mekong delta.

10. Qiang Zhai, "Transplanting the Chinese Model: Chinese Military Advisors and the First Vietnam War, 1950–1954," *Journal of Military History*, vol. 57, no. 4 (October 1993), pp. 689–715.

11. Zhai, "Transplanting," pp. 707–8.

12. Zhai, "Transplanting," pp. 710–1.

13. Chen Jian, *Mao's China and the Cold War*, Chapel Hill: University of North Carolina Press, 2001, p. 140.

14. Huang Hua, *Huang Hua Memoirs*, Beijing: Foreign Languages Press, 2008, p. 137.

15. This discussion follows Qiang Zhai, "China and the Geneva Conference of 1954," *China Quarterly*, no. 129 (March 1992), pp. 103–22. Also, Chen Jian, *Mao's China*, pp. 138–43. Also see Alfred D. Wilhelm, Jr., *The Chinese at the Negotiating Table*, Washington, DC: National Defense University Press, 1994.

16. Chen Jian, *Mao's China*, p. 142.

17. Some scholars have argued that Chinese and Soviet pressure forced the VWP to accept proposals against their will. Chen Jian argues that Zhou persuaded Ho, who persuaded the VWP Politburo. The two positions do not seem to be contradictory.

18. Regarding Hanoi's charges of Chinese "betrayal" at Geneva in 1954, see *Chinese Aggression against Vietnam: the Root of the Problem*, Hanoi: Foreign Languages Publishing House, 1979. Also *The Truth about Vietnam-China Relations over the Last Thirty Years*, Hanoi: Ministry of Foreign Affairs, 1979.

19. Chen Jian, *Mao's China*, p. 143.

20. This discussion generally follows Yafeng Xia, *Negotiating with the Enemy, U.S.-China Talks during the Cold War, 1949–1972*, Bloomington: Indiana University Press, 2006, pp. 76–105. Also Kenneth T. Young, *Negotiating with the Chinese Communists: The United States Experience, 1953–1956*, New York: McGraw Hill, 1968.

21. The most famous of these was Qian Xuesen, a leader in high-speed aerodynamics and rocket propulsion and one of the founders of the Jet Propulsion Lab in the United States in 1943. After Germany's surrender, Qian was a member of the mission that investigated Germany's rocket programs. In June 1950, Qian's US security clearance was revoked, and within two weeks Qian declared his desire to return to China. The US government detained him for five years at various locations. Once back in China, Qian became a leading figure in China's rocket program, designing its first generation of ballistic missiles.

22. Xia, *Negotiating*, p. 78–9.

23. This section follows Thomas E. Stolper, *China, Taiwan and the Offshore Islands*, Armonk, NY: M. E. Sharpe, 1985. Also, Nancy B. Tucker, *Dangerous Strait: the U.S.-Taiwan-China Crisis*, New York: Columbia University Press, 2005.

24. Stolper, *Offshores*, p. 39.

25. *China's Foreign Relations*, p. 524.

26. *China's Foreign Relations*, p. 525.

27. Xia, *Negotiating*, pp. 84–5.

28. Xia, *Negotiating*, pp. 87–8.

29. Xia, *Negotiating*, p. 89.

30. This is the central thesis of John W. Garver, *The Sino-American Alliance; Nationalist China and U.S. Cold War Strategy in Asia*, Armonk, NY: M. E. Sharpe, 1997.

31. Kuo-kang Shao, "Chou En-lai's Diplomatic Approach to Non-aligned States in Asia, 1953–60," *China Quarterly*, No. 78 (June 1979), pp. 324–38.

32. Huang Hua, *Memoirs*, p. 155.

33. Huang Hua, *Memoirs*, pp. 156–7.

34. Huang Hua, *Memoirs*, p. 160. Also George M. Kahin, *The Asian-African Conference, Bandung, Indonesia, April 1955*, Ithaca, NY: Cornell University Press, 1956.

35. Huang Hua, *Memoirs*, p. 161.

36. John Rowland, *A History of Sino-Indian Relations: Hostile Coexistence*, Princeton: Van Nostrand, 1967, pp. 84–6.

37. *China's Foreign Relations*, p. 215.

38. *China's Foreign Relations*, pp. 207–8.

39. Anwar H. Syed, *China and Pakistan: Diplomacy of an Entente Cordiale*, Amherst: University of Massachusetts Press, 1974, pp. 55–62. J. P. Jain, *China, Pakistan, and Bangladesh*, New Delhi: Radiant, 1974, p. 25.

40. Regarding India and US containment, see Dennis Kux, *India and the U.S.: Estranged Democracies*, Washington, DC: National Defense University Press, 1993, pp. 87–143.

41. A recent survey of Nehru's effort to befriend China is Johan Loov, *A Game of Chess and a Battle of Wits: The Making of India's Forward Policy 1961–1962*, London: Bloomsbury, 2014,

42. A imperial representative was installed in Lhasa circa 1720 along with a guard of several hundred. That small force constituted no threat to either British India or the Tibetan ruler, the Dalai Lama.

43. I develop these ideas more fully in Garver, *Protracted Contest, Sino-Indian Rivalry in the Twentieth Century*, Seattle: University of Washington Press, 2001, pp. 50–3.

44. Carlos P. Romulo, *The Meaning of Bandung*, Chapel Hill: University of North Carolina Press, 1956, pp. 10–21.

45. Regarding US policy at this juncture, see David Allan Mayers, *Cracking the Monolith: U.S. Policy Against the Sino-Soviet Alliance, 1949–1955*, Baton Rouge: Louisiana State University Press, 1986. Gordon H. Chang, *Friends and Enemies: The United States, China, and the Soviet Union, 1948–1972*, Stanford: Stanford University Press, 1990.

Chapter 5. The Sino-Soviet Schism

1. This interpretation of the Great Leap Forward follows Frank Dikötter, *Mao's Great Famine, the History of China's Most Devastating Catastrophe, 1958–1962*, New York: Walker, 2010. Alexander V. Pantsov and Steven I. Levine, *Mao: The Real Story*, New York: Simon and Schuster, 2012. Thomas A. Christensen, *Useful Adversaries: Grand Strategy, Domestic Mobilization, and Sino-American Conflict, 1947–1958*, Princeton: Princeton University Press, 1996. Kenneth Lieberthal, "The Great Leap Forward and the Split in the Yan'an Leadership, 1958–1965," in *The Politics of China*, edited by Roderick MacFarquar, 3rd ed., Cambridge: Cambridge University Press, 2011, pp. 87–146.

2. Christensen, *Useful Adversaries*, pp. 214–15.

3. This is a key argument of Dikötter, *Mao's Famine*. Dikötter's study is based on local archives in China, which often contained very frank descriptions of the unfolding famine.

4. The speech and the response by Western communist parties is in *The Anti-Stalin Campaign and International Communism*, New York: Columbia University Press, 1956.

5. Wu Lengxi, *Shinian lunzhan, zhong su guanxi huiyilu, 1956–1966* (Ten-year polemical war, a memoir of Sino-Soviet relations), Vol. 1, Beijing: Zhongyang wenxuan chubanshe, 1999, pp. 3–5. The US embassy in Moscow quickly obtained and released a copy of the speech. On the Sino-Soviet polemical debates of the 1950s and 1960s, see Donald S. Zagoria, *The Sino-Soviet Conflict 1956–1961*, New York: Atheneum, 1969.

6. Wu, *Shinian lunzhan*, pp. 2–5. Wu was the CCP's record keeper on relations with the Soviet Union during this period and provides a very detailed account of interactions.

7. Wu, *Shinian lunzhan*, pp. 23–4.

8. *The Historical Experience of the Dictatorship of the Proletariat*, Beijing: Foreign Languages Press, 1961, pp. 2, 18–9.

9. François Fejtő, *A History of the People's Democracies: Eastern Europe since Stalin*, Middlesex: Penguin, 1974, p. 105. Documents on the 1956 events in both Poland and Hungary are in Paul E. Zinner, *National Communism and Popular Revolt in East Europe*, New York: Columbia University Press, 1956.

10. Flora Lewis, *A Case History of Hope*, New York: Doubleday, 1958, pp. 182–5.

11. Wu, *Shinian lunzhan*, pp. 35–6.

12. Wu, *Shinian lunzhan*, p. 39.

13. Wu, *Shinian lunzhan*, Vol. 1, pp. 51–7.

14. Zinner, *National Communism*, pp. 485–98.

15. Regarding the formation of the Sino-Albanian entente in 1956–1957, see Daniel Tretiak, "The Founding of the Sino-Albanian Entente," *China Quarterly*, no. 10 (April–June 1962), pp. 123–43.

16. Wu, *Shinian lunzhan*, pp. 60–1.

17. Wu, *Shinian lunzhan*, pp. 68–73.

18. In *The Historical Experience of the Dictatorship of the Proletariat*, pp. 32–3, 39.

19. Wu, *Shinian lunzhan*, p. 68.

20. This section follows Yitzhak Shichor, *The Middle East in China's Foreign Policy, 1949–1979*, London: Cambridge University Press, 1979, pp. 60–9.

21. Shichor, *Middle East*, pp. 41, 45, 49, and 61.

22. Shichor, *Middle East*, p. 49.

23. Wu Lengxi, *Shinian lunzhan*, pp. 93–6.

24. Dikötter, *Mao's Famine*, p. 12.

25. Wu Lengxi, *Shinian lunzhan*, pp. 101–2.

26. Nikita Khrushchev, *Khrushchev Remembers: The Last Testament*, Boston: Little Brown, 1974, pp. 256–7.

27. Quoted in O. Edmund Clubb, *China and Russia: The Great Game*, New York: Columbia University Press, 1971, p. 422.

28. Wu, *Shinian lunzhan*, pp. 118–9.

29. Wu, *Shinian lunzhan*, p. 121.

30. Quoted in Dikötter, *Mao's Famine*, p. 13.

31. Dikötter, *Mao's Famine*, p. 12.

32. *Khrushchev Remembers*, pp. 254–5. Wu, *Shinian lunzhan*, pp. 130–1. Khrushchev says that on the eve of the Moscow conference Mao gave a speech at Moscow State University declaring "The socialist camp must have one head, and that head can only be the USSR." This was, Khrushchev noted, "the most unqualified endorsement of Soviet hegemony over the bloc . . . by any conference delegate."

33. The December 1957 declaration and the April 1960 declaration "Long Live Leninism" discussed below are both available at www.marxists.org/history.

34. Wu, *Shinian lunzhan*, pp. 128–9.

35. Khrushchev, *Khrushchev Remembers*, pp. 254–5.

36. Quoted in Dikötter, *Mao's Famine*, p. 14.

37. Lucian W. Pye, *Mao Tse-tung: The Man in the Leader*, New York: Basic Books, 1978, p. 309.

38. Li Zhisui, *The Private Life of Chairman Mao: The Memoirs of Mao's Personal Physician*, New York: Random House, 1999, pp. 109–10. This is discussed more fully in John W. Garver, "Mao's Soviet Policies," *China Quarterly*, no. 173 (March 2005), pp. 199–213.

39. This follows Pantsov and Levine, *Mao*.

40. Statement by the Chinese government, August 15, 1963, in *Peking Review*, August 16, 1963, pp. 7–15.

41. Liu Xiao, *Chushi sulian ba nian* (Eight years as ambassador to the Soviet Union), Beijing: Dangshi ziliao chubanshe, 1986, p. 60.

42. John Wilson Lewis and Xue Litai, *China's Strategic Seapower: The Politics of Force Modernization in the Nuclear Era*, Stanford: Stanford University Press, p. 13.

43. Lewis and Xue, *China's Strategic Seapower*, p. 13.

44. Wu, *Shinian lunzhan*, pp. 158–9.

45. Li, *Private Life of Chairman Mao*, p. 261.

46. "The origin and development of the differences between the leadership of the CPSU and ourselves," *Renmin ribao*, September 6, 1963, in *The Polemic on the General Line of the International Communist Movement*, Beijing: Foreign Languages Press, 1965, p. 77.

47. Gorshkov was a strong advocate of Soviet naval power, appointed by Khrushchev to head the Soviet navy only the year before (1957), and would go on over the next several decades to turn the Soviet navy into a potent global fleet.

48. Sergei N. Khrushchev, *Nikita Khrushchev and the Creation of a Superpower*, University Park: Pennsylvania State University Press, 2000, pp. 267–8.

49. Constanine Pleshakov, "Nikita Khrushchev and Sino-Soviet Relations," in *Brothers in Arms; the Rise and Fall of the Sino-Soviet Alliance, 1945–1963*, Stanford University Press, 1998, pp. 226–45.

50. This account follows Wu, *Shinian lunzhan*, pp. 163–73. Also Vladislav M. Zubok, "The Mao-Khrushchev Conversations, 31 July–3 August 1958 and 2 October 1959," in *CWIHP Bulletin*, Issue 12/13 (Fall/Winter 2001), pp. 244–72.

51. Within a short time, the radio station became moot when satellites provided the Soviet Union a superior method of communication with submarines.

52. Khrushchev, *Khrushchev Remembers*, pp. 260–1.

53. Wu, *Shinian lunzhan*, p. 173.

54. Henry Kissinger, *On China*, New York: Penguin, 2011, p. 360.

55. Key sources on the Taiwan Strait crisis are Thomas E. Stolper, *China, Taiwan, and the Ofshore Islands*, Armonk: M. E. Sharpe, 1985. Tang Tsou, *The Embroilment Over Quemoy: Mao, Chiang, and Dulles*, Institute of International Studies, University of Utah Press, 1959. Chen Jian, *Mao's China and the Cold War*, Chapel Hill: University of North Carolina Press, 2001. Regarding US policy and nuclear weapons, see H. W. Brands, "Testing Massive Retaliation, Credibility and Crisis Management in the Taiwan Strait," *International Security*, vol. 12, no. 4 (Spring 1988), pp. 124–51.

56. Wu, *Shinian lunzhan*, p. 175.

57. In February, Syria and Egypt merged to form a unitary state, the United Arab Republic, as the first step toward formation of a pan-Arab state. The union lasted only till 1961. Communist strength was quite strong in Syria, and Nasserism was strongly socialist, Arab nationalist, and anti-imperialist (if also anticommunist). Then on July 14 a clique of Army officers in Iraq overthrew the monarchy that had ruled that country under British auspices since 1921. Arab nationalist sentiment had been fanned by Iraq's alignment with Britain during the 1956 war, and the new military leadership moved toward alignment with Nasser and withdrawal from the Baghdad Pact (a withdrawal that occurred in March 1959). Days of mob violence against "traitors" and Westerners followed the military coup in Iraq. It seemed as if a pan-Arab union was forming. Lebanon threatened to be swept into the Nasserist vortex.

58. Shichor, *Middle East*, pp. 65–73.

59. Quoted in Shichor, *Middle East*, p. 73.

60. Wu, *Shinian lunzhan*, p. 182.

61. Wu, *Shinian lunzhan*, p. 178.

62. Wu, *Shinian lunzhan*, p. 180.

63. Chen Jian, *Mao's China and the Cold War*, p. 189.

64. Beijing denounced as false Gromyko's account of his 1958 talks with Mao and Zhou when his memoir was published in 1988. Prominent Soviet China specialist Mikhail Kapitsa, who accompanied Gromyko to Beijing, substantiated Gromyko's account. A. Doak Barnett, *China and the Major Powers*, Washington: Brookings Institution, 1977, p. 36. The Soviet documents discussed by Vladislav M. Zubok in "Khrushchev's Nuclear Promise to Beijing During the 1958 Crisis," CWIHP *Bulletin*, issue 6–7 (Winter 1995/1996), pp. 219, 226 (which reply to Chinese suggestions that the Soviet Union might remain passive while US atomic bombs fell on China) also make sense only if Gromyko's account is generally sound.

65. Wu, *Shinian lunzhan*, p. 180.

66. Chen Jian, *Mao's China and the Cold War*, p. 189.

67. Zubok, "Khrushchev's Nuclear Promise," pp. 219, 226.

68. "Communication of the CPSU CC to the CCP CC, 27 September 1958," in CWIHP *Bulletin*, issue 6–7 (Winter 1995–1996), pp. 226–27. Also Zubok, "Khrushchev's Nuclear Promise to Beijing," pp. 219, 226.

69. Zubok, "Khrushchev's Nuclear Promise," note 6, p. 227. An older but long dominant interpretation of Soviet-Chinese relations during the 1958 crisis maintained that Khrushchev's letters to Eisenhower came only after Zhou's September 6 call for US-PRC ambassadorial talks began to reduce tension, and that Mao was disappointed with Moscow's tardy support. See Barnett, *China and the Major Powers*, p. 346 note 40.

70. Christensen, *Useful Adversaries*, pp. 221–2.

71. "Speech on the International Situation," September 5, 1958, in *Mao Zedong on Diplomacy*, Beijing: Foreign Languages Press, 2007, pp. 264–69.

Chapter 6. Sino-Indian Conflict and the Sino-Soviet Alliance

1. Steven A. Hoffmann, *India and the China Crisis*, Berkeley: University of California Press, 1990.

2. P. B. Sinha and A. A. Athale, *History of the Conflict with China, 1962*, New Delhi: History Division, Ministry of Defense, Government of India, 1992, p. 28. Leaked and published online by the *Times of India* in December 2002. Available at www.bharat-rakshak.com.

3. Regarding the 1959 uprising, see Tsering Shakya, *The Dragon in the Land of Snows*, London: Pimlico, 1999. Frank Moraes, *The Revolt in Tibet*, New Delhi: Srishti, 1960.

4. Wu Lengxi, *Shinian lunzhan, zhong su guanxi huiyilu, 1956–1966* (Ten-year polemical war, a memoir of Sino-Soviet relations), Vol. I, Beijing: Zhongyang wenxian chubanshe, 1999, pp. 197–9.

5. Quoted in John Garver, "China's Decision for War with India in 1962," in *New Directions in the Study of China's Foreign Policy*, edited by Alastair Ian Johnson and Robert S. Ross, Stanford: Stanford University Press, 2006, pp. 86–130, p. 94.

6. "The Revolution in Tibet and Nehru's Philosophy," in *Concerning the Question of Tibet*, Beijing: Foreign Languages Press, 1959, pp. 239–76.

7. Garver, "China's Decision," p. 95.

8. For an assessment of Nehru's probable knowledge of CIA Tibetan operations, see John W. Garver, "India, China, the United States, Tibet, and the Origins of the 1962 War," *India Review*, vol. 3, no. 2 (April 2004), pp. 171–82.

9. Wu, *Shinian lunzhan*, pp. 210–4.

10. Wu, *Shinian lunzhan*, pp. 226–7.

11. Khrushchev, *Khrushchev Remembers*, p. 269.

12. Wu, *Shinian lunzhan*, p. 205.

13. Donald Zagoria, *Sino-Soviet Conflict, 1956–1961*, New York: Atheneum, 1969, pp. 241–2.

14. A good collection of documents from Khrushchev's visit is *Khrushchev in America*, New York: Crosscurrents, 1960.

15. "Memorandum of Conversation N. S. Khrushchev and Mao Zedong, Beijing, 2 October 1959," IHCWP *Bulletin*, issue 12, no. 13 (Fall–Winter 2001), pp. 262–70.

16. Ibid.

17. Khrushchev seems to be alluding here to the September 1958 Soviet reply to Mao's offer to dilute the Soviet obligation to come to China's assistance in the event of war with the United States.

18. The Far Eastern Republic was nominally independent but actually a Bolshevik puppet state set up following Japan's intervention in the Russian Far East during the Russian Civil War and designed as a buffer between Bolshevik Russia and Imperial Japan's interventionist military forces. It was dissolved by the Bolsheviks in 1922 following Japan's withdrawal from eastern Siberia.

19. "Memorandum of conversation N. S. Khrushchev and Mao Zedong," pp. 268–9.

20. William Taubman, *Khrushchev: The Man and His Era*, New York: W. W. Norton, 2003, p. 394.

21. This section follows Wu, *Shinian lunzhan*, pp. 236–47.

22. Wu, *Shinian lunzhan*, pp. 290, 207–10.

23. Wu, *Shinian lunzhan*, pp. 279–91.

24. Wu, *Shinian lunzhan*, pp. 336–7.

25. Wu, *Shinian lunzhan*, p. 337.

26. Zagoria, *Sino-Soviet Conflict*, p. 3.

27. Sydney Klein, *The Road Divides: Economic Aspects of the Sino-Soviet Dispute*, Hong Kong: International Studies Group, 1966, pp. 66–7.

28. Ibid.

29. O. Edmund Clubb, *China and Russia: The "Great Game,"* New York: Columbia University Press, p. 446.

30. My Georgia Tech colleague Lu Hanchao has investigated the impact of Mao's casual comments about cuisine on China's agricultural policy during the same period. Hanchao Lu, "The Tastes of Chairman Mao: The Quotidian as Statecraft in the Great Leap Forward and Its Aftermath," *Modern China* (2013), pp. 1–34. Available at http://mcx.sagepub.com/content/early/2013/12/29/0097700413517640.abstract.

31. Chinese imports from the Soviet Union fell from US$950 million in 1959 to US$233 million in 1962, a level far below any year since 1950. Chu-yuan Cheng, *Economic Relations between Peking and Moscow, 1949–63*, New York: Praeger, 1964, p. 63. Trade between the Soviet Union and China would reach a low point in 1970 before starting to recover.

Chapter 7. Reviving Revolutionary Momentum

1. Frank Dikötter, *Mao's Great Famine*, New York: Walker, 2010, p. 118.

2. This section follows Niu Jun, "1962: The Eve of the Left Turn in China's Foreign Policy," Working Paper No. 48, October 2005, Cold War International History Project, Woodrow Wilson International Center for Scholarship.

3. A substantial number of CPSU leaders in the mid-1920s, most notably Nikolai Bukharin, favored continuation of the family-farming-oriented New Economic Policy for a longer period. Stalin insisted on pushing forward with collectivization against all opposition, either within the elite or from the farmers themselves.

4. Qiang Zhai, *China and the Vietnam Wars, 1950–1975*, Chapel Hill: North Carolina University Press, 2000, pp. 114–5.

5. *Who's Who in Communist China*, Hong Kong: Union Research Center, 1966, pp. 404–6.

6. Qiang Zhai, *China and the Vietnam Wars*.

7. This account follows Sergey Radchenko, *Two Suns in the Heaven, The Sino-Soviet Struggle for Supremacy, 1962–1967*, Stanford: Stanford University Press, 2009, pp. 46–7.

8. Regarding the August 1962 Tenth Plenum, see Roderick MacFarquhar, *The Origins of the Cultural Revolution*, Vol. 3, *The Coming of the Cataclysm, 1961–1966*, New York: Columbia University Press, 1997, pp. 281–5.

9. Wu Lengxi, *Shinian lunzhan, zhong su guanxi huiyilu, 1956–1966* (Ten-year polemical war, a memoir of Sino-Soviet relations), Vol. 2, Beijing: Zhongyang wenxian chubanshe, p. 540.

10. Radchenko, *Two Suns*, p. 49.

11. Quoted in Radchenko, *Two Suns*, pp. 50–1.

12. Radchenko, *Two Suns*, pp. 56–64.

13. This document is available in *The Polemic on the General Line of the International Communist Movement*, Beijing: Foreign Languages Press, 1965. This collection of

documents also contains the Soviet letter of February 1962 and all nine "critical articles" issued by the CCP between September 1963 and July 1964. Another good compendium of documents from this period is John Gittings, *Survey of the Sino-Soviet Dispute: A Commentary and Extracts from the Recent Polemics, 1963–1957,* Oxford: Oxford University Press, 1968.

14. Quoted in Radchenko, *Two Suns,* p. 59.

15. Radchenko, *Two Suns,* pp. 59–60.

16. Quoted in Radchenko, *Two Suns,* p. 60.

17. Wu, *Shinian lunzhan.*

18. Witold S. Sworakowski, *World Communism, A Handbook, 1918–1965,* Stanford, CA: Hoover Institution Press, 1973.

19. The biography of Mao by Alexander V. Pantsov and Steven I. Levine, *Mao, The Real Story* (New York: Simon and Schuster, 2012), breaks new ground by drawing on Comintern archives to lay out the large amounts of cash doled out by Moscow to the CCP during its long struggle for power. A good study of Soviet support for the Communist Party USA is Harvey Klehr, John Earl Haynes, and Kyrill M. Anderson, *The Soviet World of American Communism,* New Haven: Yale University Press, 1998.

20. Wu, *Shinian lunzhan,* p. 779.

21. Wu, *Shinian lunzhan,* pp. 778–9.

22. Wu, *Shinian lunzhan,* p. 850.

23. This account of the "Malinovsky incident" is drawn from Wu, *Shinian lunzhan,* pp. 850–79.

24. Wu, *Shinian lunzhan,* p. 861.

25. MacFarquhar, *The Coming of the Cataclysm,* p. 309.

26. P. B. Sinha and A. A. Athale, *History of the Conflict with China, 1962,* New Delhi: History Division, Ministry of Defense, Government of India, 1992. Leaked and published online by the *Times of India* in December 2002. Available at www.bharat-rakshank.com.

27. Key sources on the Sino-Indian territorial dispute are Neville Maxwell, *India's China War,* New York: Doubleday Anchor, 1972. Steven A. Hoffmann, *India and the China Crisis,* Berkeley: University of California Press, 1998. Primary materials are *Chinese Aggression in War and Peace: Letters of the Prime Minister of India,* Information Office, Government of India, December 1962. *Premier Chou En-lai's Letter to the Leaders of Asian and African Countries on the Sino-Indian Boundary Question (November 15, 1962),* Beijing: Foreign Languages Press, 1962.

28. Johan Loov, *A Game of Chess and a Battle of Wits: The Making of India's Forward Policy 1961–1962,* London: Bloomsbury, 2014.

29. Allen S. Whiting, *The Calculus of Chinese Deterrence: India and Indochina,* Ann Arbor: University of Michigan, 1975, p. 58.

30. D. K. Palit, *War in High Himalayas: The Indian Army in Crisis, 1962,* New Delhi: Lancer, 1991, pp. 177–8.

31. Shi Bo, ed., *Zhong yin dazhan jishi* (Record of events in the China-India war), Beijing: Da di chubanshe, quoted in John W. Garver, "China's Decision for War with India in 1962," in *New Directions in the Study of China's Foreign Policy,* Stanford: Stanford University Press, 2006, p. 108.

32. Sinha and Athale, *History of the Conflict with China,* p. xx.

33. Ibid., p. 430 note 13.

34. Lei Yingfu, *Zai zuigao tongshuaibu dang canmou: Lei Yingfu huiyilu* (Serving on the staff of the high command: Memoir of General Lei Yingfu), Nanchang: Baihuazhou wenyi chubanshe. Quoted in Garver, "China's Decision," p. 108.

35. Wang Bingnan, *Zhong mei huitan jiu nian huigu* (Recollection of nine years of Sino-American talks), Beijing: Shijie zhishi chubanshe, 1985, pp. 85–90.

36. Garver, "China's Decision," p. 115.

37. Lei Yingfu memoir, quoted in Garver, "China's Decision," p. 120.

38. The first detailed study of Establishment 22 was Kenneth Conboy and James Morrison, *The CIA's Secret War in Tibet*, Lawrence: University of Kansas Press, 2002, pp. 171–97.

39. John Garver, "The Indian Factor in Recent Sino-Soviet Relations," *China Quarterly*, no. 125 (Summer 1991), pp. 55–85.

40. John Garver, *The China-India-U.S. Triangle: Strategic Relations in the Post-Cold War Era*, Seattle, WA: National Bureau of Asian Research, 2002.

41. The United States, on the other hand, did not seize Chinese territory, although it did participate in territorial "concessions" set up in China's east coast cities. This relatively non-aggressive history of the United States during China's "century of national humiliation" has been stressed to China by US leaders from Franklin Roosevelt and Harry Truman to Richard Nixon to George H. W. Bush. On the history of Russo-Chinese relations, see O. Edmund Clubb, *China and Russia: The "Great Game,"* New York: Columbia University Press, 1971. Harry Schwartz, *Tsars, Mandarins, and Commissars*, New York: Doubleday Anchor, 1973. Aitchen K. Wu, *China and the Soviet Union*, London: Methuen, 1950.

42. Accounts of the Sino-Soviet border conflict: Tai Sung An, *The Sino-Soviet Territorial Dispute*, Philadelphia: Westminster Press, 1973. Dennis J. Doolin, *Territorial Claims in the Sino-Soviet Conflict: Documents and Analysis*, Stanford: Hoover Institution, 1965.

43. "Munich" here refers to the 1938 British and French sacrifice of Czechoslovakia to Nazi Germany in hopes of satisfying Hitler's territorial demands and thus averting war.

44. Quoted in An, *Territorial Dispute*, p. 76.

45. Quoted in An, *Territorial Dispute*, p. 82.

46. An, *Territorial Dispute*, p. 82.

47. This section draws from William Burr and Jeffrey T. Richelson, "Whether to 'Strangle the Baby in the Cradle," *International Security*, vol. 25, no. 3 (Winter 2000/10), pp. 54–99. Also Gordon H. Chang, *Friends and Enemies: The United States, China, and the Soviet Union, 1948–1972*, Stanford University Press, 1990.

48. This interpretation comes from Radchenko, *Two Suns*, pp. 65–6.

49. See Walter C. Clemens, *The Arms Race and Sino-Soviet Relations*, Hoover Institution Press, 1968. Morton H. Halperin, *China and the Bomb*, London: Pall Mall Press, 1968. Morton H. Halperin and Dwight H. Perkins, *Communist China and Arms Control*, New York: Praeger, 1965. Alice Langley Hsieh, "The Sino-Soviet Nuclear Dialogue: 1963," in *Sino-Soviet Military Relations*, edited by Raymond L. Garthoff, New York: Praeger, 1966, pp. 150–70.

50. *Peking Review*, August 15, 1963, p. 7.

51. *Saturday Evening Post*, September 28 and October 26, 1963. Quoted in Burr and Richelson, *Strangle*, p. 74.

52. Wu, *Shinian lunzhan*, pp. 745, 753.

53. Barry Naughton, "The Third Front: Defense Industrialization in the Chinese Interior," *China Quarterly*, no. 115 (September 1988), pp. 351–86.

54. Anwar H. Syed, *China and Pakistan: Diplomacy of an Entente Cordiale,* Amherst: University of Massachusetts Press, 1974.

55. Regarding Operation Gibraltar, see Mohammed Musa, *My Version: India-Pakistan War, 1965,* Lahore: Wajidalis, 1983. S. M. Burke, *Pakistan's Foreign Policy,* London: Oxford University Press, 1973, pp. 326–8. Russel Brines, *The Indo-Pakistan Conflict, 1965,* London: Pall Mall, 1968, pp. 301–3.

56. Regarding China and the 1965 India-Pakistan war, see Garver, *Protracted Contest,* pp. 194–9.

57. Golam W. Choudhury, *India, Pakistan, Bangladesh and the Major Powers: Politics of a Divided Subcontinent,* New York: Free Press, 1975, pp. 183–5.

58. *Survey of the China Mainland Press,* September 3, 1965, no. 3531, p. 34.

59. Peter Van Ness, *Revolution and Chinese Foreign Policy: Peking's Support for Wars of National Liberation,* Berkeley: University of California Press, 1970, p. 97.

60. Choudhury, *India, Pakistan,* pp. 189–91.

61. This is the conclusion of Golam Choudhury based on a close study of Pakistani materials. For a discussion of Choudhury's conclusions and the historiography of China and the 1965 war, see Garver, *Protracted Contest,* p. 411 note 47.

62. Choudhury, *India, Pakistan,* p. 191.

Chapter 8. Revolutionary China's Quest to Transform Southeast Asia

1. The document is available at many websites, e.g., https://www.marxists.org/reference/archive/lin-biao/1965/09/peoples_war/cho5.htm. The contrast between this statement, issued under Lin Biao's name, and another statement written to commemorate the twentieth anniversary of Germany's surrender of Germany in May 1965 and issued by PLA chief of Staff Luo Ruiqing led many Western analysts to discern conflicting policy prescriptions between Lin and Luo. Much scholarly attention was devoted to analyzing this supposed "strategic debate." Eventually, Chinese scholars ascertained that both statements were closely edited, or even written, by Mao Zedong.

2. "More on the Historical Experience of the Dictatorship of the Proletariat," editorial in *Renmin ribao,* December 29, 1956, in *The Historical Experience of the Dictatorship of the Proletariat,* Beijing: Foreign Languages Press, 1956, p. 28.

3. Chin Peng, *My Side of History,* Singapore: Media Matters, 2003, pp. 426, 430. Chin Peng was the long-time secretary general of the Communist Party of Malaya. This is his memoir.

4. Chen Peng, *My Side,* p. 440.

5. William J. Duiker, *The Communist Road to Power in Vietnam,* Boulder, CO: Westview, 1981, pp. 186–8.

6. Qiang Zhai, *China and the Vietnam Wars, 1950–1975,* Chapel Hill: University of North Carolina Press, 2000, p. 112.

7. Mao's theory of "protracted people's war" outlined three states. In the first, "strategic defensive" stage, revolutionary forces should concentrate on education, agitation, and organizational work to build solid base areas. In the second state, of strategic stalemate, revolutionary forces would undertake some "mobile operations" but still avoid direct confrontation with enemy main units. Only in the final stage of "strategic offense" would the revolutionary forces wage big battles with enemy main forces and seize enemy-held cities.

8. Lien-Hang T. Nguyen, *Hanoi's War: An International History of the War for Peace in Vietnam*, Chapel Hill: University of North Carolina Press, 2012. This discussion of CCP-VWP debates over strategy follows Nguyen.

9. According to Lien-Hang T. Nguyen, Le Duan's and Nguyen Chi Thanh's "south first" group was opposed by a "north first" faction, which included most VWP elders—Ho, Giap, Pham Van Dong—who favored socialist construction in the north and lower intensity war in the south. The military prescriptions of this "north first" group tended to converge with Beijing's prescriptions. This clash in preferred military strategies did not become intense, according to Nguyen, until 1967–1968, in the lead-up to the Tet Offensive.

10. Zhai, *China and Vietnam Wars*, p. 113.

11. Zhai, *China and Vietnam Wars*, p. 116.

12. See Duiker, *The Communist Road to Power*. Nguyen, *Hanoi's War*.

13. "Statement against U.S.-Ngo Dinh Diem Clique's Aggression in South Vietnam and Massacre of the South Vietnamese People," August 29, 1963, *Mao Zedong on Diplomacy*, Beijing: Foreign Languages Press, 2007, pp. 385–6.

14. Zhao, *China and Vietnam Wars*, pp. 118–20.

15. Regarding China's policies during the Laotian crisis of 1961–1962, see Chae Jin Lee, "Chinese Communist Policy in Laos: 1954–1964," PhD diss., University of California in Los Angeles, 1966. Brian Crozier, "Peking and the Laotian Crisis: An Interim Appraisal," *China Quarterly*, no. 6 (July–September 1961), pp. 128–37.

16. The official name of the second province is Houa Phan, but it is commonly named after its main city, Sam Neua.

17. Brian Crozier, "Peking and the Laotian Crisis: A Further Appraisal," *China Quarterly*, no. 11 (July–September 1962), pp. 116–23.

18. Regarding US policy, see Roger Hilsman, *To Move a Nation*, New York: Delta, 1976, pp. 91–155.

19. Arthur Lall, *How Communist China Negotiates*, New York: Columbia University Press, 1968, pp. 140–51. Lall was India's representative to the conference.

20. Burma was renamed Myanmar in 1989.

21. *China's Foreign Relations: A Chronology of Events*, Beijing: Foreign Languages Press, 1989, pp. 207–8.

22. John W. Garver, *The Sino-American Alliance: Nationalist China and American Cold War Strategy in Asia*, Armonk: M. E. Sharpe, 1997, pp. 148–66.

23. Bertil Lintner, *The Rise and Fall of the Communist Party of Burma*, Ithaca, NY: Cornell University Press, 1990, pp. 22–57. This account of CCP-BCP ties follows Lintner.

24. Zhou Degao, *Wo yu zhonggong he jiangong* (Me and the Chinese communists and the Kampuchean communists), Hong Kong: Tiantu shuwu chubanshe [n.d.; 2007?]. Zhou was an ethnic Chinese journalist who served as a key liaison between the Chinese embassy and the Kampuchean Communist Party during the 1950s and 1960s. This is his memoir.

25. Zhou, *Wo yu zhonggong*, p. 111.

26. Ben Kiernan, *How Pol Pot Came to Power*, New Haven: Yale University Press, 2004, p. 203.

27. Kiernan, *How Pol Pot*, pp. 222–3.

28. Zhou, *Wo yu Zhonggong*, p. 75.

29. Kierman, *How Pol Pot*, pp. 223, 249.

30. Melvin Gurtov, "The Foreign Ministry and Foreign Affairs during the Cultural Revolution," *China Quarterly*, no. 40 (October–December 1969), pp. 84–5.

31. Zhou, *Wo yu zhonggong*, pp. 105, 108.

32. Zhou, *Wo yu zonggong*, p. 151.

33. Ibid.

34. "The Malayan Communist Party in the Federation of Malaya," report by a British Government intelligence agency, National Archives of Australia, April 1956. The Cold War in Asia (1945–1990), Asia Research Institute, University of Singapore. http://www.ari.nus.edu.sg/docs/SEA-China-interactions-Cluster/TheColdWarInAsia/1956%20Report%20on%20Malayan%20Communist%20Party%20in%20the%20Federation%20of%20Malaya.pdf. Accessed November 20, 2013.

35. Chin Peng, *My Side*, p. 253.

36. Ibid., p. 355.

37. Ibid.

38. Ibid., p. 338.

39. Ibid., pp. 335–7, 370.

40. Ibid., pp. 370, 396.

41. Ibid., p. 352.

42. Ibid., p. 353.

43. Ibid., p. 354.

44. Ibid., pp. 367–8.

45. Ibid., p. 405.

46. Ibid., p. 433.

47. Ibid., p. 408.

48. Ibid., pp. 411, 436.

49. Ibid., p. 429.

50. Ibid., p. 434.

51. Ibid., p. 435.

52. Ibid., p. 450.

53. Lee Kuan Yew, *From Third World to First*, New York: Harper Collins, 2011, p. 111.

54. Evolution of Singapore, a Digital Journal. Accessed November 15, 2012. Thinkquest web site was discontinued as of July 1, 2013.

55. Chin Peng, *My Side*, p. 405.

56. Ibid., p. 409.

57. Ibid., pp. 437–8.

58. Ibid., p. 112.

59. Internal Security Department, Government of Singapore. http://www.mha.gov.sg.

60. Chin Peng, *My Side*, p. 439.

61. Regarding China's Indonesia policies at this juncture, see Sheldon W. Simon, *The Broken Triangle: Peking, Djakarta, and the PKI*, Baltimore: Johns Hopkins Press, 1969. David Mozingo, *Chinese Policy toward Indonesia, 1949–1967*, Ithaca, NY: Cornell University Press, 1976. Donald Hindley, "The Indonesian Communist Party and the Conflict in the International Communist Movement," *China Quarterly*, no. 19 (July–September 1969), pp. 99–119.

62. Mozingo, *Chinese Policy*, p. 209.

63. Mozingo, *Chinese Policy*, p. 203.

64. Simon, *Broken Triangle*, p. 70.

65. Victor Fic, *Anatomy of the Jakarta Coup: October 1, 1965*, New Delhi: Abhinav Publications, 2004, pp. 83–6. The 1965 Djakarta coup is a controversial matter. Some scholars maintain that the PKI and China had no involvement in the abduction and murder of six high-ranking generals that touched off subsequent events. That coup, these scholars insist, was 100 percent a matter of intra-army rivalries. This has also been the position of the PKI. Fic has long been the leading scholar arguing that the PKI and China were deeply involved in events leading up to those murders. Fic's conclusions in the work cited here are based on Indonesian post-coup interrogations, post-coup PKI self-criticisms, interviews with coup participants, and some newspaper reports. The explanation offered here follows Fic's. Fic's book contains an overview of the historiographical debates surrounding the 1965 coup.

66. Fic, *Anatomy*, pp. 106–8.

67. Fic, *Anatomy*, pp. 106–11.

68. United States Central Intelligence Agency, *Indonesia—1965: The Coup That Backfired*, Washington, DC: Central Intelligence Agency, 1968, pp. 130–1.

69. Simon, *Broken Triangle*, pp. 100–1, 106.

70. Fic, *Anatomy*, pp. 90–9.

71. Fic, *Anatomy*, p. 96. Fic's source for this dialogue is an April 1966 article in Singapore's *Straits Times*, bolstered by references in several PKI documents to an earlier agreement between Sukarno and "the neighbor" (code for China) and between Aidit and "the Grandfather" (code for Mao). The latter document is from the PKI Central Committee, signed by Aidit to all party members, dated November 1965. It was obtained by Fic from a Indonesian lieutenant colonel in April 1971. Fic, *Jakarta Coup*, pp. 290, 324–327. The "North Shenxi" reference would seem to be to the Zheng Feng campaign of 1942–1944, which scholars generally agree was vicious.

72. Aidit's November 1965 letter from China to surviving PKI members in Indonesia refers to "the political agreement between [Sukarno] and the neighbor [China]." Fic, *Anatomy*, pp. 324–7.

73. CIA, *Indonesia—1965*, pp. 172–4.

74. Interview in April 1971 by Victor Fic with Indonesian Air Force officer involved in shipment. *Anatomy*, pp. 296–7.

75. CIA, *Indonesia—1965*, pp. 172–4.

76. This was a putative report from the British ambassador, Andrew Gilchrist, to London about US-British planning for an army coup to oust Sukarno and delivered to Sukarno by post. Ambassador Gilchrist denied any knowledge of the report, and it has long been recognized as a forgery. The CIA research report pointed to Subandrio, Aidit, and China as the "three prime suspects." CIA, *Indonesia: 1965*, pp. 192–7. Revelations by a Czech operative involved in this disinformation operation, and reviewed by Fic, establish convincingly that the forgery was Czech and Soviet in origin. See Fic, *Anatomy*, pp. 287–8, 349–50.

77. For a record of Indonesian violations of China's diplomatic immunities and China's protests of these, see *China's External Relations*, pp. 272–5.

78. Fic, *Anatomy*, p. 292.

79. A firsthand, authoritative, and detailed account of the incorporation of these territories, and Singapore, into the new state of Malaysia, along with fierce communist

opposition to that amalgamation, is Ghazali Shafie, *Ghazali Shafie's Memoir on the Formation of Malaysia*, Kuala Lampur: Ampang Press, 1998. Shafie was one of Malaysia's founding fathers.

80. Fujio Hara, "The North Kalimantan Communist Party and the People's Republic of China," *The Developing Economies*, vol. 43, no. 4 (December 2005), pp. 489–513.

81. Hara, "North Kalimantan", p. 503.

82. Tho Phianwitthaya [nom de guerre of Wirat Angkhathawon], "An Internal History of the Communist Party of Thailand," translated by Chris Baker, *Journal of Contemporary Asia*, vol. 33, no. 4 (2003), pp. 510–41. The author was a leading theorist of the CPT.

83. Phianwitthaya, *Internal History*, p. 527.

84. Ibid., p. 528.

85. William R. Heaton, "China and Southeast Asian Communist Movements: The Decline of Dual Track Diplomacy," *Asian Survey*, vol. 22, no. 8 (August 1982), pp. 779–800, p. 781.

86. Daniel Lovelace, *China and People's War in Thailand*, Berkeley: University of California Press, 1971, pp. 48–9.

87. Chin Peng, *My Side*, pp. 426, 428.

88. Lovelace, *China and People's War*, p. 66.

89. Heaton, "China and Southeast," p. 782.

90. Phianwitthaya, *Internal History*, p. 511.

91. Leif Rosenberger, "Philippine Communism and the Soviet Union," *Survey*, vol. 39, no. 1 (Spring 1985), pp. 113–45.

92. This account follows Gregg R. Jones, *Red Revolution: Inside the Philippine Guerrilla Movement*, Boulder, CO: Westview Press, 1989, p. 51, 62, 72–83. Jones' account is based on interviews with former leaders of the Communist Party of the Philippines.

93. Subir Bhaumik, "The External Linkages in Insurgency in India's Northeast," in *Insurgency in Northeast India*, edited by P. Pakem, New Delhi: Omsons, 1997, pp. 89–100. Bertil Lintner, "Appendix: Missions to China by Insurgents from India's North-East," in *India and Chinese Foreign Policy in Comparative Perspective*, New Delhi: Radiant Publishers, 1998, p. 433–8.

94. *Kessings Contemporary Archive*, 27, no. 43 (1981), p. 31153.

95. Mozingo, *Chinese Policy toward Indonesia*, p. 239. Jay Taylor, *China and Southeast Asia: Peking's Relations with Revolutionary Movements*, New York: Praeger, 1976, p. 99. Andrew H. Wedeman, *The East Wind Subsides: Chinese Foreign Policy and the Origins of the Cultural Revolution*, Washington, DC: Washington Institute Press, 1987, pp. 191–2.

Chapter 9. Countering the United States in Vietnam

1. See Qiang Zhai, *China and the Vietnam Wars, 1950–1975*, Chapel Hill: University of North Carolina Press, 2000. Chen Jian, *Mao's China and the Cold War*, Chapel Hill: University of North Carolina Press, 2001.

2. Leo Tansky, "Chinese Foreign Aid," *People's Republic of China: An Economic Assessment*, Joint Economic Committee, US Congress, 92nd Congress, 2nd Session, May 18, 1972, pp. 371–83.

3. Standard histories of the Vietnam War include George C. Herring, *America's Longest War: The United States and Vietnam, 1950–1975*, New York: Knopf, 1986. Anthony James Joes, *The War for South Viet Nam, 1954–1975*, Westport, CT: Praeger, 2001.

4. Regarding the US strategy of gradual escalation, see John E. Muller, "The Search for the 'Breaking Point' in Vietnam," *International Studies Quarterly*, vol. 24, no. 4 (December 1980), pp. 497–519.

5. This section follows Allen S. Whiting, *The Chinese Calculus of Deterrence: India and Indochina*, Ann Arbor: University of Michigan Press, 1975.

6. This is a key thesis of Whiting, *Chinese Calculus.*

7. Zhai, *China and the Vietnam Wars*, pp. 130–1.

8. Quoted in Whiting, *Chinese Calculus*, pp. 173–4.

9. Ibid.

10. Quoted in Whiting, *Chinese Calculus*, pp. 174–5.

11. Whiting, *Chinese Calculus*, p. 177. Zhai, *China and the Vietnam Wars*, p. 132.

12. Zhai, *China and the Vietnam Wars*, p. 133.

13. Zhai, *China and the Vietnam Wars*, p. 134.

14. Zhai, *China and the Vietnam Wars*, p. 135.

15. Whiting, *Chinese Calculus*, p. 180.

16. Zhai, *China and the Vietnam Wars*, p. 137.

17. Lee Kuan Yew, *From Third World to First*, New York: Harper Collins, 2000, p. 596.

18. Whiting, *Chinese Calculus*, p. 188.

19. Zhai, *China and the Vietnam Wars*, p. 143.

20. Whiting, *Chinese Calculus*, p. 179.

21. Yafeng Xia, *Negotiating with the Enemy: U.S.-China Talks during the Cold War, 1949–1972*, Bloomington: Indiana University Press, 2006, pp. 124–30. Kenneth T. Young, *Negotiating with the Chinese Communists: The United States Experience, 1953–1967*, New York: McGraw Hill, 1968, pp. 208–75.

22. Xia, *Negotiating*, p. 129.

23. Allen Whiting analyzed in detail China's deterrent rhetoric in its various gradations of intensity of warning. Whiting, *Calculus of Chinese Deterrence.*

24. Xia, *Negotiating*, p. 127.

25. Operations by semi-clandestine US army "long-distance reconnaissance patrols" into Laos were exceptions to this.

26. See Harry Summers, *On Strategy: A Critical Analysis of the Viet Nam War*, New York: Dell, 1982.

27. As discussed in chapter 3, recent scholarship on China's entry into the Korean War indicates that Mao was strongly inclined to intervene in the war long before the Incheon landing reversed the fortunes of war in Korea, allowing US/South Korean forces to push north.

28. See Zhai, *China and the Vietnam Wars*, p. 152. Chen, *Mao's China*, p. 230.

29. A central argument of Lien-hang T. Nguyen's work is that there was chronic debate within the VWP between a "south first" and a "north first" group, the former favoring focus on liberation of the south and the latter favoring socialist industrialization of the north. Lien-Hang T. Nguyen, *Hanoi's War: An International History of the War for Peace in Vietnam*, Chapel Hill: University of North Carolina Press, 2012.

30. Zhai, *China and the Vietnam Wars*, pp. 152–3.

31. Zhai, *China and the Vietnam Wars,* p. 153.

32. Zhai, *China and the Vietnam Wars*, p. 153.

33. Chen, *Mao's China*, pp. 230–1.

34. This discussion follows Nguyen, *Hanoi's War*.

35. The offensives that began with the Tet holiday in March 1968 continued throughout the year, with consistently devastating consequences for the attacking forces.

36. "Conversations," p. 105. Quoted in Nguyen, *Hanoi's War*, p. 95.

37. Nguyen, *Hanoi's War*, p. 117.

38. Nguyen, *Hanoi's War*, pp. 50, 81.

39. "Meeting between Chen Yi and Le Duc Tho," Beijing, October 17, 1968. Quoted in Nguyen, *Hanoi's War*, pp. 126–7.

40. Zhai, *China and the Vietnam Wars*, p. 179.

41. Nguyen, *Hanoi's War*, p. 128.

42. Zhai, *China and the Vietnam Wars*, pp. 173–4. Also Qiang Zhai, "Beijing and the Vietnam Peace Talks, 1965–68: New Evidence from Chinese Sources," Woodrow Wilson International Center for Scholars, Working Paper No. 18, June 1997. Available online at http://wilsoncenter.org/sites/default/files/ACFB46.pdf.

43. John Garver, "Sino-Vietnamese Conflict and the Sino-American Rapprochement," *Political Science Quarterly*, vol. 96, no. 3 (Fall 1981), p. 451.

44. Henry Kissinger, *White House Years*, Boston: Little Brown, 1979, pp. 716, 735, 757–8.

45. Quoted in Garver, "Sino-Vietnamese Conflict," p. 454.

46. Ibid., pp. 454–5.

47. Quoted in Garver, "Sino-Vietnamese Conflict," p. 448.

48. Tad Szulc, "How Kissinger Did It: Behind the Vietnam Cease-Fire Agreement," *Foreign Policy*, no. 15 (Summer 1974), p. 45.

49. Chou En-lai, "Report on the International Situation," *Issues and Studies* 13 (January 1977), p. 122.

50. *Chinese Aggression, Why and How It Failed*, Hanoi: Foreign Languages Publishing House, 1979, p. 33.

51. Kissinger, *White House Years*, pp. 735, 749.

52. Ibid, p. 1052.

53. Ibid, pp. 1073, 1087.

54. At least this is Nixon and Kissinger's argument. See Richard Nixon, *No More Vietnams*, New York: Avon, 1985. Richard Nixon, *The Memoirs of Richard Nixon*, Vol. 2, New York: Warner Books, 1978, pp. 433–6. Henry Kissinger, *Years of Upheaval*, Boston: Little, Brown, 1982, pp. 302–38.

Chapter 10. The Cultural Revolution

1. The standard PRC periodization used during the post-Mao era defines the entire 1966 through 1976 period as the Cultural Revolution. This makes sense, since throughout that decade Mao's radical policies dominated. China began to turn away from Mao's totalitarian project only in 1976, after Mao's death. Most non-PRC specialists, including this author, distinguish the 1966–1969 period with its Red Guard uprising from the post–Red Guard Maoist period, referring to this four-year period as the Cultural Revolution.

2. Peter Van Ness, *Revolution and Chinese Foreign Policy: Peking's Support for Wars of National Liberation*, Berkeley: University of California Press, 1970, p. 217.

3. Regarding the utopian strain in Mao's thinking, see Maurice Meisner, *Mao Zedong, a Political and Intellectual Portrait*, Cambridge: Polity, 2007, pp. 140–92.

4. Quoted in Alexander V. Pantsov and Steven I. Levine, *Mao: The Real Story*, New York: Simon and Schuster, 2012, p. 509.

5. This interpretation is drawn from Van Ness, *Revolution and Chinese Foreign Policy*.

6. Quoted in Van Ness, *Revolution and Chinese Foreign Policy*, p. 217.

7. Regarding the assault on the British mission, see Edward Rice, *Mao's Way*, Berkeley: University of California Press, 1974, pp. 379–80. John Dickie, *The British Consul: Heir to a Great Tradition*, New York: Columbia University Press, 2008.

8. Established in the early eighteenth century as a terminus for the important tea caravan trade between China and Russia, this large piece of land is among the largest diplomatic compounds in the world, established long before the maritime European countries were allowed to set up diplomatic missions in China's capital circa 1860.

9. Anthony Grey, *Hostage in Peking*, New York: Doubleday, 1971, p. 89.

10. Grey, *Hostage*, p. 51.

11. Barbara Barnouin and Yu Changgen, *Chinese Foreign Policy during the Cultural Revolution*, London: Kegan Paul International, 1998, pp. 72–3, 205–6.

12. *Peking Review*, no. 30 (1967). Quoted in Barnouin and Yu, *Chinese Foreign Policy*, p. 75.

13. The film is available at many sites on the internet.

14. Rice, *Mao's Way*, pp. 379–80.

15. Ibid.

16. This account is drawn from Barnouin and Yu, *Chinese Foreign Policy*, pp. 1–33. Also Melvin Gurtov, "The Foreign Ministry and Foreign Affairs during the Cultural Revolution," *China Quarterly*, no. 40 (October–December 1969), pp. 65–102.

17. Barnouin and Yu, *Chinese Foreign Policy*, p. 16.

18. Barnouin and Yu, *Chinese Foreign Policy*, p. 27.

19. Gurtov, "Foreign Ministry," p. 80.

20. Gurtov, "Foreign Ministry," p. 92.

21. Gurtov, writing in 1969, argues that Chen Yi survived politically after making a severe self-criticism in February 1968.

22. Ben Jones, *The French Revolution*, London: University of London Press, 1967, pp. 93–5.

23. This discussion follows Thomas M. Gottlieb, *Chinese Foreign Policy Factionalism and the Origins of the Strategic Triangle*, Santa Monica, CA: Rand Corporation, Nov. 1977, R-1902-NA.

24. "Personal file of Wang Ming," quoted in Pantsov and Levine, *Mao*, p. 539. A central argument of the Pantsov and Levine volume is that Mao was as "pro-Soviet" as any other CCP leader.

25. Gao Wenqian, *Zhou Enlai: The Last Perfect Revolutionary*, New York: Public Affairs, 2007, p. 6.

26. Pantsov and Levine suggest that a "Xian Incident"–style kidnapping of Mao by the Wuhan leaders was in Mao's mind at this juncture. The "Xian Incident" occurred in late 1936 when two Chinese warlords seized Chiang Kai-shek and demanded he shift policy and join with the CCP to confront Japan.

27. Gottlieb, *Foreign Policy Factionalism*, pp. 50–1.

28. Sources on the 1969 border clashes are: Neville Maxwell, "The Chinese Account of the 1969 Fighting at Chenpao," *China Quarterly*, no. 56 (October–December 1973), pp.

730–9. Thomas W. Robinson, "The Sino-Soviet Border Dispute: Background, Development and the March 1969 Clashes," *American Political Science Review*, vol. 66, no. 4 (December 1972), pp. 1175–202. Harold Hinton, *Bear at the Gate: Chinese Policymaking under Soviet Pressure*, Stanford: Hoover Institute Press, 1971, and "Conflict on the Ussuri: A Clash of Nationalisms," *Problems of Communism*, vol. 20, nos. 1 and 2 (January –April 1971), pp. 48–59.

29. Allen S. Whiting, *The Chinese Calculus of Deterrence*, Ann Arbor: University of Michigan Press, p. 232. Whiting's study deals primarily with India in 1962 and Indochina in 1965, but he suggests that the same logic applied to the Soviet border in 1969.

30. Pantsov and Levine, *Mao*, p. 538.

31. John Garver, *China's Decision for Rapprochement with the United States*, Boulder, CO: Westview, 1982, pp. 65–7.

32. "CCP Central Committed Order for General Mobilization in Border Provinces and Regions," *Cold War International History Project Bulletin*, no. 11 (Winter 1998), pp. 168–9.

33. Arkady Shevchenko, *Breaking with Moscow*, New York: Ballantine, 1985, pp. 165–8. Pantsov and Levine, *Mao*, p. 538.

34. Garver, *China's Decision*, pp. 68–9.

35. Interview with Allen S. Whiting, December 16, 1978. Whiting was a fellow at the Rand Corporation and an advisor to Henry Kissinger during the 1969 crisis. See Garver, *China's Decision for Rapprochement*, p. 82, note 55.

36. Golam W. Choudhury, *Brezhnev's Collective Security Plan for Asia*, Washington, DC: Center for Strategic and International Studies, 1976, p. 12. Choudhury was an advisor to the Pakistani government at that time.

37. Quoted in Garver, *Rapprochement*, p. 75.

38. John Wong, "Chinese Demand for Southeast Asian Rubber, 1949–1972", *China Quarterly*, no. 63 (September 1975), pp. 490–514.

39. Letter, Zhou Enlai to Alexei Kosygin, September 18, 1969, *IHCWP Bulletin*, no. 11 (Winter 1998) , pp. 171–2.

40. "Zhou Enlai's Talk at a Meeting of the Chinese Delegation Attending the Sino-Soviet Border Negotiations," October 7, 1969, ibid., pp. 172–3.

41. This section follows Roderick MacFarquhar and Michael Schoenhals, *Mao's Last Revolution*, Cambridge: Belknap, 2006, pp. 316–20.

Chapter 11. Rapprochement with the United States

1. George Lefebvre, *The Thermidorians*, New York: Vintage, 1964. R. R. Palmer, *Twelve Who Ruled: The Year of the Terror in the French Revolution*, New York: Atheneum, 1965.

2. It was formerly widely believed by Sinologists that Lin Biao was opposed to Mao's decision to improve relations with the United States. Mao and Zhou later told foreign leaders (Nixon, Albania's Hoxha, etc.) that Lin had opposed the opening to the United States. Recent scholarship based on fuller investigation of Chinese materials indicates that this long-held view must be discarded. There is no evidence that Lin was involved in or expressed any opposition to Mao's clear guidance of Chinese foreign policy at this juncture or any other time. Apparently Mao and Zhou found it expedient to mislead foreigners about what Lin's rebellion entailed. See Alexander V. Pantsov and Steven I. Levine, *Mao: The Real Story*, New York: Simon and Schuster, 2012, pp. 540–54. Yafeng

Xia, "China's Elite Politics and Sino-American Rapprochement, January 1969–February 1972," *Journal of Cold War Studies*, vol. 8, no. 4 (Fall 2006), pp. 3–28.

3. I elaborate this notion in *Foreign Relations of the People's Republic of China*, New York: Prentice Hall, 1993, pp. 155–7.

4. Richard M. Nixon, "Asia after Vietnam," *Foreign Affairs*, October 1967. Available online at https://www.foreignaffairs.com/articles/asia/1967-10-01/asia-after-viet-nam.

5. Chen Jian, *Mao's China and the Cold War*, Chapel Hill: University of North Carolina Press, 2001, p. 245. This section draws heavily on Chen's work. Also Jonathan D. Pollack, "The Opening to America," in *The Cambridge History of China*, Vol. 15, *The People's Republic of China*, Part 2, *Revolution within the Chinese Revolution, 1966–1982*, edited by Roderick MacFarquar and John King Fairbank, Cambridge: Cambridge University Press, 1991, pp. 402–72.

6. Neither Nixon nor Kissinger in their memoirs mentions *Renmin ribao*'s publication of the inauguration speech. See Richard Nixon, *The Memoirs of Richard Nixon*, Vol. 2, New York: Warner, 1978, pp. 7–12. Henry Kissinger, *White House Years*, Boston: Little, Brown, 1979, pp. 684–91.

7. Chen, *Mao's China*, pp. 245–6.

8. John K. Knaus, *Orphans of the Cold War: America and the Tibetan Struggle for Survival*, New York: Public Affairs, 1999, p. 297.

9. Bruce A. Elleman, "High Seas Buffer: The Taiwan Task Force, 1950–1979," *Naval War College Newport Paper*, No. 38 (2012), Center for Naval Warfare Studies, p. 133.

10. Li Zhisui, *The Private Life of Chairman Mao: The Memoirs of Mao's Personal Physician*, New York: Random House, 1994, p. 514.

11. Henry A. Kissinger, *On China*, New York: Penguin Press, 2011, p. 218. This account of Sino-US rapprochement follows Kissinger's.

12. *China and U.S. Foreign Policy*, Washington: Congressional Quarterly, 1972, p. 18.

13. Yafeng Xia, "China's Elite Politics," p. 11.

14. Yafeng Xia, "China's Elite Politics," p. 11.

15. Ambassador Han Xu later recounted how his encounter with Snow's *Red Star Over China* altered his thinking about China and communism in Beijing in 1937. Ruan Hong, *The Diplomat From China*, Beijing: Foreign Languages Press, 2007, p. 23.

16. Pantsov and Levine, *Mao*, p. 557.

17. Kissinger, *On China*, pp. 230–1.

18. Zhuang Zedong's account is at http://www.uschina.usc.edu/w_usct/showarticle.aspx?articleID=10957.

19. Kissinger, *On China*, pp. 252–3.

20. Regarding the Nixon visit, see Margaret MacMillan, *Nixon and Mao: The Week that Changed the World*, New York: Random House, 2007.

21. Quoted in Kissinger, *On China*, p. 259.

22. Yafeng Xia, "China's Elite Politics," pp. 211–2.

23. Alan D. Romberg, *Rein In at the Brink of the Precipice: American Policy toward Taiwan and U.S.-PRC relations*, Washington, DC: Henry L. Stimson Center, 2003. This section on Taiwan draws heavily on Romberg's book.

24. Quoted in Romberg, *Rein In*, p. 30.

25. Huang Hua, *Huang Hua Memoirs*, Beijing: Foreign Languages Press, 2008, p. 231.

26. Yafei Xia, "China's Elite Politics," p. 25.

27. Huang Hua, *Memoirs*, p. 225.

28. Romberg, *Rein In*, p. 42.

29. Romberg, *Rein In*, p. 45.

30. Quoted in Romberg, *Rein In*, p. 46.

31. Regarding China's diplomatic offensive at this juncture, see Joseph Camilleri, *Chinese Foreign Policy: The Maoist Era and Its Aftermath*, Seattle: University of Washington Press, 1980. Samuel S. Kim, *China, the United Nations, and the World Order*, Princeton: Princeton University Press, 1979.

32. Hoxha left an extensive diary on Albania's ties with China. Enver Hoxha, *Reflections on China*, Vol. 1, *1962–72, Extracts from the Political Diary*, Tirana: 8 Nentori, 1979. (Vol. 2 covers the period 1973 to 1977.)

33. Ibid., p. 437.

34. Ibid., pp. 482–3.

35. Ibid., pp. 555–62.

36. Ibid., pp. 596, 601, 603, 678–80, 746–50.

37. Ibid., pp. 658–8.

38. Ibid., pp. 746–50.

39. Ibid., p. 748.

40. William J. Barnds, *India, Pakistan, and the Great Powers*, New York: Praeger, 1972, p. 479. The absence of Red Guards in the Islamabad embassy was conveyed to me by retired Chinese senior diplomat Zhang Wenjin in an interview in May 1990.

41. G. W. Choudhury, *India, Pakistan, Bangladesh, and the Major Powers: Politics of a Divided Subcontinent*, New York: Free Press, 1975, pp. 192–3. Syed, *China and Pakistan*, pp. 125–6. S. M. Burke, *Pakistan's Foreign Policy: A Historical Analysis*, London: University Press, 1973, pp. 361–4.

42. R. Rama Rao, "Pakistan Re-Arms," *India Quarterly*, vol. 27, no. 2 (April–June 1971), pp. 140–8.

43. At the time of writing, China is constructing a railway along the general alignment of the Karakoram Highway. Regarding the highway, see Mahnaz Z. Ispahani, *Roads and Rivals: The Political Uses of Access in the Borderlands of Asia*, Ithaca, NY: Cornell University Press, 1989.

44. Henry A. Kissinger, *White House Years*, Boston: Little Brown, 1979, pp. 906–15.

45. Choudhury, *India, Pakistan*, p. 211.

46. Sultan M. Khan, *Memories and Reflections of a Pakistani Diplomat*, London: Center for Pakistan Studies, 1997, 304–7.

47. Richard Sisson and Leo E. Rose, *War and Secession: Pakistan, India and the Creation of Bangladesh*, Berkeley: University of California Press, 1990, pp. 249–50.

48. Mehrunnisa Ali, "China's Diplomacy during the Indo-Pakistan War, 1971," *Pakistan Horizon* (Karachi), vol. 25, no. 1 (1972): 53–62.

49. Sisson and Rose, *War and Secession*, pp. 250–1.

50. Sisson and Rose, *War and Secession*, pp. 250–1. Choudhury, *India, Pakistan*, p. 213.

51. "Pakistan Delegation in China," *Peking Review*, November 12, 1971, p. 23.

52. Kissinger, *White House Years*, p. 910.

53. This intelligence report that India's Indira Gandhi planned to strike west after settling events in the east was apparently wrong. Nixon's decision to deploy an aircraft carrier battle group to threaten India as a result of this incorrect intelligence was subsequently

a source of great criticism of Nixon's management of foreign affairs. The US naval demonstration against India at this juncture was also one of several instances in which the United States aligned with China against India—episodes that remain deep in the Indian political consciousness.

54. "Top Secret Memorandum of Conversation," in William Burr, *The Kissinger Transcripts: The Top Secret Talks with Beijing and Moscow*, New York: New Press, 1998, pp. 48–57.

55. Unfortunately, Huang Hua in his memoir says nothing about his talks with Kissinger. Huang Hua, *Memoirs*, pp. 262–4.

56. The Chinese protest is in *Survey of China Mainland Press*, no. 5041–5044, December 29–30, 1971, pp. 79–80.

57. Kissinger, *White House Years*, p. 912.

58. Kissinger, *White House Years*, p. 906.

59. Regarding this special Tibetan force, see Kenneth Conboy and James Morrison, *The CIA's Secret War in Tibet*, Lawrence: University of Kansas Press, 2002, pp. 219, 225.

Chapter 12. Countering Soviet Encirclement and Trying to Preserve Mao's Legacy

1. This section follows Gao Wenqian, *Zhou Enlai: The Last Perfect Revolutionary*, New York: Public Affairs, 2007, p. 17. Gao was the official biographer of Zhou Enlai at the Research Office of the CCP Central Documentation for over a decade. His account is based on extensive and largely previously unavailable documents from that office which he smuggled out of China.

2. Gao Wenqian, *Zhou Enlai*, p. 238.

3. Gao Wenqian, *Zhou Enlai*, pp. 238–9.

4. Gao Wenqian, *Zhou Enlai*, p. 242.

5. Andrew Mertha, *Brothers in Arms: Chinese Aid to the Khmer Rouge, 1975–1979*, Ithaca, NY: Cornell University Press, 2014, p. 2.

6. Mertha, *Brothers in Arms*, p. 5.

7. This section follows Henry Kissinger, *Years of Upheaval*, Boston: Little Brown, 1982, pp. 340–67.

8. Zhou's prognosis regarding Khmer Rouge rule in Cambodia was similar to his estimate of the eventual outcome of Pakistani's brutal repression in Eastern Pakistan in 1971—Indian intervention and Bangladeshi independence.

9. Kissinger, *Years of Upheaval*, p. 367.

10. Mertha, *Brothers in Arms*, pp. 5–6.

11. Gao Wenqian, *Zhou Enlai*, p. 243.

12. Gao Wenqian, *Zhou Enlai*, p. 258.

13. Gao Wenqian stresses the point that Deng was Mao's man, not Zhou's as is often commonly assumed. Mao feared Zhou would undo Cultural Revolution policies if he outlived him. Deng was one person Mao thought could run China's economy, and intended to replace Zhou with Deng—if Deng could convince him of his loyalty to the Cultural Revolution "achievements." Mao, according to Gao, envisioned a duumvirate succession arrangement: Zhang Chunqiao would run propaganda, culture, and continue political struggle, while Deng would replace Zhou in running the economy and state administration.

14. Henry Kissinger, *On China*, New York: Penguin Press, 2011, pp. 314–20.

15. *Zhou Enlai junshi wenxuan* (Zhou Enlai's military documents), Beijing: Renmin chubanshe, 1997, pp. 566–7.

16. *Zhou Enlai nianpu, 1949–1976* (Chronicle of Zhou Enlai, 1949–1976), Beijing: Zhongyang wenxian chubanshe, 1997, pp. 644–5. Other members of the group were Maoist radicals Wang Hongwen and Zhang Chunqiao, plus General Chen Xilian.

17. China's claim is laid out in *China's Indisputable Sovereignty over the Xixia and Nansha Islands*, Beijing: Ministry of Foreign Affairs, January 30, 1980. For an overview of the issue, see Michael Leifer, "Chinese Economic Reform and Security Policy: The South China Sea Connection," *Survival*, vol. 37, no. 2 (Summer 1995), pp. 44–58.

18. Nayan Chanda, *Brother Enemy: The War after the War*, New York: Collier, 1986, pp. 20–1.

19. John W. Garver, "China's Push Through the South China Sea: The Interaction of Bureaucratic and National Interests," *China Quarterly*, no. 132 (December 1992), p. 999–1028.

20. Henry Kissinger, *The White House Years*, Boston: Little Brown, 1979, p. 1114.

21. Chanda, *Brother Enemy*, p. 19.

22. Michael A. Palmer, *Guardians of the Gulf: A History of America's Expanding Role in the Persian Gulf, 1833–1992*, New York: Free Press, 1992, p. 281.

23. "Huang Hua's Report on the World Situation," Part III, *Issues and Studies*, vol. 14, no. 1 (January 1978), pp. 110–1.

24. On the united front against Soviet expansionism, see Henry Kissinger, *On China*, New York: Penguin Press, 2011, pp. 275–93. William R. Heaton, Jr., *A United Front Against Hegemonism: Chinese Foreign Policy in the 1980s*, National Defense University, National Security Affairs Monograph. Series 80–3, March 1980. Jonathan Pollack, *The Lessons of Coalition Politics: Sino-American Security Relations*, Santa Monica, CA: Rand Corporation, 1984.

25. Deng's Three World speech is available at www.marxists.org/reference/archive/deng-xiaoping/1974/04/10.htm.

26. Robert Sutter, *China Watch, Toward Sino-American Rapprochement*, Baltimore: Johns Hopkins University Press, 1978, p. 115.

27. J. D. Armstrong, *Revolutionary Diplomacy: Chinese Foreign Policy and the United Front Doctrine*, Berkeley: University of California Press, 1977.

28. Kissinger, *On China*, p. 276.

29. Sutter, *China Watch*, pp. 114–5.

30. "U.S. Secretary of State Kissinger in Peking," *Peking Review*, October 24, 1975, pp. 8–10.

31. "Vice-Premier Teng Hsiao-ping's Toast," *Peking Review*, December 5, 1975, pp. 8–9.

32. Kissinger, *On China*, pp. 286, 290–1.

33. This account of PRC-Japan rapprochement follows Cha-Jin Lee, *Japan Faces Chin:, Political and Economic Relations in the Postwar Era*, Baltimore: Johns Hopkins University Press, 1976, p. 123. See also Akira Iriye, "Chinese-Japanese Relations, 1945–90," *China Quarterly*, no. 124 (December 1990), pp. 624–38.

34. In a speech given at Guam Island in the Pacific in July 1969, six months after becoming president, Nixon proclaimed that the era of US military intervention in Asia was over, and that in the future the United States would rely on friendly Asian powers to play key roles in Asian security affairs. Perhaps the main pro-US Asian power to volunteer for

duty under this doctrine was Iran, but Japan was an obvious candidate. The doctrine was also called the "Nixon Doctrine."

35. Michael H. Armacost and Kenneth B. Pyle, "Japan and the Engagement of China: Challenges for U.S. Policy Coordination," *NBR Analysis*, vol. 12, no. 5 (December 2001), p. 17.

36. Lee, *Japan Faces China*, p. 129.

37. Lee, *Japan Faces China*, p. 129.

38. Lee, *Japan Faces China*, p. 124.

39. Lee, *Japan Faces China*, p. 124.

40. Kissinger, *On China*, p. 283.

41. PRC officials have consistently denied providing assistance to Pakistan's nuclear weapons efforts. Evidence strongly suggests, however, that there was such assistance starting in 1974 and continuing into the 1980s. For a fuller exposition of the evidence, see John Garver, *Protracted Contest: Sino-Indian Rivalry in the Twentieth Century*, Seattle: University of Washington Press, 2001, pp. 324–36.

42. The report was obtained under a Freedom of Information Act request and conveyed by Kyodo news agency. *Asian Recorder*, September 17–23, 1975, p. 25081.

43. B. K. Kumar, "Nuclear Nexus between Peking and Islamabad: An Overview of Some Significant Developments," *Issues and Studies* 21 (August 1985), pp. 140–50.

44. Zulfikar Ali Bhutto, *If I Am Assassinated*, New Delhi: Vikas, 1979. The reference to the June 1976 agreement is on page 221. Bhutto develops his anti-nuclear coup conspiracy hypothesis on pp. 107, 137–8, 168–9.

45. Herbert Krosney, *The Islamic Bomb: The Nuclear Threat to Israel and the Middle East*, New York: Time Books, 1981, p. 218. Also Judith Miller, "U.S. Is Holding Up Peking Atom Talks," *New York Times*, September 19, 1982, p. 11.

46. Reuters, March 31, 1996. There is an interesting contrast between China's assistance to Pakistan's nuclear weapons effort in the 1970s and its rejection of a 1965 Indonesian request for similar assistance. See Robert M. Cornejo, "When Sukarno Sought the Bomb: Indonesia's Nuclear Aspirations in the Mid-1960s," *Nonproliferation Review* 7 (Summer 2000), pp. 31–43. Jay Taylor, *China and Southeast Asia: Peking's Relations with Revolutionary Movements*, New York: Praeger, 1976, pp. 104–8.

47. John Garver, *China and Iran: Ancient Partners in a Post-Imperial World*, Seattle: University of Washington Press, 2006, pp. 154–5, 223–6.

48. This section follows Garver, *China and Iran*, pp. 29–56.

49. US construction of facilities on the island began in 1971.

50. A recent and authoritative biography of the shah which draws intriguing parallels between his modernization effort and China's post-1978 drive is Abbas Milani, *The Shah*, London: Palgrave Macmillan, 2011. For an exegesis of those similarities based on Milani's biography, see John Garver, "China and the Iran Model," *China Currents*, forthcoming.

51. "Chinese Foreign Minister Honored at Tehran Dinner," Xinhua, June 14, 1973, quoted in Garver, *China and Iran*, p. 51, p. 332 n. 47.

52. This interpretation may, of course, be challenged on the grounds that Ji's declaration simply intended neutrality and noninvolvement in power rivalry in the Gulf. I think the evidence suggests rather that Beijing sees Iran as a rising regional and friendly power with which China should, gradually and over an extended period of time, build a strategic partnership.

53. See, Garver, *China and Iran*, pp. 103–4.

54. Mohammad Reza Pahlavi, *The Shah's Story*, London: Michael Joseph, 1980, p. 147

55. Kissinger, *Years of Upheaval*, pp. 690–1.

56. This section follows Philip Brick, "The Politics of Bonn-Beijing Normalization, 1972–84," *Asian Survey*, vol. 25, no. 7 (July 1985), pp. 773–91.

57. Huang Hua to UN General Assembly, November 11, 1975. "Soviet 'Disarmament' Proposals: Camouflage for War Preparations," *Peking Review*, November 21, 1975, pp. 10–1.

58. "European Press on 'European Security Conference,'" *Peking Review*, August 15, 1975, pp. 22–3.

59. This is a quote from the British Broadcasting Corporation publication *The Listener* 94 (1975), p. 131.

60. Again this discussion follows Philip Brick.

61. "Chancellor Schmidt Visits China," *Peking Review*, November 7, 1975, pp. 4–5.

62. "Vice Premier Teng Hsiao-ping's Speech," *Peking Review*, November 7, 1975, pp. 7–8.

Chapter 13. Opening to the Outside World

1. Deng Xiaoping, "The Whole Party Should Take the Overall Interest into Account and Push the Economy Forward," March 5, 1975, *Selected Works of Deng Xiaoping*, Vol. 2 (1975–1983), Beijing: Foreign Languages Press, 1995, pp. 16–9.

2. Deng Xiaoping, "Carry Out the Policy of Opening to the Outside World and Learn Advanced Science and Technologies from Other Countries," October 10, 1978, *Selected Works*, Vol. 2, pp. 143–4.

3. Ezra Vogel, *Deng Xiaoping and the Transformation of China*, Cambridge, MA: Belknap Press, 2011, pp. 120–31.

4. For a discussion of how American hopes and beliefs have dominated US perceptions of China, see Richard Madsen, *China and the American Dream: A Moral Inquiry*, Berkeley: University of California Press, 1998. Madsen's central thesis is that Americans have tended to see in China what they wanted to see.

5. This section follows Yan Sun, *The Chinese Reassessment of Socialism, 1976–1992*, Princeton: Princeton University Press, 1995, pp. 22–34. Hu Qiaomu was the theoretician who first worked out this perspective.

6. Quoted in Yan Sun, *Chinese Reassessment*, p. 31.

7. Vogel, *Deng Xiaoping*, p. 224.

8. Regarding the politics of the post-Mao transition, see Richard Baum, *Burying Mao: Chinese Politics in the Age of Deng Xiaoping*, Princeton: Princeton University Press, 1994. Also Yan Sun, *Chinese Reassessment*.

9. Regarding this process, see Barry Naughton, *Growing Out of the Plan, Chinese Economic Reform, 1978–1993*, Cambridge: Cambridge University Press, 1996.

10. This section follows Zheng Wang, *Never Forget National Humiliation: Historical Memory in Chinese Politics and Foreign Relations*, New York: Columbia University Press, 2012, pp. 89–94.

11. Regarding Deng's 1974 New York visit, see Vogel, *Deng Xiaoping*, pp. 83–7.

12. Vogel, *Deng Xiaoping*, pp. 118–9.

13. Deng Xiaoping, "Emancipate the Mind, Seek Truth from Facts and Unite as One in Looking to the Future," December 13, 1978, *Selected Works of Deng Xiaoping*, Vol. 2 (1975–1982), Beijing: Foreign Languages Press, 1995, pp. 150–63.

14. This discussion of the 1978 foreign investigation missions follows Vogel, *Deng Xiaoping*, pp. 218–46.

15. Susan Shirk, *The Political Economy of Economic Reform in China*, Berkeley: University of California Press, 1993.

16. Regarding the revolutionary consequences of rural private enterprise, see Yasheng Huang, *Capitalism with Chinese Characteristics, Entrepreneurship and the State*, Cambridge: Cambridge University Press, 2008.

17. Quoted in Vogel, *Deng Xiaoping*, p. 210.

18. Huang Hua, *Huang Hua Memoirs*, Beijing: Foreign Languages Press, 2008, pp. 315–6.

19. Huang Hua, *Memoirs*, p. 317.

20. Huang Hua, *Memoirs*, p. 320.

21. Deng's delegation diplomacy is discussed by Huang Hua, *Memoirs*, pp. 420–1, and Vogel, *Deng Xiaoping*, pp. 294–310.

22. Huang Hua, *Memoirs*, p. 321.

23. Huang Hua, *Memoirs*, p. 322.

24. Huang Hua, *Memoirs*, p. 326.

25. Huang Hua and Ezra Vogel both deal with Deng's Japan visit. Huang Hua, *Memoirs*, pp. 331–7. Vogel, *Deng Xiaoping*, pp. 298–304.

26. Vogel, *Deng Xiaoping*, p. 301.

27. Vogel, *Deng Xiaoping*, p. 304.

28. Vogel, *Deng Xiaoping*, p. 304.

29. Vogel, *Deng Xiaoping*, p. 300.

30. *Zhongguo tongji nianjian 1989* (China statistical almanac 1989), Beijing: Zhongguo tongji chubanshe, 1989, p. 636.

31. "Overview of Official Development Assistance (ODA) to China," June 2005. Ministry of Foreign Affairs, Japan. Wang Jingru, "Japan's ODA to China: An Analysis of Chinese Attitudes towards Japan," master's thesis, National University of Singapore, 2010. Available at http://www.scholarbank.nus.edu.sg/handle/10635/14543.

32. Akira Iriye, "Chinese-Japanese Relations, 1945–90," *China Quarterly*, no. 124 (December 1990), p. 629.

33. See Alexander Eckstein, *Communist China's Economic Growth and Foreign Trade*, New York: McGraw Hill, 1966.

34. This section follows Susan L. Shirk, *How China Opened its Door: The Political Success of the PRC's Foreign Trade and Investment Reforms*, Washington, DC: Brookings Institution, 1994. Weijian Shan, "Reforms of China's Foreign Trade System, " *China Economic Review*, vol. 1, no. 1 (1989), pp. 33–55.

35. Shirk, *How China Opened*, p. 45.

36. Huang Yasheng, *Capitalism with Chinese Characteristics: Entrepreneurship and the State*, Cambridge: Cambridge University Press, 2008. Naughton, *Growing Out of the Plan*.

37. David Zweig, *Freeing China's Farmers: Rural Restructuring in the Reform Era*, Armonk, NY: M. E. Sharpe, 1997, pp. 274–95.

38. Except for the joint USSR-PRC companies set up in 1950 in Xinjiang and China's Northeast.

39. Regarding the comingling of European and East Asian trade systems, see Jack E. Wills, "Maritime Asia, 1500–1800: The Emergence of European Domination," *American Historical Review*, vol. 98, no. 1 (1993), pp. 83–105. Also John E. Wills, *Pepper, Guns, and Parleys: The Dutch East Asian Company and China, 1622–1681*, Cambridge: Harvard University Press, 1974. Tonio Andrade, *The Lost Colony: The Untold Story of China's First Great Victory over the West*, Princeton: Princeton University Press, 2011.

40. An exploration of the impact of these north-south differences in Chinese national identities is Edward Friedman, *National Identity and Democratic Prospects in Socialist China*, Routledge, 1995.

41. Ezra Vogel, *One Step Ahead in China: Guangdong under Reform*, Cambridge: Harvard University Press, 1990.

42. Xi Zhongxun, a native of Shaanxi province, was the father of Xi Jinping, who would become China's paramount leader in 2102. Regarding the creation of the SEZ, see Vogel, *Deng Xiaoping*, p. 394–399.

43. A. Doak Barnett, *The Making of Foreign Policy in China, Structure and Process*, SAIS Papers in International Affairs, Number 9, Boulder, CO: Westview, 1985, pp. 20–5.

44. Vogel, *Deng Xiaoping*, pp. 415–7.

45. General information on China's SEZs is available at http://www.en/wikipedia.org/ wiki/ Special_Economic_Zones_of_China.

46. Vogel, *Deng Xiaoping*, pp. 418–21.

47. Chu-yuan Cheng, *Economic Relations Between Peking and Moscow, 1949–63*, New York: Praeger, 1964, p. 39.

48. David M. Lampton, *A Relationship Restored: Trends in U.S.-China Educational Exchanges, 1978–1984*, Washington, DC: National Academy Press, 1986, pp. 30–35.

49. Institute of International Education. Open Door Data Base, http://www.iie.org/ Research-and-Publications/Open-Doors/Data/International-Students/All-Places-o f-Origin/2012-14.

50. http://www.iie.org/Research-and-Publications/Open-Doors/Data/ International-Students/Leading-Places-of-Origin.

51. Niu Jun, *Juece yu jiaoliang* (Choices and contests), Beijing: Jiuzhou chubanshe, 2012, p. 84.

52. Deng Xiaoping, "Peace and Development Are the Two Outstanding Issues of the World Today," March 4, 1985, *Selected Works of Deng Xiaoping*, Vol. 3 (1982–1992), Beijing: Foreign Languages Press, 1994, pp. 110–2.

53. This section follows William R. Heaton, "China and Southeast Asian Communist Movements: The Decline of Dual Track Diplomacy," *Asian Survey*, vol. 22, no. 8 (August 1982), pp. 779–800.

54. Heaton, "Decline of Dual Track Diplomacy."

55. Chin Peng, *My Side of History*, Singapore: Media Matters, 2003, pp. 457–8.

56. Chin Peng, *My Side*, p. 460.

57. Bertil Lintner, *The Rise and Fall of the Communist Party of Burma*, Ithaca, NY: Cornell University Press, 1990.

58. Regarding the development of the Irrawaddy Corridor, see John Garver, *Protracted Contest: Sino-Indian Rivalry in the Twentieth Century*, Seattle: University of Washington Press, 2001.

59. *China's Foreign Relations: A Chronology of Events*, Beijing: Foreign Languages Press, 1989, pp. 391–2.

60. Enver Hoxha, *Reflections on China,* Vol. 2, *1973–1977,* Tirana, Albania: 8 Nentori, 1979, p. 715.

61. See Bob Avakian, *From Ike to Mao and Beyond,* Chicago: Insight Press, 2005, pp. 351–72.

Chapter 14. China's Pedagogic War with Vietnam

1. On the 1979 war, see Harlan W. Jenks, "China's 'Punitive' War against Vietnam: A Military Assessment," *Asian Survey,* vol. 15, no. 8 (August 1979), pp. 801–5. Gerald Segal, *Defending China,* New York: Oxford University Press, 1985. Xiaoming Zhang, "China's 1979 War with Vietnam: A Reassessment," *China Quarterly,* December 2005, no. 184, pp. 851–74.

2. Zhang, "China's 1979 War," p. 861.

3. Zhang, "China's 1979 War," p. 866.

4. Quoted in Zhang, "China's 1979 War," p. 868.

5. For a similar lament by a Burmese general of the eighteenth century, see John Garver, *Protracted Contest: Sino-Indian Rivalry in the Twentieth Century,* Seattle: University of Washington Press, 2001, p. 246.

6. Zhang, "China's 1979 War," p. 867.

7. Lee Kuan Yew, *From Third World to First,* New York: Harper Collins, 2000, p. 596.

8. Nayan Chanda, *Brother Enemy: The War after the War,* New York: Harcourt Brace Jovanovich, 1986, p. 261.

9. Zhang, "China's 1979 War."

10. Ezra Vogel, *Deng Xiaoping and the Transformation of China,* Cambridge: Belknap Press, 2011, pp. 258–9. Deng also visited Malaysia, but was less frank there in explaining Chinese policies.

11. It is interesting that Deng presided over the Paracel operation in 1974 shortly after his first rehabilitation and over the 1979 Vietnam War shortly after his second rehabilitation.

12. Quoted in Chanda, *Brother Enemy,* pp. 321–2.

13. Kiernan, *How Pol Pot,* pp. 320–55.

14. R. J. Rummel, *Statistics of Democide: Genocide and Mass Murder since 1900,* Charlottesville, VA: Center for National Security Law, 1997, ch. 4, "Statistics of Cambodian Democide, Estimates, Calculations, and Sources." Available online at https://www.hawaii.edu/powerkills/SOD.CHAP4.HTM.

15. Chanda, *Brother Enemy,* p. 109.

16. This discussion follows Chanda, *Brother Enemy.*

17. Chanda, *Brother Enemy,* pp. 96–9.

18. Chanda, *Brother Enemy,* pp. 35–6, 94–5.

19. Chanda, *Brother Enemy,* pp. 196–7, 215, 218–9.

20. Chanda, *Brother Enemy,* p. 216.

21. Chanda, *Brother Enemy,* p. 255.

22. Chanda, *Brother Enemy,* pp. 16–7.

23. Chanda, *Brother Enemy,* pp. 17–8.

24. Chanda, *Brother Enemy,* p. 93.

25. Chanda, *Brother Enemy,* p. 201, also p. 434 n. 17.

26. Deng laid out this view during a November 1978 visit to Singapore and discussion with that country's president, Lee Kuan Yew: Lee Kuan Yew, *From Third World to First*, New York: Harpers Collins, 2000, pp. 595–6.

27. See Robert S. Ross, *The Indochina Tangle: China and Vietnamese Policies, 1975–1979*, New York: Columbia University Press, 1988. Also, Chanda, *Brother Enemy*.

28. Chanda, *Brother Enemy*, pp. 256–7.

29. *Beijing Review*, June 16, 1978, pp. 12–6. Quoted and analyzed in Chanda, *Brother Enemy*, p. 27 and p. 417 n. 27. The interval between the peace agreement of January 1973 and PAVN's initial probing operation in October 1974 was twenty months.

30. Chanda, *Brother Enemy*, pp. 26–7.

31. Vogel, *Deng Xiaoping*, pp. 273–4.

32. Lee Kuan Yew, *From Third World to First*, p. 596.

33. Ross, *Indochina Tangle*, pp. 128–9.

34. Chanda, *Brother Enemy*, pp. 188–90.

35. Chanda, *Brother Enemy*, pp. 239, 234.

36. Chanda, *Brother Enemy*, pp. 237, 239.

37. Chanda, *Brother Enemy*, p. 239.

38. Chanda, *Brother Enemy*, p. 232.

39. Chanda, *Brother Enemy*, p. 247.

40. Chanda, *Brother Enemy*, pp. 240–1.

41. Nayan Chanda points out that Hanoi's harsh anti-Chinese policies were not unpopular with many ordinary Vietnamese. The student volunteers who ransacked Cholon homes and shops were quite enthusiastic about their work.

42. Chanda, *Brother Enemy*, pp. 20–1.

Chapter 15. The Strategic Triangle and the Four Modernizations

1. Regarding China's role in the war against Japan, see Barbara Tuchman, *Stilwell and the American Experience in China, 1911–1945*, New York: Macmillan, 1970. Michael Schaller, *The U.S. Crusade in China, 1938–1945*, New York: Columbia University Press, 1979.

2. Henry Kissinger, *On China*, New York: Penguin, 2011, pp. 348–9.

3. Studies of the US-PRC normalization negotiations include Harry Harding, *Fragile Relationship: The United States and China since 1972*, Washington, DC: Brookings, 1992. Jim Mann, *About Face: A History of America's Curious Relationship with China, From Nixon to Clinton*, New York: Knopf, 1999.

4. Huang Hua, *Memoirs*, Beijing: Foreign Languages Press, 2008, pp. 345–6.

5. There were deep divisions within the administration over alignment with China against the Soviet Union. Secretary of State Cyrus Vance was opposed to this, fearing it would injure American-Soviet relations. National Security Advisor Brzezinski and Secretary of Defense Harold Brown were the main advocates of a tilt toward Beijing. Carter generally and increasingly adopted the Brzezinski and Brown approach. See Zbigniew Brzezinski, *Power and Principle: Memoirs of the National Security Advisor, 1977–1981*, New York: Farrar Straus Giroux, 1983, pp. 196–233, 403–25.

6. Huang Hua, *Memoirs*, p. 347.

7. Shirley A. Kan, *China/Taiwan: Evolution of the "One China" Policy; Key Statements from Washington, Beijing, and Taipei*, Congressional Research Service Report for Congress, RL30341, updated March 12, 2001.

8. The text of all three Sino-US joint communiqués plus unilateral statements ancillary to those communiqués are available in Harding, *Fragile Relation*, pp. 373–90.

9. "Our Principled Position on the Development of Sino-U.S. Relations," January 4, 1981, *Selected Works of Deng Xiaoping*, Vol. 2 (1975–1982), Beijing: Foreign Languages Press, 1995, pp. 369–72.

10. Ezra F. Vogel, *Deng Xiaoping and the Transformation of China*, Cambridge: Belknap, 2011, p. 372.

11. Harding, *Fragile Relation*, pp. 380–1.

12. Harding, *Fragile Relation*, p. 381.

13. Richard H. Solomon, *U.S.-PRC Political Negotiations, 1967–1984, An Annotated Chronology (U), December 1985*, Rand, R-3298. Secret. Declassified June 18, 1994. *Chinese Political Negotiating Behavior, 1967–1984, an Interpretative Assessment (U)*, Rand, December 1985. Secret. Declassified May 18, 1994.

14. Huang Hua, *Memoirs*, p. 326.

15. Vogel, *Deng Xiaoping*, p. 330.

16. Vogel, *Deng Xiaoping*, pp. 331–2.

17. Vogel, *Deng Xiaoping*, p. 332.

18. Vogel, *Deng Xiaoping*, p. 333.

19. Deng Xiaoping, "Emancipate the Mind, Seek Truth from Facts and Unite as One in Looking to the Future," *Selected Works of Deng Xiaoping*, Vol. 2 (1975–1982), Beijing: Foreign Languages Press, 1995, pp. 150–63.

20. Brzezinski, *Power*, pp. 196–7.

21. This account of the Deng-Carter talks is from Brzezinski, *Power*, pp. 406–10.

22. Jimmy Carter, *White House Diary*, New York: Farrar Straus Giroux, 1995, p. 285.

23. Brzezinski, *Power*, pp. 412, 414.

24. Brzezinski, *Power*, p. 467. In the event, the Soviets abstained from intervention when the Polish army agreed to itself impose a more repressive regime on Poland.

25. Brzezinski, *Power*, pp. 420–1.

26. Brzezinski, *Power*, p. 421.

27. Ji Chaozhu, *The Man on Mao's Right: From Harvard Yard to Tiananmen Square, My Life Inside China's Foreign Ministry*, New York: Random House, 2008, p. 301.

28. Quoted in Kissinger, *On China*, p. 357.

29. Nayan Chanda, *Brother Enemy: The War after the War*, New York: Collier Books, 1986, pp. 363–406.

30. Chanda, *Brother*, p. 379, also p. 454 n. 24.

31. Huang Hua, *Memoirs*, pp. 385–7.

32. Huang Hua, *Memoirs*, pp. 386–7.

33. Chanda, *Brother*, p. 381.

34. Interview with Dr. Zbigniew Brzezinski, June 13, 1997, National Security Archive. http://www.gwu.edu/~usarchiv/coldwar/interviews/episode-17/brzezinski.html.

35. George Crile, *Charlie Wilson's War: The Extraordinary Story of the Largest Covert Operation in History*, New York: Atlantic Monthly Press, 2002, pp. 167–8.

36. Huang Hua, *Memoirs*, pp. 391–5, 393.

37. Huang Hua, *Memoirs*, p. 393.

38. John Garver, "The Indian Factor in Recent Sino-Soviet Relations," *China Quarterly*, no. 125 (Summer 1991), p. 62.

39. Quoted in Garver, "Indian Factor," p. 63.

40. Garver, "India Factor," p. 63.

41. Peter Tomsen, *The Wars of Afghanistan: Messianic Terrorism, Tribal Conflicts, and the Failure of Great Powers*, New York: Public Affairs, 2011, p. 267. Tomsen was a long-serving diplomat who served three years in the mid-1980s as deputy chief of the US mission in Beijing. Also Crile, *Charlie Wilson's War*, pp. 268–89, 465–6.

42. Yitzhak Shichor, "The Great Wall of Steel: Militancy and Strategy in Xinjiang," in *Xinjiang: China's Muslim Borderlands*, edited by S. Frederick Starr, Armonk, NY: M. E. Sharpe, 2004, pp. 120–60, 148–9.

43. Shichor, "Great Wall," pp. 148–9. Also Jeffry T. Richelson, *Foreign Intelligence Organizations*, Cambridge: Ballinger, 1988, pp. 291–2.

44. Huang Hua, *Memoirs*, p. 359. This account of the 1979–82 renegotiations follows Huang's account. The text of the TRA is readily available online, for instance at http://www.ait.org.tw/en/taiwan-relations-act.html. Regarding the TRA, see Ramon A. Myers, ed., *A Unique Relationship: The United States and the Republic of China under the Taiwan Relations Act*, Stanford: Hoover Institution Press, 1989. Robert L. Dowen, *The Taiwan Pawn in the China Game*, Washington, DC: Center for Strategic and International Studies, 1979.

45. Harding, *Fragile Relationship*, pp. 112–3.

46. Deng Xiaoping, "Our Principled Position on the Development of Sino-US Relations," *Selected Works*, Vol. 2, pp. 369–72.

47. Huang Hua, *Memoirs*, pp. 366–7.

48. Huang Hua, *Memoirs*, p. 376,

49. This section follows James Lilley, *China Hands: Nine Decades of Adventure, Espionage, and Diplomacy in Asia*, New York: Public Affairs, p. 2004, p. 232. The "summary" to Volume 2 of Richard Solomon's 1985 study of PRC negotiating behavior said that the purpose of the volume was to "provide the basis for briefing senior American officials prior to their first negotiating encounters with PRC counterparts, establish control over the documentary record of US-PRC political exchanges during the 'normalization' phase of the relation." Solomon, part II, p. v.

50. James Mann, *About Face: A History of America's Curious Relationship with China, from Nixon to Clinton*, New York: Knopf, 1999, pp. 124–5.

51. Lilley, *China Hands*, p. 248.

52. Huang Hua, *Memoirs*, p. 376.

53. Harding, *Fragile Relationship*, p. 384.

54. Huang Hua, *Memoirs*, p. 376.

55. Brzezinski, *Power and Principle*, p. 426.

56. Huang Hua, *Memoirs*, p. 365.

57. Huang Hua, *Memoirs*, pp. 364–8.

58. Huang Hua, *Memoirs*, p. 378.

59. Dating the PRC-US strategic partnership is problematic. Either 1972 or 1979 can be seen as starting points. Selection of 1982 as end point reflects Beijing's adoption of its "independent foreign policy" and George Shultz's more skeptical approach to the utility of triangular linkage. From another perspective, however, the strategic partnership continued all the way to spring 1989.

Chapter 16. Normalization with the Asian Powers

1. Huang Hua, *Huang Hua Memoirs*, Beijing: Foreign Languages Press, 2008, p. 500.

2. Qian Qichen, *Waijiao shiji* (Ten diplomatic episodes), Beijing: Shijie zhishi chubanshe, 2003, pp. 3–4.

3. Qian, *Waijiao shiji*, pp. 4–8.

4. Huang Hua, *Memoirs*, pp. 498–9. Qian, *Waijiao shiji*, pp. 6–7.

5. Huang Hua, *Memoirs*, pp. 503–15.

6. Qian, *Waijiao shiji*, p. 11.

7. Qian, *Waijiao shiji*, p. 21–2. *Chinese Foreign Relations: A Chronology of Events (1949–1988)*, Beijing: Foreign Languages Press, 1989, pp. 474–5.

8. Qian, *Waijiao shiji*, p. 231.

9. Huang Hua, *Memoirs*, p. 517.

10. Qian, *Waijiao shiji*, pp. 27–8.

11. *China Foreign Relations*, p. 479.

12. *Foreign Broadcast Information Service, Daily Report China* (hereafter FBIS, DRC), February 6, 1989, p. 16.

13. Qian, *Waijiao shiji*, pp. 36–7.

14. Mikhail Gorbachev, *Memoirs*, New York: Doubleday, 1995, pp. 488–9. Gorbachev does not say *where* Deng proposed to revise history and redraw borders. It may have been Mongolia, where Deng raised China's claim with President George H. W. Bush during the latter's brief visit to Beijing in early 1989.

15. Gorbachev, *Memoirs*, p. 490.

16. G. S. Iyer, "Mao's Smile Revisited: Some Observations," December 2, 2009, C3S Paper No. 413, South Asia Analysis Group, http://www.southasiaanalysis.org. Press reports at the time stated that Mao smiled at Mishra while making these comments, but these reports were apparently erroneous.

17. See G. S. Bajpai, *China's Shadow over Sikkim: The Politics of Intimidation*, New Delhi: Lancer Publishers, 1999, pp. 183–95.

18. *China's Foreign Relations*, p. 266.

19. Iyer, "Mao's Smile."

20. Re US-Indian ties see, Dennis Kux, *India and the United States: Estranged Democracies*, Washington, DC: National Defense University Press, 1993.

21. John Garver, "Chinese-Indian Rivalry in Indochina," *Asian Survey*, vol. 27, no. 1 (November 1987), pp. 1205–19.

22. Nayan Chanda, *Brother Enemy: The War after the War*, New York: Collier, 1982, p. 356.

23. Quoted in John Garver, *Protracted Contest: Sino-Indian Rivalry in the Twentieth Century*, Seattle: University of Washington Press, 2001, p. 219.

24. FBIS, DRC, June 3, 1981, pp. 3–4.

25. Jeffrey Smith and Jody Warrick, "A Nuclear Power's Act of Proliferation," *Washington Post*, November 13, 2009. The authors elaborate on the multiple reasons for crediting the authenticity of the document.

26. Smith and Warrick, "A Nuclear Power's Act of Proliferation."

27. There is also extensive information on China's nuclear cooperation with Pakistan and other countries in Adrian Levy and Catherine Scott-Clark, *Deception: Pakistan, the United States and the Secret Trade in Nuclear Weapons*, New York: Walker and

Company, 2007. While the contours of China's nuclear and ballistic missile cooperation with Pakistan and via Pakistan with Libya and Iran are clear, the logic underlying those activities is not. It is *possible* that Beijing at this juncture still viewed nuclear proliferation as constraining hegemonistic powers and moving the world toward multipolarity. But purely commercial incentives probably played a role.

28. See Garver, *Protracted Contest*, p. 101.

29. Garver, *Protracted Contest*, p. 102.

30. *China's foreign Relations*, p. 268.

31. John W. Garver, "The Indian Factor in Recent Sino-Soviet Relations," *China Quarterly*, no. 125 (Summer 1991), pp. 55–85, 80.

32. Garver, *Protracted Contest*, p. 97.

33. This, of course, is a surmise. I develop this argument in John Garver, "The Unresolved Sino-Indian Border Dispute: An Interpretation," *China Report*, vol. 47, no. 2 (2011), pp. 99–113.

34. Unless otherwise indicated, this account follows John Garver, *China and Iran: Ancient Partners in a Post-Imperial World*, Seattle: University of Washington Press, 2007, pp. 63–93.

35. The congruence between He Ying's statement and Beijing's distancing itself in late 1982 from close anti-Soviet triangular cooperation with the United States suggests that improving relations with Iran, as well as with India, with which Beijing had similar problems because of its close alignment with the United States, may have been factors motivating the 1982 adjustment in Beijing's triangular alignment. Beijing's 1982 triangular adjustment was largely in the realm of public, rhetorical diplomacy, while the substance of Beijing's anti-hegemony cooperation, in Cambodia and Afghanistan, continued unimpaired. I develop this argument in Garver, *China and Iran*, pp. 72–4.

36. This discussion of IRI-PRC nuclear cooperation follows Garver, *China and Iran*, pp. 139–65.

37. Garver, *China and Iran*, pp. 143–5.

38. Garver, *China and Iran*, pp. 87–93.

39. Mike M. Mochizuki, "China-Japan Relations: Downward Spiral or a New Equilibrium?" in *Power Shift: China and Asia's New Dynamics*, edited by David Shambaugh, Berkeley: University of California Press, pp. 135–50. Chae-Jin Lee, *China and Japan: New Economic Diplomacy*, Stanford: Hoover Institution Press, 1984. Donald W. Klein, "Japan and Europe in Chinese Foreign Relations," in *China and the World: Chinese Foreign Policy Faces the New Millennium*, Boulder, CO: Westview Press, 1998, pp. 133–50.

40. Allen S. Whiting, *China Eyes Japan*, Berkeley: University of California Press, 1989, pp. 46–51.

41. Ibid.

42. Tang Jiaxuan, *Jin yu xu feng* (Heavy storms and gentle breeze), Beijing: Shijie zhishi chubanshe, 2009, pp. 2–9. Tang was foreign minister from 1998 to 2003. His university major was Japanese, and most of his foreign ministry assignments dealt with Japanese affairs.

43. Whiting, *China Eyes Japan*, pp. 59–60.

44. Whiting, *China Eyes Japan*, pp. 54–55.

45. Regarding the early modern period, see Marius B. Jansen, *China in the Tokugawa World*, Cambridge: Harvard University Press, 1992.

46. Regarding the 1894–1895 war as a hegemonic war, see S. C. M. Paine, *The Sino-Japanese War of 1894–1895; Perceptions, Power, and Primacy*, New York: Cambridge University Press, 2003.

47. *China's Foreign Relations*, pp. 227–38.

48. Klein, "Japan and Europe," p. 139.

49. *China's Foreign Relations*, pp. 227–38.

50. Whiting, *China Eyes Japan*, pp. 46–51.

51. Whiting, *China Eyes Japan*, p. 49.

52. James Reilly, *Strong Society, Smart State: The Rise of Public Opinion in China's Japan Policy*, New York: Columbia University Press, 2012, pp. 60–5.

53. *China's Foreign Relations*, p. 231. The quotations are in this China Foreign Ministry book.

54. This professor led four groups of Georgia Tech students to Yasukuni during the 2000s; it was a valuable experience for all concerned.

55. Quote in Whiting, *China Eyes Japan*, p. 56.

56. This discussions of the 1985 anti-Japan demonstrations follows Richard Baum, *Burying Mao: Chinese Politics in the Age of Deng Xiaoping*, Princeton: Princeton University Press, 1995, pp. 190–3.

57. This pattern of state-society interaction is laid out in Reilly, *Strong Society, Smart State*.

58. Baum, *Burying Mao*, pp. 189–90.

59. Whiting, *China Eyes Japan*, pp. 66–79.

60. Whiting, *China Eyes Japan*, pp. 70–1.

61. Whiting, *China Eyes Japan*, pp. 73–5.

62. Baum, *Burying Mao*, pp. 198–201.

Chapter 17. 1989: The CCP's Near Escape and Its Aftermath

1. David Shambaugh, *China's Communist Party: Atrophy and Adaptation*, Berkeley: University of California Press, 2008, pp. 42–53.

2. "White Paper on Political Democracy," October 19, 2005, available at www.china-daily.com.cn/english/doc/2005-10/19/content_486206.htm.

3. *The Tiananmen Papers*, compiled by Zhang Liang, edited by Andrew J. Nathan and Perry Link, New York: Public Affairs, 2001, p. 86. Hereafter cited as *Tiananmen Papers*.

4. *Tiananmen Papers*, p. 88.

5. *Tiananmen Papers*, p. 87.

6. *Tiananmen Papers*, p. 107.

7. Zhao Ziyang, *Prisoner of the State: The Secret Journal of Zhao Ziyang*, New York: Simon and Schuster, 2009, p. 257.

8. Zhao, *Prisoner of the State*, pp. 256–60.

9. *Tiananmen Papers*, p. 108.

10. *Tiananmen Papers*, p. 188.

11. *Tiananmen Papers*, p. 192.

12. Chongqing would become a provincial-level municipality in 1997, making thirty-three.

13. *Tiananmen Papers*, p. 133.

14. *Tiananmen Papers*, p. 205.

15. *Tiananmen Papers*, p. 209.

16. Zhao, *Prisoner of the State*, pp. 256–68.

17. Richard Madsen, *China and the American Dream, a Moral Inquiry*, Berkeley: University of California Press, 1998.

18. This is the central idea of Lucian Pye, *The Spirit of Chinese Politics: A Psychocultural Study of the Authority Crisis in Political Development*, Cambridge: MIT Press, 1968.

19. *Tiananmen Papers*, pp. 338–48.

20. *Tiananmen Papers*, p. 338.

21. *Tiananmen Papers*, p. 342.

22. *Tiananmen Papers*, p. 345.

23. *Tiananmen Papers*, p. 357.

24. *Tiananmen Papers*, pp. 358–9.

25. Zheng Wang, *Never Forget National Humiliation: Historical Memory in Chinese Politics and Foreign Relations*, New York: Columbia University Press, 2012. This discussion follows Zheng Wang.

26. Ibid., p. 99.

27. Ibid., p. 99.

28. Regarding contemporary party organization, see Richard McGregor, *The Party: The Secret World of China's Communist Rulers*, New York: Harper Perennial, 2010.

29. Zhong Jingwen, editor, *Aiguo zhuyi jiaoyu cidian* (Dictionary for patriotic education), Dalian chubanshe, 1991, p. 33.

30. James Lilley, *China Hands: Nine Decades of Adventure, Espionage, and Diplomacy in Asia*, New York: Public Affairs, 2004, p. 155.

31. http://web.archive.org/web/20070928104212/www.anti-communistanalyst.com/12222004.ntml.

32. Sources analyzing this debate are Richard Baum, *Burying Mao: Chinese Politics in the Era of Deng Xiaoping*, Princeton: Princeton University Press, 1994, pp. 313–40. Joseph Fewsmith, "Reaction, Resurgence, and Succession: Chinese Politics since Tiananmen," in *The Politics of China; the Eras of Mao and Deng*, edited by Roderick MacFarquhar, 2nd ed., Cambridge University Press, 1997, pp. 472–531. Harry Harding, *A Fragile Relationship: The United States and China since 1972*, Washington, DC: Brookings, 1992, pp. 235–59.

33. Baum, *Burying Mao*, pp. 341–56.

34. Baum, *Burying Mao*, p. 353.

35. Fewsmith, "Reaction," pp. 472–531.

36. Fewsmith, "Reaction," p. 485.

37. Allen S. Whiting, "Chinese Nationalism and Foreign Policy after Deng," *China Quarterly*, no. 142 (June 1995), p. 307.

38. Whiting, "Chinese Nationalism," p. 308.

39. Baum, *Burying Mao*, pp. 344–5.

Chapter 18. The Diplomacy of Damage Control

1. This section follows David Armstrong, *Revolution and World Order: The Revolutionary State in International Society*, Oxford: Clarendon Press, 1993. Also Robert H. Jackson, *Quasi-States: Sovereignty, International Relations, and the Third World*, Cambridge: Cambridge University Press, 1990. The PRC view of human rights has been

stated in several White Papers. All PRC White Papers are available at www.gov.cn/english/official/2005-08/17/content_24165.htm.

2. Michael H. Hunt, "Chinese National Identity and the Strong Stage," in *China's Quest for National Identity*, edited by Lowell Dittmer and Samuel Kim, Ithaca, NY: Cornell University Press, 1993, pp. 62–79.

3. Jackson, *Quasi-States*.

4. *The Tiananmen Papers*, compiled by Zhang Liang, edited by Andrew J. Nathan and Perry Link, New York: Public Affairs, 2001. pp. 397, 417. Hereafter cited as *Tiananmen Papers*.

5. *Tiananmen Papers*, p. 417.

6. Xu Jiatun's Memoirs, JPRS-CAR-93-45, March 8, 1994, p. 41. Xu Jiatun was the CCP chief in Hong Kong in the 1980s. He is dealt with in chapter 22.

7. Zhou Enlai never legally adopted Li, but served for all intents and purposes as his adoptive father. In the long and bitter struggle to gain power, caring for orphans of comrades killed in the struggle was part of the revolutionary ethos.

8. Alice Miller, "The CCP Central Committee's Leading Small Groups," *China Leadership Monitor*, no. 26 (Fall 2008), available at http://www.hoover.org/sites/default/files/uploads/documents/CLM26AM.pdf.

9. *Foreign Broadcast Information Service, Daily Report China*, November 28, 1990, pp. 6–8.

10. China's diplomatic activities are chronicled in *Zhongguo waijiao* (China's diplomacy), an annual almanac published by the Foreign Ministry.

11. Robert Benjamin, "Lee Peng and his Nation Make a Big Comeback—U.N. Meeting with Bush Will Cap Successful Tour," *Seattle Times*, January 30, 1992.

12. *Zhongguo waijiao, 1991*, p. 41.

13. This episode is discussed in John Garver, *Protracted Contest: Sino-Indian Rivalry in the Twentieth Century*, Seattle: University of Washington Press, 2011, pp. 157–61.

14. *Zhongguo waijiao, 1992*, p. 90.

15. Uli Schmetzer, "China Softly Bends in Winds of Change," *Chicago Tribune*, August 12, 1990.

16. Qian Qichen, *Waijiao shiji* (Ten episodes in diplomacy), Beijing: Shijie zhishi, 2003, p. 192.

17. Ming Wan, *Human Rights in Chinese Foreign Relations: Defining and Defending National Interests*, Philadelphia: University of Pennsylvania Press, 2001, pp. 88–9.

18. *Zhongguo waijiao, 1991*, p. 42.

19. Ming Wan, *Human Rights*, pp. 88–9.

20. Gilbert Rozman, "China's Changing Images of Japan, 1989–2001: The Struggle to Balance Partnership and Rivalry," *International Relations of the Asia-Pacific*, vol. 2 (2002), pp. 95–129.

21. *Zhongguo waijiao 1991*, p. 13.

22. Rozman, "China's Changing Images," p. 195.

23. David Holley, "British Leader Visits Beijing, Easing Sanctions," *Los Angeles Times*, September 3, 1991, available at http://articles.latimes.com/1991-09-03/news/mn-2070_1_hong-kong-airport.

24. These included suspension of military-to-military exchanges and cooperation, suspension of sales of military and police equipment, and recommendations to international financial organizations of indefinite delay of all further loans to China.

25. Ezra Vogel, *Deng Xiaoping and the Transformation of China*, Cambridge: Harvard University Press, 2011, p. 649.

26. *Tiananmen Papers*, p. 423.

27. *Tiananmen Papers*, p. 424.

28. Vogel, *Deng Xiaoping*, pp. 648–49.

29. George Bush and Brent Scowcroft, *A World Transformed*, New York: Knopf, 1998, pp. 99–100.

30. Bush and Scowcroft, *World Transformed*, p. 106.

31. Quoted in David M. Lampton, *Same Bed Different Dreams: Managing U.S-China Relations 1989–2000*, Berkeley: University of California Press, 2001, p. 29.

32. Henry Kissinger, *On China*, New York: Penguin Press, 2011, pp. 428–36. Vogel, *Deng Xiaoping*, p. 653.

33. Following the Scowcroft visit, the United States announced the sale of three commercial satellites and the renewal of support for World Bank loans to China for humanitarian projects.

34. The kowtow, or *ketou* in Chinese, was the ritual prostration of foreign envoys before the august presence of the emperor of China, symbolizing the subordination of foreign rulers to the Son of Heaven. This was a rite that ordered state relations in East Asia, off and on depending on China's actual power, for two millennia.

35. Fang Lizhi, "My 'Confession,'" *New York Review of Books*, June 23, 2011.

36. Fang Lizhi, "My 'Confession.'"

37. Qian, *Waijiao shiji*, pp. 184–6.

38. Qian, *Waijiao shiji*, p. 77.

39. Qian, *Waijiao shiji*, pp. 187–9.

Chapter 19. The Crisis Deepens

1. *Neues Deutschland*, East Berlin, April 5, 1988, *Foreign Broadcast Information Service, Daily Report, China* (hereafter *FBIS-CHI*), April 7, 1988, p. 12.

2. Xinhua, April 4, 1991, in *FBIS-CHI*, April 5, 1991, p. 7.

3. Moscow television, May 17, 1989, *FBIS-CHI*, May 18, 1989, p. 15.

4. John Garver, "China, German Unification and the Five Principles of Peaceful Coexistence," *Journal of East Asian Affairs*, vol. 8, no. 1 (Winter/Spring 1994), pp. 135–72.

5. *FBIS-CHI*, September 27, 1989, p. 14.

6. *FBIS-CHI*, September 26, 1989, p. 9.

7. Xinhua, October 9, 1989, *FBIS-CHI*, October 10, 1989, p. 19.

8. Quoted in Gottfried-Karl Kinderman, "The Peaceful Reunification of Germany," *Issues and Studies* 27, no. 3 (March 1991), pp. 61–2.

9. *Der Weg zur deutschen Einheit* (The road to German unity), Berlin: Volker Köhler, 1990. History of the German unification process, Reichstag Museum, Berlin, FRG.

10. He Po-shih, "CCP Issues Successive Emergency Circulars Ordering Entire Party to Guard against Changes," *Dangdai* (Contemporary era) (Hong Kong), September 15, 1991, in *FBIS-CHI*, September 24, 1991, p. 7.

11. "Quarterly Chronicle," *China Quarterly*, no. 121 (March 1990), p. 178.

12. Xinhua, *FBIS-CHI*, September 11, 1989, p. 15.

13. Xinhua, *FBIS-CHI*, September 11, 1989, p. 15.

14. Xinhua, *FBIS-CHI*, November 2, 1989, p. 13.

15. *FBIS-CHI*, November 2, 1989, p. 13.

16. "Quarterly Chronicle," *China Quarterly*, no. 121 (March 1990), p. 178.

17. Xinhua, *FBIS-CHI*, October 26, 1989, pp. 9–10.

18. Willy Wo-lap Lam, *South China Morning Post*, November 18, 1989, *FBIS-CHI*, November 20, 1989, pp. 24–5.

19. Xinhua, *FBIS-CHI*, November 24, 1989, p. 13.

20. Seth Faison, *South China Morning Post*, November 19, 1989, *FBIS-CHI*, November 22, 1989.

21. Andrei Ujică produced an interesting documentary movie of Ceauşescu's rise and fall, including his final "trial," *The Autobiography of Nicolae Ceauşescu*, 2010. (Material about the film can be found at www.the-autobiography.com.) Ceauşescu's interactions with CCP leaders figure prominently in the film.

22. Benjamin Yang, *Deng: A Political Biography*, Armonk, NY: M. E. Sharpe, 1998, p. 257.

23. This follows Robert L. Suettinger, *Beyond Tiananmen: The Politics of U.S.-China Relations 1989–2000*, Washington, DC: Brookings Institution Press, 2003, p. 104.

24. This follows Richard Baum, *Burying Mao: Chinese Politics in the Era of Deng Xiaoping*, Berkeley: University of California Press, 1994, pp. 303–6.

25. Baum, *Burying Mao*, p. 304.

26. Baum, *Burying Mao*, p. 313.

27. "Quarterly Documentation," *China Quarterly*, no. 122 (June 1990), p. 363.

28. "Zhonggong yifen zhongyao jimi wenjian quanwen" (Complete text of several important secret CCP documents), *Zheng ming* (Contention), Hong Kong, no. 151 (May 1, 1990), pp. 8–10.

29. *Zheng ming*, May 1, 1990, p. 5.

30. Tsai Yung-mei, "Beijing's Reactions to the Great Changes in the Soviet Union, *Kaifang* (Openness) (Hong Kong), September 15, 1991, *FBIS-CHI*, September 30, 1991, p. 16.

31. [Yevgeni Bazhanov], "Policy by Fiat: Inside Story; Kremlin Twisted Its Facts on China," *Far Eastern Economic Review*, vol. 155, no. 23 (June 11, 1992), pp. 16–8.

32. Xinhua, September 13, 1989. *FBIS-CHI*, September 13, 1989, p. 4.

33. Xinhua, September 23, 1989, *FBIS-CHI*, September 25, 1989, pp. 4–5.

34. Tsai Yung-mei, "Beijing's Reactions."

35. Xinhua, April 25, 1990, *FBIS-CHI*, April 25, 1990, pp. 15–6. Beijing Radio, April 25, 1990, *FBIS-CHI*, April 26, 1990, pp. 17–8.

36. Xinhua, April 1, 1991, *FBIS-CHI*, April 2, 1991, pp. 9–10.

37. Xinhua, March 27, 1991, *FBIS-CHI*, March 27, 1991, p. 2.

38. Xinhua, April 4, 1991, *FBIS-CHI*, April 5, 1991, p. 7.

39. Xinhua, May 17, 1991, *FBIS-CHI*, May 21, 1991, p. 10.

40. Shih Chun-yu, "China, Soviet Union Agree to Expand Co-operation," *Da gong bao*, May 18, 1991, *FBIS-CHI*, May 21, 1991, pp. 14–5.

41. Yeh Lu-ching, "CPC Holds Up Communism on Its Own, Launches Protracted War against Capitalism," *Dangdai*, no. 6, September 15, 1991, *FBIS-CHI*, September 1991, p. 23.

42. "Trends," *FBIS-CHI*, March 6, 1991, p. 18.

43. Yeh Lu-ching, "CPC Holds Up Communism."

44. He Po-shih, "CCP Issues Successive Emergency Circulars," p. 7.

45. Yeh Lu-ching, "CPC Holds Up Communism."

46. Tsai Yung-mei, "Beijing's Reactions."

47. *Qingbao* (Intelligence), Hong Kong, September 5, 1991, *FBIS-CHI*, September 9, 1991, p. 10.

48. Yeh Lu-ching, "CPC Holds Up Communism." Tsai Yung-mei, "Beijing's Reactions." He Po-shih, "CCP Issues Successive Emergency Circulars."

49. Beijing Radio, August 21, 1991, *FBIS-CHI*, August 22, 1991, p. 7.

50. He Po-shih, "CCP Issues Successive Emergency Circulars."

51. Gao Di's speech is in "Quarterly Chronicle," *China Quarterly*, no. 130 (June 1992), pp. 482–90.

52. Wang Wenli, *Heping yanbian zhanlue, ji qi duice* (Strategy of peaceful evolution and counterstrategies), Beijing: Shijie zhishi chubanshe, 1992.

53. Ibid., p. 190.

54. Jeremy Page, "China Spins New Lesson From Soviet Fall," *Wall Street Journal*, December 11, 2013. Jane Perlez, "Strident Video by Chinese Military Casts U.S. as Menace," *New York Times*, October 31, 2013. (The program was available in November 2013 at https://www.youtube.com/watch?v=m_81sjicoswb but was later removed.)

55. David M. Lampton, *Same Bed, Different Dreams: Managing U.S.-China Relations 1989–2000*, Berkeley: University of California Press, 2001.

Chapter 20. Constraining Unipolarity in an Unbalanced International System

1. FBIS-CHI, November 28, 1990.

2. James Mann, *About Face: A History of America's Curious Relationship with China, from Nixon to Clinton*, New York: Knopf, 1999, pp. 282–3.

3. Mann, *About Face*, pp. 276–7.

4. Robert Suettinger, *Beyond Tiananmen: The Politics of U.S.-China Relations, 1989–2000*, Washington, DC: Brookings Institution Press, 2003, p. 179. According to Suettinger, this was the first time a US leader had undertaken to lay out a broad outline of post–Cold War strategy. This would have given it additional weight in CCP eyes.

5. David M. Lampton, *Same Bed, Different Dreams: Managing U.S.-China Relations, 1989–2000*, Berkeley: University of California Press, 2001, p. 44.

6. Suettinger, *Beyond Tiananmen*, pp. 179, 182–3.

7. Lampton, *Same Bed*, p. 44. Robert Suettinger believes that Beijing's courtship of US business at this juncture was not a deliberate policy decision, but the result of "crossing the river by feeling the stones." *Beyond Tiananmen*, p. 183. The CCP's long tradition of exploiting contradictions and united front work makes it likely that this was the result of a conscious decision.

8. Polly Lane, "Chinese Order Will Bolster Boeing," *Seattle Times*, April 9, 1993.

9. Mary Gwinn, "China Trade in Jeopardy," *Seattle Times*, May 20, 1993.

10. Lampton, *Same Bed*, p. 44.

11. Mann, *About Face*, p. 292.

12. Lampton, *Same Bed*, p. 40.

13. Mann, *About Face*, p. 284.

14. Lampton, *Same Bed*, p. 43.

15. Mann, *About Face*, pp. 299–300.

16. Warren Christopher, *Chances of a Lifetime*, New York: Scribner, 2001, pp. 238–9.

17. Christopher, *Chances of a Lifetime*, pp. 302–3.

18. Mann, *About Face*, p. 311.

19. Qian Qichen, *Waijiao shiji* (Ten diplomatic episodes), Beijing: Shijie zhishi, 2003, pp. 43–67.

20. Qianyun Yang, "China and Peaceful Settlement of Cambodian Issues," *Asian Culture and History*, vol. 2, no. 2 (July 2010), pp. 25–9. Available at http://www.ccsenet.org/journal/index.php/ach/article/view/6577/5170 .

21. Richard H. Solomon, *Exiting Indochina: U.S. Leadership of the Cambodian Settlement and Normalization of Relations with Vietnam*, Washington, DC: United States Institute of Peace, 2000, p. 21.

22. Qian, *Waijiao shiji*, p. 61.

23. Qian, *Waijiao shiji*, pp. 44–6.

24. Solomon, *Exiting Indochina*, p. 46.

25. US-SRV relations were normalized in August 1995.

26. This section follows Joel Wit, Daniel Poneman, and Robert Gallucci, *Going Critical: The First North Korean Nuclear Crisis*, Washington, DC: Brookings Institution Press, 2004

27. Suettinger, *Beyond Tiananmen*, p. 179.

28. Wit, Poneman, and Gallucci, *Going Critical*, pp. 157–87.

29. Wit, Poneman, and Gallucci, *Going Critical*, p. 343.

30. The caveat "major" excludes the People's Democratic Republic of Korea, Cuba, and the Socialist Republic of Vietnam.

31. Regarding Sino-Russian ties at this juncture, see, Lowell Dittmer, "China and Russia: New Beginnings," in *China and the World*, 3rd ed., edited by Samuel S. Kim, Boulder, CO: Westview Press, 1994. Roxane D. V. Sismanidis, "China, the Soviet Collapse, and the Post-Soviet States," *Washington Journal of Modern China* 1, no. 2 (Spring 1993), pp. 53–83.

32. Quoted in John Garver, "Sino-Russian Relations," in *China and the World; Chinese Foreign Policy Faces the New Millennium*, edited by Samuel S. Kim, Boulder, CO: Westview, 1998, pp. 114–32, 115.

33. Yevgeni Bazhanov, "Russia and Taiwan," Bericht des BIOS Nr. 29/1996. Available at http://www.ssoar.info/ssoar/bitstream/handle/document/4251/ssoar-1996-bazhanov-russia_and_taiwan.pdf?sequence=1.

34. The normalization communiqué is in FBIS-CHI, December 18, 1992, pp. 7–9.

35. Quoted in Garver, "Sino-Russian Relations," p. 116.

36. Ahmed Rashid, *Jihad: The Rise of Militant Islam in Central Asia*, New York: Penguin, 2003.

37. Bates Gill, "Shanghai Five: An Attempt to Counter U.S. Influence in Asia?" May 4, 2001. Brookings. Available at http://www.brookings.edu/research/opinions/2001/05/04china-gill.

38. Hung P. Nguyen, "Russia and China: Genesis of an Eastern Rapallo," *Asian Survey*, no. 33, issue 3 (March 1993), pp. 285–99.

39. "Zhong e fazhan mianxiang 21 shijide zhanlue xuezuo huoban guanxi" (China and Russia developing a relation of strategic cooperative partnership facing the 21st century), *Heping yu fazhan* (Peace and development), Peace and Development Research Center, January 8, 1997.

40. "Joint Statement by the People's Republic of China and the Russian Federation on the Multipolarization of the World and the Establishment of a New International Order," April 23, 1997, in *Beijing Review*, May 12–18, 1997, pp. 7–8.

41. *New York Times*, July 17, 2001, available at http://www.nytimes.com/2001/07/17/international/17RTEX.html.

42. Joseph Y. S. Cheng and Zhang Wankun, "Patterns and Dynamics of China's International Strategic Behavior," *Journal of Contemporary China*, vol. 11, no. 31 (2002), pp. 235–60.

43. This section follows M. Taylor Fravel, "China's Attitude toward U.N. Peacekeeping Operations since 1989," *Asian Survey*, 1996.

44. Bates Gill and James Reilly, "Sovereignty, Intervention and Peacekeeping: The View from Beijing," *Survival*, vol. 42, no. 3 (Autumn 2000), pp. 41–59.

45. Fravel, "China's Attitude."

46. Fravel, "China's Attitude," p. 1110.

47. Fravel, "China's Attitude," p. 1115.

48. Sheila Tefft, "China Resents US Resolution on Its Bid for 2000 Olympics," *Christian Science Monitor*, July 29, 1993, available at http://www.csmonitor/1993/0729/29061.html.

49. Patrick Tyler, "There's No Joy in Beijing as Sydney Gets Olympics," *New York Times*, September 29, 1993, available at http://www.nytimes.com/1993/09/24/sports/olympics-there-s-no-joy-in-beijing-as-sydney-gets-olympics.html.

50. Robert McG. Thomas Jr., "Olympics: China Boycott Threat is Denied," *New York Times*, September 18, 1993, available at http://www.nytimes.com/1993/09/18/sports/olympics-chinese-boycott-threat-is-denied.html.

51. "A Billion Broken Hearts," *Newsweek*, October 4, 1993, p. 73, available at http://www.newsweek.com/billion-broken-hearts-194212.

52. Willy Wo-lap Lam, *The Era of Jiang Zemin*, New York: Prentice Hall, 1999, p. 271.

53. John Garver, *China and Iran: Ancient Partners in a Post-Imperial World*, Seattle: University of Washington Press, 2007, pp. 191–3.

54. Garver, *China and Iran*, pp. 175–7.

55. Garver, *China and Iran*, p. 192.

Chapter 21.   China and America in the Persian Gulf

1. For a recent appraisal of China-Middle East relations, see Jon B. Alterman and John W. Garver, *The Vital Triangle: China, the United States and the Middle East*, Washington, DC: Center for Strategic and International Studies, 2008. Also P. R. Kumaraswamy, ed., *China and the Middle East: The Quest for Influence*, New Delhi: Sage, 1999. Geoffrey Kemp, *The East Moves West: India, China and Asia's Growing Presence in the Middle East*, Washington, DC: Brookings Institution, 2010. Studies of China's Middle East policies prior to the rise of its energy imports are Lillian Craig Harris, *China Considers the Middle East*, London: I. B. Tauris, 1993. Hashim S. H. Behbehani, *China's Foreign Policy in the Arab World, 1955–75*, London: Kegan Paul, 1981.

2. See Michael A. Palmer, *Guardians of the Gulf: A History of America's Expanding Role in the Persian Gulf, 1833–1992*, New York: The Free Press, 1992.

3. The "tanker war" which led to IRI mining of Gulf sea lanes was an offshoot of the Iran-Iraq war. Iran began attacking Gulf oil traffic as part of its struggle against Iraq. This

led to US military punishment of Iran for its interference with Gulf oil traffic. Several maritime clashes between US and IRI naval forces, including one significant battle, resulted.

4. "Li: Gulf Crisis Should Be Resolved by Peaceful Means," *Beijing Review*, September 10–16, 1990, p. 7.

5. Rui Bian, "Haiwan jumian poqie, meiguo junshi jieru kenengxing zengjia" [The Gulf situation in urgency, possibility of US military interference increasing], *Renmin ribao*, August 12, 1990.

6. "Li: Gulf Crisis Should be Resolved by Peaceful Means," p. 7.

7. For the US perspective, see James A. Baker, *The Politics of Diplomacy: Revolution, War and Peace, 1989–1992*, New York: Putnam, 1995, pp. 275–76. George H. W. Bush and Brent Scowcroft, *A World Transformed*, New York: Knopf, 1998, pp. 302–4.

8. Shu Zhong, "Several Questions Calling for Deep Thought," *Shijie zhishi* (World knowledge), March 1, 1991, in FBIS-CHI-91-066, April 5, 1991, pp. 1–2.

9. Li Qinggong, "Special Article: Bush's State of the Union Address and the New U.S. Global Strategy," *Shijie zhishi*, March 1, 1991, p. 5.

10. "Fiendish Plot," *Far Eastern Economic Review*, January 31, 1991, p. 6.

11. "Fiendish Plot," p. 6.

12. Xiaohong Liu, *Chinese Ambassadors: The Rise of Diplomatic Professionalism since 1949*, Seattle: University of Washington Press, 2001, p. 179.

13. James Tyson, "Iraq Seeks China's Help at the UN," *Christian Science Monitor*, February 21, 1991, p. 3

14. Ellis Joffe, "China Alter the Gulf War: Lessons Learned." Yitzhak Shichor, "China and the Gulf Crisis: Escape from Predicaments," *Problems of Communism*, November–December 1991, pp. 80–90.

15. "Chinese Watchers," *Far Eastern Economic Review*, March 14, 1991, p. 9.

16. Lena Sun, "China Boosts Arms Budget 12 Percent," *Washington Post*, March 27, 1991, p. 28.

17. Liu Jinglian, "Reflections on the Gulf War and Lessons Drawn From It." Unpublished paper prepared for November 1991 conference on China and the 1991 Gulf War convened by the Center for National Security Studies of Los Alamos National Laboratory, Los Alamos, New Mexico.

18. The PLA follows the Soviet model of a chain of political officers paralleling the command chain and charged with ensuring the loyalty of the military to the Communist Party. That chain of political commissars is called the political control system.

19. David Shambaugh, *Modernizing China's Military: Progress, Problems, and Prospects*, Berkeley: University of California Press, 2002.

20. See *China-Iraq Ties: Military Assistance for Oil*, Virtual Information Center, Headquarters, US Commander in Chief Pacific, February 23, 2001.

21. Yitzhak Shichor, "Decisionmaking in Triplicate: China and the Three Iraqi Wars," in *Chinese National Security Decisionmaking Under Stress*, edited by Andrew Scobell and Larry M. Wortzel, Washington, DC: National Defense University, Strategic Studies Institute, 2005, pp. 191–228.

22. UN Security Council Debate, October 17, 2002. Available at http://www.iraqwatch.org/un/unscresolutions/PVRs-debates/un-scstatements-101702.htm.

23. Kuang Ji, "Security or Hegemony?" *Beijing Review* 15 (April 10, 2003), p. 43.

24. Zhou Yihuang, "U.S. Attack on Iraq: Killing Three Birds with One Stone," *Jiefangjun bao*, September 16, 2002. Foreign Broadcast Information Service, Daily Report China, World News Connection document # 0H32AYZ03ZIPVY.

25. In Chinese, a *weng* is the three-sided defense wall protruding beyond the normal city wall and defending a city gate in ancient times. Sometimes the outer gate was left open, inviting the enemy "gentlemen" in, where arrows would rain down on them from four sides.

26. Quoted in Garver, *China and Iran: Ancient Partners in a Post-Imperial World*, Seattle: University of Washington Press, 2006, p. 107.

27. See Garver, *China and Iran*, pp. 249–52.

28. See Garver, *China and Iran*, pp. 155–62.

29. See Alterman and Garver, *Vital Triangle*, pp. 42–7.

Chapter 22. The Recovery of Hong Kong

1. See Michael Enright and Edith Scott, "China's Quiet Powerhouse," *Far Eastern Economic Review*, May 2005, pp. 27–34.

2. The Portuguese first landed at Macao in 1513, and in 1535 Portuguese ships were granted the right to anchor at Macao.

3. S. C. M. Paine, *The Sino-Japanese War of 1894–1895: Perceptions, Power and Primacy*, Cambridge: Cambridge University Press, 2003.

4. Xu Jiatun, Hong Kong memoir, in *Joint Publication Research Service—China Area Report* (JPRS-CAR), 93-050, July 16, 1993, p. 12. Cited below as "Xu Jiatun memoir." Xu was Beijing's top representative in Hong Kong during the 1980s.

5. David C. Wolf, "'To Secure a Convenience': Britain Recognizes China—1950," *Journal of Contemporary History*, vol. 18 (1983), pp. 299–326.

6. Robin McLaren, *Britain's Record on Hong Kong*, London: Royal Institute of International Affairs, Chatham House, 1987, p. 7.

7. See Nicholas Eftimiades, *Chinese Intelligence Operations*, Annapolis, MD: Naval Institute Press, 1994, pp. 30–1, 69, 79.

8. Xu Jiatun memoir, 93-050, July 16, 1993, p. 7.

9. Eftimiades, *Chinese Intelligence*, p. 79.

10. McLaren, *Britain's Record*, p. 6.

11. Professor Liu Xuepeng of Kennesaw State University pointed this out to me on April 29, 2013.

12. Christopher Howe, "Growth, Public Policy and Hong Kong's Economic Relationship with China," *China Quarterly*, no. 95 (September 1983), pp. 529–33.

13. McLaren, *Britain's Record*, p. 6.

14. Xu Jiatun memoir, 94-010, February 10, 1994, p. 8.

15. Xu Jiatun memoir, 93-050, July 6, 1993, p. 12.

16. "Our Basic Position on the Question of Hong Kong," September 24, 1982, in *Deng Xiaoping on the Question of Hong Kong*, Beijing: Foreign Languages Press, 1993, pp. 1–5. Zhao Ziyang, Thatcher's equivalent in government, made the same point. McLaren, "Britain's Record," p. 11.

17. Deng Xiaoping, *On the Question of Hong Kong*, pp. 1–2.

18. Ibid., p. 2.

19. Ibid., pp. 4–5.

20. Ibid., p. 3.

21. Xu Jiatun memoir, 93-050, July 16, 1993, p. 14.

22. McLaren, *Britain's Record*, pp. 11–2.

23. "China Lauds Thatcher but H.K. Activists Cry Betrayal," *Bangkok Post*, April 10, 2013. Available at http://www.bangkokpost.com/news/asia/344758/china-lauds-thatcher-but-h-k-activists-cry-betrayal.

24. Xu Jiatun memoir, 93-050, July 16, 1993, p. 14.

25. Ching-fen Hu, "Taiwan's Geopolitics and Chiang Ching-kuo's Decision to Democratize Taiwan," *Stanford Journal of East Asian Affairs*, vol. 5, no.1 (Winter 2005), pp. 26–37.

26. Deng Xiaoping, "One Country, Two Systems," June 22–23, 1984, in *Deng on the Question of Hong Kong*, pp. 6–11.

27. *China Quarterly*, no. 100 (December 1984), pp. 920–2.

28. Xu Jiatun memoir, 93-050, July 16, 1993, p. 5; 94–015, Mar. 8, 1994, p. 43.

29. Xu Jiatun memoir, 93-050, July 16, 1993, pp. 14–5.

30. Xu Jiatun memoir, 93-050, July 16, 1993, p. 17; September 21, 1993, p. 3.

31. Xu Jiatun memoir, 93-050, July 16, 1993, p. 1.

32. Xu Jiatun memoir, 93-050, July 16, 1993, p. 3.

33. Xu Jiatun memoir, 93-050, July 16, 1993, pp. 2, 7, 11.

34. Xu Jiatun memoir, 93-050, July 16, 1993, p. 17.

35. Xu Jiatun memoir, 91-050, September 21, 1993, p. 1.

36. Xu Jiatun memoir, 91-101, February 10, 1994, p. 11

37. McLaren, *Britain's Record*, p. 14.

38. Mark O'Neill, "Former Hong Kong Boss Explains His Defection," *Asia Sentinel*, August 8, 2007.

39. Hu had in fact selected Xu, then serving as party secretary of rapidly opening and reforming Jiangsu province, to head the CCP's Hong Kong apparatus. Carol Lee Hamrin and Suisheng Zhao, *Decision-making in Deng's China: Perspectives from Insiders*, Armonk, NY: M. E. Sharpe, 1995, p. 107.

40. Xu Jiatun memoir, 94-105, March 8, 1994, pp. 8–9; 94–017, March 17, 1994, pp. 17–8.

41. Xu Jiatun memoir, 94-105, March 8, 1994, p. 35.

42. O'Neill, "Former Hong Kong Boss Explains His Defection."

43. Qian Qichen, *Waijiao shiji* (Ten diplomatic episodes), Beijing: Shijie zhishi chubanshe, 2003, p. 332.

44. McLaren, *Britain's Record*, p. 20.

45. McLaren, *Britain's Record*, p. 20.

46. Xu Jiatun memoir, 94–101, February 10, 1994, p. 8.

47. Qian, *Waijiao shiji*, p. 384.

48. McLaren, *Britain's Record*, p. 24.

49. Percy Cradock, *Experiences of China*, London: John Murray, 1999, pp. 230–1.

50. Qian, *Waijiao shiji*, pp. 325–6.

51. *Zhongguo waijiao gaijian, 1991* (Overview of Chinese Diplomacy 1991), Beijing; Shijie zhishi chubanshe, 1991, p. 278.

52. The text of the Basic Law is available at http://www.basiclaw.gov.hk/en/basiclaw-text/index.html.

53. Qian, *Waijiao shiji*, p. 384. "Through train" meant a continuity of institutional arrangements before and after reversion. Absence of a "through train," such as eventually came about, meant that arrangements under British rule prior to July 1, 1997, were set aside and Chinese-created institutional arrangements took over.

54. As late as 2008–2012, with LegCo made up of thirty directly elected geographic constituencies and thirty "functional constituencies," the functional constituencies and the number of voters in these constituencies included these: agriculture and fisheries (electorate of 159); insurance (144); transport (178); legal (6,111); medical (10,606); finance (140); financial services (580); first industrial district (715); second industrial district (790). Geographical constituencies, on the other hand, ranged from a low of 440,335 to a high of 943,161 registered voters.

55. Christopher Patten, *East and West: China, Power and the Future of Asia*, New York: Times Books, 1998, pp. 53–4.

56. Patten, *East and West*, p. 56.

57. Qian, *Waijiao shiji*, pp. 335–6.

58. Qian, *Waijiao shiji*, p. 340. The text of Deng's talk with Thatcher is cited in note 16 above.

59. McLaren, *Britain's Record*, p. 29.

60. Cradock, *Experiences*, pp. 226, 228. McLaren, "Britain's Record," pp. 20, 26.

61. Steven Tsang, *A Modern History of Hong Kong*, London: I. B. Tauris, 2004, p. 238.

62. This section follows Robert Suettinger, *Beyond Tiananmen: the Politics of U.S.-China Relations 1989–2000*, Washington, DC: Brookings, 2003, pp. 314–7.

Chapter 23. Military Confrontation with the United States

1. That phrase was used by Clinton's vice presidential running mate, Al Gore.

2. Regarding the 1995–1996 crisis, see Robert L. Suettinger, *Beyond Tiananmen, the Politics of U.S.-China Relations 1989–2000*, Washington, DC: Brookings Institution Press, 2003, pp. 200–63. James Mann, *About Face: A History of America's Curious Relationship with China, from Nixon to Clinton*, New York: Knopf, 1999, pp. 315–38. John Garver, *Face Off: China, the United States, and Taiwan's Democratization*, Seattle: University of Washington Press, 1997.

3. James Lilley, *China Hands: Nine Decades of Adventure, Espionage, and Diplomacy in Asia*, New York: Public Affairs, 2004, p. 377.

4. Suettinger, *Beyond Tiananmen*, p. 203.

5. Unless otherwise indicated, this account of the PLA's lobbying campaign is drawn from Garver, *Face Off*, pp. 47–66.

6. See Shirley A. Kan, *China/Taiwan: Evolution of the "One China" Policy—Key Statements from Washington, Beijing, and Taipei*, No. 7-5700, RI 30341, Washington, DC: Congressional Research Service, August 26, 2013.

7. "1994 Taiwan Policy Review," available at www.fapa.org/generalinfo/TPR1994.html.

8. Garver, *Face Off*, pp. 41–5.

9. Garver, *Face Off*, pp. 44–5.

10. Suettinger, *Beyond Tiananmen*, p. 215.

11. Suettinger, *Beyond Tiananmen*, p. 223.

12. Suettinger, *Beyond Tiananmen*, pp. 221–7.

13. Ching-fen Hu, "Taiwan's Geopolitics and Chiang Ching-kuo's Decision to Democratize Taiwan," *Stanford Journal of East Asian Affairs*, vol. 5, no. 1 (Winter 2005), pp. 26–44.

14. See Kan, *China/Taiwan.*

15. For an analysis of the politics of Taiwan's "China policies," see Richard C. Bush, *Untying the Knot: Making Peace in the Taiwan Strait*, Washington, DC: Brookings Institution, 2005.

16. John Garver, *Sino-American Alliance: Nationalist China and U.S. Cold War Strategy in Asia*, Armonk, NY: M. E. Sharpe, 1997, pp. 230–47.

17. The People's Power movement in the Philippines overthrew dictator Ferdinand Marcos in February 1986. In South Korea, a student uprising in June 1987 forced the military to abandon its long-time rule and embrace civilian and democratically constituted government.

18. It must be noted, however, that by the late nineteenth century some Chinese thinkers were reconceptualizing Confucianism to transfer sovereignty from the virtuous Son of Heaven to the people. See Liang Chi-chao, *History of Chinese Political Thought*, London: Kegan Paul, 1930, chapter "On Democratic Ideals," pp. 150–2. The CCP's narrative of the Chinese tradition is contested by prominent Chinese thinkers.

19. Suettinger, *Beyond Tiananmen*, p. 207.

20. Suettinger, *Beyond Tiananmen*, p. 232.

21. *Dagong bao* (Hong Kong), August 3, 1995. Translated in *FBIS-CHI*, August 8, 1995, pp. 4–5. As of early 2014 the text of this letter had not been released. Regarding the controversies over this letter, see Suettinger, *Beyond Tiananmen*, pp. 232–3.

22. *New York Times*, November 18, 1995; February 7, 1996.

23. East Asia Wireless File, BBC, December 14, 1995, p. 28.

24. Suettinger, *Beyond Tiananmen*, pp. 249, 251.

25. The description of the 1996 exercises draws heavily on *Chinese Exercise Strait 961: 8–25 March 1996*, Office of Naval Intelligence, May 1996.

26. *Wenhui bao*, March 5, 1996. In FBIS-CHI, March 11, 1996, p. 15.

27. Television transcript of Tim Russert interview by Secretary of State Warren Christopher, *Meet the Press*, Burrelle's Transcripts.

28. Quoted in Suettinger, *Beyond Tiananmen*, p. 256.

29. Department of Defense news briefing, March 12, 1996, available at http://www.defense.gov/transcripts/transcript.aspx?transcriptid=443.

30. *South China Morning Post*, March 18, 1996. *FBIS-CHI*, March 18, 1996, p. 5.

31. *Dagong bao*, March 12, 1996. *FBIS-CHI*, March 12, 1996, pp. 11–2.

32. Seuttinger, *Beyond Tiananmen*, pp. 246–7. Garver, *Face Off*, pp. 111–7.

33. The most convenient and detailed source tracking improvement of PLA capabilities is the Annual Report to Congress on PRC military power published by the US Department of Defense at the direction of the US Congress. The 2013 report is available at www.defense.gov/pubs/2013_china_report-final.pdf.

34. Regarding the international reaction to PLA exercises, see Garver, *Face Off*, pp. 134–47.

35. *Zhongguo waijiao* 1997 (China's diplomacy, 1997) (covers year 1996), Beijing: Shijie zhishi chubanshe, 1997, p. 571.

Chapter 24. China's Long Debate over Response to the US Challenge

1. For media discussion of the program, see Jeremy Page, "China Spins New Lessons from Soviet Fall," *Wall Street Journal*, December 11, 2013. Jane Perlez, "Strident Video by Chinese Military Casts U.S. as Menace, " *New York Times*, October 31, 2013.

2. For an overview of the US debate, see Owen Harries, "A Year of Debating China," *National Interest*, no. 58 (Winter 1999/2000), p. 141. For a Chinese view of the debate, see Qingguo Jia, "Frustration and Hope: Chinese Perception of the Engagement Policy Debate in the United States," *Journal of Contemporary China*, vol. 10, no. 27 (2001), pp. 321–30. One of the most provocative US contributions was Richard Bernstein and Ross H. Munro, "The Coming Conflict with America," *Foreign Affairs*, March–April 1997, pp. 18–32.

3. This discussion follows Robert L. Suettinger, *Beyond Tiananmen: The Politics of U.S.-China Relations 1989–2000*, Washington, DC: Brookings, 2003, pp. 264–78, 312.

4. Suettinger, *Beyond Tiananmen*, p. 278.

5. Suettinger, *Beyond Tiananmen*, p. 284.

6. Suettinger, *Beyond Tiananmen*, p. 323.

7. Suettinger, *Beyond Tiananmen*, pp. 313–5.

8. James Mann, *About Face: A History of America's Curious Relationship with China, from Nixon to Clinton*, New York: Knopf, 1999, pp. 355–6.

9. Suettinger, *Beyond Tiananmen*, p. 318.

10. Joint U.S.-China Statement, October 29, 1997, available at http://www.state.gov/www/regions/cap971029-usc-utstml.html.

11. This section relies on Robert Lawrence Kuhn, *The Man Who Changed China: The Life and Legacy of Jiang Zemin*, New York: Crown Publishers, 2004, pp. 324–49.

12. Kuhn, *Jiang Zemin*, p. 330.

13. This discussion of Clinton's 1998 visit is from Robert Suettinger, *Beyond Tiananmen*, pp. 343–6.

14. Suettinger, *Beyond Tiananmen*, p. 347.

15. David M. Lampton, *Same Bed, Different Dreams: Managing U.S.-China Relations 1989–2000*, Berkeley: University of California Press, 2001, pp. 329–31.

16. "Handling the Falungong Case," *Chinese Law and Government*, vol. 35, no. 1 (January–February 2002), pp. 53–72. This is an account of CCP deliberations written by a liberal party member and critical of the hard-line rule of Jiang and Li Peng. The guest editor of these documents, Andrew Nathan, credits their veracity.

17. Ibid., p. 62.

18. Ibid., p. 68.

19. Lampton, *Same Bed*, p. 57.

20. Andrew J. Nathan, "Guest Editor's Introduction," *Chinese Law and Government*, vol. 35, no. 1 (January–February 2002), p. 15.

21. Lampton, *Same Bed*, p. 58.

22. "The Bombing of China's Embassy in Yugoslavia," in "Zhu Rongji in 1999 (1)," *Chinese Law and Government*, vol. 35, no. 1 (January–February 2002), pp. 73–99, p. 74. The account of the Politburo meeting comes from this source.

23. Stanley O. Roth, "The Effects on U.S.-China Relations of the Accidental Bombing of the Chinese Embassy in Belgrade," testimony before the Subcommittee on East Asia

and Pacific Affairs, Senate Foreign Relations Committee, Washington, DC, May 27, 1999. In *U.S. Department of State Dispatch*, vol. 10, no. 5 (June 1999), pp. 16–7.

24. Lampton, *Same Bed*, p. 60.

25. As told to the author during a visit to the joint venture in summer 1999.

26. This section follows David M. Finkelstein, "China Reconsiders Its National Security: The Great Peace and Development Debate of 1999," *Project Asia*, Regional Assessment, Alexandria, VA: CNA Corporation, December 2000. Also Suettinger, *Beyond Tiananmen*, pp. 373–5.

27. "Bombing of China's Embassy," *Chinese Law and Government*, p. 75

28. Joseph Y. S. Cheng and King-Lun Ngok, "The 2001 'Spy' Plane Incident Revisited: The Chinese Perspective," *Journal of Chinese Political Science*, vol. 9, no. 1 (April 2004), pp. 63–83. Sheng Lijun, "A New U.S. Asia Policy? Air Collision, Arms Sale, and China-U.S. Relations," *Trends in Southeast Asia*, no. 8 (June 2001), Institute of Southeast Asian Studies, Singapore.

29. Cheng and Ngok, " 'Spy' Plane," pp. 65–6.

30. Sheng Lijun, "Air Collision," p. 11.

31. Cheng and Ngok, " 'Spy' Plane, p. 67.

32. Cheng and Ngok, " 'Spy' Plane," p. 73.

33. Cheng and Ngok, " 'Spy' Plane," p. 73.

34. See John Garver, "Sino-American Relations in 2001: The Difficult Accommodation of Two Great Powers," *International Journal*, Spring 2002, pp. 283–310.

35. Garver, "Difficult Accommodation," p. 304.

36. Regarding Pakistan-Taliban links, see Ahmed Rashid, *Taliban: Militant Islam, Oil and Fundamentalism in Central Asia*, New Haven: Yale University Press, 2001.

37. Charles Hutzler, "China's Quiet, Crucial Role in the War," *Wall Street Journal*, December 28, 2001.

38. Xinhua, September 30, 2001, in FBIS-CHI-2001-0930.

39. Musharraf in his memoir says nothing about this episode. Indeed, he says exceedingly little about Pakistan's relations with China overall. In spite of the importance of Pakistan's ties with China, and in spite of dwelling at great length on Pakistan's tumultuous ties with the United States, Musharraf touches in his memoirs on China at only a few points regarding economic ties. This fits with a broader pattern of extreme reticence by both Beijing and Islamabad in discussing their strategic entente cordiale. See Pervez Musharraf, *In the Line of Fire: A Memoir*, New York: Free Press, 2006.

40. It is sometimes argued that Beijing welcomed the US effort to clear Afghanistan of the Taliban and al-Qaeda, which threatened subversion in Xinjiang. I doubt this. China already had a very effective mechanism for limiting Taliban injury to China—Pakistan's good offices with the Taliban.

41. Kenneth Lieberthal and Wang Jisi, "Addressing U.S.-China Strategic Mistrust," John L. Thornton China Center Monograph No. 4 (March 2012), Washington, DC: Brookings Institution, 2012, pp. vii–viii, 8–9.

42. Chen Dongxiao, "Zhong mei guanxi de jiben yinsu yu bianliang [Basic factors and variables in Sino-US relations]," *Qiu Shi*, No. 2 (February 2010), available at http://www.qstheory.cn/gj/zgwj/201002/t20100202_20343.htm. The author would like to thank D. S. Ragan for tracking down this citation.

43. Quoted in Bruce Stokes, "Chinese Checkers," *National Journal*, vol. 42, no. 8 (February 20, 2010), pp. 18–27.

44. See Jeffry Bader, *Obama and China's Rise*, Washington, DC: Brookings Institution, 2012.

45. Quoted in Stokes, "Checkers," p. 20.

46. Remarks by the president at the US-China Strategic and Economic Dialogue, July 27, 2009, available at https://www.whitehouse.gov/the-press-office/remarks-president-uschina-strategic-and-economic-dialogue.

47. "Openness Sought for China Town Hall Forum Clashes with China's Controls," *New York Times*, November 17, 2005. "Beijing Limits Obama's Exposure," *Wall Street Journal*, November 17, 2009. "Another Clue to How China Managed Obama's Visit," *New York Times*, December 5, 2009.

48. U.S.-China Joint Statement, November 17, 2009, available at http://www.whitehouse.gov/the-press-office/us-china-joint-statement.

49. Stokes, "Chinese Checkers," p. 25.

50. Chris Green, "Copenhagen: Snubs, Skulduggery, and Sleepless Nights," *The Independent*, December 19, 2009, available at http://www.independent.co.uk/environment/climate-change/copenhagen-snubs-skulduggery-and-sleepless-nights-1845092.html. Also Lenore Taylor, "China's Climate Stonewall," *The Australian*, December 21, 2009, available at http://www.theaustralian.com.au/news/features/chinas-climate-stonewall/story-e6frg6z6-1225812228240.

51. Scott Snyder and See-won Byun, "Cheonan and Yeonpyeong, The Northeast Asian Response to North Korea's Provocations," *RUSI Journal*, vol. 156, no. 2 (April 2011), available at http://asiafoundation.org/resources/pdfs/201104SnyderandByun.pdf. Also Bonnie Glaser and Brad Glosserman, "China's Cheonan Problem," ETH Zurich, ISN, June 22, 2010, available at http://csis.org/files/publication/pac1031.pdf.

52. Jeremy Page, "China Warns U.S. as Korea Tensions Rise," *Wall Street Journal*, November 26, 2010. Patrick Goodenough, "U.S. Navy Exercise in Waters Near China Reportedly Canceled," CNS News, October 25, 2010, available at http://www.cnsnews.com/news/article/us-navy-exercise-waters-near-china-reportedly-canceled.

53. Rowan Callick, "Cheonan Sinking Brings Larger Spat to Surface," *The Australian*, July 27, 2010, available at http://www.theaustralian.com.au/opinion/columnists/cheonan-sinking-brings-larger-spat-to-surface/story-e6frg7e6-1225897171800.

54. "Why China Opposes US-South Korean Military Exercises in the Yellow Sea," *People's Daily Online*, July 16, 2010, available at http://en.people.cn/90001/90780/91342/7069743.html

55. Gillian Wong, "Chinese Navy to Hold Live-Ammunition Drills in Yellow Sea following US-South Korean Joint Exercises," *Seattle Times*, August 29, 2010, available at http://www.seattletimes.com/nation-world/chinese-say-navy-will-hold-drills-in-yellow-sea/.

56. Stephen Kaufman, "Clinton Urges Legal Resolution of South China Sea Dispute," July 23, 2010, available at http://www.state.gov/secretary/20092013clinton/rm/2010/07/145095.htm.

57. Associated Press, "US Warship Visits Former Foe Vietnam: China Warns US to Stay Out of Yellow Sea," Fox News, August 10, 2010, available at http://www.foxnews.com/world/2010/08/10/warship-visits-foe-vietnam-china-warns-stay-yellow-sea/.

58. "China Appears to Criticize US-South Korean Military Exercise," CNN World, November 26, 2010, available at http://www.cnn.com/2010/WORLD/asiapcf/11/26/koreas.crisis/.

59. Glaser and Glosserman, "China's Cheonan Problem."

60. Snyder and Byun, "Cheonan and Yeonpyeong."

61. "Remarks by President Obama to the Australian Parliament," The White House, Office of the Press Secretary, November 17, 2011, available at http://www.whitehouse.gov/the-press-office/2011/11/17/remarks-president-obama-australian-paraliament.

62. Hillary Clinton, "America's Pacific Century," *Foreign Policy*, November 2011.

63. Ng Tze-wei, "It's Dinner Diplomacy for Hu in Washington," *South China Morning Post*, January 19, 2011.

64. Kathrin Hille, "Boost for US-China Military Relations," *Financial Times*, December 10, 2010.

65. Chris Buckley, "PLA Researcher Says US Aims to Encircle China," November 28, 2011, available at http://www.reuters.com/article/2011/11/28/us-china-usa-pla-idUSTRE7AR07Q20111128.

66. Elizabeth Bumiller, "U.S. Will Counter Chinese Arms Buildup," *New York Times*, January 9, 2011. Julian Barnes, "Gates Arrives in Beijing for Talks," *Wall Street Journal*, January 10, 2011.

67. Julian E. Barnes and Jeremy Page, "China Snubs US Defense Pitch," *Wall Street Journal*, January 11, 2001.

68. Barnes and Page, "China Snubs."

69. Elisabeth Bumiller and Michael Wines, "China Tests Jet as Gates Visits," *New York Times*, January 12, 2011. Daniel Dombey, "China Tests Stealth Jet during Gates Visit," *Financial Times*, January 12, 2011.

70. Ng Tze-wei, "It's Dinner Diplomacy."

71. Priscilla Jiao, "Hu's Trip Stops Presses in Beijing," *South China Morning Post*, January 21, 2011, available at http://www.scmp.com/article/736295/hus-trip-stops-presses-beijing.

72. Lingling Wei, "China Publicly Cuts Off North Korean Bank," *Wall Street Journal*, May 8, 2013.

73. Jane Perlez, "North Korea Envoy Visiting Beijing amid Concerns about US-China Relations," *New York Times*, May 23, 2013.

74. Thomas Catan, "Next Up After US-China Talks: The Details," *Wall Street Journal*, June 10, 2013.

75. Jane Perlez, "Chinese Editor Suspended for Article on North Korea," *New York Times*, April 2, 2013.

76. Jeremy Page, "China Conflicted on Its Stance Toward the North," *Wall Street Journal*, April 2, 2013.

77. Jane Perlez, "Some Chinese Are Souring on Being North Korea's Best Friend," *New York Times*, February 17, 2013.

78. Jeremy Page, "New China Leader Courts Military," *Wall Street Journal*, March 5, 2013.

Chapter 25. China's Emergence as a Global Economic Power

1. See Kevin P. Gallagher and Roberto Porzecanski, *The Dragon in the Room: China and the Future of Latin American Industrialization*, Stanford: Stanford University Press, 2010.

2. Ben Simpfendorfer, *The New Silk Road: How a Rising Arab World is Turning Away from the West and Rediscovering China*, New York: Palgrave Macmillan, 2009.

3. Re parity purchasing power: rather than measuring the size of economies by taking the total circulation of goods and services measured in a country's own currency and comparing that economy to other economies by exchanging currencies at existing exchange rates, parity purchasing power adjusts for differing costs of comparable goods in different countries. In the United States, for example, higher education and medical care are very expensive, while the same items in China are much cheaper. A basked of essential goods is thus compared in terms of what they cost consumers in different countries, and the size of the overall economy adjusted accordingly. Because so many items cost less in China than in other countries, PPP makes China's larger when compared to other high-price economies. Economists generally believe PPP gives a more accurate comparison of overall size.

4. Thomas G. Rawski, *Economic Growth in Prewar China*, Berkeley: University of California Press, 1989, pp. 344–51.

5. "On Sino-US Trade Balance," March 1997, Information Office of the State Council, *White Papers of the Chinese Government (2) (1996–1999)*, Beijing: Foreign Languages Press, 2000, p. 217–18.

6. World Bank, World Development Indicators databank. www.databank.worldbank.org/data/views/variableselection/selectvariables.aspx?.

7. World Development Indicators.

8. John Mearsheimer, *The Tragedy of Great Power Politics*, New York: W. W. Norton, 2001, p. 398.

9. In the mid-fifteenth century, the Europeans, led by Portugal's Prince Henry the Navigator, began the systematic design of ships of large cargo capacity that could navigate safely and reliably on the high seas of the world's oceans. Within a century or so, seaborne trade in bulk cargos (sugar, tea, tobacco, fibers) began to tie together previously remote regions of the globe.

10. Regarding the Silk Road, see Valerie Hanson, *The Silk Road: A New History*, New York: Oxford University Press, 2012. Frances Wood, *The Silk Road*, Berkeley: University of California Press, 2002. Susan Whitfield, *Along the Silk Road*, Berkeley: University of California Press, 1999. Li Qingxin, *Maritime Silk Road*, Beijing: China Intercontinental Press, 2006. Also, *The Silk Road on Land and Sea*, Beijing: China Pictorial, 1989.

11. G. F. Hudson, *Europe and China; a Survey of their Relation from the Earliest Times to 1800*, Boston: Beacon, 1961; chapter 3, pp. 68–102, deals with the silk trade.

12. Regarding this early modern East Asian maritime trading system, see John E. Wills Jr., "Maritime Asia, 1500–1800: The Interactive Emergence of European Domination," *American Historical Review*, vol. 98, no. 1 (1993), pp. 83–105. John E. Wills Jr., "Was There a Vasco da Gama Epoch? Recent Historiography," in *Vasco da Gama and the Linking of Europe and Asia*, edited by Anthony Disney and Emily Booth, New Delhi: Oxford University Press, 2000, pp. 350–60. Tonio Andrade, *Lost Colony: The Untold Story of China's First Great Victory over the West*, Princeton: Princeton University Press, 2011.

13. Rawski, *Economic Growth in Prewar China*, p. 344.

14. Chalmers Johnson, *MITI and the Japanese Miracle: The Growth of Industrial Policy, 1925–1975*, Stanford: Stanford University Press, 1982.

15. The general idea was that Japan cooperated with the US security system in Asia in exchange for wide access to markets under US protection.

16. Singapore and Hong Kong were fully orientated to participate in global trade, thus conforming to the standard East Asian practice, but lacked the strong state guidance of markets characteristic of Japan, South Korea, and Taiwan.

17. Yasheng Huang, *Capitalism with Chinese Characteristics: Entrepreneurship and the State*, Cambridge: Cambridge University Press, 2008.

18. This discussion is based on Import and Export Values by Category of Commodities, China Statistical Yearbook, University of Michigan China database, available at http://chinadataonline.org/member/macroy/macroytshow.asp?code=A1307.

19. Studies of China's resource diplomacy include *Sino-U.S. Energy Triangles: Resource Diplomacy Under Hegemony*, edited by David Zweig and Yufan Hao, London: Routledge, 2015. "A Ravenous Dragon: Special Report on China's Quest for Resources," *The Economist*, March 15, 2008. Jill Shankleman, *Going Global: Chinese Oil and Mining Companies and the Governance of Resource Wealth*, Woodrow Wilson International Center, n.d. [2011], available at http://www.wilsoncenter.org/publication/going-global-chinese-oil-and-mining-companies-and-the-governance-resource-wealth. R. Evan Ellis, *U.S. National Security Implications of Chinese Involvement in Latin America*, Strategic Studies Institute, National Defense University, June 2005. Eurasia group, "China's Overseas Investments in Oil and Gas Production," report prepared for U.S.-China Economic and Security Review Commission, October 16, 2006, available at http://www.uscc.gov/Research/china%E2%80%99s-overseas-investments-oil-and-gas-production.

20. A fascinating account of this in majority Muslim lands is in Simpfendorfer, *The New Silk Road*.

21. World Bank, World Development Indicators databank.

22. The Republic of China was a founding member of GATT in 1947 but withdrew in 1950. The People's Republic of China was invited to join GATT circa 1950, but was not interested in joining what the CCP then deemed a "rich men's club." Li Lanqing, *Breaking Through: The Birth of China's Opening-Up Policy*, London: Oxford University Press, 2009, pp. 375–8.

23. Alice Miller, "Dilemmas of Globalization and Governance," in *The Politics of China; Sixty Years of the PRC*, 3rd ed., edited by Roderick MacFarquhar, Cambridge: Cambridge University Press, 2011, pp. 528–99.

24. This section follows Wang Yong, "China's Domestic WTO Debate," *China Business Review*, January–February 2000, pp. 54–62.

25. Penelope B. Prime, "China Joins the WTO: How, Why, and What Now," *Business Economics*, April 2002, pp. 26–32. Yong Wang, "Why China Went for WTO," *China Business Review*, July–August 1999, pp. 42–5.

26. Li Lanqing, *Breaking Through*, p. 378.

27. Li Lanqing, *Breaking Through*, p. 379.

28. Li Lanqing, *Breaking Through*, p. 380.

29. Li Lanqing, *Breaking Through*, p. 380.

30. Li Lanqing, *Breaking Through*, pp. 381–2.

31. Li Lanqing, *Breaking Through*, p. 381.

32. Miller, "Dilemmas of Globalization," p. 558.

33. Zong Hairen, "Visit to the United States," *Chinese Law and Government*, vol. 35, no. 1 (January/February 2002), pp. 36–52. Zong is a pseudonym for a member of Zhu Rongji's pro-reform faction who, according to Andrew Nathan, who edited Zong's papers, leaked this information to weaken Jiang Zemin, whom he saw as treating Zhu unfairly. Nathan credits the veracity of Zong's account.

34. Li Lanqing, *Breaking Through*, p. 43–45. It is possible but unlikely that this package of concessions was decided on by Zhu without Jiang's consent, as Jiang later implied after Zhu's offer met with a US rebuff and failure. Zong Hairen argues that Jiang's later disassociation of himself from Zhu's package of concessions and attribution of responsibility for that package to Zhu was an attempt to shift blame and embarrassment from himself to Zhu. It seems very unlikely to this author that Zhu would have submitted such a bold package of concessions without clearing it with at least Jiang if not the entire Politburo.

35. Li Lanqing, *Breaking Through*, p. 39.

36. Zong, "Visit to the United States," p. 40.

37. Miller, "Dilemmas of Globalization."

38. Zong, "Visit to the United States," p. 46.

39. Zong, "Visit to the United States," pp. 45–6.

40. Zong, "Visit to the United States," p. 50. The Twenty-one Demands" were a set of Japanese demands on China in 1915 that would have very greatly strengthened Japanese influence in China. Their presentation and subsequent disclosure played an important role in the eruption of popular nationalist movements a few years later.

41. Zong, "Visit to the United States," p. 50.

42. Regarding the organization of science and technology under the Soviet model, see Denis F. Simon and Detlef Rehn, *Technological Innovation in China: The Case of the Shanghai Semiconductor Industry*, Cambridge, MA: Ballinger, 1988. Also Charles Howe, "Technical Progress and Technology Transfer in a Centrally Planned Economy: The Experience of the USSR, 1917–1987," in *Chinese Technology Transfer in the 1990s*, edited by Charles Feinstein and Christopher Howe, Cheltenham, UK: Edward Elgar, 1997, pp. 62–81.

43. Regarding the military sector, see Evan A. Feigenbaum, *China's Techno-warriors: National Security and Strategic Competition from the Nuclear to the Information Age*, Stanford: Stanford University Press, 2003. John W. Lewis and Xue Litai, *China Builds the Bomb*, Stanford: Stanford University Press, 1988, and *China's Strategic Seapower: The Politics of Force Modernization in the Nuclear Age*, Stanford: Stanford University Press, 1994.

44. Regarding the reorganization of the 1980s and 1990s, see Shulin Gu, *China's Industrial Technology: Market Reform and Organizational Change*, London: Routledge, 1999. Samuel P. S. Ho and Ralph W. Huenemann, *China's Open Door Policy: The Quest for Foreign Technology and Capital*, Vancouver: University of British Columbia Press, 1984.

45. Regarding China's technology acquisition efforts during the late Mao period, see Hans Heymann Jr., "Acquisition and Diffusion of Technology in China," in *China: A Reassessment of the Economy, A Compendium of Papers Submitted to the Joint Economic Committee of the Congress of the United States*, July 10, 1975, 94th Congress, 1st Session, Washington, DC: Government Printing Office, 1975, pp. 701–4. Nai-Ruenn Chen, "Economic Modernization in Post-Mao China: Policies, Problems, and Prospects," in *Chinese Economy Post-Mao: A Compendium of Papers Submitted to the Joint Economic Committee of the Congress of the United States*, Volume I, Policy and Performance, 95th Congress, 2nd Session, Washington: Government Printing Office, November 9, 1978, pp. 192–5.

46. An important early instance of this is recounted in James Mann, *Beijing Jeep: A Case Study of Western Business in China*, Boulder, CO: Westview, 1997.

47. Keith Maskus, "Assessing Coherence of the Intellectual Property Rights Regime in China," in "China and India," special issue, *Indian Journal of Economics and Business*,

2006, pp. 1–13. Mark Liang, "Chinese Patent Quality: Running the Numbers and Possible Remedies," *John Marshall Review of Intellectual Property Law*, no. 478 (2012), available at http://repository.jmls.edu/cgi/viewcontent.cgi?article=1282&context=ripl. "Patents, Yes; Ideas, Maybe," *The Economist*, October 14, 2010.

48. Nicholas Eftimiades, *Chinese Intelligence Operations*, Annapolis, MD: Naval Institute Press, 1994.

49. "China's Cyber Activities that Target the United States," *2009 Report to Congress of the U.S.-China Economic and Security Review Commission*, 111th Congress, 1st Session, November 2009, Washington, DC: US Government Printing Office, 2009, pp. 167–83. Josh Rogin, "The Top 10 Chinese Cyber Attacks (That We Know Of)," The Cable, *Foreign Policy*, January 22, 2010, available at http://foreignpolicy.com/2010/01/22/the-top-10-chinese-cyber-attacks-that-we-know-of/. Brian Prince, "McAfee: Night Dragon Cyber-Attack Unsophisticated but Effective," *IT Security and Network Security News*, February 10, 2011, available at http://www.eweek.com/c/a/Security/McAfee-Night-Dragon-Cyber-Attack-Unsophisticated-But-Effective-303870. Sean Noonan, "China and Its Double-edged Cyber-sword," Stratfor, December 9, 2010, available at https://www.stratfor.com/weekly/20101208-china-and-its-double-edged-cyber-sword. Seymour M. Hersh, "The Online Threat," *New Yorker*, November 1, 2010. James Glanz, "Vast Hacking by a China Fearful of the Web," *New York Times*, December 5, 2010. John Markoff, "Researchers Spy on Computer Spies, Tracing Data Theft to China," *New York Times*, April 6, 2010. Mandiant Intelligence Center Report, February 2013, available at http://intelreport.mandiant.com/.

50. "Indigenous Innovation and Intellectual Property Rights," *2011 Report to Congress of the U.S.-China Economic and Security Review Commission*, 112th Congress, 1st Session, November 2011, Washington, DC: US Government Printing Office, 2011, pp. 70–87.

51. "China's 12th Five-Year Plan and Technology Development and Transfer to China," *2011 Report to Congress*, pp. 88–103. James McGregor, *China's Drive for 'Indigenous Innovation': A Web of Industrial Policies*, Global Intellectual Property Center, Global Regulatory Cooperation Project US Chamber of Commerce, n.d. [2010], available at https://www.uschamber.com/sites/default/files/legacy/reports/100728chinareport_0.pdf.

52. World Development Indicators.

53. Bob Davis, "How China Chases Innovation," *Wall Street Journal*, September 30, 2013.

54. Dan Breznitz and Michael Murphree, *Run of the Red Queen: Government, Innovation, Globalization, and Economic Growth in China*, New Haven: Yale University Press, 2011.

55. Galina Hale, Bart Hobijn, "The U.S. Content of 'Made in China,'" *FRBSF* [Federal Reserve Bank of San Francisco] *Economic Letter*, August 8, 2011.

Chapter 26. Reassuring and Unnerving the Neighbors: Japan

1. Regarding Japan's post–Cold War defense strategy and posture, see Reinhard Drifte, *Japan's Security Relations with China since 1989: From Balancing to Bandwagoning?*, London: Routledge, 2003. Richard J. Samuels, *Securing Japan: Tokyo's Grand Strategy and the Future of East Asia*, Ithaca, NY: Cornell University Press, 2007.

2. Wen-chung Liao, *China's Blue Waters Strategy in the 21st Century*, Chinese Council of Advanced Policy Studies, September 1995, Taipei, Taiwan.

3. Ikira Ireye argued that a critical point in Japan's path toward aggression in China came in 1922 when the Anglo-Japanese alliance was dissolved.

4. Tang Jiaxuan, *Jing yu xu feng* (Stormy rain and warm breezes), Beijing: Shijie zhishi chubanshe, 2006, pp. 2–8.

5. This section follows Gilbert Rozman, "China's Changing Images of Japan, 1989–2001: The Struggle to Balance Partnership and Rivalry," *International Relations of Asia-Pacific*, vol. 2 (2002), pp. 95–129.

6. Rozman, "China's Changing Images," p. 106.

7. Wang Jingru, "Japan's ODA to China: An Analysis of Chinese Attitudes towards Japan," master's thesis, National University of Singapore, 2004, p. 32, available at http://scholarbank.nus.edu.sg/handle/10635/14543.

8. Rozman, "China's Changing Images," p. 107.

9. Rozman, "China's Changing Images," p. 110.

10. Christopher Hughes, "Japan in the Politics of Chinese Leadership Legitimacy," *Japan Forum*, vol. 26, no. 2 (2008), pp. 245–66.

11. Rozman, "China's Changing Images," p. 111.

12. Robert Lawrence Kuhn, *Jiang Zemin: The Man Who Changed China*, New York: Crown, 2004, pp. 371–4. This account of Jiang's 1978 visit follows Kuhn.

13. Kuhn, *Jiang Zemin*, p. 374.

14. For an exposition of Japan's racialist self-conception of its role in that era, see John W. Dower, *War Without Mercy: Race and Power in the Pacific War*, New York: Pantheon, 1986.

15. Rozman, "China's Changing Images," pp. 113–4.

16. Rozman, "China's Changing Images," pp. 117–8. Peter H. Gries tracks the same shifts in "China's 'New Thinking' on Japan," *China Quarterly*, no. 184 (2005), pp. 831–50.

17. Japan's imperialist ideology in the 1930s–1940s was that Japan was leading the struggle of the nonwhite peoples of Asia to liberate themselves from the oppression of the "White Powers" of both the Russian Soviet and Western capitalist stripe. The aim was peace, prosperity, and liberation from oppression by the White Powers for all the peoples of Asia—under Japanese leadership. This imperialist narrative (with less emphasis on the final factor) still underpins the museum display at the museum associated with the Yasukuni Shrine in Tokyo.

18. See Gries, "China's 'New Thinking.'"

19. Matt Pottinger, "Our Goal," *Far Eastern Economic Review*, August 19, 2004, p. 24.

20. Joseph Kahn, "Riot Police Called In to Calm Anti-Japan Protests in China," *New York Times*, April 10, 2005. Norimitsu Onishi, "Tokyo Protests Anti-Japan Rallies in China," *New York Times*, April 11, 2005. Joseph Kahn, "If 22 Million Chinese Prevail at UN, Japan Won't," *New York Times*, April 1, 2005.

21. Joseph Kahn, "China Urges Caution for New Round of Anti-Japan Protests," *New York Times*, April 16, 2005.

22. Raymond Bonner, "China and Japan Leaders Pledge to Improve Relations," *New York Times*, September 24, 2005.

23. Hughes, "Japan in the Politics of Chinese Leadership Legitimacy."

24. Gries, "China's 'New Thinking.'"

25. Hughes, "Japan in the Politics of Chinese Leadership Legitimacy."

26. The Joint Communique of May 7, 2008, is available at http://news.xinhuanet.com/english/2008-05/08/content_8124331.htm.

27. Regarding the history and legal claims of the dispute, see Han-yi Shaw, *The Diaoyutai/Senkaku Islands Dispute: Its History and an Analysis of the Ownership Claims of the PRC, the ROC, and Japan*, Occasional Papers/Reprints Series, Contemporary Asian Studies, no. 3–1999 (152). Hungdah Chiu, *An Analysis of the Sino-Japanese Dispute over the T'iaoyutai islets (Senkaku Gunto*, Occasional Papers Series, Contemporary Asian Studies, no. 1–1999 (150).

28. Mariko Senchanta, "China Warns Japan in Tussle over Natural Gas Field," *Financial Times*, July 2, 2004.

29. James Brooke, "Drawing the Line on Energy," *New York Times*, March 29, 2005.

30. "Japanese Oil Drill Plan Stokes Tension with Beijing," *Financial Times*, April 14, 2005.

31. Howard French, "Chinese Government Permits Rare Protests against Japan," *New York Times*, April 17, 2005.

32. Howard French and Norimitsu Onishi, "Japan's Rivalry with China Is Stirring a Crowded Sea," *New York Times*, Sept. 11, 2008.

33. Peter Dutton, "Scouting, Signaling, and Gatekeeping: Chinese Naval Operations in Japanese Waters and the International Law Implications," *China Maritime Studies*, no. 2 (February 2009), US Naval War College.

34. "Japanese Demand Beijing Apology," *Financial Times*, November 13, 2004. Joseph Ferguson, "Submarine Intrusion Sets Sino-Japanese Relations on Edge," *China Brief*, vol. 4, issue 23 (November 24, 2004). Also Minxin Pei and Michael Swaine, "Simmering Fire in Asia," *Policy Brief*, no. 44 (November 2005). Carnegie Endowment for International Peace.

35. "Koizumi and Hu Fail to Defuse Disputes," *Financial Times*, November 23, 2004.

36. "Trends in Chinese Government and Other Vessels in the Waters Surrounding the Senkaku Islands and Japan's Response," Ministry of Foreign Affairs, Tokyo, February 18, 2015, available at http://www.mofa.go.jp/region/page23e_000021.html.

37. Yuka Hayashi, "Spat Tests Japan's New Leaders," *Wall Street Journal*, September 24, 2010.

38. The video is available at https://www.youtube.com/watch?v=T3qgj2RU1Ww. The video clearly shows the Chinese trawler accelerating, turning toward the Japanese Coast Guard ship, hitting the rear of the Japanese vessel, and then attempting to flee the scene.

39. A chronology of the episode is available in *New York Times*, September 25–26, 2010.

40. Edward Wong, "Chinese Civilian Boats Roil Disputed Waters," *Wall Street Journal*, October 6, 2010.

41. Martin Fackler, "Japan Rejects Apology to China," *New York Times*, September 26, 2010.

42. Martin Fackler, "Arrest in Disputed Seas Rile China and Japan," *New York Times*, September 20, 2010. Rebecca Blumenstein, Gordon Fairclough, and Yuka Hayashi, "Japan Caves In on China; Looks to U.S.," *Wall Street Journal*, September 24, 2010, available at http://www.wsj.com/articles/SB10001424052748703384204575511033698480628. Martin Fackler, "Japan Retreats in Test of Will with the Chinese," *New York Times*, September 25, 2010.

43. James T. Areddy, "China Signals More Cuts in Its Rare-Earth Exports," *Wall Street Journal*, October 20, 2010.

44. Hiroko Tabuchi, "Block on Minerals Called Threat to Japan's Economy," *New York Times*, September 29, 2010.

45. Christopher H. Sharman, *China Moves Out: Stepping Stones Toward a New Maritime Strategy*, China Strategic Perspectives, Center for Study of Chinese Military Affairs, Washington, DC: National Defense University, April 2015, pp. 28–9.

46. Chico Harlan and William Wan, "Japan to Release Chinese Boat Captain," *Washington Post*, Sept. 24, 2010, available at http://www.washingtonpost.com/wp-dyn/content/article/2010/09/24/AR2010092401149.html.

47. Keith Bradsher and Martin Fackler, "Across China, Protests Erupt Against Japan," *New York Times*, August 20, 2012. Brian Spegele, "Anti-Japan Protests Mount in China," *Wall Street Journal*, September 17, 2012.

48. Spegele, "Anti-Japan Protests Mount in China."

49. Jane Perlez, "In Crisis with Japan, China Adjusts Strategy but Does not Back Down," *New York Times*, September 30, 2012.

50. Howard French, "China's Dangerous Game," *The Atlantic*, November 2014, pp. 96–109.

51. Michael D. Swaine, Mike M. Mochizuki, Michael L. Brown, Paul S. Giarra, Douglas H. Paal, Rachel Esplin Odell, Raymond Lu, Oliver Palmer, and Xu Ren, *China's Military and the U.S.-Japan Alliance 2030: A Strategic Net Assessment*, Washington, DC: Carnegie Endowment for International Peace, 2013, available at http://carnegieendowment.org/files/net_assessment_full.pdf.

52. Beijing's use of the Senkakus to attempt to "exploit the contradictions" in Japan-US relations echoes its use of the 1958 Quemoy crisis to exploit the contradictions in US–Nationalist Chinese ties.

53. Mure Dickie and Kathrin Hille, "Nuclear Dispute Sours Ties between Tokyo and Beijing," *Financial Times*, May 18, 2010.

54. See Drifte, *Japan's Security Relations* and Samuels, *Securing Japan*.

55. Defense of Japan 2013, www.mod.go.jp/e/publ/w_paper/pdf/2013.

56. Ibid., p. 42.

57. James R. Holmes, "Japan's Maritime Thought: If not Mahan, Who?," in *Asia Looks Seaward: Power and Maritime Strategies*, edited by Toshi Yoshihara and James R. Holmes, Westport: Praeger Security International, 2008, pp. 146–68. Yamaguchi Noboru, "Evolution of Japan's National Security Policy under the Abe Administration," Asan Forum, April 11, 2014, available at http://www.theasanforum.org/evolution-of-japans-national-security-policy-under-the-abe-administration/.

58. Yuka Hayashi, "Japan Refocuses Its Defense With an Eye Toward China," *Wall Street Journal*, December 17, 2010. Martin Fackler, "Japan Plans Military Shift to Focus More on China," *New York Times*, December 13, 2010. Martin Fackler, "With an Eye on China, Japan Builds Up Military," *New York Times*, March 1, 2011. Also Bjorn Elias Gronning, "Japan's Shifting Military Priorities: Counterbalancing China's Rise," *Asian Security*, vol. 10, no. 1 (2014), pp. 1–21.

59. Wu Jian, "The Shadow of a Hawkish Japan," *China Daily*, December 22, 2010.

Chapter 27. Reassuring and Unnerving the Neighbors: India

1. Quoted in John W. Garver, *Protracted Contest: Sino-Indian Rivalry in the Twentieth Century*, Seattle: University of Washington Press, 2001, p. 226.

2. A "realist" sees states using power to advance their interests. Moral objectives such as a quest for justice typically play a subordinate role, from a realist perspective.

3. Two works exemplify this Indian realist critique: Arun Shourie, *Are We Deceiving Ourselves Again? Lessons the Chinese Taught Pandit Nehru but Which We Still Refuse to Learn*, New Delhi: SAA Publications, 2008. Shourie is one of India's prominent public intellectuals. Jaswant Singh, *Defending India*, London: Macmillan, 1999. Singh was a key leader in the BJP government led by A. B. Vajpayee that took power in 1998 and conducted the nuclear bomb tests. This book was essentially the manifesto on which the BJP took power in 1998 and set Indian policies in a new direction.

4. Quoted in Garver, *Protracted Contest*, pp. 229–30.

5. Regarding US-Pakistani maneuvering over Pakistan's nuclear program and the Khan ring, see Adrian Levy and Catherine Scott-Clark, *Deception: Pakistan, the United States, and the Secret Trade in Nuclear Weapons,* New York: Walker, 2007.

6. Regarding China's 1975 decision, see page 334. Regarding the 1982 decision, see page 449.

7. John W. Garver, "The Security Dilemma in Sino-Indian Relations," *India Review*, vol. 1, no. 4 (October 2007), pp. 1–30.

8. John W. Garver, "The Diplomacy of a Rising China in South Asia," *Orbis*, Summer 2012, pp. 391–411.

9. This is the central thesis of *Protracted Contest*.

10. *The Military Balance 2013*, chap. 6, , London: Institute for Strategic Studies, 2014, p. 260.

11. John W. Garver, "The China-India-U.S. Triangle: Strategic Relations in the Post-Cold War Era, *NBR Analysis*, vol. 13, no. 5 (October 2002). Hereafter cited as "Triangle."

12. The statement is available at www.fas.org/nuke/control/npt/docs/210a.htm.

13. Garver, "Triangle," p. 17.

14. Garver, "Triangle," p. 18.

15. *Strategic Survey, 1996*, London: IISS, 1996, pp. 202–3.

16. Quoted in Garver, "Triangle," p. 19.

17. Quoted in Garver, "The Restoration of Sino-Indian Comity Following India's Nuclear Tests," *China Quarterly*, no. 168 (2001), p. 868.

18. Ibid.

19. This follows, Garver, "Restoration of Comity," pp. 870–5.

20. See Garver, "Triangle," p. 26.

21. Regarding this US process of recalculation, see Strobe Talbott, *Engaging India: Diplomacy, Democracy and the Bomb*, Washington, DC: Brookings Institution Press, 2004.

22. Regarding Sikkim's status, see Garver, *Protracted Contest*, pp. 171–2.

23. *Zhongguo waijiao, 2002* (China's diplomacy, 2002), Beijing: MFA, 2002, p. 105.

24. Quoted in John Garver and Fei-ling Wang, "China's Anti-encirclement Struggle," *Asian Security*, vol. 6, no. 3 (2010), p. 242.

25. The quest for economic growth and the increasing political influence of Indian-Americans in the US were also important factors driving the new relationship.

26. Quoted in Garver, "Triangle," p. 39.

27. Quoted in Garver and Wang, "Anti-encirclement Struggle," p. 244.

28. Quoted in Garver and Wang, "Anti-encirclement Struggle," p. 247.

29. This and many other articles in China's war-scare effort of 2005–2009 are discussed in Garver and Wang, "China's Anti-encirclement Struggle," pp. 249–51.

30. Samuels, *Securing Japan*, pp. 86–108.

31. Daniel Twining, "The Indo-Japanese Strategic Partnership: Asia's Response to China's Rise," *The Asan Forum*, December 6, 2013, available at http://www.theasanforum.org/the-indo-japanese-strategic-partnership-asias-response-to-chinas-rise/.

32. Pranamita Baruah, "Changing Contours of the Japan-India Defense Relations," *Global Politician*, March 4, 2010, available at http://defence.pk/threads/changing-contours-of-the-japan-india-defense-relations.49721/.

33. This and other joint Japan-Indian statements are available on the Japan MFA website, http://www.mofa.go.jp.

34. Joint Declaration on Security Cooperation between Japan and India, October 22, 2008, available at http://www.mofa.go.jp/region/asia-paci/india/pmv0810/joint_d.html.

35. Action Plan to Advance Security Cooperation Based on the Joint Declaration on Security Cooperation between Japan and India, December 29, 2009, available at http://www.mofa.go.jp/region/asia-paci/india/pmv0912/action.html.

36. "Joint Statement Vision for Japan-India Strategic and Global Partnership in the Next Decade," October 25, 2010, available at http://www.mofa.go.jp/region/asia-paci/inda/pm1010/jointt_st.html.

37. Andrew S. Erickson and Austin M. Strange, *No Substitute for Experience: Chinese Antipiracy Operations in the Gulf of Aden*, China Maritime Studies Institute Monograph No. 10, U.S. Naval War College, November 2013.

38. Ananth Krishnan, "China's 'Maritime Silk Road' to Focus on Infrastructure," *The Hindu*, April 20, 2014. Pu Zhendong, "State Councilor Urges Cooperation in China's Silk Road Projects," *China Daily*, November 4, 2014.

39. Kanwal Sibal, "China's Maritime 'Silk Road' Proposals Are not as Peaceful as They Seem," *Daily Mail India*, February 25, 2014, available at http://www.dailymail.co.uk/indiahome/indianews/article-2566881/Chinas-maritime-silk-road-proposals-not-peaceful-seem.html.

40. Prakash Panneerselvam, "India-Japan Maritime Security Cooperation (1999–2009): A Report," *JMSDF Staff College Review*, May 2003, pp. 67–114, available at http://www.mod.go.jp/msdf/navcol/SSG/review/eng_2/2-4.pdf. "Japan-India Relations (Basic Data," Ministry of Foreign Affairs, Japan, July 4, 2014, http://www.mofa.go.jp. "Defense Chronology," Ministry of Defense, Japan, available at http://www.mod.go.jp/e/publ/w_paper/pdf/2007/46DefenseChronology.pdf.

41. Wei Wei, "Asian Imperatives," Indian Express, January 10, 2014. Posted on the website of the PRC embassy in India, available at http://in.china-embassy.org.in/eng/embassy_news/t1117500.htm.

42. Ananth Krishnan, "China Hopes India-Japan Ties Will Be 'Conducive' to Peace," *The Hindu*, January 27, 2014.

43. Gordon Fairclough, "India-China Border Standoff," *Wall Street Journal*, October 30, 2014, available at http://www.wsj.com/articles/india-china-border-standoff-high-in-the-mountains-thousands-of-troops-go-toe-to-toe-1414704602.

44. "Q&A: China, India Experts Address Border Dispute," *Wall Street Journal*, October 30, 2014, available at http://www.wsj.com/articles/q-a-china-india-experts-address-border-dispute-1414704782.

45. James T. Areddy, "India's Modi Urges New Tack for Beijing," *Wall Street Journal*, May 16–17, 2015.

46. Chris Buckley and Ellen Bary, "Modi Urges China to Rethink Policies that Strain Ties," *New York Times*, May 16, 2015.

Chapter 28. China's Quest for Modernity and the Tides of World History

1. The name "Wilhelmine" derives from the fact that two of the three emperors of that period were named Wilhelm. The third, Friedrich, ruled for less than a year.

2. F. L. Carsten, *The Origins of Prussia*, Oxford: Clarendon Press, 1954.

3. Hendrick Spruyt, *The Sovereign State and Its Competitors: An Analysis of Systems Change*, Princeton: Princeton University Press, 1994.

4. Richard J. Evans, "Introduction: Wilhelm II's Germany and the Historians," in *Society and Politics in Wilhelmine Germany*, New York: Barnes and Noble, 1978, pp. 11–23.

5. See Gordon A. Craig, *The Politics of the Prussian Army, 1640–1945*, London: Oxford University Press, 1975.

6. David Shambaugh, *Modernizing China's Military*, Berkeley: University of California Press, 2002.

7. Modern History Sourcebook: Tables Illustrating the Spread of Industrialization, Fordham University, available at http://legacy.fordham.edu/halsall/mod/indrevtabs1.asp . The American share in 1913 was 35.8 percent of world total manufacturing.

8. For an overview of Bismarck's diplomacy and its abandonment by Wilhelm II, see Henry Kissinger, *Diplomacy*, New York: Simon & Schuster, 1994, pp. 137–200.

9. Imanuel Geiss, *German Foreign Policy, 1871–1914*, New York: Routledge and Kegan Paul, 1976, p. 78. See also, Eckart Kehr, *Economic Interest, Militarism and Foreign Policy*, Berkeley: University of California Press, 1977.

10. Quoted in Geiss, *German Foreign Policy*. This interpretation of World War I as the result of a deliberate German decision to break out of encirclement and achieve domination on the continent of Europe entailed rebuttal of an earlier thesis that saw the war as essentially an accident, resulting from mobilization schedules and alliances. See Fritz Fischer, *Germany's Aims in the First World War*, New York: Norton, 1967. Fisher's thesis has been challenged by much subsequent scholarship and is now often considered too simplistic. My own view is that while any phenomenon is more complex that any scholarly framework can grasp, Fisher nonetheless identified an important process.

11. Peter H. Gries, "Nationalism and Chinese Foreign Policy," in *China Rising*, edited by Yong Deng and Fei-ling Wang, New York: Rowman and Littlefield, 2005, pp. 103–15.

12. Christopher H. Hughes, "Japan in the Politics of Chinese Leadership Legitimacy: Recent Developments in Historical Perspective," *Japan Forum*, vol. 20, no. 2 (2008), pp. 245–66.

13. Susheng Zhao, "Chinese Intellectual's Quest for National Greatness and Nationalistic Writing in the 1990s," *China Quarterly*, no. 152 (December 1997), pp. 725–45.

14. Kenneth Lieberthal and Wang Jisi, *Addressing U.S.-China Strategic Distrust*, John L. Thornton China Center Monograph Series, Number 4, Washington, DC: Brookings Institution, March 2002. This overview is drawn from Wang Jisi's presentation on pages 7–19.

15. Lieberthal and Wang, *Addressing*, p. 11.

16. This section draws on Andrew J. Nathan and Andrew Scobell, "How China Sees America; the Sum of Beijing's Fears," *Foreign Affairs*, vol. 91, no. 5 (September/October 2012), pp. 32–47.

17. Robert Zoellick, "Whither China: From Membership to Responsibility," September 21, 2005, available at www.2001-2009.state.gov/s/d/former/zoellick/rem/53682.htm.

18. James Steinberg, "China's Arrival: The Long March to Global Power," September 24, 2009, available at www.state.gov/s/d/former/steinberg/remark/2009/169332.htm.

19. Again this follows Nathan and Scobell, "How China Sees America."

20. White Paper on Political Democracy, October 2005, available at www.china.org. cn/english/2005/oct/145718.html#2.

21. Zheng Wang, *Never Forget National Humiliation: Historical Memory in Chinese Politics and Foreign Relations*, New York: Columbia University Press, 2012, p. 190. This section follows Zheng.

22. Zheng Wang, *Never Forget*, pp. 164–90.

23. Susan Shirk, *China: Fragile Superpower*, New York: Oxford University Press, 2007.

24. James Reilly, *Strong Society, Smart State: The Rise of Public Opinion in China's Japan Policy*, New York: Columbia University Press, 2012.

25. Shirk, *Fragile*, p. 3.

26. Jeremy Page, "China's Army Extends Sway," *Wall Street Journal*, October 4, 2010.

27. Shirk, *Fragile*, p. 76.

28. Susan Shirk, *Political Economy of Reform in China*, Berkeley: University of California Press, 1993, pp. 70–82.

29. The other surviving communist party states are Cuba, Vietnam, and North Korea.

30. The failure of liberal institutions to achieve German unification after the revolution of 1848 was a major factor inclining Germans to embrace unification under distinctly illiberal Prussia twenty-three years later. Thus 1848 can be counted as the first failure of democracy in Germany. Either 1914 or 1933 can be counted as the second failure of German democracy. Only after 1945, on its third attempt, did Germany establish a successful and stable democracy.

31. This follows Odd Arne Westad, *Restless Empire: China and the World Since 1750*, New York: Basic Books, 2002, pp. 242–5.

32. Fritz Stern, *The Politics of Cultural Despair: A Study in the Rise of the Germanic Ideology*, Berkeley: University of California Press, 1961.

33. "On the Diplomacy of the People's Republic of China," March 2002, in *Selected Writings of Li Shenzhi*, Dayton: Kettering Foundation Press, 2010, p. 149. Li also served as foreign affairs advisor to Zhou Enlai during the Bandung era of China's diplomacy and was a founding father of American studies in China after 1978.

34. Richard Madsen, *China and the American Dream: A Moral Inquiry*, Berkeley: University of California Press, 1998.

35. A TED Talk by Eric X. Li posted online by YouTube in June 2013 made this argument very cogently: "A Tale of Two Political Systems," available at https://www.ted.com/talks/eric_li_atale.

INDEX

Abe, Shinzo, 181, 719, 756
Abrams, Creighton, 289
Acheson, Dean, 63, 66, 73, 100
Adams, John, 298
Afghanistan, 543, 729, 739, 748, 779
  PRC-US cooperation for resistance war in,
    413, 416–419, 425–427
  relationship with USSR, 338, 344, 403,
    429–430, 439, 559
  US war on terrorism, 658–661, 669, 752
agriculture, 49, 131–132, 167, 351, 389, 760
  collectivized, 9, 51–54, 57, 112, 778
  Four Modernizations and, 320, 349, 369, 647
  Great Leap Forward, 142–144, 162–163, 189
Aidit, D. N., 220–223, 226
airplane collision, 2001, 633–657
Albania, 40, 173, 264
  fallout from PRC rapprochement with US,
    205–208, 381–382
  Sino-Soviet disagreement, 120–121, 160, 173
alliance, USSR-PRC,
  Soviet assistance to China, 54–58
  Korean war and, 62–66
  withdrawal of Soviet advisors, 156
al-Qaeda, 657–660
Albright, Madeleine, 640, 650, 745
Alsop, Stewart, 188
Andropov, Yuri, 170
Angola, 325, 490, 557
Antonov, Sergei, 156
Argentina, 425, 491, 586, 589, 592, 675
Arkhipov, Ivan, 432
Atatürk, Kemal Mustafa, 337
Australia, 327, 555, 585, 750, 752
Austria, 208, 275, 487, 508, 762, 764
Austria-Hungary, 764
Axen, Herman, 507

Baker, James, 503, 537
Balkans, The, 764
Balladur, Édouard, 533
Bandung era, 92–112, 103, 105–106, 108–109,
    122, 124
  Bandung Conference, 105–109
  de-Stalinization, 92
  India and, 109–112

  relaxation of international tensions, 93
  Taiwan, 100–105
Bangladesh, 464, 491, 754, 779
  1971 crisis in, 436
  formation of, 227, 308–311
  PRC relations with, 438, 442–443, 739
Bao Dai, 99
Bao Tong, 481
Battle of Portland Place, 270
Beijing Massacre, 466–471, 518, 554, 579, 597
  Tiananmen Square, demonstrations in,
    458–459
  turn to Third World after, 490–494
  Western response to, 486–488
Belgium, 275, 360, 487
Belgrade, US bombing of embassy in, 646–650,
    657, 693, 772–773, 775
benevolent authoritarianism, Confucian
    tradition of, 16, 784
Beria, Lavrenti, 84
Berlin Wall, 509
Bessmertnykh, Alexander, 518–519
Bhutan, 147–148, 178, 313, 435, 440, 743
Bhutto, Zalfikar Ali, 194, 312–313, 334–336, 417
"big cake strategy," 531
"big power chauvinist errors," 36, 65, 115, 436
Bismarck, Otto von, 763–765
Bo Yibo, 49, 52, 114, 467, 470, 523
Bogra, Mohammed Ali, 109
Bolshevism, 38, 43, 124, 129, 464, 544
  Marxism-Leninism and, 6–8, 171, 518
Borneo, 218–219, 221, 223, 228
Bosnia, 552
Botswana, 490
Brandt, Willy, 341, 343
Brazil, 487, 491, 664, 675, 679–680, 685
Brezhnev, 174–175, 250, 419, 430–431
  Doctrine, 278, 280
Britain, 153, 219, 327
  Geneva Conference, 95, 105–106
  Red Guard attack on mission, 269–271
  reversion of Hong Kong from, 578–606
  ties with, PRC, 40, 94, 304, 497
Brown, Harold, 418
Brunei, 199, 223, 228, 624
Bukharin, Nikolai, 52